THE ABCs OF D

ASPEN COLLEGE SERIES

THE ABCs OF DEBT

A CASE STUDY APPROACH TO DEBTOR/CREDITOR RELATIONS AND BANKRUPTCY LAW

Fourth Edition

STEPHEN P. PARSONS, J.D.

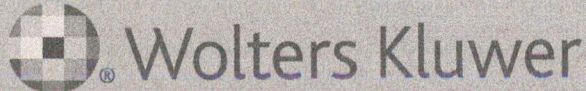

Wolters Kluwer

Published by Wolters Kluwer in New York.

Wolters Kluwer Legal & Regulatory US serves customers worldwide with CCH, Aspen Publishers, and Kluwer Law International products. (www.WKLegaledu.com)

To contact Customer Service, e-mail customer.service@wolterskluwer.com, call 1-800-234-1660, fax 1-800-901-9075, or mail correspondence to:

Wolters Kluwer
Attn: Order Department
PO Box 990
Frederick, MD 21705

Printed in the United States of America.

1 2 3 4 5 6 7 8 9 0

ISBN 978-1-4548-7350-1

Library of Congress Cataloging-in-Publication Data has been applied for.

About Wolters Kluwer Legal & Regulatory US

Wolters Kluwer Legal & Regulatory US delivers expert content and solutions in the areas of law, corporate compliance, health compliance, reimbursement, and legal education. Its practical solutions help customers successfully navigate the demands of a changing environment to drive their daily activities, enhance decision quality and inspire confident outcomes.

Serving customers worldwide, its legal and regulatory portfolio includes products under the Aspen Publishers, CCH Incorporated, Kluwer Law International, ftwilliam.com and MediRegs names. They are regarded as exceptional and trusted resources for general legal and practice-specific knowledge, compliance and risk management, dynamic workflow solutions, and expert commentary.

This book is dedicated to the memory
of Mr. and Mrs. William H. Parsons:

Bill and Juanita
Mom and Dad

Some debts can never be repaid

Summary of Contents

Contents

Preface

Approach

There are two fundamental premises underlying this book. The first is that the specialized study of bankruptcy requires an adequate foundation in other aspects of debtor/creditor relations that are too often ignored or treated only superficially in bankruptcy texts. Grasping bankruptcy concepts and procedures is challenging enough for those who understand loans, lines of credit, installment sales, consensual security arrangements involving real and personal property, surety and guarantor arrangements, statutory and equitable liens, and the priority issues that arise in all those debtor/creditor relationships. Without that foundation, the student undertaking the study of bankruptcy is at a serious disadvantage. Debt collection is another fundamental aspect of debtor/creditor relations that deserves much more attention than it usually receives in texts for this field. This book is unique in that it comprehensively addresses the topics of how consumer and business debt is created and collected (Part A) preparatory to the in-depth study of the consumer bankruptcy case under Chapter 7 or Chapter 13 of the Code (Part B) and the business bankruptcy under Chapter 11 of the Code (Part C).

The second fundamental premise of this book is that bankruptcy and related areas of debtor/creditor law are best taught using a realistic, **case-study** approach. While most current bankruptcy texts avoid the error of teaching too much theory, many err in utilizing a piecemeal approach, in which topics such as the automatic stay, adequate protection, turnover and avoidance powers, cramdown and impairment options, postpetition debt, the use of cash collateral, the assumption or rejection of executory contracts, etc., are presented in isolation, making it difficult for the student to understand when and how such concepts come into play in a particular bankruptcy case. This book is unique in that it uses realistic, current case studies to introduce, explain, and illustrate bankruptcy law and procedure. Students see how a bankruptcy case unfolds, from the moment a debtor makes contact with a lawyer until the case is closed. That chronological, step-by-step approach is used to study cases filed under Chapter 7, Chapter 13, and Chapter 11. This book aspires not just to teach students "about" bankruptcy, but to teach them how to "do" bankruptcy.

Organization of the Book

The text is divided into three parts:

Part A: The Creation and Collection of Debt Prior to Bankruptcy (Chapters Two through Five)

Part B: Consumer Bankruptcy under Chapter 7 and Chapter 13 of the Code (Chapters Six through Sixteen)

Part C: Business Bankruptcy under Chapter 11 of the Code (Chapters Seventeen through Twenty)

Following an introductory chapter that explains the learning approach to be used and debuts the three case studies utilized throughout Parts A and B of the text, Part A addresses the important distinctions between consumer and business debt and between secured and unsecured debt. Emphasis is placed on the creation, perfection, and enforcement of consensual security interests in real and personal property as well as the personal guaranty as a form of security for debt. An entire chapter is devoted to the often neglected subject of nonconsensual liens, both possessory and nonpossessory. Prelitigation efforts to collect delinquent debt are considered in Part A including comprehensive coverage of the Fair Debt Collection Practices Act as well as state legislative and tort remedies for abusive collection tactics. Part A concludes with a thorough examination of the judicial collection process and methods of executing on a final judgment and includes a discussion of the role of exemptions, jointly owned property, and trust arrangements as they impact on execution.

Part B of the text focuses on the consumer bankruptcy case including the Chapter 7 liquidation proceeding for a consumer debtor and the Chapter 13 debt adjustment case for an individual with regular income. We begin with an overview of the Bankruptcy Code, modern bankruptcy practice, and the organization and jurisdiction of the U.S. bankruptcy courts. Two realistic bankruptcy case studies are introduced and used throughout Part B, one a case under Chapter 7 and the other a case under Chapter 13. Complete **Case Files** for both case studies are provided for students on the companion website to the textbook at http://aspenlawschool.com/books/Parsons_Debt4e/ and referred to throughout the chapters that make up Part B. The case studies utilized in Part B illustrate how consumer cases under Chapters 7 and 13 of the Code are handled from beginning to end. Bankruptcy concepts and procedures are addressed as they actually arise in real cases. The case files accessible on the companion web site allow students to actually see completed petitions, schedules, statements, motions, objections, notices, and orders, all of which are routinely drafted by paralegals for review by an attorney and filed in bankruptcy cases.

Part C of the text focuses on the business bankruptcy case under Chapter 11 of the Code. It also utilizes a realistic business bankruptcy case study with complete case files accessible to students on the companion web site. As with the Chapter 7 and 13 cases in Part B, the Chapter 11 case in Part C is studied step-by-step from filing of the petition through order closing the case.

The companion website to the text also contains numerous **To Learn More (TLM)** activities for each chapter. The TLMs are designed to challenge and enable the student to do further research on issues raised in the text or to consult additional resources for further learning. Some of the TLMs are historical (e.g., Debtor/creditor tensions in the newly independent United States were a major factor in the decision to convene the meeting in Philadelphia that became the Constitutional Convention of 1787). Some are policy oriented (e.g., Debt collection work is increasingly being outsourced to India and countries in South America; the financial services industry spent more than $100 million lobbying for the passage of BAPCPA in the eight years it was under consideration by Congress). Most require the student to locate and apply local law or procedure to the general topics raised in the text (e.g., Does your state regulate the interest rate that can be charged by payday loan companies? What property exemptions are recognized in your state?). As every instructor knows, it is not enough for students to learn what the law is generally around the country—they need to know the law of their particular state. It is not enough for them to learn the different procedures bankruptcy courts or trustees across the nation may follow—they need to know the procedures followed by the bankruptcy courts and trustees in the federal district where they will work.

The **Instructor's Manual (IM)** contains material that the instructor can use to assign optional **Drafting Exercises** to students as well. There are four optional exercises to accompany Part A of the text relating to the pre-bankruptcy creation and collection of debt and ten to accompany Parts B and C of the text, including five for a Chapter 7 consumer bankruptcy case, two for a Chapter 13 case, and three for a Chapter 11 business reorganization case.

Key Features

As noted, the book utilizes realistic, current case studies. The first three case studies are introduced in Chapter One and are used throughout Part A. The characters in each case study are given sufficient history, personality, and context that they become real people for students, not just names on a page. Debt-related problems happen to real people in the real world, and students should be taught to see clients as real people with unique stories and circumstances. Following the same three case studies throughout Part A enables students to get to know these clients and their financial circumstances. Three additional case studies with case files are utilized in Parts B and C of the text to illustrate bankruptcy concepts and procedures studied there. The companion website to the text contains exhaustive case files to accompany all three bankruptcy case studies utilized in Parts B and C.

Each chapter begins with a short list of **Key Concepts.** Numerous **Examples** are provided throughout each chapter, along with timely and relevant **Illustrations.** In addition, a number of **Problem-Hypothetical (P-H)** activities appear throughout each chapter, presenting the student with the opportunity to immediately apply what is being read in the text. Similarly, a number of **Ethical Considerations (EC)** appear periodically, drawing the student's attention to a relevant ethical or professional challenge presented by the topic under discussion. New to the fourth edition are the more than twenty **Highlighted Cases** sprinkled through the text that give students the opportunity to see how courts have applied the concepts being studied in actual cases. Each highlighted case is followed by **Real-Life Application Exercises** challenging students to apply the analysis and rule announced in the highlighted case. Also new to the fourth edition are periodic **Information Boxes,** providing students with interesting historical information to supplement the text. At the end of each chapter is a comprehensive **Chapter Summary,** 10 to 15 open-ended **Review Questions,** and a list of **Words and Phrases to Remember.**

In addition to the Drafting Exercises previously mentioned, the IM contains suggested approaches to teaching with the text including testing and grading, suggested answers to the P-H and Real-Life Application Exercises that follow the Highlighted Cases, answers to the end of chapter review questions, and a comprehensive test bank with answer key.

A note on the dates used in the text: To keep the dates as current as possible, the illustrations and case file documents utilize a dating system in which YR00 is always the current year. YR-1 is last year, YR-2 is two years ago, YR+1 is next year, YR+2 is two years from now, and so on.

New for the Fourth Edition

The fourth edition has been substantially revised and reorganized to enable more efficient and focused instruction. The pre-bankruptcy chapters in Part A of the text have been revised and streamlined with extraneous material previously included in them moved to the To Learn More feature located on the companion website for optional use by the instructor. The bankruptcy chapters included in Parts B and C of the text are now organized around **consumer bankruptcy** under which heading both Chapter 7 and Chapter 13 bankruptcy cases are considered in Part B and **business bankruptcy** where Chapter 11 business reorganization is the focus of Part C. With these revisions it should be easier to cover the material in a single semester and the bankruptcy material is more clearly presented in a way that emphasizes the important consumer/business bankruptcy distinction.

The forms used in the three bankruptcy case studies utilized in Parts B and C of the text and available to the student on companion website have all been updated to comply with the important December 2015 amendments to the official bankruptcy forms. Likewise, the dollar amounts utilized for allowed federal exemptions, the standardized means test expenses, debtor qualifications to file under certain chapters, and other Bankruptcy Code provisions subject to the triennial dollar adjustment mandate of §104 have all been updated to reflect the amounts that went into effect on April 1, 2016. Examples and P-Hs throughout the book have been freshened and updated as have all statistics cited regarding consumer and business bankruptcy filings. As mentioned in the Key Features section of this Preface, major new features for this edition include the Highlighted Cases followed by Real-Life Application Exercises, the Key Concepts that now appear at the beginning of each chapter, and the entertaining Information Box feature.

The new edition has been updated to include discussion of every bankruptcy decision of the U.S. Supreme Court announced since the last edition appeared, including *Bank of America, N.A., v. Caulkett* which put the kibosh on the lien stripping option in a Chapter 7 case, *Law v. Siegel* which nixed the idea of surcharging a debtor's homestead exemption to pay administrative costs of trustee, *Harris v. Viegelahn* which quashed the practice of including undistributed funds in the hands of a Chapter 13 standing trustee in the property of debtor's Chapter 7 estate when the debtor converted the case from Chapter 13 to Chapter 7, as well as *Executive Benefits Ins. Agency v. Arkison*, and *Wellness International Network, Ltd., v. Sharif* which together, while not resolving the thorny constitutional jurisdiction issues raised for bankruptcy courts by *Stern v.* Marshall, at least work around them in such a way that bankruptcy courts can continue to function. In addition to new Supreme Court decisions, there are numerous citations to new lower court decisions throughout Parts B and C of the text as questions about the 2005 BAPCPA amendments to the bankruptcy code are slowly but surely being dealt with.

Textbook Resources

The companion website at http://aspenlawschool.com/books/Parsons_Debt4e/ includes additional resources for students and instructors, including:

- Study aids to help students master the key concepts for this course. Visit the site to access interactive StudyMate exercises such as flash cards, matching, fill-in-the-blank, and crosswords. These activities are also available for download to an iPod or other hand-held device.
- Instructor resources to accompany the text
- Links to helpful websites and updates.

Instructor resources to accompany this text include a comprehensive Instructor's Manual, Test Bank, PowerPoint slides, and sample exercises for use with Best Case bankruptcy software. All of these materials are available for download from our companion website.

Appreciation

The author wishes to thank the law students at the Appalachian School of Law in Grundy, Virginia, and the paralegal students in the Walters State Paralegal Program in Morristown, Tennessee, for serving as the amenable guinea pigs for the development of the materials and approach used here. Appreciation is also expressed to the many clients who entrusted the author with various debtor/creditor issues over the past 30 years—especially those who paid their bill.

And, as always, love and appreciation for the patience and support of the home team: Marcia, Andrew, and Emily Grayce.

Stephen P. Parsons

September 2016

Chapter One:

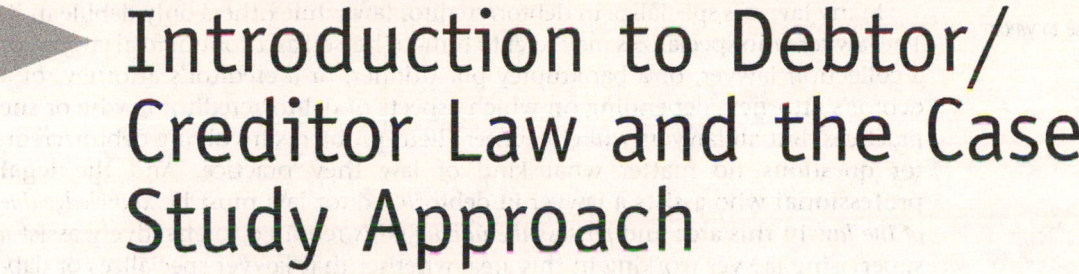

Introduction to Debtor/ Creditor Law and the Case Study Approach

KEY CONCEPTS

- The study of debtor/creditor law involves consideration of the various laws relating to the creation and collection of debt and to the discharge or reorganization of debt in bankruptcy
- Consumer debt refers to indebtedness incurred for personal, family, or household purposes while business debt refers to debt incurred in the operation of a business
- A debt obligation may be fixed or contingent, liquidated or unliquidated, secured or unsecured, current or future, and disputed or undisputed
- The study of debtor/creditor relations involves numerous areas of the law including contracts, the Uniform Commercial Code, consumer protection, business associations, property law both real and personal, tort law, and criminal law

A. The Scope of Debtor/Creditor Law

This text will cover three distinct but related topics in the following order:

Part A: The creation and collection of consumer and business debt prior to bankruptcy

Part B: The consumer bankruptcy under Chapter 7 or 13 of the Bankruptcy Code

Part C: The business reorganization proceeding under Chapter 11 of the Bankruptcy Code

Debt The obligation of one person or entity, enforceable at law, to pay money, tender property, or provide services to another person or entity now or in the future.

Debt is the central, unifying theme of this study. The word "debt" can have a variety of meanings, some legal and some only moral—look at the dedication page of this book for an example of the latter. But for our purposes, debt is the obligation of one person or entity, enforceable at law, to pay money, tender property, or provide services to another person or entity now or in the future. Most debt involves the obligation to pay money.

A study of debt is just one aspect of the broader legal topic of **commercial law**, that is, the law of commerce or doing business. Commercial law encompasses not just the creation and management of debt but many other legal aspects of doing business that are beyond the scope of our study. Here we will focus on **debtor/creditor law**, that is, the various laws relating to the rights and obligations

Debtor Person liable for a debt.

Creditor One to whom a debt is owed.

Consumer debt Debt incurred for personal, family, or household purposes.

existing between the person who owes a debt (the **debtor**) and the one to whom the debt is owed (the **creditor**).

Many lawyers specialize in debtor/creditor law while others only dabble in it. The lawyer who specializes may refer to him- or herself as a commercial lawyer, or a collection lawyer, or a bankruptcy practitioner, or a creditor's attorney, or a debtor's attorney, depending on which aspects of debtor/creditor law he or she practices. But all lawyers will encounter client problems involving debtor/creditor questions no matter what kind of law they practice. And the **legal professional** who assists a lawyer in debtor/creditor law must be *knowledgeable of the law* in this area and *possess the unique skills* required to effectively assist a supervising lawyer working in this area, whether that lawyer specializes or dabbles (see Section E of this chapter).

In the course of our study you will learn that there are numerous ways to categorize debt. For introductory purposes, let's start with one of the basic categorizations, the difference between consumer debt and business debt. **Consumer debt** refers generally to indebtedness incurred for personal, family, or household purposes. Such debt may include a home mortgage, an apartment lease, a car loan, credit card debt, school loans, utility bills, medical bills, insurance premiums, alimony or child support obligations, federal and state income taxes, state and local property taxes, and the like. **Business debt** refers generally to indebtedness incurred for business purposes. Such debt may include the lease or a mortgage on a business location as well as the business's obligations for utility bills, insurance premiums, business taxes, employee withholding and salaries, materials and equipment purchased, services provided, and so forth. Businesses also incur debt by borrowing money or obtaining credit to purchase business assets or to otherwise fund the operation of the business.

A debt may be **current**, meaning that it is owed at this moment, or it may be **future**, meaning that the obligation exists now but need not be satisfied until sometime in the future. A debt may be **liquidated**, meaning that we know its dollar value to the penny, or it may be **unliquidated**, meaning that we do not yet know its dollar value. A debt may be **fixed** or **noncontingent**, meaning that nothing else needs to happen for the obligation to exist, or it may be **contingent**, meaning that it will only exist if and when another event occurs. A debt may be **disputed** by the debtor in whole or part or it may be **undisputed**. A debt to pay money may be **unsecured**, meaning that upon default of the debtor's obligation to pay, the creditor's only resort is to seek a court judgment against the debtor, or the debt may be **secured**, which means that upon default, the creditor may be able to seize certain designated real or personal property to satisfy the obligation. We will learn much more about these various categories of debt as we proceed.

B. ▶ Introduction to the Case Studies

Throughout our study of debtor/creditor topics we will utilize *case studies*: hypothetical cases involving realistic debtors with realistic debt problems. The three case studies we will use throughout Parts A and B of the text are introduced in this chapter. If your instructor elects to do so, these case studies may also be utilized in Part C of the text when you are assigned to prepare appropriate bankruptcy filings for one or more of the case study debtors.

Illustration 1-a: CASE STUDY #1: NICHOLAS (NICK) AND PEARL MURPHY

MEMORANDUM

TO: Paralegal
FROM: Supervising attorney
RE: Nicholas and Pearl Murphy

Nick and Pearl Murphy are a married couple residing in Capital City. They have been married for 12 years and have two children, Lynette, who is 9, and Lyndon, who is 11. By an earlier marriage, Nick has a third child, Robbie, who is 15. Nick himself is 40 years old and Pearl is 39. Nick, who dropped out of high school and later earned his GED, has a degree from State Technical School and has worked in the local office of Overland Truck Services, Inc. for five years. Effective January 1 of this year he was promoted to manager of the office making $60,000 a year. Pearl has a bachelor's degree from State University in elementary education and worked as a teacher for the Capital City public school system, full-time, until August 1, YR-3 when she underwent an emergency appendectomy and suffered complications leaving her with chronic stomach and bowel problems. Pearl was unable to work full-time for more than a year following the surgery. She was able to work some last year as a substitute teacher and returned to work full-time in January of this year.

Nick and Pearl own their home, which they purchased ten years ago for $125,000. First Bank of Capital City holds the mortgage on the Murphys' home, which has a current balance of $92,500. The Murphys make a monthly mortgage payment of $993 to First Bank. The couple owns two vehicles. Nick drives a five-year-old Ford F-150 truck that has 75,000 miles on it and is paid for. Pearl drives a five-year-old Honda Accord, which the Murphys bought used three years ago. They still owe $8,900 on the Honda and make monthly payments of $310 to Friendly Finance Company. Friendly Finance holds a security interest in the car to secure payment of the obligation. The Murphys have two credit cards, a Master Card with a maximum limit of $5,000 and a Visa with a limit of $3,000. The couple has maxed out both cards and pays only the minimum balance due on the cards each month. They also have an installment sales contract with Shears Department Store for the purchase of living room furniture on which there is a $4,592 balance owing.

Less than two months before Pearl's emergency appendectomy, the Murphys took out a home improvement loan from the Teachers Credit Union in Capital City in the amount of $35,000 to add two new rooms to their house. The credit union took a second mortgage on the house to secure repayment of the loan. The construction had barely begun when Pearl had her surgery and was never finished. Most of the money borrowed from the credit union went to pay off expenses arising from Pearl's illness. The credit union loan is to be paid back over ten years at $406 per month. The Murphys are currently three payments in arrears to the credit union and it is threatening foreclosure on their home. Nick is obligated by court order to pay his ex-wife, Sharon Murphy, $400 per month as child support for Robbie until the boy turns 18.

The Murphys are in a financial crisis due to continuing medical expenses related to Pearl's condition and the loss of her full-time income. Pearl's insurance covered most of the expenses related to the original surgery but the costs related to the complications and continuing treatment and medications have far exceeded the insurance policy's coverage. At this point, Pearl's unpaid medical bills total $28,000 and her monthly medications cost $325 out of pocket. They used up all their savings while she was not working and now are too far behind to catch up.

The clients involved in our first case study have a number of issues arising out of consumer debt. Meet Nick and Pearl Murphy (Illustration 1-a). Throughout Parts A and B of the text, we will refer to the Murphys' file as "Case Study #1" in order to illustrate typical consumer issues in debtor/creditor law and to learn how those issues are analyzed and resolved by the competent attorney assisted by the able legal professional.

We will have much more to say about the Murphys' financial circumstances throughout the text. But be aware that their various debts are all typical consumer debts. Moreover, unexpected medical costs and improvident credit card use that we see in the case study, together with unexpected job loss and divorce, are leading causes of consumer insolvency and bankruptcy.

P-H 1-a: How many different consumer debts do the Murphys have based on the summary in Illustration 1-a?

P-H 1-b: What follow-up questions would you want to ask at this point concerning the Murphys' financial circumstances?

EC 1-a: Is there any ethical problem presented by one lawyer representing both Mr. and Mrs. Murphy in connection with their financial woes? Would your answer change if the couple was separated or divorcing? Why?

Oftentimes clients present debtor/creditor issues involving a mix of consumer and commercial debt. Meet Abelard (Abe) Mendoza (Illustration 1-b), whose case presents such a mix. Throughout the text, we will refer to the Mendoza file as "Case Study #2" in order to illustrate typical mixed consumer/commercial issues in debtor/creditor law and to learn how those issues are analyzed and resolved by the competent attorney assisted by the able paralegal.

We will have much more to say about Mr. Mendoza's financial circumstances throughout the text. But note that his personal and family finances are inter-mingled with his business concerns. He has also made a series of poor financial decisions that are all too typical of the unsophisticated small business owner. These decisions have left him vulnerable and now he needs sound legal advice.

P-H 1-c: How many different types of consumer debts does Mr. Mendoza have based on the summary in Illustration 1-b? How many types of commercial debts?

P-H 1-d: What follow-up questions would you want to ask at this point concerning Mr. Mendoza's financial circumstances?

P-H 1-e: Make a list of things Mr. Mendoza should have done differently that might have prevented his present difficulties.

EC 1-b: If your lawyer supervisor agrees to undertake representation of Mr. Mendoza, and his son David later comes to the same lawyer seeking representation on the criminal charge only, can that lawyer ethically undertake David's defense? Can the lawyer ethically undertake representation of both David and Mr. Mendoza regarding their financial woes? If your lawyer supervisor had represented City County Bank in connection with a school loan to David and the later, fraudulent business loan to David, can the lawyer now undertake representation of Mr. Mendoza?

Illustration 1-b: CASE STUDY #2: ABE MENDOZA

MEMORANDUM

TO: Paralegal
FROM: Supervising attorney
RE: Abelard Mendoza

Abelard (Abe) Mendoza immigrated legally to the United States from Mexico 35 years ago and later became a U.S. citizen. He married and raised two daughters and a son in Capital City. He and his wife, Maria, also built a successful construction company, known as Mendoza Construction. The business was owned by Mr. Mendoza and his wife and was never incorporated. Two years ago Mr. Mendoza lost his wife to cancer and now, at age 58, his life revolves around his children.

Mr. Mendoza's youngest child is his son, David, who is now 28. In school, David was always a good student and showed talent in the sciences. However, he has had trouble deciding exactly what he wants to do for a career. He received a bachelor's degree from State University, followed by a masters in biology from the same university. He spent 18 months in a doctoral program at UCLA before dropping out, then two more years in medical school before leaving that.

David borrowed money in connection with every phase of his higher education and his parents co-signed one promissory note and executed a separate guaranty agreement promising to repay one other note if David failed to do so. (A sample guaranty agreement can be seen in "To Learn More activity 2-2", accessible on the companion web site of the textbook at http://aspenlawschool.com/books/Parsons_Debt4e/.) All those obligations are now past due and David is unable to pay them so the creditors are demanding payment from Abe. The two separate notes reflecting David's educational loans for which Mr. Mendoza is liable exceed $60,000.

A year before his wife became ill, and while their annual income from the construction company was in excess of $300,000, Mendoza and his wife purchased a new home in Capital City. They borrowed $500,000 from Security Trust Bank in Capital City and gave the bank a mortgage in the land and house as security for repayment. The monthly payments on that mortgage are $2,500.

Last year Mr. Mendoza decided to turn the construction business over to his son, David. Mendoza himself now works as the project manager on the City Heights Condominium project, a $200 million development along the river that flows through downtown Capital City, under contract with the owner of the project, City Heights Limited Partnership. The project has not been going well. The owner is in constant dispute with the general contractor on the job. Scheduled cash advances have been withheld from the general contractor because of the disputes and unpaid subcontractors and suppliers are threatening to place liens on the property. Mendoza fears he will be named as a defendant in numerous lawsuits arising out of the project. Soon after turning the construction business over to David Mendoza, Abe was audited by the Internal Revenue Service for the first time ever, and the government has just issued an assessment against him for unpaid income taxes for three prior tax years, plus penalties and interest, totaling $50,000. To make matters worse, recently Mr. Mendoza discovered that the bookkeeper he had hired after his wife's death (she always kept the books for the business, as well as for the family finances) has been systematically embezzling ever since she came to work for him. It looks like she has drained more than $100,000 of cash out of the company bank account, which was used to fund ongoing business operations. Mendoza had no security bond or fidelity insurance from which to recoup the loss and the woman has disappeared along with the stolen cash.

As if matters were not already bad enough, yesterday Mendoza learned that his son David procured a loan in the amount of $350,000 last year from the City County Bank in Capital City using false financial statements listing assets he did not actually have and omitting numerous debts he did have. Apparently David, unknown to Mr. Mendoza, invested the money in a real estate scheme with some friends. The investment failed and the money is gone. City County Bank has already sued David and is demanding that Mr. Mendoza pay the money back pursuant to the guaranty he signed in favor of City County Bank in connection with two of David's school loans. Mr. Mendoza also fears that David will be criminally prosecuted as a result of the fraudulent financial statements.

Illustration 1-c: CASE STUDY #3: TOMORROW TODAY, INC.

MEMORANDUM

TO: Paralegal
FROM: Supervising attorney
RE: Tomorrow Today, Inc.

Tomorrow Today, Inc. (TTI) is an advanced technology company, the brainchild of Rosemary Chin, Donald Brabson, and Howard Kine. The three were college classmates at Stanford. Chin holds a doctorate in physics, Brabson is a mechanical engineer, while Kine is a computer software genius. They created TTI together their first year out of college and remain the only shareholders in the corporation. For the first several years of its existence, TTI enjoyed great success with contracts for the development of computerized traffic control systems for large urban areas and high-speed mass transit systems for the government of Japan.

Five years ago TTI procured a contract with Lockland Hughes Corporation, a major weapons manufacturer for the U.S. Department of Defense and the European Union, to develop a futuristic sounding defensive military device called MIES (Mobile Infantry Energy Shield). The theory behind MIES is that soldiers in the field can carry a portable computerized device, probably located in the helmet, having the ability to detect a moving projectile headed toward the soldier and instantaneously project an energy field around the soldier sufficient to block the projectile, deflect its line of flight, or at least disperse its explosive impact sufficiently to protect the soldier. The device, if it can be proven practical, has the potential to revolutionize infantry combat, particularly in urban warfare.

TTI has invested most of its resources in the MIES contract. That contract called for delivery of a working prototype 18 months ago. Despite major advances and promising tests, the prototype was not ready then and Lockland Hughes gave TTI a contract extension that expires in 12 months. Lockland Hughes has made it clear it will not extend its contract with TTI again beyond that 12-month deadline.

But TTI has run into financing problems. Five years ago, when it procured the MIES contract, TTI obtained a $10 million line of credit from its primary lender, United Bank of America (UBA) to finance research and development. TTI, of course, granted UBA a security interest in most of its assets as security for the loan. At the time, TTI had $5 million in cash of its own. It went through its cash and the full line of credit during the first three years of development and had to go to a second lender, Bank of Europa (BE), for an additional $7.5 million line of credit, which it has now exhausted. Like UBA, BE took a security interest in most of the assets of TTI. That security interest is second or junior to UBA's.

Under the terms of the UBA line of credit, TTI has been making interest-only payments, but the entire principal amount of $10 million is now due and payable, and TTI does not have it. Similarly, the entire $7.5 million principal amount of the BE line of credit becomes due and payable three months from now. TTI believes it is within six months of having a working prototype of the MIES ready to deliver to Lockland Hughes. Once it does so, its contract with Lockland Hughes calls for payment of a $30 million lump sum to TTI with the expectation of a long-term exclusive contract for mass production of MIES if Lockland Hughes can sell the idea to the U.S. government.

In order to complete its production of MIES according to this projected schedule, TTI needs more cash, at least $5 million. Both UBA and BE have refused TTI's requests for further loans and UBA is demanding immediate repayment of its loan and is threatening repossession of the TTI assets constituting collateral if payment is not forthcoming.

TTI has 20 employees at various levels, not including the three principals in the company. It leases office space in downtown Capital City and pays $2,000 a month for that space. It also leases a 100-acre test site in Nevada and pays $5,000 a month for it. TTI is current on its office lease payments but is two months behind on its test site lease.

To learn about nonconsumer or business debt, let's get to know Tomorrow Today, Inc. (Illustration 1-c). Throughout the text, we will refer to the Tomorrow Today, Inc. file as "Case Study #3" in order to illustrate typical commercial issues in debtor/creditor law and to learn how those issues are analyzed and resolved by the competent attorney assisted by the able paralegal.

P-H 1-f: There is one aspect of this commercial transaction that involves the personal assets of the owners of TTI. What is that?

P-H 1-g: What follow-up questions would you want to ask at this point concerning TTI's financial circumstances?

P-H 1-h: Make a list of all the categories of natural persons and businesses whose future might be dramatically impacted by what happens with TTI.

EC 1-c: Assume that you work for an attorney whose firm represents UBA, and the firm has been instructed to declare TTI in default on its obligation to UBA and to repossess TTI assets. You are aware that your attorney supervisor has been dating Rosemary Chin. Should your attorney supervisor report that relationship to the firm? Would it matter that your attorney supervisor will not be working directly on the TTI matter?

We will have much more to say about TTI's financial circumstances throughout the text. But note that this is a sophisticated commercial transaction involving many millions of dollars. A lot is on the line for all the parties involved.

C. ▶ Sources of Law Governing Debtor/Creditor Relations

In the text we will consider the creation of consumer and business debt, the collection of that debt, and the discharge or reorganization of that debt in bankruptcy. The first two of these, the creation of debt and collection of debt, are controlled primarily by **state law**, not **federal law**. As we consider those two topics in upcoming chapters we will refer to state **statutes** (legislative enactments) and **case law** (court decisions) and sometimes to state **agency rules and regulations** to determine what is permissible. And since these topics are controlled primarily by state law you must always keep in mind that the law may differ from state to state. We will see this particularly in connection with the collection of debt. The collection methods authorized by various states vary markedly.

To say that the law regarding the creation and collection of debt is primarily state law does not mean that federal law doesn't come into play there at all. It does. For example, when we consider the collection of debt in Chapter Four, we will take a close look at an important federal statute, the Fair Debt Collection Practices Act, which imposes strict regulations on those regularly involved in debt collection. But overall, state law is primary and federal law only supplementary in these two topics.

On the other hand, the third topic, the discharge or reorganization of debt in bankruptcy, involves the Bankruptcy Code found in Title 11 of the U.S. Code. The U.S. Bankruptcy Code regulates most types of bankruptcy filings throughout the country and restricts the administration of those filings to a specialized federal court: the United States Bankruptcy Court.

But that is not to say that all aspects of bankruptcy law are federal. We will learn for example that not all entities can take advantage of the Bankruptcy Code—a few must dissolve themselves under state liquidation laws. And we will see that in a typical case filed under the Bankruptcy Code, numerous questions arise that are controlled by state law. Just as a quick example, the Bankruptcy Code allows individual debtors to declare some property exempt from being seized and distributed to creditors. The Code allows states to elect to have state exemption laws to apply in federal bankruptcy proceedings filed in those states rather than the exemption laws set out in the Code itself, and a number of states have in fact made that election. But overall, federal bankruptcy law is primary and state law only secondary in connection with this third topic.

Sound confusing? It won't be for long.

D. ▶ The Relation of Debtor/Creditor Law to Other Areas of the Law

Debtor/creditor law is closely related to the study of the law of **contracts**. As we will see in Chapter Two, the primary source of debt is a contractual relationship between the debtor and creditor.

EXAMPLE

> If you go to the bank and borrow money to purchase a car, you will sign a **promissory note** (see Illustration 2-a) legally obligating yourself to repay the amount borrowed to the lender together with an agreed amount of interest. That note is a contract between you (the debtor) and the lender (the creditor).

We will not restudy the law of contracts in this course. But remember that a study of contracts teaches you the basics of (1) how contracts are negotiated, entered into, and often committed to writing by attorneys; (2) how contracts are enforced or not enforced by the courts in the event of a dispute; and (3) the kinds of remedies a court may award if it finds a breach of contract. This course is an extension of that area of law.

An important aspect of the study of contract law is the **Uniform Commercial Code** (UCC) adopted in all 50 states. Especially important for the practice of debtor/creditor law are Articles 2 and 2A of the UCC, governing contracts for the sale or lease of personal property; Article 9, governing the creation and perfection of consensual security interests in personal property of a debtor; and Articles 3 and 4 governing negotiable instruments such as promissory notes. We will have multiple occasions to reference various sections of the UCC as we continue our study.

Federal and state **consumer protection laws** can have a dramatic impact on the debtor/creditor relationship. We will have occasion to mention a number of such laws including the Fair Credit Reporting Act, the Fair Debt Collection Practices Act, and the Equal Credit Opportunity Act.

This course of study also involves the law of **business organizations** because debtor/creditor issues often arise in the context of a business operation whether as a sole proprietorship; a corporation; a limited liability company; a general partnership; a limited partnership; a joint venture; or some other more specialized business form recognized by a state (e.g., professional limited liability companies and limited liability partnerships recognized in some states for certain licensed professions or trades). Business owners/operators incur debt all the time: They borrow money from a bank or other lender to finance their operations or expand them; they purchase materials/supplies or receive services on credit with a promise to pay within an agreed period of time (e.g., receiving goods along with a 30-day invoice); they lease (another contract) premises in which to do business or lease vehicles or equipment with an accompanying obligation to pay the lease payments as they come due; and so forth. Businesses often become creditors, too, by selling their product or services to customers (the debtors) and agreeing to accept payment in the future. And, of course, financial services businesses (e.g., banks, savings and loans, credit unions, loan companies, and credit card companies) are in the business of loaning money to their customers—creating and collecting debt *is* their business.

Government agencies and departments, and quasi-governmental entities such as regulated public utilities also perform a business function, albeit for the benefit of the public rather than for private owners. Though they are nonprofit entities, they too borrow, often by way of selling **debt securities** known as **bonds** to the public, backed by the full faith and credit of the issuing government entity. They purchase real and personal property as well as services on credit and thus incur debt like any for-profit business.

EXAMPLE

> From Case Study #1 (Illustration 1-a), Nick Murphy's employer, Overland Truck Services, Inc., is a corporation. Pearl Murphy's former full-time employer is the school district, a governmental entity. She substitute teaches for a private school, likely a charitable nonprofit corporation. As a private tutor she is self-employed, or we might call her tutoring business a sole proprietorship. The law of business organizations teaches us these distinctions.

P-H 1-i: Look again at Case Study #2 (Illustration 1-b). While Mrs. Mendoza was alive, in what kind of business arrangement did she and her husband own the construction company? After she died, how did Mr. Mendoza own the business? What kind of business organization is the owner of the City Heights Condominium Project?

P-H 1-j: Look again at Case Study #3 (Illustration 1-c). What kind of business organization is TTI? Lockland Hughes? UBA? BE?

We will not restudy the law of business organizations in this course. But remember that the study of business organizations provides you with the basic understanding of how people conduct business, and how those various business arrangements are created, operated, and regulated. This course is an extension of that area of the law as well.

P-H 1-k: Go through all three case studies introduced in Illustrations 1-a, 1-b, and 1-c and determine which business entities mentioned are properly identified as a creditor and as a debtor.

P-H 1-l: Have you studied business organizations yet? If so, refresh your recollection by summarizing the advantages and disadvantages in formation, taxation, and operation of a business as a sole proprietorship, or as a general partnership, or as a limited partnership, or as a corporation, or as a limited liability company. What is an S corporation?

Debtor/creditor law is also closely related to the study of **property law**, including both **real property** and **personal property**. We will not restudy the law of real or personal property in this course but remember the basic distinction between real property (land and things permanently attached to it like buildings, vegetation, and minerals) and personal property (things that are moveable and not realty). Remember as well what are called **intangible property interests**, which are rights recognized at law involving no ownership or possessory rights in tangible property real or personal—things such as **contract rights** (the right to receive performance under a contract) and **choses in action** (the right to sue on a cause of action such as in tort). Your study of these subjects should have provided you with the basic understanding of how title to real, personal, and intangible property is obtained and transferred, the rights and obligations of ownership of property, and how the courts enforce those various rights. In Chapter Two we will consider the topic of consensual liens: how security interests are created and enforced in real and personal property.

The topics we consider in this course will also, on occasion, require us to deal with some aspects of **tort law**.

EXAMPLE

Nick and Pearl Murphy from Case Study #1 (Illustration 1-a) have a medical malpractice action sounding in negligence for Pearl and in loss of consortium for Nick pending against the doctor who performed Pearl's emergency appendectomy and the hospital where the surgery was performed. This pending tort suit will become an asset of their estate if and when they file for bankruptcy relief.

The topics we consider in this course will sometimes require us to deal with some aspects of **criminal law**, too.

E X A M P L E

> As was noted in Case Study #2 (Illustration 1-b), David Mendoza is in danger of being charged with criminal fraud in connection with the loan he procured from City County Bank.

E X A M P L E

> As we will see when we begin our study of bankruptcy law in Part C of this text, if David Mendoza were to file for bankruptcy relief, his fraud might prevent him from discharging the debt he owes to City County Bank.

This section should enable you to appreciate that although the law is usually studied by various specialized areas, it is actually an interrelated whole. A lawyer who is handling a client matter in the debtor/creditor area, and the legal professional assisting the lawyer, must also be knowledgeable of the law in a number of related areas.

P-H 1-m: Speaking hypothetically only, if Case Study #1 (Illustration 1-a) included the fact that Nick and Pearl Murphy were in the middle of a divorce, what other area of the law would the lawyer and the assisting legal professional need to be familiar with in order to advise either of them?

P-H 1-n: Speaking hypothetically only, if the estate of Abe Mendoza's deceased wife in Case Study #2 (Illustration 1-b) was still being administered, what other area of the law would the lawyer and the assisting legal professional need to be familiar with in order to advise Mr. Mendoza?

P-H 1-o: Speaking hypothetically only, if TTI in Case Study #3 (Illustration 1-c) was a publicly traded company, what other area of the law would the lawyer and the assisting legal professional need to be familiar with in order to properly advise it?

E. ▶ The Role of the Assisting Legal Professional in Debtor/Creditor Practice and the Skills Needed

Hopefully you are beginning to see that there are a number of different roles that a paralegal or associate attorney may play in a debtor/creditor scenario depending on which lawyer they are assisting. The legal professional may be assisting the creditor's lawyer by attempting to collect past-due debt from the debtor, or she may be assisting the debtor's lawyer attempting to negotiate an extension of time for the debtor to pay the debt or attempting to negotiate a

Illustration 1-d:
LEGAL PROFESSIONAL
SKILLS NEEDED TO
WORK EFFECTIVELY IN
THE DEBTOR/ CREDI-
TOR AREA INCLUDE
THE ABILITY TO:

- Interview clients and witnesses;
- Conduct an asset search;
- Conduct a factual investigation;
- Draft the basic legal documents regularly used in debtor/creditor practice;
- Conduct legal research on debtor/creditor issues, both state and federal;
- Communicate effectively with clients, witnesses, opposing counsel, and court personnel; and
- Organize and maintain client files.

formal settlement of the dispute whereby the debtor pays less than is owed. The legal professional may be assisting the lawyer who files for bankruptcy relief for the debtor, or the lawyer representing a creditor in the bankruptcy case, or the bankruptcy trustee appointed by the bankruptcy court to administer the bankruptcy case. Keep in mind that as you learn more about the law of debtor/creditor relations you are also learning about more potential career opportunities in areas of legal specialty.

Whatever role the assisting legal professional plays in a debtor/creditor drama, the supervising attorney will expect that assistant to have a firm grasp of the law of debt creation, debt collection, and debt discharge or reorganization, the topics we cover in this text. But the supervising attorney will also expect that person to have certain legal professional skills in order to assist effectively. Those skills are listed in Illustration 1-d.

As in any area of the law, the more knowledgeable the assisting legal professional is and the more skills the assistant has developed, the more job opportunities that person will encounter and the greater job security that person will enjoy.

CHAPTER SUMMARY

The scope of debtor/creditor law includes a consideration of three distinct topics: how debt is created, how debt is collected when it goes unpaid, and how debt may be reorganized or discharged in a bankruptcy case. One primary way debt is commonly categorized is to distinguish between consumer debt and commercial or business debt. There are a number of different sources of law related to debtor/creditor issues, including primarily statutes, case law, and agency rules and regulations. The study of debtor/creditor relations overlaps with several other areas of the law related to the broad area of commercial law and there are a number of specific skills the trained legal professional must have in order to effectively assist the supervising attorney specializing in debtor/creditor issues. This chapter also introduced you to the three case studies to be used in Parts A and B.

REVIEW QUESTIONS

1. What is the distinction between consumer debt and commercial or business debt?
2. Is bankruptcy law primarily federal or state law?
3. What is the difference between liquidated and unliquidated debt?
4. Is the law controlling the creation and collection of debt primarily federal or state law?
5. What is the difference between a debt obligation being contingent or fixed?
6. List three other areas of law that are involved in the study and practice of debtor/creditor relations.
7. List seven different legal professional skills that come into play in debtor/creditor law.
8. Of the legal professional skills you listed in response to Question 7, are any more or less important than the others?
9. Explain the difference between statutes, case law, and agency rules and regulations, as well as the difference between state and federal law.
10. From the following list of debt obligations, indicate which would be properly categorized as consumer debt, business debt, or a mix of the two:

   a. Tomorrow Today, Inc. borrows money from each of its three shareholders.
   b. Abe Mendoza purchases groceries using his credit card.
   c. Nick and Pearl Murphy borrow money from a bank to consolidate their debts and grant the bank a third mortgage on their house.
   d. Rosemary Chin purchases a 70-inch, high-definition, flat-screen TV for her game room to be paid for over 36 months in equal installments.
   e. Tomorrow Today, Inc. purchases the same flat-screen TV on the same terms to place in the employee lounge in its office building.
   f. Tomorrow Today, Inc. borrows money and Rosemary Chin grants the lender a security interest in her new flat-screen TV as security for the loan.
   g. Nick and Pearl Murphy borrow money to take the family on a vacation to Hawaii.
   h. Abe Mendoza leases his personal truck to Mendoza Construction for $200 per month.

WORDS AND PHRASES TO REMEMBER

agency regulations
bond
business debt
business organizations
case law
chose in action
commercial law
consumer debt
consumer protection laws
contingent debt

contract rights
creditor
criminal law
current debt
debt
debt securities
debtor
debtor/creditor law
disputed debt
federal law

fixed debt
future debt
intangible property interests
legal professional
liquidated debt
noncontingent debt
paralegal skills
personal property
promissory note
property law

real property
secured debt
state law
statutes
tort law
Uniform Commercial Code (UCC)
undisputed debt
unliquidated debt
unsecured debt

TO LEARN MORE: A number of TLM activities to accompany this chapter are accessible on the companion web site for this textbook at http://aspen lawschool.com/books/Parsons_Debt4e/.

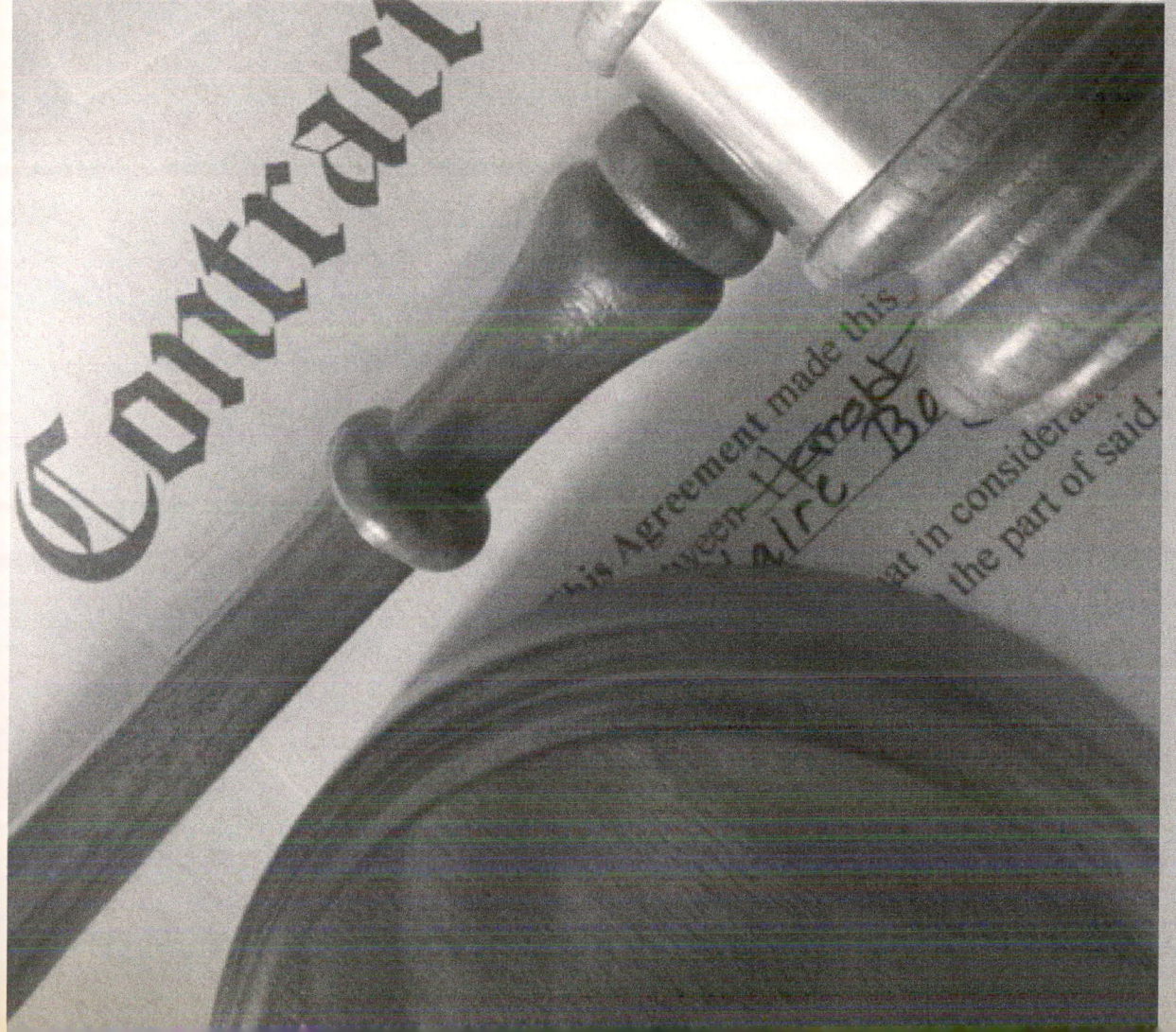

THE CREATION AND COLLECTION OF CONSUMER AND BUSINESS DEBT PRIOR TO BANKRUPTCY

Chapter Two:

▶ # Secured and Unsecured Debt

KEY CONCEPTS

- Debt can be created consensually by the making of a loan or extension of credit by a creditor to a debtor or nonconsensually by governmental mandate or court judgment
- A debt supported by nothing but the debtor's bare promise to pay is an unsecured debt
- A secured debt is one in which the creditor has rights to specific real or personal property of the debtor in addition to the debtor's promise to pay
- The creation and perfection of consensual security interests in personal property owned by a debtor is controlled by Article 9 of the Uniform Commercial Code (UCC)
- The creation and perfection of a consensual mortgage interest in a debtor's real property is controlled by the applicable state recording statute
- A consensual suretyship or guaranty arrangement is a form of security for the creditor
- Predatory lending in the form of payday loans and car title loans is a significant contributor to consumer debt

A. ▶ How Consumer and Business Debt Are Created

Consider the various kinds of debt incurred by the typical American consumer. There is debt directly related to housing—a monthly lease or mortgage payment. There is debt related to transportation—a monthly car payment or two. There is debt related to normal living expenses—food and clothing for the family, educational expenses for the kids, child care expenses for the youngest, gas for the cars, utility bills, cell phone, cable or direct streaming TV, and internet service provider. There is probably credit card debt. There may be debt for insurance premiums—life insurance, health insurance, renters or homeowners insurance. There is debt for income and property taxes. If there has been a legal separation or divorce, there may be debt for child support or alimony. A long-term debt obligation may have been undertaken with an educational loan, a loan related to a business venture, or even a loan to fund that once-in-a-lifetime vacation. There may be debt owed primarily by another but for which the consumer is liable as well by reason of having co-signed a promissory note. There may be debt associated with supporting an aging relative or a

17

struggling adult child. At any given time, there may be unexpected debt—medical bills, car and home repair bills, adverse court judgments for tortious conduct, involuntary liens placed on real or personal property—that place the consumer on or over the edge of default as to other obligations. Does any of this sound familiar?

Consider the various kinds of debt likely to be carried by a business. There is debt related to the business location(s)—either a rental obligation or a mortgage on purchased property as well as overhead related to utilities and insurance on the premises. There may be debt related to the purchase and upkeep of vehicles, equipment, and fixtures. There are accounts payable related to the order of supplies or inventory or for advertising. There are debts related to employees including not just salary and fringe benefits provided, but required payroll tax withholdings for state and federal income, Social Security, and Medicare taxes, as well as unemployment and workers' compensation insurance. There may be outstanding loans taken by the business to fund normal business operations or to expand business. There are likely outstanding balances on one or more business credit cards used by some employees in the performance of their tasks. There may be regular bills for professional advice from accountants, lawyers, and the like. There may be bills for professional or trade memberships or certifications. There will be income, use, or property taxes due on a regular basis. If the business has issued bonds or other debt securities in order to raise capital, there is the obligation to pay those as they come due long or short term. The owners and officers of an incorporated business may have signed personal guaranties so that the debt of the business is also a liability of the individual owners/officers. At any given time, there may be unexpected events—vehicle or workplace accidents, failing equipment, business interruptions due to weather or human events, loss of a key person, unexpected business downturns, legal claims or lawsuits alleging breach of contract or violation of employee rights or tortious conduct—that place the business on or over the edge of default as to other obligations. If you are now or ever have been a business owner, does any of this sound familiar?

As you ruminate over this summary of typical consumer and business debt and try to not get depressed, consider in general how debt is created. Most debt is created consensually, by contract. Such contracts may be verbal and fairly informal though certainly enforceable (e.g., hiring a plumber who leaves an invoice to be paid within 30 days of finishing the work, the doctor's bill that arrives weeks after the treatment, agreements to pay the babysitter at the end of the evening, the loan to a friend, relative or co-worker on a "pay it back when you can" basis). Other agreements creating debt obligations are reduced to formal written contracts in either paper or electronic format (credit card agreements; cell phone, cable TV, internet service provider contracts; construction contracts; employment agreements; a business's purchase of inventory or materials from a supplier; loans and lines of credit from banks and other financial services companies).

Promissory note A contract containing an enforceable promise by one person to repay another person the principal amount owed together with a stated amount of interest.

In contracts involving the borrowing of money or the extension of a line of credit, the operative contractual document that is executed is the **promissory note**. In a promissory note the debtor formally promises to repay the amount borrowed over a certain period of time at a designated rate of interest.

EXAMPLE

Nick and Pearl Murphy borrow $110,000 from First Bank of Capital City (FBCC) to purchase their home on Cherry Street in Capital City. FBCC requires the Murphys to sign a promissory note setting forth the terms under which the Murphys agree to repay the loaned amount to FBCC. The note signed by the Murphys in favor of FBCC is set out in Illustration 2-a. The Murphys are the borrowers (or simply debtors) and FBCC is the lender (or simply creditor). As a negotiable instrument, promissory notes are governed by Article 3 of the UCC. In Article 3 terms, the Murphys are the **makers** of the note (the ones who sign it and promise to pay; also called the **payors**) and FBCC is the **payee** (the one who is to be paid) on the note. As the original payee, FBCC is also the **holder** of the note but may sell and assign it to a subsequent holder. The note will state the principal amount borrowed (often referred to simply as the principal) and the agreed term over which the makers promise to repay it (e.g., 5 years, 10 years, 30 years) and it will state the rate of **interest** (per year) the makers promise to pay on the unpaid principal. Interest is the cost of using a lender's money.

Interest The cost of using another person's money (e.g., 5%, 7%, 10%) **per annum**.

EXAMPLE

To finance its operations over the next 12 months, Tomorrow Today, Inc. (TTI from Case Study #3, Illustration 1-c) borrows the amount of $1 million from FBCC and signs a **promissory note** agreeing to repay the amount borrowed within 30 days following the end of the business year plus a stated rate of interest per annum. Debt is created.

Per annum Per year.

Line of credit A loan in which the borrowed funds are not immediately advanced to the borrower but are put at the disposal of the borrower to draw down on as needed.

As an alternative to borrowing a certain sum of money from a lender all at once on a given day, an individual or business may enter into a contractual **extension of credit** from a lender as by an approved credit card authorizing purchases up to a certain dollar limit; or by an approved **line of credit loan** (also called **revolving credit**) authorizing the borrower to draw down on the line of credit as needed; or by the purchase of goods and services with payment due within some period of time following delivery of the goods or performance of the service.

EXAMPLE

Recall from Illustration 1-c that five years ago, when it began work on the MIES project, TTI obtained a $10 million line of credit from United Bank of America. And TTI went through that line of credit over a three-year period. What that means is that TTI drew funds from the approved $10 million line of credit, not all at once, but as needed from time to time. It might have drawn $500,000 at the beginning of its work on the MIES project, then $250,000 six months later, and so on. That's how a line of credit works.

Illustration 2-a: PROMISSORY NOTE

PROMISSORY NOTE

January 12, YR-10   At Capital City, Yourstate

1. MAKERS' PROMISE TO PAY: In return for a loan in the principal amount of one hundred and fifteen thousand dollars ($115,000) that we, Nicholas W. Murphy, and wife, Pearl E. Murphy (hereinafter the "Makers"), have received from First Bank of Capital City (hereinafter the "Lender"), the Makers do hereby promise to repay to Lender the principal amount of $115,000 plus interest as set forth in Paragraph 2.

2. INTEREST: Interest will be charged on unpaid principal until the principal amount has been paid in full. Makers will pay interest on unpaid principal at the rate of 8.00% per year from the date of the making of this Promissory Note until the date the principal is paid in full. Interest hereunder shall be computed on the basis of a three hundred sixty (360) day year. Notwithstanding anything herein to the contrary, in no event shall interest payable hereunder be in excess of the maximum rate allowed by applicable law.

3. TERM AND PAYMENT: Makers will repay the principal amount to Lender with interest as provided in Paragraph 2 by making three hundred and sixty (360) consecutive monthly payments of $843.83 each beginning February 1, YR-10 and continuing on the first day of each month thereafter until completed. Payment shall be made at 111 Broad Street, Capital City, Yourstate, or at such other place as the Lender or its successor(s) or assign(s) shall stipulate.

4. RIGHT OF ASSIGNMENT: Lender has the express right to assign or sell this Promissory Note in which case the assignee or buyer, as Holder, shall have all the rights of Lender under this Promissory Note including this right of assignment. Makers are prohibited from transferring this Promissory Note or any obligations under it without the prior written consent of Lender or its successor(s) or assign(s).

5. DEFAULT: If Lender fails to receive payment from Makers of any monthly payments called for in Paragraph 3 by the tenth day of any month in which a payment is due, or if default is made in the payment of the indebtedness hereunder at maturity, or in the event of default in or breach of any of the terms, provisions or conditions of this Promissory Note or any instrument evidencing or securing the indebtedness evidenced hereby, or any other instrument evidencing indebtedness from Makers, or either of them, to Lender, Makers will then be in DEFAULT. In that event, at the option of the Lender, the entire amount of the indebtedness will become immediately due and payable. Further in that event, the whole of the unpaid principal and any accrued interest shall, to the extent permitted by law, bear interest at the highest lawful rate then in effect pursuant to applicable law, or at the rate provided herein in the event no highest applicable rate is then in effect. Furthermore in that event, Lender shall be entitled to pursue all remedies available to it at law and/or equity to collect all amounts due under this Promissory Note and Makers shall pay all costs and expenses of collection, including court costs and a reasonable attorneys' fee, incurred by or on behalf of Lender in collecting the amounts due under this Promissory Note to the extent not prohibited by applicable law. Lender's failure to declare a default due to Makers' failure to make any monthly payment as called for in this Promissory Note shall not waive or otherwise prejudice Lender's right to declare a default in connection with Makers' failure to make any other monthly payment as called for in this Promissory Note.

6. SECURED NOTE: All amounts due from Makers under the terms of this Promissory Note and all extensions, modifications, renewals or amendments thereof is secured by a Mortgage of even date with the Promissory Note on certain real property located at 3521 West Cherry Street in Capital City, Yourstate, a more complete description of which is set forth in said Mortgage.

7. RIGHT TO PREPAY: Makers have the right to make payments on the Promissory Note before the due date as determined in Paragraph 3 without premium or other prepayment charge. All prepayments will be applied first to principal until the principal amount is paid in full.

8. WAIVERS: Makers expressly waive the right of presentment and notice of dishonor, and notice of non-payment, protest, notice of protest, bringing of suit, and diligence in taking any action to claim the amounts owing hereunder and are and shall be jointly and severally, directly and primarily liable for the amount of all sums owing and to be owing under the terms of this Promissory Note and agree that this Promissory Note, or any payment hereunder, may be extended from time to time without affecting such liability. "Presentment" means the right to require the Lender or its successor(s) or assign(s) to demand payment of amounts due. "Notice of dishonor" means the right to require Lender or its successor(s) or assign(s) to give notice to other persons that amounts due have not been paid.

9. NATURE OF REMEDIES: The remedies of the Lender as provided in this Promissory Note, or in the Mortgage securing this Promissory Note, or in any other instrument evidencing or securing this Promissory Note, shall be cumulative and concurrent, and may be pursued singularly, successively, or together, at the sole discretion of the Lender, and may be exercised as often as occasion therefor shall arise. No act or omission of the Lender, including specifically any failure to exercise any right, remedy, or recourse, shall be deemed to be a waiver or release of the same, such waiver or release to be effected only through a written document executed by the Lender and then only to the extent specifically recited therein. A waiver or release with reference to any one event shall not be construed as continuing, as a bar to, or as a waiver or release of, any subsequent right, remedy or recourse as to a subsequent event.

10. TIME OF THE ESSENCE: Time is of the essence of this Promissory Note.

11. GOVERNING LAW: This Promissory Note, the Mortgage securing this Promissory Note and any other instrument securing this Promissory Note shall be governed by and construed under the laws of the State of Yourstate.

12. CONSTRUCTION OF TERMS: Where used herein the singular shall refer to the plural, the plural to the singular, and the masculine or feminine shall refer to any gender. If Maker is composed of more than one person or entity, "Makers" as used herein shall refer to any and all persons or entities constituting Makers, as the circumstances may require.

13. TERMS BINDING ON SUCCESSORS: The provisions of this Promissory Note shall be binding upon the parties, their heirs, successors, and assigns.

14. SEVERABILITY OF TERMS: The provisions of this Promissory Note are severable such that the invalidity or unenforceability of any provision hereof shall not affect the validity or enforceability of the remaining provisions.

WITNESS OUR HANDS ON THE DATE ABOVE WRITTEN:

_____
Nicholas W. Murphy (Maker)

_____
Pearl E. Murphy (Maker)

EXAMPLE

Nick and Pearl Murphy buy a new washer and dryer from Shears Department Store and agree to pay off the purchase price in installments over the next 24 months. Debt has been created by the extension of credit by Shears (the seller or creditor) to the Murphys (the buyers or debtors). This debt will likely be secured by Shears retaining a security interest in the washer and dryer until payment is complete.

EXAMPLE

Abe Mendoza fills out an application for a Visa credit card to be issued by a local bank and the application is approved. The card is mailed to Mendoza along with notification that he has a $2,500 credit limit on the card. The bank issuing the Visa card has agreed to provide Mendoza with up to $2,500 credit. Debt is created when he uses the card.

A common line of credit loan in consumer lending is the **home equity loan.** **Equity** is the debtor's ownership interest in property measured by the difference between the market value of the property and the balance of any outstanding indebtedness for which the property serves as collateral. It is sometimes referred to as **owner's equity**.

EXAMPLE

We saw in Illustration 1-a that Nick and Pearl Murphy bought their home ten years ago for $125,000 and they still owe First Bank of Capital City (FBCC) $92,500 on the first mortgage. Three years ago, shortly before Pearl's botched appendectomy, the appraised value of the house had increased to $140,000 and the balance on mortgage to FBCC had been reduced to $99,000 leaving them about $41,000 of owner's equity in the home, the difference between its value and the amount owed on the mortgage against it. At that time the Murphys decided to add two rooms onto the house and arranged a $35,000 home equity line of credit from Teacher's Credit Union (TCU). TCU took a second mortgage on the house to secure repayment of the loan. TCU was willing to do so because the appraised value of the house ($140,000) was sufficient to cover the balance then owed to FBCC ($99,000) plus the amount of its loan ($35,000).

Usury Charging an illegal rate of interest for a loan.

Amortized Payments calculated on an installment note so that each installment payment of principal and interest is equal despite the declining principal balance.

P-H 2-a: Look at the promissory note of Nick and Pearl Murphy in Illustration 2-a and answer the following questions:

1. What is the interest rate the lender is charging the Murphys on the borrowed funds during the repayment period? Generally speaking, the rate of interest charged on a loan can be whatever the parties agree. But many states have criminal statutes that set the maximum legal rate of interest that can be charged in different types of financial transactions. If the creditor attempts to charge in excess of the statutory rate, it is considered **usury** and the creditor can be prosecuted criminally. What is the significance of the last sentence of Paragraph 2 of the note?

2. The Murphys' note is to be repaid over a term of 30 years or 360 months. The note is also **amortized** meaning the payments have been calculated in a way to

make them equal in total amount over the 360 months of the term even though each individual installment includes a differing amount of principal and interest. What monetary advantage would there be to a home purchaser choosing a repayment term of 25, 20, or 15 years rather than 30 years? Recall that Tomorrow Today, Inc. (TTI) from Case Study #3 (Illustration 1-c) needs to borrow an additional $5 million in order to finish the prototype of the MIES. Based on the information given to you about TTI and the MIES project in Illustration 1-c, over what term should TTI seek to repay this $5 million loan, if it is able to locate a willing lender? Why did you choose the term you did?

3. Payments on the Murphys' note are made in installments due each month of the term and include some amount of principal and interest. It is an **installment note.** But the installments need not be monthly. Not uncommonly in business transactions, the note will call for quarterly or annual payments. Or it may be unamortized and call for payments of interest only until the end of the term or for no payments at all until the end of the term when all principal and interest come due (called a **balloon note** because the payment balloons at the end of the term). Assume a lender advertises a home mortgage loan with this attractive feature: Three times a year, the borrower, making monthly installment payments, can reduce his or her payment by paying interest only (no principal) that month. So, for example, if the borrower's monthly payments of principal and interest total $1,200 and next month $650 of that payment will go to interest and $550 to reduce the principal balance, for that month, the borrower may make a payment of only $650 and not be in default. Borrower does not have to make the $550 payment on principal that month. And the borrower can do this up to three times a year at his or her option. Why would that option be facially appealing to a borrower? Why would it likely be unwise for the borrower to exercise that option?

4. Look at Paragraph 7 of the note. Can the Murphys make a payment on the note before it becomes due? What is the advantage to them of doing so? Why would a lender prohibit the maker from making early payments or impose a fee or penalty on the maker for doing so as some notes do?

5. The Murphys' note is a **fixed rate note**—the interest rate does not change throughout the term of the note. But the interest rate specified in the note could be variable, that is, it could change periodically (e.g., every quarter, six months, or annually) based upon some agreed formula or index such as U.S. Treasury Bill rates or the **prime rate** (the interest rate that commercial banks charge their best customers). **Variable rate notes** (also called **adjustable rate notes**) are common in both consumer and business transactions.

6. Look at Paragraph 4 of the Murphys' note. Can the lender assign this note and the right to receive payments from the Murphys to another holder? Can the Murphys assign this note and thus delegate the obligation to make payments due under the note to another? Why would the lender/payee want this one-sided **non-assignment** clause in the note?

7. Is the Murphys' note a secured or unsecured obligation? Look at Paragraph 6 of the note.

Prime rate The interest rate that commercial banks charge their best customers.

Variable rate note A promissory note containing a rate of interest that varies during the term of the loan.

Credit report A compilation of the debt history and bill-paying record of a consumer.

Credit reporting agencies Companies in the business of compiling credit reports and providing them to creditors and other authorized persons.

Before a lender loans money or extends credit to a borrower, the lender will typically want to access the borrower's **credit report** to determine the borrower's **credit worthiness**. A credit report is a compilation by a **credit reporting agency** (CRA) of the debt history and bill-payment record of a borrower. There are 30-some-odd true CRAs around the country but only three nationally recognized agencies:

- Experian (www.experian.com)
- Equifax (www.equifax.com) and
- TransUnion (www.transunion.com)

These three CRAs maintain records on more than 200 million Americans compiled from more than 10,000 information providers. To Learn More (TLM) activity 2-1, accessible on the companion web site to this textbook at http://aspenlawschool.com/books/Parsons_Debt4e/, contains supplementary material on the credit reporting process and regulation of CRAs under the **Fair Credit Reporting Act** for those who want to know more about this important subject.

Not all debt is created by consensual agreement. State and local governments and the federal government have various legislative enactments or **statutes** (**ordinances** in the case of local governments) and various **agency rules and regulations** that will operate to create debt as a matter of law (without consent of the debtor or any court action). The tax laws are a prime example. If you have income taxable by the federal or state governments, or if you own real property subject to state or local property taxes, debt is created without your consent. If you don't pay those taxes as they become due, the government entity that assessed the taxes will take legal action to collect them from you. We will learn how that happens when we consider tax liens in the next chapter.

Other examples of debt created by law arise from the fact that many federal, state, and local agencies and departments given oversight over commercial and public activities are empowered to create debt by assessing fines and penalties pursuant to statute or agency rule or regulation.

EXAMPLE

You are late for work and so you drive faster than you should. A city police officer stops you and gives you a speeding ticket or citation for violating the relevant city ordinance setting the speed limit on the street where you were stopped. That citation from the city government creates debt. At this point, since you might be able to contest liability in court, we would say that the citation represents contingent contested debt, but debt just the same.

EXAMPLE

The Environmental Protection Agency (EPA) inspects the paper mill in your city and finds that the mill is violating the Clean Air Act and EPA regulations promulgated under it. A $500-a-day fine is assessed by the EPA against the mill until the violation stops.

Debt can also be created by court judgment. Recall that Nick and Pearl Murphy (Illustration 1-a, Case Study #1) have a professional malpractice claim for Pearl and a loss of consortium claim for Nick pending against the doctor who

Final judgment An order or decree entered by a court finally resolving the issues before it.

Judgment creditor/ debtor Once a final judgment is entered by a court awarding a money judgment to one party, the party to whom the judgment is awarded is the judgment creditor and the one against whom it is awarded is the judgment debtor.

performed Pearl's appendectomy and the hospital where that surgery was performed. The Murphys are asking for a total of $1.5 million in damages from the two defendants in their tort suit. While the lawsuit is pending, the Murphys only have a liability claim against the defendants, an intangible property interest known as a chose in action as we considered in Chapter One. Prior to entry of final judgment on their claim, the obligation of Dr. Craft and Capital City Hospital to the Murphys is properly categorized as contingent, disputed, and unliquidated. But if the Murphys prevail in their lawsuit, the court will enter a **final judgment** in their favor against one or both defendants. At that point the Murphys will be considered **judgment creditors** as to any defendant against whom they obtain a judgment. And each defendant against whom the judgment is entered is considered a **judgment debtor**. Debt has been created, but note that it was not created by contract or by law; it was created by court judgment.

 B.

Distinguishing Secured and Unsecured Debt

A debt supported by nothing more than the debtor's bare promise to pay is an **unsecured debt**. If the debtor defaults on the obligation, the remedy of the creditor will be to file a collection lawsuit in the appropriate court, obtain a final judgment against the debtor, and then to utilize authorized methods of executing on the final judgment in order to seize the assets of the debtor and liquidate (sell) them in order to satisfy the final judgment. Judicial debt collection is a topic we will examine in Chapter Five.

A lot of consumer and business debt is unsecured: most credit card debt and most debt related to the routine purchase of goods and services, for example. But a creditor asked to make a loan of money or extend a line of credit to a consumer or business debtor may require more than the debtor's bare promise to repay. The creditor demands additional security for the repayment of the debt and bargains for the debtor to grant the creditor a security interest in the debtor's real (e.g., the consumer debtor's home or the business debtor's office or factory) or personal property (e.g., the consumer debtor's family vehicle or the business debtor's inventory, equipment, vehicles, accounts receivable, and cash) that authorizes the creditor to take possession of and sell the designated property in the event of default and apply the proceeds to the balance owed. This is a **secured debt**.

Mortgage The consensual security interest in real property granted by a debtor to a creditor that entitles the creditor upon default to take possession of and sell the realty and apply the proceeds to the balance owed.

Security interest An interest granted by a debtor to a creditor in real or personal property of the debtor authorizing the creditor to seize and sell the collateralized property to satisfy the debt obligation in the event of a default.

Generally, if the property in which the security interest is granted is realty, we say the creditor has a **mortgage** in the real property; the debtor is the **mortgagor** and the creditor is the **mortgagee**. If the designated property is personal property, we simply say the creditor holds a security interest in the property. In either event (realty or personalty), there is a consensual **lien** or **encumbrance** on the property of the debtor in favor of the creditor. The property, real or personal, on which the lien is granted, is sometimes referred to as the **collateral** securing the obligation.

Assuming the collateral has value, the secured creditor is in a much more favorable position than the unsecured creditor when default occurs. The secured creditor can take possession of and liquidate that property more quickly and inexpensively than the unsecured creditor can. And if the secured creditor has properly perfected his security interest in the collateral, he enjoys a priority position as to it that prevents any unsecured creditor or any other secured creditor with a junior position in the collateral from taking it before him. Perfection of a security interest and priority disputes are discussed in more detail below where we consider consensual security interests in personalty and realty separately. As we will see later in our study, the favorable position enjoyed by the properly perfected secured creditor in the collateral continues into a bankruptcy case filed by the debtor.

C. ▶ Consensual Security Interests in Personal Property of the Debtor

Issues regarding the creation, attachment, and perfection of security interests in personal property in consumer cases are governed by Article 9 of the Uniform Commercial Code (UCC) adopted with some variations in all 50 states. Since Secured Transactions is a separate and often required course, only a quick summary of that statutory scheme is offered here.

1. Creation and Attachment of a Security Interest in Personal Property

Creation and attachment of a security interest in personal property is governed in the first instance by UCC §9-203, which in general requires that the debtor must have rights in the property named as collateral (the **nominated property** or the **collateralized property**) and the power to transfer those rights (i.e., you can't grant a security interest in property you have no ownership interest in), that the creditor must give value in exchange for the granting of the interest in the property named as collateral, and that the debtor must sign or otherwise authenticate a **security agreement** containing an adequate description of the collateral.

EXAMPLE

> When Nick and Pearl Murphy bought their living room furniture from Shears and arranged to pay for it over 48 months, Shears retained a security interest in the furniture to secure payment of the purchase price in the security agreement that is set out in Illustration 2-b). This is a secured debt and the security interest retained by Shears is controlled by Article 9 since the collateral is personal property.

Lenders often require business borrowers to grant a security interest in all debtor's personal property as security for loans or other financial obligations in which case we say the lender holds a **blanket lien** on the assets of borrower.

EXAMPLE

> Assume Company A arranges a $20 million line of credit from Bank. To obtain the loan, Company A grants Bank a security interest in "all debtor's assets, including without limitation equipment, inventory, furnishings, supplies, vehicles, cash on hand, bank accounts, accounts receivable, and fixtures." Bank has been granted a blanket lien on the personal assets of Company A.

Illustration 2-b: SECURITY AGREEMENT BETWEEN NICK AND PEARL MURPHY AND SHEARS DEPARTMENT STORE

Installment Sale and Security Agreement

This Agreement is made and entered into this 10th day of May, YR-1, by and between Shears Department Store (Seller) and Nicholas W. Murphy and wife, Pearl E. Murphy (Buyers) who reside at 3521 West Cherry Street, Capital City, Yourstate. The Seller agrees to sell and the Buyers agree to buy the following, hereinafter referred to as the Merchandise, on the terms set forth in this Agreement:

> 1 Comfort Tone couch ($2,499); 2 Comfort Tone Spread Eagle Chairs @ $550 each ($1,100); 1 Comfort Tone Loveseat ($950); 1 American Federal Coffee Table ($350); 2 American Federal End Tables @ $200 each ($400).

1. **Price and Payment**. The total net purchase price of the Merchandise is $5,299. Buyers, having elected to pay for the Merchandise in installments as set forth in this Agreement, agree to pay Seller or its assigns the time price of the Merchandise which is $6,122.40 in 48 equal monthly installments at Seller's offices at P.O. Box 22234 Atlanta, GA 404456 or at any other address which Seller may direct in writing delivered to Buyers. The time price of the Merchandise represents the net purchase price paid over 48 monthly installments at an annual percentage rate of 7%.

Payable in 48 consecutive monthly installments of $127.55 each, except the last installment shall be the balance due.

First installment due June 1, YR-1 and each subsequent installment due on the first day of the following month.

2. **Warranties**. No representations or statements have been made by Seller concerning the Merchandise except as stated in this Agreement, and no warranty, express or implied, by Seller, arises apart from this writing. Buyers warrant that the Merchandise is purchased for use primarily for personal, family, or household purposes.

3. **Retention of security interest**. Until all installment payments, and all other amounts due under this Agreement, have been paid, Seller shall retain a security interest in the Merchandise and any and all equipment, parts, accessories, attachments, additions, and other Merchandise, and all replacements of them, installed in, affixed to, or used in connection with the Merchandise and, if Buyers sell or otherwise dispose of the Merchandise or any portion of it in violation of the terms of this Agreement, in the proceeds of such sale or disposition.

4. **Events of default**. The occurrence of any of the following shall constitute a default under this Agreement: (1) failure of Buyers to perform any obligation or Agreement specified in this Agreement, or if any warranty or representation made under this Agreement by Buyers should prove to be materially incorrect; (2) the sale or other transfer of title to the Merchandise by Buyers including the granting of any security interest in the Merchandise by Buyers without the prior written consent of Seller; (3) the institution of any proceeding in bankruptcy, receivership or insolvency against Buyers; (4) the issuance of execution process against any property of Buyers or the entry of any judgment against Buyers or any assignment for benefit of creditors; (5) when Seller shall in good faith and upon reasonable grounds believe that the prospect of performance of any obligation of Buyers under this Agreement, or of performance or payment of any obligation secured by this Agreement, by Buyers is materially diminished.

5. **Remedies on default**. In the event of a default, or if Seller or Seller's assignee shall consider the payment of the balance of the installment payments insecure, Seller shall have the right to: (1) obtain judgment for the amount of the installments delinquent under the Agreement plus interest at 6% on such delinquent payments from due date and reasonable attorney's fees without prejudicing Seller's right to subsequently obtain

judgment for additional, or the balance of, the installments or to exercise other rights contained in this Agreement or at its option, declare all unpaid installments and other moneys due or to become due under this Agreement immediately due and payable and to obtain judgment for the total amount of unpaid installments due plus interest of 6% on delinquent payments from due date and reasonable attorney's fees; (2) enter any premises and without breach of the peace take possession of the Merchandise; and (3) exercise the rights on default of a secured party under the Uniform Commercial Code. Seller shall have the right to take immediate possession of the Merchandise wherever found, with or without legal process, and to sell or otherwise dispose of the Merchandise. Unless the Merchandise is perishable or threatens to decline speedily in value or is of a type customarily sold on a recognized market, Seller will give Buyers at least five days notice by mail of the time and place of any public sale of the Merchandise or the time after which any private sale or other intended disposition is to be made. The requirements of reasonable notice shall be met if such notice is mailed, postage prepaid, to the address of the Buyers shown at the beginning of this Agreement or such other address of Buyers as may from time to time be shown on Seller's records, at least five days prior to such action. Buyers will pay any deficiency that may remain after exercise of such rights plus expenses of retaking, holding, preparing for sale, selling, or the like, including Seller's reasonable attorney's fees. All of Seller's rights under this Agreement are cumulative and no waiver of any default shall affect any later default.

6. **Miscellaneous terms and provisions**. (1) Loss or damage to the Merchandise will not release Buyers. (2) Repairs to the Merchandise and equipment or accessories placed on the Merchandise shall be at Buyers' expense and shall constitute component parts of the Merchandise, subject to the terms of this Agreement. (3) If any part of this Agreement is adjudged invalid, the remainder will not be invalidated by this. (4) Seller may assign this Agreement but Buyers shall not. Seller's assignee shall have all of the rights, powers and remedies of Seller but shall be subject to none of Seller's obligations. (5) Buyers will not assert against any assignee of this Agreement any defense which Buyers may have against Seller. (6) If there be more than one signer of this Agreement, their obligations shall be joint and several and each specifically waive presentment or demand and agree that any extension or extensions of time of payment of this Agreement or any installment or part installment may be made before, at or after maturity by Agreement with any one or more of the parties, and they waive any right which they may have to require the holder to proceed against any person. (7) This Agreement will be governed by the laws of the State of Yourstate, and all obligations of Buyers shall bind their heirs, executor, administrator or successors.

7. **Exclusive statement of Agreement**. This writing contains the full, final, and exclusive statement of the Agreement between the parties and no Agreement or warranty shall be binding on the Seller unless expressly contained in it.

_____

Nicholas W. Murphy

_____

Pearl E. Murphy

Shears Department Store, Inc.

By: _____

Wally Cousins, V-P

Once the security agreement is properly executed the security interest of the creditor has attached to the collateral and will be enforced upon default by the debtor. **Attachment** of a security interest controls the rights to the collateral as between the debtor and the creditor but not the rights of other creditors who may seek possession of the collateralized property in order to satisfy an obligation the debtor owes to them. In order to gain priority over other creditors as to the collateral, the creditor must **perfect** its security interest in that collateral.

2. The Scope of a Security Interest in Personal Property: The Floating Lien

Proceeds of the Collateral

Article 9 provides that the security interest granted in collateral extends not only to the named collateral itself, but also to the **proceeds** of that collateral.

EXAMPLE

Assume that in the security agreement between TTI and Bank of Europa (Case Study #3, Illustration 1-c), TTI grants BE a security interest in all its equipment. Assume TTI later sells a piece of equipment and receives money for that sold equipment. If TTI then defaults on repayment and BE seizes the remaining collateralized equipment, can it also seize the money received for the equipment sold? Yes, because the money is proceeds of equipment that was collateral and is also subject to BE's security interest. Another way to say this is that the security interest of BE attached to the money as soon as it was in the possession of TTI as the proceeds of the sold equipment. What if TTI swaps the equipment pledged as collateral to BE for new equipment instead of receiving money for the pledged equipment? Does BE's security interest attach to the new equipment? Yes, because the new equipment will be considered proceeds of the pledged equipment. Proceeds do not have to be money.

Although the security agreement often specifies that the proceeds of pledged collateral are also subject to the creditor's security interest, it doesn't have to. Article 9 provides for the *automatic attachment* of the security interest to proceeds whether that is stated in the security agreement or not.

After-acquired Property

After-acquired property is property the debtor acquires *after* the security agreement has been executed. Article 9 authorizes the security agreement to provide that the creditor's security interest will attach to **after-acquired property** as soon as the debtor acquires an interest in it, and no new or additional security agreement needs to be executed to accomplish that attachment. See Illustration 2-c.

Illustration 2-c: AFTER-ACQUIRED PROPERTY LANGUAGE IN A SECURITY AGREEMENT

Debtor (TTI) grants to Secured Party (BE) a security interest in all inventory, equipment, appliances, furnishings, and fixtures now or hereafter placed upon any business premises utilized by Debtor or used in connection with Debtor's business and in which Debtor now has or hereafter acquires any ownership interest.

Assume the security agreement between TTI and BE contains the language you see in Illustration 2-c. Now assume that after executing the security agreement, TTI purchases new inventory to sell or a brand new piece of equipment to use in its business. Neither the new inventory nor the new piece of equipment is proceeds of any previously pledged property. Are the new inventory and new piece of equipment subject to BE's security interest? Yes, because of the "hereafter" phrases in the security agreement in Illustration 2-c.

Future advances A loan or credit extended to a debtor that is subject to a previously created security interest in property of the debtor.

Future Advances or Other Indebtedness

Article 9 allows a security agreement to secure debt other than the specific debt being secured by the security agreement—that is, to **future advances** of money or credit to the debtor or to other indebtedness of the debtor to the creditor. See Illustration 2-d.

Illustration 2-d: FUTURE ADVANCES/OTHER INDEBTEDNESS CLAUSE IN A SECURITY AGREEMENT

> The security interest granted by Debtor (TTI) to Secured Party (BE) in Paragraph 2 of this Agreement shall secure all advances made by Secured Party under the line of credit referenced herein and any and all other indebtedness or liability that Debtor now owes or shall ever owe to Secured Party, its successors, and assigns, whether as principal obligor or as guarantor or co-signer.

Assume that the security agreement between TTI and BE contains the language shown in Illustration 2-d. Assume further that TTI pays off its borrowings under the line of credit with BE. Five years later, BE merges with Bank of North America (BNA). A year after that TTI takes out a $10 million loan from BNA secured, TTI thinks, only by a mortgage TTI gives BNA. TTI then defaults on the debt to BNA and is surprised when BNA acts to repossess all the personal property TTI pledged to BE all those years ago. Can BNA do that? Yes. It is the "successor" to BE, and the security agreement between BE and TTI effectively pledged the personal property as security—not just for the BE line of credit, but all future debts TTI might ever owe to BE or its successors.

Like after-acquired property clauses, future advances clauses must be specifically set out in the security agreement to be effective. Future advances clauses are common and very dangerous to the unsuspecting, unsophisticated borrower. Moreover, future advances clauses are commonly used, not just in security agreements, but in other contracts evidencing debt, such as promissory notes, mortgages, and guaranty agreements.

P-H 2-b: Assume the Murphys pay off their debt to Shears for the purchase of the living room furniture that is secured by that furniture. But later they run up other charges with Shears for which no specific security interest is granted and are unable to pay. Shears wants to repossess the furniture in satisfaction of those later debts. Look at paragraph 3 of Illustration 2-b. Does that security agreement contain a future advances clause? Can Shears repossess the furniture now?

P-H 2-c: Does either the promissory note signed by the Murphys to borrow money to buy their house (Illustration 2-a) or the mortgage they gave on the house to secure that note (Illustration 2-e) contain a future advances clause?

The concept of a security interest in collateral extending to proceeds of the collateral, to after-acquired property, or to future advances is sometimes referred to as the **floating lien** concept of security law. In each situation, the security interest granted moves or floats from one item of property to another or from one debt to another.

3. Perfection and Priority of a Security Interest in Personal Property

How a Security Interest in Personal Property Is Perfected

For most kinds of personalty, the creditor perfects its security interest by filing a **financing statement** (also known as a UCC-1) that complies with UCC §9-502 with the local (county) or state office designated in UCC §9-501 thus giving public notice (and constructive notice to the world) of its interest in the collateral. Alternatively, the creditor can perfect its security interest by taking physical possession of the collateral (e.g., jewelry, stock certificates, or certificates of deposit given as collateral and left with creditor) in which case we say that the property has been **pledged** to the creditor pursuant to UCC §9-313. If the collateral is property for which the state issues a **certificate of title** (e.g., automobiles, watercraft, motor homes), perfection of the security interest is achieved by noting the creditor's interest on the certificate of title itself rather than by filing a financing statement. See UCC §9-311.

EXAMPLE

If Tomorrow Today, Inc. borrows money from Bank and grants Bank a security interest in its accounts receivables, equipment, supplies, inventory, and cash to Bank to secure the loan, TTI will execute a security agreement creating Bank's security interest in the named collateral. At that point, Bank's security interest in the collateral has attached and if TTI defaults on repayment of the loan, Bank can repossess and sell the collateral. However, to perfect its security interest in the collateral Bank must file a financing statement in the proper public office designated in the state's version of Article 9. If the security agreement also grants Bank a security interest in its vehicles, Bank will perfect by having its interest noted on the certificates of title to the vehicles. If the security agreement also grants Bank a security interest in certificates of deposit owned by TTI and those certificates are in the Bank's possession, they are pledged to the Bank and the security interest of Bank in the CDs is automatically perfected.

Purchase money security interest A consensual security interest granted to one who has sold property to the debtor or loaned the purchase price for the property to the debtor.

A particular perfection issue that arises frequently in consumer bankruptcy cases is the **purchase money security interest** (PMSI) in consumer goods. Per UCC §9-103 a purchase money security interest arises in favor of a *vendor* who sells goods to a buyer on credit and retains a security interest in the goods to secure payment of the purchase price or a *lender* who loans a debtor money to enable purchase of goods and takes a security interest in the goods purchased with the loan.

E X A M P L E

> Nick and Pearl Murphy purchased living room furniture from Shears Department Store on credit and Shears had them execute the Installment Sale and Security Agreement seen in Illustration 2-b. Shears has a security interest in the furniture to secure payment of the purchase price. Shears has a PMSI in the furniture since it was the vendor extending the credit to the Murphys to enable the purchase. Had a bank loaned the money to the Murphys for the purchase, it too would have a PMSI in the furniture. On the other hand, if Nick and Pearl had already owned the furniture but grant a security interest in it to Bank in exchange for a loan, Bank would not have a PMSI in the furniture and would have to file a financing statement in order to perfect its security interest in the furniture.

UCC §9-309(1) provides that a PMSI in consumer goods is **automatically perfected** upon attachment without the filing of a financing statement by the secured creditor. Thus in the last example, Shears is automatically perfected in the living room furniture as soon as the Murphys purchase the furniture and sign the security agreement. This is true because Shears is a vendor being granted a security interest in property it sold to the Murphys on credit and because the property sold is consumer property.

P-H 2-d: Assume that after the Murphys purchase the furniture on credit from Shears and grant Shears a security interest in the furniture, they then borrow money from Bank and grant Bank a security interest in the same furniture. Does Bank have a PMSI in the furniture per UCC §9-103? Is Bank's security interest in the furniture automatically perfected per UCC §9-309(1)? If not, can it perfect its security interest in the furniture and, if so, how will it do so? Which creditor of the Murphys holds the senior lien in the furniture and which holds the junior lien?

Priority Among Competing Claims to the Collateral

It is difficult to understate the significance of the determination of whether and when a secured creditor is perfected in collateral. If the creditor's security interest in the collateral has been created and attached, that means, as between the creditor and the debtor, the creditor can exercise its rights against the collateral in the event of default. Whether the creditor's security interest is also perfected matters not at all in such a dispute. But perfection does matter when there is another party pursuing the collateral—an unsecured creditor now holding a final judgment and seeking to execute on the property or a second secured creditor granted a security interest in the same collateral as the first creditor. And it is not unusual at all for a debtor to grant a security interest in its property to more than one creditor. TTI may grant a security interest in its personalty to Bank #1 today and six months later borrow from Bank #2 and grant Bank #2 a security interest in the same collateral. (Or, in the context of realty, to be considered in the next section, homeowners may grant a mortgage in their home to Bank #1 when they purchase the home and years later grant a mortgage in the same home to Bank #2 when they take out a home equity loan.) When two or more creditors hold security interests in the same collateral, **priority** belongs to the security interest that is first perfected.

EXAMPLE

Assume Bank #1 takes a security interest in TTI's accounts receivables, equipment, supplies, inventory, and cash but fails to file a financing statement to perfect its security interest. Six months later TTI borrows money from Bank #2 and grants Bank #2 a security interest in the same collateral. Bank #2 promptly files a financing statement perfecting its security interest in the collateral. A week later, Bank #1 discovers that its security interest is unperfected and files a financing statement. If TTI now defaults on both loans, the security interest of Bank #2 in the collateral will prevail over that of Bank #1 because Bank #2 was the first to perfect its security interest. We would say that Bank #2 is the **senior lien holder** on the collateral and Bank #1 is the **junior lien holder** on the collateral even though the security interest of Bank #1 was first in time. It was first to attach but, alas, not the first to perfect. If neither Bank #1 nor Bank #2 had ever perfected its security interest, Bank #1 would prevail upon default since its interest was the first to attach.

To summarize, the priority rules for competing security interests in the same collateral are as follows:

- If neither of the security interests is perfected, the first security interest to attach (be created) will have priority.
- If one security interest is perfected and the other is not, the perfected security interest has priority over the unperfected security interest, regardless of which was the first to attach.
- If both security interests are perfected, the first to perfect has priority regardless of the first to attach.

P-H 2-e: The UCC-1 form currently used in the Commonwealth of Virginia can be viewed online at www.scc.virginia.gov/publicforms/489/ucc-1.pdf or from the link at http://www.scc.virginia.gov/clk/uccfile.aspx. Access that form and answer the following questions. If you were completing this form in connection with TTI's having granted Bank a security interest in its accounts receivables, equipment, supplies, inventory, and cash, on what line of the form would you enter the name of the debtor? The name of the creditor? A description of the collateral? If your instructor so directs, locate the version of UCC Article 9 in your state and determine in what public office Bank would properly file its financing statement. Many states now permit the electronic filing of UCC-1s so they can be filed on the same day as the security agreement is entered into. Determine if your state allows electronic filing of UCC-1s.

UCC Article 9 grants other priority advantages to creditors whose security interest in collateral qualifies as a PMSI. Under UCC §9-324(a), a creditor who holds a PMSI in goods "other than inventory or livestock" is granted priority over an earlier perfected security interest if the PMSI is perfected when the debtor takes possession of the collateral "or within 20 days thereafter." The 20-day **relation-back period** for perfection gives the creditor holding a PMSI in most kinds of personal property a decided advantage in achieving priority.

EXAMPLE

> Assume Sarah owns a business and purchases a laptop computer on credit to use exclusively in the business. Sarah grants the seller a security interest in the laptop to secure payment of the purchase price. Since seller is financing the purchase of the laptop, it holds a PMSI in it. But the laptop is not consumer goods in the hands of Sarah since it was purchased for business use only so there is no automatic perfection under UCC §9-309(1). Assume Sarah takes possession of the laptop the day of the purchase. Under state law the security interest in the laptop is perfected by filing a financing statement, but this is not done by seller until five days after the sale. Meanwhile, Sarah procures a short term loan from a lender and grants lender a security interest in some of her business assets including the laptop that is perfected by leaving the assets in possession of lender. Who has priority? Since seller's financing statement was filed within 20 days of when Sarah took possession, seller will prevail over lender under UCC §9-324(a). Seller's perfected status relates back to the date Sarah took possession and constitutes a superior lien to that of the lender. [This example assumes that the state would not treat the laptop as inventory under §9-102(a)(48)(D).]

UCC §9-317(e) contains a similar provision with regard to a PMSI that can be perfected by filing a financing statement where the secured creditor perfects by filing a financing statement within 20 days after the debtor receives delivery of the collateral. The perfected PMSI will relate back to the time the security interest attached and defeat the claim of any intervening buyer, lessee, or lien creditor of the collateral.

EXAMPLE

> Assume Dave owns a car repair shop. On October 1 he purchases a set of tools from Hand Tool Supply (HTS) to use in his business. Dave buys them from HTS on credit, grants HTS a security interest in the tools that same day, and takes them to his workshop. Since HTS sold the tools to Dave on credit it has PMSI in the tools but since they are not consumer goods in the hands of Dave, HTS's interest in them is not automatically perfected under §9-309(1). Assume HTS does not file a financing statement covering the tools until October 10. Meanwhile, on October 5, a judgment creditor of Dave's executes on its judgment by seizing the tools. Under state law the judgment creditor is a lien creditor in the tools as of October 5. In this priority struggle, HTS will prevail over the lien creditor under UCC §9-317(e). Its filing of the financing statement on October 10 was within the 20-day window and relates back to the date its security interest in the tools attached, October 1. The lien of the judgment creditor did not attach until October 5.

Unlike UCC 9-324(a), UCC 9-317(e) does not grant the holder of the PMSI priority over an earlier consensual lien in the collateral, only the claims of intervening buyers, lessees, or lien creditors.

EXAMPLE

> If Dave borrowed money from Bank on October 5 and delivered the tools to Bank that day as collateral, Bank's secured claim in the tools would have priority since it was automatically perfected by possession under UCC §9-313. Bank is not an intervening buyer, lessee, or lien creditor.

4. Remedies upon Default in an Obligation Secured by Personal Property

On default in the underlying debt obligation, the security agreement between the debtor and the secured creditor will typically authorize the creditor not already in possession of the collateral to declare default and repossess the collateral as is allowed by UCC §9-609(a). No judicial action is required; the creditor is entitled to use **self-help repossession** so long as it can be accomplished with no breach of the peace. If a breach of the peace is threatened or actual during attempted repossession, the creditor must resort to judicial action in which event repossession will be accomplished by court order executed by a designated public officer, usually the sheriff of the county where the property is located. See UCC §9-609(b). A creditor who engages in self-help repossession despite a threatened or actual breach of the peace may be liable for **conversion** of the property as well as other civil or criminal liability.

Self-help repossessions can be very noisy, confused, and messy when the debtor does not know the repossessor is coming. Sorting out exactly what happened after the fact can be challenging for the court and deciding the perimeters of what constitutes a threatened breach of the peace during the repossession event can be tricky.

HIGHLIGHTED CASE ●

GILES V. FIRST VIRGINIA CREDIT SERVICES, INC.
149 N.C. App. 89, 560 S.E.2d 557 (2002)

[Joann Giles entered into an installment sale contract on or about January 18, 1997 for the purchase of an automobile. The contract was assigned to First Virginia, which obtained a senior perfected purchase money security interest in the automobile. The terms of the contract required Giles to make sixty regular monthly payments to First Virginia, stipulated that Giles' failure to make any payment due under the contract within ten days after its due date would be a default, and contained a consent to self-help repossession in the event of default.

Giles became delinquent in her payments to First Virginia. At approximately 4 A.M. on June 17, 1999, Professional Auto Recovery, at the request of First Virginia, repossessed the locked automobile from Giles's front driveway by breaking into it, hotwiring it, and driving it away noisily and in great haste. A neighbor, Mr. Mosteller, heard and saw the repossessors' noisy diesel truck pull up to the debtor's house, and saw the repossessing agent run up the debtor's driveway toward the debtor's parked car. Moments later he saw the car "flying out back down the driveway making a loud noise and started screeching off." The repossessors' truck also gunned its engine and fled in a hurry. Mosteller phoned the debtor and her husband to report that their car was being stolen. The debtor and her husband, believing the car had been stolen, became agitated, and the police were called. The debtor's husband and the neighbor shouted back and forth from the front yards of their homes about what had happened and the entire neighborhood was awakened. At least two police cars arrived at the scene to investigate.

Giles and her husband sued First Virginia and Professional Auto Recovery for wrongful repossession and conversion of the vehicle. The trial court dismissed on motion for summary judgment finding that there had been no breach of the peace during the repossession. Plaintiffs appealed.]

OPINION: McGee, Judge

Our Courts have long recognized the right of secured parties to repossess collateral from a defaulting debtor without resort to judicial process, so long as the repossession is effected peaceably [Citation omitted]. . . . Our General Assembly codified procedures for self-help repossessions, including this common law restriction, in the North Carolina Uniform Commercial Code (UCC). N.C. Gen. Stat. §25-9-503 (1999), in effect at the time of the repossession in this case, reads in part,

> Unless otherwise agreed a secured party has on default the right to take possession of the collateral. In taking possession a secured party may proceed without judicial process if this can be done without breach of the peace or may proceed by action.

The General Assembly did not define breach of the peace but instead left this task to our Courts, and . . . none have clarified what actions constitute a breach of the peace. . . .

In a pre-UCC case, *Rea v. Credit Corp.*, 127 S.E.2d 225 (1962), a defaulting debtor left his locked automobile on his front lawn. An agent of the mortgagee went to the debtor's home to repossess the automobile, saw the automobile parked on the lawn, found no one at home, and asked a neighbor where the debtor was. The agent was told no one was at home and he thereafter opened the automobile door with a coat hanger and removed the automobile on a wrecker. Our Supreme Court found that this evidence could not warrant a finding by a jury that the mortgagee's agent wrongfully took possession of the automobile because no breach of the peace occurred. In *Rea*, although our Supreme Court did not define breach of the peace, it reiterated the common law rule that the right of self-help repossession "must be exercised without provoking a breach of the peace[.]" Id. at 127 S.E.2d at 227. Our Supreme Court thought the law "well stated" that

> "if the mortgagee finds that he cannot get possession without committing a breach of the peace, he must stay his hand, and resort to the law, for the preservation of the public peace is of more importance to society than the right of the owner of a chattel to get possession of it." *Rea*, 127 S.E.2d at 227.

In *Everett v. U.S. Life Credit Corp.*, 327 S.E.2d 269, 269 (1985) our Court stated that repossession can be accomplished under the statute without prior notice so long as the repossession is peaceable. Without specifically defining breach of the peace, our Court explained that "[o]f course, if there is confrontation at the time of the attempted repossession, the secured party must cease the attempted repossession and proceed by court action in order to avoid a 'breach of the peace.'" Id. at 270. This indicates, as argued by First

Virginia, that confrontation is at least an element of a breach of the peace analysis.

In that breach of the peace has not heretofore been clarified by our appellate courts, but instead only vaguely referred to, we must construe this term as the drafters intended. . . .

In a criminal case, our Supreme Court defined breach of the peace as "a disturbance of public order and tranquility by act or conduct not merely amounting to unlawfulness but tending also to create public tumult and incite others to break the peace." *State v. Mobley*, 83 S.E.2d 100, 104 (1954). . . .

We must also consider the nature and purpose of Chapter 25 of the North Carolina General Statutes, the UCC, which is to be "liberally construed and applied to promote its underlying purposes and policies." N.C. Gen. Stat. §25-1-102 (1999). . . .

The courts in many states have examined whether a breach of the peace in the context of the UCC has occurred. Courts have found a breach of the peace when actions by a creditor incite violence or are likely to incite violence. *Birrell v. Indiana Auto Sales & Repair*, 698 N.E.2d 6, 8 (Ind. App. 1998) (a creditor cannot use threats, enter a residence without debtor's consent and cannot seize property over a debtor's objections); *Wade v. Ford Motor Credit Co.*, 668 P.2d 183, 189 (1983) (a breach of the peace may be caused by an act likely to produce violence); *Morris v. First National Bank & Trust Co. of Ravenna*, 254 N.E.2d 683, 686-87 (1970) (a physical confrontation coupled with an oral protest constitutes a breach of the peace).

Other courts have expanded the phrase breach of the peace beyond the criminal law context to include occurrences where a debtor or his family protest the repossession. *Fulton v. Anchor Sav. Bank, FSB*, 452 S.E.2d 208, 213 (1994) (a breach of the peace can be created by an unequivocal oral protest); *Census Federal Credit Union v. Wann*, 403 N.E.2d 348, 352 (Ind. App. 1980) ("if a repossession is . . . contested at the actual time . . . of the attempted repossession by the defaulting party or other person in control of the chattel, the secured party must desist and pursue his remedy in court"); *Hollibush v. Ford Motor Credit Co.*, 508 N.W.2d 449, 453-55 (Wis. App. 1993) (in the face of an oral protest the repossessing creditor must desist). Some courts, however, have determined that a mere oral protest is not sufficient to constitute a breach of the peace. *Clarin v. Minnesota Repossessors, Inc.*, 198 F.3d 661, 664 (8th Cir. 1999) (oral protest, followed by pleading with repossessors in public parking lot does not rise to level of breach of the peace); *Chrysler Credit Corp. v. Koontz*, 661 N.E.2d 1171, 1173-74 (1996) (yelling "Don't take it" is insufficient).

If a creditor removes collateral by an unauthorized breaking and entering of a debtor's dwelling, courts generally hold this conduct to be a breach of the peace. *Davenport v. Chrysler Credit Corp.*, 818 S.W.2d 23, 29 (Tenn. App. 1991) and *General Elec. Credit Corp. v. Timbrook*, 291 S.E.2d 383, 385 (1982) (both cases stating that breaking and entering, despite the absence of violence or physical confrontation, is a breach of the peace). Removal of collateral from a private driveway, without more however, has been found not to constitute a breach of the peace. *Hester v. Bandy*, 627 So. 2d 833, 840 (Miss. 1993). Additionally, noise alone has been determined to not rise to the level of a breach of the peace. *Ragde v. Peoples Bank*, 767 P.2d 949, 951 (1989) (unwilling to hold that making noise is an act likely to breach the peace).

Many courts have used a balancing test to determine if a repossession was undertaken at a reasonable time and in a reasonable manner, and to balance the interests of debtors and creditors. See e.g., *Clarin v. Minnesota Repossessors, Inc.*, 198 F.3d 661, 664 (8th Cir. 1999); *Davenport v. Chrysler Credit Corp.*, 818 S.W.2d 23, 29 (Tenn. App. 1991). Five relevant factors considered in this balancing test are: "(1) where the repossession took place, (2) the debtor's express or constructive consent, (3) the reactions of third parties, (4) the type of premises entered, and (5) the creditor's use of deception." *Davenport*, 818 S.W.2d at 29. . . .

Relying on the language of our Supreme Court in *Rea*, plaintiffs argue that the "guiding star" in determining whether a breach of the peace occurred should be whether or not the public peace was preserved during the repossession. *Rea*, 127 S.E.2d at 228. Plaintiffs contend "the elements as to what constitutes a breach of the peace should be liberally construed" and urge our Court to adopt a subjective standard considering the totality of the circumstances as to whether a breach of the peace occurred. Plaintiffs claim that adopting a subjective standard for N.C. Gen. Stat. §25-9-503 cases will protect unwitting consumers from the "widespread use of no notice repossessions, clandestine and after midnight repossessions" and will protect "our State's commitment to law and order and opposition to vigilante policies, opposition to violence and acts from which violence could reasonably flow[.]" If a lender is not held to such a high subjective standard, plaintiffs contend that self-help repossessions should be disallowed altogether.

First Virginia, in contrast, argues that a breach of the peace did not occur in this case, as a matter of law, because there was no confrontation between the parties. Therefore, because the facts in this case are undisputed concerning the events during the actual repossession of the automobile, the trial court did not err in its partial grant of summary judgment.

First Virginia disputes plaintiffs' contention that a determination of whether a breach of the peace occurred should be a wholly subjective standard, because if such a standard is adopted, every determination of whether a breach of the peace occurred would hereafter be a jury question and "would run directly contrary to the fundamental purpose of the Uniform Commercial Code, which is to provide some degree of certainty to the parties engaging in various commercial transactions." Further, First Virginia argues that applying a subjective standard to a breach of the peace analysis could be detrimental to borrowers, with lenders likely increasing the price of credit to borrowers to cover the costs of having to resort to the courts in every instance to recover their collateral upon default. The standard advocated by plaintiffs would "eviscerate" the self-help rights granted to lenders by the General Assembly, leaving lenders "with no safe choice except to simply abandon their 'self help' rights altogether, since every repossession case could [result] in the time and expense of a jury trial on the issue of 'breach of the peace[.]'" Finally, First Virginia argues that a subjective standard would be detrimental to the judicial system as a whole because "[w]ith a case-by-case, wholly subjective standard . . . the number of lawsuits being filed over property repossessions could increase dramatically[.]"

. . . [W]e find that a breach of the peace, when used in the context of N.C. Gen. Stat. §25-9-503, is broader than the criminal law definition. A confrontation is not always required, but we do not agree with plaintiffs that every repossession should be analyzed subjectively, thus bringing every repossession into the purview of the jury so as to eviscerate the self-help rights duly given to creditors by the General Assembly. Rather, a breach of the peace analysis should be based upon the reasonableness of the time and manner of the repossession. We therefore adopt a balancing test using the five factors discussed above to determine whether a breach of the peace occurs when there is no confrontation.

In applying these factors to the undisputed evidence in the case before us, we affirm the trial court's determination that there was no breach of the peace, as a matter of law. Professional Auto Recovery went onto plaintiffs' driveway in the early morning hours, when presumably no one would be outside, thus decreasing the possibility of confrontation. Professional Auto Recovery did not enter into plaintiffs' home or any enclosed area. Consent to repossession was expressly given in the contract with First Virginia signed by Joann Giles. Although a third party, Mr. Mosteller, was awakened by the noise of Professional Auto Recovery's truck, Mr. Mosteller did not speak with anyone from Professional Auto Recovery, nor did he go outside until Professional Auto Recovery had departed with the Giles' automobile. Further, neither of the plaintiffs was awakened by the noise of the truck, and there was no confrontation between either of them with any representative of Professional Auto Recovery. By the time Mr. Mosteller and plaintiffs went outside, the automobile was gone. Finally, there is no evidence, nor did plaintiffs allege, that First Virginia or Professional Auto Recovery employed any type of deception when repossessing the automobile.

There is no factual dispute as to what happened during the repossession in this case, and the trial court did not err in granting summary judgment to First Virginia on this issue.

Giles v. First Virginia Credit Services, Inc.: Real Life Applications

1. Would the result in this case have been different if the activities of the repossessors had awakened the debtor or the neighbor and the one awakened had shouted at them out of a window something like, "Stop, thief! I've called the police"? See *Robinson v. Citicorp National Services, Inc.*, 921 S.W.2d 52 (Mo. Ct. App. 1996), and *Chrysler Credit Corp. v. Koontz*, 661 N.E.2d 1171 (1996). If the debtor's husband had raced outside with a firearm while the repossessors were pulling away from the property? If he or the neighbor had fired a firearm at the fleeing repossessors? If a sleeping child had been in the car unseen by the repossessor when the car was driven off? See *Chapa v. Traciers & Associates*, 267 S.W.3d 386 (Tex. App. 2008). If the repossessor had violated a driving ordinance in the course of repossession? See *Wallace v. Chrysler Credit Corp.*, 743 F. Supp. 1228 (W.D. Va. 1990).

2. The vehicle in *Giles* was sitting in the debtor's driveway when it was repossessed. Would the result have been different if the car had been sitting in a garage with the garage door up? With the garage door down but unlocked? With the garage door down and locked? See *Pantoja-Cahue v. Ford Motor Credit Co.*, 872 N.E.2d 1039 (Ill. 2007).

3. The law firm you work for represents a local financial institution that makes consumer loans. The client sent agents out to a debtor's home at 2 A.M. to effect a self-help repossession of a boat in which client held a security interest to secure a loan that is seriously in default. The repossessors backed away when the debtor heard them hitching up the boat and began shouting at them to stop and threatening to "blow them away" if they wouldn't. However, the agents have now reported that the debtor just drove away from his property leaving the boat where it was. The client wants to know if it's okay to send the agents back to the debtor's home before daylight to complete the repossession. How should your supervising lawyer advise this client? See *Wade v. Ford Motor Credit Co.*, 668 P.2d 183 (Kan. 1983).

4. The client from Question 3 comes up with another idea. It would like to use harmless subterfuge to effect self-help repossession. The idea is to have an employee contact a debtor who is in default by phone to advise that the manufacturer of the collateralized property is offering a free cleaning or servicing of the product for promotional purposes. Owners only have to bring the item to a designated place at a designated time to receive the free cleaning or servicing. Of course once the owner turns the property over to the agents of client, they will be told it is now repossessed. Should your supervising attorney sign off on this idea? *Compare Ford Motor Credit Co. v. Byrd*, 351 So. 2d 557 (Ala. 1974), and *Cox v. Galigher Motor Sales Co.*, 213 S.E.2d 475 (W. Va. 1975).

5. The client from Question 3 calls your supervising attorney in a panic. It seems that a company the client recently contracted with to do repossessions successfully repossessed a car earlier in the night. However, it seems a ten-year-old child of the debtor was asleep in the back seat of the car when it was towed away from debtor's home. The repossessing agents did not see the child. The car was towed to an enclosed storage area patrolled by a German Shepard guard dog, which bit the child when the child emerged sleepily from the car sometime later. Since the company hired by the client was an independent contractor, the client wants to know whether it can be held liable for any tortious conduct the contractor may have committed and, if so, what tortious conduct might be alleged on these facts. See *Sanchez v. MBank of El Paso*, 792 S.W.2d 530 (Tex. App. 1990), aff'd, 836 S.W.2d 151 (Tex. 1992).

Note that the Giles' lawsuit alleging the tort of conversion was brought against the creditor as well as its repossessing agent, Professional Auto Recovery. Though normally there is no vicarious liability of a principal for the torts of an independent contractor, there is a well-recognized exception in the self-help repossession context, where the duty on the creditor to preserve public safety during the repossession is deemed nondelegable to the independent contractor. See *General Finance Corp. v. Smith*, 505 So. 2d 1045 (Ala. 1987).

Following default and repossession, the creditor will normally sell (by public or private sale) or otherwise dispose of the property and apply the proceeds to the indebtedness owed. The disposition of the property must be accomplished in a **commercially reasonable manner** per UCC §9-610 and appropriate notices given to the debtor, co-obligors, and secondary (junior) secured parties or lien holders as required by UCC §§9-611-614.

E X A M P L E

> If TTI defaults on its obligations to the bank holding a secured interest in its equipment, the repossessing bank might sell those assets by public sale via an advertised auction. Or it might arrange for a private sale to another company. Either way is permissible so long as the notice requirements to the debtor are complied with and the sale is conducted in a commercially reasonable manner.

Where the collateral has been repossessed and disposed of, UCC §9-615 controls the order in which the proceeds are applied. The expenses of repossession and disposition are paid first. Then the proceeds are applied to the balance owed the repossessing creditor then to any subordinate or junior secured creditors or lien holders in the collateral. Any remaining proceeds are paid to the debtor.

If it is a junior lien holder who declares default and repossesses the collateral, none of the proceeds need be paid to the senior secured creditor but that senior creditor will retain its security interest in the collateral notwithstanding the sale or other disposition per UCC §§9-617(3) and 622(a)(3)(4).

E X A M P L E

> Assume TTI has granted a security interest in its equipment to both Bank #1 and Bank #2 and both banks are properly perfected in the equipment with Bank #1 holding the senior lien and Bank #2 the junior lien. TTI defaults on its loan from Bank #2 but not on its loan from Bank #1. Bank #2 can repossess and sell the equipment and apply the proceeds to what it is owed but whoever purchases the equipment in the foreclosure sale will take the equipment subject to the continuing security interest of Bank #1.

Nonrecourse A provision in a promissory note or security agreement stipulating that the secured creditor who elects to exercise its right to repossess the collateral must look exclusively to the collateral for satisfaction and cannot sue the debtor for any deficiency.

Where the collateral has been repossessed and disposed of and a deficiency balance remains owing, the secured creditor may institute legal action against the debtor to obtain a judgment for the **deficiency balance** owing. For example, if Shears repossesses and sells the living room furniture of the Murphys following default but the foreclosure sale only produces half of what is owed, Shears may sue the Murphys seeking a judgment for the balance owed *unless* the underlying promissory note or security agreement is **nonrecourse**. A nonrecourse note or security agreement stipulates that the secured creditor who elects to exercise its right to repossess the collateral must look exclusively to the collateral for satisfaction—it cannot sue the debtor for any deficiency.

It is not unusual in deficiency lawsuits for the debtor to raise defenses alleging that the secured creditor did not comply with the requirements of Article 9 in the repossession process (e.g., the creditor did not give proper notice under UCC §9-611 or did not dispose of the property in a commercially reasonable manner per UCC §9-610). There may also be a counterclaim in which the debtor seeks to recover damages for the lost property based on causes of action for **conversion** and/or **wrongful repossession**. In some states, where the debtor is able to show noncompliance by the secured creditor in a consumer transaction, the creditor is absolutely barred from recovering on the deficiency. In effect there is a **non-rebuttable presumption** that had the secured creditor complied with the requirements no deficiency would have resulted. See, e.g., *Coxall v. Clover Commercial Corp.*, 781 N.Y.S.2d 567 (N.Y. Cty. Civ. Ct. 2004). In other courts, the established noncompliance by the consumer debtor only raises a **rebuttable presumption** that the deficiency would not have resulted had the creditor complied, and the **burden of persuasion** shifts to the creditor to rebut the presumption by showing that the deficiency would remain even if the repossession and sale had been properly conducted. See, e.g., *Central National Bank v. Butler*, 294 A.D.2d 881, 882, 741 N.Y.S.2d 643 (4th Dept. 2002). And see UCC §9-626(b). In nonconsumer business repossessions, the finding of a noncompliance by the creditor only raises the rebuttable presumption per UCC §9-626(a).

D. ▶ Consensual Security Interests in Real Property of the Debtor

Both consumer and business debtors often own an interest in real property when they file for bankruptcy relief and typically there is at least one and sometimes multiple mortgages on that property at the time of filing. The law concerning the creation, attachment, and perfection of mortgages in real property is governed by the laws of the state where the property lies. For our purposes, what follows is a brief summary of how those laws work.

1. Creation of a Mortgage in Real Property

The legal document by which a mortgage in real property is created is called a **mortgage** or **mortgage deed** or, in some states, a **deed of trust** or **security deed**. The security interest in the real property that the owner/mortgagor conveys to the creditor/mortgagee is called a **right of foreclosure** or **power of sale** and authorizes the mortgagee to take possession of the property upon default and to then sell it, applying the proceeds to the debt owed. In most states, it is understood that the mortgagor maintains legal title to the property, while the mortgagee holds equitable title to it—that is, the right to take possession of and sell the property in the event of default.

Illustration 2-e shows the mortgage executed by Nick and Pearl Murphy to secure the loan from First Bank of Capital City (FBCC) to buy their residence on West Cherry Street in Capital City, Yourstate. The mortgage in Illustration 2-e secures the promissory note seen in Illustration 2-a.

In a common scenario, consumers purchase a home, borrow a portion of the purchase price from a lender, sign a promissory note evidencing the obligation to repay the amount borrowed (often called a **mortgage note**), and convey a mortgage interest in the property purchased to the lender to secure repayment of the note. Sometimes there is no lender involved in the transaction. Instead the

Illustration 2-e: MORTGAGE

THIS MORTGAGE is made on the 12th day of January, YR-10 between Nicholas W. Murphy and wife, Pearl E. Murphy, who reside at 3521 West Cherry Street, Capital City, Yourstate, hereinafter referred to collectively as "Borrower", and First Bank of Capital City, located at 1111 Main Street, Capital City, Yourstate, the original lender. The word "Lender" means the original Lender and anyone else who takes this Mortgage by transfer, sale, or assignment.

1. The debt secured: The debt secured by this Mortgage is evidenced by Borrower's promissory note dated the same date as this Mortgage, hereinafter referred to as Note, which provides for payments over 360 months in principal plus interest at 8% per annum in monthly payments of $843.83 in accordance with the terms of the Note. All terms of the Note are hereby made part of this Mortgage. This Mortgage secures to Lender: (a) the repayment of the debt evidenced by the Note, with interest, and all renewals, extensions, and modifications; (b) the payment of all other sums, with interest, advanced under Section Seven hereof to protect the security of this Mortgage; and (c) the performance of Borrower's covenants and agreements under this Mortgage and the Note. This Mortgage also secures any other indebtedness now or hereafter owing from Borrower to Lender, however or whenever created.

2. The property mortgaged: For the purposes set forth in Paragraph 1, Borrower irrevocably grants and conveys to Lender the interest and rights described in Paragraph 3 in the following described property located in Capital County, Yourstate: [legal description omitted from illustration] . . . which has the address of 3521 West Cherry Street, Capital City, Yourstate, and is hereinafter referred to as the "Property Address", together with all the improvements now or hereafter erected on the property, and all easements, rights, appurtenances, rents, royalties, mineral, oil and gas rights and profits, water rights and stock and all fixtures now or hereafter a part of the property. All replacements and additions shall also be covered by this Mortgage. All of the foregoing is referred to in this Mortgage as the "Property." This Mortgage covers property which is or may become so affixed to real property as to become fixtures and also constitutes a fixture filing under the laws of Yourstate.

3. Rights given to Lender: Borrower mortgages the Property to Lender and gives Lender the rights stated in this Mortgage and also those rights the applicable law does or in the future may give to lenders who hold mortgages on real property in Yourstate. When Borrower pays all amounts due to the Lender under the Note and this Mortgage, the Lender's rights under this Mortgage will end. The Lender will then cancel and release this Mortgage at Borrower's expense.

4. Borrower's covenants: Borrower covenants, promises, and warrants as follows:

a. Note and Mortgage. Borrower will comply with all the terms of the Note and this Mortgage.

b. Payment. Borrower will pay all amounts required by the Note and this Mortgage.

c. Ownership. Borrower is lawfully seized of the estate in the Property hereby conveyed and has the right to grant and convey the Property and that the Property is unencumbered, except for encumbrances of record, and that Borrower warrants and will defend generally the title to the Property against all claims and demands, subject to any encumbrances of record.

d. Taxes. Borrower will pay all taxes, assessments, and other government charges made against the Property when due. That Borrower will not claim any deduction from the taxable value of the Property because of this Mortgage. The Borrower will not claim any credit against the principal and interest payable under the Note and this Mortgage for any taxes paid on the Property.

e. <u>Insurance</u>. Borrower will keep the improvements now existing or hereafter erected on the Property insured against loss by fire, hazards included within the term "extended coverage" and any other hazards for which Lender requires insurance. This insurance shall be maintained in the amounts and for the periods that Lender requires. The insurance carrier providing the insurance shall be chosen by Borrower subject to Lender's approval which shall not be withheld unreasonably. All insurance policies and renewals shall be acceptable to Lender and shall include a standard mortgage clause. Lender shall have the right to hold the policies and renewals. If Lender requires, Borrower shall promptly give to Lender all receipts of paid premiums and renewal notices. In the event of loss, Borrower shall give prompt notice to the insurance carrier and Lender. Lender may make proof of loss if not made promptly by Borrower. Unless Lender and Borrower otherwise agree in writing, insurance proceeds shall be applied to restoration or repair of the Property damaged, if the restoration or repair is economically feasible and Lender's security is not lessened. If the restoration or repair is not economically feasible or Lender's security would be lessened, the insurance proceeds shall be applied to the sums secured by this Mortgage, whether or not then due, with any excess paid to Borrower. If Borrower abandons the Property, or does not answer within 30 days a notice from Lender that the insurance carrier has offered to settle a claim, then Lender may collect the insurance proceeds. Lender may use the proceeds to repair or restore the Property or to pay sums secured by this Mortgage, whether or not then due. The 30-day period will begin when the notice is given.

f. <u>Tax and Insurance Escrow</u>. Subject to applicable law or to a written waiver by Lender, Borrower shall pay to Lender on the day monthly payments are due under the Note and this Mortgage, until the Note is paid in full, a sum ("Funds") equal to one-twelfth of: (a) yearly taxes and assessments that may attain priority over this Mortgage; (b) yearly leasehold payments or ground rents on the Property, if any; (c) yearly hazard insurance premiums; and (d) yearly mortgage insurance premiums, if any. These items are called "escrow items." Lender shall give to Borrower, without charge, an annual accounting of the Funds showing credits and debits to the Funds and the purpose for which each debit to the Funds was made. The Funds are pledged as additional security for the sums secured by this Mortgage. If the amount of the Funds held by Lender is not sufficient to pay the escrow items when due, Borrower shall pay to Lender any amount necessary to make up the deficiency in one or more payments as required by Lender. Upon payment in full of all sums secured by this Mortgage, Lender shall promptly refund to Borrower any Funds held by Lender.

g. <u>Repairs</u>. Borrower will keep the Property in good repair, neither damaging nor abandoning it. Borrower will allow Lender or Lender's agent to inspect the Property upon reasonable notice.

h. <u>Lawful use</u>. Borrower will use the Property in compliance with all laws, ordinances and other requirements of any governmental authority.

i. <u>Rent</u>. Borrower will not rent the Property without the prior written consent of Lender and, in the event of such consent, will not accept any rent from any tenant for more than one month in advance.

j. <u>Other liens</u>. Borrower will not mortgage or otherwise pledge the Property as security for any other obligation without the prior written consent of Lender. Borrower will not take any action that could foreseeably result in any nonconsensual lien or claim being made against the Property.

5. Application of payments: Unless applicable law provides otherwise, all payments received by Lender shall be applied: first, to late charges due under the Note; second, to prepayment charges due under the Note; third, to any other amounts payable under Paragraph 4 of this Mortgage; fourth, to interest due; and last, to principal due.

6. Condemnation: If all or part of the Property is taken for public use, all compensation for such taking shall be paid to Lender. The Lender may use such compensation to repair or restore the Property or to reduce the amount owed on the Note and this Mortgage which application will not delay or postpone any other or further payment due from Borrower under the Note and this Mortgage.

7. Payments made for Borrower: If Borrower fails to keep the property insured, or to pay taxes or other assessments against the property as promised or to keep the property in good repair or to make other payments as promised in the Note and this Mortgage, Lender may make such payments for Borrower in which event said payments will be added to the principal due under the Note and will bear interest at the same rate provided in the Note and will be secured by the terms of this Mortgage and Borrower will repay Lender such amounts upon demand.

8. Default: The Lender may declare the Borrower to be in default on the Note and this Mortgage if (a) Borrower fails to make any payment required by the Note or this Mortgage within ten (10) days after it is due; (b) Borrower fails to comply with any other covenant or obligation under the terms of the Note or this Mortgage; (c) the ownership of the Property is changed for any reason without the prior written consent of Lender; the holder of any lien, whether consensual or nonconsensual, initiates foreclosure proceedings; or (d) bankruptcy, insolvency or receivership proceedings are begun by or against any Borrower.

9. Payments due upon default: Upon default, all amounts due under the Note and this Mortgage will become immediately due and payable and Borrower will pay the full amount of all unpaid principal, interest and other amounts due under the Note and this Mortgage. Borrower will also pay Lender all Lender's costs of collection, including court costs and reasonable attorney's fees.

10. Lender's rights upon default: Upon default, Lender will have all rights given by law now or at the time of default or as set forth in the Note and this Mortgage, including the right to do one or more of the following: (a) take possession of the Property, including the collection of rents and profits; (b) have a court appoint a receiver to accept rent for the Property to which Borrower expressly consents; (c) institute a foreclosure action which will result in sale of the Property to reduce Borrower's obligations under the Note and this Mortgage; and (d) file suit against Borrower for any balance owed by Borrower to Lender.

11. No waiver by Lender: Extension of the time for payment or modification of amortization of the sums secured by this Mortgage granted by Lender to Borrower or any successor in interest of Borrower shall not operate to release the liability of the original Borrower or Borrower's successors in interest. Any forbearance by Lender in exercising any right or remedy under the Note or this Mortgage shall not be a waiver of or preclude the exercise of any right or remedy.

12. Successors and assigns bound: The covenants and agreements of the Note and this Mortgage shall bind and benefit the successors and assigns of Lender and Borrower.

13. Each Borrower liable: Borrower's covenants and agreements shall be joint and several.

14. Notices: All notices must be given in writing and personally delivered or sent by certified mail, return receipt requested, to the address given in this Mortgage. Address changes may be given by notice to the other party.

15. No oral changes: This Mortgage can only be changed by a subsequent agreement in writing signed by both all Borrowers and the Lender.

16. Signatures: By their signatures below, Borrower and Lender evidence their acceptance of and agreement to the terms of this Mortgage effective the date above written.

owner of a home or other real property will **self-finance** or **owner finance** the buyer by conveying title to the buyer, allowing the buyer to take immediate possession, and agreeing to accept payment of all or a portion of the purchase price over some agreed period of time. In a self-financing transaction, the buyer will execute a promissory note in favor of the seller for the balance owed and grant the seller a mortgage in the property to secure the future payments. This type of mortgage is usually called a **purchase money mortgage**.

Usually, when a consumer or business first purchases realty there is little or no owner's equity in it since the amount borrowed and still owed on the mortgage is equal or close to the actual value of the house. **Owner's equity** is the market value of property in excess of the balance owed on it. Over time, as the balance due on the note underlying the mortgage is paid down, the owner's equity in the property should increase. Changes in the market value of the property can also have an impact on the amount of equity that exists in property.

EXAMPLE

Assume a husband and wife purchase a home for $300,000, its appraised value, and borrow $280,000 from Bank to finance the purchase. The remaining $20,000 of the purchase price they provide from savings. The buyers execute a promissory note payable to Bank promising to repay the money borrowed over 30 years in equal monthly installments at a stated rate of interest. The buyers also execute a mortgage deed in favor of Bank granting Bank a mortgage interest in the home purchased. At the time the transaction closes, the buyers have only $20,000 of owner's equity in the property. However, if after five years the owners have made payments on the underlying obligation reducing the balance owed to $225,000, they will have $75,000 of owner's equity in the home. And if during the same five years the value of the house has risen to $350,000, they will have $125,000 of equity in the home.

It is not uncommon in consumer transactions for homeowners who have built up sufficient equity in their home to obtain a second loan equal to all or some percentage of the equity and grant a mortgage interest in the property to the second lender even though the property is subject to the first mortgage and payments on that first mortgage are still being made to the first lender. A secured loan based on the owner's equity in a home is called a home equity loan.

EXAMPLE

If the consumers in our last example have built up owner's equity of $125,000 in their home after five years, they may choose to borrow against that equity by taking out a home equity loan even though the original loan is still being paid down and the first mortgage is still in place. The second lender is unlikely to loan an amount equal to the entire owner's equity, however. That would be far too risky since property values can fall as well as rise. Instead, the lender will have the property appraised and confirm the balance owed on the first mortgage in order to ensure that there will be sufficient equity remaining in the property after it makes the home equity loan. So on confirmed equity of $125,000 the second lender might make a loan of half that amount. State or federal regulations governing the lender may also control how much of the existing equity can be loaned.

Another variation increasingly common in consumer transactions is the **reverse mortgage**, in which a homeowner aged 62 or older borrows against the equity built up in the residence and receives that equity from the lender in either a lump sum or in installment payments. The loan is repaid when the homeowner dies or no longer lives in the home and the home is sold.

Business debtors owning an interest in realty subject to a mortgage may also use existing equity in the realty to obtain additional loans or credit resulting in a second or even third mortgage being placed on the property. Thus it is not unusual for real property owned by either consumer or business debtors to be subject to more than one mortgage simultaneously. It is possible that the first mortgage on the property prohibits the owner from using the property as security for any other indebtedness without the written consent of the mortgagee and if the owner does so it constitutes an act of default under the first mortgage. But if the first mortgage does not prohibit subsequent mortgaging of the property, or if the mortgagee consents to a subsequent mortgage notwithstanding the prohibition, the owner may mortgage the property as security for a second or even third debt, thus creating a second mortgage or a third mortgage on the property. Often the first mortgage is referred to as the **senior mortgage**, or **senior lien**, and the subsequent ones as a **junior mortgage**, or a **junior lien**.

The security interest of a creditor in real property conveyed in a mortgage instrument is created and attaches when (1) the mortgagor obtains an interest in the real property that can be conveyed as security; (2) value is given by the mortgagee in exchange for the security interest; and (3) the appropriate mortgage document is properly executed. As that point, as between the owner and the secured creditor, the creditor has the right of sale or the power of foreclosure in the event of default. But when the dispute is between multiple creditors and the question is which competing claim has priority over the others, we are again faced with the question of who was first to perfect its mortgage interest.

2. Perfection and Priority of Mortgages in Real Property

Priority between plural mortgages is determined by which kind of **recording statute** is in effect in the state where the property lies. Most states have **race-notice statutes**, whereby priority is created by being the first to record a mortgage in the public office responsible for maintaining land records (in different jurisdictions that may be the office of the Registrar of Deeds, Register of Deeds, Recorder, or the city or county clerk) while having no actual notice of any prior unrecorded claim to the property. The recording of the mortgage serves as constructive notice to the world of the recording mortgagee's claim.

A few states have **pure notice statutes**, which give priority to a prior unrecorded mortgage so long as subsequent mortgagees have actual notice of the prior unrecorded mortgage. A very few states have **race statutes**, which give priority to the first mortgage recorded regardless of actual notice.

With this recording system to establish priority among mortgages in mind, reconsider the nomenclature of senior and junior mortgages discussed above. That phraseology can refer to which mortgage interest was created and attached first, or it can refer to which mortgage interest has priority under the applicable recording statute.

3. Remedies upon Default in an Obligation Secured by a Mortgage in Real Property

The main idea behind a mortgage is that if the mortgagor defaults on the underlying debt evidenced by a promissory note, the mortgagee can take possession of the mortgaged property, sell it, and apply the proceeds to the satisfaction of the debt. This process is called **foreclosure**. Almost universally, the promissory note secured by the mortgage will contain an **acceleration of indebtedness clause** authorizing the mortgagee to declare all amounts due from the mortgagor immediately due and payable. Thus, the foreclosure can proceed in order to produce funds sufficient to pay off the entire indebtedness and other charges and expenses authorized by the note and mortgage. A typical default clause in a mortgage note can be seen in Paragraph 8 of Illustration 2-e. A typical acceleration of indebtedness clause can be seen in Paragraph 9 of that illustration.

As we will **see**, many a bankruptcy is triggered by a foreclosure begun on the debtor's realty, particularly in consumer cases when the individual debtor's home is in danger. Various states have authorized two different procedures for foreclosure: **power of sale foreclosure** and **judicial foreclosure**. Almost all states that authorize a power of sale foreclosure permit judicial foreclosure as an alternative. But almost half the states mandate judicial foreclosure and permit no alternative.

Power of Sale Foreclosure

A slight majority of the states allows mortgage instruments to convey a power of sale to the mortgagee. States allowing a power of sale use either a deed of trust or a security deed form of mortgage.

Upon default of an instrument granting a power of sale, the mortgagee (or a trustee for the mortgagee named in the mortgage instrument or a substitute trustee appointed after default) may institute foreclosure proceedings without first having to obtain any judicial or administrative approval. The mortgagee must be careful to comply with statutes governing the power of sale foreclosure. These statutes typically require the trustee to prepare a **notice of sale**, containing details of the intended public sale of the property (e.g., description of the property, time and place of the sale) and to provide the notice of sale to the mortgagor, any junior mortgage holders, and any other parties known to have an interest in the property (e.g., guarantors of the underlying debt). In addition to sending the notice of sale to designated interested parties, the trustee is typically required either to post the notice in a public place for some designated period of time before the sale (usually four to six weeks) or to run for a designated number weeks prior to sale an advertisement in the classified section of a newspaper of general circulation in the county where the land to be sold lies.

EXAMPLE

First Bank of Capital City holds the first mortgage on the home of Nick and Pearl Murphy. If the Murphys had conveyed a power of sale to FBCC and then defaulted on their payments, FBCC or a trustee acting for it may have initiated a power of sale foreclosure using the notice of foreclosure sale set forth in Illustration 2-f.

Illustration 2-f: NOTICE OF FORECLOSURE SALE

WHEREAS, Nicholas W. Murphy and wife, Pearl E. Murphy, by Deed of Trust (the "Deed of Trust") dated January 12, YR-10, of record in Mortgage Book 99, Page 077 in the Register's Office of Capital County, Yourstate, conveyed to Howard J. Sands, Trustee, the hereinafter described real property to secure the payment of a certain Promissory Note (the "Note") described in the Deed of Trust, which Note was payable to First Bank of Capital City;

WHEREAS, default has been made in the payment of the Note; and

WHEREAS, the owner and holder of the Note has demanded that the hereinafter described real property be advertised and sold in satisfaction of indebtedness and costs of foreclosure in accordance with the terms and provisions of the Note and Deed of Trust.

NOW, THEREFORE, notice is hereby given that Trustee, pursuant to the power, duty and authority vested in and conferred upon me, by the Deed of Trust, will on May 1, YR00 at 9 A.M. at the front door of the Capital County Courthouse in Capital City, Yourstate, offer for sale to the highest bidder for cash, and free from all legal, equitable and statutory rights of redemption, exemptions of homestead, rights by virtue of marriage, and all other exemptions of every kind, all of which have been waived in the Deed of Trust, certain real property located in Capital County, Yourstate, described as follows: [property description deleted from illustration]. . . . Being the same property conveyed to Nicholas W. Murphy and wife, Pearl E. Murphy, by deed from Francis H. Harmon, of record in Deed Book 813, Page 908 in the Register's Office for Capital County, Yourstate; and further conveyed by the Deed of Trust to the Trustee, of record in Mortgage Book 99, Page 077 in the Register's Office for said County.

The address of the above-described property is 3521 West Cherry Street, Capital City, Yourstate.

DATED this February 1, YR00.

Francis H. Harmon, Trustee

Following the foreclosure sale in a power of sale foreclosure, title to the property is conveyed to the new owner through a **trustee's deed**. Proceeds of the sale will be applied first to satisfy the costs of the sale (e.g., advertising, site preparation, and auctioneer's fee), second to pay any taxes or special assessments still owed on the property, and third to pay the balance owed senior and other mortgage holders. Finally, any balance left goes to the borrower. The minimum bid set at a foreclosure sale is normally equal to the amount owed to the foreclosing mortgagee. If no third-party bid on the property at the foreclosure sale exceeds that minimum amount, the foreclosing mortgagee is entitled (and in some states required) to enter a bid on the property itself in an amount equal to the amount owed, a common practice known as **bidding in** or **credit-bidding**, which means the creditor takes absolute title to the property in exchange for extinguishment of the indebtedness and for no additional payment. If there is equity in the property, then the purchasing mortgagee captures the equity.

P-H 2-f: There is quite a bit of variation among the states regarding how proceeds of a foreclosure sale are to be distributed. In some states, after the balance owed to the foreclosing mortgagee has been paid, excess proceeds must go to other creditors of the mortgagor/debtor before any are paid to him. Some states allow the mortgagee to credit-bid at an amount less than the total amount owed on the property, although this may raise questions of good faith or unconscionability if the mortgagee is allowed to (see discussion of arrearages, below) and does then pursue the debtor for any balance remaining on the account. Many states authorize a special court proceeding wherein disputes over distribution of sales proceeds can be resolved within some designated time period following the sale (e.g., six months or one year). Research and determine how your state distributes proceeds from foreclosure.

Until the foreclosure sale occurs, all states recognize an **equity of redemption** right in the mortgagor, that is, the right of the mortgagor to redeem the property from foreclosure by paying all amounts due to the mortgagee. On the designated day and time, if the mortgagor has not exercised his equity of redemption, the trustee or a public official (e.g., the county sheriff) will conduct the foreclosure sale. The property will be sold to the highest bidder. The mortgagee is allowed to bid in the amount of the debt owed to it as the purchase price.

If holders of junior mortgages were given proper notice of the foreclosure sale, their mortgage interests in the real property are extinguished by the foreclosure sale under the laws of most states such that the purchaser at foreclosure will take title free and clear of those claims even if the proceeds of sale are insufficient to pay off both the foreclosing and junior mortgages. If the proceeds of the sale produced an excess (there was more than enough money made on the sale to pay all the debts and expenses owed to the foreclosing mortgagee), that excess will go to the junior interests or to the mortgagor. The foreclosing mortgagee holding excess funds often initiates a civil lawsuit called an **impleader action**, naming the junior interest holders and the mortgagor as parties; pays the excess funds into the clerk of the court where the impleader action is filed; and requests the court to determine who is entitled to what share of those excess funds. The foreclosure of a junior mortgage will have no effect on a senior mortgage.

EXAMPLE

Assume Bank #1 holds a senior mortgage in a debtor's home. Bank #2 holds a second mortgage in the home to secure a home equity line of credit. Bank #3 holds a third mortgage in the home to secure payment of a small construction loan the owners have taken out. Owners are in default to Bank #2, which forecloses giving proper notice to Bank #3. Latisha purchases the home at the foreclosure sale, which did not raise enough to satisfy the balance owed to Bank #2 so Bank #3 received nothing. Latisha will take title to the home subject only to the mortgage of Bank #1. As senior mortgagee, the foreclosure by a junior mortgagee cannot disturb the interest of Bank #1. On the other hand, the mortgages of both Bank #2 and Bank #3 were eliminated by the foreclosure. The foreclosure by Bank #2 eliminates both its own and all junior mortgage interests so long as statutory notice was given to the junior mortgagees. The fact that the foreclosure sale brought insufficient funds to pay off either the foreclosing mortgagee or a more junior mortgagee does not affect this result.

In addition to the mortgagor's equity of redemption right, already discussed, some states provide the mortgagor with a **statutory right of redemption**. Such statutes authorize the mortgagor, for a period of time after the foreclosure sale (six to twelve months is typical), to buy back the property for the foreclosure sale price. Some of the states that recognize the right of statutory redemption permit the mortgagor to waive that right in the mortgage document.

Judicial Foreclosure

Judicial foreclosure is initiated by the mortgagee filing a lawsuit alleging default in a debt properly secured by the mortgage and the right to foreclose and asking the court to issue an order that the property be sold to pay the indebtedness secured. Judicial foreclosure is mandated in states that do not recognize a power of sale foreclosure and is an option available to the mortgagee in states that do.

The mortgagee initiating the judicial foreclosure will name the mortgagor, junior mortgage holders, and others with an interest in the property as parties so that all alleged claims and defenses can be fully litigated in the action. If the court finds for the mortgagee and orders the property sold, required notice will be given, the property levied on or seized by the sheriff or other public official, and the sale conducted publicly by auction (a **sheriff's sale** or **referee's sale**). Title to the new owner is then conveyed by a **sheriff's deed** or **referee's deed**. Distribution of proceeds from a judicial sale will be strictly governed by statute, but generally follows the scheme discussed in connection with power of sale foreclosure.

Many attorneys prefer the judicial foreclosure over the power of sale foreclosure, even in states authorizing the latter, because of the finality of the court decision. In a nonjudicial power of sale foreclosure, there is always the possibility the mortgagor will file suit contesting the right of the mortgagee to proceed or contesting the propriety of a foreclosure sale already conducted. All those issues should be resolved by the court in the judicial foreclosure prior to the sale. The rights and priorities of junior mortgage holders will be resolved there, too, negating the need for a subsequent impleader action.

Another consideration in choosing between a judicial foreclosure and a power of sale foreclosure is the possibility that the property sold at foreclosure may not bring enough to satisfy the full amount owed—there is a **deficiency balance**. In a judicial foreclosure, the court in most instances can enter a judgment against the mortgagor for the deficiency (a **deficiency judgment**) without a separate lawsuit being filed. In a power of sale foreclosure, however, the mortgagee must file a lawsuit following the foreclosure sale in order to obtain a deficiency judgment. Some states recognize an **election of remedies** doctrine, prohibiting the mortgagee from obtaining a deficiency judgment following a power of sale foreclosure. The mortgagee is held to have elected its sole remedy by proceeding with the foreclosure and cannot bring a deficiency action if the price received on foreclosure did not fully satisfy the debt.

Another source of controversy over a deficiency balance can arise when the foreclosing mortgagee enters a credit-bid on the property at the foreclosure sale for less than the total amount owed and then seeks a judgment against the debtor for the deficiency balance in jurisdictions where that is allowed. In many states, a mortgagee who enters a credit-bid on the property cannot then sue for a deficiency. Where a credit-bidding mortgagee is allowed to sue for a deficiency, there is often an issue as to whether the value of the property exceeded the amount of the credit-bid entered by the mortgagee.

Of course, if the underlying promissory note or mortgage is **nonrecourse**, the creditor cannot pursue a deficiency judgment against the mortgagor since a nonrecourse note limits the creditor's remedy to the collateral and bars any further action against the debtor for a deficiency judgment regardless of whether a judicial or power of sale foreclosure was authorized. A further consideration in electing between a judicial foreclosure and a power of sale foreclosure is that purchasers of the property at the foreclosure sale often have more confidence in the title they receive to the property by foreclosure deed when the sale is the result of a court order. On the other hand, a downside to judicial foreclosure is the delay in the mortgagee being able to move ahead with a foreclosure sale by reason of having to file the lawsuit, effect service of process on the mortgagee, and await a hearing date.

THE SERVICEMEMBERS CIVIL RELIEF ACT (SCRA)

The SCRA, found at U.S.C.A. App. §501, et seq., as revised in 2003, restricts foreclosure of properties owned by active-duty members of the military. Check the web site of the U.S. Department of Housing and Urban Development for a summary of the protections from foreclosure provided to our active-duty service members: http://portal.hud.gov/hudportal/HUD?src=/program_offices/housing/sfh/nsc/qasscra1.

P-H 2-g: Using the state foreclosure laws comparison table at www.foreclosureforum.com/basics.html and the handy links to state foreclosure laws at www.biggerpockets.com/rei/state-foreclosure-laws/, determine if your state allows both power of sale and judicial foreclosure or mandates judicial foreclosure. Is the initial step in a foreclosure proceeding in your state issuing a notice of default, publication, or filing a complaint? How quickly can a foreclosure be finalized following that initial step? How long following foreclosure can the debtor pursue his or her right of redemption in your state? Can the foreclosing creditor pursue a deficiency judgment following foreclosure?

Alternatives to Foreclosure

Foreclosure is not a happy solution for anyone, including the foreclosing creditor. Unless the real estate market is hot, the foreclosed property may sit empty for months or years with the attendant risks of deterioration in value and vandalism. Taxes still have to be paid and insurance maintained on the property. There are always costs associated with the foreclosure sale, reducing the take of the creditor and increasing the potential liability of the debtor. Foreclosure is often devastating to the credit rating of the debtor. For these and other reasons, the debtor and creditor may agree to any one of several alternatives to foreclosure:

- **Temporary Forbearance:** The creditor agrees to temporarily lower or suspend mortgage payments without declaring default and foreclosing.

- **Mortgage Modification:** The creditor agrees to permanently modify the mortgage terms by extending the term of repayment and thus reducing the amount of the periodic payments or by reducing the interest rate, or even by forgiving a portion of the principal.
- **Short Sale:** The creditor allows the homeowner time to sell the property and agrees to accept the net proceeds of the sale in full satisfaction of the indebtedness even though the sale may not bring enough to cover the entire indebtedness and even if the underlying note is not nonrecourse.
- **Deed in Lieu of Foreclosure:** The debtor agrees voluntarily to transfer title to the property to the creditor in exchange for cancelling the mortgage loan. The creditor may also agree to forgive any deficiency balance remaining when the property is finally resold.
- **State and Federal Mortgage Assistance Programs:** A number of states, such as Pennsylvania (www.phfa.org/consumers/homeowners/hemap.aspx), have established programs to assist qualified homeowners in making their house payments or offering incentivized forbearance or modification proposals to lenders. Similarly, the federal government has established its **Making Home Affordable Program**, a summary of which can be seen at http://www.makinghomeaffordable.gov/pages/default.aspx.

E. Consensual Suretyship and Guaranty Arrangements as a Form of Security for Debt

A **surety agreement** is where one person agrees to make himself liable for the debt of another. The surety is sometimes referred to as an **accommodation party**. A surprising number of consumer bankruptcies involve a consumer having co-signed a promissory note as an accommodation to another; a form of suretyship. Parents often co-sign promissory notes on loans made to children, siblings sometimes co-sign for each other, even friends co-sign for each other. For example, a Report on Private Student Loans prepared for Congress by the CFPB and Department of Education in 2012 (available online at http://files.consumer-finance.gov/f/201207_cfpb_Reports_Private-Student-Loans.pdf) reported the surprising finding that in 2011, 90 percent of private student loans were co-signed. Correspondingly, a September 2014 report by the U.S. Government Accountability Office (available online at www.gao.gov/products/GAO-14-866T) found that liability for student loan debt carried by Americans aged 65 to 74 increased from $2.8 billion in 2005 to $18.2 billion in 2013.

EXAMPLE

Assume David Hayes, 20 years old, wants to borrow $10,000 from a bank to finance the purchase of a car. If David is not deemed a sufficient credit risk by the bank, it may require David to provide a credit worthy co-signer on the note. John and Mary Hayes, David's parents, co-sign the promissory note payable to the bank and the loan is made to David. Although the loan was made for the benefit of David, his parents have agreed to make themselves **primarily liable**, along with David, on the note. David is the principal debtor on the note, while John and Mary are sureties as co-signers. Both are primarily liable on the note along with David.

To say that the co-signer is primarily liable on a debt along with the principal debtor means that the creditor can look to the co-signer for payment of the debt whether or not the principal debtor is able to pay and whether or not the creditor first seeks to collect the debt from the principal debtor. If the co-signer were only **secondarily liable** on the debt, the creditor would have to seek collection first from the principal debtor and only then could the creditor seek collection from the co-signer. But the co-maker of a promissory note makes him- or herself primarily liable on the debt along with the principal debtor. Thus, in the last example, if David fails to repay the note as it comes due, the bank or subsequent holder of the note is not required to pursue collection from David before pursuing collection from John and Mary even though David is the principal debtor on the note. It is no defense to the holder's collection action against John and Mary that David is able to pay but didn't. Nor is it a defense that the holder did not pursue David at all on the obligation before commencing collection against the co-signers.

Co-signing a note is only one way to create a surety arrangement on a debt. Another way is for the accommodation party to execute a separate **surety agreement**, or **surety bond**, promising to be responsible for the debt. Surety agreements and bonds are far more common in business transactions than in consumer transactions and may make the accommodation party either primarily or secondarily liable.

Another type of surety arrangement in which a party makes him- or herself liable for the debt of another is the **guaranty agreement**. (A sample guaranty agreement can be seen in To Learn More activity 2-2, accessible on the companion web site of the textbook at http://aspenlawschool.com/books/Parsons_Debt4e/.) By executing a guaranty agreement, the guarantor makes him- or herself secondarily liable for the debt of the principal debtor. Typically, in a guaranty arrangement, the guarantor is only secondarily liable, not primarily liable.

EXAMPLE

Assume John and Mary Hayes did not co-sign David's promissory note. Instead they executed a personal guaranty on David's behalf. If David fails to repay the note that his parents guaranteed but did not co-sign, the parents are only secondarily liable. The holder of the note will be required to pursue collection from David as the principal debtor before pursuing collection from John and Mary, who only promised to pay the guaranteed debt in the event that David defaulted on it. The holder of the note must prove the default and nonpayment by David as a condition precedent to collecting from the parents as guarantors.

Issues often arise in actions brought against an **accommodation party** like a co-signer or guarantor as to whether that party can raise the same defenses to liability that the principal debtor can raise. Generally, an accommodation party can raise any defense to liability that the principal debtor could raise, including failure of consideration, fraud, duress, breach of contract, breach of warranty, and so on. However, the surety or guarantor cannot raise personal defenses available to the principal debtor. A **personal defense** is a defense unique to the circumstances of the principal debtor that do not go to the merits of the underlying transaction. Personal defenses would include discharge in bankruptcy or lack of capacity to contract due to age or disability, and the like.

EXAMPLE

Assume that John and Mary Hayes have guaranteed the promissory note signed by their son, David. Later David files a bankruptcy case and discharges any legal obligation he might have for the note, but had he been sued by the lender he was prepared to show by way of defense that he never received the funds from the lender. As you know from your study of contract law, we would call that defense a failure of consideration. When the bank sues John and Mary Hayes on their guaranty, they can raise the failure of consideration defense just as David could have but they cannot raise David's discharge of the note obligation in bankruptcy as a defense to their liability on the guaranty. That is a personal defense. Likewise if David were only 17 years old when he signed the note and could raise incapacity due to age if sued on it, John and Mary as guarantors could not raise that defense; it is personal to David.

Another important principle of surety/guaranty law is that if the creditor and principal debtor agree to make any material change in the terms of the original obligation for which the surety/guarantor is potentially liable, and do so without obtaining the prior consent of the surety/guarantor to that material change, the obligation of the surety/guarantor will be discharged by operation of law. That is because the material change alters the risk that the surety/guarantor agreed to assume.

EXAMPLE

Assume the note that John and Mary Hayes have guaranteed is due but David cannot pay. David and the lender agree that David will have six months more time to pay than the note allows but will pay a 0.25 percent higher rate of interest in exchange for the extension. No one advises John and Mary of this alteration in the obligation or obtains their consent. David defaults on the obligation even with the extension, and the lender seeks collection from John and Mary. On these facts, John and Mary are likely discharged from any liability on the guaranty due to the material change.

Some states make a distinction between a gratuitous surety and a compensated surety in applying this doctrine of discharge by material change. A **gratuitous surety** is one who receives no compensation for serving as surety whereas a **compensated surety** is one that receives a fee or other compensation for agreeing to serve as surety or guarantor. In those states that make this distinction, an accommodation surety will be relieved from its obligation whether the material change in the obligation puts it at greater risk or not, but a compensated surety will be relieved only if the material change causes it harm or puts it at demonstrably greater risk.

EXAMPLE

Assume the lender on the note guaranteed by John and Mary agrees to give David an additional year to pay it but does not increase the amount of the principal or the interest rate payable on the note. We can argue over whether this material change puts the guarantors at greater risk or not, but for accommodation sureties it doesn't matter, so John and Mary will be relieved of their obligation as guarantors.

P-H 2-h: If John and Mary had agreed to sign the guaranty of David's note in exchange for his promise to paint their house, would that make them compensated sureties? If so, does the bank giving David an additional year to pay the note but not increasing the principal amount due or altering the interest rate due on the note put them at demonstrably greater risk such that they should be discharged? What are the arguments either way on that? Is it an easier case for them if the bank agrees to the one-year extension in exchange for an increase of 1 percent on the interest rate payable on the note? Is it a harder case for them if the extension agreed to by the bank is only for a week? Is that even a material change that might cause a surety to be discharged?

Consensual surety and guaranty arrangements should not be confused with legal rules that sometimes make one person liable for the debt of another as a matter of law.

EXAMPLE

In community property states a debt incurred during the marriage by only one spouse is the responsibility of both as a matter of law since the creditor can reach the community property of the couple (both assets and income) to satisfy that debt. Even in common law states, certain debts may be deemed the responsibility of both spouses as a matter of law: medical expenses and obligations for necessary food, clothing, and shelter are examples. Parents or legal guardians of minor children may be deemed liable as a matter of law for debts incurred by minor dependent (unemancipated) children though such obligations may be voidable by reason of the minor child's legal incapacity unless they were incurred for necessities such as food, clothing, or shelter.

F. ▶ Predatory Lending to Consumer Debtors

In recent years the **payday loan**—also called variously a cash advance, check advance, postdated check loan, deferred deposit check loan, or deferred presentment loan—has become a significant and controversial source of debt for primarily low-income consumers, and a major contributor to the web of permanent financial distress in which many such consumers live. The payday loan is a short-term loan for a small amount under terms that charge the borrower an astronomically high interest rate, sometimes camouflaged as a transaction fee or finance charge. Though not technically a secured transaction, the pay-day lender does obtain a prospective right to access and extract funds from the debtor's checking account to repay the obligation.

EXAMPLE

Assume Marta Carlson needs $100 cash right now but her checking account is empty and she doesn't get paid again until the end of the month, 14 days away. She goes to a check-cashing business and writes a check payable to the company for $115 and receives a cash loan of $100. Marta is told to postdate the check to the last day of the month and the company promises to hold and not cash the $115 check until that date, when her next paycheck will, presumably, be deposited. Fourteen days later the company cashes the $115 check. The check pays them back the $100 they loaned Marta plus $15, which they receive as "interest" or "fees" or "finance charges."

Marta just paid $15 to borrow $100 for 14 days. That's a full 15 percent charge for using someone else's money for only two weeks. Annualized, Marta is paying 391 percent per annum interest for that loan. And, if Marta extends or rolls over her loan for another 10- or 14-day term, the same charge is imposed a second time. If Marta asks for another 14 days to pay back the $100 she borrowed, the charge will be an additional $15 for a total of $30 paid in interest and fees to borrow $100 for 28 days. That's a full 30 percent charge to use someone else's money for less than a month. If she rolls over the loan a second time, for an additional 14 days, the finance charge goes to 45 percent of the amount borrowed, and so on. The loan shark in the alley could do no better.

Closely related to the payday loan is the **car title loan**, where the consumer conveys a security interest in his or her vehicle to the lender in exchange for a short-term loan at a double- or triple-digit rate of annualized interest.

In the mid-1990s there were only a few hundred payday and car title loan companies scattered around the country. Today there are thousands of storefront operations and online sites as well. Most commonly, store locations are in or near low-income neighborhoods and, until recently, around military bases. In the 2007 Defense Authorization Act, Congress capped rates on such loans made to military personnel at 36 percent per annum, resulting in a migration of payday and title loan companies away from military bases. In addition, the Servicemembers Civil Relief Act (SCRA), U.S.C.A. App. §501, et seq. authorizes military personnel going on active duty to reduce interest due on pre–active duty monetary obligations to 6 percent per annum if active duty would materially affect their ability to pay a higher interest rate.

As payday loan businesses proliferated, legislation was passed in many states specifically exempting such businesses from state usury statutes, which would otherwise control small loans and limit them to the lower double-digit range (e.g., 25% per annum). These statutory or regulatory exemptions are called **safe-harbor provisions** for the benefit of the financial services companies operating these businesses. Approximately a dozen states have enacted legislation regulating payday and car title loan companies to some extent, capping the interest rate that can be charged and/or limiting the number of rollovers per customer per year.

EXAMPLE

Virginia's Payday Loan Reform Act (well summarized at https://www.scc.virginia.gov/bfi/files/pay_guide.pdf) took effect on January 1, 2009. The bill caps interest rates lenders may charge at 36 percent per annum. Lenders must give borrowers two pay periods to repay a loan. Lenders are limited to making one loan at a time to borrowers, who must wait one day after repaying a loan to take out another. Borrowers who take out at least five loans in a six-month period must either wait 45 days before getting another loan or extend the payment term on the fifth loan to two months or more. Anyone taking a two-month extension option has to wait another two months before getting a new loan. An extended payment plan is available once a year, followed by a three-month cooling off period. Lenders that falsely threaten criminal prosecution for failure to make good on the check used to obtain the loan are subject to a fine three times the cost of the loan.

P-H 2-i: The Consumer Federation of America (www.consumerfed.org) and Center for Responsible Lending (www.responsiblelending.org) are nonprofits that provide excellent resources regarding predatory lending. Determine if your state has adopted any statutory or regulatory rules limiting the interest rate or fees these companies can charge or otherwise regulating their behavior. Determine if your state has a usury statute or regulation that applies to financial services offered to consumers and, if so, whether your state has adopted a safe-harbor provision exempting any such services from the usury rule.

WHO USES PAYDAY AND CAR TITLE LOANS?

Though the median annual income for a payday/car title borrower is less than $25,000, a 2010 investigation by National Public Radio's Planet Money ("Inside a Payday Loan Shop" at www.npr.org/sections/money/2010/05/the_tuesday_podcast_payday_len.html) revealed that a significant number of regular users of payday loan shops are solidly middle class. Payday and car title loans are often justified by the financial services industry as providing a quick, convenient, short-term loan source. However, 80 percent of payday and car title loan customers renew or roll over their loan once or more. In fact, the average payday/car title loan customer takes out a loan nine times per year, a debt trap that keeps such debtors perpetually in debt and quickly paying more in interest and fees than was borrowed..

Payday and car title loans are, needless to say, controversial. Consumer advocates consider them **predatory lending** that takes advantage of unsophisticated, and sometimes desperate, lower-income consumers. Business advocates consider them a fair lending practice, subject, like other loans, to provisions of the federal Truth in Lending Act (TILA) and Regulation Z (12 C.F.R. Part 226) promulgated under TILA, requiring lenders to disclose in writing the finance charge (a dollar amount) and the annual percentage rate (APR) to the consumer.

After releasing its formal research report on payday lending in March 2014 (available online at http://files.consumerfinance.gov/f/201403_cfpb_report_payday-lending.pdf) and a subsequent report on car title loans in May 2016 (available online at http://files.consumerfinance.gov/f/documents/201605_cfpb_single-payment-vehicle-title-lending.pdf) the Consumer Financial Protection Bureau released its first proposed formal regulations of these loans in June 2016. The proposed regulations, to be found at 12 CFR part 1041 when finalized, which were issued subject to public comment and later finalization would require that a lender reasonably determine that the consumer has the ability to repay the loan before making it, limit the number of times a loan can be renewed (three times in most cases) and the number of months in a year the debtor can owe the lender for the loan (nine months in most cases), restrict the making of new loans to a consumer who has or recently had other outstanding loans, require lenders to provide advance notice to the consumer before attempting to withdraw payment from the consumer's account, and prohibit the lender from attempting to withdraw payment from a consumer's account after two consecutive attempts have failed unless the consumer specifically consents to further attempts.

P-H 2-j: Go to the CFPB web site at www.consumerfinance.gov/ and see if the agency's proposed regulations have been finalized at this time and, if so, how the final language compares to the summary provided in the text. Do you think the proposed FRCB regulations of payday and car title loans goes far enough? Too far?.

Payday and car title loans are the best known examples of predatory consumer lending, but there are many others. In a **pawn shop loan**, somewhat similar to the car title loan, the consumer takes out a short-term loan (usually 30 days) and puts up some kind of personal property (e.g., jewelry, gun, computer, appliance, antique) as security for repayment of the loan. The property so collateralized is left in the physical possession of the pawn shop lender (thus it is "pledged"). The loan is made in an amount equal to a reduced value of the property pledged (usually 30-50%). If the borrower does not repay the loan by the due date, the pawn shop can sell the property for its full value and keep it. If the loan plus accrued interest and other charges (e.g., storage and transaction fees) is paid, the borrower can recover possession of the property pledged. Like other short-term consumer loans, pawn shop loans are often renewed or extended indefinitely with payment of accrued interest.

Buy Here Pay Here used car transactions are often subject to predatory credit terms and questionable business practices. Catering to low-income Americans who cannot qualify for a conventional car loan, these used car dealers offer the convenience of financing a car purchase through the dealer including granting the dealer/seller a security interest in the car purchased. This may seem like a good deal, except that the interest rate charged is often a multiple of the current rates of conventional loans, often 30 percent per annum or more.

Same as Cash financing offers, seen often in ads for the purchase of furniture, appliances, and other consumer goods, may contain hidden dangers for unsophisticated buyers. Seeming to offer an extended term for payment of the purchase price with no interest charged ("No interest for 24 months! Same as cash!"), the transaction may actually be a deferred interest trap containing a nasty surprise for the consumer. Typically in these transactions, if full payment is not made within the free term, then an interest rate much higher than conventional rates (40 percent per annum is not unusual) is assessed on the entire purchase price (even though a portion of the price has been paid) and the interest due is calculated over the entire period since purchase, including what the consumer thought was the interest-free period. These deals are often criticized as well for not making it clear what the length of the free term actually is and for not disclosing in advance the interest rate to be charged.

Delayed title transactions such as **rent-to-own** (RTO) contracts can pose risks for consumers. In such transactions the contract will provide that title to the property remains with seller until the buyer makes the final lease payment.

The obvious risk to the consumer buyer in such a situation is that he is acquiring no equity or ownership interest in the property as he makes the payments. If he defaults at any point during the payment term, the contract is terminated and he receives no refund of payments made. The buyer builds up no equity in the property to which he is entitled upon default as he would be if title was conveyed at the beginning of the transaction and seller retained only a security interest in the property. Consumer advocates argue that RTOs should be treated as sales on credit with title passing to the buyer at the time of contracting subject only to a security interest in the seller. In the absence of legislation at the federal or state level, courts in a few states have so held. See, e.g., *Perez v. Rent-A-Center, Inc.*, 186 N.J. 188, 892 A.2d 1255 (2006).

CHAPTER SUMMARY

Most debt is created consensually, by contract, as in a traditional loan of money or the establishment of a line of credit or the purchase of goods and services on credit. But other debt is created by government regulation as in taxes and administrative fines and penalties. And final court judgments also create debt where there was none as in tort litigation.

A basic distinction in debtor/creditor law is between secured and unsecured debt. Both consumer and business debtors routinely grant lenders and other creditors consensual security interests in their personal and real property. The creation and enforcement of a security interest in personal property is governed by Article 9 of the UCC. The creation of a security interest in personalty requires that the debtor enter into a security agreement at which time the equitable interest of the creditor attaches to the collateral. The security interest in most personalty is perfected by filing a financing statement with the appropriate governmental department but perfection can also be attained by the creditor retaining possession of the collateral and a purchase money security interest in consumer goods is automatically perfected without regard to filing or possession. Perfection determines the secured creditor's priority status versus other secured and unsecured creditors who may seek recourse to the collateral to satisfy their claims against the debtor. A security interest in realty is created by a mortgage instrument, called a deed of trust in many states. Perfection of a mortgage interest in realty is achieved by compliance with the state's recording statute.

Another form of consensual security for debt is seen in the law of suretyship and guaranty, arrangements whereby a surety or guarantor agrees to be responsible for the debt of another. A true surety, such as the co-signer of a note, is primarily liable along with the debtor for whom the loan or credit was extended whereas a guarantor is only secondarily liable.

A special problem involving both secured and unsecured debt is predatory lending to primarily low-income consumers including the payday loan, a short-term loan to a debtor paid by a postdated check timed to be deposited as soon as the debtor's next paycheck is deposited and charging a double- or triple-digit rate of interest; the car title loan where the consumer conveys a security interest in his or her vehicle to the lender in exchange for a short-term loan at a double- or triple-digit rate of interest; and other similar arrangements such as the pawn shop loan, buy here pay here vendor financing, same as cash incentives, and risky rent-to-own transactions.

REVIEW QUESTIONS

1. Name three different ways that debt can be created.
2. Who is the "maker" of a promissory note? Who is the "payee" of the note?
3. Define "debtor" and "creditor" and explain the difference between the two.
4. What is an acceleration clause in a promissory note?
5. What does it mean to say that a promissory note is nonrecourse?
6. When does a security interest in personal property "attach" to the collateral? When does a security interest in real property "attach" to the realty?
7. What is a purchase money security interest and what is the significance of it in the context of the perfection of a security interest in some personal property?
8. Explain why an unperfected security interest in personal or real property leaves the collateral vulnerable to the claims of other secured or unsecured creditors of the debtor seeking recourse to it to satisfy their claims.
9. What are the three kinds of recording statutes for realty used by the various states and how do they differ?
10. Explain the difference between a surety being primarily liable along with the debtor for the obligation and a guarantor being only secondarily liable for the obligation. Other than payment of the underlying obligation, how can a guarantor be relieved of the guaranty obligation?
11. Why are payday loans and car title loans considered predatory lending by consumer advocates? Which involves the granting of a security interest in the debtor's property?
12. For each of the following scenarios, identify (i) the way this debt was created (by contract, assignment, law, or court judgment); (ii) whether the debt or claim is liquidated, unliquidated, or partially liquidated; and (iii) whether the debt is contingent or noncontingent.
    a. John Client has been audited by the IRS and assessed $50,000 in back income taxes. The IRS disallowed almost all of his business deductions taken over the past three tax years. Client insists the deductions are all proper.
    b. Sally Client has pled guilty to the crime of shoplifting and has been ordered by the court to pay $500 in restitution to the merchant from whom she stole. Client is relieved she got no jail time and plans no appeal.
    c. Richard Client bought a car from Honest Jack's Used Cars for $15,000. Later, he learned that Honest Jack had run back the mileage odometer on the car before selling it to him. The car showed only 60,000 miles when Client bought it, but it actually had 160,000 miles on it. The car that he paid $15,000 for is actually worth only $5,000. Client sues, asking for the difference in the value of the car plus punitive damages.
    d. Mary Client agreed to paint Fred's house for $1,000. She finished the job and Fred was happy with it but said he had no money to pay her.

e. JoAnne is a make-up artist. One of her clients is the famous TV anchor-woman, Wendy City. JoAnne got sick yesterday and was unable to be at the studio yesterday evening to do Wendy's makeup. But JoAnne called her friend, Phyllis, who agreed to do Wendy's makeup that evening. However, Phyllis forgot and didn't show. Wendy went on the air with no makeup and is now furious. Wendy sues Phyllis asking for $1 million for harm to her reputation as a result of having to do the broadcast without makeup. Phyllis admits she is liable for not showing up but denies that Wendy has suffered any harm.

WORDS AND PHRASES TO REMEMBER

acceleration of indebtedness clause
accommodation party
adjustable rate note
after-acquired property
agency rules and regulations
amortized payments
automatic perfection
balloon note
bidding in
burden of persuasion
buy here pay here
car title loan
certificate of title
collateral
collateralized property
commercially reasonable manner
compensated surety
conversion
credit-bid
deed in lieu of foreclosure
deed of trust
deficiency balance
deficiency judgment
encumbrance
election of remedies
equity
equity of redemption
extension of credit
Fair Credit Reporting Act
final judgment
financing statement
fixed rate note
floating lien
foreclosure
future advances
gratuitous surety

guaranty (agreement)
holder
home equity loan
impleader action
installment note
interest
judicial foreclosure
judgment creditor
judgment debtor
junior lien holder
junior mortgage
lien
line of credit loan
maker
Making Home Affordable Program
mortgage
mortgage deed
mortgage modification
mortgage note
mortgagee
mortgagor
nominated property
non-assignment clause
non-rebuttable presumption
nonrecourse note
notice of sale
ordinances
owner's equity
owner finance
payday loan
payee
payor
perfection
pledged property
predatory lending
proceeds

power of sale (foreclosure)

primarily liable

prime rate

promissory note

purchase money mortgage

purchase money security interest (PMSI)

pure notice recording statute

race recording statute

race-notice recording statute

rebuttable presumption

recording statute

referee's deed

referee's sale

relates back

rent-to-own

repossession

reverse mortgage

revolving credit

right of foreclosure

same as cash

secondarily liable

security agreement

security deed

self-help repossession

self-finance

senior lien holder

senior mortgage

sheriff's deed

sheriff's sale

short sale

statutes

statutory right of redemption

surety (agreement, bond, compensated versus accommodation)

temporary forbearance

trustee's deed

Uniform Commercial Code (UCC)

usury

variable rate note

wrongful repossession

TO LEARN MORE: A number of TLM activities to accompany this chapter are accessible on the companion web site for this textbook at http://aspen lawschool.com/books/Parsons_Debt4e/.

Chapter Three:

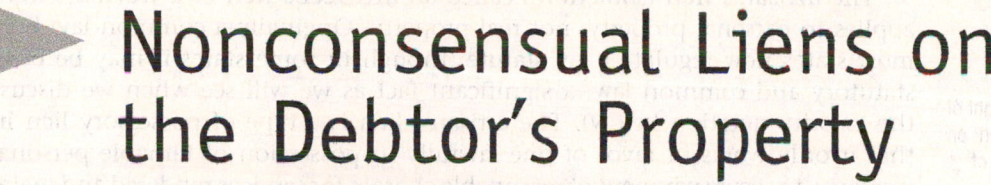

Nonconsensual Liens on the Debtor's Property

KEY CONCEPTS

- States recognize a number of involuntary nonconsensual liens that may attach to a debtor's property by statute or common law
- A nonconsensual lien is a possessory lien if it requires the creditor asserting the lien to have possession of the property encumbered by the lien
- Commonly asserted possessory liens in consumer cases include the artisan's lien and the landlord's lien
- Nonpossessory liens that may be asserted on a debtor's property include the healthcare services lien, federal or state tax liens, the child care lien, the mechanics' or materialman's lien on real property, and the lien *lis pendens* on real property
- The judicial lien is an involuntary lien granted by statute to one who obtains a final judgment against the judgment debtor, and extends to the nonexempt property of the debtor

Statutory lien A nonconsensual lien created by statute rather than by contract or court order.

Common law lien A nonconsensual lien recognized by case law; sometimes called an **equitable lien**.

To be distinguished from consensual security interests granted by a consumer in his personal or real property are a variety of **nonconsensual liens** recognized in every state by statute or common law. Where created by statute they may be referred to generally as **statutory liens**. Where they are still recognized by case law, they are referred to as **common law liens** or **equitable liens**. Whether the nonconsensual lien that attaches to a debtor's real or personal property will be recognized as valid when the debtor files for bankruptcy relief and what priority it will be given relative to other claims to the same property are both questions that commonly arise in debtor/creditor disputes outside of bankruptcy as, as we will see, continue when the debtor files for bankruptcy relief. In this chapter, we will consider the most commonly recognized nonconsensual liens.

 A.

Possessory Liens on Personal Property

Possessory lien A lien that depends on the lien holder having possession of the property.

Lien holder The creditor who holds a nonconsensual lien.

Some nonconsensual liens are **possessory liens**, which means the **lien holder** must have possession of the property in which the lien is claimed. Others are **nonpossessory liens**, which means that the lien holder need not have possession of the property in order to assert the lien. In this section we consider the most significant possessory liens.

Nonpossessory lien A lien that arises even though the lien holder does not have possession of the property.

Artisan's lien The right of one who performs work on the personal property of another to retain possession of the property as security for payment and to sell the property and apply the proceeds to the amount due.

1. The Artisan's Lien

The **artisan's lien** (sometimes called an **artificer's lien** or a **worker's lien**) applies to personal property, not real property. Originally a common law lien, most states now regulate it by statute (though in some states it may be both statutory and common law, a significant fact as we will see when we discuss the priority question below). The artisan's lien is a type of possessory lien in that it only works in favor of one lawfully in possession of tangible personal property, to secure payment of reasonable charges for services rendered and materials supplied. A typical artisan's lien statute defines artisans to include "persons with whom are left goods or products to be repaired, developed, processed, or improved." And such persons are declared to have a lien on goods that have been left with them for repair or improvement to the extent of the artisan's charges related to the goods. There are any number of businesses that may be entitled to assert an artisan's lien, including:

vehicle/small engine mechanics	pet groomers
	computer repair technicians
jewelers	aircraft maintenance technicians
cobblers	upholsterers
tailors	appliance repairers
picture framers	metal fabricators
dry cleaners	cotton ginners
printers and bookbinders	veterinarians

Some states cover all such businesses under a single artisan's lien statute, whereas others have a variety of business-specific lien statutes (e.g., a vehicle repair lien and a separate launderer's lien).

EXAMPLE

Assume Nick and Pearl Murphy take the living room couch that is pledged to Shears Department Store and have it recovered by Martha's Fabric Service. When the Murphys arrive to pick up their recovered couch, a dispute arises over the charge for recovering the couch. The Murphys refuse to pay and Martha refuses to return their couch unless they do. She intends to sell the couch if the Murphys don't pay. Martha is asserting an artisan's lien in the couch.

P-H 3-a: Assume Yourstate has a statutory definition of "artisan" that is identical to the one given in the first paragraph of this section. On the facts given, does Martha's Fabric Service qualify as an artisan under the statute?

P-H 3-b: Assume Nick Murphy is buying gas for his car at a local gas station. When he is finished pumping the gas, the station owner asks Nick to pay a nickel per gallon more than the posted price because he was getting ready to change the price anyway. Nick refuses to pay the extra nickel per gallon and the station operator won't let him drive the car off until he pays. He says he's claiming an artisan's lien in the car. Does the station owner appear to qualify as an "artisan" under the statutory language?

Normally, the artisan retains possession of the property hoping the owner will pay the bill owed or negotiate a settlement of it. But if that does not happen, the artisan, after some statutory period time (e.g., 90 days or six months) can enforce the lien by selling the property in satisfaction of the debt. To enforce the lien, the artisan must give written notice to the owner and anyone else she determines claims an interest in the property (e.g., if she knows of a co-owner or a secured party in the property). The purpose of the notice is to enable the owner, or other person having an interest, to pay the debt and recover the property prior to sale.

The notice typically must describe the property, itemize the services performed by the artisan, state the amount owed, and demand payment by a stated date from the date of the notice. Assume Nick and Pearl Murphy take a couch to an upholsterer for recovering. A dispute arises over the upholsterer's work or the amount of his bill and he refuses to return the couch to them and they refuse to pay. Illustration 3-a shows the artisan's lien notice the upholsterer might send to the Murphys regarding the couch.

Illustration 3-a: NOTICE OF ARTISAN LIENOR'S INTENT TO SELL

<u>Notice of Artisan Lienor's Intent to Sell</u>

TO: Nick and Pearl Murphy [Address]

For the past three months I have retained possession of your Shears 10' living room couch (the property) as I am empowered to do under Yourstate Statutory Code §66-11-205 (the statute) to secure my charges, amounting to $225, due as a reasonable, customary, and usual compensation for the recovering service that I provided in connection with the couch.

You are hereby notified to come forward and pay these charges. On your failure to do so within ten (10) days after this notice has been given to you, I shall sell the property at public sale and apply the proceeds to the payment of such charges, paying over the balance, if any, to you or to the person entitled to it, or holding you liable for any deficiency.

Dated: June 1, YR-1

Martha's Fabric Services, Lienor
By: _____
    Martha S. Fillers, Owner

In some states, the artisan must also advertise, for some statutory number of times (e.g., twice for two consecutive weeks), the intended sale of the item in a newspaper of general circulation in the county where the sale is to be held. In most states, the sale can be public or private. In some states, judicial foreclosure action is required to authorize the sale, and, in others, self-help foreclosure and sale is allowed if the statutory notice requirements have been satisfied. The proceeds of sale are applied first to cover the costs of the notice and any advertisement, then the claim of any other lien holder in the property over which the artisan's lien does not have priority, and then to the amount owed the artisan. Any surplus proceeds are returned to the owner.

The artisan's lien, like any possessory lien, remains perfected so long as the claimant maintains possession of the property subject to it. If the holder of the artisan's lien relinquishes possession of the property, the lien is extinguished.

2. The Landlord's Lien

Landlord's lien Where recognized, right of landlord to seize and sell tenant's personal property left on the premises to satisfy unpaid rent; requires express consent.

The landlord's lien operates on property of the tenant located on the leased premises if the tenant has defaulted in his obligations to pay the landlord. Absent proof of abandonment, most states require express and conspicuous consent to the lien in the lease agreement or the granting of an Article 9 security interest to the landlord before the landlord can seize a tenant's property for nonpayment of rent. Certain property of the debtor is usually exempted from seizure by the landlord and the landlord must leave written notice of entry and provide an itemized list of items taken. The landlord can sell the seized property by giving statutory notice so many days before the sale (e.g., 30 days) and the property may be redeemed by the tenant prior to sale by paying all amounts owed for rent and expenses. If no landlord's lien was reserved in the lease agreement, the landlord must rely on abandonment of the premises by the tenant and take judicial action. On proof of **abandonment** the court will issue what is often called a **warrant of distress** (from the old common law action for distress or distrain), authorizing the removal of the tenant's property from the premises to the street but in most states it cannot be sold by the landlord.

P-H 3-c: Locate the landlord's lien statute in your state and answer the following questions. What property is made exempt from the lien? If the lien is not created but the tenant in arrears abandons the premises, can the landlord sell the tenant's property or merely remove it from the premises?

---

3. The Warehouseman's Lien

Warehouseman's lien The right of a party who has transported or stored personal property of another to retain possession of and sell that property to satisfy an unpaid obligation.

The **warehouseman's lien** recognizes the right of a party who has transported or stored a commodity (e.g., oil or corn), an animal, or other personal property that belongs to another to declare a lien on such commodity or goods still in the warehouse's possession to secure payment for unpaid transportation or warehousing charges.

EXAMPLE

> An oil refinery in Texas may purchase oil from an international seller. The oil is shipped and delivered to a storage facility that takes possession of and then stores the oil until the buyer can pick it up. In the consumer context, a garage keeper may agree to let the owner of a vehicle store his vehicle in the garage keeper's facility. Or, a self-service storage business may lease storage units to consumers and other customers in which to store their property. Or, a pet hotel may keep an owner's pet while the owner is on vacation. Or, a shipping company transports goods on behalf of a seller. In any of these situations, whether commercial or consumer, if the agreed fee for transport or storage is not paid when due, then the party transporting or storing the other's property may refuse to turn over the property to the party demanding possession, assert the lien in the property, and retain it until payment is made.

The warehouseman's lien existed at common law and the common law lien is still recognized in many states. However, it has been made statutory in UCC §7-209. And UCC §7-210 controls the procedure for enforcing the lien and requires notice to all parties having an interest in the goods.

P-H 3-d: Locate the version of UCC §7-210 in effect in your state. What information is the required notice to contain? How long must the warehouse wait after notice is given before the goods can be sold? Can the sale be executed by either public (auction) or private sale? Must the goods be sold by the warehouse at their absolute best price or is a commercially reasonable price good enough?

In states that still recognize the warehouseman's lien at common law, it may apply only to those that store goods and not to those that transport them. But those states will likely recognize a separate lien for those that transport goods, usually called a **carrier's lien**, and it will work the same way as the warehouseman's lien.

4. The Article 2 Buyer's Lien

UCC §2-711(3) creates a nonconsensual possessory lien in favor of a buyer in a transaction for the sale of goods. It arises wherein a buyer of goods who receives shipment of the goods from the seller and who then properly rejects the goods or properly revokes his acceptance of the goods is authorized to declare a nonconsensual security interest in goods in his possession until the seller reimburses him for any down payment made to seller for the goods and any expenses incurred in inspection, transportation, care, and custody of the goods. This buyer can refuse to return the goods to the seller until those obligations are paid, and if the seller refuses to pay, then the buyer can sell the goods to recover the costs.

EXAMPLE

> Henrietta orders a new computer from Bell Computers. She pays for it in advance. The computer is delivered to Henrietta but she quickly discovers that it doesn't work. She notifies Bell Computer that she is rejecting the computer and demands a refund of her money. Bell demands that she return the computer to Bell before refunding her money. Henrietta may be able to refuse that demand, declare a UCC §2-711(3) lien in the computer, and sell it to recoup her costs if refund is not forthcoming.

P-H 3-e: Locate the version of UCC §2-711(3) in effect in the state where you plan to practice. What is the procedure for a buyer to follow in this situation when he or she wants to sell the goods in which the lien is asserted?

Attorney's or accountant's retaining lien The right of a licensed professional to retain possession of a client's personal property until the client pays the amount owed or provides other security.

5. The Attorney's or Accountant's Retaining Lien

Many states recognize an attorney's or accountant's retaining lien (or benefiting other licensed professionals) authorizing the professional to retain possession of a client's books, papers, securities, money, or other property (but not to dispose of as by sale, because it is a "passive" or "retention" lien only (see, e.g., *Brauer v. Hotel Associates, Inc.*, 192 A.2d 831, 833-834 (N.J. 1963)), until the client pays his bill or posts adequate security to cover it. Similarly, a banker's lien may authorize a bank or other financial institution to assert the lien in a customer's property in the bank's possession (e.g., cash on deposit or certificates of deposit) and to take it to satisfy debts owed the bank.

6. The Vendor's Lien

Many states recognize a vendor's lien in favor of a party that sells personal property but retains possession of it until the full purchase price is paid (sometimes called a **layaway** or **layby** arrangement), usually enforceable as if an Article 9 consensual security interest had been granted by the buyer to the seller in the goods.

7. Other Possessory Liens

There are any number of other possessory liens recognized by various states. For example, a **banker's lien** may authorize a bank or other financial institution to assert the lien in a customer's property in the bank's possession (e.g., cash on deposit in checking or savings accounts or certificates of deposit) and to take it to satisfy obligations owed to the bank by the debtor (e.g., an unpaid loan, an overdrawn checking account, etc.). Or the state may recognize a **hotel operator's lien** imposed on a guest's personal property stored on the hotel premises, including automobiles and baggage, to secure reasonable room rents.

8. Priority of Possessory Liens

Interestingly, UCC §9-333 gives possessory liens priority over prior consensual security interests in the property subject to the lien whether the prior security interest is perfected or not. That section provides that "a possessory lien on goods has priority over a security interest in the goods unless the lien is created by a statute that expressly provides otherwise." Note the important caveat at the end: The possessory lien has priority *unless* the statute creating the possessory lien says it doesn't.

EXAMPLE

Look at the warehouseman's lien created in UCC §7-209. Subsection (c) contains a "provides otherwise" clause of the type referenced in UCC §9-333 that prevents the warehouseman's lien created by §7-209 from achieving priority over a prior, properly perfected consensual security interest unless the holder of that security interest expressly or impliedly approved the debtor's submitting the goods to another's lien claim as by shipment or storage of the goods. The possessory warehouseman's lien will, however, defeat a prior unperfected security interest in the property.

In fact, most statutory possessory liens will provide expressly that the lien does not attain priority over preexisting and properly perfected mortgages, security interests, or other liens on the property unless notice is given to the creditors holding such preexisting claims and they consent in writing. For example, a typical artisan's lien statute may read, "A lien under this section shall be subject to all prior liens of record, unless notice is given to all lien holders of record and written consent is obtained from all lien holders of record to the making, repairing, improving, or enhancing the value of any personal property and in this event the lien created under this section shall be prior to liens of record."

P-H 3-f: Assume that the Murphys purchased the couch later recovered by Martha's from Shears Department Store on credit and Shears retained a purchase money security interest (PMSI) in it. Between Martha's Fabric Service, asserting an artisan's lien in the couch, and Shears Department Store, asserting a consensual security interest in the couch, who has the priority position under the statutory language in the preceding example? Might the result turn on whether the security interest of Shears is a lien "of record"? If Shears filed a financing statement to perfect its security interest in the couch, it is of record. But if Shears did not file a financing statement and is depending on perfection by way of a purchase money security interest in consumer goods, Martha's artisan's lien may be deemed senior. Locate the artisan's lien statute in effect in your state practice. Does it expressly provide that prior perfected security interests have priority over it? How would the dispute between Shears and Martha's Fabric Service be decided under that statute?

Note that UCC §9-333 says that a possessory lien will have priority "unless the lien is created by a statute that expressly provides otherwise. . . ." Many states still recognize one or more common law possessory liens, leaving the question of whether the priority scheme mandated by UCC §9-333 applies to those common law liens.

●

CHARTER ONE AUTO FINANCE V. INKAS COFFEE DISTRIBUTORS REALTY

57 UCC Rep. Serv. 2d 672, 39 Conn. L. Rptr. 110 (Conn. Super. Ct. 2005)

OPINION: Shapiro, Judge

Plaintiff Charter One Auto Finance (Charter) was assigned a retail installment contract (contract) in which the defendant, Inkas Coffee Distribution Realty and Equipment LLC (Inkas) purchased a 2001 Ford F250 (the motor vehicle) for $36,340.00, which was to be paid in 60 monthly installments. Charter was granted a security interest in the motor vehicle on or about September 20, 2000 which lien was duly noted on the certificate of title of the motor vehicle. Inkas is currently in default under the contract for failure to make payments due for July 4, 2001 to the present. Inkas' debt to Charter, exclusive of legal fees and costs was $33,391.57. The reasonable value of the motor vehicle was $24,350.00.

Connecticut International Parking, LLC (Connecticut International) is engaged in the business of storing motor vehicles at its open air parking lot located in East Granby, Connecticut. On or about May 10, 2001, Inkas delivered the motor vehicle to Connecticut International pursuant to an oral agreement to store it. Pursuant to that agreement, Inkas agreed to pay Connecticut International its standard rate of $9.25 per day for storage.

Pursuant to the oral agreement, Connecticut International took and maintained lawful possession of the motor vehicle from May 10, 2001 through May 16, 2004, and incurred $9,851.00 for storage fees during that period. Also, while the motor vehicle was in its possession, Connecticut International maintained and cared for it by regularly checking it. Connecticut International started and moved the motor vehicle on at least a monthly basis to ensure that its engine, mechanical system, and tires would remain in operating condition. Connecticut International did not send any notices to Charter during the period in which the motor vehicle was in Connecticut International's possession.

On or about April 16, 2004, Charter, claiming that it had lien rights in the motor vehicle, demanded that Connecticut International deliver it to Charter. Connecticut International offered to deliver the motor vehicle to Charter upon proof of Charter's rights, but demanded that Connecticut International be paid for the storage charges owed to it. Charter refused the demand and obtained an order of replevin for the motor vehicle pursuant to which a bond was posted.

Connecticut International believes it is entitled to recover the sum of $9,851.00, plus interest. By virtue of its prior perfected security interest in the motor vehicle, Charter believes that it is not obligated to pay Connecticut International. Inkas filed for bankruptcy, which case was dismissed in December 2001. Charter and Connecticut International stipulated also, upon information and belief that Inkas is unable to pay either of them.

In its complaint, Charter One seeks replevin, which, as noted above, already has occurred, and other relief, including money damages and attorney's fees. Connecticut International filed a two-count counterclaim seeking a determination of the rights of the parties, and various other forms of relief . . . .

Charter One's recorded security interest of September 20, 2000 pre-dated the date, May 10, 2001, when Connecticut International took and maintained lawful possession of the motor vehicle and when storage fees began to be incurred. The pivotal legal issue in this matter is whether or not a common-law possessory lien has priority over a previously recorded security interest.

Connecticut law long has recognized a common-law possessory lien. In *Leavy v. Kinsella*, 39 Conn. 50, 53 (1872), concerning the keeping of two pigs, our Supreme Court stated that "in general all bailees for hire have a lien on the thing bailed for the amount of their compensation, and common carriers and innkeepers have peculiar claims to their liens, because they cannot refuse to incur the expense cast upon them by their customers. And here the defendant may ground his right to a lien upon similar principles of justice and equity."

Subsequently, in a matter involving the keeping and feeding of a horse, the Supreme Court reiterated, "A lien is the right which a creditor has of detaining in his possession the goods of his debtor until the debt is paid. To the common-law idea of a lien it is necessary that the creditor should have the actual possession of the goods over which the lien is claimed, and that the debt should have been incurred in respect to the very goods detained." *Fishell v. Morris*, 57 Conn. 547, 551, 18 A. 717 (1889). The court noted also that such a common law lien is distinct from that created by a statute. See id., at 552. "In all cases where statutes have created any right of security on the property of a debtor in the nature of a lien, not depending on possession, they have provided carefully for a registration of the transaction." Id. See *State v. Marsala*, 59 Conn. App. 755 A.2d 965, cert. denied, 762 A.2d 902 (2000).

In addition to the common law underpinnings of the possessory lien, General Statute §49-61(a), concerning an artificer's lien, provides a mechanism by which a personal property owner may apply to the Superior Court to dissolve a bailee for hire's lien upon substitution of bond. Subsequent subsections of General Statute 49-61 provide for a procedure by which, as to a motor vehicle, a bailee for hire may give notice of his lien and for a sale of the property. See General Statute §49-61(b)-(e). [I]n view of the court's finding as to Connecticut International's priority status as a common-law possessory lien-holder, it need not determine whether Connecticut International has any lien rights under §49-61.

The similarity between a possessory lien for the keeping of a horse and one for storing and maintaining a motor vehicle is obvious. While the passage of time and the development of the automobile may now have made the latter a more common occurrence than the former, the legal principles underlying such a possessory lien remain intact.

In seeking summary judgment, Charter One . . . argues that the decisional law on the common law possessory lien . . . is unavailing "since [those cases] simply did not involve prior lienholders." See Charter One's memorandum of law, p. 7.

The court concludes that Connecticut's UCC provides that such a possessory lien has priority over a previously recorded security interest. Our legislature revised Article 9 of the UCC, effective on October 1, 2001. However, at the time the relative priorities of the claims were established, Connecticut General Statute §42a-9-310 provided as follows: "When a person in the ordinary course of his business furnishes services or materials with respect to goods subject to a security interest, a lien upon goods in the possession of such person given by statute or rule of law for such materials or services takes priority over a perfected security interest unless the lien is statutory and the statute expressly provides otherwise." In discussing the wording of Section 9-310, White & Summers notes that, "State statutory and common-law liens are excluded from the scope of Article 9, with the exception of the section 9-310 priority rule." J. White & R. Summers, Uniform Commercial Code (4th Ed. 1995) §30-12, p. 93 . . . .

Applying §9-310's priority rule, it is undisputed here that, in the ordinary course of its business, Connecticut International furnished services with respect to the motor vehicle. Until the motor vehicle was replevied by Charter One, Connecticut International was lawfully in possession of the motor vehicle. By operation of the common law, it was entitled to a possessory lien. This possessory lien is not premised on a statute; accordingly, the "unless" part of §9-310s rule is inapplicable. Also, the court is unaware of a statute which expressly provides that a perfected security interest has priority over such a common law possessory lien and Charter One has not cited any. Pursuant to former §42a-9-310, Connecticut International's possessory lien has priority over Charter One's perfected security interest . . . .

In view of the court's conclusion as to the priority status of Connecticut International's common-law possessory lien, the court need not determine the applicability of any statutory lien rights which Connecticut International may have had. See General Statutes §49-61 (artificer's lien), discussed above, and General Statute §42a-7-209 (warehouseman's lien).

Accordingly, judgment as to liability may enter for Connecticut International as to its claim on the replevin bond and for unjust enrichment.

Charter One Auto Finance v. Inkas Coffee Distributors Realty: Real Life Applications

1. Because of the dates on which the transactions in this case occurred, it was decided based on the version of Article 9 in effect in Connecticut prior to the 2001 revisions to Article 9; thus the reference in the opinion to Connecticut General Statute Annotated (C.G.S.A.) §42a-9-310. The 2001 revision to Article 9 adopted in Connecticut that same year (and now in all states) revised and renumbered C.G.S.A. §42a-9-310 as C.G.S.A. §42a-9-333. Locate the current wording of the revised Connecticut statute. Would the case likely be decided

the same way under the revised statute? How would it likely be decided under the wording of UCC §9-333 now in effect in your state?

2. Assume the law firm you work for represents Bank in each of the following scenarios. Identify the possessory lien, *if any*, that the other party might assert to gain priority over Bank and state how your supervising attorney will likely advise the client as to how a court will likely rule. If necessary, identify what additional information you will need to make that determination.

    a. Debtor has given Bank a security interest in her car and Bank has perfected by noting its security interest on the title. Debtor is in default and Bank wishes to repossess but debtor's son has possession of the car at his college in Canada.

    b. Same situation as in Question a except that debtor has left the car at Mike's Repair Shop for maintenance and has not yet paid Mike.

    c. Same situation as in Question a except that debtor left car with neighbor for safekeeping for a month while debtor travels. Neighbor agreed to keep the car as a favor. Different result if debtor promised to pay neighbor $10 a day?

    d. Debtor lives in a resort area that attracts tourists and makes and sells hand carved items from local hardwoods that are sold in arts and crafts stores in the area. Debtor has a loan from Bank properly secured and perfected in part by the carvings debtor makes and sells. Debtor enters a contract to sell 100 carvings to Craft Store and delivered the carvings to Craft Store last week. However, the carvings delivered to Craft Store were defective and Craft Store rejected the carvings but retained possession until debtor refunds the prepaid purchase price. Debtor is in default to Bank and Bank wishes to repossess all the collateralized assets of debtor including the rejected carvings. See UCC §2-711(3).

B. Nonpossessory Liens on Real and Personal Property

A number of statutory and common law liens do not require that the creditor asserting the lien have possession of the property subject to the nonconsensual lien. In this section we consider the major nonconsensual nonpossessory liens on real or personal property.

1. The Attorney's Charging Lien

Attorney's charging lien A nonpossessory lien imposed on a judgment or settlement amount due the client for the amount owed the attorney.

In contrast to the attorney's retaining lien mentioned in the previous section, which authorizes an attorney to retain possession of, but not sell, a client's books, papers, or other properties until the attorney is paid, most states recognize a separate lien, called the attorney's charging lien either by statute, common law, or both (for a good discussion of the distinction between the two liens, see *Starks v. Browning*, 20 S.W.3d 645, 650 (Tenn. Ct. App. 1999)). The charging lien is a nonpossessory lien imposed on any judgment rendered in the client's favor or on settlement proceeds due to the client in which the attorney has an

Illustration 3-b: NOTICE OF ATTORNEY'S CHARGING LIEN IN RETAINER AGREEMENT

> The parties agree that the attorney hereby claims a lien on any and all property of the client that is or may come into the possession of the attorney in connection with this representation and on any judgment or settlement amount that is or may become payable to the client as a result of this representation.

interest (e.g., an undistributed contingency fee). To enforce the lien in most states, the attorney must give written notice of the lien, record a notice of lien in the designated public records office, and file suit against the client to enforce the lien. Often the attorney's retainer agreement with the client will include a notice of the lien, using language similar to Illustration 3-b.

2. The Healthcare Services Lien

Healthcare services lien A nonpossessory lien imposed on amounts due to a patient from a third party responsible for the patient's medical condition to secure amounts owed to the healthcare provider.

Most states authorize a **healthcare services lien** to be asserted by a wide range of licensed healthcare professionals (e.g., physicians, dentists, optometrists, therapists) and providers (e.g., hospitals, clinics, EMS services, rehabilitation services) against any claim or cause of action that the patient may have against a third party who may be liable to the patient for injuries related to the healthcare service provided. The lien goes by various names in different states: medical lien, hospital lien, personal injury lien, to name a few. The lien is satisfied out of the proceeds of any judgment, award (as by arbitration), or settlement that the patient receives from the third party. Typically, a limit is imposed on the percentage of the patient's recovery that the lienholders as a class can take (e.g., 40%). Though the procedures for enforcing the healthcare services lien vary considerably among the states, the claimant is typically required to file or record a verified (sworn) statement setting forth the name and address of the patient and the claimant; the dates of the patient's treatment or admission and discharge; the amount claimed to be due for the healthcare or hospital care provided; and to the best of the claimant's knowledge, the names and addresses of those claimed by such patient to be liable for damages arising from the patient's illness or injuries. The statement must be filed or recorded in a designated public office (e.g., the county recorder's office or the county trustee's office for the county in which the services were provided) within a designated period of time (e.g., no later than 30 days after the services were provided).

Notice of the lien must then be given to each person believed to be liable on account of the illness or injury, and to the patient or the patient's attorney, usually by providing them with a copy of the sworn statement asserting the lien. Such notice can be mailed by certified or registered mail or hand delivered. At this point, the lien has been properly created and perfected. Thereafter, no settlement, judgment, or award resulting from the patient's claim against the responsible third party is free of the lien unless the lien holder joins in the settlement or executes a release of the lien.

If the healthcare professional or provider fails to file the lien in a timely manner or otherwise fails to follow the prescribed procedures to create and perfect it, that entity will be deemed to have waived the rights to the lien for the amounts the entity could have asserted in it (but not for charges for future services). Of course, a healthcare services lien can be granted by the patient by contract at any time, in which case a waiver will not be an issue.

EXAMPLE

Assume a person is involved in a car accident and receives medical services from the local hospital at a total cost of $10,000. The patient plans to file suit against the other driver. If the hospital for some reason fails to file and perfect its lien in a timely manner, it has waived the statutory or common law lien. However, the hospital may include the lien in the contract that the patient signs as part of the patient services rendered. Or, after waiver has occurred, the hospital may negotiate a contractual lien with the patient. The patient may do this to keep the hospital from filing suit against him to collect the amount owed while the suit against the other driver is still pending.

If the patient accepts any payment on the claim against the third party without obtaining a release or satisfaction of the healthcare services lien, the lien holder is entitled to enforce the lien by judicial action. In most states, that suit may be against the patient, the patient's attorney, or any other creditor of the patient who received proceeds impressed with the lien.

EXAMPLE

Assume that, following her botched appendectomy, Pearl Murphy is treated at Mercy Hospital in Capital City (not the hospital she sued; that was Capital City Hospital (CCH)) and incurs there a bill of $2,500, which insurance does not cover and which she and Nick have been unable to pay. Mercy Hospital properly files and gives notice of a hospital lien for that amount by sending copies of its verified statement to the Murphys and their attorney. Then the Murphys agree to a settlement of their lawsuit against CCH and Dr. Craft in the amount of $300,000. Once those settlement funds are in the hands of the Murphys' attorney for distribution, they are impressed with the hospital lien of Mercy Hospital. The Murphys' attorney must be careful to pay Mercy Hospital out of those funds. If she fails to do so, the hospital is entitled to enforce its lien by suing the Murphys and their attorney to collect the amount of the lien wrongfully denied it.

As the previous example shows, attorneys handling claims for plaintiffs must make arrangements to either satisfy or compromise a healthcare services lien before distributing funds paid in judgment or settlement.

EXAMPLE

Assume that an injured person has incurred $10,000 in hospital bills and the hospital properly creates and perfects a lien in that amount. His lawyer, who has taken the patient's case against a responsible third party on a one-third contingency basis, negotiates with the attorney for that party, but there are potentially valid defenses to his client's claim and the best the lawyer can settle the claim for is $15,000. Paying the hospital's lien in full would leave only $5,000 to be distributed to the client and the attorney and the attorney was expecting one-third of any settlement, which would eat up the remaining $5,000. Of course, the attorney and his client could simply reject the settlement offer and take their chances at trial. But what if the attorney is convinced that they will likely lose at trial and, even in a best-case scenario, recover no more than the $15,000 being offered. The attorney for the patient may negotiate with the hospital to accept 50 percent of its lien amount and release the rest. If the hospital agrees, the lien will be released and the funds will be distributed, $5,000 to the hospital, about $5,000 to the attorney, and the balance to the patient. What would be the incentive for the hospital to agree to compromise its lien claim in that situation?

3. Mechanic's and Materialman's Liens on Real Property

Mechanic's lien A statutory lien on realty available to a party who has supplied labor for the improvement of the realty.

Materialman's lien A statutory lien on realty available to a party who has supplied materials for the improvement of the realty.

A **mechanic's and materialman's lien** (sometimes called a **construction lien** or **supplier's lien**) is a nonpossessory lien that can be placed on real property to secure payment to one who has performed labor on the property (the mechanic) or supplied materials (the materialman) to repair or improve it. For convenience, we will refer to it as the mechanic's lien. The mechanic's lien is typically asserted by contractors (including both general contractors and subcontractors), laborers, and suppliers of materials for the job. In some states, surveyors, architects, and engineers who have worked on the project may also be entitled to the lien's protection.

EXAMPLE

Assume that Santiago's Concrete Service (SCS) enters a contract with Adams Construction Company (ACC) to pour concrete slabs for a house that ACC is building for the owner, Sofia Rodriguez. SCS supplies the concrete, pours the slabs, and sends ACC an invoice for its work. However, a dispute has arisen between ACC and Sofia and ACC tells SCS it does not have the money to pay SCS until that dispute is cleared up. To protect itself, SCS files a mechanic's lien on Sofia's lot where the concrete was poured.

State law varies in the procedures for creating a mechanic's lien. In most states, the contractor or supplier wishing to assert the lien must send a written notice of nonpayment to the owner of the property and the general contractor within some specified time frame. Let's assume the law of the state where Sofia's property is located requires the formal notice of nonpayment to be sent "within 90 days of the last day of the month when the goods or services were supplied," which is a typical provision. The notice of nonpayment that SCS sends to Sofia might look like what you see in Illustration 3-c.

Next, the contractor or supplier must file (the statute may say "record" or "register") a notice of lien or abstract of lien in a designated public records office (often the office where land records are recorded or filed) and send a copy of it (usually by registered or certified mail) to the owner, general contractor, and any other claimant of record (e.g., a bank holding a mortgage on the property). A typical state statute provides that the notice of lien or abstract of lien must be filed "within 90 days after work on the project has been substantially completed or the contract terminated." The notice of lien filed or recorded by SCS might look like Illustration 3-d.

Illustration 3-c: NOTICE OF NONPAYMENT

NOTICE OF NONPAYMENT

TO: Sofia J. Rodriguez, Owner
       Address
       Adams Construction Company, General Contractor
       Address

FROM: Santiago's Concrete Service, Claimant
       Address

Pursuant to Yourstate Statutory Code §66-11-101, et seq., claimant hereby gives notice that it provided labor and materials for the improvement of real property located at 2100 Cactus Lane, Capital City, Yourstate as described in the instrument of record in Book 897, Page 455, Register's Office for Capital County, Yourstate and more particularly described as follows: [Property description omitted from illustration.]

The labor and material provided were as described in the subcontract between claimant and Adams Construction Company dated January 30, YR-1, and consisted of the delivery of concrete to the construction site located on the property and the construction of 2 concrete pads on the property. The claim of claimant for the labor and material provided totals $15,000. The claim of claimant for the labor and material provided remains unpaid.

The last day that claimant performed labor or provided materials was February 25, YR-1.

Dated this _____ day of April, YR-1

Santiago's Concrete Service

By: _____

Raymond Santiago, Owner

P-H 3-g: ACC is not the owner of the real property on which the house is being constructed and on which SCS would file its lien; it is only the general contractor. So why should ACC be particularly concerned about the lien being filed? As you think about this question, consider what the contract between ACC and the owner of the property probably says about the obligation of ACC to pay all subcontractors. Might ACC be in breach of its contract with the owner if SCS files this lien? And recall our consideration of surety bonds in Chapter Two. ACC likely was required to obtain a surety bond covering its obligations on the project naming owner as beneficiary. If the owner becomes liable to pay SCS as a result of this mechanic's lien, it will make a claim for compensation against the surety, which will then seek reimbursement from ACC. What other negative consequences can you think of for ACC if SCS files a mechanic's lien on the property?

Illustration 3-d: NOTICE OF LIEN

NOTICE OF LIEN

Santiago's Concrete Service ("SCS"), a sole proprietorship owned by Raymond Santiago of Capital City, Yourstate, having furnished labor and materials to improve the real property described herein pursuant to a contract with Adams Construction Company ("ACC"), for the purpose of giving notice of and/or perfecting a lien on real property and improvements to secure the amount of its claim pursuant to Yourstate Statutory Code §66-11-101, et seq., through its duly authorized officer or representative, states:

That SCS claims a lien upon all interests to which it is entitled under law in the following property situated in Capital County, Yourstate, to-wit: [Property description omitted from illustration.]

This property is also known as 2100 Cactus Lane, Capital City, Yourstate and is described in the instrument of record in Book 897, Page 455, Register's Office for Capital County, Yourstate.

That, based on information and belief, the owner of the above-described property is Sofia Rodriguez.
That, to the extent allowable under law, a lien is hereby claimed to secure an indebtedness of $15,000 for labor and materials furnished relative to the above-described real property and improvements thereon and/or owed under SCS's contract with ACC. This amount includes amounts owed under the original subcontract between SCS and ACC. This lien is also claimed to secure any other allowable interest or service charges, as well as expenses relating to the recording of this Notice in the Register's Office for Capital County, Yourstate. The last day which RCS supplied labor or materials under its contract with ACC relative to this property was February 25, YR-1.

RCS reserves the right to amend this notice of lien.

Filed this 10th day of September, YR-1

SANTIAGO'S CONCRETE SERVICE

By: _____

Raymond Santiago, Owner

[Notarization omitted from illustration.]

Substantial completion The date that construction on real property is substantially completed.

Assume again that the Yourstate notice of lien statute requires filing and notice to others "within 90 days after the project has been substantially completed or the contract terminated," a common requirement. When work on a project has reached **substantial completion** can be a contested issue in mechanic's lien cases. Knowing that, it is common for general contractors to file a **notice of completion** at the earliest reasonable date to start the clock running on the time for filing and notice of the lien.

Illustration 3-e: NOTICE OF COMPLETION

NOTICE OF COMPLETION

1. Name of owner of the land: Sofia J. Rodriguez

2. Name of person, firm or organization contracted with for the entire job or improvement or demolition: Adams Construction Company.

3. Location and description of the property: [property description omitted from illustration].

4. Date of completion of the structure, improvement or demolition: December 1, YR-1.

5. A transfer of ownership of all or a part of the real property or an interest therein and encumbrance thereon or a settlement of the claims of parties entitled to the benefits of Yourstate Statutory Code §66-11-101, et seq., will take place not earlier than thirty days from the date of the filing of this notice of completion.

6. The name and address of the person, firm or organization to which parties entitled to the benefits of the said law may send notice of claims are as follows: Adams Construction Cpmpany, c/o Andrea C. Collins, Attorney at Law, 111 City Tower, Capital City, Yourstate 55677.

DATED the 1st day of December, YR-1

Adams Construction Company, General Contractor

By: _____

Fred W. Adams, President

[Notarization omitted from illustration.]

EXAMPLE

Assume that as the construction project on Sofia Rodriguez's house moves to a conclusion, Sofia and ACC fear there may be more liens coming from other unpaid subcontractors and suppliers. The project is now in the *punch-list* phase: The contractor is completing a punch-list of minor finishing tasks. Sofia or ACC will want to go ahead and record a notice of completion in the office of county land records that will serve as constructive notice of substantial completion and set the 90-day clock ticking for the filing of additional liens. Illustration 3-e shows how the notice of substantial completion on this project might look.

P-H 3-h: Assume that Raymond Santiago, the owner of SCS, comes into the law office where you work on June 1, YR-1, at the beginning of his dispute with ACC over nonpayment of the SCS invoices. He's there to consult concerning his remedies for nonpayment of his invoices. What questions are you or the supervising lawyer going to need to ask him to see if he has the right to file a mechanic's or materialman's lien? Which public records will you need to check to see what has or has not been recorded there?

Once the notice of lien has been duly filed, it is only good for a certain number of days. In many states, a mechanic's lien created by a subcontractor or supplier is good for only 90 days. The same lien created by a general contractor may be good for a longer period, up to a year. What that means is that the party who has created the lien must file suit to enforce the lien before it expires. And the suit to enforce the lien, like the judicial foreclosure on a consensual mortgage, asks the court for an order directing the sale of the property and distribution of proceeds in order of priority to the various creditors. It is not unusual for multiple mechanics' liens to be filed on a parcel where several subcontractors have not been paid. The question of priority among multiple holders of such a lien is a question of who was first to perfect their mechanics' lien.

As with consensual security interests in personal property and mortgages on real property, a mechanics' lien must be created and attach before it can be perfected. There is wide variation among the states as to the answer to this question. In some states, the lien comes into existence and attaches as soon as the contract for services or materials is executed. In other states, it comes into existence the moment services are actually provided or materials delivered to the real property. In some other states, the lien comes into existence only when the contractor or supplier asserting the lien gives the owner and contractor (if it is a subcontractor asserting the lien) formal notice of nonpayment. And in still other states, the lien does not arise until the contractor or supplier files (registers or records) the required notice of lien in the county or city land records office (or other designated local or state office) where the improved property is located and gives formal notice to the owner and other appropriate parties of the filing. There is also considerable variation among the states as to how a mechanics' lien is perfected. In most states, the lien is deemed perfected when the notice of lien is properly filed (recorded or registered) in the proper county or city office of land records and served on the owner and other appropriate parties. However, if the holder of the lien does not thereafter file suit to enforce the lien within the statutorily allowed time after filing (e.g., 90 days for a subcontractor or supplier, one year for a general contractor), the lien will have no priority at all and will be unenforceable for any purpose. Both the creation and perfection are forfeited. In a minority of states, the holder of the lien must actually file the lawsuit to enforce the lien in order for it to be deemed perfected.

A serious question arises regarding what priority a properly created and perfected mechanics' lien has against an existing and properly perfected consensual mortgage on the liened property.

EXAMPLE

Assume that Sofia had borrowed money from Bank on March 1, YR-1, and granted Bank a mortgage in the property that was properly recorded in the land records office that same day, perfecting it. When SCS files its notice of lien at any time after March 1, YR-1, and files suit to enforce it within the statutory time allowed, common sense might suggest that its lien on the property will be junior to the previously created and perfected mortgage in favor of Bank. But that is not necessarily the outcome here. It depends on the language of the controlling statute.

Mechanics' lien statutes commonly provide that such a lien, once created, "relates back to the date when the services or materials were first supplied." If that is the case, then the mechanics' lien of SCS in the preceding example will be treated as having attached and been perfected not when the notice of lien was

Relation back The retrospective effect given to some liens giving them priority from a date prior to their technical perfection.

filed or on the date the lawsuit to enforce the lien was filed, but on February 25, YR-1, prior to the creation of the Bank's mortgage. This **relation-back** feature of a mechanic's lien is not recognized in all states, and where it is not, the mechanic's lien will only have priority from the date it is perfected. In other states, the relation-back feature is present but cannot attain priority over a previously perfected construction loan.

In other states, the relation-back feature is present and goes all the way back, not to the date the contractor first performed work on the site, but to "the effective date of the lienor's contract" or "to the visible commencement of [any] operations" on the site. But usually these generous relation-back features are available only for general contractors or architects, not subcontractors or suppliers. In any state, whatever date the mechanic's lien is deemed to be effective and perfected, it will defeat a prior unperfected mortgage or other unsecured claim to the property. In any event, the relation-back feature of statutory liens can create some dramatic priority clashes.

Real property owned by the federal, state, or local government is normally not subject to attachment by mechanic's lien—a **sovereign immunity** concept. And state statutory liens cannot be asserted in federally funded construction projects. To protect subcontractors and suppliers on federal projects, where the contract price exceeds $100,000, the **Miller Act**, 40 U.S.C. §3131, requires general contractors performing public works projects to provide a **performance bond** (sometimes called a **performance and payment bond**) guaranteeing the faithful performance of the job and payment of all labor and materials obligations to subcontractors and suppliers on the project. Many state and municipal governments similarly require contractors on public works projects to be bonded.

In some states, mechanic's liens may be available to those who have contributed labor or materials to the improvement of personal property.

4. Lien *Lis Pendens*

Lien *lis pendens* Lien on real property asserted by one claiming an ownership interest in the property.

A **lien *lis pendens*** (lien pending the suit) is a statutory lien that may be created in favor of one having a claim against a particular parcel of real property. The purpose of the lien is to put potential purchasers of the property and creditors on formal notice of the lien holder's claim against the property until such time as a lawsuit regarding that claim can be litigated in court. This lien is not available against personal property.

In most states, to create a lien *lis pendens*, the claimant must file an abstract (or notice) of lien *lis pendens* in the designated public office (usually the county office where land records are filed or recorded). The abstract typically must contain the names of the parties to the suit, a description of the real estate affected, its ownership, and a brief statement of the nature of the claim and the amount of the lien sought to be fixed. The lawsuit regarding the claim is normally filed simultaneously with the abstract so that the abstract can reference the pending suit. Some states require the lawsuit to be filed before the abstract; others require the suit to be filed within a stated number of days after the abstract is filed (e.g., five days).

The filing or recording of the abstract or notice puts the world on constructive notice of the lien holder's claim to the property and has the practical effect of creating a cloud on the title to the property, preventing its sale or further encumbrance, until a lawsuit to enforce the lien can be filed and litigated.

Constructive trust An equitable remedy pursuant to which one who has wrongfully obtained title to or possession of real or personal property is deemed to hold that property in trust for the benefit of the true owner.

A lien *lis pendens* can only be filed when the lien holder has a claim to an interest in the property encumbered with the lien. It cannot be filed against any real property owned by the person with whom the lien holder has a dispute just because there is a dispute, and it cannot be used to secure property in a contract or tort action in which the property is not in dispute.

Assertion of a constructive trust in real property as a result of theft or fraud is a common basis for filing a lien *lis pendens*. A **constructive trust** is an involuntary trust declared by a court to exist in (real or personal) property owned or controlled by one person who must then hold it for the benefit of another in order to prevent an injustice. Other common grounds for assertion of a lien *lis pendens* are a genuine dispute over ownership, fraudulent conveyance, and enforcement of an equitable vendor's lien.

EXAMPLE

While Abelard Mendoza was owner of Mendoza Construction his bookkeeper, Hilda Montgomery, embezzled funds from the company over a period of years before being discovered and fired. Assume Mendoza files suit against Montgomery to recover. He learns in discovery that Montgomery used the embezzled funds to purchase a parcel of real property and Mendoza amends his complaint to allege that Montgomery holds title to the parcel in a constructive trust for his benefit. Mendoza's lawyer may simultaneously file an abstract of lien *lis pendens* as seen in Illustration 3-f.

The holder of a lien *lis pendens* has no right per se to foreclose on the lien. The claimant's rights in the property will be litigated in the lawsuit filed and are subject to the court's ruling. The owner of the property may sell or encumber the property after the lien *lis pendens* is created and before the lawsuit is over, unless the court issues a restraining order or a prejudgment attachment, freezing title to the property pending the suit. However, any purchaser or mortgagee will take title subject to the senior claim of the lien holder in the property.

5. Tax Liens

A **tax lien** is one imposed by law on the property of the delinquent taxpayer in favor of the governmental taxing authority to secure payment of the taxes owed as well as interest and penalties assessed on the delinquent tax. Tax liens operate in favor of the federal, state, and local governments.

The Federal Tax Lien

A federal tax lien can be imposed for nonpayment of income, estate, gift, excise, or other taxes owed to the federal government. The Federal Tax Lien Statute is found at 26 U.S.C. §§6321-6323. Section 6321 states:

> If any person liable to pay any tax neglects or refuses to pay the same after demand, the amount (including any interest, additional amount, addition to tax, or assessable penalty, together with any costs that may accrue in addition

Illustration 3-f: ABSTRACT OF LIEN *LIS PENDENS*

IN THE CAPITAL COUNTY YOURSTATE CIRCUIT COURT

ABELARD MENDOZA, d/b/a) MENDOZA CONSTRUCTION) Plaintiff) v.) HILDA MONTGOMERY) Defendant)	DOCKET NO. 15-98777

ABSTRACT OF LIEN LIS PENDENS

Pursuant to Yourstate Statutory Code §66-10-212, notice is hereby given of a suit filed in the Circuit Court for Capital County, Yourstate, bearing Case No. 15-98777, where Abelard Mendoza, d/b/a/ Mendoza Construction is the Plaintiff, and Hilda Montgomery is the Defendant (the "Lawsuit"). A certified copy of the complaint in the Lawsuit is attached to this Abstract.

The Lawsuit is a complaint on behalf of Plaintiff alleging embezzlement and theft of funds which Plaintiff alleges were wrongfully used by Defendant to purchase the real property described below entitling Plaintiff to have a constructive trust declared in that real property for the amount of his funds used to purchase it.

The real property that is the subject of the Lawsuit is located at 765 Western Heights Blvd. in Capital City, Yourstate and is more particularly described as follows: [Legal description of property is omitted from the illustration.]

Plaintiff is asserting a lien lis pendens upon the property in the amount of its claim against Defendant totaling $100,000 plus any prejudgment interest that may be awarded in the Lawsuit.

Respectfully submitted,

_____

Carlton W. Fisk,
Attorney for Plaintiff

---

thereto) shall be a lien in favor of the United States upon all property and rights to property, whether real or personal, belonging to such person.

The tax lien does not arise until an assessment is made by the IRS (§6201), sometimes following an audit of the taxpayer's tax return. Once the tax liability has been assessed, the IRS sends the taxpayer a Notice and Demand for Payment, essentially a formal bill telling the taxpayer how much tax is owed. The notice will advise the taxpayer that he has ten days within which to pay the assessment. If the taxpayer fails to pay within the ten-day period, the tax lien attaches automatically to all real and personal property owned by the taxpayer and to all the taxpayer's "rights to property" (e.g., accounts receivables, or salary). The date of attachment is retroactive to the date of the assessment. Internal Revenue Code §6322 (26 U.S.C. §6322) provides:

> Unless another date is specifically fixed by law, the lien imposed by section 6321 shall arise at the time the assessment is made and shall continue until the liability for the amount so assessed (or a judgment against the taxpayer arising out of such liability) is satisfied or becomes unenforceable by reason of lapse of time.

The U.S. Supreme Court, in *Glass City Bank v. United States*, 326 U.S. 265 (1945), held that the federal tax lien applies not only to property owned by the taxpayer at the time of the assessment, but to all property acquired by the taxpayer during the life of the lien. This is the important after-acquired property scope of a federal tax lien. A federal tax lien has an effective term of ten years and can be renewed for another ten-year term during a period of up to 30 days following expiration of the original term (26 U.S.C. §6323).

As between the federal government and the taxpayer, the lien is effective as of the date of attachment. However, to perfect the tax lien and thus attain priority status over other subsequent claimants to the taxpayer's property, the federal government must properly file a Notice of Federal Tax Lien (NFTL). 26 U.S.C. §6323 allows states to designate the public office where the NFTL is to be filed, and many states have adopted the Revised Uniform Federal Tax Lien Registration Act or the more recent Uniform Federal Lien Registration Act, which make such designations (e.g., NFTLs on personal property of corporations, partnerships, and trusts to be filed in the Office of the Secretary of State; NFTLs on real property to be filed in the public office for filing land records for the county in which the property is located). Absent designation by the state of a specific public office for filing a NFTL, it is to be filed with the U.S. District Court for the federal district in which the property is located.

It is important to understand that although the effective date of attachment of a federal tax lien is retroactive to the date of the assessment, the effective date of perfection of the lien will be the date the notice of lien is properly filed, not the date of assessment.

If the taxpayer wishes to sell property subject to a federal tax lien, he can apply to the IRS for a discharge of tax lien on that property so the buyer can take free and clear of the lien. Obviously, the IRS is not going to agree to that unless the taxpayer/seller agrees that the IRS will receive all or some agreed part of the proceeds of sale. A discharge certificate is also issued when the taxpayer pays off the indebtedness (26 U.S.C. §6325). The IRS can also agree to withdraw a lien from property if the taxpayer consents to pay the indebtedness in agreed-upon installments. The IRS can also agree to subordinate its tax lien in certain property to another creditor.

The federal government may **levy** (execute) on its tax lien without court action by issuing a Notice of Intent to Levy to the taxpayer. The Notice of Intent to Levy must be provided to the taxpayer at least 30 days before the levy occurs (26 U.S.C. §6331). The federal tax levy can also include a garnishment or wage attachment.

The IRS maintains a helpful web site explaining how the federal tax lien works at www.irs.gov/Businesses/Small-Businesses-&-Self-Employed/Understanding-a-Federal-Tax-Lien.

State and Local Tax Liens

State and local governments may also assert tax liens on property of a taxpayer for the failure to pay state income taxes or state or local property taxes on real or personal property. Probably the most common scenario giving rise to a state or local tax lien is a property owner's failure to pay the property tax on real estate. In most states, the procedure for creating and perfecting the lien is similar to that used in federal tax liens. The government entity asserting the lien must give notice to the taxpayer of the delinquency, identify the property in question, state the amount owed, provide a due date, and state the intent to subject the real property in question to a tax lien. The notice must also go to any mortgage holder of record in the property since its interest may be affected by a foreclosure on the tax lien. If the debt is not paid by the due date, the government must then file a notice of lien with the appropriate public office, perfecting the lien.

In many states, the state tax lien is given superpriority status over not just subsequent claims against the property but also over preexisting, perfected security interests, whether consensual or nonconsensual. And 26 U.S.C. §6323(b) allows states to assert priority of a state or local tax lien over a previously existing federal tax lien. In states electing to exercise that priority, a statute such as the one shown in Illustration 3-g is common.

Illustration 3-g: TYPICAL STATE STATUTE CLAIMING SUPERPRIORITY STATUS FOR TAX LIEN

> The taxes assessed by the state of Yourstate, a county, or municipality, taxing district, or other local governmental entity, upon any property of whatever kind, and all penalties, interest, and costs accruing thereon, shall become and remain a first lien upon such property from January 1 of the year for which such taxes are assessed.

If payment is not made after the required notice has been given to the debtor and the notice of tax lien filed, the state or local government may foreclose or execute on its lien. In some states, the government entity is permitted to proceed with nonjudicial self-help foreclosure or seizure of the burdened property. In others, a judicial foreclosure is required, which, we have learned, means the government must file a lawsuit and obtain a court order allowing sale. There usually is a statutory right of redemption in favor of the taxpayer either up until the time of sale or, in some states, for a designated period after the sale (e.g., one year).

6. The Lien for Unpaid Child Support

As part of the **Personal Responsibility and Work Opportunity Reconciliation Act of 1996 (PRWORA)**, Congress required the states, as a condition to receiving federal funding for job training and other programs intended to reform public assistance programs in this country, to establish new procedures for enforcing child support orders. The statute, 42 U.S.C. §666(a)(4), now requires all states to have laws or procedures pursuant to which child support arrearages become liens, by operation of law, against all real and personal property owned by an obligor who either resides or owns property in that state.

7. The Judicial Lien

In the next chapter we will consider prebankruptcy collection efforts a creditor can take against a debtor against whom he obtains a final money judgment. As part of that study we will examine the various ways that the judgment creditor can execute on the property of the debtor in order to satisfy the judgment focusing on the writ of execution, writ of garnishment, and judgment lien on real property. With variations in state law, we will see that at some point in the execution process the judgment creditor is recognized as having a **judicial lien**, essentially a nonconsensual security interest in the debtor's property on which he is executing.

HIGHLIGHTED CASE ●

MUGGLI DENTAL STUDIO V. TAYLOR
142 Wis. 2d 696, 419 N.W.2d 322 (Ct. App. 1987)

OPINION: NETTESHEIM, Judge.

Following a court trial, a judgment was entered in favor of the Muggli Dental Studio (the studio) against Dr. Ted Taylor. An execution was then issued against Dr. Taylor's personal property and the Manitowoc County Sheriff's Department levied against such property. This appeal relates to the sufficiency of the levy by the sheriff and whether the levy operated to create a priority lien in favor of the studio. The trial court ruled against Dr. Taylor on these questions. Dr. Taylor appeals pro se. We reject Dr. Taylor's arguments and affirm the trial court's post-judgment order.

Dr. Taylor first contends that the levy was ineffective to accomplish a seizure of his property. He cites sec. 815.19, Stats., which provides in part that "[p]ersonal property shall be bound from the time it is seized." In *Brown v. Pratt*, 4 Wis. 513 (1855), the supreme court held that a levy upon personal property is not valid unless the officer has the property in his view and under his control. Id. at 519. However, the effectiveness of a levy will not be defeated by failing to remove the property from the site of the execution. See *Johnson v. Iron Belt Mining Co.*, 78 Wis. 159, 162-63, 47 N.W. 363, 364 (1890).

Testimony at the post-judgment proceeding established that sheriff's deputy Edward Stuhr went through a checklist to assure himself that the items to be levied upon were, in fact, present. Officer Stuhr then informed Dr. Taylor that the items should be considered as tagged and seized and were not to be disposed of in any manner. The trial court determined that the officer's actions sufficiently exerted control over the property such that a seizure occurred.

We conclude that a determination of whether a levy is legally effective to bind the property presents this court with a mixed question of fact and law. We separate the factual findings of a trial court from the conclusions of law and apply the appropriate standard to each. *Geis v. City of Fond du Lac*, 140 Wis. 2d 205, 209, 409 N.W.2d 148, 150 (Ct. App. 1987). A trial court's findings of fact will not be disturbed on appeal unless they are clearly erroneous. *Laribee v. Laribee*, 138 Wis. 2d 46, 54, 405 N.W.2d 679, 683 (Ct. App. 1987). However, an appellate court must decide questions of law without deference to the trial court's decision. *Cobb State Bank v. Nelson*, 141 Wis. 2d 1, 5, 413 N.W.2d 644, 645-46 (Ct. App. 1987).

The testimony established that Deputy Stuhr had Dr. Taylor's property in his view and under his control at the time of the alleged levy. The testimony also established that the officer informed Dr. Taylor that the property was considered seized and not subject to disposition. These findings are not clearly erroneous. See sec. 805.17(2), Stats.

We also conclude that these facts sufficiently establish an effective levy for purposes of sec. 815.19, Stats. Removal of the seized property from the situs of the execution is not necessary. See *Johnson*, 78 Wis. at 162-63, 47 N.W. at 364.

Dr. Taylor next alleges that the lien created in favor of Muggli by the levy does not have priority over a security interest held by Dr. Taylor's father (Taylor, Sr.). In 1982, the Citizens Lakeshore Bank obtained a security interest in Dr. Taylor's property by virtue of a financing statement filed at that time. Prior to the levy in this case, Taylor, Sr. paid this debt for Dr. Taylor. However, Taylor, Sr.'s financing statement was not filed until January 2, 1987. The levy in this case occurred on December 9, 1986.

When it is the intention of the parties to create a security interest, the case is governed by ch. 409, Stats. *Clark Oil and Refining Co. v. Liddicoat*, 65 Wis. 2d 612, 620, 223 N.W.2d 530, 534-35 (1974); sec. 409.102(1)(a), Stats. Chapter 409 sets out rules of priority. A lien creditor has priority over a person holding an unperfected security interest. Sec. 409.301(1)(b), Stats. To perfect a security interest in the property in question, a financing statement must be filed or the collateral must be in the possession of the secured party. Sec. 409.302, Stats.

Here, because Taylor, Sr.'s financing statement was not filed until after the levy of execution by the studio and also because Taylor, Sr. did not have the collateral in his possession, Muggli, the lien creditor, has priority over the holder of the unperfected security interest. *Clark Oil*, 65 Wis. 2d at 621, 223 N.W.2d at 535; sec. 409.301(1)(b), Stats. Taylor, Sr.'s subsequent perfection has no impact on these priority rules . . . .

Accordingly, we affirm the order of the trial court.

POST-CASE FOLLOW-UP

Muggli raises the question of whether the officer serving the writ of execution has exercised sufficient dominion and control over the property for there to have been an effective levy on the property at all. In most cases the executing officer will take actual physical possession of the property and remove it to a secure place for storage until sale. For items too large or heavy to move, stickers or tags will be placed on the property declaring the levy and seizure. But when items that are removable are left in place by the executing officer, the issue of whether such constructive possession results in an effective levy is raised. Some jurisdictions agree with *Muggli Dental Studio* that actual removal of the property is not essential to levy and that constructive possession can be recognized. See, e.g., *U.S. Leather, Inc. v. Mitchell Mfg. Group, Inc.*, 276 F.3d 782 (6th Cir. 2002) (constructive possession of physical assets of business by obtaining consent of debtor's attorney that property would be left in place subject to later sale by executing officer); *Harbour Towne Marina Assn. v. Geile (In re Fees of Court Officer)*, 564 N.W.2d 509 (Mich. App. 1997) (constructive possession of boat left in dock where executing officer attached a writ of execution to the boat, gave a copy to the marina manager, seized the ship's log, and prepared a notice of sale); and *Credit Bureau of Broken Bow v. Moninger*, 284 N.W.2d 855 (Neb. 1979) (officer serving writ placing hand on truck and announcing in the presence of the debtor, "I execute on the pickup for the County of Custer" held sufficient levy). Other jurisdictions require the officer to either take actual possession or to retain a custodian on site to ensure the property is not removed. See, e.g., New York City Marshal's Handbook, Chapter II, Section 4-2.

Muggli Dental Studio v. Taylor: Real Life Applications

1. The court in *Muggli* says that a determination of whether a levy is legally effective to bind the property presents this court with a mixed question of fact and law. What are the questions of fact subject to review in *Muggli*? What is the question of law to be decided?

2. What would be the result in this case if the debtor's father, Taylor Sr., had the collateral in his possession when the writ of execution was served?

3. The debtor's father in this case, Taylor Sr., apparently paid the secured indebtedness his son owed to Citizens' Lakeshore Bank (CLB), the original creditor, then took a security interest in the same collateral to secure his son's new indebtedness to him. If Taylor Sr. had not paid off that secured debt to CLB, would Muggli's judicial lien have been deemed superior to the security interest of CLB in the collateral?

4. Assume that a week after the deputy served the writ of execution on the debtor, Dr. Taylor, and informed him that "the items should be considered as tagged and seized and were not to be disposed of in any manner," Dr. Taylor is happily continuing to use the collateral in his dental practice. A client of the firm where you work, a new dentist, visits Dr. Taylor's practice that day and, with no knowledge of the levy, purchases all the collateral for use in starting up her own dental practice. When a priority dispute over the collateral arises between Muggli Dental, claiming to be a judicial lien creditor, and your firm's client, who will prevail? See UCC §9-320(a). If your client loses, what are your client's causes of action against Dr. Taylor?

When a debtor files for bankruptcy relief and a bankruptcy trustee is appointed, §544 of the Bankruptcy Code grants that trustee the status of a judicial lien creditor in all the property of the debtor. Called the "strong-arm clause" of the Bankruptcy Code, this section means the bankruptcy trustee will take property of the debtor for the benefit of the bankruptcy estate over the claim of any creditor asserting a prior security interest in the same property if that creditor's security interest in the property was not perfected prior to filing of the bankruptcy petition. We'll look at the strong-arm clause in much more detail later.

Another judicial lien question that arises in a bankruptcy case is whether such a lien, even though valid under state law, can be set aside under any circumstances. We will deal with these questions when we begin our study of how a bankruptcy case proceeds, but you cannot understand the argument for a client in the bankruptcy case unless you understand what judicial liens are and when they attach under the relevant state law.

8. The Vendor's Lien on Real Property

Vendor's lien In context of real property, a lien afforded to sellers of property on the real property sold to assure payment of the purchase price.

A **vendor's lien** (also called a **mortgage lien**), a lien recognized in some states by statute or common law or both, is afforded to sellers of real property on the real property sold in the event the buyer fails to make payment when due. It is referred to as an equitable lien or special lien and is not dependent on the seller retaining possession of the property.

Equitable lien A lien created by court rulings rather than by statute; also called a common law lien.

This lien scenario arises most commonly where the seller of land self-financed the sale by agreeing to accept direct payment(s) from the buyer rather than requiring the buyer to obtain financing to pay the seller in full at closing, but failed to have the buyer convey a consensual mortgage in the property to the seller to secure payment (a **purchase money mortgage**). It might also arise where an owner of land agreed to convey a mortgage in the land to a creditor and then refused to cooperate in finalizing the mortgage. Or it might arise when one in possession of property and believing herself to be the owner makes permanent improvements to property, enhancing its value, and then is dispossessed by the true owner.

Purchase money mortgage A mortgage held by the seller rather than a third-party lender. A form of self-financing by seller.

Where it is recognized, this lien authorizes the holder to pursue recovery of the real property in the hands not only of the buyer but also of anyone who has purchased the property from the buyer with actual or constructive notice that the purchase price to the seller has not been paid. The lien is typically created by recording the contract of sale or other documentation establishing the transaction and obligation in the county office where land records are to be filed. It must be enforced by lawsuit.

EXAMPLE

Assume your law firm represents an owner of real property very eager to sell it. The owner has found a buyer, but the buyer is unable to qualify for a traditional mortgage loan from any lender, owing to poor credit or questions about whether the buyer's projected income flow is sufficient. The owner decides to assume the risk that the lenders will not and agrees to self-finance this purchase by the buyer. However, the owner fails to require the buyer to grant the owner a purchase money mortgage. If the buyer defaults, then the owner may be able to assert the equitable vendor's lien to retake possession of the property notwithstanding the absence of a mortgage. If the buyer has not only defaulted but also transferred an interest in the property to someone else (e.g., has resold it or granted a security interest in it to a third party), the owner may be able nonetheless to assert the lien against the property in the hands of that third party

> if the owner can show that the third party knew or should have known that a balance was still owed to the owner on the initial sale at the time the third party received an interest in the property.

In the personal property context, equitable liens are essentially identical to **constructive trusts** (that you study in your course on property law) and arise under the same circumstances. A constructive trust is a court-imposed trust relationship in which one who has obtained title to property in a wrongful manner is declared to hold title to the property as a trustee for the benefit of the true owner. In many states, the constructive trust theory is available in real property transactions like the one used in the last example so if the vendor's lien is not recognized in those states, the constructive trust theory should be available as an alternative.

P-H 3-i: If your law firm represents the original owner of the realty in the last example and can assert both a vendor's lien and constructive trust theory to regain possession, which provides that owner with the greatest protection while the lawsuit is pending? Could the owner also file a lien *lis pendens* on this property?

CHAPTER SUMMARY

In this chapter we have considered nonconsensual or involuntary liens that can be placed on real and personal property. Nonconsensual liens are also known as statutory liens because they are created by state or federal statute. In some states, some nonconsensual liens are still enforced as common law or equitable liens created by case law. Some nonconsensual liens are possessory liens, requiring that the party claiming the lien have possession of the property subject to the lien. These include the artisan's lien, the warehouseman's lien, the UCC Article 2 buyer's lien, the attorney's or accountant's charging lien, and the vendor's lien. UCC §9-333 gives possessory liens priority over prior consensual security interests in the property subject to the lien whether the prior security interest is perfected or not unless the statute creating the lien expressly provides otherwise.

Other nonconsensual liens are nonpossessory including the attorney's charging lien, the healthcare services lien, the mechanics' and materialman's lien on real property, the lien *lis pendens* on real property, federal and state tax liens, the lien for unpaid child support, the judicial lien, and the vendor's lien on real property. The manner of creating and perfecting the various nonpossessory liens varies.

REVIEW QUESTIONS

1. Explain the difference between a consensual lien and a nonconsensual lien on property.
2. Explain the difference between a possessory lien and a non-possessory lien.

3. Explain the difference between a statutory lien and a common law lien.
4. Explain when a possessory lien has and doesn't have priority over a prior perfected consensual security interest in the liened property.
5. Who is and is not an artisan for purposes of the artisan's lien statute? Give examples of kinds of businesses that qualify to assert an artisan's lien in personal property.
6. What do we mean by the "date of substantial completion" and why is that a frequent subject of dispute in construction contracts?
7. Explain the relation-back feature of some state mechanics' lien statutes. What difference might it make whether the lien holder is a general contractor or a subcontractor or a supplier on the project?
8. Why must an attorney representing an injured plaintiff be careful to ascertain outstanding medical and hospital bills before settling the client's claim?
9. Explain why the date a federal tax lien attaches to a debtor's property is not the same as the date the tax lien is deemed perfected.
10. Can a lien *lis pendens* be filed against the real property of any debtor who owes money to a creditor? Why or why not? Can a lien *lis pendens* be filed against personal property?
11. What is a constructive trust? How is it different from a statutory lien?

WORDS AND PHRASES TO REMEMBER

abandonment
abstract of lien *lis pendens*
Article 2 buyer's lien
artificer's lien
artisan's lien
assessment
attachment
attorney's charging lien
attorney's (or accountant's)
   retaining lien
audit
banker's lien
carrier's lien
child support lien
common law lien
consensual lien
construction lien
constructive notice
constructive trust
contractual lien
cotton ginner's lien
discharge certificate
discharge of tax lien
equitable lien
garage keeper's lien
healthcare services lien

hospital lien
hotel operator's lien
involuntary lien
judicial lien
landlord's lien
layaway
layby
levy
lien holder
lien *lis pendens*
materialman's lien
mechanic's lien
Miller Act
newspaper of general circulation
nonconsensual lien
notice of completion
notice of lien
notice of lien *lis pendens*
notice of nonpayment
nonpossessory lien
performance (and payment) bond
Personal Responsibility and
   Work Opportunity Reconciliation
   Act of 1996
possessory lien
purchase money mortgage

relation back
Revised Uniform Federal Tax Lien
   Registration Act
sovereign immunity
statutory lien
substantial completion
supplier's lien

tax lien
Uniform Federal Lien
   Registration Act
vendor's lien in real property
warehouseman's lien
warrant of distress
worker's lien

TO LEARN MORE: A number of TLM activities to accompany this chapter are accessible on the companion web site for this textbook at http://aspenlawschool.com/books/Parsons_Debt4e/.

Chapter Four:

Nonjudicial Debt Collection

- Most prebankruptcy debt collection activities targeted at consumer debtors are regulated by the Fair Debt Collection Practices Act and analogous state legislation
- The FDCPA creates a private right of action in favor of the debtor against the debt collector who violates its provisions
- Overly aggressive debt collection practices can give rise to various tort causes of action on behalf of the debtor as well as to criminal charges against the debt collector
- Disputes over debt obligations can be resolved without litigation by private settlement negotiations, mediation, or arbitration

A. ▶ The Fair Debt Collection Practices Act

According to the **Consumer Financial Protection Bureau** (CFPB), in the continuing aftermath of the housing crisis and Great Recession, approximately 30 million individual Americans (about 1 in 10) are being pursued by a debt collector on any given day for debt that averages $1,500 per debtor. The statistic does not include businesses being pursued for overdue debt on any given day. Debt collection is a big business in America today.

Debt collection practices have historically been subject to a great deal of abuse. Before such practices were prohibited, it was common for creditors or their representatives to harass, embarrass, and humiliate debtors until a bill was paid. Insulting letters were common. Threats were made to sue, to commit violence, to get the debtor fired, to pursue the debtor for the rest of his life. Profanity, browbeating, insults, and name calling (deadbeat, bum, cheat, thief, liar, etc.) were common both in correspondence and conversations. Telephone calls could be made as frequently as the debt collector wished and at any time, night or day. Personal visits to the debtor's house or workplace to demand payment could be made at any time, night or day. Relatives, neighbors, friends, employers, and co-workers of the debtor could be contacted and told of the debt, embarrassing the debtor and putting pressure on the debtor to pay. Creditors could undertake these debt collection efforts themselves or hire a business that specialized in debt collection. Or they could hire an attorney to do it for them.

In 1977, because of the growing amount of debt in our consumer society and the growing awareness of excessive debt collection practices by creditors and the debt collection industry, Congress passed the **Fair Debt Collection Practices Act** (FDCPA), 15 U.S.C. §1601, et seq. In this section we will summarize of how the FDCPA works.

1. Whom the FDCPA Regulates

The FDCPA regulates those defined by the statute (§803(6)) as **debt collectors**. Persons acting for businesses, "the principal purpose of which" is to collect debts owed to a consumer debtor are included, as is any individual who "regularly collects or attempts to collect" debts owed to a consumer debtor. This can include **third-party collection agencies** retained by the creditor to collect debt owed to the creditor by the debtor. It can also include **debt buyers** (also called **asset buyers**), who purchase delinquent credit card, auto loan, and other accounts from creditors for a fraction of the face value of the debt and then seek to collect it themselves. According to the Federal Trade Commission, between 2006 and 2009 the top nine debt buyers purchased 90 million consumer accounts valued at about $143 billion. Though a perfectly legal industry in itself, controversy continues to swirl around collection tactics used by some debt buyers including the fabrication of missing documentation on debts purchased in bulk and the filing of time barred claims in collection lawsuits unlikely to be defended and in the bankruptcy proceedings of the debtors (see *Crawford v. LVNV Funding LLC*, highlighted later in this section).

HISTORY OF THE DEBT BUYING INDUSTRY

There has always been some market for debts that a creditor has given up on and is considering writing off as uncollectible. But the industry boomed as a result of the Savings and Loan crisis of the 1980s (read the history at www.fdic.gov/bank/historical/history/167_188.pdf) when 118 state and federally insured savings and loan (S&L) institutions holding $43 billion in assets failed in a 2-year period. The Federal Deposit Insurance Corporation (FDIC), which insured deposits in those institutions, took over those failing S&Ls and made good all amounts on deposit at the expense of the taxpayers. The Resolution Trade Corporation (RTC) was then formed by the FDIC and began to actively seek buyers willing to purchase the assets of closed S&Ls, including both current and delinquent accounts. Auctions were held around the country at which performing and nonperforming accounts were bundled and sold to the highest bidder with no opportunity by the bidder to evaluate the specific accounts in the bundle purchased. Thus was birthed the modern debt or asset buying industry.

The statute excludes creditors themselves from the definition of debt collector since the creditor would be attempting to collect his own debt and not debt owed to another. However, the creditor himself can qualify as a debt collector under the statute if he "uses any name other than his own which would indicate that a third person is collecting or attempting to collect such debts" (§803(6)). And even where a creditor may not be regulated by the FDCPA, the creditor must be aware of potential tort liability arising from its collection activities as discussed later in this chapter.

EXAMPLE

Recall that Nick and Pearl Murphy are obligated to Shears Department Store for their purchase on credit of living room furniture. If Shears collects its debts in its own name, it is not considered a debt collector within the meaning of the FDCPA. But if Shears sets up a subsidiary to collect its account receivables and calls it Credit Collectors, Inc., that subsidiary will be a regulated debt collector under the FDCPA even though it only collects debt owed to Shears. But before you conclude that Shears can engage in any collection tactic it wants in collecting its own debt under its own name, you will want to check to see (1) if state law imposes more stringent statutory regulation on collection activities than the FDCPA, and (2) if tort theories recognized by relevant state law limit certain collection activities (see Section B).

EC 4-a: Although creditors can undertake their own prelitigation debt collection efforts, they may not be able to represent themselves in a civil lawsuit based on the debt. Generally, individuals can represent themselves in court. When a person chooses to represent himself and not have a lawyer do it, we call that appearing before the court **pro se**. However, a corporation or other entity that is a party to a lawsuit cannot appear pro se and must be represented by counsel. Why? Because someone must come into the courtroom and speak for the entity (an officer or other employee of a corporation, for example). In doing so, that someone is technically practicing law because they are representing another (the entity) in a legal matter without a law license And that constitutes the unauthorized practice of law. As a result, entity creditors, while they can engage in prelitigation collection efforts without counsel, cannot file a collection lawsuit without one. An individual debtor on the other hand, including a sole proprietor who is not considered a separate entity from his business, can both engage in prelitigation collection efforts without counsel and appear pro se (in his or her own behalf) in a collection lawsuit.

What about attorneys who are hired by a client to engage in prelitigation debt collection efforts? Are they debt collectors for purposes of the statute's regulation? The statute does not expressly include attorneys hired by creditors in the definition of debt collectors and for years after it was passed no one thought attorneys were regulated by the statute, but in *Heintz v. Jenkins*, 514 U.S. 291 (1995), the Supreme Court held that the FDCPA applies to attorneys who "regularly" engage in consumer-debt-collection activity, even when that activity consists of litigation.

Unfortunately, the Supreme Court in *Heintz* did not provide guidance on how frequently an attorney must undertake collection work before he or she is considered one who "regularly" attempts to collect consumer debt. The few post-*Heintz* decisions out there from lower courts seem to interpret "regularly" as debt collection that amounts to a substantial percentage of a lawyer's total business or that is a substantial amount of work in and of itself. See, e.g., *Garrett v. Derbes*, 110 F.3d 317, 318 (5th Cir. 1997) ("[I]f the volume of a person's debt collection activity is great enough, it is irrelevant that these services only amount to a small fraction of his total business activity; the person still renders them 'regularly.'"); *Fox v. Citicorp Credit Servs., Inc.*, 15 F.3d 1507, 1513 n.5 (9th Cir.

1994) (attorney liable as a debt collector where at least 80 percent of his legal fees came from the collection of debts); *Camara v. Fleury*, 285 F. Supp. 2d 90, 95 (D. Mass. 2003) (attorney and law firm not debt collectors where only 4.57 percent of the firm's business involved debt collection activities); *Ditty v. CheckRite, Ltd., Inc.*, 973 F. Supp. 1320, 1336 (D. Utah 1997) (attorney a debt collector where collection represented one-third to one-half of the firm's income).

P-H 4-a: (1) You work for a lawyer who has been in practice for only six months. The lawyer handled one small collection matter during that time but made no effort to comply with the FDCPA. Now a second small collection matter has been referred to the lawyer, this one for a different client. Is it time for your lawyer to begin complying with the FDCPA? (2) Would your answer to (1) change if the collection matter your lawyer handled in the first six months of practice was a large one and accounted for half of the office's income for the period? (3) Would your answer to (1) change if your lawyer had handled five collection matters in your first six months of practice but all of them were pro bono? (4) Would your answer to (1) change if the collection matter your lawyer handled in the first six months of practice was an attempt to collect from a business debtor and not a consumer debtor?

---

2. Activities Regulated by the FDCPA

The FDCPA regulates attempts to collect debt from "any natural person obligated or allegedly obligated to pay any debt" (§803(3)). Thus, the FDCPA does not regulate attempts to collect debt from a debtor who is not a natural person, such as a corporate debtor. It only regulates attempts to collect debts from natural persons who are called consumers under the statute. There are five categories of collection activity regulated by the FDCPA:

- Locating the consumer debtor
- Communicating with the consumer debtor
- Harassing or abusing the consumer debtor
- Making false or misleading representations
- Using unfair or unconscionable means

Locating the Consumer Debtor

Pursuant to §804 of the FDCPA, a debt collector contacting someone other than the consumer herself in order to locate the consumer must properly identify himself but avoid stating that he works for a debt collection company unless specifically asked. The debt collector must state that he is looking for information to help him locate the consumer but cannot mention that the consumer owes a debt. The debt collector must not contact the same person more than once unless that person invites a subsequent contact or unless the debt collector reasonably believes the person previously contacted now has more correct information. Communications from the debt collector seeking contact information for the debtor that are placed in writing must not be by postcard (where anyone handling the card can read the message) and nothing on the envelope or in the contents of the message can disclose that the sender is a debt collector or that the debtor owes a debt.

P-H 4-b: What is the policy at work behind the limitations on locating the consumer debtor outlined in §804 of the FDCPA? Are these limitations fair to the debt collector? Should there be more stringent prohibitions of the debt collector making location contacts?

Communicating with the Consumer Debtor

Pursuant to §805 of the FDCPA, the debt collector cannot make contact with the consumer at any unusual time or place or at any time and place the creditor knows or should know would be inconvenient to the consumer. Absent information to the contrary, the debt collector is to assume that a convenient time for contacting the consumer is between 8 A.M. and 9 P.M. in the consumer's time zone.

If the debt collector knows that the consumer is represented by an attorney, contact must be with that attorney unless the consumer's attorney will not respond or consents to direct contact with the consumer. Contacting a consumer at work is prohibited if the debt collector knows the employer disallows such contacts.

Contacting third persons regarding the consumer's obligation is strictly limited. The debt collector is allowed to contact only the consumer himself, the consumer's attorney, the creditor, the creditor's attorney, the debt collector's attorney, or credit reporting agencies. Note carefully the definition of consumer in §805(d), however. For purposes of restrictions on contacting the consumer himself, consumer is defined to include not just the individual who owes the debt, but his spouse, parent (if he is a minor), guardian, executor, or administrator.

Finally, if the consumer advises the debt collector verbally or in writing that he refuses to pay the debt or does not want to be contacted any further, the contact must stop, other than the limited right of the debt collector to confirm that contact will cease or that other remedies may be or are going to be pursued.

P-H 4-c: Assume that one of the medical bills incurred by Pearl Murphy (Illustration 1-a) since her botched appendectomy is from Capital City Medical Equipment (CCME) in the amount of $1,200. A debt collector hired to collect the bill, which is owed by Pearl but not by Nick, calls the Murphy home at 7:30 P.M. Nick Murphy answers and advises the caller that his wife is not at home. Can the debt collector say whatever she has to say to Nick Murphy as the spouse of the debtor without violating the statute? What specific provisions of the FDCPA tell you the answer? Now, assume it is not Nick Murphy who answers, but the Murphys' 11-year-old son, Lyndon. Can the debt collector say whatever she has to say to the son without violating the statute? What specific provisions of the FDCPA tell you the answer?

Harassing or Abusing the Consumer Debtor

Pursuant to §806 of the statute, the debt collector cannot use or threaten to use violence or other criminal means to harm the person, reputation, or property of the consumer or anyone else. The debt collector cannot use profanity or obscene language, cannot include the consumer's name on any published list of persons who haven't paid their debts, cannot disclose the debt by publicly advertising its sale or assignment, and cannot make anonymous phone calls or continuous phone calls intended to harass.

P-H 4-d: Assume the debt collector contacting Pearl Murphy on the debt she owes CCME contacts Pearl by phone at home at 6 P.M. but becomes angry when Pearl will not commit to pay the debt. The debt collector says if payment isn't forthcoming, she will ruin Pearl in the community and embarrass her children at their schools. When Pearl hangs up on the debt collector, she calls Pearl right back and keeps calling back every ten minutes until 9 P.M. How many violations of the FDCPA do you see?

EC 4-b: If the caller in P-H 4-d was a paralegal in your state and she was acting with the approval of her supervising attorney, how many ethical violations would have been committed by the supervising attorney? How many violations by the paralegal of paralegal ethics promulgated by the National Association of Legal Assistants (NALA) or by the National Federation of Paralegal Associations (NFPA) or by your state? If this paralegal was certified by NALA or NFPA or by your state, could this behavior threaten her certification?

Making False or Misleading Representations

Pursuant to §807 of the FDCPA, a debt collector cannot use "any false, deceptive, or misleading representation or means" in collecting a debt. The statute gives a number of nonexclusive examples of such prohibited acts, including

- the use of any language, clothing, or symbols that would suggest that the debt collector is affiliated with a governmental entity or a credit reporting agency, or that he is an attorney when he is not;
- saying anything false about the debt or the amount owed;
- suggesting that nonpayment of the debt is a crime or that it will result in the debtor or a co-debtor being arrested or imprisoned;
- suggesting that nonpayment will result in the debtor's property being taken other than as the law allows; or
- using any false name or false paper.

P-H 4-e: Assume that the debt collector contacting Pearl Murphy is not an attorney. She calls the Murphys' house during permitted hours and talks with Nick Murphy, who tells the debt collector that Pearl is out of town. The debt collector hears whispering in the background and believes that Pearl is actually there at home. The debt collector calls several times over the next week and receives the same response and continues to believe that Pearl is in fact there, listening in on Nick's end of the conversation. Finally the debt collector calls the Murphy house and, when Nick answers, the caller disguises her voice and identifies herself as a police officer calling Pearl to talk with her about a crime that has been committed about which she may have knowledge. Pearl comes immediately to the phone. How many violations of §807 do you recognize?

Using Unfair or Unconscionable Means

Pursuant to §808 of the FDCPA, the debt collector "may not use unfair or unconscionable means" to collect a debt. The statute gives a number of nonexclusive examples of such practices, including

- collecting any amount not actually owed, or communicating with the consumer by postcard;
- using an envelope for communication with the consumer that identifies the sender as a debt collector;
- accepting a postdated check and then depositing or threatening to deposit it early; or
- soliciting a postdated check for the very purpose of attempting to cash it before funds are available in order to allege a criminal act by the consumer.

Courts have expanded the scope of what is unfair or unconscionable under §808. For example, in *Phillips v. Asset Acceptance, LLC*, 736 F.3d 1076 (7th Cir. 2013), the court held that a debt collector governed by the FDCP who threatens to sue or actually sues on a time barred claim violates the Act. But what if the debtor files a case in bankruptcy and the debt collector files a formal claim in the bankruptcy case based on a time barred debt? Every bankruptcy practitioner knows that this is a very common practice by debt buyers, those companies that purchase charged-off debts (mostly credit card debt) at a steep discount from major banks and then aggressively pursue the debtors into litigation usually with little or no effort at negotiation or compromise. Often such aggressive litigation tactics prove the proverbial last straw compelling the debtor to file for bankruptcy protection. The debt buyers have routinely filed formal claims in the bankruptcy case notwithstanding the claim being time barred. Finally a court has spoken regarding whether this tactic is a violation of the FDCPA.

HIGHLIGHTED CASE   ● **CRAWFORD V. LVNV FUNDING, LLC (IN RE CRAWFORD)**
758 F.3d 1254 (11th Cir. 2014)

[Crawford owed $2,037.99 to the Heilig-Meyers furniture company. Heilig-Meyers charged off the debt in 1999, and in 2001, LVNV Funding, LLC, acquired the debt. The last transaction on the account occurred October 26, 2001 and the debt became unenforceable under the three-year Alabama statute of limitations in October 2004. Crawford filed for Chapter 13 bankruptcy in February 2008. LVNV filed a proof of claim to collect the debt even though the limitations period had expired. Crawford filed a counterclaim against LVNV via an adversary proceeding pursuant to Bankruptcy Rule 3007(b) alleging that LVNV's attempting to claim Crawford's time barred debt violated the FDCPA. The Bankruptcy Judge dismissed Crawford's counterclaim and the decision was affirmed on appeal by the district court. Crawford appeals.]

OPINION: GOLDBERG, J.

A deluge has swept through U.S. bankruptcy courts of late. Consumer debt buyers—armed with hundreds of delinquent accounts purchased from creditors—are filing proofs of claim on debts deemed unenforceable under state statutes of limitations. This appeal considers whether a proof of claim to collect a stale debt in Chapter 13 bankruptcy violates the Fair Debt Collection Practices Act . . . .

The FDCPA is a consumer protection statute that "imposes open-ended prohibitions on, inter alia, false, deceptive, or unfair" debt-collection practices. . . . Finding "abundant evidence" of such practices, Congress passed the FDCPA in 1977 to stop "the use of abusive, deceptive, and unfair debt collection practices by many debt collectors." 15 U.S.C. §1692(a). Congress determined that "[e]xisting laws and procedures" were "inadequate" to protect consumer debtors. Id. at 1692(b). . . .

[T]he FDCPA regulates the conduct of debt-collectors, which the statute defines as any person who . . . "regularly collects . . . debts owed or due or asserted to be owed or due another." 15 U.S.C. §1692a(6). Undisputedly, LVNV and its surrogates are debt collectors and thus subject to the FDCPA.

To enforce the FDCPA's prohibitions, Congress equipped consumer debtors with a private right of action, rendering "debt collectors who violate the Act liable for actual damages, statutory damages up to $1,000, and reasonable attorney's fees and costs." *Owen v. I.C. Sys., Inc.*, 629 F.3d 1263, 1270 (11th Cir. 2011) (citing 15 U.S.C. §1692k(a)). . . . To determine whether LVNV's conduct, as alleged in Crawford's complaint, is prohibited by the FDCPA, we begin "where all such inquiries must begin: with the language of the statute itself." [Citation omitted.]

Section 1692e of the FDCPA provides that "[a] debt collector may not use any false, deceptive, or misleading representation or means in connection with the collection of any debt." 15 U.S.C. §1692e. Section 1692f states that "[a] debt collector may not use unfair or unconscionable means to collect or attempt to collect any debt."

Because Congress did not provide a definition for the terms "unfair" or "unconscionable," this Court has looked to the dictionary for help. "The plain meaning of 'unfair' is 'marked by injustice, partiality, or deception.'" *LeBlanc v. Unifund CCR Partners*, 601 F.3d 1185, 1200 (11th Cir. 2010) (quoting Merriam-Webster Online Dictionary (2010)). Further, "an act or practice is deceptive or unfair if it has the tendency or capacity to deceive." Id. . . . We also explained that "[t]he term 'unconscionable' means 'having no conscience'; 'unscrupulous'; 'showing no regard for conscience'; 'affronting the sense of justice, decency, or reasonableness.'" Id. (quoting Black's Law Dictionary 1526 (7th ed. 1999)). We have also noted that "[t]he phrase 'unfair or unconscionable' is as vague as they come." Id. . . .

Given this ambiguity, we have adopted a "least-sophisticated consumer" standard to evaluate whether a debt collector's conduct is "deceptive," "misleading," "unconscionable," or "unfair" under the statute. . . . The inquiry is not whether the particular plaintiff-consumer was deceived or misled; instead, the question is "whether the 'least sophisticated consumer' would have been deceived" by the debt collector's conduct. . . . The "least-sophisticated consumer" standard takes into account that consumer-protection laws are "not made for the protection of experts, but for the public—that vast multitude which includes the ignorant, the unthinking, and the credulous." . . . "However, the test has an objective component in that while protecting naive consumers, the standard also prevents liability for bizarre or idiosyncratic interpretations of collection notices by preserving a quotient of reasonableness." *LeBlanc*, 601 F.3d at 1194. . . .

Given our precedent, we must examine whether LVNV's conduct—filing and trying to enforce in court a claim known to be time-barred—would be unfair, unconscionable, deceiving, or misleading towards the least-sophisticated consumer. See id. at 1193-94. . . .

The reason behind LVNV's practice of filing time-barred proofs of claim in bankruptcy court is simple. Absent an objection from either the . . . debtor or the trustee, the time-barred claim is automatically allowed against the debtor pursuant to 11 U.S.C. §502(a)-(b) and Bankruptcy Rule 3001(f). As a result, the debtor must then pay the debt from his future wages as part of the Chapter 13 repayment plan, notwithstanding that the debt is time-barred and unenforceable in court.

That is what happened in this case. LVNV filed the time-barred proof of claim in May of 2008, shortly after debtor Crawford petitioned for Chapter 13 protection. But neither the bankruptcy trustee nor Crawford objected to the claim during the bankruptcy proceeding; instead, the trustee actually paid monies from the . . . estate to LVNV. . . . It wasn't until four years later, in May 2012, that debtor Crawford . . . objected to LVNV's claim as unenforceable.

LVNV acknowledges, as it must, that its conduct would likely subject it to FDCPA liability had it filed a lawsuit to collect this time-barred debt in state court. Federal circuit and district courts have uniformly held that a debt collector's threatening to sue on a time-barred debt and/or filing a time-barred suit in state court to recover that debt violates §§1692e and 1692f. . . .

As an example, the Seventh Circuit has reasoned that the FDCPA outlaws "stale suits to collect consumer debts" as unfair because (1) "few unsophisticated consumers would be aware that a statute of limitations could be used to defend against lawsuits based on stale debts" and would therefore "unwittingly acquiesce to such lawsuits"; (2) "the passage of time . . . dulls the consumer's memory of the circumstances and validity of the debt"; and (3) the delay in suing after the limitations period "heightens the probability that [the debtor] will no longer have personal records" about the debt. *Phillips v. Asset Assistance*, 736 F.3d 1077, 1079 (7th Cir. 2013) . . . .

These observations reflect the purpose behind statutes of limitations. . . . Statutes of limitations "protect defendants and the courts from having to deal with cases in which the search for truth may be seriously impaired by the loss of evidence, whether by death or disappearance of witnesses, fading memories, disappearance of documents, or otherwise." *United States v. Kubrick*, 444 U.S. 111, 117 (1979). . . .

The same is true in the bankruptcy context. In bankruptcy, the limitations period provides a bright line for debt collectors and consumer debtors, signifying a time when the debtor's right to be free of stale claims comes to prevail over a creditor's right to legally enforce the debt. A . . . debtor's memory of a stale debt may have faded and personal records documenting the debt may have vanished, making it difficult for a consumer debtor to defend against the time-barred claim.

Similar to the filing of a stale lawsuit, a debt collector's filing of a time-barred proof of claim creates the misleading impression to the debtor that the debt collector can legally enforce the debt. The "least sophisticated" Chapter 13 debtor may be unaware that a claim is time barred and unenforceable and thus fail to object to such a claim. Given the Bankruptcy Code's automatic allowance provision, the otherwise unenforceable time-barred debt will be paid from the debtor's future wages as part of his Chapter 13 repayment plan. Such a distribution of funds to debt collectors with time-barred claims then necessarily reduces the payments to other legitimate creditors with enforceable claims. Furthermore, filing objections to time-barred claims consumes energy and resources in a debtor's bankruptcy case, just as filing a limitations defense does in state court. For all of these reasons, under the "least-sophisticated consumer standard" in our binding precedent, LVNV's filing of a time-barred proof of claim against Crawford in bankruptcy was "unfair," "unconscionable," "deceptive," and "misleading" within the broad scope of §1692e and §1692f . . . .

[W]e disagree with the contention that LVNV's proof of claim was not a "collection activity" aimed at Crawford and, therefore, not "the sort of debt-collection activity that the FDCPA regulates." As noted earlier, the broad prohibitions of §1692e apply to a debt collector's "false, deceptive, or misleading representation or means" used "in connection with the collection of any debt." 15 U.S.C. §1692e . . . . [L]VNV's filing of the proof of claim fell well within the ambit of a "representation" or "means" used in "connection with the collection of any debt." It was an effort "to obtain payment" of Crawford's debt "by legal proceeding." In fact, payments to LVNV were made from Crawford's wages as a result of LVNV's claim . . . .

LVNV also argues that considering the filing of a proof of claim as a "means" used "in connection with the collection of debt" for purposes §§1692e and 1692f of the FDCPA would be at odds with the automatic stay provision of the Bankruptcy Code, 11 U.S.C. §362(a)(6). We disagree. The automatic stay prohibits debt-collection activity outside the bankruptcy proceeding, such as lawsuits in state court . . . . It does not prohibit the filing of a proof of claim to collect a debt within the bankruptcy process. Filing a proof of claim is the first step in collecting a debt in bankruptcy and is, at the very least, an "indirect" means of collecting a debt.

Just as LVNV would have violated the FDCPA by filing a lawsuit on stale claims in state court, LVNV violated the FDCPA by filing a stale claim in bankruptcy court.

Because we hold that LVNV's conduct violated the FDCPA's plain language, we vacate the district court's dismissal of Crawford's complaint and remand for further proceedings.

POST-CASE FOLLOW-UP

In re Crawford highlights a significant problem being experienced with debt buyers. According to the Office of the Comptroller of the Currency, the five banks that issue the great majority of credit cards used by Americans sell more than 80 percent of their charged-off credit card debt to fewer than 20 national debt buyers. During 2013, debt buyers filed between 10 million and 15 million debt collection lawsuits against consumers rather than attempting a workout. A 2014 study conducted by the Center for Consumer Recovery, *A Study of the Causes of Consumer Bankruptcy,* available online at www.centerforconsumerrecovery.org/ResourceCenter/CenterForConsumerRecovery2013BankruptcyStudySummary.pdf, found that many consumers, while in arrears and struggling, are not hopelessly in debt and could ultimately manage their past-due debt with the cooperation of their creditors but decide to file for bankruptcy relief out of collection fatigue: exhaustion from the constant bombardment of debt collection activities, especially debt collection litigation, aimed at them by debt buyers. The study suggested that 78 percent of consumers who filed for bankruptcy relief in 2013 did so as result of collection litigation instigated against them by a debt buyer. Worse, debt buyers are notorious for filing collection lawsuits and proofs of claim in consumer bankruptcy cases where there is a known defense to the debtor's obligation, such as a statute of limitations having run. But if the civil collection suit is decided by default, the defense is never raised and the judgment becomes final. And in a Chapter 13 bankruptcy case, as we will see, a proof of claim filed by a creditor is automatically allowed unless specifically objected to by the debtor or the Chapter 13 trustee within a certain timeframe.

As Judge Goldberg said in *In re Crawford*, the filing of such stale claims in Chapter 13s by debt buyers has become a "deluge." Thus for the Eleventh Circuit to find that the FDCPA applies to proofs of claim filed in a bankruptcy case is huge. And to find that a proof of claim containing any information that could be construed as untrue (like not mentioning that the statute of limitations has run for pursuing payment via litigation) makes it "unfair," "unconscionable," "deceptive," and "misleading" under §1692(e) and §1692(f) is groundmoving. Debt buyers may never be able to operate the same way again.

Not all courts are likely to be convinced by the reasoning of *Crawford* and may see an important distinction between the filing of a collection suit by the creditor based on the time barred debt and the filing of a proof of claim on that time barred debt in a bankruptcy case instituted by the debtor. The former seems clearly to be an attempt to collect debt from the debtor while the latter can be characterized as a response to the debtor's action on the debt and at most an effort to collect from the estate of the debtor, not the debtor himself. See, e.g., *Elliott v. Cavalry Investments, LLC,* 2015 WL 133745 (S.D. Ind. 2015) (recognizing the issue but refusing to decide it on summary judgment).

Crawford v. LVNV Funding, LLC (In re Crawford):
Real Life Applications

1. How certain does a defense to a debt obligation have to be for it to constitute a violation of the FDCPA if the debt collector files suit to collect or files a claim in the debtor's bankruptcy? For example, if the debtor had advised the debt collector that it would defend any lawsuit based on unconscionability or capacity or mutual mistake, etc., must the debt collector not pursue the claim? What's the difference between these defenses and the statute of limitation defense?
2. If there was a genuine dispute over whether the statute of limitations had run, could the debt collector file suit to collect or file a claim in the bankruptcy proceeding?
3. Debt buyers are controversial but does that mean it would be unethical for your law office to represent them in their debt collection activities? What, if any, ethical considerations should go through an attorney's or paralegal's mind when representation is sought by an aggressive debt buyer who is known to file time barred claims and hope for default in a civil suit or absence of objection to a bankruptcy claim?

LEAST SOPHISTICATED CONSUMER OR REASONABLE CONSUMER?

Though the statute does not expressly require it, a number of federal circuits, including the Eleventh Circuit as mentioned in *Crawford*, have determined that §§804-808 of the FDCPA are to be applied using the **least sophisticated consumer standard** rather than a **reasonable consumer standard**. See, e.g., *Smith v. Consumer Credit, Inc.*, 167 F.3d 1052, 1054 (6th Cir. 1999); *Swanson v. Southern Oregon Credit Service, Inc.*, 869 F.2d 1222, 1225 (9th Cir. 1988); and *Jeter v. Credit Bureau, Inc.*, 760 F.2d 1168, 1179 (11th Cir. 1985). The least sophisticated standard is intended to protect even naïve or overly trusting consumers from deceptive debt collection practices.

P-H 4-f: See if your federal circuit has adopted the least sophisticated consumer standard for interpreting the abuse provisions of the FDCPA. If not, does your circuit follow the reasonable consumer standard or some other standard that it has articulated? If your state regulates debt collection practices, what standard have your state courts adopted for applying the state act?

---

3. The "Initial Communication" and §809 Demand Letter

Section 809(a) of the FDCPA provides that within five days following the initial communication between the debt collector and the debtor, the debt collector must send to the debtor a written communication that contains the following:

- the amount of the debt [§809(a)(1)];
- the name of the creditor owed [§809(a)(2)];
- a statement that the debt will be assumed valid unless the debtor disputes the debt within 30 days of receipt of the written communication [§809(a)(3)];
- a statement that if the debtor, within the 30-day period, notifies the debt collector in writing that the debt is disputed in whole or in part, the debt collector will then obtain verification of the debt (including a copy of any judgment upon which the debt is based) and mail it to the debtor [§809(a)(4)]; and
- a statement that if the debtor, within the 30-day period, requests in writing the name of the original creditor, the debt collector will provide that name if it is different from the current creditor [§809(a)(5)].

Section 809(b) provides that if the debtor does, in a timely writing, either dispute the debt or request the name of the original creditor in writing, debt collection activities must cease until verification of the debt and/or name of the original creditor has been mailed to the debtor. Section 809(c) provides that the failure of a debtor to dispute a debt cannot be used against him as an admission of liability for the debt in a subsequent collection lawsuit.

The scheme contemplated by §809 is that the initial communication between the debtor and the debt collector will be verbal (e.g., by phone call). Then within five days of that verbal communication, the §809 letter must be sent.

EXAMPLE

Pearl Murphy, from Case Study #1 (see Illustration 1-a) owes Capital City Medical Equipment Co. (CCME) $1,200 for medical supplies provided during her illness. If that debt had been turned over to a debt collector and the initial communication between the debt collector and Pearl Murphy is a phone call, the debt collector must send the §809 letter within five days of the phone call.

Section 809 permits the initial communication with the debtor to be in writing so long as that writing complies with the requirements of that section. If the initial communication is in writing and complies with §809, no additional written communication within five days is required. In many law offices doing collection work and at some debt collection agencies, the initial communication is indeed in writing and lawyers typically refer to that first writing as the **demand letter**. Consequently, it is important that the demand letter comply with the requirements of §809. Illustration 4-a shows a demand letter from an attorney for CCME to Pearl Murphy seeking to collect the $1,200 debt she owes CCME.

Illustration 4-a: DEMAND LETTER

ROYAL AND ASSOCIATES
Attorneys and Counselors at Law
115 Commerce Street
Capital City, Yourstate
(555) 961-9087

July 1, YR-1

Ms. Pearl E. Murphy
3521 West Cherry Street
Capital City, Yourstate

In re: Indebtedness of $1,200 to Capital City Medical Equipment

Dear Ms. Murphy:

Your name has been brought to our attention to collect from you the entire balance of a debt you owed Capital City Medical Equipment (CCME) in the amount of $1,200 under the terms of that certain Medical Equipment Rental Agreement (the Agreement) that you executed on February 1, YR-1. A bill for the $1,200 that you owe CCME under the terms of the Agreement was sent to you on May 15, YR-1, and CCME advises us that you have failed and refused to pay any portion of that amount within 30 days of receipt of the bill as you are obligated to do under the terms of the Agreement.

If you want to resolve this matter without a lawsuit, you must, within 30 days of the date of this letter, either pay the entire amount owed or call the undersigned at the number shown above and work out arrangements for payment with us. If you do neither of these things, we have been authorized to file suit on behalf of CCME for the collection of this debt.

Federal law gives you thirty (30) days after you receive this letter to dispute the validity of the debt or any part of it. If you do not dispute it within that period, we will assume that it is valid. If you do dispute it by notifying us in writing to that effect we will, as required by the law, obtain and mail to you proof of the debt. And if, within the same period, you request in writing the name and address of your original creditor, if the original creditor is different from the current creditor CCME, we will furnish you that information also. The law does not require us to wait until the end of the 30-day period before suing you to collect this debt. If, however, you request proof of the debt or the name and address of the original creditor within the 30-day period that begins with your receipt of this letter, the law requires us to suspend our efforts until we have mailed information to you.

Please make arrangements immediately to pay this debt. I trust you will give this matter priority attention.

Sincerely,

_____
Edmond T. Royal, Attorney at Law

Section 809 is primarily concerned with giving the debtor the opportunity to validate or dispute the debt, and its provisions can be a bit tricky. Note that §809(a)(3) advises the debtor that the debt will be assumed valid unless the debtor disputes it within 30 days, but it does not expressly require the debtor to dispute the debt in writing to avoid that assumption. On the other hand, §809(a)(4),

Validation notice Required language in communication from a debt collector governed by the FDCPA to a debtor regarding the debtor's right to demand verification of the debt.

referred to as the **validation notice**, provides that if the debtor does dispute the debt in writing within 30 days, the debt collector will obtain verification of the debt and provide it to the debtor. And §809(b) requires that collection efforts stop until the verification has been mailed to the debtor.

The reference to a writing in the §809(a)(4) validation notice requirement but its absence in the §809(a)(3) right to dispute provision has led to confusion among the courts. If the debtor wishes to dispute the debt, must he put his dispute in writing or is that only an option? Even if the debtor is not required to state his dispute of the debt in writing, can a §809 letter require him to do so in order to avoid the assumption that the debt is valid? There is a split of authority among the federal circuits as to whether a §809 demand letter does requires or can require the debtor to dispute the debt in writing to avoid the assumption of validity. Compare *Graziano v. Harrison*, 950 F.2d 107, 112 (3d Cir. 1991) (debtor must dispute debt in writing) with *Camacho v. Bridgeport Financial, Inc.*, 430 F.3d 1078, 1080-1082 (9th Cir. 2005) (§809 does not impose a writing requirement on debtors).

Regardless of whether §809(a)(3) requires or can be used to require the debtor to provide written dispute of the debt, it is clear that the obligation of the debt collector to provide the debtor with verification of the debt under §809(a)(4) is triggered only by receiving written notice from the debtor sent within the 30-day window that the debt is disputed in whole or part. Neither verbal notice nor dispute nor untimely notice of dispute will trigger that obligation.

Section 809(a)(5) requires inclusion of a statement in the demand letter that, upon the debtor's written request within the 30-day period, the debt collector will provide the debtor with the name and address of the original creditor, if different from the current creditor. Remember, as you learned in your Contracts course, contracts creating a debt obligation are often assigned by one creditor to another. Therefore, the creditor identified in the demand letter may not be the original creditor. Section 809(a)(5) provides the debtor with a means of contacting the original creditor.

EXAMPLE

Assume that Pearl Murphy has made a number of small payments to CCME on the debt she owes. She receives a demand letter written by a debt collector on behalf of AAA Finance Company (AAA) advising that AAA is now the creditor to whom the debt is owed and that she should pay the balance of $950 to AAA to satisfy the claim. Pearl thinks she only owes $800 on the bill and attempts to contact CCME, only to find that it has changed its phone number and apparently its name, too, because she can't find it in the phone book. Pearl may want to exercise her rights under §809(a)(5) to learn how to contact CCME if it is still in business.

Notwithstanding the language required to be included in a demand letter, nothing in the FDCPA requires a creditor to wait 30 days after sending the demand letter to file suit to collect the debt. Theoretically, the creditor could cause the demand letter to be sent today and file suit tomorrow without violating the FDCPA. One exception to that is §809(b). Under that provision, if the debtor does exercise his right under §809(a)(4) to timely notify the debt collector in writing that the debt is disputed in whole or part, or under §809(a)(5) to request the name and address of the original creditor, collection efforts must stop—but only until the information requested by the debtor has been mailed to him. Then collection efforts, including the filing of a lawsuit, can resume.

EXAMPLE

Assume that AAA causes the demand letter to be sent to Pearl. Pearl receives the letter today. A week later, AAA decides to file suit and authorizes its attorney to do so. The next day, however, Pearl's letter requesting the name and address of the original creditor arrives. Filing the suit or any other collection action must be delayed until Pearl's request is complied with. Once it is, the suit may then be filed. What if the attorney for AAA filed the lawsuit the day before Pearl's letter arrived? In that case, there is no violation of the FDCPA by filing the suit because the attorney did not know Pearl's letter was coming. However, the collection lawsuit must not move forward until the response is in the mail.

P-H 4-g: Look at the demand letter in Illustration 4-a. Compare the letter with §§809(a)(1)-(5) of the FDCPA and identify the exact language in the letter that complies with each of the provisions of §§809(a)(1)-(5).

P-H 4-h: Redraft the letter in Illustration 4-a to make it comply with any additional or different requirements on collection letters imposed by the law of your state.

What if a debt-collecting attorney makes no contact with the debtor before filing the collection lawsuit? Could the filing of the lawsuit via service of a complaint and summons be the §809(a) initial communication triggering inclusion of the validation notice and other requirements of that section and constituting an FDCPA violation if not included? For years there was a split on this issue but in 2006 Congress amended §809 to specifically provide that "a communication in the form of a formal pleading in a civil action shall not be treated as an initial communication for purposes of subsection (a) of this section."

P-H 4-i: Assume Department Store is owed $1,000 by Consumer who files for bankruptcy relief. Department Store has not undertaken any debt collection efforts against Consumer other than sending his monthly bill. (Recall that creditors seeking to collect their own debt are not debt collectors under FDCPA.) However, now that Consumer is in bankruptcy, Department Store has its outside counsel file a routine proof of claim for it in the bankruptcy case. After *In re Crawford*, supra, could filing that proof of claim without including the validation notice or other statements required by §809(a) be a violation of the FDCPA? Would filing that proof of claim under circumstances where Department Store knows the claim is inaccurate or unjustified be a violation?

Private right of action The right granted by a regulatory statute to the injured party to maintain a civil lawsuit for damages apart from governmental regulatory action.

4. Penalties for Violating the FDCPA

The FDCPA authorizes a **private right of action** on behalf of the consumer debtor for any violations of its provisions. Pursuant to §813, a debt collector found to have violated these provisions may be civilly liable to the consumer/debtor for the debtor's actual damages, plus a statutory penalty of up to $1,000 per violation, plus the attorney's fee incurred by the debtor, and court costs. The debtor has one year from the date of the alleged violation to initiate the civil lawsuit in state or federal court to recover such private damages.

It is a defense to the debt collector in the debtor's suit under the FDCPA if the debt collector can show by a preponderance of the evidence (more likely than not) that the violation "was not intentional and resulted from a bona fide error notwithstanding the maintenance of procedures reasonably adapted to avoid any such error." §813(c). In *Jerman v. Carlisle, McNellie, Rini, Kramer & Ulrich, LPA*, 559 U.S. 573 (2010), the U.S. Supreme Court held that this **bona fide error defense** of the FDCPA does not include mistakes of law regarding the requirements of the statute. The defendant law firm in *Jerman*, seeking to collect a debt for a client, demanded that the debtor dispute the validity of the debt in writing. When the debtor sued, the trial court, affirmed by the Sixth Circuit, chose to follow the view expressed in *Camacho v. Bridgeport Financial, Inc.*, supra, that §809(a)(3) does not impose a writing requirement on debtors and ruled that the defendant's demand that he do so was a violation of the FDCPA. The defendant law firm asserted the bona fide error defense on the grounds that it had mistakenly but in good faith construed §809 to require that the debtor dispute the debt in writing. Although the Supreme Court rejected defendant's mistake of law as being within the bona fide error defense of §813(c), it did not resolve the lingering question of whether §809(a)(3) should be interpreted to require a debtor to put the dispute of the debt in writing since that precise issue was not raised in the appeal. See *Jerman*, supra, at 578.

Unfair or deceptive act or practice Prohibited conduct by debt collectors under the FDCPA.

The FDCPA is administered in the first instance by the **Federal Trade Commission** (FTC), and any violation can be deemed by the FTC to be an **unfair or deceptive act or practice** by the debt collector under the Federal Trade Commission Act (FTCA). Such a finding authorizes the FTC to enforce compliance with the FDCPA on debt collectors and to assess fines and penalties for noncompliance. In an extreme case, the FTC could order a debt collector to stop doing business. The FTC maintains a helpful information site regarding the FDCPA at www.ftc.gov/bcp/edu/pubs/consumer/credit/cre18.shtm.

When it was created in 2010, the Consumer Financial Protection Bureau (CFPB) was granted supervisory and enforcement authority over large collectors of consumer debt, those with receipts of more than $10 million per year in debt collection activities. That includes about 175 debt collection companies, which collectively account for more than 60 percent of the consumer debt collection business. In October 2012 the CFPB issued its Debt Collection Examination Procedures Manual (http://files.consumerfinance.gov/f/201210_cfpb_debt-collection-examination-procedures.pdf) to alert debt collectors to the procedures and standards that the CFPB will use to determine if regulated debt collectors are following the law.

P-H 4-j: Look at the Background section of the CFPB Manual (pages 1-3) mentioned in the text. What federal statutes other than the FDCPA impact the activities of debt collectors? Look at Module 7 of the manual. What kinds of abusive litigation practices does the CFPB seem to be concerned about? What kinds of abusive repossession practices? What concerns does it seem to have about collecting time barred debt?

P-H 4-k: Go to the CFPB web site at www.consumerfinance.gov/ and use the search feature there to (1) locate recent press releases by the bureau regarding consumer debt collection, and (2) determine if the bureau has promulgated any specific regulations governing the debt collection industry.

B. ▶ State Regulation of Debt Collection Practices

A number of states have passed their own debt collection practices statutes and regulations, usually enforced by a state agency charged with consumer protection or by the state attorney general (www.naag.org/). In other states, there is no specific debt collection regulation but relief may be had by debtors under the state's generic consumer protection act, which provides remedies for any unfair or deceptive trade practice directed at a consumer. Most states enacting specific debt collection regulation closely track the federal law concerning what constitutes a violation and remedies. In a few such states, however, the regulation of debt collection activity is even more stringent than the federal FDCPA, or state law imposes more substantial penalties than the FDCPA.

EXAMPLE

California's Fair Debt Collection Practices Act (California Civil Code §1788, et seq.), known generally as the Rosenthal Act, regulates creditors collecting their own debt, which the FDCPA does not. The California act also places more limitations than the FDCPA does on a debt collector contacting the debtor's employer. Many states also require debt collectors to be licensed or registered by the state, a level of regulation not imposed by the FDCPA.

P-H 4-l: The Privacy Rights Clearinghouse maintains a web site with links to state debt collection laws at www.privacyrights.org/fs/fs27plus.htm. Is your state listed there? If so, what agency or government department enforces your state law? Is there a private right of action allowed for violation of your state law? Must debt collectors be licensed in your state? Does your statute appear to impose more stringent limitations on debt collectors than do those in the FDCPA, summarized below? If your state attorney general's office enforces your state debt collection law, locate that office from the web site of the National Association of Attorneys General (www.naag.org/). Does your attorney general's web site mention abusive debt collection practices? Does it provide a convenient way to file a complaint regarding such practices?

C. ▶ Tort, Criminal, and Ethical Considerations in Debt Collection

Attorneys engaging in debt collection work, assisting paralegals, debt collection companies, and creditors themselves (even if not regulated by the FDCPA) must also be aware of several tort theories that debtors may assert against them in order to recover damages for wrongful conduct arising out of collection practices. Some behavior that is tortious may also be considered criminal. Such tort liability or criminal exposure can exist whether or not the collection practice complained of violates the FDCPA and without regard to whether the debtor actually owes the debt or not.

EXAMPLE

> A debt collector who publishes a false statement concerning the debtor to third persons may be sued for **defamation**. A debt collector who resorts to physical attack on the debtor may prosecuted for **assault** and **battery** or sued in tort for that behavior. A debt collector who threatens criminal prosecution or other harm to the debtor or someone close to the debtor unless a debt is paid may face civil or criminal allegations of **extortion** or **blackmail**.

Other causes of action that can arise in nonjudicial debt collection include the following:

- **Intentional infliction of emotional distress** (outrageous conduct). See, e.g., *Moorhead v. J.C. Penney*, 555 S.W.2d 713 (Tenn. 1977) (decided before enactment of the FDCPA), and *Perk v. Worden*, 475 F. Supp. 2d 565 (E.D. Va. 2007).
- **Invasion of privacy**. See, e.g., *Kuhn v. Account Control Technology*, 865 F. Supp. 1443 (D. Nev. 1994), and *Sofka v. Thal*, 662 S.W.2d 502 (Mo. 1983).
- **Malicious harassment**, civil or criminal. See, e.g., *Sams v. State*, 271 Ga. App. 617, 610 S.E.2d 592 (2005).
- **Conversion**, **trespass to chattel**, or **theft**. See, e.g., *Darcars Motors of Silver Springs, Inc. v. Borzym*, 379 Md. 249, 841 A.2d 828 (2004).

Debt collection activities of an attorney found to be in violation of the FDCPA or actionable under state tort or criminal law may also be grounds for disciplinary action against the attorney involved since it will likely constitute a violation of legal ethics. For example, Rule 4.4 of the American Bar Association Rules of Professional Conduct prohibits an attorney from threatening criminal prosecution in order to induce payment to a client. Such conduct could therefore not only be construed as civil or criminal extortion or blackmail as discussed in the last section, but could result in disciplinary action against the attorney. Rule 4.4 states:

In representing a client, a lawyer shall not:
. . .

(b) threaten to present a criminal charge, or to offer or to agree to refrain from filing such a charge, for the purpose of obtaining an advantage in a civil matter.

Likewise, paralegals certified by the state in which they work or by paralegal organizations such as the National Association of Legal Assistants (NALA) or the National Federation of Paralegal Associations (NFPA) may lose their certification as a result of engaging in such conduct.

EC 4-c: Review the NALA Code of Ethics (www.nala.org/code.htm) and the NFPA Model Code of Ethics and Professional Responsibility (http://www.paralegals.org/displaycommon.cfm?an = 1&subarticlenbr = 133) and determine the various provisions of such codes that might be violated by a paralegal involved in conduct prohibited by the FDCPA or that is tortious or criminal as described in this chapter.

P-H 4-m: Patty Paralegal, paralegal for Edmond Royal, the attorney representing CCME, is directed by Royal to contact Pearl Murphy in order to inquire if she will voluntarily repay the debt she owes to CCME. When Patty cannot reach Pearl, she calls Nick Murphy at Overland Truck Services, where he is employed as manager. Overland Truck does not have a policy prohibiting such calls to the workplace. Patty calls and gets the receptionist. When she asks to speak with Nick Murphy, the receptionist asks what matter she is calling about and Patty says she is calling on behalf of the law office "to confirm a debt owed by Mr. and Mrs. Murphy" to a client. In fact, under Yourstate state law, one spouse is not legally responsible for the sole debts of the other spouse so Nick has no legal responsibility for Pearl's obligation to CCME (in some states he would as a matter of law). Word that Nick doesn't pay his bills spreads from the receptionist to every nook and cranny of the business, and eventually to the regional supervisor who is Nick's boss. The regional supervisor asks Nick what is going on and why he isn't paying his bills. Nick explains that the debt is his wife's and not his and the circumstances of Pearl's condition. What provisions of the FDCPA has Patty violated? What tort has she possibly committed? What should she have said to the Overland Truck receptionist instead of what she did say?

P-H 4-n: Assume that Pearl Murphy writes a check to the local food store to pay for the week's groceries. The check bounces (payment is refused on presentment to the drawee bank due to insufficient funds) because Pearl made an error in balancing her checkbook. The food store owner posts the check on the checkout counter where everyone passing through can clearly see the name of both Nick and Pearl Murphy printed on the check and the "Insufficient Funds" bank stamp on the face of it. Has the store owner violated any provision of the FDCPA? Has the store owner possible committed a tortious act against Pearl and/or Nick?

P-H 4-o: Assume the owner of CCME sees Nick and Pearl Murphy shopping at the mall. He approaches them and begins to demand his money. Nick steps in front of his frightened wife, and the owner pushes Nick out of the way and points his finger in Pearl's face so close to her that she flinches. Shouting as loud as he can he calls her a "no-good deadbeat" causing several shoppers to turn and stare, then he walks away. Has the CCME owner violated any provision of the FDCPA? Has he possibly committed any tortious or criminal act?

Illustration 4-b: PROMINENT DEBT COLLECTION ORGANIZATIONS

- ACA International, the Association of Credit and Collection Professionals (http://www.acainternational.org/)
- Commercial Collection Agency Association (CCAA) (http://commercialcollectionagenciesofamerica.com/)
- International Association of Commercial Collectors, Inc. (IACC) (www.commercialcollector.com/iacc/)
- The Equipment Leasing and Finance Association (ELFA) (www.elfaonline.org/)
- The Finance, Credit, and International Business Association (FCIB) (www.fcibglobal.com/)

P-H 4-p: Assume that Pearl Murphy finally writes a check to CCME to pay off her debt there. Unfortunately, the check bounces for lack of sufficient funds on deposit in the checking account. The owner of CCME calls Pearl and demands immediate payment in cash or he will have her arrested for passing a bad check. Has the owner of CCME committed any tortious or criminal act? Would your answer change if Pearl was later charged with passing a bad check and found guilty?

After considering so many abuses of debt collection activity, it is good to remind ourselves that debt collection is an honest way to make a living—a necessary and honorable trade. As always, it is the bad apples that give the barrel that sour smell. There are a number of organizations made up of members of the debt collection community who are all dedicated to the ethical and professional practice of their trade. Illustration 4-b lists a number of the more prominent ones.

P-H 4-q: Check the web site of ACA International, the Association of Credit and Collection Professionals, at www.acainternational.org/. Based in Minneapolis, ACA International is one of the largest organizations of those involved in the debt collection industry: creditors, third-party collection agencies, asset buyers, and attorneys involved in debt collection. Check out the organization's Code of Conduct at www.acainternational.org/files.aspx?p=/images/12909/acacodeofconduct20140318.pdf. Do you see concern in the code about complying with FDCPA provisions and otherwise behaving honorably? Check the sites of other organizations listed in Illustration 4-b. Do you see references anywhere to forthcoming regulations by the CFPB?

D. ► Resolution of a Disputed Debt or Liability Claim by Alternative Dispute Resolution (ADR)

Where traditional debt collection activities are unsuccessful or where the debt obligation is contested by the debtor, the creditor may resort to judicial process by filing a collection lawsuit, which we will consider in the next chapter. But where the debt is contested, the parties may first attempt **alternative dispute resolution** (ADR)—i.e., alternative to litigation in a court of law—before proceeding to litigation. Litigation can be time-consuming, expensive, and stressful. It often produces unexpected results because of the specialized and (to the layperson) often quirky rules of procedure and evidence that govern it.

The most common forms of ADR are privately negotiated settlement, mediated settlement, and arbitration.

1. Privately Negotiated Settlement

Negotiation Dialogue between parties or their representatives, with or without the aid of a mediator, aimed at reaching an agreed compromise of a dispute.

The parties to a disputed debt or liability claim may **negotiate** a settlement of the dispute. The negotiation may occur between the parties themselves or between the respective attorneys for the parties. If the negotiations are successful, a written **settlement agreement** will typically be executed by the parties and the obligations of that agreement may displace the terms of the original contract or the liability claim.

EXAMPLE

In their malpractice claim against Dr. Craft and Capital City Hospital (CCH), Pearl and Nick Murphy may be prepared to file a lawsuit seeking the recovery of $1.5 million. But they may be able to successfully negotiate a settlement of the claim of the lump sum payment of $500,000. That obligation and the timing of the payment will be set forth in a signed settlement agreement. The obligation of Dr. Craft and CCH to pay the Murphys $500,000 as set forth in the settlement agreement will displace the claim of the Murphys against either the doctor or CCH. In the settlement agreement, the Murphys will surrender and release all such claims in exchange for the settlement amount.

EXAMPLE

Capital City Medical Equipment Company (CCME) is prepared to file suit against Pearl Murphy on the Medical Equipment Lease Agreement she signed seeking to recover $1,200 plus interest and attorney's fees. Before suit is filed, the attorneys may negotiate a settlement whereby Pearl agrees to pay $600 in six monthly installments. A settlement agreement will be signed by the parties that may displace the obligations of the original lease agreement—Pearl will promise to make the monthly payments and CCME will promise to release its claim for breach of the lease agreement. However, because payment of the settlement amount is going to be delayed under this agreement, CCME will probably insist that its claim will not be released unless and until Pearl makes all of the agreed settlement payments, and if she defaults on any payment she is promising to make in the settlement agreement, then her obligations under the original lease agreement will survive and authorize CCME to sue her for any balance owed under it. That settlement agreement might look like Illustration 4-c.

Illustration 4-c: SETTLEMENT AGREEMENT WITH RELEASE

This Compromise and Settlement Agreement ("the Settlement Agreement") is made by and between Capital City Medical Equipment Company ("CCME") and Pearl E. Murphy ("Murphy"). On February 2, YR-1, Murphy entered into a Medical Equipment Lease Agreement (the "Lease Agreement") with CCME pursuant to which CCME leased and provided to defendant certain items of medical equipment set out in the Lease Agreement. CCME alleges that Murphy has breached her obligations under the Lease Agreement and now owes CCME $1,200 under the terms of the Lease Agreement plus interest and attorney's fees. Murphy disputes that she has breached her obligations under the terms of the Lease Agreement or that she owes any amount to CCME under the terms of the Lease Agreement.

No lawsuit is presently pending between the parties. The parties to this Settlement Agreement wish to reach a full and final settlement of all claims and defenses arising out of the facts recited above and the various disputes between the parties arising out of the Lease Agreement.

The parties to this Settlement Agreement, in consideration of the mutual covenants and agreements to be performed, as set forth below, agree as follows:

1. Murphy agrees to pay CCME the sum of $600 in six equal monthly installments of $100 each. Payments are to be made on the first day of each month for six consecutive months beginning September 1, YR-1.

2. Upon receipt of the sixth and final payment referenced in Paragraph 1 of the Settlement Agreement, CCME will execute the release attached as Exhibit 1 to this Settlement Agreement. However, if Murphy fails to make the payments referenced in Paragraph 1 of this Settlement Agreement in the amounts and at the times designated, the parties agree that the obligations of Murphy under the Lease Agreement shall remain in full force and effect and shall then be fully enforceable by CCME and this Settlement Agreement shall not be any bar to the right of CCME to seek all available legal and equitable relief for Murphy's alleged breach of that Lease Agreement.

3. The parties agree that the terms of this Settlement Agreement bind the parties and their respective heirs, executors, administrators, successors, and assigns.

Dated: _____

_____
Pearl E. Murphy
Capital City Medical Equipment Company
By: _____

Exhibit 1 to Compromise and Settlement Agreement

Release of Claims

Capital City Medical Equipment Company ("CCME"), having confirmed that Pearl E. Murphy ("Murphy") has fulfilled all her obligations under that certain Compromise and Settlement Agreement entered into between CCME and Murphy on the _____ day of _____, YR-1, does hereby voluntarily and knowingly execute this Release of Claims ("Release") with the express intention of effecting the extinguishment of obligations, as designated in this Release. CCME with the intention of binding itself, its successors, and assigns, does hereby release and discharge Pearl E. Murphy, her heirs, executors, administrators, and assigns, from all claims, demands, actions, judgments, and executions that the CCME ever had, or now has, or may have, against Pearl E. Murphy created by or arising out of, that certain Medical Equipment Lease Agreement (the "Lease Agreement") dated February 2, YR-1.

Dated: _____

Capital City Medical Equipment Company

By: _____

A disputed debt or liability claim can be settled at any time, even after a lawsuit has been filed over the dispute. In fact, trial judges will frequently inquire of the parties to a pending suit whether settlement negotiations have taken place and encourage the parties to attempt them. Of course, the judge cannot order parties to settle. However, Rule 26(f) of the Federal Rules of Civil Procedure (FRCP) now authorizes the U.S. district courts to require the parties to meet and discuss a number of things about the case, including "the possibilities for promptly settling or resolving the case." This procedure is frequently used in the federal courts and in many state courts.

P-H 4-r: Check the rules of civil procedure in your state and see if they contain an equivalent of FRCP 26(f).

If the parties settle a pending lawsuit, the settlement will still be reduced to a written settlement agreement, as seen in Illustration 4-c, and a release executed by any party seeking judgment against another. But something must be done as well with the pending lawsuit. If the settlement calls for one party to make a **lump sum** payment to the other, then the settlement agreement will typically call for execution of the release and dismissal of the pending lawsuit by the plaintiff with **prejudice** (meaning it can never be refiled) upon receipt of the lump sum payment. Where the settlement agreement calls for a **structured settlement** involving payments to be made over time by a reliable third party (such as a financial services company under the terms of an annuity), the settlement agreement will typically call for the dismissal of the pending lawsuit with prejudice and execution of the release immediately upon the execution of the settlement agreement. The plaintiff then looks exclusively to the reliable third party for payment of the settlement amount. But what if the settlement agreement calls for one party to the pending lawsuit to make future payments to the other? Is the party who is to receive the future payments expected to dismiss its lawsuit with prejudice and trust the other party to make the payments? Not usually. In that situation, execution of the release and dismissal of the pending lawsuit will be delayed until the final payment is made.

EXAMPLE

If CCME files suit against Pearl Murphy using the complaint seen in Illustration 4-c and the case is then settled, the settlement agreement, instead of reciting that no lawsuit is pending between the parties, will say something like, "There is now pending, based on the claim of CCME against Murphy based on the Lease Agreement, Case No. 00-7799 in the Circuit Court for Capital County, Yourstate ('the Case'). And in addition to promising to execute the release when Pearl finishes with the settlement payments, CCME will promise, as well, "to file a dismissal with prejudice of the Case."

Alternatively, a party who agrees to accept future payments or performance from the other party may ask that the paying party consent to the entry of a **consent decree** (also referred to as a **final judgment by consent** or an **agreed final judgment**) in the pending lawsuit. The basis of the obligation between the parties then becomes that final court judgment.

P-H 4-s: What would happen if Pearl and Nick settled their malpractice lawsuit against defendant Dr. Craft and accepted an agreed amount of money from him in that settlement but continued their lawsuit against co-defendant Capital City Hospital? And what if the settlement agreement between Croft and Nick and Pearl provided that Croft was "loaning" some or all of the settlement funds to the couple to use in their continuing lawsuit against CCH, and that if there were any recovery by them against CCH, then the loan would have to be repaid? Such agreements are called **loan receipt agreements** or **Mary Carter agreements** from *Booth v. Mary Carter Paint Co.*, 202 So. 2d 8 (Fla. App. 1967). For a good discussion of how they work, read *Banovz v. Rantanen*, 649 N.E.2d 977 (Ill. App. 1995), and then determine if your state allows such agreements in personal injury or other tort litigation. If so, must the settlement agreement be disclosed to the remaining defendants? Can those defendants offer proof of the Mary Carter agreement into evidence if one of the settling parties testifies in order to impeach that witness by showing an interest in the outcome of the case?

2. Mediation

Mediation A form of alternative dispute resolution in which an impartial person serving as mediator uses back and forth dialogue with the disputing parties to assist them in reaching a settlement.

The parties may employ the services of a **mediator** to assist them in reaching a negotiated settlement. **Mediation** is a form of ADR in which the mediator, a neutral third party to the dispute, seeks to facilitate a negotiated settlement between disputing parties. The mediator will listen to both sides, serve as a communication link between the disputing parties, and will encourage both sides to be reasonable and move toward a realistic settlement. The mediator has no authority to compel a settlement or to make any ruling in the favor of either party, nor does the mediator report the content of the discussions to the judge.

Mediation has become a popular and successful ADR tool. States now give trial judges the authority to order the parties to engage in good faith mediation and to select the mediator from a list of **court approved mediators**. Many federal district courts have adopted similar procedures by local rule, and some state appellate courts and federal circuit courts of appeals have mediation procedures for cases on appeal (see, e.g., **mediation conference** procedures for the Sixth Circuit at www.ca6.uscourts.gov/internet/mediation/aboutmediationconferences.htm).

If a case is successfully mediated, the mediated agreement will be reduced to a written settlement agreement, as already discussed.

3. Arbitration

Arbitration A form of ADR in which the disputing parties agree that a third-person arbitrator, or panel of arbitrators, may hear the dispute informally and render a decision. May be binding or nonbinding.

Arbitration is a different form of ADR in which the disputing parties agree that a third-person **arbitrator**, or **panel of arbitrators**, will hear the dispute and render a decision (the **arbitrator's award**). Like mediation, arbitration is considered to be a less expensive and less time-consuming method of resolving disputes than formal litigation.

Federal Arbitration Act Federal statute governing arbitration in cases affecting interstate commerce or maritime issues.

The **Federal Arbitration Act (FAA)**, 9 U.S.C. §1, et seq., governs the procedures and enforcement of arbitration awards involving **interstate commerce** or **maritime issues**. Most contracts containing mandatory binding arbitration clauses *do* involve interstate commerce and thus are subject to the FAA. Contracts

Illustration 4-d: CONTRACTUAL ARBITRATION CLAUSE

In the event of a dispute between the parties over the interpretation of this Agreement or any purported performance or failure to perform by either party, the parties agree, in lieu of litigation, to submit said dispute to binding arbitration pursuant to the rules of the American Arbitration Association.

with arbitration clauses that affect *only* **intrastate commerce** are not governed by the FAA and state law controls them. Nonetheless, 35 states have adopted some version of the FAA and 14 other states have adopted similar procedures by miscellaneous statutory and regulatory enactments.

Arbitration can be binding or nonbinding under the FAA and similar state statutes. **Nonbinding arbitration**, as the phrase suggests, means that either party dissatisfied with the arbitration award can still resort to formal litigation to resolve the dispute. **Binding arbitration** means that neither party dissatisfied with the arbitration award can thereafter resort to formal litigation to resolve the dispute. A binding arbitration award can only be attacked subsequently in court if the arbitration process itself was flawed or corrupted in some way, as by the arbitrators failing to follow the rules of the arbitration process or by proof of partiality or bias on the part of the arbitrators.

Parties to a dispute can elect to arbitrate their dispute at any time. More typically, though, arbitration is mandated by the contract between the parties that gave rise to the dispute. It is increasingly common for both commercial and consumer contracts to contain mandatory binding arbitration clauses such as that seen in Illustration 4-d.

EXAMPLE

Assume that the Medical Equipment Lease Agreement between Pearl Murphy and CCME seen as an exhibit to the complaint in Illustration 4-c contains the arbitration clause shown in Illustration 4-d. The arbitration panel finds in favor of CCME and awards it $1,500. Because the contract clause said the arbitration was binding, and assuming the arbitration clause itself is enforceable in the state, Pearl's only judicial recourse now will be to challenge the integrity of the arbitration process, not the underlying indebtedness.

The FAA *mandates* a presumption that an award arising out of the arbitration is valid and enforceable as a final judgment of a court unless the other party, within 90 days, files an action challenging the integrity of the arbitration process (e.g., fraud or prejudice) or seeks to vacate or modify the award based on some material error (e.g., an obvious miscalculation of figures). We will have more to say about final judgments in Chapter Five.

Over the past generation, the U.S. Supreme Court (SCOTUS) has identified a strong congressional policy arising from the Federal Arbitration Act (FAA), 9 U.S.C. §1, et seq., in favor of enforcing contractual arbitration agreements that has been applied to drastically limit the power of state law or even private agreement of the parties to limit or negate such agreements. In essence the Supreme Court has ruled in numerous contexts that state common law, statutes, or regulations raised as a defense to the enforcement of an arbitration agreement are preempted by the FAA to the extent that they "apply only to arbitration or that derive their meaning from the fact that an agreement to arbitrate is at issue." *AT&T Mobility v. Concepcion*, 563 U.S. 633, 639 (2011). See, e.g., *Volt Info. Scis. Inc. v. Bd. of Trs. of Leland Stanford Junior University*, 489 U.S. 468 (1989) (parties to an arbitration agreement involving an interstate transaction that would normally be governed by the FAA cannot choose in the agreement to be governed instead by state law); *Doctor's Assocs. v. Cassarotto*, 517 U.S. 681 (1996) (a state cannot require that a contract containing an arbitration clause also contain special notice requirements to ensure that the clause is conspicuous and clear); *Preston v. Ferrer*, 552 U.S. 346 (2008) (a state cannot prohibit the arbitration of a particular kind of claim); *Hall Street Associates, LLC v. Mattel, Inc.*, 552 U.S. 576 (2008) (a contract containing an arbitration clause may not grant a court discretion to engage in a broader review of the arbitration award than allowed by the FAA); *Stolt-Neilsen S.A. v. AnimalFeeds International Corp.*, 559 U.S. 662 (2010) (a member of a class cannot be compelled to submit to a class action arbitration when he has not agreed to do so); *AT&T Mobility v. Concepcion*, 563 U.S. 333 (2011) (state rule declaring class arbitration waivers unconscionable in consumer contracts preempted by FAA); *American Exp. Co. v. Italian Colors Restaurant*, 133 S. Ct. 2304 (2013) (plaintiffs have no right to litigate a statutory claim for antitrust violation via a class action notwithstanding a mandatory arbitration clause and no-class action arbitration clause in order to achieve the "effective vindication" of their statutory right to sue).

Notwithstanding the FAA and its broad construction by SCOTUS, a few federal statutes specifically restrict the use of mandatory binding arbitration clauses in predispute contracts. Those include:

- The Motor Vehicle Franchise Contract Arbitration Fairness Act, 15 U.S.C. §1226, prohibits automobile manufacturers from requiring their franchisees to agree to binding arbitration on a predispute basis.
- The John Warner National Defense Authorization Act for Fiscal Year 2007, Subtitle F §670, 10 U.S.C. §987, prohibits creditors from requiring military personnel and dependents to arbitrate consumer credit disputes.
- The Farm Bill of 2008, 7 U.S.C. §97(c), requires that growers and producers of livestock or poultry be provided an opportunity to decline to be bound by arbitration provisions on predispute basis.
- The Department of Defense Appropriations Act of 2009 amended U.S.C. §1303 by including the "Franken Amendment," detailed in 48 C.F.R. §§222.7400-7405, restricts the use of mandatory arbitration agreements by prohibiting defense contractors from requiring employees or independent contractors to agree to arbitrate claims for violation of civil rights or for sexual assault or harassment.
- The Dodd-Frank Wall Street Reform and Consumer Protection Act provides the new Bureau of Consumer Financial Protection authority to study and regulate mandatory predispute arbitration with respect to consumers' use of financial products or services.
- Dodd-Frank grants the Securities Exchange Commission authority to issue rules prohibiting or limiting the use of predispute agreements with respect to securities claims brought by customers or clients of brokers or dealers and rules prohibiting or limiting the use of predispute agreements

with respect to securities claims brought by customers or clients of investment advisors.

- Dodd-Frank prohibits lenders from imposing mandatory arbitration in residential mortgages or home equity loans.
- Dodd-Frank restricts the enforcement of provisions waiving rights or requiring arbitration in civil cases alleging retaliation by a government agency wherein fraud is reported.

P-H 4-t: In May 2016 the CFPB, acting pursuant to the authority granted it by Dodd-Frank as referenced in Exhibit 18.1, proposed a new rule to be codified as 12 CFR Part 1040 prohibiting class action arbitration waivers in a wide range of consumer contracts. The new regulation (viewable online at www.gpo.gov/fdsys/pkg/FR-2016-05-24/pdf/2016-10961.pdf) will cover most consumer financial products offered by banks and nonbanks including most secured or unsecured loans, credit cards, automobile leases, credit monitoring and debt adjustment services, as well as deposit account and check cashing services. Such contracts can still contain mandatory arbitration clauses but cannot prohibit the arbitrating consumer from instituting or participating in class action arbitration with similarly situated consumers. The new rule effectively reverses the decision in Concepcion for the consumer contracts covered by the rule. In 2015 the CFPB delivered to Congress a comprehensive report on the role of mandatory arbitration clauses in consumer contracts. Review the 2015 report at http://files.consumerfinance.gov/f/201503_cfpb_arbitration-study-report-to-congress-2015.pdf and decide if further federal regulation is needed in this area. The CFPB's proposed no class action waiver rule referenced in the text was scheduled to become final in August 2016 though opposition was expected. Visit the CFPB web site at www.consumerfinance.gov/ and determine if it has become final.

E. ▶ The Debt Settlement Industry

One consequence of American consumers having taken on such great amounts of debt in the last generation has been the explosion of the **debt settlement industry** in the guise of **credit counseling agencies** (CCAs) (sometimes called debt management, debt relief, debt settlement, debt negotiation, or credit repair companies). Some nine million Americans seek credit counseling each year. These companies offer to assist debt-strapped individuals and businesses to avoid bankruptcy by negotiating a **debt management plan** (DMP) with the client's creditors. Ideally, the DMP will lower the client's required payments by extending the time for repayment, eliminate or reduce late fees and interest rates, and, in rare cases, even reduce the principal amount owed. The CCAs also provide clients financial literacy and budget counseling.

At the end of the twentieth century, there were approximately 200 CCAs around the country, most of which were legitimate businesses assisting consumers and small businesses on a not-for-profit basis and charging minimal fees. A decade later, with the effects of the Great Recession still lingering, more than a thousand CCAs exist, many of which are for-profit. Though most CCAs are perfectly legitimate, the industry is now rife with complaints of false and deceptive promises regarding results to be obtained, charging excessive fees (often in advance and regardless of results obtained), charging undisclosed fees, and simply failing to provide promised services.

Since 2003, the Federal Trade Commission (FTC) has instituted at least six administrative actions against CCAs, including one of the largest, AmeriDebt, Inc., under the auspices of the Telemarketing and Consumer Fraud and Abuse Prevention Act of 1994 (15 U.S.C. §6101, et seq.) and the attorneys general in a number of states have brought suit against CCAs using their state consumer protection acts and antifraud laws. A number of states have legislated licensing and/or disclosure requirements on CCAs or prohibitions on up-front fees, and four states (Connecticut, Louisiana, Wyoming, and North Dakota) prohibit for-profit CCAs entirely. In 2003 the IRS began to crack down on for-profit CCAs masquerading as not-for-profit and in 2006 Congress amended the Internal Revenue Code (IRC) to add what is now 26 U.S.C. §501(q) imposing a number of requirements on CCAs wishing to receive tax-exempt status as nonprofit businesses, including a dictate that fees be reasonable and prohibiting fees based on a percentage of a client's debt or DMP payments unless state law expressly permits.

P-H 4-u: One of the leading trade associations for CCAs is the United States Organizations for Bankruptcy Alternatives (www.usoba.org/). Visit the USOBA site and see if you can determine the association's general position on industry regulation. What are its requirements for CCA membership in its association?

CHAPTER SUMMARY

In this chapter we have considered prelitigation debt collection activities. Such activities are governed primarily by the Fair Debt Collection Practices Act (FDCPA), though many states have enacted their own debt collection regulation, which may be more stringent. The FDCPA regulates the activities of debt collectors engaged in collecting debt from consumer debtors. Under the statute, debt collectors include persons acting for businesses, the principal purpose of which is to collect debts owed to another, as well as individuals who regularly collect or attempt to collect debts owed to another. Attorneys may be considered debt collectors under the FDCPA if they regularly attempt to collect debts for their clients.

The FDCPA regulates the extent to which a debt collector can gather information regarding the location of a debtor or have communications with a debtor and prohibits harassment or abuse of a debtor or the making of false or misleading representations to a debtor or utilizing other unfair or unconscionable means to collect debt. The FDCPA creates a private right of action for the consumer debtor against the debt collector violating its provisions in which the debtor can obtain his actual damages plus a statutory penalty of $1,000 as well as attorney's fees.

The Federal Trade Commission administers the FDCPA and is authorized to impose certain fines and penalties on violators and to order them to stop doing business in extreme cases. Within five days following the initial communication between the debt collector and the debtor, the debt collector must send a written communication to the debtor containing a number of provisions including the identity of the creditor, the amount owed, and a validation notice. It is essential that demand letters used by attorneys, who may be debt collectors under the FDCPA, comply with these statutory requirements.

Whether or not regulated by the FDCPA, those involved in collection work must be aware of various tort liabilities that may result from inappropriate collection activities. Viable tort theories in the debt collection area include the intentional infliction of emotional distress (outrageous conduct), defamation, invasion of privacy, assault, battery, and conversion. There may be criminal culpability as well, including criminal assault and battery, fraud, theft, or extortion (blackmail). Conduct that might render one engaged in debt collection criminally culpable or civilly liable may constitute an ethical violation as well.

Today there are more than a thousand credit counseling agencies around the country offering debt management or credit repair services to consumers.

REVIEW QUESTIONS

1. Who is a "debt collector" under the FDCPA?
2. Under what circumstances will an attorney be considered a debt collector under the FDCPA?
3. How does the FDCPA define who is a consumer debtor for purposes of making contact with that debtor? What restrictions does the FDCPA place on a debt collector in contacting that debtor?
4. What restrictions does the FDCPA impose on a debt collector needing to contact persons to determine the location of the debtor?
5. What kinds of conduct does the FDCPA consider to be harassing or abusive by the debt collector?
6. Provide as many examples as you can of what might constitute false or misleading representations by a debt collector seeking to collect a debt.
7. Provide as many examples as you can of what might constitute unfair or unconscionable means of collecting debt.
8. What federal agency administers the FDCPA and what are the governmentally imposed penalties for its violation?
9. What is a private right of action? What damages might a debtor recover from a debt collector who has violated the FDCPA in a private right of action?
10. Summarize the requirements imposed on debt collectors following the "initial communication" with the debtor. Why do these requirements apply so readily to the demand letter?
11. Under what tort theories might a debt collector or creditor be liable to a debtor separate and apart from the FDCPA? Of what crimes might a debt collector be guilty in connection with wrongful collection activities?
12. Why are credit counseling agencies controversial?

WORDS AND PHRASES TO REMEMBER

agreed final judgment
alternative dispute resolution (ADR)
arbitration (binding and nonbinding)
arbitrators
arbitrator's award
assault
asset buyers
battery
blackmail
bona fide error defense
composition agreement
consent decree
conversion
credit counseling agency
debt buyers
debt collector
debt management plan
debt settlement industry
defamation
demand letter
dismissal with prejudice
extension agreement
extortion
Fair Debt Collection Practices
   Act (FDCPA)
Fair Trade Commission (FTC)
Federal Arbitration Act (FAA)

final judgment by consent
intentional infliction of emotional
   distress
interstate commerce
intrastate commerce
invasion of privacy
least sophisticated consumer standard
loan receipt agreement
lump sum settlement
malicious harassment
Mary Carter agreement
mediation
mediator
negotiation
panel of arbitrators
private right of
   action
pro se
reasonable consumer standard
release
settlement agreement
structured settlement
theft
third-party collection agency
trespass to chattel
unfair or deceptive act or practice
validation notice

TO LEARN MORE: A number of TLM activities to accompany this chapter are accessible on the companion web site for this textbook at http://aspen-lawschool.com/books/Parsons_Debt4e/.

Chapter Five:

The Judicial Collection Process and Execution on a Final Judgment

KEY CONCEPTS

- One in whose favor a final court judgment for money is entered is the judgment creditor and the one against whom it is entered is the judgment debtor
- The ability of a judgment creditor to satisfy the money judgment by executing on the real and personal property of the debtor is impacted by applicable exempt property statutes, rules regarding concurrent ownership of property, and various trust arrangements
- States recognize a variety of different methods for executing on a final judgment including most commonly the writ of execution, the judgment lien, and the writ of garnishment
- Every state recognizes a judgment creditor's right to seek the recovery of property of the judgment debtor fraudulently transferred to defeat the creditor's rights in it

A.   Entry of a Final Judgment

When pre-judicial debt collection efforts fail, the creditor may choose to file a civil lawsuit to collect the amount owed or to liquidate the claim as in a tort action. Upon obtaining a **final judgment** in the civil lawsuit, the creditor can then utilize the various methods available for **execution** on that judgment.

The decision to file a collection lawsuit is not always automatic for the unpaid creditor. There are often considerations such as weighing the likely costs of suing relative to the size of the claim; the time and expense required to pursue a judicial remedy; the likelihood of the debtor raising valid defenses to the debt or claim; whether there might be questions of personal jurisdiction over the defendant in the court where the debtor could most conveniently and economically file the suit; and whether the debtor may in fact have no assets on which to execute if and when a final judgment is obtained. Such a debtor is referred to by practitioners as being **judgment proof**.

Judgment proof Condition of a debtor who has no assets that might be seized to satisfy a final judgment.

Not every creditor needs to utilize the judicial collection process to collect what is owed. Creditors who are secured in property of the debtor may rely instead on self-help repossession of personal property collateral under Article 9 of the UCC or self-help foreclosure on mortgaged real property where state law allows. But even secured creditors who foreclose or repossess may be left with a deficiency balance owing to them after the collateral is sold and may choose a collection action in order to obtain a final judgment on that deficiency, which can then be satisfied by execution on noncollateralized assets of the debtor. Moreover, where binding arbitration is mandated by contract or statute or is agreed to postdispute, judicial review on behalf of the losing party is limited to an attack on the validity of the arbitration process itself. But judicial collection action is available to the prevailing party in the arbitration proceeding in order to enforce an unpaid award.

It is beyond the scope of our study to review the rules of civil procedure regarding pleadings, service of process, pretrial discovery, pretrial motion practice, trial process, entry of final judgment, as well as the related topics of subject matter and personal jurisdiction of the courts. Needless to say, the supervising lawyer and assisting legal professionals must be thoroughly versed in the applicable civil rules and procedures. We will observe here that very frequently in debt collection actions involving contracts where the amount owed is liquidated, the final judgment is obtained fairly quickly by **default judgment** (under Rule 55 of the Federal Rules of Civil Procedure in federal lawsuits and analogous state rules of procedure in state court actions) since the debtor does not dispute the underlying debt or the amount—he simply cannot pay it. But where the underlying contractual obligation or the amount of it is contested or in tort claims where liability is denied, civil litigation may be hotly contested, expensive, and time-consuming.

Many a consumer bankruptcy filing is triggered by a final judgment entered against the consumer in a civil lawsuit in favor of a preexisting creditor or a plaintiff who has brought an unliquidated claim against the consumer in tort or other theory. Because the prevailing plaintiff, now a **judgment creditor**, has the right to execute on his final judgment against the consumer defendant, now the **judgment debtor**, the assets of the consumer are in peril. In this section we will consider how the judgment creditor goes about enforcing the final judgment in his favor.

Default judgment A final judgment rendered against a defendant in a civil suit who fails to file an answer to the complaint or to otherwise defend.

Judgment creditor The party to a lawsuit awarded a final judgment for money against another party.

Judgment debtor The party to a lawsuit against whom a final judgment for money is awarded.

B. Postjudgment Motions or Appeal as Delaying Execution on a Final Judgment

In the normal case, execution on a final judgment cannot begin immediately upon its entry by the court. Both the federal and state rules recognize a brief grace period following entry of final judgment during which execution is suspended as the judgment debtor decides whether to appeal or makes arrangements to pay the judgment. In some states, where judgment is entered by default, there is no grace period and execution can begin immediately.

P-H 5-a: Look at Federal Rule of Civil Procedure 62(a). What is the grace period under the federal rule between entry of the final judgment and when execution can begin? How does your equivalent state rule of procedure compare?

Posttrial motions such as a motion for judgment as a matter of law (known in some states as a motion for directed verdict), for new trial, to alter or amend a judgment, for relief from a judgment, or (in a bench trial only) for amended findings and conclusions may be filed, which will delay execution until the trial court has ruled.

P-H 5-b: Review Rules 50, 52, 59, and 60 of the Federal Rules of Civil Procedure. How quickly after entry of final judgment should the motions listed in the text be filed in order to be considered? Look at FRCP 62(b). If such a postjudgment motion is filed, how long does it delay the prevailing party's right to execute on its judgment? How do the equivalent state rules of procedure in your state compare to the federal procedure?

The timely filing of one of these motions may also extend the time the judgment debtor has to file an appeal of the final judgment.

P-H 5-c: Review Rule 4(a)(1) of the Federal Rules of Appellate Procedure (FRAP). How long after entry of a final judgment must a notice of appeal be filed under federal procedure? Review FRAP 4(a)(4). If a timely motion of the type listed in that rule is filed in the trial court, how long is the time to file a notice of appeal extended? How do the equivalent state rules of procedure in your state compare to the federal procedure?

The timely filing of a **notice of appeal** by the losing party may postpone the judgment creditor's right to begin execution on the judgment if a **stay bond** (also called a **supersedeas bond**) is applied for timely and approved. Stay bonds may involve the posting of cash or equity interest in real property with the clerk of the trial court or by providing a surety to stand good for the bond amount in the event the appeal affirms the final judgment of the trial court. The amount of the stay bond is in the court's discretion but in final money judgments the amount is usually set at the full amount of the judgment amount plus an amount equal to interest for the anticipated period of the appeal (e.g., nine months or a year) to compensate the judgment creditor for the lost use of the judgment amount during the pendency of the appeal.

P-H 5-d: Review FRCP 62(d) and FRAP 8(a). Is a motion for stay of execution pending appeal ordinarily to be made in the trial court or the appellate court? Can a supersedeas bond be given after filing a notice or appeal or must it be given before? When does the stay of execution actually take effect? How do the equivalent state rules of procedure in your state compare to the federal procedure?

If an appeal is filed but no stay of execution is ordered, execution on the final judgment can proceed notwithstanding the ongoing appeal.

E X A M P L E

> If Pearl and Nick Murphy obtain a final judgment in the amount of $1,000,000 against Dr. Craft and Capital City Hospital in Pearl's medical malpractice case and the defendants decide to appeal, they will need to obtain an order staying execution pending appeal in order to prevent Nick and Pearl from executing on the judgment while the appeal proceeds. They will file a motion for stay of execution and tender a stay bond for approval by the trial judge in the form of cash, property, or surety in the amount set by the judge. On a final judgment of $1,000,000 and if the appeal is expected to take a year, the required bond amount may be set at $1,050,000 (the full judgment amount plus 5% interest for one year).

C. ▶ Discovery in Aid of Execution (Postjudgment Asset Discovery)

Execution The right of a judgment creditor to seize a judgment debtor's property and liquidate (sell) it in order to apply the proceeds to satisfaction of the amount owed by judgment.

Discovery in aid of execution Formal discovery undertaken postjudgment to locate assets of the debtor available for execution in satisfaction of the judgment.

Once a final judgment is entered, the judgment creditor seeking to **execute** on the judgment can utilize some or all of the formal discovery methods recognized in the rules of civil procedure to locate assets of the judgment debtor that may be available for execution in satisfaction of the final judgment. This is called **discovery in aid of execution** or **postjudgment asset discovery**. FRCP 69(a)(2) authorizes the judgment creditor to obtain postjudgment discovery in aid of execution from the debtor or any other person using discovery procedures authorized by either the federal rules or the rules of the state where the court is located.

The right to engage in postjudgment discovery in aid of execution is automatic under the federal rules and under the rules of most states. In some states, however, the judgment creditor must first attempt execution (by one of the methods discussed later in this section) and then seek court permission to engage in postjudgment discovery. In a very few states the creditor must first attempt execution and then initiate a second lawsuit by filing a creditor's bill alleging the failure of execution to locate sufficient assets to pay the judgment.

The most common discovery methods used in postjudgment asset discovery are interrogatories, document requests, and depositions. Such discovery may be used to obtain information from third persons, as well as from the judgment debtor, and subpoena power is available to compel attendance of such third parties at depositions, and the production of documents and things that might be in their possession. (To Learn More activity 5-1, accessible on the companion web site to the textbook at http://aspenlawschool.com/books/Parsons_Debt4e/, contains a set of postjudgment interrogatories.)

D. ▶ Property Exempt from Execution

Exempt property Real and personal property of a judgment debtor that a judgment may not execute on in satisfaction of a final judgment.

Every state declares some property of the judgment debtor **exempt** from execution. The judgment creditor can only execute on nonexempt property. The federal government also mandates that various types of federal government benefits are exempt from execution on final judgments entered in either federal or state court. A summary of those exempt federal benefits is set out in Illustration

Illustration 5-a: FEDERAL GOVERNMENT BENEFITS EXEMPT FROM EXECUTION

- Social Security benefits
- Supplemental Security Income (SSI) benefits
- Veterans' benefits
- Civil service and federal retirement and disability benefits
- Service members' pay
- Military annuities and survivors' benefits
- Student assistance
- Railroad retirement benefits
- Merchant seamen's wages
- Longshoremen's and harbor workers' death and disability benefits
- Foreign service retirement and disability benefits
- Compensation for injury, death, or detention of employees of U.S. contractors outside the United States
- Federal Emergency Management Agency federal disaster assistance

---

5-a. There are exceptions. The federal benefits listed in Illustration 5-a may be seized to pay delinquent federal taxes or student loans or to satisfy state child support or spousal support obligations (see 42 U.S.C. §407 and 20 C.F.R. 404.970).

In addition to mandated exemption of these federal benefits, §206(d) of the Employee Retirement Income Security Act of 1974 (ERISA) mandates that states exempt qualified pension, profit-sharing, SEP, and 401-k plans with exceptions for Qualified Domestic Relations Orders, tax levies, and payment of criminal fines and penalties. (Individual retirement accounts (IRAs) and private annuities do not receive such federal protection, though states may choose to exempt them.) Section 525 of the Internal Revenue Code mandates the exemption of proceeds in college savings plans up to a maximum of $25,000.

Subject to these federal mandates, state property exemption laws apply generally to executions undertaken to enforce both state and most federal court final judgments.

EXAMPLE

> Assume that a creditor in New York files suit against a Florida resident in a U.S. District Court in New York based on diversity of citizenship and takes a final judgment against that defendant. When the judgment creditor seeks to execute on property owned by the judgment debtor in New York, it will be New York state law that controls the property exemption issue. However, where you are dealing with enforcement of a federal tax lien or other lien created by federal law (e.g., to collect unpaid federal or federally guaranteed student loans) state exemption laws will not protect a debtor's property from the reach of such federal liens; state exemption laws are preempted by federal law authorizing the lien (see *United States v. Bess*, 357 U.S. 51 (1958), and *Commissioner v. Stern*, 357 U.S. 39 (1958)). You must look to federal exemption law in such situations (see, e.g., property exempted from federal tax lien by 26 U.S.C. §6334).

When a final judgment is entered in one state and the debtor owns property in another state, the law of the state where the property is located will control the exemption issue.

EXAMPLE

> If a judgment creditor holding a final judgment issued by a New York state court (or U.S. District Court in New York) seeks to execute on property owned by the judgment debtor in Florida, the Florida exemption laws will control the disposition of that Florida property, not New York exemption laws.

1. The Homestead Exemption

Forty-six of the 50 states currently recognize a **homestead exemption**, allowing the debtor to retain some or all owner's equity in the family home or domicile (the primary home or domicile when the debtor owns more than one). There is, however, tremendous variation among the states in the dollar amount of the allowed exemption. In Texas, for example, the constitutional homestead exemption is unlimited in dollar amount, though subject to certain acreage limits, while in Tennessee, by statute, the homestead exemption is limited to owner's equity of $5,000 for an individual owner and $7,500 (total) for a married couple unless the owner has a minor child, in which case the exemption is $25,000. Minnesota, on the other hand, falls somewhere in the middle of those extremes, allowing a $200,000 statutory homestead exemption for urban property and $500,000 for rural property, subject to acreage limits and subject to adjustment for inflation every other year. Quite a difference.

P-H 5-e: Assume that Nick and Pearl Murphy had filed a medical malpractice suit against Dr. Samuel Craft for botching Pearl's appendectomy procedure and obtain a final judgment against Dr. Craft for $500,000. Dr. Craft is single and owns his home. He purchased the home five years ago for $1.2 million and has a mortgage on it in favor of Capital City Bank (CCB), with a current balance owed of $900,000. The home is appraised today at $1.5 million. Check the Asset Protection Book's State Information site at www.creditorexemption.com/ and determine what Dr. Craft's homestead exemption would be if his home was in Texas or Minnesota or North Carolina, or your state.

If a debtor's equity in the homestead exceeds the applicable homestead exemption, the executing creditor can force the property to be sold, pay the debtor the homestead amount, and apply the rest to the debt.

EXAMPLE

> Assume Dr. Craft's home is in a state that allows a $50,000 homestead exemption. When the Murphys execute on their judgment and the property is sold for $1.5 million, the first $900,000 will go to pay off the existing mortgage to CCB, assuming it is properly perfected giving it senior status and the first right to proceeds of the collateralized property. The next $50,000 will go to Dr. Craft as his homestead exemption amount. The Murphys can then apply the balance of $650,000, minus the costs of sale, to satisfy the judgment owed them.

As the preceding example illustrates, an executing judgment creditor will not have a claim to the debtor's property that is superior to a previously secured and perfected interest (the CCB mortgage in Murphy/Craft example). That example

Illustration 5-b: COMMON STATE PERSONAL PROPERTY AND INCOME SOURCE EXEMPTIONS

- Household furniture, up to a designated dollar amount of current value or equity (e.g., $5,000)
- Vehicles, up to a designated dollar amount of current value or equity
- Equipment or tools used by the debtor in a trade or business
- Necessary and proper clothing and personal possessions, such as the family Bible or Koran, family photographs/portraits, pets, school books
- Livestock, up to a designated dollar amount of current value or equity
- Any personal property, up to a designated dollar amount of current value or equity (e.g., $10,000 of value and the debtor can choose the property to be exempted)
- IRAs (including Roths) and private annuities
- State or local government employee retirement funds (often including teachers, police officers, firefighters, etc.)
- Disability or unemployment payments
- Child support or alimony payments
- Life insurance policies covering the life of the debtor on which the debtor's spouse or children are the sole beneficiaries
- Proceeds of a disability policy or annuity constituting compensation of debtor for his personal injury or the personal injury or death of one upon whom the debtor was dependent

also illustrates that exemptions do not apply to a creditor to whom the debtor has granted a security interest in the property.

EXAMPLE

Assume that Dr. Craft owes CCB $1.5 million and the entire indebtedness is secured by a mortgage on his home. If Craft defaults on his obligation to CCB and the bank forecloses on the home and sells it for $1.5 million, all of the proceeds of sale will go to retire the indebtedness owed to CCB. What about Dr. Craft's $50,000 homestead exemption? It doesn't apply between him and the bank since he voluntarily mortgaged the property in which he would have had the exemption. Creditors consensually secured in property that the debtor could otherwise claim as exempt are not bound by those exemptions.

In many states, the homestead exemption is declared inapplicable to mechanics' and materialman's liens filed against the property claimed as homestead, to family support obligations, and to tax obligations.

2. Personal Property/Income Source Exemptions

States also exempt various types and dollar amounts of personal property or income sources from execution. The variation of personal property/income exemptions among the states is significant. We have already seen in Illustration 5-a and the text following that federal law mandates that states exempt some categories of personal property and income sources. Illustration 5-b sets out other commonly recognized personal property/income source exemptions adopted by the states.

As we saw with the homestead exemption in real property, no exemption can be claimed by the debtor in personal property in which a security interest has been granted when it is the secured creditor seeking to repossess and sell that property.

EXAMPLE

If a department store sought to repossess living room furniture in which it was granted a security interest by a consumer buyer to secure the debt the consumer owed to the department store, the consumer could not claim an exemption in the furniture to block the repossession. However, if a creditor not holding a security interest in the furniture obtained a final judgment against a consumer and sought to execute on the furniture, the consumer could likely assert an exemption in it for household furniture up to the allowed dollar amount of such exemption.

3. Applicability of Property Exemptions to Government Claims

As previously noted, the federal government enforcing a federal tax lien or other obligation to the federal government (e.g., federal student loan, or farm or small business loan) is not subject to any state property exemption law affecting real or personal property due to the Supremacy Clause of the U.S. Constitution (Article VI, Paragraph 2). However, in 26 U.S.C. §6334, Congress has created specific exemptions applicable to execution on a federal tax lien, which include

- workers' compensation benefits
- unemployment benefits
- necessary clothing and schoolbooks
- furniture and personal effects up to a total value of $6,250
- necessary books and tools of the trade up to a total value of $3,125
- income or wages equal to the applicable standard deduction allowed the debtor for federal income tax purposes

Though 26 U.S.C. §6334 appears to also exempt Social Security benefits from execution on a federal tax lien, subsequent legislative enactments suggest otherwise, and the IRS has taken the position that such benefits are subject to levy (see 20 C.F.R. 404.970).

The federal government may also offset (deduct) amounts owed to any federal agency from Social Security payments or income tax refunds due the debtor.

EXAMPLE

Assume an individual defaults on a federal student loan administered by the U.S. Department of Treasury or on a small business loan administered by the U.S. Small Business Administration. Either of those federal agencies could have amounts withheld from the individual's Social Security check (including SSI payments) or tax refund to satisfy the obligation.

The homestead exemption will not defeat a state or local tax lien arising out of unpaid property taxes on the homestead property.

Exempt property issues arise in consumer bankruptcy cases as well. Individual consumer debtors are allowed to exempt certain property from their creditors in those cases. And as we will learn, the state and federal exemption laws summarized in this section are by no means irrelevant in the context of a bankruptcy case.

P-H 5-f: Now might be a good time to locate the exemption statutes for your state. What is the homestead exemption there? Are there any exceptions to the applicability of that exemption? What personal property exemptions are recognized?

E. ▶ The Effect of Concurrent Ownership of Property on Creditor Execution Efforts

Concurrent ownership raises questions regarding the right of the judgment creditor of only one of the concurrent owners to execute on the ownership interest of that owner of the property.

EXAMPLE •

> Assume Nick and Pearl Murphy concurrently own their home and there is equity in the home. Assume CCME has taken a final judgment against Pearl. CCME is now a judgment creditor of Pearl, but not Nick. The issue raised is whether CCME can execute on Pearl's share of the equity in the home. Assume that Pearl and her brother Paul concurrently own a valuable antique vase. CCME has a judgment against Pearl but not Paul. The issue raised is whether CCME can execute on Pearl's ownership interest in the vase.

Of course, if the final judgment is entered against all the concurrent owners of property, the judgment creditor can execute on the property. In our example, if CCME has a final judgment against both Nick and Pearl, it could execute on the equity in the home despite the concurrent ownership. If CCME has a final judgment against both Pearl and her brother Paul, it could execute on the vase despite the concurrent ownership.

But whether the judgment creditor holding a final judgment against only one concurrent owner of property can execute on the interest of that one owner of the property depends on what type of concurrent ownership it is. There are several.

1. Property Owned by a Married Couple

Tenancy by the entireties A form of joint ownership of property between a husband and wife where each has only a right of survivorship.

In many states, married couples can choose to own property together as **tenants by the entireties**, a form of concurrent ownership in which each spouse has only a **right of survivorship** in the property. On the death of one spouse, the survivor takes the entire ownership interest as a matter of law. So long as both spouses are alive, neither can transfer their individual interest in the property (which is only the right of survivorship) either consensually (as by selling, granting a securing interest in, or gifting it to another) or nonconsensually as in judgment execution. States recognizing the tenancy by the entireties limit it to property owned *only* by the married couple (no third party can be on the title—but see the joint tenancy below) and most such states presume the entireties arrangement when only the spouses are on the title to the property. However, spouses in these states can choose to own property together as tenants in common (discussed below) if the choose.

E X A M P L E

> Assume that CCME executes on the final judgment in its favor against Pearl Murphy. If Pearl and Nick own their home as tenants by the entireties, CCME, as the judgment creditor of Pearl only, cannot force the homestead to be sold as part of the execution (unless the jurisdiction makes such medical bills the obligation of both spouses as a matter of law).

Community property A form of concurrent ownership between husband and wife in which each spouse is deemed to own an undivided interest in all property acquired during the marriage.

Ten states (Arizona, California, Idaho, Louisiana, Nevada, New Mexico, Texas, Washington, Wisconsin, and optionally by election of the spouses in Alaska) along with Puerto Rico are **community property** jurisdictions. In those states and territory there is a presumption that all property acquired by either spouse during the marriage is wholly owned by both spouses (regardless of how it is titled) so that all such property can be executed on to satisfy a judgment against either spouse. The presumption also results in debts incurred by only one spouse being deemed the obligation of both. The presumption of ownership does not apply to property owned by either spouse prior to marriage or to property inherited by only one spouse during marriage (though such property may become community property after the marriage is so treated by the parties). And some community property states limit the presumption of debt in some instances. For example, Texas prohibits judgment liens from attaching to community property that is titled only in the non-debtor's name. Furthermore, the presumption of community ownership of property can be rebutted by proof that the spouses agreed in good faith and with no intent to defraud that certain property in fact be separately owned.

Tenancy in common A form of concurrent ownership in which each owner has an undivided percentage interest in the property. There is no right of survivorship.

2. Tenancy in Common

A **tenancy in common** is a form of concurrent ownership in which each owner has an undivided interest in the property owned. If the judgment debtor owns property concurrently with a spouse or anyone else as tenants in common, the undivided interest of the judgment debtor in the property can be partitioned or sold as part of the execution process.

E X A M P L E

Partition action A lawsuit asking a court to segregate or divide the undivided ownership interest of one concurrent owner of property so it can be seized by that owner's creditors.

> Assume that Pearl and her brother Paul own a one-acre parcel of unimproved land as tenants in common with Pearl having an undivided, one-third interest in the property and Paul an undivided two-thirds interest. CCME, as the judgment creditor of Pearl, can execute on Pearl's undivided one-third interest in the property, ask a court to partition it from Paul's two-thirds interest, and then sell her partitioned portion of the land and apply the proceeds in satisfaction of the judgment. If the parcel cannot be partitioned (perhaps the parcel only has value as a whole), the entire parcel will be sold and Pearl's share of the proceeds (one-third in this example) paid to the executing creditor. If Pearl and Paul also own the antique vase as tenants in common, it cannot be partitioned as realty can, so it will be sold and Pearl's share of the proceeds paid over to the executing creditor.

3. Joint Tenancy

Joint tenancy A form of concurrent ownership in which each owner holds an equal, undivided share and there is a right of survivorship.

In a **joint tenancy**, the concurrent owners each own an equal, undivided interest in the property and there is a right of survivorship as in a tenancy by the entireties. That means that when one joint tenant dies, the surviving joint tenants will take the decedent's interest in the property rather than it passing through her will or to her heirs by intestate succession. The joint tenancy is different from the tenancy by the entireties, however, in that, prior to death, a joint tenant may transfer her interest in the property to another by sale, pledge, or gift. The transferee of the joint tenant's interest does not become a joint tenant in the property but a tenant in common only. The joint tenancy is broken by the transfer. Significantly for our purposes, judgment creditors of a single joint tenant, like creditors of a single tenant in common, can execute on the joint tenant's interest in the property jointly owned.

EXAMPLE

> Assume Pearl and her two brothers, Paul and Peter, concurrently own the antique vase as joint tenants. CCME, as the judgment creditor of Pearl only, can execute on Pearl's undivided interest in the vase, force it to be sold, and have her one-third of the proceeds paid over to it.

P-H 5-g: Determine if the state where you plan to practice is a common law or a community property law state for purposes of concurrent ownership of property. How would your state decide the issues of concurrent ownership arising when CCME executes on the final judgment it has against Pearl Murphy only, assuming (1) Pearl and her husband Nick own an undeveloped acre of land worth $100,000, title to which is in both names? (2) Pearl owns the undeveloped acre together with her brother and title is in both names? (3) Pearl owns the undeveloped acre together with her husband and her brother and title is in all three names? (4) Pearl inherited cash from a deceased relative three years ago and has always kept it in a certificate of deposit in her name only?

F. Trust Arrangements That May Defeat Creditor Execution Efforts

Trust A legal arrangement where the owner of property conveys legal title to property into the hands of a trustee charged with holding and administering the property for the benefit of named beneficiaries.

A **trust** is an arrangement whereby the owner of property (called variously the grantor, trustor, or settlor) conveys title in the property to a designated trustee to be held by the trustee for the benefit of another party, called the trust beneficiary. The property placed in trust is called the trust principal or the trust property or the trust res. There are many different kinds of trusts, but we will focus only on two that have special consequences for efforts to execute on a final judgment.

1. Spendthrift Trust

Spendthrift trust A trust that prohibits alienation of trust property to protect the property from dissipation by the beneficiary or seizure by creditors.

A **spendthrift trust** is a trust established to provide certain benefits to a designated beneficiary from time to time that prohibits the beneficiary from selling or pledging as security any of the trust principal or any future distributions to be received from the trust. The idea behind the spendthrift trust is to protect the beneficiary from his own poor judgment by limiting his access to trust principal or interest. In most states, the spendthrift trust has the added benefit to the beneficiary of preventing his creditors from executing on assets of the trust unless and until they are distributed to the beneficiary.

EXAMPLE

Assume Pearl Murphy's parents had created a spendthrift trust containing a one-acre parcel and naming her as the sole beneficiary. Assume further that the land is income producing because coal is mined from beneath it. Under the spendthrift provisions of the trust, Pearl could not sell or mortgage her interest in the land or the income from it while either is held in trust for her, nor could her creditor CCME seize the land or income still held in the trust to satisfy its judgment against Pearl. If and when payments of interest were made to Pearl by the trustee of the trust or if the land itself was conveyed to her at the conclusion of the trust, then those payments or the land could be seized.

The reason that qualified retirement plans are exempt from execution is that §206(d)(1) of ERISA requires that in order to be qualified, a retirement plan must include an anti-assignment clause and prohibit alienation of plan assets by the beneficiary. This section is known as the **federal spendthrift clause** and has been construed to defeat both the claims of creditors of the beneficiary and the beneficiary's own worst instincts to spend the assets on anything other than retirement.

2. Domestic Asset Protection Trust

Domestic asset protection trust A trust in which the settlor can convey his own property into trust, name himself as the beneficiary to receive distributions of principal or interest as proscribed in the trust document, yet prevent his creditors from seizing trust assets not yet distributed.

A **domestic asset protection trust** (DAPT) (sometimes called a **self-settled trust**) is an arrangement whereby the settlor can convey his own property into trust, name himself the beneficiary to receive distributions of principal or interest as proscribed in the trust document, and yet prevent his creditors from seizing trust assets not yet distributed. Previously available only as questionable **foreign asset protection trusts** or **offshore trusts** under the laws of other nations (typically a Caribbean island), approximately 14 states have authorized DAPT by statute. To obtain the protection of the trust assets from creditors of the settlor/beneficiary, the conveyance of the property into trust must be irrevocable (i.e., the settlor cannot ever withdraw the assets from the trust; he can only receive the distributions from the trust as a named beneficiary); and the settlor cannot also serve as trustee of the trust (although most states allow the settlor to remove a trustee and appoint someone else to serve).

Like any trust arrangement, a DAPT is subject to legal attack if the creation of the trust itself can be demonstrated to be a fraudulent transfer as to creditors. However, in order to protect known creditors at the time the trust is created, states that recognize DAPT have a built-in statutory period that delays the effective date of protection of the trust res from execution (e.g., 2-3 years). The states will also except some creditors from the ban on execution, like child support or alimony claimants, divorcing spouses, and, in some states, preexisting tort claimants.

P-H 5-h: Determine if your state recognizes the spendthrift trust or the domestic asset protection trust. If Pearl Murphy was the beneficiary of a spendthrift trust holding real property, at what point could her creditors seize either income generated by the property or the real property itself? If Pearl creates a DAPT holding real property in a state that recognizes such trusts and names herself as sole beneficiary, can she also serve as trustee? Can she replace a named trustee? Must the trust be irrevocable? Can she receive income distributions from the trust during her life? How much time must elapse following creation of the trust until it is exempt from creditors? Are there some creditors who are not barred from reaching the principal of the trust in execution?

G. Methods of Executing on a Final Judgment

In this section we will consider the three most common methods of executing on a final judgment under state law. Recognize, however, that there is tremendous variation among the states regarding the specific methods of execution allowed, the procedures that must be followed, and the relevant nomenclature used for the execution process. Consequently, the material presented here is necessarily general.

1. The Judgment Lien

Judgment lien A judicial lien created on all real property owned by a judgment debtor in the county where the final judgment is recorded or docketed.

The judgment creditor can create an involuntary lien on any real property owned by the judgment debtor by filing a **judgment lien**. Commonly, the judgment lien is created by obtaining a certified copy of the final judgment from the clerk of the court that issued the judgment and then recording, filing, or registering that certified copy in the designated public office for the filing of land records. Illustration 5-c sets out a typical statute dealing with the procedure for creating a judgment lien.

In some states the judgment lien is created by recording a writ of execution (discussed in the next section) along with a notice of levy. Such states may also require that the writ of execution be served first on the personal property of the debtor and returned before being recorded as a lien on the real property of the debtor. However it is effected, the judgment lien becomes a cloud on the title to

Illustration 5-c: TYPICAL STATUTE REGARDING PROCEDURE FOR CREATING A JUDGMENT LIEN

Judgments and decrees in any court of record and judgments in excess of five hundred dollars ($500) in any court not of record in this state shall be liens upon the debtor's land from the time a certified copy of the judgment or decree shall be registered in the lien book in the register's office of the county where the land is located. Such lien shall be valid against any person having, or later acquiring, an interest in such property who is not a party to the action wherein such judgment is issued.

any real property owned by the debtor in the county where the judgment is recorded, just as a consensual mortgage would.

EXAMPLE

Assume that Nick and Pearl Murphy obtain a certified copy of their final judgment against Dr. Samuel Craft and properly record it in the county where Craft's home is located. Assume also that Dr. Craft is single and owns a home in Capital County, which he purchased five years ago for $1.2 million on which he has an existing mortgage in favor of Capital City Bank (CCB) with a current balance owed of $900,000. As of the moment of recording their judgment, the Murphys have a lien against Dr. Craft's home in Capital County in the amount of the final judgment plus the postjudgment interest, which is continuing to accumulate. It is just as if Dr. Craft had conveyed a second mortgage to the Murphys in that amount. Of course, if CCB has properly perfected its first mortgage, the judgment lien in favor of the Murphys will be second, or junior, to that first mortgage. But if Dr. Craft now seeks to sell his home, both the CCB mortgage and the Murphys' judgment lien are of public record, and any buyer must either pay them off or take title to the property subject to those two liens. (See the last sentence of the statute in Illustration 5-c.)

P-H 5-i: Assume Dr. Craft also owns real property in Silver County, which is another county in Yourstate. Carefully read the language of the statute in Illustration 5-c. If the Murphys record their judgment lien in Capital County only, does that subject the Silver County property to the lien? If not, what must the Murphys do to create a judgment lien on the Silver County property owned by Dr. Craft? Since the final judgment on which the Murphys are executing was entered by a court in Capital County, Yourstate, does that mean it cannot be recorded in another county to create a judgment lien on property there? What if Dr. Craft owns real property in another state?

Not only does a judgment lien create a cloud on title to the debtor's real property, effectively preventing its sale, but the judgment creditor holding the judgment lien can also foreclose on the lien, sell the real property subject to it, and apply the proceeds to the judgment amount owed. Since no consensual power of sale has been conveyed by the debtor to the judgment creditor, the lien holder must seek a judicial foreclosure either by applying to the court for an order of sale or by having the sheriff seize the property by writ of attachment or writ of execution (discussed below in this section) and then conducting a sheriff's sale. Illustration 5-d sets forth a typical state statute authorizing this procedure.

When the real property is sold, the proceeds will be applied first to the expenses incurred in the sale and then to the amount of the judgment, including accrued postjudgment interest. Of course, if there are other liens on the property

Illustration 5-d: TYPICAL STATUTE AUTHORIZING FORECLOSURE ON A JUDGMENT LIEN

As long as a judgment lien is effective, no levy is necessary; the judgment creditor may move for an order of sale. Otherwise a levy occurs when the sheriff exercises control over the judgment debtor's realty.

Illustration 5-e: TYPICAL STATUTE REGARDING TERM OF JUDGMENT LIEN AND REVIVAL OF LIEN

> Once a judgment lien is created by registration, it will last for the time remaining in a ten-year period from the date of final judgment entry in the court clerk's office and for any extension granted by the court. For the extension of the lien to be enforceable, the judgment creditor must register the court's order extending the judgment lien.

Illustration 5-f: TYPICAL STATUTE REGARDING TERMINATING AN INVOLUNTARY LIEN ON PROPERTY FOLLOWING SATISFACTION OF INDEBTEDNESS

> Upon satisfaction of the judgment, the judgment debtor may demand that the judgment creditor record in the register's office a termination statement to supersede any lien *lis pendens* or judgment lien of record. If the judgment creditor fails to register a termination statement within ten days after demand, the judgment creditor shall be liable to the judgment debtor for $100 and for any loss caused to the judgment debtor by failure to register.

senior to the judgment lien or if there are any exemptions, those must be satisfied in full before any proceeds are applied to the judgment amount.

EXAMPLE

> If the Murphys create a judgment lien on Dr. Craft's home in Capital County and then obtain an order of sale, proceeds of the sale will be applied first to the expenses of the sale, then to pay off the balance in full of the mortgage held by CCB, and only then to the Murphys. This is so because the CCB mortgage on the property is senior to the Murphys' judgment lien.

In most states, a judgment lien will attach to any real property the judgment debtor acquires after the judgment lien has been created so long as it is still in effect.

EXAMPLE

> Assume that the Murphys create their judgment lien in Capital County today. Six months from now, Dr. Craft purchases an interest in an empty lot in a residential area of the county. The Murphys will have an automatic lien against Dr. Craft's interest in that lot without having to re-record their judgment. The judgment lien created today will attach to the property acquired in six months if it has not been satisfied in the interim.

The preceding example raises the question of how long a judgment lien is valid. States differ, but a common term of validity is ten years from the date the lien was created. The judgment lien holder typically has the option to revive the judgment lien before the end of that term either by re-recording the original judgment or by obtaining an order from the court granting an extension of the judgment and then recording (registering or filing) that order of extension. Illustration 5-e sets out a typical statute regarding this procedure.

If a judgment debtor pays off the indebtedness owed to the judgment creditor after a judgment lien has been created on the debtor's property (or after a lien *lis pendens* has been created on it), the now-satisfied judgment creditor will record (register or file) a release of lien or termination statement. Illustration 5-f sets out a typical state statute regarding this procedure.

Similarly, if the judgment creditor has created a judgment lien on the debtor's property and the debtor thereafter obtains a stay of execution pending appeal, the trial court may order the judgment creditor to remove the lien pending the outcome of the appeal.

In some states, the judgment lien is deemed to attach to the judgment debtor's personal property when the lien has been properly filed (or recorded or registered) in the public office responsible for UCC filings.

P-H 5-j: Locate the statutes of your state regarding how a judgment lien is created, authorizing foreclosure on a judgment lien, regarding the effective term of a judgment lien and its revival, and termination of the lien on satisfaction of the underlying judgment.

HIGHLIGHTED CASE ●   ## CURRIER V. FIRST RESOLUTION INVESTMENT CORP.
762 F.3d 529 (6th Cir. 2014)

[In May 2012, First Resolution brought an action against Currier to collect charged-off credit card debt of $1,000.51 plus interest. A default judgment was entered by the court after Currier's counsel failed to appear at an October 1, 2012 hearing. Currier filed a motion to vacate the default judgment and asked for an extension of time to file an answer. As of that date, the judgment against Currier was not final under Kentucky law. After obtaining the default judgment, First Resolution filed a judgment lien against Currier's home. Under Kentucky law, a judgment lien can only arise from a final judgment so the lien was invalid. On October 29, 2012, a judge granted Currier's motion to vacate the default judgment. Even though First Resolution knew the judgment would be vacated, it did not release the lien until November 5. Currier sued First Resolution in federal court, alleging that the invalid lien violated various provisions of the FDCPA. Finding that a violation of state law is not a per se violation of the FDCPA and that the invalid lien was not a threat, the district court dismissed the claims. Currier appealed.]

OPINION: Stranch, Circuit Judge.

Congress passed the FDCPA to address the widespread and serious national problem of debt collection abuse by unscrupulous debt collectors . . . . The Act prohibits a wide array of specific conduct, but it also prohibits, in general terms, any harassing, unfair, or deceptive debt collection practice, which enables "the courts, where appropriate, to proscribe other improper conduct which is not specifically addressed." . . . [S]ee generally 15 U.S.C. §§1692d-1692f . . . . To determine whether conduct fits within the broad scope of the FDCPA, the conduct is viewed through the eyes of the "least sophisticated consumer." Id. This standard recognizes that the FDCPA protects the gullible and the shrewd alike while simultaneously presuming a basic level of reasonableness and understanding on the part of the debtor, thus preventing liability for bizarre or idiosyncratic interpretations of debt collection notices. Id.

Currier alleges that filing and failing to release the invalid lien against her home violated multiple provisions of the FDCPA, "including, but not limited to": 15 U.S.C. §1692f, which prohibits using "unfair or unconscionable means . . . to collect any debt"; §1692f(1), which prohibits the "collection of any amount . . . unless such amount is expressly authorized by the agreement creating the debt or permitted by law"; and §1692e(5), which prohibits "threat[ening] to take any action that cannot legally be taken or that is not intended to be taken." First Resolution admits . . . that Currier has alleged that: she is a "consumer" within the meaning of the Act; the debt arose for personal, family, or household purposes; and First Resolution is a "debt collector." See 15 U.S.C. §§1692(e), 1692a(3), 1692a(5)-(6). We conclude that Currier sufficiently alleged conduct that falls within the broad scope of practices prohibited by the FDCPA. . . .

First Resolution raises a defense to the FDCPA claims—that the invalid lien was not a violation of the FDCPA because a violation of state law is not a per se violation of the FDCPA. Our sister circuits have indeed concluded—usually in the context of licensing violations—that not every technical violation of state debt collection law rises to the level of unfair or otherwise prohibited conduct under the FDCPA. See, e.g., *LeBlanc v. Unifund CCR Partners*, 601 F.3d 1185, 1192 (11th Cir. 2010) (holding that debt collector's failure to have a proper license, a violation of state law, is not a per se violation of the FDCPA but that it may support a violation of the FDCPA); *Carlson v. First Revenue Assurance*, 359 F.3d 1015, 1018 (8th Cir. 2004) (holding that a debt collector's failure to have the proper license was not the kind of "false or misleading" practice barred by §1692e); *Wade v. Reg'l Credit Ass'n*, 87 F.3d 1098, 1100-01 (9th Cir. 1996) (holding that sending a debtor correct notice of debt and risks to her credit was not a violation of the FDCPA even though debt collector was not licensed in debtor's state). A sister circuit has also rejected the contention that using the proper state procedure to freeze a debtor's bank account after receiving a valid final judgment was unfair under §1692f where the debt collector unknowingly froze an account that contained exempt funds. *Beler v. Blatt, Hasenmiller, Leibsker & Moore, LLC*, 480 F.3d 470, 472, 473-74 (7th Cir. 2007). There, the court said that the FDCPA is not an enforcement mechanism for state laws and it declined to create a hearing requirement in the state system. Id. at 473-74.

We agree that Congress did not turn every violation of state law into a violation of the FDCPA. But that does not mean that a violation of state law can never also be a violation of the FDCPA. The proper question in the context of an FDCPA claim is whether the plaintiff alleged an action that falls within the broad range of conduct prohibited by the Act. The legality of the action taken under state law may be relevant, as it is in this case. See *LeBlanc*, 601 F.3d at 1192 (considering the state law violation relevant to the FDCPA analysis). If the judgment lien had been valid under state law for the month that First Resolution held it, we could not say that it was an unfair debt collection practice even though it was coercive in nature. But the same action becomes unfair when accomplished by using a state mechanism that does not authorize it.

First Resolution also argues that it cannot be held liable under the FDCPA because it did not have reason to know that the lien was invalid at the time it mailed the notice of judgment lien. According to this version of events, the normal rule that a successful plaintiff in Kentucky court must wait 10 days to execute on a judgment did not apply here because the default judgment stated that "[t]his is a final judgment" and "execution may issue forthwith." See Ky. Rev. Stat. Ann. §426.030 (setting a waiting period "unless ordered by the court"). Although the motion to vacate unquestionably rendered the judgment non-final, First Resolution contends that it did not know about the motion until the end of the day on October 8, 2012, after it had already mailed the notice of judgment lien. See *Pers. Bd. v. Heck*, 725 S.W.2d 13, 18 (Ky. Ct. App. 1986) ("A motion [to vacate a judgment] converts a final judgment to an interlocutory judgment.").

This argument fails for two reasons. First, whether or not First Resolution had reason to believe that the lien was valid when filed is an issue of fact that is not relevant at the motion to dismiss stage. Second, even if First Resolution's version of the facts were construed to be part of a bona fide error defense, we note that it would not establish all the elements of such defense. See 15 U.S.C. §1692k(c) . . . . To qualify for this defense, a debt collector must prove by a preponderance of the evidence that the violation was unintentional, that it was the result of a bona fide error, and that the debt collector maintained procedures to avoid the error. *Hartman v. Great Seneca Fin. Corp.*, 569 F.3d 606, 614 (6th Cir. 2009). Although First Resolution alleges that the invalid lien began as an unintentional bona fide error, it admits that it learned of Currier's motion to vacate the judgment on the same day it filed the judgment lien and nonetheless failed to release the lien for a month. And it has alleged nothing to show that it maintains a procedure to avoid the error. In Kentucky, a losing party has only 10 days after entry of the final judgment to file a motion to vacate the judgment. Ky. R. Civ. P. 59.05. The error at issue could have been avoided if First Resolution had established a practice of waiting to file a judgment lien until 10 days after obtaining a judgment or of checking the docket before filing a lien. It could also have maintained a procedure for immediate correction of error. But First Resolution admits that it had implemented none of these procedures. First Resolution is not entitled to the bona fide error defense. . . .

Currier v. First Resolution Investment Corp.:   Real Life Applications

1. Assume a debt collector obtains a final judgment in a collection lawsuit against a consumer named John Alex Smith and causes a judgment lien to be issued attaching property of Smith. One day later, the debt collector learns that service of process of the complaint on Smith at the beginning of the lawsuit was defective because the summons served contained a clerical typo misspelling the name of the defendant as John Alec Smith. Under state law this makes the final judgment later obtained in the lawsuit invalid. What should the debt collector do to avoid potential liability under the FDCPA?

2. If you are assigned to interview the debt collector client, what questions do you want to ask to evaluate whether the bona fide error defense might be available in the event of a FDCPA claim?

3. *Currier* also illustrates a debt collector's assertion of the bona fide error defense discussed in the last chapter. What is the three-part test for that defense used in the Sixth Circuit according to the *Hartman v. Great Seneca* case cited in *Currier*? Between the debtor and the debt collector, which party has the burden of proof when the bona fide error defense is raised? What part(s) of the test did First Resolution fail to establish?

2. The Writ of Execution

The method of execution most commonly used to seize nonexempt personal property of the debtor is the **writ of execution**, sometimes called a **writ of fieri facias**. The writ is typically applied for from the clerk of the court that rendered the final judgment. Illustration 5-g sets forth an application for writ of attachment that CCME might file once its judgment against Pearl Murphy becomes final and executable.

The clerk issues the writ, which is then delivered to the sheriff (or other government officer charged with executing it), and directs the sheriff to seize property of the debtor to satisfy the indebtedness. The writ of execution issued on behalf of CCME against Pearl Murphy might look like what is shown in Illustration 5-h.

Rule 69 of the Federal Rules of Civil Procedure provides that in executing on a final judgment entered in the U.S. District Court, the practice and procedure of the state in which the district court is held may be utilized. Thus, writs of execution issued by the U.S. District Court Clerk can be directed to the U.S. Marshal or to the county sheriff. In some states, a writ of execution can only authorize the seizure of a debtor's personal property. As noted earlier, in other states it can authorize the seizure of either the debtor's personal or real property. And in those latter states, there may be an order of priority in which the debtor's property

Illustration 5-g: APPLICATION FOR WRIT OF EXECUTION

The Plaintiff hereby makes application to the Clerk of the Circuit Court to issue a writ of execution in the above styled case to satisfy a judgment against the defendant Pearl E. Murphy in the amount of $2,247.70 entered on September 20, YR-1. The balance of the judgment that remains unsatisfied after the defendant is credited with payments made on said judgment is $2,247.70 plus postjudgment interest accruing on said amount from September 20, YR-1, through the date of payment.

This 1st day of November, YR-1

_____

Attorney's signature

Illustration 5-h: WRIT OF EXECUTION

To the Sheriff of Capital County, Yourstate:

On September 20, YR-1, a judgment was entered in the docket of this court in favor of Capital City Medical Equipment Company as judgment creditor and against Pearl E. Murphy as judgment debtor, for $2,247.70 the full amount of which is due on the judgment as entered together with interest on the judgment amount at 10% per annum, or $.62 per day, from the date of entry of the judgment to the date of issuance of this writ, to which must be added court costs of $255 and the commissions and costs of the officer executing this writ.

You are hereby commanded to satisfy the judgment with interest, commissions, and costs as provided by law, out of the personal property of the debtor. If sufficient personal property cannot be found, then this judgment may be satisfied out of the debtor's real property or if the judgment is already a lien on real property, then out of the debtor's real property. You are to make return of this writ within not less than 10 days nor more than 60 days after satisfaction of this judgment, with what you have done endorsed on this writ.

Dated: November 1, YR-1

_____

[Clerk]

By: _____

[Deputy Clerk]

Marshalling of assets Requirement that a judgment creditor executing on property of the judgment debtor seize and exhaust property in a certain order.

Levy Seizing or taking control of a debtor's property pursuant to a lien or writ of execution.

Till tap The direct seizure of cash from the cash register of a business pursuant to a writ of execution.

Sheriff's sale The sale by public auction or private sale of property of a debtor levied on pursuant to a writ of execution.

can be seized. A typical mandated order of priority is that the sheriff must first attempt to satisfy the execution out of the debtor's personal property, and only if that property is insufficient can the sheriff then seize the debtor's real property. This mandatory ranking or order of priority in seizing the debtor's property is often called the **marshalling of assets**.

In executing the writ, the sheriff (or U.S. Marshal in a federal case) will locate and **levy** on (take possession of) property of the debtor. This may include cash, in which case the sheriff will be careful not only to inventory the cash on the return (discussed below) but to specify how the cash was applied. When cash is taken from the cash register of a debtor, that is sometimes called a **till tap**. If personal property is seized pursuant to the writ, the sheriff will store it, and then sell it either by advertised auction (often called a **sheriff's sale**) or, in some states, by a private sale if the sheriff concludes that will bring more money.

Of course, the debtor may be able to claim some property as exempt from execution. In most instances, the sheriff takes personal property into his possession by moving it to a storage facility. But if that is not practical, the sheriff may leave the property in place, secure it with chains and locks as needed, and post a prominent notice advising anyone reading it that the property is in the possession of the sheriff and is not to be disturbed. The same will be done when real property is seized.

EXAMPLE

Assume a writ of execution is issued on a docked boat. The sheriff might move the boat to another facility but, if that is not feasible, the sheriff might leave the boat in the dock, disable it from being operated, chain and lock it to the dock so it cannot be towed away, and place yellow tape across the entrance to it along with a posted notice of the seizure and penalties for trespassing or tampering. If the sheriff seizes a house next to the dock, a similar procedure will be followed. The house will be securely locked, yellow tape placed across all entrances, and a written notice posted. The sheriff executing the writ must make a **return of the writ** to the clerk of the court. That means physically returning the executed writ to the clerk, stating the date(s) it was executed, and itemizing the assets seized (sometimes called the **inventory**).

Nulla bona Return made by sheriff on writ of execution when no executable property found.

Lien of levy The lien existing in favor of a judgment creditor against the property of the judgment debtor seized pursuant to a writ of execution.

If the writ was executed but no assets were found, it will be returned **nulla bona** (with nothing found). The writ must be served within some number of days after it is issued by clerk (e.g., 60 days) and is deemed void if not timely returned. The lien that now exists on the seized property in favor of the judgment creditor is called a **lien of levy** in some states. Illustration 5-i sets out a typical state statute regarding the creation of a lien of levy.

States typically require the sheriff to conduct the sheriff's sale of the property within some designated time period following levy and to give prior public notice of the sale. Some states require specific notice of the sale to the debtor. A typical statute setting forth the procedure for notice and sale is shown in Illustration 5-j.

Once the judgment debtor's assets seized pursuant to the writ are sold, the proceeds will go first to pay the sheriff's administrative expenses involved in seizing, storing, and selling the property, and then to pay court costs assessed against the judgment debtor, and then to satisfy the judgment of the levying creditor (unless another creditor has a priority position in the property), and then to satisfy any other consensual or nonconsensual lien existing in the property. Any excess proceeds go to the debtor.

Illustration 5-i: STATE STATUTE CREATING LIEN OF LEVY

(1) Levy. A levy is effective when the sheriff with a writ of execution exercises control over the judgment debtor's personalty.

(2) Lien of Levy. A lien of levy in the judgment creditor's favor is effective when the sheriff levies on the judgment debtor's personalty. The first judgment creditor to deliver a writ of execution to the sheriff, as shown by record in the clerk's office, has priority over other judgment creditors as to the property levied upon. A lien of levy remains effective until the property is sold or otherwise released from the sheriff's control.

Illustration 5-j: STATE STATUTE SETTING FORTH PROCEDURE FOR NOTICE AND SALE

The sheriff shall sell personalty by auction. At least ten days before the sale, a notice, generally describing the personalty and stating the time, place, and terms, shall be published in a newspaper of general circulation at the judgment creditor's expense, taxable as court costs. If the personalty is perishable, no notice of sale is required.

Bona fide purchaser for value One who purchases property in good faith with no actual or constructive knowledge of a defect in title.

In most states, the purchaser of property at the sheriff's sale is considered a **bona fide purchaser for value** and his title cannot be disturbed, even by a late exemption claim from the owner, who is now nothing but a prior owner as to the property.

3. The Writ of Garnishment

Writ of garnishment A court order directing a person in possession of the property of a debtor (e.g., an employer) to deliver that property to the clerk of the court for payment to a judgment creditor.

The method of execution used to obtain nonexempt personal property that belongs to the debtor or that is owed to the debtor from a third person (rather than from the debtor herself) is the **writ of garnishment**. Typical targets of a garnishment are the employer of the judgment debtor (called a **wage garnishment**), a financial institution holding funds of the judgment debtor in a checking or savings account (a **bank garnishment**), or anyone who owes the judgment debtor money (e.g., tenants of the judgment debtor who owe him rent). Like the writ of execution, the writ of garnishment is applied for by the judgment creditor to the clerk of the court that rendered the final judgment.

EXAMPLE

Assume that Pearl Murphy, a substitute teacher, has a paycheck due at the end of the month from the Capital City School District. Assume that CCME is ready to execute on its final judgment by default against Pearl. If the attorney for judgment creditor CCME decides to garnish that paycheck, the application for writ of garnishment might look something like what is shown in Illustration 5-k.

Illustration 5-k: APPLICATION FOR WRIT OF GARNISHMENT

State of Yourstate   )
County of Capital   )

Capital City Medical Equipment Company, Judgment Creditor, makes oath that the Judgment Debtor's last known address is 3521 West Cherry Street, Capital City, Yourstate, and the Judgment Creditor's address for mailing any notice required by Yourstate Statutory Code §26-2-204 is 413 Richardson Avenue, Capital City, Yourstate.

The Judgment Creditor hereby makes application to the Clerk of the Circuit Court to issue a writ of garnishment in the above styled case to satisfy a judgment entered against the Defendant herein on September 20, YR-1, in the amount of $2,247.70 plus interest on the judgment amount at 10% per annum, or $.62 per day, from the date of entry of the judgment to the date of issuance of this writ, plus court costs of $255.
This 1st day of November YR-1

Capital City Medical Equipment Company
By: _____

Mark Andrews, Manager
[Notarization omitted from illustration.]

Serve the garnishment execution on: Capital City Public School system at the following address: 1211 Post Road, Capital City, Yourstate.

The party who is served with the writ of garnishment is called the **garnishee.** In some states, the writ served on the garnishee advises that party of its duty to turn over the property of the debtor in its possession, or to pay the wages or other amounts owed to the debtor, to the clerk of the court that issued the writ. The clerk will then deliver the property or pay the funds over to the judgment creditor. In other states, the writ orders the garnishee to hold any funds it has in its possession payable to the judgment debtor and to await further order of the court before paying them over. The writ of garnishment served on the Capital City Public School System pursuant to the application seen in Illustration 5-k might look something like what is shown in Illustration 5-l.

In some states, the judgment creditor may also be obligated to provide the judgment debtor with notice of the garnishment (sometimes called notice of levy). Typically, the garnishment lien attaches to the property of the debtor held by the garnishee as soon as the garnishment is served on the garnishee.

As reflected in the language of Illustration 5-l, the garnishee typically has a duty to respond to a writ of garnishment by making a personal appearance in the court issuing the writ or, more commonly, by filing a written answer within some designated time period (ten days under the terms of Illustration 5-l) acknowledging that it does hold property of the judgment debtor or funds due her and describing the property or funds. Thereafter the garnishee must turn over property of the debtor or pay over the garnished funds owed to the debtor within some designated time period (30 days under the terms of Illustration 5-l or upon receipt of further court order). If the garnishee answers the garnishment by saying the judgment debtor is no longer employed by the garnishee or that the garnishee no longer has funds of the judgment debtor, the judgment creditor can typically engage in discovery from the garnishee (deposition, interrogatory, or document request) to obtain more information on the location of the judgment debtor or his property.

Disposable income The after-tax income of a garnishee, a statutory percentage of which is subject to garnishment.

Each state regulates how much of a debtor's paycheck may be garnished (e.g., maximum of 25 percent), and that amount is typically calculated based on the debtor's **disposable income**, which is defined, generally, as after-tax income. Most states also permit the judgment debtor whose employer or other income source has been garnished to move the court for permission to pay the judgment amount in installments less than what the payments would be from the garnishment. When such a **motion to pay judgment in installments** (sometimes referred to informally as a **slow pay motion**) is filed, the burden is on the judgment debtor to demonstrate to the court that his income sources are insufficient to live on with the garnished amounts deducted. The judgment debtor will ask the court to set an alternative amount of payments in equity.

P-H 5-k: Determine if your state allows a judgment debtor to apply to pay a judgment in installments. If so, what are the grounds for such a motion and what is the judgment debtor's burden of proof?

If the garnishee fails to respond to the writ of garnishment by answer or appearance or fails to pay over the property or funds as it is obligated to do, many states make the garnishee itself liable to the judgment creditor for either

Illustration 5-l: WRIT OF GARNISHMENT

TO: Capital City Public School system,
1211 Post Road
Capital City, Yourstate

TAKE NOTICE: The earnings of your employee, Pearl E. Murphy ("Employee"), are hereby garnisheed and attached in satisfaction of a judgment rendered in favor of plaintiff, Capital City Medical Equipment Company, against Employee in this action on September 20, YR-1, in the amount of $2,742.70 plus interest on the judgment amount at 10% per annum, or $.62 per day, from the date of entry of the judgment to the date of issuance of this writ, plus court costs of $255. Capital City Medical Equipment Company, Judgment Creditor, makes oath that the Judgment Debtor's last known address is 321 West Cherry Street, Capital City, Yourstate and the Judgment Creditor's address for mailing any notice required by Yourstate Statutory Code §26-2-204 is 413 Richardson Avenue, Capital City, Yourstate.

YOU ARE HEREBY COMMANDED to appear in person or by sworn affidavit before the Clerk of the Circuit Court of Capital County, Yourstate (the "Clerk") within ten (10) days of your receipt of this writ and to then and thereby answer this garnishment under oath as to:

(1) Whether you are or were at the time this garnishment was issued, indebted to the Employee; if so, how and to what amount;

(2) Whether you have in your possession or under your control any property, debts, or effects belonging to the Employee, at the time of serving this garnishment, or have at the time of answering, or have had at any time between the date of service and the time of answering; if so, the kind and amount;

(3) Whether there are, to such garnishee's knowledge and belief, any and what property, debts, and effects in the possession or under control of any other, and what, person; and

(4) Such other questions as may be put to you by the court or the judgment creditor as may tend to elicit the information sought.

YOU ARE HEREBY FURTHER COMMANDED to calculate the portion of Employee's wages that are payable to the Clerk pursuant to this garnishment as set forth in Yourstate Statutory Code §26-2-205 and to pay said amounts to the Clerk within 30 days of the date of this writ and thereafter as they become due and payable to Employee. THE MAXIMUM PART OF THE AGGREGATE DISPOSABLE EARNINGS OF AN INDIVIDUAL FOR ANY WORK WEEK WHICH IS SUBJECTED TO GARNISHMENT MAY NOT EXCEED:

(A) Twenty-five percent (25%) of his disposable earnings for that week, minus two dollars and fifty cents ($2.50) for each of his dependent children under the age of sixteen (16) who reside in the state of Yourstate as provided in §26-2-102; or

(B) The amount by which his disposable earnings for that week exceed thirty (30) times the federal minimum hourly wage at the time the earnings for any pay period become due and payable, minus two dollars and fifty cents ($2.50) for each of his dependent children under the age of sixteen (16) who reside in the state of Yourstate, whichever is less.

"Disposable earnings" means that part of the earnings of an individual remaining after the deduction from those earnings of any amounts required by law to be withheld.

BE ADVISED that, pursuant to §26-2-207, you are liable for failure to withhold the proper garnishment amount from the Employee's wages and for failure to pay these moneys to the Clerk.

Clerk

Illustration 5-m: STATE STATUTE REGARDING GARNISHEE'S LIABILITY

> If the garnishee fails to timely answer or pay money into court, a conditional judgment may be entered against the garnishee and an order served requiring the garnishee to show cause why the judgment should not be made final. If the garnishee does not show sufficient cause within ten days of service of the order, the conditional judgment shall be made final and a writ of execution may issue against the garnishee for the entire judgment owed to the judgment creditor, plus costs.

the value of the property that should have been delivered to the court clerk pursuant to the garnishment or for the entire amount of the debt. What happens procedurally is that, upon default by the garnishee, a conditional judgment against the garnishee is applied for by the attorney for the judgment creditor and issued by the court. The garnishee then has ten days to request a hearing and show cause why the conditional judgment should not be made final. Illustration 5-m sets out a typical statute regarding this aspect of garnishment law.

Garnishments typically have an effective time limit on them (e.g., six months from date of issue) and may need to be renewed until the judgment is satisfied. As with the judgment lien and writ of execution, proper service of a writ of garnishment creates a judicial lien in favor of the executing judgment creditor.

P-H 5-l: Locate the procedures for the judgment lien, writ of garnishment, writ of execution, or other method for executing on a judgment authorized in your state. Compare the procedures set out in them to the procedures described in the text.

The lien that the executing judgment creditor obtains through any of these methods is deemed a judicial lien since it arises from the judicial process. As we saw in Chapter Three, Section B, the judicial lien creditor is granted priority over a prior unsecured interest in the same property (see the highlighted case *Muggli Dental Studio v. Taylor*).

EXAMPLE

Assume that on November 4 Pearl Murphy borrows money from First City Bank (FCB) and grants FCB a security interest her jewelry to secure repayment of that loan. FCB perfects its security interest in the jewelry by filing a financing statement the same day. If the sheriff seizes the jewelry on November 5, the lien of levy in favor of CCME will be subordinate, or junior, to the consensual lien of FCB in the jewelry, and if the sheriff sells the jewelry, the proceeds will go first to repay in full FCB before they are applied to the CCME judgment. However, if FCB failed to properly perfect its lien in the jewelry before the sheriff seized it on November 5, then CCME's lien of levy will be superior to the FCB security interest in the jewelry.

H. ▶ Priority Among Competing Judicial Liens Created by Execution on the Debtor's Property

Competing claims to priority among two or more judicial lien creditors are typically given priority on a first to attach basis but state laws differ on when the lien created by the writ is deemed to attach. Depending on the type of execution involved it may be one of the following:

- Date of the actual levy—the date on which the sheriff took possession of particular property and what constitutes possession (physical seizure or symbolic as by posting a notice) can vary depending on the state;
- Date of delivery of writ—the date on which writs of execution are delivered to the sheriff for service;
- Date of service of a writ of garnishment to the bank, employer, or other third party holding property of the judgment debtor;
- For a judgment lien, date of recordation of judgment or delivery of the judgment to the appropriate filing or recording officer.

EXAMPLE

Assume the writ of execution in Illustration 5-k is issued by the clerk and delivered to the sheriff on November 2. On November 3, before the sheriff has attempted execution on the writ delivered to him on November 2, a second writ of execution is delivered to the sheriff on behalf of a second judgment creditor of Pearl Murphy, directing the sheriff to seize her assets in satisfaction of that judgment as well. When the sheriff seizes Pearl's property, which judgment creditor gets paid first? If the statute in Illustration 5-i is in effect in the state, the writ delivered on November 2 will have priority and must be satisfied in full before proceeds of sale can be applied to the writ delivered on November 3.

Property that the debtor can exempt from execution and property that has no equity for the executing creditor because it is subject to a prior perfected security interest should not be executed on. As mentioned in the earlier discussion on exempt property, states have different procedures by which a debtor can advise the court of property he claims as exempt, and public records (e.g., UCC filings and vehicle title registrations records) should be consulted if possible to identify property already subject to an unchallengeable prior security interest. When such property does get inadvertently seized in execution the debtor or secured creditor can file a motion with the court from which the execution issued contesting the seizure.

DEBTOR'S PRISON

For many years debtors could be imprisoned for nonpayment of private debts. The practice was prohibited at the federal level by 1833. Most states also enacted such bans in their constitutions or by statute. Regarding incarceration for nonpayment of public debt, *Williams v. Illinois*, 399 U.S. 235 (1970), held it a violation of equal process for a state to subject a convicted defendant to a period of imprisonment beyond the statutory maximum solely because he is too poor to pay an accompanying fine. *Tate v. Short*, 401 U.S. 395 (1971), held it an equal protection violation for a state to convert the penalty under a fine-only

---

statute to a jail term solely because the defendant cannot immediately pay the fine in full. And *Bearden v. Georgia*, 461 U.S. 660 (1983), held that a court cannot revoke a defendant's probation for failure to pay an imposed fine and restitution, absent evidence and findings that the defendant has the means to pay or was somehow responsible for the failure to pay or that alternative forms of punishment were inadequate.

But imprisonment for private debt may not really be a thing of the past due to the employment of the **pay or appear** tactic by judgment creditors. The creditor notices the judgment debtor to a postjudgment deposition and if the debtor fails to attend has the judge find the debtor in contempt of court. A **capias**, or **bench warrant**, for the arrest of the defendant (informally called a **body attachment**) is issued by the court pursuant to which the debtor is taken into custody until there is a court hearing or the debtor posts bond (which often she cannot do). Debtor's prison redux?

P-H 5-m: In 2012, Illinois passed the Debtors' Rights Act requiring judges to make an affirmative finding of the debtor's ability to pay out of nonexempt sources of income before using a pay or appear provision in an order and requiring proof that a debtor received actual notice of a postjudgment deposition. Determine if pay or appear is a problem in the state where you plan to practice and, if so, whether the state legislature has addressed the problem.

I. ▶ Continuing Execution on a Final Judgment

Often, a final judgment cannot be immediately satisfied in full by execution. The judgment debtor may not have sufficient nonexempt income or assets that can be located and taken. But, of course, that could always change in the future: The judgment debtor could become employed or better employed, or acquire nonexempt assets or receive them by gift or inheritance. And that raises the question of how long the judgment creditor can continue to execute on the judgment. States differ in the term of viability granted a final judgment but, whatever the term, the term of enforceability can be renewed or extended if proper procedures are followed. Illustration 5-n sets out a typical statutory term of viability and the procedure for extension or renewal.

Commonly, a final judgment is entered in one state and the judgment debtor has assets in another state. Most states have adopted some version of the **Uniform Enforcement of Foreign Judgments Act** (UEFJA). Under the UEFJA, the judgment creditor seeking to enforce the foreign judgment must petition a court in the state where enforcement is sought for permission to register the judgment in that state for purposes of executing on it. Normally, the court in which the "petition for permission to register foreign judgment" is filed or

Illustration 5-n: STATE STATUTE REGARDING TERM OF VIABILITY OF A FINAL JUDGMENT AND THE PROCEDURE FOR EXTENSION OR RENEWAL

> Within ten years from entry of a judgment, the judgment creditor whose judgment remains unsatisfied may move the court for an order requiring the judgment debtor to show cause why the judgment should not be extended for an additional ten years. A copy of the order shall be mailed by the judgment creditor to the last known address of the judgment debtor. If sufficient cause is not shown within thirty (30) days of mailing, another order shall be entered extending the judgment for an additional ten years. The same procedure can be repeated within any additional ten-year period until the judgment is satisfied.

registered in a court of record in the county where the property to be executed on is located. The petition must be accompanied by an attested copy of the final judgment from the clerk of the court that issued it. Many states also require that the petition be verified by the person signing it.

The clerk of the court where the petition is filed will issue a summons to be served on the judgment debtor along with a copy of the petition and all exhibits. Typically, no execution can begin on the foreign judgment until the judgment debtor has been served with the summons and petition and has been given some time (e.g., 30 days following service) to file a response raising a defense to the validity of the foreign judgment. The judgment debtor cannot relitigate the underlying debt or liability claim because that was decided by the court that issued the final judgment. The judgment debtor may be in a position to attack the underlying validity of the final judgment, however, by arguing that the court that entered the final decree lacked subject matter jurisdiction over the case or personal jurisdiction over the debtor.

P-H 5-n: Determine if the state where you plan to practice has adopted the UEFJA.

J. The Inclusion of Prejudgment Interest in Final Judgments and the Creditor's Entitlement to Postjudgment Interest

In some circumstances the prevailing plaintiff in a collection lawsuit is entitled to have prejudgment interest added to the principal amount owed and included in the final judgment amount. And almost always a judgment creditor is entitled to receive postjudgment interest on the judgment amount. In this section we will consider these two different but equally important aspects of interest.

1. Prejudgment Interest

A plaintiff suing a consumer debtor to collect a preexisting liquidated amount is normally entitled to have interest that has accrued on the debt up until the date the final judgment is entered (**prejudgment interest**) included in the judgment amount. Illustration 5-o shows a typical state statute establishing applicable rates of prejudgment interest.

Illustration 5-o: TYPICAL PREJUDGMENT INTEREST STATUTE

> Prejudgment interest, i.e., interest as an element of, or in the nature of, damages may be awarded by courts or juries in accordance with the principles of equity at any rate not in excess of a maximum effective rate of six percent (6%) per annum. In addition, contracts may expressly provide for the imposition of the same or a different rate of interest to be paid after breach or default within the limits set by [other applicable provisions].

The statute posits two different ways of calculating the rate of prejudgment interest where a plaintiff is deemed entitled to it. Where the parties have an enforceable contract specifying a rate of post-breach interest to be applied to the amount owed, the courts will typically enforce that contractual rate.

EXAMPLE

> If the Medical Equipment Lease Agreement between Pearl Murphy and CCME specifically provides for CCME to receive interest at a stated rate (e.g., 10% per annum) on late payments or in the event of a default by Pearl, the trial judge will likely order the prejudgment interest calculated at the contract rate in the final judgment. Of course, if the contractual rate of interest is deemed usurious or otherwise unenforceable (e.g., due to public policy, unconscionability, absence of notice and mutuality), the court will not apply it.

Where there is no such contractual provision (or it is deemed unenforceable) but the court deems the plaintiff is entitled to prejudgment interest, the statutory rate is applied.

The generally recognized rule among the states for when prejudgment interest should be awarded, established either by statute or case law, is that prejudgment interest can be awarded as part of the final judgment where the loss was certain or readily ascertainable as of a particular time and can be measured with mathematical certainty by objective and admissible facts and figures.

An award of prejudgment interest is most clearly appropriate where the defendant owes the plaintiff a known, liquidated amount: an amount that is readily ascertainable and quantifiable based on a preexisting contract.

EXAMPLE

> Under the Medical Equipment Lease Agreement between CCME and Pearl Murphy, Pearl owes CCME $1,200 that should have been paid within 30 days of the billing. The amount owed is liquidated and the court will award CCME prejudgment interest on that $1,200 from the date of breach through the date of final judgment. An award of prejudgment interest in such situations is deemed necessary to fully compensate the plaintiff who has lost the use of the principal amount owed since the ascertainable date of breach.

In most states, where there is an underlying agreement from which the amount owed was readily ascertainable and quantifiable, it does not matter that liability was vigorously disputed—the priority is that the prevailing plaintiff be fully compensated for the loss including the loss of use of the amount owed from the time it was owed. See, e.g., *Royal Elec. Constr. Corp. v. Ohio State Univ.*, 652 N.E.2d 687 (Ohio 1995). In a few states, however, if liability under a preexisting agreement is contested, prejudgment interest is deemed inappropriate. See, e.g.,

Theobald v. Nasser, 784 So. 2d 142 (Miss. 2001) (where damages are disputed by the parties and the contract contained no liquidated damages clause, damages were not ascertainable until determined by trial court), and *Lincoln Benefit Life Co. v. Edwards*, 243 F.3d 457 (8th Cir. 2001) (applying Nebraska law) (interest accrues on the unpaid balance of any liquidated claim from the date the cause of action arose through the date of judgment only when no reasonable controversy exists as to either plaintiff's right to recover or as to the amount of such recovery).

Where recovery is had on a quasi-contract or unjust enrichment theory rather than express or implied contract, courts are split. Some allow prejudgment interest in such cases while others do not. Compare *LTD v. American Bridge Co.*, 2010 WL 703077 (N.D. Ohio 2010) (allowed) and *Clear One Communications, Inc. v. Chiang*, 432 Fed. Appx. 770, 776 (10th Cir. 2011) (not allowed).

In tort claims involving personal injury, wrongful death, defamation, false imprisonment, malicious prosecution, assault and battery involving determination of claims for pain and suffering, loss of enjoyment of life, emotional distress, harm to reputation, etc., courts deem it inequitable to award prejudgment interest even though the claimant ultimately prevails. In such cases the damages are deemed incomplete and continuing, and peculiarly within the province of the jury to assess at the time of the trial. The amount of the loss in such cases is not knowable until the finder of fact renders a decision.

EXAMPLE

In Nick and Pearl Murphy's medical malpractice action against Dr. Craft, they may request prejudgment interest be awarded on the jury verdict from the date of the negligence. But a court is very unlikely to grant such a request because neither the basis for liability nor the amount of the damages was established prior to the entry of judgment.

On the other hand, if the tort action involves harm to property, prejudgment interest is allowable in many jurisdictions even though the amount of damage is contested and not determined (liquidated) until trial. See, e.g., *Harlan Sprague Dawley, Inc. v. S.E. Lab Group, Inc.*, 644 N.E.2d 615 (Ind. 1994) (prejudgment interest allowed on final judgment in products liability action resulting in death of lab rats even though value of rats not determinable until trial and even though value disputed at trial). And a handful of states have adopted statutes authorizing awards of prejudgment interest in any civil tort case where the party prevailing at trial made a timely offer of settlement according to terms specified in the statute. See, e.g., the Indiana Tort Prejudgment Interest Statute at Ind. Code §34-51-4-1, et seq.

Prejudgment interest is normally denied to awards for lost future profits on the grounds that such awards are not provable with sufficient mathematical certainty. See, e.g., *Clear One Communications, Inc. v. Chiang*, supra at 774 (the very nature of lost future profits injects an air of uncertainty and speculation into the calculation of damages, because a jury must speculate when it determines what profits would have been generated had the defendant not acted wrongfully). To be distinguished are awards based on lost profits incurred prior to defendant's breach. See, e.g., *Encon Utah, LLC v. Fluor Ames Kraemer, LLC*, 210 P.3d 263, 274 (Utah 2009) (affirming award of prejudgment interest on lost profits for work that the plaintiff had performed under a fixed-price contract).

The common law rule was that prejudgment interest could not be **compounded**. See Restatement (Second) of Contracts §354, cmt. a (1981). Today,

Illustration 5-p: TYPICAL POSTJUDGMENT INTEREST STATUTE

> Interest on judgments, including decrees, shall be computed at a rate equal to 1% plus the average interest rate paid at auctions of 5-year United States treasury notes during the 6 months immediately preceding July 1 and January 1, as certified by the state treasurer, and compounded annually provided, that where a judgment is based on a note, contract, or other writing fixing a rate of interest within the limits provided in [other applicable provisions] for that particular category of transaction, the judgment shall bear interest at the rate so fixed.

some states allow compounding by statute. The decision of whether to allow prejudgment interest is committed to the sound discretion of the trial judge and is reviewed for abuse of discretion. See *Hughes Aircraft Co. v. United States*, 86 F.3d 1566 (Fed. Cir. 1996).

Procedurally, in many states, entitlement to prejudgment interest must be demanded in the party's pleadings whereas in others the request for postjudgment interest can be made by motion following judgment.

2. Postjudgment Interest

In many states **postjudgment interest** begins to accrue, at a statutory rate, on money judgments as a matter of law. A typical postjudgment statute is shown in Illustration 5-p.

Because the right to postjudgment interest is statutory, a creditor does not have to ask for it in the complaint. Once the judgment is final and can be executed on, postjudgment interest can be collected, calculated at the statutory rate, from the date of the judgment until payment. Further, as the statute in Illustration 5-p suggests, many states allow parties to agree by contract to a rate of postjudgment interest different from the statutory rate, so long as the agreed rate does not violate the state's usury laws.

P-H 5-o: Locate the statutes, regulations, or court rulings regarding prejudgment and postjudgment interest in your state. Under what circumstances will prejudgment interest be allowed and in what amount? Will your state enforce contractual provisions for prejudgment interest and are there any legal or public policy limitations on such provisions? Are there pleading or other procedural requirements for recovering prejudgment interest? Is postjudgment interest automatically collectible following entry of a final judgment in your state? Is the rate of postjudgment interest set by law or up to the discretion of the judge?

K. ▶ Avoiding the Fraudulent Transfer of a Debtor's Property

What if the judgment creditor undertaking execution on its judgment discovers that the judgment debtor has transferred ownership of nonexempt assets to a third party? Counsel for the judgment creditor will examine the asset transfer to determine if it can be set aside as a **fraudulent transfer**. Of course, a fraudulent transfer action can also form the basis of an original cause of action by a plaintiff to recover property in which he or she has an existing ownership interest. It can also be asserted in a motion for **prejudgment attachment** in a pending civil case in state court where the plaintiff discovers prior to entry of final judgment that the defendant is concealing or disposing of assets in order to defeat anticipated execution by the plaintiff once the judgment is entered.

In any context in which it is asserted, what distinguishes a fraudulent transfer action is that title to the property has been previously transferred or conveyed to someone other than the debtor. The transferee is therefore a proper and necessary party to the action to set aside the transfer.

EXAMPLE

If the Murphys are executing on their judgment against Dr. Craft and discover that he gave nonexempt assets to his brother the day after the judgment was entered, the Murphys might seek to have the gift set aside as a fraudulent transfer. Once the gift transferred is reversed and the assets retitled in Dr. Craft, they can be executed on. Because the Murphys would be asking the court to take action against property then titled in Dr. Craft's brother, the brother would have to be made a party to the fraudulent conveyance action.

In more than 40 states, fraudulent transfer law and procedure is governed by the **Uniform Fraudulent Transfer Act** (UFTA). Under the UFTA, a transfer of the transferor's property may be fraudulent as to a creditor of the transferor if the creditor can show either intentional fraud or constructive fraud in connection with a transfer occurring within four years preceding the date the action is commenced (one year if transfer is to an insider for an antecedent debt, see UFTA §9).

1. Transfers Made with Intent to Defraud

The UFTA provides the creditor with relief if it can be shown that the transfer was made with the "intent to defraud, hinder or delay" the creditor. With regard to what constitutes a transfer of property, §1(12) of the UFTA defines transfer as "every mode, direct or indirect, absolute or conditional, voluntary or involuntary, of disposing of or parting with an asset or an interest in an asset, and includes payment of money, release, lease, and creation of a lien or other encumbrance."

Under this broad definition, a fraudulent transfer could include not just selling property for less than it is worth, but also (1) making a gift of property; (2) changing of beneficiary designation on an insurance policy; (3) renouncing an inheritance in a decedent's estate; (4) pledging the property as collateral to secure a debt to another creditor; or (5) allowing foreclosure or repossession of collateralized property.

Of course, just because a defendant in a collection or liability suit transfers property does not make the transfer fraudulent. The fraudulent intent must be proven by the plaintiff. Proving fraudulent intent is difficult. Who knows the intent of a person in his own mind and heart?

Because of the difficulty of proving fraudulent intent, the courts, beginning with the venerable *Twyne's Case*, 3 Coke 80, 76 Eng. Rep. 809 (1601), developed what came to be called **badges of fraud**, circumstances or indicia surrounding the

Badges of fraud In the law of fraudulent transfer, certain recognized circumstances from which the inference may fairly be drawn that a transfer was made with intent to defraud creditors.

Illustration 5-q: THE BADGES OF FRAUD AS THEY NOW APPEAR IN §4(B) OF THE UFTA

- The transfer or obligation was to an insider.
- The transferor retained possession or control of the property transferred after the transfer.
- The transfer or obligation was disclosed or concealed.
- Before the transfer was made or obligation was incurred, the transferor had been sued or threatened with suit.
- The transfer was of substantially all the transferor's assets.
- The transferor absconded.
- The transferor removed or concealed assets.
- The value of the consideration received by the transferor was not reasonably equivalent to the value of the asset transferred or the amount of the obligation incurred.
- The transferor was insolvent or became insolvent shortly after the transfer was made or the obligation was incurred.
- The transfer occurred shortly before or shortly after a substantial debt was incurred.
- The transferor transferred the essential assets of the business to a lienor who transferred the assets to an insider of the transferor.

Insolvent The inability to pay debts as they come due or the state of having total liabilities in excess of total assets.

transfer that were relevant and provable as tending to show the fraudulent intent. Those badges of fraud have now been incorporated into the UFTA and are set forth in Illustration 5-q.

2. Transfers Made with Constructive Fraud

Constructive fraud A means of finding fraud based on inference from circumstances rather than proof of actual intent.

As an alternative to proving fraudulent intent, §4(a)(2) of the UFTA allows a court to find a fraudulent transfer has occurred (1) if the debtor transfers the property without receiving **reasonably equivalent value** in exchange for the transfer, and (2) the debtor is **insolvent** at the time of the transfer or becomes insolvent as a result of the transfer or (for an entity debtor) is left with unreasonably small capital to continue in business as a result of the transfer. This is **constructive fraud** (sometimes called **presumed fraud**). Unlike the intentional fraudulent transfer, no actual intent to defraud need be proven.

Note the "and" in the definition of constructive fraud under §4(a)(2) of the UFTA. There are two mandatory findings required to apply the constructive fraud theory. Whether the debtor receives reasonably equivalent value for a transfer is a question of fact based on the circumstances of the case.

Fair market value The price at which property would change hands between a willing buyer and a willing seller neither being under compulsion.

Reasonably equivalent value is normally determined using the **fair market value** of the property involved as of the date of the transfer. Fair market value is generally considered to be the price at which the property would change hands between a willing buyer and a willing seller, neither being under any compulsion to buy or to sell and both having reasonable knowledge of relevant facts. See *United States v. Cartwright*, 411 U.S. 546, 551 (1973).

Balance sheet test of insolvency A test of insolvency whereby a debtor's liabilities exceed his assets.

Under §§2(a) and (b) of the UFTA, insolvency, the second requirement of constructive fraud, can be established by using either the **balance sheet test of insolvency** (the sum of the debtor's debts is greater than all of the debtor's assets,

Equity test of insolvency When the debtor is not paying his or her debts as they become due.

at a fair valuation) or the **equity test of insolvency** (the debtor is not paying his debts as they become due).

Later we will revisit fraudulent transfer and the issue of what constitutes reasonably equivalent value in the context of a bankruptcy case in which a debtor has made a prepetition fraudulent transfer of property.

3. Remedies for Fraudulent Transfer

In a fraudulent transfer action, the most common remedy sought by the plaintiff is to have the court void or set aside the fraudulent transfer and order that title to the property be returned to the debtor. If the fraudulent transfer claim is made in a prejudgment attachment context, the plaintiff may also seek to attach the property, pending final resolution of the suit. If the fraudulent transfer claim is being made in a postjudgment context, the plaintiff/judgment creditor likely is seeking to execute on the property once it is returned to the debtor in order to satisfy the judgment.

Section 7 of the UFTA provides a number of different remedies that the court can impose once it finds a fraudulent transfer has occurred including the right to:

- Avoid the transfer or obligation to the extent necessary to satisfy the creditor's claim;
- Attach the asset transferred or other property of the transferee;
- Obtain an injunction against further disposition by the debtor or a transferee, or both, of the asset transferred or of other property;
- Obtain the appointment of a receiver to take charge of the asset transferred or of other property of the transferee;
- Obtain any other relief the circumstances may require; and
- If the creditor has already obtained a judgment against the debtor, levy execution on the asset transferred or its proceeds.

P-H 5-p: Determine if the state where you plan to practice adopted the UFTA. If not, determine if fraudulent transfer is governed by some other statute or by case law in that state.

CHAPTER SUMMARY

Creditors unable to collect a debt through nonjudicial debt collection activity may file suit and secure a final judgment against the debtor. Where there is no defense to the obligation such final judgment is likely to be taken by default. Most collection suits are brought in state court.

The creditor granted a final judgment against a debtor may have to wait until the expiration of a grace period before executing on the judgment against the debtor's assets and such grace period may be extended by posttrial motions or an appeal of the judgment by the debtor during which execution is stayed. A judgment creditor seeking assets of the debtor on which to execute may engage in postjudgment discovery in aid of execution in the form of interrogatories, document requests, and depositions.

Every state declares some personal property of the debtor exempt from execution by judgment creditors. Likewise, every state allows the debtor to exempt some amount of equity in the debtor's homestead. Concurrent ownership of property by the debtor with another may limit the ability of the judgment creditor to seize such property in execution. This is particularly true where the debtor owns property jointly with a spouse and the debtor's interest in marital property is indivisible or limited to a right of survivorship. Property held as tenants in common can be partitioned and the judgment debtor's interest liquidated. Assets of spendthrift trusts and, in some states, domestic asset protection trusts cannot be executed on where the judgment debtor is a beneficiary.

States authorize various methods for a judgment creditor to execute on the judgment. A judgment lien can be created on the judgment debtor's real property normally by recording a certified copy of the final judgment in the land records where the property lies. The writ of execution issued by the court and served by the sheriff authorizes the seizure of debtor's personal property creating a lien of levy on that property, which is then sold by the sheriff and the proceeds applied to the expenses of execution and the underlying judgment. The writ of garnishment issued by the court is served on third parties who may hold money or other assets of the judgment debtor, such as employers and financial institutions, and such assets must be delivered to the court for distribution to the judgment creditor.

A final judgment may include an award of prejudgment interest at the contract or a statutory rate where the amount owed was readily ascertainable and quantifiable as in a contract dispute. Prejudgment interest is not generally included on judgments arising from claims of tortious conduct. All states authorize the recovery of postjudgment interest at a statutory rate from the date of judgment until paid.

Execution on final judgments may involve claims of fraudulent transfer against the debtor and transferees of property. Most states have adopted the UFTA, which allows recovery of transfers of debtor's property made either with actual intent, in which case intent can be inferred from the traditional badges of fraud, or by constructive fraud where the debtor was insolvent at the time of transfer and received less than reasonably equivalent value of the property.

REVIEW QUESTIONS

1. What does it mean to say that a judgment debtor is "judgment proof"?
2. Explain how a posttrial motion or appeal by the judgment debtor can affect the timing of execution on a final judgment.
3. What is a supersedeas bond and what is the procedure for obtaining approval of one?
4. Name five federal benefits that states must exempt from execution.
5. In which of the following properties might a judgment debtor claim a homestead exemption: (a) debtor's car; (b) debtor's camping tent and equipment; (c) debtor's house?

6. In which of the following properties will a judgment debtor be *unable* to claim an exemption: (a) a car worth $10,000 owned outright by the judgment debtor; (b) a car worth $10,000 in which Bank has a security interest to secure debt with a balance of $12,000; (c) a car worth $10,000 in which Bank has a security interest to secure debt with a balance of $7,000?

7. Explain the difference between property owned as tenants in common and as joint tenants. Explain the difference between spouses owning property as tenants by the entireties or as community property.

8. What is a spendthrift trust, and what difference does it make if a debtor is the beneficiary of such a trust?

9. Explain the difference between a writ of garnishment, a writ of execution, and a judgment lien.

10. Under what circumstances will a trial judge include prejudgment interest in the final judgment amount if no underlying contract between the parties created a right to such interest?

11. What is the role of the badges of fraud in proving a defendant had an actual intent to defraud in making a property transfer?

12. What are the two elements of proving constructive fraud under the UFTA?

WORDS AND PHRASES TO REMEMBER

badges of fraud	insolvent
balance sheet test (of insolvency)	inventory
bank garnishment	joint tenancy
bench warrant	judgment creditor
body attachment	judgment debtor
bona fide purchaser for value	judgment lien
capias	judgment proof
community property	levy
concurrent ownership	lien of levy
constructive fraud	marshalling of assets
debtor's prison	motion to pay judgment
default judgment	in installments
discovery in aid of execution	notice of appeal
disposable income	nulla bona
domestic asset protection trust	offshore trust
equity test (of insolvency)	pay or appear
execution (on a final judgment)	postjudgment asset discovery
exempt property	postjudgment interest
fair market value	prejudgment attachment
federal spendthrift clause	prejudgment interest
final judgment	presumed fraud
foreign asset protection trust	reasonably equivalent value
fraudulent transfer	return (of the writ)
garnishee (garnishor)	right of survivorship
garnishment	self-settled trust
homestead exemption	sheriff's sale

slow pay motion
spendthrift trust
stay bond
supersedeas bond
tenancy in common
tenants by the entirety
till tap
trust

Uniform Enforcement of Foreign
   Judgments Act (UEFJA)
Uniform Fraudulent Transfer Act
   (UFTA)
wage garnishment
writ of execution
writ of fieri facias
writ of garnishment

TO LEARN MORE: A number of TLM activities to accompany this chapter are accessible on the companion web site for this textbook at http://aspen lawschool.com/books/Parsons_Debt4e/.

CONSUMER BANKRUPTCY

Introduction

How debt is discharged or reorganized in the bankruptcy process will be our topic in Parts B and C of the textbook. In this Part B we will introduce the Bankruptcy Code and examine the two types of bankruptcy cases that are most commonly filed across the country, both of which are consumer bankruptcy cases: the Chapter 7 liquidation proceeding for an individual debtor with primarily consumer debts and the Chapter 13 debt adjustment for an individual with regular income. In Part C we will consider the Chapter 11 business bankruptcy in detail.

Chapter Six:

▶ Introduction to Bankruptcy

Illustration 6-a: TIMELINE OF DEBT PUNISHMENT/FORGIVENESS A...

KEY CONCEPTS

- Today's Bankruptcy Code seeks to strike a balance between the notion that a debtor ought to pay what he or she owes and the idea that some debtors are entitled to a fresh start
- The Bankruptcy Code is located in Title 11 of the U.S. Code and authorizes six different types of bankruptcy cases
- A consumer bankruptcy case is one commenced under Chapter 7 or Chapter 13 involving a debtor with primarily consumer debts
- In addition to the Bankruptcy Code itself, the Federal Rules of Bankruptcy Procedure and the Official Bankruptcy Forms are among important sources of law that apply in a bankruptcy case
- U.S. bankruptcy courts are located in each federal district and have referral subject matter jurisdiction over bankruptcy cases from the U.S. district courts
- U.S. bankruptcy courts have nationwide in personam jurisdiction based on minimum contacts with the United States rather than the forum state
- Issues that arise in a bankruptcy case are decided as either contested matters or adversary proceedings
- All U.S. bankruptcy courts utilize electronic filing

A. ▶ A Brief History of Debt Relief and Bankruptcy Laws

A fundamental premise underlying modern American bankruptcy law is that, in certain circumstances, debtors are entitled to some form of relief from their debts that will provide them with a **fresh start**. As stated by the U.S. Supreme Court:

> [I]t gives to the honest but unfortunate debtor . . . a new opportunity in life and a clear field for future effort, unhampered by the pressure and discouragement of preexisting debt. *Local Loan Co. v. Hunt*, 292 U.S. 234, 244 (1934).

The basic human compassion in that premise is moderated by a second fundamental premise underlying our laws: One who incurs a debt ought to pay it. Striking the balance between these two premises has never been easy or simple. Not all human societies have even attempted to strike such a balance. Look through the timeline set out in Illustration 6-a to get an idea of the ebb and flow of attitudes and practices toward debt punishment/forgiveness.

Illustration 6-a: TIMELINE OF DEBT PUNISHMENT/FORGIVENESS ATTITUDES AND PRACTICES

2400-1600 B.C.E.—**Clean Slate** proclamations by various kings of ancient Sumeria, Assyria, and Babylon mandate the periodic forgiveness of debt and the restoration of land given as security or persons sold for debt. E.g., Code of Hammurabi §117 (circa 1754 B.C.E.): "If any one fail to meet a claim for debt, and sell himself, his wife, his son, and daughter for money or give them away to forced labor, they shall work for three years in the house of the man who bought them and in the fourth year they shall be set free."

1400 B.C.E.—Moses' law mandates a **Sabbatical Year** every seven years, when all debts are to be forgiven. At the end of every seventh Sabbatical Year (thought to be every 50th year) a **Year of Jubilee** is declared when debts are forgiven, slaves freed, and land taken for nonpayment of debt is returned to former owners or their heirs (other than the houses of laypersons within walled cities).

1000 B.C.E.—By this time, credit arrangements are firmly established as basis of commerce by and among Assyria, Babylon, and Egypt.

500 B.C.E.—Ancient Greece has no bankruptcy relief laws. Debtors, their families, or servants can be reduced to serfdom or even slavery for unpaid debt (debt slavery). Crises develop when such portion of the farming class is in jail or enslaved that there aren't enough workers to tend the crops. Crisis temporarily relieved in Athens by the Seisachtheia (burden-shaking) laws of Solon in 594 B.C.E. that cancel existing debt, mandate the return of debtor's forfeited property, and end debt slavery. Other Greek city-states limit the term of debt slavery to five years and protect debtors from severe abuse (*protection of life and limb*).

250 B.C.E.—In the days of the Roman Republic, debtors, or their families or servants, can be sold into slavery, imprisoned, and even killed by creditors. (It is said that in Roman times, creditors not only divided the debtor's property, but they also took him to the public plaza and bodily divided him.)

100 C.E.—Under the Caesars, the Roman Empire adopts some debt collection laws, including the appointment of a trustee to sell off a merchant debtor's assets after the merchant ceases business still owing money. The trustee is called the *curator bonorum* (caretaker) of the debtor's property for the benefit of creditors. Practice of *cession bonorum* (cesstion of goods) allows debtor to surrender property to creditor to avoid imprisonment.

1285—England's *Statute of Merchants* allows imprisonment of merchant debtors.

1400—In Italian city states, the defaulting merchant's trade bench or selling counter is destroyed to publicly announce his failure, literally *banca rotta* (broken bench), which may be the source of our modern word, *bankruptcy*.

1542—The state of being bankrupt is made an official crime in England, mandating a hearing before the chancellor, and is punishable by confiscation of property and imprisonment.

1570—Under Queen Elizabeth I of England, the first official bankruptcy law is passed by Parliament. It is exclusively a creditor's device, involuntary for the debtor. The creditor can formally declare a merchant bankrupt and seek official relief, including confiscation of property, imprisonment, and corporal punishment, the last of which could include having the debtor pilloried (a form of public humiliation that involved having hands and head locked in place by wooden stock) or having an ear cut off. In Padua, Italy, the bankrupt is required to appear nearly naked in the Palace of Justice and to slap his buttocks three times against "The Rock of Shame" while loudly proclaiming, "I declare bankruptcy!"

1705—England's *Statute of Queen Anne* marks the first attempt at a humane reform of bankruptcy law. At the request of the debtor and with creditors' consent, debt can be discharged following liquidation of assets. The death penalty for the debtor is allowed for committing fraud in bankruptcy but is only known to have been enforced five times.

1788—The U.S. Constitution is ratified, including Article I, §8, which authorizes Congress "[t]o establish . . . uniform laws on the subject of bankruptcies throughout the United States." In its first session, Congress considers adopting a bankruptcy law but demurs. Without federal rules, states follow their colonial practices based on English precedent, including imprisonment and pillorying.

1800—The Panic of 1797 in America leads to the imprisonment of thousands of debtors by the states, including the "Financier of the Revolution," Robert Morris. As a result, Congress passes the first federal bankruptcy law. It allows only creditors to declare a person bankrupt. Debts can be discharged after liquidation of the debtor's assets if he has been cooperative and two-thirds of his creditors consent. Repealed in 1803.

1833—Federal imprisonment for debt is abolished in the United States by act of Congress (now 28 U.S.C. §2007). Individual states begin to follow suit.

1841—The economic depression of 1837 results in Congress passing its second bankruptcy law, which for the first time permits debtors, including nonmerchants, to voluntarily file for bankruptcy relief. Due to high administrative costs, questions of constitutionality, and the discontent of creditors, the law is repealed in 1843.

1867—Following the turmoil of the Civil War, northern creditors want a system to collect from southern debtors. Congress passes a third bankruptcy law to enable them to do so, but it is repealed in 1878, again due to high administrative costs, an unwieldy bureaucracy, and little return to creditors.

Bankruptcy Act The predecessor of the current Bankruptcy Code. Enacted in 1898 and superseded in 1978.

1898—The economic panic of 1893 results in passage of the landmark Nelson Act, initiating the modern effort to balance debtor/creditor interests. The law, formally called the **Bankruptcy Act**, acknowledges the new credit economy, provides for a debtor-initiated discharge of debts, allows debtors to keep significant exempt property, and establishes the **bankruptcy referee** (predecessor of the modern bankruptcy judge) as the designated officer of the U.S. district court to administer the law.

Bankruptcy referee Office created under Bankruptcy Act of 1898. Predecessor to the modern bankruptcy judge.

1938—The Chandler Act amends the existing Bankruptcy Act to allow reorganizations in bankruptcy for both individual and business debtors (today known as Chapter 13 and Chapter 11 bankruptcies, respectively), enabling debtors with the means to repay all or a part of their debts under court supervision as an alternative to liquidation. For the first time, bankruptcy becomes a viable option to achieve economic survival rather than the failure of liquidation.

Bankruptcy Reform Act The 1978 statute that introduced the current Code. Also the name of the 1994 statute that amended the Code.

1978—The **Bankruptcy Reform Act** substantially rewrites the nation's bankruptcy law. Now formally known as the **Bankruptcy Code**, the law contains the current chapter numbering (Chapter 7, Chapter 13, Chapter 11, etc.), bankruptcy judges are given expanded judicial powers to administer bankruptcy cases, Chapter 11 business reorganizations are made more feasible, and states are given the option to "opt out" of the Code's property exemptions and apply their own exemption laws instead.

1982—The U.S. Supreme Court decides *Northern Pipeline Construction Co. v. Marathon Pipeline Co.*, 458 U.S. 50 (1982), declaring the Bankruptcy Reform Act of 1978 unconstitutional. The Court rules that Congress had overstepped its bounds in granting bankruptcy judges, created under Article I of the Constitution, powers of Article III judges in administering the Code. The Court grants Congress a grace period to amend the Bankruptcy Reform Act to cure the defect.

1984—The Bankruptcy Amendments and Federal Judgeship Act finally address the *Northern Pipeline* decision, reconstituting bankruptcy courts and judges as units of the U.S. district courts, with bankruptcy proceedings officially "referred" to bankruptcy courts under the standing orders of the district courts.

1986—The Code is amended to create the Chapter 12 proceeding for family farmers with regular income on a test basis and to make permanent the U.S. Trustee system to help administer bankruptcy cases, a system that had been tested on a pilot basis since 1978.

1994—The **Bankruptcy Reform Act of 1994** further amends the Code to clarify when bankruptcy courts can conduct jury trials, to expedite bankruptcy proceedings, to encourage individual debtors to use Chapter 13 to reschedule their debts rather than Chapter 7 to liquidate, and to aid creditors in recovering claims against bankrupt estates.

1996—For the first time ever, one million Americans file for bankruptcy in a single year.

2005—After over a decade of study and debate, Congress passes the **Bankruptcy Abuse Prevention and Consumer Protection Act** (BAPCPA), a significant amendment to the Code, intended to reduce the number of individual consumer bankruptcies and encourage repayment by making it more difficult for individual debtors to file for Chapter 7 liquidation relief and to force more of them to file for Chapter 13 reorganization. The Chapter 12 family farmer proceeding is made permanent and expanded to include family fishermen. The Chapter 15 proceeding is added to provide a mechanism for dealing with bankruptcy proceedings across international borders.

2011—The U.S. Supreme Court decides *Stern v. Marshall*, 131 S. Ct. 2594 (2011), reviving *Northern Pipeline* concerns over the constitutional power of Article I bankruptcy courts to decide core proceedings.

B. An Overview of the Bankruptcy Code and the Types of Bankruptcy Proceedings

As noted in the timeline above, the current bankruptcy law in this country is the United States Bankruptcy Code adopted by Congress in the Bankruptcy Reform Act of 1978 and located in Title 11 of the United States Code. We will refer to it as the **Bankruptcy Code** or just the **Code** (e.g., "§547 of the Code" instead of "11 U.S.C. §547"). The Code was enacted pursuant to Article I, §8, of the U.S. Constitution, which states that "Congress shall have the power to establish uniform laws on the subject of bankruptcies throughout the United States."

The Bankruptcy Code should be seen as a formal system of compulsory debt adjustment that seeks to balance the interests of both the debtor and his creditors. The interests of the debtor seeking bankruptcy relief are (1) to stop or at least delay debt collection efforts of creditors and then (2) to obtain some form of long-term, court-sanctioned debt relief, which may take the form of either the permanent discharge of some or all the debt or the reorganization of the debt obligations to make them more manageable for the debtor. When a debtor files for bankruptcy relief, the primary concern of creditors is to obtain payment of as much of the debt as possible as quickly as possible. The Code then is best understood as a statutory scheme created by Congress to regulate and balance these competing interests and, ideally, to produce a workable result that is palatable (if only barely sometimes) to both debtors and creditors.

Illustration 6-b lists and identifies the subject matter of each chapter of the Code. Three of these chapters contain definitional, administrative, and procedural types of rules (Chapters 1, 3, and 5), while six of them set forth specific types of bankruptcy cases that qualifying debtors can file (Chapters 7, 9, 11, 12, 13, and 15). We use the Code's chapter designation to identify and describe the type of bankruptcy case that a debtor files (e.g., "John and Carol Jones have filed a Chapter 7 case" or "ABC, Inc. is in Chapter 11").

Illustration 6-b: THE CHAPTERS OF THE BANKRUPTCY CODE

Chapter 1—General Provisions
Chapter 3—Case Administration
Chapter 5—Creditors, the Debtor, and the Estate
Chapter 7—Liquidation
Chapter 9—Adjustment of Debts of a Municipality
Chapter 11—Reorganization for a business or individual with business debt
Chapter 12—Adjustment of Debts of a Family Farmer or Fisherman with Regular Annual Income
Chapter 13—Adjustment of Debts of an Individual with Regular Income
Chapter 15—Ancillary and Other Cross-Border Cases

EXAMPLE

> If Abe Mendoza (Case Study #2; see Illustration 1-b) found it necessary to file a liquidation type bankruptcy proceeding under Chapter 7 of the Code, we would say that he has "filed a Chapter 7" or he is "in Chapter 7." If Nick and Pearl Murphy (Case Study #1; see Illustration 1-a) elected to file a Chapter 13 case as individuals with regular income seeking, not liquidation, but merely an adjustment of their debts, we would say that they have "filed a Chapter 13" or that they are "in Chapter 13." If Tomorrow Today, Inc. (TTI) (Case Study #3; see Illustration 1-c) elected to file a Chapter 11 case seeking to reorganize its debts in bankruptcy, we would say that it "filed a Chapter 11" or it is "in Chapter 11."

Illustration 6-c sets forth a brief summary of each of the six different types of bankruptcy proceeding authorized by the Code.

The vast majority of bankruptcy cases filed today are Chapter 7 liquidations or Chapter 13 adjustments of debts for individuals with regular income. Next in frequency come Chapter 11 business reorganization proceedings, followed by Chapter 12 family farmer/fisherman proceedings. Chapter 15 cross-border cases are still rare in most jurisdictions but are increasing in number. Chapter 9 municipality filings are fortunately rare though there have been several in the wake of the Great Recession that have received noticeable publicity including Jefferson County, Alabama, in 2011; Stockton, California, in 2012; and the city of Detroit in 2013.

Illustration 6-d contains a brief summary of the definitional, administrative, and procedural chapters of the Code. In general, the provisions in these chapters apply to all six types of bankruptcy proceedings summarized in Illustration 6-c.

P-H 6-a: To become more familiar with the chapters of the Code dealing with definitional, administrative, and procedural matters, consult the Code and find the answers to the following questions. (If you're not using a paper copy of the Code, you can access it online from Cornell Law School's Legal Information Institute at www.law.cornell.edu/uscode/text/11.) Find these answers and indicate the specific Code provision (e.g., §101(2)) that provides the answer. The table of contents at the beginning of each Code chapter might be a good place to start to locate the answers quickly.

- Locate the section in Chapter 1 of the Code controlling who can be a debtor in a Chapter 7 case to determine if a railroad can file for bankruptcy relief under Chapter 7 or Chapter 11 of the Code.
- Locate the section in Chapter 3 of the Code that tells you under which chapters of the Code an involuntary bankruptcy case may be commenced and what document has to be filed to commence an involuntary bankruptcy case.
- Locate the section in Chapter 5 of the Code authorizing a bankruptcy trustee to avoid a prepetition fraudulent transfer of property by the debtor and designating the prepetition time period during which transfers are subject to such an avoidance claim by the trustee.

Illustration 6-c: BRIEF SUMMARY OF THE SIX TYPES OF BANKRUPTCY PROCEEDINGS

Liquidation proceeding The sale or other disposition of a debtor's nonexempt assets for the purpose of distribution to his creditors in exchange for a discharge of most unpaid debt.

A **Chapter 7 bankruptcy** is a **liquidation proceeding**. All of the debtor's non-exempt property is turned over to a *bankruptcy trustee* appointed by the bankruptcy court administering the case. The bankruptcy trustee will sell that property (thus the "liquidation") and distribute the proceeds to the various creditors of the Chapter 7 debtor based on claims they have filed with the court and that the trustee will have reviewed and verified. The debtor thus loses all his or her property that is nonexempt in the liquidation proceeding, but in exchange receives a permanent **discharge** from future liability for most (but not all, as we shall see) of the debts that remain unpaid. Chapter 7 is the classic **fresh start**, or **clean slate**, bankruptcy.

Reorganization proceeding The rearrangement of a debtor's finances under a court-approved plan as an alternative to liquidation.

A **Chapter 11 bankruptcy** is not a liquidation proceeding like a Chapter 7. Instead it is a **reorganization proceeding** designed for a business or individual with business debt. In a Chapter 11, the debtor (or creditors) will propose a **plan of reorganization** pursuant to which, if approved by the bankruptcy court, the debtor will restructure the debts and sometimes the assets of its business and repay some or all of its debts out of future income. Some assets may be sold or abandoned and some obligations discharged or adjusted as part of the reorganization.

A **Chapter 13 bankruptcy** is also a reorganization-type proceeding, but Chapter 13 is designed not for a business, like Chapter 11, but for an "individual with regular income" and thus is more accurately referred to as a **debt adjustment proceeding**. The individual debtor will propose a debt adjustment plan of three to five years in duration for court approval. If the plan is approved, the debtor will use income received during the plan to pay off all or part of her debts. Some debt may be liquidated as part of the adjustment.

A **Chapter 9 bankruptcy** is designed specifically for "municipalities," which are defined in §101(40) of the Code to include political subdivisions of a state such as cities, counties, towns, villages, and public agencies or instrumentalities of a state such as taxing districts, municipal districts, school districts, or public utilities. This is a highly specialized type of bankruptcy and, fortunately, one that very rarely occurs.

Ancillary proceeding A bankruptcy case filed in a bankruptcy court in the United States that is related to the primary case filed in another country.

A **Chapter 12 bankruptcy** proceeding is a reorganization proceeding designed for debtors who qualify as **family farmers** or **family fishermen**. It is somewhat similar to a Chapter 13 proceeding but not so frequently used.

Cross-border cases A bankruptcy case involving debtors, assets, and creditors in more than one country.

A **Chapter 15 bankruptcy** proceeding is a special **ancillary proceeding** filed in a bankruptcy court in the United States after the primary proceeding has been commenced in a foreign country. It provides mechanisms for dealing with insolvency cases involving debtors, assets, and creditors in more than one country (**cross-border cases**) and allows adjudication of those interests located in the United States.

Illustration 6-d: BRIEF SUMMARY OF THE DEFINITIONAL, ADMINISTRATIVE, AND PROCEDURAL CHAPTERS OF THE CODE

- Chapter 1 of the Code contains general provisions, definitions, and rules of construction that govern the bankruptcy case.
- Chapter 3 of the Code sets out the procedures for commencing the bankruptcy case and administering it.
- Chapter 5 of the Code contains specific provisions pertaining to the rights and responsibilities of the debtor and creditors in the bankruptcy case, as well as indicating what property is to be included in the bankruptcy estate.

 C.   **Distinguishing Between Consumer and Business Bankruptcy Cases**

Debtor in bankruptcy A person who files a petition under the Code.

Business bankruptcy case A bankruptcy case in which the debtor is an entity or an individual with primarily business debts.

Consumer bankruptcy case A bankruptcy case in which the debtor is an individual with primarily consumer debts.

Consumer debt Debt incurred for personal, family, or household purposes.

Both individuals and business entities that file for bankruptcy relief are properly referred to as the **debtor** or the **debtor in bankruptcy** under the Code (see §§101(13) and (41)). However, organizations that compile statistics regarding annual bankruptcy filings (e.g., the American Bankruptcy Institute and the Administrative Office of the Federal Courts; see Illustration 6-l) commonly distinguish between **business bankruptcy cases** and **consumer bankruptcy cases**. Moreover, many lawyers and even paralegals specialize in either consumer or business bankruptcy but not both. That is why it is important to understand the distinction between consumer and business cases and why we will study Chapter 7 and Chapter 13 consumer cases separately from the Chapter 11 business reorganization.

Business bankruptcies include cases filed by business entities (corporations, including limited liability companies, and partnerships) or individuals with primarily business debt, whereas consumer bankruptcies include cases filed by individuals with primarily consumer debt. Section 101(8) of the Code defines **consumer debt** as follows:

> The term "consumer debt" means debt incurred by an individual primarily for a personal, family, or household purpose.

Thus, a consumer bankruptcy case is one filed by a debtor with primarily consumer debts whereas a business bankruptcy case is one filed by an entity or an individual with primarily business debts. Generally, business bankruptcy cases are filed as Chapter 7 liquidations or Chapter 11 reorganizations while consumer bankruptcies are filed as Chapter 7 liquidations or Chapter 13 debt adjustment proceedings.

Why does it matter in a bankruptcy case whether the case is a consumer or business bankruptcy filing? It matters for two reasons. First, in a bankruptcy case, the Code treats certain (not all) consumer debts differently than it does nonconsumer debts. We will see examples of this in later chapters as we walk through how a consumer bankruptcy case actually works, but if you just can't wait, take a peek at 11 U.S.C §523(a)(2)(C), which makes certain consumer debts nondischargeable in a bankruptcy case. Don't try to figure out how that section works now—we'll come to it later—just note that some consumer debts are treated differently in the Code than other debts.

Second, the difference between consumer and business debt matters because the Code also contains certain rules for debtors holding "primarily consumer debts" as opposed to debts that are not primarily consumer debts. Again, we will see examples of this in later chapters, but if you still can't wait, go ahead and look at 11 U.S.C. §707(b), which authorizes a bankruptcy judge to dismiss or convert a Chapter 7 case filed by "an individual debtor . . . whose debts are primarily consumer debts" if there is a finding of abuse. There is much to learn regarding this notion of abuse and we will consider it in later chapters, but for now, simply note that it applies only to cases where the debtor is an individual with primarily consumer debts. And there can be disputes over whether a particular debt is incurred primarily for personal, family, or household use.

P-H 6-b: Assume that Mary Jones purchases 200 loaves of bread from a supplier on credit. She purchases them intending to use them all in her sandwich shop business, a sole proprietorship. The next day she decides to use 110 of the loaves to make food for a family reunion. Then, not yet having paid the supplier what she owes, Mary files a petition in bankruptcy. Is that debt to the supplier consumer or business debt? What arguments would you make either way based on what you know at this point?

The Code's differing treatment of consumer debt and its different rules for individual debtors with primarily consumer debt is only part of the reason that consumer bankruptcy has become an area for specialized practice and study. The other part of the story is the staggering amount of consumer debt that exists in the United States, and the number of individual debtors who find it necessary to file for bankruptcy relief in any given year because they cannot manage their consumer debt. According to the Federal Reserve Bank of New York's Household Debt and Credit Report, in mid-2015 Americans collectively owed $8.1 trillion to creditors on home mortgages. Approximately 176 million of us carry credit cards on which we collectively owe about $712 billion, an average of more than $15,000 in credit card debt per American household. Forty-seven percent of households roll over a credit card balance over from month to month instead of paying off the balance, usually incurring an annualized double-digit interest rate charge on the rolled-over balance for doing so. And in 2012 came the startling news that total student loan debt owed by Americans exceeds total credit card debt for the first time. By 2015 total student debt topped $1.2 trillion and the delinquency rate was 11.5 percent.

P-H 6-c: Do your own research to update the consumer debt figures provided here. What are the consumer debt statistics for the state where you plan to practice and how do they compare to the national numbers? A good place to start is the latest quarterly Household Debt and Credit Report from the Federal Reserve Bank of New York (www.newyorkfed.org/). You would also do well to familiarize yourself with the history of the explosion in consumer spending and consumer debt in this country during the twentieth century via eased monetary policy to make more money available to financial lenders, expanded mortgage lending, installment purchasing, credit cards, subprime lending, the relaxation of usury rules, etc. Two good sources include *Debtor Nation*, by Louis Hyman (Princeton University Press, 2011) and *Financing the American Dream: A Cultural History of Consumer Credit*, by Lendol Calder (Princeton University Press, 1999).

It is this tremendous surge in consumer spending and resultant consumer debt that spurred the dramatic increase in bankruptcy filings in the modern era. In 1980 there were approximately 300,000 total bankruptcy filings in the United States. But the rise in consumer debt caused that number to swell to more than 1 million per year by 1996. In 2005 filings exceeded 2 million for the first time ever, although that number was inflated by filings intended to beat the October 17, 2005, effective date of the **Bankruptcy Abuse Prevention and Consumer Protection Act of 2005** (BAPCPA) (pronounced "bap-SEE-pah"), which made sweeping changes in the Code for both consumer and business cases. Its most dramatic effect was to impose new restrictions on consumers seeking to file Chapter 7 liquidation cases, with the intended effect of forcing more of them to file Chapter 13 reorganization cases instead. (The numerous significant features of BAPCPA will be discussed in upcoming chapters.)

After BAPCPA went into effect, filings for 2006 fell sharply to a little over 600,000, then climbed back to 850,000 in 2007 as debtors' lawyers became acquainted with the BAPCPA changes. With the bursting of the real estate bubble in 2007, the consequent mortgage foreclosure crisis, and the onset of what is now generally referred to as the Great Recession, filings surged to 1.1 million for calendar year 2008, 1.47 million for 2009, and approximately 1.6 million for 2010 before drifting lower in the years since. By 2014 annual filings had fallen below a million. Illustration 6-e charts the total number of bankruptcy filings for the period from 1980 to 2014.

Illustration 6-e: TOTAL BANKRUPTCY FILINGS FROM 1980 TO 2014

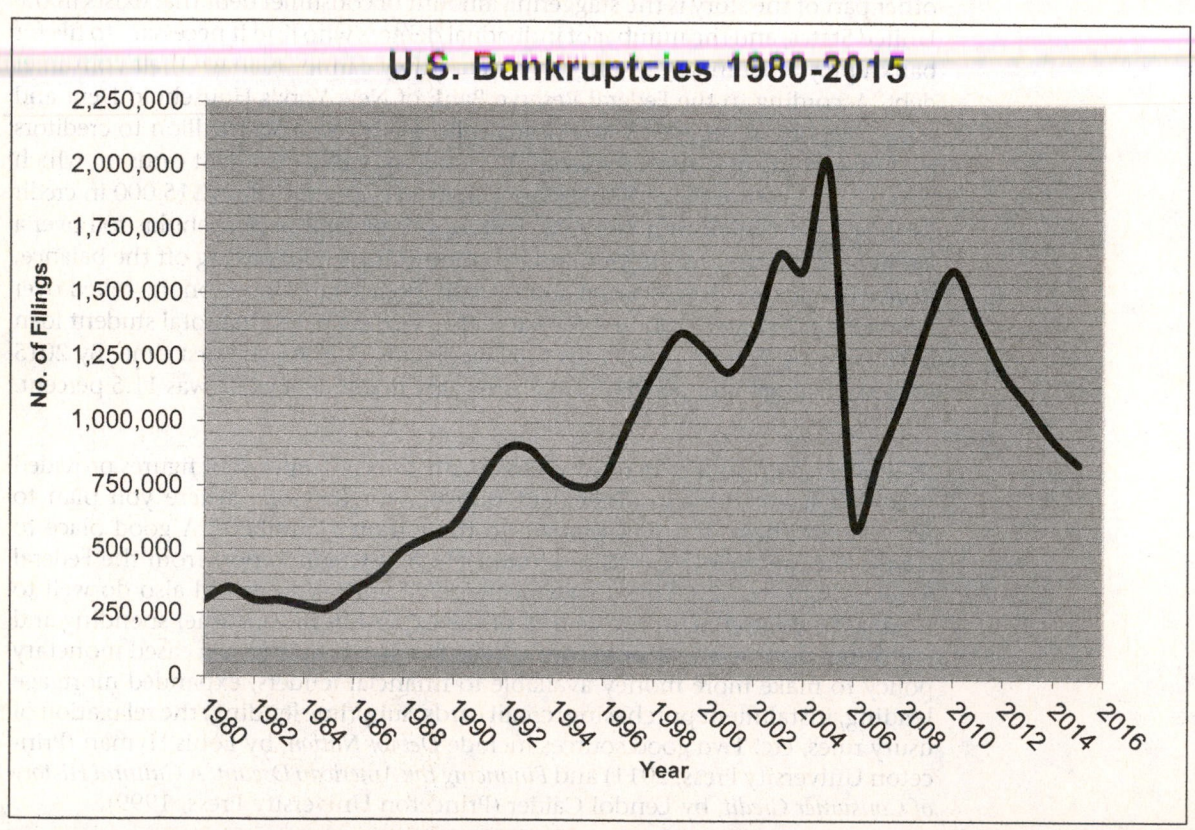

The vast majority of bankruptcy filings since 1980 that you see charted in Illustration 6-e are consumer bankruptcy cases, i.e., they are cases filed under Chapter 7 or Chapter 13 by individuals with primarily consumer debt. According to statistics compiled by the Administrative Office of the Federal Courts (www.uscourts.gov/report-name/bankruptcy-filings), in calendar year 2015 there were 844,495 total bankruptcy cases filed, of which only 24,735 or about 3 percent were categorized by bankruptcy court clerks as business bankruptcies. The balance of filings (97%) were categorized as consumer bankruptcies.

P-H 6-d: From the Administrative Office web site at www.uscourts.gov/ or some other authoritative source, locate the national bankruptcy filing statistics through the most recent quarter: What percentage were business filings? What percentage consumer filings? What percentage of the consumer case filings were Chapter 7s? What percentage were Chapter 13s? Check the filings for your state for the same period: How do the percentages of business versus consumer case filings in your state compare to the national percentages? Is the ratio of Chapter 7s to Chapter 13s among consumer case filings similar to the nationwide ratio?

Do not conclude that the tremendous disparity between the number of consumer and business bankruptcy filings means that consumer bankruptcies are somehow more important than business bankruptcies. Business bankruptcies commonly involve more debt, more assets, more creditors, more disputes, and more issues generally than do consumer bankruptcy cases. In addition, the vast majority of Chapter 11 filings are business bankruptcies, and the rules and procedures governing Chapter 11 cases are in many ways more detailed and complex than those governing Chapter 7 and 13 cases. Moreover, a business bankruptcy is likely to have significant consequences for a wider range of people than a consumer bankruptcy—like the difference between the ripple caused by throwing a brick versus that caused by throwing a pebble in a pond. In a consumer bankruptcy, the debtor, his family, and his creditors will certainly be impacted, but in a business bankruptcy you may also have business employees, suppliers reliant on the business, and indeed an entire community impacted by the case. Business bankruptcy filings commonly precipitate consumer filings by impacted individuals.

D. ▶ Brief Profile of Consumers Who File for Bankruptcy

According to the now classic study of American consumers by Teresa Sullivan, Elizabeth Warren, and Jay Westbrook, *The Fragile Middle Class: Americans in Debt* (Yale University Press, 2001), more than 90 percent of consumer bankruptcies are triggered by sudden job loss or downsizing, unexpected medical expenses, or loss of a spouse by divorce, separation, or death. Since that study, we have experienced the mortgage foreclosure crisis, which severely complicated the finances of millions of middle-class homeowners, and the Great Recession, which dramatically exacerbated sudden job loss as a bankruptcy trigger.

People with children at home are nearly three times as likely to file bankruptcy as people with no children. A single woman raising a child alone is more than four times as likely to file bankruptcy as a single woman with no children. Divorced fathers also file with much greater frequency than men with no children. Unmanageable prescription drug expenses and other medical costs are a primary reason that older Americans file for relief. More than one-half of Chapter 7 cases filed by Americans of all ages involve excessive medical bills (see Illustration 6-f).

The easy availability of credit cards, the popularity of payday loans, and the failure of some debtors to constrain or manage the resulting debt, even without individual or family emergencies, are significant factors in bankruptcy filings as well. The substantial role of credit card debt in bankruptcy filings can be seen in Illustration 6-f, which sets forth a comprehensive profile of consumers filing for bankruptcy relief.

In the past 30 years, approximately one in seven American households has filed for some type of bankruptcy relief. Illustration 6-g lists the five states with the highest per capita rate of bankruptcy filings in 2015.

Illustration 6-f: PROFILE OF CONSUMERS FILING FOR BANKRUPTCY RELIEF

- Average age: 38
- Median income: $20,172
- Total median assets: $37,000
- Homeowners: 50%
- Median value of homes owned by debtors who are homeowners: $90,000
- Median non-home assets: $9,657
- Median total debt-to-income ratio: 3.04 (the median debtor owes 3.04 times more total debt than his annual income)
- Median non-mortgage debt-to-income ratio: 1.48 (the median debtor owes 1.48 times more non-mortgage debt than his annual income)
- Percentage of median non-mortgage debt represented by credit card debt: 50%
- Percentage of debtors who owe more than a year's income in credit card debt: 21.8%
- Percentage of debtors who owe more than $10,000 in credit card debt on date of filing: 56.2%
- Percentage of debtors who owe more than $20,000 in credit card debt on date of filing: 34.6%
- Married couples: 44%
- Single women: 30%
- Single men: 26%
- Slightly better educated than the general population —
- Sustained job loss or downsizing that contributed to filing 66%
- Have not experienced a contributing medical problem, job loss, or divorce < 9%

Illustration 6-g: STATES WITH THE HIGHEST BANKRUPTCY FILINGS PER CAPITA (PER 1,000 RESIDENTS) IN 2015

1.	Tennessee	5.73
2.	Alabama	5.36
3.	Georgia	5.02
4.	Illinois	4.34
5.	Utah	4.28

P-H 6-e: Are you good at math? If a debtor owes 3.04 times more total debt than her annual income and her net annual income is $25,000 per year, (1) how much total debt does she owe? and (2) assuming she has 25 percent of her net annual income available to pay off her existing debt, how long will it take her to pay it off, disregarding mounting interest charges?

E. ► Important Sources of Law for Bankruptcy Practice

In addition to the Code itself, there are a number of legal sources that play a critical role in bankruptcy practice and the legal professional working in the bankruptcy field must be familiar with them.

1. The Federal Rules of Bankruptcy Procedure

Federal Rules of Bankruptcy Procedure The formal rules supplementing the Code and governing proceedings in bankruptcy cases.

In addition to the Code itself, Congress has adopted the **Federal Rules of Bankruptcy Procedure**. We will refer to the federal rules frequently, as they comprise the procedural rules that provide guidance and detail regarding how to comply with the Code requirements in all six types of bankruptcy cases.

P-H 6-f: To become more familiar with the Federal Rules of Bankruptcy Procedure, consult those rules and find the answers to the following questions (if you're not using a paper copy of the rules, you can access them online from the Federal Judiciary web site at www.uscourts.gov/rules-policies/current-rules-practice-procedure). Find these answers and indicate the specific rule (e.g., Bankruptcy Rule 1007) that provides the answer. The table of contents at the beginning of each part of the bankruptcy rules would be a good place to start to locate the answers quickly.

- Consult Part I of the rules specifying to whom the filing fee is paid when a bankruptcy case is commenced.
- Consult Part V of the rules to determine what days the bankruptcy courts and bankruptcy court clerk's offices are open.
- Consult the definitions in Part IX of the rules to determine whether the Federal Rules of Evidence apply in cases under the Code.

2. The Official Bankruptcy Forms

In addition to the Code and the bankruptcy rules, Congress has adopted **Official Bankruptcy Forms**. The official forms are drafted by the **Administrative Office of the U.S. Courts** (www.uscourts.gov/) and that office is constantly revising the forms to comply with changes in the Code or the bankruptcy rules, new court decisions, or recommendations from judges and practitioners. Bankruptcy Rule 9009 provides that the official forms "shall be observed and used."

P-H 6-g: To become more familiar with the official forms, locate the particular form requested in the list below (if you don't have a paper copy of the official forms, you can access them online from the Federal Judiciary web site at www.uscourts.gov/forms/bankruptcy-forms). Indicate the specific official form requested by its number and name (e.g., Official Form 318: Discharge of Debtor in a Chapter 7 Case).

1. Voluntary Petition for Individual filing for Bankruptcy
2. Schedule A/B: Property (Individual)
3. Statement of Your Financial Affairs (non-individuals)
4. Proof of Claim
5. Notice of Chapter 13 Case

3. The Federal Rules of Civil Procedure

The **Federal Rules of Civil Procedure** (FRCP) control the procedure in all types of civil proceedings in bankruptcy courts. As we will see, some disputes that arise in a bankruptcy case that must be resolved by the bankruptcy judge are treated by the Code and the bankruptcy rules as mini-lawsuits, which we will learn to call adversary proceedings. The FRCP govern the procedure in adversary proceedings in bankruptcy court, just as they would in any civil trial before a federal judge. If you do not have a paper copy of the FRCP, you can access them online at www.uscourts.gov/rules-policies/current-rules-practice-procedure or www.law.cornell.edu/rules/frcp/.

4. The Federal Rules of Evidence

The **Federal Rules of Evidence** (FRE) govern the admissibility of evidence at hearings conducted in all federal courts, including the U.S. Bankruptcy Courts. Whenever the bankruptcy judge conducts a hearing where evidence is presented (called an **evidentiary hearing**), the FRE will control the presentation of that evidence. If you do not have a paper copy of the FRE, you can access them online at www.uscourts.gov/rules-policies/current-rules-practice-procedure or www.law.cornell.edu/rules/fre/.

5. Local Court Rules

Bankruptcy Rule 9029(a)(1) provides in pertinent part as follows:

> Each district court acting by a majority of its district judges may make and amend rules governing practice and procedure in all cases and proceedings within the district court's bankruptcy jurisdiction which are consistent with—but not duplicative of—Acts of Congress and these rules and which do not prohibit or limit the use of the Official Forms . . . . A district court may authorize the bankruptcy judges of the district . . . to make and amend rules of practice and procedure which are consistent with—but not duplicative of—Acts of Congress and these rules and which do not prohibit or limit the use of the Official Forms.

Local court rules The written rules of procedure and practice that prevail in a particular court.

Pursuant to the authority granted by Bankruptcy Rule 9029(a)(1), bankruptcy courts around the country have adopted their own **local court rules**. These local rules are important and will control the way that the particular court processes bankruptcy cases in accordance with the Code and bankruptcy rules.

EXAMPLE

In some bankruptcy courts, by local rule, the party filing a motion for the judge to decide is required to arrange a date for the motion to be heard and to notify the other interested parties. In other bankruptcy courts, by local rule, the party need only file the motion and the clerk of the court will arrange the date for the motion to be heard.

EXAMPLE

When a creditor files a proof of claim in a debtor's bankruptcy case in accordance with the Code and bankruptcy rules, some bankruptcy courts require by local rule that a copy of the filing be sent directly to the bankruptcy trustee by the creditor. Others require by local rule that the bankruptcy court clerk send a copy of the proof of claim to the bankruptcy trustee after it has been filed with the clerk by the creditor.

P-H 6-h: Locate the local rules for the U.S. bankruptcy court located in the federal district where you plan to practice. See if you can locate a rule there dealing with:

- the allowed attorney's fee for an attorney representing a debtor in a Chapter 13 case;
- the availability of electronic filing of documents with the court;
- the procedure for conversion of a case from a Chapter 13 to a Chapter 7;
- the procedure for amendment of a Chapter 13 plan; and
- the approved manner for payment of filing and other fees (e.g., by credit card, personal check, etc.).

6. Miscellaneous Provisions of the U.S. Code

Although, as we have noted, the Bankruptcy Code is found in Title 11 of the U.S. Code, other provisions of the U.S. Code come into play in bankruptcy cases. Most notably, Title 28 of the U.S. Code contains provisions identifying the various federal districts where bankruptcy courts are located (§152), the procedures for the appointment of bankruptcy judges (§152), the procedures for the referral of bankruptcy cases from the district court to the bankruptcy court (§159), and other details concerning the duties of bankruptcy judges. Title 28 also sets out the extent of bankruptcy jurisdiction (§1334) and venue (§§1408-1412). And it contains provisions creating and regulating the U.S. Trustee system (§§581-589), discussed in more detail below.

Title 18 of the U.S. Code contains provisions regarding the offenses of bankruptcy fraud (§157), embezzlement against a bankruptcy estate (§153), false oaths and claims (§152), and other federal crimes that may arise in bankruptcy cases.

7. State Law

Though the Bankruptcy Code is a federal statute, state law plays a major role in the administration of a bankruptcy case. In *Butner v. United States*, 440 U.S. 48 (1979), the Supreme Court held that, while the Code itself rather than state law governed questions regarding the administration of a bankruptcy case, questions regarding the nature or extent of an interest in property claimed by a debtor or creditor in the bankruptcy case are to be determined by the controlling state law, not federal law.

Property interests are created and defined by state law. Unless some federal interest requires a different result, there is no reason why such interests should be analyzed differently simply because an interested party is involved in a bankruptcy proceeding. Uniform treatment of property interests by both state and federal courts within a State serves to reduce uncertainty, to discourage forum shopping, and to prevent a party from receiving "a windfall merely by reason of the happenstance of bankruptcy. The justifications for application of state law are not limited to ownership interests; they apply with equal force to security interests, including the interest of a mortgagee in rents earned by mortgaged property."

Id. at 55.

EXAMPLE

The question of where the debtor resides for purposes of deciding the proper bankruptcy court in which to file his or her case is a question of state law. Whether a debt created by contract is valid and collectible will be determined by state law. Whether a creditor is properly secured and perfected in personal property of the bankrupt debtor will be determined by the state's version of Article 9 of the UCC. Whether a creditor holds a mortgage in the debtor's real property will be determined by state law. Whether a creditor holds a valid nonconsensual lien in property of the bankrupt will be determined by state law. On the other hand, whether a debtor is entitled to file for relief under a particular chapter of the Code is controlled by the Code itself. What priority a creditor's claim has in the Code's distribution scheme is controlled by the Code itself. Whether a claim is dischargeable in bankruptcy is determined by the Code.

> **P-H 6-i:**   Recall the Code's definition of what constitutes a consumer debt in 11 U.S.C. §101(8). Recall too the example we used of Mary Jones who purchases 200 loaves of bread to use in her sandwich shop but who then takes 110 of them home to use in preparing food for a family reunion. Mary has now filed a Chapter 7 bankruptcy case and there is a motion to dismiss her case under 11 U.S.C. §707(b) for abuse by an individual filing a case with primarily consumer debt. If a question arises concerning whether Mary owes this particular debt to the supplier who sold her the loaves of bread, what law will control: state contract law or §707(b) of the Code? If there is a question of whether her debts, including this one, are primarily consumer debts for purposes of §707(b), what law will control, state contract law or the Code provision? Would it change your answer to the second question if state law also defined what is or is not a consumer debt?

F. ▶ Number and Location of the U.S. Bankruptcy Courts

Congress has divided the United States geographically into 94 different federal districts. Each of those federal districts, in turn, lies within a larger federal circuit, over which sits one of the 13 U.S. circuit courts of appeal. In each of the 94 federal districts, there are one or more district judges presiding over a U.S. district court. And in each of those 94 federal districts, there are one or more bankruptcy judges presiding over a U.S. bankruptcy court.

> **P-H 6-j:**   Go to the Court Links web site of the Administrative Office of the Federal Courts (www.uscourts.gov/about-federal-courts/federal-courts-public/court-website-links) and locate the bankruptcy court in your federal district and division. On your computer, bookmark this web site for future use.

G. ▶ Jurisdiction, Appellate Process, and Decision-Making Procedures in Bankruptcy Court

1. Subject Matter Jurisdiction of the Bankruptcy Courts

Subject matter jurisdiction A court's power to hear and decide certain types of cases.

The subject matter jurisdiction of the U.S. bankruptcy courts is a complex and multi-layered subject. It is challenging even for experienced practitioners to grasp. Moreover, it is still evolving, as the Supreme Court continues to sort out significant constitutional and statutory interpretation issues that have a dramatic and practical impact on the scope of that jurisdiction. Your ability to grasp this challenging topic will be enhanced by first learning the mechanics of how consumer bankruptcy cases work. This is so because the statutes, rules, and court rulings regarding bankruptcy jurisdiction are encountered in the context of those mechanics and can be even more challenging if the student is not already grounded in bankruptcy vocabulary and procedures.

Having said that, in true chicken or egg fashion, it will enhance your study of the mechanics of the consumer bankruptcy case to have some rudimentary understanding of bankruptcy jurisdiction as you begin. The following synopsis of subject matter jurisdiction is intended to serve that purpose.

28 U.S.C. §1334(a) grants the U.S. district courts (not the U.S. bankruptcy courts) "original and exclusive" jurisdiction over cases under Title 11 (the Bankruptcy Code). 28 U.S.C. §1334(b) then grants the district courts "original but not exclusive jurisdiction" over civil proceedings "arising under title 11, or arising in or related to cases under title 11." Proceedings that are "arising in or related to" cases under Title 11 are generally understood to include any issues that could conceivably have an impact on the property of the estate to be administered in the bankruptcy case. See *In re Wood*, 825 F.2d 90 (5th Cir. 1987). So the U.S. district courts are given "original and exclusive" jurisdiction over all bankruptcy cases filed under Title 11 but "original but not exclusive" jurisdiction over issues that arise in or are related to bankruptcy cases filed under Title 11.

This "original but not exclusive" jurisdiction allows a district court to delegate the authority to handle proceedings arising in or related to bankruptcy cases to a lower court that answers to it while retaining jurisdiction over the bankruptcy cases themselves. 28 U.S.C. §151 provides: "In each judicial district, the bankruptcy judges in regular active service shall constitute a unit of the district court to be known as the bankruptcy court of that district." Thus, bankruptcy courts in each federal district across the country serve as units or adjuncts of the district courts in those districts.

28 U.S.C. §157(a) specifically authorizes the district courts to refer bankruptcy cases to the bankruptcy courts in their districts. Consequently, the bankruptcy courts, as adjuncts or units of the district courts per 28 U.S.C. §151, obtain jurisdiction over bankruptcy cases only by referral from the district courts. Bankruptcy courts have **referral jurisdiction** from the district courts over bankruptcy cases. And the district court that has referred jurisdiction to a bankruptcy court (usually done routinely and automatically by standing court order of the district) has the discretion to **revoke the reference** at any time on its own motion or upon the motion of any party in interest for cause shown per 28 U.S.C. §157(d).

This scheme is made necessary by the historical fact that while the district courts are deemed Article III courts (established under Article III of the U.S. Constitution), bankruptcy courts are deemed only Article I courts (created by Congress for a narrow legislative purpose under Article I of the Constitution). As Article I courts, the bankruptcy courts cannot enter binding final judgments in all of the proceedings that are referred to them by the district courts. The proceedings in a bankruptcy case referred to the bankruptcy court in which it has the power, as an Article I court, to enter a binding final judgment are called **core proceedings**. Proceedings that arise in a bankruptcy case referred to the bankruptcy court in which the court may not enter a binding final judgment are called **non-core proceedings**.

28 U.S.C. §157(b)(1) provides that the bankruptcy court may enter a final judgment or dispositive order in a core proceeding but §157(c)(2) provides that the bankruptcy court may *not* do so in a non-core proceeding *unless* all the parties consent. When the matter before the bankruptcy court is non-core, §157(c)(1) limits the power of that court to making proposed findings of fact and conclusions of law for review de novo by the district court.

Referral jurisdiction A description of the subject matter jurisdiction of U.S. bankruptcy courts since such jurisdiction depends on referral from the U.S. district courts.

Core proceedings A proceeding in a bankruptcy case in which the bankruptcy court is authorized to enter a final judgment or order per 28 U.S.C. §157(b)(2).

Non-core proceedings A proceeding in a bankruptcy case in which the bankruptcy court is not authorized to enter a final judgment or ordered unless the parties consent.

Illustration 6-h: TYPES OF PROCEEDINGS ARISING IN A BANKRUPTCY CASE DESIGNATED AS CORE PROCEEDINGS (BASED ON 28 U.S.C. §157(b)(2))

- Matters concerning the administration of the estate
- Allowance or disallowance of claims against the estate
- Estimation of claims or interests for purposes of confirming a plan under Chapter 11, 12 or 13
- Counterclaims by the estate against persons filing claims against the estate
- Allowance or disallowance of exemptions of property from the estate
- Orders in respect to obtaining credit
- Orders to turn over property of the estate
- Proceedings to determine, avoid, or recover preferential transfers
- Motions to stay, annul, or modify the automatic stay
- Proceedings to determine, avoid, or recover fraudulent transfers
- Determinations as to the dischargeability of particular debts
- Objections to discharge
- Determinations as to the validity, extent, or priority of liens
- Confirmation of plans
- Orders approving the use or lease of property, including the use of cash collateral
- Orders approving the sale of property (other than property resulting from claims brought by the estate against persons who have not filed claims against the estate)
- Other proceedings affecting the liquidation of assets of the estate or the adjustment of the debtor/creditor relationship or the equity security holder relationship
- Recognition of foreign proceedings and other matters under Chapter 15 of the Code

So what is a core proceeding in a bankruptcy case and what isn't? 28 U.S.C. §157(b)(2) designates a number of specific matters that arise in a bankruptcy case as core proceedings. In deciding disputes involving any of those enumerated matters, the bankruptcy court can enter a final order or judgment per the statutory scheme. Illustration 6-h lists the proceedings designated as core by Congress.

The matters listed in §157(b)(2) do not constitute an exclusive list of core proceedings ("Core proceedings include, but are not limited to . . .") and courts commonly disagree over whether a particular matter excluded from the list is to be treated as core or non-core. When a matter is determined to be non-core and the parties will not consent to the bankruptcy court entering a final order on the matter, one of two things can happen. First, the bankruptcy court can go ahead and hear the matter as non-core, which means it can only enter **proposed findings and conclusions** for the district court's review or, second, one of the parties can move to revoke the reference to the bankruptcy court as to that non-core matter and the district court will then hear and decide it. Remember, district courts retain overall jurisdiction over bankruptcy cases filed in their district and may revoke the jurisdiction they referred to the bankruptcy courts at any time per 28 U.S.C. §157(d).

Pursuant to 28 U.S.C. §157(b)(5), bankruptcy courts may not conduct trials involving personal injury or wrongful death regardless of whether they qualify as core proceedings and may not even make proposed findings in them as in a non-core proceeding. The U.S. district court is to hear and decide such claims.

2. Constitutional or "Gap" Jurisdictional Issues in a Bankruptcy Case

As observed in the last section, the referral jurisdiction scheme and distinction between core and non-core proceedings that now characterize bankruptcy court jurisdiction have been made necessary by distinction between the Article III district courts and the Article I bankruptcy courts. A little background regarding this distinction will prove helpful.

Article III of the Constitution mandates that "[t]he judicial power of the United States shall be vested in one Supreme Court and in such inferior courts as the Congress may from time to time ordain and establish." The **Article III courts** are the U.S. Supreme Court, the 13 U.S. circuit courts of appeals, and the 94 U.S. district courts. The judges of these courts are selected by the constitutionally mandated process of nomination by the president and confirmation by the U.S. Senate, and they enjoy lifetime tenure since Article III says that they "shall hold their offices during good behaviour." It has long been understood that only Article III courts, constituting the judicial branch of the federal government, can enter final orders that determine issues involving life, liberty, or property rights (see, e.g., *American Ins. Co. v. 356 Bales of Cotton*, 1 Pet. 511 (1828) (commonly referred to as *Canter*) and *Ex parte Bakelite Corp.*, 279 U.S. 438 (1929)).

Congress has in fact created a number of "inferior" courts pursuant to the mandate of Article III. These are referred to as **Article I courts** (since it is Article I of the Constitution that details the powers of the legislative branch) or **legislative courts** (since they are created by the legislative branch and not by the Constitution). Since they are created by Congress for some specialized legislative purpose Article I courts do not enjoy plenary Article III powers and the judges of those courts do not enjoy lifetime tenure. More specifically, Article I courts, like the bankruptcy courts, cannot be empowered to decide disputes between private parties controlled by state law (called actions involving **private rights**). The Supreme Court has described private rights claims as those involving "the liability of one individual to another under the law as defined." See *Stern v. Marshall*, 131 S. Ct. 2594, 2612 (2011). Instead, Article I courts can only decide designated disputes between the government and persons subject to its authority (called actions involving **public rights**). In *Stern*, the Supreme Court defined a public right claim as one that "derives from a federal regulatory scheme, or in which resolution of the claim by an expert governmental agency is essential to a limited regulatory objective within the agency's authority." Id. at 2613.

In *Northern Pipeline Constr. Co. v. Marathon Pipeline Co.*, 458 U.S. 50 (1982), the Supreme Court held that the Bankruptcy Reform Act of 1978 violated the separation of powers doctrine of the Constitution by purporting to give bankruptcy courts the power to enter final orders determining issues regarding property in disputes between private parties controlled by state law, i.e., claims involving private rights, a power reserved by the Constitution for the Article III courts. It was in response to *Northern Pipeline* that Congress passed the 1984 Amendments Act amending Title 28 to accomplish two major objectives: (1) to make it clear that subject matter jurisdiction over bankruptcy matters resides in the Article III district courts, and (2) to authorize those courts to refer that jurisdiction to the Article I bankruptcy courts. Congress believed and hoped that this referral jurisdictional scheme would satisfy the constitutional defect in bankruptcy court jurisdiction.

With the 1984 Amendments Act creating the referral jurisdiction scheme we have considered and designating certain actions as core in 28 U.S.C. §157(b)(2), Congress probably thought it had adequately addressed the problems raised by *Northern Pipeline* and that all would thereafter be well. However, a post-*Northern Pipeline* aftershock came along with *Stern v. Marshall.*

In *Stern*, a claim was filed in a Chapter 11 case alleging that the debtor had defamed the claimant. The claimant also asked that the claim be declared non-dischargeable in bankruptcy. The debtor objected to the claim asserting truth as a defense and also included a counterclaim against the creditor alleging tortious interference with a promised inheritance. The bankruptcy court entered a final order dismissing the defamation claim and finding for the debtor on her counterclaim. Even though 28 U.S.C. §157(b)(2)(C) specifically lists counterclaims by the estate against persons filing claims against the estate as core proceedings, the Supreme Court on appeal held that the bankruptcy court lacked constitutional power to enter a final order on the tortious interference claim because it was a dispute involving private not public rights.

After *Stern*, it is clear that Congress's creation of the core/non-core distinction in 28 U.S.C. §157(b) as a basis for determining the bankruptcy court's power to enter a final order or judgment is inadequate. An action may be designated as core in §157(b), but if it involves a dispute over private not public rights notwithstanding such designation, the bankruptcy court will still be unable to enter a final order or judgment and will be limited to entry of proposed findings and conclusions for review by the district court. There is thus a "gap" between the jurisdictional scheme of §157(b) and what the Constitution allows because of the private versus public rights distinction involving Article III and Article I courts. Claims that trigger this analysis are sometimes called **Stern claims** and are said to raise **gap jurisdiction** scrutiny.

Gap jurisdiction (also called **Stern claims**) Issues arising in a bankruptcy case that although core are deemed to lie outside the referral jurisdiction of the bankruptcy court because they involve a determination of private rather than public rights.

For some time after *Stern*, chaos reigned in bankruptcy practice as judges and practitioners struggled to determine the scope of that holding and which core proceedings (other than counterclaims by debtors against creditors of the estate raising state law claims like tortious interference as in *Stern* itself) might trigger gap jurisdictional issues. However, two subsequent Supreme Court decisions have gone a long way toward restoring order in this area.

In *Executive Benefits Ins. Agency v. Arkison*, 134 S. Ct. 2165, 2174 (2014), the Supreme Court confirmed that a bankruptcy court that lacks constitutional jurisdiction to enter a final judgment in a core proceeding may nonetheless utilize the procedure set forth in 28 U.S.C. §157(c)(1) for non-core proceedings and enter proposed findings of fact and conclusions of law in cases involving Stern claims. And in *Wellness International Network, Ltd. v. Sharif*, 135 S. Ct. 1932 (2015), the Court held that the procedure set forth in 28 U.S.C. §157(c)(2), which authorizes a bankruptcy court to enter a final order or judgment in a non-core proceeding where all parties consent, *is* available in cases involving Stern claims.

As a result of *Wellness*, procedures have been adopted in federal districts around the country whereby parties are required to specify whether they consent to the bankruptcy court entering a final order or judgment in any matter that may be non-core or any core matter that might otherwise raise *Stern* jurisdictional issues.

3. Personal Jurisdiction of the Bankruptcy Courts

Personal jurisdiction The due process requirement that a defendant have sufficient minimum contacts with a forum to enable a court in that forum to enter a final order binding on a named defendant.

Whereas subject matter jurisdiction has to do with the power of a court to hear and decide a particular kind of case, **personal jurisdiction** (also called **in personam** jurisdiction) has to do with the power of a court to enter a binding order on a particular defendant.

The notion of personal jurisdiction in state courts is intertwined with the demands of **due process** required by the Fourteenth Amendment to the U.S. Constitution. In order to satisfy the dictate of due process, it must be shown that **minimum contacts** exist between a defendant and the forum state such that maintenance of the suit does not offend traditional notions of fair play and substantial justice. *International Shoe Co. v. Washington*, 326 U.S. 310, 316 (1945). Thus, in the ordinary civil lawsuit in state court, the personal jurisdiction question is determined by whether the defendant resides in or is otherwise present in the forum state, or has consented to the jurisdiction of the forum state or, if neither present nor consenting, has sufficient minimum contacts with the forum state to satisfy due process.

When the civil suit is filed in a federal court, Rule 4(k)(1)(A) of the Federal Rules of Civil Procedure generally limits in personam jurisdiction of the federal courts over defendants to that which a court of general jurisdiction in the forum state would have, so the minimum contacts analysis proceeds just as it would if the case was pending in a state court of the forum state. Significantly, however, FRCP 4(k)(1)(C) states that the general rule established by FRCP 4(k)(1)(A) making in personam jurisdiction of federal courts co-extensive with that of the courts of the forum state does not apply where extraterritorial service of process is "authorized by a federal statute." And Bankruptcy Rule 7004(d) is just such a statute. It provides, "The summons and complaint and all other process except a subpoena can be served anywhere in the United States."

Bankruptcy Rule 7004(f) then provides:

If the exercise of jurisdiction is consistent with the Constitution and laws of the United States, serving a summons or filing a waiver of service in accordance with this rule or the subdivisions of Rule 4 F. R. Civ. P. made applicable by these rules is effective to establish personal jurisdiction over the person of any defendant with respect to a case under the Code or a civil proceeding arising under the Code, or arising in or related to a case under the Code.

Thus, the Code not only authorizes **nationwide service of process**, but such nationwide service is also made the basis for the bankruptcy court's reach of personal jurisdiction. See, e.g., *Nordberg v. Granfinanciera, S.A.*, 835 F.2d 1341, 1344 (11th Cir. 1988), rev'd on other grounds, 492 U.S. 33 (1989) ("Bankruptcy Rule 7004(d) provides for nationwide service of process and thus is the statutory basis for personal jurisdiction in this case"). This is not to say that due process is necessarily made co-extensive with service of process. Note the first phrase in Bankruptcy Rule 7004(f); even where service of process is accomplished, the exercise of jurisdiction must satisfy the due process demands of the Fifth Amendment requiring minimum contacts between the defendant and the forum. However, in bankruptcy cases the "forum" is not the particular state in which the bankruptcy court sits, it is the United States in general, and what is required to satisfy due process under the Fifth Amendment is quite different than under the Fourteenth. See, e.g., *Brown v. C.D. Smith Drug Co.*, 1999 WL 709992 (D. Del. 1999), where the court found a bankruptcy court in Delaware had personal jurisdiction over defendants in Missouri to pursue claims made by the trustee of the debtor against the defendants arising under Missouri law:

> Because the present case is "related to" a bankruptcy proceeding and because service of process was effected pursuant to a federal rule having the force of federal law, it is the Fifth, not the Fourteenth, Amendment that is at issue. The Supreme Court has not addressed whether the Due Process Clause of the Fifth Amendment also requires personal jurisdiction over out-of-state defendants to comport with notions of fairness and substantial justice; however, the majority of lower federal courts to have considered the issue have concluded that out-of-state defendants need only have minimum contacts with the United States in order to satisfy Fifth Amendment due process. In reaching this conclusion, courts have reasoned that the fairness requirement imposed by the Fifth Amendment relates only to whether the sovereign has the power to exercise jurisdiction, not to the fairness of suit in a particular forum provided by the sovereign.

Id. at *3-4.

See also *In re Tandycrafts, Inc.*, 317 B.R. 287, 289 (Bankr. D. Del. 2004) (Mexican corporation that provided trucking services from Mexico to cities in the United States and maintained a post office in Texas to receive payments had sufficient contacts with the United States to justify a bankruptcy court in Delaware asserting personal jurisdiction over it), and *In re Uni-Marts, LLC*, 399 B.R. 400 (Bankr. D. Del. 2009) (nonresident principal of debtor alleged to have committed tortious act in Pennsylvania subject to personal jurisdiction of bankruptcy court in Delaware).

4. Appellate Procedure in a Bankruptcy Case

Where the bankruptcy court exercising its referral jurisdiction enters a final judgment, the appeal lies to the district court that referred jurisdiction pursuant to 28 U.S.C. §158(a). The standard of review utilized by the district court in considering whether to reverse a final judgment entered by the bankruptcy court is de novo as to questions of law but clearly erroneous as to findings of fact and due regard is given to the opportunity of the bankruptcy court to judge the credibility of the witnesses. See, e.g., *In re Nosek*, 544 F.3d 34, 43 (1st Cir. 2008). A party unhappy with the decision of the district court may then appeal that ruling to the appropriate U.S. circuit court pursuant to 28 U.S.C. §158(d) where the same standard of review will prevail. A party unhappy with the decision of the circuit court of appeals may file an application for writ of certiorari to the U.S. Supreme Court.

Bankruptcy Appellate Panel A court made up of bankruptcy judges in a federal circuit to hear the appeal of rulings by other bankruptcy judges in that circuit in lieu of the district court. Utilized in only five federal districts.

In five federal circuits (the First, Sixth, Eighth, Ninth, and Tenth), appeals of final judgments entered by bankruptcy courts may go to a special panel of bankruptcy judges selected from the entire federal circuit instead of to the district court *if* all parties consent. These are **Bankruptcy Appellate Panels** (BAPs) authorized by 28 U.S.C. §158(b). Decisions of the BAP are appealable directly to the circuit court per 28 U.S.C. §158(d), effectively bypassing the district court.

5. Decision-Making Procedures in Bankruptcy Court

The particular procedures authorized by the Code and the bankruptcy rules for decision making in a bankruptcy case are unusual and challenging to master. In a bankruptcy case there are myriad issues that a bankruptcy judge may have to decide. The Code and the bankruptcy rules recognize two broadly different procedures for deciding those issues: Some are decided as **contested matters** and others are decided as **adversary proceedings**.

Contested Matters

Contested matter A proceeding arising in a bankruptcy case that is initiated by motion or objection or statement of intent to act.

Adversary proceedings Certain disputes defined by Bankruptcy Rule 7001 that arise in a bankruptcy case and are conducted according to procedures governing a formal civil lawsuit.

Most issues that arise in a bankruptcy case are considered contested matters and that procedure is governed by Bankruptcy Rule 9014. A contested matter is the simpler and quicker process for deciding an issue that arises in a case. It requires a hearing before the bankruptcy judge but not a full-blown trial as does an adversary proceeding. At the hearing on the contested matter, the bankruptcy judge may consider written briefs filed by the contesting parties and the oral arguments of counsel. If necessary, the court may also listen to the sworn testimony of witnesses. But contested matter procedure can become confusing because the Code and bankruptcy rules provide that some contested matters are initiated by filing a **motion**, some by filing an **objection**, and some by filing what is called a **notice of intended action** that is then followed by an objection to that intended action.

Briefly, a motion in bankruptcy procedure is essentially the same as you learned it in Civil Procedure: It is a written request made to a court seeking an order granting the moving party affirmative relief regarding the subject of the request (e.g., a motion to lift automatic stay or a motion for additional time to file bankruptcy schedules that accompany a petition). An objection is very similar. It is a written request to a court seeking an order denying another party some relief or adjusting the rights of the other party in some way in connection with the subject of the request (e.g., an objection to a debtor's claimed property exemption). Bankruptcy Rule 9013 governs the required content of motions and objections as well as who is to be served with copies.

The oddest of the three methods of initiating a contested matter is the notice of intended action. In some situations the Code and bankruptcy rules allow a party to simply give notice that it intends to take some action rather than filing a motion to obtain court permission to do it (e.g., the intent of a bankruptcy trustee to abandon property of the estate as having no value to the estate as authorized by §554 of the Code and Bankruptcy Rule 6007(a)). If a notice of intended action is given and no objection to it is made within the time allowed, the action can be taken with no formal order of the court. No hearing will be scheduled or conducted. Only if a timely objection to the intended action is made will a hearing be scheduled and held and an order entered allowing or disallowing the intended action (e.g., Bankruptcy Rule 6007(a) requires that an objection to a notice of intent to abandon property be filed and served within 14 days).

Importantly, not only are notices of intended action authorized by the Code governed by the **"after notice and a hearing"** procedure, a number of (but by no

Illustration 6-i: ADMINISTRATIVE ACTIONS ACCOMPLISHED BY MOTION, OBJECTION, OR NOTICE OF INTENDED ACTION THAT ARE SUBJECT TO THE "AFTER NOTICE AND A HEARING" PROCEDURE OF THE CODE

- Under §554 of the Code, the bankruptcy trustee may notice the intent to abandon property of the estate, "after notice and a hearing."
- Under §363(b) and Bankruptcy Rule 6004, the bankruptcy trustee may notice the intended use, sale, or lease of property of the estate in other than the ordinary course of business "after notice and a hearing."
- Under §362, a motion for relief from the automatic stay may be approved "after notice and a hearing."
- Under §324(a), a motion to remove the bankruptcy trustee for cause may be approved "after notice and a hearing."
- Under Bankruptcy Rule 9019, a motion to compromise or settle a dispute may be approved "after notice and a hearing."
- Under §§707(a) and (b), a motion to dismiss or convert a Chapter 7 case to a case under Chapter 13 or 11 on certain grounds may be approved "after notice and a hearing."
- Under §1112(b), a motion to dismiss or to convert a Chapter 11 case to a case under Chapter 7 on certain grounds may be approved "after notice and a hearing."
- Under §§1208(c) and (d), a motion to dismiss or to convert a Chapter 12 case to a case under Chapter 7 on certain grounds may be approved "after notice and a hearing."
- Under §502(b), the objection to a claim is to be decided "after notice and a hearing."
- Under Bankruptcy Rule 4003(c), an objection to a claimed exemption is to be decided "after hearing on notice," which some, but not all, courts treat as after notice and a hearing.

means all) matters properly raised by motion or objection are as well. But whereas any action authorized by the Code to be accomplished by notice of intended action will be governed by the "after notice and a hearing" procedure, only those motions and objections specifically designated as to be accomplished "after notice and a hearing" will be subject to that procedure. Thus, when a notice of intended action is authorized by the Code or where the Code specifically makes a motion or objection subject to the "after notice and a hearing" procedure, that means that written notice of the intended action, motion, or objection *must* be given to parties required to receive it. However, a hearing on the matter will be conducted *only* if a party in interest objects within the time allowed to the intended action or to the relief requested in the motion or objection. If no party in interest contests the motion or objection made or no party in interest objects to the notice of intent in the time allowed for a response, either the court will grant the motion or objection, or the action that was the subject of the notice of intent can go forward. A list of various actions accomplished by motion, objection, or notice of intended action that are subject to the "after notice and a hearing" procedure is set out in Illustration 6-i.

It bears repeating that the "after notice and a hearing" procedure *only* applies to matters properly raised by motion, objection, or notice of intended action when the Code specifically says that it does. If a matter is properly raised by motion, etc., but is not made specifically subject to the "after notice and a hearing" procedure, it will be treated automatically as a contested matter and a hearing will be scheduled.

EXAMPLE

Look at the Motion for Additional Time to File Schedules, Statement of Affairs, etc., filed by Marta Carlson (Document 5 in the Carlson case file introduced in Section M below). This motion is authorized by §521(i)(3) and Bankruptcy Rule 1007(c) but it is not designated there as an "after notice and a hearing" matter. Instead, Bankruptcy Rule 1007(c) provides that the time to file can be extended by motion and for "cause shown." So when Marta's lawyer files this motion, it automatically will be treated as a contested matter and a hearing will be scheduled as the notice of motion indicates. Compare the Objection to Claim filed by the bankruptcy trustee in Marta's case (Document 28 in the Carlson case file). Section 502(b) designates this as an "after notice and a hearing" matter, so if the creditor, Pine Ridge Nursing Home, does not file a written response to the objection to its claim, the court may rule on the objection without a hearing. All this is explained to Pine Ridge in the notice of objection and hearing accompanying the objection.

P-H 6-k: Review the Motion for Order of Contempt for Violation of Automatic Stay filed by Marta Carlson against Pine Ridge Nursing Home and the accompanying Notice of Motion (Document 24 in the Carlson case file). Can you tell by looking at the Notice of Motion whether this motion is subject to the "after notice and a hearing" procedure?

Adversary Proceedings

Issues that arise in a bankruptcy case that are not designated as contested matters will be resolved instead as adversary proceedings. An adversary proceeding is essentially a formal civil lawsuit initiated within the bankruptcy case and decided there. Part VII of the Bankruptcy Rule (Rules 7001 through 7087) apply in adversary proceedings and those rules incorporate most of the formal FRCP to such actions. Thus, they must be commenced by filing a complaint and accomplishing service of process. Motions under FRCP 12 or 56 may be made; counterclaims, cross claims, and third-party complaints filed; formal discovery had; and formal trials conducted.

One rule of civil procedure that is not incorporated into Part VII of the Bankruptcy Rule governing adversary proceedings is FRCP 38 regarding the demand for a jury trial. That is because per 28 U.S.C. §157(e) a bankruptcy court is authorized to conduct a jury trial when demanded *only* when all parties consent and the district court specifically designates the bankruptcy court to conduct that trial. Generally, when a party to a bankruptcy dispute desires a jury trial, the reference will be revoked either at the request of a party or by the district court acting *sua sponte* and the case tried to a jury by the district court.

Bankruptcy Rule 7001 lists the types of disputes that must be treated as adversary proceedings, and they are summarized in Illustration 6-j.

Illustration 6-j: DISPUTES THAT MUST BE RESOLVED AS ADVERSARY PROCEEDINGS

- A proceeding to bar the debtor from receiving a discharge in bankruptcy or to revoke a discharge previously granted
- A proceeding to declare a particular debt nondischargeable
- A proceeding to determine the validity, extent, or priority of a lien on property of the debtor
- A proceeding to recover money or property from a third party
- A proceeding to obtain an injunction or other equitable relief
- A proceeding to obtain approval to sell property in which both the debtor and a nondebtor have an interest
- A proceeding to subordinate a creditor's claim or interest to other claims
- A proceeding to revoke an order confirming a plan in a Chapter 11, 12, or 13 case

H. ▶ Other Important Players in a Bankruptcy Case

Needless to say, the bankruptcy judge is a key player in the administration of a bankruptcy case. But here let's briefly consider the other key actors in the drama.

The party that files the bankruptcy proceeding is of course the debtor. In the forms that the debtor files in connection with the bankruptcy case all creditors must be identified and those creditors are certainly significant actors in the bankruptcy drama. Beginning with the petition in bankruptcy the debtor files to begin the case, all documents in a bankruptcy case are filed with the office of the **bankruptcy court clerk** in most federal districts, though a few require filing with the district court clerk. The court clerk is the administrative officer for the court in which the case is pending. The clerk's office will maintain all records regarding the case and is responsible for sending out various notices regarding actions taken or to be taken in the case (e.g., notice to listed creditors of the filing of the case, notice of the first meeting of creditors, notice of upcoming hearings on disputed matters).

Bankruptcy court clerk Administrative officer of the bankruptcy court whose office receives and maintains all filings in pending cases and sends out required notices.

Most debtors hire attorneys to help them prepare and file the necessary papers and to represent them throughout the bankruptcy proceeding. Creditors also often retain attorneys to assist them in processing their claim through the bankruptcy proceeding. These debtor's attorneys and creditor's attorneys are certainly key players in the case.

In most but not all federal districts, there is another government official involved in bankruptcy cases: the **U.S. Trustee** (never to be confused with the bankruptcy trustee discussed below). The U.S. Trustee is given responsibilities under §586 of the Code and various bankruptcy rules to perform duties such as:

U.S. Trustee Government official appointed in most federal districts responsible for overseeing bankruptcy trustees and monitoring pending bankruptcy cases.

- to determine who is eligible to serve as a bankruptcy trustee;
- to oversee and monitor the work of the bankruptcy trustees;
- to monitor pending cases; and
- to make recommendations to the bankruptcy judge on contested issues that arise before the bankruptcy judge.

The U.S. Trustee program is administered and overseen by the U.S. Department of Justice (www.usdoj.gov/ust). In North Carolina and Alabama, there are no U.S. Trustees, but bankruptcy administrators perform the same tasks in those states, overseen by the Administrative Office of the U.S. Courts (www.uscourts.gov).

In most bankruptcy cases (and always in Chapter 7 and 13 cases), as soon as the petition is filed, beginning the case, the U.S. Trustee (or the bankruptcy judge in districts where there is no U.S. Trustee) will appoint a **bankruptcy trustee** to administer the case. As we shall see later, the bankruptcy trustee is given broad powers under the Code and is responsible to the court and to the creditors of the estate for his actions. Sometimes the bankruptcy trustee finds it appropriate to hire an attorney to represent him in some proceeding in the case, like an adversary proceeding.

Bankruptcy trustee Individual appointed by the bankruptcy court to administer a bankruptcy case according to the Code and to provide accounting to the court.

In the course of administering a bankruptcy case, the services of a number of different professionals and businesspeople may be utilized by the bankruptcy trustee, the debtor, or creditors. Those may include auctioneers, realtors, appraisers, insurance agents, bankers, economists, accountants, and repossession and storage services.

Party in interest One who has sufficient interest in a matter before the court to be deemed to have standing to be heard by the court on the matter.

A number of Code provisions refer to the right of a party in interest to take some action in a bankruptcy case. For example, §502(a) authorizes a **party in interest** to object to the claim filed in a case by a creditor of the debtor. Bankruptcy Rule 4003(b) authorizes a party in interest to object to a debtor's claim of exempt property. Curiously, neither the Code nor the bankruptcy rules define who is a party in interest, leaving courts to make that determination based on the particular right to act being granted by the Code. But, generally speaking, a party in interest is a person or entity who has sufficient interest in a matter before the court to be deemed to have standing to be heard by the court on the matter. For most matters, the debtor, the bankruptcy trustee, the U.S. Trustee or bankruptcy administrator, and creditors or other third parties (e.g., persons who are not in bankruptcy but who are jointly liable with the bankruptcy debtor on certain obligations or nondebtor owners of an entity in bankruptcy) who may be affected by the action taken will be deemed parties in interest.

I. ▸ Electronic Filing in Bankruptcy Court

Every bankruptcy court in the country now employs electronic case filing instead of paper filing for all or most documents. A few courts still require the petition itself to be filed in paper, but most have gone completely paperless. The various parties in interest to the bankruptcy case will use **electronic case filing**: The petition, supporting schedules, statements and lists, motions, objections, reports, applications, etc., are submitted electronically, the court's orders are entered electronically, and all notices and other communications from the court to case participants are distributed electronically. Needless to say, lawyers and those assisting them in the bankruptcy field must become familiar with the e-filing system utilized in bankruptcy courts.

The electronic system used in all bankruptcy courts is known as **Case Management/Electronic Case Files** (CM/ECF). The way the system works is that documents created in a lawyer's office by word processing software are saved in a portable document format (PDF). The attorney then logs in by computer to the local court's CM/ECF system using a log-in name and password provided by the court clerk, identifies the case in which the document is to be submitted, attaches the PDF file containing the document to be filed in the case, and presses a "submit" button. In the clerk's office, the CM/ECF immediately sends the lawyer's office by e-mail an **electronic receipt** confirming receipt of the document filed. The receipt can be saved or printed by the lawyer's office. The CM/ECF system allows 24-hour, 7-day-a-week filing for case participants. Once a party has made an appearance in a pending case, the party then receives electronic notification of case activity (other filings, entry of orders, etc.) by means of a **Notice of Electronic Filing** (NEF), which allows the recipient a one-time look at the document filed and the opportunity to copy or save it. The system also allows the payment of filing fees by credit card.

In order to be able to view all documents in a case (any case) at any time and as frequently as desired (rather than the one-free-look allowed by CM/ECF), lawyers must subscribe to **Public Access to Court Electronic Records** (PACER). Members of the public may also subscribe to PACER. To avoid having to pay for access to electronic records, lawyers or members of the public may also go physically to the office of the bankruptcy court clerk and view files on screens made available there. A charge will be made, however, for documents copied.

Notices from the bankruptcy court to case participants is also done electronically through **Electronic Bankruptcy Noticing** (EBN), which allows attorneys and others to receive notices from the bankruptcy court by e-mail link, e-mail with PDF attachment, or fax.

P-H 6-l: Go to www.pacer.gov/ and choose one or more of the video tutorials available there explaining how the CM/ECF, PACER, and EBN systems work.

If a party in interest is entitled to notice or service of a motion or other document filed in the case but does not participate in CM/ECF, notice or service on that party must then be accomplished by sending a paper copy by first class mail or hand delivery. Typically, a party filing a motion or other document will utilize electronic filing and then examine the electronic receipt to make sure all parties entitled to notice received it by the electronic filing. If any party did not receive it electronically, that party is then served with paper copy by hand delivery or first class mail. The **certificate of service** included on the document filed will advise that service was accomplished electronically or by hand delivery or mailing.

J. Bankruptcy Software

Attorneys who represent bankruptcy debtors utilize **bankruptcy software** programs to expedite the preparation of the numerous schedules and statements required in every case. A good software program can save time for the debtor's attorney and assist legal professionals by automatically filling in repetitive information, performing calculations, and formatting the documents in a way that complies with electronic filing requirements. Some programs allow for unlimited use and some are limited to one-time use. A number of bankruptcy software

Illustration 6-k: A SAMPLING OF BANKRUPTCY SOFTWARE PROVIDERS

- BestCase (www.bestcase.com)
- TopForm (www.fastcase.com/topform/)
- BankruptcyPRO (www.bankruptcy-pro.com/)
- Bankruptcy Case Software (www.nationallawforms.com/bankruptcy/software-bankruptcy.htm)
- NextChapter (www.nextchapterbk.com/)
- New Hope (www.bankruptcysoftware.com)
- Blumberg Blankrupter (www.blumberg.com/)
- Standard Legal (www.standardlegal.com)

---

providers and their web sites are listed in Illustration 6-k. A number of the web sites provide a free online demonstration and/or permit the free download of forms that can be used for demonstration purposes.

K. Web-Based Resources for Learning About Bankruptcy

There are a number of excellent web sites providing free access to current news and information of interest to bankruptcy professionals, as well as bankruptcy-specific legal research. Illustration 6-l lists a number of these.

Illustration 6-l: USEFUL BANKRUPTCY INFORMATION SITES

The Bankruptcy Code, Rules, Forms, and General Information:

- Title 11 of the U.S. Code (http://uscode.house.gov/ or www.law.cornell.edu/uscode/text/11)
- Rules of Bankruptcy Procedure (www.uscourts.gov/rules-policies/current-rules-practice-procedure)
- Official Bankruptcy Forms (www.uscourts.gov/forms/bankruptcy-forms)
- Administrative Office of the Federal Courts' Federal Judiciary Home Page (www.uscourts.gov)
- United States Trustees Program (administered by the U.S. Department of Justice) (www.usdoj.gov/ust)
- Administrative Office of the U.S. Courts, Bankruptcy Basics (www.uscourts.gov/services-forms/bankruptcy/bankruptcy-basics)
- Electronic Bankruptcy Noticing Center (www.ebnuscourts.com)
- Cornell University Law School's Legal Information Institute's Bankruptcy Information Page (www.law.cornell.edu/search/site/bankruptcy)
- FindLaw's Internet Guide to Bankruptcy Law (http://corporate.findlaw.com/law-library/the-internet-guide-to-bankruptcy-law.html)
- Bernstein's Dictionary of Bankruptcy Terminology (https://bernsteinlaw.com/resources/dictionary-of-bankruptcy-terminology/)
- NOLO Bankruptcy in Your State (www.thebankruptcysite.org/topics/bankruptcy-your-state)

Organizations Concerned with Bankruptcy Practice:

- American Bankruptcy Institute (www.abiworld.org)
- National Bankruptcy Conference (www.nationalbankruptcyconference.org)
- The American College of Bankruptcy (www.amercol.org)
- National Association of Bankruptcy Trustees (www.nabt.com/faq.cfm)

- National Association of Chapter 13 Bankruptcy Trustees (www.nactt.com)
- National Association of Consumer Bankruptcy Attorneys (www.nacba.org)
- National Consumer Law Center (www.nclc.org)
- The Commercial Law League of America (www.clla.org)

Bankruptcy Blogs and Other News and Information Sites:

- ABA Journal Blawg Directory (www.abajournal.com/blawgs/topic/bankruptcy+law)
- ABI Blog Exchange (http://blogs.abi.org/)
- Bankruptcy Attorneys on the Web (www.bestcase.com/bkattys.htm)
- Bankruptcy Law Network (www.bankruptcylawnetwork.com)
- Bankruptcy Lawyers Blog (http://blog.startfreshtoday.com)
- Bankruptcy Litigation Blog (http://www.bankruptcylitigationblog.com/)
- LAW 360: Bankruptcy (www.law360.com/bankruptcy)
- Becker & Posner Blog (http://www.becker-posner-blog.com/)
- The Atlanta Bankruptcy Blog (www.thebklawyer.com/thebkblog/)
- Credit Slips Blog on Credit, Finance and Bankruptcy (www.creditslips.org/creditslips)
- The Daily Bankruptcy News (http://bkinformation.com/news/dailynews.htm)
- SheppardMullin Finance and Bankruptcy Blog (http://www.bankruptcylawblog.com/)
- In the (Red)® Business Bankruptcy Blog (http://bankruptcy.cooley.com/)
- New Generation Research (NGR) (http://newgenerationresearch.com/)
- Wall Street Journal Bankruptcy Beat Blog (http://blogs.wsj.com/bankruptcy/)
- Weil Bankruptcy Blog (http://business-finance-restructuring.weil.com/)

L. ▶ Alternatives to Filing for Bankruptcy Relief

A debtor facing the prospect of filing for bankruptcy relief may seek legal advice as to possible alternatives. There may be several, although whether they are preferable to filing for bankruptcy relief when all consequences are considered is for the debtor and his attorney to decide.

1. The Assignment for Benefit of Creditors

In an **assignment for the benefit of creditors** (commonly called an ABC), the debtor conveys his nonexempt property to an assignee, often a lawyer or accountant, who will liquidate the property and then distribute the proceeds pro rata to the claimants. The ABC does not discharge the balance remaining on any indebtedness, as a bankruptcy proceeding might, and so its usefulness is limited. But if the debtor has reason to believe that his creditors will not file suit to collect the deficiencies, the ABC may be a cheaper, quicker route than bankruptcy.

EXAMPLE

If Abe Mendoza is in danger of being sued by his various creditors and losing his home to foreclosure, he may well be a candidate for a Chapter 7 liquidation bankruptcy. But before filing that, he might consider transferring all his non-exempt assets to a cooperating attorney as part of an ABC. This would be especially appealing if the exempt property statutes would allow him to exempt the equity in his home and his other creditors would not likely file suit against him for any deficiencies owed after the liquidation and distribution of his other assets.

In some states, ABCs are regulated by statute and, in others, by common law decision. Once the property has been assigned by the debtor to the assignee as part of an ABC, the property is exempt from execution by individual creditors (other than creditors secured in the property). And, typically, the assignee of the ABC takes title to the property as a lien creditor with a superior claim to any prior unsecured claim to the property (see UCC Article 9, §§309(12) and 317). Some states allow the ABC to prefer some creditors over others in the distribution, while others forbid any such preference.

2. The Composition and Extension Agreements

Composition agreement A contract made between a debtor and his or her creditors pursuant to which partial payment is made and accepted in full satisfaction of all claims.

As discussed in Chapter Four, Section E, in connection with the rising debt settlement industry, a **composition agreement** is a private, voluntary arrangement between a debtor and his or her creditors, pursuant to which the creditors agree to take a stated partial payment in full satisfaction of their claims. The composition agreement is often accompanied by an **extension agreement**, whereby the participating creditors agree to give the debtor additional time to make the agreed payments. Like the ABC, the composition and extension agreements might be preferable to bankruptcy in terms of cost and time, but they are contingent on the cooperation of creditors. The agreements will typically stipulate that if the debtor defaults on any promised payment, the original debt will be revived in full.

EXAMPLE

TTI (Case Study #3; see Illustration 1-c) might well be a candidate for an expensive, drawn-out Chapter 11 reorganization in order to stay in business. Before filing that Chapter 11, though, the attorney for TTI might contact the company's various creditors to see if a composition agreement might be reached with all of them, including an extension of time to repay scheduled debt. Some or all of the creditors might even be willing to take less than 100 cents on the dollar of debt owed in exchange for having the company avoid a Chapter 11, which will be expensive and drawn out for them as well.

There is a hidden danger for consumer debtors in a composition plan that includes a write-off by the creditor of a portion of the debt owed. Unless the written-off portion of the debt was legitimately contested, it may be deemed taxable income to the debtor for tax purposes.

EXAMPLE

Assume Pearl Murphy (or a CCA acting on her behalf) finally convinces CCME that she simply cannot pay the full $1,200 she owes it and the creditor agrees to take three payments of $300 each ($900 in total) in full satisfaction of the debt. Pearl may be surprised later to receive an IRS Form 1099-C listing the $300 forgiven portion of the debt as reportable taxable income to her.

3. The Receivership

Receivership Proceeding in which a person is appointed to take control of a debtor's property and manage it under court supervision.

A **receivership** action is a lawsuit in which the court is asked to appoint a **receiver** to take legal control of the debtor's property, along with the power to manage that property. In most states, receivership actions are controlled by statute, and there are also some federal receivership laws, notably for railroads and securities businesses. Receiverships can be chosen voluntarily by qualifying debtors, but creditors can also seek the receivership for dissenting debtors. This is an important aspect of receivership law for creditors of certain debtors like churches, political committees, or other nonprofit organizations, which cannot be forced into involuntary bankruptcy.

Like an ABC, once the assets of the debtor are placed in receivership, they are immune from attachment or execution by individual creditors. The receiver will act on behalf of all the creditors to liquidate the assets and distribute the proceeds pro rata to creditors. Disputes among creditors as to the validity of their claims will be resolved by the court that ordered the receivership.

4. The Bulk Sale Transfer Act

Bulk Sale Transfer Act Article 6 of the UCC providing a nonbankruptcy procedure for the sale of all of the assets of a business outside the ordinary course of business. Repealed in most states.

A handful of states have adopted Article 6 of the Uniform Commercial Code (UCC), which is known as the **Bulk Sale Transfer Act** (BSTA). The BSTA requires a business that is selling "all or substantially all" of its assets "outside of the ordinary course of business" to give prior written notice of the sale to its creditors. A sale outside the ordinary course of business is usually defined as the sale of more than one-half of a business's assets at one time or to one buyer. In a typical BSTA statute, the notice given to creditors must advise of the assets being sold, the price, the identity of the buyer, the expected payout (i.e., "pro rata" or "share and share alike"), and must be given at least 45 days before the sale. The creditors of the seller then have six months following the date of the sale to submit claims to the buyer of the business assets. The buyer is then required to pay the creditors of the seller on some fair basis.

The BSTA became popular at the beginning of the twentieth century as a means to avoid a businessperson selling all of his assets and disappearing without paying his business creditors. With the popularity of the Uniform Enforcement of Foreign Judgments Act, which we considered in Chapter Five, the need for the BSTA has diminished and today only a few states still have it. The BSTA applies primarily to the payment of unsecured creditors. Creditors secured in property of the debtor/seller will typically have the right to repossess the pledged property in the event of default so it is not available to be sold in the bulk sale.

| P-H 6-m: | Determine if your state still has the BSTA in its version of the UCC. |

5. Dissolution of a Business Entity Under State Law

Every state has laws under which a business entity such as a corporation, limited liability company, or partnership may simply dissolve and go out of business. Such laws contain detailed procedures for the entity to elect **dissolution**, give notice to the state and to creditors, wind up its business, and distribute its assets in an orderly fashion and according to a strict priority (e.g., creditors of a business entity being dissolved under state law are to be paid in full before any distribution of assets to owners). Creditors of a business entity may have standing to compel an **involuntary dissolution** on certain grounds such as insolvency of the entity, failure to pay its debts as they come due, or fraud by management. The state may also have authority to compel dissolution for failure of the entity to pay taxes and assessments or other grounds.

P-H 6-n: Locate the statutes in your state governing the dissolution of a corporation. What is the procedure to be followed by a corporation seeking to dissolve? What notices must be given? What are the timeframes for wind up and distribution? What is the order of priority for distribution of assets? Can creditors compel an involuntary dissolution under your state laws? Can the state itself compel dissolution?

P-H 6-o: Do not confuse the right of creditors to compel a debtor corporation or partnership to dissolve under state law with the right of a creditor to sue the entity to collect past-due debt. And do not confuse either of those with the right of one or more shareholders of a corporation to bring a **derivative action** under state law on behalf of the corporation against the officers and directors for mismanagement. Such derivative actions are based on the **fiduciary duty** (duty of care, loyalty, and honesty) that officers and directors owe to the corporation and to its shareholders. Check the corporate act of your state and determine the procedure for the filing of a shareholder derivative action.

P-H 6-p: What about corporate creditors? Can those creditors initiate a derivative action against the officers and directors on behalf of the corporation? Most states say yes, when the corporation becomes insolvent. See, e.g., *N. Am. Catholic Educ. Programming Foundation, Inc. v. Gheewalla*, 930 A.2d 92, 101-102 (Del. 2007) (when a corporation becomes insolvent, its creditors replace the shareholders as the principal constituency injured by breaches of duty, reducing the entity's value). See if your state follows *Gheewalla* on this point either by statute or case law.

P-H 6-q: If creditors of an insolvent corporation can file a derivative action against the officers and directors on behalf of an insolvent corporation, does it follow that those officers and directors owe a fiduciary duty to each individual creditor of the corporation that would permit each such corporate creditor to sue the officers and directors for breach of that duty? The majority rule is no. See *Gheewalla*, supra, at 101-102 (no fiduciary duty owed by officers and directors to individual corporate creditors who are in a position to protect their interests through contract with the corporation). See if your state follows *Gheewalla* on this point.

P-H 6-r: The universal rule that when a business entity is being dissolved under state law, all creditors of the entity are to be paid in full before there is any distribution of assets to owners is known as the **trust fund doctrine**. For an interesting case discussing the doctrine, see *Sanford v. Waugh & Co., Inc.*, 328 S.W.3d 836 (Tenn. 2010). Does the trust fund doctrine apply even before dissolution begins if an entity is insolvent? Does it apply to a technically solvent corporation that chooses to dissolve? Does the doctrine allow a creditor of a corporation to gain possession of corporate property conveyed to a third party in violation of the doctrine if that third party was not a good faith purchaser for value? Does your state recognize the trust fund doctrine by case law or statute?

6. Dissolution or Reorganization of Certain Businesses Denied the Right to File for Bankruptcy Relief

The Code denies some types of businesses the right to file for bankruptcy relief—commercial banks chartered by a state or by the federal government, credit unions, savings banks, savings and loan associations, and insurance companies being notable examples per Code §109(b)(2). A railroad company can file for Chapter 11 reorganization but not for Chapter 7 liquidation per Code §§109(b)(1) and (d). So what happens when such an entity needs reorganization or liquidation and is denied the right to file under the Code? The financial institutions mentioned will be placed into involuntary receivership by the chartering authority—the state banking commissioner in the case of state-chartered institutions; the Office of the Comptroller of the Currency for national banks; and the Office of Thrift Supervision for federal savings banks, credit unions, and savings and loan associations. Insurance companies and railroads are dealt with under state law.

M. ▶ Introduction to the Consumer Bankruptcy Case Studies

To learn how Chapter 7 and Chapter 13 consumer bankruptcy cases work we will reference two fictitious but realistic case studies: the Chapter 7 case of Marta Rinaldi Carlson filed in 2016 in a U.S. bankruptcy court in Minnesota and the Chapter 13 case of Roger and Susan Matthews filed in 2016 in a U.S. bankruptcy court in Pennsylvania. (Minnesota and Pennsylvania were selected for use in these case studies primarily because neither state has opted out of the federal exemptions for individual filers, as will be discussed in Chapter Eight.)

In Appendix A you will find the original assignment memorandum prepared by a supervising attorney directing a paralegal to assist in filing the Chapter 7 case for Marta Carlson and the case file index illustrating the various filings that were subsequently made in the course of Ms. Carlson's Chapter 7 case. On the companion web site to this textbook at http://aspenlawschool.com/books/Parsons_Debt4e/, you will find all the documents listed in the Carlson case file index.

In Appendix B you will find the original assignment memorandum prepared by a supervising attorney directing a paralegal to assist in filing a Chapter 13 case for the Matthews, the initial prepetition budget for the Matthews, and the case file index illustrating the various filings that were made in the course of the Matthews' Chapter 13 case. On the companion web site to this textbook at http://aspenlawschool.com/books/Parsons_Debt4e/, you will find all the documents listed in the Matthews case file index.

As we work our way through the upcoming material on Chapter 7 and Chapter 13 bankruptcies, we will reference the Carlson and Matthews files frequently as a practical way of illustrating the points being made—much as a supervising attorney training you in an area of the law might show you a closed case file to learn from. Some of the Carlson and Matthews filings are reproduced in the text itself for more convenient scrutiny, but all of the filings in both cases are available to you on the companion web site so bookmark it for easy reference.

CHAPTER SUMMARY

The U.S. Bankruptcy Code governs the bankruptcy options and procedures for most individuals and entities in this country. The Code authorizes six different types of bankruptcy proceedings for qualifying debtors and contains definitions and rules for case administration and procedure. Business bankruptcies are cases filed by corporations (including limited liability companies) and partnerships or by individuals with primarily business debts. Nonbusiness or consumer bankruptcies are cases filed by individuals with primarily consumer debts. Consumer debt is debt incurred for primarily a personal, family, or household purpose.

Since 1980 bankruptcy filings have soared from 300,000 to more than a million per year though they have levelled off to just below a million in recent years. More than 95 percent of filings are consumer bankruptcies. Divorce, lost employment, and unmanageable medical bills are the primary causes of consumer bankruptcy though easy availability of credit and irresponsible spending play a role as well.

The Federal Rules of Bankruptcy Procedure supplement the Code and provide detailed guidance on numerous procedural aspects of a bankruptcy case. Congress has also approved Official Bankruptcy Forms for use in bankruptcy cases across the country. Each bankruptcy court has its own local rules that further supplement the Code, the Bankruptcy Rules, and the official forms. Though the Code itself governs the administration of a bankruptcy case, questions regarding the nature or extent of an interest in property claimed by a debtor or creditor are governed by state law.

U.S. bankruptcy courts are located in each of the 94 federal districts across the country and function as adjuncts of the U.S. district courts in those districts by reason of referral jurisdiction. Bankruptcy courts are authorized to enter final orders and judgments in core proceedings that arise in a bankruptcy case but can only enter proposed findings and conclusions for consideration by the district judge in non-core proceedings unless the parties consent. The appeal of a final order or judgment entered by a bankruptcy court is first to the district court and then to the appropriate circuit court of appeal of bankruptcy appellate panel in districts that have them.

Some matters that arise for decision in a bankruptcy case are treated as contested matters initiated by motion, objection, or notice of intended action. Other matters must be initiated formally as adversary proceedings in which most of the Federal Rules of Civil Procedure apply. All bankruptcy courts around the country utilize electronic case filing.

In addition to the U.S. bankruptcy judge, key players in a bankruptcy case include the debtor, the creditors, the bankruptcy trustee, the U.S. Trustee, attorneys and other professionals who may be hired by these various parties in interest and the bankruptcy clerk's office.

Alternatives to bankruptcy include an assignment for benefit of creditors where the debtor assigns nonexempt property to a designated assignee, who liquidates it and distributes the proceeds to creditors pro rata. A composition agreement is a private voluntary arrangement between a debtor and his or her creditors pursuant to which the creditors agree to take a stated partial payment in full satisfaction of their claims. A receivership is a court proceeding in which the court is asked to appoint a receiver to take legal control of the property of the debtor along with the power to manage that property. A few states still retain the Bulk Sale Transfer Act (BSTA), Article 6 of the Uniform Commercial Code, which provides a statutory scheme for a business selling all or substantially all of its assets outside the ordinary course of business. Every state provides a statutory or regulatory scheme for the dissolution of a business entity and federal or state law provide schemes for the dissolution of entities not qualified to file as debtors under a chapter of the bankruptcy code.

REVIEW QUESTIONS

1. Where are the bankruptcy laws located within the U.S. Code? What authorizes Congress to enact bankruptcy legislation? Why do we call the Bankruptcy Code a system of compulsory debt adjustment? What is meant by the phrase "fresh start" in the bankruptcy context?
2. Identify and briefly describe the six different types of bankruptcy proceedings authorized under the Code. Indicate which types are most and least commonly filed. Identify and briefly describe the contents of the other chapters of the Code.
3. Explain the difference between a business bankruptcy filing and a consumer bankruptcy filing.
4. How does the Bankruptcy Code define consumer debt?
5. Approximately what percentage of bankruptcy filings nationwide are consumer bankruptcies? Business bankruptcies?
6. Describe the circumstances of the typical consumer debtor who files for Chapter 7 relief.
7. What are local court rules?
8. What title of the U.S. Code contains the Bankruptcy Code? What title of the U.S. Code defines the various federal districts around the country where U.S. bankruptcy courts are located? What title of the U.S. Code contains federal criminal laws related to bankruptcy?
9. What is meant by referral jurisdiction?
10. What is the difference in a bankruptcy court's power to enter an order or final judgment in a core versus a non-core proceeding in a bankruptcy case?
11. What is a Stern claim? What is gap jurisdiction?

12. What is the significance of the Supreme Court's 2015 decision in *Wellness*?

13. When a bankruptcy court enters a final judgment on a matter, to which court can the ruling be appealed?

14. What is the significance of personal jurisdiction of the bankruptcy court being based on the Fifth rather than the Fourteenth Amendment? Is due process still required? What does due process mean under the Fifth Amendment?

15. Explain the difference between an assignment for benefit of creditors and a composition/extension agreement?

WORDS AND PHRASES TO REMEMBER

Administrative Office of the
  U.S. Courts (AO)
adversary proceeding
ancillary proceeding
Article I courts
Article III courts
assignment for the benefit of creditors
  (ABC)
Bankruptcy Abuse Prevention and
  Consumer Protection Act of 2005
  (BAPCPA)
Bankruptcy Act
Bankruptcy Appellate Panels (BAPs)
Bankruptcy Code
bankruptcy court clerk
bankruptcy judge
bankruptcy referee
bankruptcy software
bankruptcy trustee
Bankruptcy Reform Act of 1994
Bulk Sale Transfer Act (BSTA)
business bankruptcy case
Case Management/Electronic Case
  Files (CM/ECF)
certificate of service
clean slate
composition agreement
consumer bankruptcy case
consumer debt
contested matter
core proceeding
cross-border case
debt adjustment proceeding
debtor (in bankruptcy)

derivative action
discharge proceeding
due process
Electronic Bankruptcy Noticing (EBN)
electronic case filing
electronic receipt
evidentiary hearing
extension agreement
family farmer
family fisherman
Federal Rules of Bankruptcy
  Procedure
Federal Rules of Civil
  Procedure (FRCP)
Federal Rules of Evidence (FRE)
fiduciary duty
fresh start
gap jurisdiction
involuntary dissolution
legislative courts
liquidation proceeding
local court rules
minimum contacts
motion
nationwide service of process
non-core proceeding
Notice of Electronic Filing (NEF)
notice of intended action
objection
Official Bankruptcy Forms
party in interest
personal jurisdiction
plan of reorganization
private rights

Public Access to Court Electronic
    Records (PACER)
public rights
proposed findings and conclusions
receiver
receivership
referral jurisdiction

reorganization proceeding
revoke the reference
Sabbatical Year
Stern claim
trust fund doctrine
U.S. Trustee
Year of Jubilee

TO LEARN MORE: A number of TLM activities to accompany this chapter are accessible on the companion web site for this textbook at http:// aspenlawschool.com/books/Parsons_Debt4e/.

Chapter Seven:

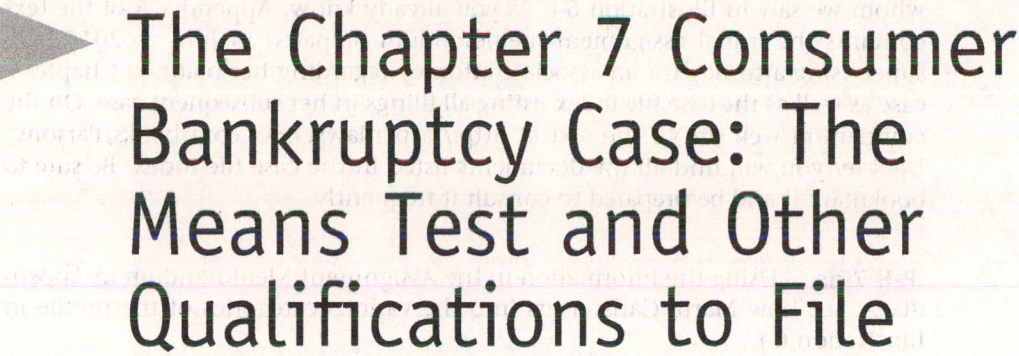

The Chapter 7 Consumer Bankruptcy Case: The Means Test and Other Qualifications to File

KEY CONCEPTS

- The basic qualifications to file a Chapter 7 case are set out in §109 of the Code
- An individual debtor cannot file a Chapter 7 case who has received a discharge in Chapter 7 within eight years or a discharge under Chapter 13 within six years
- An individual with primarily consumer debts cannot file a Chapter 7 case unless he or she satisfies the means test
- An individual debtor filing a Chapter 7 case must receive prepetition credit counseling

Introduction

Approximately 70 to 75 percent of all bankruptcy filings nationwide are Chapter 7 liquidation cases and about 98 percent of those are consumer bankruptcies filed by individuals with nonbusiness debt. Chapter 7 is a liquidation proceeding in which a bankruptcy trustee is authorized to locate and take possession of the nonexempt assets of the debtor, **liquidate** (sell) those assets, and distribute the proceeds to creditors of the estate per a distribution formula established by the Code. Either an individual or an entity may be a Chapter 7 debtor but, as we will see, that is not to say that *any* individual or entity can file for the Chapter 7 fresh start.

Most debts remaining unpaid after the distribution and not formally reaffirmed by the debtor in the bankruptcy proceeding will be permanently **discharged** by order of the bankruptcy court. Thus, the basic idea in a Chapter 7 is that the debtor makes all of her nonexempt assets available to her creditors in exchange for a discharge of most of her unpaid debts. We will learn, however, that some debts cannot be discharged in a Chapter 7 and some Chapter 7 cases do not result in any discharge at all.

For our study of Chapter 7 in this and the next four chapters, we will focus on the case of an individual who in many ways fits the profile of a typical debtor whom we saw in Illustration 6-f. As you already know, Appendix A of the text contains the initial assignment memorandum prepared in June 1, 2016 by a supervising attorney for an associate attorney regarding her planned Chapter 7 case as well as the case file index listing all filings in her subsequent case. On the companion web site to the text at http://aspenlawschool.com/books/Parsons_Debt4e/ you will find all the documents listed in the case file index. Be sure to bookmark it and be prepared to consult it frequently.

P-H 7-a: Using the information in the Assignment Memorandum in Appendix A, see how Marta Carlson fits into the various categories of the profile in Illustration 6-f.

A. ▶ The Basic §109 Qualifications

Section 109(a) of the Code provides that "only a person that resides or has a domicile, a place of business, or property in the United States, or a municipality" can file as a debtor under any of the six chapters of the Code. Regarding who can file for Chapter 7 relief, §109(b) says any "person" can, and "person" is defined by §101(41) to include both individuals (natural persons) and business entities, such as corporations (including limited liability companies) and partnerships, but not governmental units. However, §109(b) specifically prohibits railroads, insurance companies, commercial banks chartered by federal or state governments, savings banks, savings and loan associations, credit unions, and some other financial institutions from filing for Chapter 7 liquidation relief. (As discussed in Chapter Six, Section L, such entities are liquidated under state law or specialized federal regulation, and railroads may file for Chapter 11 reorganization.)

EXAMPLE

If Abe Mendoza (Case Study #2, Illustration 1-b) decides to file for Chapter 7 relief, he will qualify under §109 because he is an individual. If Tomorrow Today, Inc. (TTI) (Case Study #3, Illustration 1-c) decides to file for Chapter 7 relief, it will qualify because it is a corporation. But if Security Trust Bank, which holds the mortgage on Abe Mendoza's home, decides to file for Chapter 7 relief, it will not qualify and will have to seek relief under separate statutory authority involving both state and federal law. If the municipality of Capital City itself decides to file for Chapter 7 relief, it will not qualify and will have to seek relief under Chapter 9 of the Code.

B. ▶ The §727(a) Prior Discharge Limitations

Pursuant to §727(a), a debtor qualified to file a Chapter 7 case under §109 cannot receive a discharge in Chapter 7 if he or she previously received a discharge in a Chapter 7 or Chapter 11 case within *eight years* preceding the filing of the petition or in a Chapter 13 or Chapter 12 case within *six years*.

EXAMPLE

If Marta Carlson had received a discharge in Chapter 13 in YR-4, she could not now file under Chapter 7. As we will see when we study Chapter 13 bankruptcy, she might be able to file another Chapter 13 but not a Chapter 7 because of the six-year prohibition.

C. ▶ The Prepetition Credit Counseling Requirement for All Individual Debtors

Prepetition Events occurring prior to the filing of a petition for relief in bankruptcy.

Section 109(h)(1) of the Code provides that no individual (either individual consumer or individual business debtors) may be a debtor under any chapter of the Code unless, within 180 days before filing the petition (**prepetition**), the individual receives "an individual or group briefing" (which can be by phone or Internet) from "an approved nonprofit **budget and credit counseling agency**" that outlines "the opportunities for available credit counseling" and assists the individual "in performing a related budget analysis." The court may grant an exemption to the prepetition credit counseling requirement based on the debtor's sworn statement that he needed emergency relief and did not have time to complete it prepetition, but the exemption expires 30 days *after* the petition is filed, and so the counseling must be completed by that time. The briefing is not required if the court determines that the debtor is incapacitated (mentally), disabled (physically), active military in a combat zone, or where the U.S. Trustee determines that there are insufficient approved agencies to provide the required counseling. Debtors themselves must pay any costs associated with this required counseling but the cost is not prohibitive and the counseling can often be accomplished by phone or Internet.

Fortunately, not just any credit counseling agency can provide these required services (see the discussion of CCAs and the current problems with some of them in Chapter Four, Section E). CCAs desiring to provide these services to debtors sufficient to satisfy the §109(h)(1) requirement must be *nonprofit* and certified by the U.S. Trustee, and to become and remain certified they must successfully complete in-depth preliminary and subsequent examinations by the office of the U.S. Trustee. The current list of CCAs certified by the U.S. Trustee to provide these services can be seen at www.usdoj.gov/ust/eo/bapcpa/ccde/cc_approved.htm. The bankruptcy court clerks are also required by §111 of the Code to maintain a list of approved CCAs.

The individual debtor's compliance with the prepetition credit counseling requirement is demonstrated by the completion of Part 5 of the individual debtor's Chapter 7 petition, Official Form 101. (See Document 2 in the Carlson case file.)

D. ▶ The §707(b) Means Test and Presumption of Abuse Limitation for Individual Consumer Debtors

1. Introduction to the Means Test and the Presumption of Abuse

Recall that in Chapter Six, Section C, we distinguished between **business bankruptcy cases** and **consumer bankruptcy cases**, defining the latter as the

Consumer debt Debt incurred for personal, family, or household purposes.

Presumption of abuse The presumption of inappropriate filing of a Chapter 7 case for the debtor who fails the *means test*.

Means test A test for Chapter 7 filers introduced by BAPCPA intended to determine whether the debtor has sufficient *disposable income* to enable the debtor to repay some or all of his debts in a Chapter 13 case.

case of an individual with primarily consumer debts. And recall that §101(8) of the Code defines **consumer debt** as "debt incurred by an individual primarily for a personal, family or household purpose."

Section 707(b)(1) authorizes the court to dismiss a Chapter 7 case filed by a consumer debtor if it finds that the granting of relief would be an "abuse of the provisions of this chapter." Section 707(b)(2)(A)(i), as amended by BAPCPA, raises a **presumption of abuse** if the debtor fails a **means test** created by that section. The means test essentially compares the debtor's average monthly income to the median family income of a household the size of the debtor's in the state where the debtor resides. If the debtor's income is equal to or less than the state median income figure, the debtor can file for Chapter 7 relief. If the debtor's income (calculated with the debtor's spouse if the spouse is not filing) exceeds the state median income figure for a household of similar size, the presumption of abuse arises and the debtor cannot file for Chapter 7 relief. Debtor's income from the following sources is included in the calculation:

- wages, salary, tips, bonuses, overtime, and commissions
- gross income from a business, profession, or a farm
- interest, dividends, and royalties
- rental and real property income
- regular child support or spousal support
- unemployment compensation
- pension and retirement income
- workers' compensation
- annuity payments
- state disability insurance

Debtor's income from the following sources is excluded from the calculation:

- tax refunds
- Social Security retirement benefits
- Social Security Disability Insurance
- Supplemental Security Income
- Temporary Assistance for Needy Families

The object of the means test is to identify **"can-pay" debtors** and to funnel them into Chapter 13 filings, where the excess disposable income is made available to pay all or a portion of the debtor's debts.

HIGHLIGHTED CASE ●

IN RE HLAVIN

394 B.R. 441 (Bankr. S.D. Ohio 2008)

[The Debtors accumulated debt from general expenses and pursuing unsuccessful business ventures. They also purchased a home and obtained a loan secured by a first mortgage. They later obtained a second loan secured with a second mortgage on the home. As of the petition date, the aggregate amount owed on the home loans combined with other consumer debts would constitute 59 percent of the Debtors' liabilities if the home loans were classified as consumer debts. The number of their nonconsumer debts exceeds the number of their consumer debts regardless of how the loans are classified. After the Debtors' petition in Chapter 7 bankruptcy was filed, the U.S. Trustee (UST) requested dismissal of their bankruptcy case for abuse under 11 U.S.C. §707(b)(1), which applies only if the Debtors have "primarily consumer debts." The Debtors responded with a motion for partial summary judgment raising two issues: whether a debt secured by a mortgage in a debtor's real property is a consumer debt within the meaning of §101(8) and what standard should be applied to determine whether the debts are primarily consumer debts.]

OPINION: Hoffman, Jr., Bankruptcy Judge

The Debtors argue that the Home Loans—which they concede were incurred primarily for a Consumer Purpose—are non-consumer debts because they are secured by the Home Mortgages. The UST's response is that a debt incurred primarily for a Consumer Purpose is a consumer debt even though it is secured by a debtor's real property.

Second, the Debtors argue that they have primarily non-consumer debts because their business-related debts outnumber their consumer debts and were the primary cause of their filing for bankruptcy. For its part, the UST contends that numerosity should not be outcome determinative. Rather, the UST argues, an individual's liabilities should be found to be primarily consumer debts if the dollar amount of consumer debt exceeds 50% of the total debt.

Under §707(b)(1), the Court "may dismiss a case filed by an individual debtor under [Chapter 7] whose debts are primarily consumer debts if it finds that the granting of relief would be an abuse of the provisions of [Chapter 7]." 11 U.S.C. §707(b)(1). To determine whether the Debtors' liabilities are primarily consumer debts, the Court must first decide the threshold issue of whether a loan incurred primarily for a Consumer Purpose is a consumer debt if it is secured by a debtor's real property.

The Bankruptcy Code defines consumer debt as "debt incurred by an individual primarily for a personal, family, or household purpose." 11 U.S.C. §101(8). Nothing in §101(8) suggests that a debt meeting this definition nonetheless mutates into a non-consumer debt merely because it is secured by real property. Rather, under the plain language of §101(8), a debt incurred by an individual primarily for a Consumer Purpose is a consumer debt regardless of whether it is secured or unsecured. And the Court must follow the plain statutory language. Indeed, the majority of courts have held that a debt secured by a debtor's real property is a consumer debt if it is incurred primarily for a Consumer Purpose.

The Debtors do not argue that the Home Loans were incurred for a business purpose or for any purpose other than a Consumer Purpose. Nor do they argue that the language of §101(8) is ambiguous. Rather, their argument rests on statements made by two members of Congress that "[a] consumer debt does not include a debt to any extent the debt is secured by real property." 124 Cong. Rec. H11,089 (daily ed. Sept. 28, 1978) (statement of Rep. Edwards); 124 Cong. Rec. S17,406 (daily ed. Oct. 6, 1978) (statement of Sen. DeConcini). The Debtors also rely on several older decisions in which courts, following this legislative history, have held that a debt secured by the debtor's real property is never a consumer debt. *See In re Restea,* 76 B.R. 728, 734 (Bankr. D.S.D. 1987); *In re Stein,* 18 B.R. 768, 769 (Bankr. S.D. Ohio 1982). Legislative history, however, does not override the plain language of a statute. *See, e.g., U.S. v. Ron Pair Enters., Inc.,* 489 U.S. 235, 241 (1989) ("The language before us expresses Congress' intent with sufficient precision so that reference to legislative history is hardly necessary.").

In light of the plain language of §101(8)—and the Supreme Court pronouncements regarding the application of clear statutory language—the Court concludes that loans incurred primarily for a Consumer Purpose are consumer debts even though they are secured by mortgages on a debtor's real estate. Thus, the Court finds that the Home Loans are consumer debts.

Anticipating the Court's ruling that the Home Loans constitute consumer obligations, the Debtors contend that they nonetheless have primarily non-consumer debts because the number of such debts exceeds the number of their consumer liabilities. Taking the contrary position, the UST argues that the Debtors have primarily consumer debts because the aggregate dollar amount of their consumer debt exceeds 50% of their total liabilities.

Courts have interpreted the phrase "primarily consumer debts" in several different ways. The majority view is that a debtor's liabilities are primarily consumer debts if the aggregate dollar amount of such debts exceeds 50% of the debtor's total liabilities.

There are a number of minority approaches. Some courts consider the relative dollar amount of consumer and non-consumer debt and, if those amounts are "approximately equal," the number of consumer and non-consumer debts as well. See *In re Bell,* 65 B.R. 575, 577-78 (Bankr. E.D. Mich. 1986). Other courts hold that a debtor has primarily consumer debts only if the dollar amount of such debts exceeds 50% of the debtor's total liabilities and the consumer debts outnumber the non-consumer debts. See *In re Vianese,* 192 B.R. 61, 68 (Bankr. N.D.N.Y. 1996). Still other courts hold that a debtor has primarily consumer debts only if the amount of consumer debt actually being discharged and not reaffirmed exceeds 50% of the debtor's total liabilities. See *Restea,* 76 B.R. at 734.

[The court concludes it cannot find that the meaning of the phrase "primarily consumer debts" as used in §707(b)(1) is unambiguous and must look to legislative history, policy rationales, and the context in which the statute was passed.]

In summarizing the context in which §707(b)(1) was passed, and the policy rationale motivating its enactment, the Sixth Circuit has explained:

> Section 707(b) was among the consumer credit amendments to the Bankruptcy Code enacted in 1984. These amendments were passed in response to an increasing number of Chapter 7 bankruptcies filed each year by non-needy debtors. Under prior practice, aside from potential §523(a) exceptions, §707(a) dismissals, and §727(a) objections to discharge, debtors enjoyed an unfettered right to a "fresh start" under Chapter 7, in exchange for liquidating their nonexempt assets for the benefit of their creditors. Section 707(b) introduces an additional restraint upon a debtor's ability to attain Chapter 7 relief. Bankruptcy judges now have discretion to dismiss a consumer case when the filing is abusive.
>
> In essence, §707(b) allows a bankruptcy court to deal equitably with the unusual situation where an unscrupulous debtor seeks to enlist the court's

assistance in a scheme to take unfair advantage of his creditors; it serves notice upon those tempted by unprincipled accumulation of consumer debt that they will be held to at least a rudimentary standard of fair play and honorable dealing.

In re Krohn, 886 F.2d 123, 125-26 (6th Cir. 1989). In short, §707(b)(1) was passed in part to protect creditors against abusive Chapter 7 filings.

Based on the context in which §707(b)(1) was passed and the policy concerns it was intended to address, the Court adopts the majority view and concludes that a debtor has "primarily consumer debts" if the aggregate amount of his or her consumer debt exceeds 50% of the total debt. To hold otherwise and determine the primary nature of debts based on the relative number of consumer versus non-consumer obligations could lend itself to pre-bankruptcy manipulation. For example, a debtor with total consumer debts of $50,000 owed on five credit cards could attempt to avoid §707(b)(1)'s abuse analysis by consolidating the $50,000 of debt onto one credit card, leaving the debtor with only one consumer debt to weigh against a larger number, but lesser amount, of non-consumer debts. If this same debtor owes several small tax debts to multiple taxing authorities—which the Sixth Circuit has held is non-consumer debt, . . . then the debtor would have a greater number of non-consumer debts than consumer debts. If a bankruptcy court were to determine the nature of the debts based on numerosity, then the debtor would not be subject to scrutiny under §707(b)(1)—contrary, it would seem, to Congress's aim of addressing the perceived abuse of Chapter 7. By contrast, if the primary nature of a debtor's liabilities is measured by the relative amount of debt, then a prospective debtor planning ahead to avoid a Chapter 7 dismissal might do so by paying down consumer debt, consistent with the policies behind §707(b)(1).

For these reasons, the Court concludes that the appropriate method for ascertaining §707(b)(1)'s applicability is to determine whether the aggregate amount of a debtor's consumer debt exceeds 50% of his/her total liabilities. If so, then §707(b)(1) applies. Application of this methodology here leads to the inescapable conclusion that the Debtors' obligations are primarily consumer debts.

For the foregoing reasons, the Court holds that a loan incurred primarily for a Consumer Purpose is a consumer debt even if it is secured by a mortgage on a debtor's real property. The Court also concludes that a debtor has "primarily consumer debts" if the aggregate amount of consumer debt exceeds 50% of the total debt. The Court accordingly finds that the Debtors are not entitled to judgment in their favor as a matter of law.

POST-CASE FOLLOW-UP

Determine whether your federal district or circuit has ruled on whether a debt secured by a home mortgage can be considered a consumer debt for purposes of §101(8). If so, does it follow the majority rule announced in *Hlavin*? Has your district or circuit ruled on the question of how to determine whether a debtor's debts are "primarily consumer debts" within the meaning of §707(b)(1)? If so, does it follow the approach utilized in *Hlavin*, one of the alternative approaches mentioned in that case, or some other approach?

In re Hlavin: Real Life Applications

1. Why was it the debtors and not the bankruptcy trustee who argued that their home mortgage is not a consumer debt?

2. Would the result in *Hlavin* have been different if the loans secured by the debtors' home had originally been taken out to fund a failed business venture? What if they had been taken out for home improvement or a vacation but then actually used to fund a business venture? Would it matter if they told the bank the money was being borrowed for home improvement or vacation but intended it to be used to fund a business venture? What if the home loans had been taken out for mixed personal/business reasons?

3. If the debtors in *Hlavin* had 30 different consumer debts totaling $75,000 and only one business debt totaling $76,000, would that court find that they had "primarily consumer debts" under §707(b)(1)? What would be the result if a court utilized one of the alternative approaches to this question mentioned in *Hlavin*?

Entity debtors and individual debtors whose debts are primarily business rather than consumer debts are not subject to the means test. Veterans suffering from a 30 percent or higher permanent disability and whose indebtedness arose primarily during active duty or while performing a homeland defense activity are expressly exempted from the means test, as are certain members of the National Guard and armed forces reserves who were called to duty for at least 90 days following September 11, 2001, pursuant to the **National Guard Reservists Debt Relief Act of 2008.**

EXAMPLE

> The vast majority of Marta Carlson's debt, as described in the Assignment Memorandum in Appendix A, will qualify as consumer debt. One exception might be the indebtedness to Dreams Come True Finance Company, which was incurred to fund a business venture for her ex-husband. Since Marta is an individual consumer debtor, she will have to satisfy the means test of §707(b) in order to maintain a Chapter 7 filing.

P-H 7-b: What happens if a debtor files a petition in Chapter 13 (which requires a calculation of disposable income for purposes of a Chapter 13 plan but does not involve a means test) and then converts the case to one in Chapter 7? Will that debtor have to satisfy the means test in order to proceed in Chapter 7? There is actually a split on this question with a majority of courts following what is called the "common sense" view that the means test must still be satisfied because Congress intended all Chapter 7 debtors to do so (see, e.g., *In re Kellett*, 379 B.R. 332 (Bankr. D. Or. 2007), but a strong minority follow the "plain language" view, saying that the debtor converting a Chapter 13 case over need not satisfy the means test because, literally read, §707(b) only requires the test in consumer cases "filed" under Chapter 7 and a converted Chapter 13 case was not filed under Chapter 7 (see, e.g., *In re Layton*, 480 B.R. 392 (Bankr. M.D. Fla. 2012)). How have the bankruptcy or district courts of your federal district or circuit decided this issue?

To determine if the presumption of abuse arises in the consumer debtor's Chapter 7 case the debtor must complete Official Bankruptcy Form 122A-1, **Chapter 7 Statement of Your Current Monthly Income** (all official bankruptcy forms are available at www.uscourts.gov/forms/bankruptcy-forms).* If the debtor claims exemption from having to satisfy the presumption of abuse because his or her debts are not primarily consumer debts or because of qualifying military service, the debtor must still complete Form 122A-1 but will attach Statement of Exemption from Presumption of Abuse Under §707(b)(2) (Form 122A-1Supp) to the form.

If Form 122A-1 demonstrates that the nonexempt consumer debtor's current monthly income is below the applicable median income, that debtor's filing does not raise the presumption of abuse; that debtor can proceed in Chapter 7. However, if the debtor's Form 122A-1 demonstrates that the debtor's current monthly income is higher than the applicable median income figure, then the debtor must also complete Form 122A-2, **Chapter 7 Means Test Calculation** to determine if the presumption of abuse arises. This one- or two-step process for running the presumption of abuse gauntlet is illustrated in the following sections of this chapter.

The means test and the forms used to complete it are new with BAPCPA and many questions concerning how it works remain unanswered. As we work through Marta Carlson's Form 122-A, we will look at a number of recent cases beginning to interpret the test. Additionally, the U.S. Trustee Program has issued its own Statement on Legal Issues Arising Under the Chapter 7 Means Test that can be accessed at www.justice.gov/sites/default/files/ust/legacy/2015/03/03/ch7_line_by_line.pdf and can be consulted with profit as we venture through Form 122A.

2. Comparing the Debtor's Current Monthly Income to the State Median Family Income Using Form 122A-1

Current monthly income The monthly income of a consumer debtor calculated by averaging the debtor's income from all sources during the six months preceding the filing of the petition.

Median family income State-by-state income statistics compiled by the U.S. Census Bureau based on household size and adjusted annually.

As already stated, the means test for determining whether the presumption of abuse arises in a consumer debtor's case is a one- or two-step process. As a first step the debtor completes Form 122A-1 to compare the debtor's annualized **current monthly income** (CMI) to the annualized **median family income** for a similar size household in the debtor's state of residence. Section 707(b)(7) provides that if the debtor's current monthly income is equal to or less than the applicable median family income, no presumption of abuse arises and the means test is satisfied for that debtor. Marta Carlson's Form 122A-1 is

---

*Note: The official forms used in this discussion and in the accompanying bankruptcy case studies are those in use in 2016 when the fictitious Chapter 7 case of Marta Carlson was filed. The bankruptcy forms are frequently amended, however, and consequently the ones used here may not be what is used currently when you read this.

set out in Illustration 7-a and can also be seen as Document 19 in her case file available on the companion web site at http://aspenlawschool.com/books/ Parsons_Debt4e/.

The median family income numbers are published by the **U.S. Census Bureau** by state and household size and are updated annually.[†] The web site of the U.S. Trustee Program (at www.justice.gov/ust/means-testing) sets forth the Census Bureau's current tables for median family income and you should bookmark this site.

P-H 7-c: Our fictitious Chapter 7 client, Marta Carlson, resided in Minnesota and filed her bankruptcy case there. There are three persons in Marta's household and her bankruptcy case was filed in June 2016. Go to the U.S. Trustees web site (at www.justice.gov/ust/means-testing) and locate the Census Bureau's current tables for median family income for a household of three in the state of Minnesota as of June 2016. This is the median family income figure that was used on her Form 122A-1 to compare with her annual income to determine if she passed the means test. The median income figures from the Census Bureau are adjusted annually and Marta's case was filed using the correct median income figure for Minnesota as of June 2016. If Marta's case was being filed in Minnesota today, what would the relevant median income figure be for a household of three? If Marta was a resident of your state, what would the relevant median income figure be today?

To determine the debtor's annual income, we first calculate the debtor's current monthly income (CMI), defined in §101(10A) to include the average monthly income from all sources that the debtor has received during the six months preceding the filing of the petition (known as the **look back period**), regardless of whether such income is taxable as well as any amounts paid by a third party for the household expenses of the debtor. The sixth month to be included in the look back period is the month immediately preceding the date the case is filed.

EXAMPLE

If a Chapter 7 petition is filed on September 15, the applicable look back period for calculating the debtor's CMI will be income from all sources received from March through August of that year. Income from those six months will be averaged to arrive at the current monthly income figure. So if the debtor had income totaling $26,400 during the look back period, the applicable CMI will be $4,400 ($26,400 divided by six). Marta Carlson filed her Chapter 7 petition on June 6, 2016 (see Document 2 in the Carlson case file) so her look back period is December 2015 through May 2016.

The debtor's CMI is calculated in Part 1 of Form 122A-1 (see Illustration 7-a).

---

† **Note:** Since the median income figures from the Census Bureau are adjusted annually, Marta's form uses the correct median income figure for Minnesota as of June 2016, but that figure may be different when you read this.

Illustration 7-a: MARTA CARLSON'S FORM 122A-1

Fill in this information to identify your case:

Debtor 1 Marta   Rinaldi   Carlson
          First Name   Middle Name   Last Name

Debtor 2
(Spouse, if filing) First Name   Middle Name   Last Name

United States Bankruptcy Court for the: District of Minnesota

Case number 16-7-XXXX
(If known)

Check one box only as directed in this form and in Form 122A-1Supp:

☑ 1. There is no presumption of abuse.

☐ 2. The calculation to determine if a presumption of abuse applies will be made under *Chapter 7 Means Test Calculation* (Official Form 122A–2).

☐ 3. The Means Test does not apply now because of qualified military service but it could apply later.

☐ Check if this is an amended filing

Official Form 122A—1

Chapter 7 Statement of Your Current Monthly Income   12/15

Be as complete and accurate as possible. If two married people are filing together, both are equally responsible for being accurate. If more space is needed, attach a separate sheet to this form. Include the line number to which the additional information applies. On the top of any additional pages, write your name and case number (if known). If you believe that you are exempted from a presumption of abuse because you do not have primarily consumer debts or because of qualifying military service, complete and file *Statement of Exemption from Presumption of Abuse Under § 707(b)(2)* (Official Form 122A-1Supp) with this form.

Part 1:	**Calculate Your Current Monthly Income**

1. **What is your marital and filing status?** Check one only.

   ☑ **Not married.** Fill out Column A, lines 2-11.

   ☐ **Married and your spouse is filing with you.** Fill out both Columns A and B, lines 2-11.

   ☐ **Married and your spouse is NOT filing with you.** You and your spouse are:

   ☐ **Living in the same household and are not legally separated.** Fill out both Columns A and B, lines 2-11.

   ☐ **Living separately or are legally separated.** Fill out Column A, lines 2-11; do not fill out Column B. By checking this box, you declare under penalty of perjury that you and your spouse are legally separated under nonbankruptcy law that applies or that you and your spouse are living apart for reasons that do not include evading the Means Test requirements. 11 U.S.C. § 707(b)(7)(B).

Fill in the average monthly income that you received from all sources, derived during the 6 full months before you file this bankruptcy case. 11 U.S.C. § 101(10A). For example, if you are filing on September 15, the 6-month period would be March 1 through August 31. If the amount of your monthly income varied during the 6 months, add the income for all 6 months and divide the total by 6. Fill in the result. Do not include any income amount more than once. For example, if both spouses own the same rental property, put the income from that property in one column only. If you have nothing to report for any line, write $0 in the space.

	Column A Debtor 1	Column B Debtor 2 or non-filing spouse
2. **Your gross wages, salary, tips, bonuses, overtime, and commissions** (before all payroll deductions).	$ 3,888.88	$
3. **Alimony and maintenance payments.** Do not include payments from a spouse if Column B is filled in.	$ 0.00	$
4. **All amounts from any source which are regularly paid for household expenses of you or your dependents, including child support.** Include regular contributions from an unmarried partner, members of your household, your dependents, parents, and roommates. Include regular contributions from a spouse only if Column B is not filled in. Do not include payments you listed on line 3.	$ 0.00	$

5. **Net income from operating a business, profession, or farm**

	Debtor 1	Debtor 2
Gross receipts (before all deductions)	$	$
Ordinary and necessary operating expenses	– $	– $
Net monthly income from a business, profession, or farm	$ 0.00	$	Copy here →	$ 0.00	$

6. **Net income from rental and other real property**

	Debtor 1	Debtor 2
Gross receipts (before all deductions)	$	$
Ordinary and necessary operating expenses	– $	– $
Net monthly income from rental or other real property	$ 0.00	$	Copy here →	$ 0.00	$

7. **Interest, dividends, and royalties** $ 0.00 $

Debtor 1   Marta   Rinaldi   Carlsor   Case number *(if known)* 16-7-XXXX
_____   First Name   Middle Name   Last Name

	Column A Debtor 1	Column B Debtor 2 or non-filing spouse

8. **Unemployment compensation**

   Do not enter the amount if you contend that the amount received was a benefit
   under the Social Security Act. Instead, list it here: .... ↓

For you	$_____
For your spouse..............................	$_____

   Column A: $ 0.00   Column B: $_____

9. **Pension or retirement income.** Do not include any amount received that was a
   benefit under the Social Security Act.

   Column A: $ 0.00   Column B: $_____

10. **Income from all other sources not listed above.** Specify the source and amount.
    Do not include any benefits received under the Social Security Act or payments received
    as a victim of a war crime, a crime against humanity, or international or domestic
    terrorism. If necessary, list other sources on a separate page and put the total below.

    _____ $ 0.00 $_____

    _____ $ 0.00 $_____

    Total amounts from separate pages, if any.   + $ 0.00   + $_____

11. **Calculate your total current monthly income.** Add lines 2 through 10 for each
    column. Then add the total for Column A to the total for Column B.

    $ 3,888.88   + $_____   = $ 3,888.88

    Total current
    monthly income

Part 2:   Determine Whether the Means Test Applies to You

12. **Calculate your current monthly income for the year.** Follow these steps:

    12a.   Copy your total current monthly income from line 11.....................................Copy line 11 here → $ 3,888.88

           Multiply by 12 (the number of months in a year).   x 12

    12b.   The result is your annual income for this part of the form.   12b. $ 46,666.56

13. **Calculate the median family income that applies to you.** Follow these steps:

    Fill in the state in which you live.   MN

    Fill in the number of people in your household.   3

    Fill in the median family income for your state and size of household. .... 13. $ 80,900.00

    To find a list of applicable median income amounts, go online using the link specified in the separate
    instructions for this form. This list may also be available at the bankruptcy clerk's office.

14. **How do the lines compare?**

    14a. ■ Line 12b is less than or equal to line 13. On the top of page 1, check box 1, *There is no presumption of abuse.*
            Go to Part 3.

    14b. ☐ Line 12b is more than line 13. On the top of page 1, check box 2, *The presumption of abuse is determined by Form 122A–2.*
            Go to Part 3 and fill out Form 122A–2.

Part 3:   Sign Below

By signing here, I declare under penalty of perjury that the information on this statement and in any attachments is true and correct.

✗ /s/ Marta Rinaldi Carlson   ✗ _____
_____
Signature of Debtor 1   Signature of Debtor 2

Date 06/17/2016   Date _____
     MM / DD / YYYY   MM / DD / YYYY

If you checked line 14a, do NOT fill out or file Form 122A–2.

If you checked line 14b, fill out Form 122A–2 and file it with this form.

Official Form 122A-1   **Chapter 7 Statement of Your Current Monthly Income**   page **2**

Determining Marta's current monthly income during her applicable look back period is a fairly simple calculation since she is the sole debtor and currently has only one source of income, her salary from TTI. According to the Assignment Memorandum in Appendix A, her annual salary during 2015 was $40,000 ($3,333.28 per month). Beginning January 1, 2016 her salary was increased to $48,000 per year or $4,000 per month. So her total income during the lookback period was $23,333.28 ($3,333.28 for December 2015 plus $20,000 for the first five months of 2016). Averaged over the six months of the look back period that is $3,888.88 per month and that is the figure she enters on Line 2 of her Form 122A-1.

But calculating the debtor's CMI is not always simple. If a husband and wife file a joint petition, then the income of both spouses must be reported in Columns A and B of Part 1 respectively. If a married debtor files, but a spouse from whom the debtor is either living separately or is legally separated does not, the debtor must check the appropriate box on Line 1 of the form and the income of the nonfiling spouse need not be reported. But if a married debtor files and a spouse living in the same household and from whom the debtor is not legally separated does not file, the debtor must check the appropriate box on Line 1 of the form and include the nonfiling spouse's income in column B of Part 1 of the form. There is a presumption in the latter circumstance, but not the former, that the income of the nonfiling spouse is available to support the debtor's household. If in fact any of the reported income of the nonfiling spouse is not available on a regular basis to help with household expenses of the debtor or the debtor's dependents, that will be reported if necessary on Form 122A-2.

If Marta was receiving alimony from her ex-husband, she would report that on Line 3. If she was receiving child support payments from her ex-husband, she would include those on Line 4. If Marta owned and operated a business, she would include net income from that business on Line 5. If she was leasing a house or apartment and had rental income, she would include net income from that rental on Line 6. If she had received interest income on a savings or checking account or other source, she would include that income on Line 7. If she had lost her job but received unemployment compensation, she would report that on Line 8. If she had received pension or retirement income during the relevant six-month period, she would report that on Line 9. If Marta's parents had been helping her out with occasional payments during the past six months, those payments would have to be reported on Line 10.

P-H 7-d: Note that Social Security payments do not have to be reported on the form. Why do you think that is? If Marta was receiving regular financial assistance from her parents, would she be required to include that on Form 122A-1 and, if so, on what line? If she was receiving monthly annuity payments as part of the settlement of a prior personal injury case, would she be required to include those payments on the form and, if so, on what line?

Once the CMI itemized in Part 1 of the form has been totaled on Line 11, we then take that total to Part 2 of the form where it is annualized by being multiplied by 12 on Line 12 (CMI × 12).

EXAMPLE

> Look at Illustration 7-a or Document 19 in the Marta Carlson case file. Her total CMI from the past six months is $3,888.88 based on her salary from TTI, and we annualize that to get $46,666.56 for her annual income for purposes of the form (even though that is less than her actual current income of $48,000).

Next we determine the median family income figure for a household the size of debtor's in the debtor's state of residence using the Census Bureau's tables posted on the U.S. Trustee Program's web site mentioned above. On Line 13 of the form the debtor indicates the state in which he or she resides and the number of people in debtor's household.

Then we compare the debtor's annualized monthly income number with the median family income number for a household of debtor's size in debtor's state of residence using the Census Bureau's tables. If the debtor's annual income is *equal to* or *less than* the applicable median family income for his state, he is what practitioners call a **below median debtor** and the presumption of abuse does not arise in his case. The below median debtor has passed the means test and need not complete Form 122A-2. Instead, the debtor will merely complete the verification in Part 3 of Form 122A-1 and indicate on the first page of the form that the presumption of abuse does not arise in his case.

EXAMPLE

> Look at Illustration 7-a or Document 19 in the Marta Carlson case file. Marta's annualized monthly income is $46,666.56. The median family income for a household of three living in Minnesota as of June 2016 was $80,900. Since her annualized monthly income is less than the state median income for her size household, the presumption does not arise. She is a below median debtor and has passed the means test. She will indicate in the box on the top right side of page 1 of the form that the presumption does not arise. (Remember that the median income figures from the Census Bureau are adjusted annually and may be different from the illustration and document in the case file when you read this.)

The Code itself provides little guidance in determining who should be included in a debtor's "household" for inclusion on Line 13 of Form 122A-1 in calculating the median family income from the Census Bureau's tables as part of the means test. Should individuals living in the debtor's home but who are unrelated to the debtor by blood or marriage be included? Should individuals living there who are not dependents of the debtor be included? Should persons who are occasional but not continuous residents of the household be included?

HIGHLIGHTED CASE

IN RE HERBERT
405 B.R. 165 (Bankr. W.D.N.C. 2008)

OPINION: Hodges, Bankruptcy Judge.

This matter is before the court on the Motion to Dismiss filed by the Bankruptcy Administrator ("BA"). The sole issue presented by the BA's motion is the definition of the phrase "household size" as it is used on Form B22A [now Form 122A-1]. Having considered the pleadings and the arguments of counsel, the court denies the BA's Motion to Dismiss and finds that the debtor may claim a household size of 11 on Form B22A.

BACKGROUND

The debtor filed a Chapter 7 petition on March 28, 2008. He lives with his girlfriend and nine children. One of the children is the debtor's biological daughter with his girlfriend, and the remaining eight children are the girlfriend's children from a previous relationship.

The debtor, his girlfriend, their child, and the girlfriend's eight children have lived together for several years, and the debtor has supported the girlfriend and her children during that time because their biological father is incarcerated. The debtor has claimed all of the children as dependents on his tax returns and he has attempted to adopt the eight children, but their father will not consent to the adoption.

With respect to his bankruptcy schedules, the debtor claims all nine children as dependents on Schedule I. Specifically, he lists one as his daughter and the other eight as stepchildren. [A]lthough the debtor lists the 8 children as his stepchildren, they do not legally fall within that category because he and his girlfriend are not married. See Black's Law Dictionary 255 (8th ed. 2004) (defining stepchild as the "child of one's spouse by a previous marriage.").

In addition, the debtor claims a household size of 11 on line 14(b) of Form B22A and an applicable median family income of $111,469.00. The household size of 11 includes the debtor, his girlfriend, and the nine children living in the house.

The debtor listed Current Monthly Income for §707(b)(7) of $9,125.00, which includes $1,600.00 his girlfriend receives for food stamps each month. Therefore, his Annualized Current Monthly Income on line 13 of Form B22A is $109,500.00, which is less than the applicable median family income of $111,469.00 for a household size of 11 in North Carolina. Therefore, the debtor was not required to complete the remaining portions of Form B22A.

The BA moved to dismiss the debtor's case on the basis that the debtor is entitled to claim only a household size of 2, which includes himself and his daughter. Therefore, the BA argues that the debtor's applicable median family income should be $49,259.00, which is the applicable median family income for a household size of 2 in North Carolina. And if the debtor's applicable median family income is $49,259.00, it would appear he has sufficient disposable income to pay unsecured creditors some portion of their claims over 60 months. For that reason, the BA moved to dismiss the case pursuant to 11 U.S.C. §707(b) as an abuse of Chapter 7.

DISCUSSION

The facts in this case are not in dispute. Thus, the sole issue to be determined by the court is what number the debtor should use for household size when completing Form B22A. Unfortunately, the phrase is not defined in either the Bankruptcy Code or on Form B22A.

. . .

One of the leading cases to have considered the definition of "household size" is *In re Ellringer*, 370 B.R. 905 (Bankr. D. Minn. 2007). In *Ellringer*, the court held that the Census Bureau's definition of household is the most appropriate one because §101(39A)(A) defines median family income as "the median family income both calculated and reported by the Bureau of the Census." See *Ellringer* at 910. The Census Bureau defines "household" as "'all of the people, related and unrelated, who occupy a housing unit.'" See *Ellringer* at 911 (quoting the U.S. Census Bureau, Current Population Survey (2004), http://www.census.gov/population/www/cps/cpsdef.html). The *Ellringer* court concluded that using the Census Bureau's definition "ensures that a household in the means test will have the same number of members as the calculation of median family income." See id. at 910-911. This approach has been referred to as the "heads on beds" approach, and it does not take into consideration financial contributions of the household member, dependency, or the relationship of the household member to the debtor.

[T]he *Ellringer* court found that Congress meant two different things by family size and household size on Form B22A. In addition, the court noted that Congress elected to use the broader term "household size" on line 14(b) of Form B22A in recognition of the fact that there may be instances in which two unrelated, non-dependent individuals should be treated as a household for purposes of the means test. See id. at 911. Using the "heads on beds" approach, the court concluded that the debtor resided in a household size of 2. Included in that number was the debtor's roommate of several years with whom she owned her home as joint tenants; was jointly liable for the mortgage; had a joint bank account; and jointly owned a 2002 Ford Focus. See id. at 910.

Another leading case to interpret the phrase household size is *In re Jewell*, 365 B.R. 796 (Bankr. S.D. Ohio 2007). In *Jewell*, at the time the debtors[] filed their case, they lived with their two dependent children, an adult daughter, Crystal, her three minor children, and an adult son, Chris. Crystal and her children had lived with the debtors for approximately six months at the time the debtors filed their petition. Crystal did not help pay any of the household expenses, and the debtors provided Crystal and her children funds for medical care, gas, and other needs. See *Jewell* at 798.

The other adult child, Chris, never left home, but he attended college and had a full-time job. He neither contributed to the household expenses nor accepted financial assistance from the debtors. Finally, the two dependent children were both employed, but they did not contribute financially to the household expenses. See id.

In their second amended Form B22A, the debtors claimed a household size of 8, which resulted in their Annualized Current Monthly Income being less than the applicable median family income in Ohio. As a result, they were not required to calculate the monthly disposable income on Form B22A. The United States Trustee moved to dismiss the case for abuse pursuant to 11 U.S.C. §707(b)(2)(A) on the basis that the debtors were claiming a household size larger than that to which they were entitled. See id.

The United States Trustee argued that the court should look to the Internal Revenue Manual (the "IRM") as guidance for determining the definition of household size. See id. at 800. The IRM in turn states that the number of household members allowed for purposes of determining the applicable

National Standards should generally be the same as the number of household members allowed as dependents on a tax return. See id. The *Jewell* court rejected this approach as being too narrow because it fails to recognize those instances when a debtor may be actually providing support for a household member. See id. at 801. In that regard, the court noted that even the IRS acknowledges that there may be reasonable exceptions to the general rule stated above. See id.

The *Jewell* court also rejected the Census Bureau definition of household or the "heads on beds" approach argued by the debtors because the court found that it is inconsistent with the purpose of Form B22A, which is a "means test" designed to determine disposable income. See *Jewell* at 800. Specifically the court found that:

> Such a definition is inconsistent with the methodology and purpose of Official Form 22A for calculating a debtor['s] disposable income in that it does not include the element of a debtor's support of the person who puts the head on the bed. If a person lives in the home with the debtor but the debtor does not support that person, then inclusion of that person for purposes of calculating the applicable median family income and disposable income would give rise to a faulty calculation and would result in an inaccurate figure for both.

See id. The court also noted that the purpose for which the Census Bureau determines household size is "radically different" than the purpose of Form B22A. See id.

The *Jewell* court ultimately held that the debtors could claim a household size of 8, which included the debtors, the two dependent children, Crystal, and her three children. See id. at 802. The court concluded that Crystal and her three children should be counted as part of the household because they had been dependent on the debtors for support during the six months prior to the filing of the case. See id. at 801. On the other hand, the court did not include the debtors' adult son, Chris, who it considered to be "merely a head on a bed." See id. Although the debtors occasionally provided Chris funds, the court emphasized that he did not regularly receive financial assistance from the debtors, and they did not provide him support in the form of food and clothing. Neither did the debtors claim Chris as a dependent on their tax returns. See id.

This court is persuaded to follow the reasoning in *Jewell* because it seems the most consistent with the purpose of Form 22A, which, as the *Jewell* court noted, is a means test designed to determine a debtor's disposable income. While this court agrees with the *Ellringer* court to the extent it recognizes that there will be instances in which unrelated, non-dependent individuals should be treated as part of a household, the "heads on bed" approach adopted by that court is too broad because it includes anybody who may be residing under the debtor's roof without regard to their financial contributions to the household or the monetary support they may be receiving from the debtor. Neither does it take into consideration their dependency or relationship to the debtor. On the other hand, the court declines to adopt the standards of the Internal Revenue Manual for purposes of determining household size because they do not account for the situation in which a debtor may be supporting an individual without declaring that person as a dependent on his tax return.

And although the *Jewell* court did not delineate hard and fast guidelines for calculating household size, it looked primarily to the debtors' financial support of their household members to determine whether those individuals should be included within the household size for purposes of Form B22A. This approach recognizes that debtors have a variety of different living arrangements that defy being pigeonholed into a neat formula for purposes of defining household size. In that regard, this court notes that it will consider the issue of household size on a case by case basis with key considerations being the debtor's history of support of a household member as well as the debtor's good faith.

Applying that analysis to this case, the court finds that the debtor has a household size of eleven. The reality of this debtor's situation is that he is—and has been for several years—supporting his girlfriend, their daughter, and her eight children. That support, while voluntary, has been consistent and of long standing. It is not contrived or concocted for the purpose of this bankruptcy filing. But, rather, appears to be simply the fact of this debtor's life.

The court is satisfied that the debtor's applicable median family income should be calculated based upon that reality rather than on some artificial construct. Consequently, the court concludes that this debtor's "household size" is determined by the actual number of people supported by the debtor; and that his applicable median family income should be calculated based on a "household size" of 11.

It is therefore ORDERED that the BA's Motion to Dismiss is DENIED.

POST-CASE FOLLOW-UP

Note that the motion to dismiss the debtor's case in *In re Herbert* was brought by a bankruptcy administrator, not the U.S. Trustee. Do you recognize why that is? If not, go back and read the discussion of the U.S. Trustee position in Chapter Six, Section H.

In re Herbert: Real Life Applications

1. Which of the three methods of determining household size did the court adopt in *In re Herbert* (Census Bureau or heads on beds method, the dependency on the debtor method, or the Internal Revenue Manual method)? What was debtor's household size determined to be based on the method adopted? What would it have been under each of the other two methods mentioned?

2. Assume the law office for which you work is filing a Chapter 7 case for Roscoe Millan, a recently divorced man of 45. Roscoe has three children who live with his ex-wife but who stay with him on weekends. He pays child support to his ex-wife faithfully though under the divorce decree she claims the children as dependents on her tax return. Roscoe's brother lives with him and since the brother only works part-time, Roscoe provides all the food in the apartment

and only occasionally charges the brother rent. The brother's 14-year-old stepson has been living with them for three months as well since he had an argument with his mother, who has custody of him. He could move back in with his mom any day. What household size should you claim for Roscoe on his Form 122A-1 using the heads on beds method of calculating it? The dependency on the debtor method? The Internal Revenue Manual method?

3. The opinion in *In re Ellringer*, 370 B.R. 905 (Bankr. D. Minn. 2007), cited in *Herbert*, contains an excellent defense of the head on beds approach to determining household size. Which approach do you find most appropriate given the language of the Code and Form 122A-1 itself and the purposes to be accomplished by the means test?

---

3. The Means Test for the Above Median Debtor: Determining That Debtor's Disposable Monthly Income to Determine the Feasibility of Funding a Chapter 13 Plan Using Official Form 122A-2

If the debtor's annualized CMI is greater than the applicable median family income figure, the debtor is an **above median debtor** and must take a second step to determine whether the presumption of abuse arises in his or her case by completing Form 122A-2. The purpose of Form 122A-2 is to determine if the debtor will have sufficient **disposable monthly income** to fund a Chapter 13 reorganization plan. Specifically, we calculate the debtor's disposable income by deducting from his current monthly income a mix of actual and standardized expenses based on the **National Standards for Allowable Living Expenses** and **Local Standards for Transportation and Housing and Utilities Expenses** published by the **Internal Revenue Service**. Section 707(b)(2)(A)(i) provides that if the debtor has sufficient disposable income to pay $12,850 over five years, or as little as $214 a month to creditors (as of April 2016; the dollar amounts will be adjusted again in March 2019 per §104), the presumption of abuse arises and the case must be dismissed or converted (with the debtor's consent) to a Chapter 13 case. If the debtor does not have sufficient income to pay that much to creditors, then the means test is satisfied (the presumption of abuse does not arise).

To see how this calculation for the above median debtor works, let's assume that Marta Carlson's salary at TTI is $84,000 a year and had been during the entire look back period. In that case, she is an above median debtor and will not satisfy the means test using Form 122A-1. She will have to complete Form 122A-2 as well. Marta's alternative Form 122A-1 based on the assumption of higher income can be seen Illustration 7-b. (It can also be viewed as Extra Material Item #1 in her case file available on the companion web site at http://aspenlawschool.com/books/Parsons_Debt4e/.) (Since the median income figures are adjusted annually, if the applicable median income figure for a household of three in Minnesota exceeds the $84,000 used in her alternative Form 122A-1 seen in Illustration 7-b at the time you are reading this, then raise Marta's hypothetical income to $5,000 in excess of that number.)

Illustration 7-b: MARTA CARLSON'S FORM 122A-1 ASSUMING ANNUAL INCOME OF $84,000

Fill in this information to identify your case:

Debtor 1   Marta   Rinaldi   Carlson
            First Name   Middle Name   Last Name

Debtor 2
(Spouse, if filing) First Name   Middle Name   Last Name

United States Bankruptcy Court for the: District of Minnesota

Case number   16-7-XXXX
(If known)

Check one box only as directed in this form and in Form 122A-1Supp:

☐ 1. There is no presumption of abuse.

☑ 2. The calculation to determine if a presumption of abuse applies will be made under *Chapter 7 Means Test Calculation* (Official Form 122A–2).

☐ 3. The Means Test does not apply now because of qualified military service but it could apply later.

☐ Check if this is an amended filing

Official Form 122A—1

Chapter 7 Statement of Your Current Monthly Income

12/15

Be as complete and accurate as possible. If two married people are filing together, both are equally responsible for being accurate. If more space is needed, attach a separate sheet to this form. Include the line number to which the additional information applies. On the top of any additional pages, write your name and case number (if known). If you believe that you are exempted from a presumption of abuse because you do not have primarily consumer debts or because of qualifying military service, complete and file *Statement of Exemption from Presumption of Abuse Under § 707(b)(2)* (Official Form 122A-1Supp) with this form.

Part 1:	Calculate Your Current Monthly Income

1. **What is your marital and filing status?** Check one only.

   ☑ **Not married.** Fill out Column A, lines 2-11.

   ☐ **Married and your spouse is filing with you.** Fill out both Columns A and B, lines 2-11.

   ☐ **Married and your spouse is NOT filing with you.** You and your spouse are:

      ☐ **Living in the same household and are not legally separated.** Fill out both Columns A and B, lines 2-11.

      ☐ **Living separately or are legally separated.** Fill out Column A, lines 2-11; do not fill out Column B. By checking this box, you declare under penalty of perjury that you and your spouse are legally separated under nonbankruptcy law that applies or that you and your spouse are living apart for reasons that do not include evading the Means Test requirements. 11 U.S.C. § 707(b)(7)(B).

Fill in the average monthly income that you received from all sources, derived during the 6 full months before you file this bankruptcy case. 11 U.S.C. § 101(10A). For example, if you are filing on September 15, the 6-month period would be March 1 through August 31. If the amount of your monthly income varied during the 6 months, add the income for all 6 months and divide the total by 6. Fill in the result. Do not include any income amount more than once. For example, if both spouses own the same rental property, put the income from that property in one column only. If you have nothing to report for any line, write $0 in the space.

		Column A Debtor 1	Column B Debtor 2 or non-filing spouse
2.	**Your gross wages, salary, tips, bonuses, overtime, and commissions** (before all payroll deductions).	$ 7,000.00	$
3.	**Alimony and maintenance payments.** Do not include payments from a spouse if Column B is filled in.	$ 0.00	$
4.	**All amounts from any source which are regularly paid for household expenses of you or your dependents, including child support.** Include regular contributions from an unmarried partner, members of your household, your dependents, parents, and roommates. Include regular contributions from a spouse only if Column B is not filled in. Do not include payments you listed on line 3.	$ 0.00	$

5. **Net income from operating a business, profession, or farm**

	Debtor 1	Debtor 2			
Gross receipts (before all deductions)	$____	$____			
Ordinary and necessary operating expenses	– $____	– $____			
Net monthly income from a business, profession, or farm	$ 0.00	$____	Copy here →	$ 0.00	$____

6. **Net income from rental and other real property**

	Debtor 1	Debtor 2			
Gross receipts (before all deductions)	$____	$____			
Ordinary and necessary operating expenses	– $____	– $____			
Net monthly income from rental or other real property	$ 0.00	$____	Copy here →	$ 0.00	$____

7.	**Interest, dividends, and royalties**	$ 0.00	$____

Debtor 1 **Marta**   **Rinaldi**   **Carlson**   Case number *(if known)* _16-7-XXXX_
          First Name   Middle Name   Last Name

	Column A Debtor 1	Column B Debtor 2 or non-filing spouse
8. **Unemployment compensation** Do not enter the amount if you contend that the amount received was a benefit under the Social Security Act. Instead, list it here: .... ↓	$ _____0.00_____	$ _____
For you .... $_____		
For your spouse .... $_____		
9. **Pension or retirement income.** Do not include any amount received that was a benefit under the Social Security Act.	$ _____0.00_____	$ _____
10. **Income from all other sources not listed above.** Specify the source and amount. Do not include any benefits received under the Social Security Act or payments received as a victim of a war crime, a crime against humanity, or international or domestic terrorism. If necessary, list other sources on a separate page and put the total below.		
_____	$ _____0.00_____	$ _____
_____	$ _____0.00_____	$ _____
Total amounts from separate pages, if any.	+ $ _____0.00_____	+ $ _____

11. **Calculate your total current monthly income.** Add lines 2 through 10 for each
column. Then add the total for Column A to the total for Column B.

$ __7,000.00__ + $ _____ = $ __7,000.00__
                                              Total current
                                              monthly income

Part 2:   **Determine Whether the Means Test Applies to You**

12. **Calculate your current monthly income for the year.** Follow these steps:

   12a.   Copy your total current monthly income from line 11. .... Copy line 11 here ➜ $ __7,000.00__

             Multiply by 12 (the number of months in a year).   x 12

   12b.   The result is your annual income for this part of the form.   12b. $ __84,000.00__

13. **Calculate the median family income that applies to you.** Follow these steps:

   Fill in the state in which you live. | MN |

   Fill in the number of people in your household. | 3 |

   Fill in the median family income for your state and size of household. .... 13. $ __80,900.00__

   To find a list of applicable median income amounts, go online using the link specified in the separate
instructions for this form. This list may also be available at the bankruptcy clerk's office.

14. **How do the lines compare?**

   14a. ☐ Line 12b is less than or equal to line 13. On the top of page 1, check box 1, *There is no presumption of abuse.*
         Go to Part 3.

   14b. ■ Line 12b is more than line 13. On the top of page 1, check box 2, *The presumption of abuse is determined by Form 122A-2.*
         Go to Part 3 and fill out Form 122A-2.

Part 3:   **Sign Below**

By signing here, I declare under penalty of perjury that the information on this statement and in any attachments is true and correct.

✗ _/s/ Marta Rinaldi Carlson_____   ✗ _____
   Signature of Debtor 1   Signature of Debtor 2

Date _06/17/2016___   Date _____
    MM / DD / YYYY   MM / DD / YYYY

   If you checked line 14a, do NOT fill out or file Form 122A-2.

   If you checked line 14b, fill out Form 122A-2 and file it with this form.

Official Form 122A-1   **Chapter 7 Statement of Your Current Monthly Income**   page 2

Observe that in Lines 13 and 14 of Part 2 of Marta's alternative Form 122A-1 that assumes the higher income, her annualized current monthly income exceeds the median family income figure for her household of three. Accordingly, in the box at the top right of page one of the form she has checked the box indicating that the calculation to determine if the presumption of abuse arises in her case is to be made under Form 122A-2.

Before we look at what Marta Carlson's Form 122A-2 would look like (on the assumption she had annual income of $84,000), note that while some of the living expense standards published by the IRS and utilized in Form 122A-2 are national (food, clothing, and healthcare) others (housing, utilities, and transportation) are local. Thus, to illustrate how Form 122A-2 works, we have located our fictional Marta Carlson in Roseville, Ramsey County, Minnesota.

In addition, though many of the expenses we will see used in that form come from the IRS living expense standards, others do not. Some of the deductions allowed in Form 122A-2 are unique to the individual debtor. So some of the expenses we will see on Marta's Form 122A-2 are based on her actual expenses as described in the Assignment Memo in Appendix A to the text.

Now we're ready to consider what her Form 122A-2 as would look like had she had annual income of $84,000 and been required to file that form. You can see her hypothetical Form 122A-2 in Illustration 7-c. (It can also be viewed as Extra Material Item #2 in her case file available on the companion web site at http://aspenlawschool.com/books/Parsons_Debt4e/.) The form sets out Marta Carlson's Form 122A-2 using the applicable data for that county as of June 2016 (remember, those numbers are adjusted annually), her listed actual expenses, and a presumed income of $84,000 from TTI.

Part 1 of Form 122A-2: The Marital Adjustment

Marta does not utilize the **marital adjustment** on Lines 2-3 of Part 1 of the form because she is not married. But recall from our earlier discussion that a married debtor who does include the income of a nonfiling spouse on Form 122A-1 can adjust his or her annualized monthly income figure from that form by deducting in Part 1 of Form 122A-2 as much of the nonfiling spouse's income as is not actually made available for household expenses. The reason that the nonfiling spouse's income is not available for household expenses must be stated on Line 3 by explaining the non-household support use that was made of that income. The most common reason is that the nonfiling spouse is required to pay taxes or spousal or child support from an earlier marriage.

Part 2 of Form 122A-2: Deductions from the Debtor's Annualized Monthly Income

Part 2 of the Form 122A-2 allows the debtor to deduct a variety of expenses from his annualized monthly income computed in Form 122A-1. On Line 5 the debtor enters the number of persons used to calculate the expenses to be deducted in Part 2. Why doesn't Line 5 of Form 122A-2 simply ask for the number of people in debtor's "household" as it did on Line 13 of Form 122A-1? Because §707(b)(2)(A)(ii)(I) provides that the debtor's monthly expenses calculated on Form 122A-2 using this combination of actual and standardized expenses shall include such expenses "for the debtor, the dependents of the debtor, and the spouse of the debtor in a joint case, if the spouse is not otherwise a dependent." So the expense number in the form may be calculated for the debtor and his or her dependents who make up the "household" but also for dependents of the debtor who reside elsewhere (e.g., a dependent aging parent who still lives on her own). A dependent on Form 122A-2 is the same as a dependent on the debtor's Schedule J, Your Expenses (to be discussed in the next chapter), though the expenses listed on Schedule J are all actual expenses and are not derived from the IRS standards. Generally, the debtor must provide at least 50 percent of the support for a person for that person to be considered a dependent of the debtor.

On Line 6 the debtor enters his or her deduction for food, clothing, housekeeping supplies, personal care products, and related services calculated, not from his actual expenses, but from the IRS national standards for such expenses accessible at the web site of the U.S. Trustee Program. (Remember when comparing the current IRS national and local standard amounts that they are adjusted annually. Illustration 7-c reflects the applicable amounts as of June 2016.)

On Line 7, the debtor again accesses the IRS national standards to deduct an amount for projected out-of-pocket healthcare costs including medical services, prescription drugs, and medical supplies for each member of the debtor's family.

P-H 7-e: Access the U.S. Trustee Program's web site and determine the current IRS national standard for the food and clothing, etc., deduction and for the out-of-pocket healthcare expenses deduction for a household of your size.

On Line 8 the debtor utilizes the IRS local standards for projected housing operation expenses such as homeowner's or renters insurance and utilities (gas, electric, water, etc.) Due to the wide variation in such expenses around the country, the IRS standards are organized by state and county as well as by household size. Thus, the IRS local standards are used for this line.

On Line 9a the debtor again uses the local standards to enter the figure for household mortgage or rent expense. The figure used from the local standards may not be the actual expense the debtor incurs for these items, of course. On Line 9b the debtor enters the actual average monthly expense incurred for mortgage or rent payments and the local standard figure entered on Line 9a must be reduced by the amount of the debtor's actual monthly mortgage payment with the result entered on Line 9c. That may seem unfair, but the debtor will be able to receive a deduction for his future mortgage payments on Line 33 as discussed below.

EXAMPLE

The applicable IRS local standard for nonmortgage housing and utility expenses in Ramsey County, Minnesota where Marta Carlson resides is $526 (as of June 2016) so she enters that amount on Line 8. The local standard for mortgage/rental expense is $1,420 so she enters that amount on Line 9(a). But the two mortgages on her residence require her to pay a total of $1,442 per month (see the Assignment Memo in Appendix A) so she must enter that actual monthly payment total on Line 9b and deduct it from the amount on Line 9a. Since the amount of her actual monthly payments ($1,442) exceeds the local standard for mortgage/rental expense ($1,420 as of June 2016), she enters zero on Line 9c. But on Line 33b she will enter and receive a deduction for her actual mortgage payments.

If the debtor contends that the IRS local standards for housing do not accurately reflect his real expense for housing and utility expenses (e.g. a debtor lives in a remote location and pays a premium for utility service), he can enter an adjustment to be made to such deduction (i.e., increase it) on Line 10. The bankruptcy trustee will question that entry closely so the debtor will need to document his contention.

On Line 11 the debtor indicates the number of vehicles the debtor owns and operates. If the debtor owns and operates one or more vehicles, the debtor will then utilize the IRS local standards for vehicle operation transportation to deduct an amount for the expense of operating up to two vehicles. This figure is entered on Line 12. The IRS local standards are actually arranged by region of the country.

EXAMPLE

Marta Carlson operates one vehicle and so indicates on Line 11 of her Form 122A-2. The IRS local standards for the Midwest Census Region where Ramsey County, Minnesota is located designate $217 for operating costs of one vehicle (as of June 2016) so that is the amount entered on her Line 12.

On Line 13 the debtor utilizes the IRS local standards for vehicle ownership/lease expense for up to two vehicles. However, as with the mortgage expense standard entered on Line 9, the local standard amount for vehicle ownership/lease expense must be reduced by the average actual monthly payment the debtor makes on a vehicle that is subject to a security interest. Again, that initially seems unfair, but the debtor will be able to enter and deduct future payments on the secured vehicle on Line 33 discussed below.

EXAMPLE

Marta Carlson only has one vehicle and so indicates on Line 13. She enters the IRS local standard for ownership costs for one car in the Midwest Census Region, which as of June 2016 was $517. But since she makes monthly payments totaling $210 on her car to a secured creditor, Automotive Financing, Inc. (AFI) (see the Assignment Memo in Appendix A), she must deduct the amount of that actual payment from the IRS standard figure leaving a balance of $307 entered on Line 13c. However, on Line 33b she will enter and deduct the amount of her monthly payment to AFI.

Illustration 7-c: MARTA CARLSON'S FORM 122A-2 ASSUMING ANNUAL INCOME OF $84,000

Fill in this information to identify your case:

Debtor 1	Marta First Name	Rinaldi Middle Name	Carlson Last Name
Debtor 2 (Spouse, if filing)	First Name	Middle Name	Last Name

United States Bankruptcy Court for the: District of Minnesota

Case number 16-7-XXXX
(If known)

Check the appropriate box as directed in lines 40 or 42:

According to the calculations required by this Statement:

☑ 1. There is no presumption of abuse.

☐ 2. There is a presumption of abuse.

☐ Check if this is an amended filing

Official Form 122A–2

Chapter 7 Means Test Calculation

04/16

To fill out this form, you will need your completed copy of *Chapter 7 Statement of Your Current Monthly Income* (Official Form 122A-1).

Be as complete and accurate as possible. If two married people are filing together, both are equally responsible for being accurate. If more space is needed, attach a separate sheet to this form. Include the line number to which the additional information applies. On the top of any additional pages, write your name and case number (if known).

Part 1: Determine Your Adjusted Income

1. Copy your total current monthly income.......................... Copy line 11 from Official Form 122A-1 here ➜ .... $ 7,000.00

2. **Did you fill out Column B in Part 1 of Form 122A–1?**

  ☑ No. Fill in $0 for the total on line 3.

  ☐ Yes. Is your spouse filing with you?

    ☐ No. Go to line 3.

    ☐ Yes. Fill in $0 for the total on line 3.

3. **Adjust your current monthly income by subtracting any part of your spouse's income not used to pay for the household expenses of you or your dependents.** Follow these steps:

  On line 11, Column B of Form 122A–1, was any amount of the income you reported for your spouse NOT regularly used for the household expenses of you or your dependents?

  ☐ No. Fill in 0 for the total on line 3.

  ☐ Yes. Fill in the information below:

State each purpose for which the income was used For example, the income is used to pay your spouse's tax debt or to support people other than you or your dependents	Fill in the amount you are subtracting from your spouse's income	
_____	$_____	
_____	$_____	
_____	+ $_____	
Total...	$_____ 0.00	Copy total here ➜ − $_____ 0.00

4. **Adjust your current monthly income.** Subtract the total on line 3 from line 1. $ 7,000.00

Debtor 1   Marta _____ Rinaldi _____ Carlson _____   Case number *(if known)* 16-7-XXXX _____
            First Name   Middle Name   Last Name

Part 2:   Calculate Your Deductions from Your Income

The Internal Revenue Service (IRS) issues National and Local Standards for certain expense amounts. Use these amounts to answer the questions in lines 6-15. To find the IRS standards, go online using the link specified in the separate instructions for this form. This information may also be available at the bankruptcy clerk's office.

Deduct the expense amounts set out in lines 6-15 regardless of your actual expense. In later parts of the form, you will use some of your actual expenses if they are higher than the standards. Do not deduct any amounts that you subtracted from your spouse's income in line 3 and do not deduct any operating expenses that you subtracted from income in lines 5 and 6 of Form 122A–1.

If your expenses differ from month to month, enter the average expense.

Whenever this part of the form refers to *you*, it means both you and your spouse if Column B of Form 122A–1 is filled in.

5. **The number of people used in determining your deductions from income**

    Fill in the number of people who could be claimed as exemptions on your federal income tax return, plus the number of any additional dependents whom you support. This number may be different from the number of people in your household. | 3 |

National Standards   You must use the IRS National Standards to answer the questions in lines 6-7.

6. **Food, clothing, and other items:** Using the number of people you entered in line 5 and the IRS National Standards, fill in the dollar amount for food, clothing, and other items. $ 1,249.00

7. **Out-of-pocket health care allowance:** Using the number of people you entered in line 5 and the IRS National Standards, fill in the dollar amount for out-of-pocket health care. The number of people is split into two categories—people who are under 65 and people who are 65 or older—because older people have a higher IRS allowance for health care costs. If your actual expenses are higher than this IRS amount, you may deduct the additional amount on line 22.

    People who are under 65 years of age

    7a.   Out-of-pocket health care allowance per person $ _____ 60.00

    7b.   Number of people who are under 65   x _____ 3

    7c.   **Subtotal.** Multiply line 7a by line 7b. $ _____ 180.00   Copy here ➡ $ _____ 180.00

    People who are 65 years of age or older

    7d.   Out-of-pocket health care allowance per person $ _____

    7e.   Number of people who are 65 or older   x _____

    7f.   **Subtotal.** Multiply line 7d by line 7e. $ _____ 0.00   Copy here ➡   + $ _____ 0.00

    7g.   **Total**. Add lines 7c and 7f... $ _____ 180.00   Copy total here ➡ $ _____ 180.00

Official Form 122A–2   Chapter 7 Means Test Calculation   page **2**

Debtor 1 __Marta__ __Rinaldi__ __Carlson__   Case number *(if known)* __16-7-XXXX__
First Name   Middle Name   Last Name

Local Standards   You must use the IRS Local Standards to answer the questions in lines 8-15.

Based on information from the IRS, the U.S. Trustee Program has divided the IRS Local Standard for housing for bankruptcy purposes into two parts:

- Housing and utilities – Insurance and operating expenses
- Housing and utilities – Mortgage or rent expenses

To answer the questions in lines 8-9, use the U.S. Trustee Program chart.

To find the chart, go online using the link specified in the separate instructions for this form.
This chart may also be available at the bankruptcy clerk's office.

8. **Housing and utilities – Insurance and operating expenses:** Using the number of people you entered in line 5, fill in the dollar amount listed for your county for insurance and operating expenses. .... $ _____526.00_____

9. **Housing and utilities – Mortgage or rent expenses:**

   9a. Using the number of people you entered in line 5, fill in the dollar amount listed for your county for mortgage or rent expenses....................................... $ __1,420.00__

   9b. Total average monthly payment for all mortgages and other debts secured by your home.

   To calculate the total average monthly payment, add all amounts that are contractually due to each secured creditor in the 60 months after you file for bankruptcy. Then divide by 60.

Name of the creditor	Average monthly payment
Capital Savings Bank	$ 965.00
Dreams Come True Financing Company	$ 477.00
_____	+ $ _____
Total average monthly payment	$ 1,442.00

   Copy here → − $ __1,442.00__ Repeat this amount on line 33a.

   9c. Net mortgage or rent expense.
   Subtract line 9b (*total average monthly payment*) from line 9a (*mortgage or rent expense*). If this amount is less than $0, enter $0. .... $ _____0.00_____ Copy here → $ _____0.00_____

10. If you claim that the U.S. Trustee Program's division of the IRS Local Standard for housing is incorrect and affects the calculation of your monthly expenses, fill in any additional amount you claim. $ _____

    Explain why: _____
    _____

11. **Local transportation expenses:** Check the number of vehicles for which you claim an ownership or operating expense.

    ☐ 0. Go to line 14.
    ☑ 1. Go to line 12.
    ☐ 2 or more. Go to line 12.

12. **Vehicle operation expense:** Using the IRS Local Standards and the number of vehicles for which you claim the operating expenses, fill in the *Operating Costs* that apply for your Census region or metropolitan statistical area. $ __217.00__

Debtor 1   __Marta__   __Rinaldi__   __Carlson__   Case number *(if known)* __16-7-XXXX__
         First Name   Middle Name   Last Name

13. **Vehicle ownership or lease expense:** Using the IRS Local Standards, calculate the net ownership or lease expense for each vehicle below. You may not claim the expense if you do not make any loan or lease payments on the vehicle. In addition, you may not claim the expense for more than two vehicles.

    Vehicle 1   Describe Vehicle 1:   __YR-4 Toyota Camry__

13a. Ownership or leasing costs using IRS Local Standard. .... $ __517.00__

13b. Average monthly payment for all debts secured by Vehicle 1.
      Do not include costs for leased vehicles.

      To calculate the average monthly payment here and on line 13e, add all amounts that are contractually due to each secured creditor in the 60 months after you filed for bankruptcy. Then divide by 60.

Name of each creditor for Vehicle 1	Average monthly payment
Automotive Financing, Inc.	$ 210.00
_____	+ $ _____

      Total average monthly payment $ __210.00__   Copy here ➔   – $ __210.00__   Repeat this amount on line 33b.

13c. Net Vehicle 1 ownership or lease expense
      Subtract line 13b from line 13a. If this amount is less than $0, enter $0. .... $ __307.00__   Copy net Vehicle 1 expense here ..... ➔ $ __307.00__

    Vehicle 2   Describe Vehicle 2:   _____

13d. Ownership or leasing costs using IRS Local Standard. .... $ _____

13e. Average monthly payment for all debts secured by Vehicle 2.
      Do not include costs for leased vehicles.

Name of each creditor for Vehicle 2	Average monthly payment
_____	$ _____
_____	+ $ _____

      Total average monthly payment $ _____   Copy here ➔   – $ _____   Repeat this amount on line 33c.

13f. Net Vehicle 2 ownership or lease expense
      Subtract line 13e from 13d. If this amount is less than $0, enter $0. .... $ __0.00__   Copy net Vehicle 2 expense here ... ➔ $ __0.00__

14. **Public transportation expense**: If you claimed 0 vehicles in line 11, using the IRS Local Standards, fill in the *Public Transportation* expense allowance regardless of whether you use public transportation. $ __0.00__

15. **Additional public transportation expense:** If you claimed 1 or more vehicles in line 11 and if you claim that you may also deduct a public transportation expense, you may fill in what you believe is the appropriate expense, but you may not claim more than the IRS Local Standard for *Public Transportation*. $ __0.00__

Debtor 1   Marta   Rinaldi   Carlson   Case number *(if known)* 16-7-XXXX
            First Name   Middle Name   Last Name

Other Necessary Expenses   In addition to the expense deductions listed above, you are allowed your monthly expenses for the following IRS categories.

16. **Taxes:** The total monthly amount that you will actually owe for federal, state and local taxes, such as income taxes, self-employment taxes, Social Security taxes, and Medicare taxes. You may include the monthly amount withheld from your pay for these taxes. However, if you expect to receive a tax refund, you must divide the expected refund by 12 and subtract that number from the total monthly amount that is withheld to pay for taxes. $ 1,583.00

    Do not include real estate, sales, or use taxes.

17. **Involuntary deductions:** The total monthly payroll deductions that your job requires, such as retirement contributions, union dues, and uniform costs.

    Do not include amounts that are not required by your job, such as voluntary 401(k) contributions or payroll savings. $ 0.00

18. **Life insurance:** The total monthly premiums that you pay for your own term life insurance. If two married people are filing together, include payments that you make for your spouse's term life insurance. Do not include premiums for life insurance on your dependents, for a non-filing spouse's life insurance, or for any form of life insurance other than term. $ 0.00

19. **Court-ordered payments:** The total monthly amount that you pay as required by the order of a court or administrative agency, such as spousal or child support payments. $ 0.00

    Do not include payments on past due obligations for spousal or child support. You will list these obligations in line 35.

20. **Education:** The total monthly amount that you pay for education that is either required:

    ■ as a condition for your job, or

    ■ for your physically or mentally challenged dependent child if no public education is available for similar services. $ 0.00

21. **Childcare:** The total monthly amount that you pay for childcare, such as babysitting, daycare, nursery, and preschool. $ 100.00

    Do not include payments for any elementary or secondary school education.

22. **Additional health care expenses, excluding insurance costs:** The monthly amount that you pay for health care that is required for the health and welfare of you or your dependents and that is not reimbursed by insurance or paid by a health savings account. Include only the amount that is more than the total entered in line 7. Payments for health insurance or health savings accounts should be listed only in line 25. $ 720.00

23. **Optional telephones and telephone services:** The total monthly amount that you pay for telecommunication services for you and your dependents, such as pagers, call waiting, caller identification, special long distance, or business cell phone service, to the extent necessary for your health and welfare or that of your dependents or for the production of income, if it is not reimbursed by your employer.   + $ 0.00

    Do not include payments for basic home telephone, internet and cell phone service. Do not include self-employment expenses, such as those reported on line 5 of Official Form 122A-1, or any amount you previously deducted.

24. Add all of the expenses allowed under the IRS expense allowances. $ 4,882.00
    Add lines 6 through 23.

Debtor 1   Marta   Rinaldi   Carlson   Case number *(if known)* 16-7-XXXX
            First Name   Middle Name   Last Name

Additional Expense Deductions   These are additional deductions allowed by the Means Test.
                                     Note: Do not include any expense allowances listed in lines 6-24.

25. **Health insurance, disability insurance, and health savings account expenses.** The monthly expenses for health
    insurance, disability insurance, and health savings accounts that are reasonably necessary for yourself, your spouse, or your
    dependents.

Health insurance	$ 85.00	
Disability insurance	$ 0.00	
Health savings account	+ $ 0.00	
Total	$ 85.00	Copy total here➔ .... $ 85.00

    Do you actually spend this total amount?

    ☐ No. How much do you actually spend? $_____
    ☑ Yes

26. **Continuing contributions to the care of household or family members.** The actual monthly expenses that you will
    continue to pay for the reasonable and necessary care and support of an elderly, chronically ill, or disabled member of
    your household or member of your immediate family who is unable to pay for such expenses. These expenses may
    include contributions to an account of a qualified ABLE program. 26 U.S.C. § 529A(b). $ 0.00

27. **Protection against family violence.** The reasonably necessary monthly expenses that you incur to maintain the safety
    of you and your family under the Family Violence Prevention and Services Act or other federal laws that apply. $ 0.00

    By law, the court must keep the nature of these expenses confidential.

28. **Additional home energy costs.** Your home energy costs are included in your insurance and operating expenses on line 8.

    If you believe that you have home energy costs that are more than the home energy costs included in expenses on line
    8, then fill in the excess amount of home energy costs. $ 0.00

    You must give your case trustee documentation of your actual expenses, and you must show that the additional amount
    claimed is reasonable and necessary.

29. **Education expenses for dependent children who are younger than 18.** The monthly expenses (not more than $160.42*
    per child) that you pay for your dependent children who are younger than 18 years old to attend a private or public
    elementary or secondary school. $ 150.00

    You must give your case trustee documentation of your actual expenses, and you must explain why the amount claimed is
    reasonable and necessary and not already accounted for in lines 6-23.

    *   Subject to adjustment on 4/01/19, and every 3 years after that for cases begun on or after the date of adjustment.

30. **Additional food and clothing expense.** The monthly amount by which your actual food and clothing expenses are
    higher than the combined food and clothing allowances in the IRS National Standards. That amount cannot be more than
    5% of the food and clothing allowances in the IRS National Standards. $ 0.00

    To find a chart showing the maximum additional allowance, go online using the link specified in the separate instructions for
    this form. This chart may also be available at the bankruptcy clerk's office.

    You must show that the additional amount claimed is reasonable and necessary.

31. **Continuing charitable contributions.** The amount that you will continue to contribute in the form of cash or financial
    instruments to a religious or charitable organization. 26 U.S.C. § 170(c)(1)-(2).   + $ 0.00

32. **Add all of the additional expense deductions.** $ 235.00
    Add lines 25 through 31.

Debtor 1 **Marta**   **Rinaldi**   **Carlson**   Case number (if known) 16-7-XXXX
          First Name   Middle Name   Last Name

Deductions for Debt Payment

33. For debts that are secured by an interest in property that you own, including home mortgages, vehicle loans, and other secured debt, fill in lines 33a through 33e.

To calculate the total average monthly payment, add all amounts that are contractually due to each secured creditor in the 60 months after you file for bankruptcy. Then divide by 60.

		Average monthly payment
Mortgages on your home:		
33a. Copy line 9b here .... →		$ 1,442.00
Loans on your first two vehicles:		
33b. Copy line 13b here. .... →		$ 210.00
33c. Copy line 13e here. .... →		$ _____

33d. List other secured debts:

Name of each creditor for other secured debt	Identify property that secures the debt	Does payment include taxes or insurance?	
_____	_____	☐ No ☐ Yes	$ _____
_____	_____	☐ No ☐ Yes	$ _____
_____	_____	☐ No ☐ Yes	+ $ _____

33e. Total average monthly payment. Add lines 33a through 33d..........	$ 1,652.00	Copy total here → $ 1,652.00

34. Are any debts that you listed in line 33 secured by your primary residence, a vehicle, or other property necessary for your support or the support of your dependents?

☐ No. Go to line 35.
☑ Yes. State any amount that you must pay to a creditor, in addition to the payments listed in line 33, to keep possession of your property (called the *cure amount*). Next, divide by 60 and fill in the information below.

Name of the creditor	Identify property that secures the debt	Total cure amount		Monthly cure amount
Capital Savings B.	Residence	$ 1,930.00	÷ 60 =	$ 32.16
Dreams Come Tru	Residence	$ 1,431.00	÷ 60 =	$ 23.85
Automotive Fin.	YR-4 Toyota	$ 420.00	÷ 60 =	+ $ 7.00

Total	$ 63.01	Copy total here → $ 63.01

35. Do you owe any priority claims such as a priority tax, child support, or alimony — that are past due as of the filing date of your bankruptcy case? 11 U.S.C. § 507.

☑ No. Go to line 36.
☐ Yes. Fill in the total amount of all of these priority claims. Do not include current or ongoing priority claims, such as those you listed in line 19.

Total amount of all past-due priority claims	$ 0.00 ÷ 60 =	$ 0.00

Debtor 1   Marta   Rinaldi   Carlson   Case number (if known) 16-7-XXXX
            First Name   Middle Name   Last Name

36. **Are you eligible to file a case under Chapter 13?** 11 U.S.C. § 109(e).
    For more information, go online using the link for *Bankruptcy Basics* specified in the separate
    instructions for this form. *Bankruptcy Basics* may also be available at the bankruptcy clerk's office.

    ☐ No. Go to line 37.

    ☑ Yes. Fill in the following information.

    Projected monthly plan payment if you were filing under Chapter 13 $ _____ 1,700

    Current multiplier for your district as stated on the list issued by the
    Administrative Office of the United States Courts (for districts in Alabama and
    North Carolina) or by the Executive Office for United States Trustees (for all   x 0.07
    other districts).

    To find a list of district multipliers that includes your district, go online using the
    link specified in the separate instructions for this form. This list may also be
    available at the bankruptcy clerk's office.

    Average monthly administrative expense if you were filing under Chapter 13 $ _____ 122.40   Copy total $ _____ 122.40
                                                                                               here ➡

37. **Add all of the deductions for debt payment.**
    Add lines 33e through 36. .... $ 1,837.40

Total Deductions from Income

38. **Add all of the allowed deductions.**

    Copy line 24, *All of the expenses allowed under IRS* $ _____ 4,882.00
    expense allowances ....

    Copy line 32, *All of the additional expense deductions*.......... $ _____ 235.00

    Copy line 37, *All of the deductions for debt payment*.............   + $ _____ 1,837.41

    Total deductions $ _____ 6,954.41   Copy total here .... ➡ $ 6,954.41

Part 3:   Determine Whether There Is a Presumption of Abuse

39. **Calculate monthly disposable income for 60 months**

    39a. Copy line 4, *adjusted current monthly income* ..... $ _____ 7,000.00

    39b. Copy line 38, *Total deductions*..........   – $ _____ 6,954.41

    39c. Monthly disposable income. 11 U.S.C. § 707(b)(2). $ _____ 45.59   Copy $ _____ 45.59
          Subtract line 39b from line 39a.   here ➡

          For the next 60 months (5 years)...   x 60

    39d. **Total**. Multiply line 39c by 60. .... $ 2,735.40   Copy $ 2,735.40
                                                                                                  here ➡

40. **Find out whether there is a presumption of abuse.** Check the box that applies:

    ☑ **The line 39d is less than $7,700*.** On the top of page 1 of this form, check box 1, *There is no presumption of abuse.* Go
       to Part 5.

    ☐ **The line 39d is more than $12,850*.** On the top of page 1 of this form, check box 2, *There is a presumption of abuse.* You
       may fill out Part 4 if you claim special circumstances. Then go to Part 5.

    ☐ **The line 39d is at least $7,700*, but not more than $12,850*.** Go to line 41.

    * Subject to adjustment on 4/01/19, and every 3 years after that for cases filed on or after the date of adjustment.

Official Form 122A–2   **Chapter 7 Means Test Calculation**   page **8**

Debtor 1   **Marta**   **Rinaldi**   **Carlson**   Case number *(if known)* 16-7-XXXX
                First Name   Middle Name   Last Name

41. 41a. Fill in the amount of your total nonpriority unsecured debt. If you filled out *A Summary of Your Assets and Liabilities and Certain Statistical Information Schedules* (Official Form 106Sum), you may refer to line 3b on that form................................ $_____

                                                                                                                                    x .25

   41b. 25% of your total nonpriority unsecured debt. 11 U.S.C. § 707(b)(2)(A)(i)(I).
         Multiply line 41a by 0.25. .... $_____   Copy
                                                                                                                                        here → $_____

42. Determine whether the income you have left over after subtracting all allowed deductions is enough to pay 25% of your unsecured, nonpriority debt.
   Check the box that applies:

   ☐ **Line 39d is less than line 41b.** On the top of page 1 of this form, check box 1, *There is no presumption of abuse*. Go to Part 5.

   ☐ **Line 39d is equal to or more than line 41b.** On the top of page 1 of this form, check box 2, *There is a presumption of abuse*. You may fill out Part 4 if you claim special circumstances. Then go to Part 5.

Part 4:   Give Details About Special Circumstances

43. Do you have any special circumstances that justify additional expenses or adjustments of current monthly income for which there is no reasonable alternative? 11 U.S.C. § 707(b)(2)(B).

   ☐ No. Go to Part 5.

   ☐ Yes. Fill in the following information. All figures should reflect your average monthly expense or income adjustment for each item. You may include expenses you listed in line 25.

   You must give a detailed explanation of the special circumstances that make the expenses or income adjustments necessary and reasonable. You must also give your case trustee documentation of your actual expenses or income adjustments.

Give a detailed explanation of the special circumstances	Average monthly expense or income adjustment
_____	$_____
_____	$_____
_____	$_____
_____	$_____

Part 5:   Sign Below

By signing here, I declare under penalty of perjury that the information on this statement and in any attachments is true and correct.

✗ /s/ Marta Rinaldi Carlson   ✗ _____
   Signature of Debtor 1   Signature of Debtor 2

   Date 06/17/2016   Date _____
        MM / DD / YYYY   MM / DD / YYYY

THE OWNERSHIP EXPENSE DEDUCTION

May a debtor take the expense deduction for vehicle ownership allowed in Line 13 if the vehicle is paid for and is subject to neither a lease nor a secured debt? That issue has arisen under BAPCPA and Form 122A-2 (as well as Form 122C, used in Chapter 13 cases, as we will see later). Lower courts were badly split on this issue until the Supreme Court held in *Ransom v. FIA Card Services, N.A.*, 131 S. Ct. 716 (2011), that a debtor cannot use the IRS Local Standards Transportation Ownership Costs for a car that is owned free of debt or lease obligations. Although *Ransom* involved a Chapter 13 debtor and Form 122C, the decision is controlling in Chapter 7 cases involving Form 122A-2 as well. The debtor who owns and operates a vehicle that is not rented or subject to a security interest can still take the vehicle operation expense on Line 12.

If the debtor does not own and operate a vehicle but does incur public transportation expenses (e.g., subway train or city bus), that figure determined from the local standards is entered on Line 14. And if a debtor has both private vehicle expenses includable on Line 11 and public transportation expenses, the latter actual expense may be entered on Line 15 up to the amount of the local standards figure.

On Lines 16-31 the debtor is allowed to enter and deduct his average monthly expenses actually incurred on items related to the IRS standards but not expressly covered by them, including taxes (other than real estate and sales taxes) (Line 16); payroll deductions for items such as retirement contributions, union dues, and uniform costs (Line 17); term life insurance for policies covering the debtor's life only (Line 18); court-ordered payments such as child support or alimony (in their full amount, not averaged) (Line 19); education expenses for the debtor that are a condition of employment or for a physically or mentally challenged dependent child for whom no such public education service is available (Line 20); child care (Line 21); unreimbursed healthcare expenses in excess of the amount entered on Line 7 and not including health insurance premiums (Line 22); and telecommunication expenses in excess of home phone and cell phone service but only to the extent necessary to the health and welfare of the debtor or his dependents (Line 23). These amounts are based on averages of the debtor's actual expenses and not based on IRS standards.

EXAMPLE

Marta Carlson's average monthly withholding for income, Social Security, and Medicare taxes is $1,583, and she enters that amount on Line 16. She does not include real estate taxes because those are included in her mortgage payments listed on Lines 9 and 33. Sales taxes are excluded too since they are part of the calculation used for other deductions such as the IRS national standards for food and clothing, etc., deducted on Line 6. She has not deducted any of her educational expenses on Line 20, concluding that they are not a "condition" of her continued employment at TTI. She is not currently incurring child care expenses so there is no deduction on Line 21. She has incurred additional healthcare expenses for her daughter (see the Assignment Memo in Appendix A) and in recent months has been paying an average of $900 a month on those obligations, even though she is in arrears on her mortgages and car payment. She was able to deduct $180 of that amount on Line 7 using the guidelines so the additional $720 she has actually been spending is the amount she enters on

Line 22. She can expect to be challenged on such a large deduction for this item and should have documentation ready to support it. She is currently incurring $100 per month in child care expense and enters that amount on Line 21.

Line 25 allows the debtor to deduct premiums paid monthly for health and disability insurance or payments into a health savings account, items that were excluded from Line 7.

EXAMPLE

> On Line 22 Marta Carlson entered an amount equal to the average payment she has been making on unreimbursed healthcare expenses for herself and the two children, but health insurance premiums she pays for the TTI group coverage are not included there. The monthly premium for that group coverage ($85) is included on Line 25.

Line 26 allows the debtor to enter and deduct extraordinary expenses incurred for the care and support of a member of the debtor's household or a member of the debtor's immediate family who is elderly, chronically ill, or disabled.

EXAMPLE

> If Marta Carlson's elderly mother was still living and was a member of her household, Marta might be able to deduct any extra expenses incurred for her mother's upkeep here (e.g., having someone stay with her during the day). Or if her chronically ill daughter was incurring expenses other than medical costs Marta has deducted on Line 22 (e.g., expensive foods for a special diet), those could be deducted on Line 26. This is again the kind of unusual deduction a bankruptcy trustee will examine closely and the debtor must have supporting documentation.

On Line 27 a debtor who has been the victim of domestic violence or stalking and who qualifies for protection under the **Family Violence Prevention and Services Act** may deduct expenses related to keeping the family safe (e.g., home security system).

If the average monthly amount the debtor actually expends on utilities exceeds the IRS local standard for that item used on Line 8, the debtor may deduct the excess on Line 28 but will need to provide documentation if challenged.

On Line 29 the debtor with minor children may deduct average monthly school costs actually incurred in connection with their attendance at a public or private elementary or secondary school up to a current maximum of $160.42 per child (that amount will be next adjusted in April 2019).

EXAMPLE

> Marta Carlson has calculated that she spends an average of $75 a month on each of her two children for special equipment or supplies or field trips. Thus, she has deducted a total of $150 here. Such expenses must be documented and must be beyond routine costs of sending children to school (e.g., normal school clothes and supplies).

If the average monthly amount the debtor *actually* spends on food and clothing and other items exceeds the amount allowed by the IRS national standard for such items that was entered on Line 6, a debtor may deduct the excess on Line 30 up to a maximum of 5 percent of the IRS standard but will need to provide documentation if challenged.

On Line 31 the debtor may enter and deduct charitable contributions the debtor plans to "continue" making. This wording suggests that the debtor must have a legitimate and provable history of making such contributions to justify this deduction from annualized monthly income and the amount must be reasonable.

Section 707(b)(1) says that in making the determination of whether to dismiss a Chapter 7 case for abuse, "the court may not take into consideration whether a debtor has made, or continues to make, charitable contributions. . . ." That language could be construed to mean that the form's limitation of this deduction to continuing contributions is inappropriate and that a bankruptcy judge may not limit the amount of such deductions if they are bona fide. A form, even an official form, cannot vary the terms of a bankruptcy rule or the Code itself. Bankruptcy Rule 9009 states, "The forms shall be construed to be consistent with these rules and the Code." See *In re Meyer*, 355 B.R. 837, 843 n.6 (Bankr. D.N.M. 2006) ("[O]ne looks to the statute to determine what the law is, and then interprets the form in light of the statute's dictate."). There is little case law interpreting §707(b)(2) or the apparent inconsistency of the form language, probably since statistics suggest that few Chapter 7 debtors claim the charitable deduction and only about 2 percent claim a charitable deduction of more than 5 percent of their gross income.

WHO CAN DEDUCT A CHARITABLE CONTRIBUTION EXPENSE AND IN WHAT AMOUNT?

The issue of limiting a debtor's deductions for charitable contributions to a religious organization raises First Amendment Free Exercise Clause issues that have never been completely resolved. In the Religious Liberty and Charitable Donation Clarification Act of 2006, Congress made clear its intent in the Religious Liberty and Charitable Contribution Protection Act of 1998 that debtors in bankruptcy be allowed to claim charitable contribution expenses as part of their adjustment of income as part of the means test. Such contributions cannot be disallowed as being not reasonably necessary to the support of the debtor and his dependents as part of the Chapter 7 means test. Notwithstanding that, per the language of the form, listed contributions must be "continuing." A debtor who has rarely if ever made charitable contributions may not enter an amount here on the grounds that he or she intends to begin making those contributions without drawing a challenge. Moreover, trustees will generally limit the amount claimed to 10 to 15 percent of the debtor's gross income (and §1325(b)(2)(A)(ii) specifically limits this deduction to 15 percent of the debtor's gross income for purposes of determining a Chapter 13 debtor's disposable income). Though there is no such statutory limitation on the charitable contribution deduction in the Chapter 7 means test, the U.S. Trustee Program has taken the position that such contributions by a Chapter 7 debtor should not be allowed in excess of 15 percent of gross income (see Statement of U.S. Trustee at www.justice.gov/sites/default/files/ust/legacy/2015/03/03/ch7_line_by_line.pdf).

The additional expense deductions allowed in Lines 16-31 are totaled on Line 32.

On Line 33 the debtor may enter and deduct scheduled monthly payments on debt secured by the debtor's real or personal property. This entry was discussed in connection with Lines 9 and 13 above.

EXAMPLE

On Line 33 of her Form 122A-2, Marta Carlson enters her scheduled monthly payments for both mortgages and the payment to AFI secured by her automobile. Commonly in a Chapter 13 case, the debtor will propose a plan to continue paying the mortgage debt on his house and the secure debt on at least one car in order to keep those items of property, and those continued payments are what are contemplated here. Remember, the purpose of having the above median debtor complete Form 122A-2 as part of the Chapter 7 means test is to determine if that debtor might have enough remaining disposable income after making such payments to fund a Chapter 13 plan.

P-H 7-f: An issue has arisen under the new means test regarding whether a debtor may deduct secured payments for her home or vehicles on Line 33 of Form 122A-2 where the debtor intends to surrender such property rather than keep it (as Marta Carlson plans to do per her Debtor's Statement of Intent, which is Document 18 in the Carlson case file). We will consider the surrender of property in more detail in the next chapter, but it essentially means that the debtor intends to stop paying for the property and relinquish possession of it to the secured creditor. The courts have split on this issue. *In re Rivers*, 466 B.R. 558 (Bankr. M.D. Fla. 2012), held that the question of whether a Chapter 7 debtor satisfied the means test or triggered the presumption of abuse is to be decided on the basis of the debtor's financial circumstances as of the date the petition is filed and that since the debtor has not as of that date abandoned property subject to a security interest the debtor can indeed enter payments on such secured debt on Line 33 notwithstanding an intent to surrender the property postpetition. Compare *In re Fredman*, 471 B.R. 540 (Bankr. S.D. Ill. 2012), which disallowed the deduction rejecting the "mechanical approach" of *Rivers* in favor of a "forward looking approach" to the means test, which takes into account "changes in the debtor's income or expenses that are known or virtually certain at the time of confirmation" including the intent to surrender. The forward looking approach of *Fredman* is probably the majority rule on this issue but determine if the courts of your federal district or circuit have ruled on it and which rule is followed there.

As we will see when we study the Chapter 13 bankruptcy, if a debtor in such a proceeding desires to keep possession of property subject to a mortgage or security interest, the debtor must not only continue to make scheduled payments but must propose a plan to pay off any arrearages in such debt during the term of the plan. With that aspect of Chapter 13 in mind, and again keeping in mind that the purpose of having the above median debtor complete Form 122A-2 as part of the Chapter 7 means test is to determine if that debtor might have enough remaining disposable income after making such payments to fund a Chapter 13 plan,

Line 34 requires the debtor to state the amount of any arrearage owed on such property (the **cure amount**). The cure amount is then divided by 60 because in a Chapter 13 such arrearages must be paid as part of a plan that can run no more than 60 months.

EXAMPLE

> At the time she files her petition, Marta Carlson is two payments in arrears on the mortgage held by Capital Savings Bank for a total of $1,930. If she proposed a Chapter 13 plan to cure that arrearage over 60 months she would pay $32.16 a month for that purpose. She is three payments in arrears on the mortgage held by Dreams Come True Finance Company for a total of $1,431. Over a 60-month plan she would pay $23.85 to cure that arrearage. She is two payments behind to AFI on her secured car debt for a total of $420 and would need to make 60 payments of $7 per month to cure that arrearage. Those are the cure amounts she lists on Line 34.

We will learn later that there are some creditors who hold claims that enjoy a priority over others in a bankruptcy case when it comes to distributing proceeds in a Chapter 7 or making payments in a Chapter 13 reorganization (e.g., those to whom child support or alimony payments are owed). If the debtor is in arrears on such priority claims at the time a Chapter 13 petition is filed, those priority claims must be paid in full in the debtor's plan. On Line 35 of Form 122A-2 the Chapter 7 debtor enters the monthly payments that he or she would propose in a Chapter 13 plan to bring those priority claims current over the term of a plan not longer than 60 months.

In a Chapter 13 case, once a proposed plan is approved, the debtor will make payments, usually monthly, to a Chapter 13 trustee who will then distribute the payments among the creditors of the debtor as called for in the plan. The trustee will receive a fee for doing so that is a percentage of the payments distributed. That fee is an administrative expense of the Chapter 13 case. We will learn more about this later when we study Chapter 13 in earnest, but, for now, on Line 36 of Form 122A-2 the Chapter 7 above median debtor lists a projected monthly payment he or she would make into a Chapter 13 plan and the projected monthly administrative expense is calculated using the appropriate multiplier, which as of June 2016 in the District of Minnesota was 7.2 percent.

EXAMPLE

> The attorney for Marta Carlson projects that in a Chapter 13 case her plan would call for her to pay $1,700 per month (which as we will see when we study the Chapter 13 bankruptcy would include payments on debtor's secured debt such as mortgage and car payments and would by no means all go to satisfy unsecured claims of debtor's creditors). Based on an applicable current multiplier of 7.2 percent this results in a projected monthly administrative expense on such a plan of $122.40.

On Line 37 the debtor enters the total for all debt payment deductions claimed on Line 33-36 of the form and on Line 38 the debtor enters the grand total for all deductions claimed in Part 2 of the form.

Part 3 of Form 122A-2: Determination of the Presumption

In Part 3 of Form 122A-2, the above median debtor subtracts all deductions claimed in Part 2 of the form from the adjusted current monthly income figure entered on Line 4 of the form. (This figure is the monthly income figure calculated in Form 122A-1 as modified by the marital adjustment of Part 1 of Form 122A-2.) The result is entered on Line 39c and constitutes the monthly disposable income figure for the debtor; that is, the amount the debtor would have available on a monthly basis (after paying living expenses) to pay unsecured creditors in a Chapter 13 plan over the next five years. On Line 39d we then multiply that number by 60, again because the typical Chapter 13 plan would run 60 months.

EXAMPLE

Marta Carlson's deductions from Part 2 of her Form 122A-2 total $6,954.41 leaving her a monthly disposable income figure of $45.59. Over the life of a five-year Chapter 13 plan, then, she would have a total of $2,735.40 of disposable income available with which to fund the plan ($45.59 × 60) and that is the figure entered on Line 39d of her form.

Recall that the means test for the above median debtor is controlled by §707(b)(2)(A)(i), which provides that if the debtor has *more than* $12,850 (the current figure, to be adjusted again in 2019) in disposable income after payment of living expenses that can be applied to pay unsecured claims over the course of a five-year plan under Chapter 13 ($214 a month), the presumption of abuse arises and that debtor may not continue in Chapter 7. That debtor will check the second box on Line 40 of the form, note in the box at the top right hand side of page 1 that the presumption of abuse does arise, and can expect the U.S. Trustee to seek dismissal of the Chapter 7 case. (In the next section we will discuss the debtor's right to challenge that presumption of abuse in the face of a motion to dismiss.)

If the debtor's disposable income totaled on Line 39d is less than $7,700 (the current figure, to be adjusted again in April 2019), the presumption of abuse does not arise. That debtor will check the first box in Line 40, note in the box at the top right hand side of page 1 that the presumption does not arise, complete the verification in Part 5 of the form, and can expect to proceed in Chapter 7.

However, if the debtor has *less than* $12,850 but *more than* $7,700 in disposable income, we have to ask one more question before we can conclude that the presumption does not arise: Is the debtor's total disposable income over the projected 60 months of the plan *also less than* 25 percent of the debtor's nonpriority unsecured debts? The above median debtor whose total disposable income falls in this range will check the third box on Line 40 and must complete Lines 41-42 of the form to determine if his or her disposable income is less than 25 percent of the nonpriority unsecured debts.

We mentioned earlier that some creditor claims enjoy a priority in a bankruptcy case. Unpaid taxes and past-due child support are frequent examples in consumer bankruptcy cases. We will consider priority and nonpriority claims in more detail in Chapter Eleven, Section B. But understand now that if the total disposable income of an above median debtor completing Form 122A-2 is more than $7,700 but less than $12,850, that disposable income figure must also be compared in Line 41 to the debtor's nonpriority claims if any. If the disposable income figure is also less than 25 percent of such nonpriority claims, the presumption does not arise. That debtor will check the first box on Line 42 of the form, note on page 1 of the form that the presumption does not arise, complete the verification in Part 5 of the form, and can expect to proceed in Chapter 7. But if that debtor's disposable income figure exceeds 25 percent of his or her nonpriority claims as calculated on Line 41, the presumption of abuse will arise. That debtor must check the second box on Line 42 of the form, and note on page 1 of the form that the presumption does arise in the case. Like the debtor whose disposable income figure was in excess of $12,850, a motion to dismiss filed by the U.S. Trustee can be expected.

EXAMPLE

Even assuming Marta Carlson was an above median debtor making $84,000 per year, she does not trigger the presumption of abuse. She has total disposable income over the projected five years of a Chapter 13 plan totaling $2,736.40 as noted on Line 39d of her Form 122A-2. Since that is less than $7,700, the presumption does not arise in her case. She has checked the first box on Line 40 of her form, noted on page 1 that the presumption does not arise in her case, and completed the verification in Part 5 of the form. She is ready to proceed in Chapter 7, assuming there is no challenge by the trustee to her income stated in her Form 122A-1 or her deductions taken in Part 2 of her form 122A-2.

P-H 7-g: If Marta's ex-husband had been paying her $1,000 per month in child support for the six months preceding her filing and continuing to assume she was making $84,000 per year at TTI, would the presumption of abuse arise in her case using Form 122A-2? What if her jurisdiction disallowed the deduction from income of her mortgage payments on the house and her car payments on the YR-04 Toyota Camry on Line 33 of her form 122A-2 since she plans to surrender the house and car to the creditors secured in those assets (see *In re Fredman*, supra)? Would the presumption of abuse then arise in her case, requiring her to file under Chapter 13 or not at all?

4. The Right to Challenge the Presumption of Abuse by Showing Special Circumstances

Special circumstances Unique financial circumstances of a Chapter 7 debtor involving additional expenses or adjustments of current monthly income for which there is no reasonable alternative that may be sufficient to rebut the presumption of abuse.

The presumption of abuse is just that—a presumption. That means that if the debtor cannot satisfy the means test using Form 122A-1 for the below median debtor or Form 122A-2 for the above median debtor, the debtor may still challenge the presumption by filing a motion with the bankruptcy court and presenting proof of **special circumstances** sufficient to rebut the presumption of abuse. Section 707(b)(2)(B) defines special circumstances as those that "justify either additional expenses or adjustments of current monthly income for which there is no reasonable alternative" and gives examples such as a serious medical condition of the debtor or a dependent or a call to active duty in the military that is likely to impact on future income or future expenses in a way not disclosed on either form.

Line 43 in Part 4 of Form 122A-2 is where the debtor for whom the presumption of abuse is raised may indicate the special circumstances that should result in a reconsideration of either the income debtor as reported on Form 122A-1 or expenses deducted on Form 122A-2. But note that the debtor is not allowed to adjust the results of the raising of the presumption using Form 122A-2 based on the circumstances entered on Line 43. The presumption is still raised and the debtor will have to ask the bankruptcy court pursuant to §707(b)(2)(B) to reverse the presumption of abuse based on those special circumstances so that the debtor can proceed in Chapter 7. An evidentiary hearing will be required for the court to consider the motion.

In connection with a debtor's claim of special circumstances under §707(b)(2)(B), Line 13 of debtor's **Schedule I: Your Income**, to be discussed in the next chapter, provides debtor the opportunity to identify changes to income the debtor is expecting in the year following the filing of the petition. Similarly, Line 24 of debtor's **Schedule J: Your Expenses** provides debtor the opportunity to identify changes to expenses the debtor is expecting in the next year. Certainly, any debtor planning to rely on the §707(B)(2)(B) special circumstances exception to the presumption of abuse should reference the circumstances in those schedules. In fact, the U.S. Trustee or any other party in interest examining the consumer debtor's Forms 122A-1 and 122A-2 will compare the income and expense information set out on those forms with the same or similar information provided on that debtor's Schedules I and J. The one assisting the debtor in preparing those various forms and schedules must be sure they are consistent.

P-H 7-h: The BAPCPA changes are still new enough that we do not know what other circumstances may or may not satisfy the special circumstances test of §707(b)(2)(B). For example, if the debtor shows she is facing the possibility of a layoff that will dramatically reduce the income reported on Form 122A-1, will that suffice or would the court expect the debtor to file a Chapter 13 and then convert the case to a Chapter 7 if the layoff actually occurred and no substitute employment could be found? Or if the debtor is in the process of adopting a child that will result in a dramatic increase in expenses not reported on Form 122A-2? Research the cases in your federal district or circuit to see what factual scenarios regarding special circumstances may have been decided.

---

5. The U.S. Trustee's Duty to Report on the Presumption of Abuse and the Right to Challenge the Debtor's Conclusion That the Presumption of Abuse Does Not Arise

Code §704(b)(1)(A) requires the U.S. Trustee, in all Chapter 7 cases involving individual debtors, to file a statement with the court within ten days following the first meeting of creditors advising as to whether the presumption of abuse arises under §707(b). The UST's statement is sent to creditors by the clerk of the court within seven days thereafter per §704(b)(1)(B).

Within 30 days of filing the notice with the court, the UST must file a motion to dismiss (or convert to Chapter 13 with the debtor's consent) based on the presumption of abuse or explain to the court why it does not consider such motion appropriate. If the UST's motion to dismiss is not filed within the 30-day window, it is thereafter barred.

Even if a debtor concludes on either Form 122A-1 or 122A-2 that the presumption of abuse does not arise in his or her case, that conclusion is *not* binding on the U.S Trustee or the court. The bankruptcy trustee, the U.S. Trustee, any party in interest (e.g., a creditor) or the bankruptcy court acting *sua sponte* (on its own motion) may challenge the debtor's numbers and seek dismissal of the case under §707(b)(1). Motions to dismiss are contested matters and require an evidentiary hearing.

FINAL THOUGHTS ON THE BAPCPA MEANS TEST

A primary purpose of BAPCPA was to push more debtors away from Chapter 7 liquidation and toward Chapter 13 repayment plans. Its primary tool to accomplish that goal was the presumption of abuse. Has it worked? Studies to date suggest no. One study suggested that no more than 1 percent of Chapter 7 debtors failed the means test and triggered the BAPCPA presumption of abuse. See Clifford J. White III, *Making Bankruptcy Reform Work: A Progress Report in Year 2*, 26 Am. Bankr. Inst. J. 16 (June 2007), reporting that only 7.9 percent of Chapter 7 debtors who have above median incomes triggered Step 2 of the test, and of those, only 9.5 percent triggered the presumption of abuse. An empirical study reported in Robert M. Lawless, Angela K. Littwin, Katherine M. Porter, John A.E. Pottow, Deborah K. Thorne & Elizabeth Warren, *Did Bankruptcy Reform Fail? An Empirical Study of Consumer Debtors*, 82 Am. Bankr. L.J. 349, 361 (2008), demonstrates that between 2001 (pre-BAPCPA) and 2007 (post-BAPCPA) the inflation-adjusted median income of Chapter 7 and Chapter 13 filers did not change. These studies are consistent with reports of many practitioners who say that not only do the vast majority of above median debtors not trigger the presumption, the few that do are clients they would have steered toward a Chapter 13 filing even without the BAPCPA changes.

If the means test of BAPCPA has not accomplished its purpose of curing abuse by directing more debtors into Chapter 13, it has certainly increased the complications and expense of filing Chapter 7 cases for debtors and of administration of those cases by the courts. See the 2008 Report of the U.S. Government Accountability Office on Dollar Costs Associated with BAPCPA at www.gao.gov/new .items/d08697.pdf, reporting an increase in the average cost to a debtor for filing Chapter 7 from $921 to $1,477 attributable to BAPCPA.

The 2011 Consumer Bankruptcy Fee Study Final Report funded by the American Bankruptcy Institute and the National Conference of Bankruptcy Judges (available online at https://bapcpastudy.wordpress.com/2011/12/09/ the-consumer-bankruptcy-fee-study-final-report/) concluded that BAPCPA has made the bankruptcy system more time-consuming and costlier for debtors. That study found a significant increase in post-BAPCPA total direct access costs (TDAC) for consumers in both Chapter 7 and Chapter 13 cases.

While the 2011 report found the difference in actual returns to unsecured creditors in consumer cases before and after BAPCPA to be "statistically insignificant," the 2013 Consumer Bankruptcy Creditor Distribution Study sponsored by those same organizations (available online at http://abi-org.s3.amazonaws.com/Endowment/Research_Grants/Creditor_Distributions_ABI_Final.pdf) determined that under BAPCPA unsecured creditors are actually receiving less than they did under the pre-BAPCPA regime ("BAPCPA does not appear to have achieved the primary objective of its proponents as unsecured distributions as a percentage of unsecured claims declined nationally by a statistically significant 3.2 percentage points in the post-BAPCPA time period. Moreover, unsecured distributions as a percentage of total distributions declined by 2.5 percentage points, a result that was also statistically significant").

We noted earlier that the requirement to satisfy the means test to avoid the presumption of abuse is only imposed on the individual debtor with primarily consumer debts. It is not imposed on an individual debtor who has primarily business debts. This disparity in the treatment of the consumer debtor is one of the major criticisms of BAPCPA: Why should the presumption of abuse be applied only to consumer debtors able to fund a Chapter 13 plan and not to individual debtors with primarily business debt? However, as we will see in Chapter Twelve, Section C, §707 contains other abuse provisions that may be used to dismiss the case of *any* Chapter 7 debtor, whether an individual or an entity, and whether involving primarily consumer or business debts.

CHAPTER SUMMARY

Chapter 7 is a liquidation proceeding in which a bankruptcy trustee appointed by the court locates and takes possession of the nonexempt assets of the debtor, liquidates those assets, and distributes the proceeds to creditors of the estate per a distribution formula established by the Code. In Chapter 7 most debts left unpaid by an individual debtor are permanently discharged and the debtor receives a fresh start. The vast majority of bankruptcy cases filed each year are Chapter 7 cases, and the very great majority of those are consumer bankruptcy cases.

An individual debtor may not proceed in Chapter 7 if he received a discharge in a Chapter 7 or Chapter 11 case within eight years preceding the filing of the petition or in a Chapter 13 or Chapter 12 case within six years of filing the petition. Unless exempted, an individual debtor must certify that he or she has completed a prepetition budget and counseling session within 180 days prior to filing the bankruptcy petition.

Individual consumer debtors must also satisfy the means test introduced by BAPCPA in 2005 in order to proceed in Chapter 7. Utilizing Form 122A-1, the means test compares the debtor's annualized monthly income to the median family income for a similar size household in the debtor's state of residence. If the debtor's income is equal to or less than the applicable median income, no presumption of abuse arises in the case and he may proceed in Chapter 7.

If the debtor's income exceeds the applicable median income, the consumer debtor must complete Form 122A-2, which is a detailed itemization of expenses to determine if he has sufficient projected disposable income over the next 60 months to fund a Chapter 13 plan of reorganization. Some of the expenses listed on Form 122A-2 are the debtor's actual expenses but others are standardized expenses based on national or local figures published by the IRS. If the above median income debtor does not have sufficient projected disposable income to fund a Chapter 13 plan, the presumption of abuse still does not arise and he may proceed in Chapter 7. If, however, the debtor's income exceeds the applicable median income and the debtor does have sufficient projected income to fund a Chapter 13 plan of reorganization, the presumption of abuse arises and the case must be either converted to a Chapter 13 or dismissed, unless the debtor can show special circumstances justifying the case continuing in Chapter 7.

Where the above median consumer debtor's Forms 122A-1 and 122A-2 trigger the presumption of abuse, the debtor can ask the court to remove the presumption by showing special circumstances involving less income than indicated on Form 122A-1 or greater expenses than indicated on Form 122A-2. The consumer debtor's determination that the presumption of abuse does not arise using Forms 122A-1 and 122A-2 can be challenged by a party in interest or the court *sua sponte*.

Within 10 days following the first meeting of creditors the U.S. Trustee must file a statement with the court regarding whether the presumption of abuse arises and must file any motion to dismiss on that basis within 30 days of filing that statement. Where the presumption of abuse arises and is not rebutted the Chapter 7 case will be dismissed or, on request of the debtor, be converted to Chapter 13.

REVIEW QUESTIONS

1. If a debtor has received a discharge under Chapter 7, how long must he or she wait to file another Chapter 7 case?
2. When was the means test and presumption of abuse introduced in the Bankruptcy Code? To which Chapter 7 debtors does the means test apply?
3. What is the difference between an above median debtor and a below median debtor for purposes of the means test?
4. Name three sources of income that are excluded from the Chapter 7 debtor's calculation of income for purposes of the means test. What is the look back period?
5. Why do we care about the state median family income in connection with the means test?
6. What agency publishes the state median family income figures for the various states and how often are they adjusted? What agency publishes the national and local standards for expenses used in the means test calculation? How often are they adjusted?
7. What is the marital adjustment and who may take advantage of it?
8. What is the role of national and local standards for expenses in applying the means test for the above median debtor?
9. May the above median debtor deduct vehicle or home ownership expenses as part of the means test? What Supreme Court case tells you the answer to this question?
10. What is the "cure amount" and what role does it play in determining the expenses of the above median debtor completing the means test?
11. What kind of special circumstances might a Chapter 7 debtor show to rebut the presumption of abuse in his case?

12. Who has the standing to challenge the debtor's determination that the presumption of abuse does not arise in his case?

13. What are the options of a Chapter 7 debtor in whose case the presumption of abuse arises and is not rebutted?

14. Who determines which CCAs can provide the required prepetition credit counseling to individual Chapter 7 debtors?

WORDS AND PHRASES TO REMEMBER

above median debtor

below median debtor

budget and credit counseling agency

business bankruptcy case

can pay debtor

Chapter 7 Means Test Calculation

Chapter 7 Statement of Your Current Monthly Income

consumer bankruptcy case

consumer debt

cure amount

current monthly income

discharged

disposable monthly income

Family Violence Prevention and Services Act

Internal Revenue Service

liquidate

Local Standards for Transportation and Housing and Utilities Expenses

look back period

marital adjustment

means test

median family income

National Guard Reservists Debt Relief Act of 2008

National Standards for Allowable Living Expenses

prepetition

presumption of abuse

Schedule I: Your Income

Schedule J: Your Expenses

special circumstances

sua sponte

U.S. Census Bureau

TO LEARN MORE: A number of TLM activities to accompany this chapter are accessible on the companion web site for this textbook at http://aspen lawschool.com/books/Parsons_Debt4e/.

Chapter Eight:

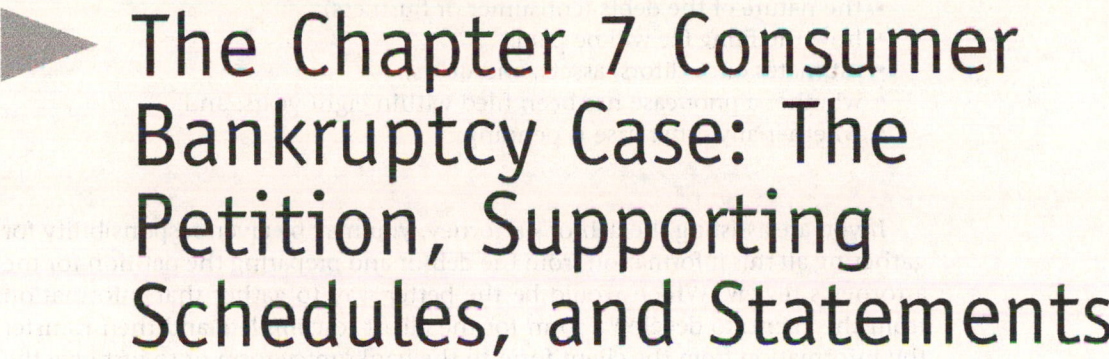

The Chapter 7 Consumer Bankruptcy Case: The Petition, Supporting Schedules, and Statements

KEY CONCEPTS

- A bankruptcy case begins with the filing of a petition in bankruptcy
- The petition is accompanied by a number of schedules, statements, and lists that require the attorney for the debtor to obtain substantial financial and other information from the debtor
- By signing the petition for a debtor client, the attorney certifies to the court that after reasonable inquiry he has no knowledge that any information on the petition, schedules, and statements is incorrect
- Attorneys for debtors in bankruptcy are considered Debt Relief Agencies and must comply with the Code's requirements for DRAs concerning advertising and mandatory disclosures to clients

 A. **The Petition Commencing the Case**

1. The Voluntary Petition

Petition The document filed to initiate a bankruptcy case under the Code.

Order for relief The formal beginning of a bankruptcy case triggered by the filing of a voluntary petition or by court order following an involuntary petition.

A bankruptcy case under any chapter is commenced by the filing of the bankruptcy **petition** per §301(a) of the Code and Bankruptcy Rule 1002. The voluntary petition for individuals filing for bankruptcy is Official Form 101. Per §301(b), the filing of the petition constitutes an **order for relief** under the Code, a term used often in the Code as we will see.

P-H 8-a: Go to www.uscourts.gov/forms/bankruptcy-forms and view the voluntary bankruptcy petition for individuals, Form 101. Scroll down through the voluntary petition form and note the kinds of information that have to be provided there. Just some of the information to be provided includes:

- not just the debtor's full name, but all other names used in the preceding eight years;
- the address where the debtor's principal assets are located;

- the type of debtor (individual, corporation, partnership, etc.);
- the chapter of the Code the filing is under (7, 11, 13, etc.);
- the nature of the debts (consumer or business);
- how the filing fee will be paid;
- estimates of creditors, assets, and debts;
- whether a prior case has been filed within eight years; and
- whether any other case is pending.

If you are assisting the debtor's attorney, you may be given responsibility for gathering all this information from the debtor and preparing the petition for the attorney's review. Which would be the better way to gather that information from the client: to develop a form for the client to complete and then transfer the information from the client form to the bankruptcy form or to just give the client a copy of the bankruptcy form with instructions to complete it by hand and then transfer the information to the form to be filed with the court? Law offices do it both ways.

2. The Joint Petition, Consolidation, and Joint Administration

Joint administration Where two or more related bankruptcy cases are ordered to be administered by the same trustee to save administrative costs.

Consolidation The merging of two or more bankruptcy cases involving the same debtor into one.

A married couple may file a **joint petition** (see §302 of the Code), in which case they will identify themselves as debtor and joint debtor (with the Supreme Court having struck down the Defense of Marriage Act in *United States v. Windsor*, 133 S. Ct. 2675 (2013), this should now include same-gender couples married under the laws of a state recognizing same-gender marriage). When a married couple file a joint petition, only one set of schedules (discussed below) is required. Other closely related debtors cannot file a joint petition, but the court may order the **joint administration** of related cases, pursuant to Bankruptcy Rule 1015(b). And if two or more petitions are pending in the same court involving the same debtor, the court may order those cases **consolidated** pursuant to Bankruptcy Rule 1015(a).

EXAMPLE

Assume a brother and sister are partners in a business. They both decide to file for bankruptcy relief. Even though the two debtors are closely related and share the same income sources and debts, they cannot file a joint petition. However, once both of them have filed individual petitions, the court may order the joint administration of their cases. If the business partnership files a separate petition, its case may be ordered jointly administered with those of the two partners. If a corporation were in bankruptcy and one of its subsidiaries filed a separate petition in the same court, the court might order joint administration if the assets and obligations of the two corporations are intertwined and creditors will not be prejudiced. If a debtor files a voluntary petition and his creditors then file an involuntary petition (discussed below) against him in the same court, the court might consolidate the two cases into one.

Marta Carlson is a divorced, single woman. Her individual voluntary petition for Chapter 7 relief is shown in Document 2 in the Carlson case file.

3. Proper Venue for Filing the Petition

Lines 5 and 6 of Part 1 of the voluntary petition form deal with **venue**. In a bankruptcy case, venue has to do with which bankruptcy court the case should be filed in or, more specifically, which federal district the case should be filed in. The general venue rule in bankruptcy cases is that the petition should be filed in the bankruptcy court in the district where the debtor has resided or had his or her principal place of business for the 180 days preceding filing (see 28 U.S.C. §1408). If the debtor has resided or had his or her primary place of business in more than one district during that timeframe, then venue is proper in whichever district the debtor has had such contacts for the longer part of the past 180 days.

Notwithstanding proper venue, pursuant to 28 U.S.C. §1412 a court can transfer an entire case or any particular proceeding within a case (e.g., the trial of a preference action) to another federal district "in the interest of justice and for the convenience of the parties." Factors considered by the courts on a motion to transfer venue focus on the economic and efficient administration of the case including the location of the debtor and creditors, the location of assets of the estate, and the likely impact of the transfer decision on administrative expenses. Where change of venue is sought for only a particular proceeding in a case, most but not all courts recognize a "strong presumption" in favor of maintaining venue where the bankruptcy case is pending. See, e.g., *In re Onco Invest. Co.*, 320 B.R. 577 (Bankr. D. Del. 2005), but compare *Brown v. C.D. Smith Drug Co.*, 1999 WL 709992 (D. Del. 1999).

Motions for change of venue are uncommon in consumer bankruptcy cases.

4. Signatures on the Petition

The Debtor's Signature

Pursuant to Bankruptcy Rule 1008, the debtor(s) must sign the voluntary petition under oath (see Part 7 at the bottom of page 6 of the voluntary petition), which means the debtor is subject to penalties of **perjury** for a deliberate misstatement or omission on the petition and supporting schedules. If the debtor is filing the petition without the assistance of an attorney (**pro se**), the debtor must also answer the questions asked on page 8 in Part 7 of the form and sign there as well. The questions on page 8 of the form are not answered by the pro se debtor under oath but are sobering nonetheless in their import since they alert the debtor to the complexity of the bankruptcy process and the dangers of proceeding pro se (the reference in this section of the form to the debtor having received nonattorney assistance is discussed below).

The Signature and Certification of the Attorney for the Debtor

The attorney for the debtor will sign the voluntary petition as well (see Part 7 at the top of page 7 of the voluntary petition). Pursuant to Bankruptcy Rule 9011, based on Rule 11 of the Federal Rules of Civil Procedure, an attorney's signature on anything filed with the court constitutes a certification to the court that "to the best of the attorney's knowledge, information and belief formed after an inquiry reasonable under the circumstances,"

- the filing is not done for any improper purpose (e.g., to harass or delay);
- the factual allegations or denial of an opponent's factual contentions have or likely will have evidentiary support; and
- all legal contentions are warranted by existing law or a nonfrivolous argument for what the law should be.

BAPCPA, however, added a new dimension to the attorney's signature on the petition. New §707(b)(4)(D) of the Code provides as follows:

> The signature of an attorney on the petition shall constitute a certification that the attorney has no knowledge after an inquiry that the information in the schedules filed with such petition is incorrect.

Note that this certification by the attorney extends not just to the information on the petition itself but to information contained on the debtor's many schedules filed with the petition. What exactly is the "inquiry" required of debtor's attorney regarding the information his client provides to him? Is the attorney being asked to guarantee the accuracy of his client's information? Is the attorney responsible if the client misstates or falsifies information that appears in the petition and schedules? Can an attorney not simply rely on the veracity and accuracy of the information his client gives him? What exactly are the penalties to be imposed on the debtor's attorney if he is deemed by the court to have breached the certification? Neither the Code nor the Bankruptcy Rules answer these questions and case law is still threshing it out. One oft-cited decision construed the new inquiry requirement to mean that the attorney's inquiry need only be "a reasonable one" to "be tested objectively" and stressed that the debtor's attorney "is not a guarantor of the accuracy of any information contained in bankruptcy documents prepared . . . with information provided by that debtor." See *In re Withrow*, 391 B.R. 217, 227 (Bankr. D. Mass. 2008).

> Accordingly, it seems to this Court that the answers to at least the following questions are germane to a Rule 9011 and §707(b)(4)(C) analysis: (1) did the attorney impress upon the debtor the critical importance of accuracy in the preparation of documents to be presented to the Court; (2) did the attorney seek from the debtor, and then review, whatever documents were within the debtor's possession, custody or control in order to verify the information provided by the debtor; (3) did the attorney employ such external verification tools as were available and not time or cost prohibitive (e.g., on-line real estate title compilations, on-line lien search, tax "scripts"); (4) was any of the information provided by the debtor and then set forth in the debtor's court filings internally inconsistent—that is, was there anything which should have obviously alerted the attorney that the information provided by the debtor could not be accurate; and (5) did the attorney act promptly to correct any information presented to the Court which turned out, notwithstanding the attorney's best efforts, to be inaccurate. These questions can be further simplified and reduced to one question, their common denominator: Did the attorney do his or her level best to get it right?

Id. at 228.

P-H 8-b: In the case of *In re Dean*, 401 B.R. 917 (Bankr. D. Idaho 2008), the debtor's attorney advised his clients to perfect a relative's security interest in their motor home before filing a bankruptcy petition, then took their word for it that it had been done. It wasn't and the debtors lost their mobile home in the bankruptcy case. The court found that since the security filing was easily verifiable by the attorney and had not been done, the attorney had violated his duty of inquiry under §707(b)(4)(D). The court entered a **turnover order** directing him to **disgorge** (refund) the fee paid to him by the debtors. See if the courts of your federal district or circuit have decided a case under Bankruptcy Rule 9011 as supplemented by new §707(b)(4)(D).

Section 342(b) of the Code, added by BAPCPA, requires that consumer debtors be provided with written notice explaining all the options for filing bankruptcy (usually Chapters 7, 11, 12, and 13 for the individual debtor) and the differences between each type of filing. Section 342(b) seems to literally place the requirement of providing consumer debtors with written notice of their filing options and differences between the various bankruptcy filings on the clerk of the bankruptcy court. However, since debtor's attorneys are considered debt relief agencies as discussed in the next section, they are required to comply with the notice requirement of §342 as well. For that reason, the signature of the attorney on the top of page 7 in Part 7 of the petition will certify that this requirement has been met. The clerk will provide the §342 notice only if the debtor is pro se.

The signature of the debtor in Part 7 of the petition at the bottom of page 6 acknowledges receipt of the information contained in the §342 notice. The fee agreement between Marta Carlson and her attorney is accompanied by the required §342 notices and is included in her case file as Document 1 (viewable on the companion web site at http://aspenlawschool.com/books/Parsons_Debt4e/).

The Signature of a Debt Relief Agency (DRA) Providing Assistance in a Consumer Debtor Case: The Debtor's Attorney as a DRA

BAPCPA introduced the concept of a **debt relief agency** (DRA) to the Code. Section 101(12A) defines a DRA in part as one "who provides any bankruptcy assistance to an assisted person in return for the payment of money or other valuable consideration. . . ." An **assisted person** is defined in §101(3) as an individual debtor with primarily consumer debts. Sections 526-528 of the Code impose a number of restrictions on DRAs including the requirement that they identify themselves as such in all advertising, make certain detailed disclosures to clients in writing, provide consumer debtors with the §342 notice explaining all the options for filing bankruptcy and the differences between each type of filing, and abstain from advising clients to incur more debt in contemplation of the bankruptcy filing. The Code authorizes a number of sanctions that can be imposed on DRAs for violation of those restrictions including forfeiture of fees and other charges to assisted persons, liability to such persons for actual damages, and attorney's fees.

Of course, there are numerous private, nonattorney businesses that are engaged in providing financial advice to consumers for a fee to whom this definition applies. We have met them before in the guise of **credit counseling** agencies discussed in Chapter Four, Section E. But an immediate issue arose after BAPCPA became law as to whether debtor's attorneys would be considered DRAs. Of particular concern was the §526(a)(4) prohibition on a DRA advising an assisted person to incur more debt in contemplation of bankruptcy, something attorneys routinely do (e.g., to refinance debt at a lower rate, pay certain bills, or purchase a reliable car). In *Milavetz, Gallop & Milavetz v. United States*, 559 U.S. 229 (2010), the U.S. Supreme Court held that lawyers *are* DRAs under the Code, but in response to an argument that the restriction of §526(a)(4) violated the free speech rights of attorneys, construed that section to prohibit only giving advice to a client to load up on debt so that it can be discharged in bankruptcy, advice that would likely be unethical and possibly fraudulent anyway.

The Signature of the Bankruptcy Petition Preparer

Bankruptcy petition preparer Prepares a bankruptcy petition for a fee. Not an attorney or working under the supervision of an attorney.

Section 110 of the Code authorizes nonattorneys to assist debtors in preparing the petition and supporting schedules and to receive a fee for doing so. However, the nonattorney **bankruptcy petition preparer** (BPP) is subject to numerous limitations and requirements. The BPP is strictly prohibited from providing the client with any legal advice, including advice concerning the petition or what chapter of bankruptcy to file under, and the BPP must disclose those limitations in writing to the client per Official Form 119. The pro se debtor who utilizes the assistance of a BPP in preparation of the bankruptcy petition or supporting schedules must disclose that in response to the question asked in Part 7, page 8 of the petition, and the completed Form 119 must then be attached to the petition. The debtor must sign Part 1 of Form 119 acknowledging receipt of a copy of the form that contains the required disclosures.

The BPP must sign Form 119 under oath subject to penalties of perjury. The BPP is also subject to the forfeiture of any fee deemed excessive or the entire fee collected for failure to comply with the requirements imposed on the BPP, plus an additional $500 penalty for failure to comply with a turnover order (the court order to disgorge and refund fees received from the debtor), and possible criminal prosecution under 18 U.S.C. §156 for the knowing disregard of a bankruptcy law or rule.

Code §110(h) authorizes the U.S. Judicial Conference to set maximum fees that BPPs may charge and the various offices of the United States Trustee across the country have done so.

P-H 8-c: Review the Bankruptcy Petition Preparer Guidelines issued by the U.S Trustee's Office for the Middle District of California in 2014 at www.justice.gov/sites/default/files/ust-regions/legacy/2014/03/10/bpp_guidelines.pdf. What is the maximum fee that a BPP may charge a client in the district? Does the charge include expenses for copying, postage, courier services, etc.? Does the charge include filing fees for the debtor's petition? What exactly do these guidelines say that a BPP can do for a client that is not possibly the prohibited practice of law by the BPP?

BPPs are also considered DRAs per the definition of Code §101(12A) and must comply with those provisions as well.

5. The Filing Fee

Per Bankruptcy Rule 1006, the **filing fee** is normally paid to the clerk of the bankruptcy court at the time the petition is filed, although the Code does permit a debtor to pay the fee in installments. In that event, the debtor must file Form 103A, Application to Pay Filing Fee in Installments, along with the petition. The number of installments is limited to four, and the debtor must make the final installment no later than 120 days after filing the petition. However, that time limit can be extended to 180 days on motion and for cause shown. In Chapter 7 cases only, the debtor may request waiver of the fee entirely by filing Form 103B with the petition, but as you can see by reading that form, that remedy is only available to the very poor.

P-H 8-d: Go to www.uscourts.gov/forms/bankruptcy-forms and view Official Form 103B, Application for Waiver of the Chapter 7 Filing Fee, and then answer these questions:

- What is the current filing fee for a Chapter 7 bankruptcy petition?
- How close to the poverty line does the debtor have to be in order to qualify for waiver of the fee?
- Is the application signed by the debtor under penalties of perjury?
- If the debtor is assisted in completing this form by a NABPP, does that person have to sign the application?
- What is the current official poverty line for a family of four?

---

6. The Involuntary Petition

The vast majority of bankruptcy cases are filed voluntarily, meaning the debtor him or herself makes the decision to file for relief. But §303 of the Code does permit a debtor to be forced into a Chapter 7 (or a Chapter 11 to be considered later) bankruptcy by creditors filing an **involuntary petition**. Three creditors with unsecured claims totaling at least $15,775 (as of April 2016; to be next adjusted in April 2019 per §104) may join in the petition. If the debtor has fewer than 12 unsecured creditors, then a single creditor with a claim of at least $15,775 can initiate the involuntary petition. The involuntary proceeding is available only in Chapters 7 or 11. The involuntary petition for an individual is Official Form 105.

Bankruptcy Rules 1010 through 1013 provide that when an involuntary petition is filed it must be served on the debtor along with a summons, just as would happen in a civil lawsuit under the Federal Rules of Civil Procedure. Once the debtor is served with the petition and summons, he must file an answer to the petition within 21 days raising any defenses or objections he has to the petition. If he fails to do so, the court will enter an order for relief on the involuntary petition by **default** and the case will proceed. Bankruptcy Rule 1011(a) allows a nonpetitioning partner to contest an involuntary petition against the partnership but does not allow a nonpetitioning creditor or other **party in interest** to contest an involuntary petition. Recall from the introduction of this term in Chapter Six

Party in interest One who has sufficient interest in a matter before the court to be deemed to have standing to be heard by the court on the matter.

that a party in interest is one who has sufficient interest in a matter before the court to be deemed to have standing to be heard by the court on the matter.

P-H 8-e: Look at §101 of the Code and Bankruptcy Rule 9001. Is "party in interest" defined in either place? Assume an individual debtor files a Chapter 7 petition but contends he does not need to complete the means test because most of his debts are nonconsumer debts. Given the informal definition of the phrase suggested in the text, who would be a party in interest with sufficient interest to be given standing to contest this matter? The debtor? A business partner of the debtor? The U.S. Trustee? The bankruptcy trustee appointed to administer the case? All the creditors of the debtor? If a creditor of the debtor is a corporation, the individual shareholders, officers, or directors of the creditor? The debtor's parents or other family members who are not creditors or business partners of the debtor? The local media? The debtor's noncreditor nosey neighbor?

Evidentiary hearing A court hearing at which sworn testimony is taken and exhibits may be offered subject to the Federal Rules of Evidence.

If the involuntary petition is properly answered and contested, the court will then conduct an **evidentiary hearing** where live testimony is given and relevant exhibits introduced, all subject to the Federal Rules of Evidence. At the hearing, the court must decide whether to enter an order for relief allowing the involuntary case to proceed or to dismiss the petition. The creditors filing the involuntary petition have the **burden of proof** at the hearing to demonstrate that sufficient grounds exist to justify proceeding with the bankruptcy case over the debtor's objection. To satisfy their burden, the creditors must demonstrate that one or both of the following grounds are present:

- the debtor is not generally paying its bona fide debts as they come due; or
- within 120 days preceding the filing of the involuntary petition, a receiver, assignee, or custodian has taken possession of all or substantially all of the debtor's property.

The first ground, that the debtor is not paying his debts as they come due, is the ground most frequently asserted in an involuntary case. Consider why creditors force a debtor into bankruptcy: Because the creditors are unsecured or under-secured in specific property of the debtor, they are not being paid, and they cannot gain access to the debtor's assets without suing him and obtaining a judgment, which could take months or years. And those creditors fear that the debtor will have dissipated his assets by then, so there will be no property to execute on to satisfy the judgment when it is finally rendered. Forcing the debtor into a liquidation bankruptcy is seen as the quickest and surest way to stop the debtor from further dissipating his assets and to force a distribution of the remaining assets for the benefit of all the creditors.

Creditors must proceed with caution in filing an involuntary petition. If the petition is contested and dismissed, then §303(i) of the Code permits the bankruptcy court to award court costs and attorney's fees to the debtor for contesting the petition. And if the judge finds that the petition was filed in bad faith, then the court may award the debtor consequential damages (e.g., lost profits to the business caused by the filing) and even punitive damages.

B. ▶ Schedules, Statements, and Other Documents That Accompany the Petition

As required by §521 of the Code and Bankruptcy Rule 1007, the consumer debtor must file a number of schedules, statements, and other documents in addition to the voluntary petition and its exhibits. Section 521, as amended by BAPCPA, is dense, poorly structured, and not well worded. However, the BAPCPA changes have now been in effect long enough for bankruptcy practitioners and judges to figure out with some confidence what is required.

This section will summarize the schedules, statements, and other documents that must be prepared and filed in support of the Chapter 7 petition. Where there is an official form for the required schedules, statements and the like, that form is referenced in the summary. Remember that the official forms can be accessed and viewed at www.uscourts.gov/forms/bankruptcy-forms if you do not have them in paper form.

The schedules, statements, and other documents filed by Marta Carlson in connection with her Chapter 7 case are set forth in the Carlson case file (accessible at the companion web site). As you read the description of each schedule below, compare that description to the Carlson filings in her case file. Keep in mind as you review these schedules, statements, and other documents that if you work as an assisting legal professional for the debtor's attorney, you will be preparing them for review by the supervising attorney using information supplied by the debtor/client. If you are the assisting legal professional for a creditor or creditor's attorney, the bankruptcy trustee, or the U.S. Trustee, you will be reviewing them for the accuracy of the information and to summarize them for your supervisor.

1. The List of Creditors

Section 521(a)(1) of the Code and Bankruptcy Rule 1007(a)(1) require that the debtor file a list of creditors. (See Document 4 in the Carlson case file.) There is no official form for this list, but most bankruptcy courts provide practitioners with a matrix form accessible from the court's web site. The list will serve as a mailing matrix by the clerk's office to provide creditors notice of the bankruptcy filing and of other proceedings in the case.

2. Schedule A/B, Property (Official Form 106A/B)

On this form the debtor must list, by description and location, all real and personal property in which the debtor owns an interest. In Part 1 of the form the debtor lists each parcel of real property by street address, describes the property (e.g., unimproved land, single family home, timeshare, etc.), states whether others have an interest in the property, identifies the interest held (fee simple, life estate, leasehold, etc.), and states the estimated value of the entire property and the value of the debtor's interest in it.

On this form the debtor must also list, describe, and place a value on personal property owned by the debtor including vehicles (Part 2), personal and household items (Part 3), financial assets (Part 4), non-realty business related property (Part 5), and farm or fishing-operation property (Part 6). There is a comprehensive "other" category in Part 7 of the form for property not listed elsewhere in it.

(See Document 7 in the Carlson case file.)

3. Schedule C, The Property You Claim as Exempt (Individuals) (Official Form 106C)

How Exemptions Work

In Chapter Five, Section D we considered exempt property in the context of a judgment creditor executing on a judgment. Similarly, the Code allows an individual bankruptcy debtor to claim certain property as exempt. Exemptions are not available to Chapter 7 entity debtors (corporations and partnerships) since they go out of business at the end of the liquidation and do not retain assets. Individual debtors are required to set forth the property they claim as exempt on Schedule C: The Property You Claim as Exempt, which is Official Form 106C. Illustration 8-a sets out Marta Carlson's Schedule C.

The Chapter 7 bankruptcy trustee cannot seize the property that is fully exempt and sell it for the benefit of the creditors. Instead the debtor will retain possession of the fully exempt property.

EXAMPLE

In her Schedule C (Illustration 8-a and Document 8 in the Carlson case file) Marta Carlson has claimed her jewelry to be fully exempt under §522(d)(4). It is worth $1,350 and that Code section currently allows her to exempt such property up to $1,600. If her valuation of the jewelry is correct, she has fully exempted it and the trustee cannot seize it.

If the debtor is unable to fully exempt property, the trustee may seize it and sell it in order to realize the equity in the property for the benefit of the estate. But the debtor is entitled to receive the exempted value following the sale.

EXAMPLE

In her Schedule C Marta Carlson has claimed exemptions totaling $5,025 in her YR-4 Toyota Camry. But the vehicle is worth $8,500 so she is unable to fully exempt it. Once the trustee determines there is equity for the estate in that property, the trustee will seize the car and sell it. But Marta will have to be paid her exempt amount of $5,025 from the proceeds of the sale.

If a creditor is properly secured and perfected in the property claimed as exempt, the debtor's claimed exemption normally cannot defeat that secured claim (subject to an exception for judicial liens discussed later in this section) and there is no equity for the estate in the property to the extent of the secured claim.

EXAMPLE

Automotive Finance, Inc. (AFI) has a claim in the amount of $1,750 secured by the YR-4 Toyota Camry in which Marta also claims an exemption of $5,025. If the trustee seizes and sells the vehicle, AFI's secured claim must be paid in full first from the proceeds, then Marta's exemption claim. Only after those two superior claims are satisfied can the trustee take the balance of the proceeds of the sale into the estate for the benefit of creditors.

Illustration 8-a: MARTA CARLSON'S SCHEDULE C

Fill in this information to identify your case:

Debtor 1   Marta   Rinaldi   Carlson
           First Name   Middle Name   Last Name

Debtor 2
(Spouse, if filing) First Name   Middle Name   Last Name

United States Bankruptcy Court for the: District of Minnesota

Case number   16-7-XXXX
(if known)

☐ Check if this is an
amended filing

Official Form 106C

Schedule C: The Property You Claim as Exempt   04/16

Be as complete and accurate as possible. If two married people are filing together, both are equally responsible for supplying correct information. Using the property you listed on *Schedule A/B: Property* (Official Form 106A/B) as your source, list the property that you claim as exempt. If more space is needed, fill out and attach to this page as many copies of *Part 2: Additional Page* as necessary. On the top of any additional pages, write your name and case number (if known).

For each item of property you claim as exempt, you must specify the amount of the exemption you claim. One way of doing so is to state a specific dollar amount as exempt. Alternatively, you may claim the full fair market value of the property being exempted up to the amount of any applicable statutory limit. Some exemptions—such as those for health aids, rights to receive certain benefits, and tax-exempt retirement funds—may be unlimited in dollar amount. However, if you claim an exemption of 100% of fair market value under a law that limits the exemption to a particular dollar amount and the value of the property is determined to exceed that amount, your exemption would be limited to the applicable statutory amount.

Part 1:   Identify the Property You Claim as Exempt

1. Which set of exemptions are you claiming? *Check one only, even if your spouse is filing with you.*
   ☐ You are claiming state and federal nonbankruptcy exemptions. 11 U.S.C. § 522(b)(3)
   ☑ You are claiming federal exemptions. 11 U.S.C. § 522(b)(2)

2. For any property you list on *Schedule A/B* that you claim as exempt, fill in the information below.

Brief description of the property and line on *Schedule A/B* that lists this property	Current value of the portion you own Copy the value from *Schedule A/B*	Amount of the exemption you claim *Check only one box for each exemption.*	Specific laws that allow exemption
Brief description: Primary Residence Line from Schedule A/B: 1.1	$255,000.00	☑ $ 11,825.00 ☐ 100% of fair market value, up to any applicable statutory limit	11 U.S.C. § 522(d)(1)
Brief description: YR-4 Toyota Camry Line from Schedule A/B: 3.1	$8,500.00	☑ $ 5,025.00 ☐ 100% of fair market value, up to any applicable statutory limit	11 U.S.C. § 522(d)(2) and (d)(5)
Brief description: Washing machine Line from Schedule A/B: 6	$350.00	☑ $ 350.00 ☐ 100% of fair market value, up to any applicable statutory limit	11 U.S.C. § 522(d)(3)

3. Are you claiming a homestead exemption of more than $160,375?
   (Subject to adjustment on 4/01/19 and every 3 years after that for cases filed on or after the date of adjustment.)
   ☑ No
   ☐ Yes. Did you acquire the property covered by the exemption within 1,215 days before you filed this case?
      ☐ No
      ☐ Yes

Official Form 106C   Schedule C: The Property You Claim as Exempt   page 1 of __

Debtor 1   Marta   Rinaldi   Carlson   Case number *(if known)* 16-7-XXXX
            First Name   Middle Name   Last Name

Part 2:   Additional Page

Brief description of the property and line on *Schedule A/B* that lists this property	Current value of the portion you own Copy the value from *Schedule A/B*	Amount of the exemption you claim *Check only one box for each exemption*	Specific laws that allow exemption
Brief description: Clothes dryer Line from *Schedule A/B*: 6	$ 250.00	☑ $ 250.00 ☐ 100% of fair market value, up to any applicable statutory limit	11 U.S.C. § 522(d)(3)
Brief description: Other furnishings Line from *Schedule A/B*: 6	$ 6,500.00	☑ $ 6,500.00 ☐ 100% of fair market value, up to any applicable statutory limit	11 U.S.C. § 522(d)(3)
Brief description: Electronics Line from *Schedule A/B*: 7	$ 900.00	☑ $ 900.00 ☐ 100% of fair market value, up to any applicable statutory limit	11 U.S.C. § 522(d)(3)
Brief description: Clothes Line from *Schedule A/B*: 11	$ 1,000.00	☑ $ 1,000.00 ☐ 100% of fair market value, up to any applicable statutory limit	11 U.S.C. § 522(d)(3)
Brief description: Doll collection Line from *Schedule A/B*: 8	$ 15,125.00	☑ $ 15,125.00 ☐ 100% of fair market value, up to any applicable statutory limit	11 U.S.C. § 522(d)(3) & $11500 of unused exemption from 11 U.S.C. § 522(d)(1)
Brief description: Retriever dog (Max) Line from *Schedule A/B*: 12	$ 50.00	☑ $ 50.00 ☐ 100% of fair market value, up to any applicable statutory limit	$50 of unused exemption from 11 U.S.C. § 522(d)(1)
Brief description: Cash Line from *Schedule A/B*: 16	$ 50.00	☑ $ 50.00 ☐ 100% of fair market value, up to any applicable statutory limit	$50 of unused exemption from 11 U.S.C. § 522(d)(1)
Brief description: Deposits Line from *Schedule A/B*: 17	$ 250.00	☑ $ 250.00 ☐ 100% of fair market value, up to any applicable statutory limit	$250 of unused exemption from 11 U.S.C. § 522(d)(1)
Brief description: TTI 401(k) Line from *Schedule A/B*: 21	$ 7,600.00	☑ $ 7,600.00 ☐ 100% of fair market value, up to any applicable statutory limit	11 U.S.C. § 522(d)(10)(E)
Brief description: Support arrearage Line from *Schedule A/B*: 29	$ 15,000.00	☑ $ 15,000.00 ☐ 100% of fair market value, up to any applicable statutory limit	11 U.S.C. § 522(d)(10)(D)
Brief description: Line from *Schedule A/B*:	$	☐ $ ☐ 100% of fair market value, up to any applicable statutory limit	
Brief description: Line from *Schedule A/B*:	$	☐ $ ☐ 100% of fair market value, up to any applicable statutory limit	

Official Form 106C   Schedule C: The Property You Claim as Exempt   page 2 of __

P-H 8-f: On her Schedule C, Marta Carlson has claimed an exemption in her home of $11,825, less than the maximum **homestead exemption** currently allowed under §522(d)(1). As you can see on her Schedule D (Document 9 in the Carlson case file), she has two mortgages on the property and those two secured claims together total $180,000. The home is valued by Marta on her Schedules A/B and D at $255,000. Assume her bankruptcy trustee seizes the home and sells it for that price and incurs no sales commission in doing so. Using the last example, in what order will the proceeds of sale be distributed? If the trustee incurs a 6 percent realtor's commission on the sale of the home, that expense will come out of the estate's share of the proceeds. We will learn later that the realtor's postpetition commission will be treated as a priority administrative claim in the bankruptcy case.

The Federal Exemptions and Right of States to Opt Out

The Code contains a uniform set of federal exemptions for individual debtors set out in §522(d). In a case where husband and wife are joint debtors, §522(m) provides that each debtor may claim the stated exemption separately, a process practitioners call **doubling** or **stacking**. As mandated by §104, the dollar value of the federal exemptions is adjusted in April of every third year. The last adjustment was on April 1, 2016, and the next will be on April 1, 2019.

EXAMPLE

As of April 1, 2016, the federal homestead exemption allowed under §522(d)(1) is $23,675. If a husband and wife both own the homestead and they are joint bankruptcy debtors, they may each claim the full exemption amount and, together, exempt $47,350 of equity in their home.

Illustration 8-b summarizes the federal exemptions.

Section 522(b) allows states, acting through their legislatures, to **opt out** of using the federal exemptions set out in §522(d) and to require use of the applicable state exemption laws instead. More than 30 states have opted out of the federal exemptions. In those states, bankruptcy filers must use the state exemption laws that control in executions on final judgments. In states that have not opted out of the federal exemptions, §522(b) permits the individual bankruptcy filer to choose between the federal exemptions and the applicable state exemptions. The filer in those states cannot pick and choose among the federal and state exemption provisions, however. He must use *only* the federal exemptions or *only* the state exemptions. And a husband and wife filing a joint petition in those states must *both* use the federal exemptions or *both* use the state exemptions.

P-H 8-g: In her Schedule C, Marta Carlson has utilized the federal exemptions of §522(d). Minnesota is one of the few states that has not opted out of the federal exemptions so Marta had the option of using the federal exemptions or the Minnesota state exemption laws. If she had filed in an opt out state, she would be unable to use the federal exemptions and could only have used the state exemption laws of the opt out state. Go through each exemption she has claimed and be sure you understand why she is claiming each exemption listed. Has she cited the proper subsection of §522(d) in connection with each claimed exemption?

P-H 8-h: Locate the exemption statutes of your state and compare them with the federal exemptions set forth in §522(d) of the Code. Which appear more generous to debtors? Which appear more reasonable to you? If your state has opted out of the Code exemptions to use its own exemptions, do you think that was a good idea? If it has not, should it?

P-H 8-i: In *Rousey v. Jacoway*, 544 U.S. 320 (2005), the Court held that assets in Individual Retirement Accounts (IRAs) are exempt under §522(d)(10)(E) as payments "on account of age" notwithstanding they can be accessed prior to age 59 1/2. This decision has broad implications for the baby boomer generation, providing millions of Americans nearing retirement with increased protection of their earnings. Read the Pew Research report on baby boomers at www.pewresearch.org/daily-number/baby-boomers-retire/. How many baby boomers are turning 65 each day? How many will retire over the next 20 years or so?

Illustration 8-b: SUMMARY OF §522(d) FEDERAL EXEMPTIONS (ALL DOLLAR VALUES STATED ARE AS OF APRIL 1, 2016)

> - $23,675 of equity in the residence of the debtor and used by the debtor or a dependent (§522(d)(1))
> - $3,775 of equity in one vehicle (§522(d)(2))
> - $12,625 of equity (not to exceed $600 per item) in household goods and furnishings, appliances, wearing apparel, books, animals, crops, or musical instruments held for personal, family, or household use by the debtor or a dependent (§502(d)(3))
> - $1,600 of equity in jewelry used by the debtor or a dependent (§502(d)(4))
> - $1,250, plus up to $11,850 of any unused balance of the homestead exemption of §522(d)(1) (§522(d)(5)) (known as the **wild card exemption**)
> - $2,375 of equity in implements or tools of the trade or professional books of the debtor or a dependent (§522(d)(6))
> - An unlimited amount in unmatured life insurance policies owned by the debtor, excluding credit life contracts (§522(d)(7))
> - $12,625 in cash value of an insurance policy (e.g., a whole life policy) (§522(d)(8))
> - An unlimited amount in prescription health aids for the debtor or a dependent (§522(d)(9))
> - An unlimited amount in Social Security, welfare, disability, unemployment, or veteran's benefits and in alimony, child support, or separate maintenance, to the extent reasonably necessary to support the debtor or a dependent, and in qualified pension and profit sharing plans (§522(d)(10))
> - An unlimited amount as crime victim's reparation benefits and wrongful death recovery or life insurance benefits if the debtor was a dependent of the deceased, to the extent reasonably necessary for the support of the debtor or a dependent, and up to $23,675 in recovery on a personal injury claim involving the debtor or a dependent, and compensation for lost future earnings of the debtor or one on whom the debtor was a dependent, to the extent reasonably necessary for the support of the debtor or a dependent (§522(d)(11))
> - An unlimited amount in any retirement fund exempted from taxation by the IRS (e.g., 401(k), 403(b), and IRA plans) (§522(d)(12))

Wild card exemption Practitioner's phrase for §522(d)(5) allowing an individual debtor a general exemption in any property up to a stated value.

EC 8-a: The right of states to opt out of the federal exemption scheme and apply their own exemptions in bankruptcy cases filed in the federal courts within that state is a striking example of variation allowed in the application of what was intended to be a uniform national bankruptcy process imposed by federal law. The exemptions a debtor in one state might enjoy are quite different from those a debtor in another state will have to settle for. Is this right in a moral/ethical sense? Does it encourage forum shopping, in the sense that a financially challenged debtor might change his state of residence in advance of a foreseeable bankruptcy filing? Is it ethical for an attorney to advise a client to do that?

Another consideration in determining what exemptions apply in a particular case is §522(b)(3)(A), which provides that it is the law of the debtor's domicile that will determine what exemptions apply in his case but only if he has been domiciled there 730 days (two years) prior to the date the petition is filed. If he has not been domiciled in any one state for the requisite 730 days, then the law of the state where he was domiciled for the 180 days preceding the 730-day period will determine the exemptions.

EXAMPLE

Assume a debtor files for bankruptcy relief in a U.S. bankruptcy court in California. The debtor moved to California from Texas six months ago. She had lived in Texas five years before moving to California. Though California is now the debtor's domicile, she has not lived there 730 days preceding the filing of the petition, and so California exemption laws will not control her Schedule C exemptions. Because she lived in Texas for the requisite 180 days preceding the 730-day period, Texas exemption laws will control her Schedule C exemptions.

Applicable exemptions will control property of the debtor wherever it is located. (Compare the rule for controlling exemption law in the enforcement of final judgments, as discussed in Chapter Five, Section D.)

EXAMPLE

Assume the debtor from the previous example owns property in Colorado. Texas exemption laws will control her right to exempt any such property on her Schedule C, not Colorado law.

Limitations on the Homestead Exemption: The 1,215-Day Rule

There is an important limitation on the right of a debtor in bankruptcy to claim the homestead exemption (for the debtor's principal residence) in a state that has opted out of the federal exemptions. As we considered in Chapter Five when studying state exemption laws in the context of a judgment debtor executing on a final judgment, some states have very generous homestead exemptions, far more generous than the federal homestead exemption, which is limited to $23,675 for a sole individual debtor or $47,350 for a husband and wife filing as joint debtors (per §522(d)(1) as of April 1, 2016).

EXAMPLE

A bankruptcy debtor residing in a state that allows an unlimited homestead exemption and which has opted out of the federal exemptions could theoretically exempt all the equity in his principal residence just as he could exempt it from executing judgment creditors. Thus, that bankruptcy debtor could emerge from a Chapter 7 liquidation with his debts discharged and not lose his home.

1,215-day rule Rule limiting amount of homestead exemption for principal residence purchased less than 1,215 days before petition in bankruptcy filed.

However, §522(p)(1), added by BAPCPA, provides that if the bankruptcy debtor has not owned the principal residence for more than 1,215 days preceding the filing of the petition, debtor cannot exempt more than $160,375 of equity in it (as of April 1, 2016) regardless of the applicable homestead exemption. This is the **1,215-day rule**.

EXAMPLE

Assume the debtor in the previous example bought his home 24 months before filing for bankruptcy relief and has a total of $250,000 of equity in the home. He has owned the home only 730 days. So even though the state where he resides allows an unlimited homestead exemption, and even though that state has opted out of the federal exemptions for bankruptcy cases, the debtor will be limited to a homestead exemption of no more than $160,375.

Section 522(p)(2)(B) does say that the limitation of §522(p)(1) does not apply to any equity the debtor has in his current principal residence that was transferred from a prior principal residence so long as the prior residence was acquired outside of the 1,215-day limit and was in the same state.

EXAMPLE

Assume the debtor in our previous example bought his first home six years (2,190 days) before filing for bankruptcy relief. Then 24 months ago he sold that first residence and used $225,000 of the equity he realized from that sale to purchase the current home. At the time he files his petition in bankruptcy, he has a total of $250,000 equity in his home. That debtor can exempt all of the $225,000 equity he transferred from his first home to the second but not the additional $25,000 of equity he has accumulated since the purchase of the second home less than 1,215 days before filing. But note that if the first home of the debtor had been located in a different state from the second home, debtor would not get the benefit of this exception to the 1,215-day rule.

Valuing Property Claimed as Exempt

Schedule C requires the debtor to state the value of the property claimed as exempt and the dollar amount of the claimed exemption. That can be confusing.

EXAMPLE

As you can see on her Schedule C, Marta Carlson claims an exemption in her four-year-old Toyota Camry. She is the sole owner of the vehicle and it is valued at $8,500 so that is the value of the portion she owns and she so indicates on the form. The Camry is collateral for the debt owed to Automotive Financing, Inc., which has a balance of $1,750 owed at the time the petition is filed so there is a total of $6,750 of equity in the car ($8,500 − $1,750 = $6,750). However, Marta decides to exempt only $5,025 of that equity and that is the dollar amount of the exemption for the Camry that she enters on the schedule. To reach that exemption amount she combined the $3,775 exemption for motor vehicles authorized by §522(d)(2) with the $1,250 wildcard exemption of §522(d)(5) (both values as of April 1, 2016). If Marta's claimed exemptions in the vehicle are approved and it is sold, the proceeds will be applied first to pay off the claim of AFI, totaling $1,750, which is secured by the vehicle, and second to pay Marta $5,025 as her total exemption in the vehicle. The balance will then be used by the bankruptcy trustee for estate administration costs or distribution to creditors.

P-H 8-j: Marta has a total of $6,750 of equity in the YR-4 Toyota Camry ($8,500 value minus the $1,750 owed to AFI). She could have exempted all of that equity using §522(d)(2), the wildcard exemption of §522(d)(5), plus a portion of her homestead exemption under §522(d)(1) as is allowed by §522(d)(5). If she had chosen to do that, what would be the maximum homestead exemption she could have claimed under §522(d)(1)?

EXAMPLE

Note that on her Schedule C, Marta has claimed only $11,825 of the §522(d)(1) homestead exemption in connection with her residence even though there is $75,000 owner's equity in the home ($255,000 value minus $180,000 balance owed on two mortgages). But note from her Schedule C that she uses a portion of her §522(d)(1) homestead exemption to exempt her cash ($50), her bank account balance ($250), her pet dog ($50), and her doll collection ($11,500). That borrowing of the unused portion of the §522(d)(1) homestead exemption is expressly authorized by the wild card exemption of §522(d)(5). But Marta's use of those amounts leaves only $11,825 available for her homestead exemption. What does that use of the homestead and wild card exemptions by Marta tell you about the priority she places on that doll collection?

Fair market value The price that a willing buyer would pay a willing seller for an item, neither being under a compulsion to sell or buy.

Section 522(a)(2) and Schedule C require the debtor to list the **fair market value** of property claimed as exempt, "as of the date of the filing of the petition." Undefined in the Code, fair market value has been held to mean the estimated price that a willing buyer would pay to a willing seller for the item, neither being under a compulsion to sell or buy and both having reasonable knowledge of the underlying facts (see *United States v. Cartwright*, 411 U.S. 546 (1973)). So debtor cannot use a lower "fire sale value" or "distress value" for exempted property even though debtor may be in desperate straits financially.

The Right to Object to a Claimed Exemption

The bankruptcy trustee appointed to administer the Chapter 7 case does not have to accept the debtor's Schedule C exemptions. Bankruptcy Rule 4003 authorizes the trustee or other party in interest to object to the debtor's claimed exemptions. The objection may contend that the debtor is not entitled to exempt a particular item of property listed on Schedule C or that the value assigned by the debtor to an item of property claimed as exempt is too low. (Recall the discussion in Chapter Six, Section G, regarding how disputes in bankruptcy court are resolved using motions, objections, notices of intended action, or adversary proceedings.) Challenges to a debtor's claimed exemptions are common and we will consider them further in Chapter Ten, where we consider the various actions that a bankruptcy trustee may take to identify and take possession of property of the estate for the benefit of creditors.

EXAMPLE

In her Schedule C, Marta claims her jewelry as exempt, assigning it a value of $1,350, which is $250 below the maximum exemption amount for jewelry allowed by §522(d)(4) ($1,600 as of April 2016). If that valuation is correct, she will be able to keep the jewelry because it has no value in excess of the allowed exemption. But if the bankruptcy trustee can prove that the jewelry is actually worth $5,000, he will object to Marta's valuation in that exemption and if he prevails on his objection, will take possession of it as property of the estate, sell it, give Marta $1,600 of the proceeds as her maximum exempt amount, and then use the balance for estate administration costs or distribution to creditors.

EXAMPLE

Look at Document 32 in Marta Carlson's case file. The bankruptcy trustee is objecting to her valuation of the doll collection and arguing that it has a value in excess of her exempted value leaving equity in the estate. The trustee intends to recover that doll collection from Marta's sister who currently has possession of it (see Document 31) and sell it for the benefit of the estate. Assume that the court finds that the doll collection is worth $31,000 and the trustee recovers and sells it. How will the proceeds of the sale be distributed?

What happens if a debtor claims as exempt the full value of property having an actual value in excess of the maximum dollar amount of the exemption applicable to that property but no timely objection is filed? The U.S. Supreme Court has held that absent a timely objection, the property claimed as exempt will be excluded from the estate and retained by the debtor even if the exemption's actual value exceeds what the Code permits. See *Taylor* v. *Freeland & Kronz*, 503 U.S. 638, 642-643 (1992) (debtor who listed expected proceeds of pending employment discrimination lawsuit as exempt on Schedule C entitled to keep all those proceeds even though the dollar amount of recovery exceeded all allowable exemption amounts where trustee failed to file timely objection to claimed exemption).

On the other hand, what happens if a debtor assigns a specific dollar amount to property claimed as exempt thinking that is its full value but the property turns out to have a higher value than that claimed? In *Schwab v. Reilly*, 560 U.S. 770 (2010), the Supreme Court held that a debtor is only entitled to the dollar amount of the exemption *actually claimed* on Schedule C, *not* the full value of the exempted property where that value turns out to be more than the claimed exempted amount even though the debtor *intended to* and *could have* exempted the full value of the property and was merely *mistaken* as to its true value. Moreover, the Court held that in such situations the failure of the trustee to file a timely objection to the exemption on the basis of the incorrect value is no bar to the trustee treating the dollar value of the property in excess of the claimed exemption amount as **property of the estate** (a concept to be considered in depth in Chapter Ten, Section B).

P-H 8-k: In a practical sense, what does the result in *Taylor* mean for the trustee examining a debtor's claimed exemptions? And what does the result in *Schwab* mean for the legal professional assisting the debtor client in filling out the debtor's Schedule C? Look at the Notice of Chapter 7 Bankruptcy Case issued in Marta's case (Document 23 in her case file) and at the Trustee's Objection to Claimed Exemption filed regarding the doll collection (Document 32). When was the first meeting of creditors held in Marta's case? Was the trustee's objection to her claimed exemption timely filed under Bankruptcy Rule 4003(a)?

A debtor's right to claim property as exempt is sacrosanct even where the debtor uses the bankruptcy process in bad faith and to commit a fraud on creditors. See *Law v. Siegel*, 134 S. Ct. 1188 (2014) (bankruptcy court inappropriately surcharged debtor's homestead exemption to pay administrative costs of trustee incurred in multi-year litigation that concluded in a finding that debtor had listed a fictitious second mortgage on his home to create the appearance of there being no equity for the estate in the home; a bankruptcy court may not exercise its authority under §105(a) to "carry out" the provisions of the Code or its inherent power to sanction abusive litigation practices by taking action otherwise prohibited by the Code such as §522(k), which makes exempt property "not liable for payment of any administrative expense").

The Right to Avoid a Judicial Lien in Property Claimed as Exempt

As noted earlier, if a debtor has granted a consensual **security interest** in property that could be exempt in bankruptcy, the secured creditor's claim to the property will be superior to the debtor's claimed exemption in the property.

EXAMPLE

> If the debtor in our series of homestead exemption examples has obtained a home equity loan for an amount equal to all his equity in the principal residence and granted the lender a mortgage interest in the residence to secure repayment, the debtor will have no equity in the home to exempt when he files a petition in bankruptcy. His right of homestead exemption will not defeat the mortgagee's secured position in the home.

The same is true as to **statutory liens** in the debtor's property (see Chapter Three). They are superior to a claimed exemption in the property that is subject to a properly perfected nonconsensual statutory lien.

EXAMPLE

> If the debtor in our series of homestead exemption examples enters into a contract to sell his principal residence but that contract subsequently falls through, the frustrated buyer who believes the debtor has breached the contract of sale may file a **lien *lis pendens*** on the property and file suit to enforce it. The lien *lis pendens* is a statutory lien. If the debtor then files a petition in bankruptcy, his right of homestead exemption will not defeat the claim of the holder of the lien *lis pendens*.

Judicial lien Any lien resulting from court proceedings.

Interestingly though, §522(f)(1)(A) empowers the debtor to avoid a **judicial lien** on his or her property to the extent that the lien impairs an exemption the debtor would otherwise have in the property. Judicial liens are defined by §101(36) as liens obtained by judgment, levy sequestration, or other legal or equitable process and include those postjudgment execution remedies we considered in Chapter Five, Section G. Bankruptcy Rule 4003(d) provides that a proceeding to avoid a judicial lien to preserve an exemption is to be initiated by motion, not adversary proceeding.

EXAMPLE

If the debtor in our series of homestead exemption examples has a judgment entered against him for $100,000 and the judgment creditor has created and perfected a judgment lien on the debtor's principal residence by recording the judgment, when the debtor files his bankruptcy petition he may avoid that judgment lien under §522(f)(1)(A) to the extent it impairs his exemption. So if the debtor has $250,000 of equity in his home, all of which state law allows him to exempt as homestead, and has owned it more than 1,215 days so that the 1,215-day rule does not limit his right to claim all his owner's equity as exempt, he can avoid the creditor's judgment lien on the property entirely and claim the full exemption.

Domestic support obligation An obligation to pay alimony, child support, or maintenance.

Section 522(f)(1)(A) does provide, however, that a judicial lien resulting from a **domestic support obligation** (child support, alimony, or maintenance recoverable by a spouse, former spouse, or child of the debtor) cannot be avoided by the debtor.

EXAMPLE

If the creditor holding the judgment lien in the previous example is the ex-spouse of the debtor and the judgment is for unpaid child support, the debtor will be unable to avoid that lien on the principal residence.

Section 522(f)(1)(B) also authorizes the individual Chapter 7 debtor to avoid a nonpossessory, nonpurchase money security interest in certain household items and tools of the trade to the extent the lien impairs an exemption. We will illustrate that section later in connection with the Chapter 13 case (see Chapter Fifteen, Section B).

P-H 8-l: If your state has opted out of the federal exemptions, compare your state's exemptions to Marta Carlson's schedules. What property could she exempt on her Schedule C under the exemption laws of your state?

4. Schedule D, Creditors Holding Claims Secured by Property (Official Form 106D)

On Part 1 of Schedule D the individual debtor must list every creditor who claims a security position in the debtor's property, along with detailed information about any co-debtors, the value of the property, the amount of the claim, whether the claim is contingent, unliquidated, or disputed, and whether there is any portion of the claim that is not secured. (See Document 9 in the Carlson case file.) In Part 2 of the form the debtor lists any person to be notified of a particular listed debt other than the creditor named in Part 1 of the form. For example, if a contract giving rise to the debt obligation listed in Part 1 has been assigned from an original creditor to the current creditor listed in Part 1 but the debtor remains liable to the original creditor on the assigned obligation, the original creditor should be listed in Part 2 of the form. Or, if a debt has been assigned for collection to a debt collector listed in Part 1, the original creditor should be listed in Part 2.

5. Schedule E/F, Creditors Holding Unsecured Priority and Nonpriority Claims (Official Form 106E/F)

When it is time for the bankruptcy trustee to distribute proceeds of the estate to the various creditors of the estate, some creditors get paid in full before others are paid anything, pursuant to §726 of the Code. We will examine the distribution process and order of priority in detail in Chapter Eleven, Section B. But note here that, certain unsecured creditor claims are designated as priority claims by §507 of the Code and, as such, enjoy a high priority in the distribution process under §726. The debtor is required to list §507 priority claims in Part 1 of Schedule E/F.

There are a number of claims designated as priority claims in §507. In consumer bankruptcy cases like Marta's, the ones most commonly present are

- Domestic support obligations of the debtor, per §507(a)(1)(A)
- Prepetition deposits of money for the lease or purchase of real property or consumer services up to $2,225 per claimant, per §507(a)(7)
- Various tax claims including income and property taxes assessed at varying times before the petition was filed, per §507(a)(8)
- Personal injury or wrongful death claims arising out of DUI, per §507(a)(10)

Marta Carlson's Schedule E/F is Document 10 in her case file. She lists no priority claims. Recall from the Assignment Memorandum in Appendix A and Line 29 of her Schedule A/B that Marta's ex-husband, Eugene, is $15,000 in arrears on his child support obligation to Marta. Were Eugene to file a bankruptcy case he would list that obligation on his Schedule E as an unsecured priority claim. He would also list that claim on his list of creditors naming Marta as the creditor.

In Part 2 of Schedule E/F, the debtor must list all other creditors who have unsecured claims. The debtor must also state whether each claim is disputed or undisputed, contingent or not, and whether it is liquidated or unliquidated. It is important to note that a debtor must list a claim even if the debtor disputes all or part of it.

As we learned in Chapter One, a contingent claim is one that hasn't fully matured yet, an unliquidated obligation is one that has not yet been reduced to a sum certain, and a disputed claim is one not agreed to and yet to be determined.

EXAMPLE

> In her Schedule E/F (Document 10 in the Carlson case file) Marta lists the claim of Pine Ridge Nursing Home against her in the amount of $45,290 but designates it as disputed and contingent on the outcome of the lawsuit Pine Ridge has filed against her. She also lists it as unliquidated. Although that claim is liquidated in the sense that Pine Ridge is seeking a sum certain against Marta, she lists it as unliquidated because the exact amount that she might ultimately owe, if anything, might be less than the full amount sought.

6. Schedule G, Executory Contracts and Unexpired Leases (Official Form 106G)

Executory contract A contract that has not been fully performed by either party to it.

An **executory contract** is one that is ongoing and on which both parties still owe some performance. Those ongoing contracts and unexpired leases may give rise to additional claims by the other party to the contract if the debtor intends to discharge continuing obligations under the contract in a Chapter 7. (In a reorganization case under Chapters 11, 12, or 13 of the Code they are also important to know about because the debtor's plan will have to deal with them in some way.) Marta Carlson's Schedule G lists executory contracts common to consumer debtors. (See Document 11 in the Carlson case file.)

7. Schedule H, Co-debtors (Official Form 106H)

Co-debtor Two or more debtors liable for the same debt.

What happens if the bankruptcy debtor wants to discharge a debt on which someone else is also liable as a **co-debtor**? Of course, the co-debtor may have also filed bankruptcy and, if the co-debtor is a spouse of the debtor, the co-debtor may be a joint petitioner in the same bankruptcy case. But if the co-debtor has not also filed for bankruptcy relief, is that co-debtor still liable for the debt even though this debtor has filed for bankruptcy relief? Yes. A Chapter 7 discharge releases only the debtor from the discharged debts. The liability of a co-debtor to a creditor is not affected by that discharge. (See Document 12 in the Carlson case file.)

In the next chapter we will see that the filing of the bankruptcy petition triggers an automatic stay, prohibiting creditors of the debtor from continuing to pursue collection of the debts owed to them. However, in a Chapter 7 case, a co-debtor does *not* benefit from the automatic stay and collection efforts can continue against the co-debtor unless he or she is also a joint petitioner or has filed his or her own bankruptcy case. In Chapter Thirteen we will learn that in a Chapter 13 case under the Code some co-debtors do enjoy the benefit of the automatic stay.

EXAMPLE

> In her Schedule H (Document 12 in the Carlson case file) Marta identifies her ex-husband, Eugene, as a co-debtor on obligations that originated during the marriage. Note that those obligations on which Eugene is a co-debtor were also listed on her Schedule D if secured and on her Schedule E/F if unsecured (Documents 9 and 10 in the Carlson case file) and a co-debtor noted. But since this is a case under Chapter 7 and not Chapter 13, Eugene does not receive the protection of the automatic stay, and so those creditors can continue collection efforts against him. And though Marta may receive a discharge from those obligations, Eugene will not unless he files his own bankruptcy case.

8. Schedule I, Your Income (Official Form 106I)

Debtors who are individuals (not entities) must complete this form whether they are consumer debtors or business debtors. We noted in the last chapter the interplay between the data set forth on the Schedule I and the consumer debtor's income or anticipated change of income noted on the debtor's means test forms. Line 13 of Schedule I now includes the debtor's statement disclosing reasonably anticipated increase or decrease in income over the 12-month period following the date of filing the petition required by Code §521(a)(1)(B)(vi). If Marta had a reasonable expectation that her ex-husband would resume making child support payments or making up those arrearages in the upcoming 12 months she would indicate that expectation on Line 13 of the form. But apparently Eugene's leukemia makes that prospect unlikely.

This statement is required of all individual debtors (both those with primarily consumer and business debts). (See Marta Carlson's Schedule I in Document 13 in the Carlson case file.)

9. Schedule J, Your Expenses (Official Form 106J)

Schedule J is a companion form to Schedule I, requiring individual debtors to list their average monthly expenses. We noted in the last chapter the interplay between the data set forth on the Schedule J and the consumer debtor's expenses or anticipated change in expenses noted on the debtor's means test forms. Line 24 of Schedule J now includes the debtor's statement disclosing reasonably anticipated increase or decrease in expenditures over the 12-month period following the date of filing the petition required by Code §521(a)(1)(B)(vi). (See Marta Carlson's Schedule J in Document 14 in the Carlson case file.)

If husband and wife have filed a joint petition but maintain separate households, they must use Schedule J-2 to report the living expenses separately.

10. Summary of Assets and Liabilities and Certain Statistical Information (Official Form 106-Summary)

This form requires the debtor to enter the totals from Schedules A/B through J and to summarize them. Individual consumer debtors (not individual business debtors or entity debtors) must provide additional information as well including whether the debtor's debts are primarily consumer debts. (See Marta Carlson's Summary in Document 15 in the Carlson case file.)

11. Declaration Concerning Debtor's Schedules (Official Form 106-Declaration)

On this form, the individual debtor will sign, declaring under penalties of perjury that the information contained on the various schedules is true and correct to the best of the debtor's knowledge, information, and belief. If the petition and schedules were prepared by a nonattorney bankruptcy petition preparer (NABPP), that person must also sign under oath, not that the information is true, but that the preparer has complied with all his obligations under the Code. (See Document 16 in the Carlson case file.)

If you are the legal professional assisting the debtor in gathering and entering all the information contained in the various schedules, you have a large responsibility in making sure the debtor's declaration is true.

12. Statement of Financial Affairs (Official Form 107)

The **statement of financial affairs** is a comprehensive form that the debtor must complete and file along with the schedules and which is due, like the schedules, within 14 days of filing the petition, per Bankruptcy Rule 1007(b) and (c). The form requires disclosure of different types of financial information than was disclosed in the schedules.

EXAMPLE

> The Statement of Financial Affairs makes inquiries concerning payments to creditors in the 90-day and one-year period prior to filing the petition, lawsuits to which the debtor has been a party, as well as any garnishments, repossessions, or seizures of the debtor's property within one year preceding the filing, and gifts made within one year of filing.

We will see in Chapter Ten that this information relates to powers given the bankruptcy trustee to avoid (cancel) certain transfers of the debtor's property made within a certain number of months of the bankruptcy filing and to bring the transferred property back into the bankrupt estate. (See Marta Carlson's Statement of Financial Affairs in Document 17 in the Carlson case file.)

The statement of financial affairs also has questions regarding safety deposit boxes, closed financial accounts, current and former businesses, former spouses, the location of financial records, and so on. The bankruptcy trustee is entitled to know where all the debtor's property is or may be located and is empowered to search thoroughly for undisclosed assets of the debtor that may be in someone else's possession. As part of that task, the trustee may want to obtain and review the debtor's financial records to make sure all property and income is accounted for. We consider the Chapter 7 bankruptcy trustee's duties in more detail in Chapter Nine, Section B.

13. Statement of Intention for Individuals Filing Under Chapter 7 (Official Form 108)

If an individual Chapter 7 debtor has listed property in which a creditor has a security interest, §521(a)(2) of the Code requires the debtor to state in this form whether he or she intends to **surrender** the property to the secured creditor or try to retain it. By stating the intent to surrender the collateralized property on Form 108, the debtor is giving notice that debtor will voluntarily relinquish possession of the property to the creditor. As we will see, a Chapter 7 debtor's statement of intent to abandon is not the end of the matter, however, since the bankruptcy trustee may assert an interest in it for the benefit of the estate if the property has value in excess of the amount owed or if the trustee can avoid the lien (to be considered in Chapter Ten). And even if the trustee decides to formally **abandon** the collateralized property to the creditor (to be considered in Chapter Eleven) as having no value to the estate, the creditor must make sure the automatic stay of §362 (to be considered in Chapter Nine) has been lifted before proceeding to repossess the property. All of this in due time.

An individual Chapter 7 debtor may seek to retain collateralized property if the debtor intends to avoid the lien and exempt the property as discussed above in connection with Schedule C, or if the debtor intends to either **redeem the property** or **reaffirm the debt**, topics that will be considered in Chapter Eleven. But, for now, understand that the individual debtor must state his or her intent in this form. The debtor's statement of intent must be filed within 30 days after the petition is filed or before the first meeting of creditors, whichever is earliest. (See Marta Carlson's Statement of Intent in Document 18 in the Carlson case file.)

EXAMPLE

In her Statement of Intent, Marta Carlson indicates that she intends to surrender both her home and her YR-4 Toyota Camry. She apparently has made other arrangements regarding where to live (maybe she will rent a place she can afford or move in with a friend or relative) and how to get around (maybe someone is going to give or loan her a car or she's planning to buy something more affordable). But note that in her Schedule C she still claims an exemption in that property she is surrendering. So once the home and vehicle are sold by either the creditors secured in those items or the bankruptcy trustee (who may want to sell them since there is equity for the estate in both the home and the vehicle) and the secured claims satisfied out of the proceeds, the amount of her exemption amounts will have to be paid to her before they go to the benefit of the estate.

If the individual debtor is a party to an unexpired lease, the debtor must state his or her intent on this form to either discharge the obligation under the lease or to reassume that obligation.

14. Statement About Your Social Security Numbers (Official Form 121)

This form is required of all individual debtors (those with primarily consumer or business debt). (See Document 20 in the Carlson case file.) To protect the privacy of the debtors, it is filed with the bankruptcy court clerk separately from the petition, schedules, and statements and is withheld by the clerk from the publicly accessible case file.

15. Disclosure of Compensation of Attorney for the Debtor (Official Form 2030)

This disclosure using Official Form 2030 is required of all debtors whether individuals or entities pursuant to Code §329(a) and Bankruptcy Rule 2016(b). (See Document 21 in the Carlson case file.) This is not the same as requiring the fee agreement itself to be in writing. However, since the attorney for a consumer debtor is considered a debt relief agency (see discussion of *Milavetz* in Section A, supra), §528(a)(1) effectively requires that the attorney/client fee agreement in consumer debtor cases be in writing. Otherwise the Code does not require fee agreements between debtors and attorneys to be in writing but state professional rules governing attorneys may so require. Whether required or not, having the fee agreement in writing is always a good idea for both the attorney and the client.

Furthermore, although Form 2030 requires the disclosure of attorney's fees in a Chapter 7 case, such fees need not be approved by the bankruptcy court, as we will learn is required in Chapter 11, 12, or 13 cases. Thus, the fee that debtor's attorneys charge their Chapter 7 clients is determined for the most part by the marketplace. However, §329(b) gives the bankruptcy court authority in any case filed under Title 11, in the event a debtor or other party in interest objects to the attorney's fee, to cancel the fee agreement or to order the attorney to disgorge (refund) as much of a fee already paid that it finds excessive. The test in such a case is whether the fee charged by the attorney "exceeds the reasonable value of any such service." And as we saw in the *In re Dean* case summarized in P-H 8-b, the court can order a disgorgement of fees by an attorney for misconduct or failure to comply with requirements of the Code.

P-H 8-m: Does your state require attorneys to place their fee agreements with clients in writing? Check the advertisements of debtor's attorneys in your local media or, if your instructor so directs, contact an attorney who handles Chapter 7 cases for debtors or the bankruptcy court clerk and find out what is currently the typical fee for handling a Chapter 7. How does that fee compare with what is charged in surrounding areas? In more urban or more rural areas of your state? How frequently are §329(b) challenges asserted to debtor's attorney's fee agreements?

Attorneys representing debtors in Chapter 7 cases typically get their full fee in advance to eliminate the risk that their claim as a creditor for the unpaid portion of the fee will be discharged.

16. Copies of All Payment Advices or Other Evidence of Payment Received from Any Employer Within 60 Days Before the Filing of the Petition

This is required of all individual debtors (both consumer and business). (See Document 22 in the Carlson case file.)

17. Copy of the Debtor's Last Federal Income Tax Return

This is required of all individual debtors (both consumer and business) and is to be provided to the bankruptcy trustee (not filed with the clerk with the petition) no later than seven days before the first meeting of creditors (the first meeting of creditors will be discussed in the next chapter). In addition, a copy of all tax returns filed during the case, including tax returns for prior years that had not been filed when the case began, must be supplied. Section 521(e)(2)(B) calls for mandatory dismissal of the case if the debtor fails to comply with this requirement and cannot show that failure to comply was beyond his control.

P-H 8-n: Official Form 2000, Required Lists, Schedules, Statements and Fees, contains a convenient list of the required schedules, statements, lists, and other documents. Review Form 2000. Has Marta Carlson has filed all the necessary schedules, statements, lists, and other documents required of a consumer debtor in a Chapter 7 case?

18. Other Required Filings Mandated by Local Court Rules

The **local court rules** of particular bankruptcy courts may mandate other filings and should always be consulted. In addition, local court rules may mandate use of a designated form for providing some of the information mandated by §521 and Bankruptcy Rule 1007 but that does not have an official form.

P-H 8-o: Check the local rules of the bankruptcy court in your district to see if they contain any information in addition to that mandated by §521 and Bankruptcy Rule 1007 to be provided by the debtor filing a Chapter 7 petition. If so, see if the local rules or the court's web site provides a form for use in providing that information.

C.   The Timeframe for Filing the Supporting Schedules, Statements, and Lists and Bankruptcy Rule 9006 for Computing Time Deadlines

The list of creditors must be filed with the petition. The required schedules and statements usually are filed then as well, but §521(a) and Bankruptcy Rule 1007(c) allow the schedules, statement of affairs, and most other documents to be filed within 14 days after the petition without penalty, and the statement of intent by an individual debtor may be filed within 30 days after the petition. In addition, those grace periods may be extended by motion filed with the bankruptcy court and cause shown per Bankruptcy Rule 1007(c). (See Documents 5 and 6 in the Carlson case file.)

There is a limit to the time extension the court can grant a debtor to comply with his obligation to file the various schedules, however. Section 521(i)(1) of the Code provides that if the debtor fails to file the required schedules within 45 days following the date the petition is filed, the petition is to be "automatically dismissed effective on the 46th day after the date of the filing of the petition." This section could be read to mean that bankruptcy judges have no discretion to grant extensions beyond 45 days and that the failure to comply with the 45-day filing requirement cannot be forgiven or cured. To date, however, two circuits have found an ambiguity between the apparent mandate of §521(i)(l) and the arguably conflicting language of §521(a)(1)(B) directing the debtor to file the various schedules and statements "unless the court orders otherwise" and construed the sections to mean that bankruptcy courts retain discretion to waive or excuse the failure to file the required information within the 45-day window notwithstanding the automatic dismissal language (see *In re Acosta-Rivera*, 557 F.3d 8 (1st Cir. 2009), and *In re Warren*, 568 F.3d 1113 (9th Cir. 2009)).

Bankruptcy Rule 9006 is the primary source for guidelines governing the computation of time periods for all actions mandated or allowed under the Code. It helps practitioners deal with issues like those raised in P-H 8-p.

P-H 8-p: What happens if the last day to file something falls on a weekend or legal holiday? Which legal holidays are recognized for purposes of extending a deadline? Does the *last day* to file something end at midnight that day or when the clerk's office closes for that day? What happens if the clerk's office is unexpectedly closed for weather or other eventuality on the day something is due?

D. ▶ The Importance of Reporting Accurate and Complete Information

It is critical to both the debtor and the attorney that all information reported in the petition, schedules, statements, and other documents filed in connection with a bankruptcy case be accurate and complete. As we will learn in Chapter Twelve, failing to list a creditor in the debtor's schedules can result in that creditor's claim not being discharged. And we will learn in the same chapter that providing inaccurate or incomplete information can result in denial of any discharge at all or revocation of a discharge already granted. If the debtor is found to have acted intentionally with regard to the withheld, incomplete, or inaccurate information, there could be state or federal criminal charges brought against the debtor and anyone who knowingly assisted him or her, including charges of **bankruptcy fraud** or making **false oaths and claims** under 18 U.S.C. §§157 or 152.

P-H 8-q: Do you understand why both federal and state prosecutors might file charges arising out of a bankruptcy case pending in a bankruptcy case in your state? What is the federal interest? What is the state interest?

CHAPTER SUMMARY

A Chapter 7 case by an individual debtor is commenced by filing a voluntary petition with a bankruptcy court having proper venue. Venue is proper in the federal district where the debtor has resided or had his or her primary place of business for the past 180 days. Husbands and wives may file a joint petition. The bankruptcy court may order two or more cases involving debtors with related assets and debt obligations to be jointly administered and two or more cases involving the same debtor to be consolidated. In certain circumstances, creditors of a debtor may force him into bankruptcy by filing an involuntary petition for the debtor. In addition to the petition, the debtor must file a number of supporting schedules of assets and liabilities, a statement of affairs, a list of creditors, and a number of other supporting statements, most of which must be filed within 14 days of the date the petition is filed.

The debtor signs the petition under oath subject to penalties of perjury. The attorney for the debtor also signs the petition certifying that the attorney has no knowledge after an inquiry that the information in the petition and supporting schedules is incorrect. If the debtor is assisted by a nonattorney bankruptcy petition preparer, that BPP and the debtor must complete, sign, and file a form containing certain disclosures.

The individual Chapter 7 debtor is entitled to claim certain property as exempt using federal exemptions set forth in the Code or the exemptions laws of his state of residence unless the state has elected to opt out of the federal exemptions in which case the debtor must use the state exemptions. Husbands and wives who are joint debtors can double or stack the exemptions in jointly owned property. Property cannot be exempted to the extent it is subject to a valid security interest, consensual or nonconsensual, except that the debtor can avoid a judicial lien in property in order to preserve an exemption in that property.

BAPCPA has placed limitations on an individual debtor's right to claim all of the equity in his principal residence as exempt if he has owned it fewer than 1,215 days before filing his petition. The debtor's schedules must indicate whether creditor claims are secured or unsecured, liquidated or unliquidated, contested or uncontested, contingent or noncontingent, or entitled to any priority treatment under the Code. It is essential that the information contained in the debtor's petition, schedules, and supporting statements be accurate and complete.

REVIEW QUESTIONS

1. Who may file a joint bankruptcy petition?
2. Explain the difference between the consolidation of two or more bankruptcy cases and the joint administration of two or more bankruptcy cases.
3. Who signs the Chapter 7 bankruptcy petition of an individual debtor and why? Which signatures are under oath?
4. Summarize the circumstances under which creditors may force a debtor into an involuntary bankruptcy proceeding. What is the procedure followed after the filing of an involuntary petition?
5. What is venue and what bankruptcy court is the proper venue for a bankruptcy filing?
6. What or who is a bankruptcy petition preparer and how is its involvement in a pro se case disclosed to the court?
7. Name one thing an individual debtor must do during the 180 days preceding the filing of the Chapter 7 petition.
8. Explain the opt out feature of the Code for purposes of claimed exemptions.
9. May a debtor claim as exempt property in which debtor has granted a creditor a perfected security interest? Property in which a creditor claims a perfected statutory lien? Property in which a creditor claims a judicial lien?
10. What is the homestead exemption? What is the 1,215-day rule and how does it limit the debtor's right to claim the homestead exemption?

11. What is the debtor's statement of intent and does it apply to secured or unsecured property of the debtor?

12. Why is it important for the debtor and the debtor's attorney and assisting legal professional to make sure that the information contained in the petition, schedules, and statements is accurate and complete? What possible criminal liability is present for a debtor who knowingly enters false information on a bankruptcy petition or supporting schedule?

WORDS AND PHRASES TO REMEMBER

abandon property

assisted person

bankruptcy fraud

bankruptcy petition preparer

burden of proof

co-debtor

consolidation

credit counseling agencies

debt relief agency

default

disgorge

domestic support obligation

doubling

evidentiary hearing

executory contract

fair market value

false oath and claims

filing fee

homestead exemption

involuntary petition

judicial lien

joint administration

joint petition

lien *lis pendens*

local court rules

opt out

order for relief

party in interest

perjury

petition

priority claims

property of the estate

pro se

reaffirm debt

redeem property

stacking

statement of financial affairs

statutory lien

surrender

turnover order

venue

wild card exemption

1,215-day rule

TO LEARN MORE: A number of TLM activities to accompany this chapter are accessible on the companion web site for this textbook at http://aspen-lawschool.com/books/Parsons_Debt4e/.

Chapter Nine:

The Chapter 7 Consumer Bankruptcy Case: The Order for Relief, Bankruptcy Trustee, First Meeting of Creditors, and Automatic Stay

Once the bankruptcy petition is filed, the case is commenced and very important consequences flow from that fact for both the debtor and his creditors. From the very moment the case is filed the provisions of the Code and the Bankruptcy Rules are set in motion. Filing a bankruptcy petition is somewhat like turning the ignition switch in a car. The machine roars to life as numerous systems inside begin to operate—warming up, lighting up, lubricating, rotating, inspecting themselves, preparing to perform. In this chapter, we will see how the various systems that make up the great machine of bankruptcy procedure roar to life with the filing of the Chapter 7 petition and then methodically grind forward to administer the case.

KEY CONCEPTS

- Immediately upon the filing of a Chapter 7 petition, the bankruptcy court will appoint a bankruptcy trustee to administer the case
- Most Chapter 7 consumer cases are no-asset cases in which there are no nonexempt assets to be liquidated and no distribution to unsecured creditors
- Upon filing of the petition an automatic stay goes into effect causing most collection-type activities against the debtor to stop
- A creditor may ask the court to lift the automatic stay if one of the statutory grounds for lifting is present
- Actual and punitive damages can be awarded against a creditor who willfully violates the automatic stay
- A first meeting of creditors is to be held within 21-40 days of the order for relief

A. ▸ The Order for Relief

Petition The document filed to initiate a bankruptcy case under the Code.

Order for relief The formal beginning of a bankruptcy case triggered by the filing of a voluntary petition or by court order following an involuntary petition.

The Chapter 7 case is commenced by the filing of the bankruptcy **petition** per §301(a) of the Code and Bankruptcy Rule 1002. Per §301(b), the filing of the petition constitutes an **order for relief** under the Code, a term used often in the Code as we will see. The Code and a number of the Official Bankruptcy Forms refer to the order for relief as if it were something separate from the petition. For example, §341(a) says, "Within a reasonable time after the order for relief in a case under this title, the United States trustee shall convene and preside over a meeting of creditors." Some courts do enter a formal order for relief after the petition is filed. But in most districts the petition itself is treated as the order for relief and no separate order is entered by the court. When an **involuntary petition** is filed and granted, a separate order for relief will be entered (see Official Forms 105 and 205). In this chapter, we refer interchangeably to the filing of the petition, the commencement of the case, and entry of the order for relief.

Local rules Supplemental rules of procedure and practice that prevail in a particular court.

P-H 9-a: Determine if the bankruptcy court in your federal district enters a formal order for relief upon filing of the petition or if it allows the petition itself to serve that purpose. The **local rules** of that court will probably give you the answer. If the court does utilize a separate order for relief, see if the court's web site provides a form for that order, or obtain one from the court clerk.

B. ▸ The Chapter 7 Bankruptcy Trustee

Section 701 of the Code provides that "promptly after the order for relief under this chapter" (i.e., Chapter 7), the **U.S. Trustee** is to appoint a person to serve as **bankruptcy trustee** in the Chapter 7 case. Section 586(a)(1) of Title 28 directs the U.S. Trustee in each federal district to "establish, maintain, and supervise a panel of private trustees that are eligible and available to serve as trustees in cases under Chapter 7." It is from this **trustee panel** that the U.S. Trustee will select the bankruptcy trustee for each Chapter 7 case. Persons selected to serve on the panel of trustees may be lawyers, accountants, retired bankers, and other businesspeople. In the notice to creditors of the filing of the case (discussed below), creditors are advised of the identity of the person appointed to serve as trustee. (See Document 23 in the Carlson case file.)

P-H 9-b: Locate the bankruptcy trustee panel for the federal district where you plan to practice. This information might be available on the web sites of the bankruptcy courts in the district. The U.S. Trustee web site has a Private Trustee Locator page that will assist you as well at www.justice.gov/ust/chapter-7-12-13-private-trustee-locator.

It is rare for creditors to *not* accept the initial choice of trustee made by the U.S. Trustee, but §702 authorizes them to elect someone else to serve as trustee at the first meeting of creditors (discussed in Section E). Thus, the trustee appointed by the U.S. Trustee serves only in an interim capacity until after that meeting. Section 324 of the Code authorizes the court to remove a trustee for *cause*. Though cause for removal is not defined in the Code and is, fortunately, a rare event, cause for removal can be anything from dishonesty to dilatoriness to inability to work with the debtor.

The creditors may form a **creditors' committee** to work closely with the trustee and to represent the creditors before the court (see §705). Creditors' committees are unusual in a Chapter 7 consumer case but common in a Chapter 11, so we will consider them in detail when we study the Chapter 11 case.

Bankruptcy trustees must be **bonded** because they are handling the property of the estate. They are responsible not only to the debtors, the creditors of the estate, and the U.S. Trustee who selects and supervises them, but also to the bankruptcy judge before whom they will appear as the representative of the estate (see §323(a)). Sometimes the duty the bankruptcy trustee owes to the estate and its creditors is described as a **fiduciary duty** involving the obligations of reasonable care, trust, and loyalty. However, the trustee enjoys a **quasi-judicial immunity** from personal liability for actions taken pursuant to his authority as trustee or according to court order. See *Lonneker Farms, Inc. v. Klobucher*, 804 F.2d 1096, 1097 (9th Cir. 1986) (bankruptcy trustee receives "derived judicial immunity" because he performs "integral part of the judicial process"). Even with regard to third persons unconnected to the bankruptcy estate the bankruptcy trustee enjoys absolute immunity for actions taken within the scope of the position. See, e.g., *In re Bryan*, 308 B.R. 583, 587 (Bankr. N.D. Ga. 2004) (Chapter 7 trustee sued by individual concerning whom trustee had initiated an unlicensed practice of law inquiry with state bar had absolute immunity from allegations of slander and libel since trustee acted in his capacity as trustee and in accordance with his statutory duty to protect assets of the estate from dissipation via frivolous pleading drafted with plaintiff's assistance), and *In re Heinsohn*, 247 B.R. 237, 244 (E.D. Tenn. 2000) (trustee sued for malicious prosecution and defamation by a nondebtor prosecuted and acquitted of bankruptcy fraud upon referral of charges by the trustee had absolute immunity from suit).

1. Duties of the Bankruptcy Trustee

The duties of the Chapter 7 trustee are set out in §701 of the Code. Illustration 9-a summarizes those duties. We will examine many of these duties in detail as we move through the administration of the case.

Once a Chapter 7 case is filed, the bankruptcy trustee becomes the primary actor in the case. Bankruptcy Rule 2015 requires the trustee to file a complete **inventory of the property of the estate** within 30 days following his appointment, to keep detailed records of the receipt and disposition of property of the estate, and to provide interim reports (often quarterly) regarding affairs of the estate. Section 345 of the Code requires the trustee to invest cash belonging to the estate in government insured accounts or certificates unless the court otherwise orders. All records of the trustee's handling of estate property are open to examination by the debtor, creditors, the U.S. Trustee, and the court.

Illustration 9-a: DUTIES OF THE BANKRUPTCY TRUSTEE IN A CHAPTER 7 CASE

> **Property of the estate** All property in which the debtor holds a legal or equitable interest at the commencement of a bankruptcy case.

- To investigate the financial affairs of the debtor
- To locate and take possession of all nonexempt property of the debtor (called **property of the estate** under the Code)
- To preserve the property of the estate and then liquidate it (in a Chapter 7) for the benefit of the creditors of the estate, or abandon it if it has no value to the estate
- To examine the exempt property claims of the debtor and challenge them if there are disputes as to the legitimacy of the claimed exemption or the value claimed by the debtor
- To examine the claims of creditors in an asset case, allow those that appear properly supported, and to challenge and disallow those that are not
- To raise objections to discharge of the debtor if grounds for such objection are present
- To distribute property of the estate in the order of priority dictated by the Code
- To prepare and file reports with the U.S. Trustee and the court, fully disclosing actions taken with regard to the debtor and the property of the estate (see Bankruptcy Rule 2015)

Serving as a bankruptcy trustee is a challenging task. Working as a legal professional on the trustee's staff demands a high level of expertise, an honest character, and a substantial capacity for working under pressure.

2. Compensation of the Bankruptcy Trustee

Sections 326 and 330 of the Code govern the trustee's fees. In general, the trustee is entitled to reasonable compensation based on the nature of the services rendered to the estate, their market value, and the time spent. A minimum payment is allowed a trustee under §330(b), which comes in part from the filing fee. In a no-asset case (discussed in the next section), that may be the only compensation the trustee receives. Where there are assets in the estate to be distributed to creditors, the trustee also receives as compensation a percentage of the value distributed, within certain limits established by §326. The trustee's fee is considered an **administrative expense** and is given a significant priority in the distribution of the estate, as discussed in Chapter Eleven, Section B.

3. Hiring Professional Persons to Assist the Bankruptcy Trustee

Section 327 of the Code and Bankruptcy Rule 2014 authorize the bankruptcy trustee to hire professional persons such as attorneys, accountants, appraisers, auctioneers, real estate agents, or other professionals to assist the trustee with administering the estate.

E X A M P L E

If the bankruptcy trustee is going to initiate an adversary proceeding, the trustee will usually hire an attorney to represent him or her in that litigation. When the time comes to liquidate property of the estate, the trustee may conduct a public auction and need to retain the services of an auctioneer for that purpose. If the trustee encounters complicated financial dealings by the debtor or other party that the trustee lacks the sophistication to understand, the trustee may need an accountant or other financial professional to assist. If the trustee has a question regarding the value of realty, the trustee may need an appraiser to tell determine the likely value and, later, a real estate agent to help sell it.

Professionals can only be hired with the authorization of the bankruptcy court. So the trustee will file a motion with the court for authorization to do so and obtain a court order approving the hiring.

EXAMPLE

In the Marta Carlson case, the bankruptcy trustee has decided that Marta's home needs to be appraised to determine its potential value to the estate. He has filed a motion for authorization to hire a real estate appraiser, which is shown in Document 29 in the Carlson case file. The order granting that authorization is shown in Document 30.

Bankruptcy Rule 6003 provides that, absent a showing of immediate and irreparable harm, the court cannot grant an application for permission to hire a professional person during the first 21 days following the filing of the petition.

Section 327(a) requires that any professional hired by the trustee be a **disinterested person** and not hold or represent an **adverse interest** to the estate. The term "disinterested" is defined in 11 U.S.C. §101(14) as pertaining to a person who (1) "is not a creditor, an equity security holder, or an insider"; (2) "is not and was not, within 2 years before the date of the filing of the petition, a director, officer, or employee of the debtor"; and (3) "does not have an interest materially adverse to the interest of the estate or of any class of creditors or equity security holders, by reason of any direct or indirect relationship to, connection with, or interest in, the debtor, or for any other reason." Professionals have an adverse interest to the estate if they "(1) possess or assert any economic interest that would tend to lessen the value of the bankruptcy estate or that would create either an actual or potential dispute in which the estate is a rival claimant; or (2) possess a predisposition under circumstances that render such a bias against the estate." *In re AroChem Corp.*, 176 F.3d 610, 623 (2d Cir. 1999).

EXAMPLE

The trustee in Marta Carlson's case could not hire an appraiser who was also a creditor of Marta's estate. That appraiser would not be disinterested (unless it agreed to waive its claim against the estate). The trustee could not hire as an attorney a lawyer who also represents Pine Ridge Nursing Home, which has a lawsuit pending against her at the time she files. That lawyer represents an adverse interest to Marta's estate.

The compensation of professionals is governed by §328 and Bankruptcy Rule 2016. Under §328, the trustee is authorized to employ professionals on any reasonable terms, including retainer, hourly rate, fixed fee, or contingency. In order to be paid, however, Rule 2016 requires the professional seeking payment to file a **fee application** containing a description of services performed, payments to date, and any fee sharing agreements. Most bankruptcy courts have local rules and customized forms governing fee applications. In practice, bankruptcy courts want to see a sufficiently detailed description of all services performed, dates, attorney names, the amount of time spent, and other relevant information so that the court can be satisfied that payment of estate funds to the professionals is commensurate with the value received by the estate.

To the extent the court finds the fee application excessive in light of the benefit to the estate, the court has authority under §328(a) to modify or deny the compensation requested. If the court finds that the professional seeking compensation was not a disinterested person or held or represented an interest adverse to the estate, compensation may be denied under §328(c).

Per §331, professionals may apply to the court for compensation on an interim basis, but not more than once every 120 days. While this is better than waiting until the end of a case, for many professionals waiting four months to be paid can be a serious burden. Accordingly, many courts will enter orders allowing professionals to file interim fee applications on a monthly basis, such as a final fee order at the end of the case. Interim fee orders commonly include a **holdback provision** of 5 to 20 percent of the requested fee until the final order.

 ## C.   The No-Asset Case

No-asset case A Chapter 7 liquidation case in which there are no assets available for liquidation and distribution to creditors.

The first thing the newly appointed trustee will do in a Chapter 7 case is review the petition and supporting schedules to make an initial determination as to whether the case is an **asset case** or a **no-asset case**. A no-asset case is one in which all of the debtor's assets are either properly exempted (meaning the debtor can keep the property, despite the bankruptcy proceeding) or subject to validly perfected prepetition security interests or liens that give the secured creditors a priority claim to the collateralized property over the claim of the bankruptcy trustee. Approximately 90 percent of all Chapter 7 cases nationwide are no-asset cases.

> **NOTE ON THE MARTA CARLSON CASE STUDY**
>
> A review of Marta Rinaldi Carlson's schedules in the Carlson case file will quickly disclose that hers is an asset case and, in that sense, her Chapter 7 case is atypical. But we use a Chapter 7 asset case study in order to illustrate various aspects of case administration that would not arise in a no-asset case. Working through a no-asset case will not teach you how to handle an asset case. Working through an asset case will teach you how to handle both.

Since bankruptcy trustees are compensated out of the filing fee paid by the debtor and a percentage of property located and sold for the benefit of creditors in the case, the trustee's compensation can be dramatically impacted by whether a case is an asset case or a no-asset case.

Before finally concluding that the case is a no-asset one, the bankruptcy trustee will question the debtor at the first meeting of creditors and do any further investigation he or she deems appropriate. As suggested in the list of the trustee's duties in Illustration 9-a, that may include a close review of the debtor's claimed exemptions and the values asserted by the debtor and a close review of the claims of listed secured creditors. If the trustee concludes that the case is a no-asset one, the trustee will file a **no-asset report** with the bankruptcy court and a **discharge in bankruptcy** will be issued promptly and the case closed (see Chapter Twelve).

D. ▶ Notice to Creditors of Filing of Case

Pursuant to §342 of the Code, upon the filing of the petition, the bankruptcy court clerk will issue a **Notice of Chapter 7 Bankruptcy Case** (sometimes called a **notice of commencement**) to the creditors and the U.S. Trustee. Section 342(d) provides that if the case is filed by a consumer debtor, the notice is to be given no later than ten days after the petition is filed. This notice is Official Form 309 and there is a separate notice form for cases filed under Chapters 7, 11, 12, or 13. (Remember that all official bankruptcy forms are available at www.uscourts.gov/forms/bankruptcy-forms.) There are also different notice of filing forms for Chapter 7 cases, depending on whether the debtor is an individual or an entity and on whether the case is an asset case or a no-asset case.

Marta Carlson's Chapter 7 case is by an individual with assets so the clerk has used Form 309B because the case does appear to be an asset case and a proof of claim deadline is established (see Document 23 in the Carlson case file). Observe that the first page of the notice provides the creditor with the name, address, and phone number of the bankruptcy trustee appointed in the case. As we move through the other aspects of case administration, refer back to the notice to see how it advises creditors of the various aspects of case administration that apply to them.

E. ▶ The First Meeting of Creditors

Pursuant to §341 of the Code and Bankruptcy Rule 2003, the U.S. Trustee is required to call a meeting of creditors within 21 to 40 days following the order for relief in a Chapter 7 case. This **first meeting of creditors** is required in a case filed under any chapter of the Code, but the timing of the meeting varies (e.g., 21 to 40 days after the order for relief in Chapter 7s and 11s; 21 to 35 days in a Chapter 12; and 21 to 50 days in a Chapter 13). Practitioners often refer to the first meeting of creditors as the **341 meeting**.

The notice of filing of the case advises creditors of the date and time set for the 341 meeting.

The 341 meeting is conducted by the bankruptcy trustee. This is not a court hearing and the bankruptcy judge is not present. The debtor is put under oath and must answer questions regarding his assets and financial affairs. Frequently, nonexempt property of the debtor is turned over to the bankruptcy trustee at this meeting: keys to cars, houses, lockboxes, and the like. There are often questions about assets or liabilities the debtor has or hasn't listed in his schedules, or issues discussed regarding the valuation of property claimed as exempt. All these matters may be inquired into at the 341. Since the debtor is under oath, it is important that he answer truthfully and candidly.

Illustration 9-b: QUESTIONS THE BANKRUPTCY TRUSTEE IS REQUIRED TO ASK THE CHAPTER 7 DEBTOR AT THE FIRST
MEETING OF CREDITORS

- Debtor's awareness of the consequences of receiving a discharge in bankruptcy, including the effect on credit history
- Debtor's ability to file for relief under another chapter of the Code
- Debtor's awareness of the effect of a discharge of debt under Chapter 7
- Debtor's awareness of the effect of reaffirming debt rather than discharging it

Section 341(d) requires that the bankruptcy trustee examine a Chapter 7 debtor on several matters at the 341 meeting. Those required topics are set forth in Illustration 9-b.

MAY A NONATTORNEY AGENT OF A CREDITOR ASK QUESTIONS AT THE 341 MEETING?

One question that has arisen historically in 341 meetings is whether a nonattorney employee of a creditor can attend and ask questions of the debtor on behalf of the creditor. Some courts have allowed that and some have not on the grounds that asking questions on behalf of another at the 341 hearing is the practice of law. Under that view, an individual creditor could appear and ask questions himself at the hearing, but if he sends an agent to speak for him, that agent must be an attorney. Since corporations are not natural persons like the individual creditor and must always be represented by an agent, the practical effect of this view is to require entity creditors such as corporations to always be represented by counsel at the 341 meeting, adding to the expense of the proceeding for that creditor. BAPCPA revised §341(c) to provide that a creditor holding a consumer debt (one related to personal or household goods) may be represented at the meeting by an employee or agent of the creditor who need not be an attorney.

A closely related question is whether a paralegal or legal assistant for the attorney representing a creditor can attend and ask questions of the debtor in lieu of the attorney herself. In some districts that has been prohibited as constituting the practice of law.

P-H 9-c: Research the court rulings of your federal district or circuit (or the ethical rules/opinions for attorneys in your state) to determine the prevailing rule there, or check the local rules of your bankruptcy court to see if that issue is addressed there.

Within ten days following the 341 meeting, the U.S. Trustee is required by §704(b)(1) to file a report with the bankruptcy court advising whether any presumption of abuse should arise in the case because of the means test of §704(b). The clerk then provides a copy of that statement to creditors within five days. If the U.S. Trustee concludes that the presumption of abuse is still present, he is required to file a motion to dismiss the case or convert it to a Chapter 13 within 30 days of filing the §704(b)(1) report. The §704(b)(1) report filed by the U.S. Trustee in Marta Carlson's case can be seen in Document 26 in the Carlson case file.

The 341 meeting is not the only time that a debtor can be examined under oath in a case. If at any time there is a dispute about the debtor's 341 meeting testimony or if any new issue arises in the case requiring sworn testimony of the debtor or anyone else, Bankruptcy Rule 2004 authorizes any party in interest to file a motion with the courts asking permission to conduct a sworn examination of the debtor or any other witness. This is called a **Rule 2004 examination**.

EXAMPLE

Assume that the bankruptcy trustee in Marta Carlson's case is considering an objection to the claim of Pine Ridge Nursing Home based on the debtor's dispute of that debt. The trustee may want to examine Marta further on this dispute and he may want to examine one or more persons from Pine Ridge as well. To accomplish those examinations, the trustee may utilize Rule 2004.

Official Form 2540 contains the subpoena form to compel a witness's attendance at a 2004 examination.

F. ▶ The Automatic Stay

Automatic stay The prohibition on creditors continuing collection efforts against a debtor that arises automatically upon the debtor's filing of a bankruptcy petition.

The **automatic stay** is one of the most important events in a bankruptcy case. Section 362(a) of the Code provides that the filing of a bankruptcy petition automatically stays (stops) any action by a creditor to collect on the indebtedness owed to him by the debtor or any action by the creditor to improve his position vis-à-vis other creditors (e.g., by obtaining a postpetition security interest in the debtor's property). A stay mandates the following:

- All informal collection efforts against the debtor must stop.
- All pending collection lawsuits must stop.
- All efforts to collect on a final judgment previously entered must stop.
- All efforts to obtain a security interest must stop.
- All efforts to repossess or foreclose on the debtor's property pursuant to a consensual or nonconsensual lien must stop.

EXAMPLE

According to the Assignment Memorandum in Appendix A, Pine Ridge Nursing Home has filed suit against Marta Carlson to collect on amounts allegedly owed on the personal guaranty she signed. If that case is scheduled to go to trial tomorrow, the trial must be continued (postponed). If motions are scheduled to be heard in that case tomorrow, the motions will have to be postponed. If the judge has just entered a judgment in favor of Pine Ridge Nursing Home, it must take no action to collect on the judgment lest it be found in violation of the automatic stay. According to the Assignment Memorandum in Appendix A, the Dreams Come True Financing Company has declared the loan to Marta to be in default and is preparing to foreclose on her home. With the filing of the bankruptcy petition, that foreclosure proceeding must stop.

The rationale behind the automatic stay provision is that once the debtor has filed the petition seeking bankruptcy relief, he is immediately entitled to the protections afforded by the Code, and his property is also immediately subject to the procedures outlined in the Code. Consequently, the automatic stay serves to freeze actions against the debtor's property at the commencement of the case so that the bankruptcy procedure can control what happens to the debtor and his property from that point on.

1. Exceptions to the Automatic Stay

Per §362(b)(21), the filing of a petition in bankruptcy does not operate as a stay if the debtor is ineligible under §109(g) to be a debtor in the kind of case filed. See, e.g., *In re Brown*, 2013 WL 2318414 (Bankr. E.D. Va. May 28, 2013) (no violation of the stay when mortgagee proceeded with postpetition foreclosure on Chapter 13 debtors' home where debtors were ineligible under §109(g) to file the Chapter 13 case). Section 362(b) of the Code sets out a number of other exceptions to the automatic stay—specific types of collection activities that *can* continue and are not stayed by the filing of the petition. A number of these are actions involving domestic disputes. Illustration 9-c lists various domestic disputes that, per §362(b), are not automatically stayed by the filing of a bankruptcy petition.

Per §362(b)(10), a landlord's eviction action against a debtor involving a **non-residential lease** is not stayed where the eviction is based on expiration of the agreed lease term either before or after the bankruptcy petition is filed. The stay will apply to such eviction action if it is based on some other ground (e.g., non-payment of rent). Per §§362(b)(22) and (23), a landlord's eviction action against a debtor involving a **residential lease** is not stayed where:

- the landlord has obtained a prepetition judgment of eviction;
- the landlord certifies that the basis of the eviction action is the debtor's endangerment of the property; or
- the landlord certifies that the basis of the eviction action is the debtor's illegal use of controlled substances on the property.

Illustration 9-c: DOMESTIC ACTIONS NOT SUBJECT TO THE §362 AUTOMATIC STAY

- To establish paternity
- To establish or modify an order for domestic support obligations
- Concerning child custody or visitation
- To dissolve a marriage, except to the extent that such proceeding seeks to determine the division of property that is property of the estate
- Regarding domestic violence
- To collect a domestic support obligation from property that is not property of the estate
- To withhold income of the debtor or intercept a tax refund due the debtor in order to satisfy a domestic support obligation under state law
- To withhold or restrict a driver's license or a professional, occupational, or recreational license for non-payment of domestic obligations under state law
- To report nonpayment of a domestic obligation to a credit reporting agency

Per §362(b)(1), neither state nor federal criminal actions against a debtor are stayed by the filing of a petition. Per §362(b)(4), regulatory actions against a debtor by any governmental unit that involve protecting public health and safety (e.g., a state department of health acting to shut down debtor's business for violations of state fire code or state food handling regulations) are not stayed.

Though §362(a)(8) provides that tax disputes pending in U.S. Tax Court when the petition is filed are stayed, §362(b)(9) provides that state or federal government actions to audit a debtor for tax liability, to issue tax deficiency notices, to demand tax returns, or to issue a past-due tax assessment and demand payment are not stayed. Other actions to collect a tax from the debtor will be stayed, as will any other action to create, perfect, or enforce a tax lien. Section 362(b)(18) does exempt from the stay an action by a governmental unit to create or perfect a statutory tax lien arising from a property tax or special assessment on debtor's real property, but only where such tax or assessment becomes due after the petition is filed.

Though most foreclosure actions are subject to the stay, §362(b)(8) does except from the stay foreclosure actions initiated by the U.S. Department of Housing and Urban Development (HUD) on properties consisting of five or more living units.

Recall from Chapter Three, Section A, our consideration of nonconsensual statutory liens and how they are created and perfected and how the date on which such a lien is deemed to exist or deemed to be perfected may be impacted by the **relation-back** feature of the state statutes regulating those liens. What does that have to do with the automatic stay? Well, actions by a creditor to create, perfect, or renew a security interest in the debtor's property are subject to the automatic stay of §362(a), with an important exception. Section 362(b)(3) excepts from the operation of the automatic stay the creation or perfection of a security interest where applicable state law authorizes a grace period (such as the relation-back feature of nonconsensual statutory liens) for determining the effective date or date of perfection of a prepetition security interest.

EXAMPLE

Assume a state's mechanic's lien statute provides that such a lien is created and perfected by filing of a notice of lien and giving owner of the real property written notice of the filing. The statute also provides that the lien, once created, "relates back to the date when the services or materials were first supplied." Now suppose a subcontractor provides services for the improvement of the owner's real property on March 1. Payment is not made when due, and on June 10 the subcontractor's lawyer is preparing to file the required notice of lien and to give the owner notice of the filing when she learns that the owner filed a bankruptcy petition on June 9. Does the automatic stay prevent filing and service of the notice of lien? No. Because the statute contains the relation-back feature and will deem the lien created and perfected on March 1 (prepetition), §362(b)(3) allows the attorney to file and serve the notice of lien postpetition without violating the stay.

EXAMPLE

Recall from Chapter Two, Section C, the discussion of perfecting a security interest in personal property by filing a **financing statement** (UCC-1) pursuant to **Article 9** of a state's version of the **Uniform Commercial Code** (UCC). For most kinds of collateral, perfection is accomplished by filing a financing statement (UCC-1) in the designated state or local government office. Per UCC §9-515, once filed, a financing statement is valid for only a stated number of years (typically five years), but can be renewed under state law by filing a **continuation statement** within six months of the expiration of the original five-year term. What if a creditor filed a financing statement properly perfecting a security interest in personal property of the debtor four years and five months ago and is now preparing to file a continuation statement when debtor files a bankruptcy petition? Does the automatic stay bar the creditor from filing the continuation statement? No, because the security interest existed prepetition and filing the continuation statement during the six-month grace period created by state law merely continues (relates back to) the security interest that was created prepetition. Section 362(b)(3) allows the creditor to file the continuation statement postpetition without violating the stay.

In addition to recognizing state law grace periods or relation-back periods impacting on when a security interest is created or perfected, §362(b)(3) creates its own relation-back period for perfecting a security interest postpetition without violating the stay. By referencing §547(e)(2)(A) (a section of the Code that we will look at in more detail in the next chapter), §362(b)(3) allows a security interest to be perfected postpetition in a consensual prepetition transfer of property to the debtor so long as the perfection is completed within 30 days of the transfer.

EXAMPLE

Assume a borrower purchases a house on June 1 and borrows money from the bank to make the purchase. At the closing on June 1, the borrower provides the bank with a mortgage on the house to secure repayment of the amount borrowed. The bank does not record the mortgage (an act required to perfect its secured position in the property, as we learned in Chapter Two) until June 3. Meanwhile, the borrower files a bankruptcy petition on June 2. Has the bank violated the automatic stay by recording the mortgage instrument on June 3? No. Per §362(b)(3), the bank has the 30 days following transfer of the property to the debtor on June 1 allowed by §547(e)(2)(A) to perfect its secured position in the property without running afoul of the statute.

P-H 9-d: Assume a debtor has filed for Chapter 7 bankruptcy relief. In his schedules he lists the following pending actions to collect indebtedness. Determine which ones are automatically stayed by §362(a):

- lawsuit by his former business partner alleging fraud by debtor
- criminal prosecution of debtor by the state for that fraud
- child custody dispute with debtor's ex-wife
- hearing on property division in divorce action in state court brought by debtor's ex-wife

- eviction action brought by landlord of the apartment where debtor resides seeking to evict him for playing loud music; no judgment entered when petition filed
- repossession by bank on debtor's business assets
- foreclosure by bank on debtor's home
- repossession by bank on car owned by debtor's ex-wife who is not in a bankruptcy proceeding herself

2. Enforcing the Automatic Stay and Sanctions for Violation

As the name implies, the automatic stay is truly automatic; it goes into effect upon the filing of the petition.

In most bankruptcy courts, the procedure for obtaining damages or other relief for violation of the automatic stay is for the debtor to file a **motion** in his bankruptcy case alleging the violation and seeking appropriate sanctions. A motion creates a **contested matter** in the bankruptcy case that the bankruptcy judge will hear and decide. In a minority of federal districts, allegations of violation of the automatic stay must be brought as formal **adversary proceedings**, essentially mini-lawsuits within the bankruptcy case. (You may want to review the distinctions in these procedures as discussed in Chapter Six, Section G.)

P-H 9-e: Determine which procedure the bankruptcy courts of your federal district require that a debtor use to allege violation of the automatic stay.

Contempt Power of a court to declare one subject to the court's order in violation of it and to assess penalties.

The typical remedies sought against a creditor accused of violating the automatic stay are for the court to **enjoin** (stop) any continuing violation by the creditor, to declare any actions taken by the creditor in violation of the stay **void** and of no effect (e.g., to cancel the repossession of a vehicle and order the vehicle returned to debtor), and, if the violation of the stay was done with knowledge that a bankruptcy case was pending, to declare the creditor in **contempt** of the bankruptcy court since the automatic stay is a court order that has been violated by the creditor.

EXAMPLE

The notice of filing sent to creditors specifically references the danger of proceeding with postpetition collection activities. (See the first page of the Notice of Chapter 7 Bankruptcy Case issued in Marta Carlson's case, Document 23 in the Carlson case file.)

Punitive damages Damages intended to punish the wrongdoer in order to deter similar conduct in the future.

For any "willful violation" of the stay, §362(k)(1) provides that the court may also award the individual debtor his **actual damages** caused by the violation of the stay, **court costs**, **attorney's fees** incurred by the debtor, and "in appropriate circumstances" even **punitive damages** (damages intended to punish the wrongdoer).

EXAMPLE

> Pine Ridge Nursing Home filed a motion for summary judgment in its collection lawsuit after receiving notice of Marta Carlson's bankruptcy filing. Marta's attorney responded with a motion for order of contempt for violation of the automatic stay (see Document 24 in the Carlson case file). Following the hearing on the motion, the court found Pine Ridge Nursing Home in contempt and ordered it to pay Marta's attorney's fee incurred in making the motion and enjoined any further violation of the stay (see Document 25 in the Carlson case file).

Not surprisingly, there is much dispute over what constitutes a "willful violation" of the stay under §362(k)(1).

HIGHLIGHTED CASE

IN RE BUTZ
444 B.R. 301 (Bankr. M.D. Pa. 2011)

[Freda Butz, an individual bankruptcy debtor, received a computer-generated printout from one of her creditors, People First Federal Credit Union, five weeks after filing a joint petition with her husband and four weeks after Credit Union had received notice of the filing. The statement identified the balance owed and included language saying, "Your account is 10 or more days past due. Please remit the amount due immediately. If you feel an error has been made please contact us." The debtor filed a complaint with the bankruptcy court alleging that Credit Union had committed a willful violation of the automatic stay under §362(k) and sought actual damages. The debtor then filed a motion for summary judgment on the complaint. Credit Union defended the motion on the grounds that the statement was not an effort to collect a prepetition debt and was instead informational only and did nothing more than advise the debtor of the status of her account, which the Credit Union had properly marked internally as a not-for-collection account. The Credit Union also defended on the grounds that the statement was not a willful violation of the automatic stay since it was an automatically computer-generated statement routinely sent to all Credit Union customers.]

OPINION: OPEL, Bankruptcy Judge:

Generally, to prove a violation of the automatic stay, a debtor/plaintiff must show both that the defendant (1) knew of the automatic stay, and (2) acted willfully to violate the stay. A "willful" violation is a condition precedent to receiving damages under §362(k). "It is a willful violation of the automatic stay when a creditor violates the stay with knowledge that the bankruptcy petition has been filed." *In re Lansdale Family Restaurants, Inc.*, 977 F.2d 826, 829 (3d Cir. 1992) . . . . Courts in the Third Circuit have consistently recognized that "willfulness" under §362(k) does not require a finding of a creditor's specific intent to violate the stay. *In re Nixon*, 419 B.R. 281, 288 (Bankr. E.D. Pa. 2009).

The Defendant admits receiving notice of the bankruptcy filing when it received the Notice of 341 Meeting of Creditors on May 5, 2010. The

Defendant also admits that it sent the Statement to the Plaintiff on June 14, 2010. With these admissions, I find that there are no genuine issues of material fact in this case. I find that the Defendant had notice of the bankruptcy filing when it mailed the Statement to the Plaintiff on or about June 14, 2010.

Since the Defendant admits it had notice of the bankruptcy when it sent the Statement, the question I must now decide is whether sending the Statement was a willful violation of the automatic stay. The Defendant has explained that it sent the Statement to the Plaintiff because she continues to conduct post-petition business with the Credit Union and has both a savings account and a line of credit. Mr. Kurtz, the Defendant's Asset Recovery Supervisor, stated in his Affidavit that monthly, the Defendant mails what it calls a "combined statement" to the Plaintiff, and its other customers. The combined statement outlines the activity and balances of the line of credit and the savings account. Paragraph 6 of the Affidavit states "Defendant is unable to segregate loans from savings or checking accounts for purposes of mailing [s]tatements to Plaintiff or any other members of the Credit Union." Kurtz Aff. 6. Finally, Mr. Kurtz verified that the Statement was only sent when the Plaintiff's line of credit became past due, and clarified that the Defendant's system is programmed to forward one notice only, regardless of whether or not payment is tendered.

To further substantiate its position, the Defendant contends that it took several actions which demonstrate that it complied with the requirements of the automatic stay. Upon receipt of the Notice of the 341 meeting, the Defendant states that the Plaintiff's line of credit was immediately marked as "no collection activity." The Defendant also reported the line of credit to the three major credit bureaus as included in a Chapter 13 bankruptcy. Finally, through the Defendant's internal procedures, the line of credit was charged off in July 2010.

In determining whether or not sending the Statement was a violation of the stay, the Defendant's other acts, which appear to be harmonious with the stay, are irrelevant to the analysis. Sending the Statement itself was either a violation of the stay, or it was not. The Statement is addressed to the Plaintiff and includes her member number; it is a preprinted form with several blank boxes for the computer to fill with the appropriate member specific information. The Statement indicates that payments are due monthly and it is dated "6/14/10." It states, "Your account is 10 or more days past due. Please remit the amount due immediately. If you feel an error has been made please contact us." It further states a loan balance of "4809.76," that the last payment was made on "4/19/10," the loan paid through date is "5/25/10" and an amount due of "125.00." Finally, there is a line to indicate the "amount paid" and the form is perforated such that a Credit Union member may separate a portion of the statement to presumably return with a payment.

Tasked to evaluate the Statement, I conclude that it is, in part, an invoice demanding payment on the account. The Defendant's arguments that the Statement is a simple notice to keep the Plaintiff informed of the status of her account is unpersuasive. If the Statement were only an informative notice, it would not use the language, "Your account is 10 or more days past due. Please remit the amount due immediately." Nor would it state "125.00" in the amount due box. Finally, if the Statement was only informative, and not for collection purposes, the computer would not have been triggered to send it only after when the Plaintiff's line of credit became past due as explained by Mr. Kurtz. I find that by sending the Statement to the Plaintiff, the Defendant violated the automatic stay under §362(a).

Similarly, the Defendant's position that it was necessary for the computer to send such statements to the Plaintiff, as it does all other customers, is unpersuasive. When considering the willfulness of acts which violate the stay, courts have rejected the so called "computer did it" defense. See *In re Wingard*, 382 B.R. 892, 902 (Bankr. W.D. Pa. 2008) . . . . Where there is actual notice of the bankruptcy, the defendant has the burden of proving that it took steps to prevent violations of the stay. See *In re Rijos*, 263 B.R. 382, 392 (1st Cir. BAP 2001). The computer did it defense has been characterized as a non-starter "since intelligent beings still control the computer and could have altered the programming appropriately." *In re McCormack*, 203 B.R. 521, 524 (Bankr. D.N.H. 1996).

The supposed necessity in this case is of the Defendant's own creation; it arises because of the Credit Union's own internal policies and procedures. The Defendant has an obligation to shape its policies and procedures such that they are harmonious with the legal requirements placed upon it by the Bankruptcy Code and otherwise. "Sophisticated commercial enterprises have a clear obligation to adjust their programming and procedures and their instruction to employees to handle complex matters correctly." *McCormack*, 203 B.R. at 525.

I find that the Defendant's act of sending the Statement to the Plaintiff was a willful violation as described in §362(k). Therefore, the Plaintiff is entitled to judgment as a matter of law on the issue of violation of the automatic stay. A hearing must still be held to determine if the Plaintiff is entitled to recover any damages.

POST-CASE FOLLOW-UP

Butz illustrates the widely accepted view that in order to prove a willful violation of the automatic stay under §362(k), the debtor is not required to show that the creditor acted with the specific intent to violate the stay. "The willfulness requirement refers to the deliberateness of the conduct and the knowledge of the bankruptcy filing, not to a specific intent to violate a court order." *In re Wagner*, 74 B.R. 898, 903 (Bankr. E.D. Pa. 1987). "The question is not whether the creditor intended to violate the stay, but whether the creditor intended the act." *In re Kinsey*, 349 B.R. 48, 52 (Bankr. D. Idaho 2006). Of course, the willful action taken by the creditor must be an attempt to collect a debt in a way forbidden by §362(a). For example, if a creditor does send a postpetition notice to a debtor regarding a prepetition debt for genuinely informational or account status purposes only, there is no violation even though sending the notice was willful and done with knowledge of the filing. See, e.g., *In re Schatz*, 452 B.R. 544, 549-550 (Bankr. M.D. Pa. 2011).

In re Butz: Real Life Applications

1. Since the court in *Butz* rejected the "computer made me do it" defense and stressed that creditors have an obligation to shape their policies and procedures to make them harmonious with legal requirements such as the automatic stay, what recommendations should the attorney for that creditor make to the client regarding changes it needs to make (1) to its computerized records system, and (2) instructions to its employees regarding an alternative system for identifying accounts subject to the automatic stay and preventing even routine billing of such accounts?

2. Even where a creditor has policies and procedures in place designed to avoid violating the stay, inadvertent violations can occur, giving rise to the issue of whether the creditor should be deemed to have acted willfully. Should "oops" be a defense in the following scenarios?

   a. ABC Collection Company purchases charged-off consumer debt and quickly files suit to obtain judgment, usually by default. ABC uses Quick Serve, Inc., to achieve service of process on defendants in its collection lawsuits. ABC has in place a policy and procedures to pull unserved process for debtors upon receipt of notice of their filing for bankruptcy so that process is not delivered to Quick Serve for service on those debtors. Where process has already been delivered to Quick Serve when notice of bankruptcy filing is received the procedure is to immediately contact Quick Serve by phone and e-mail to prevent service of process that would violate the automatic stay. Today, ABC receives notice that Martha Jones has filed a case in Chapter 7. The procedures are followed but her process papers cannot be located in the office. On the assumption that the process papers have already been forwarded to Quick Serve, ABC contacts Quick Serve, notifies it of the bankruptcy filing, and instructs it to not serve Martha. Quick Serve acknowledges receipt of the information but thereafter has Martha served with process. Has ABC violated the stay? See *In re Kinsey*, 349 B.R. 48, 52 (Bankr. D. Idaho 2006).

   b. Fast Collect Corp. has purchased a debt owed by "Mike P. Campion" and has filed suit against him to collect it. While the collection suit is pending, Fast Collect receives notice that "Michael P. Campion" has filed a petition in Chapter 7. Using its recently updated software system, it notes the Michael P. Campion bankruptcy filing in its Mike P. Campion file and the collection lawsuit is stayed. Three months later Fast Collect purchases another debt owed by "Michael P. Campion." When the new account is entered into Fast Collect's computer system, it does not find a match with the Mike P. Campion file because the software searches only for similarities between last names and the first three letters of the first name. Not recognizing that Michael P. Campion is the same person as Mike P. Campion and is in a Chapter 7 case, Fast Collect files suit against Campion. Has Fast Collect violated the stay? See *In re Campion*, 294 B.R. 313 (9th Cir. B.A.P. 2003).

3. The *Butz* court says that a violation of the automatic stay occurs only where the creditor commits the willful act with "knowledge of the automatic stay." The creditor in *Butz* admitted to having actual knowledge of the bankruptcy filing prior to

the statement being sent and as a commercial lender clearly knew that such filing triggered the automatic stay. But there can be disputes regarding whether a creditor has the requisite knowledge to substantiate a finding of violation.

a. Is it a defense if the creditor knows that a bankruptcy petition has been filed but is not familiar with the automatic stay? See *In re Wagner*, 74 B.R. 898 (Bankr. E.D. Pa. 1987).

b. Is it a defense if a creditor hears through the grapevine that a debtor has or may have filed for bankruptcy relief but the creditor has not received any official notice from the debtor or the bankruptcy court? See *In re Rhyne*, 59 B.R. 276 (Bankr. E.D. Pa. 1986), and *In re Flack*, 239 B.R. 155, 163 (Bankr. S.D. Ohio 1999).

c. Is it a defense if a creditor learns of a debtor's bankruptcy filing but continues collection efforts after an attorney tells him (mistakenly) that the automatic stay does not go into effect until formal notice is received from the court? See *In re Ashby*, 36 B.R. 976 (Bankr. D. Utah 1984).

d. Is it a defense if a creditor continues collection efforts after learning of a debtor's bankruptcy filing but does so believing in good faith that his debt is not one subject to the automatic stay and in fact the law is sharply divided on the point? See *United States v. Norton*, 717 F.2d 767 (3d Cir. 1983), and *In re Wilson*, 19 B.R. 45 (Bankr. E.D. Pa. 1982).

e. Is it a defense if the debt that is owed to the creditor is a nondischargeable debt such as a student loan? See *In re Walker*, 336 B.R. 534 (Bankr. M.D. Fla. 2005), but compare *In re Billingsley*, 276 B.R. 48, 53 (Bankr. D.N.J. 2002).

f. Is it a defense if the creditor itself has no knowledge of the bankruptcy filing but an agent or affiliate of the creditor does when the willful act occurs? See *Green Tree Servicing, LLC v. Taylor*, 369 B.R. 282 (Bankr. S.D. W. Va. 2007) (attorney of creditor given notice), and *Haile v. New York State Higher Educ. Servs. Corp.*, 90 B.R. 51, 55 (Bankr. W.D.N.Y. 1988) (collection agency retained by creditor given notice).

Safe-harbor provision A provision in a statute or regulation that exempts a person from liability for certain conduct.

A SAFE HARBOR FOR CREDITORS VIOLATING THE AUTOMATIC STAY?

Section 342(g)(1), added by BAPCPA, provides that if the creditor designates a person or organizational subdivision to receive bankruptcy notices and has a reasonable procedure to deliver notices to such person or subdivision, then a notice has not been "brought to the attention" of the creditor until the designated person or subdivision receives the notice. Early indications are that this very pro-creditor **safe-harbor provision** is not being well received by bankruptcy courts, which generally take violations of the automatic stay very seriously. Several decisions interpreting §342(g)(1) have held that even where the creditor has designated someone to receive notice for them, if the creditor otherwise had actual notice of the bankruptcy filing (as opposed to constructive or imputed knowledge), the creditor cannot rely on that safe-harbor provision. See *In re Murray*, 2013 WL 6800881 (Bankr. N.D. Cal. 2013), and *In re Davis*, 498 B.R. 64, 69 (Bankr. D.S.C. 2013).

If a creditor continues with collection efforts after the filing of the petition but does not have any actual or constructive notice of the filing of a bankruptcy case by the debtor, much less the automatic stay itself, the court will not hold the creditor in contempt but will likely set aside any actions taken by the creditor after the filing of the petition. There still has been a violation of the stay but not a willful violation (see a good discussion of the difference in *In re Taylor*, 369 B.R. 282, 286-287 (S.D. W. Va. 2007).

EXAMPLE

> If Pine Ridge Nursing Home had filed its motion for summary judgment after Marta's petition was filed but before receiving notice, the judge likely would not have imposed sanctions on Pine Ridge but instead would have ordered the motion stricken until the stay is lifted, as discussed below.

In many federal districts, the debtor must prove willfulness by only a **preponderance of the evidence**. See, e.g., *In re Johnson*, 501 F.3d 1163 (10th Cir. 2007). Others hold the debtor to a **clear and convincing** standard. See, e.g., *In re Bennett*, 135 B.R. 72 (Bankr. S.D. Ohio 1992).

P-H 9-f: Determine which standard of proof the bankruptcy courts in your federal district or circuit employ in willful violation cases.

Section 362(k)(2), added by BAPCPA, provides a creditor accused of willfully violating the automatic stay with a defense wherein the action taken by the creditor involved collateralized personal property and the secured creditor can show that it believed in **good faith** that debtor had failed to file a timely §521(a)(2) **statement of intent** (Form 108, discussed in Chapter Eight, Section B) with regard to such property (see Document 18 in the Carlson case file).

P-H 9-g: What are the implications of the good faith defense of §362(k)(2) regarding the importance of timely filing the debtor's statement of intent and being sure to include on it all property of the debtor that is collateral for an obligation?

Upon a showing of willful violation of the stay, the debtor is entitled to recover actual damages but has the burden of proving such damages apart from the proof of willful violation. Note that in *In re Butz* the court, having found a willful violation, reserved the question of whether the debtor could prove actual damages for a later hearing. Actual damages sought by debtors for violation of the automatic stay are typically **economic loss** that can be shown to be causally related to the stay violation (e.g., lost income, lost future profits, lost use of property wrongfully withheld from debtor, lost value of property wrongfully seized and not returned).

EXAMPLE

A debtor who has to miss work in order to attend a court hearing made necessary by the stay violation may ask for her lost income; a debtor who has to lease a rental car because the creditor seized or kept his in violation of the stay may seek that rental expense; a debtor whose vehicle is wrongfully repossessed in violation of the stay but sold to a good faith purchaser for value may seek the value of the lost vehicle; a debtor who is a house painter and who lost job opportunities due to his vehicle or trade tools being seized or kept in violation of the stay may seek lost profits from those jobs.

Though §362(k)(1) literally says that upon the finding of a willful violation the debtor shall recover "actual damages including . . . attorney's fees," there is a split of authority over whether that includes attorney's fees incurred by the debtor in prosecuting the stay violation itself as opposed to attorney's fees incurred by the debtor in avoiding the consequences of the stay violation itself (e.g., seeking dismissal of a collection lawsuit filed in state court postpetition in violation of the stay). Compare *Sternberg v. Johnston*, 595 F.3d 937 (9th Cir. 2010), cert. denied, 131 S. Ct. 102 (2010) (Congress legislates against the backdrop of the "American Rule" pursuant to which each party is responsible for its own attorney's fees; once the stay violation has ended, any fees the debtor incurs after that point in pursuit of a damage award would not be to compensate for "actual damages" under §362(k)(1)) and *In re Durby*, 451 B.R. 664 (1st Cir. B.A.P. 2011) (since most decisions pre-BAPCPA held attorney's fees for prosecuting the stay violation recoverable under old §362(h), Congress's failure to change the language of the provision indicates an intent that they be recoverable and policy supports that construction; what good is it to be entitled to damages and attorney's fees for a violation of the automatic stay if it costs a debtor much more in unrecoverable fees to recover such damages and recoverable attorney's fees).

P-H 9-h: Determine if the decisions in your federal district or circuit allow the debtor to recover attorney's fees under §362(k)(1) for prosecuting the stay violation. Based on the order entered on Marta Carlson's motion for order of contempt for violation of the automatic stay against Pine Ridge Nursing Home (Documents 24 and 25 in the Carlson case file), which view does that court follow?

Another question that has divided the courts is whether actual damages recoverable for a willful violation under §362(k)(1) include only economic loss to the debtor or can include **emotional distress** damage as well. As you learned when studying torts, claims for emotional distress are often suspect due to their subjective nature. Compare *Fleet Mortg. Group, Inc. v. Kaneb*, 196 F.3d 265, 269 (1st Cir. 1999) (emotional distress recoverable under §362(k) if supported by "specific information" rather than "generalized assertions") with *Aiello v. Providian Fin. Corp.*, 239 F.3d 876, 880 (7th Cir. 2001) (emotional distress compensable under §362(k) only if accompanied by economic loss) and *United States v. Harchar*, 331 B.R. 720 (N.D. Ohio 2005) (when §362(h) was enacted in 1984, Congress was concerned not with providing debtors compensation for emotional harms, but with providing explicit statutory authorization for contempt, the only previously available remedy for a stay violation, and awarding damages for emotional harm was never commonplace under the bankruptcy court's traditional contempt procedures; the problems of proof, assessment, and appropriate compensation attendant to awarding damages for emotional distress are troublesome enough in the ordinary tort case, and should not be imported into civil contempt proceedings).

P-H 9-i: Determine if the courts of your federal district or circuit have ruled on whether damages for emotional distress are recoverable for a willful violation of the automatic stay under §362(k)(1) and, if so, whether proof of economic damages is required as a condition to the recovery of emotional distress damages.

Section 362(k)(1) also provides that the debtor who demonstrates a willful violation of the stay can recover punitive damages "in appropriate circumstances." This phrase is universally understood by the courts to require proof of something more than a willful violation of the stay by the offending creditor, although the something more that is required is stated variously by different courts. *In re Taylor*, 369 B.R. 282 (S.D. W. Va. 2007), involved a willful violation of the automatic stay and an award of actual damages to an individual debtor where a creditor who had been awarded a prepetition writ of possession to the debtor's mobile home and whose lawyer had been given notice of the bankruptcy filing thereafter entered the mobile home twice, once to post a "for sale" sign and a second time to verbally instruct debtor to leave the home. The debtor in *Taylor* also sought punitive damages. In the course of deciding what standard to apply to determine the punitive damage claim, the *Taylor* court provided a good summary of the various standards utilized:

> The relevant statute provides for punitive damages "in appropriate circumstances." 11 U.S.C. §362(k). There is a lack of uniform guidance on what is meant by "appropriate circumstances." Several standards have been adopted by the various courts that have considered the question. (Taylor Br. at 17-19).
>
> One group uses "**maliciousness or bad faith**" as the guide. See *Crysen/Montenay Energy Co. v. Esselen Associates*, 902 F.2d 1098, 1104-05 (2d Cir. 1990); *Atlantic Business and Community Corp.*, 901 F.2d 325, 329 (3d Cir. 1990); *In re Rutherford*, 329 B.R. 886, 898 (Bankr. N.D. Ga. 2005); *In re Calvin*, 329 B.R. 589, 604 (Bankr. S.D. Tex. 2005); *In re Harris*, 310 B.R. 395, 400 (Bankr. E.D. Wis. 2004); *In re Bivens*, 324 B.R. 39, 42 (Bankr. N.D. Ohio 2004). Another group of cases uses "**arrogant defiance of federal law**" as the touchstone. See *In re Curtis*, 322 B.R. 470, 486 (Bankr. D. Mass. 2005); *In re Bishop*, 296 B.R. 890, 898 (Bankr. S.D. Ga. 2003); *In the Matter of Mullarkey*, 81 B.R. 280, 284 (Bankr. D.N.J. 1987).
>
> Other courts have used **egregious, vindictive or intentional misconduct** as the standard. *Lovett v. Honeywell*, 930 F.2d 625, 628 (8th Cir. 1991); *In re McHenry*, 179 B.R. 165, 168 (9th Cir. BAP 1995); *Davis v. IRS*, 136 B.R. 414, 423, n. 20 (E.D. Va. 1992); *In re Hampton*, 319 B.R. 163, 174 (Bankr. E.D. Ark. 2005); *In re Cullen*, 329 B.R. 52, 57-58 (Bankr. N.D. Iowa 2005); *In re Jackson*, 309 B.R. 33, 40 (Bankr. W.D. Mo. 2004); *In re Bivens*, 324 B.R. 39, 42 (Bankr. N.D. Ohio 2004); *In re Smith*, 296 B.R. 46, 56 (Bankr. M.D. Ala. 2003); *In re Hedetneimi*, 297 B.R. 837, 843 (Bankr. M.D. Fla. 2003); *In re Siharath*, 285 B.R. 299, 305 (Bankr.

D. Minn. 2002); *In re Briggs*, 143 B.R. 438, 464 (Bankr. E.D. Mich. 1992). Still other courts have used a **multi-factor approach** and considered the following four factors: (1) the nature of the defendant's conduct; (2) the defendant's ability to pay; (3) the motives of the defendant; and (4) any provocation by the debtor. *Heghmann v. Indorf (In re Heghmann)*, 316 B.R. 395, 405 (1st Cir. BAP 2004) . . . ; *In re B. Cohen & Sons Caterers, Inc.*, 108 B.R. 482, 487-88 (E.D. Pa. 1989)).

One point that seems clear from the different standards articulated is that "punitive damages usually require more than mere willful violation of the automatic stay." *Heghmann*, 316 B.R. at 405. It is elsewhere suggested that "the Bankruptcy Code does not attempt to delineate what 'appropriate circumstances' means, leaving it to the sound discretion of the bankruptcy court." Id.; *In re Smith*, 296 B.R. 46, 56 (Bankr. M.D. Ala. 2003).

Id. at 289 (bolding supplied).

P-H 9-j: Determine what standard for the award of punitive damages under §362(k) is utilized by the courts of your federal district or circuit.

It is not just the offending creditor who may be tagged with damages and costs in a proceeding alleging willful violation of the stay. Attorneys and those assisting them who represent the creditor are at risk as well.

EXAMPLE

In *Eskanos & Adler, P.C. v. Leetien*, 309 F.3d 1210 (9th Cir. 2002), sanctions for willful violation were imposed on the attorney for the creditor for failing to immediately dismiss a suit against the debtor after being notified of the bankruptcy filing. In *In re Repine*, 536 F.3d 512 (5th Cir. 2008), an attorney was assessed actual and punitive damages for willful violation of the stay where he caused property of the bankrupt debtor's estate to be attached to pay a child support obligation after receiving notice of the bankruptcy filing. (Remember from Illustration 9-b that postpetition actions to "establish or modify" domestic support obligations are not subject to the automatic stay and neither are actions to collect such obligations taken against property that is not property of the estate.)

EC 9-a: Legal professionals assisting debtor's attorneys may be assigned the task of notifying creditors by phone immediately after the petition has been filed in order to stop a lawsuit, foreclosure, or repossession from going forward. Verbal notification provided prior to the receipt of the formal notice of filing is sufficient to put a creditor on notice of the automatic stay and trigger a contempt finding. Legal professionals working for a creditor, a collection agency, or a creditor's attorney must be careful to understand the significance of a bankruptcy filing and know to *stop* all collection efforts immediately. Otherwise that legal professional, the supervising attorney, and the client may be found in contempt of the bankruptcy court. What ethical problems might that raise for the attorney? For a certified paralegal?

There are some special rules added by BAPCPA pertaining to the automatic stay for the individual debtor (not the entity debtor) who has previously filed a case under Chapters 7, 11, or 13 and had it dismissed within one year preceding the filing of the current case. If an individual debtor filing today has filed a different bankruptcy case within one year preceding this filing and had the preceding filing dismissed, then the automatic stay goes into effect, but only for 30 days, pursuant to §362(c). To extend the stay, that debtor must file a **motion for extension of stay** with the court. A hearing will be conducted and the court will decide whether to extend the stay or not. The burden in such a hearing is placed on the debtor to show by **clear and convincing evidence** that this bankruptcy case has been filed in **good faith** and that the debtor is entitled to the stay per §362(c)(3).

Good faith Generally, honesty in fact and compliance with the letter and spirit of the Code.

If the individual debtor has filed *two* bankruptcy cases within the year preceding the filing of this one, whether Chapters 7, 11, or 13, and both have been dismissed, there is no automatic stay at all upon the filing of the third petition. In such case, the debtor must file his motion for automatic stay immediately upon filing his petition and carry his burden of showing a good faith filing by clear and convincing evidence per §362(c)(4).

EC 9-b: One purpose of BAPCPA was to stop debtor abuse of the Code. Do you see why repeated bankruptcy filings by a debtor triggering the automatic stay provision might be a tactic to unfairly delay or complicate a creditor's efforts to collect on a legitimate debt? Do you think these BAPCPA provisions are fair and reasonable? What ethical implications might there be for an attorney who cooperates with a debtor client to make repeated filings for the primary purpose of delaying collection efforts by triggering the automatic stay with no real intent to see the bankruptcy case through?

3. Lifting the Automatic Stay

The automatic stay created by §362(a) does not necessarily last for the duration of the case as against secured creditors of the debtor in a Chapter 7 liquidation. A creditor who is properly secured and perfected in property of the debtor will typically have a superior claim to it over that of the bankruptcy trustee unless the value of the secured property exceeds the amount of the creditor's claim. (See further discussion of this struggle for priority in Chapter Ten, Section E.)

EXAMPLE

Recall from the Assignment Memorandum in Appendix A that Marta Carlson has two mortgages on her home, one in favor of Capital City Savings Bank (CCSB) with a balance of $142,500, and one in favor of Dreams Come True Finance Company (DCT) with a balance of $37,500. Marta is in default on the debt owed to DCT and, prior to the bankruptcy, it declared foreclosure and initiated foreclosure proceedings. But DCT's plan to foreclose is delayed by Marta's filing of the Chapter 7 petition, triggering the automatic stay. If DCT files a motion to lift the stay, the bankruptcy trustee will object. Do you see why? Assuming the property is worth $255,000, as the realtor has estimated to Marta, if it sells for that amount, the first $142,500 would go to CCSB, holder of the first mortgage. The next $37,500 would go to DCT, holder of the second mortgage. Per §522(d)(1) of the Code and her Schedule C, Marta would take the next $11,825 as her federal homestead exemption in the home (see Illustration 8-b). But that leaves $63,175 to which the bankruptcy trustee will be entitled, subject to expenses of sale, and the bankruptcy judge will not lift the stay and allow repossession. Instead, it will order the stay kept in place and allow the bankruptcy trustee to liquidate the property and distribute the proceeds as indicated.

If the value of the secured property is less than the amount of the debt, however, and the security interest of the creditor is properly perfected and superior to any claim the bankruptcy trustee can make to the property, then the trustee will not object to the lifting of the stay.

EXAMPLE

As indicated in Marta's Schedule D (Document 9 in the Carlson case file), she owes $900 to Shears Department Store for a washer and dryer she purchased nine months ago. Shears is perfected in the washer and dryer for the entire amount of the indebtedness and the washer and dryer together are valued at only $600. Thus, if Marta is in default on her obligation to Shears and it seeks the lifting of the stay to repossess the washer and dryer, the bankruptcy trustee will not object. He will, of course, review the claim of Shears closely and the paperwork offered in support of its perfected security interest before conceding the superiority of Shears' claim to the property.

Section 362(d) sets out the procedure available to a creditor for lifting the automatic stay so that it can proceed against the property of the debtor. In most circumstances the creditor will file a **motion to lift stay**, per Bankruptcy Rule 4001. If the motion is contested, the bankruptcy judge will conduct a hearing on the motion at which the creditor has the burden of showing that one of the two grounds set forth in §362(d)(1) for lifting the stay is present.

Grounds for Lifting the Automatic Stay for Cause: Debtor in Default to Secured Creditor

The most common scenario for a motion to lift stay in a consumer bankruptcy case is where a secured creditor moves to lift the stay so that it can repossess or foreclose on the property securing the debt. The secured creditor will allege as "cause" to satisfy §362(d)(1) that the debtor is in default and that the contract between the parties entitles the creditor to repossess or foreclose on the collateral upon default. Often such motions to lift stay are routinely granted by the court on adequate proof of perfection and default. But not always. As we will learn in Chapter Eleven, several options may be available to the Chapter 7 debtor to retain the collateral notwithstanding the bankruptcy. We've already seen one of those options in Chapter Eight, Section B, where we considered the debtor's right under §522(f)(1)(A) to avoid a judicial lien on his or her property to the extent that the lien impairs an exemption the debtor would otherwise have in the property.

EXAMPLE

Assume a debtor owns a home worth $200,000. Bank holds a mortgage on the home and is owed $100,000 leaving Debtor with $100,000 in owner's equity. Debtor files a Chapter 7 case but Bank does not move to lift the automatic stay and foreclose because Debtor is current on his payments to Bank. Bank will be happy for debtor to reaffirm his debt to Bank secured by the home and for the obligation to ride through the bankruptcy case undisturbed (we will consider the reaffirmation and ride through options in Chapter Eleven). Assume the applicable state homestead exemption enables Debtor to exempt all of his $100,000 owner's equity in the home so the bankruptcy trustee appointed in his Chapter 7 case cannot reach it. However, assume further that another creditor of Debtor has filed suit prepetition, obtained a final judgment, and caused a judicial lien to attach to Debtor's home in the amount of $50,000. The judicial lien creditor now files a motion to lift the automatic stay so it can foreclose on its judicial lien, sell the home, and distribute the proceeds first to the Bank, which has a priority position, then to itself, then any remaining proceeds to Debtor. If Debtor acts to avoid the judicial lien on the grounds that it impairs his right to exempt all of his equity in the home, the bankruptcy court will likely deny the motion to lift stay.

In the example, note that the judicial lien creditor winds up being treated effectively as an unsecured creditor. Of course, an unsecured creditor could file a motion to lift stay and ask the court to allow it to proceed with its collection efforts but it will not be granted absent exceptional circumstances (e.g., the debt is a contingent unliquidated claim pending in a state court action where it can be conveniently decided). And certainly if the unsecured debt is one that is going to be discharged in the bankruptcy there is no reason to let collection efforts proceed. Having said that, as we have seen, there are a number of domestic or other collection activities against a debtor involving unsecured debt as well as criminal or governmental regulatory actions against a debtor that are not subject to the automatic stay at all (see Illustration 9-b).

Grounds for Lifting the Automatic Stay for Cause: Lack of Adequate Protection

Adequate protection Must be provided by the bankrupt estate to a secured creditor whose interest in the collateral is threatened by the debtor's continued possession and use of the collateralized property.

Another ground for lifting the stay in §362(d)(1) is lack of **adequate protection**. That means that the secured creditor's interest collateral is not being adequately protected because the collateral securing the obligation to the creditor or its value is at risk for some reason. Maybe it is at risk because the debtor does not have it insured so that if it is damaged or stolen the creditor effectively loses its security for the debt. Maybe it is at risk because the debtor is misusing it or not properly protecting it. Maybe the debtor is now current on his payment obligations but the creditor has reason to believe he will not remain so (due to job loss, etc.). Maybe it is at risk due to rapid depreciation of the collateral (e.g., the creditor is secured by the debtor's shares of stock in a company that is failing).

EXAMPLE

Recall from the Assignment Memorandum in Appendix A that Marta Carlson owns a Toyota Camry with a book value of $8,500 and that she owes a balance on it of $1,750 to Automotive Financing, Inc. (AFI), which holds a security interest in the car. If Marta had let her insurance policy on the Toyota lapse because she could not afford the premiums, AFI would consider itself at risk (e.g., Marta could total the car leaving AFI with no security). The bankruptcy trustee will consider the interests of the estate at risk as well since there is $1,725 of equity in the car for the estate (the value of the car minus the amount owed to AFI and Marta's §522(d)(2) exemption of $5,025). Either of these parties in interest would have standing to ask that the stay be lifted so that the car could be taken into custody and protected from risk of loss until it could be sold.

Of course, if the debtor can satisfy the court that the creditor is adequately protected (insurance is obtained; the misuse has ended; the debtor gives proof of ability to pay; the value of the collateral is not really falling), the motion will be denied.

We will revisit the concept of adequate protection when we study the Chapter 11 business reorganization, where it comes up not only in connection with lifting the automatic stay but also in connection with motions to use property of the estate (see Chapter Eighteen, Section D).

Ground for Lifting the Automatic Stay: No Equity and Collateral Not Needed in a Reorganization

Section 362(d)(2) provides another basis for a secured creditor to move to lift stay to enable repossession or foreclosure. The stay can be lifted under §362(d)(2) where:

- the debtor has no equity in the property (more is owed on it than it is worth), and
- the debtor does not need it for an effective reorganization.

Since Chapter 7 is a liquidation proceeding and not a reorganization as in Chapters 11, 13, and 12, the second criterion, that the debtor does not need it for an effective reorganization, is obviously satisfied. But the creditor seeking to lift the stay on this second ground must also show that there is no equity in the property.

EXAMPLE

Assume Marta Carlson owed AFI $10,000 on the Toyota Camry that is worth only $8,500. She is not in a reorganization proceeding and has no equity in the vehicle. Even if she is not currently in default to AFI, that creditor may be in a position to ask that the stay be lifted under §362(d)(2). But is the creditor likely to do so long as it is being paid?

Of course, where the undervalue of the collateral is the basis for the motion to lift stay, the debtor may be able to cure the problem by applying payments to bring the amount owed in line with the current value of the collateral. But for a debtor in such distress that a bankruptcy filing has been deemed necessary, that option may not be realistic. As we will see in a business bankruptcy, however, the business debtor may be able to propose such a solution to avoid lifting of the stay.

Hearings on motions to lift stay are often hotly contested on the critical valuation/equity issues raised by these provisions and experts often are called to testify for the competing parties. Where the valuation issue is complex or particularly close, the contesting parties may choose to settle the issue rather than risk a hearing before the bankruptcy judge. But often there is simply no practical basis on which to settle and the dispute goes to the judge on a win-lose basis. If the stay is lifted as to the secured creditor, it will be allowed to repossess or foreclose on the property just as it would have if the debtor had not filed for bankruptcy relief.

4. Expiration of the Automatic Stay for Secured Personal Property of the Individual Chapter 7 Debtor

BAPCPA created a creditor-friendly automatic expiration of stay on personal property only, in Chapter 7 consumer cases only. The procedure, set out in §521(a)(6), provides that the automatic stay in personal property of the individual Chapter 7 consumer debtor automatically expires 45 days after the first meeting of creditors unless the debtor enters into a reaffirmation agreement with the creditor or redeems the property from the security interest. (We consider reaffirmation agreements and the redemption option in Chapter Eleven, Section C.)

The effect of §521(a)(6) is to save the secured creditor the trouble and expense of having to file a motion to lift stay and of having to establish one of the grounds of §362(d) in order to prevail on such motion. It effectively shifts the burden to the debtor to file a motion seeking to extend the stay and to show the court why the stay should not be automatically lifted. It also forces the debtor to take the initiative to file that motion within 45 days after the first meeting of creditors. Likewise, if the bankruptcy trustee believes there is equity for the Chapter 7 estate in the collateralized property, the trustee must file a motion with the court to retain the property in the estate before that deadline runs.

EXAMPLE

Since Marta Carlson is an individual consumer debtor in a Chapter 7, §521(a)(6) applies in her case. So if Shears wishes to repossess the washer and dryer (personal property in which it is secured), instead of filing its own motion under §362(d) seeking an order lifting the stay, it can simply wait until the §521(a)(6) deadline expires and then repossess the property. The stay will have expired automatically. The Code is unclear as to whether the bankruptcy court must enter a formal order lifting the stay upon the expiration of the 45 days; in practice, some do and some don't. The attorney must check the local rules of the court or learn the informal local practice.

5. Effect of Individual Debtor's Surrender of Collateralized Property on the Automatic Stay

In Chapter Eight, Section B, we learned that one of the statements that an individual Chapter 7 debtor must file with her petition is a statement of intent with regard to collateralized property, indicating whether the debtor will **surrender** that property to the secured creditor or seek to retain it. If the debtor indicates an intent to surrender that property, the secured creditor must still take appropriate action to have the automatic stay lifted or await the automatic lifting of the stay before taking possession of the property. And, of course, the creditor must await the decision of the bankruptcy trustee regarding whether to **abandon** the collateralized property to the creditor as being of no interest to the estate (to be considered in Chapter Eleven, Section A) or to assert an interest in the property for the benefit of the estate by avoiding the lien (to be considered in Chapter Ten, Section E) or by contending that there is equity in the property for the estate (i.e., it is worth more than is owed the creditor).

However, if an individual debtor fails to file the required statement of intent with regard to collateralized personal property, §362(h)(1) provides that the automatic stay is lifted as to such personal property and it is no longer to be considered property of the estate. We have already seen that §362(k)(2) provides a creditor accused of willfully violating the automatic stay as to such property with a good faith defense.

6. The Automatic Stay and Utility Services

An issue that can arise in any bankruptcy case, but that is most common in consumer cases, involves a debtor who is in arrears to a public utility (water, gas, electric, etc.) at the time the petition is filed. Section 366(a) prohibits the utility from discontinuing service to the debtor postpetition, notwithstanding the arrearage. The utility may, however, demand a reasonable deposit or security as **adequate assurance** of future performance and may discontinue service after 20 days following the filing of the petition if the deposit or security is not provided per §366(b). Disputes over what is a "reasonable" deposit are resolved by the court.

CHAPTER SUMMARY

Upon the filing of the petition, an order for relief is entered or deemed entered. In a Chapter 7 case, a bankruptcy trustee is appointed from the panel of trustees overseen by the U.S. Trustee. The trustee's duties include locating and taking possession of the nonexempt property of the debtor to be liquidated, liquidating that property, and distributing the proceeds to creditors in the order of priority mandated by the Code. Approximately 90 percent of all Chapter 7 consumer cases are no-asset cases. Upon filing of the petition, a notice of filing of case is sent by the court clerk to creditors, advising of the filing and providing deadlines and other information regarding the case, including the automatic stay. A first meeting of creditors is scheduled within 21-40 days of the filing of the petition.

An automatic stay on efforts to collect most obligations owed by the debtor goes into effect when the order for relief is entered. A creditor or its representative that violates the stay can be found in contempt of the court and enjoined. For a willful violation of the stay actual and punitive damages may be assessed. Secured creditors properly perfected in property of the debtor will move the court to lift the stay and allow them to repossess or foreclose on the collateral where the debtor is in default on the underlying obligation, or where the secured interest of the creditor is not adequately protected, or where there is no equity in the property for the estate and it is not needed in a reorganization. In consumer bankruptcy cases the automatic stay expires as to collateralized personal property 45 days after the first meeting of creditors unless the debtor enters a reaffirmation agreement with the creditor. If the individual debtor fails to file a timely statement of intent regarding collateralized personal property, the automatic stay is deemed lifted and the property is no longer property of the estate.

A public utility cannot discontinue service to a debtor upon filing of the petition notwithstanding the existence of an arrearage in the debtor's account but the utility may demand a reasonable deposit or security as adequate assurance of future performance and discontinue service after 20 days following the filing of the petition if the deposit or security is not provided.

REVIEW QUESTIONS

1. Explain how the panel of trustees operates. Who can serve as a bankruptcy trustee? Who appoints them? What does it mean that they are bonded and why is that required? On what basis can a bankruptcy trustee be removed from a case?

2. Summarize the duties of a bankruptcy trustee in a Chapter 7 case. Give examples of various kinds of professional persons that a trustee might request permission to hire to assist in the administration of a case, and explain why the trustee might need the assistance of each professional mentioned.

3. What is a no-asset case? What difference does that make for unsecured creditors of the debtor? What difference does that make in the fee of the bankruptcy trustee?

4. Summarize the different information provided to creditors in the notice of filing of case sent to creditors.

5. Give examples of collection efforts that are subject to the automatic stay. Give examples of collection efforts that are not subject to it. How is the automatic stay enforced? What are likely penalties for violating the stay? What changes did BAPCPA make to the operation of the automatic stay for some individual debtors?

6. What do we mean by saying that there is equity in an item of property? What do we mean by asking if the estate has equity in collateralized property of the debtor?

7. Explain how the 45-day automatic expiration rule works in an individual debtor's Chapter 7 case.

8. Explain the difference between a debtor's surrender of property of the estate and the bankruptcy trustee's abandonment of such property.

9. List questions that the bankruptcy trustee must ask the debtor at the first meeting of creditors. List other questions the debtor is likely to be asked at the meeting.

10. What is a Rule 2004 examination and how is it different from the first meeting of creditors?

WORDS AND PHRASES TO REMEMBER

abandon (property)   adequate protection
actual damage   administrative expense
adequate assurance   adversary proceeding

adverse interest
Article 9 (UCC)
asset case
attorney's fees
automatic stay
bankruptcy trustee
bonded
clear and convincing
contempt
contested matter
continuation statement
court costs
creditors' committee
discharge in bankruptcy
disinterested person
economic loss
emotional distress
enjoin
fee application
fiduciary duty
financing statement
first meeting of creditors
good faith
holdback provision
order for relief
Inventory of the property of the estate

involuntary petition
motion
motion for extension of stay
motion to lift stay
no-asset case
no-asset report
nonresidential lease
notice of filing of the case (notice of
    commencement)
petition
preponderance of the evidence
property of the estate
punitive damages
quasi-judicial immunity
relation back
residential lease
Rule 2004 examination
safe-harbor provision
statement of intent
surrender (property)
trustee panel
void
Uniform Commercial Code (UCC)
U.S. Trustee
341 meeting

TO LEARN MORE: A number of TLM activities to accompany this chapter are accessible on the companion web site for this textbook at http:// aspenlawschool.com/books/Parsons_Debt4e/.

Chapter Ten:

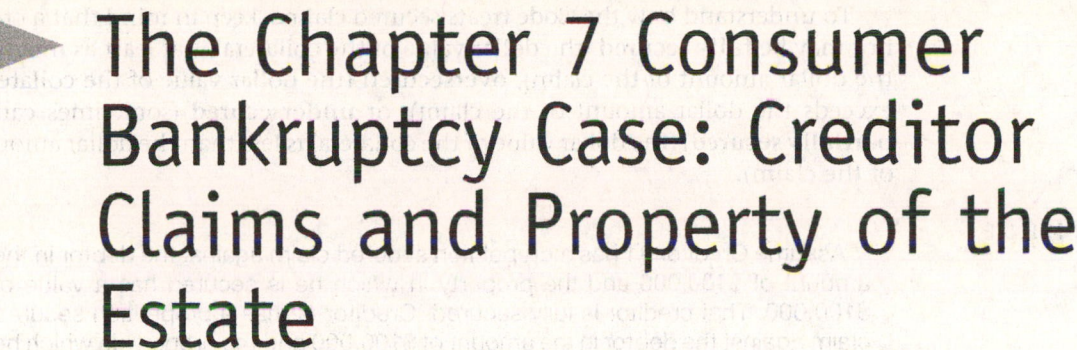

The Chapter 7 Consumer Bankruptcy Case: Creditor Claims and Property of the Estate

KEY CONCEPTS

- Unsecured creditors must file a proof of claim in order to participate in any distribution to creditors in a Chapter 7 and a claim is deemed allowed if no timely objection is made
- The failure of a secured creditor to file a timely proof of claim does not impair its secured position in the property of the debtor
- Undersecured claims are bifurcated into the secured and unsecured parts and a proof of claim must be filed for the unsecured portion to participate in distribution
- The right to setoff is recognized as between the debtor and creditors in the bankruptcy case
- Generally, postpetition interest is not payable on creditor claims
- Property of the estate includes all property in which the debtor has a legal or equitable interest at the time the petition is filed
- The bankruptcy trustee may challenge a debtor's claimed exemptions in order to increase the property of the estate
- The Code provides the bankruptcy trustee with the power to compel turnover of property of the estate in the hands of the debtor, custodians, or other third persons
- The Code provides the bankruptcy trustee with a wide range of powers to avoid prepetition transfers of the debtor's property

A. ▶ Creditor Claims

1. Distinguishing Between Secured and Unsecured Claims in Bankruptcy: Bifurcation of the Undersecured Claim

When a creditor files a claim against a debtor in a bankruptcy case, the claim will be treated as an **unsecured claim** if the creditor is unsecured and as a **secured**

claim to the extent the creditor holds a consensual or nonconsensual security interest or lien in any of the debtor's property.

To understand how the Code treats secured claims, keep in mind that a creditor may be **fully secured** (the dollar value of the collateral is at least as much as the dollar amount of the claim), **oversecured** (the dollar value of the collateral exceeds the dollar amount of the claim), or **undersecured** (sometimes called **partially secured**) (the dollar value of the collateral is less than the dollar amount of the claim).

EXAMPLE

Assume Creditor #1 has a prepetition secured claim against the debtor in the amount of $100,000 and the property in which he is secured has a value of $100,000. That creditor is fully secured. Creditor #2 has a prepetition secured claim against the debtor in the amount of $100,000 and the property in which he is secured has a value of $125,000. That creditor is oversecured. Creditor #3 has a prepetition secured claim against the debtor in the amount of $100,000 and the property in which he is secured has a value of $75,000. That creditor is undersecured, or only partially secured.

Section 506(a)(1) of the Code provides that a secured claim in bankruptcy is only secured up to the value of the collateral at the time the petition is filed. For the wholly secured and oversecured creditor that presents no problem—their secured claim will be valued at the full amount of the indebtedness. But for the undersecured creditor that means his secured claim will be allowed only up to the value of the collateral, and as to the balance of what he is owed over the value of the collateral, his claim will be treated as unsecured. Thus, §506(a) effectively **bifurcates** the undersecured claim into its secured and unsecured portions. Practitioners sometimes refer to this mandated bifurcation as a **strip down** or **write down** of an undersecured claim to the value of the collateral. Note that the undersecured creditor does not forfeit the unsecured portion of its claim, but the creditor can only pursue that claim through the bankruptcy process as an unsecured claim.

EXAMPLE

As a result of the bifurcation mandated by §506(a), Creditor #3 in our last example will have a secured claim of $75,000 and an unsecured claim of $25,000 in the bankruptcy proceeding.

There are numerous consequences of this bifurcation of an undersecured claim in a bankruptcy case, including how the collateral securing the claim is to be valued. We will consider each consequence and valuation issue as we come to it in our study of Chapters 7, 13, and 11 throughout the remainder of the text.

Proof of claim The writing that a creditor submits as evidence of its claim against the estate.

Claims bar date The deadline set for creditors in a case to file proofs of claim.

2. The Proof of Claim

The notice of commencement of a Chapter 7 case advises the creditors whether to file a written **proof of claim** and, if so, the deadline (called the **claims bar date**) by which such claim must be filed. If a case is a no-asset one, creditors will be advised not to file a proof of claim since no distribution (payout) to creditors is anticipated. Since the Marta Rinaldi Carlson case is an asset case, the notice of filing in the case does advise creditors of a filing deadline for proofs of claim (see Document 23 in the Carlson case file).

Section 501(a) of the Code authorizes the filing of the proof of claim. Official Form 410 is the proof of claim form. In some districts, the court clerk will attach a copy of the form to the notice of commencement. In other districts, the creditor must download the form from the clerk's web site or obtain one from the clerk's office. Pursuant to Bankruptcy Rules 3001 and 3002, the proof of claim form must be completed by the creditor, signed, and mailed or delivered to the bankruptcy court clerk or the bankruptcy trustee or both, as the form directs.

Bankruptcy Rule 3001 requires that if the claim is based on a writing (e.g., promissory note, written contract, security agreement, mortgage), a copy of the writing must be attached to the proof of claim.

EXAMPLE

> The proof of claim filed by Pine Ridge Nursing Home in Marta Carlson's Chapter 7 case is Document 27 in the Carlson case file. Note that the guaranty she executed, which forms the basis of the claim, is attached.

If the creditor asserts a security interest in any property of the debtor, proof of perfection of that interest must accompany the claim form.

Bankruptcy Rule 3001 and Official Form 410 require creditors to provide certain specific information where claims are filed in cases of individual debtors, including:

- an itemized statement of interest, fees, expenses, or other charges sought in addition to the principal indebtedness;
- if a security interest is asserted in debtor's property, the amount of any arrearage (amount needed to cure any default) as of the date of the petition;
- if a mortgage is asserted in debtor's principal residence, an attachment (Form 410A) must accompany the proof of claim, providing details of the outstanding loan as of the date the petition is filed; and
- if the claim is based on a revolving or open-end consumer credit account (like a credit card or department store account), a statement containing details of the last transaction, payment, and posting on the account.

Per Bankruptcy Rule 3002(c), the proof of claim in a Chapter 7, Chapter 13, or Chapter 12 case must be filed not later than 90 days after the first date set for the meeting of creditors (the 341 meeting) unless one of six enumerated exceptions applies. The exceptions pertain to claims of governmental units, infants and incompetent persons, recipients of avoided transfers, parties to executory contracts or unexpired leases, foreign creditors, and claims in Chapter 7 cases that began as no-asset cases. A governmental unit, however, has 180 days to file a claim from the "date of the order for relief," which is normally the date the petition was filed.

A timely filed proof of claim can be amended freely "where the purpose is to cure a defect in the claim as originally filed, to describe the claim with greater particularity or to plead a new theory of recovery on the facts set forth in the original claim." *In re South Atlantic Financial Corp.*, 767 F.2d 814, 819 (11th Cir. 1985). However, an amendment requested after the claims bar date will not be allowed where it attempts to add a new claim that could have been filed timely. See, e.g., *In re Chavis*, 160 B.R. 804, aff'd 47 F.3d 818 (6th Cir. 1995) (IRS amendment to add new tax years was untimely and disallowed). Pursuant to §726(a)(1), **priority claims** (discussed in Chapter Eleven, Section B) are to be allowed if filed on or before ten days after the date the trustee mails a summary of the final report to creditors or the date on which final distribution in the case is commenced, whichever is earlier. And §726(a)(2)(C) provides that any late-filed unsecured claim will be allowed if the filing was late due to the creditor's lack of notice or actual knowledge of the case filing and the claim is filed in time to permit payment. If the initial notice to creditors did not require that a proof of claim be filed (e.g., the case was initially thought to be a no-asset one) but a later notice is given to that effect, the proof of claim must be filed within 90 days of the later notice.

It is important that creditors in a Chapter 7 who wish to participate in any distribution from the estate file the proof of claim and file it within the time allowed. If an unsecured creditor fails to file a proof of claim, the bankruptcy trustee will *not* include that creditor in a distribution. If the proof of claim is filed late (after the claims bar date), the trustee may object to it on that basis under §502(b)(9) or seek to have it subordinated (made inferior or junior in status) to other claims of equal rank, pursuant to the **equitable subordination** doctrine of §510 (discussed in more detail in Chapter Eleven, Section B).

The failure of a secured creditor to file a timely claim does *not* impair its secured position in the property of the debtor per §506(d)(2). So, technically, if the creditor is fully secured in the collateralized property (the value of the collateral equals or exceeds the amount owed), there will be no detriment to the late filing of the claim or the failure to file a claim at all. But despite that technicality, the secured creditor, as a practical matter, should always file a proof of claim and attach proof of his security interest in the debtor's property and the perfected status of that interest in order to prove that status to the trustee, who otherwise will be looking to take that property for the benefit of the estate.

Furthermore, if the secured creditor is undersecured, failing to file a claim or filing a claim late could result in the lost opportunity to participate in any distribution the creditor might otherwise have received on the unsecured portion of his claim.

EXAMPLE

Assume that Marta Carlson owed Automotive Financing, Inc. (AFI) $10,000 on debt secured by the Toyota Camry that is worth only $8,500. When the automatic stay is lifted, AFI will repossess and sell the car. But even if the sale brings the maximum value of the car, AFI would still be owed $1,500. Pursuant to §506(a), AFI's claim is secured only up to the value of the collateral and is unsecured as to the balance owed in excess of that value. As we have seen, §506(a) effectively bifurcates the claim of the undersecured creditor into its secured and unsecured portions. Consequently, the $1,500 balance owed to AFI over the value of its collateral will be treated as a general unsecured claim in Marta's bankruptcy case. If there is a distribution from the estate to general unsecured creditors, AFI will participate *only* if it files a timely proof of claim.

3. Objections to Claims

Claims docket The official registry of claims filed in a bankruptcy case.

As claims are filed, they will be entered on a **claims docket** by the clerk of the court. One of the duties of the bankruptcy trustee is to examine the proofs of claim filed by creditors to determine if they are valid (see Illustration 9-a). Section 502(a) provides that unless an **objection to claim** by the trustee or other **party in interest** is filed, the claim will be deemed allowed.

Sections 502(b)(d)(e) and (k) set forth several grounds for objecting to a claim. The most general of these grounds is §502(b)(1), which authorizes an objection if the claim is *unenforceable against the debtor under the terms of the underlying agreement or due to controlling law*. Thus, the trustee's (or other party in interest's) examination will include a determination of whether the claim is valid at all, whether it is made in the correct amount, whether the creditor is properly secured in property of the estate, or whether the debtor has any counterclaim or other offset (discussed below) to the claim. In addition, a creditor who is in possession of debtor's property or who is the transferee of a voidable transfer from the debtor (to be considered in Sections D and E) and who refuses to turn the property over or pay the amount of the voidable transfer upon proper demand by the trustee may have its claim disallowed pursuant to §502(d).

If a claim is filed as a secured one, the trustee will examine the claim not only to make sure the claim is in fact secured but to determine if the security interest is properly perfected. As we will see in Section E, below, if the security interest of the creditor is not properly perfected prior to the filing of the bankruptcy petition, the Code empowers the trustee to avoid the creditor's security interest or lien in the collateral and take the property for the benefit of the estate.

P-H 10-a: The schedules filed by the debtor will assist the trustee in the examination of the claims of creditors. Recall that Schedules D and E/F, on which the debtor lists secured claims and unsecured nonpriority claims, require the debtor to list whether the debtor disputes the claim. The debtor's dispute of the claim may form the basis of the trustee's challenge to that claim. The debtor's basis for disputing the claim may be a subject of inquiry at the 341 meeting. The initial task of reviewing the debtor's schedules and the creditors' proofs of claim in the bankruptcy trustee's office may be assigned to the assisting legal professional. Assume you are that legal professional. Review the schedules filed by Marta Carlson to identify claims that you might recommend to the trustee for close examination for possible dispute when the proofs of claim are filed.

EC 10-a: In addition to questioning the debtor at the 341 meeting regarding possible objections to claims, the bankruptcy trustee may also request other assistance from the debtor. Thus, there may be several unofficial meetings between personnel in the trustee's office and the debtor and the debtor's attorney. The assisting legal professional in the trustee's office may be charged with contacting the debtor or his attorney to obtain all kinds of information or further detail. Assume you are that legal professional. What ethical and professional considerations must you remember when you are given such responsibilities?

If the bankruptcy trustee concludes that any claim, secured or unsecured, is invalid in whole or in part, Bankruptcy Rule 3007 requires that the trustee file a written **objection** to the claim.

E X A M P L E

> The bankruptcy trustee in Marta Carlson's Chapter 7 filed an objection to the claim of Pine Ridge Nursing Home. You can see that objection in Document 28 in the Carlson case file.

Pursuant to §502(b) and Bankruptcy Rule 3007, the creditor whose claim is objected to must receive a 30-day notice of the objection and of the proposed hearing date (see Official Form 20B and Document 28 in the Carlson case file). An objection to a creditor's claim is designated a **core proceeding** by 28 U.S.C. §157(b)(2) (see Illustration 6-h) so the bankruptcy court can hear and enter a final order in the matter. Since most objections to claims are controlled by the **after notice and a hearing procedure** (discussed in Chapter Six, Section G), the objection will be treated as a disputed matter and an evidentiary hearing conducted only if the creditor contests the objection. If the creditor does not contest the objection, it will be sustained without a hearing. If the objection to the creditor's claim involves an attack on the validity or sufficiency of the creditor's claimed security interest in property of the debtor, however, the trustee must initiate an **adversary proceeding** to set aside that security interest as required by Bankruptcy Rule 7001 (see Illustration 6-j and further discussion in Section E below).

Though it is most often the bankruptcy trustee who initiates an objection to a creditor's claim, note that §502(a) authorizes any party in interest to do so. If a trustee refuses to file such an objection, then another creditor who could be benefited by the disallowance of the contested claim may do so. In some situations, the Chapter 7 debtor himself may file an objection to a claim, as we will consider in Chapter Eleven, Section C.

The Code does not set out a timeframe in which an objection to a creditor's claim must be made. Normally, such objections will be made prior to **distribution of the estate** to creditors (discussed in Chapter Eleven, Section B), but there is no time bar to a trustee who, having made a distribution to a creditor, seeks to recover it based on information learned after the distribution. Even after a case has been closed, a trustee may move to reopen it in order to object to a creditor's claim, recover the distribution to that creditor, and redistribute to others. Of course, attempts by a trustee to object to a claim after distribution may be met with defenses such as **waiver** (the voluntary relinquishment of a known right), **promissory estoppel** (the preclusion of one from acting now because he earlier made promises on which others reasonably relied, to their detriment), **equitable estoppel** (the preclusion of one from acting now because his earlier wrongful or dishonest actions or inactions worked to the detriment of others), or **laches** (the neglect of a claim or right for an inordinate period of time under the circumstances).

The validity and enforceability of most contracts as well as questions regarding attachment and perfection of security interests are controlled by state law. Thus, this topic of creditor claims and their validity is another example of how prominent a role state law plays in the administration of a bankruptcy case in a U.S. bankruptcy court.

Waiver The voluntary relinquishment of a known right.

Promissory estoppel The preclusion of one from acting now because he earlier made promises on which others reasonably relied to their detriment.

Equitable estoppel The preclusion of one from acting now because his earlier wrongful or dishonest actions worked to the detriment of others.

4. The Right to Setoff as Affecting a Creditor's Claim

Laches Neglect of a claim or right for an inordinate period of time.

The doctrine of **setoff** is recognized in most states by common law or by statute. The idea behind the doctrine is a simple one: If two persons are indebted to each other, the debt of either is offset by the amount of the debt of the other.

EXAMPLE

> Assume that Pete borrows $2,000 from Sally. Later, Pete does $1,000 worth of work for Sally. If Sally ever sues Pete for the $2,000 he owes her, the debt will be offset by what Sally owes Pete, so Sally will obtain a judgment for only $1,000. And if the value of Pete's services to Sally is $2,000, the debts mutually offset, so neither owes the other anything. If the value of Pete's work is $2,200, the debt he owes Sally for the loan is completely offset and Sally owes Pete $200. Or, assume Pete has an unsecured loan from Bank and also has a savings account at Bank. That savings account is in the nature of a loan by Pete to Bank. If Pete misses a payment on the loan obligation he owes to Bank, the Bank can set off what Pete owes it against what it owes Pete by transferring the amount of the missed payment from the Pete's savings account.

Section 553 of the Code provides that the right to setoff recognized under nonbankruptcy law (common law or statute) is alive and well in the bankruptcy context and it works in favor of both the debtor and creditors.

EXAMPLE

> If Pete from the last example files under Chapter 7 and Sally files a proof of claim for the $2,000 Pete owes her, Sally's claim can be offset by the $1,000 she owes Pete.

P-H 10-b: Go to www.uscourts.gov/forms/bankruptcy-forms and locate Parts 1 and 2 of Official Form E/F where the debtor lists creditors holding unsecured claims. Does the form allow the debtor to state whether a creditor's claim is subject to possible offset?

EXAMPLE

> When Pete files under Chapter 7 he will list the unsecured loan of Bank on his Schedule E/F, list the balance in his savings account at Bank as an asset in Part 4 of his Schedule A/B, and he may seek to exempt the balance in his savings account on his Schedule C. If the Code did not honor the right to setoff in bankruptcy, Bank could find itself in the position of having its unsecured claim against Pete for the loan completely discharged while Pete is able to exempt and keep the money in his savings account at Bank. But not only does §553 provide that the right to setoff will be recognized in the bankruptcy case, §506(a) mandates that a setoff claim that can be asserted against property of the estate under nonbankruptcy law be treated as a secured claim. The right to setoff is not an actual type of security interest in real or personal property, but the Code mandates that it be treated as such in this context. Since the Bank has a right to setoff against the funds in the savings account under nonbankruptcy law, it will be treated as secured in that account up to the amount it is owed and that will prevent Pete from exempting the savings account balance.

P-H 10-c: If Pete does list the savings account as exempt property in his Schedule C, what procedural action should Bank take to assert its setoff interest and prevent Pete from successfully exempting that property?

---

5. Interest on Creditor Claims in Chapter 7 Cases

Interest on Unsecured and Undersecured Claims

Section 502(b)(2) disallows claims made for **unmatured interest**. That phrase refers to interest that is not yet due and owing to the creditor at the time the petition is filed and is sometimes called **postpetition interest**. Unsecured claims may include charges for **prepetition interest** that were due and owing on the date the petition was filed but are not entitled to receive postpetition interest.

> **EXAMPLE**
>
> Marta owed an unsecured debt to Capital City Bank (CCB) on her Visa credit card in the amount of $8,200 at the time her petition and Schedule E/F were filed (Document 10 in the Carlson case file). A portion of that $8,200 may include prepetition interest charges by CCB for a carryover balance or for late payments on the account. If the underlying card agreement permits CCB to make such interest charges, it can include them in its claim. But if CCB files a proof of claim stating a claim for not just the $8,200 balance owed at the time of the petition filing but adding a claim for interest that has accrued since the petition was filed, the trustee will object to that portion of the claim, pursuant to §502(b)(2). If Marta had not filed her petition, the interest would have continued to accrue, but once she files her petition, the unsecured creditor cannot seek to recover it on a claim made in her bankruptcy case.

A secured creditor who is undersecured in the property of the debtor securing the claim is in the same situation as the unsecured creditor, like CCB in the previous example as to interest.

> **EXAMPLE**
>
> Assume that Marta owes AFI $10,000 on the Toyota Camry that is worth only $8,500. Assume that the automatic stay is lifted, and AFI repossesses and sells the car for $8,500. Pursuant to §506(a)(1), AFI now has a bifurcated, general unsecured claim for the $1,500 balance but *may not* include postpetition interest in that claim per §502(b)(2). The fact that AFI was a secured creditor as to part of its claim does not change its treatment under §502(b)(2) for the unsecured portion of its claim.

In the very rare case, there may be sufficient assets in a Chapter 7 case to pay all expenses of administration and all the claims of creditors in full and still have cash left over. In that case, §726(a)(5) allows the trustee to pay postpetition interest on unsecured creditors' claims (see Illustration 11-a).

Interest, Fees, and Other Charges on Oversecured Claims

If a creditor is not just fully secured but oversecured in the collateral at the time the petition is filed (i.e., the value of the collateral not only equals but exceeds the amount of the claim), then §506(b) allows the creditor to include in its claim postpetition interest up to the value of the collateral, as well as other fees, costs, and charges but only if those fees, costs, and charges are authorized by the underlying agreement or by state law and only up to the value of the collateral.

EXAMPLE

> Capital Savings Bank (CSB) holds the first mortgage on Marta's residence. The principal amount of its claim at the time the petition is filed is $142,500 and the residence securing the debt is valued at $255,000. CSB is fully secured in the residence because its value exceeds the principal amount of the debt. Section 506(b) allows CSB to file a claim in Marta's Chapter 7 case for the principal amount owed ($142,500) plus (if the underlying mortgage agreement allows) unpaid postpetition interest, fees, and charges up to the value of the collateral ($225,000). And CSB's right to do this would not be affected by the fact that another creditor, Dreams Come True Finance Company, is also secured in the residence. CSB has a first position in the property and its claim will take priority up to the full amount allowed by the Code.

As previously noted, the failure of a secured creditor to file a timely proof of claim does not impair its secured position in the property of the debtor per §506(d)(2). It can still seek to lift the stay on the collateral and sell it in full satisfaction of its claim or, if there is equity for the estate in the property in excess of the creditor's claim, simply wait for the trustee to sell the property, at which time its full claim plus postpetition interest, fees, and charges will be paid to it, per §506(d)(2). For this reason, many bankruptcy courts do not require fully secured creditors to file formal proofs of claim and instead require only that the creditor informally make available to the trustee the documentation demonstrating that the creditor holds a perfected security interest in the property.

EXAMPLE

> The local rules of the bankruptcy court handling Marta's Chapter 7 case might not require Capital Savings Bank to file a formal proof of claim but to, instead, provide the trustee with a copy of the mortgage or deed of trust establishing its secured, perfected position in the residence.

B. ▶ Property of the Estate

Property of the estate All property in which the debtor holds a legal or equitable interest at the commencement of a bankruptcy case.

What constitutes the **property of the estate** is one of the most important concepts in bankruptcy law. Section 541(a) of the Code provides that the commencement of a case under any chapter of the Code creates such estate and that it consists of all property in which the debtor holds a **legal** or **equitable interest** at the time of commencement. Section 541(b) contains some minor exceptions to this very broad definition of what constitutes property of the estate. What property makes up the bankruptcy estate is critical because it is from this pool of assets that the claims of the creditors will be satisfied. The question of what is or is not property of the estate under §541 is ultimately a federal question governed by that statute though the underlying question of whether the debtor has a sufficient legal or equitable ownership interest in property to bring it within the federal definition will normally be governed by applicable state law. See In re Yonikus, 996 F.2d 866, 869 (7th Cir. 1993).

E X A M P L E

Recall the discussion in Chapter Five, Section E, of property owned by a married couple. If the spouses own property as tenants by the entireties and only one of them files for bankruptcy relief, both spouses have only a right of survivorship in marital property while alive so that the interest of the non-filing spouse in such property which will not then become property of the estate and the tenancy cannot be severed by the bankruptcy trustee in hopes of reaching a greater interest in the property than the filing spouse has—the right of survivorship. On the other hand, if the same spouses own property in a community property state, all the community property may be deemed property of the estate even though only on spouse files since each spouse is deemed to own it entirely. (Note that Official Form A/B specifically asks who has an ownership interest in the property listed and whether it is community property.) Unless the filing spouse can exempt that property, the bankruptcy trustee will take and sell it. If the filing spouse cannot exempt marital property in a community property state, it's best if the two spouses file jointly so they can stack their exemptions and protect as much marital property as possible.

You may want to review the discussion of concurrently owned property as well as property held in trust. The same challenges presented to the prepetition judgment creditor seeking to seize debtor's property to satisfy the judgment at least initially confront the bankruptcy trustee seeking property to liquidate for the benefit of all unsecured creditors of the estate.

Generally, property acquired by the debtor *after* the commencement of the Chapter 7 case does *not* belong to the estate because that will be the property available to the debtor for his **fresh start**. But read the following example to get a feel for how truly broad the concept of "property of the estate" is.

E X A M P L E

If the debtor inherits property up to 180 days *after* the petition is filed, that property belongs to the estate. The debtor is considered to have had an equitable interest in the inheritance at the time he filed. The same is true as to insurance proceeds received within 180 days of filing. If the debtor is the beneficiary of a trust, the trust property to which the debtor is entitled now belongs to the estate unless the trust was set up as a spendthrift trust. If the debtor has earned a paycheck or commission at the time he files the petition, that property belongs to the estate even though it is not paid until after the petition is filed. Stock or bonds held for the debtor by a brokerage house belong to the estate. Any debts owed to the debtor by another when the case is filed become the property of the estate. If the debtor has the right to file a lawsuit at the time the petition is filed, the claim underlying the lawsuit now becomes the property of the estate and the bankruptcy trustee has standing to pursue the lawsuit in the place of the debtor. If the debtor holds a mortgage on the property of another, the mortgage and all the rights under it, including the right to foreclose in the event of default, become the property of the estate. If the debtor buys a lottery ticket before filing the petition and wins after filing the petition, the proceeds belong to the estate since the ticket became property of the estate upon filing. If stock owned by the debtor at the time the petition is filed splits after the filing, the estate gets the benefit of the stock split.

Property held in trust by the debtor as trustee (as opposed to property held in trust for the debtor as beneficiary) raises some difficult questions since the debtor as trustee does have legal title to such property under trust law but not equitable title. However, §541(d) makes it clear that such property interest becomes property of the estate "only to the extent of the debtor's legal title to such property, but not to the extent of any equitable interest in such property the debtor does not hold." Since the beneficiaries of the trust have the equitable interest in the trust res and that equitable interest is not subject to the claims of the debtor's creditors, no equitable interest in the res becomes property of the estate when the trustee files. "Where the debtor holds bare legal title without an equitable interest, the estate acquires bare legal title without any equitable interest." *In re N.S. Garrott & Sons*, 772 F.2d 462, 466 (8th Cir. 1985).

EXAMPLE

Assume Chris establishes an express trust and names his children as beneficiaries. He names his sister Alexia as trustee. If Alexia files a petition in bankruptcy, the property in the trust does not become property of the estate and subject to being liquidated by the bankruptcy trustee for the benefit of Alexia's creditors. Alexia had only the bare legal title to the property subject to the trust and that is all that passes to the estate upon the filing of the petition.

Of course, some of the property of the estate will be claimed as exempt by the debtor and retained by him. And creditors holding a perfected security interest in property of the estate may have a priority claim to it over the trustee (see the next section). Additionally, the bankruptcy trustee may consider some of the property of the estate to have no value to the estate and abandon it pursuant to §554 (see discussion in Chapter Eleven, Section A). But otherwise the property of the estate comes under the control of the bankruptcy trustee at the time the case is commenced and will be liquidated by the trustee for the benefit of all creditors of the estate. As we have seen, however, the trustee may contest the validity of a secured creditor's claim to certain property of the debtor as collateral, hoping to defeat the allegedly perfected security interest and seize that collateral as property of the estate. With the same goal in mind, the trustee may challenge exemptions claimed by the individual debtor, as we consider in the next section.

Property in which the debtor has a legal or equitable interest may not be in the debtor's possession when the case is commenced. It may be held by another. That does not prevent it from becoming property of the estate. The definition in §541(a) specifically says that qualifying property belongs to the estate "wherever located and by whomever held."

EXAMPLE

Salary the debtor has earned as of the filing of the petition may be held by the employer. A car the debtor owns may be loaned to a family member or friend. Funds of the debtor in checking and savings accounts will be held by the financial institution.

Contingent, disputed, and unliquidated claims that the debtor has against third parties are property of the estate, and the trustee has standing, pursuant to §704(a)(1), to pursue those claims to judgment for the benefit of the estate. Normally, that will be done by filing an adversary proceeding against the third party where the trustee is seeking to recover money or property from a third party (see Chapter Six, Section G, and Illustration 6-j) and such actions are typically core proceedings (see Illustration 6-h) such that the bankruptcy judge can enter a final order in them.

EXAMPLE

There is an important exception to the bankruptcy court's jurisdiction to hear and decide a Chapter 7 trustee's suit to liquidate a claim that is property of the estate. Recall that Nick and Pearl Murphy (Illustration 1-a, Case Study #1) have a professional malpractice claim for Pearl and a loss of consortium claim for Nick against the doctor who performed her botched appendectomy and the hospital where the surgery was performed. If the couple files a joint petition in Chapter 7 before that claim is resolved, the claims themselves are assets that they must list on their Schedule A/B and assign a value to them. At that point the claims are contingent on their prevailing, disputed because the doctor and hospital are not admitting liability, and unliquidated because we do not know yet the dollar amount, if any, of any settlement or verdict to be rendered on the claims. But the claims are assets that become property of the estate unless properly exempted and the trustee may decide to pursue the claims for the benefit of the estate. However, since these claims are in the nature of a personal injury action, 28 U.S.C. §157(d) mandates that the claims be tried in the U.S. district court rather than in a bankruptcy court adversary action. U.S. district courts have subject matter jurisdiction to hear such cases even without diversity of citizenship between the parties under 28 U.S.C §1334(b). As a practical matter, however, personal injury and wrongful death cases that arise in a bankruptcy case are normally tried in the state court having jurisdiction under the discretionary **abstinence for comity** provision of 28 U.S.C. §1334(c)(1) or the **mandatory abstinence** provision of §1334(c)(2). Thus, in the Murphys' bankruptcy case, the trustee is likely to ask for and receive permission from the court to pursue the Murphys' malpractice claim in state court. Since the claim is property of the estate, only the trustee now has the right to file suit on it. The Murphys will be nominal (in name only) plaintiffs in that lawsuit, and proceeds from any judgment or settlement of the claim will become property of the estate.

P-H 10-d: Read 28 U.S.C. §§1334(c)(1) and (2). What is the difference between the abstinence for comity and mandatory abstinence provisions?

C. Challenging the Debtor's Claimed Exemptions in Order to Increase Property of the Estate

Per §522(a)(2) of the Code, the individual Chapter 7 debtor sets out his or her claimed exemptions on Schedule C at their fair market value as that phrase has been interpreted by the U.S. Supreme Court in *United States v. Cartwright*, 411 U.S. 546 (1973). The bankruptcy trustee will not automatically accept the debtor's claimed exemptions or their valuation but instead will carefully examine the exemptions on Schedule C, to see if a challenge can be made to either (1) the property claimed as exempt, or (2) the valuation of the exempt property by the debtor.

EXAMPLE

> Assume a Chapter 7 debtor owns a house and lot. He owes a secured creditor $200,000 on the house, lists its fair market value on Schedule C as $220,000, and claims the $20,000 of equity in the house as exempt as a homestead under Code §522(d)(1). If the trustee in his case discovers that this is actually a rental house owned by the debtor and not a residence for the debtor or a dependent, the trustee may object to the claimed exemption on the grounds that the equity in that house and lot cannot be exempted at all under §522(d)(1). On the other hand, if the house and lot are used as a residence by the debtor, but the trustee discovers the fair market value is $250,000, the trustee may object, not to the exemption itself, but to the low valuation of the exempted property by the debtor. After all, if that house and lot are worth $250,000 that means the debtor has $50,000 of equity in it—not just $20,000. And since, under §522(d)(1), the debtor may currently exempt only $23,675 of that equity (as of April 2016), the trustee wants to claim the balance of the equity as property of the estate.

The bankruptcy trustee in Marta Carlson's case is challenging her valuation of the doll collection she claims as exempt (see Document 32 in the Carlson case file). Bankruptcy Rule 4003(b) authorizes not just the bankruptcy trustee but any other party in interest to object to a debtor's claimed exemption or its value, but most commonly it is the trustee who files the objection. Bankruptcy Rule 4003(b) requires that any objection to a debtor's claimed exemptions be made within 30 days following the first meeting of creditors or within 30 days following any amendment to Schedule C, although that time period can be extended by motion and for cause shown. Bankruptcy Rule 4003(b)(2) allows a year beyond the date the case is closed to object to an exemption fraudulently claimed. Section 522(l) of the Code provides that if no timely objection to a claimed exemption is made, the exemption is **deemed allowed**.

Due to this "deemed allowed" feature of §522(l), bankruptcy trustees and creditors must examine a debtor's claimed exemptions closely and timely move the court to extend the time for objecting if there is any question at all about the nature of property claimed as exempt or the value attached to it by debtor. Moreover, the U.S. Supreme Court held in *Taylor v. Freeland & Kronz*, 503 U.S. 638 (1992), that the 30-day deadline for objections (or any extensions thereof granted by the court) is to be strictly construed. In a hearing on an objection to a debtor's exemption, Bankruptcy Rule 4003(c) places the *burden* of showing why the debtor is not entitled to the claimed exemption on the objecting party.

As we saw in Chapter Eight, *Taylor v. Freeland & Kronz* effectively mandates that where the *actual value* of property the debtor claims as fully exempt is unknown or undetermined as of the first meeting of creditors, the trustee files a timely objection just in case the exempted property may turn out to have more value than the dollar limit of the exemption claimed. Otherwise, the excess value of exempted property that could have been captured as property of the estate will be lost to the estate. Conversely, *Schwab v. Reilly*, 130 S. Ct. 2652 (2010), effectively mandates that debtors seeking to exempt property up to the full dollar value of an available exemption amount for that property must make that intention expressly clear on their Schedule C, even if they suspect that the actual full value of the property may be less than that available exemption amount. Otherwise, the trustee may be able to capture for the estate the actual value of the property sought to be exempted in excess of the debtor's designated exemption amount for the property even though the trustee fails to file a timely objection to the claimed exemption amount.

P-H 10-e: Go back to Chapter Eight, Section B, and reread the summaries of *Taylor v. Freeland & Kronz* and *Schwab v. Reilly* or read the opinions themselves. Why did the trustee's failure in *Taylor* to file a timely objection to the debtor's exemption bar him from including the dollar amount of the debtor's settlement in excess of the allowable exemption amount in the property of that estate when the trustee's similar failure in *Schwab* did *not* bar him from including the excess dollar value of the exempted property over the amount the debtor designated as exempt in the property of that estate? What distinguishes these two cases? Do you see how the trustees in both cases were trying to increase the property of their respective estates at the expense of the debtors' claimed exemptions?

Per 28 U.S.C. §157(b)(2), disputes over the debtor's claimed exemptions are core proceedings that the bankruptcy court can hear and decide. Under Bankruptcy Rule 4003(c), an objection to a claimed exemption is a contested matter and need not be resolved through an adversary proceeding.

 D.   # The Trustee's Powers to Compel Turnover of Property of the Estate

The Code also grants the bankruptcy trustee broad power to locate and take possession of property of the estate from the debtor and from third parties who refuse to turn it over. There are three **turnover** provisions in the Code empowering the bankruptcy trustee to compel a person or entity holding property of the estate to deliver that property to him.

Turnover The surrender of estate property to the trustee by the debtor or other person.

1. The Debtor's Duty to Turn Over Property to the Bankruptcy Trustee

Section 521(a)(4) of the Code imposes an obligation on the debtor to turn over to the trustee "all property of the estate and any recorded information, including books, documents, records, and papers relating to property of the estate." If the debtor fails to comply with a turnover demand from the trustee, the trustee will file a motion to compel the turnover, which is treated as a contested matter, not an adversary proceeding. The debtor's failure to comply with this duty is also a basis for the trustee to ask the court to deny the debtor a discharge of his debts pursuant to §727 or to dismiss the case pursuant to §707 (discussed in detail in Chapter Twelve).

2. The Duty of Third Persons to Turn Over Property of the Estate

Section 542 of the Code empowers the trustee to compel third persons (who are not *custodians* within the meaning of §101(11)) holding the property of the debtor to turn it over to him or to account for its value if the property no longer exists. Since the trustee is seeking to recover money or property from a third party in such an action, it must be brought as an adversary proceeding pursuant to Bankruptcy Rule 7001 rather than by motion (see Illustration 6-j).

EXAMPLE

Prior to filing her Chapter 7 petition Marta Carlson loaned her doll collection to her sister, Evelyn Rinaldi, as disclosed in her Schedule A/B (see Document 7 in the Carlson case file). Marta placed a value of $15,125 on the doll collection in her Schedule A/B and claimed the entire collection exempt on her Schedule C (Document 8). The trustee concluded, however, that the doll collection was in fact worth $30,000 to $35,000, more than Marta could exempt, meaning that there was equity for the estate in the doll collection in excess of Marta's exemption. Following the first meeting of creditors, the trustee contacted Evelyn and demanded the return of the doll collection, not to Marta, but to the trustee. Evelyn refused and the trustee filed an objection to Marta's claimed exemption (Document 32) and a complaint (Document 31) instituting an adversary action against Evelyn pursuant to §542 and Bankruptcy Rule 7001, seeking the return of the doll collection or a money judgment for its value.

3. The Duty of Custodians to Turn Over Property of the Estate

Custodian A person authorized to have possession of a debtor's property for a specific purpose as in a trustee, receiver, or assignee for the benefit of creditors.

If the property of the estate is in the hands of a **custodian**, including an assignee for the benefit of creditors or a trustee or receiver appointed as part of a prebankruptcy effort to work out the debtor's financial problems, §543 of the Code empowers the bankruptcy trustee to compel that custodian to deliver the property held to him or to account for its proceeds.

EXAMPLE

If Marta Carlson had attempted an assignment for benefit of creditors prior to filing her petition in bankruptcy, the trustee designated to hold her property as part of that assignment would be the target of the bankruptcy trustee's §543 turnover demand.

If the custodian fails to turn over the property, the trustee can enforce the §543 turnover demand by filing an adversary proceeding. In addition, a third person or custodian who refuses to turn over property to the trustee pursuant to a §§542 or 543 demand and who is also a creditor of the estate can have his claim set off per §553 or disallowed per §502(d).

E. ▶ The Trustee's Avoidance Powers Regarding Property of the Estate

The bankruptcy trustee not only has power to demand the turnover of property of the debtor, but to set aside certain voluntary and involuntary transfers of the debtor's property to others that occurred before the petition was filed. In Code parlance, the trustee can *avoid* these prepetition transfers. Thus, we speak of the **avoidance powers** of the trustee. There are several of them. Since all of these avoidance actions involve the trustee's effort to determine the validity, extent, or priority of a lien on the debtor's property or to recover money or property from a third party, they must be brought as adversary proceedings pursuant to Bankruptcy Rule 7001 and not by motion (see Illustration 6-j). As with the targeted party in a turnover action, if the party targeted by the trustee's avoidance action is also a creditor of the estate and fails to consent to the avoidance or pay the amount demanded by the trustee, that creditor may have its claim set off per §553 or disallowed per §502(d).

> **Avoidance powers** Trustee's powers to set aside certain prepetition transfers of property of the estate.

1. The Power to Avoid Unperfected Security Interests in the Debtor's Property

Section 544(a) of the Code, known as the **strong-arm clause**, provides that, as of the moment the case is commenced by the filing of the petition, the bankruptcy trustee has the status of a *perfected secured creditor* in *all* the property of the estate, whether as a judicial lien creditor (§544(a)(1)) or as a judgment creditor who has had a writ of execution issued in his favor (§544(a)(2)) or as the holder of a consensual mortgage or deed of trust in the real property of the debtor (§544(a)(3)). This makes the trustee a **supercreditor** of the debtor. Note that this status given the trustee is a legalized fiction: The trustee need not take any action to become a judicial lien creditor or judgment creditor or mortgagee, as we considered those concepts in Part A of the text. Instead, the Code simply declares him to have that legal status as of the date the petition is filed.

> **Strong-arm clause** Practitioner's phrase for the trustee's avoidance powers under §544 of the Code.

The most dramatic result of that supercreditor status is that the trustee can defeat

- the claim of any unsecured creditor to the property of the debtor; or
- the claim of any secured creditor whose security interest in the property was not properly perfected prior to the filing of the petition.

EXAMPLE

Recall from the Assignment Memorandum in Appendix A that Marta Carlson has two mortgages on her home, one in favor of CSB with a balance of $142,500 and one in favor of DCT with a balance of $37,500. If the trustee determines that CSB failed to properly record its mortgage or deed of trust prior to the filing of the bankruptcy petition, he would initiate an adversary proceeding by filing a complaint, pursuant to §544(a) and Bankruptcy Rule 7001, seeking to avoid the security interest CSB claims in the home. If the trustee prevailed in avoiding CSB's lien in the home, that would mean that when the home was sold, DCT would be paid first out of the proceeds (assuming it did properly record its mortgage or deed of trust, thus perfecting its secured interest in the home). Marta would receive her homestead exemption next, and the rest of the proceeds would go to the trustee to be used for the benefit of all other creditors of the estate. CSB would still be a creditor, of course, but its claim would now be an unsecured claim, not a secured claim.

Prepetition security interests in both the personal and real property of the debtor that were not properly perfected are subject to the avoidance powers of the trustee under §544(a). However, §546(b) recognizes the right of a creditor to perfect its security interest in property of the estate postpetition so long as, under applicable law (usually the law of the state where the debtor or the property is located), the creditor's interest relates back to a date prior to the commencement of the case.

Recall the discussion of UCC §9-324 in Chapter Two, Section C, regarding a creditor who holds a **purchase money security interest** (PMSI) in goods other than inventory or livestock being granted priority over an earlier perfected security interest if the PMSI is perfected when the debtor takes possession of the collateral or within 20 days thereafter. And recall there the discussion of §9-317(e) providing that a PMSI that can be perfected by filing a financing statement is deemed perfected as of the date the security interest attaches to the goods so long as the financing statement is filed within 20 days of delivery of the goods to the debtor. At this time you may want to review the examples of these UCC sections that were provided in Chapter Two, Section C. Where applicable, these relation back provisions will work to the benefit of the secured creditor against the bankruptcy trustee when the debtor files for relief by allowing the creditor to perfect its security interest postpetition under §546(b) and giving effect to these state law provisions that treat the creditor as perfected as of a date prior to the filing of the bankruptcy petition.

EXAMPLE

Assume Sarah owns a business and purchases a laptop computer on credit to use exclusively in the business on October 1. That same day Sarah grants the seller a security interest in the laptop to secure payment of the purchase price and takes possession of the laptop. Under state law, the security interest in the laptop is perfected by filing a financing statement, but this is not done by seller when Sarah files a petition in Chapter 7 on October 5 and a bankruptcy trustee is appointed. Since Seller's interest in the laptop is unperfected as of the date the petition is filed it looks like the trustee will be able to use the strong arm clause of §544 to avoid the security interest of Seller and treat its claim as unsecured. But

Illustration 10-a: PREPETITION STATUTORY LIENS SUBJECT TO AVOIDANCE UNDER §545

- A statutory lien that only goes into effect upon the debtor's insolvency or financial distress, or upon the bankruptcy filing or the commencement of a nonbankruptcy insolvency proceeding against the debtor (§545(1))
- A statutory lien that would not be enforceable under applicable state law against a bona fide purchaser of the property for value as of the date the case was commenced (§545(2))
- Landlord liens (§545(3))

---

under §546(b) Seller can file a financing statement postpetition and the relation back feature of UCC §9-324 (the applicable state law) will treat the security interest of Seller as perfected as of October 1 so long as the financing statement is filed within 20 days of the date Sarah took possession of the laptop. [This example assumes state law would not treat the laptop as inventory since the relation back feature of UCC §9-324 does not apply to inventory.]

Section 546(c) recognizes the superiority of the rights of a seller of goods to reclaim such goods from possession of a debtor/buyer who has taken possession of the goods within 45 days of the commencement of the case and at a time when the debtor was insolvent (compare the right of reclamation outside of bankruptcy given a seller of goods for buyer's insolvency under UCC §2-702). To exercise this **reclamation right** in the goods, the seller must give the trustee a written demand for reclamation of the goods within 20 days following commencement of the case. This right of reclamation is deemed superior to the trustee's strong-arm power under §544(a) as to those goods even though the seller is not perfected in them.

2. The Power to Avoid Statutory Liens in Property of the Estate

Recall our study of nonconsensual statutory liens in Chapter Three: the artisan's lien, the landlord's lien, the mechanics' lien, and so on. Section 545 of the Code grants the bankruptcy trustee a very limited power to avoid prepetition statutory liens asserted against the property of the debtor. Most statutory liens are not subject to this particular avoidance power of the trustee. The ones that are subject to avoidance are listed in Illustration 10-a.

EXAMPLE

Assume that the state has a statute providing that car repair businesses having an unpaid bill for car repair have a lien on any car repaired for the amount owed if the owner of the car filed for bankruptcy relief before paying the debt in full. If Marta owed a repairperson for work on her car when she filed the petition, the trustee could avoid that statutory lien on Marta's car under §545(1).

EXAMPLE

Assume that the state has a statute providing that car repair businesses having an unpaid bill for car repair have an automatic lien on any car repaired for the amount owed if the debt was not paid within 30 days of the repair but only if the business gives notice of its lien by certified mail. If, under state law, a bona fide purchaser of the car from Marta could take the car free from that lien by purchasing it before the 30 days ran out or before the statutory notice was given, the bankruptcy trustee could likewise defeat the lien under §545(2) if Marta filed her petition before the 30 days ran out or before the statutory notice was given.

EXAMPLE

Assume Marta rented her home instead of owning it and that, pursuant to state law, her landlord was asserting a lien against her personal property in the home for the amount of the unpaid rent. The bankruptcy trustee may avoid that landlord's lien pursuant to §545(3).

Actions brought by the trustee to avoid a statutory lien in the debtor's property pursuant to §545 are adversary proceedings.

3. The Power to Avoid a Fraudulent Transfer of Property of the Estate

Section 548 of the Code authorizes the trustee to set aside any **fraudulent transfer** of the debtor's property made within two years preceding the filing of the petition. Such transactions operate as a fraud against the debtor's creditors because the debtor's estate is depleted without exchanging property of similar value from which the creditors' claims can be satisfied. If applicable state law (such as the Uniform Fraudulent Transfer Act (UFTA), considered in Chapter Five, Section K) allows more than two years for a fraudulent transfer action to be instituted, the trustee may utilize that longer statute of limitations (e.g., UFTA §9 recognizes a four year statute of limitations for most transfers).

Like the Uniform Fraudulent Transfer Act (UFTA), considered in Chapter Five, Section K, §548 defines a fraudulent transfer to include not just a transfer made with actual intent to "hinder, delay or defraud" a creditor per §548(a)(1)(A) but also constructive fraud. The constructive fraud concept is governed by §548(a)(1)(B) and requires a showing that the transfer was made for less than the **reasonably equivalent value** and one or more of the following:

Insolvent The inability to pay debts as they come due or the state of having total liabilities in excess of total assets.

- The transfer was made at a time when the debtor was **insolvent** (see §101(32));
- it caused the debtor to become insolvent;
- it left the debtor undercapitalized for current or planned business transactions;
- it was made at a time the debtor had or planned to incur other debts beyond its ability to pay; or
- it was to or for the benefit of an **insider** (see §101(31) and further discussion in the next section) not in the ordinary course of business.

EXAMPLE

Assume that Marta Carlson, instead of loaning her doll collection to her sister, Evelyn Rinaldi, had made a gift of it to the sister after deciding to file for bankruptcy but before the actual petition was filed. This gift would be disclosed in Marta's Statement of Financial Affairs (Document 17 in the Carlson case file) because it was made within one year of filing. The circumstances of this "gift" would look very suspicious to the trustee searching for property of the estate, and the purported gift might well be attacked as a fraudulent transfer both because it was made when Marta was insolvent and it was arguably made with actual intent to defraud.

The phrase "reasonably equivalent value" is not defined in the Code. It is normally determined using the **fair market value** of the property involved as of the date of the transfer. Fair market value has been defined by the Supreme Court to be the price at which the property would change hands between a willing buyer and a willing seller, neither being under any compulsion to buy or to sell and both having reasonable knowledge of relevant facts (*United States v. Cartwright*, 411 U.S. 546, 551 (1973)).

Applying a strict fair market value standard to determine reasonable equivalence does not always work, however, particularly where the benefit received by the transferee is indirect or intangible. See, e.g., *Mellon Bank N.A. v. Metro Commcns., Inc.*, 945 F.2d 635, 644-645 (3d Cir. 1991) (value of transfer was the intangible benefit of improving debtor's ability to borrow capital), and *In re Jumer's Castle Lodge, Inc.*, 338 B.R. 344 (C.D. Ill. 2006) (debtor received more in value than it transferred, since transfer made it more attractive to investors and financiers). The most that can be said about reasonable equivalence, then, is that it "should depend on all the facts of each case an important element of which is market value. Such a rule requires case-by-case adjudication with fair market value of the property transferred as a starting point" (*In re Morris Commcns., Inc.*, 914 F.2d 458, 466-467 (4th Cir. 1990)).

Actions brought by the trustee to avoid alleged fraudulent transfers of the debtor's property pursuant to §548 are adversary proceedings.

4. The Power to Avoid Preferential Transfers of Property of the Estate

Perhaps the most breathtaking example of avoidance powers given the bankruptcy trustee is the **preferential transfer** provision of §547. This section allows the trustee to set aside any transfer of the debtor's property made within 90 days preceding the filing of the petition if the following additional elements are present:

- The transfer was "to or for the benefit of a creditor."
- The transfer was made for or on account of an antecedent (preexisting) debt.
- The debtor was insolvent at the time of the transfer.
- The transfer would enable the creditor to receive more than it would have received if the transfer had not been made.

EXAMPLE

One of Marta's unsecured debts is to Crisis Counseling Center (CCC) for the counseling services rendered to her son, Chris (see the Assignment Memorandum in Appendix A and Document 12 in the Carlson case file). The total amount owed to CCC was $1,250 and let's say it was due and payable on February 1, 2016. Assume that Marta did finally make a payment of $700 to CCC on May 15 before filing her Chapter 7 petition on June 6, 2016. The bankruptcy trustee will demand that CCC return that $700 payment as a preferential transfer. It was a payment made by the debtor within 90 days of the date the petition was filed, was a payment to a creditor on account of a preexisting debt, was paid at a time when Marta was insolvent, and that payment would enable CCC to receive more than it would have had the payment not been made. If CCC refuses to return the money to the trustee, he will institute an adversary proceeding, pursuant to §547 and Bankruptcy Rule 7001, to recover it as a preferential transfer.

Consider why allowing CCC to keep the $700 payment in the previous example would enable it to receive more than it would have had the payment not been made. If the payment had not been made, CCC would file a proof of claim in the bankruptcy case as an unsecured creditor for the full amount owed, $1,250. When the time comes for a distribution to unsecured creditors, it is very unlikely that they will all receive 100 cents on each dollar owed. Instead they will probably receive some percentage of what they are owed. But if CCC is allowed to keep the $700 payment, it is getting 100 cents on the dollar from the debtor for that portion of the debt, more than it would receive had the payment not been made.

P-H 10-f: When Marta filed her bankruptcy petition in June 2016 she was seriously in arrears in her payments to DCT, holder of the second mortgage on her home. She had failed to make the payments due on March 1, April 1, and May 1, 2016. However, on May 15, 2016 she did pay DCT $954 to cover the missed payments that were due March 1 and April 1. This May 15 payment is disclosed in Part 3 of Marta's Statement of Financial Affairs (Document 17 in the Carlson case file). Will the bankruptcy trustee demand that DCT return the $954 payment it received from Marta on May 15 to the trustee as a preferential transfer? It was a payment made by the debtor within 90 days of the date of the petition, to a creditor on account of a preexisting debt, at a time when Marta was insolvent. But the last element is missing. Based on the estimated value of the real property securing the debt owed to DCT, it is going to receive the full amount Marta owes it from the proceeds of the sale of the property even though it is a junior lien holder in the property. Thus, her May 15 payment does not satisfy the last element of the preferential transfer definition because the payment does not enable the creditor to receive more from the estate than it would have had the payment not been made. If the trustee discovers some defect in CSB's perfected status and succeeds in avoiding CSB's secured position in the home using the strong-arm clause, will the trustee also be able to recoup the May 15 payment to this creditor as preferential?

P-H 10-g: Assume that the May 15 payment is made to DCT as described above, but assume further that the real property securing that DCT debt is not worth as much as what DCT is owed. Will the May 15 payment to DCT now be deemed preferential?

To be preferential, the payment also has to have been made on account of an **antecedent debt**. An antecedent debt is a preexisting one.

EXAMPLE

> If Marta made a car payment to AFI on May 15 but it was an installment payment that was only then due from her, that payment cannot be considered preferential. It was a payment for a current debt, not a preexisting one.

To be preferential, the payment must also have been made while the debtor was **insolvent**. Recall from Chapter Five, Section K, that under the UFTA, there are two definitions of fraud, the **balance sheet test** (the sum of the debtor's debts is greater than all of the debtor's assets, at a fair valuation) and the **equity test** (the debtor is not paying his debts as they become due). Section 101(32) of the Code defines insolvency using *only* the balance sheet test. Thus, when insolvency is at issue in a bankruptcy case, as in a preference action, valuation of the assets of the debtor as part of the balance sheet test of insolvency is often vigorously contested.

Balance sheet test A test of insolvency whereby a debtor's liabilities exceed his or her assets.

Section 547(f) aids the trustee or other party asserting preferential transfer by creating a rebuttable **presumption of insolvency** during the 90-day preferential transfer period. Pursuant to Rule 301 of the Federal Rules of Evidence, which controls presumptions that arise in federal courts, the effect of the presumption of insolvency is to effectively shift the burden of coming forward with evidence of solvency to the creditor being sued. Though the burden of proof regarding insolvency always remains on the trustee alleging the preferential transfer, the presumption will be sufficient to satisfy that element for the trustee unless the transferee presents sufficient evidence to rebut the presumption. If the presumption is effectively rebutted by the transferee, then the burden of persuasion is on the trustee to present other evidence of insolvency. For a good discussion of how the presumption works, see *In re Koubourlis*, 869 F.2d 1319, 1321-1322 (9th Cir. 1989).

Forcing a creditor to return a payment received from a debtor within 90 days of the petition being filed may not seem fair to the creditor. After all, the creditor receiving the payment may not even have known the debtor was insolvent when the payment was made. The creditor was legitimately owed the money and did nothing illegal or unethical to collect the payment. But the policy behind the preferential transfer avoidance power given the bankruptcy trustee is that it is not fair to all creditors for one to be "preferred" by receiving a payment or other transfer of the debtor's property so close to the date of filing bankruptcy when the debtor was already insolvent. So every transfer of property by the debtor within the 90-day window is immediately suspect and will be closely examined by the trustee to see if the elements of a preference are present. The trustee's duty is to all the creditors of the estate, so the trustee will aggressively pursue each preferential transfer.

When payments from the debtor must be returned to the trustee as preferential, the creditor's only remedy is to file a proof of claim for the amount of the preferential transfer returned and stand in line with other general unsecured creditors hoping that there is eventually a distribution from the estate. Of course, how much the general unsecured creditors ultimately receive will depend on the total assets located by the trustee, and they may ultimately get only pennies on each dollar owed. We will consider the distribution to creditors in the next chapter.

A preferential transfer need not involve the payment of money by the debtor. 11 U.S.C. §101(54) defines "transfer" as follows:

The term "transfer" means—

(A) the creation of a lien;
(B) the retention of title as a security interest;
(C) the foreclosure of a debtor's equity of redemption; or
(D) each mode, direct or indirect, absolute or conditional, voluntary or involuntary, of disposing of or parting with—

(i) property; or
(ii) an interest in property.

Using this broad definition, the transfer of any property interest of the debtor within 90 days of filing may trigger a claim of preference if the other elements of §547 are satisfied.

EXAMPLE

Assume that Marta transferred her doll collection to her sister a month before the petition was filed but did so in payment of an old debt she owed her sister. The transfer of the doll collection is a transfer of the debtor's property within 90 days of filing to a creditor in payment of an antecedent debt and made when the debtor was insolvent. It is a preferential transfer within the meaning of §547 and the doll collection will have to be returned to the estate. If Evelyn no longer has the doll collection (e.g., it was stolen, sold, or lost), she will have to return its dollar value to the trustee. Evelyn can file a claim with the estate for the debt owed her by Marta.

EXAMPLE

Assume that to keep the CCC from suing her for the amount she owes, Marta had agreed on May 15, 2016, to give CCC a security interest in all her personal property. And assume she signed a proper security agreement to create that security interest and that CCC filed a proper financing statement to perfect its secured position in that property. When she files her petition on June 6, the trustee will seek to avoid the security interest Marta granted CCC on the grounds that it was preferential. What "property" did the debtor convey to CCC on September 15? The security interest in her personal property is a type of property interest and is subject to avoidance as preferential.

In addition to the standard 90-day preferential transfer provision, §547 allows the bankruptcy trustee to avoid preferential transfers to insiders of the debtor made within one year preceding the date the petition was filed. 11 U.S.C.

Insider A person in close relationship with a debtor such that the person may be assumed to have superior access to information and be subject to special treatment.

§101(31) contains an extensive definition of who is an insider, but essentially an insider is a person in close relationship with a debtor such that he may be assumed to have superior access to information and be subject to special treatment.

P-H 10-h: Assume that Marta transfers her doll collection to her sister, Evelyn, six months before the bankruptcy petition is filed in payment of an old debt. The transfer occurred more than 90 days prior to the filing of the petition, but using the definition in §101(31), can the trustee avoid the transfer of the doll collection to Evelyn on the basis that she was an insider as to the debtor? What if the debtor is a partnership and the questioned transfer was made to a partner six months before the partnership files its bankruptcy case? To a receptionist who works for the partnership as an employee only? To the wife of a partner? What if the debtor is a corporation and the transfer was to a shareholder? An officer? A director? To an attorney who does legal work for the corporation?

The §547(c)(1) Equivalent Value Exception to the Trustee's Right to Avoid Preferential Transfers

Contemporaneous exchange for equivalent value A transaction supported by adequate present consideration.

Section 547(c)(1) recognizes an important exception to the trustee's right to avoid and recover preferential transfers where the transfer was intended as and in fact was a **contemporaneous exchange for equivalent value**.

EXAMPLE

Assume that Marta Carlson had ordered a new car on January 2, 2016, from AAA Chevrolet. The purchase price was $15,000 and was to be paid on delivery. The car is delivered on April 1, 2016, and Marta pays AAA cash for it. She is insolvent at the time she does so. When she files her bankruptcy petition on June 6, 2016, the trustee will look at the April 1 payment and see a transfer of the debtor's property made within the 90-day preference window to a creditor in payment of a preexisting debt made at a time when the debtor was insolvent, all of which enables the creditor to receive more than it would have had the payment not been made. Looks like a preferential payment all right. But if the car purchased was in fact worth $15,000, it is not preferential because the transfer of cash was in exchange for something of "equivalent value," the $15,000 car, which is now property of the estate. So this transfer would not be preferential under the Code and the trustee could not set it aside.

EXAMPLE

Assume that the car Marta purchases from AAA for $15,000 is actually worth only $12,000. That's not equivalent value. On those facts, the trustee would likely succeed in his preference claim against AAA to recover the full $15,000 for the estate. Could AAA get the car back under those circumstances? Not unless it retained a perfected security interest in the car, which it would not do if it received cash in full payment. That car is property of the estate. File your proof of claim, AAA, and get in line with the other unsecured creditors.

The §547(c)(2) Ordinary Course of Business Exception to the Trustee's Right to Avoid Preferential Transfers

Ordinary course of business or financial affairs In general, following the typical, usual practices engaged in by a business.

Section 547(c)(2) recognizes a second important exception to the trustee's right to avoid and recover preferential transfers where the transfer was in payment of a debt incurred in the **ordinary course of business or financial affairs** of the debtor and transferee and the transfer itself was made either (and note this alternative for the transfer) in the ordinary course of business or financial affairs of the debtor and transferee or was made according to ordinary business terms. Thus, the debt at issue must have been incurred in the ordinary course of business or financial affairs of both the debtor and the transferee and the transfer must be made in the ordinary course of business or financial affairs of both the debtor and the transferee (§547(c)(2)(A)), *or* according to ordinary business terms (§547(c)(2)(B)).

EXAMPLE

Assume that the bankruptcy debtor is the proprietor of a grocery business. Sixty days before filing his bankruptcy petition the debtor orders inventory for his store, which is delivered five days later, together with an invoice stating that payment is due within ten days of receipt of the goods. The debtor pays the invoice from his supplier within the ten days even though he is insolvent at the time. Then he files a case in bankruptcy. That payment to the supplier is immediately suspect because it was made within the 90-day preferential window. But there is nothing extraordinary about the payment because the debtor only paid what was owed and he paid it on time. The debt was created in the ordinary course of the debtor's business as well as the supplier's business (note that to qualify for the exception the debt must be created in the ordinary course of business of both the debtor and the transferee) and it was paid (that's the transfer) in the ordinary course of both the debtor's and the transferee's business (note that to qualify for the exception under §547(c)(2)(A) the transfer must be made in the ordinary course of business or financial affairs of both the debtor and the transferee). This transfer is probably not preferential and the supplier can keep the money.

It has long been understood that whether a debt is created or a transfer made in the ordinary course of the debtor's and transferee's business is a subjective inquiry focusing on what is "ordinary" for those particular parties. See, e.g., *In re Fred Hawes Organization, Inc.*, 957 F.2d 239 (6th Cir. 1992).

EXAMPLE

Assume that our bankruptcy debtor who owns the grocery business pays the invoice 12 days after the goods are delivered, two days late under the terms of the invoice. That payment is now likely to be found preferential and the trustee will recover it for the estate. Do you see why? Because payments made late will not be considered "ordinary" unless the debtor and transferee have an established course of dealing whereby past payments have been made late and accepted by the transferee without complaint. If that course of dealing exists, then the late payment may be in the ordinary course of business as between the debtor and transferee.

Even the slightest deviation from normal business behavior or practice of a debtor and transferee may render a payment extraordinary and thus unqualified for the ordinary course of dealing exception to the preferential transfer statute.

EXAMPLE

Assume that our bankrupt grocer pays the invoice on time, within ten days. However, the supplier has heard rumors that the debtor may be in financial trouble and so he demands payment of this invoice by cashier's check. Previously, the supplier has always allowed payment by personal check. Even if the debtor makes the payment on time, if he does so by cashier's check, that's not the usual practice and the transfer will be deemed preferential and recoverable by the trustee when the debtor files his petition.

But note that per §549(c)(2)(B) the transfer part of the challenged transaction can qualify for the exception either by having been made in the ordinary course of business or financial affairs of the debtor and the transferee, *or* by having been made according to "ordinary business terms." Unlike "ordinary course of business," "ordinary business terms" is understood to involve an objective inquiry focusing not on ordinary business terms between the debtor and the transferee, but on ordinary business terms in the relevant business or industry. See, e.g., *In re Nowlen*, 452 B.R. 619, 621-622 (Bankr. E.D. Mich. 2011).

EXAMPLE

Assume our bankrupt grocer cannot pay the invoice within the ten days of delivery when it is due although he has always paid this supplier on time in the past. This time debtor calls the supplier and asks for five additional days to pay even though he knows he will be late in doing so. Debtor makes the payment on the fifteenth day after delivery, paying by check as he always has, and then files bankruptcy. Must the transferee supplier disgorge the payment to the trustee as preferential? This payment was not in the ordinary course of business of the debtor and supplier since they had no course of dealing allowing debtor to pay late. But supplier may be able to successfully defend against the preference action if he can show that payment by check is a standard method of payment in the industry and that there is an industry custom of allowing customers such as debtor to occasionally make a payment slightly late. By making such argument, supplier transferee is arguing that the payment he received from debtor was according to ordinary business terms in the industry.

The §547(c)(3) Enabling Loan Exception to the Trustee's Right to Avoid Preferential Transfers

Under §547(c)(3), the bankruptcy trustee cannot avoid a transfer that creates a security interest in property to secure payment of the loan or credit that enabled the debtor to purchase the property and the security interest "is perfected on or before 30 days after the debtor receives possession of such property." The **enabling loan exception** is asserted frequently in consumer bankruptcy cases where the consumer debtor purchases a vehicle (or other consumer item) shortly before filing the bankruptcy petition and grants the seller or lender a security interest in the vehicle.

EXAMPLE

Joe and Alice, husband and wife, purchase a used car from Carla's Used Cars on March 1. They purchase the car on credit and sign a purchase and security agreement requiring them to pay in installments over 36 months. The agreement grants Carla's a security interest in the car to secure payment of the debt. Joe and Alice drive home in their new car and apply the next day for new title, which is issued by the state on March 21 with the security interest of Carla's properly noted thereon; Carla's security interest in the car is now perfected under state law. Joe and Alice then file for Chapter 7 bankruptcy on April 10 and are able to claim as exempt all of their property not subject to security interests so it appears to be a no-asset case. The bankruptcy trustee will examine this transaction to see if there might be a basis to set aside the transfer of the security interest in the car from Joe and Alice to Carla's as a preference. The granting of the security interest to Carla's is a transfer within §101(54). Carla's was a creditor of the debtors when the transfer was made. The transfer occurred within the 90-day preference period. The trustee can rely on the presumption of insolvency per §547(f). Carla's is in a position to receive more than it would have received had the security interest not been granted since even if the trustee were able to sell the car for the benefit of unsecured creditors, none of them, including Carla's, is going to get anything near 100 percent of what is owed. But as a secured creditor, Carla's can expect to get most or all of what is owed. Finally, the transfer is made on account of an antecedent debt since the date of the transfer of the security interest was March 21, the date it was perfected by being properly noted on the title, whereas the debt was created on March 1. The obligation to Carla's was an antecedent debt when perfection occurred.

It appears that all the elements of a preferential transfer are present in the last example, but now look at the §547(c)(3) exception. The security interest in the car was given to Carla's to secure new credit ("new value"); the credit was given to debtors on March 1 at the time the security agreement describing the vehicle was executed; the credit was given to enable the debtors to acquire the vehicle; and they did in fact obtain title to the vehicle using the credit given. All the elements of §547(c)(3)(A) are satisfied but subsection (B) must be satisfied as well, and on the facts of our example it is—the new title noting Carla's security interest was issued by the state on March 21, fewer than 30 days after Joe and Alice took possession of the car on March 1. Since Carla's security interest in the vehicle was perfected within 30 days of debtors taking possession the enabling loan exception will defeat trustee's preference claim. (BAPCPA amended the §547(c)(3) exception in a way that favors secured creditors over the bankruptcy trustees by changing the permissible time window for perfection from 20 to 30 days.)

P-H 10-i: What is the result in the last example if the new title noting Carla's security interest in the vehicle is not issued by the state until April 5? Or if Joe and Alice grant a security interest in the vehicle on March 2 to Joe's mother to secure a loan Joe's mother made to them two years ago that was originally unsecured?

HIGHLIGHTED CASE   ●

IN RE CARPENTER

378 B.R. 274 (Bankr. D. Idaho 2007)

OPINION: PAPPAS, Bankruptcy Judge:

On July 27, 2006, Debtor filed for relief under chapter 7 of the Bankruptcy Code. Several months prior to filing his bankruptcy petition, Debtor had purchased a 2003 Chevrolet Silverado Duramax pickup truck from Defendant. Debtor and Defendant agreed Defendant would retain a security interest in the truck to secure Debtor's payment of the purchase price to Defendant at a later date.

Debtor and Defendant negotiated the purchase and sale of the Silverado in December of 2005. After settling the various terms of their arrangement, the parties decided that Debtor would draft a simple written purchase agreement, and travel from his home in Preston to Defendant's residence in Blackfoot on December 11, 2005 to sign the contract and finalize the sale.

The simple written agreement Debtor prepared was executed by the parties at Defendant's house that day. It called for Debtor to pay Defendant a total purchase price for the Silverado of $22,000, but the spaces in the agreement providing for an initial down payment and for subsequent monthly payments were left blank. The agreement provided that Debtor was to take delivery of the pickup on the date it was executed, December 11, 2005. The contract required Debtor to secure insurance coverage on the truck by December 12, 2005.

The day before the parties were to meet to sign the deal, Debtor telephoned his insurance agent to inquire about insuring the Silverado. Debtor discovered that it would be too expensive to carry insurance on both his current Ford pickup and the Silverado. Debtor therefore decided it would be best not to take delivery of pickup from Defendant, nor to insure it, until he could sell the Ford. Despite this decision, on December 11, 2005, Debtor traveled to Blackfoot with his spouse, met with Defendant, and signed the agreement as originally planned, making no changes to the contract's terms regarding the delivery date or his obligation to insure the Silverado by December 12, 2005. Debtor did not take delivery of pickup at that time, and instead returned to Preston, leaving the Silverado in Defendant's garage in Blackfoot. This arrangement was satisfactory to Defendant, and she continued her insurance coverage on the Silverado.

A few days later, Debtor found a buyer for the Ford. On December 17, 2005, after being informed of this development by Debtor, Defendant cancelled her insurance coverage on the Silverado. On December 18, 2005, Debtor closed the sale on the Ford. On December 19, 2005, Debtor called his insurance agent, cancelled the coverage on the Ford pickup, and added the Silverado to his policy.

Debtor testified at trial that, having sold the Ford and obtained insurance on the Silverado, he had hoped to return to Blackfoot to retrieve the Silverado. However, this plan proved inconvenient. With the rapidly approaching holiday season, Debtor and his wife decided it would be best to wait until after Christmas to get the Silverado. Then, on December 27, 2005, Debtor's wife broke her wrist and underwent surgery; the following week Debtor's son required dental surgery. Because of these complications, it was not until

January 4, 2006, that Debtor was able to return to Blackfoot. He took the Silverado from Defendant's garage and returned home with it.

Debtor then attempted to obtain a certificate of title to the Silverado. However, the county assessor's office informed him that to do so he needed the existing title certificate. Debtor contacted Defendant and asked her to sign off and send him the certificate. On January 27, 2006, Debtor received the title certificate from Defendant. Debtor returned to the county assessor's office with the title and other necessary paperwork, and on January 31, 2006, the Idaho Department of Motor Vehicles issued a new certificate of title for the Silverado showing Debtor as owner and noting that Defendant held a lien on the pickup.

CONCLUSIONS OF LAW AND ANALYSIS

Given these facts, two legal issues require analysis by the Court. First, was the Defendant's retention of a security interest in the Silverado a preference under §547(b)? And second, if Defendant's retention of a security interest is a preference, is the transfer insulated from avoidance by §547(c)(3)?

A. The Transfer of the Security Interest in the Silverado was an Avoidable Preference

[The court finds that the trustee/plaintiff has satisfied his burden of proving all the elements of a §547(b) preferential transfer.]

B. The Enabling Loan Exception to Preference Avoidance Does Not Apply

Plaintiff may avoid the Debtor's transfer of the security interest to Defendant unless one of the statutory safe harbors to avoidance is shown to apply to the transaction. As affirmative defenses, it is Defendant's burden to prove she is protected by one or more of the preference exceptions under §547(c) . . . . 11 U.S.C. §547(g) . . . .

Defendant acknowledges that the only provision of §547(c) that is arguably applicable is the so-called "enabling loan" exception under §547(c)(3) . . . . Under this exception, a trustee may not avoid a transfer that creates a security interest in property to secure payment of the purchase price "that is perfected on or before 30 days after the debtor receives possession of such property." 11 U.S.C. §547(c)(3)(B). Here, whether this provision shields Defendant from avoidance of her security interest depends upon when Debtor "received possession" of the Silverado.

Plaintiff argues that upon execution of the agreement by the parties, Debtor was given "constructive" possession of the pickup, and thus the 30-day time limit for perfection of Defendant's security interest began to run on December 11, 2005. Since Defendant's security interest was not perfected by noting her lien on the certificate of title to the Silverado until January 31, 2006, Plaintiff contends the enabling loan exception does Defendant no good.[5]

---

[5] Under §547(e)(1)(B) and (2), the transfer of a security interest in a debtor's personal property is deemed to occur for preference purposes at the time such transfer is perfected under applicable law as against third parties, where that perfection occurs after 30 days from the date "such transfer takes effect between the transferor and the transferee. . . ." Defendant does not dispute Plaintiff's position that the transfer of the security interest

Defendant, on the other hand, argues that the 30-day perfection period did not commence until Debtor received actual, physical possession of the Silverado on January 4, 2006. If Defendant's construction of §547(c)(3)(B) is correct, her security interest may not be avoided by Plaintiff.

The Bankruptcy Code contains no definition of the term "possession." However, this Court has interpreted the meaning of possession in the context of §547(c)(3)(B) to refer to "physical control or custody of the collateral, as opposed to the acquisition of a right of ownership." See *In re Tuttle*, 2003 WL 22221330 (Bankr. D. Idaho 2003). See also, *In re B & B Utilities, Inc.*, 208 B.R. 417, 424 (Bankr. E.D. Tenn. 1997) (quoting *In re Trott*, 91 B.R. 808, 811 (Bankr. S.D. Ohio 1988)). In *Trott*, the bankruptcy court concluded that there was "simply no reason . . . to depart from the definition of the word possession which has gained acceptance throughout the law[.]" *In re Trott*, 91 B.R. at 811. The court explained that possession, as generally understood in legal matters, meant "[t]he detention and control, or the manual or ideal custody [of something] . . . either held personally or by another who exercises it in one's place and name." Id. (citing Black's Law Dictionary 1047 (5th ed. 1979). In *Tuttle*, this Court agreed with *Trott*, noting that "to add gloss to the concept of possession [is] inconsistent with the plain language of the Code." *In re Tuttle*, 2003 WL 22221330. The Court further observed that the language of §547(c)(3)(B) "contains no qualification or condition on the nature of a debtor's possession."

In this case, from and after December 11, 2005, the date the parties executed the agreement by which Debtor purchased the Silverado and Defendant retained a security interest in it, the pickup, while still parked in Defendant's garage, was under Debtor's control. Defendant did not require that the Silverado be left with her after December 11. Instead, the arrangement was merely a convenience to Debtor. Importantly, both Defendant and Debtor testified that Debtor could have taken the Silverado at any time thereafter. Defendant never denied Debtor access to the pickup, nor did she charge Debtor to store the Silverado at her home. Moreover, during the time the Silverado remained in Defendant's garage, Defendant cancelled her insurance, and Debtor added the pickup to his insurance policy. This is consistent with the notion that, after December 11, Debtor was in control of the truck. Furthermore, as Defendant's counsel conceded during argument at trial, after the purchase agreement was executed, Defendant had the original certificate of title to the Silverado, and nothing prevented her from immediately taking the necessary steps to transfer title and perfect her security interest in the Silverado, as opposed to waiting for Debtor to have the title transfer completed.

Under these facts, the Court finds that Debtor had actual control of the Silverado as of December 11, 2005, and that from and after that date, Defendant held the pickup merely as Debtor's agent for purposes of storing it until it was convenient for Debtor to retrieve it. "If a debtor has actual physical control over the property before or at the time of an agreement granting a purchase

---

in the Silverado from Debtor to Defendant was effective between the parties when they signed the purchase agreement on December 11, 2005. Therefore, since Defendant's security was not perfected under Idaho law until the application for certificate of title was filed on January 31, 2006, see Idaho Code §49-510," for preference purposes, the transfer is deemed to have occurred on that date.

money security interest therein, the [thirty] day window for the creditor's perfection of that interest under §547(c)(3)(B) begins to close from the date of the agreement." *In re Tuttle*, 2003 WL 22221330.

CONCLUSION

Plaintiff has shown by a preponderance of the evidence that Defendant's retention of a security interest in the Silverado was a preferential transfer for the purpose of §547(b). Because Debtor had "possession" of the pickup by virtue of his right to control it from and after December 11, 2005, even though it remained stored at Defendant's premises, and because Defendant did not perfect her security interest until January 31, 2006, the exception to avoidance in §547(c)(3) does not protect Defendant. Plaintiff is therefore entitled to avoid Defendant's security interest.

POST-CASE FOLLOW-UP

Not all courts might have reached the same result on the possession issue as in *Carpenter*. Though the concept of constructive possession or right of possession to property not literally in a debtor's hands is generally recognized, the debtor's decision to delay taking actual possession until the Ford truck was sold and his delay in securing insurance to cover the Silverado truck could have persuaded a court that the debtor was willfully postponing taking physical control. See, e.g., *In re Ashworth*, 227 B.R. 801 (Bankr. S.D. Ohio 1998) (debtor's delay in making first payment and acquiring insurance for mobile home defeated claim to have taken possession). *Carpenter* provides a reminder of the critical role that state law plays in bankruptcy practice, a principle established by the Supreme Court in *Butner v. United States*, discussed in Chapter Six, Section E. Though the preferential transfer statute is federal, what constitutes perfection of a security interest in contested property under §547(c)(3)(B) will be governed by applicable state law. For a dramatic example of the difference this can make, read *In re Conklin*, 511 B.R. 688 (Bankr. D. Idaho 2014), another enabling loan exception case involving a vehicle, decided by the same bankruptcy judge who authored *Carpenter* and also controlled by Idaho law regarding registration of vehicles. In *Conklin* the certificate of title evidencing the creditor's security interest was not issued until 34 days after the debtor took possession, but the creditor's security interest was deemed perfected on the thirtieth day following possession when the application for title was received by the state. A 2007 change in the Idaho vehicle registration statute was decisive.

In re Carpenter: Real Life Applications

1. Locate the vehicle registration statute in your state. How would *In re Carpenter* have been decided under that statute?

2. Assume that each of the following transfers has been found to be preferential. What issues might arise if the creditor/transferee asserts the enabling loan exception of §547(c)(3) as a defense?

   a. Debtor leased a vehicle three years ago and the lease contained an option to purchase for $5,000 at the conclusion of the lease on June 1. On May 25 debtor borrowed $5,000 from Bank to exercise the option to purchase and granted Bank a security interest in the vehicle. On June 1 debtor paid the $5,000 to lessor, kept the vehicle, and an application for title in debtor's name was initiated the same day. Bank's security interest was perfected by being noted on title issued to debtor on June 30. Debtor filed a Chapter 7 petition on September 1. See *In re Moon*, 262 B.R. 97 (Bankr. D. Or. 2001).

   b. Debtor purchased a used vehicle from co-worker on credit on June 1 by promising to pay for the car in 12 monthly installments beginning July 1. Co-worker signed title over to debtor on June 1 and gave him possession that day as well. Debtor made the first promised payment on July 1 but missed the August payment. Co-worker then demanded a security interest in the vehicle to secure future payments. Debtor agreed and the security interest of the co-worker was noted on the title on August 3, perfecting it under state law. Debtor filed a Chapter 7 petition on August 30.

   c. Debtor borrowed $20,000 from Bank on June 1 to purchase a mobile home. The June 1 agreement granted Bank a security interest in the mobile home to secure repayment of the loan. On the same day, the loan proceeds were paid to the mobile home dealer/seller and debtor received the keys to the mobile home. An application for title was initiated that day as well. Due to some unforeseen delays the mobile home was not delivered to debtor's property by dealer until July 30. The certificate of title noting Bank's security interest in the mobile home was issued by the state on July 3, properly perfecting Bank's interest under state law. After delivery of the mobile home to debtor's property, debtor had to have the mobile home leveled and tied down, the tires removed, steps and skirting installed, and utilities connected; because of this, debtor did not move in until August 10. Debtor filed a Chapter 7 petition on August 20. See *In re Winnett*, 102 B.R. 635 (Bankr. S.D. Ohio 1989).

Section 547(c) contains a number of other exceptions to the preferential transfer, some of which are pertinent to the consumer bankruptcy debtor:

- Transfers that constitute the fixing of a statutory lien that is avoidable under §545 are not preferential per §547(c)(6).
- To the extent a transfer during the preference period was for a bona fide domestic support obligation (e.g., child support or alimony) it is not considered preferential per §547(c)(7).

- In cases involving consumer debtors, transfers having an aggregate value of less than $600 are not preferential per §547(c)(9).

5. Avoidance of Postpetition Transfers

Section 549 grants the trustee the power to avoid unauthorized transfers of property of the estate made after commencement of the case. An exception is the postpetition transfer of real property to a good faith purchaser without knowledge of the filing who pays a fair equivalent value, unless a copy of the petition or notice of the bankruptcy filing was previously filed or recorded where the deed of transfer would be recorded. The trustee's action under §549 must be commenced within two years after the date of the transfer or before the case is closed or dismissed, whichever is earlier.

6. Recovery of Avoided Transfer from the Party for Whose Benefit It Was Made

Section 550(a)(1) of the Code provides that if a transfer is avoided under one of these avoidance powers, the trustee can recover the property itself or the value of such property from either the **initial transferee** or the party for whose benefit the transfer was made.

EXAMPLE

Assume that Marta Carlson's May 15 payment was not made to DCT but instead was made to her parents who held the mortgage on her sister's house to satisfy a past-due mortgage payment owed by the sister to her parents. Assuming all the requirements for constructive fraudulent transfer under §548(a)(1) are present (made while the debtor was insolvent and for less than reasonably equivalent value), the trustee could pursue the parents as transferees of the payment under §548 or, if the transfer is avoided, may pursue recovery from the sister under §550. He might well do this if the parents are unable to pay. The sister is "the entity for whose benefit such transfer was made." Don't be thrown off by the use of the word "entity" in §550(a)(1). Section 1101(15) of the Code defines entity to include "person" and §1101(41) defines person to include an individual as well as nongovernmental entities.

Section 550(a)(2) also allows the trustee to recover the property or its value from a transferee other than the initial transferee (called an immediate or mediate transferee of the initial transferee) unless per §550(b)(1) that subsequent transferee gave value for the transfer in good faith and without actual or constructive knowledge of the voidability of the transfer.

EXAMPLE

Assume that Marta Carlson's parents, after receiving the May 15 preferential payment from Marta, transfer the funds to their son, Marta's brother, as a gift. The son is an immediate transferee under §550(a)(2) who likely took without knowledge of the voidability of the original transfer but did not do so for value. The son may be a target of the trustee if neither the parents nor the sister can pay.

> **P-H 10-j:** If Marta Carlson's parents, sister, and brother are all potentially liable to the trustee under §§548 and 550, does that mean the trustee can recover the full amount of the avoided transfer from each of them? See §550(d). If the brother, upon receipt of the funds from his parents and before having knowledge that the transfers are voidable, transfers the funds to his girlfriend as a gift, may the trustee pursue recovery from the girlfriend in the event neither the parents, nor the sister, nor the brother can pay? See §550(b)(2).

7. Time Limitations on the Trustee's Right to Bring an Avoidance Action

Section 546(a) establishes a time limitation on the right to bring an avoidance action under any of the provisions we have just considered other than §549. Under all the other avoidance sections the suit must be commenced within two years from the order of relief or one year from the date a trustee is first appointed, whichever is later. And, in any event, it must be filed before the case is closed, which could occur earlier than either of those two events.

CHAPTER SUMMARY

In a Chapter 7 asset case, unsecured creditors must file a proof of claim by the claims bar date in order to participate in any distribution from the estate. Late filed claims are permitted prior to distribution if the creditor had no notice or actual knowledge of the filing. The failure of a secured creditor to file a timely proof of claim does not impair its secured position in the property of the debtor. However, since the Code treats claims as secured only up to the value of the collateral at the time the petition is filed, an undersecured creditor must file a proof of claim in order to participate in any distribution as to the unsecured portion of its claim.

The bankruptcy trustee reviews submitted claims and may object to their allowance, raising a contested matter. Claims are deemed allowed if no objection is filed by the trustee or other party in interest. There is no time bar for the filing of objections to claims.

The right to setoff is recognized in bankruptcy cases where the debtor and creditors have claims against each other. A creditor may include matured prepetition interest in his claim. Generally, unsecured and undersecured creditors are not entitled to receive postpetition interest on their claims. Fully secured creditors any include postpetition interest in their claims as well as postpetition fees, costs, and charges if the underlying agreement allows, up to the value of the collateral.

Property of the bankruptcy estate includes all property in which the debtor has a legal or equitable interest at the time the case is commenced wherever located and by whoever held at the time. Some property the debtor becomes entitled to within 180 days of filing the petition is considered property of the estate. If the debtor is the trustee of a trust, only his or her legal interest in the trust res becomes property of the estate, not the equitable interest of beneficiaries in the res.

The bankruptcy trustee may challenge the debtor's claimed exemptions by objection to increase the property of the estate and objection must normally be filed within 30 days following the first meeting of creditors. Where the value of a claimed exemption is listed on Schedule C as contingent or unknown, timely objection must be made or the estate forfeits any later-determined value of the property in excess of the exemption allowance. A debtor who understates the value of an exemption on the Schedule C is bound by that value.

The bankruptcy trustee is empowered to compel the turnover of property of the estate by the debtor or third persons, including legal custodians of that property. Using the strong-arm clause of the Code, the trustee can defeat the claim of any unsecured creditor to the property of the debtor or the claim of any secured creditor whose claim to the debtor's property was not perfected prior to the filing of the petition. The trustee is also empowered to set aside certain prepetition transfers of the debtor's property, including some statutory liens, fraudulent transfers made within two years preceding the filing of the petition, and preferential transfers of debtor's property made within the 90 days preceding the filing of the petition and within one year of that date for insiders. All such actions are adversary proceedings except the turnover action against the debtor, which is initiated by motion creating a disputed matter.

In a preference action the trustee must show that the transfer was made to or for the benefit of a creditor within the requisite time period for or on account of an antecedent debt while the debtor was insolvent and enabled the transferee creditor to receive more than it would have had the transfer not been made. There is a rebuttable presumption of the debtor's insolvency during the preference period to aid the trustee. Any transfer of the debtor's property or an interest of the debtor in that property may be preferential including the creation of a consensual or nonconsensual lien on the debtor's property.

An exception to a preferential transfer claim is recognized for transfers for which the debtor received equivalent value. An exception is also made for transfers made in satisfaction of a debt that was incurred in the ordinary course of business or financial affairs of the debtor and transferee where the transfer itself was made either in the ordinary course of business or financial affairs of the debtor and transferee or was made according to ordinary business terms. An exception is also recognized for transfers creating a security interest in property to secure payment of an enabling loan where the security interest was perfected within 30 days after the debtor received possession of such property.

The bankruptcy trustee can also avoid an unauthorized postpetition transfer of property of the estate unless the transfer was for equivalent value and without notice. Avoidance actions by the trustee can be maintained against the transferee or other party for whose benefit the transfer was made.

REVIEW QUESTIONS

1. Why does a creditor in a no-asset case not need to file a proof of claim?
2. What is the risk to an unsecured creditor of not filing a proof of claim in an asset case? What is the risk to an undersecured creditor? What is the risk to a fully secured creditor?

3. Explain the procedure the trustee must follow in objecting to a creditor's claim, including the timeframe for making the objection.
4. What is the right to setoff outside of bankruptcy? How might a right to setoff reduce or eliminate a creditor's claim in bankruptcy? How might it actually strengthen a creditor's claim against certain property of the debtor's?
5. Under what circumstances is a creditor entitled to recover postpetition interest on its claim?
6. What do we mean by property in which the debtor holds a legal or equitable interest for purposes of determining what is or is not property of the estate? Give examples.
7. Describe the turnover powers of the bankruptcy trustee. Who might be a custodian of the debtor's property?
8. What is the strong-arm clause of the Code? What do we mean when we say that the bankruptcy trustee is a supercreditor of the debtor? What does that mean for unsecured claims to the debtor's property? For secured claims not properly perfected prepetition?
9. What are the four elements of a preferential transfer? How is insolvency determined for purposes of a preferential transfer? Who will be considered an insider for purposes of a preferential transfer claim and what difference does it make?
10. Explain the exchange for reasonably equivalent value in connection with fraudulent transfers. What is fair market value?

WORDS AND PHRASES TO REMEMBER

abstinence for comity	initial transferee
adversary proceeding	insider
antecedent debt	insolvent
avoidance powers	laches
balance sheet test	legal interest (in property)
(for insolvency)	mandatory abstinence
bifurcated claim	objection to claim
claims bar date	ordinary course of business or
claims docket	financial affairs
contemporaneous exchange for	oversecured claim
equivalent value	partially secured claim
core proceeding	party in interest
custodian	postpetition interest
deemed allowed	preferential transfer
distribution of the estate	prepetition interest
enabling loan exception	presumption of insolvency
equitable interest (in property)	priority claim
equitable estoppel	proof of claim
equitable subordination	promissory estoppel
equity test (for insolvency)	property of the estate
fair market value	purchase money security interest
fresh start	reasonably equivalent value
fully secured claim	reclamation right

secured claim
setoff
strong-arm clause
strip down
supercreditor

turnover powers
unmatured interest
unsecured claim
waiver
write down

TO LEARN MORE: A number of TLM activities to accompany this chapter are accessible on the companion web site for this textbook at http://aspenlawschool.com/books/Parsons_Debt4e.

The Chapter 7 Consumer Bankruptcy Case: Liquidation, Distribution, and the Debtor's Right to Retain Possession of Property

In this chapter we consider how the bankruptcy trustee liquidates the property of the estate in an asset case in order to generate a distribution of proceeds to the unsecured creditors. We will learn the order of priority in which creditors receive that distribution. There are a number of ways that Chapter 7 debtors can manage to retain possession of property in which the debtor has granted a creditor a security interest notwithstanding the bankruptcy case and we will examine those in depth.

KEY CONCEPTS

- In liquidating property of the estate the bankruptcy trustee may sell property by public or private sale, may obtain authority to sell encumbered property free and clear of liens, or may abandon property of no value to the estate
- Allowed claims against the estate are paid by the trustee in an established order of priority
- The debtor may be permitted by the court to reaffirm a debt in bankruptcy rather than discharge it or may redeem collateralized property by paying the value of the collateral to the secured creditor
- In some districts the debtor may be able to retain collateral by ride through without court approval or to strip down the balance owed on a secured claim to the collateral's then current value

A. ▶ Liquidating Property of the Estate

In a Chapter 7 asset case, the trustee will liquidate nonexempt property of the estate and distribute the proceeds in an order of priority we consider in Section B, below. First, we consider how the trustee liquidates the property of the estate. Of course, if the trustee determines the filing to be a no-asset case and files a no-asset report, that means there is no nonexempt property to liquidate and the case will be closed quickly.

1. Abandonment of Property of the Estate

If a timely objection to the debtor's claimed Schedule C exemptions is not made, that property is **deemed abandoned** by the trustee and the estate has no further interest in it. Abandonment is the formal relinquishment of property of the estate by the trustee.

Pursuant to §554 and Bankruptcy Rule 6007, the trustee can abandon any other property of the estate that is

- of inconsequential value to the estate, or
- burdensome to the estate.

Abandonment of Secured Property

Abandonment The formal relinquishment of property of the estate by the trustee.

The most common example of **abandonment** arises in connection with property in which a security interest has been granted as security for debt. If the security interest is perfected and the trustee cannot avoid it as considered in the last chapter, the secured claim will be allowed under §502. And if there is no equity for the estate in the collateralized property (i.e., the amount of the allowed claim equals or exceeds the value of the collateral), that property is of no value to the estate and will be abandoned to the creditor. If the value of the collateral abandoned to the creditor is equal to the full amount of the allowed claim, the claim of the creditor is fully satisfied by that abandonment. On the other hand, if the value of the abandoned collateral is insufficient to satisfy the full amount of the allowed claim (i.e., the creditor is undersecured or partially secured), the creditor's claim is bifurcated pursuant to §506(a)(1). The trustee will abandon the collateral to the undersecured creditor in full satisfaction of the secured portion of the creditor's bifurcated claim. But the creditor still has a general unsecured claim (as opposed to a priority unsecured claim) for the balance owed in excess of the value of the collateral.

If there is equity for the estate in the collateralized property (i.e., the creditor is oversecured; the value of the property exceeds the amount owed), the trustee will usually not abandon the property to the creditor. Instead, the trustee will sell the property himself, pay the creditor the full amount of his allowed secured claim from the proceeds (which may sometimes include post-petition interest and fees per §506(b) as we saw in Chapter Ten), and will then include the excess proceeds of the sale in the property of the estate available to other creditors.

Abandonment of Other Property of the Estate

Any property of the estate may be abandoned by the trustee whether it is collateral for a security interest or not, if the trustee concludes that it is burdensome to the estate.

EXAMPLE

Assume the property of the estate includes a claim the debtor has made against a local clothes cleaning business alleging that the cleaner lost a shirt worth $20. The cleaner denies liability on the claim and refuses to settle. The trustee may conclude that it will cost the estate more to litigate that small claim than it is worth and abandon the claim as burdensome to the estate.

Procedure for Abandonment

Section 554 abandonment is governed by the Code's "after notice and a hearing" procedure, which means the trustee must give notice to all parties in interest of his intent to abandon and a hearing is conducted only if an objection is made within 14 days following notice (the "after notice and a hearing" procedure of the Code is discussed in Chapter Six, Section G, and see Illustration 6-i).

Recall that in Chapter Eight, Section B, we learned that an individual Chapter 7 debtor must file Form 108 Statement of Intention for Individuals Filing Under Chapter 7 with regard to property in which a security interest has been granted, indicating whether he or she will surrender that property to the secured creditor or seek to retain it. If the debtor does indicate an intent to surrender collateralized property, the secured creditor must still await the trustee's decision as to whether to abandon that property as having no benefit to the estate or to assert an interest in it for the benefit of the estate as by avoiding the creditor's security interest or lien as we considered in the last chapter or by contending that there is **equity** in the property for the estate (i.e., it is worth more than the amount owed the creditor). And even if the trustee does decide to abandon, the secured creditor must also take appropriate action to have the automatic stay of §362 lifted per the procedures discussed in Chapter Nine, Section F.

As a practical matter, the trustee will make the decision as to whether to abandon collateralized property or challenge the lien at or shortly after the first meeting of creditors. By then the individual Chapter 7 debtor will have filed his statement of intent with regard to the property so his intent to surrender the property or not will be known to all parties. Some secured creditors will await the decision of the debtor and trustee regarding surrender and abandonment before filing a motion to lift stay while others will file a motion to lift stay as soon as the petition is filed and they receive notice of the case.

EXAMPLE

The bankruptcy trustee in Marta Carlson's case has identified a few items to be abandoned, some collateral for debt, some not (see Document 34 in the case file). Note how the notice of hearing that accompanies the notice of intent to abandon contemplates a hearing only if an objection is filed within 14 days following the filing of the notice of intent to abandon.

2. Sale of Property Free and Clear of Liens

When a creditor has a perfected security interest in some property of the estate but there is still equity for the estate in that property (i.e., the creditor is over-secured), the trustee may seek a **sale of property free and clear of liens**, pursuant to §363(f) and Bankruptcy Rule 6004(c). The property is sold and the security interest then attaches to the proceeds of sale up to the amount of the secured claim. Permission for a sale free and clear of liens is obtained by filing a motion subject to the "after notice and a hearing" procedure.

EXAMPLE

Recall from the Assignment Memorandum in Appendix A that Marta Carlson has two mortgages on her home, one in favor of Capital Savings Bank (CSB) with a balance of $142,500 and one in favor of Dreams Come True Finance Company (DCT) with a balance of $37,500. In her Schedule C (Document 8 in the Carlson case file) Marta has claimed a homestead exemption of $11,825 in the home. No objection has been filed to these secured claims or to Marta's claimed exemption amount. The home has appraised for $255,000 and the trustee has filed a motion for permission to sell the home free and clear of liens (Document 35 in the Carlson case file). If permission is granted by the court and the sale brings the full $255,000, the proceeds will be distributed as follows: the realtor's 6 percent fee ($15,300) as an administrative expense; $142,500 to pay off CSB; $37,500 to pay off DCT; $11,825 to Marta for her exemption; and the balance of $47,875 will go to the estate. But by order of the court, that sale will extinguish the liens of CSB and DCT in the property, as well as Marta's exemption in it. It is a sale free and clear of liens.

Pursuant to §524(e), discharge of a debt in bankruptcy does not also discharge any nonbankruptcy party who might be liable on the debt, such as a guarantor. Thus, when property of the state is sold free and clear of liens, that sale will have no effect on the remaining liability of any nonbankruptcy guarantor of the debt. See, e.g., *In re Applewood Chair Co.*, 203 F.3d 914 (5th Cir. 2000) (sale of property pursuant to bankruptcy court's order approving sale has no effect on guarantor's liability).

EXAMPLE

Assume Marta's brother, who is not in bankruptcy, had guaranteed the debt Marta owed to DCT secured by her home and the guaranty agreement contained an "other indebtedness clause" covering not only the secured indebtedness on the home but the second unsecured obligation as well. Assume Marta had a second unsecured obligation to DCT at the time of her bankruptcy in the amount of $7,000. Marta will discharge that second unsecured debt to DCT in her Chapter 7 bankruptcy case but per §524(e) her brother will not be relieved of his obligation as guarantor on that debt. DCT may still pursue him on that obligation to collect. Assume further that following her discharge in bankruptcy (in which Marta will have discharged all her then existing obligations to DCT) Marta borrows $5,000 from DCT to purchase a used car. Again, per §524(e), Marta's brother will be liable as a guarantor on the $5,000. Nothing that happened in Marta's bankruptcy case, including the sale of the home that secured one of her debts to DCT that her brother had guaranteed, will discharge his obligations to DCT on the guaranty. State guaranty law may have something to say about his continuing obligation as guarantor, but bankruptcy law will not.

Section 363(k) preserves the right of a creditor secured in the property to be sold in the bankruptcy case to bid on the property at the sale and in doing so to receive credit against the purchase price for the amount of its unpaid claim, a practice known as **credit-bidding** (or **bidding in**).

EXAMPLE

Credit-bidding (or bidding in) The practice of a creditor secured in property foreclosed on or repossessed bidding the amount owed at the foreclosure/repossession sale and receiving credit for the amount owed against the sales price.

> If Marta's trustee receives permission to sell her home free and clear of liens, either or both of the secured creditors have the right under §363(k) to bid at the sale. If CSB chose to credit-bid at the sale and the amount of its winning bid was $151,050 (an amount equal to the $142,500 balance owed to it, plus $8,550 representing the 6 percent realtor's fee), CSB would only have to pay cash in the amount of $8,550 because the amount CSB is owed is credited against the bid amount.

The Code gives a secured creditor this right as a means of assuring that the property is not sold at a price less than what is owed to the creditor. After all, the sale is going to extinguish the creditor's security interest in the property.

EXAMPLE

> If a third party appears at the sale and bids in at the $255,000 appraised value, then neither CSB nor DCT is likely to bid—the sale will bring enough to satisfy both their claims. But what if the high bid by a third party at the sale is only $125,000? If that bid is accepted, CSB is going to receive only a portion of what it is owed and DCT, whose lien on the property is junior to CSB's, will get nothing. So both CSB and DCT will likely be ready to credit-bid as necessary to protect their respective interests.

3. Sale of Other Property of the Estate

Section 363(b)(1) and Bankruptcy Rule 6004(a) permit the trustee to notice his intent to sell other property of the estate using the "after notice and a hearing" procedure. No hearing will be conducted unless an objection is filed not less than five days before the date of the proposed sale per Bankruptcy Rule 6004(b). If an objection is filed, it becomes a contested matter and a hearing will be conducted.

The sale of property of the estate can be accomplished by public or private sale. Bankruptcy Rule 2002(c) requires that the notice of a proposed sale, use, or lease of property include:

- the time and place of a public sale;
- the terms and conditions of a private sale; and
- the time fixed for filing objections.

A public sale is by **auction**, properly advertised and usually conducted by an auctioneer retained as a professional, pursuant to §327 and Bankruptcy Rule 2014. If the order authorizing the hiring of the professional person did not specifically approve the manner of his compensation, the trustee must obtain court approval for that compensation before paying the professional from the assets of the estate.

P-H 11-a: Look at the motion for permission to hire a real estate appraiser filed by the trustee in Marta Carlson's case (Document 29 in the Carlson case file) and the order approving that hiring (Document 30 in the Carlson case file). Based on the order approving the motion, can the trustee go ahead and pay the appraiser's fee without further court action?

Section 363 and other sections of the Code deal with other ways the bankruptcy trustee may need to utilize property of the estate, some of which include:

- operating an ongoing business of the debtor;
- leasing estate property; or
- pledging property of the estate as collateral to raise cash or obtain credit.

These options can be utilized in a Chapter 7 consumer case though they arise more routinely in business reorganization cases.

EXAMPLE

If Marta Carlson owned a rental house that the trustee planned to liquidate but a realtor advised waiting six months until the area real estate market improved, the trustee might choose to lease the house for that six months.

P-H 11-b: Bankruptcy trustees are increasingly using the Internet to liquidate property of the estate. The trustee's notice of intent to sell will have to disclose that means of public sale. To learn more, go to www.marketassetsforsale.com/index.cfm and note the kinds of property being offered for sale by bankruptcy trustees around the country. See if you can find a property listing for a case pending in the federal district where you plan to practice.

4. Continuing Operation of a Business Debtor as Part of the Liquidation

When an individual debtor who owns an ongoing business as a proprietor files for Chapter 7 liquidation, the bankruptcy trustee may determine that it is in the best interest of the creditors to continue operating the business for a certain period of time postpetition in order to maximize the value of the property of the estate and the ultimate payout to creditors. It is unusual for this to occur in a Chapter 7 liquidation but §721 of the Code authorizes the trustee to seek court permission to operate the business postpetition for this purpose.

When a liquidating business does continue to operate postpetition under Chapter 7, there are a number of operational motions that will need to be made to deal with matters such as using property of the estate postpetition, which could put that property at risk of deterioration or loss; using property—such as cash—postpetition in which a security interest has been given to one or more creditors; obtaining postpetition financing, thus increasing the total indebtedness of the business; and so on. These operational concerns are similar to those that routinely arise in a Chapter 11 reorganization in which the business debtor is not liquidating but continuing to operate under the postpetition protection of the Code. We will not consider these operational concerns until we look at Chapter 11 in detail.

B. ▶ Distribution of the Estate to Creditors and the Order of Priority

Administrative expenses Actual and necessary expenses incurred postpetition to preserve the property of the estate and to administer the case.

Once the bankruptcy trustee has liquidated the other property of the estate, including the settlement of allowed secured claims as discussed in the last section, the proceeds will be distributed to pay **administrative expenses** of the case and claims of creditors in a certain order of priority. Administrative expenses are defined in §503(b)(1)(A) as "the actual, necessary costs and expenses of preserving the estate, including wages, salaries, or commissions for services rendered after the commencement of the case" and include:

- the trustee's fee;
- fees of professionals hired by the trustee;
- certain taxes incurred by the estate;
- "actual and necessary" costs and expenses of preserving the estate, which can include wages, salaries, and commissions incurred after the commencement of the case; and
- "actual and necessary" expenses incurred by creditors who file an involuntary petition in the case or who, with court permission, recover property for the estate transferred or concealed by the debtor.

Section 507 priority claims Unsecured claims entitled to a priority in payment over general unsecured claims under §507.

Section 507 establishes an order of priority for various administrative expenses and other claims. Section 726 then mandates the particular order in which distributions on claims not secured by property of the estate are to be made by the Chapter 7 trustee. Secured claims have the highest priority to the extent of the value of the collateral per §506(a)(1). See also *Hartford Underwriters Ins. Co. v. Union Planters Bank*, 530 U.S. 1, 5 (2000), and *United Sav. Assn. of Tex. v. Timbers of Inwood Forest Associates, Ltd.*, 484 U.S. 365, 378-379 (1988). **Section 507 priority claims** (see itemization of such claims in Part B of Illustration 11-a) have the next priority followed by the claims of general unsecured creditors, and then certain miscellaneous claims. Illustration 11-a summarizes the order of distribution mandated by the Code.

Each class of claims listed in Illustration 11-a is entitled to be paid in full before the next class in priority receives anything. For example, if all property of the estate is subject to a properly perfected security interest, no other claims will be paid. If all the available uncollateralized assets are exhausted in paying §507 priority claims, general unsecured creditors will receive nothing. If all available assets are exhausted paying priority and general unsecured claims that were timely filed, general unsecured claims not timely filed will receive nothing.

Within a particular class of claims not involving secured claims, the distribution will be *pro rata*.

Illustration 11-a: ORDER OF PRIORITY FOR PAYMENT OF CREDITOR CLAIMS

A. Secured claims

1) Allowed fully secured or oversecured claims are satisfied entirely out of the secured property up to its value, per §§506(a) and (b)

2) Allowed partially secured (undersecured) claims are satisfied out of the secured property up to the value of the secured property and the deficiency is treated as a general unsecured claim, per §506(a)(1)

B. Section 507 priority claims

1) The bankruptcy trustee's fee and expenses attributable to payment of domestic support obligations of the debtor, per §507(a)(1)(C)

2) Domestic support obligations of the debtor, per §507(a)(1)(A)

3) Administrative expenses authorized by §503(b), per §507(a)(2)

4) Allowed §502(f) unsecured claims arising in an involuntary case between the time the petition is filed and the time the trustee is appointed (called the **gap period**), per §507(a)(3)

5) Claims for employee's wages, salaries, or commissions and some benefits earned within 180 days prior to the filing of the petition not to exceed $10,000 per claim, per §507(a)(4)

6) Claims for unpaid contributions to any employee benefit plan arising from services rendered within 180 days prior to filing of the petition not to exceed $10,000 per claim, per §507(a)(5)

7) Certain farmer and fishermen claims up to $10,000 each, per §507(a)(6)

8) Prepetition deposits of money for the lease or purchase of real property or consumer services up to $2,225 per claimant, per §507(a)(7)

9) Various tax claims including income and property taxes assessed at varying times before the petition was filed, per §507(a)(8)

10) Certain claims arising out of federal depository insurance, per §507(a)(9)

11) Personal injury or wrongful death claims arising out of DUI, per §507(a)(10)

C. General (i.e., nonpriority) unsecured claims, per §726, including deficiency claims of partially secured creditors whose collateral was insufficient to cover the entire debt per §506(a)(1)

1) General unsecured claims timely filed, per §726(a)(2)

2) General unsecured claims untimely filed, per §726(a)(3)

D. Claims for fines, penalties, forfeiture, or punitive damages other than compensation for actual pecuniary loss, per §726(a)(4)

E. Interest at the legal rate on priority and general unsecured claims, per §726(a)(5)

F. Remaining surplus, if any, returned to debtor, per §726(a)(6)

EXAMPLE

> Assume the trustee has $10,000 available to distribute to general unsecured claimants. But there is a total of $100,000 owed to all the creditors in that classification. The distribution will be *pro rata*, with each unsecured creditor receiving ten cents on the dollar for its claim regardless of whether its claim was larger or smaller than others in the same class. The holder of a $10 claim will receive $1 and the holder of a $100 claim will receive $10.

A general unsecured debt that is not dischargeable (nondischargeable claims are discussed in the next chapter) still participates in the distribution under §726.

EXAMPLE

> The educational loans that Marta Carlson owes to Columbiana Federal Savings & Loan, in the amount of $5,000, and Capital City Bank in the amount of $10,000, are unsecured nonpriority but nondischargeable debts. Even though Marta cannot discharge those debts and will remain liable for them, those creditors will participate with other general unsecured creditors in any distribution to that class of creditors.

P-H 11-c: Assume the following expenses and claims are present in an estate and that the trustee has funds to pay most but not all of them: unpaid federal income taxes for the past two tax years; unpaid unsecured bills from the debtor's suppliers; unpaid child support; unpaid Social Security withholdings on the debtor's employees; an unpaid student loan; and travel expenses of the bankruptcy trustee. Arrange the list in the order of priority mandated by §726.

Subordination The treatment of a claim in a less favored way than others either by consent of the creditor or by court order where the creditor has either filed a claim after the claims bar date or has acted dishonestly.

Section 510 provides for the **subordination** of a claim to others of equal rank under certain circumstances. Section 510(a) provides that a prepetition **subordination agreement** will be enforced in bankruptcy if it is otherwise valid under nonbankruptcy law. A subordination agreement is most commonly used where the owner of property needs to refinance property on which there is an existing mortgage. The new lender will not agree to loan funds unless the existing mortgagee agrees to take a second or junior position to the new lender, who will take a first mortgage position in the property after it makes the loan.

Why would the original mortgagee voluntarily agree to subordinate its mortgage position to the new lender? Well, if the owner/mortgagor is in arrears on its payments to the original mortgagee, the original mortgagee might have a lot to gain by allowing the refinancing even though it gives up its priority position (i.e., the deficiencies get paid off and future payments are more likely due to the refinancing). Often, to induce the original mortgagee to agree to the subordination, the pot is sweetened in some way (e.g., by increasing the interest rate on that obligation).

Alternatively, the court may order involuntary **equitable subordination** of all or part of a creditor's claim pursuant to §510(c). Equitable subordination is most typically exercised where the creditor has engaged in inequitable or dishonest conduct that resulted in unfair advantage to him or prejudice to other creditors.

EXAMPLE

> Assume a creditor holding a senior security interest in property of the estate misrepresents the value of its secured claim to a creditor holding a junior secured position in the same property. If that misrepresentation causes the junior creditor to be prejudiced in some way, the court may order the senior claim equitably subordinated to the junior claim.

C. The Debtor's Right to Retain Property in a Chapter 7 Case: Reaffirmation, Redemption, Exemption, Ride Through, and Lien Stripping

1. The Reaffirmation Agreement

Recall that the individual Chapter 7 debtor must file a statement of intent with regard to his or her secured property. One option is to surrender the collateral to the secured creditor and discharge the balance of the debt. Another option, provided by §524(c) of the Code, permits the Chapter 7 debtor to agree with the creditor to retain the collateral and reaffirm the secured debt. The typical reaffirmation situation involves a debt secured by the debtor's home or vehicle and the debtor does not want to lose possession of that collateralized property.

EXAMPLE

> Assume that a Chapter 7 debtor owns a car that is worth $6,000 and on which he owes $6,500 to the creditor who holds a security interest in it. There is no equity in the car for the debtor to exempt and no equity for the estate either since the creditor's secured claim against the car exceeds its value. The trustee will abandon this property for the estate. The debtor could allow the creditor to repossess the car and discharge the $6,500 debt he owes the creditor. But the debtor needs a car, and he would like to keep this one. The debtor may therefore enter into a reaffirmation agreement with the creditor in which he agrees to remain legally liable for the debt following his discharge in bankruptcy.

Debtors may choose to reaffirm a dischargeable debt in the full amount owed and according to the original terms of the obligation. Or they may negotiate with the creditor to reaffirm only a portion of the balance owed or on more favorable terms (e.g., lower monthly payments, longer amortization, or lower interest rate).

It is important that the individual debtor seeking to reaffirm a secured debt indicate that on his or her statement of intent since, as we saw in Chapter Nine, Section F, if an individual debtor fails to list collateralized personal property in his or her statement of intent, the automatic stay is lifted as to such property per §362(h)(1). If the debtor's original statement of intent indicated the intent to surrender the collateralized property and the debtor later decides to reaffirm the debt and keep the property, the statement of intent must be amended.

Reaffirmation agreement The bankruptcy debtor's agreement with a creditor, subject to court approval, to pay the creditor a debt that could have been discharged in bankruptcy.

Section 524(c) requires that in order to reaffirm a debt the debtor and creditor must enter into a written **reaffirmation agreement**. The bankruptcy court must review the agreement and has the power to disapprove it. The reaffirmation agreement will provide that the debtor will remain liable and pay all or a portion of the money owed, even though the debt would otherwise be discharged in the bankruptcy. In return, the creditor promises that it will not repossess or take back the automobile or other property so long as the debtor continues to pay the debt.

EXAMPLE

Recall that Marta Carlson owes Shears Department Store $900 and the debt is secured by her washer and dryer, worth only $600 together. Marta would like to reaffirm her debt to Shears in order to keep her washer and dryer. Although Marta claimed an exemption in the washer and dryer in her Schedule C (Document 8 in the Carlson case file) under §522(d)(3), that alone will not entitle her to keep possession of that property since she has given Shears a security interest in the washer and dryer that she cannot avoid in bankruptcy. So Marta decides to enter a reaffirmation agreement with Shears, promising to pay the entire indebtedness in exchange for Shears allowing her to keep the washer and dryer. That reaffirmation agreement is set out in Illustration 11-b (and Document 36 in the Carlson case file). The court still has to approve the agreement.

The procedure for obtaining the approval of a reaffirmation agreement set out in §524(c) and Bankruptcy Rule 4008 is quite complex. Section 524(c) says that the reaffirmation agreement must be entered into before the discharge is entered by the court in order to be valid and that the agreement must be signed by the parties and filed with the court. But Bankruptcy Rule 4008 supplements the timeframe of the statute by requiring that the signed reaffirmation agreement be filed with the court within 60 days following the 341 meeting. Section 524(k) requires that a reaffirmation agreement contain an extensive set of disclosures. Among other things, the agreement must advise the debtor of the amount of the debt being reaffirmed and how it is calculated, and that reaffirmation means that the debtor's personal liability for that debt will not be discharged in the bankruptcy.

The disclosures also require the debtor to sign and file a statement of his or her current income and expenses that shows that the balance of income available to after paying living expenses is sufficient to pay the reaffirmed debt. If the balance is not enough to pay the debt to be reaffirmed, there is a **presumption of undue hardship**, and the court may decide not to approve the reaffirmation agreement. If the court is inclined to disapprove the reaffirmation agreement because the presumption of hardship is present or for any other reason, the court must conduct a hearing and give the debtor and creditor an opportunity to overcome the presumption of undue hardship or to otherwise convince the court that the agreement is in the debtor's best interest.

Illustration 11-b: REAFFIRMATION AGREEMENT BETWEEN MARTA CARLSON AND SHEARS DEPARTMENT STORE

Form 2400A (12/15)

Check one.
☐ **Presumption of Undue Hardship**
☑ **No Presumption of Undue Hardship**
See Debtor's Statement in Support of Reaffirmation,
Part II below, to determine which box to check.

UNITED STATES BANKRUPTCY COURT

District of Minnesota

In re _____Marta Rinaldi Carlson_____,   Case No. 10-7-XXXX
                    Debtor

                                              Chapter 7

REAFFIRMATION DOCUMENTS

Name of Creditor: Shears Department Store

☐ Check this box if Creditor is a Credit Union

PART I. REAFFIRMATION AGREEMENT

Reaffirming a debt is a serious financial decision. Before entering into this Reaffirmation Agreement, you must review the important disclosures, instructions, and definitions found in Part V of this form.

A. Brief description of the original agreement being reaffirmed: Appliance purchase agreement

For example, auto loan

B. ***AMOUNT REAFFIRMED***: $_____900.00_____

   The Amount Reaffirmed is the entire amount that you are agreeing to pay. This may include unpaid principal, interest, and fees and costs (if any) arising on or before ___07/07/2016___, which is the date of the Disclosure Statement portion of this form (Part V).

   See the definition of "Amount Reaffirmed" in Part V, Section C below.

C. The ***ANNUAL PERCENTAGE RATE*** applicable to the Amount Reaffirmed is ___6.5000___ %.

   See definition of "Annual Percentage Rate" in Part V, Section C below.

   This is a *(check one)* ☑ Fixed rate   ☐ Variable rate

If the loan has a variable rate, the future interest rate may increase or decrease from the Annual Percentage Rate disclosed here.

D. Reaffirmation Agreement Repayment Terms *(check and complete one)*:

☑ $ __45.00__ per month for __20__ months starting on __08/01/2016__ .

☐   Describe repayment terms, including whether future payment amount(s) may be different from the initial payment amount.

E. Describe the collateral, if any, securing the debt:

Description: Shears washer and dryer
Current Market Value $ 600.00

F. Did the debt that is being reaffirmed arise from the purchase of the collateral described above?

☑ Yes. What was the purchase price for the collateral? $ 1,200.00

☐ No.   What was the amount of the original loan? $

G. Specify the changes made by this Reaffirmation Agreement to the most recent credit terms on the reaffirmed debt and any related agreement:

	Terms as of the Date of Bankruptcy	Terms After Reaffirmation
Balance due *(including fees and costs)*	$ 900.00	$ 900.00
Annual Percentage Rate	6.5000 %	6.5000 %
Monthly Payment	$ 45.00	$ 45.00

H. ☐ Check this box if the creditor is agreeing to provide you with additional future credit in connection with this Reaffirmation Agreement. Describe the credit limit, the Annual Percentage Rate that applies to future credit and any other terms on future purchases and advances using such credit:

PART II.   DEBTOR'S STATEMENT IN SUPPORT OF REAFFIRMATION AGREEMENT

A. Were you represented by an attorney during the course of negotiating this agreement?

Check one.   ☐ Yes   ☑ No

B. Is the creditor a credit union?

Check one.   ☐ Yes   ☑ No

C. If your answer to EITHER question A. or B. above is "No," complete 1. and 2. below.

    1.   Your present monthly income and expenses are:

        a. Monthly income from all sources after payroll deductions
        (take-home pay plus any other income) $ 3,888.00

        b. Monthly expenses (including all reaffirmed debts except
        this one) $ 3,550.00

        c. Amount available to pay this reaffirmed debt (subtract b. from a.) $ 338.00

        d. Amount of monthly payment required for this reaffirmed debt $ 45.00

        *If the monthly payment on this reaffirmed debt (line d.) **is greater than** the amount you have available to pay this reaffirmed debt (line c.), you must check the box at the top of page one that says "Presumption of Undue Hardship." Otherwise, you must check the box at the top of page one that says "No Presumption of Undue Hardship."*

    2.   You believe that this reaffirmation agreement will not impose an undue hardship on you or your dependents because:

        Check one of the two statements below, if applicable:

        ☑   You can afford to make the payments on the reaffirmed debt because your monthly income is greater than your monthly expenses even after you include in your expenses the monthly payments on all debts you are reaffirming, including this one.

        ☐   You can afford to make the payments on the reaffirmed debt even though your monthly income is less than your monthly expenses after you include in your expenses the monthly payments on all debts you are reaffirming, including this one, because:

        Use an additional page if needed for a full explanation.

D. If your answers to BOTH questions A. and B. above were "Yes," check the following statement, if applicable:

        ☐   You believe this Reaffirmation Agreement is in your financial interest and you can afford to make the payments on the reaffirmed debt.

Also, check the box at the top of page one that says "No Presumption of Undue Hardship."

PART III.   CERTIFICATION BY DEBTOR(S) AND SIGNATURES OF PARTIES

I hereby certify that:

(1)   I agree to reaffirm the debt described above.

(2)   Before signing this Reaffirmation Agreement, I read the terms disclosed in this Reaffirmation Agreement (Part I) and the Disclosure Statement, Instructions and Definitions included in Part V below;

(3)   The Debtor's Statement in Support of Reaffirmation Agreement (Part II above) is true and complete;

(4)   I am entering into this agreement voluntarily and am fully informed of my rights and responsibilities; and

(5)   I have received a copy of this completed and signed Reaffirmation Documents form.

SIGNATURE(S) (If this is a joint Reaffirmation Agreement, both debtors must sign.):

Date ___07/07/2016___   Signature ___/s/ Marta Rinaldi Carlson___
                                                    Debtor

Date _____   Signature _____
                                           Joint Debtor, if any

Reaffirmation Agreement Terms Accepted by Creditor:

Creditor ___Shears Department Store___   ___411 Woodlands Place, Roseville, MN. 55113___
                    Print Name   *Address*

___Martha Adkins, Regional Credit Mgr.___   ___/s/ Martha Adkins___   ___07/07/2016___
    Print Name of Representative   *Signature*   *Date*

PART IV.   CERTIFICATION BY DEBTOR'S ATTORNEY (IF ANY)

To be filed only if the attorney represented the debtor during the course of negotiating this agreement.

I hereby certify that: (1) this agreement represents a fully informed and voluntary agreement by the debtor; (2) this agreement does not impose an undue hardship on the debtor or any dependent of the debtor; and (3) I have fully advised the debtor of the legal effect and consequences of this agreement and any default under this agreement.

☐   A presumption of undue hardship has been established with respect to this agreement. In my opinion, however, the debtor is able to make the required payment.

Check box, if the presumption of undue hardship box is checked on page 1 and the creditor is not a Credit Union.

Date _____   Signature of Debtor's Attorney _____

                            Print Name of Debtor's Attorney _____

As curious as it may sound, it is not unusual for the debtor's attorney to abstain from representing the debtor in connection with a reaffirmation agreement. This is so because if the attorney chooses to represent the client in connection with the agreement, the attorney must certify in writing that the attorney advised the debtor of the legal effect and consequences of the agreement, including a default under the agreement. The attorney must also certify that the debtor was fully informed and voluntarily entered into the agreement and that reaffirmation of the debt will not create an undue hardship for the debtor or the debtor's dependents. It is no small thing for a debtor with a history of severe financial problems to reaffirm a debt that he could discharge in bankruptcy. There may be disagreements between the debtor and the attorney regarding whether it is in the best interests of the debtor to reaffirm. Even if it appears to be at the time, it may not turn out well if the debtor reaffirms, then defaults later and can no longer discharge the debt. The attorney who has certified that reaffirmation will not create an undue hardship for the debtor could face malpractice charges if it does.

If the debtor who enters the reaffirmation agreement and files it with the court is not represented by counsel in connection with the agreement, a hearing on the proposed reaffirmation agreement will be held, and the bankruptcy judge will decide whether to approve the agreement. However, in many districts, if the debtor is represented by an attorney in connection with the reaffirmation agreement, and the presumption of undue hardship is not present, the reaffirmation agreement may become effective without court approval. Even if the debtor is represented by counsel, if the presumption of hardship arises in connection with the proposed reaffirmation agreement, a hearing will be held and the judge will decide whether the reaffirmation is in the best interests of the debtor.

P-H 11-d: Look at Marta Carlson's reaffirmation agreement with Shears again. Did the presumption of hardship arise in connection with that agreement? Did her attorney represent her in connection with the reaffirmation agreement? Check the local rules of the bankruptcy court in your federal district. If Marta was a debtor in that court, would a hearing be needed on her reaffirmation agreement?

Some bankruptcy judges are reluctant to allow debtors to reaffirm debts absent a showing of real need.

EXAMPLE

> If a debtor wanted to reaffirm debts on three different vehicles when he needed only one or two for personal and business purposes, many judges would limit the debtor to the one or two vehicles needed. And reaffirming a debt on that recreational Jet Ski or bass boat? The debtor and the lawyer recommending reaffirmation of such debts should be prepared to be lectured by these judges on the inadvisability of coming out of bankruptcy with such debts.

Sometimes debtors see reaffirmation as a way to salvage their credit history or their relationship with a particular creditor, even though it is not essential to do so and the obligation is unsecured by any property of the debtor.

EXAMPLE

A debtor may have a long-standing credit account with a local or national department store where the debtor likes to shop. Even though the balance owed the department store is unsecured and the debtor could discharge it, the debtor chooses to reaffirm the debt just to keep the credit account with the department store in good standing.

Of course, a debtor who has received a discharge may repay any debt voluntarily whether or not a reaffirmation agreement exists and this does sometimes occur.

EXAMPLE

A debtor may formally discharge a debt arising from a family loan but still feel a moral obligation to pay the debt. The creditor whose debt has been discharged will not be able to sue or otherwise take action to collect that debt; it has been discharged.

A debt that is reaffirmed in bankruptcy, even if it was otherwise dischargeable in the bankruptcy proceeding, is valid and enforceable following the debtor's discharge.

P-H 11-e: What risk is presented by a Chapter 7 debtor who receives a discharge agreeing to reaffirm a debt that could have been discharged in the proceeding? How soon can the debtor file another Chapter 7 case?

---

2. The Right to Redeem Personal Property

Another option available to the Chapter 7 debtor to retain secured property arises from §722, which allows an individual consumer debtor in Chapter 7 the right to **redeem** tangible personal property (not realty) intended primarily for personal, family, or household use (consumer property) from a lien securing such property where the property has been claimed as exempt by the debtor under §522 or has been abandoned by the trustee under §554.

This **right of redemption** is exercised by the debtor paying the amount of the allowed secured claim to the creditor. Recall that §506(a)(1) provides that a secured creditor's claim is only a secured claim up to the value of the collateral. The creditor's claim is unsecured (and probably dischargeable) as to all amounts owed over that value. The value of personal property securing a claim for purposes of determining the secured portion of the claim is defined in §506(a)(2), added by BAPCPA, as the replacement value of the goods on the date the petition is filed without deduction for sale or marketing costs. For goods acquired for personal, family, or household purposes (consumer goods), such as those subject to §722 redemption, replacement value means *the price a retail merchant would charge for property of that kind, given its age and condition.*

EXAMPLE

Marta Carlson owes Shears Department Store $900 and the debt is secured by her washer and dryer, which she values at only $600 together. In her Schedule C (Document 8 in the Carlson file), she has exempted the total $600 value of the washer and dryer from any claim of the trustee. The trustee has abandoned this property for the estate because there is no equity in it since both Shears' lien and Marta's claimed exemption in the property are superior to his claim (see Document 34 in the Carlson case file). It is tangible consumer property within the meaning of §722 since it is property used for personal, family, or household purposes. As an alternative to reaffirming her debt to Shears, Marta could seek to redeem this property from the lien by paying the debtor "the full amount of the allowed secured claim."

Of course, Shears may not agree that Marta's valuation of the washer and dryer at $600 is accurate. Shears may contend that the value she has placed on the washer and dryer is the liquidation value of the property but not the replacement value, which is the required valuation under §506(a)(2). The court may have to decide the valuation dispute. But if the court does find the replacement value of the washer and dryer to be less than the full amount of the debt ($900) and Marta can exempt that value in her Schedule C, then Marta can redeem the property by paying Shears that replacement value. The balance owed to Shears becomes an unsecured claim that can be discharged if there are insufficient nonexempt assets in the estate available to pay it. Of course, Marta will have to come up with the $600 or other dollar amount determined to be the replacement value of the collateral to pay Shears and that may be difficult for someone already in bankruptcy.

BEFORE THERE WAS BAPCPA THERE WAS *RASH*

Prior to BAPCPA's addition of the new §506(a)(2), the Supreme Court had adopted the replacement value rule in *Associates Commercial Corp. v. Rash*, 520 U.S. 953 (1997). *Rash* rejected the debtor's argument that the present value of the collateral under §506(a)(1) should be the liquidation or foreclosure value of the property, which is essentially what the property would sell for in a rushed, even emergency, situation, likely to produce far less than its retail value. So the replacement value of the washer and dryer that Marta Carlson might like to redeem from the lien of Shears would be not what a consumer would sell it for in a garage sale, and not what a consumer who needed quick cash would sell it for to a neighbor or friend, and not what it would be sold for wholesale, but instead what a retail merchant would ask for it given its present age and condition.

In actual practice, the codification of the *Rash* replacement value rule in §506(a)(2) is highly beneficial to the secured creditor and has made it more difficult for Chapter 7 consumer debtors to utilize the §722 right of redemption in consumer property. Some debtors can exempt enough cash to redeem an automobile of modest value. Some are able to borrow from relatives or friends. And there are lenders who specialize in making bankruptcy redemption loans, particularly for vehicles. See, for example, www.globeacceptance.com/ and www.722redemption.com/ and http://rightsizefunding.com/. Such companies typically offer redemption loans for periods of two to six years at high interest rates commensurate with high risk of lending to a borrower whose credit rating is wrecked. Of course, those lenders will take a security interest in the redeemed vehicle safe in the knowledge that the debtor who just received a discharge in Chapter 7 has severely limited options for seeking further bankruptcy relief during the term of the redemption loan. But all things considered, it is now the rare case in which a right to redeem is exercised by the debtor. Instead, debtors will opt if possible for a debt reaffirmation for property they would like to keep.

As with the intent to reaffirm a debt, the individual debtor's intent to redeem collateralized property must be noted on his statement of intent.

3. Debtor's Right to Avoid Liens Impairing an Exemption

In Chapter Eight, Section B, we learned that an individual debtor can exempt certain real and personal property from the bankruptcy trustee. In most situations, however, an exemption cannot prevail over a perfected security interest of a creditor in the property sought to be exempted. Thus, exemptions are mostly claimed in unsecured property. However, §522(f)(1)(A) of the Code empowers the individual debtor to avoid a **judicial lien** on property to the extent that the lien impairs an exemption the debtor would otherwise have in the property. Judicial liens are defined by §101(36) as liens obtained by judgment, levy sequestration, or other legal or equitable process and include prejudgment remedies such as prejudgment attachment as well as the postjudgment execution remedies we considered in Chapter Five.

EXAMPLE

Assume that an individual Chapter 7 debtor owns a residence worth $200,000 that is encumbered by a mortgage in favor of the bank in the amount of $150,000. If the jurisdiction allows the debtor a $30,000 homestead exemption, then there would be only $20,000 in nonexempt equity in the residence. If another creditor of the debtor had taken a prepetition final judgment against the debtor in the amount of $40,000 and filed a judgment lien against the debtor's residence in that amount, once the debtor files in Chapter 7 he can avoid $20,000 of that judgment lien on the residence, the amount by which the judgment lien impairs his exemption based on the value of the property.

Section 522(f)(1)(A) prohibits a judicial lien resulting from a domestic support obligation (child support, alimony, or maintenance recoverable by a spouse, former spouse, or child of the debtor) from being avoided by the debtor.

Section 522(f)(1)(B) also authorizes the debtor to avoid a nonpossessory, non-purchase money security interest in certain household items and tools of the trade to the extent the lien impairs an exemption (to be illustrated later in connection with the Chapter 13 case). Moreover, §§522(g), (h), and (i) authorize the Chapter 7 debtor to initiate turnover, avoidance, or setoff actions if the trustee refuses to do so in order to assert an exemption in property recovered.

As with the intent to reaffirm a debt and the right to redeem, the individual debtor's intent to avoid one of these liens in order to claim an exemption must be noted on the statement of intent. Per Bankruptcy Rule 4003(d), the proceeding to avoid judicial lien impairing an exemption is brought by motion, not adversary proceeding. Rule 4003(d) also recognizes the creditor's right to object to such a motion by challenging the exemption claimed by the debtor.

4. The Ride Through Option

Before BAPCPA, many federal circuits recognized an additional option for a Chapter 7 debtor to retain secured property following discharge. A typical scenario was this: The debtor owns a car worth $10,000 and owes $10,500 on it to the creditor holding a security interest in the car to secure payment of the debt. The bankruptcy trustee has abandoned the car since there is no equity in it for the estate. The debtor is not in default on the payments to the creditor and the creditor has not repossessed and does not want to do so. The debtor needs the car but is unable to redeem it. So the debtor asks the court for permission to reaffirm the debt. The court refuses the application to reaffirm, finding that it is not in the best interests of the debtor (perhaps he has another car and the judge concludes that all he needs is one car, or perhaps he is reaffirming other debts that the court believes will put him at high risk of default on the car note if it is reaffirmed as well so the presumption of hardship is not overcome). What happens now? The debtor is in no position to redeem the vehicle. Must the debtor surrender the car he would like to keep, is paying for, and that the creditor would like him to keep and continue paying for?

Prior to 2005, five federal circuits recognized that a debtor had an additional option. With the acquiescence (rather than formal agreement, as in a reaffirmation) of the creditor, the debtor could allow the debt to the secured creditor to be formally discharged but keep the car and continue making the payments. This option was called a **ride through** or **pay through** (or, if the collateral was a vehicle, a **drive through** or **pay and ride**) by practitioners because the debtor's possession of the collateral was riding through and beyond the bankruptcy case. This arrangement was quite favorable to the debtor because the underlying debt to the creditor was discharged. If at any time before the debtor completed the payments due the creditor the debtor no longer wanted the car (or if it were wrecked), debtor could simply surrender it back to the creditor and have no further liability on the debt—it had been discharged. Of course, the lien on the property survived the bankruptcy case even if the underlying debt did not; if there were a postdischarge default by the debtor, the creditor could repossess. However, with ride through, that was the creditor's sole remedy upon default; there was no right to sue for a deficiency judgment since the underlying debt had been discharged in the bankruptcy proceeding.

Ride through (or **pay through** or **pay and ride**) Informal arrangement whereby a Chapter 7 debtor retains possession of collateral through and beyond the bankruptcy case by continuing to make payments to the secured creditor.

THE RATIONALE FOR THE RIDE THROUGH PRE-BAPCPA

The rationale for the ride through option was that §521(a)(2), the Code provision requiring the individual debtor to file his statement of intent regarding property, was not limited by that section to the options of surrender, exemption, redemption, or reaffirmation. Though the ride through option was not expressly granted in the Code, it was a long-recognized practice and, because it was not prohibited by §521(a)(2), was allowed in these circuits for debts secured by both personal property (e.g., vehicles) and real property (e.g., home mortgages). Although debtors often sought reaffirmation before choosing the ride through option, doing so was not a necessary prerequisite to ride through. Read *In re Waller*, 394 B.R. 111 (Bankr. D.S.C. 2008), highlighted below, for a discussion of the pre-BAPCPA ride through practice and a list of the federal circuits that recognized it.

In 2005 BAPCPA added §362(h)(1), stating that, in an individual bankruptcy case, the automatic stay terminates with respect to personal property securing an obligation of the debtor and such property is no longer deemed property of the estate if the debtor does not file a statement of intention in a timely manner or does not perform the stated intention (surrender, redemption, or reaffirmation) by the statutory deadline—30 days after the petition is filed or before the first meeting of creditors, whichever is earliest per §521(a)(2).

Section 362(h)(1) has been interpreted as eliminating the ride through option concerning collateralized personal property leaving the debtor the options of reaffirming the debt or redeeming the property if possible under §722 in order to retain possession. See, e.g., *In re Jones*, 591 F.3d 308, 311-312 (4th Cir. 2010). But what about debts secured by the debtor's real property? Is ride through still an option for a Chapter 7 consumer debtor to retain possession of his or her mortgaged home?

HIGHLIGHTED CASE ●

IN RE WALLER
394 B.R. 111 (Bankr. D.S.C. 2008)

OPINION: DUNCAN, Bankruptcy Judge.

This matter is before the Court on two Reaffirmation Agreements between Steven Alan Waller, Monique Tonia Waller ("Debtors"), and South Carolina State Housing Finance and Development Authority ("Creditor"), which were filed by Creditor on August 21, 2008. The Court has jurisdiction over this matter under 28 U.S.C. §§157(b) and 1334(a) and (b). Pursuant to Fed. R. Civ. P. 52 made applicable to this proceeding by Fed. R. Bankr. P. 7052, the Court makes the following Findings of Fact and Conclusions of Law:

FINDINGS OF FACT

1. On May 21, 2008, Debtors jointly filed a voluntary petition under chapter 7 of the United States Bankruptcy Code.

2. Debtors owe Creditor on two notes secured by a first and second mortgage on their residence located at 630 Greenwich Drive, Aiken, South Carolina.

3. Debtors' Schedule I, Current Income of Individual Debtors, reflected that Mr. Waller is employed while Mrs. Waller is unemployed, with the potential for seasonal employment. According to Schedule I, Debtors' monthly take home pay is $2,163.00. Debtors' Schedule J, Current Expenditures of Individual Debtors, lists their average monthly expenses as $3,382.00. Together Schedules I and J demonstrate a deficit in the Debtors' monthly net income of $1,219.00.

4. Creditor, through counsel, filed two reaffirmation agreements between Debtors and Creditor on August 21, 2008. The first agreement sought to reaffirm Debtor's first mortgage in the amount of $105,372.93. The second agreement sought to reaffirm Debtors' second mortgage in the amount of $2,009.99. Both agreements were filed on an outdated form requiring a hearing for proper determination of the whether the reaffirmation agreements created a presumption of undue hardship on the Debtors. The matter was set for a hearing on September 16, 2008.

5. Debtors, through counsel, filed two amended reaffirmation agreements using the current official form on September 11, 2008. The amended reaffirmation agreements indicated a presumption of undue hardship. The amended reaffirmation agreements differed from Debtors' schedules I and J indicating that Mrs. Waller is now employed.

6. A hearing was held on September 16, 2008. Debtors stated at the hearing that they were current on their payments with Creditor on both mortgages and were current at the time of filing for chapter 7 relief. Creditor did not appear at the hearing.

7. Additionally, Debtors indicated that Mrs. Waller was now working part-time in the golf shop at Woodside Plantation Country Club and occasionally serves as a substitute teacher in the local school district.

8. Debtors' income from teaching is sporadic, unreliable, and insufficient to rebut the presumption of undue hardship.

9. Reaffirmation of debts secured by real estate, when the debtors are current with the payments, is not in Debtors' best interest.

CONCLUSIONS OF LAW

An individual chapter 7 debtor receives a discharge from all debts save those specified in 11 U.S.C. §727(a), those within the scope of §523(a), and those subject to an agreement for reaffirmation pursuant to §524(c). The discharge of debt is the foundation for a debtor's fresh start. Exceptions to discharge are narrowly construed. . . . The Bankruptcy Abuse Prevention and Consumer Protection Act of 2005 ("2005 Amendments") amended the Bankruptcy Code and extensively revised those provisions relating to reaffirmation of a debt. The Bankruptcy Code has always permitted only those reaffirmation agreements that do not impose an undue hardship on the debtor or a dependant of the debtor. A separate provision of the 2005 Amendments deals with a debtor's options for property used as collateral for debts.

Debtors who are current with payments on debts secured by real property are not limited to the options of surrender, reaffirmation, or redemption found in

§521(a)(2), but may also choose to continue with the payments and retain possession of the property. This option, commonly known as "ride-through," was embraced by a number of federal judicial circuits, prior to the enactment of the 2005 Amendments and applied to both real property and personal property. . . .

This Court recently confirmed the viability of the "ride-through" option for debts secured by real property. *In re Wilson*, 372 B.R. 816, 820 (Bankr. D.S.C. 2007). In *Wilson*, the Court noted the changes made to the Bankruptcy Code by the 2005 Amendments and stated that the changes apply only to debts secured by personal property. *Id.* at 818. The relevant language of §521(a)(2)(C) provides that "nothing in subparagraphs (A) and (B) of this paragraph shall alter the debtor's or the trustee's rights with regard to such property under this title, except as provided in section 362(h)." 11 U.S.C. §521(a)(2)(C). Section 362(h) employs limiting language that terminates the automatic stay as to *personal property* when the debtor fails to state an intention to surrender, reaffirm, redeem, or does not perform the stated intention within a prescribed period. *Wilson* at 818, *citing,* 11 U.S.C. §362(h). The plain language of §§521(a)(2)(C) and 362(h) "limits their application to a debtor's rights with regard to personal property." *Id.*

It is presumed that Congress enacts legislation "with knowledge of the law, including knowledge of the interpretation that courts have given to an existing statute." . . . For this reason, the right of debtors to continue current payments on debts secured by real property and retain the collateral established in *Belanger* remains intact. *Id., See also, Wilson* at 819. Congress curtailed the ride-through option for debts secured by personal property but not with regard to debts secured by real property. . . . "Limiting a debtor to the three choices of surrender, redeem, or reaffirm for real property would impair the debtor's ability to obtain a fresh start, which is one of the primary purposes of bankruptcy law." . . .

In this case, the Reaffirmation Agreements are not in Debtors' best interest because Debtors can retain the real property without reaffirming the debt. For this reason, approval of the Reaffirmation Agreements is denied.

POST-CASE FOLLOW-UP

Be sure you understand why formal reaffirmation of debt in bankruptcy favors the creditor: The debtor is contractually back on the hook for a debt it could have discharged and may not meet the qualifications for filing a second bankruptcy case for some time. Reaffirmation poses real risks for debtors. On the other hand, ride through, where it is still an option for debts secured by real property, favors the debtor. The underlying debt is discharged in the bankruptcy case and only the creditor's security interest in the property and the debtor's obligation to remain current in her payments and comply with any other contractual obligations related to the collateralized property, such as maintaining insurance on it, remain. Ride through poses real risks for the creditor and the creditor's consent to it is not required. Of course, a creditor unhappy with the ride through will watch for any postdischarge breach by the debtor in order to foreclose on the property. See, e.g., *In re Wilson*, 372 B.R.

816 (Bankr. D.S.C. 2007). Not all courts agree that ride through is permitted on debt secured by realty post-BAPCPA. Those courts rejecting the idea are typically those that rejected ride through as an option for both personal and real property pre-BAPCPA. See, e.g., *In re Linderman*, 435 B.R. 715 (Bankr. M.D. Fla 2009) (pre-BAPCPA, the Eleventh Circuit construed the language of §521(a)(2)(A) to prohibit ride through regardless of the property involved, personal or real; BAPCPA merely confirms that ride through is not available for debts secured by personal property—it does not impliedly make it available for debts secured by real property).

In re Waller: Real Life Applications

1. The law firm you work for represents consumer debtors in Chapter 7 cases who have the following debts. The jurisdiction follows *In re Waller*. Which of those debts might qualify for ride through treatment?

    a. Debtor owns a boat in which Bank holds a security interest to secure a loan with a balance of $5,000. Debtor is current on the payments to Bank.

    b. Debtor owns a boat in which Bank holds a security interest to secure a loan with a balance of $5,000. Debtor is in arrears on the payments to Bank.

    c. Debtor owns a home that is mortgaged to Bank to secure a loan with a balance of $50,000. Debtor is current on the payments to Bank.

    d. Debtor owns a home that is mortgaged to Bank to secure a loan with a balance of $50,000. Debtor is not current on the payments to Bank.

2. For each of the debts listed in Question 1 that do not qualify for ride through treatment, what alternatives might your supervising attorney recommend to the debtors to enable them to keep the collateral through the bankruptcy case?

P-H 11-f: Determine if the courts of your federal district or circuit allow post-BAPCPA ride throughs for debts secured by mortgages on the debtor's real property.

But has BAPCPA totally eliminated the ride through option for debts secured by personal property? Maybe not. Some courts are construing §521(a)(2) and new §362(h) together to mean that what the debtor must do is *request* the court to reaffirm the debt secured by personal property. If a timely notice of intent to reaffirm is filed and a timely application to reaffirm the debt is requested but not approved, those courts are saying the requirements of §362(h) are complied with and the debtor may still choose ride through with the acquiescence of the creditor. Called a **back door ride through** by practitioners, the procedure is being recognized in those federal districts where pre-BAPCPA ride through was recognized. See, e.g., *In re Chim*, 381 B.R. 191 (Bankr. D. Md. 2008), and *In re Moustafi*, 371 B.R. 434 (Bankr. D. Ariz. 2007).

In bankruptcy courts where ride through is still deemed an option, debtors will often state their intent to pursue that option on their statement of intent even though the official form does not contain that option. And in many bankruptcy courts where the controlling law says ride through is not a viable option, it has been and still is done informally between debtor and acquiescing creditor. After all, who is to complain if the creditor does not? The trustee has abandoned the property as having no value to the estate. For the same reason no other creditor will care, having no interest in the collateral. The debtor is delighted to keep the property and the creditor is delighted to keep receiving payments. All's well that ends well?

IPSO FACTO CLAUSES IN BANKRUPTCY

An *ipso facto* (Latin for "by the act itself") clause in a contract is one that makes the act of one party becoming insolvent, acknowledging insolvency, filing a bankruptcy case or state law receivership proceeding (or having one filed involuntarily for the party), or making an assignment for the benefit of creditors an act of default by that party. Many states disallow *ipso facto* clauses in consumer contracts. Section 365(e) of the Code together with §541(c) effectively make *ipso facto* clauses in executory contracts ineffective postpetition. However, BAPCPA added §521(d), which makes *ipso facto* clauses in contracts enforceable when

- an individual debtor fails to comply with §362(h)(1)(A) by filing the required statement of intent as to a debt secured by personal property within the time allowed by §521(a)(2); or
- an individual debtor in Chapter 7 fails to reaffirm or redeem a debt secured by personal property within 45 days following the 341 meeting as required by §521(a)(6).

In other words, even if the debtor is not otherwise in default under the contract with the secured creditor, if the debtor fails to reference the debt on his statement of intent and then to reaffirm or redeem in a timely manner and if the contract contains an *ipso facto* clause, these sections authorize the creditor to utilize that clause to declare the debtor in default, have the automatic stay lifted (it is automatically terminated by §362(h)(1) for failure to file the timely statement of intent regarding debts secured by personal property), and repossess the collateral. The continuing postpetition effect of an *ipso facto* clause in a contract where the debtor rides through on a debt secured by personal property is unclear. See, e.g., *In re Wilson*, 372 B.R. 816 (Bankr. D.S.C. 2007) (creditor unhappy with proposed ride through on debt secured by real property could not declare default by debtor by reason of *ipso facto* clause in mortgage since §521(d) allowing enforcement of such clauses refers to them in agreements covered by §521(a)(6) and §362(h), which address only personal property liens. Section 521(d) only preserves the enforceability of *ipso facto* clauses in personal property loans).

P-H 11-g: Determine if your state allows *ipso facto* clauses in consumer contracts.

---

5. The Lien Stripping Option

Recall the bifurcation of an undersecured claim mandated by §506(a) pursuant to which the value of a secured claim is stripped down to the value of the collateral and bifurcated between its secured and unsecured portion. Section 506(d) provides that a lien is void "[t]o the extent that [it] secures a claim against the debtor that is not an allowed secured claim." How do those two provisions work in the following scenario? The creditor is owed $250,000 and the debt is secured by a perfected mortgage on the debtor's residence. The residence is valued at only $200,000, so the creditor is undersecured. The Chapter 7 trustee decides there is no equity in the residence for the estate and abandons it to the debtor.

Lien stripping (or **strip down** or **write down**) A proposal made on an undersecured claim to reduce the balance due on a secured claim to the value of the collateral property so that the Chapter 7 debtor can maintain possession of the collateral via redemption or pay through based on the reduced value.

Can debtor use §§506(a) and (d) to ask the court to reduce the lien of the creditor on the residence to the $200,000 value? In this **lien stripping** scenario, note that the debtor is not simply asking for what §506(a) already does—bifurcate the bankruptcy claim of this undersecured creditor into a secured claim for $200,000 and an unsecured claim for $50,000. The debtor is asking that the secured position of creditor in the residence be limited to the $200,000 present value and the obligation declared unsecured for all amounts above $200,000. The creditor is left with an unsecured claim for the amounts owed in excess of the value of the property. This is an effort to **strip down** or **write down** the lien not just for purposes of treating the creditor's claim in a distribution but to actually void the balance of the secured debt.

EXAMPLE

Assume a Chapter 7 debtor owns a home secured by a mortgage having a balance of $200,000 but the home is only valued at $180,000 when the petition is filed. We know that this creditor is undersecured and that pursuant to §506(a) its claim is bifurcated: Its claim is secured in the amount of $180,000 and unsecured in the amount of $20,000. If the debtor can succeed in having the court void the mortgage on the $20,000, consider the consequences. The trustee may abandon the residence as having no equity for the estate. The creditor may then effectively redeem the property by paying the secured creditor only the $180,000 secured value and discharge the unsecured $20,000 balance even though §722 limits the right of redemption to certain personal property. Or the debtor may remain current on the payments to the creditor and retain possession via a pay through, paying only the $180,000 secured balance as it comes due. If at any time property values go back up, say to $220,000, the debtor could then sell the residence for the increased value, pay off the $180,000 secured balance, and retain the balance of the proceeds. In other words, any increase in equity after the mortgage is stripped down accrues to the debtor.

Sections 506(a) and (d) could certainly be read as allowing if not intending the kind of strip down illustrated in the last example. But in *Dewsnup v. Timm*, 502 U.S. 410 (1997), the Supreme Court, while recognizing some ambiguity in the meaning of the provisions, held it was not allowable. The reasoning is that

Congress intended the two sections to be read independently of each other and that the claim bifurcation feature of §506(a) does not mandate or authorize an otherwise legitimate security interest to be otherwise stripped down or voided under §506(d), regardless of the value of the collateral. To read §§506(a) and (d) to allow stripping of the lien down to the value of the collateral would run afoul of the basic notion imbedded in §502 that properly perfected liens pass through bankruptcy unaffected. The Court adopted the view that

> the words "allowed secured claim" in §506(d) need not be read as an indivisible term of art defined by reference to §506(a), which by its terms is not a definitional provision. Rather, the words should be read term-by-term to refer to any claim that is, first, allowed, and, second, secured. Because there is no question that the claim at issue here has been "allowed" pursuant to §502 of the Code and is secured by a lien with recourse to the underlying collateral, it does not come within the scope of §506(d), which voids only liens corresponding to claims that have not been allowed and secured. This reading of §506(d) . . . gives the provision the simple and sensible function of voiding a lien whenever a claim secured by the lien itself has not been allowed.

Id. at 515-516.

The Court was bothered by the idea that the debtor would benefit by any post–strip down increase in the value of the collateral and decided to preserve the pre-Code rule reflected in §502 that liens on real property should pass through bankruptcy unaffected unless a Code provision expressly said otherwise.

Notwithstanding the decision in *Dewsnup*, some courts continued to allow a lien strip under §§506(a) and (d) in the following scenario: Creditor #1 is owed $250,000 and the debt is secured by a mortgage on debtor's residence. The residence is valued at only $240,000, meaning that Creditor #1 is undersecured. *Dewsnup* says that the lien of Creditor #1 cannot be stripped down to the value of the collateral. However, Creditor #2 is owed $30,000 by our debtor and that debt is secured by a second mortgage on the debtor's residence, junior to the mortgage held by Creditor #1. Both mortgages are properly perfected but if the residence is sold, all the proceeds of sale will go to Creditor #1 and none to Creditor #2. Creditor #2 is not just undersecured, it is wholly underwater—there is no equity in the collateral for Creditor #2. In that scenario, some courts said *Dewsnup* did not apply to protect Creditor #2 and that the debtor could not just strip down, but **strip off** the second mortgage since the secured claim of Creditor #2 was valueless. The rationale was that under §506(a) the junior lien was completely unsecured and could thus be stripped off under §506(d). *Dewsnup* was distinguishable because, unlike the undersecured creditor in *Dewsnup* (and Creditor #1 in our example), Creditor #2 arguably had no allowed secured claim at all. Thus, the lien-preserving imperative of §502 the Supreme Court held preeminent in *Dewsnup* was irrelevant as to Creditor #2.

Following *Dewsnup*, disallowing the strip down of a partially undersecured lien, the lower courts were divided on whether §§506(a) and (d) nonetheless allowed the complete strip off of a wholly undersecured lien. That division was put to rest when the Supreme Court ruled in *Bank of America, N.A. v. Caulkett*, 135 S. Ct. 1995 (2015), that *Dewsnup*'s interpretation of §506(d) disallowed the strip off of a wholly underwater second lien as well.

Dewsnup's construction of "secured claim" resolves the question presented here. *Dewsnup* construed the term "secured claim" in §506(d) to include any claim "secured by a lien and . . . fully allowed pursuant to §502." Id., at 417. Because the Bank's claims here are both secured by liens and allowed under §502, they cannot be voided under the definition given to the term "allowed secured claim" by *Dewsnup* . . . . The debtors do not ask us to overrule *Dewsnup*, but instead request that we limit that decision to partially—as opposed to wholly—underwater liens. We decline to adopt this distinction.

Id. at 1999-2000.

P-H 11-h: Assume the law office you work for represents a Chapter 7 debtor who owns a home that has been valued at $200,000. Bank #1 holds the first mortgage on the home and the balance owed Bank #1 is $210,000. Bank #2 holds the second mortgage on the home and the balance owed Bank #2 is $25,000. Client is current on the loan from Bank #1 but three payments behind on the loan from Bank #2. Only the lack of equity in the home prevented Bank #2 from instituting a prepetition foreclosure action. Nonetheless, Client is desperate to retain possession of the home if possible.

a. Will the fact that Client can claim a homestead exemption of $100,000 be of any use in this case?
b. What will the bankruptcy trustee probably do with the home as far as the bankruptcy estate is concerned?
c. After *Dewsnup* and *Caulkett*, what options does Client have to retain possession of the home postdischarge?
d. If a search of the public records revealed that Bank #1 in the above scenario did not properly perfect its mortgage interest in the home prepetition, how does that change your analysis? Does the homestead exemption matter now? What is the bankruptcy trustee likely to do now? Have the options Client has to retain possession postdischarge changed?

CHAPTER SUMMARY

The bankruptcy trustee can abandon property of the estate that is of inconsequential value or burdensome to the estate on notice and a hearing. Property that is burdened by a perfected security interest but in which there is equity for the estate may be sold by the trustee free and clear of all liens with prior permission of the court. The trustee will liquidate other property of the estate by selling it at public or private sale.

Assets of the estate are distributed by the trustee to satisfy administrative expenses of the case and creditor claims in a mandated order of priority. Allowed secured claims have the highest priority as to their respective collateralized property of the estate up to the value of such collateral. Section 507 priority claims such as trustee's fees, domestic support obligations, and administrative expenses enjoy the next priority followed by general unsecured claims. Each priority class of claims is entitled to be fully satisfied before a lower class receives anything. Within a particular priority classification, distribution is *pro rata* among unsecured creditors in the class. A court may order equitable subordination of a creditor's claim upon a finding of inequitable or dishonest conduct that resulted in unfair advantage to the creditor or prejudice to other creditors.

A Chapter 7 debtor may attempt to retain collateralized property that the trustee has abandoned on behalf of the estate by consensual reaffirmation of the debt. Reaffirmation agreements must be approved by the bankruptcy judge. If an attorney advises the debtor in connection with negotiation of a reaffirmation agreement, the attorney must certify that the debtor was fully informed and voluntarily entered into the agreement and that reaffirmation will not create an undue hardship for the debtor or the debtor's dependents.

A Chapter 7 debtor may also redeem consumer personal property that serves as collateral where the debtor could otherwise exempt or the estate has abandoned by paying the creditor the full amount of its secured claim with the collateral valued at its replacement value. The debtor may also avoid judicial liens on property to the extent they impair an exemption in such property.

In some districts the debtor may have a ride through option regarding debt secured by realty. In some districts there may also be a back door ride through option for debts secured by personalty where a reaffirmation of such debt is proposed but refused by the court. In many districts, an informal ride through is practiced by debtors and creditors without formal court sanction, enabling debtors to maintain possession of collateral.

The practice of stripping down an undersecured claim to the value of the collateral securing it or stripping off a fully undersecured claim is no longer available in a Chapter 7 case.

REVIEW QUESTIONS

1. Who surrenders property of the estate? Who abandons property of the estate?
2. Explain why a bankruptcy trustee would not sell property free and clear of liens if the lien holder was oversecured in the property.
3. What is an "administrative expense"? Name three kinds of administrative expenses.
4. Which claim has a higher priority when assets of a bankruptcy estate are distributed: a claim for a debtor's child support obligation or a claim by the debtor's credit card company?
5. In what sense do secured claims have a higher priority than administrative expenses?
6. What is a prepetition subordination agreement? Is it enforceable in a bankruptcy case? What is an *ipso facto* clause in a prepetition agreement? Is it enforceable in a bankruptcy case?
7. Explain the difference between a reaffirmation agreement and the debtor's right to redeem property.
8. Why might a debtor's lawyer refuse to represent the debtor in negotiating a reaffirmation agreement?
9. Is the ride through option still available to a Chapter 7 debtor as to a collateralized vehicle? Is it still available to a Chapter 7 debtor as to the debtor's mortgaged home?

10. Can a wholly undersecured second mortgage on the debtor's home be stripped off and the underlying obligation be treated as an unsecured claim? What Supreme Court case tells you the answer?

WORDS AND PHRASES TO REMEMBER

abandonment (of property)	pay through
administrative expense	presumption of undue hardship
auction	priority claim
back door ride through	reaffirmation agreement
bidding in	redeem
credit-bidding	ride through
deemed abandoned	right of redemption
drive through	sale of property free and clear of liens
equitable subordination	statement of intent
equity	strip down
gap period	strip off
judicial lien	subordination (agreement)
lien stripping	write down
pay and ride	

TO LEARN MORE: A number of TLM activities to accompany this chapter are accessible on the companion web site for this textbook at http://aspenlawschool.com/books/Parsons_Debt4e/.

Chapter Twelve:

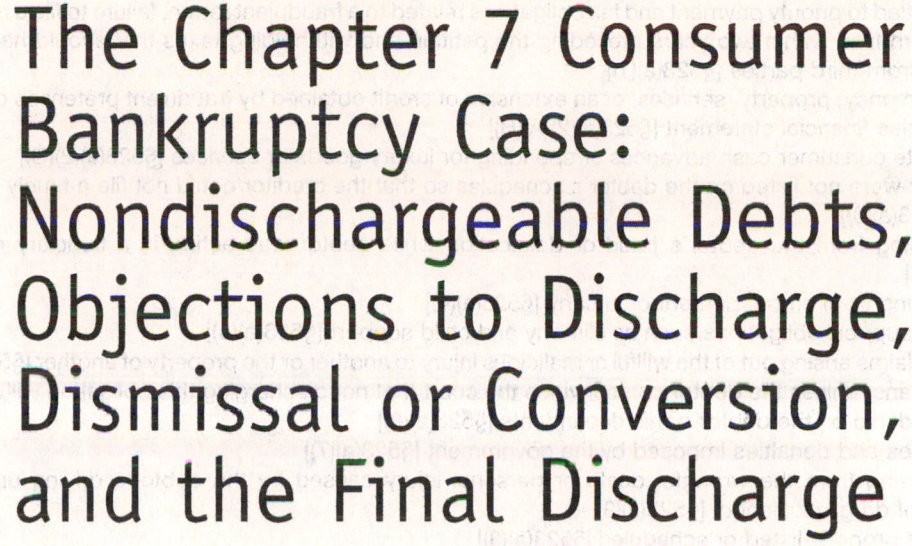

The Chapter 7 Consumer Bankruptcy Case: Nondischargeable Debts, Objections to Discharge, Dismissal or Conversion, and the Final Discharge

Not all debts that a Chapter 7 debtor has can be discharged in a bankruptcy case. In this chapter we will identify those nondischargeable debts. The Code also sets out grounds to deny a Chapter 7 debtor any discharge at all or to involuntarily dismiss the case; we will cover those important topics in this chapter too. A Chapter 7 debtor whose case is dismissed or who has a debt declared nondischargeable may choose to convert her case to one under Chapter 13 and we will consider that option here. Finally, we will examine the procedures for winding up a Chapter 7 case, including the trustee's final accounting to the court and the entry of discharge.

KEY CONCEPTS

- A number of debts are nondischargeable in a Chapter 7 bankruptcy
- A number of grounds exist to deny a Chapter 7 debtor any discharge at all or to involuntarily dismiss the case
- A debtor who originally filed under Chapter 7 can convert her case to one under Chapter 11, 12, or 13 if she qualifies as a debtor under the alternative chapter
- The final discharge granted an individual Chapter 7 debtor forever protects him from liability for discharged debts and includes a prohibition on discrimination

A. Nondischargeable Debts

Discharge Permanent relief from certain debts pursuant to order of the bankruptcy court.

The primary purpose of filing a Chapter 7 petition from the individual debtor's standpoint is to receive a **discharge** of his or her debts. Once discharged, the debtor can never again be held legally responsible for the discharged debts. This is part of the fresh start public policy behind Chapter 7. The concept of a discharge is irrelevant to an entity debtor like a corporation or partnership since the effect of

Illustration 12-a: DEBTS THAT CANNOT BE DISCHARGED IN A CHAPTER 7 BANKRUPTCY

- Taxes entitled to priority payment and tax obligations related to a fraudulent return, failure to file a return, or a late return filed within two years preceding the petition and withholding taxes that should have been collected from third parties [§523(a)(1)]
- Debts for money, property, services, or an extension of credit obtained by fraudulent pretenses or by the use of a false financial statement [§523(a)(2)(A)(B)]
- Last-minute consumer cash advances or spending for luxury goods or services [§523(a)(2)(C)]
- Debts that were not listed on the debtor's schedules so that the creditor could not file a timely proof of claim [§523(a)(3)]
- Debts arising from the debtor's fraud or defalcation while debtor was acting in a fiduciary capacity [§523(a)(4)]
- Debts arising from embezzlement or larceny [§523(a)(4)]
- Domestic support obligations such as alimony and child support [§523(a)(5)]
- Debts or claims arising out of the willful or malicious injury to another or the property of another [§523(a)(6)]
- Student loans, unless the debtor can convince the court that not discharging this obligation will work an undue hardship on the debtor or his dependents [§523(a)(8)]
- Certain fines and penalties imposed by the government [§523(a)(7)]
- Claims arising from the wrongful death or personal injury caused by the debtor's driving under the influence of drugs or alcohol [§523(a)(9)]
- Claims not properly listed or scheduled [§523(a)(3)]

liquidation for such a debtor is that it will simply cease doing business. However, not all debts can be discharged in a Chapter 7 bankruptcy by the individual debtor. Section 523(a) identifies the **nondischargeable debts** and the primary ones are summarized in Illustration 12-a.

Bankruptcy Rule 4007 provides that any creditor can file a complaint objecting to the discharge of a particular debt or the debtor himself can file a complaint to determine the dischargeability of a particular debt. Any such action is an adversary proceeding, not just a contested matter (see Illustration 6-j). Rule 4007 also provides that any complaint contesting the dischargeability of a debt must be filed within 60 days following the first meeting of creditors though the time can be extended by motion. Rule 2002(f) requires the bankruptcy court clerk, or some other person as the court may direct, to provide notice by mail of the time fixed for filing a complaint objecting to discharge of a particular debt.

1. Taxes [§523(a)(1)]

Generally speaking, income taxes (whether federal, state, local) for which the tax return was due during the three years preceding the filing of the petition cannot be discharged, nor can property taxes due within the year preceding the filing of the petition. Regardless of the tax year in question, a debtor filing a fraudulent tax return or filing with willful intent to evade taxes cannot discharge that obligation. Even for tax obligations that are dischargeable, properly recorded tax liens that attached to debtor's property prior to filing the petition survive the bankruptcy. Employer debtors who fail to withhold payroll "trust fund" taxes including FICA, Social Security (employee's share), or Medicare premiums from employee paychecks as required by law also cannot discharge those obligations. The same is true with most state sales taxes.

2. Debts Obtained by False Pretenses, False Representation, False Financial Statement, or Actual Fraud [§523(a)(2)(A)(B)]

Debts created by fraudulent means are nondischargeable.

EXAMPLE

Assume that a person obtains a loan from a bank to buy a car. She borrows $10,000 from the bank but has a kickback deal with the seller of the car to get $2,000 of the purchase price back after the deal is done. When the buyer of the car files for bankruptcy the bank can argue that the debt to it should be declared nondischargeable under §523(a) due to the fraudulent pretenses used to obtain the loan. Or assume that a real estate developer obtains a million dollar loan from a bank to develop a subdivision. Developer presents a personal financial statement to the bank as part of the loan application but materially exaggerates the value of his assets in order to qualify for the loan. If developer files bankruptcy, the entire debt may be declared nondischargeable due to the fraudulent financial statement if the lender reasonably relied on the false statement.

Does the statutory "obtained by . . . actual fraud" language of §523(a)(2)(A) mean that the debt had to be originally obtained by fraud in order to be declared nondischargeable? Can that language be fairly applied to a debt involving no fraud in its inception but subject later to a fraudulent scheme to avoid repayment?

HIGHLIGHTED CASE

HUSKY INT'L ELECTRONICS, INC. V. RITZ
136 S. Ct. 445 (2016)

[Chrysalis incurred a debt of $164,000 to Husky. Ritz, Chrysalis' director and then-part-owner, drained Chrysalis of assets available to pay the debt by transferring large sums to other entities Ritz controlled. Husky sued Ritz, who then filed for Chapter 7 bankruptcy. Husky filed a complaint in Ritz' bankruptcy case, asserting "actual fraud" under the Code's discharge exceptions, 11 U.S.C. 523(a)(2)(A). The district court held that Ritz was personally liable under state law but that the debt was not "obtained by . . . actual fraud" and could be discharged. The Fifth Circuit affirmed.]

OPINION by JUSTICE SOTOMAYOR:

The Bankruptcy Code prohibits debtors from discharging debts "obtained by . . . false pretenses, a false representation, or actual fraud." 11 U. S. C. §523(a)(2)(A). The Fifth Circuit held that a debt is "obtained by . . . actual fraud" only if the debtor's fraud involves a false representation to a creditor. That ruling deepened an existing split among the Circuits over whether "actual fraud" requires a false representation or whether it encompasses other traditional forms of fraud that can be accomplished without a false representation, such as a fraudulent conveyance of property made to evade payment to creditors. We granted certiorari to resolve that split and now reverse . . . The term "actual fraud" in §523(a)(2)(A) encompasses forms of fraud, like fraudulent conveyance schemes, that can be effected without a false representation.

Before 1978, the Bankruptcy Code prohibited debtors from discharging debts obtained by "false pretenses or false representations." §35(a)(2) (1976 ed.). In the Bankruptcy Reform Act of 1978, Congress added "actual fraud" to that list. The prohibition now reads: "A discharge under [Chapters 7, 11, 12, or 13] of this title does not discharge an individual debtor from any debt . . . for money, property, services, or an extension, renewal, or refinancing of credit, to the extent obtained by . . . false pretenses, a false representation, or actual fraud." §523(a)(2)(A).

When "'Congress acts to amend a statute, we presume it intends its amendment to have real and substantial effect.'" *United States* v. *Quality Stores, Inc.,* 572 U. S. ___, ___ (2014) (slip op., at 7). It is therefore sensible to start with the presumption that Congress did not intend "actual fraud" to mean the same thing as "a false representation," as the Fifth Circuit's holding suggests. But the historical meaning of "actual fraud" provides even stronger evidence that the phrase has long encompassed the kind of conduct alleged to have occurred here: a transfer scheme designed to hinder the collection of debt.

[F]rom the beginning of English bankruptcy practice, courts and legislatures have used the term "fraud" to describe a debtor's transfer of assets that, like Ritz' scheme, impairs a creditor's ability to collect the debt.

One of the first bankruptcy acts, the Statute of 13 Elizabeth, has long been relied upon as a restatement of the law of so-called fraudulent conveyances (also known as "fraudulent transfers" or "fraudulent alienations"). See generally G. Glenn, The Law of Fraudulent Conveyances89–92 (1931). That statute, also called the Fraudulent Conveyances Act of 1571, identified as fraud "feigned covenous and fraudulent Feoffmentes Gyftes Grauntes Alienations [and] Conveyaunces" made with "Intent to delaye hynder or defraude Creditors." 13 Eliz. ch. 5. In modern terms, Parliament made it fraudulent to hide assets from creditors by giving them to one's family, friends, or associates. The principles of the Statute of 13 Elizabeth—and even some of its language— continue to be in wide use today. See *BFP* v. *Resolution Trust Corporation,* 511 U. S. 531, 540 (1994) ("The modern law of fraudulent transfers had its origin in the Statute of 13 Elizabeth"); *id.,* at 541 ("Every American bankruptcy law has incorporated a fraudulent transfer provision"); Story §353, at 393 ("[T]he statute of 13 Elizabeth . . . has been universally adopted in America, as the basis of our jurisprudence on the same subject"); *Boston Trading Group, Inc.* v. *Burnazos,* 835 F. 2d 1504, 1505–1506 (CA1 1987) (Breyer, J.) ("Mass. Gen. Laws ch. 109A, §§1–13 . . . is a uniform state law that codifies both common and statutory law stretching back at least to 1571 and the Statute of Elizabeth"). The degree to which this statute remains embedded in laws related to fraud today clarifies that the common-law term "actual fraud" is broad enough to incorporate a fraudulent conveyance.

Equally important, the common law also indicates that fraudulent conveyances, although a "fraud," do not require a misrepresentation from a debtor to a creditor. As a basic point, fraudulent conveyances are not an inducement-based fraud. Fraudulent conveyances typically involve "a transfer to a close relative, a secret transfer, a transfer of title without transfer of possession, or grossly inadequate consideration." BFP, 511 U. S., at 540–541 (citing Twyne's Case, 3 Co. Rep. 80b, 76 Eng. Rep. 809 (K. B. 1601)); O. Bump, Fraudulent Conveyances: A Treatise Upon Conveyances Made by Debtors To Defraud Creditors 31–60 (3d ed. 1882)). In such cases, the fraudulent conduct is not in dishonestly inducing a creditor to extend a debt. It is in the acts of concealment and hindrance. In the fraudulent-conveyance context, therefore, the opportunities for a false representation from the debtor to the creditor are limited. The debtor may have the opportunity to put forward a false representation if the creditor inquires into the whereabouts of the debtor's assets, but that could hardly be considered a defining feature of this kind of fraud.

Relatedly, under the Statute of 13 Elizabeth and the laws that followed, both the debtor and the recipient of the conveyed assets were liable for fraud even though the recipient of a fraudulent conveyance of course made no representation, true or false, to the debtor's creditor. The famous Twyne's Case, which this Court relied upon in BFP, illustrates this point. See Twyne's Case, 76 Eng.Rep., at 823 (convicting Twyne of fraud under the Statute of 13 Elizabeth, even though he was the recipient of a debtor's conveyance). That principle underlies the now-common understanding a "conveyance which hinders, delays or defrauds creditors shall be void as against [the recipient] unless . . . th[at] party . . . received it in good faith and for consideration." Glenn, Law of Fraudulent Conveyances §233, at 312. That principle also underscores the point that a false representation has never been a required element of "actual fraud," and we decline to adopt it as one today . . . .

It is of course true that the transferor does not "obtai[n]"debts in a fraudulent conveyance. But the recipient of the transfer—who, with the requisite intent, also commits fraud—can "obtai[n]" assets "by" his or her participation in the fraud. See, *e.g.*, *McClellan* v. *Cantrell*, 217 F. 3d 890 (CA 7 2000); see also *supra,* at 6. If that recipient later files for bankruptcy, any debts "traceable to" the fraudulent conveyance, see *Field,* 516 U. S., at 61; *post,* at 3, will be nondischargable under §523(a)(2)(A). Thus, at least sometimes a debt "obtained by" a fraudulent conveyance scheme could be nondischargeable under §523(a)(2)(A). Such circumstances may be rare because a person who receives fraudulently conveyed assets is not necessarily (or even likely to be) a debtor on the verge of bankruptcy, but they make clear that fraudulent conveyances are not wholly incompatible with the "obtained by" requirement . . .

We therefore reverse the judgment of the Fifth Circuit and remand the case for further proceedings consistent with this opinion.

POST-CASE FOLLOW-UP

In his dissent to this 7-1 majority decision, Justice Thomas challenges the majority's conclusion that a debt can be "obtained by" actual fraud where there was no fraud in the creation of the debt itself but where there was a subsequent fraudulent conveyance by the debtor in which the recipient of the transfer participates because if that transferee later files for bankruptcy relief, the debt transferee owes as a fraudulent schemer might be nondischargeable under §523(a)(2)(A). Thomas responds, "But §523(a)(2)(A) does not exempt from discharge any debts 'traceable to the fraudulent conveyance.' Instead, §523(a)(2)(A) exempts from discharge 'any debt for' goods that are 'obtained by' actual fraud." Who do you think gets this interpretation of the statute right? In briefs filed with the Supreme Court in this case, Husky and its supporters urged the court to adopt this expansion of the actual fraud exception of §523(a)(2)(A) to include a post-debt creation fraudulent transfer for an important policy reason: it would prohibit debtors using the Bankruptcy Code as an "engine of fraud." On the other hand, a group of consumer bankruptcy attorneys urged the court to not adopt this expansion of actual fraud nondischargeability because it would render debtors who are self-employed or owners of small businesses and who often transfer funds informally between personal and business accounts more vulnerable to §523(a)(2)(A) challenges arising from alleged post-debt creation fraudulent transfers. Which policy argument do you find more persuasive? Husky does not stand for the proposition that any post-debt creation transfer of assets by the debtor will make the debt non-dischargeable—fraudulent transfer must still be proven. But the case does represent a fascinating expansion of the actual fraud concept of §523(a)(2)(A) that may motivate more unsecured creditors to look for questionable asset transfers by the debtor and to contest dischargeability of their claim on that basis. Finally, note the many references in the majority opinion to English common law and acts of parliament. That's a good reminder that many of our laws in the 21st century, including fraud, have roots going back to English law.

Husky Int'l Electronics, Inc. v. Ritz: Real Life Applications

1. Terry incurs borrows money from Alice. There is no fraud involved in the transaction. Before Terry repays Alice, Terry conveys his property available to pay Alice to Frank for less than its ordinary value in order to deprive Alice of payment. Terry then files for bankruptcy under Chapter 7 and seeks to discharge the obligation to Alice. Alice contends the debt owed to her by Terry is nondischargeable under §523(a)(2)(A). Under the rule of Husky, did Terry obtain the loan from Alice using actual fraud within the meaning of §523(a)(2)(A)? If Alice makes a claim against Frank for liability to her for fraudulent transfer and Frank responds by filing under Chapter 7, is Alice's claim against Frank dischargeable?

2. Assume the same facts as in #1 except that Frank is unaware actually or constructively that the property Terry conveys to him is undervalued and has no idea that Terry is conveying the property to him in order to defraud Alice. Under the rule of Husky, is the debt that Terry owes to Alice nondischargeable in Terry's bankruptcy per §523(a)(2)(A)?

3. Presumption of Fraud in "Last-Minute" Consumer Purchases of Luxury Goods or Services [§523(a)(2)(C)]

Luxury goods or services Goods or services not reasonably necessary for the maintenance or support of the debtor or a dependent.

Section 523(a)(2)(C) creates a rebuttable presumption that consumer debts aggregating more than $500 owed to a single creditor for **luxury goods or services** purchased within 90 days preceding the petition are fraudulent and nondischargeable. The phrase "luxury goods or services" is not defined but expressly does not include goods or services reasonably necessary for the maintenance or support of the debtor or a dependent.

The same section also makes **cash advances** aggregating more than $750 obtained within 70 days preceding the petition on an open end credit plan nondischargeable. The policy behind these consumer provisions is to punish last-minute spending sprees by unethical debtors. But the presumption of fraud is rebuttable by the debtor.

EXAMPLE

Assume that in the 90 days preceding the filing of her bankruptcy petition Marta Carlson charged almost $1,000 on her Capital City Bank Visa card for an iPod, several video games, and tuition to a three-week science camp for her son, Chris. In her bankruptcy case, CCB may seek to have these charges declared nondischargeable under §523(a)(2)(C) as luxury goods and services. At the trial, Marta testifies that each of those purchases was necessitated by the emotional problems suffered by her son and all represented efforts on her part to provide him with healthy diversions and positive experiences to improve his emotional state. If the court concludes that these charges were reasonably necessary for the maintenance or support of Chris, she may be allowed to discharge them. How do you think the court will rule?

4. Debts Arising from Fraud or Defalcation in a Fiduciary Capacity [§523(a)(4)]

A **fiduciary capacity** arises when the debtor occupies a position of trust and confidence as to another person who relies on the debtor to exercise competence, honesty, and loyalty. Some courts construe this "fraud or defalcation in a fiduciary capacity" language narrowly and hold it only applies to express or implied trusts (see, e.g., *In re Burress*, 245 B.R. 871 (Bankr. D. Colo. 2000)). Other courts construe the language more broadly to apply to any person entrusted with the property or confidential affairs of others raising an expectation of loyalty and care (e.g., attorneys, trustees, brokers, bankers) (see, e.g., *In re McDade*, 282 B.R. 650 (N.D. Ill. 2002)). If an obligation arises out of fraud or defalcation (dishonesty) by the debtor acting in such capacity, that obligation may not be dischargeable in bankruptcy.

EXAMPLE

Assume an accountant (or lawyer or trustee) is sued for lying to a client regarding the investment of the client's money entrusted to the accountant for safe investment, and a prepetition judgment is entered against the accountant for fraud. If the accountant files in Chapter 7 to discharge that judgment, it may be deemed nondischargeable since it arose out of the accountant's fraud in a fiduciary capacity, depending on whether the bankruptcy court follows *Burress* or *McDade* in interpreting the scope of §523(a)(4).

There has also been a question regarding the degree of culpability that should be required to bar the fiduciary from discharging an obligation arising from defalcation of his or her obligation. Should a knowing, intentional violation of the fiduciary duty be required in order to block discharge, or is a negligent or technical but innocent violation of duty that results in loss to the beneficiary enough? The lower courts were split on this issue until the Supreme Court decision in *Bullock v. BankChampaign, N.A.*, 133 S. Ct. 1754 (2013), holding that defalcation does require a culpable state of mind beyond mere negligence, which can consist of knowledge of, or gross recklessness in respect to, the improper nature of the relevant fiduciary behavior.

5. Debts Arising from Embezzlement or Larceny [§523(a)(4)]

Regardless of whether a fiduciary capacity is involved, any obligation arising out of embezzlement or larceny cannot be discharged in bankruptcy.

EXAMPLE

Assume a bookkeeper employee steals from the employer. The employer files a civil suit based on the embezzlement and obtains a final judgment against the bookkeeper. The final judgment obligation arising from that embezzlement will be nondischargeable if the former employee files for Chapter 7 relief.

6. Domestic Support Obligations [§523(a)(5)]

Section 101(14A) of the Code defines **domestic support obligations** generally as debts for "alimony, maintenance or support" of a spouse, former spouse, or child of the debtor. Generally, these obligations must arise from a court decree of divorce or separation or from a property settlement agreement. Both domestic support obligations and other debts to a former spouse or child of the debtor arising in the course of a divorce or separation are exempted from discharge by §523(a)(5)(15).

7. Debts Arising from Willful or Malicious Injury to the Person or Property of Another [§523(a)(6)]

In *Kawaauhau v. Geiger*, 523 U.S. 57, 61-62 (1998), the Supreme Court made it clear that a judgment of liability arising out of mere negligent or even reckless conduct does not fall within this exception to discharge. Nor do judgments based on intentional torts where all that is proven (or required) is an intent to perform the intentional act. What is required is that the debtor intended the harm or injury itself. As the courts have interpreted *Geiger*: "A debtor is responsible for a 'willful' injury when he or she commits an intentional act the purpose of which is to cause injury or which is substantially certain to cause injury." *In re Jennings*, 670 F.3d 1329, 1334 (11th Cir. 2012). The debtor need not have held any personal animosity against the creditor, but must have intended the consequences of his act.

The courts disagree regarding whether the "substantially certain" aspect of the debtor's intent for purposes of §523(a)(6) is to be measured subjectively or objectively. Compare *In re Ormsby*, 591 F.3d 1199, 1206 (9th Cir. 2010) (requiring creditor to show that "debtor believes that injury is substantially certain to result from his own conduct"), with *In re Shcolnik*, 670 F.3d 624, 630 (5th Cir. 2012) (finding willfulness where creditor showed an "objective substantial certainty of harm"). Determine how the courts of the federal district or circuit where you plan to practice measure substantial certainty for purposes of §523(a)(6). Most courts also interpret *Kawaauhau* to require that the debtor have committed an intentional tort recognized under state law. See, e.g., *Lockerby v. Sierra*, 535 F.3d 1038 (9th Cir. 2008) (A debt arising from a willful breach of contract by debtor is not nondischargeable under §523(a)(6) unless accompanied by conduct that would give rise to a tort action under state law).

8. Student Loans [§523(a)(8)]

At one time, student loan debt could be discharged in bankruptcy as easily as an auto loan or credit card debt. Congress implemented the prohibition on discharge of student loans in 1976 after widespread reports of new college and professional school graduates (including doctors and lawyers) filing Chapter 7 cases to discharge their considerable (and often taxpayer guaranteed) student loan debt before undertaking successful and even lucrative careers.

Until BAPCPA in 2005, the prohibition on discharge only applied to a federal student loan, meaning an educational loan made, subsidized, or guaranteed by the government or made under a program funded by either a governmental unit or a nonprofit institution. In one of its more controversial provisions, BAPCPA expanded the nondischargeability provision to include private student loans (meaning loans made by for-profit lenders, not subsidized or guaranteed by the government and thus not subject to government regulation on amount, interest rate, or fees) as well. Thus, today neither a public nor a private student loan can be discharged absent a showing of undue hardship.

The only exception to the prohibition on discharge of student loans is a showing by debtor that disallowing discharge of the student loan obligation will cause **undue hardship** to the debtor and debtor's dependents. "Undue hardship" is an undefined term in the Code but has always been construed by the courts as a demanding standard. In the oft-cited case of *In re Briscoe*, 16 B.R. 128, 131 (Bankr. S.D.N.Y. 1981), the court said, "Dischargeability of student loans should be based upon the certainty of hopelessness, not simply present inability to fulfill financial commitment." That "certainty of hopelessness" test was cited with approval in the leading case of *Brunner v. New York State Higher Educ. Serv. Corp.*, 831 F.2d 395, 396 (2d Cir. 1987), which held that in order to establish undue hardship the debtor must show:

- that the debtor cannot maintain, based on current income and expenses, a "minimal" standard of living for herself and her dependents if forced to repay the loan;
- that additional circumstances exist indicating that this state of affairs is likely to persist for a significant portion of the repayment period of the student loan; and
- that the debtor has made good faith efforts to repay the loan.

In *Brunner* the Second Circuit said of Congress's decision to exempt student loan debt from discharge in bankruptcy: "In return for giving aid to individuals who represent poor credit risks, it strips these individuals of the refuge of bank-ruptcy in all but extreme circumstances." It was, "a conscious Congressional choice to override the normal 'fresh start' goal of bankruptcy."

P-H 12-a: Determine if the courts of your federal district or circuit follow *Brunner* and the certainty of hopelessness test in applying the undue hardship standard for discharge of student loan debt. If not, what standard do they apply? Marta Carlson has two educational loans (see the Assignment Memorandum in Appendix A and her Schedule E/F, Document 10 in the Carlson case file), one to Columbiana Federal Savings & Loan in the amount of $5,000 and one to Capital City Bank in the amount of $10,000. Looking at Marta's overall financial situation and that of her two children, can you construct a plausible argument under the standard used in your federal circuit that excepting these two loans from discharge would work an undue hardship on her or her dependents?

The second prong of the *Brunner* formula, requiring the debtor seeking to discharge student debt to show "additional circumstances" indicating that the debtor's inability to maintain a minimal standard of living will continue for all or a significant portion of the loan payback period, has proved to be the most difficult for debtors to meet. As summarized in *In re Nys*, 308 B.R. 436 (9th Cir. B.A.P. 2004), such circumstances may include:

- serious mental or physical disability of the debtor or the debtor's depen-dents that prevents employment or advancement;
- the debtor's obligations to care for dependents;
- lack of, or severely limited, education;
- poor quality of education;
- lack of usable or marketable job skills;
- underemployment, maximized income potential in the chosen educational field, and no other, more lucrative job skills;
- limited number of years remaining in the debtor's work life to allow pay-ment of the loan;
- age or other factors that prevent retraining or relocation as a means for payment of the loan;
- lack of assets, whether or not exempt, which could be used to pay the loan;
- potentially increasing expenses that outweigh any potential appreciation in the value of the debtor's assets and/or likely increases in the debtor's income; and
- lack of better financial options elsewhere.

HOW HARD IS THE HARDSHIP TEST, REALLY?

Maybe the undue hardship test is not as intimidating in the application as it sounds in theory. A 2012 study found that four out of ten debtors who sought partial or total discharge of student debt in bankruptcy were successful notwithstanding the undue hardship test. Remarkably, the study found that only one-tenth of 1 percent of bankruptcy debtors with student loan debt even attempted to discharge it. See Jason Iuliano, *An Empirical Assessment of Student Loan Discharges and the Undue Hardship Standard*, 86 Am. Bankr. L.J. 495 (Sept. 25, 2012). If this is a subject that interests you, read the study and determine the common characteristics of the debtors whose student debt was discharged in whole or part.

The U.S. Department of Education (DOE) has instituted a new **Income Based Repayment (IBR) Plan** that caps the required monthly payment on a federal student loan obligation at an amount calculated based on the former student's income and family size. The qualifying former student is given 25 years to repay the loan rather than the standard 10 years and any amounts still owing after 25 years will be forgiven under the plan. The DOE also offers a **Public Service Loan Forgiveness (PSLF) Plan**, pursuant to which graduates who choose to work as public school teachers or in other government positions or for nonprofit organizations can repay their student loans at reduced amounts and receive forgiveness of the balance after only ten years. You can read up on these DOE repayment options at http://studentaid.ed.gov/.

The availability of such school loan management programs has raised the question of whether the failure of a debtor to enroll in such a program means the debtor cannot satisfy the third prong of the *Brunner* test—that debtor has made a good faith effort to repay his or her student loans. Some courts have come close to adopting a per se rule to the effect that a debtor who could have but chose not to participate in such a program cannot satisfy the good faith requirement. See, e.g., *In re Gibson*, 428 B.R. 385, 391-392 (Bankr. W.D. Mich. 2010) (debtor who declined to participate in DOE IBR plan did not use good faith efforts to repay her loans). But most courts, while giving weight to the debtor's decision to participate in such programs or not, have rejected any per se rule. See, e.g., *In re Barrett*, 487 F.3d 353 (6th Cir. 2007) (although debtor's decision to forgo participation in the program is not a per se indication of a lack of good faith, the decision is probative of debtor's intent to repay the student loans), and *In re Bene*, 474 B.R. 56, 71-72 (Bankr. W.D.N.Y. 2012) (debtor's decision not to participate outweighed by other circumstances and no bar to finding of good faith).

P-H 12-b: The law office your work for represents each of the following four Chapter 7 debtors. Rank these clients from 1 (least likely) to 4 (most likely) in terms of the likelihood of their being able to discharge all or part of their student loan debt in bankruptcy.

a. Carey has more than $100,000 in student loans from undergraduate and graduate work. Her master's and PhD degrees are in History and she was planning on a university level academic career but has had no success in landing even an instructor's position at that level in the two years since she received her PhD. She's had to settle for part-time teaching at the local high school while she lives with her parents. She considered the IBR program mentioned in the text but was scared away from it after learning that any portion of the student loan eventually written off by participation in such a program could be deemed taxable income to her (cancellation of debt (COD) income) in the year it is written off. She's been making very small payments on her student loan debt, usually about one-fourth of what is owed in each installment. It is all she can afford.

b. Clarissa has more than $100,000 in student loans from undergraduate and graduate work. She received her master's degree in early childhood education three years ago. A month before that she was diagnosed with Hodgkin's lymphoma and has been in the fight of her life since. She has undergone three rounds of radiation and chemotherapy that, together with the powerful medications she must take, have left her unable to handle any employment for the present. She lost her home and her vehicle and lives with and depends on her sister. Currently, the disease does not seem to be worsening and it is still possible that she might be declared cancer free at some point but doctors will not do that until it has been at least five years since the last chemotherapy. Even in the best case scenario she will have lost a decade in her career that she cannot recover. She has not made any payments on her student loan obligation and has not participated in any government programs to defer or manage such debt.

c. Clay has more than $100,000 in student loans from undergraduate and graduate work. He received his master's degree in economics 18 months ago and had a really good job offer from a national company but had to refuse it when he became ill with a rare virus he picked up on a post-graduation trip to Fiji. He came close to death several times and needed a number of blood transfusions while suffering from the virus. His medical bills from the ordeal exceed $250,000. The prognosis is finally somewhat positive. He will have mostly a full recovery but will always have breathing problems if placed under too much stress; he has a greatly enhanced chance of suffering cardiovascular problems compared to other men his age; and he faces a 25 percent chance of a relapse in the next ten years and the odds for it grow as he ages. With that prognosis, Clay expects to be back in the job market within nine months. However, the gap in his employment history resulting from the health problems together with permanent health problems and the significant risk of a relapse are likely to make it harder for him to find a position like the one he had to pass up and to permanently handicap his ability to go as far in his field as he could have both in terms of position and income. Clay's parents made payments on his student loan debt for several months following his graduation but had to stop for financial reasons. Clay has participated in every federal and state program he can qualify for to defer payment on and otherwise manage his student debt obligation.

d. Clarence has more than $100,000 in student loans from spending eight years obtaining his B.A. degree during which time he attended four different universities and changed his major six times. He's been looking for a job in his degree field (journalism, finally) for nine months since graduation without success. The fast food job he has pays minimum wage and leaves him unable to make any payment on the student loan balance.

P-H 12-c: In the last generation the cost of a college education has accelerated far faster than inflation. At the same time, most states have reduced aid to public institutions, placing more of the increasing cost on the student and her family. In 2012 the total student loan debt in the United States, for the first time, actually exceeded total consumer credit card debt, second only to total indebtedness for home loans. As of 2015 student loan debt in the United States exceeds $1.2 trillion, approximately 12 percent of which is delinquent or in default. Forty million Americans carry student loan debt, including a number of seniors who either returned to school late in life or co-signed for a child or grandchild's loan. Is it time to revisit the undue hardship standard for discharge of student loan debt and give bankruptcy judges more flexibility to modify such obligations in particular cases? Should BAPCPA's expansion of the discharge restriction to private student loans made by for-profit lenders be reconsidered? Can you think of other approaches to this vexing problem that ought to be considered?

9. Fines, Penalties, and Forfeitures Owed to the Government [§523(a)(7)]

Governmental fines and penalties imposed to punish the debtor for wrongdoing are nondischargeable if not more than three years old when the petition is filed. Examples include speeding tickets, penalties on unpaid taxes, and liability for bail bond forfeiture.

10. Personal Injury and Wrongful Death Claims Arising from DUI [§523(a)(9)]

Judgments and pending claims arising out of simple or even gross negligence are generally dischargeable in bankruptcy, but if the wrongful death or personal injury claim against the debtor arises out of the debtor's driving while intoxicated by alcohol or drugs, it will not be a dischargeable debt.

11. Unlisted Debts [§523(a)(3)]

When preparing their schedules and lists to accompany the bankruptcy petition, debtors must be very careful to list every single debt they owe, whether contingent or fixed, disputed or undisputed. Any debt not listed may not be discharged whether the error was intentional or accidental. For reasons we have discussed, attorneys and their assistants must take reasonable steps to ensure debtors' schedules are complete and accurate.

Section 523(a)(3) makes claims omitted from the debtor's lists and schedules nondischargeable, with the result that the creditor fails to file a timely proof of claim *unless* the creditor in question had other notice or actual knowledge of the bankruptcy filing. Certain claims are given protection on the same grounds for failure of the creditor to file a timely objection to discharge.

When a debtor's lawyer belatedly discovers that a claim was omitted from the debtor's lists and schedules, the thing to do is to promptly file an amended list or schedule including the claim. Bankruptcy Rule 1009 provides that a voluntary

Illustration 12-b: GROUNDS FOR DENYING A DISCHARGE TO AN INDIVIDUAL CHAPTER 7 DEBTOR

- The debtor has transferred, removed, destroyed, or concealed property with the intent to hinder, delay, or defraud a creditor or the trustee within either a year preceding the filing of the petition or after the petition was filed [§727(a)(2)]
- The debtor has concealed, destroyed, falsified, or failed to keep books and records from which his financial condition or business transactions may be ascertained unless there is justification [§§727(a)(3) & (4)(D)]
- The debtor has knowingly made a false oath or account, or presented or used a false claim in connection with the bankruptcy case [§727(a)(4)]
- The debtor has failed to satisfactorily explain any loss of assets or deficiency of assets to meet his liabilities [§727(a)(5)]
- The debtor has failed to obey a lawful order of the bankruptcy court [§727(a)(6)]
- The debtor has been previously granted a discharge in a Chapter 7 or 11 within eight years prior to filing the petition in the current case or a discharge in a Chapter 13 within six years prior to filing the petition in the current case [§§727(a)(8) & (9)]
- The debtor has failed to complete an instructional course concerning financial management [§727(a)(11)]

---

petition, list, statement, or schedule can be amended by the debtor at any time before the case is closed. If the case has been closed when the omission of a creditor from the schedules is discovered, the case may be reopened by motion pursuant to §350(b) and Bankruptcy Rule 5010, and the schedules then amended. However, the debtor will be required to pay a new filing fee for reopening the case as well as the additional attorney's fee involved.

B.   Objections to Discharge

An individual Chapter 7 debtor can be denied any discharge at all (i.e., no relief from any debts) if one of the grounds set forth in §727(a) of the Code and summarized in Illustration 12-b is established.

The bankruptcy trustee, U.S. Trustee, or any creditor is given standing to object to the debtor's discharge by filing a complaint and instituting an adversary proceeding. Bankruptcy Rule 4004 requires that a complaint to deny discharge be initiated within 60 days following the first meeting of creditors subject to extension by motion and, as with complaints objecting to discharge of a particular debt, Bankruptcy Rule 2002(f) requires the bankruptcy court clerk, or some other person as the court may direct, to provide notice by mail of the time fixed for filing a complaint objecting to discharge.

1. Dealing with Property for the Purpose of Hindering, Delaying, or Defrauding a Creditor [§727(a)(2)]

Debtors must be very careful not to play games with the bankruptcy process by hiding assets, putting them into the name of a third person prior to filing, or similar gambits. The trustee will aggressively look for that type of thing and most bankruptcy judges will have little sympathy for debtors engaged in such behavior when a denial of discharge is requested.

2. Concealing, Destroying, Falsifying, or Not Keeping Books and Records [§§727(a)(3) & (4)(D)]

Debtors must be very careful not to destroy, alter, or hide their financial records as part of an attempt to hide assets or deceive as to their value. Bankruptcy trustees know the kinds of records consumer and business debtors should have and will aggressively pursue any situation that looks suspicious. Note that it is not just concealing, destroying, or falsifying books and records that is punishable, but the failure to keep adequate records.

3. Making a False Oath or Account or Using a False Claim [§727(a)(4)]

The petition and supporting schedules and lists filed by the debtor are signed under penalty of perjury and the debtor must be sure before signing that they are accurate and complete. The failure to do so can be construed as a false oath and a discharge can be denied. In addition, the debtor is examined under oath at the first meeting of creditors (the 341 meeting) and must be careful to give truthful answers there.

4. Lack of Satisfactory Explanation of Loss of or Inadequate Assets [§727(a)(5)]

At the 341 meeting and at informal meetings with the bankruptcy trustee the debtor may be questioned closely regarding assets debtor once had but now does not. Where did those assets go? If the debtor seemed to have adequate income flow to pay his or her obligations but did not pay them, where did that income go? If the debtor cannot give a plausible explanation, deception may be suspected and the unsatisfactory explanation will form the basis of this objection to discharge.

5. Failure to Obey a Lawful Court Order or to Answer When Asked [§727(a)(6)]

Assume a debtor fails to come to his 341 meeting as required by §521 and the court orders him to be present for the rescheduled date. Assume a debtor refuses to turn over property to the trustee as required by §521 and the court orders the turnover. Assume the trustee requests a Rule 2004 examination of a debtor, the debtor fails to attend, and the court orders his attendance. The debtor in each of these scenarios must obey the court's orders. Failure to obey even one lawful order forms the basis for this objection to discharge. A pattern of refusal to obey practically guarantees the motion being granted.

The debtor must also respond to material questions put to him by the court and to testify when asked to do so whether at his 341 meeting or at a Rule 2004 examination, at any other evidentiary hearing, or in connection with discovery undertaken in an adversary proceeding. A claim by the debtor of the Fifth Amendment privilege against self-incrimination will not prevent denial of discharge on this basis if the judge has granted the debtor immunity in connection with the testimony.

6. A Prior Discharge [§§727(a)(8) & (9)]

Section 727(a)(8) stipulates that a bankruptcy court is to deny a Chapter 7 discharge if the debtor previously received a discharge in a Chapter 7 or 11 case within eight years preceding the filing of the petition.

The court will also deny a Chapter 7 discharge if the debtor previously received a discharge in a Chapter 13 or Chapter 12 case within six years preceding the petition under §727(a)(9) unless:

- the debtor paid all allowed unsecured claims in the earlier case in full; or
- the debtor made payments under the plan in the earlier case totaling at least 70 percent of the allowed unsecured claims and the debtor's plan was proposed in good faith and the payments represented the debtor's best effort.

7. Failure to Complete the Postpetition Financial Management Course [§727(a)(11)]

In addition to the prepetition credit counseling requirement imposed on individual debtors considered in Chapter Seven, Section C, §727(a)(11), added by BAPCPA, requires those debtors to complete a postpetition financial management instructional course before the discharge will be granted. Per Bankruptcy Rule 1007(c)(7), the individual debtor must also file a Certification About a Financial Management Course (Official Form 423) unless the provider of the course notifies the court that the debtor has completed the course. As with the prepetition credit counseling, the postpetition and predischarge financial management instructional course must be conducted by nonprofit budget and credit counseling agencies that are approved by the U.S. Trustee.

Credit counseling agency A nonprofit entity approved by the U.S. Trustee to provide required prepetition credit counseling or predischarge financial management services to individual debtors.

C. ▶ Involuntary Dismissal of a Chapter 7 Case

Related to the topic of the §727 objection to discharge is the possibility that a Chapter 7 case may simply be dismissed by the bankruptcy judge making the subject of discharge irrelevant. This can happen for a number of different reasons.

1. "For Cause" Dismissal for Unreasonable Delay, Nonpayment of Fees, or Failure to File Schedules Under §707(a)

Section 707(a) provides that the court may dismiss any Chapter 7 case after notice and a hearing "for cause" including:

- unreasonable delay by the debtor that is prejudicial to creditors;
- nonpayment of any required fees or charges; or
- failure to timely file the required schedules supporting the debtor's petition.

Most of the motions seeking **dismissal for cause** under §707(a) involve the latter two grounds, which are fairly objective. The first though, unreasonable delay prejudicial to creditors, is a little trickier. It seems clear that the unreasonable delay must arise from postpetition actions of the debtor, not prepetition actions that may have hindered or frustrated the creditor. See, e.g., *In re Jackson*, 258 B.R. 272, 277 (Bankr. M.D. Fla. 2000) ("[A]ny successful motion to dismiss for delay as 'cause' must be grounded on allegations of post-petition hindrance by a debtor, rather than on prepetition avoidance of service or prepetition avoidance of repossession."). And while courts make it clear that the "for cause" grounds set out in §707(a) are not exclusive, the fact that the debtor has the means to pay a creditor's claim in whole or part is not itself cause to dismiss under that provision. See, e.g., *In re Bushyhead*, 525 B.R. 136, 142, 152 (Bankr. N.D. Okla. 2015) ("The Bushyheads have sought Chapter 7 relief to discharge several debts . . . . The only remarkable aspect of this case is the Bushyheads' income. If they did not earn a lot of money, we would not be here. On that issue, Congress has spoken. The ability to pay is not cause for dismissal under §707(a).").

Courts in the Second, Third, and Sixth federal circuits have construed dismissal for cause under §707(a) to include a **bad faith filing** (or lack of good faith in filing) by the Chapter 7 debtor. See *In re Zick*, 931 F.2d 1124 (6th Cir. 1991); *In re Tamecki*, 229 F.3d 205 (3d Cir. 2000); and *In re Aiello*, 428 B.R. 296, 301-302 (Bankr. E.D.N.Y. 2010). To justify the drastic remedy of dismissing the case, the bad faith alleged and proven against the debtor must involve egregious conduct.

> Dismissal based on lack of good faith must be undertaken on an ad hoc basis. It should be confined carefully and is generally utilized only in those egregious cases that entail concealed or misrepresented assets and/or sources of income, and excessive and continued expenditures, lavish life-style, and intention to avoid a large single debt based on conduct akin to fraud, misconduct, or gross negligence.

Zick, 931 F.2d at 1129. See also *In re Lombardo*, 370 B.R. 506, 511-512 (Bankr. E.D.N.Y. 2007), identifying 14 factors to be considered in a for cause bad faith allegation under §707(a)(1).

P-H 12-d: The Eighth and Ninth Circuits held that bad faith should generally not be a basis for dismissal under §707(a). See *In re Huckfeldt*, 39 F.3d 829, 832 (8th Cir. 1994) ("framing the issue in terms of bad faith may tend to misdirect the inquiry away from the fundamental principles and purposes of Chapter 7" and concluding that dismissal under §707(a) for bad faith should be limited to extreme misconduct that was not worthy of bankruptcy protection, such as using bankruptcy "as a 'scorched earth' tactic against a diligent creditor, or using bankruptcy as a refuge from another court's jurisdiction"), and *In re Padilla*, 222 F.3d 1184, 1191 (9th Cir. 2000) ("bad faith as a general proposition does not provide 'cause' to dismiss a Chapter 7 petition under §707(a)"). Determine whether your federal circuit or district recognizes bad faith as a basis for dismissal for cause under §707(a) and, if so, what factors or tests those courts utilize in determining bad faith.

---

2. Dismissal for Abuse by Reason of Bad Faith Filing or as Evident from the Totality of the Debtor's Financial Circumstances Under §§707(b)(1) and (3)

Dismissal for cause under §707(a) is applicable to all Chapter 7 filings. In contrast, §707(b)(1) authorizing dismissal for "abuse of the provisions of this chapter" applies only to a Chapter 7 case filed by a consumer debtor. We learned in Chapter Seven, Section D, that §§707(b)(1) and (2) read together raise a **presumption of abuse** if the consumer debtor fails the **means test**. But **dismissal for abuse** under §707(b)(1) is a broader concept than the means test and its presumption of abuse.

Sections 707(b)(1) and (3) read together allow the court in all Chapter 7 cases to consider whether (1) the debtor filed the petition in bad faith, or (2) "the totality of the circumstances of the debtor's financial situation" demonstrates that it would be an abuse of the system to allow the debtor a Chapter 7 discharge. The court can look at any relevant factors in making the decision except that §707(b)(1) specifically says the court may not consider charitable contributions by the debtor.

EXAMPLE

Assume a consumer debtor files in Chapter 7 to stop foreclosure on his home. He fights the lifting of the stay on the creditor's foreclosure on his home then dismisses that case without receiving a discharge. A year and a day later (to avoid the application of the 30-day automatic stay of §362(c) discussed in Chapter Nine, Section F) he files another Chapter 7 case to prevent foreclosure and again fights the lifting of the stay for a while and dismisses this case too. Now, another year and a day later (again to avoid the application of §362(c)), he files yet another Chapter 7 to delay the latest foreclosure actions against him. Regardless of other circumstances, the bankruptcy court could conclude that this third filing is in bad faith and that the debtor is abusing the system by manipulating it only to stop foreclosures using the automatic stay while never intending to allow the case to proceed against his nonexempt assets for the benefit of his creditors. A case like that might well be dismissed under §707(b)(3).

EXAMPLE

Assume a physician just finishing her residency and carrying a substantial amount of debt from her medical education and training signs a personal services contract agreeing to provide medical services for a physician's group for three years. The physician begins performance on the agreement but is immediately sorry she entered into it. Unhappy with where she is living and working, the physician breaches the agreement after six months and moves to another location to practice. When the physician's group with which she contracted files suit, the physician files a Chapter 7 case to discharge the claims arising from the agreement. In examining the totality of the physician's financial circumstances the court may conclude that although the debtor can avoid the presumption of abuse based on the education loan debt she is still carrying, her projected income in the near future will quickly enable her to pay off that debt at which point she will not be able to rebut the presumption of abuse from the means test. Based on the totality of circumstances the court may dismiss this case.

EXAMPLE

> Assume a consumer debtor files for Chapter 7 relief where it is learned that the debtor is unable to pay his creditors because he gave almost everything he owned away to charities. Per §§707(b)(1) and (3) this arguably is not ground for dismissal based on either bad faith or abuse evident from the totality of the circumstances.

The juxtaposition of a means test and presumption of abuse from §§701(b)(1) and (2) with the abuse by reason of bad faith filing or from the totality of debtor's circumstances from §§701(b)(2) and (3) can be confusing. If an individual Chapter 7 debtor satisfies the means test and does not raise the presumption of abuse, can that debtor's case still be dismissed for abuse under §§707(b)(2) and (3)? The answer to that is clearly yes based on the language of §707(b)(3).

Another question not made clear by statutory language is whether the case of an individual consumer debtor who satisfies the means test can be dismissed for abuse under §707(b)(3) based on a finding that the debtor does in fact have the means to pay his or her debts even though that debtor satisfied the means test. Some courts have ruled that it cannot. See, e.g., *In re Walker*, 381 B.R. 620, 624 (Bankr. M.D. Pa. 2008) ("inclusion of the income and expenses calculation in §707(b)(2) precludes reconsideration of income and expenses in §707(b)(3) pursuant to the canon of negative implication"). Most courts, however, have ruled that the ability of a debtor to pay his or her debts notwithstanding having satisfied the means test is a factor that can be considered in deciding whether §707(b)(3) abuse is present. See, e.g., *Calhoun v. U.S. Trustee*, 650 F.3d 338 (4th Cir. 2011) (the means test is not conclusive, the presumption is rebuttable, and a court may still find abuse under §707(b)(3) even if there is no presumption); *In re Sonntag*, 2012 WL 1065482, *4 (Bankr. N.D. W. Va. 2012) (ability to pay alone is insufficient to find §707(b)(3) abuse but may weigh "significantly" in the court's determination of abuse under the totality of circumstances test of that section); *In re Lipford*, 397 B.R. 320 (Bankr. M.D.N.C. 2008) (ability to pay may be considered in determining §707(b)(3) abuse claim since the Chapter 7 debtor is entitled to a fresh start but not a head start), and *In re Rivers*, 466 B.R. 558 (Bankr. M.D. Fla. 2012) (a debtor's ability to repay creditors is the primary factor to consider under the totality of the circumstances analysis of §707(b)(3) but it is not the conclusive factor, and other relevant factors must be taken into account). What remains unknown is whether a finding of abuse under §707(b)(3) can be based *solely* on the debtor's ability to pay where the debtor has satisfied the means test.

Motions to dismiss under §707(b)(3) are governed by Bankruptcy Rule 1017(e), which provides that they must be filed within 60 days following the first date set for the meeting of creditors unless the time is extended on timely motion for cause.

D. Debtor's Right to Convert a Chapter 7 Case

So long as the case was originally filed as a Chapter 7 (and not converted to a Chapter 7 from another chapter of the Code), §§706(a) and (d) permit the debtor, on motion, to **convert** the case to a case under Chapters 11, 12, or 13 so long as the debtor qualifies as a debtor under the chapter of the Code to which he converts the case.

On motion, a party in interest may request the conversion of a Chapter 7 case to one under Chapter 11 and such motion is decided using the "after notice and a hearing" procedure per §706(b). But a Chapter 7 case cannot be converted to one under Chapter 12 or 13 without the debtor's request or consent per §706(c).

A case that has been or is likely to be converted from one chapter of the Code to another is commonly referred to by practitioners as one that has or is likely to go **"downstream."**

EXAMPLE

If a debtor files a shaky Chapter 13 case that is likely to be converted later to a Chapter 7 liquidation, a practitioner might say, "That is a downstream liquidation if I ever saw one."

Consider the circumstances under which a Chapter 7 consumer debtor might seek conversion of his case to one under Chapter 13. If the court is going to involuntarily dismiss the Chapter 7 case for one of the reasons we've considered, the debtor may want to covert in order to prevent the automatic stay from expiring, leaving him at the mercy of his creditors. Or if the court has ruled a particular debt nondischargeable, the debtor may want to convert to Chapter 13 in order to manage that nondischargeable debt in the confines of a three- to five-year plan, as we will discuss beginning in the next chapter.

Although the Code itself does not impose any test of good faith on the debtor's right to voluntarily convert a case from Chapter 7 to Chapter 13 or another chapter under the Code, the Supreme Court has held that debtors who have not engaged in good faith conduct do not have an unqualified right to convert a Chapter 7 case to one under Chapter 13 and that the bankruptcy court may deny the motion to convert if the court finds that the case would likely be dismissed under Chapter 13 on the basis of bad faith, a topic to be discussed in Chapter Sixteen, Section F. See *Marrama v. Citizens Bank of Massachusetts*, 549 U.S. 365 (2007).

E. ▶ The Final Discharge, Closing the Case, and Prohibition on Discrimination

The individual Chapter 7 debtor receives a final **discharge in bankruptcy** from the court under §727 of the Code (see Official Form 318, Order of Discharge). The discharge entered in Marta Carlson's case is Document 37 in the Carlson case file. In a no-asset case the discharge may be entered in as little as 30 to 60 days following filing of the petition. In asset cases it takes approximately four months. Some cases get bogged down with disputes and go on significantly longer.

The procedure for handling the final discharge varies among federal districts. In most districts the entry of the discharge is done automatically without any hearing being held. In the past bankruptcy judges routinely conducted a discharge hearing where they would endeavor to make sure the debtor understood the significance of the discharge but most judges now do not. In some districts the court requires the debtor's attorney to file a certification or affidavit stating that the attorney has reviewed the significance of the discharge with the debtor before the discharge will be granted. The local rules of the bankruptcy court will typically address how the judge handles the discharge.

P-H 12-e: Determine the discharge procedure used in the bankruptcy court in your federal district. Does the judge conduct a formal discharge hearing? Is the debtor's attorney required to make any certifications or to file an affidavit concerning discussions with his client? Check the local rules of your court or discuss this issue with the U.S. Trustee, a trustee panel member, or a bankruptcy practitioner.

The discharge releases the debtor from any further personal liability for dischargeable debts. The debtor is no longer legally required to pay those debts and the discharge operates as a permanent injunction prohibiting creditors from ever undertaking any form of collection action on the discharged debts. Look at the Explanation of Bankruptcy Discharge portion of in Official Form 318, Order of Discharge, and note the various warnings and other information set out there concerning the effect of the discharge.

If a creditor does violate the permanent injunction against attempting to collect a discharged debt the debtor can file a motion with the bankruptcy court asking that the offending creditor be enjoined for continuing to violate the discharge order and found in contempt of the court's discharge order. An injunction and a monetary fine for civil contempt is the usual result. If the case has been closed when the creditor violates the order of discharge, the debtor must move to reopen the case pursuant to §350(b) and Bankruptcy Rule 5010 in order to seek relief from the court. The filing fee is waived when a case is reopened for this purpose.

As has been mentioned, only an individual debtor actually receives a discharge in Chapter 7. An entity debtor simply goes out of business.

A discharge, once granted, can be revoked. Section 727(d) sets forth the reasons why a **revocation of discharge** can be entered by the bankruptcy court upon request of the bankruptcy trustee, U.S. Trustee, or a creditor and those are summarized in Illustration 12-c.

A request to revoke the debtor's discharge on the first ground listed in Illustration 12-c must be filed within one year of the date the discharge was granted. For the other grounds the request must be filed within a year of the date the discharge was granted or the date that the case is closed, whichever is later. If the case has been closed when the creditor seeks to revoke the discharge it must move pursuant to §350(b) and Bankruptcy Rule 5010 to reopen the case.

The granting of the discharge does not mean that the case itself is closed. Following discharge, the bankruptcy trustee may still have property of the estate to seize or liquidate and proceeds to distribute. When that process is completed and if there are no other matters pending, the trustee will file the final report and accounting required by §704(a)(9) and the case will be closed pursuant to §350(a).

Illustration 12-c: GROUNDS SUPPORTING A REVOCATION OF DISCHARGE

- The debtor obtained the discharge fraudulently
- The debtor failed to disclose the fact that he or she acquired or became entitled to acquire property that would constitute property of the bankruptcy estate
- The debtor has refused to obey any lawful order of the court
- The debtor has failed to explain misstatements discovered in an audit of the case
- The debtor has failed to provide documents or information requested in an audit of the case

---

P-H 12-f: Let's look at Marta Carlson's fresh start following her discharge in Chapter 7. What property was she able to exempt and keep for use in her fresh start? What debts does she remain liable for postdischarge? She lost her house in the liquidation so will now need a new place to live with her children. She lost her car in the liquidation and so will need a new one. She needs to make wise financial decisions now. How long will it be before she can file another Chapter 7 case?

Section 525 of the Code contains a broad prohibition on discrimination against a debtor because he has been through bankruptcy. Though §525 applies to any debtor invoking any chapter of bankruptcy relief, it is the Chapter 7 debtor who is most likely to suffer discrimination as a result of the stigma of having filed. Section 525(a) prohibits any governmental entity from denying, revoking, conditioning, or refusing to renew any license, permit, charter, or employment solely because the person or entity has been a bankruptcy debtor. Section 525(b) prohibits private employers from discriminating in employment solely because the person or someone associated with the person has been a bankruptcy debtor. And §525(c) prohibits both public and private makers of student loans from discriminating in making such a loan on that basis.

CHAPTER SUMMARY

Some debts cannot be discharged in a Chapter 7 case, including certain tax obligations, fines, and penalties owed to the government; domestic support obligations; student loans; consumer debts aggregating more than $500 owed to a single creditor for luxury goods or services purchased within 90 days preceding the petition unless the debtor can overcome the presumption of fraud; debts created by means of fraudulent pretenses or use of a fraudulent financial statement; debts arising from fraud or defalcation in a fiduciary capacity or from embezzlement or larceny; debts arising from willful or malicious injury to person or property; wrongful death or personal injury claims arising out of operation of a vehicle while intoxicated; and unscheduled claims. An action to determine dischargeability of a debt is an adversary proceeding.

For purposes of the willful or malicious injury to person or property ground for denying discharge of a debt, an intentional breach of contract does not qualify unless accompanied by tortious conduct. Student loans may be discharged if the debtor can satisfy the "undue hardship" test interpreted in most districts to involve a certainty of hopelessness standard met by showing that debtor cannot currently maintain even a minimal standard of living for himself and dependents if required to repay the loan, that such circumstances are likely to continue for all or a substantial portion of the payback period, and the debtor has made a good faith effort to repay the loan.

A number of grounds exist for the denial of any discharge to an individual Chapter 7 debtor including hiding or concealing property to hinder, delay, or defraud a creditor; concealing, destroying, or altering books and records without adequate explanation; unexplained loss of an asset; making a false oath or using a false claim; failure to obey a court order or to answer when asked; prior discharge in a Chapter 7 or 11 within eight years or in a Chapter 12 or 13 within six years; or failure to complete the postpetition financial course. An objection to discharge must be pursued as an adversary proceeding.

A Chapter 7 case can be involuntarily dismissed for cause for nonpayment of fees or costs or failure to timely file schedules or unreasonable postpetition delay by the debtor that prejudices creditors. It can also be dismissed upon a finding that the petition was filed in bad faith or that the filing is abusive considering the totality of debtor's financial circumstances notwithstanding that no presumption of abuse arose from the means test. In totality of the circumstances cases, most districts say the court can consider the debtor's ability to pay his creditors notwithstanding having passed the means test but cannot rely on that factor alone to find abuse and instead must examine all of the debtor's financial circumstances.

A Chapter 7 debtor can voluntarily convert his case to one under Chapter 13, 12, or 11 so long as the debtor qualifies for relief under the chapter to which the case is converted. Debtor may seek such conversion if the presumption of abuse arises in his case and cannot be rebutted or if the court involuntarily dismisses the Chapter 7 or denies discharge in the case or of a particular debt. If a case is dismissed because the petition was filed in bad faith, conversion may be denied.

The individual Chapter 7 debtor receives a discharge from the bankruptcy court, which operates as a permanent injunction prohibiting creditors from ever undertaking any form of collection action on the discharged debts. For a year following the discharge it can be revoked upon the showing that it was obtained by fraud, and other limited grounds for revoking a discharge also exist.

REVIEW QUESTIONS

1. List four kinds of debts that cannot be discharged in a Chapter 7 bankruptcy.
2. Explain how the presumption of fraud in "last-minute" consumer purchases of luxury goods and services arises.
3. Explain how the presumption of fraud in "last-minute" cash advances arises.
4. What is a fiduciary duty and what role does it play in determining if a debt might be deemed nondischargeable in a Chapter 7 bankruptcy?
5. Describe the undue hardship exception to the nondischargeability of educational loans. What leading case sets forth the three-pronged test for demonstrating undue hardship?

6. Can proof of reckless conduct that causes harm to person or property support an argument that a claim based on such conduct is nondischargeable? What Supreme Court case tells you the answer?

7. What is the risk to an individual Chapter 7 debtor of failing to list a particular debt or claim on the debtor's bankruptcy schedules?

8. List four grounds on which a Chapter 7 debtor can be denied any discharge at all.

9. Explain the difference between involuntary dismissal of a Chapter 7 case under §707(a) and under §707(b).

10. Explain why the case of an individual consumer debtor who has satisfied the means test and not raised the §707(b)(2) presumption of abuse may nonetheless be dismissed under §707(b)(3).

11. Can a Chapter 7 case be converted to a Chapter 13 case over the debtor's objection?

12. What is the majority rule regarding whether a Chapter 7 debtor's ability to pay his or her debts can be considered as part of the totality of the circumstances to determine if the filing is abusive under §707(b)(3) where that debtor has satisfied the means test?

WORDS AND PHRASES TO REMEMBER

bad faith filing	Income Based Repayment Plan
cash advances	luxury goods or services
convert	means test
discharge (in bankruptcy)	nondischargeable debts
dismissal for abuse	presumption of abuse
dismissal for cause	Public Service Loan Forgiveness
domestic support obligation	(PSLF) Plan
downstream	revocation of discharge
efficient breach	undue hardship
fiduciary capacity	

TO LEARN MORE: A number of TLM activities to accompany this chapter are accessible on the companion web site for this textbook at http://aspenlawschool.com/books/Parsons_Debt4e/.

Chapter Thirteen:

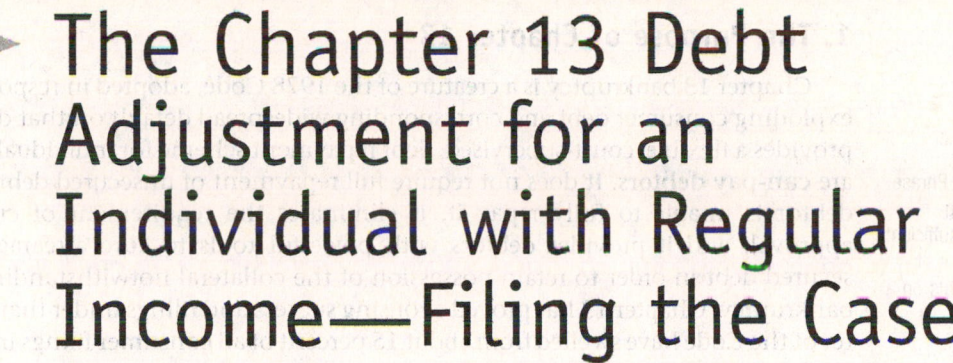

The Chapter 13 Debt Adjustment for an Individual with Regular Income—Filing the Case

In this chapter we begin our examination of the Chapter 13 bankruptcy case. We will take note of the key differences between a Chapter 7 liquidation proceeding and the Chapter 13 debt adjustment for an individual. The individual in a Chapter 13 must demonstrate a regular source of income to fund his plan and we will consider what income qualifies. We will review the petition and other documents that a debtor must file in connection with a Chapter 13 and meet the Chapter 13 standing trustee who is appointed to administer the case. The automatic stay and property of the estate concepts as well as the proof of claim requirements work slightly differently in a Chapter 13 than in a Chapter 7 and we will consider those distinctions.

KEY CONCEPTS

- Chapter 13 is a reorganization proceeding for an individual with regular income
- Any legal source of income that is sufficiently regular and stable to enable the debtor to fund his plan will qualify
- A Chapter 13 case is commenced by the filing of a petition and the debtor is required to provide the same schedules and statements as a Chapter 7 debtor
- The debtor is to file a Chapter 13 plan with the petition or within 14 days thereafter
- Each federal district has one or more standing Chapter 13 trustees who will be appointed to administer the case
- In a Chapter 13 case, nonfiling co-debtors on consumer debt enjoy the benefit of the automatic stay along with the debtor in bankruptcy
- Property of the estate in a Chapter 13 case includes nonexempt postpetition property acquired by the debtor

A. Introduction to the Chapter 13 Case

1. The Purpose of Chapter 13

Can-pay debtors Phrase generally describing debtors who have sufficient income to pay some of their unsecured debts on a deferred basis.

Chapter 13 bankruptcy is a creature of the 1978 Code, adopted in response to exploding consumer debt and corresponding widespread default on that debt. It provides a flexible, court-supervised, debt repayment scheme for individuals who are **can-pay debtors**. It does not require full repayment of unsecured debt if the debtor is unable to fully repay it, it eliminates the requirement of creditor approval, and it provides debtors with powerful tools to cure arrearages on secured debt in order to retain possession of the collateral notwithstanding the bankruptcy. Chapter 13 has proved a rousing success and filings under that chapter of the Code have swelled from about 15 percent of all consumer filings in 1978 to about one-third today.

A Chapter 13 bankruptcy case is not a liquidation proceeding like a Chapter 7 case. It is a reorganization or debt adjustment proceeding designed for an **individual with regular income** (see §109(e)). In a Chapter 13 case the debtor proposes a plan that requires the debtor to use future income to pay all or some of his or her unsecured debts in exchange for which the debtor will be able to keep all or most of debtor's nonexempt assets. Since the vast majority of individuals filing for Chapter 13 relief have primarily **consumer debts**, Chapter 13 cases are, after Chapter 7 cases filed by individual consumer debtors, the next most common type of **consumer bankruptcy case**.

The Chapter 13 plan may call for the modification of debt obligations to enable the debtor to repay what is owed on more favorable terms.

EXAMPLE

Assume a debtor borrows money and signs a promissory note calling for repayment to the creditor over five years at $100 per month. Assume the debtor files for Chapter 13 relief when he still owes 24 more payments at $100 per month, or $2,400. The debtor's Chapter 13 plan may call for the balance of the debt to be paid over 60 additional months at $40 per month. If the plan is approved by the court, the creditor must accept the extended plan payments.

The plan may also call for all or a portion of some debts to be discharged.

EXAMPLE

The Chapter 13 plan for the debtor in the last example may call for 60 payments of $20 each to the creditor, for a total of $1,200, and for the remaining $1,200 balance to then be discharged. If the plan is approved, the 60 monthly payments of $20 each will be the only payments to which the creditor is entitled and the balance will be discharged.

Of course, the debtor cannot arbitrarily alter the repayment schedule or reduce the payments due a creditor. In Chapter Fifteen we will learn what kinds of debt modification Chapter 13 allows. And in Chapter Sixteen we will consider the requirements for approval of a Chapter 13 plan by the bankruptcy court.

Wage earner plan Informal name for a Chapter 13 plan.

Pursuant to §1325(b)(4) a Chapter 13 plan must run between three to five years under the close supervision of a named trustee. Because the Chapter 13 debtor is using future income to fund the plan, the plan itself is sometimes referred to informally as a **wage earner plan**, though, as we will see, the Chapter 13 debtor need not necessarily be a wage earner. Many judges and practitioners prefer to call it a **debt adjustment plan** or just a Chapter 13 plan. Pursuant to Bankruptcy Rule 3015(b), the debtor's Chapter 13 plan is to be filed with the petition or within 14 days thereafter. Section 1326(a)(1) of the Code requires the debtor to begin making payments on the plan within 30 days following the entry for the order of relief or the filing of the proposed plan, whichever is earlier.

After BAPCPA and the new means test that we considered in Chapter Seven, the Code now contains a clear bias in favor of an individual debtor filing a Chapter 13 rather than a Chapter 7. The idea is that if the debtor is in a position to pay off even some of his debt, he should do that rather than liquidating under a Chapter 7. Thus, if the debtor filing for Chapter 7 relief triggers the presumption of abuse under that chapter and cannot rebut it, his case will be dismissed unless he voluntarily converts it to a Chapter 13. The means test and the presumption of abuse are the Code's way of not so gently pushing individual debtors toward a Chapter 13 and away from a Chapter 7.

2. Eligibility to File a Chapter 13 Case

Chapter 13 is limited to debtors with relatively small amounts of debt. Section 109(e) places strict dollar limits on how much debt a prospective Chapter 13 debtor can have. The dollar limits are subject to adjustment every third year, as mandated by §104. An individual filing for Chapter 13 relief can have no more than $394,725 in unsecured debt and $1,184,200 in secured debt. (These amounts will be adjusted next in April 2019 pursuant to §104.) Individuals with debt in excess of either the secured or unsecured debt limits can reorganize under Chapter 11, though a Chapter 11 case contains many more technicalities and is much more expensive. In order to file for Chapter 13 relief, the individual must have "**regular income**," which will be used to fund the reorganization plan. Section 101(30) defines the phrase "an individual with regular income" to mean an "individual whose income is sufficiently stable and regular to enable such individual to make payments under a plan under Chapter 13. . . ."

What is or is not "regular income" has been left largely to the courts to determine, and the courts have identified a congressional intent that the phrase be interpreted broadly. As stated in *In re Baird*, 228 B.R. 324, 327-328 (Bankr. M.D. Fla. 1999):

> The legislative history of §101(30) is unusually clear and indicates that Congress intended to expand and broadly define "individual with regular income" to include funding from diverse and nontraditional sources.

> Where the debtor is employed and has a regular wage or salary, there is rarely a problem, even if that wage or salary varies from period to period.

EXAMPLE

Assume the debtor is a used car salesperson whose monthly income depends on commissions from sales. Though his income may vary depending on how well he does from month to month, he will qualify as an individual with regular income. The same is true for a debtor who works in construction and whose income may be both seasonal and weather-dependent.

If a debtor is retired or disabled and living on a fixed income (e.g., pension, disability, or Social Security benefits), he will qualify for a Chapter 13 so long as those payments are regular and stable. A debtor who is unemployed at the time the petition is filed but who has good prospects for employment in the immediate future will also qualify.

Although the Code does not specifically prohibit illegal sources of income from being used to meet the stable and regular requirement of §109(30), disclosing such sources in a bankruptcy filing could of course subject the debtor to criminal prosecution. Moreover, as we will learn in Chapter Sixteen, §1325(a)(3) requires that, to be confirmed, a Chapter 13 plan must have been "proposed in good faith and not by any means forbidden by law." Thus, a Chapter 13 filing where income to fund the plan will be derived from illegal sources is likely to be dismissed as a bad faith filing under §1307(c) (to be discussed in Chapter Sixteen, Section F). See, e.g., *In re Arenas*, 514 B.R. 887 (Bankr. D. Colo. 2014) (motion to convert Chapter 7 case to Chapter 13 denied where any plan would be funded primarily from the cultivation and sale of marijuana under license granted by the state of Colorado but still in violation of federal law; cause existed to dismiss Chapter 13 case under §1307(c) and therefore debtor did not qualify to be debtor under Chapter 13).

What about a debtor who has no income him- or herself but has received the support or promise of support from another? Can that debtor qualify as an individual "with regular income"?

HIGHLIGHTED CASE

IN RE MURPHY
226 B.R. 601 (Bankr. M.D. Tenn. 1998)

[The Debtor shared a household with Sam Hambrick for 11 years prior to filing her Chapter 13 case. The home is owned by Hambrick and his mother. Hambrick's twin daughters also live in the house and have been raised by the Debtor. One of the twins has asthma and needs special medical attention. Hambrick nets $3,800 per month from his business. At times the Debtor worked at a market owned by Hambrick over the last 11 years until the market closed. The Debtor has not worked outside the home since then. Throughout their relationship, Hambrick deposited $800 a month into the Debtor's account. The Debtor owns a 1994 Cadillac with a scheduled value of $14,750. In July of 1998, Constance Morris took a default judgment against the Debtor for $15,000. Ms. Morris executed on this judgment during the first week of August 1998 and the sheriff seized the Debtor's 1994 Cadillac. This Chapter 13 case was filed on August 12, 1998, after seizure but before sale of the car to satisfy the judgment. The statements and schedules show the current income and expenses of the Debtor's household with Hambrick. Attached to the schedules is an affidavit of Hambrick where he agrees to make the proposed Chapter 13 payments on the Debtor's behalf. The Debtor filed a motion to partially avoid the Morris lien and a motion for turnover of the 1994 Cadillac. Ms. Morris objected arguing that the Debtor is not eligible for Chapter 13 because the Debtor does not have "regular income" as required by 11 U.S.C. §§109(e) and 101(30).]

OPINION: Lundin, Bankruptcy Judge . . .

II.

Bankruptcy Code §109(e) provides, "only an individual with *regular income* . . . may be a debtor under Chapter 13 of this title." 11 U.S.C. §109(e) (emphasis added). Section 101(30) of the Code further defines "individual with regular income" to mean "individual whose income is sufficiently stable and regular to enable such individual to make payments under a plan under chapter 13 of this title." 11 U.S.C. §101(30). The Bankruptcy Code does not define the word "income" within §101(30).

That §101(30) defines individual with regular income by reference to stability and regularity suggests that the existence of regular income is predominantly a fact question answered by examining the flow of money available to the debtor. Put another way, the Bankruptcy Code does not specifically exclude any *source* of funding from the regular income calculus; the Code does require that whatever source of income is claimed by a debtor, it must be regular and stable enough to fund a plan. The stable and regular focus of §101(30) has led several courts to state that "the test for 'regular income' is not the type or source of income, but rather its regularity and stability." [Citations omitted]. . . .

If the monthly contribution of money committed by Mr. Hambrick to the Debtor is income, the facts overwhelmingly support the finding that this Debtor's income is sufficiently regular and stable to fund a Chapter 13 plan. For 11 years Mr. Hambrick has maintained unbroken financial support to the Debtor. The Debtor has raised Mr. Hambrick's twin daughters and taken care of Mr. Hambrick's elderly parent while maintaining a home for herself, Mr. Hambrick, and Mr. Hambrick's children. Mr. Hambrick's income is substantial and regular and for many years has produced at least the amount he has committed to funding this plan. The expenses in the budget for the Debtor and Mr. Hambrick are comprehensive, modest and appropriate. Mr. Hambrick has signed an unconditional written commitment to provide the Debtor with money sufficient to fund the proposed Chapter 13 plan. Mr. Hambrick was forthright and honest in his testimony. Both Mr. Hambrick and the Debtor presented undisputed and convincing evidence of their commitment to each other and to their collective family and of their intent and ability to fund a Chapter 13 plan.

If Congress intended the word "income" in §101(30) to exclude the money Mr. Hambrick will pay to the Debtor, that less inclusive definition is not apparent in the Bankruptcy Code or its legislative history. The Code easily could but does not restrict the notion of income to wages, salary, return on investment or any of the other restrictions suggested in reported cases. *See, e.g., In re Hanlin*, 211 B.R. 147, 149 (Bankr. W.D.N.Y. 1997) (citing dictionary definitions of income). The legislative history of what is now 11 U.S.C. §101(30) is unusually clear that Congress intended to expand and broadly define "individual with regular income" to include funding from diverse and nontraditional sources. As explained in the Senate Report:

> Paragraph [(30)] defines "individual with regular income." The effect of this definition, and of its use in section 109(e), is to expand substantially the kinds of individuals that are eligible for relief under chapter 13, Adjustment of Debts of an Individual with Regular Income. Chapter XIII is now available only for wage earners. The definition encompasses all individuals with incomes that are sufficiently stable and regular to enable them to make payments under a chapter 13 plan. Thus, individuals on welfare, social security, fixed pension incomes, or who live on investment incomes, will be able to work out repayment plans with their creditors rather than being forced into straight bankruptcy. Also, self-employed individuals will be eligible to use chapter 13 if they have regular incomes.

S. Rep. No. 95-989, at 24 (1978). *See also* H. Rep. No. 95-595, at 311-12 (1977).

The examples in the legislative reports demonstrate congressional intent that regular income need not have as its source employment or the provision by the debtor of services or property to another. Income includes entitlements and benefits that can be freely given and freely taken away by governments. The legislative history of §101(30) supports the view that the touchstone for an individual with regular income is not the source of the income, but its regularity and stability.

Many reported decisions recognize that nontraditional sources of money can generate income for §101(30) purposes. Social security benefits can be regular income. *In re Cornelius*, 195 B.R. 831 (Bankr. N.D.N.Y. 1995); [other citations omitted]. Disability benefits can be regular income. *In re Tucker*, 34 B.R. 257 (Bankr. W.D. Okla. 1983); [other citations omitted]. Unemployment compensation can be regular income. *In re McMonagle*, 30 B.R. 899 (Bankr. D.S.D. 1983); [other citation omitted]. Aid to Families with Dependent Children can be regular income. *Bibb County Dep't of Family & Children's Servs. v. Hope (In re Hammonds)*, 729 F.2d 1391 (11th Cir. 1984); [other citation omitted]. A debtor who was employed, but then became unemployed may have regular income. *McMonagle*, 30 B.R. at 902-03. A self-employed debtor who essentially determines his or her own income can have regular income. See *In re Monaco*, 36 B.R. 882 (Bankr. M.D. Fla. 1983); [other citations omitted]. Odd jobs can produce regular income. *In re Cole*, 3 B.R. 346 (Bankr. S.D. W. Va. 1980). Several courts have held that a nonfiling spouse's income can be regular income for §101(30) purposes. See *In re Sigfrid*, 161 B.R. 220 (Bankr. D. Minn. 1993); [other citations omitted] . . . .

Some courts have narrowed the definition of income for §101(30) purposes by requiring that the debtor have a "legal right" to the funding or that the source have a "legal duty" to make payments to the debtor. In cases involving contributions by a significant other of the debtor, some decisions use the absence of a "legal duty of support" as the basis for finding the debtor ineligible. See *Hanlin*, 211 B.R. at 148 (parents); [other citations omitted].

What does legal duty or legal right mean in this context? By statute or common law spouses, for example, have a mutual duty or right of support.

See, e.g., *In re Antoine*, 208 B.R. 17, 20 (Bankr. E.D.N.Y. 1997) (spouse's "legal duty to provide spousal support" provides income to unemployed debtor for eligibility purposes). But the absence of similar law with respect to the support obligations of unmarried couples hardly proves the absence of income for §101(30) purposes. In states like Tennessee, in the absence of a contrary contract or overriding public interest, an employer has the right to fire an employee at will and without cause. . . . There is no "legal right" in Tennessee to continued employment—it depends on the pleasure of the employer, the quality of a debtor's work, the success of the employer's business, the weather, the economy in Asia—conditions to a debtor's right to wages that are in many ways less within a debtor's control than this Debtor's relationship to Mr. Hambrick. Yet, no one would seriously contend that the money a debtor expects to receive from employment is not income for §101(30) purposes just because the debtor has no legal right to continued employment. A definition of income for Chapter 13 eligibility purposes cannot be bottomed alone on the presence or absence of statutory or common law support obligations.

Maybe these courts mean that there is income only if a debtor has a remedy through the courts if payments stop. This notion is also too narrow for §101(30) purposes. Entitlements such as welfare and social security are income for eligibility purposes in a Chapter 13 case yet such benefit programs can be limited or abolished at the will of the legislature. And once (constitutionally) altered by the legislature, there is no recourse through the courts to force the payment of benefits.

Mr. Hambrick could employ the Debtor to take care of his twin teenagers and that employment would most likely be found to produce income for §101(30) purposes. *See In re Ellenburg*, 89 B.R. 258, 260 (Bankr. N.D. Ga. 1988) ($500 per month for "bookkeeping services for her husband" constitutes regular income). In Tennessee, Mr. Hambrick could also fire the Debtor from that employment at any time, with or without cause. Mr. Hambrick's written promise to fund this Chapter 13 plan coupled with Mr. Hambrick's convincing testimonial commitments is at least as formal and concrete as legislative largess in a welfare program or as an employer's promises of work in the typical Chapter 13 case.

Mr. Hambrick's promise to fund this plan together with continued performance by this Debtor may generate rights and obligations that are every bit as enforceable as an employment contract. Reported decisions from many jurisdictions confirm that on theories of unjust enrichment, quantum meruit, restitution and express or implied contract, unmarried individuals sharing a household have successfully enforced financial commitments by their significant others.[5] These cases are not based on marital support obligations found

---

[5] A cross section of such cases might include: *Marvin v. Marvin*, 557 P.2d 106 (1976) (allegation that woman gave up career to become companion, cook and housekeeper in exchange for man's promise of financial support stated a cause of action based on an express contract); *Levar v. Elkins*, 604 P.2d 602 (Alaska 1980) (jury verdict on express or implied contractual theory where 20 years of cohabitation included promise to provide financial support in exchange for services as a homemaker and caretaker of children); *Burns v. Koellmer*, 527 A.2d 1210 (Conn. App. 1987) (quantum meruit and unjust enrichment may support recovery between unmarried couple); *Bright v. Kuehl*, 650 N.E.2d 311, 315 (Ind. Ct. App. 1995) ("a party who cohabits with another without subsequent

in statutes. Rather, recoveries typically are allowed on contract theories. If there is an amorphous requirement of legal rights or legal duties as predicate to a finding of income for §101(30) purposes, such rights and duties are found in the promises and performance by unmarried couples like this Debtor and Mr. Hambrick. . . .

. . . IT IS ORDERED, ADJUDGED and DECREED that this Debtor is an individual with regular income eligible for Chapter 13 relief.

POST-CASE FOLLOW-UP

Most but not all bankruptcy courts interpret the "regular income" requirement broadly, as illustrated in *Murphy*. But given the fact that, nationwide, only one out of three Chapter 13 cases succeeds (see the Informational Box at the end of Chapter Sixteen), is there reason to be more demanding regarding the stability and reliability of the income source for Chapter 13 debtors? After all, a Chapter 13 plan is going to run from three to five years and approving an income source for that duration from a source with whom the debtor is in a casual or informal relationship seems risky. On the other hand, as the judge in *Murphy* noted, what employment status isn't inherently risky and possibly temporary? What do you think were the main factors in the court's approval of debtor's income source in this case? If the boyfriend had not made a "written promise" to fund debtor's plan, would the court have approved it? If the couple had been together six months (rather than eleven years), would the court have approved it?

marriage is entitled to relief upon a showing of an express contract or available equitable theory such as an implied contract or unjust enrichment."); *Wilcox v. Trautz*, 693 N.E.2d 141 (Mass. 1998) (contractual agreement between unmarried cohabitates is enforceable so long as it conforms with ordinary rules of contract law); *Hudson v. DeLonjay*, 732 S.W.2d 922 (Mo. Ct. App. 1987) (implied contract to share assets between parties living together); *Kinkenon v. Hue*, 301 N.W.2d 77 (Neb. 1981) (express oral contract regarding disposition of personal property between cohabitants); *Dominguez v. Cruz*, 617 P.2d 1322 (N.M. App. 1980) ("It is well-established that this state does not recognize common law marriage.' . . . The presence or absence of the marital state is not relevant in this action. . . . If an agreement such as an oral contract can exist between business associates, one can exist between cohabiting adults who are not married if the essential elements of the contractual relationship are present.") (internal citations omitted); *Crowe v. De Gioia*, 495 A.2d 889 (N.J. App. Div. 1985) (court should enforce contracts between unmarried parties so long as not based only on a promise to marry); *Suggs v. Norris*, 364 S.E.2d 159 (N.C. 1988) (agreements regarding finances and property of unmarried cohabiting couple whether express or implied are enforceable as long as sexual services or promises thereof do not provide the consideration); *McHenry v. Smith*, 609 P.2d 855 (Or. 1980) (enforcing oral agreements with respect to pooling income, providing companionship, cooking and homemaking); *Knauer v. Knauer*, 470 A.2d 553 (Pa. Super. 1983) (agreements between nonmarried cohabitors are enforceable in an action for breach of contract); *Brooks v. Steffes*, 290 N.W.2d 697 (Wis. 1980) (implied contract between housekeeper and former partner for personal services).

In re Murphy: **Real Life Applications**

Answer the questions about the "regular income" requirement presented in the following scenarios.

1. The law office where you work has been preparing to file a Chapter 13 case for Elliot Bernard, aged 52, who was divorced last year and is struggling financially. He called today to say that he was just fired from his job but that his 30-year-old son who is employed will make the plan payments for him "as long as he can." See *In re Baird*, 228 B.R. 324, 327-328 (Bankr. M.D. Fla. 1999).

2. Nicole Watson, aged 49, lost her IT job during the Great Recession. While she was living exclusively on unemployment compensation, your law office filed a Chapter 13 case for Nicole that has now been operating successfully for two years. However, she called today and advised that her eligibility for unemployment compensation has expired and she is still unemployed. The good news is that she's found a boyfriend who she's been living with for the past year and he provides her with support "as needed." If a challenge is made to the client regarding whether she has sufficient regular income to fund her plan, is she likely to prevail? See *In re Loomis*, 487 B.R. 296 (Bankr. N.D. Okla. 2013).

3. After Nicole Watson from Question 2 lost her eligibility for unemployment compensation and became dependent on her boyfriend for support he did make the plan payments for her. Your office notified the standing trustee of the change in the client's source of income and, fortunately, no objection was made. However, after the boyfriend has made plan payments for Nicole for six months they break up and he stops making the payments. The standing trustee in the case is threatening to file a motion to dismiss Nicole's case if the missed payments are not made up immediately and regular timely payments resumed. Nicole is distraught at the thought of her Chapter 13 case being dismissed and her creditors descending on her and taking judgments against her. She keeps saying, "He promised, he promised. I thought I was going to be okay." Is Nicole in a position to compel her ex-boyfriend to resume plan payments or to sue him for damages if he fails to do so? After reading *In re Murphy*, what theories might your supervising attorney assert against the ex-boyfriend on behalf of Nicole?

Married couples can file a **joint petition** in a Chapter 13 case, under §§109(e) and 302(a), and commonly do so because they share joint liability for debts and joint ownership of property. However, the combined debts of the joint debtors cannot exceed the monetary debt limits set by §109(e), discussed above. Only one of the spouses needs to have regular income to fund the plan in a joint case.

The most obvious requirement for Chapter 13 eligibility is that the debtor must be an individual. Thus, Chapter 13 is not available to an entity. Both individuals with primarily consumer debt and individuals with primarily business debt can file under Chapter 13. Pursuant to §1304, an individual who owns a business as a sole proprietor can file Chapter 13 since the law does not consider the owner to be a separate legal person from his business. Such a debtor is permitted by §1304 to maintain control of his business and to operate it postpetition. The standing trustee in the case (discussed below) is required by §1302(c) to monitor the business and to provide reports on its operation to the court and creditors.

Pursuant to §109(g), an individual cannot file under Chapter 13 or any other chapter if, during the preceding 180 days, a prior bankruptcy petition was either (1) involuntarily dismissed due to the debtor's willful failure to appear before the court or comply with orders of the court, or (2) voluntarily dismissed by the debtor after creditors sought relief from the automatic stay to recover property of the debtor upon which they hold liens.

EXAMPLE

In the case of *In re Brown*, 2013 WL 2318414 (Bankr. E.D. Va. May. 28, 2013), the Browns filed a Chapter 13 case and Shackleton, who held a mortgage on debtor's home that was in arrears, filed a motion to lift stay so it could foreclose on the home. The parties initially worked out an agreement and a consent order was entered giving debtors time to cure the arrearage. When debtors failed to do so the bankruptcy court lifted the automatic stay as to Shackleton. Debtors then sought and received permission to voluntarily dismiss their Chapter 13 case. One day later they filed a second Chapter 13 case. When Shackleton proceeded with the foreclosure on debtor's home without seeking a lifting of the automatic stay in the second case, debtors alleged it had violated the automatic stay. The court disagreed noting that under Code §362(b)(21), the filing of a petition does not operate as a stay if the debtor is ineligible under §109(g) to be a debtor (as we noted in Chapter Nine, Section F). Since the Browns had voluntarily dismissed their first case after Shackleton obtained a lifting of the stay they were ineligible to file a new Chapter 13 case for 180 days following that dismissal under §109(g). Since they were ineligible to be debtors in the second case the automatic stay never arose against Shackleton in that case.

P-H 13-a: Assume that each of the following debtors filed their Chapter 13 petition today. Which of them is in danger of having the case involuntarily dismissed on the grounds that they are not eligible to be debtors under Chapter 13?

a. An individual who filed another Chapter 13 case a month ago and had it voluntarily dismissed two weeks ago after a secured creditor filed a motion to lift stay but before the court had ruled on that motion.
b. An individual with $450,000 in credit card debt.
c. An individual who filed another Chapter 13 case four months ago and had it involuntarily dismissed for failure to appear and testify at his first meeting of creditors even after being explicitly ordered to do so by the bankruptcy judge.
d. An individual who owns a convenience store as a sole proprietor.
e. A corporation owned by a single shareholder and that operates a convenience store.

P-H 13-b: Vickie Long is experiencing problems paying her debts as they come due and is explaining her circumstances to your supervising attorney while you take notes. You learn that she went through a Chapter 13 more than a decade ago, when she completed a five-year plan and received a discharge. She also filed a second Chapter 13 case about 12 months ago, had a Chapter 13 plan confirmed, and was making payments under the plan including payments to the bank that holds the mortgage on her house. But when she missed some payments to Bank about two months ago, Bank filed a motion with the bankruptcy court to lift the automatic stay and foreclose. She decided then to just voluntarily dismiss her case and let Bank have the house and that's what happened. Now she rents but is still in financial trouble. Is Vickie eligible to file a third Chapter 13 case? Would it matter if Bank had threatened to file a motion to lift stay in the second case but had not done so before Vickie voluntarily dismissed that case? Would it matter if the motion to lift stay had been filed in the second case and that case was voluntarily dismissed nine months ago instead of two months ago?

Chapter 20 case Informal description of a Chapter 13 case filed soon after the debtor has received a discharge in Chapter 7.

Bankruptcy practitioners sometimes speak of a **Chapter 20 case**. There is no Chapter 20 in the Code, of course, but that phrase is used to describe the not uncommon practice of a debtor obtaining a discharge in a Chapter 7 case and then filing a Chapter 13 case shortly thereafter (7 + 13 = 20). Section 1328(f) provides that a Chapter 13 debtor cannot receive a discharge in his Chapter 13 case if he has received a discharge under Chapter 7, 11, or 12 during the four years preceding his filing of the Chapter 13 petition (we will consider discharge in a Chapter 13 case in detail in Chapter Sixteen, Section E). However, a Chapter 13 case can be filed and a plan approved even though no discharge is granted in the case (e.g., the debtor proposes a 100 percent plan involving no discharge of debt).

Why would a debtor who has received a discharge in Chapter 7 file a Chapter 13 less than four years later? Sometimes it is planned, a calculated strategy. A debtor goes through a Chapter 7 to discharge all the debt he can and then immediately files a Chapter 13 and proposes a plan that will enable him to make payments on his remaining debt on a more flexible schedule than his creditors would allow otherwise. Or he proposes a plan to take advantage of the more generous lien-stripping options that Chapter 13 allows, as we will see in Chapter Fifteen. Often the Chapter 13 filing so soon after the Chapter 7 discharge is unplanned but necessary because the debtor has fallen behind on payment schedules and needs a Chapter 13 plan to cure arrearages and perhaps even to obtain court assistance to control his own spending.

Prepetition credit counseling Counseling that an individual debtor must receive from an approved credit counseling agency as a qualification for filing.

Since the Chapter 13 filer is by definition an individual, he must comply with the **prepetition credit counseling** requirement of §109(h)(1), imposed on all individuals filing under any chapter of the Code.

For our detailed study of how a Chapter 13 proceeding works we will focus on the fictitious but realistic Chapter 13 case of Roger and Susan Matthews filed in 2016 in a U.S. bankruptcy court in Pennsylvania. (As explained in Chapter Six, Section M, Pennsylvania was selected for use in the Matthews case study primarily because it has not opted out of the federal exemptions for individual filers.) If you have not done so already, go to Appendix B at this time and read the Assignment Memorandum for Roger and Susan Matthews.

P-H 13-c: Based on the budget for Roger and Susan Matthews shown in the Assignment Memorandum in Appendix B, how much money do the Matthews have available each month to apply to the bills not being paid? How financially vulnerable are they to unexpected expenses in excess of those budgeted or to job loss? Does it appear from a quick look at their circumstances that the Matthews will be able to propose a plan that will pay 100 percent of their secured and unsecured debts over a three- to five-year period?

B. ▶ Filing a Chapter 13 Case

1. The Petition, Schedules, and Other Documents

A Chapter 13 case is commenced in the same way as a Chapter 7, by filing Official Form 101, Voluntary Petition for Individuals Filing for Bankruptcy the Matthews' joint petition in Chapter 13 is Document 1 in the Matthews case file accessible on the companion web site to the textbook at http://aspenlawschool. com/books/Parsons_Debt4e/). Per Bankruptcy Rule 1007(b), the Chapter 13 debtor, like the Chapter 7 individual debtor, must also file a list of creditors (see Document 2 in the Matthews case file), along with the various schedules of assets and liabilities, a statement of financial affairs, and the other statements and documents discussed in Chapter Eight, Section B (see Documents 3 through 13 and 15-17 in the Matthews case file), except for the Statement of Intent. Section 521(a)(2) requires the filing of Form 108 Statement of Intention only of an individual Chapter 7 debtor. The Chapter 13 debtor's proposed plan will indicate how he or she intends to deal with property that is subject to a security interest.

P-H 13-d: Review the exemptions claimed by the Matthews on their Schedule C (Document 4 in the Matthews case file). Do all of those claimed exemptions appear to comply with §522? Note that Roger Matthews is reporting a priority claim on Schedule E/F in favor of the IRS for $1,000 in back taxes he has not paid. You may want to review the discussion of priority claims in Chapter Eleven, Section B, and the treatment such claims receive in a Chapter 7 liquidation. In Chapter Fifteen we will see how they are treated in a Chapter 13. Go ahead and look at the Matthews' Chapter 13 plan (Illustration 15-b and Document 18 in the Matthews case file). The plan indicates that they are going to surrender one of their vehicles to the secured creditor. Since the Chapter 13 plan states the debtor's intent with regard to secured property, no statement of intent is required.

The Chapter 13 debtor is not required to file Form 122A as the individual Chapter 7 debtor is. Instead, the Chapter 13 debtor must file Form 122C-1, Chapter 13 Statement of Your Current Monthly Income and Calculation of Commitment Period, and the above median debtor must also file Form 122C-2, Chapter 13 Calculation of Your Disposable Income, to determine the **applicable commitment period** (i.e., required duration) of the debtor's plan and the amount of **disposable income** the debtor is expected to have available during the plan term to pay to creditors. We will consider these forms and these concepts in detail in the next chapter.

The signatures on a Chapter 13 petition involve the same considerations as those on a Chapter 7 petition. This might be a good time to review that discussion in Chapter Eight, Section A.

A Chapter 13 case can only be commenced voluntarily. The Code does not authorize an involuntary Chapter 13 filing.

2. Attorney's Fees in a Chapter 13 Case

As previously noted, in all bankruptcy cases the attorney's fee agreement between the debtor and his attorney must be in writing, per §528(a)(1). As in a Chapter 7 case, Bankruptcy Rule 2016 requires the debtor to file Official Form 2030 Disclosure of Compensation of Attorney for Debtor in a Chapter 13 case. (See Document 16 in the Matthews case file.) However, attorney's fees work differently in a reorganization case than in a Chapter 7 liquidation. In a Chapter 13 case, the fees charged by the debtor's attorney must not only be disclosed, they must also be approved by the court. And they can be paid by the debtor through the plan. If the fees are disclosed and payment is provided in the plan, the order confirming the plan (discussed in Chapter Sixteen, Section B) is a sufficient court approval of the fees. Some federal districts may require a formal application for payment of attorney's fees separate from the plan.

EXAMPLE

The Disclosure of Compensation of Attorney for Debtor filed by the Matthews' attorney discloses that $2,000 of the $3,000 fee was paid prior to filing of the petition (Document 16 in the Matthews case file), the balance of $1,000 will be paid through the plan (Document 18 in the Matthews case file), and the order confirming the plan (Document 21 in the Matthews case file) is sufficient court approval.

Sometimes attorneys for the Chapter 13 debtor are called upon to provide legal assistance not contemplated by the initial fee paid prepetition or through the plan. In that event, the attorney will be required to file an **application for additional compensation** and obtain court approval of the proposed fee.

EXAMPLE

Assume that the attorney for the Matthews discloses his initial fee agreement with the clients and a plan is confirmed that calls for that fee to be paid through the plan. A year later, the Matthews need to modify the plan due to changed circumstances (modification is discussed in Chapter Sixteen, Section D) and call on the attorney again. The original fee did not contemplate this additional work, and so the attorney will file an application for additional compensation and obtain court approval for the additional fee. Bankruptcy Rule 2016 will apply, requiring the attorney to submit a detailed, itemized statement of services rendered and expenses incurred.

Fees allowed to debtor's attorneys for Chapter 13 work vary considerably among bankruptcy courts across the country.

Illustration 13-a: UNIQUE DUTIES OF THE CHAPTER 13 STANDING TRUSTEE

- To evaluate the case to make sure it is filed in good faith and in compliance with all Code requirements
- To ensure that the debtor begins making payments under the plan as required by the Code (which often occurs before plan confirmation, as discussed later)
- To review the debtor's proposed plan for feasibility and good faith and to be heard in support or opposition to its confirmation
- To review any proposed modifications of the debtor's plan after confirmation or to propose such modification and to be heard in support or opposition to any proposed modification
- Upon approval of the plan, to collect the payments made by the debtor under the plan and to distribute those payments pursuant to the plan
- To advise the debtor on other than legal matters and to assist the debtor in performance of the plan
- If any claim for a domestic support obligation is made in the case, to advise the holder of the claim of his or her rights including the right to utilize the state child support enforcement agency to collect the amount owed

3. The Standing Chapter 13 Trustee

In most federal districts the trustee in a Chapter 13 case is not appointed from the trustee panel, as are trustees in Chapter 7 cases (see discussion in Chapter Nine, Section B). Instead, there is one individual designated by the U.S. Trustee to serve as the Chapter 13 **standing trustee** pursuant to 28 U.S.C. §586(b). The standing trustee will automatically serve as trustee in all Chapter 13 cases filed in that district. In districts with heavier Chapter 13 filings, there may be more than one standing trustee. In most districts the standing trustee also handles Chapter 12 cases.

Standing trustee A person appointed by the U.S. Trustee to serve as trustee in all Chapter 12 and 13 cases filed in the district.

Section 1302(b) assigns the Chapter 13 standing trustee many of the same duties as those of the Chapter 7 trustee (see Illustration 9-a), with the important exception that the Chapter 13 standing trustee's duties do not include the Chapter 7 trustee's duty under §704(a)(1) to "collect and reduce to money" the property of the estate. Thus, the Chapter 13 trustee will not seize nonexempt assets, liquidate them, and distribute the proceeds to creditors. In fact, per §1327(b), upon confirmation of the Chapter 13 plan all property of the estate (to be discussed in Section D) vests in the debtor, not the standing trustee, unless the plan or court order directs otherwise. Remember, Chapter 13 is an individual reorganization or adjustment of debts proceeding, not a liquidation. But §1302(b) imposes unique duties on the Chapter 13 standing trustee, and those duties are summarized in Illustration 13-a.

We will have more to say about the duties of the Chapter 13 standing trustee as we consider other aspects of administering a Chapter 13 case.

C. ▶ The Order for Relief, Notice to Creditors, and Automatic Stay Under Chapter 13

As was discussed in Chapter Nine, Section A, most bankruptcy courts treat the filing of the petition as the entry of an order for relief in the case, while some enter a formal order to that effect. Pursuant to §342, the clerk of the bankruptcy court will give immediate notice to all creditors and other parties in interest of the commencement of the case using Official Form 309I. (See Document 19 in the Matthews case file.)

Filing the petition under Chapter 13 triggers the **automatic stay** provision of §362. As we have learned, the stay arises by operation of law, with the exception of the BAPCPA limitations imposed on debtors who have filed once (stay limited to 30 days unless debtor moves for extension) or twice (no stay at all) in the year preceding the current filing. (See discussion in Chapter Nine, Section F.) As long as the stay is in effect, creditors may not initiate or continue collection demands, lawsuits, or execution on judgments. The notice of commencement to creditors advises creditors of the stay and the danger of penalties if they continue collection efforts.

Section 1301(a) of the Code provides that unless the bankruptcy court authorizes otherwise, a creditor may not seek to collect a consumer debt from any individual who is liable along with the debtor. This is the **co-debtor stay** of Chapter 13. It does not apply in Chapter 7 or 11 cases. It does not apply to co-debtors on nonconsumer debts in Chapter 13. As we have learned, consumer debts are those incurred by an individual primarily for personal, family, or household purposes (see §101(8)).

Co-debtor stay A Chapter 13 provision extending the automatic stay to individual co-debtors of the Chapter 13 debtor regarding consumer debt.

EXAMPLE

> A married person may file a Chapter 13 and the debtor's spouse, who does not file, will be protected by the stay from being pursued on any consumer debts she owes with her debtor/husband. Of course, if the spouse files as a joint debtor, they both have the benefit of the automatic stay.

The rationale behind the co-debtor stay of Chapter 13 is that persons who do not themselves receive the actual consideration for a consumer debt often volunteer to become liable for such a debt and it would be unfair to stay collection against the person who did receive the actual consideration while collection proceeded against the person who didn't.

EXAMPLE

> Assume Susan Matthews's parents co-signed the promissory note when Roger and Susan borrowed money to purchase furniture for their house. When Roger and Susan file for Chapter 13 relief, the automatic stay goes into effect on their behalf. But what about the parents? They are not in a bankruptcy proceeding. Without the co-debtor stay, the creditor could proceed with collection efforts against the parents even though they received no actual consideration (furniture) for the debt.

Sections 1301(a)(1) and (2) provide that the co-debtor stay is automatically lifted when the Chapter 13 debtor receives a discharge and the case is closed or when the case is dismissed or converted to a Chapter 7. Per §§1301(c)(2) and (d), the co-debtor stay is to be lifted on motion of the creditor and after notice and a hearing *to the extent that* the plan does not provide for paying the creditor. Twenty days after the filing of a motion to lift stay under §1301(c)(2), the stay is automatically terminated per the mandate of §1301(d) unless the debtor or co-debtor files a written objection in which case a hearing will be conducted.

EXAMPLE

Assume a married person files a Chapter 13 case but the spouse does not. The spouse initially gets the benefit of the co-debtor stay as to consumer debts. But if the debtor files a plan that calls for paying only half of that debt and the plan is confirmed, the creditor may file a motion to have the co-debtor stay lifted as to the half of the debt not to be paid under the plan. The co-debtor stay will automatically terminate 20 days after the motion is filed unless the debtor or co-debtor files a written objection. If an objection is filed, a hearing will be conducted at which the burden will be on the party filing the objection to show cause why the stay should be continued as to the co-debtor.

Per §1301(c), the co-debtor stay can also be lifted by motion of the creditor and after notice and a hearing if the creditor can show that either

- the creditor will be irreparably harmed if the stay is not lifted; or
- between the debtor and the co-debtor, the co-debtor received the actual consideration for the claim.

EXAMPLE

Assume a married person files a Chapter 13 but the spouse does not. The spouse gets the benefit of the co-debtor stay as to joint consumer debts, but if the creditor can show that the consumer item purchased was for the exclusive benefit of the spouse and not the debtor, the stay may be lifted. Or, if the creditor can show that the co-debtor is disposing of assets and will be judgment proof when the case is over, that may constitute irreparable harm to the creditor.

D. ▶ Property of the Estate in a Chapter 13 Case

Just as in a Chapter 7, all of the Chapter 13 debtor's nonexempt property becomes **property of the estate** upon filing of the petition and, as such, is subject to the control of the court, per §§1306(a) and 541(a). However, as noted earlier, the standing trustee will not take possession of and sell the property of the estate unless the debtor's plan contemplates a surrender and sale of property in which the estate has equity. Instead the debtor will retain possession of the property, subject to the terms of his plan per §1306(b).

The standing trustee in a Chapter 13 case has the same powers as a Chapter 7 trustee to challenge a debtor's claimed exemptions (Chapter Ten, Section C) and to pursue disputed, contingent, or unliquidated claims of the debtor against third parties (see Chapter Ten, Section B). The standing trustee also has the same power to compel turnover of the debtor's property from third persons and custodians holding it (see Chapter Ten, Section D) and to avoid other prepetition transfers of the debtor's property (see Chapter Ten, Section E) as a Chapter 7 trustee.

Having said all that, Chapter 13 standing trustees rarely pursue prepetition claims on behalf of the debtor even though they might increase the property of the estate. And Chapter 13 trustees only rarely exercise their turnover and avoidance powers on behalf of the estate. Remember the statutory duties of the standing trustee in a Chapter 13 do not include liquidating the estate as in a Chapter 7. Instead, the trustee's functions are to examine the debtor at the 341 hearing and review the petition, supporting schedules, and the debtor's proposed plan to determine if the case is properly filed and plan confirmation is feasible and otherwise appropriate. Following plan confirmation the trustee will receive and disburse payments to creditors and follow up on the administration of cases as needed.

The debtor may be handicapped in accomplishing that task since, other than the limited power to avoid a lien to protect an exemption (discussed in Chapter Eleven, Section C) and the power granted the debtor in §522(h) to avoid a transfer of property or recover a setoff in order to protect an exemption (discussed in more detail below), the Code does not specifically grant the Chapter 13 debtor the power to compel turnover or to avoid prepetition transfers. The standing trustee's reluctance to utilize the turnover or avoidance powers (or as we will see in the next section, to object to claims despite having standing to do so) is often a point of contention in light of the trustee's duty under §1302(b) to assist the debtor in performance under the plan (see Illustration 13-a). But, where challenged, the courts grant the standing trustee discretion in the performance of that duty and recognize that "the Trustee must balance this duty with his other duties." *In re Mallory*, 444 B.R. 553, 561-562 (S.D. Tex. 2011).

The common reluctance of a Chapter 13 standing trustee to exercise turnover or avoidance powers on behalf of the estate has also led to Chapter 13 debtors attempting to use those powers themselves and courts are split on whether the debtor has standing to do so. The narrow view of the debtor's powers reasons that since §323 designates the trustee as the representative of the estate and grants the trustee capacity to sue and be sued; since §1303, enumerating the powers of the trustee that the debtor has, does not reference the turnover or avoidance sections; and since the various turnover and avoidance sections of the Code expressly confer those powers on "the trustee," the Chapter 13 debtor does not have standing to act under such provisions without the trustee joining in. See, e.g., *In re Mitrano*, 468 B.R. 795 (E.D. Va. 2012) (only Chapter 13 trustee has standing to bring §548 fraudulent transfer action), and *In re Gardner*, 218 B.R. 338 (Bankr. E.D. Pa. 1998), and cases cited therein.

The competing view notes that under §1306(b) property of the estate is retained by the Chapter 13 debtor and since the various turnover and avoidance powers are intended to capture the property of the estate as defined in §541 the debtor should have power to utilize those powers for that purpose, at least where the standing trustee refuses to do so. See, e.g., *In re Freeman*, 72 B.R. 850, 854-855 (Bankr. E.D. Va. 1987) ("Although there is a substantial split of authority among the courts which have considered this issue, this Court is satisfied that in cases such as this one, where the trustee does not act, the debtor himself may exercise the trustee's 'strong arm' powers under §544(a)"), and *In re Willis*, 48 B.R. 295, 302-303 (S.D. Tex. 1985) (the "realities of bankruptcy practice" require allowing Chapter 13 debtors to pursue avoidance power actions).

In those districts following the narrow view that denies the debtor standing to exercise the turnover and avoidance powers on his own, the debtor may be able to convince the trustee to agree to a provision in the plan providing that the trustee will pursue the action. Sometimes debtors convince the trustee to bring the action jointly with the debtor and to retain the debtor's attorney as special counsel under §327(e) so that a single attorney represents both. In some of those districts, ironically perhaps, the courts allow the plan to delegate the standing of the trustee to bring an avoidance or turnover action to the debtor and consider this "derivative standing" of the debtor sufficient. In some districts this derivative standing is accomplished separate from the plan by a postconfirmation court order. See *In re Cohen*, 305 B.R. 886, 891 n.5 (9th Cir. B.A.P. 2004) (Even if Chapter 13 debtor lacked concurrent statutory standing with trustee to maintain avoidance action, the court has authority in a Chapter 13 case to permit a party other than trustee to bring a trustee avoidance action with explicit court approval.).

Where the debtor is allowed to maintain a turnover or avoidance action, either in the plan or a postconfirmation court order, the plan or order will typically require the debtor to pay such amounts recovered to the standing trustee per §1325(c) for distribution to creditors under the plan.

P-H 13-e: Determine if the courts of your federal district or circuit have decided the question of whether a Chapter 13 debtor may utilize the turnover and avoidance powers of the Code. If so, is the right to do so limited to situations where the standing trustee is requested to bring the action but refuses, or is standing treated as completely concurrent?

Ironically, the debtor's inability to bring property transferred prepetition back into the estate using the turnover or avoidance powers of the Code may cause the standing trustee to object to the plan on the basis that it doesn't provide unsecured creditors as much as they would receive in a Chapter 7 liquidation (a requirement for plan confirmation discussed in Chapter Sixteen). This can be a real catch-22 for Chapter 13 debtors.

There are two exceptions to this controversy over the debtor's standing to commence an avoidance or turnover action without the trustee. Section 522(h) specifically authorizes a debtor to institute an action to avoid a transfer of property or recover a setoff to the extent that the transfer would be avoidable if brought by a trustee and the debtor can claim an exemption in the property effected. And, as discussed in Chapter Eleven, Section C, an individual debtor has power to institute an action to avoid a **judicial lien** and some other liens that impair an exemption as authorized by §522(f)(1)(A).

EXAMPLE

Even in a district that did not allow a Chapter 13 debtor to file a §547 preferential transfer action on his or her own in order to increase the property of the estate and increase the payout to unsecured creditors, the debtor, pursuant to §522(h), could maintain that action but only to the extent the debtor could and intended to exempt the property to be recovered in the action. Let's say a debtor being hard pressed by a creditor on an overdue debt agrees to transfer title to his car to the creditor in partial satisfaction of the obligation. Two months later the debtor files a Chapter 13 case. The transfer of the vehicle occurred during the 90-day preference period and if debtor could recover it, he could exempt it in his bankruptcy case. A §547 preference action might be just the ticket and if the standing trustee won't bring that action, the debtor can under §522(h).

P-H 13-f: In contrast to the silence of the Code regarding a Chapter 13 debtor having the turnover and avoidance powers of the trustee, §1203 does specifically grant those powers to a Chapter 12 debtor (as discussed in Chapter Twenty, Section A) and §1107(a) grants those powers to a Chapter 11 debtor as discussed in Chapter Seventeen, Section E). Technically, the reason for that distinction is that a bankruptcy trustee is not initially appointed in a Chapter 11 case and the debtor continues to operate his business as a debtor in possession. Although there is a standing trustee in a Chapter 12 case, that debtor, too, is considered a debtor in possession and given some of the powers of a trustee. Is this an oversight in the Code's treatment of a Chapter 13 debtor? Should the standing trustee in a Chapter 13 be required to pursue turnover and avoidance actions that appear to have merit? Is the fact that most such prepetition transfers by the Chapter 13 debtor were voluntary a sufficient reason to deny him the right to exercise such powers if the standing trustee declines?

Closely related to the Chapter 13 debtor's standing to commence a turnover or avoidance action in lieu of the standing trustee doing so is the debtor's right to pursue a prepetition cause of action in contract, tort, or statutory relief (e.g., employment discrimination) when the standing trustee will not do so. Such claims are choses in action and constitute property of the estate under §541. In Chapter 7 cases trustees routinely pursue such claims if they have validity to enhance the property of the estate, but for the reasons we have discussed, standing Chapter 13 trustees will rarely do so. That leaves the question of whether the debtor him- or herself may pursue such prepetition claims when the standing trustee abstains.

Again, the courts are split. Some courts take a strict view and say that the Code gives standing to sue and be sued on claims arising prepetition only to the trustee and the debtor therefore lacks standing to bring the suit. See, e.g., *Smith v. Cumulus Broadcasting, LLC,* 2011 WL 3489820 (D.S.C. 2011), and *In re Gardner,* 218 B.R. 338 (Bankr. E.D. Pa. 1998). Other courts, likely a majority, rely on the §1306(b) mandate that the Chapter 13 debtor is to remain in possession of all property of the estate unless a confirmed plan says otherwise and on Bankruptcy Rule 6009, which authorizes a trustee or debtor in possession to enter an appearance in and prosecute any pending action or to initiate any action on behalf of the estate. In other words, these courts interpret §1306(b) to impliedly designate the Chapter 13 debtor as a debtor in possession (though the Code does not explicitly do so) and then gives the Chapter 13 debtor the benefit of the standing bestowed on the debtor in possession in Bankruptcy Rule 6009. See, e.g., *Cable v. Ivy Tech State College,* 200 F.3d 467 (7th Cir. 1999) (Chapter 13 debtor had standing to maintain prepetition ADA discrimination action as an asset of the estate); *In re Bowker,* 245 B.R. 192 (Bankr. D.N.J. 2000) (Chapter 13 debtor had standing to prosecute prepetition personal injury action as an asset of the estate); and *Olick v. Parker & Parsley Petroleum Co.,* 145 F.3d 513 (2d Cir. 1998) (Chapter 13 debtor had standing to prosecute prepetition class action alleging securities violations).

In districts that do not grant the debtor standing to pursue prepetition causes of action, the debtor may be able to negotiate with the standing trustee to include a provision in the plan calling for joint prosecution of the action or delegation of the standing to the debtor or to obtain a postconfirmation court order authorizing the same as discussed above in connection with the trustee's avoidance and turnover powers.

The definition of property of the estate is actually broader in a Chapter 13 than in a Chapter 7. Per §1306(a), what becomes property of the estate in a Chapter 13 includes postpetition property: all nonexempt property acquired by the debtor *after* the petition is filed and while the plan is in effect, including postpetition earnings and other income received by the debtor. The reason for including postpetition property, including income and earnings in the Chapter 13 estate, is that the plan is going to be funded from the postpetition income of the debtor, and that income and any other property the debtor acquires during the term of the plan must be subject to court supervision.

EXAMPLE

> Assume a Chapter 13 debtor's petition was filed one month ago and the proposed plan was confirmed today and will last for 48 months. The property of the estate will include all nonexempt property owned by the debtor as of the date the petition was filed; all income received by the debtor between the date the petition was filed and the date of confirmation; all income received by the debtor during the 48 months that the plan will run; and all nonexempt property acquired by the debtor by purchase, gift, inheritance, or otherwise during the 48 months of the plan's duration.

The rights of creditors secured in the property of the debtor when a Chapter 13 petition is filed are governed in the first instance by §506, which provides that such claim is secured up to the value of the property securing the claim. We will consider the options of a Chapter 13 debtor in dealing with secured claims in Chapter Fifteen, Section B.

E. ▶ The First Meeting of Creditors and Filing Proofs of Claim in a Chapter 13 Case

Pursuant to §341 and Bankruptcy Rule 2007(a), between 21 and 50 days after the debtor files the Chapter 13 petition the first meeting of creditors (the 341 meeting) is held. The Notice of Chapter 13 Case, Official Form 309I, will advise the creditors of the time and place of the meeting. (See Document 19 in the Matthews case file.) As in a Chapter 7 case, the Chapter 13 debtor is placed under oath at the meeting and will answer questions asked by the standing trustee and creditors. Significantly, the debt adjustment plan proposed by the debtor will be available to the trustee and creditors at the meeting because per Bankruptcy Rule 3015(b) it must be filed by the debtor with the petition or within 14 days thereafter. Most of the questions at the 341 meeting will typically relate to the plan.

As discussed in Chapter Ten, Section A, the proof of claim in a Chapter 7, Chapter 13, or Chapter 12 case must be filed not later than 90 days after the first date set for the meeting of creditors per Bankruptcy Rule 3002(c). A governmental unit, however, has 180 days from the date the case is filed to file its claim.

The failure of a secured creditor to file a timely proof of claim does not impair its secured position in the property of the debtor per §506(d)(2). So, technically, the secured creditor need not file a proof of claim to preserve its secured status in the debtor's property. The lien on the property if properly perfected will pass through the bankruptcy case unmolested and the creditor can continue to look to its collateral for satisfaction of the underlying obligation (as by, in the event of default, asking for lifting of the stay so that it can foreclose or repossess). However, §1326(c) requires the standing trustee in a Chapter 13 to make plan distributions to creditors under the confirmed plan and the standing trustee can only make those distributions on account of allowed claims. Bankruptcy Rule 3021 ("after a plan is confirmed, distribution shall be made to creditors whose clams have been allowed . . ."). Consequently, most courts read §506 and §1326 together to mean that although the secured creditor's lien on the collateral continues without the filing of a proof of claim, that secured creditor cannot receive payments under the Chapter 13 plan unless a timely proof of claim is filed. See, e.g., *In re Dumain*, 492 B.R. 140 (Bankr. S.D.N.Y. 2013). Thus, the secured creditor in a Chapter 13 case should, as a practical matter, always file a proof of claim and attach proof of its security interest in the debtor's property and the perfected status of that interest.

The timing rule for filing proofs of claim in a Chapter 13, set forth in Bankruptcy Rule 3002(c), illustrates how tricky such deadlines can become and the importance of the attorney knowing the deadlines that apply and of having a system in place to make sure those deadlines are met.

EXAMPLE

> Assume a Chapter 13 case is filed and the 341 meeting is scheduled for September 1. Then, the meeting is rescheduled for September 15. The proofs of claim are due in that case 90 days from September 1, not 90 days from September 15. If you are responsible for preparing the proof of claim for a client or if you are representing the standing trustee or the debtor, it is imperative that you know the applicable deadline.

Any party in interest may object to a claim filed by a creditor in a Chapter 13 case pursuant to §502, just as can be done in a Chapter 7 (see Chapter Ten, Section A). That objecting party is most likely to be the debtor himself. As with the exercise of avoidance powers discussed in the last section, the standing trustee in many districts leaves it to the debtor to object to creditor claims.

CHAPTER SUMMARY

A Chapter 13 bankruptcy case is a debt adjustment proceeding in which an individual with regular income formulates a plan to use future income to pay some or all of his debts over the following three to five years. Husbands and wives may be joint debtors in Chapter 13. Most courts utilize a broad definition of the regular income eligibility requirement and include both earned and unearned income of the debtor and even dependable support from a third person.

An individual cannot file under Chapter 13 if, during the preceding 180 days, a prior bankruptcy petition was either involuntarily dismissed due to the debtor's willful failure to appear before the court or comply with orders of the court, or voluntarily dismissed by the debtor after creditors sought relief from the automatic stay to recover property of the debtor upon which they hold liens. A Chapter 13 debtor cannot receive a discharge in his Chapter 13 case if he has received a discharge under Chapter 7, 11, or 12 during the four years preceding his filing of the Chapter 13 petition. A Chapter 13 may be filed less than four years following a Chapter 7 discharge if the Chapter 13 does not involve any discharge.

A Chapter 13 is commenced by filing a petition with supporting schedules. The proposed plan of reorganization must be filed by the debtor with the petition or within 14 days thereafter. Attorney's fees in a Chapter 13 must be disclosed and approved by the court.

An order for relief is entered or deemed entered with the filing of the petition, and the automatic stay goes into effect. In a Chapter 13, the automatic stay includes a stay against proceeding against nonfiling co-debtors on consumer debts. The co-debtor stay can be lifted on motion if the creditor can show it will otherwise be irreparably harmed or that the co-debtor received the actual consideration.

A Chapter 13 standing trustee will administer the case under the supervision of the U.S. Trustee. The standing trustee will ensure that the plan of reorganization is proposed in good faith and is feasible and will then collect the debtor's plan payments and distribute funds to creditors pursuant to the plan.

Property of the estate in a Chapter 13 includes both prepetition and postpetition property of the debtor for the duration of the plan. However, in a Chapter 13, the standing trustee does not take possession of, abandon, or sell property of the estate unless the plan calls for it; the debtor retains possession of his property. The Chapter 13 standing trustee may, but rarely does, pursue contested claims on behalf of the estate or exercise his turnover or avoidance powers, leaving it to the debtor to pursue such matters as state law allows. Courts are divided over whether the Chapter 13 debtor himself has standing under the Code to maintain an avoidance or turnover action other than an action to avoid a judicial lien to preserve an exemption and an action to avoid a transfer avoidable by the trustee under one of those powers and which would preserve an exemption in the debtor. Most courts hold that a Chapter 13 debtor can also institute a postpetition action based on a prepetition common law or statutory cause of action on his own in order to enhance the property of the estate.

A first meeting of creditors is conducted at which questions about the plan or objections to it are often resolved. In order to participate in distributions under the plan, both secured and unsecured creditors must file proofs of claim within 90 days following the meeting of creditors. A governmental creditor, however, has 180 days from the date the petition is filed to file its proof of claim.

REVIEW QUESTIONS

1. Why are Chapter 13 plans sometimes called "wage earner" plans? Must the Chapter 13 debtor be a wage earner? Explain the "regular income" requirement for Chapter 13 relief.
2. What are the secured and unsecured monetary debt maximums for one seeking to file for Chapter 13 relief? If a debtor does not qualify for Chapter 13 relief due to exceeding those limits, what other reorganization proceeding might the debtor choose?

3. Can a Chapter 13 be commenced involuntarily? Must a Chapter 13 debtor comply with the prepetition credit counseling requirement?

4. How are debtor's attorney's fees handled differently in a Chapter 13 than in a Chapter 7 case? If a debtor's attorney is required to do unexpected work for the debtor after the plan has been approved, what is the procedure for receiving compensation?

5. How does a Chapter 13 debtor determine the required duration of his or her plan of reorganization?

6. What do we mean by a "standing trustee" and how is that different from a "trustee panel"?

7. List all the duties of a Chapter 13 standing trustee that you can recall. Describe how the duties of a Chapter 13 standing trustee differ from those of a Chapter 7 trustee.

8. What is the co-debtor stay of Chapter 13? What is the policy behind the co-debtor stay? How can the co-debtor stay be lifted?

9. How is the property of the estate defined differently in a Chapter 13 than in a Chapter 7 and why?

10. Why might a Chapter 13 debtor have difficulty setting aside prepetition transfers of his or her property or liquidating contingent claims the debtor has against others or pursuing prepetition claims against third parties that are assets of the estate?

WORDS AND PHRASES TO REMEMBER

applicable commitment period
application for additional
    compensation
automatic stay
can-pay debtor
Chapter 20 case
co-debtor stay
consumer bankruptcy case
consumer debtor
consumer debts

debt adjustment plan
disposable income
individual with regular income
joint petition
judicial lien
order confirming plan
property of the estate
regular income
standing trustee
wage earner plan

TO LEARN MORE: A number of TLM activities to accompany this chapter are accessible on the companion web site for this textbook at http://aspen-lawschool.com/books/Parsons_Debt4e/.

Chapter Fourteen:

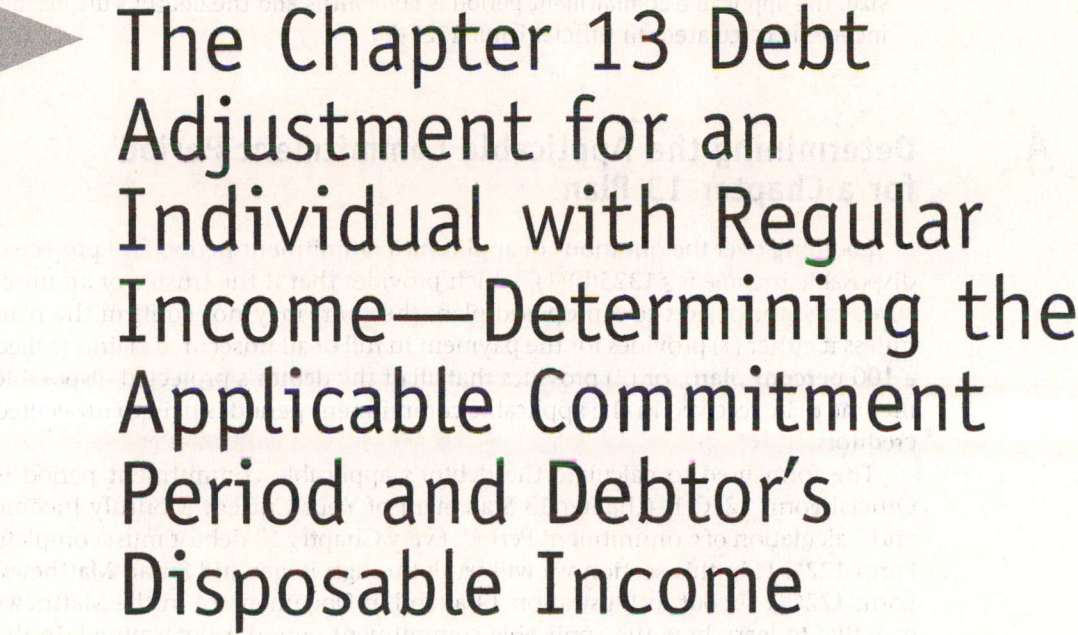

The Chapter 13 Debt Adjustment for an Individual with Regular Income—Determining the Applicable Commitment Period and Debtor's Disposable Income

Disposable income Income a bankruptcy debtor has available to pay creditors after deducting income necessary for the support or maintenance of the debtor and his dependents.

Applicable commitment period The required duration of a Chapter 13 plan, between three and five years.

Projected disposable income Income that a bankruptcy debtor is projected to have available during the term of his or her plan to pay unsecured creditors after deducting income necessary for the support or maintenance of the debtor and debtor's dependents and to pay secured creditors.

The idea behind a Chapter 13 plan is that for the term of the plan, three to five years (the **commitment period** required by §1325(b)(4)), the debtor retains enough monthly income to pay his or her basic living expenses, either surrenders secured property to the secured creditors or makes arrangements to pay the full value of secured debt on some allowed terms (to be considered in the next chapter), and then turns over the excess income, called debtor's **disposable income**, to the trustee, who will disperse that amount to unsecured creditors as called for in the plan. Thus, the first step in calculating a Chapter 13 plan is to determine the **applicable commitment period** for the debtor's plan. The second step is to determine the debtor's **projected disposable income** during the plan period. We will consider these two important steps in this chapter. In the next chapter we will look at the various ways that a Chapter 13 debtor can propose to deal with secured and unsecured debts in his or her plan.

KEY CONCEPTS

- A Chapter 13 plan must run from 36 to 60 months, and the debtor must complete Official Form 122C-1 to determine the applicable commitment period for the debtor's plan
- If the current monthly income of the Chapter 13 debtor as calculated on Official Form 122C-1 is below the applicable median income for his state and household size, the applicable commitment period is 36 months and the debtor's disposable income is determined primarily from Schedules I and J

- If the current monthly income of the Chapter 13 debtor as calculated on Official Form 122C-1 is above the applicable median income for his state and household size, the applicable commitment period is 60 months and the debtor's disposable income is calculated on Official Form 122C-2

A. ▶ Determining the Applicable Commitment Period for a Chapter 13 Plan

Looming over the questions of applicable commitment period and projected disposable income is §1325(b)(1), which provides that if the trustee or an unsecured creditor objects to a proposed plan, the court may not confirm the plan unless it either (1) provides for the payment in full of all unsecured claims (called a **100 percent plan**), or (2) provides that all of the debtor's projected disposable income to be received in the applicable commitment period is paid to unsecured creditors.

The form used to calculate the debtor's applicable commitment period is Official Form 122C-1, Chapter 13 Statement of Your Current Monthly Income and Calculation of Commitment Period. Every Chapter 13 debtor must complete Form 122C-1. In this section we will work through Roger and Susan Matthews' Form 122C-1 set out in Illustration 14-a (and in Document 14 in the Matthews case file) to learn how the applicable commitment period is determined. In the next section we will use it to learn how the debtor's projected disposable income is calculated. As set out in the Assignment Memorandum in Appendix B and explained in Chapter Six, Section M, our fictitious Chapter 13 debtors, Roger and Susan Matthews, reside in Harrisburg, Dauphin County, Pennsylvania.

Whether a debtor's commitment period can run as little as three years per §1325(b)(4)(A)(i) or must run for the maximum of five years per §1325(b)(4)A)(ii) is determined by whether the debtor's **current monthly income** is less than the **median family income** for the debtor's state and size of household. Every year the U.S. Census Bureau publishes median family income figures for households of a certain size in all 50 states. Briefly, the determination of the Chapter 13 debtor's applicable commitment period works like this: Part 1 of Form 122C-1 calculates the debtor's average current monthly income. In Part 2 of the form that income figure is annualized and compared to the applicable median family income figure for the debtor's state and household size. If the debtor is a **below median debtor** (the debtor's annualized current average monthly income is less than the applicable median family income), the commitment period is three years and that is shown in Part 3 of the form. If the debtor is an **above median debtor** (the debtor's annualized current monthly income is more than the applicable median family income figure), the commitment period is five years and that is shown in Part 3 of the form. (The determination of how a debtor's projected disposable income is to be calculated is also made in Part 2 of Form 122C-1. We will consider the disposable income calculations in the next section.)

Current monthly income (CMI) (used to determine the debtor's average current monthly income in Form 122C-1) is defined in §101(10A) to include the average monthly income from all sources that the debtor has received during the six months preceding the filing of the petition (known as the

Current monthly income The average monthly income of a debtor from all sources received during the six months preceding the filing of a bankruptcy petition.

Median family income Income statistics compiled annually by the U.S. Census Bureau for all 50 states based on household size.

Above/below median debtor Description of a debtor whose annualized current monthly income is greater or lesser than the applicable median family income.

look back period) regardless of whether such income is taxable, as well as any amounts paid by a third party for the household expenses of the debtor. The sixth month to be included in the look back period is the month immediately preceding the date the case is filed.

EXAMPLE

> If a Chapter 13 petition is filed on September 15, the applicable look back period for calculating the debtor's CMI is March through August of that year. Income from all sources received during those six months will be averaged to arrive at the current monthly income figure. So if the debtor had income totaling $26,400 during the look back period, the applicable CMI will be $4,400 ($26,400 divided by 6).

You can see the §101(10A)(A) definition of CMI summarized just above Line 2 in Part 1 of the form. After debtor enters his or her marital status on Line 1, the remainder of Part 1 of the form then requires the debtor to report the debtor's average monthly income, so defined, from a number of different categories.

Joint debtors must report their income figures separately in Columns A and B in Part 1 of the form. A debtor with a nonfiling spouse must still include that spouse's income in Column B. (Part 2 of the form includes a marital adjustment to deduct the amount of the nonfiling spouse's income that is not regularly available for household expenses of the debtor and dependents. We will examine the marital adjustment shortly.)

On Line 2 the debtor lists gross wages, salary, and tips. That gross wages, etc., figure is to be entered *without* deductions or withholdings for tax, insurance, etc.; it is a gross income figure. On Line 3 the debtor lists alimony or maintenance payments, excluding such payments if the spouse paying them is a joint debtor. On Line 4 the debtor lists child support payments received, again excluding such payments if the spouse paying them is a joint debtor. On Line 4 the debtor also lists "regular contributions" to household expenses from other sources such as parents, dependents, an unmarried partner, etc. On Line 5 the debtor who operates a business reports net income from that business (gross income minus ordinary and necessary business expenses). Similarly, on Line 6, the debtor who leases a house or apartment and had rental income for the preceding six months will report that net rental income. Line 7 requires the inclusion of **passive income** from various kinds of investments, Line 8 unemployment compensation, Line 9 retirement income, and Line 10 income from any other source excluding Social Security benefits. Remember, the amounts entered in each of the lines in Part 1 of the form are an average of the monthly amounts received during the applicable look back period.

For example, Mr. and Mrs. Matthews are joint debtors, so they list their income separately in Columns A and B of Part 1. The only source of income for either of them is the salaries they are paid by their respective employers, so they enter the six-month average of their respective salaries in Columns A and B of Line 2. In Lines 3 through 10 they enter zero, then show the subtotals and combined total in Line 11.

Illustration 14-a: FORM 122C-1 FOR ROGER AND SUSAN MATTHEWS

Fill in this information to identify your case:

Debtor 1	Roger	H.	Matthews
	First Name	Middle Name	Last Name
Debtor 2	Susan	J.	Matthews
(Spouse, if filing)	First Name	Middle Name	Last Name

United States Bankruptcy Court for the: Middle District of Pennsylvania

Case number _____
(If known)

Check as directed in lines 17 and 21:

According to the calculations required by this Statement:

☑ 1. Disposable income is not determined under 11 U.S.C. § 1325(b)(3).

☐ 2. Disposable income is determined under 11 U.S.C. § 1325(b)(3).

☑ 3. The commitment period is 3 years.

☐ 4. The commitment period is 5 years.

☐ Check if this is an amended filing

Official Form 122C-1

Chapter 13 Statement of Your Current Monthly Income and Calculation of Commitment Period

12/15

Be as complete and accurate as possible. If two married people are filing together, both are equally responsible for being accurate. If more space is needed, attach a separate sheet to this form. Include the line number to which the additional information applies. On the top of any additional pages, write your name and case number (if known).

Part 1:   Calculate Your Average Monthly Income

1. **What is your marital and filing status?** Check one only.

   ☐ **Not married.** Fill out Column A, lines 2-11.

   ☑ **Married.** Fill out both Columns A and B, lines 2-11.

   Fill in the average monthly income that you received from all sources, derived during the 6 full months before you file this bankruptcy case. 11 U.S.C. § 101(10A). For example, if you are filing on September 15, the 6 month period would be March 1 through August 31. If the amount of your monthly income varied during the 6 months, add the income for all 6 months and divide the total by 6. Fill in the result. Do not include any income amount more than once. For example, if both spouses own the same rental property, put the income from that property in one column only. If you have nothing to report for any line, write $0 in the space.

		Column A Debtor 1	Column B Debtor 2 or non-filing spouse
2.	**Your gross wages, salary, tips, bonuses, overtime, and commissions** (before all payroll deductions).	$ 3,000.00	$ 2,167.00
3.	**Alimony and maintenance payments.** Do not include payments from a spouse.	$ 0.00	$ 0.00
4.	**All amounts from any source which are regularly paid for household expenses of you or your dependents, including child support.** Include regular contributions from an unmarried partner, members of your household, your dependents, parents, and roommates. Do not include payments from a spouse. Do not include payments you listed on line 3.	$ 0.00	$ 0.00

5. **Net income from operating a business, profession, or farm**

	Debtor 1	Debtor 2			
Gross receipts (before all deductions)	$_____	$_____			
Ordinary and necessary operating expenses	– $_____	– $_____			
Net monthly income from a business, profession, or farm	$ 0.00	$ 0.00	Copy here →	$ 0.00	$ 0.00

6. **Net income from rental and other real property**

	Debtor 1	Debtor 2			
Gross receipts (before all deductions)	$_____	$_____			
Ordinary and necessary operating expenses	– $_____	– $_____			
Net monthly income from rental or other real property	$ 0.00	$ 0.00	Copy here →	$ 0.00	$ 0.00

Debtor 1   <u>Roger</u>   <u>H.</u>   <u>Matthews</u>   Case number *(if known)*_____

First Name   Middle Name   Last Name

		Column A Debtor 1	Column B Debtor 2 or non-filing spouse
7.	Interest, dividends, and royalties	$ 0.00	$ 0.00
8.	Unemployment compensation	$ 0.00	$ 0.00

Do not enter the amount if you contend that the amount received was a benefit under the Social Security Act. Instead, list it here:................... ↓

For you.. $_____

For your spouse .... $_____

9. **Pension or retirement income.** Do not include any amount received that was a benefit under the Social Security Act.

    $ 0.00 $ 0.00

10. **Income from all other sources not listed above.** Specify the source and amount. Do not include any benefits received under the Social Security Act or payments received as a victim of a war crime, a crime against humanity, or international or domestic terrorism. If necessary, list other sources on a separate page and put the total below.

_____ $ 0.00 $ 0.00

_____ $ 0.00 $ 0.00

Total amounts from separate pages, if any.   + $ 0.00   + $ 0.00

11. **Calculate your total average monthly income.** Add lines 2 through 10 for each column. Then add the total for Column A to the total for Column B.

    $ 3,000.00 + $ 2,167.00 = $5,167.00

    Total average monthly income

Part 2:   **Determine How to Measure Your Deductions from Income**

12. **Copy your total average monthly income from line 11.** .... $ 5,167.00

13. **Calculate the marital adjustment.** Check one:

☐ You are not married. Fill in 0 below.

☑ You are married and your spouse is filing with you. Fill in 0 below.

☐ You are married and your spouse is not filing with you.

    Fill in the amount of the income listed in line 11, Column B, that was NOT regularly paid for the household expenses of you or your dependents, such as payment of the spouse's tax liability or the spouse's support of someone other than you or your dependents.

    Below, specify the basis for excluding this income and the amount of income devoted to each purpose. If necessary, list additional adjustments on a separate page.

    If this adjustment does not apply, enter 0 below.

_____ $_____

_____ $_____

_____   + $_____

Total........................... $ 0.00 Copy here → — 0.00

14. **Your current monthly income.** Subtract the total in line 13 from line 12. $ 5,167.00

15. **Calculate your current monthly income for the year.** Follow these steps:

15a. Copy line 14 here →.. $ 5,167.00

    Multiply line 15a by 12 (the number of months in a year).   x 12

15b. The result is your current monthly income for the year for this part of the form. .... $ 62,004.00

Debtor 1   Roger   H.   Matthews   Case number *(if known)*_____
     First Name   Middle Name   Last Name

16. Calculate the median family income that applies to you. Follow these steps:

  16a. Fill in the state in which you live.   PA

  16b. Fill in the number of people in your household.   4

  16c. Fill in the median family income for your state and size of household. .... $ 86,112.00
       To find a list of applicable median income amounts, go online using the link specified in the separate
       instructions for this form. This list may also be available at the bankruptcy clerk's office.

17. How do the lines compare?

  17a. ☑ Line 15b is less than or equal to line 16c. On the top of page 1 of this form, check box 1, *Disposable income is not determined under*
       11 U.S.C. § 1325(b)(3). **Go to Part 3.** Do NOT fill out *Calculation of Your Disposable Income (Official Form 122C–2)*.

  17b. ☐ Line 15b is more than line 16c. On the top of page 1 of this form, check box 2, *Disposable income is determined under*
       11 U.S.C. § 1325(b)(3). **Go to Part 3 and fill out Calculation of Your Disposable Income (Official Form 122C–2)**.
       On line 39 of that form, copy your current monthly income from line 14 above.

Part 3:	**Calculate Your Commitment Period Under 11 U.S.C. § 1325(b)(4)**

18. Copy your total average monthly income from line 11. .... $ 5,167.00

19. Deduct the marital adjustment if it applies. If you are married, your spouse is not filing with you, and you contend that
calculating the commitment period under 11 U.S.C. § 1325(b)(4) allows you to deduct part of your spouse's income, copy
the amount from line 13.

  19a. If the marital adjustment does not apply, fill in 0 on line 19a. ....   – $ 0.00

  19b. **Subtract line 19a from line 18.** $ 5,167.00

20. Calculate your current monthly income for the year. Follow these steps:

  20a. Copy line 19b .... $ 5,167.00

       Multiply by 12 (the number of months in a year).   x 12

  20b. The result is your current monthly income for the year for this part of the form. $ 62,004.00

  20c. Copy the median family income for your state and size of household from line 16c. .... $ 86,112.00

21. How do the lines compare?

  ☑ Line 20b is less than line 20c. Unless otherwise ordered by the court, on the top of page 1 of this form, check box 3,
     The commitment period is 3 years. Go to Part 4.

  ☐ Line 20b is more than or equal to line 20c. Unless otherwise ordered by the court, on the top of page 1 of this form,
     check box 4, *The commitment period is 5 years*. Go to Part 4.

Part 4:	**Sign Below**

By signing here, under penalty of perjury I declare that the information on this statement and in any attachments is true and correct.

✘ /s/ Roger H. Matthews   ✘ /s/ Susan J. Matthews
     Signature of Debtor 1   Signature of Debtor 2

     Date 06/06/2016   Date 06/06/2016
         MM / DD / YYYY   MM / DD / YYYY

If you checked 17a, do NOT fill out or file Form 122C–2.
If you checked 17b, fill out Form 122C–2 and file it with this form. On line 39 of that form, copy your current monthly income from line 14 above.

Official Form 122C-1   Chapter 13 Statement of Your Current Monthly Income and Calculation of Commitment Period   page 3

P-H 14-a: The definition of CMI used in connection with Form 122C-1 in a Chapter 13 case is the same as that used in connection with Form 122A-1 utilized for the means test in a Chapter 7 case filed by an individual debtor with primarily consumer debts (see discussion in Chapter Seven, Section D). In both forms, CMI is calculated using the same definition of that term. But the two forms are used for different purposes. This is a good time to review the reason why Form 122A-1 is used in Chapter 7 cases for individual consumer debtors. There is no means test for a Chapter 13 debtor, however. If you are ready to do so, verbalize the reasons for using the Form 122A-1 form in a Chapter 7 bankruptcy case involving a consumer debtor and the different reasons for using the Form 122C-1 form in a Chapter 13 case. What is the purpose for calculating CMI in each form? If you can't verbalize that distinction yet, you certainly should be able to do so once you've finished this chapter.

In the vast majority of cases, calculating the debtor's CMI using the six-month look back period makes perfect sense because the debtor expects his or her income during the upcoming plan period to be identical or very similar to what it has been during the look back period. But occasionally that is not the case because the debtor's income during the look back period was higher or lower than what it will be during the plan period. And since, as we will see, the CMI figure is used in calculating the debtor's projected disposable income (PDI), that PDI number may be inaccurate as well.

EXAMPLE

Assume the debtor receives a one-time buyout from an employer during the look back period, causing her CMI figure calculated per §101(10A)(A) to be substantially higher than what her actual monthly income will be during the period of her plan. Or a debtor gets a new job that will significantly increase his real income during the plan period in excess of the CMI calculated using income from the look back period. Or a debtor is in the process of changing jobs when the petition is filed and the new job will pay less. For each of these debtors the CMI figure will not be an accurate forecast of the debtor's income during the plan period and any PDI calculated using the CMI figure is going to be inaccurate. And that is critical since most debtors cannot satisfy the confirmation requirement of §1325(b)(1)(A) by filing a 100 percent plan and must rely on satisfying §1325(b)(1)(B) by proposing a plan that will pay all their PDI to unsecured creditors.

In dealing with debtors like the ones in the last example, some bankruptcy courts, after BAPCPA, utilized a strict **mechanical approach** to CMI calculation that focused exclusively on income/expenses in the look back period without regard to any upcoming changes in the debtor's income or expenses. In these districts, debtors either had to delay filing until the applicable look back period encompassed the change in income or expenses (which was not always possible due to repossessions, foreclosures, or other financial emergencies) or go ahead and propose a plan based exclusively on numbers from the look back period, have it confirmed, and then file a proposed modification to the plan based on changed circumstances (to be considered in Chapter Sixteen, Section D), which would add to their attorney's fees and the administrative expenses of the case. Other courts developed a **forward-looking approach** that allowed/required debtors when doing their initial CMI calculation to consider the upcoming changes, notwithstanding the unequivocal language of §101(10A)(A).

The question of how to interpret §§1325(b)(1)(B) and 101(10A)(A) was finally resolved by the Supreme Court in *Hamilton v. Lanning*, 130 S. Ct. 2464 (2010). In *Lanning*, debtor Stephanie Kay Lanning filed for Chapter 13 bankruptcy protection in October 2006. On her Schedule I she reported monthly gross income of $1,922 per month and on her Schedule J she reported monthly living expenses of $1,772.97 leaving her with monthly disposable income of $149.03 with which to fund a plan. However, Lanning had received a one-time buyout from her former employer during the six-month look back period so that her current monthly income as calculated for Form 122C-1 purposes was inflated to $5,343.70 per month. When the debtor filed a proposed 36-month plan to pay $144 per month on her unsecured obligations, the standing trustee objected to confirmation on the grounds that she was not proposing a plan that committed all of her projected disposable income as calculated on her Form 122C-1 to the repayment of creditors, squarely presenting the issue of whether the mechanical or forward-looking approach was the correct one to use. On appeal the Supreme Court clarified that the forward-looking approach was the appropriate one to use both based on interpretation of the statutory language and well-established bankruptcy practice prior to passage of BAPCPA in 2005:

> Consistent with the text of §1325 and pre-BAPCPA practice, we hold that when a bankruptcy court calculates a debtor's projected disposable income, the court may account for changes in the debtor's income or expenses that are known or virtually certain at the time of confirmation.

Id. at 2478.

After *Lanning*, Schedule I was revised to allow the debtor to indicate (on Line 13) expected increases or decreases in income. The Schedule J form has been revised to allow the debtor to indicate (on Line 24) expected changes in expenses. And new Form 122C-2 allows the above median debtor to indicate (on Line 46) expected changes to income or expenses. Nonetheless, calculating the Chapter 13 debtor's projected disposable income is not an easy, mechanical process. It is accomplished using the data made available on Schedules I, J, and Form 122C-1 and C-2 (for the above median debtor). The lawyer for the debtor makes her best calculation from these sources in proposing the plan. Questions raised by the standing trustee or creditors regarding the accuracy of the numbers used in the calculation or the veracity of debtor's claimed upcoming changes to income or expenses (or for that matter to current income or expenses) are usually argued over and worked out at the 341 meeting. If no agreement can be reached there, an objection to confirmation is filed and the judge conducts a hearing and decides the issue.

P-H 14-b: When is an upcoming change in income or expense "known or virtually certain" so as to be properly reportable on the bankruptcy forms and fair game for use in calculating the debtor's disposable monthly income? Is a "likely" or "probable" change enough? A "maybe" change? Should those be included notwithstanding the phrase used by the court? See *In re Connor*, 464

B.R. 14 (E.D. Mich. 2012). Assume the law office you work for represents the following debtors and you are tasked with preparing their petition and forms for filing a Chapter 13 case. Answer the questions posed for each debtor:

a. A debtor who needs to file a Chapter 13 case immediately to prevent foreclosure on his home is currently employed by a local company making $2,500 per month, gross. However, he has been advised by his employer that in 60 days he will receive a promotion and a raise to $3,200 per month, which will make him an above median debtor. How will you show that anticipated change in income on the forms you are preparing for this debtor? Should you go ahead and treat him as an above median debtor and complete Form 122C-2 for him?

b. A divorced debtor has total monthly expenses for Schedule J purposes of $2,333. However, she has a 16-year-old son who has been living with her who plans to go to live full-time with his father in approximately three months. If that happens, it will reduce her monthly expenses by about $400. On the other hand, the ex-husband has been paying her child support for the boy and that may end if and when the boy goes to live with his father although there are other children of the couple living with your client, the father has not mentioned changing child support, and your client thinks he won't file a petition with the divorce court seeking a modification. Should you report one or both of these anticipated changes on the forms you are preparing for debtor and, if so, on what forms should you report them?

c. An above median debtor's income is not expected to change in the foreseeable future. Neither are her expenses, with one exception. Her aged mother has been diagnosed with Alzheimer's and the family expects she will not be able to live by herself much longer. Your client and her siblings have discussed what they will do and have tentatively agreed that the mother will live with the debtor, probably starting sometime in the next 6 to 18 months depending on how rapidly her condition deteriorates. Debtor knows her expenses will rise in that event but really has no idea by how much. Should you report this possible change on the forms you are preparing for debtor and, if so, on what forms will you report it? In drafting the debtor's proposed Chapter 13 plan, should you go ahead and reduce her projected income by some amount of anticipated expenses associated with the mother moving in or wait and amend her plan later if and when that event occurs? If you go ahead and reduce her projected monthly income available over the term of her five-year plan and propose a plan based on that projection, do you think the standing trustee or a creditor might object?

Once the average current monthly income calculated in Part 1 of Form 122C-1 has been totaled on Line 11, we then take that total to Part 2 of the form and enter it on Line 12. Chapter 13 debtors who are married but who did not file jointly and who entered the nonfiling spouse's average income in Column B of Part 1 may subtract that portion of the nonfiling spouse's income on Line 13 that was not paid on a regular basis to defer household expenses of the debtor or dependents of the debtor and enter the balance on Line 14. This is the **marital adjustment** of Form 122C-1. As we saw earlier, the income of a nonfiling spouse must be reported in Column B of Part 1 of the form. And if the income of the nonfiling spouse is regularly available for household expenses of the debtor or his dependents, it must be listed and included in the debtor's total average monthly income entered on Line 11. It is only where the nonfiling spouse's income is not regularly available for household expenses that it can be deducted from the debtor's CMI. And the reason that the nonfiling spouse's income is not available for household expenses must be stated. The most common reason is that the nonfiling spouse is required to pay spousal or child support from an earlier marriage.

The marital adjustment seen on Line 13 of Form 122C-1 is similar to that seen on Line 3 in Part 1 of Form 122A-2 as part of the Chapter 7 individual consumer debtor's means test (see discussion in Chapter Seven, Section D). Both the qualifying Chapter 13 debtor and the qualifying Chapter 7 consumer debtor can make this adjustment to CMI. But don't forget, we're calculating the debtor's CMI in each case for different reasons.

EXAMPLE

The Matthews enter the total of their joint CMI on Line 12 of their form 122C-1. No reduction is made for the marital adjustment since they are both debtors. Instead, a zero is entered on Line 13, and the total from Line 12 is carried forward to Line 14.

On Line 15 of the form, the CMI total from Line 14 is annualized by being multiplied by 12 (current monthly income × 12). Then on Line 16 we enter the **median family income** figure for a household the size of the debtor's household living in the debtor's state of residence (the size of a debtor's household for purposes of Line 16 of Form 122C-1 is the same as that determined for purposes of Line 13 of Form 122A-1 by the individual Chapter 7 debtor; recall the discussion of what persons make up a debtor's household in Chapter Seven, Section D). The median family income figures are drawn from the Census Bureau's tables and posted on the U.S. Trustee Program's web site at www.justice.gov/ust/means-testing.

P-H 14-c: Since our fictional Chapter 13 debtors live in Harrisburg, Dauphin County, Pennsylvania, the median family numbers for Pennsylvania are used as of June 2016 when they filed. There are four persons in the Matthews family. Go to the U.S. Trustee web site and locate the Census Bureau's current tables for median family income for a family of four in the state of Pennsylvania. This is the median family income figure the Matthews use on Line 16 of their Form 122C-1. (Remember that the median income figures from the Census Bureau are adjusted annually. The Matthews form uses the correct median income figure for Pennsylvania as of June 2016 but that figure may be different when you read this.) If the Matthews lived in your state and were filing their case there today, what would the applicable median income for them be?

Next we compare the debtor's annualized CMI on Line 15 with the state's median family income number on Line 16. This comparison will determine the applicable commitment period for the debtor's Chapter 13 plan. If the Chapter 13 debtor's annualized CMI is less than the applicable median family income figure, he or she is a below median debtor and §1325(b)(4)(A) provides that the debtor's plan may run anywhere from 36 months (three years) to 60 months (five years). It must run at least three years. However, if the debtor's annualized CMI is equal to or more than the applicable median family income figure, he is an above median debtor and §1325(b)(4)(A) requires that his plan run for a full five years. An important exception to these applicable time periods is found in §1325(b)(4)(B), which provides that if the plan of a below median or above median debtor calls for unsecured creditors to be paid 100 percent of what they are owed, it can run for less than the applicable period calculated under §1325(b)(4)(A). After all, those unsecured creditors are going to be pleased to receive 100 percent of what they are owed and would much rather receive it in fewer than three or five years.

The formal determination of the commitment period is done in Part 3 of the form in an arguably redundant manner using the calculations made in Parts 1 and 2 of the form. First, the average monthly income number from Line 11 of Part 1 is again entered on Line 18 of Part 3. If the debtor claimed the marital deduction on Line 13 of Part 2 that amount is again entered on Line 19 of Part 3 and subtracted from the average monthly income number on Line 18. On Line 20 the average monthly income number is again multiplied by 12 to generate the debtor's current monthly income for the year, which is entered on Line 20b. The debtor's applicable median family income figure based on state and family size that was entered on Line 16 is again entered on Line 20c. The amount of the debtor's annualized current income appearing on Line 20b is then compared with the median family income appearing on Line 20c to determine if the debtor is an above or below median debtor. If the debtor is below median, the first box on Line 21 is checked along with Box 3 at the top right of page one of the form indicating that the applicable commitment period of the debtor is three years. If the debtor is above median, the second box on Line 21 is checked along with Box 4 at the top right of page one of the form indicating that the applicable commitment period of the debtor is five years.

EXAMPLE

> The Matthews' annualized CMI falls below their state's median family income figure, making them below median debtors. They check the first box on Line 21 of their Form 122C-1 and the third box on the top right of page one of the form indicating that their commitment period is three years. They can propose a plan that will call for them to pay out their disposable income to unsecured creditors for as little as three years and no more than five. Their plan must run for at least three years.

P-H 14-d: The applicable commitment period of the Matthews is only three years but they have proposed a five-year plan (see Illustration 15-b). Can you think of reasons why a debtor might choose to do this? Might moral attitudes regarding a perceived duty to pay as much debt as possible be involved in this decision? Might practical concerns regarding the impact on the debtor's credit rating be involved? Or the debtor's desire to do business in the future with certain creditors?

B. ▶ Determining the Projected Disposable Income for a Chapter 13 Plan

You may have noticed that we did not reference Line 17 in Part 2 of Form 122C-1 in the last section. Although that form determines the applicable commitment period for both the above and below median Chapter 13 debtor, it does not determine the projected disposable income that a debtor, either above or below median income, will have available to fund the Chapter 13 plan during the applicable commitment period. It does, however, indicate whether or not the debtor's disposable income is to be calculated under §1325(b)(3). To understand the significance of that determination, let's start with the Code's definition of disposable income. Disposable income is defined by §1325(b)(2) as current monthly income (other than child support, foster care, and disability payments for a dependent child) received by the debtor, less amounts "reasonably necessary" for the maintenance or support of the debtor or dependents or to satisfy a domestic support obligation and also less charitable contributions up to 15 percent of the debtor's gross income. If the debtor operates a business, the definition of disposable income excludes those amounts that are necessary for ordinary operating expenses.

Section 1325(b)(3) then says that if the debtor is an above median debtor, what constitutes "reasonably necessary" amounts to be deducted from currently monthly income of the debtor is to be determined under §707(b)(2), the section of the Code that determines whether a Chapter 7 debtor satisfies the means test (as examined using Marta Carlson's hypothetical Form 122A-2 in Chapter Seven, Section D). In a Chapter 13 case, when the debtor's disposable income is to be determined under §1325(b)(3), that debtor must complete Form 122C-2, which we will see is very similar to the 122A-2 form used in Chapter 7 cases.

Form 122C-1, in addition to determining the debtor's applicable commitment period as discussed in the last section, also determines whether or not the debtor must calculate his disposable income using §1325(b)(3). This is what Line 17 of Form 122C-1 accomplishes. Having calculated the debtor's annualized monthly income and compared it to the median income for the applicable state and household size, the debtor whose annualized monthly income is less than the median is instructed to check Box 17a and Box 1 on the top right of page one of the form indicating that disposable income for this debtor will not be calculated under §1325(b)(3) (we will examine how it is calculated next). If the debtor's annualized monthly income exceeds the median, the debtor is instructed to check Box 17b and Box 2 on the top right of page one of the form indicating that disposable income for this debtor will indeed be calculated under §1325(b)(3). The above median debtor is also instructed to complete Form 122C-2 (we will consider the disposable income calculation for the above median debtor under §1325(b)(3) and using Form 122C-2 later in this chapter).

EXAMPLE

On their Form 122C-1 the Matthews have determined that their annualized current monthly income is less than the applicable state median for their size family. They are below median debtors. Accordingly, they check Box 17a on their form and Box 1 on the top right of page one of the form indicating that their disposable income will not be calculated using §1325(b)(3).

Before we begin to look at how disposable income is calculated for the below and above median debtor, be sure you are aware of how critical that calculation is in a Chapter 13 case. Essentially, the disposable income calculation is a determination of how much money the debtor will have available on a monthly basis to pay his unsecured creditors during the term of the plan. We are concerned with money available for unsecured creditors because the debtor is going to retain sufficient funds to support himself and his dependents during the plan and he will propose separate treatment of his various secured debts, as we will consider in the next chapter. But remember the dictate of §1325(b)(1): The Chapter 13 plan cannot be confirmed over an objection unless it proposes to pay unsecured creditors 100 percent of what they are owed or to utilize *all* of the debtor's projected disposable income to be received in the applicable commitment period to pay those unsecured creditors. That's what makes this calculation so critical.

The U.S. Trustee's office has formulated a Statement on the Trustee Program's Position on Legal Issues Arising Under the Chapter 13 Disposable Income Test that is accessible online at www.justice.gov/sites/default/files/ust/legacy/2015/03/03/chapter13_analysis.pdf. This a good site to bookmark.

1. Calculating Disposable Income for the Below Median Debtor

Once the below median Chapter 13 debtor has completed his or her Form 122C-1 we know the debtor's annualized currently monthly income figure. But that is not the same as disposable income. And the below median debtor is not required to complete Form 122C-2 as the above median debtor is. So how do we determine the disposable income figure for the below median debtor?

It is §1325(b)(2) that controls the disposable income calculation unless the debtor is above median. That section provides that the debtor will deduct amounts reasonably necessary for the maintenance or support of himself and his dependents. We begin by examining the debtor's Schedule I, Your Income, and comparing it with the CMI calculation made on the debtor's 122C-1. Note that the Schedule I provides a snapshot picture of debtor's income as of the day the petition is filed while the 122C-1 provides an average income over the six months of the look back period. But comparing the data on the two forms should provide a somewhat accurate picture of the debtor's income as of the date the case is filed and any changes in income over the preceding six months. The income information from Form 122C-1 and Schedule I is then compared with the debtor's actual expenses to determine what is reasonably necessary for the debtor and his or her dependents' maintenance and support, always remembering that such actual expenses must be reasonable under §1325(b)(2). For the below median debtor, the Schedule J, Your Expenses, is the primary source of information regarding the debtor's reasonably necessary expenses.

P-H 14-e: The Matthews' Schedules I and J are Documents 9 and 10 in their case file. For convenience the Schedule J is also set out in Illustration 14-b. Notice how much like a budget it is. Compare the Schedule J with the informal budget drawn up by their lawyer in the Assignment Memorandum in Appendix B of the text. From the budget document, can you determine where much of the Schedule J information came from?

Illustration 14-b: MATTHEWS SCHEDULE J

Fill in this information to identify your case:

Debtor 1	Roger	H.	Matthews
	First Name	Middle Name	Last Name
Debtor 2	Susan	J.	Matthews
(Spouse, if filing) First Name		Middle Name	Last Name

United States Bankruptcy Court for the: Middle District of Pennsylvania

Case number
(If known)

Check if this is:

☐ An amended filing

☐ A supplement showing postpetition chapter 13
expenses as of the following date:

_____
MM / DD / YYYY

Official Form 106J

Schedule J: Your Expenses   12/15

Be as complete and accurate as possible. If two married people are filing together, both are equally responsible for supplying correct information. If more space is needed, attach another sheet to this form. On the top of any additional pages, write your name and case number (if known). Answer every question.

Part 1:   Describe Your Household

1. **Is this a joint case?**

   ☐ No.   Go to line 2.
   ☑ Yes. **Does Debtor 2 live in a separate household?**

       ☑ No
       ☐ Yes. Debtor 2 must file Official Form 106J-2, *Expenses for Separate Household of Debtor 2*.

2. **Do you have dependents?**   ☐ No

   Do not list Debtor 1 and   ☑ Yes. Fill out this information for
   Debtor 2.   each dependent..........................

   Do not state the dependents'
   names.

Dependent's relationship to Debtor 1 or Debtor 2	Dependent's age	Does dependent live with you?
Daughter	7 yr	☐ No ☑ Yes
Daughter	11 mo	☐ No ☑ Yes
		☐ No ☐ Yes
		☐ No ☐ Yes
		☐ No ☐ Yes
		☐ No ☐ Yes

3. **Do your expenses include**   ☑ No
   expenses of people other than   ☐ Yes
   yourself and your dependents?

Part 2:   Estimate Your Ongoing Monthly Expenses

Estimate your expenses as of your bankruptcy filing date unless you are using this form as a supplement in a Chapter 13 case to report expenses as of a date after the bankruptcy is filed. If this is a supplemental *Schedule J*, check the box at the top of the form and fill in the applicable date.

Include expenses paid for with non-cash government assistance if you know the value of such assistance and have included it on *Schedule I: Your Income* (Official Form 106I).

		Your expenses
4. The rental or home ownership expenses for your residence. Include first mortgage payments and any rent for the ground or lot.	4.	$ 850.00
If not included in line 4:		
4a. Real estate taxes	4a.	$ 0.00
4b. Property, homeowner's, or renter's insurance	4b.	$ 0.00
4c. Home maintenance, repair, and upkeep expenses	4c.	$ 75.00
4d. Homeowner's association or condominium dues	4d.	$ 0.00

Official Form 106J   **Schedule J: Your Expenses**   page 1

Debtor 1   Roger   H.   Matthews   Case number *(if known)*_____
             First Name   Middle Name   Last Name

	Your expenses
5. **Additional mortgage payments for your residence,** such as home equity loans 5.	$ 700.00
6. **Utilities:**	
6a. Electricity, heat, natural gas 6a.	$ 315.00
6b. Water, sewer, garbage collection 6b.	$ 50.00
6c. Telephone, cell phone, Internet, satellite, and cable services 6c.	$ 135.00
6d. Other. Specify: _____ 6d.	$ 0.00
7. **Food and housekeeping supplies** 7.	$ 475.00
8. **Childcare and children's education costs** 8.	$ 0.00
9. **Clothing, laundry, and dry cleaning** 9.	$ 200.00
10. **Personal care products and services** 10.	$ 40.00
11. **Medical and dental expenses** 11.	$ 100.00
12. **Transportation.** Include gas, maintenance, bus or train fare. Do not include car payments. 12.	$ 150.00
13. **Entertainment, clubs, recreation, newspapers, magazines, and books** 13.	$ 50.00
14. **Charitable contributions and religious donations** 14.	$ 50.00
15. **Insurance.** Do not include insurance deducted from your pay or included in lines 4 or 20.	
15a. Life insurance 15a.	$ 0.00
15b. Health insurance 15b.	$ 0.00
15c. Vehicle insurance 15c.	$ 60.00
15d. Other insurance. Specify:_____ 15d.	$ 0.00
16. **Taxes.** Do not include taxes deducted from your pay or included in lines 4 or 20. Specify: _____ 16.	$ 0.00
17. **Installment or lease payments:**	
17a. Car payments for Vehicle 1 17a.	$ 360.00
17b. Car payments for Vehicle 2 17b.	$ 240.00
17c. Other. Specify: Vehicle 3 _____ 17c.	$ 120.00
17d. Other. Specify:_____ 17d.	$ 0.00
18. **Your payments of alimony, maintenance, and support that you did not report as deducted from your pay on line 5, *Schedule I, Your Income* (Official Form 106I).** 18.	$ 0.00
19. **Other payments you make to support others who do not live with you.** Specify:_____ 19.	$ 0.00
20. **Other real property expenses not included in lines 4 or 5 of this form or on *Schedule I: Your Income*.**	
20a. Mortgages on other property 20a.	$ 0.00
20b. Real estate taxes 20b.	$ 0.00
20c. Property, homeowner's, or renter's insurance 20c.	$ 0.00
20d. Maintenance, repair, and upkeep expenses 20d.	$ 0.00
20e. Homeowner's association or condominium dues 20e.	$ 0.00

Official Form 106J   Schedule J: Your Expenses   page 2

Debtor 1   Roger _____ H. _____ Matthews _____   Case number (if known)_____
            First Name   Middle Name   Last Name

21. **Other.** Specify: Miscellaneous _____   21. +$_____ 100.00

22. **Calculate your monthly expenses.**

  22a. Add lines 4 through 21.   22a. $_____ 4,070.00

  22b. Copy line 22 (monthly expenses for Debtor 2), if any, from Official Form 106J-2   22b. $_____ 0.00

  22c. Add line 22a and 22b. The result is your monthly expenses.   22c. $_____ 4,070.00

23. **Calculate your monthly net income.**

  23a. Copy line 12 (*your combined monthly income*) from *Schedule I*.   23a. $_____ 4,133.00

  23b. Copy your monthly expenses from line 22c above.   23b. $_____ 4,070.00

  23c. Subtract your monthly expenses from your monthly income.
       The result is your *monthly net income*.   23c. $_____ 63.00

24. **Do you expect an increase or decrease in your expenses within the year after you file this form?**

    For example, do you expect to finish paying for your car loan within the year or do you expect your
    mortgage payment to increase or decrease because of a modification to the terms of your mortgage?

    ☐ No.

    ☑ Yes.   Explain here: We intend to surrender vehicle #3 immediately. We anticipate having to incur monthly child
                            care expenses of $250 beginning in August 2016.

Official Form 106J   Schedule J: Your Expenses   page 3

Although the Schedule J now in use is a useful starting point to determine the below median debtor's disposable income, the monthly net income figure calculated on Line 23c of Schedule J likely is not that debtor's actual disposable income that must be paid to unsecured creditors. It is only the *starting point* to determine it. Why do we say that?

Expenses listed on Schedule J may be modified or even eliminated in the actual Chapter 13 plan, leaving more disposable income to apply to unsecured debts that will be paid in the plan. Collateralized obligations listed on Schedule J may change or disappear when the collateral is surrendered to the secured creditor and the remaining obligation is discharged in the plan. As we will see in the next chapter, if the value of the collateral securing a loan exceeds the balance owing on the loan, Chapter 13 may allow the debtor to strip down the balance owed to the creditor to the current value of the collateral and adjust payments accordingly in the plan. These are only two of several options a Chapter 13 debtor may be able to utilize to adjust his Schedule J expenses in the actual Chapter 13 plan.

EXAMPLE

The Matthews currently make monthly payments totaling $720 on three vehicles. If their plan proposes to reaffirm those three debts, retain possession of all three vehicles, and continue paying the monthly obligations as they come due, that will be $720 per month that will not be available to unsecured creditors during the term of the plan. However, if the Matthews' plan proposes to surrender one or more of the vehicles or other secured property and stop paying the affected secured creditors, that decision will free up additional "disposable" dollars to go to unsecured creditors each month. That decision is not reflected on Schedule J. Thus, for this reason too, the amount of monthly net income entered on Line 23c of Schedule J is only a suggestion or a starting point for the trustee to determine if the debtor is making all of his projected disposable income available to unsecured creditors as required by §1325(b).

Another reason that current Schedule J does not calculate the debtor's disposable income for plan purposes is that it does not calculate certain anticipated expenses that may arise during the term of the plan.

EXAMPLE

Line 24 of the Matthews' Schedule J indicates that they expect to begin incurring child care expenses of $250 per month in the next year. That expense will obviously have an impact on their disposable income. But note that Schedule J does not allow that anticipated future expense to be added to the average monthly expense total showing on Line 23c. In *Hamilton v. Lanning*, the Supreme Court held that upcoming changes in a debtor's income or expenses that are "virtually known or certain" can be considered in determining the debtor's disposable income. Those upcoming changes can be referenced on Line 24 of Schedule J but note that they are not included in the calculation of monthly net income total on Schedule J.

For these reasons, Schedule J does not accurately calculate the Chapter 13 debtor's disposable income. It is nothing more than a starting point to figure it out. Thus, although Line 23c on the Matthews' Schedule J shows a *monthly net income* available to them of $63 after deducting the various expenses listed on the form, that is not their disposable income for purposes of determining debtors' projected disposable income under §1325(b)(2).

In actuality, the debtor and debtor's attorney must decide on the specific terms of the plan, including how secured claims will be treated and what likely changes there will be to his income and expenses during the term of the plan before his disposable income can be determined. In Chapter Fifteen, we will look at the decisions the Matthews have made regarding those things and the actual terms of the Chapter 13 plan they put together. Only then can we determine if the plan actually proposes paying all their disposable income to unsecured creditors over the term of the plan as required by §1325(b).

2. Calculating Disposable Income for the Above Median Debtor

Let's assume for the moment that Roger Matthews has a gross salary of $50,000 per year ($4,166.66 per month) at City Plumbing Company and Susan Matthews has a gross salary of $45,000 per year ($3,750 per month) at Heart and Soul Academy. Based on those assumptions, their CMI is $7,916.66 and their annualized CMI is $95,000, which puts them above their applicable median income level in June 2016 when they filed. They are now above median debtors and will be required to propose either a five-year plan or a shorter 100 percent plan. Illustration 14-c shows what the Matthews' Form 122C-1 would look like if they had the higher incomes (this form is also included in the Matthews case file available on the companion web site of the textbook as "extra material"). As above median debtors in this alternative scenario the Matthews check the second box on Line 21 of their form and Box 4 on the top right of page one of the form, indicating that their applicable commitment period is five years. They also check Box 17b as well as Box 2 on the top right of page one of the form, indicating that their disposable income will be calculated using §1325(b)(3).

To calculate their disposable income as above median debtors the Matthews must complete Form 122C-2. Before we go through that form using the higher income assumptions for the Matthews, it may be helpful for you to review the step-by-step discussion of Marta Carlson's Form 122A-2 in Chapter Seven, Section D, Illustration 7-c, since the deductions allowed on the two forms are substantially similar and calculated in the same way. As we have noted, this is the case because §1325(b)(3) dictates that the reasonably necessary expenses of the above median Chapter 13 debtor allowed in order to determine his disposable income are to be calculated according to §707(b)(2), the same section that controls the determination of the means test for the Chapter 7 consumer debtor.

The Matthews' Form 122C-2 assuming they were above median debtors is set out in Illustration 14-d (this form is also included in the Matthews case file available on the companion web site of the textbook as "extra material").

Illustration 14-c: ALTERNATIVE FORM 122C-1 FOR ROGER AND SUSAN MATTHEWS ASSUMING ABOVE MEDIAN INCOME

Fill in this information to identify your case:

Debtor 1	Roger First Name	H. Middle Name	Matthews Last Name
Debtor 2 (Spouse, if filing)	Susan First Name	J. Middle Name	Matthews Last Name

United States Bankruptcy Court for the: Middle District of Pennsylvania

Case number
(If known) _____

Check as directed in lines 17 and 21:

According to the calculations required by this Statement:

☐ 1. Disposable income is not determined under 11 U.S.C. § 1325(b)(3).

☑ 2. Disposable income is determined under 11 U.S.C. § 1325(b)(3).

☐ 3. The commitment period is 3 years.

☑ 4. The commitment period is 5 years.

☐ Check if this is an amended filing

Official Form 122C-1

Chapter 13 Statement of Your Current Monthly Income and Calculation of Commitment Period

12/15

Be as complete and accurate as possible. If two married people are filing together, both are equally responsible for being accurate. If more space is needed, attach a separate sheet to this form. Include the line number to which the additional information applies. On the top of any additional pages, write your name and case number (if known).

Part 1:   Calculate Your Average Monthly Income

1. **What is your marital and filing status?** Check one only.

   ☐ **Not married.** Fill out Column A, lines 2-11.

   ☑ **Married.** Fill out both Columns A and B, lines 2-11.

   Fill in the average monthly income that you received from all sources, derived during the 6 full months before you file this bankruptcy case. 11 U.S.C. § 101(10A). For example, if you are filing on September 15, the 6-month period would be March 1 through August 31. If the amount of your monthly income varied during the 6 months, add the income for all 6 months and divide the total by 6. Fill in the result. Do not include any income amount more than once. For example, if both spouses own the same rental property, put the income from that property in one column only. If you have nothing to report for any line, write $0 in the space.

	Column A Debtor 1	Column B Debtor 2 or non-filing spouse
2. **Your gross wages, salary, tips, bonuses, overtime, and commissions** (before all payroll deductions).	$ 4,166.66	$ 3,750.00
3. **Alimony and maintenance payments.** Do not include payments from a spouse.	$ 0.00	$
4. **All amounts from any source which are regularly paid for household expenses of you or your dependents, including child support.** Include regular contributions from an unmarried partner, members of your household, your dependents, parents, and roommates. Do not include payments from a spouse. Do not include payments you listed on line 3.	$ 0.00	$ 0.00

5. **Net income from operating a business, profession, or farm**

	Debtor 1	Debtor 2			
Gross receipts (before all deductions)	$ _____	$ _____			
Ordinary and necessary operating expenses	– $ _____	– $ _____			
Net monthly income from a business, profession, or farm	$ 0.00	$ 0.00	Copy here ➔	$ 0.00	$ 0.00

6. **Net income from rental and other real property**

	Debtor 1	Debtor 2			
Gross receipts (before all deductions)	$ _____	$ _____			
Ordinary and necessary operating expenses	– $ _____	– $ _____			
Net monthly income from rental or other real property	$ 0.00	$ 0.00	Copy here ➔	$ 0.00	$ 0.00

Debtor 1	Roger	H.	Matthews	Case number (if known)
	First Name	Middle Name	Last Name	

	Column A Debtor 1	Column B Debtor 2 or non-filing spouse
7. Interest, dividends, and royalties	$ 0.00	$ 0.00
8. Unemployment compensation	$ 0.00	$ 0.00

Do not enter the amount if you contend that the amount received was a benefit under the Social Security Act. Instead, list it here: .... ↓

For you.. $_____

For your spouse .... $_____

9. **Pension or retirement income.** Do not include any amount received that was a benefit under the Social Security Act.

9.	$ 0.00	$ 0.00

10. **Income from all other sources not listed above.** Specify the source and amount. Do not include any benefits received under the Social Security Act or payments received as a victim of a war crime, a crime against humanity, or international or domestic terrorism. If necessary, list other sources on a separate page and put the total below.

_____	$ 0.00	$ 0.00
_____	$ 0.00	$ 0.00
Total amounts from separate pages, if any.	+ $ 0.00	+ $ 0.00

11. **Calculate your total average monthly income.** Add lines 2 through 10 for each column. Then add the total for Column A to the total for Column B.

$ 4,166.66 + $ 3,750.00 = $7,916.66

Total average monthly income

Part 2:　Determine How to Measure Your Deductions from Income

12. Copy your total average monthly income from line 11. .... $ 7,916.66

13. **Calculate the marital adjustment.** Check one:

☐ You are not married. Fill in 0 below.

☑ You are married and your spouse is filing with you. Fill in 0 below.

☐ You are married and your spouse is not filing with you.

Fill in the amount of the income listed in line 11, Column B, that was NOT regularly paid for the household expenses of you or your dependents, such as payment of the spouse's tax liability or the spouse's support of someone other than you or your dependents.

Below, specify the basis for excluding this income and the amount of income devoted to each purpose. If necessary, list additional adjustments on a separate page.

If this adjustment does not apply, enter 0 below.

_____	$_____
_____	$_____
_____	+ $_____

Total.. $ 0.00　Copy here → − 0.00

14. **Your current monthly income.** Subtract the total in line 13 from line 12. $ 7,916.66

15. **Calculate your current monthly income for the year.** Follow these steps:

15a. Copy line 14 here → .... $ 7,916.66

Multiply line 15a by 12 (the number of months in a year). x 12

15b. The result is your current monthly income for the year for this part of the form. .... $ 94,999.92

Debtor 1   Roger   H.   Matthews   Case number *(if known)*_____

       First Name   Middle Name   Last Name

---

16. **Calculate the median family income that applies to you.** Follow these steps:

     16a. Fill in the state in which you live.   **PA**

     16b. Fill in the number of people in your household.   **4**

     16c. Fill in the median family income for your state and size of household. .... $ 86,112.00

         To find a list of applicable median income amounts, go online using the link specified in the separate
         instructions for this form. This list may also be available at the bankruptcy clerk's office.

17. **How do the lines compare?**

     17a. ☐ Line 15b is less than or equal to line 16c. On the top of page 1 of this form, check box 1, *Disposable income is not determined under*
         11 U.S.C. § 1325(b)(3). **Go to Part 3.** Do NOT fill out *Calculation of Your Disposable Income* (Official Form 122C–2).

     17b. ☑ Line 15b is more than line 16c. On the top of page 1 of this form, check box 2, *Disposable income is determined under*
         11 U.S.C. § 1325(b)(3). **Go to Part 3 and fill out Calculation of Your Disposable Income (Official Form 122C–2).**
         On line 39 of that form, copy your current monthly income from line 14 above.

Part 3:   **Calculate Your Commitment Period Under 11 U.S.C. § 1325(b)(4)**

---

18. Copy your total average monthly income from line 11. .... $ 7,916.66

19. **Deduct the marital adjustment if it applies.** If you are married, your spouse is not filing with you, and you contend that
    calculating the commitment period under 11 U.S.C. § 1325(b)(4) allows you to deduct part of your spouse's income, copy
    the amount from line 13.
     19a. If the marital adjustment does not apply, fill in 0 on line 19a. ....   − $ 0.00

     19b. **Subtract line 19a from line 18.** $ 7,916.66

20. **Calculate your current monthly income for the year.** Follow these steps:

     20a. Copy line 19b. .... $ 7,916.66

         Multiply by 12 (the number of months in a year).   x   12

     20b. The result is your current monthly income for the year for this part of the form. $ 94,999.92

     20c. Copy the median family income for your state and size of household from line 16c. .... $ 86,112.00

21. **How do the lines compare?**

     ☐ Line 20b is less than line 20c. Unless otherwise ordered by the court, on the top of page 1 of this form, check box 3,
        The commitment period is 3 years. Go to Part 4.

     ☑ Line 20b is more than or equal to line 20c. Unless otherwise ordered by the court, on the top of page 1 of this form,
        check box 4, *The commitment period is 5 years.* Go to Part 4.

Part 4:   **Sign Below**

By signing here, under penalty of perjury I declare that the information on this statement and in any attachments is true and correct.

✗ /s/ Roger H. Matthews   ✗ /s/ Susan J. Matthews

   Signature of Debtor 1   Signature of Debtor 2

Date   06/06/2016   Date   06/06/2016

      MM / DD / YYYY   MM / DD / YYYY

If you checked 17a, do NOT fill out or file Form 122C–2.

If you checked 17b, fill out Form 122C–2 and file it with this form. On line 39 of that form, copy your current monthly income from line 14 above.

Official Form 122C-1   **Chapter 13 Statement of Your Current Monthly Income and Calculation of Commitment Period**   page 3

Illustration 14-d: FORM 122C-2 FOR ROGER AND SUSAN MATTHEWS ASSUMING ABOVE MEDIAN INCOME

Fill in this information to identify your case:

Debtor 1	Roger	H.	Matthews
	First Name	Middle Name	Last Name
Debtor 2	Susan	J.	Matthews
(Spouse, if filing)	First Name	Middle Name	Last Name

United States Bankruptcy Court for the: Middle District of Pennsylvania

Case number _____
(If known)

☐ Check if this is an amended filing

Official Form 122C-2

Chapter 13 Calculation of Your Disposable Income

04/16

To fill out this form, you will need your completed copy of *Chapter 13 Statement of Your Current Monthly Income and Calculation of Commitment Period* (Official Form 122C-1).

Be as complete and accurate as possible. If two married people are filing together, both are equally responsible for being accurate. If more space is needed, attach a separate sheet to this form. Include the line number to which the additional information applies. On the top of any additional pages, write your name and case number (if known).

Part 1:	Calculate Your Deductions from Your Income

The Internal Revenue Service (IRS) issues National and Local Standards for certain expense amounts. Use these amounts to answer the questions in lines 6-15. To find the IRS standards, go online using the link specified in the separate instructions for this form. This information may also be available at the bankruptcy clerk's office.

Deduct the expense amounts set out in lines 6-15 regardless of your actual expense. In later parts of the form, you will use some of your actual expenses if they are higher than the standards. Do not include any operating expenses that you subtracted from income in lines 5 and 6 of Form 122C-1, and do not deduct any amounts that you subtracted from your spouse's income in line 13 of Form 122C-1.

If your expenses differ from month to month, enter the average expense.

Note: Line numbers 1-4 are not used in this form. These numbers apply to information required by a similar form used in chapter 7 cases.

5. **The number of people used in determining your deductions from income**
   Fill in the number of people who could be claimed as exemptions on your federal income tax return, plus the number of any additional dependents whom you support. This number may be different from the number of people in your household.

   4.00

National Standards You must use the IRS National Standards to answer the questions in lines 6-7.

6. **Food, clothing, and other items:** Using the number of people you entered in line 5 and the IRS National Standards, fill in the dollar amount for food, clothing, and other items.

   $ 1509

7. **Out-of-pocket health care allowance:** Using the number of people you entered in line 5 and the IRS National Standards, fill in the dollar amount for out-of-pocket health care. The number of people is split into two categories—people who are under 65 and people who are 65 or older—because older people have a higher IRS allowance for health care costs. If your actual expenses are higher than this IRS amount, you may deduct the additional amount on line 22.

Debtor 1   Roger   H.   Matthews   Case number (if known)_____
            First Name   Middle Name   Last Name

People who are under 65 years of age

7a. Out-of-pocket health care allowance per person $_____54.00_____

7b. Number of people who are under 65   x   4

7c. Subtotal. Multiply line 7a by line 7b. $_____216.00_____   Copy here→ $____216.00____

People who are 65 years of age or older

7d. Out-of-pocket health care allowance per person $_____

7e. Number of people who are 65 or older   X_____

7f. Subtotal. Multiply line 7d by line 7e. $_____0.00_____   Copy here→   + $____0.00____

7g. Total. Add lines 7c and 7f. .... $_____216.00_____   Copy here→ .... $ 216.00

Local Standards   You must use the IRS Local Standards to answer the questions in lines 8-15.

Based on information from the IRS, the U.S. Trustee Program has divided the IRS Local Standard for housing for bankruptcy purposes into two parts:

■ Housing and utilities – Insurance and operating expenses
■ Housing and utilities – Mortgage or rent expenses

To answer the questions in lines 8-9, use the U.S. Trustee Program chart. To find the chart, go online using the link specified in the separate instructions for this form. This chart may also be available at the bankruptcy clerk's office.

8. **Housing and utilities – Insurance and operating expenses:** Using the number of people you entered in line 5, fill in the dollar amount listed for your county for insurance and operating expenses. $ 644.00

9. **Housing and utilities – Mortgage or rent expenses:**

   9a. Using the number of people you entered in line 5, fill in the dollar amount listed for your county for mortgage or rent expenses. $ 1,239.00

   9b. Total average monthly payment for all mortgages and other debts secured by your home.

   To calculate the total average monthly payment, add all amounts that are contractually due to each secured creditor in the 60 months after you file for bankruptcy. Next divide by 60.

Name of the creditor	Average monthly payment
First Bank of Capital City	$ 850.00
Capital Savings Bank	$ 700.00
_____	+ $

   9b. Total average monthly payment $ 1,550.00   Copy here→   – $ 1,550.00   Repeat this amount on line 33a.

   9c. Net mortgage or rent expense.
   Subtract line 9b (total average monthly payment) from line 9a (mortgage or rent expense). If this number is less than $0, enter $0. $ 0.00   Copy here→ .... $ 0.00

10. **If you claim that the U.S. Trustee Program's division of the IRS Local Standard for housing is incorrect and affects the calculation of your monthly expenses, fill in any additional amount you claim.** $ 0.00

    Explain why: _____

                  _____

Debtor 1   Roger   H.   Matthews   Case number (if known) _____
            First Name   Middle Name   Last Name

11. **Local transportation expenses:** Check the number of vehicles for which you claim an ownership or operating expense.

☐ 0. Go to line 14.
☐ 1. Go to line 12.
☐ 2 or more. Go to line 12.

12. **Vehicle operation expense:** Using the IRS Local Standards and the number of vehicles for which you claim the operating expenses, fill in the *Operating Costs* that apply for your Census region or metropolitan statistical area. $ 502.00

13. **Vehicle ownership or lease expense:** Using the IRS Local Standards, calculate the net ownership or lease expense for each vehicle below. You may not claim the expense if you do not make any loan or lease payments on the vehicle. In addition, you may not claim the expense for more than two vehicles.

Vehicle 1   Describe Vehicle 1:   YR-3 Ford F-150

13a. Ownership or leasing costs using IRS Local Standard .... $ 471.00

13b. Average monthly payment for all debts secured by Vehicle 1.
Do not include costs for leased vehicles.

To calculate the average monthly payment here and on line 13e, add all amounts that are contractually due to each secured creditor in the 60 months after you file for bankruptcy. Then divide by 60.

Name of each creditor for Vehicle 1	Average monthly payment
Automotive Financing, Inc.	$ 360.00
	+ $
Total average monthly payment	$ 360.00

Copy here ➡ — $ 360.00   Repeat this amount on line 33b.

13c. Net Vehicle 1 ownership or lease expense
Subtract line 13b from line 13a. If this number is less than $0, enter $0. .... $ 111.00   Copy net Vehicle 1 expense here ➡ $ 111.00

Vehicle 2   Describe Vehicle 2:   YR-4 Honda Civic

13d. Ownership or leasing costs using IRS Local Standard .... $ 471.00

13e. Average monthly payment for all debts secured by Vehicle 2.
Do not include costs for leased vehicles.

Name of each creditor for Vehicle 2	Average monthly payment
Columbiana Federal S&L	$ 240.00
	+ $
Total average monthly payment	$ 240.00

Copy here ➡ — $ 240.00   Repeat this amount on line 33c.

13f. Net Vehicle 2 ownership or lease expense
Subtract line 13e from line 13d. If this number is less than $0, enter $0. .... $ 231.00   Copy net Vehicle 2 expense here ➡ $ 231.00

14. **Public transportation expense:** If you claimed 0 vehicles in line 11, using the IRS Local Standards, fill in the *Public Transportation* expense allowance regardless of whether you use public transportation. $ 0.00

15. **Additional public transportation expense:** If you claimed 1 or more vehicles in line 11 and if you claim that you may also deduct a public transportation expense, you may fill in what you believe is the appropriate expense, but you may not claim more than the IRS Local Standard for *Public Transportation*. $ 0.00

Debtor 1   Roger   H.   Matthews   Case number (if known)_____
              First Name   Middle Name   Last Name

Other Necessary Expenses	In addition to the expense deductions listed above, you are allowed your monthly expenses for the following IRS categories.

16. **Taxes:** The total monthly amount that you actually pay for federal, state and local taxes, such as income taxes, self-employment taxes, social security taxes, and Medicare taxes. You may include the monthly amount withheld from your pay for these taxes. However, if you expect to receive a tax refund, you must divide the expected refund by 12 and subtract that number from the total monthly amount that is withheld to pay for taxes. $1,100.00
    Do not include real estate, sales, or use taxes.

17. **Involuntary deductions:** The total monthly payroll deductions that your job requires, such as retirement contributions, union dues, and uniform costs.
    Do not include amounts that are not required by your job, such as voluntary 401(k) contributions or payroll savings. $ 0.00

18. **Life insurance:** The total monthly premiums that you pay for your own term life insurance. If two married people are filing together, include payments that you make for your spouse's term life insurance.
    Do not include premiums for life insurance on your dependents, for a non-filing spouse's life insurance, or for any form of life insurance other than term. $ 0.00

19. **Court-ordered payments:** The total monthly amount that you pay as required by the order of a court or administrative agency, such as spousal or child support payments. $ 0.00
    Do not include payments on past due obligations for spousal or child support. You will list these obligations in line 35.

20. **Education:** The total monthly amount that you pay for education that is either required:
    ■ as a condition for your job, or $ 0.00
    ■ for your physically or mentally challenged dependent child if no public education is available for similar services.

21. **Childcare:** The total monthly amount that you pay for childcare, such as babysitting, daycare, nursery, and preschool. $ 0.00
    Do not include payments for any elementary or secondary school education.

22. **Additional health care expenses, excluding insurance costs:** The monthly amount that you pay for health care that is required for the health and welfare of you or your dependents and that is not reimbursed by insurance or paid by a health savings account. Include only the amount that is more than the total entered in line 7. $ 50.00
    Payments for health insurance or health savings accounts should be listed only in line 25.

23. **Optional telephones and telephone services:** The total monthly amount that you pay for telecommunication services for you and your dependents, such as pagers, call waiting, caller identification, special long distance, or business cell phone service, to the extent necessary for your health and welfare or that of your dependents or for the production of income, if it is not reimbursed by your employer.   + $ 0.00
    Do not include payments for basic home telephone, internet or cell phone service. Do not include self-employment expenses, such as those reported on line 5 of Form 122C-1, or any amount you previously deducted.

24. **Add all of the expenses allowed under the IRS expense allowances.** $4,363.00
    Add lines 6 through 23.

Additional Expense Deductions	These are additional deductions allowed by the Means Test. *Note:* Do not include any expense allowances listed in lines 6-24.

25. **Health insurance, disability insurance, and health savings account expenses.** The monthly expenses for health insurance, disability insurance, and health savings accounts that are reasonably necessary for yourself, your spouse, or your dependents.

    Health insurance $ 74.00

    Disability insurance $_____

    Health savings account + $_____

    Total $ 74.00   Copy total here ➔ .... $ 74.00

    Do you actually spend this total amount?

    ☐ No. How much do you actually spend? $_____
    ☑ Yes

26. **Continuing contributions to the care of household or family members.** The actual monthly expenses that you will continue to pay for the reasonable and necessary care and support of an elderly, chronically ill, or disabled member of your household or member of your immediate family who is unable to pay for such expenses. These expenses may include contributions to an account of a qualified ABLE program. 26 U.S.C. § 529A(b). $ 0.00

27. **Protection against family violence.** The reasonably necessary monthly expenses that you incur to maintain the safety of you and your family under the Family Violence Prevention and Services Act or other federal laws that apply. $ 0.00
    By law, the court must keep the nature of these expenses confidential.

Debtor 1   Roger   H.   Matthews   Case number (if known)_____

    First Name   Middle Name   Last Name

28. **Additional home energy costs.** Your home energy costs are included in your insurance and operating expenses on line 8.

If you believe that you have home energy costs that are more than the home energy costs included in expenses on line 8, then fill in the excess amount of home energy costs. $ __0.00__

You must give your case trustee documentation of your actual expenses, and you must show that the additional amount claimed is reasonable and necessary.

29. **Education expenses for dependent children who are younger than 18.** The monthly expenses (not more than $160.42* per child) that you pay for your dependent children who are younger than 18 years old to attend a private or public elementary or secondary school. $ __0.00__

You must give your case trustee documentation of your actual expenses, and you must explain why the amount claimed is reasonable and necessary and not already accounted for in lines 6-23.

   * Subject to adjustment on 4/01/19, and every 3 years after that for cases begun on or after the date of adjustment.

30. **Additional food and clothing expense.** The monthly amount by which your actual food and clothing expenses are higher than the combined food and clothing allowances in the IRS National Standards. That amount cannot be more than 5% of the food and clothing allowances in the IRS National Standards. $ __0.00__

To find a chart showing the maximum additional allowance, go online using the link specified in the separate instructions for this form. This chart may also be available at the bankruptcy clerk's office.

You must show that the additional amount claimed is reasonable and necessary.

31. **Continuing charitable contributions.** The amount that you will continue to contribute in the form of cash or financial instruments to a religious or charitable organization. 11 U.S.C. § 548(d)(3) and (4).   + $ __50.00__

Do not include any amount more than 15% of your gross monthly income.

32. **Add all of the additional expense deductions.** $ __124.00__
Add lines 25 through 31.

Deductions for Debt Payment

33. **For debts that are secured by an interest in property that you own, including home mortgages, vehicle loans, and other secured debt, fill in lines 33a through 33e**

To calculate the total average monthly payment, add all amounts that are contractually due to each secured creditor in the 60 months after you file for bankruptcy. Then divide by 60.

	Average monthly payment
Mortgages on your home	
33a. Copy line 9b here .... →	$ __1,550.00__
Loans on your first two vehicles	
33b. Copy line 13b here. .... →	$ __360.00__
33c. Copy line 13e here. .... →	$ __240.00__

33d. List other secured debts:

Name of each creditor for other secured debt	Identify property that secures the debt	Does payment include taxes or insurance?	
_____	_____	☐ No ☐ Yes	$ _____
_____	_____	☐ No ☐ Yes	$ _____
_____	_____	☐ No ☐ Yes	+ $ _____

33e. Total average monthly payment. Add lines 33a through 33d. .... $ __2,150.00__   Copy total here → $ __2,150.00__

Debtor 1   Roger   H.   Matthews   Case number (if known) _____
          First Name   Middle Name   Last Name

34. **Are any debts that you listed in line 33 secured by your primary residence, a vehicle, or other property necessary for your support or the support of your dependents?**

☐ No. Go to line 35.
☑ Yes. State any amount that you must pay to a creditor, in addition to the payments listed in line 33, to keep possession of your property (called the *cure amount*). Next, divide by 60 and fill in the information below.

Name of the creditor	Identify property that secures the debt	Total cure amount		Monthly cure amount
First Bank of Capital C	Residence	$ 850.00	÷ 60 =	$ 14.16
_____	_____	$ _____	÷ 60 =	$ _____
_____	_____	$ _____	÷ 60 = + $ _____

| | | Total | $ 14.16 | Copy total here ➔ | $ 14.16 |

35. **Do you owe any priority claims—such as a priority tax, child support, or alimony—that are past due as of the filing date of your bankruptcy case?** 11 U.S.C. § 507.

☐ No. Go to line 36.
☑ Yes. Fill in the total amount of all of these priority claims. Do not include current or ongoing priority claims, such as those you listed in line 19.

Total amount of all past-due priority claims. .... $ 1,000.00 ÷ 60 $ 16.67

36. **Projected monthly Chapter 13 plan payment** $ 2,200.00

Current multiplier for your district as stated on the list issued by the Administrative Office of the United States Courts (for districts in Alabama and North Carolina) or by the Executive Office for United States Trustees (for all other districts).

To find a list of district multipliers that includes your district, go online using the link specified in the separate instructions for this form. This list may also be available at the bankruptcy clerk's office.   x ____5____

Average monthly administrative expense $ 112.20   Copy total here ➔ $ 112.20

37. **Add all of the deductions for debt payment.** Add lines 33e through 36. $ 2,993.03

Total Deductions from Income

38. **Add all of the allowed deductions.**

Copy line 24, *All of the expenses allowed under IRS expense allowances* .... $ 4,363.00

Copy line 32, *All of the additional expense deductions* .... $ 124.00

Copy line 37, *All of the deductions for debt payment* .... + $ 2,993.03

Total deductions .... $ 7,480.03   Copy total here ➔ $ 7,480.03

Debtor 1   Roger   H.   Matthews   Case number (if known) _____
            First Name   Middle Name   Last Name

Part 2:   Determine Your Disposable Income Under 11 U.S.C. § 1325(b)(2)

39. Copy your total current monthly income from line 14 of Form 122C-1, *Chapter 13 Statement of Your Current Monthly Income and Calculation of Commitment Period.* .... $ 7,916.66

40. **Fill in any reasonably necessary income you receive for support for dependent children.** The monthly average of any child support payments, foster care payments, or disability payments for a dependent child, reported in Part I of Form 122C-1, that you received in accordance with applicable nonbankruptcy law to the extent reasonably necessary to be expended for such child. $ _____ 0.00

41. **Fill in all qualified retirement deductions.** The monthly total of all amounts that your employer withheld from wages as contributions for qualified retirement plans, as specified in 11 U.S.C. § 541(b)(7) plus all required repayments of loans from retirement plans, as specified in 11 U.S.C. § 362(b)(19). $ _____ 0.00

42. **Total of all deductions allowed under 11 U.S.C. § 707(b)(2)(A).** Copy line 38 here ....→ $ ___ 7,480.03

43. **Deduction for special circumstances.** If special circumstances justify additional expenses and you have no reasonable alternative, describe the special circumstances and their expenses. You must give your case trustee a detailed explanation of the special circumstances and documentation for the expenses.

Describe the special circumstances	Amount of expense
_____	$ _____
_____	$ _____
_____	+ $ _____
Total	$ _____ 0.00 Copy here → + $ _____ 0.00

44. **Total adjustments.** Add lines 40 through 43 .... $ ___ 7,480.03   Copy here →   − $ 7,480.03

45. **Calculate your monthly disposable income under § 1325(b)(2).** Subtract line 44 from line 39. $ ___ 436.63

Part 3:   Change in Income or Expenses

46. **Change in income or expenses.** If the income in Form 122C-1 or the expenses you reported in this form have changed or are virtually certain to change after the date you filed your bankruptcy petition and during the time your case will be open, fill in the information below. For example, if the wages reported increased after you filed your petition, check 122C-1 in the first column, enter line 2 in the second column, explain why the wages increased, fill in when the increase occurred, and fill in the amount of the increase.

Form	Line	Reason for change	Date of change	Increase or decrease?	Amount of change
☐ 122C–1 ☑ 122C–2	21	Family child care provider will	08/01/2016	☑ Increase ☐ Decrease	$ _____ 250.00
☐ 122C–1 ☐ 122C–2	___	_____	_____	☐ Increase ☐ Decrease	$ _____
☐ 122C–1 ☐ 122C–2	___	_____	_____	☐ Increase ☐ Decrease	$ _____
☐ 122C–1 ☐ 122C–2	___	_____	_____	☐ Increase ☐ Decrease	$ _____

Debtor 1	Roger	H.	Matthews	Case number *(if known)* _____
	First Name	Middle Name	Last Name	

Part 4:   Sign Below

By signing here, under penalty of perjury you declare that the information on this statement and in any attachments is true and correct.

X /s/ Roger H. Matthews _____   **X** /s/ Susan J. Matthews _____

Signature of Debtor 1   Signature of Debtor 2

Date 06/06/2016 _____   Date 06/06/2016 _____
MM / DD / YYYY   MM / DD / YYYY

Because of the similarity between Form 122C-2 used by above median debtors in Chapter 13 cases and Form 122A-2 used in the Chapter 7 means test by above median debtors and explained in detail in Chapter Seven, our examination of the Form 122C-2 here will be cursory. Thus, on Line 5 of Part 1 of the form, where the debtor calculates deductions from income, the Matthews first enter the number of persons whose expenses will be considered in calculating the deductions. As with Form 122A-2 for the above median debtor in a Chapter 7, the persons whose expenses can be considered on Form 122C-2 potentially include more than the persons who make up his household (compare Line 16(b) on Form 122C-1). Section 1325(b)(2)(A)(i) provides that the debtor's monthly expenses shall include such expenses "for the debtor, the dependents of the debtor, and the spouse of the debtor in a joint case, if the spouse is not otherwise a dependent."

Using the number of persons designated on Line 5 the debtor then enters the standardized expense amounts for food and clothing (Line 6) and healthcare (Line 7) using the IRS National Standards for Allowable Living Expenses posted on the U.S. Trustee Program web site at www.justice.gov/ust/means-testing for a dependency group of that size living in Pennsylvania, the debtor's state of residence, in 2016. Note that the instructions on Line 7 indicate that if the debtor's actual healthcare expenses are greater than the standard figure that can be noted on Line 22, discussed below.

The Matthews then utilize the IRS Local Standards for Transportation and Housing and Utilities Expenses to enter the standardized expenses for non-mortgage housing and utility expenses (Line 8), mortgage/rent expense (Line 9), vehicle operation expense (Lines 11 and 12), and vehicle ownership or lease expense for up to two vehicles (Line 13) in Dauphin County, Pennsylvania.

With regard to the deduction for vehicle ownership expense on Line 13 of Form 122C-2 (and Line 13 of Form 122A-2 discussed in Chapter Seven), recall that there was an issue of whether that deduction is allowable where the debtor owns the vehicle outright so there is no lease or debt secured by the vehicle. The Supreme Court resolved the issue in *Ransom v. FIA Card Services, N.A.*, 131 S. Ct. 716 (2011), holding that the deduction is not allowable for a car that is owned free of debt or lease obligations. All three vehicles owned by the Matthews are security for debt, so *Ransom* is no bar to their taking the deduction for all three vehicles. However, the ownership expense deduction can only be taken for up to two vehicles (though a debtor might seek a deduction for an additional vehicle as part of a special circumstance on Line 43 of the form, discussed below). But the Matthews have no such special circumstance to justify deducting ownership expenses for the third car. Moreover, they plan to surrender the YR-8 Chevrolet Malibu to Car World, the creditor secured in it. For all those reasons, counsel for the Matthews does not have them list ownership expenses associated with this third vehicle.

Left unanswered by *Ransom* is the question of whether a Chapter 13 debtor who plans to surrender a collateralized vehicle to the secured creditor can still claim the ownership and operation expenses for that vehicle on Lines 12 and 13 of Form 122C-2 or payments on the note secured by the vehicle on Line 33 of that form as part of the determination of his or her disposable income. The same question arises regarding the home ownership expense deduction on Line 9 and deduction of mortgage payments on Line 33 of Form 122C-2 where the debtor intends to surrender the home to the mortgagee. (Recall from Chapter

Seven the discussion of this same issue in the context of the Form 122A-2 for the above median debtor addressed in P-H 7-f.)

A majority of courts deciding this issue have been influenced by the Supreme Court's adoption of the forward-looking ("known or virtually certain changes") approach in *Hamilton v. Lanning* for the calculation of the Chapter 13 debtor's current monthly income. They hold the same forward-looking approach is to be used in connection with these parts of the Form 122C-2 such that if the debtor has indicated an intent to surrender collateral, the debtor may not claim the vehicle ownership and operation expense or the mortgage ownership expense for such collateral. See, e.g., *Darrohn v. Hildebrand*, 615 F.3d 470 (6th Cir. 2010), and *In re Liehr*, 439 B.R. 179 (10th Cir. B.A.P. 2010). But see *In re Coffin*, 435 B.R. 780, 785-786 (1st Cir. B.A.P. 2010) (acknowledging that "[i]t is generally accepted that many provisions of BAPCPA are unclear, making it difficult for courts to discern the congressional intent" and that "[i]n our view, §1325(b) is an example of a provision that is caught between the tension of BAPCPA's two goals: bankruptcy abuse prevention and consumer protection" and concluding that Congress's specifying that debtors are entitled to "applicable" monthly expense amounts with respect to the National and Local Standards, in contrast to specifying use of "actual" monthly expenses with respect to Other Necessary Expenses, manifests an intent that vehicle ownership expense be determined strictly based on the National Standards rather than on the debtor's actual expense notwithstanding intent to surrender).

P-H 14-f: The law firm you work for represents the above median Chapter 13 debtors in the following scenarios. Answer the questions posed for both debtors assuming the jurisdiction follows *Darrohn v. Hildebrand* and *In re Liehr*.

a. Client owns a vehicle that is collateral for a loan from Bank and Client has no equity in it (Bank is undersecured in the vehicle). Client would just as soon surrender the vehicle to Bank but does not have any other means of transportation. However, her brother-in-law has promised he will fix up one of his cars for her and give it to her to use next month. If he comes through on his promise, Client will surrender her vehicle; if he doesn't, Client will attempt a strip down and pay through on the vehicle. Should you report ownership and operation payments on Lines 12 and 13 of Client's Form 122C-2 or payments on the note secured by the vehicle on Line 33? You want to file the proposed plan with the petition and schedules. What should you say in the plan regarding the vehicle?

b. Clients, a married couple, own a home mortgaged to the Bank and in which they have a small amount of equity that they can exempt. But they are in disagreement about whether to try to keep the house or surrender it in bankruptcy. They are four payments behind on the mortgage note and you have explained to them that in order to keep the home their plan will have to pay the arrearages in full as well as continue to make the scheduled payments. Husband wants to let the house go and rent for a while but wife loves the house and says that any sacrifice is worth it to hold on to it. If the couple is unable to resolve this dispute over what to do with the house, what do you do in terms of whether to deduct ownership, note payments, and arrearages payments on their Form 122C-2, and what do you say about the house in their plan?

On Lines 16-23 the Matthews enter average monthly amounts (based on an average of actual payments made during the six months preceding filing of the petition) of Other Necessary Expenses related to the IRS standards but not expressly covered by them including taxes (other than real estate and sales taxes) (Line 16), involuntary deductions from paychecks for things such as union dues, uniforms, etc. (Line 17), life insurance premiums on the debtor's life (Line 18), court-ordered payments such as spousal or child support (in their full amount, not averaged) (Line 19), education expenses necessary for continued employment or for a physically or mentally challenged dependent child for whom no similar public service is available (Line 20), child care expenses (Line 21) (zero entered here by the Matthews because they are not incurring those expenses yet), unreimbursed healthcare expenses in excess of the national standard deduction allowed on Line 7 and not including insurance premiums (Line 22), and necessary additional telecommunication expenses (Line 23). The total of all expenses entered on Lines 6-23 is entered on Line 24.

On Lines 25 through 31, the Matthews can enter deductions they have for other monthly living expenses, such as health/disability insurance premiums (Line 25); reasonable and necessary costs of supporting an elderly, chronically ill, or disabled member of the household or a member of the debtor's immediate family (Line 26); expenses related to keeping the debtor's family safe where a member of the family has been the victim of domestic violence or stalking and qualifies for protection under the Family Violence Prevention and Services Act (Line 27); home energy costs in excess of the IRS standards for non-mortgage utility costs; school costs incurred in connection with a dependent child's attendance at a public or private elementary or secondary school up to a current maximum of $160.42 per child (that amount will be next adjusted in April 2019) (Line 29); food and clothing expenses in excess of the IRS standards up to a maximum of 5 percent of the combined IRS allowances (Line 30), and continuing charitable contributions not to exceed 15 percent of the debtor's gross monthly income (Line 31) (compare the treatment of this item on Line 31 of Form 122A-2 for purposes of the Chapter 7 means test as discussed in Chapter Seven, Section D). All additional living expenses entered on Lines 25 through 31 are totaled on Line 32.

On Lines 33 through 36 of the form, the Matthews can enter deductions they have for debt payments, including the average monthly scheduled payment on secured debts (Line 33) (they exclude payment on the YR-8 Chevy Malibu that they plan to surrender to Car World, as discussed earlier); monthly amounts needed over the term of the 60-month plan to cure arrearages on secured debt where the debtor intends to retain the property (such as the overdue $850 payment the Matthews owe to First Bank of Capital City secured by the residence) (Line 34); monthly amounts needed over the term of the 60-month plan to pay prepetition priority debts (such as Roger Matthews's $1,000 obligation to the IRS for back taxes) (Line 35); and the projected monthly administrative expense of the plan, calculated by multiplying the current multiplier for administrative expense established by the U.S. Trustee Program (5.1 percent or .051 as of June 2016) by the monthly amount the debtors estimate paying into their Chapter 13 plan ($2,200 for the Matthews; thus $2,200 × .051 = $112.20) (Line 36). All debt payments entered on Lines 33 through 36 are totaled on Line 37. Then all the subtotals from Lines 24, 32, and 37 are totaled and entered on Line 38.

The figure used on Line 36 of Form 122C-2 for the debtor's "projected" monthly Chapter 13 plan payment will not likely be the actual figure used in the debtor's plan. After all, many of the expenses used by the above median debtor on the form are based on the national and local standards and do not reflect actual expenses. As we have seen, the 122C forms do not themselves take into account anticipated changes in the debtor's income or expenses during the term of the plan (e.g., the Matthews will begin incurring child care expenses in August after they file in June). And even the projected payments on secured debt that appear on the form may change as the debtor makes final decisions regarding what collateralized property to keep or surrender. The figure on Line 36 is nothing more than a good faith guestimate of what the eventual monthly plan payment will be utilizing the expenses deducted using the form, and is done at this point only to calculate an additional projected expense the debtor will incur during the term of the plan—the monthly administrative expense charged by the standing trustee in the district using a percentage multiplier set by the district from time to time (but which cannot exceed 10 percent per §707(b)(2)(A)(ii)(III)).

EXAMPLE

> The figure used on Line 36 of the Matthews' Form 122C-2 (assuming they were above median debtors) is calculated beginning with their gross combined income of $7,916 and subtracting the expenses allowed on the form under the national and local standards (which, again, may not reflect their actual expenses for such items) as well as their actual expenses for tax and other deductions from their wages, health and insurance costs, charitable deductions, and payments on secured debt as projected using the form. As we will see when we look in detail at the Chapter 13 plan itself beginning with the next chapter, normal living expenses of Chapter 13 debtors are not included in the monthly plan payment made to the standing trustee but are instead paid by the debtor from month to month. What is included in the plan to be paid to and distributed by the standing trustee are the payments on secured debt (which as we will see may be modified in the plan in ways not accounted for in the Form 122C-2) including any arrearages, priority claims, administrative costs, unpaid attorney's fees of debtor's attorney, and remaining disposable income that will be distributed on allowed unsecured claims. Thus, the $2,200 figure used on their Line 36 is only their attorney's best guestimate using the figures on the form itself of what the debtors will ultimately pay into the plan. The final figure will likely be close to it but different.

In Part 2 of the form the debtor will then calculate his or her disposable income. On Line 39 the debtor inserts the CMI figure from Line 14 of Form 122C-1. On Line 40 the Matthews are then allowed to deduct from their CMI any amounts of income received and included in Part I of Form 122C-1 for child support, foster care payments, or disability payments for a dependent child. Section 1325(b)(2) expressly excludes these items from the definition of disposable income. Similarly, on Line 41 the Matthews can deduct from CMI amounts withheld by the employer from the debtor's paycheck for qualified retirement plan contributions or to repay loans from such retirement plans. Section 1322(f) expressly excludes these items from disposable income. A **qualified retirement plan** is one approved by the IRS allowing the withholding of pre-tax contributions and deferring tax on the amounts withheld until withdrawal from the plan, usually at retirement.

On Line 43 of the form the Matthews can enter deductions for expenses related to special circumstances for which there is no reasonable alternative. This **special circumstances expense** deduction derives from §707(b)(2)(B) and is the same as that allowed a Chapter 7 consumer debtor who can use it to rebut the presumption of abuse arising from the means test (see discussion in Chapter Seven, Section D). Special circumstances expenses may be unusual expenses arising from a serious medical condition or a decrease in income or increase in expenses due to a call to active duty in the military. Special circumstances expenses must be itemized, explained, and well documented.

The total adjustments (deductions) claimed by the debtor to his CMI are entered on Line 44 of the form, subtracted from the CMI figure, and the result entered on Line 45. Though the form identifies the figure on Line 45 as the above median debtor's monthly disposable income under §1325(b)(2) (the amount that must be distributed to unsecured creditors in the plan if they are not paid 100 percent), that's not exactly right. As established by the Supreme Court in *Hamilton v. Lanning*, known or virtually certain changes in the debtor's income or expenses must be taken into account even if the forms, using prepetition numbers, do not take them into account. And as we mentioned in connection with the below median debtor's Schedule J, the terms of the plan itself may alter the disposable income figure (e.g., by surrendering secured property, freeing up more disposable dollars for unsecured creditors). Every bankruptcy practitioner knows that when there is a challenge to the Chapter 13 debtor's plan based on the debtor's proposed disposable income, the court and interested parties will look just as hard at the debtor's Schedules I and J as at his Form 122C-2.

The variableness of the debtor's disposable income as calculated using Form 122C-2 is highlighted by Line 46 of the form, where the Chapter 13 debtor can list any changes in income or expenses that have occurred since the petition was filed (remember the schedules and statements supporting the petition may be filed up to 14 days after the petition itself and the income and expense numbers on Forms 122C-1 and 122C-2 are tied to the date of the petition) or which are "virtually certain" to change after the date of the petition. But there is no place on the form to deduct such claimed expenses from CMI. The debtor claiming such change in income or expenses will draft a plan reflecting such anticipated changes and then fight it out when the trustee or a creditor objects to plan confirmation on that basis.

EXAMPLE

The Matthews children are currently being kept during the day by Susan's mother, who does not charge them for that child care, but the mother is going to be unable to continue to care for the children for much longer so the Matthews expect to begin incurring child care expenses at that time. On Line 46 of their Form 122C-2 (and on Line 24 of their Schedule J) they disclose this expected change to their expenses and estimate that the child care expenses they will begin incurring will be about $250 per month. As we will see in Chapter Fifteen, the Matthews draft their Chapter 13 plan assuming that they will be incurring that child care expense. At their first meeting of creditors, the standing trustee or a creditor may question them closely regarding whether this change in expenses is "virtually certain" to occur and whether the amount allocated for that new expense is accurate and reasonable.

For reasons like this, the monthly disposable income figure listed on Line 45 of Form 122C-2 is only another starting point to determine the real disposable income figure for purposes of §1325. See *In re Risher*, 344 B.R. 833, 836-837 (Bankr. W.D. Ky. 2006) (Form 122C calculation provides a "starting point . . . a floor not a ceiling" for determination of debtor's disposable income), and *In re Grant*, 364 B.R. 656, 667 (Bankr. E.D. Tenn. 2007) ("A debtor's monthly disposable income as reflected on Form 122C is the starting point by which a court determines the debtor's projected disposable income, but this figure can be rebutted by evidence that the debtor's actual net disposable income as of the filing date, reflected on Schedules I and J, as well as other evidence that the debtor's circumstances have changed as of the effective date of the plan.").

Having stated those caveats, if none of the deductions taken by the Chapter 13 debtor on Form 122C-2 are challenged by the trustee, the number entered on Line 45 ($436.63 for the Matthews) will certainly be the *starting point* for the trustee and creditors to determine if the debtor is in fact making all of his projected disposable income available to unsecured creditors in a non–100 percent plan and to decide whether to object to plan confirmation.

EXAMPLE

> Assuming the Matthews had the higher income we have theorized on their Form 122C-2 and assuming their trustee did not challenge their calculations on that form, the trustee would likely begin her inquiry into whether their plan meets the disposable income requirement with the $436.63 figure on Line 45. But that would only be the starting point for the inquiry.

Recall that for the below median debtor, we said earlier that the monthly net income entered on Line 23c of the debtor's Schedule J is no more than a starting point determination of the debtor's disposable income. The same is true of Line 45 in the above median debtor's Form 122C-2 and for the same reasons. In both circumstances, we have to look at the debtor's final determination of how secured debt will be treated in the plan and whether there are likely to be changes to income or expenses during the term of the plan not dealt with in Schedule J or Form 122C-2. Those types of issues will ultimately determine the actual disposable income amount. In the next chapter we will see that done in the Matthews' case.

Throughout this chapter we have assumed that the commitment period for the plan of the above median Chapter 13 debtor will be 60 months and in the majority of cases it will be. But what if that debtor's calculation of disposable income on Form 122C-2 shows that debtor has none (negative disposable income) and a plan is proposed that will pay only secured creditors so that the debtor can retain possession of the property in which those creditors hold a security interest? Must that debtor nonetheless propose a five-year plan?

MUSSELMAN V. ECAST SETTLEMENT CORP.

394 B.R. 801 (E.D.N.C. 2008)

[Brooks Musselman filed a Chapter 13 petition on February 27, 2007. His Chapter 13 Statement of Current Monthly Income and Calculation of Commitment Period and Disposable Income (Form B22C) indicated that the debtor had above median income with monthly disposable income under 11 U.S.C. §1325(b)(2) of negative $255.80. Musselman's proposed plan provided for payments of $459.00 per month for 55 months. The plan did not provide for any payments to unsecured creditors. eCast held around 48 percent of the debtor's scheduled unsecured debt and objected to the debtor's proposed plan. eCast objected to the proposed term of the debtor's plan. The bankruptcy court sustained eCast's objection and the debtor appeals.]

OPINION: FLANAGAN, Chief District Judge . . . .

Where objections were raised by eCast, holder of two allowed unsecured claims, to confirmation of Musselman's Chapter 13 bankruptcy plan, initial reference is made to 11 U.S.C. §1325(b)(1) which provides:

> If the trustee or the holder of an allowed unsecured claim objects to the confirmation of the plan, then the court may not approve the plan unless, as of the effective date of the plan—
>
> (A) the value of the property to be distributed under the plan on account of such claim is not less than the amount of such claim; or
>
> (B) the plan provides that all of the debtor's projected disposable income to be received in the applicable commitment period beginning on the date that the first payment is due under the plan will be applied to make payments to unsecured creditors under the plan.

The difficulty here in application of this section of the statute involves discerning the relationship between "projected disposable income" in §1325(b)(1)(B) and "disposable income" in §1325(b)(2). "Disposable income" is defined in §1325(b)(2) as a debtor's current monthly income (defined in §101(10A)) minus certain "amounts reasonably necessary to be expended." 11 U.S.C. §1325(b)(2). "Projected disposable income" is not, however, defined in the Bankruptcy Code. As a result, this term has produced "varying interpretations as bankruptcy courts across the country struggle to ascertain what the BAPCPA amendments mean." *In re Frederickson*, 375 B.R. 829, 833 (8th Cir. BAP 2007) . . . .

Another issue to be decided concerns application of the term created by BAPCPA, "applicable commitment period." This term appears twice in Chapter 13 of the Bankruptcy Code, once in §1325(b)(1)(B) and again in §1325(b)(4). As already noted, §1325(b)(1)(B) requires that a plan provide that all "projected disposable income to be received in the applicable commitment period" be paid to unsecured creditors to be confirmed. 11 U.S.C. §1325(b)(1)(B). Section 1325(b)(4) states that the applicable commitment period "shall be" 3 years in the case of a below-median income debtor or "not less than 5 years" for an above-median debtor. 11 U.S.C. §1325(b)(4)(A). The court must decide here whether the "applicable commitment period" time requirements apply to above-median debtors with zero or negative "projected disposable income." . . .

7A . . . B. APPLICABLE COMMITMENT PERIOD

Specifically, this court must determine whether the term "applicable commitment period" has any application to debtors who have zero or negative "projected disposable income" under §1325(b)(2) . . . . [I]nterpretation by courts of "applicable commitment period" has resulted in a split.

Some courts have held that "applicable commitment period" does not apply to debtors who do not have any "projected disposable income," regardless of whether the term is temporal in nature or not. See *In re Kagenveama*, 541 F.3d at 875-78; *In re Frederickson*, 375 B.R. at 835; *In re Davis*, 392 B.R. 132, 146 (Bankr. E.D. Pa. 2008); *In re Brady*, 361 B.R. at 776-77; *In re Green*, 378 B.R. 30, 39 (Bankr. N.D.N.Y. 2007); *In re Alexander*, 344 B.R. at 750-51.

Other courts have held that "applicable commitment period" is temporal in nature and sets a fixed plan length for all debtors whose plans are governed by §1325(b). See *In re Grant*, 364 B.R. 656, 667 (Bankr. E.D. Tenn. 2007); *In re Slusher*, 359 B.R. at 305; *In re Strickland*, 2007 WL 499623, *2, 2007 (Bankr. M.D.N.C. 2007); *In re Cushman*, 350 B.R. 207, 212-13 (Bankr. D.S.C. 2006), *In re Girodes*, 350 B.R. at 35; *In re Casey*, 356 B.R. 519, 526-27 (Bankr. E.D. Wash. 2006).

Still other courts have held that "applicable commitment period" is not temporal at all, but rather serves as a multiplicative term. Under this approach, "applicable commitment period" merely sets forth the number by which "projected disposable income" is multiplied to determine how much money a debtor must pay into his plan instead of the length of time that a debtor must make payments into a plan. See *In re McGillis*, 370 B.R. at 734; *In re Fuger*, 347 B.R. 94, 99-101 (Bankr. D. Utah 2006).

This last interpretation of "applicable commitment period" is the one which the debtor here urges the court to adopt. The second one made mention of above was adopted by the bankruptcy court in this case. This court considers the first approach to be the correct one, however.

"Applicable commitment period" appears in two relevant subsections of §1325(b). The first is §1325(b)(1)(B) which provides that a debtor's plan may not be confirmed if a trustee or unsecured creditor objects unless the plan "provides that all of the debtor's *projected disposable income* to be received in the *applicable commitment period* . . . will be applied to make payments to unsecured creditors under the plan." 11 U.S.C. §1325(b)(1)(B) (emphasis added). The second is §1325(b)(4) which sets forth the definition of "applicable commitment period" for above- and below-median debtors (5 and 3 years, respectively), and provides that the "applicable commitment period" may be shorter than 5 or 3 years if "the plan provides for payment in full of all allowed unsecured claims over a shorter period." 11 U.S.C. §1325(b)(4).

Section 1325(b)(1)(B) is the only relevant section of the Bankruptcy Code that applies "applicable commitment period" to any debtors. On its face, §1325(b)(1)(B) requires "all of the debtor's projected disposable income to be received in the applicable commitment period" to go to payments to unsecured creditors. 11 U.S.C. §1325(b)(1)(B). Two threshold requirements are apparent from this language. First, a debtor must have unsecured creditors. Second, a debtor must have "projected disposable income" in order for this subsection to apply to his situation. . . . The first threshold requirement is uncontroversial.

The second is at the heart of one of the debates surrounding "applicable commitment period." A review of the legislative history suggested to the bankruptcy court that the "applicable commitment period" as defined by §1325(b)(4) drives the plan length. It followed the lead of *In re Casey*, and, as noted, rejected the second threshold requirement. While there is an intuitive appeal to such a result, the structure of §1325(b) does not permit this.

Section 1325(b)(4)'s function in the structure of §1325(b) is to define the term "applicable commitment period." Section 1325(b)(1)(B), on the other hand, puts that term into action. It delineates the situations in which the definition of "applicable commitment period" set forth in §1325(b)(4) will apply. Those situations include any cases in which a debtor has "projected disposable income" as defined in §1325(b)(2). By contrast, those situations do not include cases where debtors have no "projected disposable income" under §1325(b)(2).

When a trustee or an unsecured creditor objects to a plan, §1325(b)(1) provides that a court may not approve the plan unless, "(B) the plan provides that all of the debtor's projected disposable income to be received in the applicable commitment period . . . will be applied to make payments to unsecured creditors under the plan." 11 U.S.C. §1325(b)(1). This language requires that a debtor have "projected disposable income" as a threshold matter for the subsection to apply. If a debtor has zero or negative "projected disposable income," then there is nothing "to be received in the applicable commitment period." Id. If there is nothing for a debtor to receive in the "applicable commitment period," there is nothing to "apply to make payments to unsecured creditors under the plan." Id. If none of the subsection's provisions are relevant to a debtor's situations, then that subsection does not apply. Therefore the term "applicable commitment period" simply does not apply to Musselman. On this issue, for the reasons given, the bankruptcy court is REVERSED.

POST-CASE FOLLOW-UP

If the debtor has no projected disposable income, what did eCast have to gain as an unsecured creditor by requiring the debtor to propose a full five-year plan? How is the court's decision justified in the face of the §1325(b)(4)(A) mandate that the applicable commitment period "shall be" three years in the case of a below median income debtor or "not less than 5 years" for an above median debtor? For a well-written opinion adopting the "temporal" approach that insists that the mandate means what it says even for the above median debtor with no disposable income, see *In re Grant*, 364 B.R. 656, 667 (Bankr. E.D. Tenn. 2007) ("To state it more succinctly, the historical 'current monthly income,' determined under §101(10A) as set forth on Form 122C, will determine the 'applicable commitment period' under §1325(b)(4) without consideration of 'projected disposable income' under

§1325(b)(1)(B)."). The third approach, sometimes called the "monetary" or "multiplier" approach, is well described in *In re McGillis*, 370 B.R. 720, 734-739 (Bankr. W.D. Mich. 2007), and provides that §1325(b) does not require the debtor to propose a plan that lasts for the entire length of the applicable commitment period and may propose a plan lasting for a shorter time so long as it provides for the payment of the full amount of disposable income projected to be received over the full length of the applicable commitment period as calculated on Form 122C. Which approach makes the most sense to you in light of both the language of the Code sections and the policies at work? Is it possible that Congress never gave thought to the possibility that a debtor might not have any projected disposable income left after payment of his allowed secured debts and deduction of permissible expenses? Determine if the courts of your federal district or circuit have ruled on this issue and, if so, which approach they take.

Musselman v. eCast Settlement Corp.:   Real Life Applications

1. The law office you work for represents Fred Sauceman, an above median debtor who is planning to file a Chapter 13 case. Fred has a number of secured obligations on his home and cars, all of which are current and which he intends to keep paying as scheduled through the term of the plan and beyond so he can retain possession of those assets. He also has unsecured credit card debt. Calculation of his allowed expenses on his Form 122C-2 including those projected payments to secured creditors leaves him with zero projected disposable income, and nothing in his Schedules I and J suggests any other result. Fred would like to propose a 36-month plan calling for payment of the secured debts as they come due and paying nothing to unsecured creditors. Can that plan be confirmed if your district follows *Musselman*? If it follows the temporal approach? If it follows the monetary or multiplier approach?

2. The law office where you work represents Maria Ortega, a below median debtor, who is planning to file a Chapter 13 case. Maria has a single secured debt, her home mortgage, on which she is current and which she plans to keep paying through the term of the plan and beyond. She also has unsecured credit card debt but according to your calculations of her projected disposable income from her Form 122C-1 she will have sufficient disposable income to pay that unsecured debt in full over 24 months. Nothing in her Schedules I and J suggests otherwise. Can Maria propose a confirmable 24-month plan on these terms? See §1325(b)(4)(B).

IMPACT OF BANKRUPTCY ON THE INDIVIDUAL DEBTOR'S CREDIT RATING

An individual debtor's filing for bankruptcy can be and will be reported to credit reporting agencies and reflected in his credit history and credit score. Under the Fair Credit Reporting Act (FCRA) that regulates credit reporting agencies, a bankruptcy filing as a public record can appear on the debtor's credit history for ten years following the date of filing (15 U.S.C. §1681c) though some agencies voluntarily retain records on Chapter 13 filings for only seven years to encourage debtors to choose that option. Specific debt obligations owed by the debtor at the time bankruptcy is filed remain on the credit report for seven years following the original delinquency date of such obligation (which may have preceded the date of the bankruptcy petition and so will be removed from the report before the bankruptcy proceeding itself is removed). A debt obligation discharged in the bankruptcy case may remain on the credit report until the time to remove it expires but will be labeled "discharged in bankruptcy." The debtor's credit score that is calculated by the credit reporting agencies and used by creditors in the decision to make a new loan or extend credit (most agencies utilize the debtor's credit score calculated according to the predictive analysis formula developed by Fair Isaac Corporation or FICO, which uses a 300 to 850 scoring range) is of course impacted negatively by the bankruptcy filing and may take years to repair. Postbankruptcy, debtors may be able to secure new loans or credit but often at significantly higher interest rates due to the damage done.

CHAPTER SUMMARY

A Chapter 13 plan must propose to pay unsecured creditors 100 percent of what is owed to them or all of the debtor's projected disposable income over the term of the plan.

A Chapter 13 plan must run for a commitment period of at least three but no more than five years. To determine the debtor's applicable commitment period, Chapter 13 debtors must complete and file Official Form 122C-1, which calculates the debtor's current monthly income defined as his average monthly income from all sources received during the look back period of six months preceding the filing of the petition and comparing that CMI with the median family income figure for a household the size of the debtor's household living in the debtor's state of residence.

For the debtor whose annualized CMI is below the applicable state median, the commitment period will be three years, although that debtor may propose a plan of up to five years. The plan of an above median debtor must run for five years, unless it proposes to pay unsecured creditors 100 percent over a shorter term.

Projected disposable income for the below median debtor is calculated primarily from the debtor's Schedules I and J and Form 122C-1. The above median debtor must complete Official Form 122C-2 to calculate his projected disposable income though that debtor's Schedules I and J will be material to the determination as well. Courts are split over whether the above median debtor can deduct ownership and operation expenses on Form 122C-1 related to collateralized property, such as a home or vehicle, where the debtor intends to surrender such property.

Projected disposable income for either the below or above median debtor as calculated using the various schedules and forms filed by the debtor may be impacted by postpetition changes in the debtor's income or expenses and by plan proposals modifying secured or unsecured obligations and thus the final determination of projected disposable income must include an examination of the debtor's proposed plan.

Courts are divided over whether a debtor with negative projected disposable income can propose a plan of less than 60 months that pays only secured claims to enable the debtor to retain the collateralized property.

REVIEW QUESTIONS

1. Explain the difference between an above median debtor and a below median debtor.
2. What do we mean by the applicable commitment period and how is it affected by whether the debtor is above or below median income?
3. Explain how the disposable income of a below median Chapter 13 debtor is determined and what role Form 122C-2, Schedule I, and Schedule J play in that determination.
4. What is the significance of the Supreme Court's holding in *Hamilton v. Lanning*?
5. What is the majority rule regarding whether a Chapter 13 debtor who plans to surrender a collateralized vehicle or mortgaged home to the secured creditor can still claim the vehicle ownership and operation and home ownership expenses on Form 122C-2?
6. Why do we say that the monthly disposable income figure listed on Line 45 of Form 122C-2 is only a "starting point" to determine the actual disposable income figure for an above median debtor for purposes of §1325?
7. What limits does Form 122C-2 place on the debtor's charitable contribution deduction?
8. How long does a Chapter 13 filing stay on the debtor's credit report? A Chapter 7 filing?
9. Under what circumstances can a Chapter 13 debtor's plan run less than three years?
10. What is a 100 percent plan?

WORDS AND PHRASES TO REMEMBER

above median debtor
applicable commitment period
below median debtor
commitment period
current monthly income

disposable income
forward-looking approach
known or virtually certain
look back period
marital adjustment

mechanical approach   qualified retirement plan
median family income   special circumstances expense
passive income   100 percent plan
projected disposable income

TO LEARN MORE: A number of TLM activities to accompany this chapter are accessible on the companion web site for this textbook at http://aspen lawschool.com/books/Parsons_Debt4e/.

The Chapter 13 Debt Adjustment for an Individual with Regular Income—Treatment of Priority, Secured, and Unsecured Claims in the Plan

In this chapter we will examine how the Code requires that priority claims be treated in a Chapter 13 plan. Then we will consider how secured claims may be treated in the plan and the wide range of options the Code provides to enable the Chapter 13 debtor to modify secured debt and retain possession of the collateral. We will also discuss options for the treatment of nonpriority unsecured debt in a Chapter 13 including circumstances under which a debtor may propose a plan that pays unsecured claims less than 100 percent. In addition, we will take a practical look at how payments to creditors get made under a Chapter 13 plan with the use of wage orders, payments to creditors through the standing trustee, and sometimes with payments made outside the plan.

KEY CONCEPTS

- Generally, a Chapter 13 plan must provide for payment of all priority claims in full
- A Chapter 13 plan may propose a pay through for secured debt allowing the debtor to retain the collateral
- A Chapter 13 plan may also provide for modification of secured claims in a variety of ways including curing of arrearages, avoiding certain liens that impair exemptions, reducing certain secured claims to the value of the collateral, adjusting the amount of installment payments due during the term of the plan, selling collateralized property free and clear of liens, or abandoning collateral and surrendering it to the creditor

- A Chapter 13 plan may provide for modification of unsecured claims in a variety of ways including curing of arrearages and adjusting the amount of installment payments during the term of the plan
- A Chapter 13 plan may provide for paying unsecured claims less than 100 percent of their value and for discharging the balance if the plan calls for the payment of all of the debtor's projected disposable income over the applicable commitment period and if unsecured creditors will receive at least as much in the Chapter 13 plan as they would have received in a Chapter 7 liquidation
- The debtor's disposable income funding the plan over its term is normally paid to the standing trustee via wage order and other devices and the trustee then makes the payments to creditors
- The plan may call for some payments to be made outside the plan by the debtor or a third party other than the standing trustee

A. ▶ Treatment of Priority Claims in the Chapter 13 Plan

In Chapter Eleven, Section B, we saw that §507 designates some claims as **priority claims** for purposes of payment. Section 1322(a)(2) requires that a Chapter 13 plan provide for the payment of all §507 priority claims in full (100 percent) although the payment may be made in deferred installments over the term of the plan.

EXAMPLE

> The Matthews' Chapter 13 plan (Illustration 15-b) calls for the payment in full of a tax obligation resulting from federal income taxes assessed for tax year YR-2. That tax obligation is given a priority status by §507(a)(8) (see Illustration 11-a).

One exception to the requirement of full payment of priority claims is where the priority creditor agrees to a different treatment under the plan, which is uncommon. Another exception applies to the priority granted by §507(a)(1)(B) to domestic support obligations that have been assigned for collection to a governmental agency. Section 1322(a)(4), added by BAPCPA, provides that the plan can call for less than full payment of that priority claim if the plan runs a full five years and calls for the distribution of all the debtor's projected disposable income during that term.

B. ▶ Treatment of Secured Claims in the Chapter 13 Plan

The debtor has a number of options in deciding how to deal with secured debts in his or her proposed Chapter 13 plan, a number of which involve the right to modify the terms of a secured claim.

1. Payment of the Secured Claim in Full and Retention of the Lien: The Pay Through Proposal

Per §1322(b)(2), the plan may propose to pay a secured claim in full as called for in the underlying contract and for the creditor to retain its lien on the secured property. The secured creditor is not likely to object to such a plan because its interest is not impaired in any way, and the debtor is able to keep the property.

EXAMPLE

> The Matthews' plan calls for First Bank of Capital City (FBCC) to retain its first mortgage position in their home and for the monthly payments of $850 to continue unimpaired by the plan. FBCC should have no objection to this arrangement. So long as the Matthews make the mortgage payments, they will be able to retain the home.

Practitioners sometimes call this proposal a **pay through** (or sometimes a **ride through**) provision since the debtor is proposing to pay installments as they come due throughout the duration of the plan and beyond.

If the debtor is in arrears on payments to the secured creditor, the plan can propose to make extra payments to **cure the arrearage** during the term of the plan as discussed in more detail below along with the pay through.

2. Avoiding a Lien That Impairs an Exemption in Property of the Debtor

The Chapter 13 debtor, like the individual Chapter 7 debtor, may claim property as exempt and must file a Schedule C in order to do so. As we learned in our consideration of exemptions in Chapter 7 in Chapter Eight, Section B, a debtor cannot normally claim an exemption in property in which the debtor has granted a consensual security interest or in property subject to a statutory lien. However, we also know that §522(f)(1)(A) permits a debtor to avoid a judicial lien on property that impairs an exemption unless the judicial lien arises out of a domestic support obligation. Section 522(f)(1)(A) is available to the Chapter 13 debtor as well, as is §522(f)(1)(B), which permits the debtor to avoid even a consensual lien in household goods and furnishings, wearing apparel, appliances, tools of the trade, and other such items to the extent the lien is not a **purchase money security interest** and it impairs the debtor's right to exempt such property. Per Bankruptcy Rule 4003(d), the proceeding to avoid a lien impairing an exemption is initiated by motion, not adversary proceeding.

Purchase money security interest A consensual security interest granted to one who has sold property to the debtor or loaned the purchase price for the property to the debtor.

EXAMPLE

> The Matthews' Chapter 13 plan (Illustration 15-b) seeks to avoid the lien of Capital City Finance Company (CCFC) in Roger's plumbing tools and the couple's furniture under §522(f)(1)(b). The debt of CCFC is not a purchase money one because Roger and Susan already owned these items before he and Susan incurred the debt to CCFC and CCFC does not have possession of the items in which it claims the security interest. Consequently, the debtors should be able to avoid the CCFC lien in those goods entirely, have the $2,000 balance of the debt to CCFC treated as a general unsecured claim, and keep the items because they claim them as exempt, pursuant to §522(d)(3) (see the Matthews' Schedule C, Document 4 in their case file). If Roger had granted a security interest in a gun collection as part of the CCFC loan, there might be a question as to whether the guns constitute household goods within the meaning of that section. If Roger was a traveling salesman and had granted a security interest in his car as security for this loan, there might be a question as to whether the car was a tool of the trade for purposes of §522(f)(1)(B).

3. Curing of Arrearages Created by Prepetition Default

Curing an arrearage A Chapter 13 plan proposal to pay past due amounts to a creditor over a reasonable time within the term of the plan in order to retain collateralized property.

At the time the Chapter 13 petition is filed, a debtor frequently has defaulted on some payments due to secured creditors and owes the **arrearage**, as well as future payments. Simply promising to make all future payments is not going to appease the creditor in that situation. Pursuant to §§1322(b)(3) and (5), the debtor's plan may propose to cure the arrearage by making up the past-due payments. However, the plan must call for the arrearages to be paid

- over a reasonable time, and
- within the term of the plan.

Section 1322(b)(5) allows the curing of arrearage on debt secured by either real or personal property. This includes the debtor's principal residence, the mortgage on which is often in default due to missed payments when a debtor files for Chapter 13 relief. Foreclosure looms. Saving the residence becomes the highest priority for such a debtor and the right to cure the arrearage on the mortgage arising from the defaults is critical to the debtor's hopes. If the debtor can cure the arrearage as part of the plan and make the future payments as they come due, debtor can keep the secured property.

In the case of a debt secured by a mortgage in the debtor's principal residence, however, there is an important exception. Section 1322(c)(1) provides that curing the arrearage is only possible until such residence is sold at a foreclosure sale conducted in accordance with applicable nonbankruptcy law. Most foreclosures are conducted under state law. So what this provision means is that if the debtor does not file his Chapter 13 petition triggering the automatic stay of a foreclosure proceeding prior to the time the residence has been sold in foreclosure, it is too late to cure the arrearage and the debtor loses the house.

EXAMPLE

When the Chapter 13 petition was filed, the Matthews had failed to make their last monthly mortgage payment of $850 to FBCC (see the Assignment Memorandum in Appendix B). Their plan calls for curing that arrearage over the first 12 months of the plan, along with payment of the remaining installments as they come due. So long as a foreclosure action has not been completed by the sale of the property in foreclosure when the Matthews' Chapter 13 petition is filed, this is permissible. If the court concludes that 12 months is a reasonable time over which to cure the arrearage, the plan may be approved and the Matthews will be able to keep their house.

Note in the last example that the plan calls for curing the arrearage during the term of the plan, over the first 12 months of it. If the plan called for the arrearage to be cured over 6 years when the plan itself is only 5 years in duration, the proposal could not be approved. Under §1322(b)(5), it doesn't matter if the payment schedule on the underlying secured debt runs longer than the plan (e.g., the plan runs for 5 years and the FBCC mortgage has another 23 years to run) so long as the arrearage is cured during the term of the plan.

EXAMPLE

The mortgage payments owed by the Matthews to FBCC run for longer than the term of their plan (five years). That is no bar to their plan calling for the curing of the arrearage within a reasonable time and for continuing the payments in order to retain the secured property.

Since it is too late to cure an arrearage on a mortgage in Chapter 13 once the residence has been sold in foreclosure, questions can and do arise over exactly when a foreclosed-on residence has been sold and over whether and to what extent applicable state law should control that question.

HIGHLIGHTED CASE

IN RE MEDAGLIA
402 B.R. 530 (Bankr. D.R.I. 2009)

[This dispute arises from Robert Buonano's (the "Buyer's") "Motion for Relief from Automatic Stay in Order to Record a Deed and to Take Possession" of property that he purchased at a (prepetition) foreclosure auction on September 9, 2008. A Memorandum of Sale was executed on the same day, and the Buyer paid the required deposit of $5,000. On September 11, 2008, before the Buyer recorded his deed, the Debtor (Medaglia) filed the instant Chapter 13 case.

The Buyer argues that, under 11 U.S.C. §1322(c)(1), the Debtor's right to cure the mortgage default terminated at the moment when the Memorandum of Sale was signed, and that thereafter, the Debtor no longer had any interest in the Property. The Debtor objects to relief from stay, arguing that the foreclosure sale did not terminate his right to cure the loan default, and that such right stays "alive and well" until the foreclosure deed is recorded and delivered to the purchaser. The issue of when the right to cure a loan default on the Debtor's principal residence terminates under §(c)(1) has generated conflicting results in the bankruptcy arena.]

OPINION: VOTOLATO, Bankruptcy Judge . . .

DISCUSSION

Under Section 1322(b)(5), the Debtor may provide in his plan for the curing of any default on any unsecured or secured claim on which the last payment is due after the date on which the final payment under the plan is due. Section 1322(c)(1) states: "Notwithstanding subsection (b)(2) and applicable nonbankruptcy law . . . a default with respect to, or that gave rise to, a lien on the debtor's principal residence may be cured . . . *until such residence is sold at a foreclosure sale that is conducted in accordance with applicable nonbankruptcy law. . . .*" (emphasis added.) It is clear, to me at least, that the *notwithstanding* clause in Section 1322 trumps nonbankruptcy law regarding the cure of mortgage defaults on a debtor's primary residence. . . . And the statute itself would seem to leave no doubt that, in bankruptcy, the right to cure exists only until the property is sold at a (valid) foreclosure sale. Nevertheless, judicial disagreement has emerged over the meaning of the phrase "sold at a foreclosure sale that is conducted in accordance with applicable nonbankruptcy law." In preparing this decision, we have identified three different interpretations of Section 1322(c)(1).

The majority view (and the one I like), known as the "gavel rule," is that Section 1322(c)(1) is clear and unambiguous, and that the debtor's right to cure is cut off at the foreclosure sale. See e.g. *In re Connors*, 497 F.3d 314 (3d Cir. 2007); *In re Cain*, 423 F.3d 617 (6th Cir. 2005); *In re Smith*, 85 F.3d 1555, 1558 n. 3 (11th Cir. 1996) (dictum); *In re McCarn*, 218 B.R. 154 (10th Cir. BAP 1998); *In re Crichlow*, 322 B.R. 229 (Bankr. D. Mass. 2004). Based on our research, every appeals court, with one exception described below, and every bankruptcy appellate panel that has considered the issue, has adhered to the gavel rule.

A second line of cases focuses on the word "sold" in Section 1322(c)(1), holding that a foreclosure sale is not an event, but instead, is part of a process culminating in the delivery and recordation of the deed, with the debtor's right to cure surviving until title to the property passes to the purchaser under the relevant state law. See e.g. *In re Beeman*, 235 B.R. 519, 525 (Bankr. D.N.H. 1999).

And, finally, a solitary Court of Appeals has construed Section 1322(c)(1) to mean that the right to cure a default exists "*at least* up to the date of the foreclosure sale," and that if state law provides a redemption period that extends beyond the date of the foreclosure sale, then bankruptcy law defers to such state law, with the right to cure extended accordingly. *Colon v. Option One Mortgage Corp.*, 319 F.3d 912, 918 (7th Cir. 2003) (emphasis added).

This Court is most comfortable adopting the majority view on the ground that the language of the statute is clear, unambiguous, and needs no interpretation. I also agree that the term "foreclosure sale" describes a single, discrete event, and not merely a step in a process culminating in the recordation and delivery of a deed. . . . It is not, I think, an extreme position to take, i.e., that the property is *sold* at the foreclosure sale, and that the deed is customarily not delivered to the purchaser until after the foreclosure sale. . . . The delivery of a foreclosure deed has been described as a "ministerial act, routinely performed, which does not affect the redemption rights of the parties." . . . Further, the words "conducted in accordance with applicable nonbankruptcy law" do not expand the cure period according to state-law redemption rights, but rather describes a foreclosure sale conducted in compliance with (and not in violation of), relevant state law. . . .

Nowhere does the statute require that the cure rights under Section 1322 terminate only upon the recordation and delivery of the foreclosure deed. Such language is not part of the statute, and it is not within the Court's authority to read the statute as though it were in there. "To define the word 'sold' as the point at which a deed is transferred to the prevailing bidder subsequent to the date of the auction . . . removes the words 'foreclosure sale' from the statute." . . . Therefore, if the foreclosure sale did not violate applicable state law, it follows that when the gavel falls, the right to cure no longer exists. There is no suggestion in this case of any violation of, or noncompliance with applicable state law.

We reject the third view, also without difficulty, as nothing in Section 1322(c)(1) requires deference to whatever expansive cure rights may exist under state law. The *Colon* court finds support for its view in the legislative history and scholarly texts. *Colon*, 319 F.3d at 917-918. However, the statute does not provide or suggest that the right to cure exists *at least* until such residence is sold at a foreclosure sale. On the contrary, Section 1322(c)(1) states unequivocally: "[n]otwithstanding . . . any nonbankruptcy law . . . ." If Congress intended to place federal bankruptcy law beneath, or subject to, certain state created rights, it could have chosen a better way to do so.

Finally, even if we were to look to state law in this case, the result would be the same because under its statutory power of sale, Rhode Island law does not provide for any post-foreclosure right of redemption. In fact, R.I. Gen. L. §34-11-22 states ". . . which sale or sales . . . shall forever be a perpetual bar against the mortgagor." R.I. Gen. Laws §34-11-22 (2008). *See also, Holden v. Salvadore*, 964 A.2d 508, 516 (R.I. 2009) (noting that it was not within the power of the defendant to prevent or postpone the foreclosure sale, because the sale and foreclosure had already taken place, the plaintiff herself was the highest bidder, and plaintiff and auctioneer had executed all the appropriate documents); *140 Reservoir Avenue Associates v. Sepe Investments, LLC*, 941 A.2d 805, 811-812 (R.I. 2007) (concluding that any interest of mortgagor's successor in real estate was forever barred by the foreclosure sale, where no party challenged the validity of the sale).

Based on the foregoing discussion, the authorities cited, and the arguments of the parties, Relief From Stay is GRANTED.

POST-CASE FOLLOW-UP

Are the two views rejected by this court unreasonable interpretations of §1322(c)(1)? Couldn't Congress have intended the "process" approach or the "right of redemption" approach rather than the "gavel" approach adopted here? There is actually a fourth view, referred to as the "deed-delivery" approach, whereby the property is not sold at foreclosure until the foreclosure deed is delivered to the buyer. See, e.g., *In re Randall*, 263 B.R. 200, 201 (D.N.J. 2001). In adopting the "gavel" approach, is this court saying that the question of when a "sale" has occurred is purely a matter of federal and not state law? Is that what Congress meant by use of the phrase "notwithstanding applicable nonbankruptcy law" in §1322(c)? Under any of the approaches to this issue, doesn't §1322(c)(1) require the court to determine that a foreclosure sale has been properly conducted under applicable state (nonbankruptcy) law? Determine whether the courts of your federal district or circuit have addressed this issue and, if so, how they have ruled.

478 Chapter Fifteen: The Chapter 13 Debt Adjustment for an Individual with Regular Income—Treatment

In re Medaglia: Real Life Applications

1. The law firm you work for represents a debtor who owns a home mortgaged to Bank. Debtor is three months in arrears on his mortgage payments to bank when he comes to the firm to discuss a bankruptcy filing. Debtor tells you and the supervising attorney conducting the interview that he likes the idea of being able to cure the arrearage to Bank in his plan and of keeping his house. But he says that Bank is "about to foreclose." Your jurisdiction follows the gavel rule. Can your supervising attorney preserve Debtor's right to cure and keep by filing the Chapter 13 petition under the following scenarios?

   a. The foreclosure sale is scheduled for later today.
   b. The foreclosure sale is going on right this moment.
   c. The foreclosure sale just ended and there was a recognized high bidder on the house to whom the gavel fell but no contract or memorandum of sale will be signed until "buyer" posts earnest money, which he will be unable to do until tomorrow afternoon.
   d. The foreclosure sale was yesterday and buyer posted the required earnest money deposit and signed a memorandum of sale. However, the high bidder is a former employee of the auction company that conducted the sale and state law forbids "employees" of the auction company handling a foreclosure sale from bidding. This employee still worked for the company when it received the contract from Bank to handle the foreclosure sale; he quit the day before the sale.
   e. The foreclosure sale was last week. Buyer posted the required earnest money deposit, signed a memorandum of sale, paid the full balance owed three days later, received his deed that day, and recorded it immediately. State law requires certain disclosures to be read at the beginning of a foreclosure sale and your information is that this was not done at this sale.

Although the curing of an arrearage in secured debt does not normally require the payment of **postpetition interest** to the creditor, §1322(e) requires the payment of such interest *if* the terms of the underlying agreement itself or state law do so.

EXAMPLE

> The Matthews' plan calls for interest to be paid to FBCC on the arrearage payments. This is necessary because the promissory note between the Matthews and FBCC requires the payment of interest on arrearages.

When a Chapter 13 debtor's plan proposes to cure an arrearage on a debt secured by a mortgage on the debtor's principal residence under §1322(b)(5), Bankruptcy Rule 3002.1 imposes significant notice requirements and filing deadlines on the creditor secured by such mortgage.

EXAMPLE

The holder of the mortgage must give written notice to the debtor, the debtor's attorney, and the trustee of changes in the payment amount caused by changes in the applicable interest rate or by adjustments in the escrow account balance at least 21 days before the changes become effective. And the mortgage holder must give written itemization of any postpetition fees, expenses, or charges it alleges are due under the mortgage within 180 days after such costs were incurred. Significant penalties are imposed on the mortgage holder for noncompliance with these requirements.

4. Reducing an Undersecured Claim to Present Value: Strip Down

How Strip Down Works in General

Recall that §506(a) provides that a secured claim in bankruptcy is only secured up to the value of the collateral and is unsecured to the extent the claim exceeds that value. Consequently, the claim secured by collateral having a value equal to or greater than the amount of the claim is a fully secured claim (or even oversecured). But a claim secured by collateral having a value less than the amount of the claim is an undersecured claim (sometimes called partially secured) and it is this claim that §506(a) effectively bifurcates into its secured and unsecured portions. In significant contrast to Chapter 7, §§1322(b)(2) and 1325(a)(5) authorize a Chapter 13 debtor to utilize the bifurcation feature of §506 to propose a plan in which the debtor will retain possession of secured property while paying the undersecured creditor only the present value of the collateral as a secured claim over the term of the plan rather than the entire amount of the debt. Section 1322(b)(2) provides in pertinent part as follows:

(b) Subject to subsections (a) and (c) of this section, the plan may—

(2) modify the rights of holders of secured claims, other than a claim secured only by a security interest in real property that is the debtor's principal residence, or of holders of unsecured claims, or leave unaffected the rights of holders of any class of claims.

Section 1325(a)(5) then provides in pertinent part as follows:

(a) Except as provided in subsection (b), the court shall confirm a plan if . . .

(5) with respect to each allowed secured claim provided for by the plan . . .

(B)(i) the plan provides that—

(I) the holder of such claim retain the lien securing such claim until the earlier of—

(aa) the payment of the underlying debt determined under nonbankruptcy law; or
(bb) discharge under section 1328; and

(ii) the value, as of the effective date of the plan, of property to be distributed under the plan on account of such claim is not less than the allowed amount of such claim . . . .

The unsecured portion of the debt is then treated as a nonpriority **general unsecured claim** under the plan.

This right of the Chapter 13 debtor to reduce the amount of a secured claim to the **present value** of the property securing the claim while retaining that property is informally called a **strip down** or **write down**. It is also sometimes called **cram down** since it can be approved by the bankruptcy court without creditor approval and over creditor objection (but cram down is actually a broader concept than strip down—it describes any proposal to modify a secured creditor's rights over the creditor's objection whether involving strip down or not, and we will see examples of other cram down options the Chapter 13 debtor has later in the chapter). Technically, the secured claim is stripped down or written down to its present value per §506(a) and then crammed down on the unconsenting creditor per §§1322(b)(2) and 1325(a)(5).

E X A M P L E

> The YR-3 Ford F-150 truck that Roger drives is worth $7,500 but the Matthews still owe $9,000 for it. Thus, the claim of the creditor holding a security interest in the truck, Automotive Financing, Inc. (AFI) is undersecured on its claim. The Matthews' Chapter 13 plan (Illustration 15-b) proposes to pay AFI the $7,500 present value of the truck over the 60-month term of the plan and for debtors to retain possession of the truck. This is a strip down proposal. The balance of $1,500 owed to AFI is treated and paid as a general unsecured claim in the Matthews' plan. If AFI was fully secured or oversecured (i.e., the truck had a present value equal to or in excess of the $9,000 balance owed), the Matthews could not propose this strip down. They would have to propose paying the full $9,000 in order to keep the truck.

Note in the last example that the strip down proposal on the truck calls for the Matthews to pay the full present value of AFI's secured claim during the term of the plan. This is a strict requirement of the strip down option. The present value to which the secured claim is stripped down must be paid in full during the term of the plan.

E X A M P L E

> If the Matthews' plan called for the truck value to be stripped down to its present value of $7,500 and paid over six years, it would not be approved since the plan can only run for five years.

In Chapter Eleven, Section C, we considered whether a Chapter 7 individual debtor could use lien stripping together with a ride through option to retain possession of collateralized property while paying only the undersecured value of a claim. And we learned that the answer is no owing to the decisions in *Dewsnup v. Timm*, 502 U.S. 410 (1997), and *Bank of America, N.A. v. Caulkett*, 135 S. Ct. 1995 (2015). Be careful to not confuse that rule in Chapter 7 cases with the strip down options available in Chapter 13 cases using §§1322(b)(2) and 1325(a)(5). There are no equivalent provisions in Chapter 7.

Exclusion of the Debtor's Principal Residence from the Strip Down Option—and Some Exceptions

Pursuant to the language of §1322(b)(2) set out above ("other than a claim secured only by a security interest in real property that is the debtor's principal residence") as interpreted by the Supreme Court in *Nobleman v. American Savings Bank*, 508 U.S. 324 (1993), the right to strip down a secured claim to the present value of the collateral does not apply to a debt secured only by a security interest in real property that is the debtor's **principal residence**. Thus, in most Chapter 13 cases, the debtor is unable to modify the secured balance of the mortgage on his or her home even if the value of the home has fallen below the balance of the mortgage (i.e., the creditor is undersecured).

There are, however, a number of exceptions to the §1322(b)(2) prohibition on strip down of a claim secured by a mortgage in the debtor's primary residence. First, note that the restriction just quoted applies only to real property used as the debtor's principal residence. If the Chapter 13 debtor owns a second home that is not the debtor's principal residence, the debtor can strip down the mortgage on that second home if its value has fallen below the balance of the mortgage. This disparity in the Code gives a curious advantage to debtors who are better off (i.e., those who own two or more homes rather than one), which is troubling during a time of continuing economic distress due to the lingering effects of the Great Recession and the mortgage foreclosure crisis. To date, legislative efforts to extend the strip down option to the principal residence of Chapter 13 debtors even temporarily have failed in Congress.

Second, note also that the restriction of §1322(b)(2) applies only to a security interest in real property used as the debtor's principal residence. What if the debt is secured by a mobile home used as the debtor's principal residence? Can the mobile home ever be considered personal property and thus subject to §1322(b)(2) modification? Some courts say yes if, under state law, the mobile home is not so permanently attached to the real property on which it sits to be considered real property itself. See, for example, *In re Reinhardt*, 563 F.3d 558 (6th Cir. 2009) (mobile home used as principal residence but not considered real property under Ohio law so debt secured by it subject to modification), and *In re Ennis*, 558 F.3d 343 (4th Cir. 2009) (same result under Virginia law).

Third, what if there is a second mortgage on the debtor's primary residence that is wholly undersecured?

EXAMPLE

Assume the Chapter 13 debtor's primary residence is valued at $200,000. Bank #1 holds a first mortgage on the residence, the balance on which is $225,000. Bank #1 is undersecured in the amount of $25,000 per §506(a) so that the value of its secured claim in the residence is only $200,000. But Bank #1 is not wholly undersecured because the secured portion of its claim does have that $200,000 value. However, assume that Bank #2 holds a second mortgage on the residence, the balance on which is $30,000. Bank #2 is wholly under-secured—all the secured value of the residence ($200,000) will go to satisfy the mortgage of Bank #1. Can the Chapter 13 debtor strip down (or **strip off**, as it is sometimes called in this context) that second mortgage in his plan and treat the $30,000 owed to Bank #2 as an unsecured claim without running afoul of the §1322(b)(2) prohibition?

A majority of courts to examine this issue have concluded that a creditor whose mortgage on the debtor's primary residence is wholly unsecured (as opposed to partially undersecured) is not the holder of a secured claim under §506 and cannot qualify for the anti-modification protection of §1322(b)(2). Instead that debtor is the holder of an unsecured claim that is subject to modification under §1322(b)(2). See, e.g., *In re Lane*, 280 F.3d 663 (6th Cir. 2002), and *In re Zimmer*, 313 F.3d 1220 (9th Cir. 2002).

There is a significant minority position that relies on the Supreme Court's refusal in *Nobleman v. American Savings Bank*, supra, to allow the strip down of an undersecured (partially secured) mortgage on the debtor's primary residence since the creditor, though undersecured, still was the holder of a secured claim under §506 and it was the rights of "holders of secured claims" that are given the benefit of the anti-modification protection in §1322(b)(2). Those courts that espouse the minority approach to modification of a wholly undersecured mortgage on the debtor's primary residence reason that, like the undersecured mortgagee in *Nobleman*, the wholly undersecured mortgagee is still the holder of a secured claim and entitled to the anti-modification protection of §1322(b)(2). See, e.g., *American General Finance, Inc. v. Dickerson*, 229 B.R. 539, 542 (M.D. Ga. 1999) ("the emphasis in the statute [§1322] is on the fact that a lien exists on the property, not the value of such property").

A fourth exception to the exclusion of the debtor's principal residence from the strip down option arises from use of the word "only" in §1322(b)(2), which excludes debts secured *only* by the debtor's principal residence from strip down. So if the debt obligation is secured not only by the principal residence itself but by some other property (e.g., another parcel of real property or any personal property), that debt is subject to strip down. Of course, the fact that the debt is secured by other property makes it less likely that the debt will be undersecured.

Fifth, §1322(c)(2), added to the Code following *Nobleman*, provides as follows:

> Notwithstanding subsection (b)(2) and applicable nonbankruptcy law
>
> . . . .
>
> > (2) in a case in which the last payment on the original payment schedule for a claim secured only by a security interest in real property that is the debtor's principal residence is due before the date on which the final payment under the plan is due, the plan may provide for payment of the claim as modified pursuant to section 1325(a)(5) of this title.

Thus, if the original payment schedule for a loan secured only by the debtor's primary residence calls for the last payment to be made *before* the Chapter 13 plan expires, the plan can modify the claim using §1325(a)(5). A number of courts have construed §1322(c)(2) to mean that the amount of the secured claim to be paid in full during the term of the plan can be reduced to the extent that it *exceeds* the available equity in the residence. In other words, the secured claim can be stripped down to the present equity so long as it is paid in full during the term of the plan. The balance of the debt will be bifurcated pursuant to §506(a) and treated as a general unsecured claim.

EXAMPLE

Capital Savings Bank (CSB) holds a second mortgage in the residence of Roger and Susan Matthews, and the balance on that debt is $30,000. The CSB debt is scheduled to be paid off in 48 more months. However, the value of the house is only $120,000 and the balance owed on the first mortgage to FBCC is $100,000. That means there is only $20,000 of equity in the home available to CSB. Because the Matthews have proposed a 60-month (five-year) plan, they have proposed to reduce the claim of CSB to that $20,000 equity amount, pursuant to §1322(c)(2), and to pay it off entirely during the plan. Note that if there was $30,000 or more equity in the residence available for CSB or if the original term of the CSB loan extended beyond the term of the Matthews' plan, they could not take advantage of this strip down provision. Because the principal amount owed to CSB has been stripped down from $30,000 to $20,000, the $10,000 difference will be treated as a general unsecured claim under the plan.

The §1322(c)(2) strip down exception is usually directed at short-term home equity loans and balloon notes secured by debtor's residence wherein the lender has loaned an amount in excess of the true equity in the residence.

Strip Down of Purchase Money Claim Secured by a Motor Vehicle: The 910-Day Rule of the §1325(a) "Hanging Paragraph"

By far the most common use of this strip down power is in connection with automobiles. It is very common for debtors to owe more on their vehicles than they are worth, as the Matthews do on the YR-3 Ford F-150 truck mentioned in earlier examples, and to propose Chapter 13 plans seeking to strip down on that value. However, BAPCPA has imposed some severe limitations on the right of a Chapter 13 debtor to strip down the amount owed on a vehicle to its value. The last paragraph of §1325(a), added by BAPCPA and known to practitioners as the infamous **hanging paragraph** (so called because it "hangs" on the end of §1325(a) like an afterthought), provides as follows:

> For purposes of paragraph (5), section 506 shall not apply to a claim described in that paragraph if the creditor has a purchase money security interest securing the debt that is the subject of the claim, the debt was incurred within the 910-day period preceding the date of the filing of the petition, and the collateral for that debt consists of a motor vehicle (as defined in section 30102 of title 49) acquired for the personal use of the debtor, or if collateral for that debt consists of any other thing of value, if the debt was incurred during the 1-year period preceding that filing.

Thus, the strip down to value option cannot be used for automobiles if

- the debt secured by the automobile is a purchase money security interest (the debtor purchased the vehicle on credit from the seller or obtained the loan from the creditor to enable the purchase of the vehicle);
- the debt was incurred within 910 days (two-and-a-half years) preceding the filing of the petition; *and*
- the vehicle was acquired for the "personal use of the debtor."

EXAMPLE

> The Matthews purchased the Ford F-150 truck new almost three years ago and borrowed money from Automotive Financing, Inc. (AFI) in order to do so. Although the debt owed on the truck is therefore a purchase money security interest, and although the truck was purchased for Roger's personal use, the Matthews' plan can strip down the debt owed to AFI to the truck's value because it was purchased more than 910 days (two-and-a-half years) prior to the filing of the petition, triggering the 910-day rule of §1325(a). On the other hand, the Honda Civic was purchased only two years ago, making it a 910 vehicle, so this option is not available to the Matthews as to this vehicle even if the debt secured by it is undersecured.

Technically, what the hanging paragraph of §1325(a) says is that §506 does not to apply to 910 vehicles for purposes of the strip down provisions of Chapter 13. This is being construed by the courts to mean that claims secured by 910 vehicles cannot be bifurcated under §506(a). Thus, the creditor is entitled to receive the full value of its secured claim rather than the present value of the collateral if the debtor wishes to retain possession of the vehicle. See, e.g., *In re Dean*, 537 F.3d 1315 (11th Cir. 2008) (rejecting an early interpretation of the hanging paragraph by some courts now almost entirely rejected that reasoned that since that paragraph prevents a Chapter 13 debtor from bifurcating a 910 creditor's claim and stripping it down, it also prevents that claim from being treated as a secured claim but only as an allowed claim for entire prepetition debt, which debtors have to pay in full but without postpetition interest). In order to retain 910 vehicles, Chapter 13 debtors have to propose either a pay through on such secured claims or a payoff of the entire value of the secured claim during the term of the plan even though the claim is undersecured.

Strip Down of Purchase Money Claim Secured by Property Other Than a Motor Vehicle: The Hanging Paragraph Strikes Again

The hanging paragraph of §1325(a) also provides that any debt secured by property other than vehicles ("any other thing of value") is not subject to bifurcation under §506 and thus cannot be stripped down to value if

- it is a purchase money security interest, and
- the debt was incurred during the one-year period preceding the filing of the petition.

EXAMPLE

> Assume a debtor purchases $5,000 of household appliances on credit and grants the seller a security interest in the items purchased. Since seller extended credit to debtor for the purchase of these items of personal property, this is a purchase money security interest. Nine months later, the debtor files for Chapter 13 relief and still owes $4,000 on the debt. She would like to strip down this obligation because her household appliances that secure the debt only have a total value of $2,500. But she will be unable to do so because of the one-year rule of §1325(a). This debtor might be well advised to delay the Chapter 13 filing until the one-year period has run, if feasible.

As with 910 vehicles, if the Chapter 13 debtor wants to retain possession of secured property falling within the one-year rule, he or she will have to propose a pay through or a payoff of the entire value of the unmodified claim during the plan period.

How the Strip Down Value of Collateral Is Determined

The value of personal property securing a claim for purposes of determining the secured portion of the claim and exercising the strip down right where it is available is defined in §506(a)(2), added by BAPCPA, as the replacement value of the goods on the date the petition is filed without deduction for sale or marketing costs. For goods acquired for personal, family, or household purposes (consumer goods), replacement value means the price a retail merchant would charge for property of that kind, given its age and condition, on the date the petition is filed.

EXAMPLE

> In determining the value of the Ford F-150 truck that the Matthews are stripping down, we would determine the replacement value of that vehicle as of the date the petition is filed. Common sources for determining automobile values are the Kelley Blue Book or the National Automobile Dealers Association (NADA). Debtor's lawyers are more likely to use the former since its values are usually lower than those in NADA.

P-H 15-a: Go back and read the discussion of *Associates Commercial Corp. v. Rash*, 520 U.S. 953 (1997), and the codification by BAPCPA of the *Rash* replacement value standard in §506(a)(2) in Chapter Eleven, Section C, where we were studying the right of an individual consumer debtor in Chapter 7 to redeem property under §722. Do you see why the replacement value will almost always be greater than the liquidation or foreclosure value of the property, or the casual garage sale value of the property, or even the wholesale value, whether you're dealing with a Chapter 7 redemption or a Chapter 13 strip down?

Defining value in §506(a)(2) as replacement value has by no means ended disputes over what replacement value is with regard to many kinds of property. If the creditor or trustee will not accept the debtor's proposed strip down value, they can object to the confirmation of the plan and an evidentiary hearing may be conducted by the court on the issue of value. Experts may be called by either or both sides to testify on the value dispute. That can be time-consuming and expensive, of course. As a practical matter, determination of the value of property in a strip down is often arrived at by negotiations between the debtor and the affected creditor, usually at the first meeting of creditors. And though the replacement value standard obviously favors the creditor, the debtor often has leverage to negotiate a more favorable value since the debtor has the option to simply surrender the property to the creditor as discussed later in this section and perhaps even to discharge the balance of the debt.

Determining the "Present Value" of the Collateral for Purposes of Plan Payments

Determining the payments to be made to a secured creditor to give it the value of its collateral as calculated under §506(a) is not simply a matter of dividing the replacement value by the number of plan payments to be made. That is because the debtor is not going to pay the creditor that replacement cost as a lump sum at the beginning of the plan. Instead, the debtor is proposing to pay that amount to the creditor in installments over the time of the plan (three to five years). The secured creditor is entitled to receive the value of its collateral, but since that value is going to be paid to him over time rather than immediately, the creditor must be compensated for the delay with some amount of interest, just as a lender of money is entitled to interest until the loan is repaid in full. By adding an interest component to the installment payments of the replacement value of the collateral, we are seeking to quantify the time-price differential involved in the delayed payment to the creditor of the full replacement value of the collateral. Since the full value is being paid over time, the total amount of the debtor's plan payments to the creditor must equal the present value of the collateral. In essence, the plan payments must be discounted by a rate of interest that will ultimately provide the creditor with that present value.

When a Chapter 13 plan calls for a secured claim to be stripped down to present value and for the payments of that value to be made in installments during the term of the plan, as the Matthews are doing on their truck, §§1325(a)(5)(B)(ii) and (iii) require that

- the present value be paid in full during the term of the plan;
- the payments be made in equal installments; and
- the payments be increased to compensate the creditor for the delay in receiving the present value of the collateral in order to give the creditor adequate protection.

EXAMPLE

When the Matthews strip down on the Ford F-150 truck, they are declaring that AFI will get only the replacement value of the collateral in payment of its claim. If they simply surrendered the truck to AFI, it would be getting that replacement value immediately. But the Matthews' plan contemplates the debtors keeping the truck and paying AFI the value of its claim in installments over the term of the plan. The plan is therefore delaying AFI's receipt of the value of its claim. The Matthews' plan must increase the payments by an appropriate rate of interest to account for that delay and to adequately protect AFI by providing it with the present value of its claim.

Though the Code recognizes that the secured creditor receiving the value of its collateral in delayed payments is entitled to interest to compensate for that delay, it does not specify the appropriate interest rate to be applied to those payments. In *Till v. SCS Credit Corp.*, 541 U.S. 465 (2004), the Supreme Court rejected a creditor's argument that the appropriate rate of interest in such situations is the rate set forth in the contract between the debtor and creditor. The Court held instead that the appropriate interest rate to be used is the national prime rate (the interest rate that commercial banks charge their best customers) plus an "upward adjustment" to reflect the risk of nonpayment by the bankrupt debtors (called a "prime plus" rate by practitioners). The Court left the question of the appropriate upward risk adjustment to be decided by the lower courts based on the circumstances of each case. In most cases the risk adjustment will run one to three percentage points.

EXAMPLE

> Assume that the contract rate of interest that the Matthews agreed to pay AFI when they purchased the Ford F-150 truck was 10 percent per annum. At the time the petition is filed, the prevailing national prime rate is 6 percent. In the Matthews' plan they strip down the debt owed to AFI to its replacement value and propose to pay that value in installments through the term of the plan. Since AFI is being delayed in receiving the replacement value of the collateral to which it is entitled, the plan adds a *Till* rate of interest based on the 6 percent prime plus an upward risk adjustment factor of a half point, for a total rate of interest of 6.5 percent. This is the Matthews' proposal to give AFI the present value of its collateral. AFI may object to the half-point risk adjustment and argue for more, perhaps one to two points higher. But the plan rate will still be lower than the contract rate.

P-H 15-b: Do you see why *Till* is, in most situations, a pro-debtor decision?

Under the hanging paragraph of §1325(a), claims secured by 910 vehicles or property subject to the one-year rule cannot be stripped down; they are not controlled by the bifurcation concept of §506(a). We noted that as to such claims, the debtor, in order to keep the property, will either have to propose a pay through, in which case the **contract rate of interest** will continue to apply, or a payoff of the full value of the unmodified claim during the term of the plan. If the debtor chooses the latter, however, the creditor is being denied immediate payment of that value, again raising the question of what interest the creditor should receive on those payments in order to compensate it for the delayed receipt of value and the risk of debtor's nonpayment. Should we use the *Till* rate of prime plus in such cases? Or, since the whole basis for excepting such property from strip down is that the bifurcation of §506(a) is inapplicable to such property, is the *Till* rate that was deemed appropriate in a bifurcation and strip down context irrelevant and the contract rate the one to use?

HIGHLIGHTED CASE

IN RE WRIGHT
338 B.R. 917 (Bankr. M.D. Ala. 2006)

OPINION: WILLIAMS, JR., Bankruptcy Judge.

Centrix Funds Series CLPF ("Centrix") filed an objection to confirmation of the chapter 13 plan proposed by the debtors. At issue is whether under . . . BAPCPA the plan may modify the contractual interest rate applicable to the creditor's secured claim . . . .

FACTUAL FINDINGS . . .

On May 29, 2004, the debtors purchased a 2004 Nissan Altima. The purchase price of the vehicle was financed by Centrix, and Centrix took a security interest in the vehicle. On December 5, 2005, the debtors filed this chapter 13 case. The plan treats the claim of Centrix as fully secured. Further, the plan provides that Centrix will be paid interest on its claim at the rate of 7.75%. Centrix filed a proof of claim totaling $18,747.38. The claim reflects a contract interest rate of 17.90%.

CONCLUSIONS OF LAW

Centrix contends that it is entitled to the 17.90% contract interest rate on its secured claim. The court disagrees.

If a debtor retains lien-encumbered property under a chapter 13 plan and pays the underlying secured claim in deferred installments, the creditor is entitled to interest on the secured claim. The Code provides:

(ii) the value, as of the effective date of the plan, of property to be distributed under the plan on account of such claim is not less than the allowed amount of such claim;

11 U.S.C. §1325(a)(5)(B)(ii).

The Supreme Court in *Till v. SCS Credit Corporation*, 541 U.S. 465 (2004) addressed the issue of the appropriate rate of interest to be applied under §1325(a)(5)(B)(ii). There the Court held that the so-called formula approach, which starts with the prime national interest rate and adjusts for risk of non-payment, is the appropriate method in determining the adequate interest rate to be paid on secured claims. Id. at 478-80. In so doing, the Court specifically rejected the presumptive contract interest rate approach as the proper method to determine §1325(a)(5)(B)(ii) interest. Id. at 477.

Centrix contends that under the facts in this case *Till* no longer applies. First, Centrix maintains that *Till* is applicable only to chapter 13 plans that are "crammed down." Centrix reasons that because its claim in this case is fully secured, this is not a "cram down" case. Centrix, however, confuses the term "cram down" with the term "strip down."

"Cram down" is a term that refers to confirmation of a chapter 13 plan over the objection of the holder of a claim. *Associates Commercial Corp. v. Rash*, 520 U.S. 953, 957 (1997). The term "strip down" refers to the bifurcation of a claim into its secured and unsecured components under 11 U.S.C. §506. The secured claim is said to be stripped down to the value of the collateral.

Although *Till* interpreted 11 U.S.C. §1325(a)(5)(B)(ii) in a case involving the strip down of a secured claim, the statute itself is broader and applies to all cram down cases. Hence, the decision in *Till* is not confined merely to those cases where the value of the collateral is less than the creditor's claim. Rather, *Till* applies in all chapter 13 cases which are being confirmed over the objection of a secured creditor irrespective of the value of its collateral in relation to the amount of its claim.

Secondly, Centrix contends that *Till* has been abrogated by the BAPCPA amendments. [The opinion quotes §1325(a)]. . . . Centrix contends that this provision prevents any modification of its contractual rights, including the interest rate. The court disagrees.

This new provision prohibits the application of §506 to the claims of secured creditors having a purchase-money security interest in a debtor's personal vehicle if the debt was incurred within 910 days prior to bankruptcy. Simply put, the claims of these creditors must be treated as fully secured under the plan. However, this restriction on bifurcation does not protect these creditors from modification of other contractual rights.

The BAPCPA amendments to §1325 simply do not address the issue of the appropriate interest rate applicable to secured claims under §1325(a)(5)(B)(ii). Thus, *Till* has not been abrogated by the BAPCPA amendments.

Had Congress intended to create a complete safe harbor for the automobile lender with a purchase-money security interest, it could have expressly done so, but it did not. Indeed, the law permits modification of the rights of secured creditors. The only complete safe harbor from any modification is that provided to home mortgagees under 11 U.S.C. §1322(b)(2). See *In re Robinson*, 338 B.R. 70 (Bankr. W.D. Mo. 2006); *In re Johnson*, 337 B.R. 269 (Bankr. M.D.N.C. 2006).

CONCLUSION

For the foregoing reasons the court concludes that the plan may properly modify the contract interest rate applicable to the secured claim of Centrix. Pursuant to Fed. R. Bankr. Proc. 9021, a separate order will enter overruling Centrix's objection to confirmation of the plan.

POST-CASE FOLLOW-UP

It has become widely accepted that the *Till* rate applies to modified payments on 910 property rather than the contract rate regardless of which is higher or lower. How firmly fixed this idea is can be seen in *In re Taranto*, 365 B.R. 85 (6th Cir. B.A.P. 2007), where the contract rate on the 910 vehicle was zero percent and the plan proposed modified payments to the creditor along with that rate of interest—zero. The court ordered that notwithstanding the zero percent contract rate, creditor was to receive the *Till* rate on the modified payments rejecting debtor's argument that such rate gave the creditor a windfall and despite the fact that debtor's plan also proposed to pay the 910 creditor in full on an earlier schedule than that provided for in the contract! That outcome may seem unfair to the debtor but you have to remember that an allowed secured claim on a 910 vehicle is entitled to be paid in full with no strip down allowed. The Supreme Court in *Till* interpreted §1325(a)(5)(B) to require that the secured creditor's claim must be paid (1) in full at the time of confirmation, or (2) over time with interest to ensure the creditor receives present value as of the date of confirmation. Contract interest rate is irrelevant. Remember too that per §1325(a)(5)(A) the creditor can accept a plan calling for an interest rate different from the contract rate or the *Till* rate. The *Till* rate is used where the creditor does not consent.

In re Wright: Real Life Applications

1. Which of the following creditors are entitled to receive their contract rate of interest on plan payments, which are entitled to receive the *Till* rate of interest on such payments, and which are entitled to receive no interest on their plan payments?

   a. Debtor purchased a washing machine from creditor nine months before petition filed with purchase price to be paid over 24 months at 12 percent per annum interest. Washing machine value now is $250 and balance owed is $500. Creditor did not have debtor grant it a security interest in the washing machine to secure payment. Debtor claims full value of washing machine as exempt and proposes to keep it in 100 percent plan.

   b. Debtor purchased washing machine from creditor 15 months before petition filed with purchase price to be paid over 24 months at zero percent interest. Washing machine value now is $250 and balance owed is $400. Debtor granted security interest in the washing machine to creditor to secure payment. Debtor proposes to pay creditor $250 over 60 months of 100 percent plan.

   c. Debtor purchased washing machine from creditor 15 months before petition filed with purchase price to be paid over 24 months at 10 percent per annum interest. Washing machine value now is $250 and balance owed is $200. Debtor granted security interest to creditor in washing machine to secure payment. Debtor proposes to pay creditor $200 over 60 months of 100 percent plan and retain possession by exempting $50 equity.

   d. Debtor purchased washing machine from creditor 15 months before petition filed with purchase price to be paid over 24 months at 2 percent per annum interest. Washing machine value now is $250 and balance owed is $200. Debtor granted security interest in washing machine to creditor to secure payment. Debtor proposes to pay creditor $200 as scheduled in contract during the first nine months of the five-year 100 percent plan and retain possession by exempting $50 equity.

2. Which creditor on these two 910 vehicles is entitled to its contract rate of interest and which to the *Till* rate?

   a. Vehicle worth $10,000 and secured creditor owed $12,000. Debtor proposes to keep vehicle and pay creditor through plan by making scheduled payments at scheduled amount.

   b. Vehicle worth $10,000 and secured creditor owed $12,000. Debtor proposes to keep the vehicle but reduce scheduled payments to creditor for 24 months while other short-term obligations are paid, then increase payments to creditor in last 36 months of plan.

5. Modifying a Secured Claim by Adjusting Payments

As we have seen, when a secured claim is stripped down to the value of its collateral, that will result in a modification downward of the contractual payments to be made by the debtor to the creditor under the terms of the plan simply because less principal is being paid to that creditor on the debt. But can a Chapter 13 debtor who does not or cannot strip down a secured claim to its value propose to modify installment payments to a secured creditor by lowering those payments during the term of the plan? Sections 1322(b)(2) and 1325(a)(5) do allow such a modification with one important caveat: Per §1325(a)(5)(B)(ii), the full value of the claim must be paid during the term of the plan.

EXAMPLE

The Matthews owe Columbiana Federal Savings & Loan (CFSL) a total of $7,500 on an original loan of $12,000 made two years ago for which they obligated themselves to pay $240 per month for five years. There are currently 36 monthly payments remaining on the contract. The debt is secured by the Honda Civic automobile that Susan drives. The vehicle is a 910 vehicle since they have owned it only two years, which means they cannot strip down CFSL's secured claim to the present value of the vehicle. However, their Chapter 13 plan (Illustration 15-b) proposes to pay CFSL the full amount of the unmodified claim at the contract rate of 7.5 percent but over the full 60 months of the plan, rather than over the remaining 36 months of the contract. This will require them to pay CFSL only $150 per month over the term of the plan. CFSL will retain its lien on the automobile. The court can approve this plan even over CFSL's objection pursuant to §1325(a)(5)(B)(ii) (thus it is a cram down) because the creditor is receiving the full amount of its allowed claim during the term of the plan. Note that this saves the Matthews $90 per month over what they were paying CFSL (see the budget in the Assignment Memorandum in Appendix B).

P-H 15-c: Even though this plan provision saves the Matthews $90 a month over what they were paying CFSL, it may not mean that they come out better in the long run. How much total principal and interest would the Matthews have paid CFSL if they paid off the car over the remaining 36 months of the contract? How much will they pay CFSL in principal and interest over the 60 months of the plan?

In the last example, if the Matthews' plan proposed to not only extend the number of installment payments to CFSL but to also use a *Till* rate of interest for such payments rather than the contract rate, that would raise an unanswered question. And if the contract rate on that debt was 15 percent per annum rather than 7.5 percent, it would be very tempting for their attorney to propose a *Till* rate. But often Chapter 13 debtors will choose not to propose a lower *Till* rate for modified plan payments when they could do so because they do not wish to offend a creditor with whom they hope to do business in the future.

6. Surrender of Secured Property

Pursuant to §1325(a)(5)(C), a Chapter 13 debtor may propose to **surrender** property subject to a security interest to the secured creditor where there is no equity for the estate and where no lien avoidance action is plausible. The creditor must then move to have the automatic stay lifted in order to take possession of the property. The trustee will **abandon** the property to the creditor pursuant to §554 of the Code on the grounds that it is not needed for the reorganization. (See the discussion of abandonment in Chapter Eleven, Section A.)

As we know, §506(a) bifurcates most secured claims by providing that a secured creditor's claim is secured only up to the value of the collateral and is an unsecured claim to the extent the debt exceeds the value of the collateral. Thus, if the debtor surrenders the property securing the debt but its value is less than the amount owed (i.e., the creditor is undersecured or partially secured), the balance still owing on the debt after the property is repossessed and sold will be treated as a general unsecured claim.

EXAMPLE

The Matthews have decided to surrender the YR-8 Chevy Malibu. This surrender is referenced in their plan. Note that this relieves them of the $120 per month payment they were making to Car World (see the budget in the Assignment Memorandum in Appendix B). They owed Car World $5,000 on that debt. Upon surrender, Car World will move the court, pursuant to §362, to lift the automatic stay. Since there is no equity in the car (it is worth only $2,000 and the amount owed is $5,000), the trustee will not object to the motion to lift stay and will abandon pursuant to §554. Assuming the car is in fact worth $2,000, the $3,000 balance of the debt ($5,000 minus the $2,000 value of the car surrendered) will be treated as a general unsecured debt under the plan.

What happens when a debtor surrenders a 910 vehicle or other collateral subject to the one-year rule of the §1325(a) hanging paragraph? Since that paragraph says that such claims are not governed by the bifurcation concept of §506(a) and the debtor therefore cannot strip down the value of the secured claim to the value of the collateral, it might follow that when the debtor chooses to surrender such property, the creditor must accept that surrender as a full satisfaction of its claim rather than bifurcating its secured claim into an unsecured claim for the deficiency owing after disposition of the surrendered collateral. After all, isn't sauce for the goose sauce for the gander?

HIGHLIGHTED CASE

IN RE WRIGHT

492 F.3d 829 (7th Cir. 2007)

OPINION: EASTERBROOK, Circuit Judge.

Bankruptcy judges across the nation have divided over the effect of the unnumbered hanging paragraph that [BAPCPA] added to §1325(a) of the Bankruptcy Code. . . . Section 1325, part of Chapter 13, specifies the circumstances under which a consumer's plan of repayment can be confirmed. The hanging paragraph says that, for the purpose of a Chapter 13 plan, §506 of the Code, 11 U.S.C. §506, does not apply to certain secured loans.

Section 506(a) divides loans into secured and unsecured portions; the unsecured portion is the amount by which the debt exceeds the current value of the collateral. In a Chapter 13 bankruptcy, consumers may retain the collateral (despite contractual provisions entitling creditors to repossess) by making monthly payments that the judge deems equal to the market value of the asset, with a rate of interest that the judge will set (rather than the contractual rate). . . . This procedure is known as a "cramdown"—the court crams down the creditor's throat the substitution of money for the collateral, a situation that creditors usually oppose because the court may underestimate the collateral's market value and the appropriate interest rate, and the debtor may fail to make all promised payments, so that the payment stream falls short of the collateral's full value. . . .

The question we must decide is what happens when, as a result of the hanging paragraph, §506 vanishes from the picture. The majority view among bankruptcy judges is that, with §506(a) gone, creditors cannot divide their loans into secured and unsecured components. Because §1325(a)(5)(C) allows a debtor to surrender the collateral to the lender, it follows (on this view) that surrender fully satisfies the borrower's obligations. If this is so, then many secured loans have been rendered non-recourse, no matter what the contract provides. . . . The minority view is that Article 9 of the Uniform Commercial Code plus the law of contracts entitle the creditor to an unsecured deficiency judgment after surrender of the collateral, unless the contract itself provides that the loan is without recourse against the borrower. . . . That unsecured balance must be treated the same as other unsecured debts under the Chapter 13 plan . . . .

[D]ebtors in this proceeding, owe more on their purchase-money automobile loan than the car is worth. Because the purchase occurred within 910 days of the bankruptcy's commencement, the hanging paragraph in §1325(a)(5) applies . . . .

Debtors proposed a plan that would surrender the car to the creditor and pay nothing on account of the difference between the loan's balance and the collateral's market value. After taking the minority position on the effect of bypassing §506, the bankruptcy judge declined to approve the Chapter 13 plan, because debtors did not propose to pay any portion of the shortfall.

. . .

Like the bankruptcy court, we think that, by knocking out §506, the hanging paragraph leaves the parties to their contractual entitlements. True enough, §506(a) divides claims into secured and unsecured components. . . . Yet it is a mistake to assume, as the majority of bankruptcy courts have done, that §506 is the *only* source of authority for a deficiency judgment when the collateral is insufficient. The Supreme Court held in *Butner v. United States*, 440 U.S. 48, (1979), that state law determines rights and obligations when the Code does not supply a federal rule. . . .

The contract between the Wrights and their lender is explicit: If the debt is not paid, the collateral may be seized and sold. Creditor "must account to Buyer for any surplus. Buyer shall be liable for any deficiency." In other words, the contract creates an ordinary secured loan with recourse against the borrower. Just in case there were doubt, the contract provides that the parties enjoy all of their rights under the Uniform Commercial Code. Section 9-615(d)(2) of the UCC, enacted in Illinois as 810 ILCS 5/9-615(d)(2), provides that the obligor must satisfy any deficiency if the collateral's value is insufficient to cover the amount due.

If the Wrights had surrendered their car the day before filing for bankruptcy, the creditor would have been entitled to treat any shortfall in the collateral's value as an unsecured debt. It is hard to see why the result should be different if the debtors surrender the collateral the day after filing for bankruptcy when, given the hanging paragraph, no operative section of the Bankruptcy Code contains any contrary rule. Section 306(b) of the 2005 Act, which enacted the hanging paragraph, is captioned "Restoring the Foundation for Secured Credit." This implies replacing a contract-defeating provision such as §506 (which allows judges rather than the market to value the collateral and set an interest rate, and may prevent creditors from repossessing) with the agreement freely negotiated between debtor and creditor. Debtors do not offer any argument that "the Foundation for Secured Credit" could be "restored" by making all purchase-money secured loans non-recourse; they do not argue that non-recourse lending is common in consumer transactions, and it is hard to imagine that Congress took such an indirect means of making non-recourse lending *compulsory*.

Appearing as *amicus curiae*, the National Association of Consumer Bankruptcy Attorneys makes the bold argument that loans covered by the hanging paragraph cannot be treated as secured in any respect. Only §506 provides for an "allowed secured claim," *amicus* insists, so the entire debt must be unsecured. This also would imply that a lender is not entitled to any post-petition interest. *Amicus* recognizes that §502 rather than §506 determines whether a claim should be "allowed" but insists that only §506 permits an "allowed" claim to be a "secured" one.

This line of argument makes the same basic mistake as the debtors' position: it supposes that contracts and state law are irrelevant unless specifically implemented by the Bankruptcy Code. *Butner* holds that the presumption runs the other way: rights under state law count in bankruptcy unless the Code says otherwise. Creditors don't need §506 to create, allow, or recognize security interests, which rest on contracts (and the UCC) rather than federal law. Section 502 tells bankruptcy courts to allow claims that stem from contractual debts; nothing in §502 disfavors or curtails secured claims. Limitations, if any, depend on §506, which the hanging paragraph makes inapplicable to purchase-money interests in personal motor vehicles granted during the 910 days preceding bankruptcy (and in other assets during the year before bankruptcy).

Both the debtors and the *amicus curiae* observe that many decisions, of which *United States v. Ron Pair Enterprises, Inc.*, 489 U.S. 235, 238-39 (1989), is a good example, state that §506 governs the treatment of secured claims in bankruptcy. No one doubts this, but the question at hand is what happens when §506 does not apply. The fallback under *Butner* is the parties' contract (to the extent the deal is enforceable under state law), rather than non-recourse secured debt (the Wrights' position) or no security interest (the *amicus curiae*'s position). And there is no debate about how the parties' contract works: the secured lender is entitled to an (unsecured) deficiency judgment for the difference between the value of the collateral and the balance on the loan.

By surrendering the car, debtors gave their creditor the full market value of the collateral. Any shortfall must be treated as an unsecured debt. It need not be paid in full, any more than the Wrights' other unsecured debts, but it can't be written off *in toto* while other unsecured creditors are paid some fraction of their entitlements.

AFFIRMED.

POST-CASE FOLLOW-UP

You will recall that we considered the significance of the Supreme Court's *Butner* decision in Chapter Six, Section E. Once again we see just how significant the role of state law is in interpreting and applying provisions of the Code. How would *In re Wright* have been decided if UCC Article 9 as enacted in the state of Illinois provided that a secured creditor who chooses to repossess collateral rather than sue for the underlying debt has no recourse against the debtor for a deficiency? Would the decision have been the same if the contract between the parties had not contained explicit language stating that debtor must account to creditor for the balance owed following seizure and sale of the collateral and be liable for any deficiency? The Seventh Circuit's interpretation of the role of the hanging paragraph in the context of surrender has become the majority view but there is still disagreement. See, e.g., *In re Adams*, 403 B.R. 387, 391-392 (Bankr. E.D. La. 2009) ("The hanging paragraph, in effect, provides a 910 Creditor with a secured claim, up to the value of that claim. If a debtor intends to retain the collateral, the creditor is entitled to full payment, regardless of the value of the collateral. If, however, the debtor surrenders the collateral, the entire claim is satisfied. Once the hanging paragraph eliminates §506, the claim and collateral become indivisible."). Determine if your federal district or circuit courts have addressed this issue.

In re Wright: Real Life Applications

1. Assume your federal district follows *In re Wright* but applicable state law provides that a secured creditor who chooses to repossess collateral rather than sue for the underlying debt has no recourse against the debtor for a deficiency. The law office where you work represents the creditor who holds a security interest in a Chapter 13 debtor's 910 vehicle on which $10,000 is still owed but which is worth only $7,000. Your firm's client did not attempt repossession prior to the petition being filed.

    a. If debtor chooses to surrender this vehicle to your client, can you file an unsecured claim for the balance owed on behalf of your client?

    b. Would your answer be different if the contract between your client and the debtor had an express provision stating that the debtor would be liable for any deficiency in the event of repossession and sale of the vehicle?

2. Assume your federal district follows *In re Adams* and that the applicable state law provides that a secured creditor who repossesses and sells collateral is entitled to recover any deficiency from the debtor.

    a. If debtor chooses to surrender this vehicle to your client, can you file an unsecured claim for the balance owed on behalf of your client?

    b. Would your answer be different if the contract between your client and the debtor had an express provision stating that the debtor would be liable for any deficiency in the event of repossession and sale of the vehicle?

7. Sale of Property Free and Clear of Liens

Section 1303 of the Code authorizes a Chapter 13 debtor to ask that secured property be sold free and clear of liens pursuant to §363(f). As in a Chapter 7 liquidation, such sale will be subject to the secured creditor's §363(k) right to credit-bid for the property at the sale (see the discussion in Chapter Eleven, Section A).

EXAMPLE

> Assume a Chapter 13 debtor owns an empty lot valued at $25,000. Bank holds a mortgage on such property with a balance owed of $18,000. Debtor cannot exempt the equity and unsecured creditors will expect that equity to be paid to them. Debtor's plan will likely propose that the property be sold free and clear of liens.

C. ▶ Treatment of General (Nonpriority) Unsecured Claims in the Chapter 13 Plan

1. Curing Arrearages and Modifying the Obligation of Unsecured Debt

Sections 1322(b)(3) and (5) allow a Chapter 13 debtor to propose curing arrearages arising from default on unsecured debt just as debtor can on secured debt. If a debtor plans to propose a 100 percent plan (a plan calling for full payment of all unsecured claims, discussed in more detail below),, that plan *must* cure any arrearages owed on unsecured claims and must do so during the term of the plan.

Section 1322(b)(2) allows the Chapter 13 plan to modify the rights of unsecured creditors just as it can for secured creditors by modifying the amount of payments due or the time over which they will be paid again.

EXAMPLE

> The Matthews owe $25,000 in unsecured debt for hospital and doctor bills at the time their petition is filed. This amount is due and payable immediately to the various creditors. But their plan calls for paying these creditors some amounts in monthly installments over the term of the plan. Section 1322(b)(2) permits this modification of these unsecured obligations. Interest is not normally an issue when unsecured debt is modified in a Chapter 13 plan since the creditor's claim is not being valued by any collateral and the creditor is not being deprived of the right to possess any such collateral. Moreover, as we consider in the next section, a Chapter 13 plan may propose to pay unsecured creditors less than the full amount of their claim anyway subject to the various requirements for plan confirmation.

2. Classes of Unsecured Claims in a Chapter 13 Plan

Section 1322(b)(1) permits a Chapter 13 plan to create separate classes of unsecured claimants and to treat each class of creditors differently from one another. Classes are designated groups of creditor claims or equity interests with members of each class receiving equal treatment under the plan but different classes receiving disparate treatment. Creation of classes in a plan of reorganization is commonplace in Chapter 11 business reorganization proceedings. They are unusual in Chapter 13 plans but not unheard of.

EXAMPLE

> A debtor engaged in business may put unsecured consumer debt in one class and unsecured business debt in another. A consumer who is jointly liable with a nondebtor on a debt may choose to place that debt in a separate class for favorable treatment in order to protect the nondebtor.

The debtor is not free to create any classes of unsecured debt he or she wishes or to propose favorable treatment for some over others. If that were so, debtors would routinely put nondischargeable debts (to be discussed in the next chapter) such as student loans in one class for favorable treatment over dischargeable debts in another class, a practice that has been ruled impermissible in many cases (see, e.g., *In re Simmonds*, 288 B.R. 737 (Bankr. N.D. Tex. 2003) (mere fact that a Chapter 13 debtor's student loan debts are nondischargeable is not sufficient basis for allowing debtor to freely discriminate in favor of such debts in his or her proposed plan and discrimination was "unfair" to extent that, due to such discrimination, other unsecured creditors received less than that to which they would have been entitled over first 36 months of plan). There are three requirements imposed on classifications of unsecured debt:

- §1322(b)(1) requires that only claims that are substantially similar can be grouped in the same class;
- §1322(b)(1) provides that a plan cannot discriminate unfairly against any class; and
- §1322(a)(3) requires that claims within the same class be treated the same for purposes of payment.

The second requirement, that the plan not discriminate unfairly against any class, is the one most likely to draw objection. If a debtor's proposed plan with classes of debt draws an objection, the burden is on the debtor to show why the differing treatment of the classes is fair.

P-H 15-d: Section 1322(b)(1) expressly recognizes the right to treat a consumer debt on which a nondebtor is jointly liable with the debtor differently. And the unfairness of attempting to treat nondischargeable debt more favorably than dischargeable debt can be readily seen. What about disputed debt being treated differently than undisputed debt? If Marta Carlson, our Chapter 7 debtor, was in a Chapter 13 plan, could she place the debt her former husband was responsible for paying but didn't in one class for less favorable treatment? Could the Matthews put their credit card debt attributable to fees and penalties in one class for less favorable treatment? Or could they put some or all of their credit card debt in one class for more favorable treatment because of their desire to keep those particular credit cards? Could they classify their medical or hospital debt separately and provide for more favorable treatment in order to maintain the relationship with a particular doctor or hospital? What other classifications can you think of that might be plausible to a consumer debtor? What are the arguments that such classifications do or do not discriminate unfairly?

Section 502(b)(2) disallows claims for unmatured (postpetition) interest, and so postpetition interest need not be paid on unsecured claims in a Chapter 13 plan.

You can see from this discussion that a great deal of flexibility is possible in a Chapter 13 plan. And fashioning a plan for a debtor involves understanding the provisions of the Code, budgets, and how various financial arrangements work.

3. The Less Than 100 Percent Plan

A Chapter 13 plan may propose to pay unsecured claims in full over the term of the plan. We call that a **100 percent plan**. Such a plan may modify the original terms of payment to unsecured creditors, as discussed in the preceding section, and if the court approves the debtor's proposed plan, the creditors must accept the modified payments. Most unsecured creditors will not complain about proposed modifications if the plan does in fact pay them all they are owed during the term of the plan. As we have already seen, to be considered a 100% plan, it must also propose to fully cure any prepetition arrearages in unsecured debt.

A Chapter 13 plan is not required to propose payment of 100 percent of unsecured claims and most do not. Most are instead less than 100 percent plans. However, a plan that proposes to) to pay less than unsecured claims less than 100 percent must meet two requirements. First, pursuant to §1325(b)(1)(B), the plan must propose to pay unsecured creditors all projected disposable income over the applicable commitment period (the term of the plan). Second, pursuant to §1325(a)(4), the plan must provide that the unsecured creditors will receive at least as much under the plan as they would receive if the debtor's assets were liquidated under Chapter 7. This **liquidation analysis** is also called the **best interests test** since it determines whether it is in the best interests of unsecured creditors for debtors to be in a Chapter 13 rather than a Chapter 7. Let's consider both of these requirements in order.

The Disposable Income Requirement

To understand the disposable income requirement for a non–100 percent plan consider the following hypothetical: Assume a debtor calculates that he will have $150 per month, or $9,000, in disposable income during the term of his five-year plan. He has $45,000 in unsecured debt. He cannot propose a plan that will pay his unsecured creditors less than 100 percent of what they are owed unless his plan calls for paying all of that projected disposable income to those unsecured creditors. If his plan does call for paying the full $150 a month to unsecured creditors for the full term of the plan, it can be confirmed. But if his plan only calls for paying $125 a month to the unsecured creditors for the term of the plan, it will not be confirmed.

But we are still left with the question of how much disposable income the debtor has that must be paid in full on unsecured claims for the term of the plan. In Chapter Fourteen, Section B, we discovered that neither the debtor's Schedules I or J, even together with Forms 122C-1 and 122C-2 (if an above median debtor), precisely calculate the actual disposable income figure of a Chapter 13 debtor. These forms and schedules, we said, are merely starting points because the final calculation must await the debtor's decisions about how to treat secured claims in the plan and about likely future changes in income and expenses. So how do we, finally, determine the debtor's disposable income when debtor proposes a less than 100 percent plan? Remember, §1325(b)(1) provides that a non–100 percent plan must propose to pay *all* of the debtor's projected disposable income over the term of the plan to unsecured creditors.

The Matthews have finally made those decisions in consultation with their lawyer. They know what their income is and is likely to be over the term of the plan. They have calculated their likely living expenses over the term of the plan. As we've seen in this chapter, they've made decisions about what to do with their various secured debts. In Illustration 15-a you will find the final budget that the attorney for the Matthews has put together reflecting these decisions and what the Matthews will be able to pay out of their projected income on the secured debt they plan to reaffirm and retain through the plan, on the priority unsecured debt that they must pay in full, and on their remaining unsecured debt.

Out of a total combined net monthly income of $4,133 (after employer deductions for taxes, health insurance, etc.), the Matthews expect to have monthly living expenses of $2,135 and will keep that amount from their monthly paychecks to pay themselves. That leaves $1,998, and $1,538 of that will go each month to pay the secured debt that they plan to retain in the plan. That leaves $460 available each month to be applied to administrative expenses, priority unsecured debt, the curing of arrearages proposed in the plan, and, finally, to nonpriority (general) unsecured debt. Of that $460, only $323.86 per month will wind up being paid to nonpriority unsecured creditors and that $323.86 is the Matthews' monthly projected disposable income number. (See the detailed analysis of the Matthews' plan below.)

Illustration 15-a: MONTHLY BUDGET FOR ROGER AND SUSAN MATTHEWS UNDER PROPOSED PLAN

Net monthly income:	
Roger:	$ 2,400
Susan:	$ 1,733
Total monthly income	$ 4,133
Living expenses:	
Food	$ 500
Home maintenance	100
Clothing	175
Dry cleaning/laundry	25
Gas	150
Utilities & phone	500
Insurance (auto)	60
Medical/dental	100
Charitable contributions	50
Entertainment/recreation	50
Child care	250
Miscellaneous	175
Total monthly living expenses	$ 2,135
Payments on secured debt:	
House payments	$ 1,241
(FBCC $850)	
(CSB $091)	
Car payments	297
(AFI for Ford F-150 truck $147)	
(CFSL for Honda Civic $150)	
Total monthly secured debt payments	$ 1,538
Available to apply to administrative costs, priority claims, arrearages, and general unsecured debts	$ 460
Total monthly plan payments	$ 1,998
Unsecured debt with priority:	
IRS (U.S.) Tax bill from YR-2	$ 1,000
Attorney's fee	1,000
Unsecured debts with no priority:	
Credit cards	$35,000
Doctor & hospital	25,000
CCFC vacation debt	2,000
CSB	10,000
AFI	1,500
Car World	3,000
Total nonpriority (general) unsecured debt	$76,500

The Liquidation Analysis Requirement

Pursuant to §1325(a)(4), a non–100 percent plan must result in the unsecured creditors receiving at least as much under the plan as they would receive if the debtor's assets were liquidated under Chapter 7. This best interests test requires a comparison of the proposed payout to what unsecured creditors would have received if the debtor had filed a Chapter 7 liquidation proceeding. If creditors receive more under the Chapter 13 plan than they would have received in the liquidation, this test is met. If creditors would have received more in the Chapter 7, then this test is not met and the plan will not be confirmed.

P-H 15-e: Assume our hypothetical debtor mentioned above (who calculates that he will have $150 per month, or $9,000, in disposable income during the term of his five-year plan and who has $45,000 in unsecured debt) has assets that, in a Chapter 7, would have been liquidated by the trustee and would have produced sufficient proceeds to pay all §507(a) priority claims in full, with $5,000 left over available to be paid to his unsecured creditors. If he proposes a Chapter 13 plan paying $150 a month to his unsecured creditors over five years, can it be confirmed? If he proposes a plan paying $75 a month to his unsecured creditors over five years, can it be confirmed?

General unsecured debt that is not paid in an approved Chapter 13 plan will be discharged, just as in a Chapter 7 case, unless the obligation is of a type treated by the Code as nondischargeable, a topic to be discussed in Chapter Sixteen, Section E.

A Chapter 13 plan that is not a 100 percent plan is often referred to by the percentage of unsecured debt that it does pay.

EXAMPLE

The debtor who proposes to pay $150 a month, or $9,000 over 60 months in his plan on $45,000 of unsecured debt, has proposed a 25 percent plan. If it is approved, the $36,000 of unsecured debt not paid will be discharged. The Matthews' plan will be referred to as a 24–25 percent plan because it proposes to pay nonpriority unsecured claims slightly more than 24 percent of the amount owed (see Paragraph 9 of the plan in Illustration 15-b).

P-H 15-f: Do you see why the child care expense is included in the budget in Illustration 15-a when it was not in the initial budget shown in the Assignment Memorandum in Appendix B? Why do you think the attorney increased the "Miscellaneous" category from $100 in the initial budget to $175 in this budget and the food budget from $475 to $500? Do you understand why the total of unsecured debt listed in the budget in Illustration 15-a is higher than the total of debt listed as "not being paid" in the initial budget? Do you see why the debt owed to CCFC for the financed vacation debt is now treated as unsecured debt, even though it was originally a secured debt? Do you see why a portion of the secured debt owed to CSB, AFI, Car World, and CCFC is now regarded as unsecured debt? Based on the revised budget in Illustration 15-a, how much disposable income should be available to pay a portion of the Matthews' unsecured debts over the term of the plan?

Illustration 15-b: CHAPTER 13 PLAN OF ROGER AND SUSAN MATTHEWS

UNITED STATES BANKRUPTCY COURT
MIDDLE DISTRICT OF PENNSYLVANIA

In re Roger H. Matthews and wife,   )   Case no. 16-13-XXXX
    Susan J. Matthews   )
)   Chapter 13
    Debtors   )
)

CHAPTER 13 PLAN

1. **PLAN TERM AND PAYMENT**: The term of this plan is 60 months, during which period the Debtors will pay the Chapter 13 Trustee the total sum of $1,998 per month by wage order of both debtors.

2. **TAX REFUNDS** to be paid into the plan as follows: All refunds in excess of $500 annually during plan.

3. **PROPERTY OF THE ESTATE/INSURANCE**: Debtors' income and nonexempt assets remain property of the estate and do not vest in debtors until completion of the plan. The Chapter 13 Trustee has no obligation to insure property of the estate, which is the responsibility of the debtors.

4. **ADMINISTRATIVE EXPENSES** under 11 U.S.C. §§503 and 1326 are to be paid in full including, per §707(b)(2)(A)(ii)(III), the actual administrative expense of administering a Chapter 13 plan for the Middle District of Pennsylvania, which is currently 5.1% of projected plan payments or $101.89. The balance of attorney's fee to debtor's attorney Edmond Montgomery in the amount of $1,000 to be paid in first five months at $200 per month.

5. **PRIORITY CLAIMS**: Claims entitled to priority under 11 U.S.C. §507 are to be paid in full in deferred cash payments, including the claim of the United States of America in the amount of $1,000 for Tax YR-2 to be paid in the first 24 months in installments of $41.66 per month.

6. **POSTPETITION DEBT** cannot be incurred by the Debtors without the prior written approval of the Chapter 13 Trustee unless debt is incurred for medical expenses for the Debtors or Debtors' dependents, utilities for the Debtors' household, and/or for repairs to Debtors' vehicles that are used for transportation necessary for the Debtors' performance under the plan. If postpetition debt is incurred, it will be paid under the plan as allowed under 11 U.S.C. §1305.

7. **LIEN RETENTION**: Secured claims remain subject to objection by the Trustee if not properly documented or perfected regardless of confirmed plan treatment. Secured creditors retain their liens, which shall be released upon satisfaction of the secured amount except as modified in Paragraphs 10 or 11 below. If the title with lien released is not received by counsel for Debtors within thirty (30) days of satisfaction of the secured amount, then the creditor will be responsible for any court costs and/or legal fees incurred by the Debtors in obtaining release of the lien.

8. **TAX LIABILITY** claims for secured, priority, and unsecured debts paid per claim unless objected to.

9. **NONPRIORITY UNSECURED CLAIMS**: If no secured plan treatment is provided herein, the claim will be treated as nonpriority unsecured and, depending on the allowed claims, will be paid the resulting dividend within the designated range below; provided, however, that if the funds available exceed the specified dividend range allowed, nonpriority unsecured claims will be entitled to the greater dividend.

24-25%

10. **SECURED CLAIMS OTHER THAN MORTGAGES ON DEBTORS' HOME:**

a. YR-8 Chevrolet Malibu pledged as security for indebtedness to Car World to be surrendered to Car World and balance of debt owed to Car World to be treated as a nonpriority unsecured debt.

b. Lien of Capital City Financing Company in debtor's plumbing tools and furniture to be avoided per 11 U.S.C. §522(f)(1)(B) and exempted per 11 U.S.C. §522(d)(3). Balance owed Capital City Financing Company to be treated as a nonpriority unsecured debt.

c. Secured claim of Automotive Financing, Inc. (secured by YR-3 Ford F-150 truck) to be modified to current value of collateral ($7,500) and paid in full over 60 months of plan together with interest at 6.5% per annum in monthly installments of $147 per 11 U.S.C. §§1322(b)(2) and 1325(a). Balance owed Automotive Financing, Inc. to be treated as a nonpriority general unsecured debt.

d. Secured claim of Columbiana Federal Savings & Loan (secured by YR-4 Honda Civic) to be modified and paid in full over 60 months of plan together with interest at 7.5% per annum in monthly installments of $150 per month per 11 U.S.C. §§1322(b)(2) and 1325(a)(5).

11. **MORTGAGES ON DEBTORS' HOME**: The Debtors will retain possession of their residence located at 901 Magnolia Lane, Harrisburg, Pennsylvania as follows:

a. Arrearage on mortgage payment to First Bank of Capital City in the amount of $850 to be cured over first 12 months of plan together with interest at 8% per annum in 12 monthly installments of $74 each per 11 U.S.C. §1322(b)(5). Future mortgage payments to First Bank of Capital City to be paid through the plan in monthly installments of $850. Debtors to pay any future mortgage increases due to escrow changes. Mortgage balance and lien survive beyond the plan.

b. A second mortgage on the residence held by Capital Savings Bank with prepetition balance of $30,000. Secured claim of Capital Savings Bank to be modified to $20,000 per 11 U.S.C. §1322(c)(2) and paid in full through the plan together with interest at 6.5% per annum in 60 monthly installments of $391. Unsecured balance of $10,000 to be treated as a nonpriority general unsecured claim per Paragraph 9.

Date: 6/6/2016   /s/ Roger H. Matthews
                  Roger H. Matthews, Debtor

/s/ Susan J. Matthews
Susan J. Matthews, Debtor

/s/ Edmond J. Montgomery
Edmond J. Montgomery
Montgomery & Associates PLLC
Attorney for Debtors
912 West Court Street
Harrisburg, Pennsylvania 17101
(717) 555-1234
Bar # PA-XXX-99

UNIFORM CHAPTER 13 PLAN IN THE WORKS?

There is currently wide diversity in the format and contents of Chapter 13 plans among the federal districts. Some districts have adopted mandatory forms for such plans while others have adopted only certain required language for such plans but not an entire form. The variety of forms currently in use reflects the significant disparity in local Chapter 13 practice and custom. The U.S. Judicial Conference, the national policy-making body for the federal courts, is authorized by 28 U.S.C. §331 to review and make recommendations regarding rules of practice and procedure in the federal courts, including the bankruptcy courts. Since 2013 the Conference's Committee on Rules of Practice and Procedure has been debating whether to recommend adoption of a national uniform Chapter 13 plan matrix. The proposal has generated significant controversy among bankruptcy judges and standing trustees around the country, most of it centered on the possible disruption of the "local culture" that pervades Chapter 13 practice by adoption of a national form and associated rules. To get a flavor of the controversy, review the transcript of the Bankruptcy Rules Committee public hearing conducted on January 23, 2015, accessible from the Conference's proposed amendments page at www.uscourts.gov/rules-policies/proposed-amendments-published-public-comment. The proposed new form, which, if adopted, will become Official Form 113, can be seen in its 2015 iteration at www.bankruptcymastery.com/wp-content/uploads/2013/08/proposed-chapter-13-plan1.pdf. If adopted, the national form is expected to go into effect in late 2016 or the beginning of 2017. Go to the Conference's web site at www.uscourts.gov/ and determine the status of the national Chapter 13 form.

D. ▶ Payments Outside the Chapter 13 Plan and the Wage Order

In general, the payments that a Chapter 13 debtor is going to make to creditors under the plan will not be made by the debtor directly. Instead, the Code envisions that the portion of the debtor's income that is to be paid to creditors goes to the standing trustee, who then distributes the funds to the creditors under the terms of the plan. That portion of the debtor's income needed for regular recurring living expenses will be retained by the debtor, who will be expected to pay those living expenses as they come due. These living expense payments are considered **payments outside the plan** since the debtor pays those debts directly as they come due.

If the source of the debtor's income to fund the plan is wages or salary, the employer will be served with a **wage order** from the bankruptcy court, directing the employer to make a payroll deduction from the debtor's paycheck each pay period and to pay that amount directly to the trustee rather than to the debtor. The debtor is to receive only that portion of his or her paycheck that goes toward living expenses. The trustee receives the rest and pays it to the creditors as called

Illustration 15-c: WAGE ORDER TO EMPLOYER OF ROGER MATTHEWS

UNITED STATES BANKRUPTCY COURT MIDDLE DISTRICT OF PENNSYLVANIA

In re: Roger H. Matthews and wife, Susan J. Matthews	)	Case No. 16-13-XXXX
Debtors	)	Chapter 13

To: City Plumbing Company
411 Butler Avenue
Harrisburg, PA 17101
Re employee Roger H. Matthews
Deduction: $1,119 monthly

ORDER TO EMPLOYER TO DEDUCT AND REMIT A PORTION OF DEBTOR'S EARNINGS FOR THE VOLUNTARY PAYMENT OF DEBTS

This is an ORDER of the United States Bankruptcy Court, NOT a garnishment. It supersedes any previous order of this court issued with respect to Debtor/Employee's wages. The above named Debtor/Employee has voluntarily filed a petition and plan under Chapter 13 of the United State Bankruptcy Code seeking to pay certain debts under the protection of this Court. These debts are to be paid by the Chapter 13 Trustee from the future earnings of the Debtor/Employee. Debtor/Employee has requested an order to have his future earnings withheld and paid to the Chapter 13 Trustee. This Court is empowered under Title 11 Section 13259(c) of the United States Code to direct any entity from which the Debtor/Employee receives income to pay all or any part of such income to the Chapter 13 Trustee. Accordingly, it is hereby ORDERED, that:

Until further order of the court, you are directed to immediately begin withholding the above stated amount from the wages, salary, commission, and all other earnings or income of Debtor/Employee and to remit the same promptly to the Standing Chapter 13 Trustee no less frequently than once each month. (Make check payable to "Standing Chapter 13 Trustee" at the address shown below.)

MAIL ALL REMITTANCES WITH CASE NAME AND NUMBER TO:

Standing Chapter 13 Trustee
319 West Court Street
Harrisburg, PA 17101

ENTER: August 16, 2016

/s/ _____
United States Bankruptcy Judge

---

for by the plan. The wage order served on the employer of Roger Matthews is shown in Illustration 15-c. (Both wage orders are shown in Document 22 of the Matthews case file.)

This system means the standing trustee's office in any given federal district is handling a tremendous amount of money coming in from Chapter 13 debtors or their employers. Nationwide, Chapter 13 standing trustees collect and disburse hundreds of millions of dollars to creditors every year.

Chapter 13 plans sometimes propose that certain debts, other than regular living expenses, be paid outside the plan. This is most commonly proposed when a third person (someone other than the debtor) is making part or all of the payment.

EXAMPLE

There may be a nondebtor who is also liable on the debt and who will be making all or part of the payments to avoid his own default. Or a relative or friend of the debtor may volunteer to pay all or part of the debt for the debtor. Where a nondischargeable debt such as a student loan is being repaid on an established schedule that is not altered by the terms of the plan, the plan may propose that it be paid outside the plan.

In some federal districts it is customary for secured debt subject to a pay through proposal to be paid outside the plan since the obligation is not modified (scheduled payments will be made per the contract throughout the plan and beyond). However, if an obligation is impaired by the plan either because it is not being paid 100 percent or because it is not being paid on the terms of the original contract, that obligation normally must be made through the plan.

EXAMPLE

In some districts the Matthews' plan might call for the monthly payments to FBCC, holder of the first mortgage, to be paid outside the plan since that obligation is a pure pay through; it is not modified or impaired by the plan, involves no arrearage to be cured, and will be paid as called for in the contract during and beyond the plan. In districts where that is not customary, the plan might still propose to pay that obligation outside the plan if a nondebtor was also liable on the debt along with the Matthews or if a third party (e.g., Roger or Susan's parents) had agreed to help the couple make the payments to FBCC. On the other hand, the plan could not call for the payments to CSB, holder of the second mortgage, to be made outside the plan because that obligation is impaired by the plan with the strip down to equity value.

A desire to avoid the trustee's administrative costs for handling plan payments may also explain a proposal to make certain payments outside the plan, but many Chapter 13 trustees would object to a proposal based solely on such a rationale and some bankruptcy judges would not confirm a plan on that basis. This is the kind of thing on which there is wide variation of practice among the federal districts.

E. ▶ Analysis of the Matthews' Chapter 13 Plan

The Matthews have a combined net monthly income of $4,133. Under the terms of their plan, each month they will retain a total of $2,135 to pay their monthly living expenses as itemized in the budget in Illustration 15-a.

The balance of the Matthews' net monthly income, $1,998 ($4,133 minus $2,135) will be paid by wage order to the Chapter 13 trustee each month; the trustee will distribute those funds as follows:

$41.66 .... to the United States of America for 24 months to pay the YR-2 tax obligation in full

$200 .... to attorney Edmond Montgomery for five months on the balance of the fee owed

$850 .... to FBCC on the first mortgage

$391 .... to CSB on the second mortgage

$74 .... to FBCC for 12 months to cure the arrearage

$147 .... to AFI on the Ford F-150 truck

$150 .... to CFSL on the Honda Civic

$101.89 .... to Chapter 13 Trustee for administrative expenses ($1,998 × 5.1% multiplier)

$42.45 .... to unsecured creditors pro rata, to increase as payments of the priority tax claim, administrative expense for attorney's fee, and arrearage cure are completed during the term of the plan.

Obviously, the Matthews are not proposing a 100 percent plan. And initially only $42.45 per month will be available for distribution to unsecured creditors. But remember that the $200 per month payment to attorney Edmond Montgomery will only be made for five months, the $41.66 payment to the United States on the priority tax obligation will only be made for 24 months, and the $74 per month payment to FBCC to cure that arrearage for only 12 months. As those obligations are satisfied, the monthly *pro rata* payment to unsecured creditors will increase for the duration of the plan.

EXAMPLE

Excluding the $101.89 administrative expense to the Chapter 13 trustee that will be paid each of the 60 months of the plan, the $200 administrative expense for attorney's fees that will be paid for the first 12 months of the plan, and the $41.66 paid for 24 months on the priority claim of the United States for Roger's tax obligation (all of which must be paid in full), and recognizing that the $74 paid for 12 months to secured creditor FBCC to cure that arrearage will thereafter be available to distribute to unsecured creditors, this plan calls for a total of $18,598.20 to be paid to nonpriority, nonadministrative, unsecured creditors over the 60 months of the plan or an average of $309.97 per month. Note in Illustration 15-a that the Matthews have a total of $76,500 in nonpriority (general), unsecured debt. Thus, they are proposing a 24–25 percent plan ($18,598.20 ÷ $76,500 = 24.3%).

P-H 15-g: If the Matthews had the higher joint monthly income of $7,916.66 ($95,000 annually) that we assumed for purposes of completing a Form 122C-2 in Chapter Fourteen (see Illustration 14-d), would they be able to propose a 100 percent plan based on the analysis in the last example?

Questions regarding the debtor's income or living expenses claimed in Schedules I and J and on Form 122C-2 for the above median debtor and used to calculate the amount retained for living expenses by the debtors are typically raised and resolved at the first meeting of creditors.

EXAMPLE

At the Matthews' 341 meeting, the Chapter 13 trustee may question the inclusion of $175 in "miscellaneous" expenses in the Matthews' calculation of living expenses in their plan since only $100 was included for such expenses on their Schedule J (Document 10 in the Matthews case file). Or, the trustee might question the inclusion of the $250 for child care expenses in their projected living expenses if the couple is not yet actually incurring that expense. What modifications in the plan as proposed might the trustee demand on these issues? Since the Matthews have included an amount in their living expenses for charitable contributions, the trustee may ask for documentation that the debtor has historically made such contributions in that amount to ensure the debtor isn't just looking for a way to keep more cash from creditors. Of course, if the plan is a 100 percent plan, the trustee will have less reason for concern. Since the Matthews were below median debtors as calculated on their Form 122C-1, they did not file a Form 122C-2.

Questions regarding other aspects of the proposed plan are also raised at the 341 meeting and are often resolved there. Such meetings often take on the appearance of a settlement conference or a mediation session as the parties work to find solutions to problems raised by the trustee or creditors.

EXAMPLE

The Chapter 13 trustee for the Matthews may question the plan proposing to pay the full contract rate of interest on the strip down of the claim of CFSL when it is not doing so on the stripped down claims of either AFI or CSB. If the plan proposed to pay the first mortgage payments owed to FBCC outside the plan, the trustee might object, either because the parents' promise to help is not a sufficiently valid reason or because the trustee considers that claim impaired due to the arrearage that has to be cured. Again, attitudes and practice on such matters vary widely across the country.

Agreements made at the 341 meeting often result in debtor's proposed plan being revised prior to confirmation. (Section 13239(a) allows the debtor to modify a proposed plan prior to confirmation.) Disputes raised at the 341 meeting regarding the plan that cannot be resolved there often lead to a formal objection to confirmation being made to the court by the trustee or a creditor, and that objection can threaten the confirmation of the plan, a topic we will consider in the next chapter.

CHAPTER SUMMARY

Priority claims must be paid in full in a Chapter 13 plan, though payment may be made in deferred installments over the term of the plan.

The plan may propose to pay a secured claim in full as scheduled during the term of the plan and beyond and for the creditor to retain its lien on the secured property, an arrangement known as a pay through. Arrearages on secured claims may be cured by installment payments over a reasonable time made within the term of the plan. Interest may be required on the arrearage payments if the underlying agreement or state law requires.

As in a Chapter 7, the Chapter 13 debtor can avoid a judicial lien in property that impairs an exemption unless the lien arises out of a domestic support obligation. But in Chapter 13 the debtor may also avoid a consensual security interest in household goods and furnishings, wearing apparel, appliances, tools of the trade, and other such items to the extent the lien impairs an exemption in such property, so long as it is not a purchase money security interest.

A Chapter 13 plan may strip down the amount of an undersecured claim to the present value of the collateral, pay the full amount of the reduced secured claim over the term of the plan, treat the balance of the debt as unsecured, and retain the collateral. Claims secured only by the debtor's primary residence are excluded from the strip down option unless the last payment is due during the term of the plan. Courts are split over whether Chapter 13 strip off is available where the mortgage in the debtor's primary residence is wholly undersecured. Strip down is also disallowed for vehicles purchased for personal use by the debtor within 910 days of the filing of the petition that are subject to a PMSI and for any other property purchased by the debtor within one year of filing the petition that is subject to a PMSI.

Where strip down is allowed, the present value of the collateral is the replacement value as of the date the petition is filed. If the stripped down value will be paid to the creditor in installments, interest must be added to the payments calculated using not the contract rate but the *Till* rate, the national prime together with an appropriate risk adjustment.

The Chapter 13 plan can modify the rights of a secured creditor by adjusting downward the amount of the periodic payments the secured creditor is to receive and/or extending the payment period accordingly so long as the full present value of the secured claim is paid during the term of the plan.

A debtor may surrender collateralized property to the secured creditor as part of a plan where no lien avoidance is plausible and the standing trustee will abandon the property for the estate. Where there is likely to be equity in collateralized property for the estate, the plan may ask that such property be sold free and clear of liens.

A Chapter 13 plan may cure arrearages in unsecured claims. A 100 percent plan must include the curing of all arrearages in unsecured debt. Interest is not paid on arrearage payments of unsecured debt.

The plan may also modify unsecured obligations, including proposing to discharge some or all of them subject to the requirement that a plan must propose to pay all the debtor's projected disposable income over the term of the plan and subject to the liquidation analysis or best interest tests that requires that unsecured creditors receive more in the Chapter 13 plan than they would have received in a Chapter 7 liquidation.

During the term of the plan, funds that debtors need for regular living expenses for themselves and dependents are retained by debtors. Payments to be made to secured and unsecured creditors are channeled through the standing trustee who then distributes them to creditors according to the terms of the plan. If the debtor is employed, a wage order will issue to the employer directing the employer to make payroll deductions and remit the designated amount to the trustee. A plan may propose that certain debts, other than regular living expenses, be paid outside the plan as in a claim subject to an unaltered, unimpaired pay through proposal or where a nondebtor third party is making the payments.

Questions that the standing trustee or a creditor have concerning the debtor's proposed Chapter 13 plan will typically be raised and often resolved at the first meeting of creditors.

REVIEW QUESTIONS

1. What percentage of priority claims must be paid in the Chapter 13 plan?
2. What two liens can a Chapter 13 plan avoid in order to claim an exemption in the collateral subject to the liens?
3. What are the two requirements for curing an arrearage in a Chapter 13 plan?
4. Explain the bifurcation feature of a secured claim under §506(a) and how that impacts on the debtor's right to strip down a secured claim in a Chapter 13 plan.
5. How is the value of the secured portion of a bifurcated secured claim determined?
6. What is a pay through proposal in a Chapter 13 plan and how does it work?
7. Explain the difference between strip down and cram down as Code concepts.
8. Explain the difference between strip down and strip off as Code concepts.
9. Under what circumstances may the debtor's principal residence be subject to strip down or strip off treatment in a Chapter 13 plan?
10. What is the "hanging paragraph" and what does it have to do with a 910 vehicle?
11. What is the *Till* rate" and how does it come into play in determining the present value of collateral in a Chapter 13 case?
12. What happens to a secured creditor's claim when the Chapter 13 debtor surrenders the collateral to the creditor?
13. Explain the disposable income requirement for approval of a less than 100 percent Chapter 13 plan. Explain the liquidation analysis requirement.
14. Explain what we mean by payments outside the plan.
15. Explain what a wage order is and what the employer must do to comply with it.

WORDS AND PHRASES TO REMEMBER

abandon (property)	general unsecured claim
arrearage	hanging paragraph
best interests test	liquidation analysis
contract rate of interest	payments outside the plan
cram down	pay through
cure the arrearage	postpetition interest

present value
principal residence
priority claims
purchase money security interest
ride through
strip down

strip off
surrender (property)
Till rate
wage order
write down
100 percent plan

TO LEARN MORE: A number of TLM activities to accompany this chapter are accessible on the companion web site for this textbook at http://aspen-lawschool.com/books/Parsons_Debt4e/.

Chapter Sixteen:

The Chapter 13 Debt Adjustment for an Individual with Regular Income—Plan Confirmation, Modification, and Discharge

In this chapter we will conclude our study of the Chapter 13 bankruptcy by considering the requirements for confirmation of a Chapter 13 plan as well as the procedure for confirmation. We will examine the requirements and procedure for postconfirmation modification of a Chapter 13 plan. We will also look at what debts can be discharged in a Chapter 13 case and the timing of the Chapter 13 discharge. Finally, we will analyze the debtor's right to voluntarily dismiss his Chapter 13 case or convert it to a Chapter 7 liquidation as well as the right of a party in interest to seek an involuntary dismissal or conversion of the case.

KEY CONCEPTS

- The debtor generally must propose a Chapter 13 plan within 14 days of filing the petition and begin making payments under the plan to the standing trustee within 30 days following the entry for the order of relief or the filing of the proposed plan, whichever is earlier
- The bankruptcy court must confirm the Chapter 13 plan and the Code contains a number of requirements that must be satisfied to obtain confirmation including that the debtor has proposed the plan in good faith
- Once confirmed, a Chapter 13 plan can be modified on motion based on changed circumstances of the debtor but a modified plan must meet the same requirements for confirmation as the original plan
- A discharge of debts in Chapter 13 is granted only upon completion of the plan though an early or hardship discharge can be granted in exceptional circumstances upon a required showing
- As in a Chapter 7 case, certain debts cannot be discharged in a Chapter 13 case

A. Timing of the Chapter 13 Plan and Initial Payments

Bankruptcy Rule 3015(b) requires that the debtor's proposed Chapter 13 plan be filed at the time the petition is filed or within 14 days thereafter. Section 1323(a) permits the debtor to modify the plan at any time before confirmation. This allows the plan to be proposed prior to the 341 meeting, discussed there with creditors and the trustee, and then modified if necessary prior to the court's confirmation of the plan.

Section 1326(a)(1) of the Code requires the debtor to begin making payments on the plan within 30 days following the entry for the order of relief or the filing of the proposed plan, whichever is earlier. This means the debtor is making payments to the trustee on his or her plan even before it is confirmed. One of the duties imposed on the standing trustee is to ensure that the debtor begins making these payments (see Illustration 13-a). Per §1326(a)(2), the trustee retains these preconfirmation payments until the plan is confirmed and only then distributes them to creditors.

EXAMPLE

Under their plan (Illustration 15-b or Document 18 in the Matthews case file), the Matthews propose to pay a total of $1,998 per month into their plan. Since they filed their plan with the petition, they must begin making payments within 30 days after the filing, even though their plan is not yet confirmed. (Compare the date the plan was filed with the date the plan was confirmed in Document 21 in the Matthews case file.) The standing trustee retains these payments until the plan is confirmed and then distributes them to creditors, per the now-confirmed plan.

B. Confirmation of the Chapter 13 Plan

Section 1324 provides that the court "shall hold" a **confirmation hearing** on the plan no earlier than 20 days and no later than 45 days after the first meeting of creditors. Creditors must be given 28 days' notice of the confirmation hearing, pursuant to Bankruptcy Rule 2002(b). Notwithstanding the mandatory language of §1324, many bankruptcy judges only conduct a confirmation hearing if an objection to confirmation is filed. In those districts, absent an objection, confirmation will be automatic when the deadline for making objections passes. In addition, §1324 allows the confirmation hearing to be held earlier than 20 days following the first meeting of creditors if the court determines it would be in the "best interests" of the estate and creditors to do so and there is no objection. As a result, many bankruptcy judges conduct the confirmation hearing shortly after the first meeting of creditors if no objection is filed at that time. Others wait until the time for filing claims (the claims bar date) has expired.

P-H 16-a: Look at the Notice of Chapter 13 Case that was sent to creditors in the Matthews' Chapter 13 case (Document 19 in the Matthews case file). What is the deadline established there for filing proofs of claim in the Matthews case? Now look at the Order Confirming Chapter 13 Plan (Document 21 in the Matthews case file) to see when it was entered. Does it appear that any objection to the plan was made at or following the 341 meeting? How does the judge in the Matthews' case interpret §1324?

Illustration 16-a: CRITERIA FOR CONFIRMING A CHAPTER 13 PLAN

- The Chapter 13 petition was filed in good faith
- The Chapter 13 plan has been proposed in good faith and not by any means forbidden by law
- The plan is feasible, in the sense that the debtor will be able to make all payments called for in the plan and will be able to comply with the plan
- The debtor has filed all federal, state, and local tax returns due
- The debtor is current on all domestic support obligations
- The value to be distributed to all unsecured creditors under the plan is not less than they would have received in a Chapter 7 liquidation
- Each secured creditor has either (a) accepted the plan or (b) will receive at least the value of the collateral and have the security interest in the property continued or (c) has had the secured property surrendered to it
- All administrative and priority claims, as well as fees associated with the filing, have been paid or will be paid through the plan
- The plan otherwise complies with all provisions of the Code

Section 1325(a) sets out the criteria that the court must consider in deciding whether to confirm a plan; those criteria are summarized in Illustration 16-a.

Any **party in interest** may object to the confirmation of a proposed Chapter 13 plan. In most Chapter 13 cases, any objections to the plan by the U.S. Trustee, creditors, or the standing trustee are worked out at the 341 meeting prior to the confirmation hearing so that the confirmation hearing is perfunctory and brief. If they cannot be worked out, a formal objection to confirmation of the plan will be filed and the matter will be resolved at the confirmation hearing. Upon confirmation of the plan, the court will enter an order complying with Official Form 2300B, Order Confirming Chapter 13 Plan. (See Document 21 in the Matthews case file.)

Neither the Code nor the Official Rules establish a time deadline for filing an objection to confirmation of a Chapter 13 plan. In many districts the **local rules of court** will deal with that issue. In some districts objections to confirmation must be filed by the first meeting of creditors. In other districts objections must be filed by the date of the confirmation hearing or if no confirmation hearing is held by a date established in the notice to creditors for filing objections to avoid automatic confirmation.

When a creditor fails to object to a plan prior to confirmation the debtor may be able to argue **implied consent** from the failure to object even where there is no deadline for filing an objection. Alternatively, the creditor may be able to argue that since the plan is confirmed by court order the objecting creditor is barred from objecting postconfirmation by reason of **waiver** or the **res judicata** effect of final orders. See e.g., *In re Andersen*, 179 F.3d 1253 (10th Cir. 1999) (upholding on res judicata grounds a provision in a confirmed Chapter 13 debtor's plan that discharged student loan debt based on undue hardship even though the debtor had not obtained such a finding in the bankruptcy case). But what if the postconfirmation objection is to a provision that clearly violates the Code? Here the courts are split. See, e.g., *In re Montoya*, 341 B.R. 41 (Bankr. D. Utah 2006) (where plan wrongfully bifurcated and stripped down lien on 910 vehicle in violation of the Code and contained a clear deadline for filing objections, court would not entertain either implied consent or res judicata arguments as reasons to exclude objection filed after the deadline since one requirement of confirmation is that plan conform to all provisions of the Code). But compare *In re Pardee*, 218 B.R. 916 (9th Cir. B.A.P. 1998) (creditor's failure to object to plan at confirmation hearing constituted waiver of its right to collect postpetition interest on its claim, even though plan provision discharging that postpetition interest was contrary to the Code; preclusive effect of final orders to be honored).

P-H 16-b: Check the local rules of the bankruptcy court in your federal district and determine if there is a deadline for filing objections to confirmation of a Chapter 13 case and research to determine if the courts of your federal district have recognized an implied consent or res judicata defense to entertaining a postconfirmation objection to a Chapter 13 plan.

Most of the requirements for confirmation in §1325(a) are self-explanatory and some we have already considered (e.g., the required treatment of secured claims in §1325(a)(5) and the liquidation comparison requirement of §1325(a)(4)). But note the first two requirements in Illustration 16-a, one relating to the good faith of the debtor in filing the petition (from §1325(a)(7)), and the other relating to the plan being proposed in good faith (from §1325(a)(3)). **Good faith** is not a defined term under the Code and the concept has been left

Good faith Generally, honesty in fact and compliance with the letter and spirit of the Code.

to court interpretation. The various issues that we indicated in the previous section might be raised for discussion at the 341 meeting may, if they cannot be resolved there, give rise to an objection to confirmation on the basis of lack of good faith.

Good faith also emerges as a consideration in other contexts in Chapter 13 cases when the debtor seeks to modify a confirmed plan and as an implicit (not explicit) factor in a court's decision to dismiss a Chapter 13 case or convert it to a Chapter 7 liquidation under §1307 prior to plan confirmation (see further discussion of good faith in Section F).

HIGHLIGHTED CASE ●

IN RE HATEM
273 B.R. 900 (S.D. Ala. 2001)

OPINION: BUTLER, Chief District Judge . . . .

Prior to filing for Chapter 13 bankruptcy, Hatem had been involved in litigation in the Circuit Court of Baldwin County, Alabama, in an action styled *Elizabeth L. Kennedy v. Betty Lynn Hatem and Leroy Hatem* involving a dispute between Hatem and Elizabeth Kennedy, Hatem's mother and the appellee herein, concerning the ownership of 2.7 acres of land and a home located in Montrose, Alabama ("the property"). On March 31, 1999, the Circuit Court of Baldwin County set aside a deed executed by Kennedy, which transferred Kennedy's one-half interest in the property to Hatem, holding that the deed was void because it was the result of fraud, deception, and undue influence by Hatem and Hatem's then husband. The circuit court declared both Hatem and Kennedy once again one-half owners of the property. On January 11, 2000, the circuit court issued an order of sale of the property requiring its appraisal, sale, and equitable division. The circuit court amended its order on May 11, 2000, in order to give both Kennedy and Hatem the exclusive right to bid on the property within thirty days from the date of filing of the appraisal. On October 27, 2000, following Hatem's appeal, the Alabama Court of Civil Appeals affirmed the circuit court's orders. On November 6, 2000, the court-appointed appraiser filed its appraisal with the circuit court, establishing the value of the property at $410,000.00. Pursuant to the circuit court's order of sale, Kennedy and Hatem had thirty days from that date to submit their bids on the property.

On November 29, 2000, one week before the expiration of the bid period, Hatem filed for Chapter 13 bankruptcy. In the petition and accompanying schedules, Hatem indicated that she was the sole owner of the 2.7 acres of land and the home located in Montrose, Alabama, and that the property was subject to a mortgage in favor of Regions Bank in the amount of $54,623.00 and a vendor's lien in favor of Elizabeth Kennedy in the amount of $210,000.00, totaling $264,623.00 in secured claims on the property. Hatem also listed unsecured debt of $52,252.00, bringing her total reported liabilities to $316,875.00. Hatem listed the value of her interest in the property as $205,000.00 and her total assets, including personal property, as $215,403.00. Hatem reported a monthly income of $1,582.00 and monthly expenditures of $1,572.00.

Hatem's Chapter 13 plan proposed to pay the Trustee's commission, Hatem's attorney, and the unsecured property tax claim of $1,009.00 by making monthly payments to the Trustee of $50.00. The plan further proposed that Hatem would make monthly payments directly to Regions Mortgage, outside the plan, in the amount of $581.00 on its secured mortgage. The plan proposed no payments to Hatem's unsecured nonpriority creditors on their claims totaling $51,243.00.

Kennedy filed a motion to dismiss Hatem's Chapter 13 proceeding on the grounds that Hatem did not file the Chapter 13 petition in good faith; Hatem did not propose a Chapter 13 plan in good faith; and Hatem's sole purpose in filing the petition was to invoke the automatic stay provisions of the Bankruptcy Code to prevent the sale and division of the property by the state court. [T]he bankruptcy court found that neither Hatem's Chapter 13 petition nor her plan had been filed in good faith. In addition, the bankruptcy court found that Hatem's purported amended plan, which was proposed by Hatem at the hearing on the motion, was not feasible and likewise lacked good faith. Based on those findings, the bankruptcy court denied confirmation of Hatem's plan and dismissed Hatem's Chapter 13 case with a 180-day injunction against further bankruptcy filings. It is the bankruptcy court's finding of bad faith that is at issue in this appeal.

A Chapter 13 plan must be confirmed by the bankruptcy court if meets the six criteria set forth in 11 U.S.C. §1325(a). This appeal focuses on the third of these criteria found in §1325(a)(3), requiring that the plan be proposed in good faith. A Chapter 13 plan cannot be confirmed if it fails to satisfy the good faith requirement. *In re Waldron*, 785 F.2d 936, 939 (11th Cir. 1986) (quoting 11 U.S.C. §1325(a)(3)). That requirement "is the only safety valve available through which plans attempting to twist the law to malevolent ends may be cast out." Id.

Whether a Chapter 13 plan has been proposed in good faith is a question of fact subject to the "clearly erroneous" standard of review. *In re Saylors*, 869 F.2d 1434, 1438 (11th Cir. 1989). While the Bankruptcy Code does not define the term "good faith," the Eleventh Circuit has interpreted "good faith" as "requiring that there is a reasonable likelihood that the plan will achieve a result consistent with the objectives and purposes of the Code." *In re McCormick*, 49 F.3d 1524, 1526 (11th Cir. 1995). The petition may not be used as a device to serve some "unworthy purpose" of the petitioner. *Waldron*, 785 F.2d at 939.

In analyzing the good faith of the debtor, the court looks to the "totality of the circumstances" surrounding the plan. See *McCormick*, 49 F.3d at 1526. In *In re Kitchens*, the Eleventh Circuit set forth a nonexclusive list of factors that the bankruptcy court should consider in making a determination of good faith:

(1) the amount of the debtor's income from all sources; (2) the living expenses of the debtor and his dependents; (3) the amount of attorney's fees; (4) the probable or expected duration of the debtor's Chapter 13 plan; (5) the motivations of the debtor and his sincerity in seeking relief under the provisions of Chapter 13; (6) the debtor's degree of effort; (7) the debtor's ability to earn and the likelihood of fluctuation in his earnings; (8) special circumstances such as inordinate medical expenses; (9) the frequency with which the debtor has sought relief under the Bankruptcy Reform Act and its predecessors; (10) the circumstances under which the debtor has contracted his debts and has demonstrated bona fides, or lack of same, in dealings with his creditors; (11) the burden which the plan's administration would place on the trustee.

Kitchens, 702 F.2d 885, 888-89 (11th Cir. 1983).

The court further enumerated three additional factors for consideration, those being: substantiality of the repayment to the unsecured creditors; consideration of the type of debt to be discharged and whether such debt would be nondischargeable under Chapter 7; and the accuracy of the plan's statements of debts and expenses and whether any inaccuracies are an attempt to mislead the court. Id. at 889 . . . .

[T]he bankruptcy court found that Hatem's petition contained multiple misstatements and omissions regarding the ownership of the property, the claims against the property, and the value of the property. The court held that the admittedly erroneous information indicated either a callous disregard of a debtor's duties in filling out the Chapter 13 schedules and plan or an intentional misrepresentation of information in an attempt to secure confirmation and avoid the consequences of the state court litigation. The court further noted that Hatem had assets that, if liquidated, would be more than sufficient to pay off her indebtedness; yet, Hatem had proposed to pay nothing to her unsecured nonpriority creditors. In addition, the court noted that the timing of the filing of the petition, which was only three weeks before the property was to be sold and only one week before the expiration of Hatem's right to bid on the property, indicated that the petition was filed to forestall the court ordered sale. The court found Hatem's testimony that she was unaware of the state court orders regarding the sale of the property incredible. The court further found that Hatem's purported amended plan to obtain a mortgage on the property and buy out her mother's interest in the property, which Hatem proposed from the witness stand at the hearing, was not feasible and was merely a last ditch attempt to thwart the dismissal of the case. The court concluded that neither the petition, nor the original or amended plans, had been submitted in good faith.

After reviewing the entire record, the Court agrees. It is undisputed that Hatem's Chapter 13 petition and schedules failed to disclose Kennedy's one-half ownership interest in the subject property. It is undisputed that Hatem erroneously (if not falsely) reported that Kennedy had a secured lien on the property in the amount of $210,000.00, making Hatem's secured claims on the property, and her liabilities in general, appear much greater than they were.

It is undisputed that Hatem listed the value of her interest in the property as $205,000.00, which, in conjunction with her failure to list Kennedy as a one-half owner, made it appear that she was the sole owner of property whose value was only $205,000.00. This omission, in conjunction with the misstatement that Kennedy had a lien on the property of $210,000.00, made it appear that property worth only $205,000.00 was subject to secured debt of $264,623.00 (made up of Kennedy's purported lien and the Regions' mortgage). In fact, the property was worth $410,000.00 and was subject to secured debt of only $54,623.00.

At the confirmation hearing on January 4, 2001, Hatem and her attorney acknowledged that the information given in the petition was erroneous in many respects. The bankruptcy court noted that, although objections had been filed to the petition and plan on December 13, 2000, neither Hatem nor her attorney had made any attempt to correct or amend the misrepresentations and omissions therein. In fact, they continued to seek to have the defective plan confirmed at the hearing.

In addition . . . the timing of the filing of Hatem's Chapter 13 proceeding clearly indicated that her motive was to attempt to defeat the state court ordered sale of the property. If there were any doubt about that motive, Hatem erased it when she candidly admitted in her brief to this Court that she filed her Chapter 13 case in part "to forestall a sacrificial forced sale of her one-half undivided [interest] in the real estate in which she resides."

The Court further notes that Hatem's assets, including her personal property, totaled $215,403.00, and her liabilities (once the erroneous $210,000.00 lien was removed) totaled only $106,875.00. As the bankruptcy court found, had the state court ordered sale of the property proceeded, it would likely have generated $205,000.00 for Hatem as one-half owner of the property, which would have been more than sufficient to pay all of her creditors in full. Despite that fact, Hatem filed a Chapter 13 plan in which she proposed to pay nothing of the $51,243.00 owed to her unsecured creditors.

Considering the totality of the circumstances in this case, particularly Hatem's motivations in seeking Chapter 13 relief, her ability to pay her debts in full, her lack of effort in putting forth a proper and feasible plan, the insubstantiality of the repayment to her unsecured creditors, the degree of inaccuracy of the plan's statements of assets and debts, and the misleading nature of those inaccuracies, this Court cannot say that the bankruptcy court was clearly erroneous in its finding that Hatem filed her Chapter 13 petition and her Chapter 13 plan in bad faith. Moreover, for these same reasons and for the additional reason that Hatem completely failed to show the feasibility of her purported amended plan.

Where a bankruptcy court has properly found that a Chapter 13 petition and plan were filed in bad faith, confirmation of the plan may be denied, and the case may be dismissed. See 11 U.S.C. §1307(c)(5); *Green*, 214 B.R. at 506 n. 9 ("[b]ankruptcy courts have a duty to preserve the bankruptcy process for its intended purpose and may dismiss a Chapter 13 case which is filed in bad faith."); *In re Steele*, 34 B.R. 172, 173 (Bankr. M.D. Ala. 1983) ("[w]here the court finds that a petition and plan are not filed in good faith, confirmation may be denied and the case dismissed. . . ."). As such, the bankruptcy court properly denied confirmation of the present Chapter 13 plan and properly dismissed the Chapter 13 petition, and that judgment is due to be AFFIRMED . . . .

POST-CASE FOLLOW-UP

In retrospect this looks like a fairly egregious case of abuse: the timing of the filing to stop the state-court ordered sale of the property, the misstatements of the debtor in her schedules and testimony, the proposal to discharge unsecured debt when she had ample resources to pay it. Would you have had any ethical or professional qualms about taking this case for this debtor? Recall our discussion in Chapter Eight, Section A, regarding the duty of inquiry and certification by the attorney for the debtor who signs the petition. It is unclear whether the debtor had assistance of counsel in completing her petition and schedules and the case makes no reference to any breach of duty by an attorney but if Hatem had come to a law office where you were working, would you have recommended that the supervising attorney take this case and file a petition and schedules containing the information these did? What inquiry should an attorney have made into the circumstances of ownership and value of the property that might have altered what appeared on these schedules?

In re Hatem: Real Life Applications

1. *In re Hatem* establishes that the good faith inquiry involves looking at "the totality of circumstances surrounding the plan." Look again at the 14 total factors that the Eleventh Circuit in *Kitchens* identified as relevant to that broad inquiry. Determine if the courts of your federal district or circuit follow the **totality of the circumstances** approach to the good faith inquiry under §1325(a).

2. Using the totality of the circumstances approach to good faith and assuming both a practical and ethical component to good faith, should the following

proposed plans meet the good faith tests for confirmation found in §§1326(a)(3) and (7)?

a. Debtor has previously filed two Chapter 13 cases to obtain a stay of fore-closure on his house. Judge in those cases lifted the stay when debtor could not propose a plan to make up arrearages on mortgage and for pay through of scheduled payments. With foreclosure scheduled to occur tomorrow, debtor now files a third Chapter 13 invoking the automatic stay. Plan proposes to pay one-half of the arrearages during the term of the plan plus pay through of future scheduled payments.

b. Debtor who is current on both her secured obligations, mortgage on house and lien on vehicle, proposes Chapter 13 plan that will enable her to hold on to house and vehicle with pay through even though both secured debts are dramatically undersecured and could be stripped down. Plan proposes to pay sole unsecured creditor hospital nothing and to discharge that debt. If strip down of secured debts had been proposed, unsecured debtors could have received 20 cents on the dollar of what is owed. Would it matter if hospital had provided emergency lifesaving services to a child of the debtor? Would it matter if the debtor's ex-spouse was now married to the hospital administrator and the debtor and administrator had had physical confrontations?

c. Debtor proposed 100 percent plan though current disposable income inadequate to pay more than 40 percent of unsecured claims. Debtor explains that aged aunt likely to die soon and has promised to leave him large sum of money that will fully fund plan. Would it matter if debtor explained that he's enrolled in a "Get Rich Quick by Purchasing Foreclosed Properties" seminar and expects to be a millionaire within 12 months?

d. Debtor proposes a 10 percent plan but there is proof he turned down a significant promotion at work that would have provided sufficient income to fund a 50 percent plan. Debtor told supervisor he appreciated promotion offer but didn't feel he could do the job adequately with all this debt hanging over him. Would it matter if debtor told supervisor he didn't want to make more money just to see it go to creditors and to please consider him for promotion again when Chapter 13 case is over?

Recall that the Chapter 13 debtor is required to make the first payments on his or her proposed plan to the trustee within 30 days following the filing of the petition or the proposal of the plan, whichever is earlier, per §1326(a)(1), and that the standing trustee retains these preconfirmation payments until the plan is confirmed, per §1326(a)(2). Once the plan is confirmed, §1326(a)(2) requires the trustee to distribute funds received under the plan "as soon as is practicable."

If the court declines to confirm the plan, the debtor may propose an alternative modified plan or, pursuant to §1307(a), may convert the case to a liquidation case under Chapter 7 without the need for court permission so long as the debtor meets the eligibility criteria for that chapter. One option not open to the debtor who fails to achieve plan confirmation is an immediate appeal of that decision as of right. In *Bullard v. Blue Hills Banks*, 135 S. Ct. 1686

(2015), the Supreme Court held that a bankruptcy court order denying confirmation of a Chapter 13 plan is not a final appealable order in a case or proceeding within the scope of 28 U.S.C. §158(a) so long as the debtor retains the option to propose an alternative modified plan for confirmation. Interlocutory appeal "with leave of the court" under §158(a)(3) may still be available to the debtor unable to appeal as a matter of right due to *Bullard*.

C. ▶ Living with the Confirmed Chapter 13 Plan

Pursuant to §1327(a), the provisions of a confirmed plan bind the debtor and each creditor. Sections 1327(b) and (c) provide that, except as otherwise provided in the plan, upon confirmation, the property of the estate vests in the debtor free and clear of any claim or interest of any creditor provided for in the plan, unless the plan or the order of confirmation state otherwise. The idea is that, upon filing the petition, the bankruptcy estate is created and is subject to the control of the court per §§1306(a) and 541. However, upon confirmation, per §1306(b), right to possession of all the property not surrendered remains with the debtor, not the trustee as in a Chapter 7. And, per §1306(a), postpetition earnings and other property acquired by the debtor are considered property of the estate subject to the terms of the plan. Note carefully the exception to this automatic revesting of the property of the estate in the debtor carved out in §§1327(b) and (c): "Except as otherwise provided in the plan or the order confirming the plan." We will have more to say about this exception.

After confirmation, it is up to the debtor to make the plan succeed. The debtor must make the payments to the standing trustee either directly or through payroll deduction and must make sure that any payments to be made to creditors outside the plan are made as well, either by him- or herself or by a third party. And the debtor must accept living under the strictures of what is essentially a fixed budget for the term of the plan.

Furthermore, while confirmation of the plan entitles the debtor to retain property as long as payments are made, §1305(c) has been interpreted by the courts to mean that the Chapter 13 debtor may not incur new debt after the Chapter 13 petition has been filed without consulting with and obtaining the permission of the standing trustee. The reason for that limitation is that new debt may compromise the debtor's ability to complete the plan. The only exceptions to this requirement are recurring living expenses that were anticipated when the plan was confirmed and emergency expenses the debtor incurs without time to seek prior permission from the trustee.

EXAMPLE

> If the debtor, or a dependent, living under a confirmed plan has a medical emergency, or if a vehicle breaks down and needs immediate repair, the debt incurred is allowable and the creditor can file a postpetition claim to be paid.

A debtor incurring unapproved new debt due to an emergency situation must seek the standing trustee's ratification of the expense promptly after it has been incurred or risk a motion by the trustee of dismissal of the case (dismissal is discussed in Section F). The limitations on incurring postpetition debt are normally set out in the plan itself. (See Paragraph 6 of the Matthews' plan, Illustration 15-b and Document 18 in the Matthews case file.)

If the debtor fails to make the payments due under the confirmed plan, the court may dismiss the case or convert it to a liquidation case under Chapter 7, pursuant to §1307(c), on the motion of the trustee or an unpaid creditor. If the payments that are to be made to the standing trustee are not received as called for by the plan, the trustee's office will typically contact the debtor's lawyer or the debtor to find out what the problem is. The trustee has some discretion to work with a debtor who has gotten behind to allow the debtor time to catch up on his or her payments. When a motion to dismiss or convert the case is made due to delinquencies in payments under the plan bankruptcy judges may also exercise discretion to allow the debtor some time to make up the missed payments before granting the relief requested if they are convinced the debtor has good intentions and a reasonable chance of making up the delinquencies.

EXAMPLE

Assume that a year after confirmation of the Matthews' Chapter 13 plan Roger is laid off and their plan payments become delinquent. The trustee or creditors may move the court to dismiss or convert the case. If Roger appears before the court and explains that the layoff was due to no fault of his own, that he is desperately seeking new employment, and is confident of finding a job within 30 to 45 days, the court may stay a ruling on the motion to give him time to find a new job, make up the deficiencies, and begin making regular contributions to the plan again. The hearing on the motion will likely be continued for some number of days until Roger can return and report back to the court.

D. ▶ Modifying a Confirmed Chapter 13 Plan

Sometimes events occur that call for a plan to be modified after it has been confirmed. The debtor may lose his or her job, have to change jobs, or take time off from a job due to illness, or the debtor may incur new unexpected expenses (e.g., medical expenses due to health problems, a new child). Or the debtor may have a significant increase in income, enabling the debtor to pay more than at the time of confirmation.

Section 1329(a) authorizes the debtor, the trustee, or a creditor to file a **motion to modify plan** with the court. The matter is determined after notice and a hearing, which, as we know, means the proposed modification will be approved without a hearing unless an objection to modification is filed. Notice is provided using Official Form 2310B, Order Fixing Time to Object to Proposed Modification of Confirmed Chapter 13 Plan.

Section 1329(c) requires that, to be approved, the modified plan must comply with all the requirements of §§1322 and 1325 that we considered in connection with the original plan, including the good faith requirement. Assuming that the proposed modification does comply with those requirements, §1329(a) provides that a modification can propose to (1) increase or reduce the amount to be paid on a particular class of claims; (2) extend or reduce the time for payments called for in the plan; (3) alter the amount to be distributed to a creditor under the plan to account for payments made to that creditor outside the plan; or (4) as added by BAPCPA, reduce amounts to be paid under the plan by an amount expended by the debtor to purchase health insurance for the debtor or a dependent so long as the amounts are reasonable and necessary. Note that though a modification can extend or reduce the time for payments called for in the plan, §1329(c) provides that the plan, as modified, cannot, in any event, extend more than five years beyond the time that the first payment was due under the original plan.

EXAMPLE

Assume a debtor is operating under a confirmed plan calling for payment of a nondischargeable priority claim in full over the first 12 months of the plan (as we know from Chapter Fifteen, Section A, priority claims must be paid in full). A month later, due to an unexpected reduction in income, the debtor seeks a modification of the plan calling for payment of the priority claim in full over 60 months. That modification can be granted but the payments to that creditor under the modified plan cannot extend more than five years beyond the date that the first payment was due under the original plan (which we know from Section A of this chapter may be an earlier date than the date the original plan was confirmed).

Per §1329(a) not only the debtor, but the standing trustee or any unsecured creditor has standing to seek a modification of a confirmed plan.

EXAMPLE

If a plan is confirmed that calls for payment of 40 percent of the debtor's allowed unsecured claims and the trustee or an unsecured creditor subject to that provision learns a year later that the debtor's income has increased significantly, the trustee or unsecured creditor may seek a modification of the plan to increase the amount to be distributed to unsecured creditors in the plan.

The typical motion to modify plan is made by the debtor seeking some relief from the commitments made in the confirmed plan based on changed circumstances or on a tardy realization that the commitments taken on were too onerous. Courts take varying approaches to such requests, some requiring a showing of a **substantial and unanticipated change in circumstances** to merit modification and rejecting mere difficulty in compliance as a legitimate ground if such difficulty was reasonably foreseeable at the time the plan was confirmed. Other courts are more lenient, noting that the Code itself does not impose any such requirements on the approval of a modification request and concluding that Congress intended to leave the determination of sufficient grounds for modification to the discretion of the bankruptcy judge.

IN RE MEEKS

237 B.R. 856, 859 (Bankr. M.D. Fla. 1999)

OPINION: JENNAMANN, Bankruptcy Judge.

The Debtors filed for Chapter 13 relief on November 21, 1997. GMAC filed a claim in their bankruptcy case for $6,822.18, of which $5,888.16 was secured by the Debtors' 1988 Cadillac Deville. GMAC had a remaining unsecured claim of $934.02.

On September 22, 1998, the Debtors confirmed a Chapter 13 plan which provided that the Debtors would pay GMAC the full amount of GMAC's secured claim over 36 months rather than the 14 months remaining under the original contract. Only four months after confirmation, on January 29, 1999, the Debtors filed a Verified Motion to Modify Confirmed Chapter 13 Plan. The Debtors alleged that a new baby caused unexpected financial problems. As such, the Debtors sought permission to surrender the Cadillac to GMAC and, significantly, to also reduce their plan payments by the $174.00 per month which is the amount allocated to pay GMAC's secured claim. In addition, the Debtors wished to reclassify any remaining claim due to GMAC after the sale of the vehicle as unsecured.

The Chapter 13 Trustee consented to the modification, and the Court granted the Debtors' Motion to Modify the Plan on an ex parte basis. No notice was given to GMAC. Thereafter, GMAC brought this Motion to vacate the Modification Order.

In the meantime, GMAC sought and was granted relief from the automatic stay in order to take possession of the Cadillac. GMAC obtained possession and later sold the vehicle. After crediting all sums received from the sale, GMAC has a remaining amount due on its secured claim of $2,165.28.

The issue presented by the Motion is whether, under §1329 of the Bankruptcy Code, a Debtor may modify a confirmed Chapter 13 plan to surrender collateral subject to a security interest and then reclassify the unpaid remainder of the Creditor's claim as unsecured. GMAC argues that §1329 does not allow the reclassification of claims and that such a modification is inequitable and unfair to GMAC. The Debtors argue that §1329 does permit the reclassification of claims despite GMAC's objection.

Res Judicata Does Not Prevent Modification of Confirmed Chapter 13 Plan for Certain Specified Purposes. Section 1327(a) provides that "[T]he provisions of a confirmed plan bind the debtor and each creditor, . . . whether or not the creditor has objected to, has accepted, or has rejected the plan." U.S.C. 1327(a) (1998). Accordingly, a confirmed plan is res judicata as to any issues resolved or subject to resolution at the confirmation hearing. Among these issues is the amount of a secured claim. Under §1325(a)(5)(B)(ii), a chapter 13 plan must pay the full value of any allowed secured claim. 11 U.S.C. §1325(a)(5)(B)(ii) (1998). Accordingly, the value of a secured claim is fixed as of the effective date of the plan. *In re Dunlap*, 215 B.R. 867, 869 (Bankr. E.D. Ark. 1997).

However, §1329 specifically allows a debtor to modify a confirmed chapter 13 plan for three specific purposes. Section 1329 provides, in relevant part:

(a) At any time after confirmation of the plan but before the completion of payments under such plan, the plan may be modified, upon request of the debtor . . . to—

(1) increase or reduce the amount of payments on claims of a particular class provided for by the plan;

(2) extend or reduce the time for such payments; or

(3) alter the amount of the distribution to a creditor whose claim is provided for by the plan to the extent necessary to take account of any payment of such claim other than under the plan.

11 U.S.C. §1329(a).

In order to overcome the res judicata effect of §1327(a), some courts require a debtor to demonstrate a substantial, unanticipated change in circumstances justifying the requested modification. See, e.g., *Arnold v. Weast (In re Arnold)*, 869 F.2d 240 (4th Cir. 1989); *Dunlap*, 215 B.R. at 869; *In re Rimmer*, 143 B.R. 871, 873 (Bankr. W.D. Tenn. 1992). Generally, these courts reason that "§1329(a) should not be abused by repetitive modification and . . . the confirmation should have a significant degree of finality." *In re Klus*, 173 B.R. 51, 59 (Bankr. D. Conn. 1994).

Section 1329(a) does not contain any express requirement that an unanticipated change in circumstances is necessary to justify modification. Rather, §1329(a) specifically permits debtors and creditors to modify the plan for the limited purposes listed. The legislative history indicates that Congress created §1329 to allow debtors to modify their confirmed plan to address certain problems arising after confirmation. H.R. Rep. No. 95-595 at 265 (1977). However, Congress did not include any language indicating an intent to make a substantial change of circumstances a threshold requirement for any such modification of the plan. See *In re Powers*, 140 B.R. 476, 479 (Bankr. N.D. Ill. 1992). As the United States Court of Appeals for the Seventh Circuit stated:

The Code, in this instance §1329, does not require any threshold requirement for a modification and we will not use the legislative history to create a rule where none exists.

Matter of Witkowski, 16 F.3d 739, 742 (7th Cir. 1994). Neither this court nor other courts should require new hurdles for modification of a Chapter 13 plan which Congress neither contemplated nor enacted.

Furthermore, res judicata on its own does not create a requirement for a showing of a substantial change in circumstances. Res judicata does not apply when the plain language of a statute demonstrates that it should not apply. Id. at 744 . . . . Here, §1329(a) gives the debtor, unsecured creditors and the trustee the right to modify a confirmed plan without any threshold requirement. As such, §1329 and the entire Bankruptcy Code indicate a clear intention that res judicata does not apply to the limited modifications permitted for by §1329. See Id.

Accordingly, the Debtors need not demonstrate a substantial, unanticipated change in circumstances in order to modify their confirmed chapter 13 plan. However, neither can Chapter 13 debtors simply modify their plans willy-nilly. Section 1329(a) only permits the modification of a confirmed plan for three specific limited purposes.

[The court then disallowed the modification on the basis that none of the grounds for modification in §1329 permit the amount of an allowed secured claim to be modified by treating it as unsecured.]

POST-CASE FOLLOW-UP

For a good opinion justifying the use of the substantial and unanticipated change standard for plan modification, read *In re Mellors*, 372 B.R. 763 (Bankr. W.D. Pa. 2007) (it is proper to use a substantial and unanticipated change standard for proposed plan modifications under §1329 since §1327 providing that a confirmed plan binds the debtor and each creditor evidences Congress's intent that confirmed plans should be accorded a great deal of finality).

The rules governing plan modification are important because so many Chapter 13 plans are modified, many more than once. That is due, of course, to the mandatory length of a Chapter 13 plan, three to five years. As we all know, financial circumstances can change dramatically in that length of time. Though most modifications are sought by debtors claiming negative changed circumstances that call for paying unsecured creditors less or over a longer period than the original confirmed plan called for, there can also be positive changed circumstances enabling a debtor to pay more to unsecured creditors or to pay more quickly than the original plan called for. Though the Code does not require it, many standing trustees require Chapter 13 debtors to include language in their plan requiring the debtor to advise the trustee of both adverse and favorable changes in their income or assets, or to provide postpetition tax returns to the trustee during the term of the plan, or directing that income tax refunds over a certain amount (e.g., $1,000) be paid directly from the IRS to the trustee. Those trustees typically also require the plan to provide, as allowed by §§1327(b) and (c) discussed in Section C above, that the property of the estate will not revest in the debtor upon confirmation so that the postconfirmation income of the debtor remains property of the estate throughout the term of the plan.

In re Meeks : | Real Life Applications

Chapter 13 debtors operating under confirmed plans experience the changes set out in the list below. Using the standard for modification approval set out in *In re Meeks* determine if the modification would likely be allowed. Then make the same determination using the modification approval standard set out in *In re Mellors*.

a. Debtor living under a confirmed 100 percent plan of 36 months' duration asks that the plan be converted to five years so debtor will have more flexibility in his budget.

b. Debtor's aged parent unexpectedly comes to live with debtor significantly increasing his living expenses.
c. Debtor's unemployed adult daughter who was living with her and was pregnant at the time of plan confirmation has the baby and debtor claims increased expenses due to the newborn child.
d. Debtor's primary vehicle for family use, which was 15 years old at the time of plan confirmation, fails and cannot be fixed and debtor wants to buy a new car to replace it.
e. Debtor's primary vehicle for family use, which was five years old at the time of plan confirmation, is totaled in an accident and debtor wants to buy a new car to replace it.
f. Debtor experiences postconfirmation conversion to a new faith that requires tithing and debtor needs additional income to comply.
g. Debtor loses the job he had at the time of confirmation that paid $33,000 per year; he finds new job paying $32,000 per year but that is 10 miles further from his home.

E. ▶ The Chapter 13 Discharge

1. Timing of the Discharge

Confirmation of a Chapter 13 plan does *not* result in an immediate discharge of the debts not to be paid under the plan. Section 1328(a) of the Code provides that the discharge in a Chapter 13 is granted only upon completion of the plan. One exception to that rule is that an early discharge can be granted under §1328(b) for hardship (thus sometimes called a **hardship discharge**), if the debtor can establish the following three requirements:

Discharge Permanent relief from certain debts pursuant to order of the bankruptcy court.

1.   The failure to complete payments under the plan is beyond the control of the debtor.
2.   The payments made to unsecured creditors up to the time of discharge are at least as much as they would have received in a Chapter 7 liquidation (this is sometimes called the good faith test of §1328(b)).
3.   Modification of the plan is not feasible.

A hardship discharge is reserved for extreme cases, as where a debtor becomes permanently disabled and is unable to further fund any feasible plan. Often the reasons a debtor gives to support a request for hardship discharge are similar to those given in support of a motion to modify the plan. Granting an early discharge is a more extreme measure because it means creditors won't be paid as much as anticipated when the plan was confirmed, thus the requirement that the debtor seeking early discharge demonstrate that plan modification is not feasible. Moreover, the Chapter 13 debtor who does receive a hardship discharge gets only the discharge of debts available to a Chapter 7 debtor that we considered in Chapter Twelve and not the more expansive super discharge that Chapter 13 debtors receive upon completion of plan payments (to be discussed later in this section).

Many courts have interpreted the first element of the test for hardship discharge—that the failure to complete plan payments is beyond control of the debtor—to require a showing of **catastrophic circumstances** by the debtor. See, e.g., *In re Nelson*, 135 B.R. 304, 307 (N.D. Ill. 1991) (courts will approve a request for hardship discharge only in the presence of "catastrophic circumstances" citing K. Lundin, Chapter 13 Bankruptcy §9.8 at 9-26 (1990), a leading authority on Chapter 13 cases, as suggesting that circumstances that would justify hardship discharge have to be the "truly worst of the awfuls—something more than just the temporary loss of a job or temporary physical disability"). Not all courts agree. See, e.g., *In re Edwards*, 207 B.R. 728, 730-31 (Bankr. N.D. Fla. 1997):

> I am unable to conclude that the law requires a debtor seeking a hardship discharge under §1328(b) must demonstrate the existence of catastrophic circumstances. First, I do not believe that the language of §1328(b)(1) requires such a standard. Secondly, given the requirement of §1328(b)(2) that unsecured creditors have received at least that which they would have received in a liquidation under Chapter 7, and the limited extent of a discharge received under §1328(b), I can find no justification for exacting such a standard. Unlike the "super discharge" provided to debtors pursuant to §1328(a) upon completion of all payments under a plan, the hardship discharge under §1328(b) is the same discharge received under Chapter 7 with all of the exceptions the discharge specified in §523(a). To deny a debtor who has made every effort to comply with a Chapter 13 plan the benefits of any discharge in bankruptcy when, despite his best efforts, economic circumstances prevent him from completing his payments would punish that debtor for attempting to repay his creditors under Chapter 13 in the first place.
>
> Where a debtor is unable to complete payments under a Chapter 13 plan due to economic circumstances that did not exist nor were foreseeable at the time of confirmation of the plan, where those circumstances are beyond the debtor's control, and where the debtor has made every effort to overcome those circumstances but is unable to complete his plan payments, then I think the requirement of §1328(b)(1) has been met.

P-H 16-c: Chapter 13 debtors in the following circumstances have moved for early discharge and all satisfy the §1328(b)(2) requirement. Determine if these debtors have satisfied the §§1328(b)(1) and (3) requirements. Make that determination first using the "catastrophic circumstances" test for §1328(b)(1). Then make that determination using the *In re Edwards* test for §1328(b)(1).

a. Debtor says his girlfriend has moved out since plan confirmation and she helped him with groceries and utility payments most of the time. Debtor has not filed any motion to modify his plan.

b. Debtor who had been laid off construction jobs three times in the two years preceding his Chapter 13 filing is laid off again and now cannot find other employment despite vigorous search; has no disposable income.

c. Debtor who had steady employment when the Chapter 13 was filed and the plan confirmed is fired for stealing from her employer and cannot find other employment despite vigorous search; no disposable income.

d. Debtor who had steady employment when the Chapter 13 was filed and the plan confirmed is laid off for no fault of her own three weeks before filing the motion for early discharge. Has been vigorously searching for other employment since but no leads yet. Will run out of funds to make plan payments in another 30 days.

e. Debtor, a car salesman, has been seriously and permanently injured in a car accident. His disabilities will render him unable to ever work again. He has no pension or disability insurance. Has applied for SSI but if approved it will not provide sufficient disposable income to fund a Chapter 13 plan. Would it matter if the accident were the debtor's fault? If he was driving drunk? If he had three prior DUIs all prepetition?

Official Form 3180W is used for the normal Chapter 13 discharge and Official Form 3180WH for the hardship discharge.

2. Requirements for Receiving a Chapter 13 Discharge

In addition to completing the plan payments, receiving a discharge under Chapter 13 is contingent upon meeting other requirements as follows:

- Certification by the debtor (if appropriate) that all domestic support obligations called for in the plan or that otherwise came due prior to making such certification have been paid (§1328(a) using Official Form 2830)
- The debtor has not received a discharge in a prior Chapter 13 case (within two years preceding the order for relief in the instant case or within four years in a prior Chapter 7, 11, or 12 case; §1328(f))
- The debtor has completed the postpetition course in financial management (§1328(g); see Document 20 in the Matthews case file)

Unlike Chapter 7, creditors have no standing to object to a debtor's discharge under Chapter 13. Of course, they can object to the plan's confirmation or modification and move to dismiss or convert the case if plan payments are not being made (see discussion in Section F), but only the trustee can object to a discharge under Chapter 13.

3. Scope of the Chapter 13 Discharge: Nondischargeable Debts

Nondischargeable debt A debt that may not be discharged in bankruptcy.

The discharge releases the debtor from all unpaid claims designated for nonpayment in the plan or disallowed under §502, with limited exceptions. Sections 1328(a) and (d) set forth the debts that cannot be discharged in a Chapter 13, and those are summarized in Illustration 16-b.

Just because a debt is nondischargeable does not mean it cannot be dealt with in the Chapter 13 plan. Payments on nonpriority unsecured but nondischargeable

Illustration 16-b: DEBTS THAT CANNOT BE DISCHARGED IN A CHAPTER 13 BANKRUPTCY

- Long-term obligations, such as the home mortgage extending beyond the term of the plan and that the plan contemplated would continue to be paid [§1328(a)(1) & §1322(b)(5)]
- Unpaid taxes on returns filed two years preceding the petition or on returns not filed or for fraudulent returns [§1328(a)(1) & §523(a)(1)(B)(C)]
- Debts for money, property, services, or an extension of credit obtained by fraudulent pretenses or by the use of fraudulent financial statements [§1328(a)(1) & §523(a)(2)(A)(B)]
- Last-minute consumer cash advances or spending for luxury goods or services [§1328(a)(1) & §523(a)(2)(C)]
- Debts that were not listed on the debtor's schedules so that the creditor could not file a timely proof of claim [§1328(a)(1) & §523(a)(3)]
- Debts arising from the debtor's fraud or defalcation while acting in a fiduciary capacity [§1328(a)(1) & §523(a)(4)]
- Domestic support obligations, such as alimony and child support [§1328(a)(1) & §523(a)(5)]
- Student loans, unless the debtor can convince the court that not discharging this obligation will work an undue hardship on the debtor or his dependents [§1328(a)(1) & §523(a)(8)]
- Claims arising from the wrongful death or personal injury caused by the debtor's driving under the influence of drugs or alcohol [§1328(a)(1) & §523(a)(9)]
- Restitution or fine included on the sentence of the debtor for a crime [§1328(a)(3)]
- Restitution or damages awarded in a civil action against the debtor based on willful or malicious injury that caused personal injury or death [§1328(a)(4)]
- Postpetition debts for consumer necessities allowable under §1305(a)(2), for which trustee approval could have been sought but was not [§1328(d)]

debt can be modified during the term of the plan even though the underlying debt is not dischargeable.

EXAMPLE

Payments due from the debtor on a nondischargeable student loan debt may be modified during the term of the plan even where the entire indebtedness will not be paid off during the plan and the debt will not be discharged in the Chapter 13 proceeding. The advantage to the Chapter 13 debtor, of course, is that, if the plan is approved, the automatic stay remains in effect on such nondischargeable debt until the case is over.

Most of the nondischargeable debts you see in Illustration 16-b are identical to the debts declared nondischargeable in a Chapter 7, pursuant to §523(a). You may want to go back and read the discussion of these various nondischargeable obligations (see Chapter Twelve, Section A).

However, a slightly more generous discharge is available under a Chapter 13 than under a Chapter 7, giving rise to the practitioner's characterization of the §1328(a) discharge as a **super discharge** as compared to the Chapter 7 discharge under §727, which is limited by all the exceptions contained in §523(a). In a Chapter 13, debts or claims arising out of the willful or malicious injury to the property (but not the person) of another, referenced in §523(a)(6), and certain fines and penalties imposed by the government, referenced in §523(a)(7), can be discharged. As noted above in connection with *In re Edwards*, §1328(c) provides that a Chapter 13 debtor receiving an early hardship discharge under §1328(b) does not discharge any of the debts listed in §523(a); that debtor does not receive the super discharge of §1328(a).

EXAMPLE

> Assume an individual is sued for civil damages by another who alleges that the individual committed an intentional and malicious physical assault with a baseball bat on his automobile, totally destroying it. The case goes to trial and a verdict in the amount of $20,000 is returned for the plaintiff. A final judgment is entered on the jury's verdict. The final judgment is now enforceable. If the individual against whom the verdict has been returned consults a debtor's attorney as to whether the judgment can be discharged in bankruptcy, he will likely be told that cannot be accomplished in a Chapter 7 case but might be accomplished in a Chapter 13 case subject to the Code requirements for confirmation and discharge already discussed.

P-H 16-d: Look again at Illustration 16-a. Assume the individual described in the last example files for Chapter 13 relief and proposes a plan to pay all his creditors 100 percent over five years, except for the judgment creditor in the lawsuit described. The plan proposes to pay nothing on that claim and to discharge it. Which criterion for confirmation of a Chapter 13 plan is the judgment creditor most likely to say is not satisfied by this plan? How would you rule on that issue if you were the bankruptcy judge? Would it matter that the debtor can show that in fact all of his projected disposable income for the five years of the plan will be needed to pay the other creditors 100 percent?

The **order granting discharge** will follow Official Form 3180W, Order of Discharge.

Note that Chapter 13 does not contain a provision similar to §727, which sets out various grounds for denying any discharge at all to a Chapter 7 debtor (see Chapter Twelve, Section B). The types of conduct that might serve as a basis for denying a discharge in a Chapter 7 (fraud, dishonesty, lack of cooperation, etc.) will be relevant in the decision to confirm the Chapter 13 debtor's plan regarding whether it was proposed in good faith. They will also be relevant in deciding to dismiss or convert the Chapter 13 case, as discussed in the next section.

F. ▶ Conversion or Dismissal of a Chapter 13 Case

1. Voluntary Conversion or Dismissal

Section 1307(a) provides that the debtor can convert his or her case to a Chapter 7 liquidation at any time. Of course, the debtor wishing to convert the case will have to meet the requirements for being a Chapter 7 debtor, as stipulated in §1307(g). Conversion is accomplished by the debtor filing a **notice of conversion**. Where a Chapter 13 case is converted to Chapter 7 prior to confirmation of any plan, §1326(a)(2) directs that payments that have been made to the standing trustee but not yet distributed (recall that the debtor must begin making plan payments prior to confirmation per §1326(a)(1) and the trustee is to retain such payments until plan confirmation or denial per §1326(a)(2)) are to be returned to the debtor after deducting §503(b) administrative expenses, which are understood to include the standing trustee's fee and, in some but not all districts, the unpaid amount of the debtor's attorney's fee (recall that the attorney's fee may be paid through the plan).

Pursuant to §1307(b), the debtor may request that the court dismiss his or her Chapter 13 case at any time, and the court will grant that request unless the Chapter 13 case was itself converted from an earlier Chapter 7 or Chapter 11 case. Request for dismissal is accomplished by filing a motion for permission to dismiss the Chapter 13 case.

Where the Chapter 13 case is dismissed before confirmation but there is no conversion to Chapter 7 or any other chapter under the Code, §349, dealing generally with the effect of dismissal in any case under the Code, provides in §349(b)(3) that "[u]nless the court, for cause, orders otherwise, the dismissal . . . revests the property of the estate in the entity in which such property was vested immediately before the commencement of the case . . . ." In other words, property of the debtor goes back to the debtor upon dismissal. Do administrative claims get paid out of postpetition preconfirmation payments being held by the debtor? Usually, yes, because of the "Unless the court, for cause, otherwise orders" language of §349(b). The court will order funds held by the standing trustee returned to the debtor but, using the authority of §1326(a)(2), order payment of outstanding administrative fees first, which in some districts will include the earned but unpaid balance of the attorney's fee.

The last three paragraphs deal with what happens when there is a conversion or dismissal of a Chapter 3 case prior to plan confirmation. A question that has divided the circuits concerns what is to be done with undistributed funds in the hands of the standing trustee when a Chapter 13 debtor in good faith converts to a Chapter 7 after confirmation of his plan. In *Harris v. Viegelahn*, 135 S. Ct. 1829, 1836 (2015), the Supreme Court held that absent a bad faith conversion, §348(f) limits a converted Chapter 7 estate to property belonging to the debtor "as of the date" the original Chapter 13 petition was filed ("Conversion from Chapter 13 to Chapter 7 does not commence a new bankruptcy case. The existing case continues along another track, Chapter 7 instead of Chapter 13, without effecting a change in the date of the filing of the petition. §348(a)"). Because post–Chapter 13 petition wages do not fit that bill, such wages collected by a Chapter 13 trustee but not yet distributed to creditors pursuant to a Chapter 13 plan do not become part of a converted Chapter 7 estate and are properly paid to the debtor.

2. Involuntary Conversion or Dismissal

Sections 1307(c) and (e) provide a number of circumstances under which a party in interest (the standing trustee, U.S. Trustee, or a creditor) can move the bankruptcy court to either dismiss the Chapter 13 case or convert it to a Chapter 7, "whichever is in the best interest of creditors and the estate." Those circumstances are summarized in Illustration 16-c. **Involuntary dismissal or conversion** can be sought before or after confirmation of the Chapter 13 plan.

Illustration 16-c: GROUNDS FOR INVOLUNTARY DISMISSAL OR CONVERSION OF A CHAPTER 13 CASE UNDER §§1307(c) AND (e)

- Unreasonable delay by the debtor that is prejudicial to creditors
- Nonpayment of any required fees and charges
- Failure to timely file a plan
- Failure to commence making timely payments under the plan, as required by §1326(a)(1)
- The denial of confirmation of a plan and the denial of a request made for additional time for filing another plan or a modification of a plan
- A material default by the debtor with respect to a term of a confirmed plan
- The revocation of the order of confirmation
- The termination of a confirmed plan by reason of the occurrence of a condition specified in the plan, other than completion of payments under the plan
- Only on request of the U.S. Trustee, failure of the debtor to timely file the various schedules of assets and liabilities and statement of affairs, as required by §521
- Failure of the debtor to pay any domestic support obligation that first becomes payable after the date of the filing of the petition
- Failure of the debtor to file all tax returns due for the preceding four years by the day before the first meeting of creditors is first scheduled, as required by §1308(a)

Note that some of these grounds can arise prior to plan confirmation (e.g., failure to timely file a plan; denial of plan confirmation and failure to seek additional time to file another plan or to modify; failure to file required schedules and statements in support of the petition, etc.). When a motion to dismiss or convert is made prior to plan confirmation, the good faith of the debtor can be an issue the court will consider as part of the decision to dismiss or convert under §1307(c) (the §1307(c) grounds are not exclusive). That good faith inquiry may consider the prepetition activities of the debtor that gave rise to his or her debts, the motives of the debtor in deciding to file the Chapter 13 case, the accuracy of the disclosures made in the debtor's petition and supporting schedules, or the terms of the plan that the debtor proposes in the unconfirmed Chapter 13 plan.

However, if the motion to dismiss or convert is filed after plan confirmation, most courts will not conduct a good faith inquiry since confirmation required a finding by the court that the debtor filed the petition in good faith (§1325(a)(7)) and that the plan was proposed in good faith (§1325(a)(3)). Those courts consider that the confirmation order has res judicata effect as to the good faith issue and will focus only on the specific §1307 grounds (see, e.g., *United States v. Tucker*, 1996 WL 741510 (M.D. Fla.) (creditor's motion for summary judgment denied on issue of good faith where Chapter 13 plan was confirmed even though creditor's motion to dismiss for lack of good faith was filed and pending when confirmation occurred).

The most frequent grounds asserted in a motion to dismiss or convert is §1307(c)(4), the failure of the debtor to make the payments due under the plan either before or after plan confirmation (recall from Section A that pursuant to §1326(a)(1) the plan payments must begin within 30 days after the plan is filed or the order of relief entered, whichever is earlier without regard to confirmation). But in many cases there are good or at least plausible reasons why payments are not being made and the debtor asks for a modification in lieu of dismissal or for additional time to make up missed payments. Bankruptcy judges have considerable discretion in deciding whether to order dismissal under §1307(c)(4) and the bankruptcy court's historical role as a **court of equity**, still recognized in §105(a), is often a factor in such disputes. See, e.g., *In re Mallory*, 444 B.R. 553 (S.D. Tex. 2011) (Chapter 13 debtor who, after making plan payments for three years, unilaterally withheld plan payments from trustee for three and a half months due to debtor's contention that claim of creditor secured in debtor's home was invalid and should be challenged had insufficient defense to trustee's motion to dismiss for failure to make plan payments; equities did not favor debtor who should have moved to suspend mortgage payments until his objection to claim was decided). For the bankruptcy court's role as a court of equity, see, e.g., *In re Beaty*, 306 F.3d 915, 922 (9th Cir. 2002) ("[A] bankruptcy court is a court of equity and should invoke equitable principles and doctrines, refusing to do so only where their application would be inconsistent with the Bankruptcy Code.").

HOW MANY CHAPTER 13 CASES SUCCEED?

The available empirical data going back 20 years seems to indicate that, nationwide, only one out of every three Chapter 13 cases succeeds in the sense that the debtor pays as scheduled throughout the term of a confirmed plan and receives a discharge at the end. There is considerable variation from state to state and even district to district but nationwide that percentage looks accurate. See, e.g., *The Pretend Solution: An Empirical Study of Bankruptcy Outcomes*, 90 Tex. L. Rev. 103, 107-111 (2011) (only one in three cases filed under Chapter 13 ends in discharge); Scott F. Norberg & Andrew J. Velkey, *Debtor Discharge and Creditor Repayment in Chapter 13*, 39 Creighton L. Rev. 473, 505, n.70 (2006) ("The overall discharge rate for the debtors in the seven districts covered by the Project was exactly the oft-repeated statistic of one-third."); Gordon Bermant & Ed Flynn, *Measuring Projected Performance in Chapter 13: Comparisons Across the States*, 19 Am. Bankr. Inst. J. 22, 22 (July-Aug. 2000); Henry E. Hildebrand, III, *Administering Chapter 13—At What Price?*, 13 Am. Bankr. Inst. J. 16, 16 (July-Aug. 1994); Katherine Porter, *The Pretend Solution: An Empirical Study of Bankruptcy Outcomes*, 90 Tex. L. Rev. 103 (2011).

But not everyone agrees that an uncompleted Chapter 13 plan is necessarily a failure. See, e.g., Gordon Bermant, *What Is "Success" in Chapter 13? Why Should We Care?*, 23 Am. Bankr. Inst. J. 20, 65 (Sept. 2004) arguing that plan completion and discharge are not essential to success if the plan goes on long enough that debtor's finances are substantially reordered and the ship more or less righted.

CHAPTER SUMMARY

The Chapter 13 plan must be filed with the petition or within 14 days thereafter. The debtor must begin making payments to the trustee under the plan within 30 days of the entry of the order for relief or filing the proposed plan even if the plan has not yet been confirmed.

There are a number of criteria for confirmation of a Chapter 13 plan, and any party in interest may object to confirmation, in which event a confirmation hearing will be conducted by the court. The deadline for objections is normally set by local court rule. A creditor who fails to timely object to a plan prior to confirmation may be deemed to have accepted the plan but the court can still deny confirmation to a plan that does not comply with the Code. In deciding whether the plan has been proposed in good faith the court looks to the totality of the circumstances to determine whether the plan will achieve a result consistent with the objectives and purposes of the Code.

Upon confirmation of a Chapter 13 plan the right to possession of property of the estate not surrendered by the debtor and abandoned by the trustee remains in the debtor subject to the requirements of the plan. Earnings and other property acquired by the debtor from the commencement of the case through its conclusion are also property of the estate subject to the terms of the plan.

Once a plan is confirmed, the debtor may not incur new debt without permission of the standing trustee except for recurring living expenses or emergencies. If a debtor fails to make the payments promised under the confirmed plan, the Chapter 13 case can be dismissed or converted to a Chapter 7 liquidation. The standing trustee has discretion to work with a debtor who falls behind on plan payments, as do bankruptcy judges when a motion to dismiss or convert is filed.

A confirmed plan can be modified on motion of the debtor, trustee, or creditors, to increase or reduce plan payments, extend or reduce the time for payments. The plan as modified must comply with all Code requirements for confirmation. Some courts require the debtor to demonstrate a substantial unforeseen change of circumstance to justify a modification.

A discharge of debts not paid through the plan is granted upon completion of the plan unless the court grants an earlier hardship discharge where the debtor can show that the inability to complete plan payments is beyond his control, modification is not feasible, and unsecured creditors have received more than they would in a Chapter 7. As in a Chapter 7, some debts cannot be discharged in a Chapter 13 although Chapter 13 does recognize a super discharge in comparison to Chapter 7 in that debts arising out of the willful or malicious injury to property and certain fines and penalties imposed by the government may be discharged in Chapter 13.

A Chapter 13 debtor may voluntarily dismiss his case or convert it to another chapter of the Code so long as he meets the criteria to be a debtor under that alternative chapter. Undistributed funds in the hands of the standing trustee when a Chapter 13 debtor in good faith converts to a Chapter 7 are returned to the debtor. A number of grounds exist upon which a Chapter 13 case may be involuntarily dismissed or converted to Chapter 7, the most frequently asserted of which is failure of the debtor to make required payments to the standing trustee before or after plan confirmation.

REVIEW QUESTIONS

1. How long after the Chapter 13 petition is filed must the debtor's proposed plan be filed?
2. How soon after the first meeting of creditors is the confirmation hearing on a Chapter 13 plan to be held?

3. Explain how issues regarding implied consent, waiver, and res judicata arise in the context of the objections to confirmation of a Chapter 13 plan.

4. Explain the "totality of the circumstances" test for determining the good faith requirement for confirmation of a Chapter 13 plan.

5. What right does a Chapter 13 debtor have to incur new debt during the term of the plan?

6. Explain what typically happens when a Chapter 13 debtor fails to make scheduled plan payments to the standing trustee.

7. Describe the substantial and unanticipated change standard for Chapter 13 plan modification. What is the alternative standard used by many courts?

8. What are the three requirements for receiving a hardship discharge by a Chapter 13 debtor? What is the catastrophic circumstances requirement utilized by some courts?

9. What is the super discharge available in Chapter 13 and what makes it so super?

10. May a Chapter 13 debtor convert his or her case to one under Chapter 7? May the debtor dismiss his or her case at any time? List five grounds upon which a Chapter 13 case may be involuntarily dismissed or converted to one under Chapter 7.

WORDS AND PHRASES TO REMEMBER

catastrophic circumstances
confirmation hearing
court of equity
good faith
hardship discharge
implied consent
involuntary dismissal or conversion
local rules of court
motion to modify plan

notice of conversion
order granting discharge
party in interest
res judicata
substantial and unanticipated change
    in circumstances
super discharge
totality of the circumstances
waiver

TO LEARN MORE: A number of TLM activities to accompany this chapter are accessible on the companion web site for this textbook at http://aspen-lawschool.com/books/Parsons_Debt4e/.

THE BUSINESS BANKRUPTCY CASE

Introduction

In Part C we will focus on the Chapter 11 business reorganization proceeding. Although a business entity may simply liquidate under Chapter 7, a business seeking to reorganize will choose to file under Chapter 11. After Chapter 7 and Chapter 13 cases, Chapter 11 business reorganization proceedings are the next most commonly filed cases under the Code.

After a detailed examination of the Chapter 11 business reorganization proceeding, we will take a brief look at the three remaining types of bankruptcy cases that may be filed under the Code, all of which are types of business bankruptcies but infrequently filed: the Chapter 12 reorganization proceeding for the family farmer or family fisherman with regular income, the Chapter 9 adjustment of debts for a municipality, and the Chapter 15 cross-border bankruptcy proceeding.

Chapter Seventeen:

The Chapter 11 Business Reorganization—Filing the Case

KEY CONCEPTS

- Chapter 11 bankruptcy is a business reorganization proceeding for an entity debtor or an individual debtor with primarily business debts
- Upon filing of a Chapter 11 petition, the debtor continues to operate the business as a debtor in possession though a trustee may be appointed for cause including fraud, dishonesty, incompetence, or gross mismanagement by the DIP
- The automatic stay goes into effect upon filing a Chapter 11 petition and the U.S. Trustee appoints a creditors' committee usually consisting of the seven largest unsecured creditors of the debtor and which serves as a party in interest during the case
- The debtor has the exclusive right for 120 days following filing of the petition to file a proposed plan of reorganization but after 180 days, any party in interest may propose a plan
- The debtor in possession may utilize the turnover and avoidance powers of a bankruptcy trustee to recover property of the estate
- After the petition is filed, the debtor in possession may use or sell property of the estate in the ordinary course of its business without court approval but must obtain such approval to use or sell property other than in the ordinary course of its business
- In most Chapter 11 cases the debtor in possession will file first day motions seeking authorization to use cash collateral, to pay prepetition claims of critical vendors, to pay prepetition priority claims for employee wages and benefits, and for authorization to use current accounts

A. Overview of Chapter 11

1. The Purpose of Chapter 11

Individuals with primarily business debt and most business entities may **liquidate** under Chapter 7 of the Code. The individual Chapter 7 debtor will be able to exempt certain property as discussed in Chapter Eight, Section B, and will receive a discharge as discussed in Chapter Twelve. The entity debtor can neither exempt property nor receive a discharge of debt under Chapter 7; it will simply cease existence following liquidation of its assets. As we now know, Chapter 13 of the Code is a type of reorganization proceeding for an individual debtor with a regular source of income and thus is not available to an entity debtor. But there is a procedure under the Code for a business that does not want to liquidate its assets but only to reorganize its finances while it receives protection from the collection efforts of its creditors. That procedure is the Chapter 11 bankruptcy.

A Chapter 11 bankruptcy is known as a **business reorganization** proceeding. Although qualifying individuals may file for Chapter 11 relief, it is used mostly by **entity debtors** that need to reorganize their finances under bankruptcy court supervision as an alternative to liquidation. Chapter 11 shares the same underlying purpose of Chapter 13—to enable a debtor to reorganize—but it is much more complex. It is the difference between reorganizing the finances of an individual consumer or couple and the finances of an ongoing business that may have millions of dollars in both assets and debt; dozens or even hundreds of creditors; dozens, hundreds, or even thousands of employees; and owners eager to protect their investment in the business (their **equity interest**).

The financial affairs of a typical Chapter 11 debtor involve not only more transactions *quantity-wise* than a typical Chapter 13 debtor, but also more *quality-wise*, in the sense of legal sophistication and complexity.

EXAMPLE

Think of the shopping mall nearest to where you live. Imagine if the owner of the mall filed for Chapter 11 relief. We might discover that the "owner" of the mall is a limited partnership with a single corporate general partner and several limited partners. The corporate general partner is in turn owned by three individuals who have signed personal guaranties and mortgaged their homes to guaranty the corporate debt but not specifically the limited partnership debt. The limited partners in the limited partnership are a variety of wealthy individuals from around the state, who have not only made a capital investment in the limited partnership but who have also loaned it money and hold promissory notes issued by the limited partnership. Those notes, however, are subordinated to the master promissory note issued to the primary creditor of the company that holds a first mortgage on the mall property and a second secured position as to all personal property of the limited partnership. The corporate general partner has also issued corporate bonds to raise capital, some of which are convertible to stock in the corporation and all of which were purchased by another limited partnership. Sound like this could get complicated? How does the complexity of your personal financial situation compare with that?

As this example may suggest, those who are planning to work in the Chapter 11 area will benefit from studying accounting, business associations, and business financing.

2. Eligibility to File a Chapter 11 Case

Section 109(d) provides generally that any "person" (see Chapter Seven, Section A) qualifying to file for Chapter 7 liquidation qualifies to file for Chapter 11 as well. Thus, technically, qualified individuals, as well as most entity debtors, can file for Chapter 11 reorganization. But most individuals seeking to reorganize their financial affairs will choose Chapter 13, which we know is designed for individuals with relatively small amounts of debt. Individuals filing for Chapter 11 relief will be those with debt in excess of the Chapter 13 limits (see Chapter Thirteen, Section A) or those whose debt is primarily business debt rather than consumer debt.

EXAMPLE

In the previous example, the three individual shareholders in the corporation serving as general partner in the limited partnership that owns the mall may find it necessary to file for individual bankruptcy relief. Not only will the debt they have guaranteed likely exceed the limits imposed for filing under Chapter 13, it sounds like most of their debt is likely to be business related. For either reason, Chapter 11 would probably be the appropriate reorganization chapter for them to file under. Of course, if the limited partnership, the corporate general partner, or the individual shareholders of the corporation decide that a liquidation bankruptcy is necessary, they will file under Chapter 7.

The Small Business Debtor

One type of Chapter 11 debtor that receives special treatment under the Code is the debtor engaged in commercial or business activities who has aggregate, noncontingent, liquidated debts not exceeding $2,566,050 (this amount is adjusted every three years, with the next adjustment due April 1, 2019). Such a debtor is designated a **small business debtor**, pursuant to §101(51D), and its Chapter 11 filing will be designated a **small business case**, as defined in §101(51C), if

Small business debtor A Chapter 11 debtor engaged in commercial or business activities that has aggregate, noncontingent, liquidated debts not exceeding $2,566,050 and that elects to have its case treated as a small business case for expedited administration.

- the U.S. Trustee does not appoint a creditors' committee in the case (see Section C, below); or
- such a committee is appointed but the court concludes it is not sufficiently active to provide adequate oversight to the debtor.

The designation of a proceeding as a small business case under Chapter 11 has consequences we will refer to periodically in our study but, in general, it means that

- the period for plan formulation (see Chapter Nineteen, Section A) is reduced;
- the procedures for plan approval (see Chapter Nineteen, Section E) are somewhat simplified;
- the debtor is subject to closer supervision by the U.S. Trustee; and
- some specialized reporting requirements are required.

The Single Asset Real Estate Debtor

Single asset real estate debtor A Chapter 11 debtor whose primary business is the operation of a single piece of income-producing property and which derives substantially all of its income from that property.

A second type of Chapter 11 debtor that receives special treatment under the Code is the **single asset real estate debtor**. Per §§1121 and 362(d), a debtor whose primary business is the operation of a single piece of income-producing property and who derives substantially all of its income from that property is treated as a single asset real estate debtor (see definition in §101(51B)). Owners of an apartment complex whose income derives from apartment rentals are the best example. Such debtors are treated specially by the Code due to historical problems with their filing a Chapter 11 petition in order to trigger the automatic stay against creditors secured in the real property when there are no realistic prospects of successfully reorganizing. Essentially, §362(d) requires the single asset real estate debtor to produce an expedited plan of reorganization or to make other arrangements with such creditors to avoid lifting of the stay against the real property.

3. Overview of a Chapter 11 Case

Automatic stay The prohibition on creditors continuing collection efforts against a debtor that arises automatically upon the debtor's filing of a bankruptcy petition.

Plan of reorganization A plan proposed under Chapter 11.

The goal of a business filing for Chapter 11 relief is survival. Sometimes we refer to the **rehabilitation** of the debtor, but the reality in most instances is that the Chapter 11 case is an effort by a struggling business to avoid liquidation. Filing the Chapter 11 petition triggers the **automatic stay** of §362, which gives the debtor breathing room: time to negotiate with creditors and to come up with a **plan of reorganization** to which the creditors will consent. In contrast to a Chapter 13 plan, which can run for no more than five years, the Code does not place a limit on the duration of a Chapter 11 plan of reorganization.

Chapter 11 does not allow a debtor to win court approval of its plan of reorganization as easily as the Chapter 13 debtor. The creditors of the Chapter 11 debtor, both secured and unsecured, must be involved in the plan negotiation process and, in most instances, their approval must be obtained in a formal voting process. So critical is the involvement of creditors in a Chapter 11 case that if the debtor fails to produce a plan that can win sufficient creditor support within the **exclusivity period** granted it by the Code (see Chapter Nineteen, Section A), creditors are allowed to propose competing plans that may be approved over the debtor's objection. As part of the plan approval process, the debtor must provide a comprehensive **disclosure statement** explaining in detail its financial dealings, the sources of its financial distress, and how the proposed plan will succeed. Once a plan of reorganization meets the confirmation requirements of the Code and is confirmed by the bankruptcy court, the reorganized debtor will operate its business pursuant to the plan and with continued court monitoring and creditor input. At the conclusion of the plan, the case is closed and the debtor emerges from Chapter 11.

As the old saying goes, "there's many a slip twixt the cup and the lip," and there are multiple steps and many opportunities for failure from the filing of a Chapter 11 petition to the confirmation of a plan and from confirmation to plan consummation. A significant number of Chapter 11 cases fail somewhere along the way and convert to Chapter 7 liquidation. The various stages of a Chapter 11 proceeding are shown in Illustration 17-a, and these will form the basis for our step-by-step study of the business reorganization.

The fictitious but realistic family-owned furniture manufacturer, Banowsky Brothers Furniture, Inc., is a typical Chapter 11 debtor in most ways and we will examine its hypothetical Chapter 11 filing in the Middle District of North Carolina in order to learn how such a proceeding works. Go to Appendix C at this time and read Assignment Memorandum #1.

Illustration 17-a: THE STAGES OF A CHAPTER 11 BUSINESS REORGANIZATION PROCEEDING

1. Petition filed (voluntary or involuntary)

   - Automatic stay goes into effect, per §362
   - Debtor operates business as a debtor in possession (DIP), per §1108, unless a bankruptcy trustee is appointed prior to plan confirmation, per §1104

2. Creditors' committee appointed by U.S. Trustee, per §1102
3. Preliminary operational motions regarding use of cash collateral; use, sale, or lease of other property; payment of critical prepetition debts; and hiring of professionals
4. The first meeting of creditors
5. Plan negotiation period

   - Motions regarding postpetition financing, executory contracts, and interim compensation
   - Debtor has benefit of 120-day exclusivity period to file plan
   - Property of the estate, per §541, is identified and brought under DIP control using turnover and avoidance powers

6. Disclosure statement and proposed plan filed

   - Hearing on adequacy disclosure statement conducted
   - Disclosure statement approved or disapproved by court
   - Approved disclosure statement and proposed plan distributed to creditors, equity security holders, and U.S. Trustee

7. Solicitation of support for plan
8. Voting on plan
9. Confirmation hearing conducted on plan; objections heard
10. Order of confirmation entered on accepted plan, per §1129(a), or by cram down over objections, per §1129(b)
11. Discharge of preconfirmation debts for entity debtor upon confirmation and for individual debtor upon completion of plan payments
12. Reorganized debtor operates pursuant to confirmed plan
13. Plan consummated: case closed and debtor emerges from plan

4. The Impact of a Business Filing on Owners, Officers, and Others

Whenever a bankruptcy case is filed for a business entity such as a corporation, limited liability company, or partnership, questions arise concerning the impact of that filing on those who own the debtor business or serve as its officers or directors, not to mention its employees. Are jobs going to be lost? Is compensation going to be reduced? Will benefits be slashed? Will customers, suppliers, or others who have dealt with the debtor business be negatively impacted by the filing? What if the owners or officers of the business have personally guaranteed the debt of the business, a very common occurrence for many businesses? Upon default by the debtor business, those guarantors can expect a demand from the creditors holding the guarantees to demand payment of the entity's debts.

For all these reasons, the bankruptcy filing by a business entity often produces a domino effect. Those negatively impacted by the filing find themselves in financial peril and seek consultation as a result. It is not unusual to see multiple bankruptcy filings, particularly where individuals have personally guaranteed the debt of the entity.

P-H 17-a: Look again at Assignment Memorandum #1 in Appendix C. Do you see that the two brothers now operating this business, Charles and Timothy Banowsky, have personally guaranteed the obligation that their business owes to its largest creditor, Capital City Bank (CCB), which is currently owed $1.5 million? If the corporation defaults on that obligation, CCB can be expected to pursue both brothers on their guarantees. If Charles and/or Timothy consults with the firm for which you work regarding their options, what kinds of questions should be asked to determine if they should be advised to consider filing a bankruptcy case of their own? Which chapters of the Code might they consider filing under? What does your firm need to know in order to give that advice?

---

5. The "Prepackaged" Chapter 11

Where time and resources allow, a business may be able to negotiate a plan of reorganization with creditors *before* filing the Chapter 11 petition. If the business can win prepetition agreement from debtors for a plan of reorganization, the Chapter 11 petition can be filed, the plan submitted immediately, and confirmation obtained speedily, in the absence of creditor objections. We call such a case a **prepackaged Chapter 11**.

Prepackaged Chapter 11
A Chapter 11 proceeding in which the plan of reorganization has been drafted and informally approved by creditors prepetition.

P-H 17-b: Based on the information provided in Assignment Memorandum #1 in Appendix C, why will BBF not qualify for treatment as a small business debtor when it files its Chapter 11 petition? Why will it not be governed by the rules regarding a single asset real estate company since it only owns the one piece of real property?

B. ▶ Filing a Chapter 11 Case

1. Venue in a Chapter 11 Case

28 U.S.C. §1408 provides that a bankruptcy case may be commenced in the district

(1) in which the domicile, residence, principal place of business in the United States, or principal assets in the United States, of the person or entity that is the subject of such case have been located for the one hundred and eighty days immediately preceding such commencement, or for a longer portion of such one- hundred-and-eighty day period than the domicile, residence, or principal

place of business, in the United States, or principal assets in the United States, of such person were located in any other district; or

(2) in which there is pending a case under title 11 concerning such person's affiliate, general partner, or partnership.

For corporate debtors without affiliates, §1408(1) allows a debtor to file in its **domicile**, which means the state where it is incorporated, regardless of where its main office or other assets are located. Since many U.S. corporations are incorporated in Delaware, and because Delaware law is often viewed as corporate friendly, a large percentage of major Chapter 11 filings occur in Delaware.

Under §1408(2), corporate debtors with one or more affiliates may file in any district in which there is a pending bankruptcy case filed by one of the debtor's affiliates, even if the affiliate is a subsidiary and the subsequent filing is by the affiliate's parent.

EXAMPLE

> We have assumed for purposes of the case study featuring our fictitious Chapter 11 debtor, Banowsky Brothers Furniture, Inc. (BBF), that it is a closely held corporation that is incorporated in North Carolina and has its principal place of business and principal assets there. Thus, venue for it was controlled by §1408(1). But if BBF was a subsidiary of a larger corporation that had recently filed under Chapter 11 in Delaware, then the BBF Chapter 11 case could be filed there as well.

Forum selection is often more than just an academic exercise. On a basic level, choice of venue determines where the potentially hundreds of parties involved in a reorganization proceeding must go to court. The debtor will consider a location's convenience for its own business, the professionals employed to assist in the reorganization, as well as influential creditors. Yet the implications of venue go beyond geography: Key aspects of any Chapter 11 case may be decided by different bankruptcy judges differently; certain jurisdictions may carry a reputation as more debtor or reorganization friendly; some districts are perceived as more adept than others in handling large Chapter 11 cases; and forum court case precedent might be more favorable to issues that the debtor anticipates will arise in the case.

2. Joint Administration and Substantive Consolidation

Joint Administration

Joint administration
Where two or more bankruptcy cases involving affiliated debtors are ordered to be administered jointly to save administrative costs.

Bankruptcy Rule 1015(b) provides, inter alia, that if two or more bankruptcy petitions are pending in the same court by or against a partnership and one or more of its general partners, two or more general partners, or a debtor and an affiliate, "the court may order joint administration of the estates." The remedy of **joint administration** is permissive, not mandatory. Rule 1015(b) further states that "prior to entering an order the court shall give consideration to protecting creditors of different estates against potential conflicts of interest."

EXAMPLE

> If BBF was the subsidiary of a larger corporation that had filed under Chapter 11 in the Northern District of California, not only could the Chapter 11 petition of BBF be filed in that district, that court could also order the joint administration of the two cases.

To obtain joint administration of affiliated debtors, the filing party should file a motion for joint administration pursuant to Rule 1015(b), using the form and procedures set forth in Rule 9013. Most bankruptcy courts will also have local rules regarding motions for joint administration as well.

If the motion for joint administration is granted, then all proceedings in the lead bankruptcy case and all affiliated cases will be filed and adjudicated under the case number of the lead case. However, in the absence of any other orders, the debtor entities still retain their separate legal existence. Joint administration does not result in **piercing the corporate veil** and creditors of one debtor entity may not assert claims on the assets of affiliated debtors simply because the cases are jointly administered.

Joint administration is a valuable tool because it can greatly enhance the efficiency and judicial economy of a case.

Piercing the corporate veil Theory of liability under which the shareholders of a corporation may be held personally liable for corporate obligations for failure to maintain corporate separateness.

Substantive Consolidation

A motion for joint administration will often expressly state that it is a request "for joint administration but not substantive consolidation." This abundance of caution is warranted because while both actions will cause affiliated cases to be administered under a single case number, the effect of the two is very different.

Substantive consolidation means that the separate legal identity of affiliated debtors will be disregarded, and the assets and claims of all the debtors will be treated as one. In other words, all assets of all member debtors will be pooled together, and the claims of all creditors of all member debtors may be asserted against the pooled assets, subject to any valid security interests and the priorities of creditors under the Code.

There is no provision in the Code that specifically provides for substantive consolidation. Courts that have granted it have done so pursuant to §105(a), which permits bankruptcy courts to enter orders "necessary or appropriate to carry out the provisions" of the Bankruptcy Code.

Substantive consolidation Where two or more bankruptcy cases involving closely affiliated debtors are ordered to be consolidated into a single case and any technical distinctions between the debtors is ignored and they are treated as a single entity.

3. The Petition, Schedules, and Other Documents

A Chapter 11 case is commenced in the same way as a case under any other chapter of the Code, by filing a **voluntary petition** (Official Form 201 for a business entity and Official Form 101 for the individual debtor) with a bankruptcy court having proper venue (see the BBF Chapter 11 petition, Document 1 in the BBF case file). Though it is unusual, an **involuntary petition** can be filed by creditors who meet the requirements of §303, which we considered in Chapter Eight, Section A, in connection with an involuntary Chapter 7 petition.

Illustration 17-b: DOCUMENTS THAT MUST BE FILED WITH THE CHAPTER 11 PETITION OF AN ENTITY DEBTOR

- A list of creditors
- A corporate resolution authorizing the filing of the petition (Document 2 in the BBF case file) (a partnership will file an appropriate consent or appointment of general partner with authority to file)
- A list of the 20 largest unsecured creditors, supplied using Official Form 204 Corporate Ownership Statement containing the information described in Bankruptcy Rule 7007.1 (Document 3 in the BBF case file)
- Official Form 201A, Attachment to Voluntary Petition for Non-Individuals Filing for Bankruptcy Under Chapter 11, for **publicly traded corporations** only

P-H 17-c: Take a moment to compare the Chapter 11 petition of BBF, a corporate entity, (Document 1 in the BBF file) with the individual petitions of Marta Carlson (Document 2 in the Carlson file) and Roger and Susan Matthews (Document 1 in the Matthews file). Most of the information sought is identical but note the detailed business information requested in Part 7 of Form 201 for the entity filer including its four-digit NAICS Code. Go to www.uscourts.gov/four-digit-national-association-naics-codes and open the list of code numbers. Think of one or two different businesses that you or someone close to you has been associated with and find the appropriate NAICS Code for those businesses.

The filing fee must be paid when the petition is filed and cannot be paid in installments by a corporate debtor. Pursuant to §521 of the Code and Bankruptcy Rule 1007, at the same time it files its petition, the entity debtor must also file the items listed in Illustration 17-b.

Pursuant to §1116(1), a debtor who qualifies as a small business debtor must file with the petition its most recent balance sheet, statement of operations, cash-flow statement, and federal income tax return. The Chapter 11 *individual debtor* must file with his or her petition, or within 14 days thereafter, the various schedules of assets and liabilities including Schedules I and J, the Statement of Financial Affairs, and the other statements and documents discussed in Chapter Eight, Section B.

At the time the petition is filed, or within 14 days thereafter, the Chapter 11 *entity debtor* must also file the documents listed in Illustration 17-c. Note that the entity debtor does not file a Schedule C since only individual debtors can claim property as exempt. And Schedules I and J are not required of the entity debtor either. Those forms are designed for individual debtors and the Statement of Income and Expenses filed by the entity debtor serves in their stead (see Document 5 in the BBF case file).

The time for filing the required schedules and statements that need not accompany the petition can be extended by motion filed with the bankruptcy court, as discussed in Chapter Eight, Section C. But for small business cases, §1116(3) limits the permissive extension period to 30 days after the order for relief "absent extraordinary and compelling circumstances."

Illustration 17-c: DOCUMENTS THAT MUST BE FILED WITH THE CHAPTER 11 PETITION OR WITHIN 14 DAYS THEREAFTER BY THE ENTITY DEBTOR

- The various schedules of assets and liabilities (excluding Schedules C, I, and J, which are for individual debtors only)
- The Declaration Under Penalty of Perjury Regarding Debtor's Schedules
- A Statement of Current Income and Expenditures (Document 5 in the BBF case file)
- A Statement of Financial Affairs
- A Statement Disclosing Compensation Paid or to Be Paid to an Attorney
- A list of **equity security holders** of the debtor (Document 4 in the BBF case file). Equity security holders are the shareholders or owners of the debtor corporation. If the debtor is a limited liability company, the equity holders are the owner/members. If the debtor is a partnership, the equity holders are the partners (see §§101(9), (16), and (17))

Equity security holders
The holders of an ownership interest in an entity debtor.

C.   The Debtor in Possession and Appointing a Bankruptcy Trustee

Debtor in possession (DIP) The legal status given a debtor filing a Chapter 11 or Chapter 12 case.

A bankruptcy trustee is *not* automatically appointed upon the filing of the Chapter 11 petition, as happens in a Chapter 7 or 13. Instead, the debtor is considered the **debtor in possession (DIP)**, per §1101(1). The debtor, as DIP, retains possession and control of its assets while reorganizing, as well as the right to continue operating the business per §1108 (that section has been so construed by the courts even though it makes no mention of the DIP). Section 1107 of the Code gives the DIP essentially all the rights and powers of a **bankruptcy trustee** in a case (other than the right to compensation), including the turnover and avoidance powers that we considered in Chapter Ten, Sections D and E. The DIP can also pursue claims that are property of the estate (Chapter Ten, Section B), hire professionals as needed (e.g., attorneys, accountants, or appraisers) (see Chapter Nine, Section B), and can object to any claim made by a creditor, just as a trustee could (see Chapter Ten, Section A).

The DIP operates the business under the close supervision of the **U.S. Trustee**. The U.S. Trustee may schedule a §1116(2) **initial debtor interview** or other informal meeting with representatives of the DIP to discuss matters related to the case. The DIP usually must file a **property inventory** within 30 days and periodic **operating reports**, just as a trustee would do per §1106(a)(1) and Bankruptcy Rule 2015(a)(3). Reporting requirements for DIPs are often addressed in the **local court rules** of the particular court. The operating reports provided by the DIP will contain a detailed disclosure of all the business operations of the debtor during the period covered (receipts, disbursements, accrued expenses, changes in cash position, changes in inventory, or other assets, etc.). The operating reports will be examined closely by the U.S. Trustee and creditors to see if reorganization seems feasible or whether a motion should be made to convert the case to a Chapter 7 liquidation (discussed in Chapter Eighteen, Section C) in order to protect creditors. Creditors who see the DIP wasting its assets or going deeper into debt each reporting period will likely move for conversion of the case to a liquidation in order to stop the bleeding and maximize their return from remaining assets.

The DIP is technically considered an entity separate and apart from the prepetition business. Accordingly, the local rules or the U.S. Trustee will require the DIP to open new bank accounts in the name of the business, specifically adding "Debtor in Possession" to the name of the account. Titled assets such as vehicles may have to be retitled in the new "DIP" name.

EXAMPLE

> Prior to filing its Chapter 11 petition, all bank accounts of BBF were in the name of "Banowsky Brothers Furniture, Inc." Immediately after the petition is filed, at the direction of either the local rules or the U.S. Trustee, BBF as DIP will close out all its accounts and reopen them under the name "Banowsky Brothers Furniture, Inc., Debtor in Possession."

Another consequence of the debtor operating as a debtor in possession under §1101 as a separate legal entity from the prepetition entity and being granted the equivalent powers of a bankruptcy trustee per §1107 is that, like a bankruptcy trustee, the DIP must seek the court's permission to hire counsel to represent it pursuant to §327. Even though the attorney for the debtor has provided prepetition advice and assisted the debtor in preparing the Chapter 11 petition and schedules, once the petition has been filed the new DIP must obtain court authorization to hire the attorney to represent it in that capacity.

EXAMPLE

> Attorney Forsyth was retained by BBF prepetition and provided certain services for them under the privately negotiated fee agreement. But when BBF filed under Chapter 11, it became a different entity (BBF, Debtor in Possession), retains possession and control of property of the estate, and functions essentially as a bankruptcy trustee. Thus, the new entity must formally ask the court for authorization to retain attorney Forsyth to represent it postpetition just as a bankruptcy trustee would under §327 (see Document 6 in the BBF case file).

We will have more to say regarding the motion for authorization to hire attorneys and other professionals in Section F when we consider first day motions.

In most Chapter 11 cases a bankruptcy trustee is never appointed and the case proceeds with the DIP operating the business under the U.S. Trustee's supervision. But the bankruptcy court does have the power to appoint a bankruptcy trustee in a Chapter 11 case. Section 1104 of the Code sets out the grounds upon which the court, on request of the U.S. Trustee or a party in interest, can appoint a bankruptcy trustee in the case, which include:

- For cause, including fraud, dishonesty, incompetence, or gross mismanagement of the affairs of the debtor by current management, either before or after the commencement of the case
- If such appointment is in the interests of creditors, any equity security holders, and other interests of the estate

- As an alternative to converting the case to a Chapter 7 liquidation or dismissing it when it appears that a trustee might be able to save the reorganization from failing, if grounds exist to convert or dismiss the case under §1112 but the court determines that the appointment of a trustee or an examiner is in the best interests of creditors and the estate.

When the bankruptcy court orders a trustee to be appointed in a Chapter 11 case, the U.S. Trustee makes the appointment from the **trustee's panel**, discussed in Chapter Nine, Section B. The bankruptcy trustee is authorized by §1108 to operate the debtor's business and will expect to have the debtor's cooperation in doing so. The trustee is authorized by §1106 to perform all the normal duties of a trustee including to:

- exercise the turnover and avoidance powers;
- review and dispute claims;
- file any schedules or statements the debtor has not filed;
- file the periodic operating reports;
- hire professionals to assist in the administration of the estate;
- file any tax returns the debtor has failed to file;
- investigate the financial circumstances of the debtor and the conduct of its management in order to make a recommendation on the feasibility of reorganization;
- formulate a plan of reorganization if the debtor fails to do so;
- keep the U.S. Trustee, creditors, and the court advised as to all material developments; and
- make appropriate recommendations to the court.

As an alternative to the appointment of a trustee, the court may appoint an **examiner**, pursuant to §1104(c). An examiner does not assume responsibility for operating the debtor's business or have the powers of a trustee. Instead, the examiner will be charged with making investigations into specific aspects of the debtor's business and reporting back to the court. Examiners can also serve as mediators and even perform functions normally done by the DIP when the court lacks confidence in the debtor.

Trustee's panel Persons approved by the U.S. Trustee to serve as trustees in Chapter 7 or 11 cases in a district.

Examiner A person appointed by a bankruptcy court to investigate specific aspects of a Chapter 11 debtor's conduct or management of the estate.

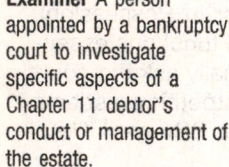

D. The Creditors' Committee

Creditors' committee A committee of creditors appointed by the U.S. Trustee in Chapter 11 cases and sometimes in Chapter 7 cases to represent the interests of all creditors.

We mentioned in the overview of a Chapter 11 case, in Section A, that creditors play a critical role in a Chapter 11 reorganization. And we learned in Section B (see Illustration 17-b) that one of the required schedules that the Chapter 11 debtor files is a list of its 20 largest unsecured creditors. Section 1102(a) of the Code requires that the U.S. Trustee appoint a committee of unsecured creditors "as soon as practicable after the order for relief." Section 1102(b)(1) suggests but does not require that this **creditors' committee** consist of the seven largest unsecured creditors. That section does require that the members of the committee be "representative of the different kinds of claims."

Illustration 17-d: FUNCTIONS OF THE CREDITORS' COMMITTEE IN A CHAPTER 11 CASE

> - To consult with the DIP or trustee concerning the administration of the case
> - To investigate the debtor's financial condition and business operations
> - To participate in the formulation of the plan of reorganization
> - To request the appointment of a trustee, if appropriate
> - To keep other creditors not on the committee advised
> - To perform "such other services as are in the interest of those represented," per §1103(c)

EXAMPLE

If the debtor owes unsecured lenders, that is a claim class with different interests than unsecured trade creditors or unsecured tort claimants. Each of these classes should be represented on the creditors' committee.

Pursuant to §§1102(b)(3) and 1103, the creditors' committee performs a number of functions, as summarized in Illustration 17-d.

The creditors' committee is a **party in interest** in the Chapter 11 case, entitled to notice of all proceedings and entitled to be heard by the court on all matters. It may hire an attorney, accountant, or other professional to assist it in its work, subject to court approval per §§1103(a) and 328. The retention, qualifications, and other requirements for such professionals are the same as with employment of professionals by the debtor or trustee. The creditors' committee may be authorized by the bankruptcy court to initiate a turnover or avoidance action if the DIP has refused a demand to do so. Under certain circumstances, it can even propose its own plan of reorganization for the debtor (see Chapter Nineteen, Section A).

Party in interest Any party having a stake in the outcome of a matter arising in a bankruptcy case.

Section 1102(a) gives the U.S. Trustee discretion to create other committees as it sees fit, including a committee of equity security holders. Sections 101(16) and (17) define an equity security holder as one holding an ownership interest in an entity debtor (a corporation or partnership) or holding a warrant or other right to purchase such an ownership interest. Equity security holders are also parties in interest in a Chapter 11 case, entitled to notice and to be heard. Chapter 11 frequently refers to **claims and interests**, a phrase encompassing not just creditors holding "claims" against the debtor, but owners holding ownership "interests." The creditor hopes to recover all of the debt owed to it in the debtor's reorganization; the owner hopes to maintain or receive the value of his investment in the debtor.

P-H 17-d: Review the U.S. Trustee's notice of appointment of creditors' committee in the BBF case (Document 10 in the BBF case file). How many creditors were appointed to the committee? Do they represent more than one class of unsecured creditors? Did the U.S. Trustee appoint more than one committee of creditors?

Pursuant to §1102(a)(3), the court may order that a creditors' committee not be appointed in a small business case. The nonappointment of such committee is one of the prerequisites for treatment of a Chapter 11 debtor under the small business case rules of the Code.

In a prepackaged bankruptcy case the creditors' committee will have been formed prepetition. Bankruptcy Rule 2007(a) authorizes the court, on motion, to approve that committee's formation and membership ex post facto in order to expedite the reorganization case.

E. ▶ Property of the Estate in a Chapter 11 Case

Executory contract An agreement that is so far unperformed by the parties to it as to constitute a material breach.

Property of the estate All property in which the debtor holds a legal or equitable interest at the commencement of a bankruptcy case.

Among the schedules and statements of assets and liabilities that the Chapter 11 debtor must file are Schedule A/B listing real and personal property in which the debtor owns an interest, Schedule B listing personal property in which the debtor owns and Schedule G for listing **executory contracts** and **unexpired leases** to which the debtor is a party or in which it has an interest (e.g., as a third-party beneficiary). The property interests listed on Schedule A/B (Official Form 206A/B), and the leases and contracts listed on Schedule G (Official Form 206G), constitute the **property of the estate** in a Chapter 11 case. Once the bankruptcy petition is filed, property of the estate must be administered and accounted for in accordance with the Bankruptcy Code, Rules, and other applicable laws and rulings for as long as the case is open.

EXAMPLE

Upon filing the Chapter 11 petition, the automatic stay of §362 stays a wide range of actions by creditors or other parties against property of the estate, such as actions to enforce claims or judgments, enforce possession, create or perfect liens, or exercise control over property of the estate. Similarly, once the petition is filed, the debtor is likewise restricted in its use of estate property under various sections of the Code, including, among others, §363(b), which prohibits the debtor from using or transferring estate property outside the ordinary course without prior court approval after notice and a hearing, and §364(c), which likewise requires the debtor to obtain court approval before granting liens against estate property for postpetition financing of the estate. Therefore, it is essential that the debtor completely and accurately identify and list all property of the estate.

As we considered in Chapter Ten, Section B, §541(a) of the Code provides that the filing of a petition in bankruptcy creates an estate consisting of "all legal or equitable interests of the debtor in property as of the commencement of the case" wherever such property is located and by whomever it is held.

Clearly, the statute is intended to be read broadly. Notwithstanding this expansive definition, the Code contains specific exceptions to property of the estate. In §541(b), these include fiduciary or executory powers that the debtor may exercise solely for the benefit of an entity other than the debtor, any nonresidential leasehold interest that expired under its stated terms prior to commencement of the case, funds in an account controlled by the debtor that are withheld from employee wages for qualified retirement plans or deferred compensation, and, in a complicated nod to the energy industry, certain interests in "liquid or gaseous hydrocarbons" (oil and natural gas) that the debtor has assigned to a third party. To see how §541(b)(4) operates in this context, see *Tow v. HBK Main St. Invs., LP (In re Tow)*, 2015 WL 1093568 (Bankr. S.D. Tex. Mar. 10, 2015) (finding that a purported assignment of gas revenues was actually a debt instrument and therefore the revenues were property of the estate).

Section 541(d) adds an additional limitation to property of the estate. That section provides that property that the debtor holds only a legal title to, but not an equitable interest, is not property of the estate.

EXAMPLE

> Suppose a creditor gave legal title to certain real property to a builder-debtor so that the debtor could obtain a construction loan and construct a building for the creditor. The debtor may have bare legal title to the real property, but the creditor has equitable title such that the real property would be excluded from property of the estate under §541(d).

P-H 17-e: Assume the law office you work for represents Standard Cable Corp., a mid-sized ($100 million annual revenue) enterprise that manufactures wire and metal cables. Standard has its own bookkeeping department, but contracts with an outside accounting firm, CPA Partners, Inc., for all its accounting and auditing work. Your firm is negotiating with Standard's senior lenders over the terms of a bankruptcy reorganization, and you have been assigned to prepare schedules of assets. Review Schedule A/B (Official Form 206A/B). Who are the people within Standard Cable and/or outside the firm that you should contact to obtain this information?

Legal interests in property are direct and immediate ownership rights, but equitable interests include causes of action, whether or not a demand has been made or a case has been filed, latent or inchoate claims, present rights to future interests, unliquidated or disputed claims, and even potential claims or interests for which a right to recovery is uncertain or elusive.

HIGHLIGHTED CASE

IN RE ONIO'S ITALIAN RESTAURANT CORP.
42 B.R. 319 (Bankr. S.D.N.Y. 1984)

[After months of nonpayment, the landlord obtained judgment, and a warrant of eviction was issued to the marshal to remove the nonpaying culinary tenant. And just when the landlord thought it had cleared the final hurdle in the laborious process of recovering its premises, the restaurant corporation filed Chapter 11, thus invoking the automatic stay and immediately stopping the eviction. The landlord's position was that because a warrant of eviction had been issued prepetition, the leasehold was not property of the bankruptcy estate. So what was left of the debtor's interest in the leasehold once it filed bankruptcy?]

OPINION: EDWARD J. RYAN, Bankruptcy Judge.

On August 3, 1984, Onio's Italian Restaurant (Onio's) filed a voluntary petition for relief under Chapter 11 of the Bankruptcy Code, and has continued as a debtor in possession. In February, 1976, Anthony Ippolito, President of Onio's, entered into an agreement with Vinellis, Inc. (Vinellis) to lease a store and basement located at 310 West 34th Street for a twelve-year period. Thereafter, Ippolito assigned the lease to Onio's, which is controlled by Ippolito.

Onio's failed to pay rent on numerous occasions, the last of which compelled Vinellis to commence a summary eviction proceeding in the Civil Court of the City of New York on April 23, 1984. On July 25, 1984, a default judgment was entered in favor of Vinellis and a warrant of eviction issued by the City Court to a New York City marshal. On or about August 3, 1984, the marshal served notice on the debtor, and sought to execute the warrant on August 13, 1984. The marshal did not proceed with the eviction on August 13, 1984, because it was presented by the debtor with a certificate of the debtor's filing under Chapter 11 of the Code.

Vinellis now moves to modify the automatic stay under §362(a) of the Code so as to proceed with the eviction. Vinellis predicates his application on the ground that under state law, the issuance of the warrant of eviction terminated any interest that the debtor may have had in the premises prior to the filing of the Chapter 11 petition. He asserts the debtor had no interest in the premises to which the automatic stay could attach at the time of filing. Vinellis argues in the alternative, that even if the debtor has some kind of possessory interest in the property, the automatic stay should be modified because Vinellis must continue to pay taxes and incur other expenses related to the property, without any expectancy of payment by the tenant.

Onio's contends that the issuance of the warrant of eviction per se did not terminate the debtor's leasehold interest. Onio's is presently proceeding in Civil Court to vacate the warrant on the ground of improper service of the landlord's petition.

Under New York law, issuance of a warrant of eviction cancels the lease agreement and annuls the landlord-tenant relationship. *New York City Housing Authority v. Torres*, 61 A.D.2d 681, 682, 403 N.Y.S.2d 527 (1st Dep.t 1978); N.Y. R.P.A.P.L. §749(3) (McKinneys 1979). On the issuance of the warrant, the tenant has no legal interest in the property. He does have an equitable interest based upon possession. *Matter of GSVC Restaurant Corp.*, 3 B.R. 491, 494 (Bankr. S.D.N.Y.), *aff'd*, 10 B.R. 300 (D.C.S.D.N.Y. 1980).

Section 362(a)(2) of the Code stays enforcement of pre-petition judgments against property of the estate. Under §541(a)(1), "property of the estate" consists of "all legal or equitable interests of the debtor in property as of commencement of the case." Thus, if the debtor holds an equitable interest in property even though without legal title, the estate acquires that equitable interest of the debtor in the property. Despite termination of the legal interest of a tenant in the premises when the warrant is issued, the tenant's equitable interest of possession allows him to petition the court to vacate the warrant after issuance, but prior to execution, "for good cause shown." *New York City Housing Authority v. Torres*, 61 A.D.2d at 682, 403 N.Y.S.2d 527; N.Y. R.P.A.P.L. §749(3). It is this equitable right to which the debtor-in-possession in these circumstances succeeds upon filing of the bankruptcy petition. In *United States v. Whiting Pools, Inc.*, 462 U.S. 198, 103 S. Ct. 2309, 76 L. Ed. 2d

515 (1983), even though the debtor's property had been seized by the Internal Revenue Service to satisfy a tax lien and the property was no longer in the debtor's possession, his residual interest in the property was held sufficient to justify use of the turnover provisions of §542(a) so as to bring the property into the estate. The Court, in so ruling, effectuated the policy of Congress of encouragement of reorganizations by including a broad range of property in the estate as defined by §541(a)(1). 103 S. Ct. at 2313.

Similarly, the debtor's bare possessory interest in the premises without legal right is a residual interest which the debtor-in-possession may utilize as part of the estate to effectuate the reorganization. The bankruptcy court has the power to stay a warrant for a reasonable time for good cause providing the debtor is in possession and pays the landlord for use and occupation. *In re Lane Foods, Inc.*, 213 F. Supp. 133 (S.D.N.Y. 1963). The warrant may be vacated in the state court. Good cause exists for the bankruptcy court to continue the automatic stay to allow the debtor-in-possession to pursue its legal remedies under state law. *In re GSVC Restaurant Corp.*, 10 B.R. 300, 302 (S.D.N.Y. 1980) (dicta).

The motion to vacate the stay is denied without prejudice pending the outcome of the litigation in the Civil Court of the City of New York. The debtor shall pay the rent due for August and September 1984 and keep current the monthly rental pending the outcome of the litigation in the local court.

POST-CASE FOLLOW-UP

As it turned out, this debtor had quite a bit more interest in the leasehold when it filed bankruptcy than the landlord expected under the broad scope of §541. *In re Onio's* is not a famous case, and had no particular impact as precedent. But it demonstrates that property of the estate comes in different forms, and attorneys for both debtors and creditors and the staff that assist them must carefully scrutinize all potential interests of the debtor, even those that on first glance may seem tenuous. In this case, New York City municipal law provided a brief window between the issuance of the eviction warrant and the actual eviction for the debtor to assert an equitable interest to possession. We can surmise that debtor's counsel had this in mind when filing the petition, because it was the bankruptcy stay that stopped the marshal from executing the eviction warrant. Onio's eventually closed, but even if a debtor does not intend to continue the business, an equitable interest in a leasehold can be a valuable asset. If the monthly rent amount is lower than comparable rents in the area, the debtor can sublease the premises at the higher prevailing rate and retain the difference between the sublease amount and the original lease amount.

| *In re Onio's Restaurant Corp.:* | **Real Life Applications** |

1. The law office you work for represents the Official Committee of Unsecured Creditors in the Chapter 11 bankruptcy case of Metro-Taste Sandwich Shops, a small restaurant chain based in Milwaukee, Wisconsin. Metro-Taste filed bankruptcy after losing ground for years to larger national fast food behemoths. Prior to filing, Metro-Taste sued one of the major chains for infringement on its trademark commercials featuring feisty senior citizens at a generic hamburger store angrily demanding "where's the meat?" Sadly, Metro-Taste ran short on funds, and prosecution of the trademark case had ceased by the time the bankruptcy was filed. Is the cause of action for infringement property of the estate? As an aside, do you think we dreamed up this scenario ourselves? Take a break and check out these amusing commercials from the 1980s: https://www.youtube.com/watch?v=riH5EsGcmTw.

2. Section 365 deals with executory contracts and unexpired leases and we will examine it in the next chapter. However, look at §365(d)(4), which was added to the Code in 2005, long after the decision in *Onio's*. Under §365(d)(4)(A), a lease of nonresidential real property will be deemed rejected (no longer property of the estate) if it is not assumed by the trustee within either 120 days of the petition date or the date a plan is confirmed. Section 365(d)(4)(B) allows the court to grant a 90-day extension of that deadline, but no further extensions unless the landlord consents. Note that in order to assume a lease, the debtor must first cure all prepetition arrearages. See §365(b)(1)(A). What effect, if any, would §365(d)(4) have had in *Onio's* if it had been in the Code at that time? How would that section have affected the strategy of debtor's counsel?

Strong-arm clause
Practitioner's phrase for the trustee's avoidance powers under §544 of the Code.

Preferential transfer A prepetition transfer of an interest in the debtor's property that results in the creditor receiving the payment or transfer being unfairly advantaged compared to other creditors. May be avoidable pursuant to §547.

Fraudulent conveyance (or transfer) A prepetition transfer of property by a debtor with actual or constructive intent to defraud creditors by delaying or hindering their collection efforts.

As noted earlier in our discussion of the debtor as debtor in possession, §1107 of the Code gives the DIP essentially all the rights and powers of bankruptcy trustee in a case (other than the right to compensation), including the turnover and avoidance powers that we considered in Chapter Ten, Sections D and E. Thus, the DIP can demand that a third party or custodian of the debtor's property turn over property of the estate to the DIP under §§542 or 543 respectively and may institute an action in the bankruptcy case to recover such property if the demand is refused.

The DIP can also utilize the **strong-arm clause** of §544(a) to set aside an improperly perfected prepetition security interest, statutory lien, or judicial lien on property of the estate or to defeat the claim by the holder of a junior security interest in such property. The DIP can utilize §545 to defeat certain enumerated prepetition **statutory liens** even though such liens are perfected (see Illustration 10-a). The DIP can set aside **preferential transfers** or **fraudulent conveyances** of property of the estate under §§547 or 548 respectively.

UNITED STATES V. WHITING POOLS, INC.
62 U.S. 198 (1983)

OPINION: Justice BLACKMUN.

Promptly after the Internal Revenue Service (IRS or Service) seized respondent's property to satisfy a tax lien, respondent filed a petition for reorganization under the Bankruptcy Reform Act of 1978, hereinafter referred to as the "Bankruptcy Code." The issue before us is whether §542(a) of that Code authorized the Bankruptcy Court to subject the IRS to a turnover order with respect to the seized property.

I

A

Respondent Whiting Pools, Inc., a corporation, sells, installs, and services swimming pools and related equipment and supplies. As of January 1981, Whiting owed approximately $92,000 in Federal Insurance Contribution Act taxes and federal taxes withheld from its employees, but had failed to respond to assessments and demands for payment by the IRS. As a consequence, a tax lien in that amount attached to all of Whiting's property.

On January 14, 1981, the Service seized Whiting's tangible personal property—equipment, vehicles, inventory, and office supplies—pursuant to the levy and distraint provision of the Internal Revenue Code of 1954. According to uncontroverted findings, the estimated liquidation value of the property seized was, at most, $35,000, but its estimated going-concern value in Whiting's hands was $162,876. The very next day, January 15, Whiting filed a petition for reorganization, under the Bankruptcy Code's Chapter 11 in the United States Bankruptcy Court for the Western District of New York. Whiting was continued as debtor-in-possession.

The United States, intending to proceed with a tax sale of the property, moved in the Bankruptcy Court for a declaration that the automatic stay provision of the Bankruptcy Code, §362(a), is inapplicable to the IRS or, in the alternative, for relief from the stay. Whiting counterclaimed for an order requiring the Service to turn the seized property over to the bankruptcy estate pursuant to §542(a) of the Bankruptcy Code. Whiting intended to use the property in its reorganized business.

B

The Bankruptcy Court determined that the IRS was bound by the automatic stay provision. Because it found that the seized property was essential to Whiting's reorganization effort, it refused to lift the stay. Acting under §543(b)(1) of the Bankruptcy Code, rather than under §542(a), the court directed the IRS to turn the property over to Whiting on the condition that Whiting provide the Service with specified protection for its interests.

The United States District Court reversed, holding that a turnover order against the Service was not authorized by either §542(a) or §543(b)(1). The

United States Court of Appeals for the Second Circuit, in turn, reversed the District Court. It held that a turnover order could issue against the Service under §542(a), and it remanded the case for reconsideration of the adequacy of the Bankruptcy Court's protection conditions. The Court of Appeals acknowledged that its ruling was contrary to that reached by the United States Court of Appeals for the Fourth Circuit in *Cross Electric Co. v. United States*, 664 F.2d 1218 (1981), and noted confusion on the issue among bankruptcy and district courts. 674 F.2d, at 145 and n.1. We granted certiorari to resolve this conflict in an important area of the law under the new Bankruptcy Code.

II

By virtue of its tax lien, the Service holds a secured interest in Whiting's property. We first examine whether §542(a) of the Bankruptcy Code generally authorizes the turnover of a debtor's property seized by a secured creditor prior to the commencement of reorganization proceedings. Section 542(a) requires an entity in possession of "property that the trustee may use, sell, or lease under §363" to deliver that property to the trustee. Subsections (b) and (c) of §363 authorize the trustee to use, sell, or lease any "property of the estate," subject to certain conditions for the protection of creditors with an interest in the property. Section 541(a)(1) defines the "estate" as "comprised of all the following property, wherever located: (1) . . . all legal or equitable interests of the debtor in property as of the commencement of the case." Although these statutes could be read to limit the estate to those "interests of the debtor in property" at the time of the filing of the petition, we view them as a definition of what is included in the estate, rather than as a limitation.

A

In proceedings under the reorganization provisions of the Bankruptcy Code, a troubled enterprise may be restructured to enable it to operate successfully in the future. Until the business can be reorganized pursuant to a plan under 11 U.S.C. §§1121-1129, the trustee or debtor-in-possession is authorized to manage the property of the estate and to continue the operation of the business. By permitting reorganization, Congress anticipated that the business would continue to provide jobs, to satisfy creditors' claims, and to produce a return for its owners. Congress presumed that the assets of the debtor would be more valuable if used in a rehabilitated business than if "sold for scrap." The reorganization effort would have small chance of success, however, if property essential to running the business were excluded from the estate. Thus, to facilitate the rehabilitation of the debtor's business, all the debtor's property must be included in the reorganization estate.

This authorization extends even to property of the estate in which a creditor has a secured interest. §363(b) and (c). Although Congress might have safeguarded the interests of secured creditors outright by excluding from the estate any property subject to a secured interest, it chose instead to include such property in the estate and to provide secured creditors with "adequate protection" for their interests. §363(e). At the secured creditor's insistence, the bankruptcy court must place such limits or conditions on the trustee's power to sell, use, or lease property as are necessary to protect the creditor. The creditor with a secured interest in property included in the estate must look to this provision for protection, rather than to the nonbankruptcy remedy of possession.

B

The statutory language reflects this view of the scope of the estate. As noted above, §541(a) provides that the "estate is comprised of all the following property, wherever located: . . . all legal or equitable interests of the debtor in property as of the commencement of the case." 11 U.S.C. §541(a)(1) . . . . Most important, in the context of this case, §541(a)(1) is intended to include in the estate any property made available to the estate by other provisions of the Bankruptcy Code. Several of these provisions bring into the estate property in which the debtor did not have a possessory interest at the time the bankruptcy proceedings commenced.

Section 542(a) is such a provision. It requires an entity (other than a custodian) holding any property of the debtor that the trustee can use under §363 to turn that property over to the trustee. Given the broad scope of the reorganization estate, property of the debtor repossessed by a secured creditor falls within this rule, and therefore may be drawn into the estate. While there are explicit limitations on the reach of §542(a), none requires that the debtor hold a possessory interest in the property at the commencement of the reorganization proceedings.

III

A

We see no reason why a different result should obtain when the IRS is the creditor. The Service is bound by §542(a) to the same extent as any other secured creditor. The Bankruptcy Code expressly states that the term "entity," used in §542(a), includes a governmental unit. §101(14) . . . . Tax collectors also enjoy the generally applicable right under §363(e) to adequate protection for property subject to their liens. Nothing in the Bankruptcy Code or its legislative history indicates that Congress intended a special exception for the tax collector in the form of an exclusion from the estate of property seized to satisfy a tax lien.

IV

When property seized prior to the filing of a petition is drawn into the Chapter 11 reorganization estate, the Service's tax lien is not dissolved; nor is its status as a secured creditor destroyed. The IRS, under §363(e), remains entitled to adequate protection for its interests, to other rights enjoyed by secured creditors, and to the specific privileges accorded tax collectors. Section 542(a) simply requires the Service to seek protection of its interest according to the congressionally established bankruptcy procedures, rather than by withholding the seized property from the debtor's efforts to reorganize.

The judgment of the Court of Appeals is affirmed.

POST-CASE FOLLOW-UP

Whiting Pools, Inc. illustrates both the §542 turnover available to the DIP in a Chapter 11 and the broad interpretation of the notion of property by including within the estate "property in which the debtor did not have a possessory interest at the time the bankruptcy proceedings commenced" and by rejecting any notion that collateralized property should not be deemed estate property even where the secured creditor was the IRS. Note that although the IRS was ordered to turn over the lawfully seized collateral to the DIP since it was still property of the estate, its lien on that collateral remained intact. As we will see in the next chapter, if the debtor desires to maintain possession of the property and use, sell, or lease it in connection with its reorganization effort, §363(e) will require it to provide the secured creditor with adequate protection or to demonstrate that the property is necessary for an effective reorganization. Otherwise the bankruptcy court will lift the automatic stay of §362 and allow repossession.

United States v. Whiting Pools, Inc.:   **Real Life Applications**

1. Earth Equipment Co. (EEC) is a secured creditor of Homewood Homes, Inc., a mid-sized ($100 million) residential home builder. Word has gotten around that Homewood is late in payments to many creditors, which EEC already knows because Homewood is three months behind on its payments for certain heavy machinery (bulldozers, forklifts, etc.). EEC is considering repossessing the machinery under state law. If EEC contacts the law office where you work, what advice should your supervising attorney give EEC regarding whether it should repossess the equipment at this time?

2. Assume that EEC does repossess the collateral from Homewood and Homewood immediately files a petition in Chapter 11 threatening a turnover action to recover possession of the collateral. There is no dispute that the collateral is still property of the estate. What argument(s) might EEC make that Homewood is nonetheless not entitled to turnover?

F. ▶ First Day Motions in a Chapter 11 Case

Section 363(c)(1) contains one of the most significant powers of the DIP. That section provides that the trustee (or the DIP exercising the powers of a trustee per

Ordinary course of business In general, following the typical usual practices engaged in by a business.

§1107) may use, sell, or lease property of the estate "**in the ordinary course of business**" without further authorization of the court. The term "ordinary course of business" is not defined in the Code, but has generally been recognized to mean the "reasonable expectations of interested parties of the nature of transactions that the debtor would likely enter in the course of its normal, daily business." *In re Watford*, 159 B.R. 597, 599 (Bankr. M.D. Ga. 1993), aff'd without opinion, 61 F.3d 30 (11th Cir. 1995). The power to use property in the ordinary course of business is important because it allows the debtor to continue its prepetition operations without constantly seeking approval of the court, while at the same time being protected from creditors under the automatic stay.

However, per §363(c)(2), **cash collateral** (cash of the debtor in which a creditor holds a security interest) is specifically excluded from the "use in the ordinary course of business" authorization of §363(c)(1) and the DIP must first obtain court approval to use that critical asset using the notice and a hearing procedure. In addition, if the DIP needs or wants to use or sell property of the estate outside the ordinary course of business, §363(b) requires the DIP to first obtain court approval again using the notice and a hearing procedure. And, as noted in the post-case follow-up to *Whiting Pools*, any time the DIP desires to use, sell, or lease collateralized property of the estate, the secured party can demand **adequate protection** of its secured interest as a condition to the intended use, sale, or lease of the collateral.

Consequently, the days immediately following the filing of a Chapter 11 petition are a critical period for the debtor hoping to successfully reorganize. Most entity debtors need to use cash collateral immediately (e.g., to order and pay for essential inventory, material, or supplies; or to pay employees; or to pay rent, utility, and other bills associated with the work location; or to make installment payments owed on existing debt). Or they need to use or sell property of the estate outside the ordinary course of business. Or they need to use, sell, or lease collateralized property of the estate triggering the right of the secured creditor to demand adequate protection. Or they are challenged by a creditor regarding whether some intended use of property is in fact within the ordinary course of the DIP's business. Thus, notwithstanding the use in the ordinary course of business authorization of §363(c)(1), the DIP cannot realistically do just whatever it wants with most of its property postpetition. It will have to seek court permission for these intended uses of property of the estate and other business decisions.

First day motions Practitioner's phrase for common and critical preliminary operational motions made by the debtor in possession at the beginning of a Chapter 11 case.

First day orders Practitioner's phrase for orders commonly sought via first day motions immediately upon filing of a Chapter 11 case.

It is for these reasons that, in most Chapter 11 cases, the debtor's attorney will file one or more motions on the same day that the petition is filed, called **first day motions** by practitioners, seeking court approval (called **first day orders** by practitioners) to use cash that is encumbered for any purpose, or to obtain new credit, or to pay critical prepetition debts, or to hire certain professionals, and so on. The Code does not *require* that these preliminary operational motions be filed on the day the petition is filed or even shortly thereafter, but circumstances usually do. Often the debtor must have quick court approval for these matters or the business will fail. Without court approval of these motions in the very earliest days of the case, the reorganization effort is stillborn.

EXAMPLE

> Assume that BBF decides to file a Chapter 11 petition to stop an anticipated repossession of its CAD/CAM systems and production equipment by New Century Automation (NCA). A week before filing, it receives notification from three essential trade creditors that unless their past due bills are all paid in full by cash or cashier's check within one week, they will stop doing business with BBF. If that occurs, BBF will be out of business. BBF files its Chapter 11 petition triggering the §362 automatic stay and delaying NCA's repossession. But BBF still needs to use its cash immediately to satisfy the three critical trade creditors and to pay its employees or it will be out of business anyway. Thus, the preliminary operational motions that the attorney for BBF files along with the petition will be as critical to its survival as stopping the repossession.

Let's examine the most common "first day motions" filed in a Chapter 11 case. The Code sections dealing with these motions refer to "the trustee" being authorized to do this or that. But remember that §1107 gives the DIP the powers of a bankruptcy trustee and that, in most Chapter 11 cases, a trustee is never appointed. So we will study these sections on the assumption that they refer to the DIP, as in practical effect they do.

1. Motion for Authorization to Use Cash Collateral

Section 363(c)(2) provides that cash collateral cannot be used by the DIP postpetition even in the ordinary course of its business unless:

Cash collateral Cash or cash equivalents that are part of the property of the estate and which are subject to a security interest in favor of a creditor.

- the creditor secured in the cash consents to the use, or
- the court authorizes the use.

Cash collateral is defined in §363(a) to mean not just bank notes on hand in a cash register but also cash held in deposit accounts, negotiable instruments (e.g., promissory notes, certificates of deposit, or uncashed checks) and securities, documents of title, or other instruments readily turned into cash and thus called **cash equivalents**. For the cash collateral rules to apply, the cash or cash equivalents must be collateralized (serving consensually or nonconsensually as security for an indebtedness). If the cash is not collateralized, it is subject to the same §363 rules as other property of the DIP (to be considered in the next chapter).

Cash equivalents Instruments easily convertible to cash, such as checks or promissory notes.

EXAMPLE

> The master loan that BBF arranged with Capital City Bank (CCB) in YR-6 required BBF to grant CCB a security interest in, not just its real property, but its inventory, accounts receivable, and cash as security for that loan. Thus, CCB is secured in the cash and cash equivalents of BBF. This will include the cash in all BBF bank accounts, any promissory notes it holds, and any uncashed checks it has. BBF has filed an application for authorization to use the cash collateral in which CCB holds a security interest (see Document 7 in the BBF case file).

If the creditor secured in the cash the DIP seeks to use postpetition will not consent and the DIP is forced to file a motion or application seeking authorization from the court to use it, §363(c)(4) obligates the DIP to keep the cash collateral in a separate account from other cash, pending the resolution of the motion.

Adequate protection The protection that must be provided by the bankrupt estate to a creditor whose interest in property is threatened by the estate's continued possession and use of the property.

The primary issue in the DIP's request for authorization to use cash collateral is always **adequate protection** of the secured creditor's interest in the cash. Sections 363(c)(3) and (e) provide that when a motion for authorization to use cash collateral is filed, the court "shall prohibit or condition such use . . . as is necessary to provide adequate protection of such interest." Adequate protection has to do with the secured creditor's right to have the value of the property in which it is secured protected or maintained throughout the case, such that the creditor has the same advantaged position as a secured creditor throughout a case as it had at the beginning. Remember that per §506(a)(1) a secured creditor's claim is only secured up to the value of the collateral as of the date the petition is filed. That is the value the secured creditor is entitled to have adequately protected if the debtor contemplates doing anything with the property other than turning it over to the creditor.

P-H 17-f: Both the DIP's need to use the cash collateral and the secured creditor's concern about its depletion should be fairly obvious. Consider BBF's position. It needs to use its cash to continue ordering inventory, making furniture, paying its employees, and meeting other obligations in order to stay in business to have any hope of reorganizing. Consider CCB's position. BBF owes it money and agreed that it could have a secured position in all its cash. To the extent this struggling debtor depletes its cash, CCB's secured position is impaired. What questions about the various uses to be made of the cash might the judge have for BBF at the hearing on its motion for authorization to use cash collateral? Will it be concerned about BBF's declining sales over the past few years? Will it be concerned about the salaries it pays its workers? What about the other overhead of BBF? What other concerns might the judge have?

What constitutes adequate protection is not comprehensively defined in the Code but §361 provides that it may be provided by:

- periodic cash payments to the creditor sufficient to compensate for the decrease in value of the collateral;
- providing the creditor with a lien on other property sufficient to compensate for the decrease in value of the collateral being used; or
- granting other such relief as will result in the creditor receiving the **indubitable equivalent** of its interest in the property.

We will consider §361 in more detail in the next chapter (including that intriguing phrase, indubitable equivalent) when we examine motions by the DIP to use other property of the estate outside of the ordinary course of its business. It is sufficient here to note that the most typical adequate protection arrangement made in cash collateral disputes is for the debtor to grant the creditor a security interest in other property as contemplated by §361(2). In many situations, this simply means granting the creditor a security interest in the same

Floating lien A security interest (lien) that attaches automatically to property of the debtor acquired after the date the security interest was created.

kinds of property acquired postpetition in which the creditor held a prepetition security interest. To understand this, recall that in Chapter Two, Section C, we learned that a security interest in personal property—like cash, inventory, and accounts receivable—is subject to the **floating lien** concept, including **after-acquired property**.

EXAMPLE

> The security agreement in which BBF granted CCB a security interest in its inventory, accounts receivable, and cash would have provided that the security interest extend not only to inventory, accounts receivable, and cash on hand at that moment, but also to the same such property as the debtor might acquire in the future.

After-acquired property Property acquired by a debtor that automatically becomes subject to a preexisting security interest (lien) of a creditor.

Section 552(a) of the Code provides, however, that the security interest of a creditor does *not* extend to property acquired by the debtor postpetition. The security interest in after-acquired property is effectively suspended with the filing of the petition and will not attach to that property. So providing adequate protection in a cash collateral dispute often involves nothing more than the DIP offering the creditor a security interest in the same property it acquires postpetition that would have been subject to the original prepetition security agreement but for the bankruptcy filing.

EXAMPLE

> If BBF proposes to grant CCB a security interest in its postpetition inventory and accounts receivable, CCB may consent to that arrangement or, if a motion is necessary, the court may approve that arrangement as adequate protection and authorize the use of cash collateral.

The procedures for motions for the authorization to use cash collateral set forth in Bankruptcy Rule 4001(b) provide that the court is *not* to conduct a final hearing on the motion any earlier than 14 days after the motion is filed and served on the various parties entitled to notice. A delay of that length could be disastrous for a DIP needing to pay employees, order and pay for new materials, and the like. Fortunately, the rules do allow the court to conduct a *preliminary hearing* prior to the expiration of the 14 days and to then authorize the use of "that amount of cash collateral that is necessary to avoid immediate and irreparable harm to the estate pending a final hearing." The typical motion for authorization to use cash collateral will allege such harm and ask for the expedited preliminary hearing (see Document 7 in the BBF case file). If relief is granted at the preliminary hearing, a final hearing on the motion will be scheduled for a date more than 14 days after the original motion was filed.

Section 363(c)(3) of the Code supplements Bankruptcy Rule 4001(b)(2) by providing that authorization to use cash collateral can be approved at the preliminary hearing "only if there is a reasonable likelihood" that the DIP will prevail at the final hearing on the motion. (Although §363(c)(3) uses the word "trustee" rather than "DIP," remember that per §1107, the DIP has all the rights, title, and power of a bankruptcy trustee in a Chapter 11 case.)

P-H 17-g: The debtor has just filed bankruptcy, and the same day filed a motion for use of cash collateral. The secured creditor will consent to the motion if the debtor provides certain now unencumbered assets as additional collateral. What concerns would unsecured creditors have about the motion and the secured creditor's position?

---

2. Motion for Authorization to Pay Prepetition Claims of Critical Vendors

The right of a creditor to pursue payment of a prepetition debt is automatically stayed upon the filing of the petition, per §362. Normally, no payment of prepetition debt is required or made in any case under the Code until the stay is lifted for a secured creditor, or property is abandoned to a creditor, or there is a distribution in a Chapter 7, or payments begin under a confirmed plan in a Chapter 13, 12, or 11. And we have learned that interest does not accrue on prepetition unsecured debts awaiting payment and accrues on prepetition secured debts only up the value of the collateral (see Chapter Ten, Section A).

But sometimes in a Chapter 11, the DIP needs authorization from the court to go ahead and pay certain prepetition debts owed to **critical vendors** (e.g., suppliers, shippers, warehousemen, workers' compensation and other insurance providers, various service or equipment maintenance companies) in order to stay in business and make reorganization feasible.

> **Critical vendors** In a Chapter 11 case, suppliers of essential goods and services to the debtor in possession whose prepetition claims must be paid promptly in order for the reorganization to proceed since such vendors may not otherwise continue to do business with the debtor.

EXAMPLE

On the date BBF filed its petition it has two vendor/suppliers threatening to stop doing business with it unless payment is made on their outstanding invoices. If these two vendors stop doing business with BBF, BBF will be unable to continue making furniture. Thus BBF filed a motion for authorization to pay the prepetition debts owed to these critical prepetition vendors (see BBF's motion in Document 8 in the BBF case file).

Interestingly, no provision of the Code deals specifically with this problem. But the courts have developed what is known as the **necessity doctrine**, pursuant to which payments of prepetition unsecured debt can be made in a Chapter 11 *if* the DIP can show that the failure to make those payments will imperil the ability of the business to survive and reorganize. (The doctrine was first suggested by the Supreme Court more than 130 years ago in *Miltenberger v. Logansport*, 106 U.S. 286 (1882), when the Court stated that "[m]any circumstances may exist which may make it necessary and indispensable to the business of the road and the preservation of the property, for the receiver to pay pre-existing debts . . . .")

The source of the court's authority to order what is obviously a postpetition preferential payment to certain unsecured creditors to the detriment of the others

> **Necessity doctrine** The court-made rule that a Chapter 11 debtor may pay certain prepetition debts to critical vendors or essential employees if necessary for the business to survive.

(and contrary to the order of claims priority established by §507) is uncertain. Some courts rely on a common law doctrine preceding the Code, while others base their rulings on the inherent **equitable powers** of a bankruptcy court arising out of §105(a), which authorizes the court to "issue any order, process, judgment that is necessary or appropriate to carry out the provisions of this title." Others find authority in §363(b)(1) since satisfaction of a prepetition debt in order to keep "critical" supplies flowing is a use of property other than in the ordinary course of administering an estate in bankruptcy. But some courts, following the lead of *In re Kmart Corp.*, 359 F.3d 866 (7th Cir. 2004), are skeptical of either statutory justification for the necessity doctrine and, while not abolishing the doctrine, have narrowed it, requiring the debtor to at least show (1) that the vendor's goods or services are essential for the debtor to continue to operate; (2) that the vendor will stop supplying the same if it is not paid; (3) that there is no other legal or practical alternative; and (4) that other creditors will not be harmed thereby. See, e.g., *In re United American, Inc.*, 327 B.R. 776, 782-783 (Bankr. E.D. Va. 2005).

3. Motion for Authorization to Pay Prepetition Priority Claims for Taxes or Employee Benefits and Wages

As with critical vendor motions, this motion draws upon the necessity doctrine, but is likely to be far less controversial since, unlike the general unsecured claims of prepetition vendors, claims for certain prepetition taxes (e.g., sales, property, or employment withholding taxes); wages, salary, or commissions; and employee benefits are **priority claims** under §507(a).

EXAMPLE

> Assume, as is usually the case, that the debtor files bankruptcy in the middle of a payment cycle, where employees are owed for wages earned before the filing, but are expected to continue working (and earning wages) before the next wage payment date, which will be postpetition. Employees must be assured that prepetition wages and benefits will be paid, or otherwise they may leave their jobs and seek employment elsewhere. Accordingly, it is a commonsense motion, and almost always granted. (Postpetition taxes, wages, and benefits are payable as **administrative expenses** under §§503(b) and 507(a)(2).)

Some priority claims related to prepetition taxes and employee wages and benefits under §507(a) are limited to claims arising within so many days of the filing of the petition. For example, §§507(a)(4) and (5) grant priority status only to wages and benefits earned within 180 days before filing, but places a cap of $12,850 per employee (as of April 1, 2016 to be adjusted again on April 1, 2019 per §104). If the estate has sufficient cash flow to pay the prepetition claims in full, the court may grant the motion without regard to these priority limits. Some courts, however, may refuse to approve prepetition payments that exceed the priority claim limits.

P-H 17-h: Look again at BBF's motion for authorization to pay prepetition priority claims for employee wages and benefits (Document 9 in the BBF case file). Why do you think the motion advises the court that none of the employees for whom payment is sought in the motion are insiders of BBF? Might creditors or the creditors' committee be more likely to object to the motion if a portion of the payment went to Charles or Timothy Banowsky or some other member of the Banowsky family? Note that the motion also asks for permission to pay various withholding obligations of BBF associated with the unpaid wages. There may be an objection to allowing payment of those withholding obligations at the beginning of the Chapter 11 case since, alternatively, they could be paid following plan confirmation as administrative expenses entitled to priority under §507(a)(8).

4. Motion for Authorization to Use Existing Accounts

Many business debtors file a first day motion for authority to use existing accounts, sometimes called a motion to approve cash management system, or something similar. As discussed earlier in this chapter, once a DIP files bankruptcy it must immediately close all prepetition bank accounts and then open new DIP accounts. The purpose of this is to distinguish between prepetition and postpetition activity. Some U.S. Trustees may even insist that the debtor imprint the words "Debtor in Possession" or "DIP," but the authority to require this is unclear. Compare *In re Young*, 205 B.R. 894, 897 (Bankr. W.D. Tenn. 1997) ("the UST does not have the statutory authority to require the debtor to imprint 'Debtor-In-Possession' on his checks") with *In re Colad*, 324 B.R. 208, 217 (Bankr. W.D.N.Y. 2005) (debtor permitted to use existing accounts, but required to order new checks with debtor in possession designation). In addition, the debtor must observe the requirements for investments and bank deposits set forth in §345.

If the DIP is a small entity with no subsidiaries and modest operations in the forum state, then closing prepetition accounts and opening new DIP accounts may seem little more than a bookkeeping annoyance. It can be a very different matter if the DIP is a large enterprise with multiple subsidiaries, bank or investment accounts, and operations nationwide or worldwide. Prepetition security interests often have been granted in the DIP's bank accounts that are subject to automatic payment instructions (such as batched electronic Automatic Clearing House (ACH) payments) with creditors, employees, and suppliers, so that changing the debtor's existing checking and payments structure is unduly debilitating. In addition, such action can be disconcerting to creditors and other parties, and heighten the sense of the debtor's troubled financial condition. Accordingly, motions seeking authorization to use existing prepetition accounts for such debtors are generally granted.

P-H 17-i: Note that the case file index contains no motion for authorization to use existing accounts. What does that tell you about what BBF, as debtor in possession, has done concerning its various bank accounts?

5. Motion for Authorization to Employ Professionals

In Chapter Nine, Section B, we discussed the employment of attorneys and other professionals (accountants, appraisers, auctioneers, etc.) by the bankruptcy trustee as authorized by §327 and Bankruptcy Rule 2014. You may want to review that material at this time. In a Chapter 11, a debtor functioning as a DIP will also need authorization to employ professionals, beginning significantly with the attorney for the debtor.

The reasons why a motion for authorization to hire attorney to represent debtor is a common first day motion in most federal districts (see the discussion of Bankruptcy Rule 6003 below) should be obvious. Very few businesses can comply with the requirements imposed by the Code on the Chapter 11 debtor without near-constant legal advice. Though a lot of the work of the attorney for the debtor is done prepetition, once the petition is filed the debtor will continue operating its business and must comply with all requirements of the Code imposed on DIPs. Literally every "business decision" it makes must now be made in light of its responsibilities as a Chapter 11 DIP. As we will see in the next two chapters, postpetition the DIP must put together a complicated disclosure statement and proposed plan of reorganization and win its approval from creditors. In the interim there may be operational motions to be filed with the bankruptcy court regarding matters that require court approval such as the use, sale, or lease of property other than in the ordinary course of business. The postpetition reporting requirements imposed on the DIP will require attorney review and approval. Postpetition assistance of counsel is vital to the DIP.

Thus, the Chapter 11 debtor will file a first day motion or application for immediate authorization to hire an attorney to represent it pursuant to 11 U.S.C. §327 and Bankruptcy Rule 2014, which contains detailed fact averments supporting the necessity for the employment, reasons for selecting the specific counsel, professional services to be rendered, potential conflicts of interest, and other information. The retention application must be accompanied by a verified statement of the proposed counsel disclosing all connections with the debtor, creditor, U.S. Trustee, and other potential conflicts of interest.

P-H 17-j: Review the Motion for Immediate Authorization to Hire Attorney filed by BBF, which is Document 6 in the BBF case file. Does it appear to comply with the requirements of Bankruptcy Rule 2014 and §327?

Since any professionals employed by the DIP must be "disinterested persons" under §327(a), they may not be employed postpetition if they are creditors of the estate. Therefore, attorneys for the debtor must ensure they are paid in full for all prepetition services prior to filing; otherwise, the balance of the prepetition fee is waived.

Once the petition has been filed, attorneys and other professionals may not be paid for any services performed on behalf of the bankruptcy estate unless they have first been retained upon application of the debtor pursuant to Rule 2014, and after an order has been entered by the court approving their employment. Bankruptcy Rule 6003 provides that the court shall not enter an order approving employment of professionals within 21 days of the petition date unless "necessary to avoid immediate and irreparable harm." Of course, Chapter 11 debtors need continuing legal representation during those 21 days. In some districts, the debtor will go ahead and file the motion seeking authorization to hire counsel as a first day motion alleging such authorization is necessary to avoid immediate and irreparable harm, confident the judge will routinely grant the motion. In other districts the practice by local rule is to file the motion for authorization immediately following the expiration of the 21-day period and the court will grant the motion *nunc pro tunc* (Latin: "now for then," or retroactively) to the date the petition was filed.

6. Administrative First Day Motions

The purpose of administrative first day motions is to streamline certain procedural requirements to accommodate the debtor's specific situation and thus reduce administrative costs. We will review some of the most common ones.

Motion for Joint Administration (But Not Substantive Consolidation)

Joint administration was discussed generally in Chapter Eight, Section A, and more specifically as to affiliated companies filing separate Chapter 11 petitions in Section B of this chapter. Bankruptcy Rule 1015(b) provides that where there are two or more petitions pending by a partnership and one or more of its general partners, or by a debtor and an affiliate, the court may order joint administration of the estates. This is done upon the debtor's motion for joint administration. Upon entry of the order, the multiple cases will then be docketed and administered under a single case number and caption of the "lead" debtor. This is almost always done by first day motion, because it avoids the necessity and expense of creating and serving duplicate documents in each separate case. First day motions for joint administration are typically granted ex parte, often before orders are entered on any other first day motions so that any remaining first day motions can be decided under the lead case. Debtors under joint administration retain their individual legal existence and are not substantively consolidated.

Motion to Establish Notice and Administrative Procedures

This motion is also sometimes called motion to establish case management procedures, or something similar. This motion seeks relief specific to the administrative circumstances of the bankruptcy case. If it is a large case, the debtor may want to establish specific notice and service procedures, allow for Internet posting or service, and set up a regular schedule of omnibus hearings for any motions to be filed in the case, along with response deadlines and related procedures. Authority to grant case management motions can be found in part in §105(d), which allows the court to "prescribe limitations and conditions as the court deems appropriate to ensure that the case is handled expeditiously and economically . . . ." Note, however, that Rule 2002 provides minimum timeframes for notice on certain types of hearings, which orders pursuant to §105(d) should observe.

Motion for Authority to Retain Notice and Claims Agent

Debtors in large cases may want to employ an outside agent to mail notices, serve documents, process proofs of claim and maintain a claims register, solicit and review plan balloting, and perform other administrative functions. 28 U.S.C. §156(c) permits the employment of such services "on or off the court's premises." In addition, Rule 2002(f) allows "some other person as the court may direct" to serve notices to various parties in the case. A motion for authority to retain notice and claims agent (or claims and noticing agent) is a common first day motion in large cases and is generally granted. For an example, see *In re Credit-Based Asset Servicing and Securitization*, 2010 WL 5136414 (Bankr. S.D.N.Y. 2010).

Motion for Extension of Time to File Schedules, Statement of Financial Affairs, or Other Documents

Section 521(a) requires the debtor to file schedules of assets and liabilities, a statement of financial affairs, and other documents. Under Rule 1007(c), these documents must be filed within 14 days of the petition date. Depending on the size of the case, this may be a monumental task that may require much more time. Rule 1007(a)(5) allows the court to grant an extension of this time "upon motion for cause shown," and with notice to the U.S. Trustee, creditors' committee, and other parties that the court may require. This is a fairly routine first day motion and is almost always granted. As with all other motions, counsel should review and comply with any local bankruptcy rules related to extensions of time.

Motion for Interim Fees Procedures

Section 330(a)(1) allows the court, after notice and hearing, to award "reasonable compensation for actual, necessary services" rendered by professional persons employed by the estate, in addition to "actual and necessary expenses." An order under §330(a) is a "final" order granted by the court at the end of the case, after all of counsel's services have been rendered and reviewed by the court. As might be expected, it can be unreasonable to require attorneys and other professionals to wait until the end of the case before being paid. For some professionals and their firms, this is simply not financially possible. Accordingly, §331 allows the court to grant compensation on an interim basis during the case "once every 120 days after an order for relief . . . or more often if the court permits . . . ." But waiting even four months to be paid can be a substantial financial burden for firms in active or large cases. Therefore, a common first day motion is a motion for interim fees procedures requesting authority to submit a monthly fee application. In such motions, it is common to ask for payment of all expenses, but only for a percentage of the fees generated during that fee cycle (80 or 90 percent is typical). As provided in §330(a)(5), an award of fees on an interim basis is subject to reexamination and possible adjustment in a final fee application hearing. Thus, to the extent that interim fees are found to exceed the final fee amount, they are subject to **disgorgement**. *In re St. Joseph Cleaners, Inc.*, 346 B.R. 430 (Bankr. W.D. Mich. 2006) (quoting *Specker Motor Sales Co. v. Eisen*, 393 F.3d 659, 663 (6th Cir. 2004)).

Disgorgement A remedy ordered by a court pursuant to which an attorney is compelled to return to the client payments previously made for legal services or expenses.

P-H 17-k: Look at the BBF case file index in Appendix C. Of the various filings you see listed there, which were filed by the debtor along with the petition? Which would qualify as "first day motions"? Check your answer by looking at the actual documents located in the BBF case file accessible on the companion web site and noting the date of filing.

---

7. Preliminary Motions in a Prepackaged Chapter 11

In a prepackaged Chapter 11, the debtor will have worked out arrangements with creditors and other parties and resolved disputes regarding these issues (the debtor's use of cash collateral; the payment of critical prepetition debt; and the hiring of professionals) before filing the petition. The debtor will then file motions asking the court to approve those arrangements on the same day the petition is filed so approval can be obtained quickly, in the absence of objection, and the case can proceed quickly.

CHAPTER SUMMARY

Chapter 11 is designed as a dynamic process in which the debtor continues to conduct its prepetition operations under protection of the automatic stay while negotiating with creditors, using its bankruptcy powers to restructure, and formulating a plan of reorganization.

A creditors' committee, usually consisting of the seven largest unsecured creditors, is appointed in a Chapter 11 case to work with the DIP, offer input, and to serve as and speak as a representative of all creditors in matters before the court.

A prepackaged Chapter 11 is one where the debtor's plan of reorganization has already been worked out and agreed to by creditors and is confirmed by the court, in the absence of objection, promptly after the case is commenced.

In Chapter 11, the DIP normally exercises the power of a trustee including the turnover and avoidance powers. However, in appropriate circumstances, a bankruptcy trustee may be appointed to operate the business and administer the bankruptcy estate.

Section 363(c) allows the DIP to use or sell property of the estate, including assets subject to a security agreement other than cash collateral, in the ordinary course of business without the need to obtain approval of creditors or the court. A debtor wanting to use cash collateral postpetition without the consent of the secured creditor or wanting to use or sell property of the estate in other than ordinary course must obtain court permission.

First day motions are motions normally filed by a DIP along with the petition seeking court approval for use of cash collateral, to pay prepetition critical vendor claims, to pay prepetition employee wages and benefits claims, to hire professionals, and regarding other administrative and operational matters.

REVIEW QUESTIONS

1. How does a Chapter 11 bankruptcy differ from a Chapter 7 bankruptcy? Why does a company that has just filed a Chapter 11 petition change the name on its bank accounts to include the company name and debtor in possession?

2. Who is eligible to file for Chapter 11 relief? Explain what is meant by the small business case and the single asset real estate debtor. How are the rules of Chapter 11 different for such debtors?

3. Does the automatic stay go into effect when a Chapter 11 petition is filed? Is a bankruptcy trustee automatically appointed? Is a first meeting of creditors held?

4. Describe how a Chapter 11 filing by an entity debtor may impact on the individual shareholders, directors, officers, and employees of the debtor.

5. What is a prepackaged Chapter 11? Describe what happens between a debtor and its creditors before the petition is filed in a prepackaged case.

6. Explain how venue works in a Chapter 11 entity filing and why forum selection can be crucial in such a case.

7. What is the difference between substantive consolidation of two or more Chapter 11 cases and joint administration of those cases?

8. What is a creditors' committee and what role does it play in a Chapter 11 case?

9. Why doesn't a Chapter 11 entity debtor file a Schedule C? What document does a Chapter 11 entity debtor file in lieu of Schedules I and J?

10. What section of the Code gives the Chapter 11 debtor in possession the authority to exercise the turnover and avoidance powers of a bankruptcy trustee?

11. Describe generally the power of a DIP to use or sell property of the estate with or without court approval. How does that work for cash collateral? For other collateralized property of the estate? For property of the estate the DIP desires to use or sell in a way that is outside its ordinary course of business?

12. What are first day motions and why are they usually so critical to the debtor's right to continue in Chapter 11?

13. When a creditor secured in the cash of a Chapter 11 debtor will not consent to its postpetition use by the DIP, how does the DIP provide that creditor with adequate protection of its secured position?

14. What is a critical vendor in the Chapter 11 context? What is the necessity doctrine that arises when a DIP asks the court for permission to pay prepetition critical vendor claims? Why is that doctrine controversial where such prepetition claims are unsecured? What two sections of the Code are relied on by various courts to justify authorizing postpetition payment of such claims?

15. Explain why a bankruptcy court will be more willing to grant a DIP's first day motion for authorization to pay claims for prepetition wages and benefits claims than a first day motion to pay prepetition critical vendor claims.

WORDS AND PHRASES TO REMEMBER

adequate protection
administrative expense
after-acquired property
automatic stay
bankruptcy trustee
business reorganization
cash collateral
cash equivalents
claims and interests
creditors' committee
critical vendors
debtor in possession (DIP)
disclosure statement
entity debtor
equitable powers
equity interest
exclusivity period
executory contracts
first day motions
first day orders
floating lien
forum selection
fraudulent conveyance
indubitable equivalent
in the ordinary course of business
initial debtor interview
involuntary petition

joint administration
liquidate
local court rules
necessity doctrine
nunc pro tunc
operating report
party in interest
piercing the corporate veil
plan of reorganization
preferential transfer
prepackaged Chapter 11
priority claim
property inventory
property of the estate
publicly traded corporations
rehabilitation
single asset real estate debtor
small business case
small business debtor
special counsel
statutory liens
strong-arm clause
substantive consolidation
trustee's panel
unexpired leases
U.S. Trustee
voluntary petition

TO LEARN MORE: A number of TLM activities to accompany this chapter are accessible on the companion web site for this textbook at http://aspen lawschool.com/books/Parsons_Debt4e/.

Chapter Eighteen:

▶ The Chapter 11 Business Reorganization— Operating the Business Prior to Plan Approval

KEY CONCEPTS

- A first meeting of creditors is conducted in a Chapter 11 and often a meeting of equity security holders as well
- Listed claims of creditors in a Chapter 11 are deemed allowed unless an objection to the claim is filed
- A Chapter 11 debtor may convert the case to one under Chapter 7 without court approval if no trustee has been appointed; a case may be dismissed or converted on the motion of a party in interest
- Section 363 of the Code grants the debtor authority to sell estate assets other than in the ordinary course of business and such assets may be sold free and clear of claims and interests (such as liens)
- Section 364 allows the debtor to obtain unsecured and secured postpetition credit, subject to terms that protect existing creditors and in certain circumstances, the liens of prepetition creditors may be primed (subordinated) in order to provide security for postpetition lenders
- Section 365 of the Code gives the debtor the power, upon approval by the court, to assume, reject, and in some cases, assign an executory contract or unexpired lease to an assignee, even if the contract or lease prohibits the same, or the nondebtor party does not consent
- Contracts dealing with the rejection or assumption of collective bargaining agreements, retiree benefits, and intellectual property are governed by special provisions of the Code
- Section 503(c) allows debtors to offer retention and performance incentives to key employees, based on certain restrictions

A. ▶ The First Meeting of Creditors in a Chapter 11

Pursuant to §342 of the Code, upon the filing of the Chapter 11 petition, the bankruptcy court clerk will issue a **Notice of Chapter 11 Case** to the creditors and the U.S. Trustee using Official Form 309F. The notice will advise of the date

Equity security holders
The holders of an ownership interest in an entity debtor.

scheduled for the §341 **first meeting of creditors**. Section 341(b) authorizes the U.S. Trustee to convene a meeting of **equity security holders** in the debtor (those holding an ownership interest in a debtor entity: shareholders of a debtor corporation, members/owners of a debtor limited liability company, or partners in a debtor partnership) as well. In a prepackaged Chapter 11, where the proposed plan of reorganization has been negotiated and approved prepetition, §341(e) authorizes the court to order that *neither* a meeting of creditors nor of equity security holders be held.

B. Creditor Claims in a Chapter 11

Proof of claim The writing that a creditor submits as evidence of its claim against the estate.

Deeming Code process where certain determinations are deemed made unless a timely objection is filed.

Pursuant to §1111(a) and Bankruptcy Rule 3003, a creditor in a Chapter 11 case is *not* required to file a **proof of claim** unless its debt was not listed in the debtor's schedules or was listed there as disputed, contingent, or unliquidated. Instead, Chapter 11 utilizes a unique "deeming" approach, pursuant to which listed claims are **deemed filed** under §1111(a) and, as in all cases under the Code, claims are **deemed allowed** under §502(a) unless an objection is filed. If a creditor required to file a proof of claim does so, then the debtor in possession (DIP) or a party in interest can object to a creditor's claim pursuant to §502, as in other cases (discussed in Chapter Ten, Section A).

Listed equity security holders need not file a **proof of interest**. Instead, Bankruptcy Rule 3003(b)(2) provides that their right to participation in the case as a party in interest, including the right to vote on the plan, is to be established from the list of equity security holders that the debtor files at the beginning of the case. (See Illustration 17-c and Document 4 in the BBF case file.) One claiming to be an equity security holder but omitted from the list would file a proof of interest.

C. Voluntary Conversion or Dismissal of a Chapter 11 Case

The debtor in a Chapter 11 case has the right to convert the case to a Chapter 7 liquidation at any time under §1112(a), unless

- a trustee has been appointed;
- the case originally was commenced by an involuntary petition; or
- the case was converted to a case under Chapter 11 other than at the debtor's request.

The Chapter 11 debtor does *not* have an automatic right to have the case dismissed. A party in interest may file a motion to dismiss or convert a Chapter 11 case to a Chapter 7 liquidation case "for cause" under §1112(b)(1). Section 1112(b)(4) lists 16 different circumstances constituting cause; those are summarized in Illustration 18-a.

Generally, if cause is established after notice and a hearing, the court must convert or dismiss the case unless it specifically finds that the requested conversion or dismissal is not in the best interest of creditors and the estate. Alternatively, the court may decide that appointment of a Chapter 11 trustee or an examiner is in the best interests of creditors and the estate as authorized by §1104(a)(3).

Illustration 18-a: WHAT CONSTITUTES "CAUSE" TO DISMISS OR CONVERT A CHAPTER 11 CASE
TO A CHAPTER 7 LIQUIDATION

- The substantial or continuing diminution of the estate with no likelihood of rehabilitation
- Gross mismanagement of the estate
- Failure to maintain insurance with resulting risk to the estate or the public
- Unauthorized use of cash collateral substantially harmful to a creditor
- Failure to comply with an order of the court
- Unexcused failure to comply with any filing requirement
- Failure to attend the 341 meeting or a Rule 2004 examination without good cause
- Failure to timely provide information or to attend meetings requested by the trustee, if any
- Failure to file tax returns or pay taxes due after the date of the order for relief
- Failure to file a disclosure statement or a plan within the time permitted
- Failure to pay any fees or charges in connection with the Chapter 11
- Revocation of an order confirming a plan
- Inability to effectuate substantial consummation of a confirmed plan
- Material default by the debtor with respect to a confirmed plan
- Termination of a confirmed plan, pursuant to a condition in the plan
- Failure of an individual debtor to pay a domestic support obligation that first becomes due after the filing of the petition

D. Operational Motions Critical to Formulating a Plan of Reorganization

If the DIP survives the flurry of activity associated with obtaining the **first day motions** considered in Chapter Seventeen, operation of the business continues as the debtor prepares its plan of reorganization (see Illustration 17-a). However, there can be quite a delay between the time the petition is filed and the time a plan of reorganization is finally proposed and between the time a plan is proposed and its confirmation. During those delays, the DIP must keep the business operating and stave off motions to dismiss or convert the case to a Chapter 7 liquidation.

There are a number of critical operational motions that frequently arise during this period of the case that may be just as "make or break" as the preliminary motions considered in Chapter Seventeen. These additional motions may be made before the plan is formally proposed as part of the DIP's ongoing operations or they may be proposed as part of the plan itself. (And, of course, the motions we considered in Chapter Seventeen may be made as part of the ongoing operation of the DIP rather than at the beginning of the case or included in its plan.) Before we look at these additional motions, let's see what decisions BBF has made regarding the future of its business. Go to Appendix C at this time and read Assignment Memorandum #2.

1. The Motion for Authorization to Use, Sell, or Lease Property in Other Than the Ordinary Course of Business

Section 363 of the Code deals with the DIP's (or trustee's if one has been appointed) right to use, sell, or lease property of the estate postpetition. With the exception of cash collateral, the special rules for which we considered in Chapter Seventeen, Section F, so long as the DIP is using, selling, or leasing its assets in the **ordinary course of business**, it can do so without court approval.

EXAMPLE

> At the time the petition is filed, it is in the ordinary course of business for BBF to continue selling its furniture in the showroom attached to the factory building (see Assignment Memorandum #1 in Appendix C). After its Chapter 11 petition is filed, it can continue to do so without court permission.

However, if the DIP wants to use, sell, or lease the assets *other than* in the ordinary course of business, §363(b)(1) requires that it file a motion for permission to do so. That motion is decided using the "after notice and a hearing" standard.

EXAMPLE

> Assume BBF, instead of continuing to sell its furniture as it has done in the past, wants to sell it in bulk to a retailer so it can begin producing different lines of furniture pursuant to the plan of reorganization it is preparing to propose. Because this is not a sale in the ordinary course of business for BBF, it can proceed only with permission granted by the court after notice and a hearing.

Sometimes there is a dispute regarding whether a proposed use, sale, or lease of property is or is not within the debtor's ordinary course of business.

EXAMPLE

> Assume that immediately after filing its Chapter 11 petition, BBF advertises a 50 percent off sale on all the furniture in its showroom attached to the factory building. Does it need court permission for this sale? A creditor concerned that BBF maximize its receipts on its existing inventory of furniture might argue that this is an extraordinary event requiring court approval because of the steep discount being offered. BBF might counter that it regularly conducts sales offering steep discounts and that this sale is nothing out of the ordinary so court permission is not required.

P-H 18-a: The usual test used to decide whether a proposed sale or other use of the debtor's property is within the ordinary course of the debtor's business is whether the parties in interest should reasonably have foreseen a transaction of the type contemplated, given both the history of the debtor's business practices (the **vertical factor**) and the normal practices within the industry (the **horizontal factor**). An informative case concerning the **reasonable foreseeability** test is *In re Dant & Russel, Inc.*, 853 F.2d 700 (9th Cir. 1988). Research the decisions in your federal district or circuit to see if they follow the two-part vertical/horizontal test or employ some other test.

When an intended use, sale, or lease of the debtor's property is found to be outside the ordinary course of its business, the court must decide whether to approve it over an objection. The factors to be considered are

- whether the proposed use, sale, or lease is on fair and reasonable terms;
- is in the best interests of the estate; and
- will not pose an unjustifiable risk to parties in interest.

These factors require factual determinations by the court based on the particular circumstances of the case.

EXAMPLE

> If BBF files a §363(b)(1) motion seeking permission to sell its inventory of furniture in bulk to a retailer in order to begin producing new product lines, the court will have to consider whether such sale is in the best interests of the estate and furthers the goal of reorganization. In the process of making that decision, the court will hear proof regarding the fairness and adequacy of the proposed sale price, the price at which the inventory furniture could be sold in the ordinary course of business, how the proceeds would be applied to the anticipated conversion to new product lines, the impact on creditors, and so forth. Often these operational motions require the court to consider the feasibility of some aspects of a debtor's plan for reorganization before the plan has been formally proposed.

Sub rosa Practitioner's term for an operating motion in a Chapter 11 that is effectively a plan of reorganization and for a plan of reorganization that is effectively a liquidation.

When the DIP files a §363(b)(1) motion seeking permission to sell all or substantially all of the assets of the business, objections are often made that such a proposal should be dealt with in the final, confirmed plan of reorganization rather than by preplan motion. The argument is that the §363(b)(1) motion is itself a *sub rosa* ("under the rose," connoting secrecy or misdirection) plan that avoids the rigorous disclosure, solicitation, voting, and confirmation process that a plan ordinarily goes through (to be considered in Chapter Nineteen). After all, selling all or substantially all the assets of a business would be a fundamental aspect of a business reorganization plan. On the other hand, the open bidding that often results from an approved §363(b)(1) sale may result in a higher return than in a sale through the confirmed plan.

E-C 18-a: When a debtor files a Chapter 11 case with the primary intent of selling all of its assets and ceasing doing business, you might think that an appropriate objection is that the entire proceeding is a *sub rosa* liquidation that should have been filed under Chapter 7. But in fact Chapter 11 does not prohibit liquidation of a debtor as its ultimate plan of reorganization nor does it require a debtor to continue doing business after confirmation of its plan. Many debtor's attorneys choose Chapter 11 for the liquidation of their business clients to avoid the automatic appointment of a Chapter 7 trustee whose fees will be charged against the proceeds of liquidation in a Chapter 7. Using Chapter 11 for liquidation isn't unethical and it may be smart lawyering.

Not only is using §363 in a Chapter 11 to effectively liquidate by selling all assets not unethical, it is increasingly common. In 2014, §363(b) sales took place in 38 percent of large public bankruptcies, an increase of 4 percent from the previous year (see UCLA-LoPucki Research Database, *363 Sales of All or Substantially All Assets in Large Public Company Bankruptcies, as a Percentage of All Cases Disposed, by Year of Case Disposition*, available online at lopucki.law.ucla.edu/tables_and_graphs/363_sale_percentage.pdf). Data for smaller enterprise bankruptcies is difficult to track, but it is estimated that effective liquidation is accomplished by way of §363 sales in approximately half of all nonpublic corporation Chapter 11 cases.

Most courts follow the leading case of *In re Lionel Corp.*, 722 F.2d 1063 (2d Cir. 1983), holding that a sale of all or substantially all of a debtor's assets via §363(b)(1) motion rather than a confirmed plan will be approved only where *sound business reasons* support such a sale, but there are many variations on that rule among the federal circuits. Common factors that courts consider in deciding whether the §363(b)(1) motion is supported by sound business reasons include:

- the likelihood that a plan of reorganization will be proposed and confirmed in the near future;
- the proceeds likely to be obtained from the proposed disposition vis-à-vis any appraisals of the property;
- whether the assets to be sold are increasing or decreasing in value;
- whether there is a valid business justification to sell the assets through a §363 sale rather than through a Chapter 11 plan;
- whether there is sufficient notice to inform all creditors and interested parties of the effect of the sale on the distributions to creditors;
- whether sales notice is the functional equivalent of a disclosure statement; and
- whether the sale recognizes the fiduciary duties owed by the debtor in possession to all creditors and interest holders.

For a helpful case applying most of these factors to evaluation of a Chapter 11 trustee's §363 motion to sell rather than to seek confirmation of a competing Chapter 11 plan proposed by creditors, see *In re GSC, Inc.*, 435 B.R. 132 (Bankr. S.D.N.Y. 2011).

When collateralized property is sold, §363(k) authorizes a secured creditor to **credit-bid** the value of its security interest at the sale by offsetting the value of its secured claim against the purchase price of the property (see discussion of credit-bidding in Chapter Eleven, Section A).

EXAMPLE

Assume a Chapter 11 debtor receives permission to sell real property valued at $500,000 on which Bank has a mortgage with a balance of $750,000. At the §363 sale, Bank can bid $500,000, the value of its secured claim under §506. If that is the high bid, Bank takes title to the property without having to pay the debtor anything. It will file an unsecured claim for the $250,000 it is still owed. Assume Bank #2 held a junior mortgage on the property with a balance owed of $300,000 and it enters the high bid of $1,000,000 for the property at auction. It would have to pay $750,000 to Bank in satisfaction of the first mortgage held by Bank but could then satisfy the balance of the $1,000,000 purchase price by credit-bidding what it is owed since, after the lien of Bank is satisfied, the secured claim of Bank #2 has value.

The Role of Adequate Protection in Connection with the Motion for Permission to Use, Sell, or Lease Encumbered Property

The right of the DIP to use, sell, or lease property in the ordinary course of its business without court permission under §363 is not affected by the fact that the property involved is encumbered by the lien of a secured creditor (except in the case of cash collateral as discussed in Chapter Seventeen, Section F). However, the intended use, sale, or lease of the encumbered property is *always* subject to the secured creditor's right to **adequate protection**, per §§363(e) and 361, whether the planned sale or other use is in the ordinary course of the debtor's business or not.

Adequate protection The right of a secured creditor to have the value of its collateral protected and maintained throughout a bankruptcy case where debtor maintains possession of that collateral postpetition.

Adequate protection involves the secured creditor's right to have the value of the property in which it is secured protected or maintained throughout the case. Since a secured creditor's claim is only secured up to the value of the collateral as of the date the petition is filed per §506(a)(1), it is that value that the secured creditor is entitled to have adequately protected.

EXAMPLE

> After it files its petition, BBF continues to "use" the CAD/CAM systems and other production equipment in which NCA holds a security interest. It is using the property in the ordinary course of its business so it need not seek court permission under §363. However, NCA may have an argument that BBF's continued use of the property will result in the impairment of the value of that property and thus the impairment of NCA's secured position. NCA is prepared to prove that on the day the petition is filed, the CAD/CAM systems and production equipment in which it is secured is worth $350,000 but that it is depreciating at $25,000 a year. Thus, if BBF uses the systems and equipment during the term of a multi-year plan, it will have lost substantial value and seriously impair NCA's secured position in it. NCA can demand adequate protection as a condition to BBF's continued use of the property, per §§363(e) and 361.

Note that in the preceding example, the burden will be on the creditor, NCA, to file a motion to bring the adequate protection issue to the court's attention because BBF is planning to use the property in the ordinary course of its business. But if BBF contemplated using the property in other than the ordinary course of its business, then the burden would have been on BBF to file a motion for permission to use it, per §363(b)(1).

What constitutes adequate protection is not defined in the Code but some guidelines as to what it may be are provided in §361. Section 361(1) says that adequate protection may be provided by periodic cash payments to the creditor sufficient to compensate for the decrease in value of the collateral.

EXAMPLE

> In the previous example, the court may order that as a condition to the continued use of the CAD/CAM systems and production equipment, BBF pay NCA $25,000 per year, an amount equal to the annual decrease in value of the collateral, which is also the extent to which NCA's secured claim is impaired by BBF's continued use of that collateral.

Section 361(2) says that the adequate protection requirement may be satisfied by the debtor providing the secured creditor with a lien on other property sufficient to compensate for the decrease in value of the collateral being used.

EXAMPLE

> The court may order that, as a condition to the continued use of the systems and equipment for a plan of three years' duration, BBF grant NCA a security interest in other property valued at $75,000, an amount equal to the annual decrease in value of the collateral, which is also the extent to which NCA's secured claim is impaired by BBF's continued use of the collateral. Of course, that would only be feasible if BBF has property with $75,000 of equity in which NCA could be granted a security interest.

Section 361(3) says that adequate protection may be provided by the debtor granting the creditor "such other relief" as will enable the creditor to realize the **"indubitable equivalent"** of its interest in the collateralized property. This is obviously an open-ended provision suggesting that, based on the facts of the case, the parties may work out, or the court may order, a unique solution to the adequate protection dilemma so long as the unquestioned value of the creditor's interest in the property is protected.

EXAMPLE

> Charles and Timothy Banowsky may offer to personally guarantee the debt of BBF to NCA, and NCA may accept these personal guarantees as adequate protection. Or, one or both of the brothers may grant NCA a mortgage in their personal residences up to the amount of the impairment of the NCA lien in the machinery. Or they may offer NCA an ownership position in a wholly new investment they are planning. Can you think of other solutions the debtor or its owners might propose to adequately protect NCA?

Administrative expense
Postpetition expenses incurred in preserving the property of the estate and in administering the estate by the trustee or debtor in possession.

Superpriority A priority granted to the holders of some claims that is superior even to other priority claims.

Section 507(b) allows a secured creditor whose adequate protection is ultimately found to be insufficient to claim an **administrative expense** for the amount of that insufficiency and gives that claim a **superpriority** among other allowed administrative expenses. (See Illustration 11-a and the discussion of administrative expenses in Chapter Eleven, Section B.) However, §361(3) stipulates that "such other relief" must be something *other than* the fact that the creditor may have an administrative claim later for the amount by which the adequate protection being proposed now ultimately proves insufficient.

EXAMPLE

> Assume that Charles and Timothy Banowsky offer the personal guarantees or mortgages as suggested in the preceding example, but NCA objects on the grounds that the impairment may be greater than what is being projected and the offer does not constitute adequate protection. BBF may want to argue that the judge should go ahead and approve the proposal since NCA will have a §507(b) superpriority administrative expense claim for the amount of any ultimate insufficiency. But §361(3) prohibits that. The adequate protection proposal must be found sufficient on its own terms without regard to the possible §507(b) claim.

The adequate protection dispute can become complicated when the debtor is in arrears to the secured creditor whose property the debtor desires to use, sell, or lease postpetition. In that situation it is natural for the creditor to ask that the DIP make up the arrearage or pay the creditor interest on the balance owed as a part of the adequate protection arrangement. However, most bankruptcy courts hold that prepetition arrearages are not a relevant issue in adequate protection decisions and are properly dealt with in the plan itself. And in *United Savings Association of Texas v. Timbers of Inwood Forest Associates, Ltd.*, 484 U.S. 365 (1988), the Supreme Court rejected a creditor's claim for interest payments on an arrearage as an adequate protection remedy based on alleged *lost opportunity* costs.

The Role of the Automatic Stay in Connection with the Motion for Permission to Use, Sell, or Lease Encumbered Property

Closely related to the issue of adequate protection when the DIP anticipates the use, sale, or leasing of encumbered property is the secured creditor's right to seek the lifting of the **automatic stay** of §362(a). We examined aspects of the automatic stay and lifting of the stay in Chapter Nine, Section F, in connection with a Chapter 7 liquidation. You may want to review that section at this time.

Frequently, a secured creditor's response to the DIP's intention to use, sell, or lease property in which the creditor is secured is a motion to lift the stay, under §362(d). In other words, the creditor not only opposes the DIP's plan to use, sell, or lease the property, it wants the stay lifted so it can repossess or foreclose on the property. Thus, bankruptcy courts frequently have two competing motions before them simultaneously: the DIP's §363(b)(1) motion and the creditor's competing §362(d) motion.

As we learned in Chapter Nine, one of the grounds for lifting the automatic stay under §362(d)(1) is lack of adequate protection, which we now know is also a consideration under §363(e) in the court's decision to permit the DIP's use, sale, or lease of the property. The adequate protection issue involves the same general analysis under both §§362(d)(1) and 363(e) such that if the court rejects the DIP's proffered adequate protection needed to satisfy §363(e), it will likely also find a sufficient ground exists to lift the stay as to the collateral under §362(d)(1).

EXAMPLE

If the court finds that the various proposals of BBF or its owners to provide NCA adequate protection for the impairment of its interest in the CAD/CAM systems and production equipment are insufficient, that finding will support both a rejection of BBF's intended use of the property under §363(e) and a lifting of the stay under §362(d)(1). Since losing that property will likely put BBF out of business, winning these operational motions is critical to BBF.

The alternative ground for lifting the automatic stay under §362(d)(2) is that

- the debtor has no equity in the property (more is owed on it than it is worth), and
- the debtor does not need it for an effective reorganization.

Note that both prongs of this test must be established by the creditor to have the stay lifted.

EXAMPLE

Under §362(d)(2), NCA will be able to show that it is owed $425,000 by BBF and that the property in which it is secured is worth only $350,000. Thus, it can satisfy the first prong of the §362(d)(2) test. But how do you think the court will rule if NCA contends that the CAD/CAM systems and production equipment is not needed by BBF for an effective reorganization? Of course, it could be that BBF in fact is not using and will not need some portion of that property, in which case the stay would likely be lifted as to that portion of the property, perhaps even with BBF's consent. Otherwise, do you see why NCA is more likely to move to lift the stay under §362(d)(1) than under (d)(2)?

For the **single asset real estate debtor**, §362(d)(3) provides generally that the automatic stay will be lifted against the real property that constitutes its primary income-producing asset within 90 days from the entry of the order for relief unless by that time the debtor has either

- proposed a plan of reorganization with a reasonable possibility of being confirmed, or
- begun making interest payments to the secured creditor based on the value of the secured property at the then-prevailing nondefault contract rate.

Bankruptcy Rule 4001(a) governs the procedure for filing a motion to lift stay pursuant to §362(d) or to condition the use, sale, or lease of property by the DIP on adequate protection pursuant to §363(e). That rule provides that either motion can be issued by the court **ex parte** (at the request of one party without the other being present) if the moving creditor alleges that immediate and irreparable injury, loss, or damage will occur unless the relief is granted without a hearing. But the order lifting stay issued ex parte will normally be **stayed** (held in abeyance) for 14 days until notice can be given to the DIP and a hearing held.

Ex parte An appearance before a court seeking relief without notice to other parties.

2. The Motion for Authorization to Incur Postpetition Debt

Operating a business after the Chapter 11 petition has been filed will typically involve the DIP incurring new or additional debt, either in the form of purchases on credit or the borrowing of funds.

EXAMPLE

A DIP operating a restaurant will need to order food items every day from suppliers. A debtor in the office supply business will need to order new inventory weekly. BBF has furniture orders yet to be filled and will need to purchase additional materials to fill those orders. If suppliers of any of these DIPs will not sell to them on credit as they ordinarily would, the DIPs may need to borrow money to pay for the needed supplies.

Postpetition Unsecured Debt Incurred in the Ordinary Course of Business

Section 364(a) authorizes the DIP to incur unsecured debt postpetition (in the form of a loan or extension of credit) without court approval so long as the debt is incurred in the ordinary course of the debtor's business. It further provides that such debt is to be treated as an administrative expense under §503(b)(1), which receives priority treatment over prepetition unsecured claims (see Illustration 11-a). This serves as an inducement to creditors to provide credit to a risky debtor postpetition but, understandably, it makes existing creditors of the struggling debtor nervous.

EXAMPLE

> In the last example, so long as the purchases of food items by the restaurant, inventory by the office supply business, and manufacturing materials by BBF are done in the ordinary course of those debtors' businesses, they will need no court approval for them. Suppliers who provide such DIPs with postpetition credit have the comfort of knowing their claims will be treated as priority administrative expense in the Chapter 11.

If a DIP has ordinarily done business with its suppliers on credit, continuing to do so will be within its ordinary course of business, even if the terms of credit change.

EXAMPLE

> Assume BBF's suppliers normally sell to it on 30-day credit terms: payment due 30 days after delivery. But after the Chapter 11 petition is filed they are more wary and require payment within ten days after delivery. Such arrangement will still be in the ordinary course of BBF's business because it is still a credit arrangement. No court approval will be needed.

Postpetition Unsecured Debt Incurred in Other Than the Ordinary Course of Business

If the DIP needs to incur unsecured debt *other* than in the ordinary course of its business, §364(b) requires that a motion for authorization to incur the debt or obtain credit be filed. The motion is governed by the "after notice and a hearing procedure."

EXAMPLE

> Assume BBF's suppliers, who have normally sold to it on credit, now demand cash on delivery so BBF arranges an unsecured line of credit with New Era Capital Alliance (see Assignment Memorandum #2 in Appendix C) to pay the suppliers. BBF will have to file a motion for authorization to obtain that loan, pursuant to §364(b), since that is not the way it has ordinarily done business.

EXAMPLE

> If BBF wants to begin purchasing teakwood and rubberwood on credit from the Hong Kong supplier (see Assignment Memorandum #2) prior to confirmation of its plan of reorganization, this postpetition unsecured credit arrangement would be outside its ordinary course of business since it had not previously purchased such wood for its manufacturing process. A motion will be required.

Anytime a motion to obtain court approval of postpetition indebtedness is required, the burden is on the DIP to show the court that the proposed transaction is made on fair and reasonable terms, is in the best interests of the estate, and will not pose an unjustifiable risk to parties in interest.

Postpetition debt incurred in other than the ordinary course of the debtor's business also receives priority treatment as an administrative expense under §503(b)(1). That may be sufficient inducement to the creditor to make the loan or extend the credit. But what if a potential creditor concludes it is not a sufficient inducement? Section 364(c)(1) authorizes the court, on motion, to approve a postpetition loan or credit transaction that gives the creditor a super-priority position over all other administrative expense claims. Since all postpetition expenses have priority as administrative expenses, this approach may induce the creditor to extend unsecured postpetition credit to the DIP by granting it a first-among-equals priority status as to its claim.

Postpetition Secured Debt

Often potential creditors refuse to extend postpetition loans or credit unless they can receive a security interest in property of the estate. Approving a postpetition debt arrangement involving the granting of a security interest to the creditor *always* requires court approval. Whether the proposed transaction will receive court approval depends in large part on how it is structured. A particular concern is how the proposed post-transaction debt arrangement will impact on prepetition creditors.

Section 316(c) provides that if the DIP is unable to obtain postpetition unsecured debt, the court can approve a secured postpetition debt arrangement in two ways, neither of which will impair the position of fully secured prepetition creditors.

First, the court can approve a transaction giving the postpetition creditor a security interest in property that is not presently encumbered.

EXAMPLE

Assume BBF requests the court to approve a postpetition loan from New Era Capital Alliance but New Era refuses to make the loan unless it is granted a security interest in some property of sufficient value. If BBF can show the court that it is unable to otherwise obtain this loan and it is in a position to grant New Era a security interest in some property not already collateralized, the court can approve the transaction.

Second, the court can approve the transaction giving the creditor a junior security interest in property that is presently encumbered.

EXAMPLE

Assume BBF requests the court to approve a postpetition credit arrangement with the Hong Kong supplier but the supplier refuses to extend the credit unless it is granted a security interest in some property. If BBF can show the court that it is unable to otherwise obtain this credit and that the supplier is willing to take a second secured position in the computerized machinery in which New Century Automation (NCA) already holds a prepetition first position, the court can approve the transaction.

Section 364(d) authorizes the court to approve a postpetition debt arrangement that grants the creditor a secured position senior to that of a prepetition secured creditor. For this reason, a lien granted to a postpetition creditor under

Priming lien A senior security interest granted to a creditor as an inducement to provide a postpetition loan or credit to a Chapter 11 debtor that will be superior to a prepetition interest in the same property.

§364(d) is sometimes referred to as a **priming lien** because it both *primes* (is deemed senior to) prepetition liens and *primes the pump* for the postpetition loan. Granting a priming lien to a postpetition creditor is obviously a dramatic step for a court to take and it is rarely granted. And it can only be granted where

- the DIP is unable to obtain postpetition unsecured debt or credit under one of the means authorized by §364, and
- the secured creditor whose prepetition lien is impaired is given adequate protection for its loss as by being granted an additional lien in other property or cash payments.

A postpetition debt arrangement not specifically addressed in the Code but approved by some courts is one that allows a prepetition creditor—secured or undersecured—to provide postpetition debt or credit to the DIP in exchange for the DIP granting the creditor a security interest covering not only the postpetition indebtedness, but also prepetition indebtedness owed to that creditor.

EXAMPLE

NCA is a prepetition creditor of BBF. NCA is owed $425,000 and is secured in property worth only $350,000. It is an undersecured creditor on the prepetition debt. If BBF seeks to purchase additional computer systems or equipment from NCA on credit, as part of its postpetition operations, NCA may condition such grant of further credit on BBF giving it a security interest in the goods to be sold to BBF, securing payment of not just the new debt being created but also the prepetition debt to the extent NCA is undersecured in it. Should the court approve that?

Cross-collateralization An arrangement whereby a creditor agrees to extend postpetition credit to a debtor in exchange for which property of the estate is offered as security for both the postpetition and prepetition claims of the creditor.

Some courts reject such **cross-collateralization** proposals for postpetition debt on the grounds that they are not specifically authorized by §364.

Any proposed postpetition debt arrangement has a potential impact on unsecured and undersecured prepetition creditors because the increased total indebtedness of the debtor threatens to dilute the return to such unsecured creditors in the event of a liquidation. Postpetition debt that involves granting a security interest in property to the postpetition creditor is of special concern to unsecured prepetition creditors because the secured creditor now has a superior claim to it. In deciding whether to approve a motion to incur postpetition debt, the court will consider the impact of the proposed arrangement on unsecured claims in its analysis of whether the proposed transaction is in the overall best interests of the estate and whether it presents an unjustified risk to all parties in interest.

Appealing Bankruptcy Court Decisions Regarding Postpetition Debt

It is not unusual for a DIP who is denied authorization of a proposed postpetition credit arrangement by the bankruptcy court to appeal that denial to the district court or the Bankruptcy Appellate Panel (BAP) (discussed in Chapter Six, Section G) in hopes of having the ruling reversed. It is also not unusual for a party in interest to appeal a bankruptcy court decision approving a proposed postpetition debt arrangement that the party opposes. Such an appeal can pose a real threat to the DIP, who desperately needs that postpetition arrangement to move forward. The bankruptcy judge has discretion at that point to stay (stop) the authorized arrangement, pending the outcome of the appeal, or to let the arrangement go forward, notwithstanding the appeal.

Section 364(e) provides that, unless the bankruptcy court stays the approved postpetition debt arrangement pending the appeal, it will be a valid and enforceable arrangement even if the bankruptcy judge's decision to authorize it is reversed or modified on appeal, so long as the creditor extended the new debt proposal in good faith. This provision reflects the Code's recognition of how absolutely critical postpetition debt arrangements can be to reorganizing debtors.

In some Chapter 11 cases, the motion to incur postpetition debt is made at the time the petition is filed and becomes the subject of one of the preliminary first day orders sought by the DIP that we considered in Chapter Seventeen.

EXAMPLE

Assume BBF files its Chapter 11 petition and, on the same day, a motion for authorization to use its cash collateral to pay certain obligations. But assume it has insufficient cash to pay all of those obligations even if that motion is granted. It may also file a motion to incur postpetition debt along with the petition and seek first day orders on both motions.

3. The Motion for Authorization to Assume or Reject Unexpired Leases or Executory Contracts

Every business filing for Chapter 11 reorganization is going to be a party to **unexpired leases** or other **executory contracts**. The widely accepted definition of an executory contract is the **Countryman definition**, named for Professor Vern Countryman. Using this definition, an executory contract is:

> a contract under which the obligation of both the bankruptcy and the other party to the contract are so far unperformed that the failure of either to complete performance would constitute a material breach excusing the performance of the other.

Vern Countryman, *Executory Contracts in Bankruptcy, Pt. 1*, 57 Minn. L. Rev. 439, 460 (1973).

Executory contract An agreement that is so far unperformed by the parties to it as to constitute a material breach.

Decisions must be made as to whether the DIP will fulfill its obligations under existing leases or other executory contracts by formally *assuming* them as part of the reorganization or will decline to fulfill its obligations under those contracts by formally *rejecting* them. For some contracts the DIP may have a third alternative, to *assign* the contract to another, discussed later in this chapter.

Section 365 governs the procedure for assuming or rejecting unexpired leases and executory contracts and seeks to balance two competing interests: the right of the DIP to make decisions in its own best interest as a reorganizing entity and the right of the other party to the contract to receive the benefit of the prepetition bargain the DIP made. Subject to these the procedural requirements of §365, the Code allows the debtor to "cherry pick" profitable contracts and leases to keep, while getting rid of unfavorable ones.

EXAMPLE

Assume that BBF at one time had a contract with Columbiana Leasing Company (CLC), pursuant to which it leased showroom space in a strip mall in which to sell its furniture at retail. The contract expired a year before BBF filed its Chapter 11 petition. BBF had paid all rental amounts it owed to CLC, and CLC had made the leased space available to BBF for the term of the lease. By the time BBF files its Chapter 11 petition, this contract has been fully performed by both parties. It is not executory, but executed.

EXAMPLE

Assume that when BBF's lease with CLC expired a year ago, BBF still owed CLC for three months' rent. CLC had continued to make the leased space available to BBF throughout the term of the lease. If BBF has not paid the past-due rent by the time it files its Chapter 11 petition, this is not an executory contract subject to §365 because CLC has fulfilled all its obligations under the contract. BBF has not, however, so BBF is, at the time its petition is filed, in breach of the contract with CLC, and CLC can make a claim as an unsecured creditor in BBF's case.

EXAMPLE

Assume that, six months before BBF's lease with CLC expired, CLC wrongfully evicted BBF, even though BBF was paying rent as it came due and otherwise complying with its obligations under the lease. When BBF files its Chapter 11 petition, this is not an executory contract subject to §365 because BBF fulfilled all its obligations under it until CLC breached it. BBF has a claim against CLC for that breach at the time it files its Chapter 11 case and that claim becomes property of the estate under §541 and can be pursued by BBF in the Chapter 11.

EXAMPLE

In fact, the lease agreement between BBF and CLC is still in effect when BBF files its Chapter 11 petition and has almost a year left in its term. BBF still has the obligation to lease the space and pay rent at $750 per month. CLC still has the obligation to lease the space to BBF. This is an executory contract subject to §365 because both parties still have duties to perform at the time the petition is filed. BBF has filed a motion for authorization to reject that lease on the grounds that it is unduly burdensome to the estate to continue that obligation as part of its reorganization (see Document 11 in the BBF case file).

Section 365 is a lengthy, convoluted section of the Code that provides detailed rules for the assumption or rejection of numerous specific types of contracts. Illustration 18-b lists the types of specific contracts that are subject to their own unique rules under §365.

Illustration 18-b: TYPES OF EXECUTORY CONTRACTS SUBJECT TO UNIQUE RULES FOR ASSUMPTION OR REJECTION UNDER §365

- Contracts for the lease of space in a shopping center [§§365(b)(3) and (h)(1)(C)]
- Contracts for the lease of aircraft terminals and gates [§§365(c)(4) and (d)(5) through (9)]
- Contracts for the lease of nonresidential real property [§§365(d)(3) and (4)]
- Contracts for the lease of nonconsumer personal property [§365(d)(10)]
- Contracts under which the debtor is the seller of an interest in a timeshare [§§365(h)(2)(i) and (j)]
- Contracts licensing the use of intellectual property [§365(n)]
- Contracts involving a commitment by the debtor to a federal depository institution [§365(o)]

The Procedure for Assuming or Rejecting a Contract and the Standards for Approval

Business judgment rule
A rule applied by the bankruptcy court to a trustee's (or DIP's) decision to assume or reject an executory contract pursuant to which the court will not interfere with the trustee's decision if it was made in good faith and reflects reasonable business judgment.

In general, and subject to specific requirements for the contracts listed in Illustration 18-b, the DIP must file a motion for the court to approve its assumption or rejection of an executory contract. Bankruptcy courts typically show some deference to a DIP's decision to assume or reject a contract. The test used in most courts in deciding whether to grant the motion to assume or reject is the **business judgment rule**, which means the court will grant the DIP's motion if it appears to have been made in good faith and reflects a reasonable business judgment that the assumption or rejection is in the best interest of the estate. When the motion seeks to reject a contract, some courts use the **undue burden** test, requiring the DIP to show that it would be unduly burdensome to the estate to have to fulfill its obligations under the contract.

EXAMPLE

BBF has filed a motion to reject the executory contract with CLC (see Document 11 in the BBF case file). In support of the motion to reject, it is prepared to show that its sales of furniture in the space leased from CLC have steadily declined and no longer represent a profitable venture for BBF and that, as part of its anticipated plan of reorganization, it will no longer be making the kind of furniture sold in the leased space. Do you think those arguments will satisfy the best judgment rule? Will they satisfy the undue burden test?

Timing of the Motion to Assume or Reject an Executory Contract

In general, §365 imposes no time limit on a debtor to decide whether to assume or reject an executory contract. Section 365(d)(2) provides that a debtor in Chapter 11 may assume or reject an executory contract or unexpired lease of residential real property or personal property "at any time before the confirmation of a plan." But the uncertainty and delay can be difficult on contractual counterparties, who have to hold their future planning in suspension, not knowing what the ultimate status of the contract will be. In recognition of this, the court may, upon request of a party in interest, set a deadline for assumption or rejection. It is not uncommon in a Chapter 11 for the nondebtor party to the contract or lease to file such a motion, often styled as a motion to compel the debtor to assume or reject executory contract (or unexpired lease).

In some instances, the Code provides for **automatic rejection** of a contract or lease if no formal motion to assume or reject is made within a specified timeframe.

> **EXAMPLE**
>
> Section 365(d)(1) provides that in a Chapter 7 case (the role of §365 in a Chapter 7 liquidation is discussed in more detail below) executory contracts (other than nonresidential real property leases) are automatically deemed rejected by the debtor unless a motion to reject or assume is made within 60 days of the order for relief. In addition, §365(d)(4) provides that an executory lease of nonresidential real property is deemed automatically rejected if the debtor does not assume or reject within the earlier of 120 days of the filing date or prior to plan confirmation. This period can be extended for an additional 90 days on motion of the DIP, but after that, the time to assume or reject an unexpired nonresidential real property lease can only be extended upon prior written consent of the landlord. §365(d)(4)(B).

Whether or not a Code provision calls for the automatic rejection of a contract on the expiration of a specified time period, there is almost always a delay between the time the petition is filed and the filing of a motion to assume or reject an executory contract. The petition is often filed in a rushed effort to stop an anticipated foreclosure or repossession and it is only afterward that the DIP is able to consider its options regarding the assumption or rejection of a contract. Section 365 is largely silent about the responsibilities of the parties to the executory contract during the period between filing and assumption or rejection. Must both parties continue to perform? Must leased property be returned by the debtor to the lessor? Section 365 clarifies this issue in connection with only two kinds of contracts and then only partially. Section 365(d)(3) requires the debtor to "timely perform" its obligations under a nonresidential lease agreement from the time the order for relief is entered but gives the debtor 60 days to begin such performance. And, §365(d)(5) obligates a Chapter 11 debtor who is a lessee in a personal property lease agreement (such as business equipment) to make all payments that arise after 60 days following the order for relief. Put another way, the DIP has 60 days to use the personal property without paying for it as a postpetition administrative expense, should it then decide to reject the lease.

During the time between filing the petition and accepting or rejecting a contract or lease, the debtor may continue to perform and accept the nondebtor's performance, but, without more, the debtor will not be presumed to have assumed the contract (see the highlighted case of *In re Whitcomb & Keller Mortgage Co.*, below).

Assuming a Contract on Which the Debtor Is in Default

Cure the default Payment of an arrearage to bring the defaulting party into compliance with its obligations under a contract.

If a DIP is not in default on an executory contract and wishes to assume the obligation as part of its reorganization, the creditor is usually more than happy to agree to the assumption. But if the DIP is in default on its obligations under the contract and still wishes to assume it, the creditor has a right to demand that something be done to **cure the default** as a condition to the assumption. Section 365(b)(1) provides that the debtor seeking to assume an executory contract of which it is in breach must do three things as a condition to approval of the assumption. The DIP must

- cure the past default or give adequate assurance that it will cure;
- compensate the creditor for any "actual pecuniary loss" resulting from the default or provide adequate assurance that it will compensate the creditor; and
- provide adequate assurance of future performance under the contract.

Section 365 does not define what *adequate assurance* is in this context, except in the case of *shopping center lease agreements* where the term is defined in detail in §365(b)(3).

EXAMPLE

Assume that BBF desires to assume its lease agreement with CLC for the shopping center space but it is in default for not paying the last three months' rent. Assume, too, that CLC can show that because BBF was in arrears on its rent payments to CLC, CLC was late with its own mortgage payment on the shopping center and incurred a $500 late fee. As a condition to assumption, BBF will have to pay CLC the past-due rent to cure the default (or somehow give assurance it will be paid) and pay CLC the $500 pecuniary loss it suffered as a result of BBF's default (or assurance of payment) and provide adequate assurance of future performance.

Where the DIP is in default on an executory contract, the other party may have the right to terminate the contract even if the DIP wishes to assume it by complying with §365(b)(1). Whether the other party can do so depends on the nature of the DIP's default. Some contracts contain a clause specifically authorizing the nondebtor party to declare default and terminate the contract on the grounds of insolvency, financial condition, or filing bankruptcy. Section 365(e)(1) prohibits the enforcement of these so-called *ipso facto* clauses postpetition. However, if the DIP is in material breach of the contract for reasons other than the violation of an *ipso facto* clause and cannot cure the arrearage owed or compensate for the damage already caused, the nondebtor party can normally declare the contract at an end and reject the proffered assumption. Most courts require the nondebtor party to the contract to file a motion to lift the automatic stay of §362(a) in order to terminate the contract (see *In re Carroll*, 903 F.2d 1266 (9th Cir. 1990)).

Ipso facto clause A provision in a contract declaring the filing of bankruptcy to be an act of default.

Consequences of the Rejection of a Contract by the DIP

If the DIP properly rejects a contract pursuant to §365, the rejection is treated as a **prepetition breach**, pursuant to §365(g)(1), and the other party to the contract will have an unsecured nonpriority claim for any prepetition amounts owed by the DIP and other damages resulting from that breach. Note, however, the special provisions of §§502(b)(6)(A) and (B) that limit damages resulting from termination of a lease to the greater of one year's rent or 15 percent of the remaining rent, but not to exceed a maximum of three years, plus unpaid rent due under the lease.

Obligations that the DIP owes to the creditor between the time the petition is filed and the time the contract is ultimately rejected and that are not paid by the debtor as an ordinary business expense under §363 are treated as §503(b) administrative expenses and will receive priority treatment under §507(a)(2).

EXAMPLE

If the motion of BBF to reject its lease agreement with CLC (Document 11 in the BBF case file) is granted, CLC will have a nonpriority unsecured claim for damages resulting from the breach, including any prepetition obligations that were not paid. However, to the extent BBF continued to occupy the premises postpetition, the landlord will have a priority administrative expense claim for the value of the premises during the time it was occupied by BBF postpetition.

If a debtor assumes an executory contract and then rejects it, the rejection is then treated as a postpetition breach by the estate and, pursuant to §365(g)(2), all damages accruing from the breach are treated as an administrative expense whether prepetition or postpetition.

EXAMPLE

Here are four scenarios that illustrate the rejection of pre- and postpetition leases and other executory contracts:

Case 1: Spoogie Co. vacated certain leasehold premises three months before the expiration of its lease, and ceased paying rent. Landlord continued to make the leased space available to Spoogie Co. throughout the term of the lease. Thereafter, Spoogie Co. filed its Chapter 11 petition. Landlord can file a nonpriority unsecured claim for three months' rent.

Case 2: Assume that six months before Spoogie Co.'s lease with Landlord expired, Landlord wrongfully evicted Spoogie Co., even though Spoogie Co. was paying rent as it came due and otherwise complying with its obligations under the lease. When Spoogie Co. files its Chapter 11 petition, Spoogie Co. has a claim against Landlord for breach of the lease. The claim for breach is property of the estate under §541 and can be pursued by Spoogie Co. in the Chapter 11.

Case 3: Assume that the lease agreement between Spoogie Co. and Landlord has two years left when Widget Co. files its Chapter 11 petition. Spoogie Co. has an initial 120 days to decide whether to assume or reject the lease, but may obtain an additional 90-day extension of that time. Spoogie Co. must decide whether to assume or reject before the end of that period, or the lease will automatically be deemed rejected unless Landlord consents to a further extension of the time.

Case 4: Assume that Spoogie Co. owes Landlord for six months of rent as of the petition date. Assume further that the lease agreement runs for another five years. If Spoogie Co. rejects the contract three months after the petition date having paid no postpetition rent, Landlord has a nonpriority unsecured claim for the six months of prepetition rent owed, plus damages for the remaining term. In addition, the Landlord has a priority administrative claim for three months of rent following the petition date.

P-H 18-b: In Case 4, and in light of §502(b)(6)(A), how will Landlord decide whether to assert a claim for one year of rent, or for 15 percent of the remaining five years?

IN RE WHITCOMB & KELLER MORTGAGE CO.
715 F.2d 375 (7th Cir. 1983)

[The debtor, Whitcomb & Keller, entered into a contract for computer services with Data-Link Systems, Inc. Sometime later it filed under Chapter 11. As of the petition date, Whitcomb & Keller owed Data-Link $12,954, which it scheduled as an unsecured claim. During the course of the bankruptcy, Data-Link continued to provide computer services to Whitcomb & Keller, which the debtor paid as an administrative expense of the estate. Later, after Whitcomb & Keller filed a motion to sell all its assets to a third party, Data-Link suddenly discontinued service, paralyzing the debtor's operations, and demanding that the court find that Whitcomb & Keller had assumed the contract due to its postpetition continued acceptance of services under the contract. The bankruptcy court entered an order restraining Data-Link from refusing to provide service, and finding that the contract had not been accepted merely because of postpetition performance. The district court affirmed and Data-Link appealed to the Seventh Circuit.]

OPINION: JAMESON, District Judge.

ACCEPTANCE OR REJECTION

Acceptance and rejection of executory contracts are governed by Section 365 of the Bankruptcy Code. Title 11 U.S.C. §365(d)(2) provides:

> In a case under Chapter 9, 11 or 13 of this title, the trustee may assume or reject an executory contract or unexpired lease of the debtor at any time before the confirmation of a plan, but the court, on request of any party to such contract or lease, may order the trustee to determine within a specified period of time whether to assume or reject such contract or lease.

In *In re American National Trust*, 426 F.2d 1059, 1064 (7 Cir. 1970), this court held that a trustee in a reorganization proceeding "is entitled to a reasonable time to make a careful and informed evaluation as to possible burdens and benefits of an executory contract," quoting from 6 Collier on Bankruptcy (14th Ed.) 576-80.

The executory contract between Data-Link and Whitcomb & Keller was in effect on October 27, 1980, when Whitcomb & Keller filed its bankruptcy petition. The contract remained in effect until Whitcomb & Keller made its decision to assume or reject the contract. Before Whitcomb & Keller made its decision, however, Data-Link ceased providing essential computer services. Whitcomb & Keller then applied for the restraining order, as it had a right to do. Similarly, the bankruptcy court had the authority to preserve the status quo until Whitcomb & Keller made its decision. The district court held that the bankruptcy court did not err in issuing the restraining order. We agree.

REQUIRING DEBTORS IN POSSESSION TO ASSUME OR REJECT EXECUTORY CONTRACT

Data-Link contends that because of the essential nature of the service it provided under the contract, the bankruptcy court, pursuant to Section 365 of the Bankruptcy Code, 11 U.S.C. §365(d)(2), should have specified a period of time within which Whitcomb & Keller was required to decide whether to assume or reject the executory contract. The parties had, of course, stipulated that the computer services were essential and that the information stored in the computer included information essential to the sale of Whitcomb & Keller's accounts. Data-Link argues that time for further inquiry into the benefits and burdens of the contract was not needed.

Data-Link interprets the purpose of §365(d) too narrowly. It is not enough that the trustee or debtor in possession recognize that the services provided under the contract are essential. Rather, §365(d) allows the trustee or debtor in possession a reasonable time within which to determine whether adoption or rejection of the executory contract would be beneficial to an effective reorganization. *In re American National Trust*, supra, 426 F.2d at 1064 (interpreting 11 U.S.C. §516(1) (repealed 1979), predecessor to §365).

The bankruptcy court addressed this issue in its order. After discussing the purpose of allowing the trustee a reasonable time to make its decision, the court noted that Data-Link was adequately protected because (1) Whitcomb & Keller had paid for all services received during the administration of its estate, and (2) the parties had stipulated that any right, lien or other interest that Data-Link might have would attach to the proceeds of the sale of Whitcomb & Keller's assets. Accordingly, the court exercised its discretion under §365(d) in denying Data-Link's request to require Whitcomb & Keller "to assume or reject the contract forthwith." We find no abuse of the bankruptcy court's discretion.

RECEIPT OF BENEFITS AND ASSUMPTION OF BURDENS

Data-Link next contends that a finding that Keller assumed the contract is necessary to avoid the inequitable result of allowing Whitcomb & Keller to derive the benefits of the contract without assuming its burdens.

In the first place, it may be noted that general principles governing contractual benefits and burdens do not always apply in the bankruptcy context. The purpose of the Bankruptcy Code is to "suspend the normal operation of rights and obligations between the debtor and his creditors." *Fontainebleau Hotel Corp. v. Simon*, 508 F.2d 1056, 1059 (5 Cir. 1975). Moreover, successful reorganization under Chapter 11 depends on relieving the debtor of burdensome contracts and pre-petition debts so that "additional cash flow thus freed is used to meet current operating expenses." H.R. Rep. No. 595, 95th Cong., 1st Sess. 221 (1977), reprinted in 1978 U.S. Code Cong. & Ad. News 5787, 5963, 6181. The post-petition services provided by Data-Link were operating expenses which Whitcomb & Keller paid in full. But merely providing such services did not alter Data-Link's position as a general unsecured creditor on its pre-petition claim. *U.S. Financial, Inc. v. Pacific Telephone & Telegraph*, 594 F.2d 1275, 1279 (9 Cir. 1979); *In re Kassuba*, 396 F. Supp. 324, 326 (N.D. Ill. 1975).

The cases upon which appellant relies are factually distinguishable. Here it is undisputed that Whitcomb & Keller paid in full for all services rendered during the administration of the estate, including the preparation of the data base tape. The only alleged breach of the executory contract relates to the indebtedness owed by Whitcomb & Keller when the petition was filed. Data-Link suffered no harm nor prejudice through the continued utilization of its computer services. Rather it presumably earned a profit from the continued use. Whitcomb & Keller's utilization of the computer services during the administration of the estate did not support a finding that Whitcomb & Keller assumed the contract or that Data-Link was entitled to a priority.

REQUIREMENTS FOR ASSUMPTION OF EXECUTORY CONTRACTS

Finally, Data-Link contends that Whitcomb & Keller's "application for the enforcement of this essential executory contract and the Bankruptcy Court's mandatory order thereon (that Data-Link must perform) constituted an assumption with Court approval."

Under §365(a) the trustee or debtor in possession, "subject to the court's approval, may assume or reject any executory contract . . . ." 11 U.S.C. §365(a) (emphasis added). Interpreting similar language in *In re American National Trust*, supra, 426 F.2d at 1064, this court declared: "'Assumption or adoption of the contract can only be effected through an express order of the judge.'" (quoting 6 Collier on Bankruptcy 576-80 (14th ed.)). No such order issued in the present case. Neither the bankruptcy court nor Whitcomb & Keller exhibited any intention of assuming the contract when the court enjoined Data-Link's termination of services. We will not infer such intention. Instead, we find the order was directed solely toward maintaining the status quo—a permissible purpose well within the bankruptcy court's power, as we have noted.

CONCLUSION

We find no abuse of the bankruptcy court's discretion. We agree with the bankruptcy court and the district court that (1) Whitcomb & Keller did not assume the executory contract; but rather (2) was entitled to and did reject the contract; and (3) Data-Link's pre-petition claim of $12,954.63 is an unsecured claim.

AFFIRMED.

POST-CASE FOLLOW-UP

The rule of *Whitcomb & Keller*—that a Chapter 11 debtor's continuing to perform and accept performance from a party to a prepetition executory contract is not, without more, an effective assumption of that contract by the debtor—is almost universally followed by bankruptcy courts around the country. The case also illustrates that the Chapter 11 debtor is not required to cure prepetition arrearages in contracts that it continues to perform postpetition but does not formally assume—the other party is entitled to adequate protection only postpetition and payment of postpetition charges as they come due is sufficient to provide that. It is only when the debtor wishes to assume the contract that arrearages must be cured or adequate assurance provided that they will be paid.

| *In re Whitcomb & Keller Mortgage Co.:* | **Real Life Applications** |

1. On what basis did the court find that Data-Link was adequately protected as to payments due from its continuing postpetition performance of this contract with debtor?

2. If the court had agreed with Data-Link that the debtor's continuing postpetition performance of the contract amounted to an effective assumption of it under §365, what would have been the necessary treatment of Data-Link's unsecured prepetition claim of $12,954.63 since debtor was assuming the contract?

Contracts That Cannot Be Rejected

Section 365(h) provides that a DIP who is the lessor of real property cannot reject that lease, although some of its obligations under the lease agreement can be rejected, such as the obligation to provide maintenance. Sections 365 (h) and (i) impose similar restrictions on the DIP's right to reject a timeshare contract in which the DIP is the seller or an installment land contract where the DIP is the seller. Section 365(n) provides that a DIP cannot reject a contract under which it has licensed another to use its patent, copyright, or other intellectual property.

EXAMPLE

Assume that one year before filing its Chapter 11 petition, BBF had entered into a contract to sell its manufacturing facility and had signed an installment agreement pursuant to which the buyer was to pay BBF in monthly installments over 20 years. That contract is executory when BBF files its Chapter 11 petition but it cannot reject it.

EXAMPLE

Assume that one year before filing its Chapter 11 petition, BBF had entered into licensing agreements with three other furniture manufacturers giving them the right, for ten years, to make furniture using a patented carving tool that BBF devised. Those contracts are executory when BBF files its Chapter 11 petition but it cannot reject them.

The Limited Right to Reject a Collective Bargaining Agreement

Collective bargaining agreement A contract between employers and labor unions specifying various conditions of employment for employees.

Consider the sad plight of a business debtor saddled with a costly union contract, also called a **collective bargaining agreement** (CBA). A CBA is a contract between employers and labor unions, typically for a short term, specifying terms for wages, hours, and other conditions of employment. Under the National Labor Relations Act of 1935 (NLRA), federal labor laws encourage collective bargaining between employers and employee representatives. 29 U.S.C. §158(d). If an employer modifies the terms of a duly negotiated CBA without following the steps set forth in the Act, it will be subject to a claim before the National Labor Relations Board. *NLRB v. Katz*, 369 U.S. 736, 747-748 (1962).

Legacy costs The obligation of an employer to its retirees including pension and healthcare obligations.

In addition to CBA, a business may also be burdened by excessive **legacy costs**, an industry euphemism for retiree pensions and healthcare plans. These expenses can constitute a substantial part of the company's expenses, and can sink a debtor's hopes for a successful reorganization or sale to a buyer if not reduced.

Section 1113(b)(1) requires that a DIP seeking to reject a collective bargaining agreement first present a proposal to the representative of the employees "based on the most complete and reliable information available at the time" which provides for "those necessary modifications in the employees' benefits and protections that are necessary to permit the reorganization of the debtor and assures that . . . all of the affected parties are treated fairly and equitably . . . ." Section 1113(b)(2) goes on to require that the parties must meet and confer "at reasonable times" and "in good faith" in attempting to reach mutually satisfactory modifications of a CBA. If the negotiations fail, the court may only approve rejection of a CBA if it finds that

- the DIP has made a proposal that meets the requirements of §1113(b)(1);
- the authorized representative of the employees has refused to accept the proposal without good cause; and
- the "balance of equities clearly favors rejection."

Section 1113 does not define the term "necessary modifications" and the courts are divided over the meaning of the phrase. The Third Circuit in *Wheeling-Pittsburgh Steel Corp. v. United Steelworkers of America*, 791 F.2d 1074, 1088-1089 (3d Cir. 1986), adopted a restrictive, pro-labor view of the provision, finding that the modification sought by the debtor must be the minimum necessary to ensure reorganization:

> The "necessary" standard cannot be satisfied by a mere showing that it would be desirable for the trustee to reject a prevailing labor contract so that the debtor can lower its costs. Such an indulgent standard would inadequately differentiate between labor contracts, which Congress sought to protect, and other commercial contracts, which the trustee can disavow at will . . . .
>
> While we do not suggest that the general long-term viability of the Company is not a goal of the debtor's reorganization, it appears from the legislators' remarks that they placed the emphasis in determining whether and what modifications should be made to a negotiated collective bargaining agreement on the somewhat shorter term goal of preventing the debtor's liquidation, the mirror image of what is "necessary to permit the reorganization of the debtor." This construction finds additional support in the conferees' choice of the words "permit the reorganization," which places the emphasis on the reorganization, rather than the longer term issue of the debtor's ultimate future.

In contrast, the probably majority approach articulated by the Second Circuit in *Truck Drivers Local 807 v. Carey Transportation, Inc.*, 816 F.2d 82, 90 (2d Cir. 1987), permits the debtor to propose modifications that facilitate the reorganization, even if they are not absolutely essential: "[T]he necessary requirement places on the debtor the burden of proving that its proposal is made in good faith, and that it contains necessary, but not absolutely minimal, changes that will enable the debtor to complete that reorganization process successfully." Id. Whichever view is utilized, courts in fact overwhelmingly approve debtor motions to reject CBAs. See, e.g., *In re Trump Entmt. Resorts, Inc.*, 2014 Bankr. LEXIS 4439 (Bankr. D. Del. Oct. 20, 2014); *In re 710 Long Ridge Road Operating Company, II, LLC* (Bankr. D.N.J. 2014); *In re Karykelon, Inc.*, 435 B.R. 663 (Bankr. C.D. Cal. 2010).

If the debtor does not reach agreement with its union and cannot reject a CBA under §1113, then it may seek to modify the CBA pursuant to the NLRB process, which can take a year or longer.

Section 1114 governs rejection of retiree healthcare plans, and adopts a similar procedure and test where the DIP seeks to reject or modify a contract involving payment of retirement benefits to company employees. If there is no union representative representing the retired employees affected, the DIP negotiates with a committee of retired employees appointed by the court.

P-H 18-c: There is no better example of the dramatic power of bankruptcy law to alter existing contract rights in a way that impacts the lives of many people than this limited right to reject a collective bargaining agreement between an employer and a duly certified union representative. An excellent article to read to learn more about the modification of collective bargaining agreements in Chapter 11 is *Collective Bargaining Agreements in Corporate Reorganizations*, by Andrew B. Dawson, Am Bankr. L.J. Volume 84, Issue 1, 2010. Locate and read that article. Do the courts seem generally receptive or hostile to such proposals? What priority seems to be given to the potential impact on current and retired employees of CBA rejection? Should the Code prohibit rejection of a CBA? Make it more difficult?

Rejection of Intellectual Property Contracts

Intellectual property is an important and increasingly complex issue in Chapter 11. The Code defines **intellectual property** (IP) in §101(35A) to include patents, copyrights, and trade secrets. However, this only includes U.S. patents and copyrights, not those of foreign origin. Note that trademarks, which are typically viewed as intellectual property in nonbankruptcy usage, are excluded from the Code definition of intellectual property as well.

Intellectual property licenses are generally considered to be executory contracts because the licensee must use the IP in accordance with the license agreement, and the licensor must refrain from suing for infringement. See, e.g., *In re Valley Media, Inc.*, 279 B.R. 105, 135 (Bankr. D. Del. 2002) ("The Third Circuit follows the general rule that intellectual property licenses, including copyright licenses, are executory contracts . . . .").

In 1988, Congress passed the Intellectual Property Licenses in Bankruptcy Act, which added §365(n) to the Code to govern assumption and rejection of IP contracts. Section 365(n) provides that in the event that the debtor as licensor rejects an IP license, the licensee may

- treat the license as terminated and assert a claim for money damages (but not specific performance), or

- continue to use the licensed IP while paying royalties due under the agreement, but waive any administrative claims for breach or setoff claims for rejection of the license.

The effect of §365(n) is to encourage and protect third-party investment and development of intellectual property. This is sound policy in an economy dependent upon advanced technology, and where new technology start-ups often contract with investors or more established firms to further develop the technology into marketable products.

As mentioned, §365(n) does not protect trademarks in the event that the debtor who owns a trademark rejects a prepetition trademark license agreement. Rejection is most likely to happen if the market value of a trademark is greater than the royalty fees paid under the license agreement because the debtor may seek to reject the license and sell the mark to another buyer for a higher royalty. So what is the consequence for the trademark licensee when the debtor rejects the license agreement in a Chapter 11? Does rejection mean the trademark license is effectively rescinded so that the licensee can no longer use it for the term of the contract?

Section 365(g) states that postpetition rejection of an executory contract shall be treated as a prepetition breach by the debtor. What that means for the licensee wishing to continue using the trademark for the term of the license, however, has divided the courts. In *Lubrizol Enterprises, Inc. v. Richmond Metal Finishers, Inc.*, 756 F.2d 1043 (4th Cir. 1985), cert. denied sub nom. *Lubrizol Enters. Inc. v. Camfield*, 475 U.S. 1057 (1986), the Fourth Circuit held that this means that the debtor recovers all interest in the trademark, including the right to exclude the nondebtor licensee from using it. On the other hand, the Seventh Circuit in *Sunbeam Prods., Inc. v. Chi. Am. Mfg., LLC*, 686 F.3d 372 (7th Cir. 2012), held that although the debtor's rejection of a trademark license freed the estate from its obligations to perform under the license, it was not equivalent to rescission of the license and did not divest the licensee of the right to continue using the trademark. For further reading on this interesting issue, see James M. Wilton & Andrew G. Devore, *Trademark Licensing in the Shadow of Bankruptcy*, 68 Bus. Law. 739 (May 2013).

4. The Motion for Authorization to Assign Contract Rights

When one party to a contract transfers his rights under the contract to another he **assigns** those rights. When one party to a contract transfers his duties under the contract to another he **delegates** those duties. Under the common law of contracts, contractual rights and duties can be freely assigned or delegated, unless

- the contract itself prohibits such assignment or delegation;
- a statute or rule prohibits such assignment or delegation;
- the contract involves the personal performance by the party seeking to delegate his performance to another;
- the contract involves a performance by the party seeking to assign his rights to another that could impact on the duty of the other party to perform; or
- the other party to the contract is a governmental entity.

Section 365(c)(1) provides that a DIP may assign its rights or delegate its duties under an executory contract *unless* such "applicable law" prohibits an assignment or delegation.

EXAMPLE

> If a federal or state law prohibited the assignment of a contract to export furniture outside the United States, BBF, as DIP could not assign a prepetition contract to manufacture and deliver furniture to China to another furniture manufacturer under §365. If BBF had a prepetition contract with a motivational speaker to come and speak to the employees in its Arizona headquarters, it could not assign the right to receive that service to another company. If BBF had a prepetition contract to manufacture and deliver furniture to an Arizona state agency, it could not assign that contract to another furniture manufacturer. If BBF had a prepetition contract requiring a California supplier to deliver materials to it in Arizona, it could not assign that contract to a manufacturer in Maine.

However, §365(f)(2) requires that the person to whom the assignment is made must provide the other party to the contract with adequate assurance that the assignee/delegate will perform.

EXAMPLE

> Assume that in lieu of rejecting its lease with CLC, BBF proposes to assign its lease of the premises to another furniture manufacturer. This assignment can be approved by the court if the furniture manufacturer to whom the lease is assigned can provide CLC with adequate assurance of performance.

Non-assignment clause
A provision in a contract that prohibits one or both parties from assigning the contract to a third party.

Though state contract law routinely enforces **non-assignment clauses** in contracts, §365(f)(1) specifically renders such contractual provisions unenforceable in bankruptcy.

Section 365(f)(2) requires that the debtor must first assume a contract or lease before it can be assigned, and that the assignee must provide the other party with adequate assurance of future performance of the contract or lease.

EXAMPLE

> Assume that BBF proposes to assign its lease agreement with CLC to another furniture manufacturer but the lease agreement itself prohibits such assignment. That non-assignment clause will not be given effect in the Chapter 11 case. However, BBF will have to formally assume the contract with CLC before assigning it and the assignee will have to provide CLC with adequate assurance of future performance of the lease.

Under general contract law, an assignor remains liable for its obligations under an assigned contract. In bankruptcy, however, §365(k) provides that an assignment relieves the DIP or trustee and the estate from any future liability on the contract. As mentioned, under §365(f)(2) the assignee must give adequate assurance of future performance, which at least partially makes up for the lack of continuing liability by the assignor under bankruptcy law.

5. The Abandonment of Property of the Estate

Abandonment The formal relinquishment of property of the estate by the trustee.

As discussed in Chapter Eleven, Section A, §554 of the Code and Bankruptcy Rule 6007 authorize the trustee to **abandon** any property of the estate that is

- of inconsequential value to the estate, or
- burdensome to the estate.

EXAMPLE

BBF has a lot of old, worn-out saws and other equipment that has no real value and that it should have gotten rid of long ago. This property may be subject to a §554 notice of intent to abandon for that reason. Or assume BBF has a piece of equipment that sprays a particular lacquer finish on some furniture. The lacquer contains a particular chemical closely regulated by the Environmental Protection Agency (EPA) that requires BBF to file quarterly reports of use to the EPA. But in fact, the equipment is not used any longer because neither BBF nor any other furniture maker still uses that lacquer. But as long as BBF owns that equipment, it must file the EPA reports. BBF may file a §554 notice of intent to abandon that equipment as either of inconsequential value or as unduly burdensome to the estate.

Abandonment is accomplished by the filing of a notice of intent and is governed by the "after notice and a hearing" procedure. No hearing will be conducted if a timely objection is not filed following notice of intent to abandon has been given.

6. The Motion for Authorization to Pay Interim Compensation

By their nature, Chapter 11 cases that survive the preliminary operational motions considered in Chapter Seventeen tend to go on for some time and involve a lot of work by the DIP's attorney and other professional persons retained by the DIP or the creditors' committee, or by the trustee, if one has been appointed. Consequently, motions for authorization to pay **interim compensation** are common. Section 331 provides that motions for interim compensation can be made not more than once every 120 days after the order for relief, though the court has discretion to permit them more frequently. Bankruptcy Rule 2016 requires that all motions for compensation and reimbursement of expenses be accompanied by a detailed statement of services rendered, time spent, and expenses incurred.

7. Motions to Approve Key Employee Retention or Incentive Agreements

Picture a sinking ship. The crew is working feverously to keep the vessel afloat, but at the height of their exertions, the captain and officers lower themselves into a sturdy life boat, row over to a nearby yacht, and comfortably motor away, leaving the hapless crew to its fate. Such can be the temptation of insiders and upper management of a distressed enterprise: Better to find a suitable alternative while you can than to risk the turmoil and uncertainty of a collapsing enterprise.

The downside for those who remain (either voluntarily or because they have no choice) is that prospects for successful reorganization may be diminished if the most experienced managers abandon ship. Of course, in some situations the opposite may be true—the senior managers who piloted the enterprise onto financial shoals would be best tossed overboard, figuratively speaking. But, if we assume a situation where top management is important or even indispensable for successful reorganization, then the debtor will look for a strategy to retain their services during the Chapter 11 process. For this, Chapter 11 debtors can request the court to approve a **Key Employee Retention Plan** (KERP) to retain key employees during the bankruptcy, or a **Key Employee Incentive Program** (KEIP) to incentivize them to successful performance in the bankruptcy.

KERPs

A KERP is a postpetition incentive program designed to retain certain key employees. A KERP typically consists of enhanced compensation through confirmation of the plan, severance payments if the employee is terminated, indemnity for postpetition conduct, and bonus payments tied to a successful reorganization. Since compensation under a KERP has priority as an administrative expense, the debtor must obtain court approval, after notice and a hearing.

In past decades, KERPs were routinely proposed and approved. But they were frequently criticized as unnecessary, collusive arrangements for the benefit of insiders. To curb these perceived abuses, Congress included §503(c) in BAPCPA imposing strict conditions on the use of KERPs.

Section 503(c)(1) applies when a postpetition compensation program proposes to make a transfer or incur an obligation for the benefit of an "insider" in order to induce the person to remain with the debtor's business. "Insider" is defined in §101(31) to include a relative or general partner of the debtor; a director, officer, or person in control of the debtor; and any relatives. If the KERP is found to benefit an insider, then it can only be approved if the debtor establishes that

- the individual has a bona fide job offer from another business at the same or greater rate of compensation;
- the services provided by the individual are "essential to the survival of the business"; and
- the compensation is not greater than ten times the amount of retention compensation given to non-management employees, or 25 percent of the individual's total compensation in the prior year.

Clearly, the evidentiary bar for approval of a KERP for insiders is high. Overall, §503(c)(1) is a departure from the business judgment standard (discussed earlier requiring only a showing that a decision was made in good faith and reflects a reasonable business purpose) that otherwise governs a DIP in making day-to-day decisions.

The requirements of §503(c)(1) apply when the proposed retention program will benefit insiders. When the retention program seeks to retain non-insiders, courts utilize the less stringent test of §503(c)(3), which allows "other transfers and obligations that are outside the ordinary course of business" to be approved when justified by the "facts and circumstances of the case." In *GT Advanced*

Technologies, Inc. v. Harrington, 2015 WL 4459562 (D.N.H. July 21, 2015), the court considered the debtor's motion to approve a retention program for non-insiders. The court focused on whether the proposed plan would serve the interests of creditors and the debtor's estate. Id. at *7. In doing so, the court used the following elements, which are known as the *Dana* factors:

- Is there a reasonable relationship between the plan proposed and the results to be obtained, i.e., will the key employee stay for as long as it takes for the debtor to reorganize or market its assets, or, in the case of a performance incentive, is the plan calculated to achieve the desired performance?
- Is the cost of the plan reasonable in the context of the debtor's assets, liabilities, and earning potential?
- Is the scope of the plan fair and reasonable; does it apply to all employees; does it discriminate unfairly?
- Is the plan or proposal consistent with industry standards?
- What were the due diligence efforts of the debtor in investigating the need for a plan: analyzing which key employees need to be incentivized, what is available, and what is generally applicable in a particular industry?
- Did the debtor receive independent counsel in performing due diligence and in creating and authorizing the incentive compensation?

Id. at *8, citing *In re Dana Corp.*, 358 B.R. 567, 576-577 (Bankr. S.D.N.Y. 2006). Other courts use the less restrictive business judgment test in determining whether to approve a KERP for non-insiders, sometimes weighing the same *Dana* factors, but asking whether the KERP is designed, in effect, to "motivate insiders to rise to a challenge or merely report to work." *In re Hawker Beechcraft, Inc.*, 479 B.R. 308, 313 (Bankr. S.D.N.Y. 2012) (citing *In re Velo Holdings*, 472 B.R. 201, 209 (Bankr. S.D.N.Y. 2012)); see also *In re Patriot Coal Corp.*, 492 B.R. 518 (Bankr. E.D. Mo. 2015) (adopting business judgment standard).

KEIPs

As an alternative to the heavy burden of qualifying a KERP, debtors have turned to Key Employee Incentive Programs (KEIPs). The purpose of a KEIP is to incentivize employees for successful postpetition performance. Since a KEIP, as stated, does not seek to retain key employees, court approval is based on the less onerous "facts and circumstances" test of §503(c)(3), rather than the strict evidentiary requirements of §503(a)(1).

In a KEIP, a firm offers bonuses contingent on the employees achieving predetermined milestones. Performance metrics can include

- preconfirmation financial performance (e.g., cash flow, cost containment, net income, etc.);
- timely plan confirmation, usually by a determined date;
- asset sales;
- payments to creditors; and
- postconfirmation financial performance.

In order for a plan to be defined as a KEIP, the debtor must show that the plan requires "affirmative action [by the insiders] beyond that contemplated prepetition." *In re Patriot Coal*, 492 B.R. at 518. Upon satisfying this burden of proof, the

KEIP is analyzed using the same standards that are applied to retention programs for non-insiders. Not surprisingly, because of the more lenient standards that apply under §503(c)(3), Chapter 11 debtors increasingly pitch their plans as KEIPs. One commentator finds this to be nothing more than a loophole around the clear intent of Congress to rein in the excessive use of bonuses paid to high-level employees in Chapter 11 bankruptcies. See Dorothy Hubbard Cornwall, *To Catch a KERP: Devising a More Effective Regulation Than §503(c)*, 25 Emory Bankr. Dev. J. 485, 506 (2009).

8. Comparison to Operational Motions in a Chapter 7 Business Liquidation

All of the motions we have considered in this section and in Chapter Seventeen, Section F could also be filed in a Chapter 7 liquidation, though they rarely are. As was noted in Chapter Eleven, Section A, in a Chapter 7 liquidation of an ongoing business, the trustee may in some cases seek permission, pursuant to §721, to continue operating the business postpetition for a while in order to maximize the value of the property of the estate and the ultimate payout to creditors. If the court authorizes the trustee to operate the business as part of its liquidation, then the same concerns about operating a business postpetition may arise in that Chapter 7 as we have considered in these two sections with regard to a Chapter 11.

E. ▶ Gathering the Property of the Estate

Recall that §1107(a) grants the DIP the powers of a bankruptcy trustee. This includes the power to pursue contingent or unliquidated claims that are assets of the estate to judgment (see Chapter Ten, Section B), to compel turnover of the debtor's property from third persons and custodians holding it (see Chapter Ten, Section D), and to avoid other prepetition transfers of the debtor's property (see Chapter Ten, Section E). If the DIP for any reason refuses to pursue such action, a creditor or the creditors' committee can seek permission from the court by motion to pursue it for the benefit of the estate, and the attorney's fees and other expenses incurred may be treated as administrative expenses, pursuant to §§503(b)(3) and (4), and receive priority treatment, per §507(a)(2) (see Illustration 11-a).

EXAMPLE

Assume that just before filing its Chapter 11 petition, BBF declared an unusual $10,000 cash dividend payable to all five shareholders. That transfer might well be recoverable as a fraudulent transfer but the shareholders operating BBF as DIP might be reluctant to sue themselves. One or more creditors might petition the court for authority to file suit for the recovery of those funds for the estate. Of course, such activity by the shareholders of BBF might also cause a creditor to move for the appointment of a trustee in the case for cause (see Illustration 17-d) or to dismiss or convert the case to a Chapter 7 for gross mismanagement (see Illustration 18-a).

CHAPTER SUMMARY

Section 363(b) allows the debtor to lease or sell capital assets and other property other than in the ordinary course of business upon notice to creditors and a hearing and approval by the court.

The sale of assets under §363(b) can potentially allow the debtor to restructure without going through the plan confirmation process (known as a *sub rosa* plan). Hence, a sale of all or substantially all of debtor's assets will only be approved if there are sound business reasons to support the sale.

Under §363(k) a secured creditor is entitled to credit-bid the value of its security interest in a §363(b) sale. Section 363(f) provides that a sale of assets under §363(b) shall be free and clear of claims or interests, as long as any one of the five conditions listed in that section are met.

Section 364 allows a debtor to obtain postpetition unsecured credit in the ordinary course. The debtor must obtain court approval to obtain credit other than in the ordinary course. If approved by the court, a postpetition creditor may be granted a lien against property of the estate, and in appropriate circumstances, a creditor may receive a priming or superpriority lien with priority over an existing prepetition lien.

Section 365 allows a debtor to assume, reject, and, under certain circumstances, assign an executory contract or unexpired lease on notice and after hearing and approval by the bankruptcy court.

Bankruptcy courts apply the debtor friendly "business judgment" rule when deciding whether to approve a motion for assumption or rejection, and only in unusual cases will considerations such as public policy come into play to challenge the debtor's prerogatives as to contracts and leases.

For most contracts and leases, the debtor may make the determination to assume or reject at any time before confirmation of a plan and mere continuance of postpetition performance is not by itself an assumption.

If a contract is rejected by the debtor, the rejection will be treated as a prepetition breach pursuant to §365(g)(1), for which the nondebtor party may assert a nonpriority claim. If the contract is assumed and later rejected, any amounts owed under the contract will be treated as an administrative claim under §365(g)(2).

A debtor must cure or give adequate assurance of curing any substantial default before it can assume an executory contract or unexpired lease.

After assuming a contract, a debtor may assign the contract to a third party even if the contract or nonbankruptcy law prohibits the assignment without consent of the nondebtor. §365(f). However, §365(c) provides that the contract may not be assumed or assigned if nonbankruptcy law excuses the nondebtor party from performing or accepting performance by anyone except the original contracting party as in personal services contracts.

Intellectual property contracts (excluding trademarks) are governed by §365(n) and allow the nondebtor licensee to continue using the licensed technology in the event the debtor rejects the contract, even though the debtor is relieved of its obligations under the license.

KERPs and KEIPs are compensation programs offered to key employees who remain with the debtor throughout the bankruptcy. Court approval of such programs is governed by §503(c) and the standards for approval are based on whether the program is aimed at insiders or non-insiders, and whether the purpose is to retain the employee or offer incentive for meeting financial performance metrics.

Chapter 11 debtors have the same power as a bankruptcy trustee to abandon property of the estate and to exercise turnover and avoidance powers.

REVIEW QUESTIONS

1. Why do most creditors not need to file proofs of claim in a Chapter 11 case? When is a creditor in a Chapter 11 required to file a proof of claim?
2. When can a Chapter 11 debtor *not* convert the case to one under Chapter 7 without court approval?
3. What is the vertical/horizontal test used in most federal districts to determine if a Chapter 11 debtor's intended use, sale, or lease of property of the estate is within its ordinary course of business?
4. What is a *sub rosa* Chapter 11 plan?
5. What role does adequate protection play in a Chapter 11 debtor's plan to use, sell, or lease collateralized property of the estate? Where adequate protection is required, how might a debtor provide it?
6. How does the Code's treatment of postpetition debt serve as an inducement to creditors to loan funds or extend credit to a Chapter 11 debtor? How do the procedures for incurring postpetition debt in the ordinary and non-ordinary course of debtor's business differ?
7. What is a priming lien? What is cross-collateralization?
8. What is the Countryman definition of an executory contract? What is the business judgment rule in the context of a Chapter 11 debtor's right to assume or reject an unexpired lease or executory contract?
9. What special requirements are placed on a Chapter 11 debtor seeking to assume a prepetition contract on which there is a deficiency owed? If a debtor continues to perform and accept performance under a contract postpetition before it has formally assumed or rejected it, is that an implied assumption of that contract? Under what circumstances can a prepetition deficiency balance owing on an executory contract become entitled to be treated as a priority administrative expense?
10. Summarize the limited right a Chapter 11 debtor has to reject a collective bargaining agreement. What are the two different approaches taken by courts to deciding whether the "necessary modifications" requirement of §1113 is satisfied?
11. Explain how state common law regarding the assignability of contract rights can prohibit a Chapter 11 debtor from assigning contract rights postpetition.
12. Explain the difference between a KERP and a KEIP. Why is it more difficult to obtain court approval of a KERP benefiting an insider to the Chapter 11 debtor rather than one benefiting a non-insider?

WORDS AND PHRASES TO REMEMBER

abandon

adequate protection

administrative expense

assign

automatic rejection

automatic stay

business judgment rule

collective bargaining agreement

Countryman definition

cross-collateralization

cure the default

deemed allowed

deemed filed

delegate

equity security holders

executory contracts

ex parte

first day motion

first meeting of creditors

horizontal factor

indubitable equivalent

intellectual property

interim compensation

ipso facto clause

Key Employee Incentive Plan

Key Employee Retention Plan

legacy costs

non-assignment clause

notice of commencement of case

ordinary course of business

prepetition breach

priming lien

proof of claim

proof of interest

reasonable foreseeability (test)

single asset real estate debtor

stayed

sub rosa

superpriority

undue burden (test)

unexpired leases

vertical factor

TO LEARN MORE: A number of TLM activities to accompany this chapter are accessible on the companion web site for this textbook at http://aspen-lawschool.com/books/Parsons_Debt4e/.

Chapter Nineteen:

The Chapter 11 Business Reorganization—The Plan of Reorganization

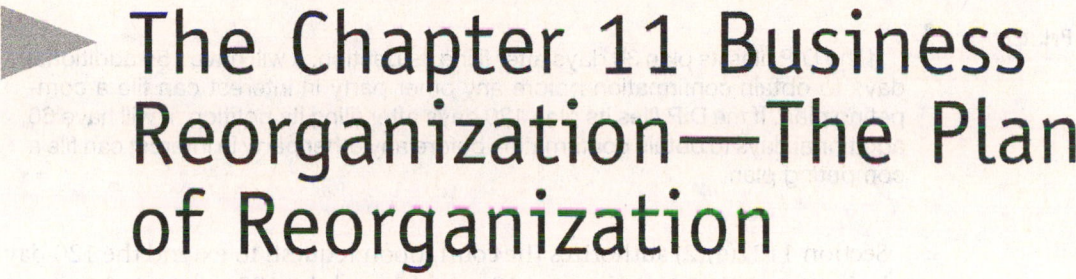

KEY CONCEPTS

- The debtor in possession has the exclusive right, during the 120 days following the order for relief, to file a proposed plan
- The plan must place creditors' claims and equity security holder interests into classes and specify which classes are impaired
- Secured claims may be modified in a Chapter 11 plan in much the same way they can be in a Chapter 13
- Prior to soliciting votes to accept or reject a plan, a debtor must submit a disclosure statement containing adequate information to enable a hypothetical investor to make an informed judgment about the plan
- Solicitation of votes must be done in good faith and classes of claims or interests that are not impaired are conclusively presumed to accept the plan
- A plan may be confirmed consensually by affirmative vote of all impaired classes under §1129(a)
- Alternatively, a plan may be confirmed by cram down so long as at least one impaired class approves it and the debtor satisfies the no unfair discrimination and fair and equitable treatment tests for all secured and unsecured classes under §1129(b)
- Upon confirmation, property of the estate immediately vests in the reorganized debtor and is free and clear of all liens, claims, and interests, except as allowed by the confirmed plan

 A. ▶ **The Exclusivity Period for Filing a Plan of Reorganization**

Exclusivity period The period of time in which a Chapter 11 debtor has the exclusive right to propose a plan of reorganization.

The Chapter 11 debtor in possession (DIP) may file a proposed plan of reorganization with the petition or at any time thereafter, per §1121(a). Section 1121(b) gives the DIP the exclusive right, during the 120 days following the order for relief, to file a proposed plan. Practitioners call this the **exclusivity period**. If the DIP does file a proposed plan during the exclusivity period, then no competing plan can be filed until 180 days after the petition is filed. This gives the DIP additional time to get its plan confirmed. Both the 120-day and 180-day periods begin to run from the day the order for relief is entered, and the 180-day period is available to the DIP regardless of at what point in the 120-day exclusivity period the DIP proposes its plan.

EXAMPLE

> If the DIP files its plan 30 days after filing its petition, it will have 150 additional days to obtain confirmation before any other party in interest can file a competing plan. If the DIP files its plan 120 days after filing its petition, it will have 60 additional days to obtain confirmation before any other party in interest can file a competing plan.

Section 1122(d)(2) authorizes the court, upon request, to extend the 120-day exclusivity period, but not beyond 18 months, and the 180-day period, but not beyond 20 months.

Exclusivity does not apply if a trustee has been appointed, in which case §1121(c) provides that any party in interest—including the debtor, trustee, creditor, equity security holder, or any committee that has been named—can file a proposed plan. And if the DIP fails to file a proposed plan during the 120-day exclusivity period or cannot get its plan confirmed within the 180 period, then those same parties in interest are free to propose a plan.

The prospect that a creditor might file a competing plan of reorganization if the DIP fails to take advantage of the exclusivity period gives those creditors leverage in negotiating the terms of a plan with the DIP. This leverage is even greater because creditors get to vote to approve or disapprove of the DIP's plan of reorganization as part of the confirmation process (see Section E). The DIP has to formulate its plan knowing that if it cannot propose it in the time allowed or win sufficient creditor approval for its confirmation, an alternative plan may be proposed that is much less advantageous to it. For all these reasons, the plan negotiation period of a Chapter 11 case (see Illustration 17-a) tends to be yet another white-knuckle time for the DIP.

P-H 19-a: By now you should appreciate how pressure-packed a Chapter 11 case can be from the time the decision is made to file, forward. What does this aspect of the business reorganization say about the professional skills needed by attorneys representing the debtor, creditors, or creditors' committees and the legal professionals assisting them? Is this an area for the inexperienced lawyer or paralegal to work without close supervision? What does it say about the importance of communication and negotiating skills? What does it say about the importance of being able to meet numerous deadlines and of beginning work early in order to do so? What does it say about the ability of all the players to perform at a high level under constant pressure?

In the small business case, §1121(e) provides for only a single 180-day exclusivity period for the small business DIP to file its plan and mandates that the plan be filed within 300 days after the order for relief. Extension of these time periods is available only if the small business DIP convinces the court by a preponderance of the evidence that a plan likely will be confirmed within a reasonable time, and any extension granted must state a new deadline.

Remember that, in a case involving a single asset real estate debtor, §362(d)(3) mandates that the automatic stay will be lifted against the debtor's real property unless, within 90 days following the order for relief, the DIP has filed a plan having a reasonable possibility of being confirmed or has commenced interest payments to the creditor in the real property. If the interest payments have commenced within the 90 days but no plan is filed by the single asset real estate debtor during that period, it will have the benefit of the 120-day and 180-day provisions of §1121(b).

In a prepackaged Chapter 11 case, the plan will typically be filed with the petition.

B. ▶ Content of the Plan of Reorganization

Section 1123 governs the contents of a plan of reorganization. Section 1123(a) contains a number of mandatory plan provisions, while §1123(b) sets out a number of optional plan provisions. We will examine some of the key mandatory and optional provisions here.

1. Classes of Claims and Interests

Classes Designated groupings of creditor claims or equity interests with members of each class receiving equal treatment.

Section 1123(a)(1) requires that the plan place creditors' claims and equity security holder interests into **classes**. Per §1122(a), the claims and interests placed in each class must be **substantially similar**. The Code does not define the phrase *substantially similar* but courts have construed it to refer primarily to the similarity of the *legal rights* arising from the nature of the claim and its priority.

EXAMPLE

Secured and unsecured creditors have different legal rights and must be placed in different classes. A secured creditor holding a first mortgage on real property has different legal rights than a secured creditor holding a junior mortgage and would normally be put in a different class. Creditors secured in realty have different legal rights than those secured in personalty. Holders of priority claims under §507 have different legal rights than those holding non-priority claims. Creditors holding disputed, nonliquid, or contingent claims have different rights than creditors whose claims are not disputed, noncontingent, and liquidated. Unsecured creditors holding trade debt (e.g., suppliers of the debtor) have different legal rights than unsecured creditors holding nontrade debt (e.g., utilities). If a corporation had issued both preferred and common stock, the legal rights of those interest holders are different and they must be placed in separate classes.

Most Chapter 11 plans place each secured claim in its own separate class. Pursuant to §1111(b)(1), an **undersecured claim** may be treated in two different classes: one class for its secured claim up to the value of the collateral, per §506(a)(1), and another class for its unsecured balance.

E X A M P L E

> New Century Automation (NCA) holds a claim of $425,000 against Banowsky Brothers Furniture, Inc. (BBF), and is secured in the CAD/CAM systems and production equipment valued at only $350,000. It is an undersecured creditor. In the BBF plan (Document 13 in the BBF case file), the secured claim of NCA valued at $350,000, per §506(a)(1), is placed in one class and the unsecured portion of its claim valued at $75,000 is placed in another.

Election of remedies
Doctrine requiring a secured creditor to choose between exercising a right of foreclosure on secured property or suing the debtor for a judgment, but disallowing both foreclosure and a suit for deficiency judgment.

This right of an undersecured creditor to have its claim bifurcated in this way under §1111(b)(1) is present in a Chapter 11 even though under the contract or state law that creditor has no recourse against the debtor for the unsecured portion of its claim. (See the discussion of the **election of remedies** and **nonrecourse** doctrines recognized in some states in Chapter Two.)

Creditors holding unique claims can be placed in a class by themselves. And §1122(b) allows for the placing of dissimilar but low-value claims in a single class, if the classification is reasonable and necessary for **administrative convenience**.

E X A M P L E

> A plan might lump together in one class all miscellaneous unsecured claims for less than $200.

P-H 19-b: Review the plan of reorganization proposed by BBF (Document 13 in the BBF case file) and identify the various classes of claims and interests it creates. Are these classifications reasonable? Are any subject to challenge as not being based on substantially similar claims or interests? Do you see why the various secured claims are treated in separate classes?

Administrative expenses
Postpetition expenses incurred in preserving the property of the estate and in administering the estate by the trustee or debtor in possession.

Gap period The period of time between the filing of a petition and entry of the order for relief.

Administrative expenses and other §507 priority claims (see Illustration 17-a) receive specialized treatment in a plan of reorganization. Section 507(a)(2) **administrative expenses** and §507(a)(3) claims arising out of the **gap period** (the period between the date of the petition and the entry of the order for relief) in an *involuntary case* must be paid in full on the effective date of the plan, per §1129(a)(9)(A). Tax claims holding §507(a)(8) priority must be paid in full within six years of assessment, per §1129(a)(9)(C). Because of the nondiscretionary treatment of such claims, some plan drafters treat them as not subject to classification and simply recite the mandated treatment. But, more typically, §507 priority claims are placed in the first class of claims designated in the plan.

P-H 19-c: Review the treatment of §507 administrative expenses in Article III of the BBF plan of reorganization (Document 13 in the BBF case file). Does Class 1 comply with the requirements of §§507(a)(2) and (8) regarding the payment of administrative expenses and priority tax claims? Do you see why if the court denies the DIP's motion to pay prepetition tax withholding claims associated with unpaid prepetition wages (see discussion in Chapter Seventeen, Section F), those claims will receive priority treatment under the plan per §507(a)(8)? Do you understand why the plan makes no specific mention of §507(a)(3) gap operating expenses (see Illustration 11-a)? Recall that if the DIP's motion for authorization to reject its contract with Columbiana Leasing Company (CLC) (Document 11 in the BBF case file) is granted, CLC will have an administrative expense claim for the December YR-1 rent that came due postpetition. When will it be paid if the BBF plan is confirmed?

2. Impaired Classes and Their Treatment

Impaired A class created in a Chapter 11 plan whose claims are not to be paid according to their contractual terms.

Section 1123(a)(2) requires that the plan specify all classes of claims and interests that are not **impaired** under the plan. If the plan does not specify a class to be unimpaired, we assume that it is impaired.

Impairment is an important concept in plan approval under Chapter 11 and we will return to it several times in this chapter. Section 1124(1) provides that a claim or interest is unimpaired if the plan does not alter the holder's underlying rights. That means a claim is impaired if the right to payment is altered either because it will not be paid in full or when due.

EXAMPLE

Assume a creditor is owed $1,000, which is due the first day of next January. If the plan calls for that creditor to be paid the full $1,000 on the date the plan is confirmed or next January 1, whichever is sooner, that claim is not impaired. If the plan calls for that creditor to be paid only $750 in full satisfaction of his claim, the claim is impaired because the creditor is receiving less than 100 percent of what is owed. If the plan calls for that creditor to receive $1,000 to be paid in installments over five years, the claim is impaired because of the delay in payment. If the original debt agreement had called for the debtor to make ten payments of $100 each but the plan calls for 20 payments of $50 each, the claim is impaired because the payment schedule is decelerated. If the debt was past due when the petition is filed and the plan calls for it to be paid in full on the date of confirmation, it is still impaired because it is not being paid when due.

However, §1124(2) provides that a claim can still be considered unimpaired if the plan calls for the cure of any default and compensation for any delay in payment.

EXAMPLE

If the debt in the previous example was past due when the petition was filed and the plan calls for it to be paid in full on the date of confirmation together with interest to compensate the creditor for the late payment, the claim is not impaired. If the debt was an installment debt on which the debtor had missed three payments when its petition was filed, and if the plan calls for the payment of the arrearage in full together with interest to compensate for the delay in paying the missed installments, as well as for the payment of future installments as called for in the original contract, the claim is not impaired.

A class of **interests** is impaired if the owners in that class will suffer any diminution of their ownership interests.

EXAMPLE

The plan of reorganization proposed by BBF provides that New Era Capital Alliance will become a shareholder in the corporation holding preferred stock with a priority right to dividends over the holders of common stock (see Articles III and IV of the BBF plan, Document 13 in the BBF case file). This proposal diminishes the ownership interests of the current shareholders and impairs all classes of interests in BBF.

Section 1123(a)(3) requires that the plan explain how every class of impaired claims and interests will be treated. Section 1123(a)(4) requires that all claims or interests within each class must receive the same treatment, whether impaired or unimpaired.

The DIP must be very careful how it defines its classes of claims and interests and how it treats impaired claims. As we will see, if one or more class of claims is impaired in a proposed plan, the DIP must win the support of at least one impaired class in order for the plan to be confirmed. Thus, if the plan calls for one or more class of claims to be impaired, as most do, the plan will be carefully designed to treat at least one class of impaired claims in a way that does not cause the members of that class to oppose the plan.

Subject to those concerns, the Code does allow the DIP considerable flexibility in fashioning proposals for treatment of claims. Sections 1123(a)(5) and (b) authorize a plan to propose that

- arrearages be paid in full, in part, or not at all;
- property be retained by the debtor, abandoned, or transferred to another person or entity;
- security interests be retained, satisfied, or modified;
- new shares of a corporate debtor be issued or that the corporation merge or consolidate with another;
- maturity dates on debt be extended or installment payments reduced and extended;
- unsecured debt be paid in full, in part, or discharged;
- claims in a particular class be paid from the proceeds of designated property to be sold;
- members of a class receive a transfer of designated property in satisfaction of their claims; or
- any other proposal not inconsistent with the Code be allowed.

P-H 19-d: How many of the classes created in the BBF plan of reorganization (Document 13 in the BBF case file) are impaired? Does the plan call for any arrearages to be cured? For property to be abandoned? For leases or other contracts to be rejected? That security interests be retained, satisfied, or modified? That maturity dates be extended? That secured debt be paid in full or part? That unsecured debt be paid in full or in part? That new security interests be issued?

3. The Right to Modify a Secured Claim in a Chapter 11 Plan

As in a Chapter 13 case, a Chapter 11 debtor can propose to treat an allowed secured claim as a **pay through** (or **ride through**), which means the obligation will not be modified and will instead be paid according to the terms of the underlying contract during the term of the plan and beyond. However, §1123(b)(5) allows a plan to modify the rights of a secured creditor other than one secured by real property that is the principal residence of an individual Chapter 11 debtor. (You may want to review and compare the discussions of a Chapter 13 right to modify a secured claim in Chapter Fifteen, Section B.) This means that

- the plan of an individual Chapter 11 debtor can avoid a lien to the extent necessary to preserve an exemption (recall that entity debtors do not claim exemptions);
- the plan can propose to cure an arrearage on a secured debt during the term of the plan, make all future scheduled payments, and retain the collateral;
- the plan can propose to pay an undersecured creditor the value of the collateral and treat the balance as unsecured debt in the plan (though Chapter 13 forbids this cram down by an individual debtor on real property used as his or her principal residence, Chapter 11 contains no limitation on the cram down like the 910-day rule and one-year rule of §1325(a) applicable in Chapter 13 cases);
- the plan can propose to pay the amount owed a secured creditor in full but lower the amount and extend the term of the installments called for in the contract so long as the present value of the secured creditor's claim is paid during the term of the plan;
- the plan may propose to surrender collateral to the secured creditor, satisfying the secured claim of the creditor and leaving the creditor with, at most, an unsecured claim for the balance owed over the value of the collateral.

Recall from our discussion of these various ways of modifying a secured claim in a Chapter 13 case that under §506(a)(1) a creditor is secured up to the value of the collateral at the time the petition is filed. And that value is determined by **replacement cost**, per §506(a)(2) and *Associates Commercial Corp. v. Rash*, 520 U.S. 953 (1997). Recall, too, that the total of the installment payments to a secured creditor in a cram down to value must be based on a **discounted present value** equal to the value of the collateral, which means the plan payments to the secured creditor must include interest sufficient to compensate the creditor for the delay in receiving the full value of its claim. Recall further that we base that interest rate on a formula based on the then-current **prime rate** with an additional risk premium to be decided by the court based on the circumstances of the case, per *Till v. SCS Credit Corp.*, 541 U.S. 465 (2004). All of this is identical to what we learned was possible in connection with a Chapter 13.

Present value Calculation of the current value of property for purposes of determining the value of a secured claim in bankruptcy.

P-H 19-e: Review Chapter Fifteen, Section B, and the BBF plan of reorganization (Document 13 in the BBF case file). Identify each proposal you see there that modifies a secured claim and be sure you understand the basis for the proposed modification.

Section 1111(b) does provide one twist on the cram down to value treatment of a secured interest in a Chapter 11 plan, which we will deal with in Section D when we look at voting on and confirming a plan of reorganization.

In those situations where one or more creditors has a perfected security interest in a portion of the property but there is still equity for the estate (i.e., the creditor is oversecured), the plan can propose that the property be the subject of a **sale free and clear of liens**, pursuant to §363(f) and Bankruptcy Rule 6004(c). The secured creditor's right to **credit-bid** (discussed in Chapter Eleven, Section A and Chapter Eighteen, Section D) in such a sale is assured by §363(k).

4. Means of Implementing the Plan

Section 1123(a)(5) requires that the plan explain the means by which the plan will be implemented.

EXAMPLE

Will there be a new infusion of capital? Is a new contract going to produce revenue to fund the plan and save the company? Is new management coming in who might turn the company around? Are cost-cutting measures going to be taken that will produce profitability? Are unprofitable assets or divisions of the company going to be sold or abandoned, which will improve the bottom line? Is a new or modified business plan going to be pursued?

These are the type of questions that must be explained in the plan. As suggested by §1123(b), the plan may also utilize a number of matters we dealt with in Chapter Eighteen, Section D, regarding operational motions. It may call for the approval of postpetition credit or loan arrangements or the rejection or assumption of existing contracts not just to stay in business, but as a key element of its reorganization plan.

P-H 19-f: Review the BBF plan of reorganization (Document 13 in the BBF case file). How is the plan to be implemented? What will be the source of new capital? Are assets being disposed of or contracts being rejected as part of the plan?

C. ► The Disclosure Statement

As we have noted, creditors and equity security holders will vote whether to accept or reject a proposed plan of reorganization. To ensure that those voting understand the plan and how it works, §1125 requires that the DIP first file, and the court approve, a **disclosure statement** (see Document 12 in the BBF case file). Bankruptcy Rule 3016(b) requires that the disclosure statement be filed along with the proposed plan. Bankruptcy Rule 3017(a) then provides that the court must hold a hearing, upon 28 days' notice following the filing of the disclosure statement, to determine whether the disclosure statement should be approved. Section 1125(b) forbids postpetition solicitation for acceptance or rejection of a plan until the court has approved the disclosure statement. In a prepackaged Chapter 11 the solicitation would have occurred prepetition. In the small business case §1125(f) authorizes the court to waive the disclosure statement requirement if it finds that the plan itself provides adequate information.

Disclosure statement A detailed summary of the Chapter 11 debtor's financial and operational history and prospects sufficient to enable holders of claims and interests to make an informed judgment of a proposed plan of reorganization.

Illustration 19-a: CATEGORIES OF INFORMATION A DISCLOSURE STATEMENT SHOULD CONTAIN

- A detailed summary of the plan
- A detailed description of how the plan will work
- Financial projections for the duration of the plan
- A *liquidation analysis* comparing the plan to the likely results of a Chapter 7 liquidation
- A discussion of the potential material federal tax consequences to the debtor or any successor of the debtor contemplated by the plan and to any hypothetical investor typical of the current holders of claims and interests
- A description of the balloting procedure to be used in voting on the plan

The disclosure statement must provide *adequate information* concerning the affairs of the debtor to enable the holder of a claim or interest to make an informed judgment about the plan. Section 1125(a)(1) provides that in determining whether the disclosure statement does provide adequate information, the court is to consider

- the complexity of the case;
- the benefit of additional information to the parties in interest; and
- the cost of providing additional information.

Illustration 19-a summarizes the specific categories of information a disclosure statement should contain.

Once the disclosure statement is filed, the court will issue a Notice of Hearing on Adequacy of Disclosure Statement to parties in interest (Official Form 312 and Document 14 in the BBF case file). At the hearing, the disclosure statement may be approved as written, modified and approved, or not approved. The plan proponent who fails to win approval of his disclosure statement at the hearing may amend and resubmit it for further hearing. Keep in mind that if the DIP has not filed a plan within the 120-day exclusivity period or has not succeeded in winning confirmation of its plan (not just approval of its disclosure statement) within the 180-day period of §1121(c)(3), there may be one or more competing disclosure statements and plans being filed and considered for approval by the court. It is unusual, but it is possible for more than one proposed plan to be presented for consideration by those entitled to vote.

EXAMPLE

Assume a DIP proposes a plan 120 days after the order for relief but cannot get its disclosure statement approved before 180 days have run. The DIP may amend and resubmit its disclosure statement, but other plans and disclosure statements may now be submitted for court consideration.

Upon approval of the disclosure statement, the court will issue an order approving the disclosure statement, establishing a deadline for filing acceptances or rejections of the plan, fixing a time for the distribution of ballots to those voting on the plan, and scheduling a date for the confirmation hearing on the plan (Official Form 313 and Document 15 in the BBF case file). Bankruptcy Rule

3017(d) requires that the DIP or other plan proponent then provide the U.S. Trustee, creditors, and equity security holders a copy of

- the plan or a court-approved summary of the plan;
- the disclosure statement approved by the court;
- notice of the time within which acceptances and rejections of the plan may be filed; and
- such other information as the court may direct, including any opinion of the court approving the disclosure statement or a court-approved summary of the opinion.

In addition, the plan proponent must mail the following items to the creditors and equity security holders entitled to vote on the plan:

- notice of the time fixed for filing objections to the plan;
- notice of the date and time for the hearing on confirmation of the plan;
- a ballot for accepting or rejecting the plan using Official Form 314; and
- if appropriate, a designation for the creditors to identify their preference among competing plans.

P-H 19-g: Review the BBF disclosure statement (Document 12 in the BBF case file). Does it contain all of the categories of information listed in Illustration 19-a? Do the contents of the disclosure statement (other than those excluded from the illustration) appear to be complete? If you were a creditor of BBF, would you be satisfied with the information contained in the disclosure statement or would you want more? What questions might you have for BBF representatives at the hearing on the adequacy of its disclosure statement?

D. ▶ Solicitation for Support or Opposition and Voting on the Plan

Under §1126(a) both creditors with allowed claims and equity security holders with allowed ownership interests are entitled to vote for or against the proposed plan of reorganization. In Chapter Eighteen, Section B, we considered how claims and interests are "deemed" allowed in a Chapter 11 case.

Proponents and opponents of the plan may solicit those entitled to vote. Such solicitation must be done in **good faith**, per §1125. Section 1126(f) provides that if a class of claims or interests is not impaired by the plan, they are **conclusively presumed** to have accepted the plan and their vote need not be solicited. Section 1126(g) provides that if a class of claims or interests is to receive nothing under the plan, it is "deemed not to have accepted" the plan and members of that class need not be solicited.

Good faith Generally, honesty in fact and compliance with the letter and spirit of the Code.

P-H 19-h: Review the proposed plan of BBF (Document 13 in the BBF case file). Are there any classes of claims or interests created in it that need not be solicited?

Each creditor or equity interest holder in a class created by the plan receives a **ballot** for accepting or rejecting the proposed plan (Official Form 314 and Document 16 in the BBF case file) along with the other materials provided to them after the hearing on the disclosure statement. They must mark the ballot indicating an acceptance or rejection of the plan and return it by the deadline prescribed by the court.

In a vote to approve or reject a Chapter 11 plan, it is the vote of each class of claims and interests that matters, not the vote of any individual member of the class. In other words, each class forms a voting block that itself accepts or rejects the plan. Section 1126(c) provides that a class of claims accepts a plan if

- at least two-thirds of the dollar amount represented in the class votes to approve, and
- more than one-half of the creditors in that class vote to approve.

EXAMPLE

If there are 20 unsecured trade creditors in a class, at least 11 must vote to approve the plan, and the dollar amount of claims held by those 11 must represent at least two-thirds of the total dollar amount of all 20 creditors in the class. If both those requirements are satisfied, we say that the class—not just the individual creditors within the class—has voted to approve the plan.

When the class is made up of equity interests, rather than creditors with claims, §1126(d) provides that the class can approve the plan by a vote that represents two-thirds of the dollar amount of the interests represented. There need not be a majority of the number of owners in the class supporting the plan.

EXAMPLE

If a class of interests includes 20 shareholders in the debtor corporation, one of whom holds 70 percent of the outstanding shares of stock in the corporation, representing 70 percent of the value of all the shares represented, that one shareholder can cause the class to accept or reject the plan even if the 19 others vote the other way.

§1111(b)(2) election The right of an *undersecured creditor* in a Chapter 11 case to demand that the plan treat its claim as secured up to the full amount owed.

Recall that the holder of an undersecured claim is entitled to treatment in two classes under the plan: one for the secured portion of its claim up to the value of the collateral under §506(a)(1) and one for the unsecured portion for the balance per §1111(b)(1). However, under §1111(b)(2) an undersecured creditor can elect to have its claim treated as secured up to the full amount owed. If the undersecured creditor makes this **§1111(b)(2) election**, then §1129(b), which sets forth the requirements for plan confirmation, requires that the plan call for the payment of the entire amount of the claim and not just an amount equal to the value of the collateral, and the plan cannot be confirmed under §1129(a)(7)(B) unless it does so.

EXAMPLE

Assume a creditor is owed $500,000 and is secured in real property having a current value of $400,000. The plan may call for treating that as a secured claim for $400,000 and an unsecured claim for $100,000. But if this undersecured creditor makes the §1111(b)(2) election, the claim must be treated as a secured claim for the entire amount owed—$500,000. And if the debtor wishes to keep the property securing the debt, the plan must call for the payment of the entire amount owed.

The effect of an undersecured creditor making the §1111(b)(2) election is to defeat the debtor's right to cram down to value. The most common situation in which a Chapter 11 creditor makes the election is where the value of the collateral is currently depressed but has potential to increase.

EXAMPLE

> Assume the real property in the preceding example is valued at $400,000 due to a depressed real estate market. But the expectation is that in one to two years the market will improve and the property will appreciate to equal or exceed the amount owed. The currently undersecured creditor will consider whether to exercise its §1111(b)(2) option.

You might think that an undersecured creditor would always exercise its §1111(b)(2) election in order to defeat a possible cram down of its secured claim to value. But that isn't the case at all. There are disadvantages to a creditor exercising this election. First, the debtor may simply surrender the property to the creditor instead of attempting to retain it. If that happens, the creditor now has to deal with disposing of the property at its depressed value and the debtor can treat any arrearage as an unsecured claim anyway. Second, a creditor who makes this election waives the right to vote on the plan as an unsecured creditor, which may be desirable leverage to have over plan approval. But because it elected to have its entire claim treated as secured, it only gets a vote in the secured class where its claim is placed. Third, the creditor making the election waives its right to participate in the distribution to holders of unsecured claims.

P-H 19-i: How has BBF treated the undersecured claim of NCA in its plan? (See Document 13 in the BBF case file.) Did it cram down that claim? How does the plan treat the secured and unsecured claims of NCA? Should NCA have exercised its §1111(b)(2) election?

E. ▶ Confirmation of the Plan

Confirmation The court's formal approval of a plan of reorganization under Chapter 11.

Cram down The right to confirm a plan of reorganization despite the opposition of some creditors.

Section 1129 governs the requirements for the court's **confirmation** of the plan of reorganization. There are two alternative methods of confirmation outlined in that section. In general, confirmation under §1129(a) contemplates that all classes of creditors and claims, including any impaired class, have approved the plan. Confirmation under §1129(b), known as **cram down confirmation**, is used when all impaired classes have not accepted the plan and confirmation is therefore not possible under §1129(a).

1. Section 1129(a) Confirmation

Confirmation under §1129(a) requires much more than approval of the plan by all classes. In fact, there is a laundry list of requirements for confirmation listed in this section but a number of them are very technical and we will consider only the ones that generally come into play.

Approval of the Plan by All Classes, Including Any Impaired Classes [§1129(a)(8)]

Recall that unimpaired classes are conclusively presumed to have accepted the plan, per §1126(f), so if there are no impaired classes, this test is met. If any class is to receive nothing, then §1126(g) provides that class is deemed not to have accepted the plan, which means that the plan cannot be confirmed under §1129(a) if any class is to be paid nothing. Consequently, the focus of this requirement is on impaired classes and whether all impaired classes have voted to approve the plan.

P-H 19-j: How many impaired classes does the BBF plan create? (See Document 13 in the BBF case file.) Has it designated any class to receive nothing? Consider the proposals contained in the plan from the standpoint of each of the secured creditors. Should they vote to accept or reject the plan? If they vote to reject, should they propose their own plan or seek to force BBF into liquidation? Will any secured creditor come out better in a liquidation than under the plan as proposed? Will any unsecured creditor? (Look at the liquidation analysis in BBF's disclosure statement, Document 12 in the BBF case file, in connection with these last two questions.) If secured or unsecured creditors argue for a more favorable payout to themselves under the plan, what is likely to be BBF's response?

Approval by at Least One Impaired Class Discounting Affirmative Votes of Insiders [§1129(a)(10)]

Insiders A person in close relationship with a debtor such that he may be assumed to have superior access to information and be subject to special treatment.

As we just saw, §1129(a)(8) requires that all classes have approved the plan, including any impaired class, so at first blush, this requirement seems inconsistent with that. But this section deals with the possibility that §1129(a)(8) was complied with only because **insiders** of the debtor who were members of an impaired class voted to approve the plan. In that event, even though all classes did in fact vote to approve the plan and §1129(a)(8) is complied with, this section requires a showing that at least one impaired class would have voted to approve without regard to those insider votes.

The Best Interests of Dissenting Creditors Test [§1129(a)(7)]

Best interest of creditors test A test for confirmation of a plan of reorganization under Chapter 11 or 13 of the Code, which requires a showing that unsecured creditors will receive at least as much under the plan as they would have received in a Chapter 7 liquidation.

This section requires that the court determine that individual creditors and owners who voted against the plan (even if their entire class approved it) receive or retain as much in the Chapter 11 reorganization as they would have in a Chapter 7 liquidation. Practitioners call this the **best interest of creditors test**, though that phrase is not used in the Code section itself.

EXAMPLE

Recall from Illustration 19-a that one part of a disclosure statement is a liquidation analysis, comparing the effect of the proposed plan on creditors with what they would receive in a Chapter 7 liquidation. The requirement of §1129(a)(7) is an extension of that analysis, applied to specific dissenting creditors.

The Feasibility Test [§1129(a)(11)]

Feasibility test A test for confirmation of a plan of reorganization requiring a showing that the debtor has a reasonable prospect of completing the plan.

What practitioners call the **feasibility test** requires that the court determine that the plan of reorganization is in fact feasible and is not likely to be followed by liquidation or another reorganization (unless a second reorganization is called for in the plan).

P-H 19-k: What kinds of contingencies does the BBF plan (Document 13 in the BBF case file) depend on? What kinds of proof would the bankruptcy court expect to hear at the confirmation hearing in order to determine the feasibility test of §1129(a)(11)?

The Lawfulness and Good Faith Tests [§§1129(a)(1)(2) and (3)]

These three sections together require that the court determine whether both the conduct of the plan proponent in connection with the formulation of the plan and the terms of the plan itself comply with the Code and, further, whether the "plan has been proposed in good faith and not by any means forbidden by law." Referred to generally as the good faith requirement, the court will consider whether the proponent has acted with honesty, integrity, and fairness in connection with the plan's formulation. If the proponent has employed dishonest, abusive, or coercive tactics, the court has the discretion to refuse confirmation.

Treatment of §507 Priority Claims [§1129(a)(9)]

Unless the holder of a claim entitled to priority treatment under §507 (see Illustration 11-a) consents to a different treatment, the plan must provide for the following treatment of such priority claims:

- Section 503(b) administrative claims allowed under §507(a)(2) and all "gap claims" arising in an involuntary case allowed under §507(a)(3) must be paid in full as of the effective date of the plan.
- Section 507(a)(8) tax claims must be paid in full in installments over a period not to exceed five years from the date of the order for relief.
- Section 507(a)(1), (4), (5), (6), and (7) claims must be paid in full.

If the classes that include the §§507(a)(1), (4), (5), (6), (7), and (8) priority claims approve the plan, the payments can be made in installments over the term of the plan. If any class including those claims rejects the plan (and confirmation is accomplished by §1129(b) discussed below), they must be paid in full as of the effective date of the plan like the §503(b) priority claims.

P-H 19-l: How many classes of priority claims does the BBF plan (Document 13 in the BBF case file) create? Does its treatment of priority claims comply with §1129(a)(9)?

2. Section 1129(b) Confirmation

Most Chapter 11 plans are successfully negotiated so that all classes vote to accept the plan and confirmation is accomplished through §1129(a). Confirmation through §1129(b) becomes necessary only when one or more classes have voted to reject the proposed plan. Even under §1129(b), however, at least one class must have voted to accept the plan because of the requirements of §1129(a)(10) (discussed above), which apply in a §1129(b) confirmation, as well as in a §1129(a) confirmation. In fact, all of the requirements for a §1129(a) confirmation must be satisfied in a §1129(b) confirmation as well except for §1129(a)(8), which requires that all classes have voted to accept the plan. But in addition to those §1129(a) requirements, a confirmation under §1129(b) has its own unique requirements.

Because §1129(b) allows a plan to be confirmed notwithstanding one or more classes having rejected it, practitioners refer to it as a cram down confirmation; the plan is being "crammed down" on the objecting classes. Under a §1129(b) confirmation, we are concerned only with those objecting classes because the other classes have voted to accept the plan. Under §1129(b) a plan can be confirmed by cram down on an objecting class if

- the requirements of §1129(a) are satisfied, other than §1129(a)(8), including approval by at least one impaired class, per §1129(a)(1);
- the court finds, pursuant to §1129(b)(1), that the plan does not **discriminate unfairly** against the objecting class; and
- the court finds, pursuant to §§1129(b)(1) and (2), that the plan is **fair and equitable** to the objecting class.

Approval by One Impaired Class

The lawyer drafting a Chapter 11 plan that will have to be confirmed by §1129(b) cram down must be careful to create at least one impaired class that will approve the plan. Otherwise, cram down on the objecting classes is not possible. As a result, the lawyer will be careful to provide sufficient sweeteners in the proposal for that impaired class so that, despite the impairment, its approval is certain.

EXAMPLE

Recall that in the discussion of classes in Section B, above, we noted that a plan might create a class of unique claims for administrative convenience, such as small, miscellaneous claims under $200. Assume a plan calls for the class containing nonpriority, unsecured trade debt creditors to receive 30 percent of their claims over the life of the plan and that the class is expected to reject the plan. To enable cram down approval under §1129(b), the plan also creates an impaired class of nonpriority, unsecured claims that includes miscellaneous, small claims under $200 on the basis of administrative convenience and calls for those claims to be paid 100 percent within 60 days following confirmation. This slightly impaired class can be expected to approve the plan, satisfying this requirement of §1129(b) confirmation.

P-H 25-m: Review the BBF plan of reorganization (Document 13 in the BBF case file). Does it appear to have structured an impaired class likely to approve the plan if cram down confirmation is needed under §1129(b)?

Of course, the plan creating this "likely-to-approve" impaired class must comply with the requirements of Chapter 11 regarding class characteristics, which we considered in Section B, above. And the treatment of the impaired class counted on for approval must pass the two remaining tests for §1129(b) confirmation discussed next.

The No Unfair Discrimination Requirement of §1129(b)(1)

The class voting to reject a plan is going to be one whose claims are impaired under the plan because classes of unimpaired claims are "conclusively presumed" to have accepted the plan, pursuant to §1126(f). So the plan obviously "discriminates" against an impaired class. The issue under §1129(b)(1) is whether the discriminating impairment is "unfair."

Most courts determine the issue of unfair discrimination by looking at

- how the objecting class is treated relative to other similar classes of claims;
- whether the motivation for the discriminatory treatment (the impairment) is reasonable or motivated by bad faith or ill will; and
- whether the discriminatory treatment appears to be reasonably necessary to a successful reorganization.

The question of unfair discrimination is a question of fact to be decided on the facts of each case.

P-H 19-n: You be the judge on this one. Examine the BBF plan (Document 13 in the BBF case file). Assume that any impaired class in the plan might vote to reject it. Based on the plan as an entirety and what you know at this point concerning BBF, does the plan appear to unfairly discriminate against any of the impaired classes? What other information would you want to have in order to make that decision? If you were examining a plan like the one mentioned in the previous example, would you find unfair discrimination in the treatment of the small claims class that is to receive 100 percent payment for administrative convenience when trade creditors are to get only 30 percent?

The resolution of the issue of fair and equitable treatment under §§1129(b)(1) and (2) turns on whether the objecting class is made up of secured or unsecured creditors.

The Fair and Equitable Requirement of §§1129(b)(1) and (2) as to Secured Claims

In order to meet the fair and equitable requirement for a cram down confirmation, the plan must ensure that an impaired, secured claim in a class objecting to the plan receives the full amount of the allowed secured claim (and recall that, pursuant to §506(a), the amount of the secured claim is limited to the value of the collateral). The plan can ensure that the objecting secured creditor receives the full amount of its secured claim in one of three ways:

- the plan can call for the secured creditor to retain its lien on the property and receive deferred cash payments per §1129(b)(2)(A)(i);
- the plan can call for selling the property free and clear of the lien and grant the creditor a lien on the proceeds of sale up to the value of its secured claim per §1129(b)(2)(A)(ii); or
- the plan can provide the secured creditor with the indubitable equivalent of its claim per §1129(b)(2)(A)(iii).

If the claim is undersecured and the creditor exercises the §1111(b)(2) election, then the plan must deal with the claim as discussed in the section above on solicitation for approval or rejection and voting on a plan.

In *Radlax Gateway Hotel, LLC v. Amalgamated Bank*, 132 S. Ct. 2065 (2012), the Supreme Court held that a Chapter 11 plan could not be confirmed using the cram down procedure of §1129(b)(2)(A), where the plan proposed to sell property pledged to an objecting creditor free and clear of the lien per §1129(b)(2)(A)(ii) but denied that creditor the right to credit-bid for the property at the sale. The creditor wanted the right to bid to purchase the property at the sale using the debt it was owed to offset the purchase price, i.e., it wanted to utilize credit-bidding. The court said that by denying the creditor the right to credit-bid on the pledged property, the plan failed to satisfy the fair and reasonable requirement since §1129(b)(2)(A)(ii) requires that any sale free and clear of liens is subject to §363(k) of the Code, which specifically preserves a creditor's right to credit-bid in a sale free and clear of liens. *Radlax* confirms that a secured creditor cannot be denied the right to credit-bid when the property in which it holds a security interest is sold in a bankruptcy proceeding, whether on motion for sale free and clear of liens or as part of a plan of reorganization.

We saw the curious phrase **indubitable equivalent** that appears in §1129(b)(2)(A)(iii) once before in Chapter Eighteen, Section D, in connection with the Chapter 11 debtor's §361(3) obligation to provide the secured creditor with adequate protection when the debtor seeks to use, sell, or lease collateralized property. The phrase comes from *In re Murel Holding Corporation*, 75 F.2d 941 (2d Cir. 1935), authored by distinguished Judge Learned Hand. It may literally be impossible to state all the ways in which the indubitable equivalent can be offered, but one common example is surrendering all or a portion of the collateral to a secured creditor or providing the creditor with a secured position in other property that is indubitably (often described as meaning by clear and convincing evidence) of the same or greater value. This form of indubitable equivalent is colorfully referred to in bankruptcy practice as **dirt for debt**. As the court in *In re Arnold and Baker Farms*, 177 B.R. 648, 655 (B.A.P. 9th Cir. 1994), aff'd, 85 F.3d 1415 (9th Cir. 1996), described it:

A dirt for debt transfer requires the debtor to transfer to a secured creditor the asset securing the original loan obligation. Conceivably, the transfer may be either a full transfer or a partial transfer of the collateral. When a debtor proposes a partial transfer of collateral pursuant to a plan, it is essential for the bankruptcy court to estimate the value of the "dirt" in order to determine how much of the collateral will ultimately be transferred to the creditor in satisfaction of the debt.

IN RE RIDDLE

444 B.R. 681 (Bankr. N.D. Ga. 2011)

OPINION: Paul W. Bonapfel, Bankruptcy Judge

Northside Bank (the "Bank") has rejected the Chapter 11 Plan filed by Green Hobson Riddle, Jr., and objected to its confirmation. At the hearing on confirmation, the Court determined that the Plan meets all requirements for confirmation in 11 U.S.C. §1129(a) except the requirement in §1129(a)(8) that all classes of impaired claims accept it, a requirement that the Debtor cannot meet in view of the Bank's rejection of the Plan as the sole member in its class. The question considered here is whether the plan is confirmable under the so-called "cram-down" provision, 11 U.S.C. §1129(b), notwithstanding the Bank's failure to accept it.

POSITIONS OF THE PARTIES

The Bank is the holder of a claim in the amount of approximately $907,000 secured by a first priority deed to secure debt on approximately 36 acres of real property generally referred to as the "Highway 411/Dodd Blvd Property" and a second priority deed to secure debt on a condominium unit generally referred to as the "Heritage Square Property." The Bank also holds a judgment lien.

The Plan proposes to surrender the Highway 411/Dodd Blvd Property, which the Plan asserts is worth $1.2 million, to the Bank by execution of a quitclaim deed to the Bank upon confirmation in full satisfaction of the Bank's claim, thereby requiring cancellation of both the second priority security deed on the Heritage Square Property and the judgment lien.

The Bank rejected the Plan and appeared at the confirmation hearing to object to its confirmation because all classes of impaired claims had not accepted it as 11 U.S.C. §1129(a)(8) requires. As secured creditors typically are, the Bank is the sole member of its class so its vote determines the vote of that class. At that hearing, the Court determined that the Plan meets all requirements for confirmation set forth in §1129(a), except the requirement of paragraph 8.

The Debtor requests that the Court confirm the plan pursuant to 11 U.S.C. §1129(b). Section 1129(b) is the so-called "cram-down" provision of Chapter 11 that permits confirmation notwithstanding the absence of acceptance by an impaired class if the treatment of the impaired, nonaccepting class "does not discriminate unfairly" and is "fair and equitable." With regard to a class of secured claims, like the Bank's, section 1129(b)(2)(A) requires that the plan meet one of three alternative conditions to be "fair and equitable." The Debtor invokes clause (iii) of §1129(b)(2)(A), which states that a plan is "fair and equitable" with regard to a class of secured claims if it provides for the secured creditor to realize the "indubitable equivalent" of its claim.

The Bank asserts that the plan does not satisfy the requirements of §1129(b) because it discriminates unfairly and because it does not provide for it to realize the "indubitable equivalent" of its claim.

SUMMARY OF FINDINGS OF FACT

The Court heard evidence at the hearing on January 27, 2011, with regard to the §1129(b)(2)(B) issues and announced its findings of fact on the record. In summary, the Court found that, properly marketed, the Highway 411/Dodd Blvd Property would likely sell for a price in the range of $1.2 million to $1.3 million, possibly more; that it would bring $990,000 at a "fire sale," *i.e.*, a sale under distressed circumstances in which the seller is under pressure to sell promptly; that selling costs would be approximately $50,000; and that, consequently, the net proceeds realizable from a "fire sale" of the property would be $940,000. To determine what the Bank could realize from the property, it is necessary to deduct unpaid ad valorem taxes that have priority over the Bank's deed to secure debt. The parties agree that the amount of unpaid ad valorem taxes is $8,981.04.

The net amount realizable from the Heritage Square Property, after satisfaction of the first priority deed to secure debt that another lender holds, is at least $100,000. The Debtor testified that release of the Bank's second priority deed to secure debt on the Heritage Square Property is necessary to permit the Debtor to use that property as collateral for additional financing for one of his companies, which, in turn, is essential to the feasibility of the Plan and his ability to pay other claims as the Plan proposes.

DISCUSSION

Section 1129(b)(1) permits confirmation of a plan over the objection of a class of creditors if the plan does not "discriminate unfairly" and is "fair and equitable" with regard to the objecting class. Section 1129(b)(2)(A) lists three alternative ways that a plan may treat a secured claim to meet the "fair and equitable" requirement. Applicable here is the third alternative, §1129(b)(2)(A)(iii), which provides that a plan is fair and equitable if it provides for the secured creditor to realize the "indubitable equivalent" of its claim.

The provision for treatment of the Bank's claim is a so-called "dirt for debt" provision that seeks to satisfy a creditor's claim to the extent of the value of real estate that the lender holds as collateral. Such a provision may, under appropriate circumstances, provide the indubitable equivalent of the lender's claim. *See, e.g., Arnold & Baker Farms v. United States (In re Arnold & Baker Farms)*, 85 F.3d 1415 (9th Cir. 1996); *Sandy Ridge Development Corp. v. Louisiana National Bank (In re Sandy Ridge Development Corp.)*, 881 F.2d 1346 (5th Cir. 1989); *In re Atlanta Southern Business Park, Ltd.*, 173 B.R. 444 (Bankr. N.D. Ga. 1994); Alan N. Resnick & Henry J. Sommer, 7 Collier On Bankruptcy §1129.04[2][c] (16th ed. 2010).

The Plan here goes beyond the concept of transferring *all* of a lender's collateral to it in satisfaction of its *secured* claim. Rather, the Plan provides for the Bank to receive only part of its collateral, the Highway 411/Dodd Blvd Property, and to lose the additional collateral it has. The theory underlying the Debtor's ability to do this is that the Bank's receipt of the Highway 411/Dodd Blvd Property provides it with enough value to satisfy its claim in full, resulting in release of other collateral that the Bank holds as additional collateral for its claim.

In order for treatment of a secured creditor's claim to qualify as being the "indubitable equivalent" of the claim, the treatment must be completely compensatory. *See, e.g., Arnold & Baker Farms v. United States (In re Arnold & Baker Farms),* 85 F.3d 1415, 1422 (9th Cir. 1996); *In re Atlanta Southern Business Park, Ltd.,* 173 B.R. 444, 448 (Bankr. N.D. Ga. 1994). In this regard, an equivalent is "indubitable" if no reasonable doubt exists that the creditor will be paid in full. *See, e.g., Arnold & Baker Farms,* 85 F.3d at 1421 (quoting *In re Walat Farms, Inc.,* 70 B.R. 330, 334 (Bankr. E.D. Mich. 1987)); *In re Freymiller Trucking, Inc.,* 190 B.R. 913, 915-16 (Bankr. W.D. Okla. 1996). When the plan proposes the transfer of some, but not all, of the collateral to the creditor in full satisfaction of the debt, the court must take a conservative approach to valuation of the collateral in order to protect the secured creditor. *Atlanta Southern Business Park,* 173 B.R. at 450.

Applying these standards here, the Court concludes that the transfer of the Highway 411/Dodd Blvd Property to the Bank provides for the realization of the indubitable equivalent of its claim. Specifically, the credible and uncontroverted evidence before the Court establishes that $990,000 is a "fire sale" value. In this regard, the "fire sale" value reflects a discount of at least $200,000 from what the property could be sold for if it were marketed in the usual way that such properties are marketed. The "fire sale" value of $990,000, then, clearly reflects a conservative approach to valuation that is the bare minimum that the property will sell for in a reasonably prompt time.

After payment of estimated selling expenses of $50,000 and satisfaction of unpaid ad valorem taxes of approximately $9,000, the remaining proceeds from such a "fire sale" would be $931,000, which is enough for the Bank to receive more than the amount now due (approximately $907,000), plus six months of interest (approximately $21,500 for 180 days at the per diem rate of $119) (a total of $928,500).

Based on the evidence before the Court, as reflected in its findings of fact, the Court concludes that no reasonable doubt exists that the transfer of the Highway 411/Dodd Blvd Property to the Bank will result in full payment of its claim. As such, the transfer provides for the realization by the Bank of the indubitable equivalent of its claim. The Plan therefore meets the "fair and equitable" requirement of §1129(b)(2)(A)(iii).

The Bank also contends that the plan discriminates unfairly because its claim is the only one that is being satisfied by the transfer of collateral. Section 1129(b)(1) requires that a plan "not discriminate unfairly" as a condition for its confirmation over its rejection by an impaired class.

This condition has little, if any, significance in the context of a secured claim. Because each secured creditor has collateral, repayment terms, and other rights that are unique to it, proper classification in a Chapter 11 plan requires a separate class for each secured claim. The propriety of the treatment of a secured claim is not generally determined by reference to the treatment of other secured claims. Nothing requires that a plan provide treatment for every secured claim with the same maturity date, rate of interest, payment schedule, or any other term. So a secured creditor must show something other than the uniqueness of its treatment to establish unfair discrimination. In any event, a provision that provides treatment for a secured creditor that provides the indubitable equivalent of its claim—in this case, payment in full—cannot be said to be "unfair."

At the same time, it is important to recognize that §1129(b), the "cram-down" subsection, "provides only a minimum requirement for confirmation . . . so a court may decide that a plan is not fair and equitable even if it is in technical compliance with the Code's requirements." *E.g., Atlanta Southern Business Park,* 173 B.R. at 448. In this regard, it could be inequitable to conclude that a plan provision such as the one under consideration here is "fair and equitable," if the provision serves no reorganization purpose. *See Freymiller Trucking,* 190 B.R. at 916. But in this case, the evidence shows that elimination of the Bank's lien on other collateral is necessary for the reorganization of the Debtor and his ability to deal with all of the claims of other creditors who have accepted the Plan. No evidence demonstrates that the Plan is inequitable or unfair.

CONCLUSIONS OF LAW

Based on the findings of fact announced by the Court at the hearings in this case and the undisputed facts that the parties have agreed on, the Court concludes that the Plan's provisions with regard to treatment of the Bank's claim provide for the Bank to realize the indubitable equivalent of its claim, that the Plan does not unfairly discriminate with regard to the Bank's claim, and that the Plan's provisions with regard to the Bank's claim are fair and equitable. Consequently, the Court concludes that the Plan meets the requirements of 11 U.S.C. §1129(b) with regard to the Bank's claim such that its acceptance of the Plan is not required.

The Court having determined at the hearings that the Plan meets all other requirements for confirmation, the Court will enter a separate Order for confirmation of the Plan.

IT IS ORDERED.

POST-CASE FOLLOW-UP

In re Riddle is a good case to see a number of the concepts we have been discussing in action. First, the debtor's plan put the Bank's claim in a class all by itself, which is commonly done with secured claims since each such claim almost always receives individual and differing treatment under the plan from other secured claims. Second, Bank's claim was impaired by the plan since it does not propose to pay Bank according to the terms of the contract between debtor and Bank. Third, the debtor initially sought confirmation under §1129(a) but could not accomplish it under that section because of the Bank's vote to reject the plan. Remember that confirmation under §1129(a) requires approval of the plan by all classes of claims, including impaired classes. Fourth, once the bankruptcy court ruled that confirmation was not to be had under §1129(a), the debtor sought alternatively to obtain cram down confirmation using §1129(b) raising the specific issue addressed in the opinion as to whether the plan satisfied the fair and equitable requirement of §§1129(b)(1) and (2) by proposing to pay Bank the full amount of its secured claim. Debtor relied on the §1129(b)(2)(A)(iii) indubitable value approach to satisfy that requirement.

In re Riddle contains a simple but comprehensive description of what indubitable value means: "In order for treatment of a secured creditor's claim to qualify as being the indubitable equivalent of the claim, the treatment must be completely compensatory . . . an equivalent is indubitable if no reasonable doubt exists that the creditor will be paid in full." Though *Riddle* involves a classic "dirt for debt" proposal, it should be remembered that indubitable value questions can arise in plan proposals having nothing to do with real estate. Where the plan proposes to provide the secured creditor with anything of demonstrable value in full or partial satisfaction of the secured claim, the fair and equitable requirement for cram down confirmation is met so long as the value offered the secured creditor is "indubitably" equivalent to the portion of the secured claim being satisfied.

In re Riddle: **Real Life Applications**

1. Be sure you understand and can articulate how the claim of Bank in *In re Riddle* was impaired by the debtor's proposed plan. As of the date the petition was filed, how much was Bank owed by the debtor? Bank as of that time was secured by two consensual liens and one nonconsensual lien. What were they? What did debtor's plan propose as to each of the two consensual liens and as to the nonconsensual lien? Did the plan propose to surrender all the property in which Bank held a security interest to Bank?

2. *Riddle* interprets the indubitable equivalent language of §1129(b)(2)(A)(iii) to require proof "beyond a reasonable doubt" that the value offered the secured creditor in debtor's plan will pay the creditor's secured claim in full. Many courts use a "clear and convincing" standard for indubitable value. Determine if the courts of your federal district or circuit have decided an indubitable value case and see what standard of proof for indubitable value is used.

3. How did the court in *Riddle* calculate the net value of the property to be surrendered to Bank as proposed in the plan? How did it conclude that the net value would actually exceed the value of the Bank's secured claim and provide it with a windfall? Did it consider both a likely non-distress and distress sale value of the property being considered? Did it deduct likely expenses associated with the property and sale of the property in its calculations?

4. Assume an appraiser for debtor testified as is summarized in the Summary of Findings of Fact in the opinion but an appraiser for Bank had testified that the real estate market in the area was "beginning to stall" and that the property "normally" would bring $1.2 to $1.3 million and be on the market 6-12 months, but in the current market "might" bring as little as $1 million and be on the market 6-18 months, and in a fire sale where it was disposed of as

quickly as possible "might" bring as little as $925,000. You are the judge. What impact will the qualifications and experience of the two opposing appraisers have on your decision regarding indubitable value? What difference will the standard of proof for indubitable value used in your district make?

P-H 19-o: Does the BBF plan (Document 13 in the BBF case file) appear to meet the fair and equitable requirement of §1129(b)(2) as to secured creditors? Which of the three methods of ensuring that secured creditors receive the full value of their secured claim authorized in §1129(b)(2)(A) is used? Would the plan meet the fair and equitable requirement if any of the secured creditors involved exercised the §1111(b)(2) election? How would you alter that plan to make it more likely to satisfy the fair and equitable requirement?

The Fair and Equitable Requirement of §§1129(b)(1) and (2) as to Unsecured Claims

The fair and equitable requirement can be satisfied as to impaired, unsecured claims in a class objecting to the plan in one of two ways. Section 1129(b)(2)(B)(i) provides that it can be satisfied by the plan paying the full amount of the claims in deferred installments over the term of the plan.

Alternatively, §1129(b)(2)(B)(ii) provides that it can be satisfied if the holders of equity interests in the debtor neither receive anything under the plan nor retain any ownership interest in the reorganized debtor. This second method of satisfying the fair and equitable requirement as to an objecting class of impaired unsecured claims is known as the **absolute priority rule**: If the unsecured claims in the objecting class are not paid in full, then "any claim or interest that is junior" to the claims in the impaired objecting class must receive nothing and retain nothing under the plan. The only interests junior to unsecured claims are the equity interest of the owners, so the effect of this rule is that the owners of the debtor must forfeit their entire ownership interest in the debtor.

Absolute priority rule The principle applicable in Chapter 11 cases that no junior class of claims or interests in a plan of reorganization should receive any distribution until senior classes are paid in full.

EXAMPLE

Assume BBF proposes a plan in which the class of trade creditors holding unsecured debt are to receive 50 percent of what they are owed. The class is impaired and votes to reject the plan. BBF cannot satisfy the fair and equitable requirement via §1129(b)(2)(B)(i) because the creditors in the objecting impaired class are not receiving 100 percent of their claims over the term of the plan. To satisfy the absolute priority rule of §1129(b)(2)(B)(ii), the plan must provide that all five shareholders in BBF forfeit their entire investment in BBF. They cannot receive any distribution as owners under the plan and they cannot retain an ownership interest in BBF under the plan. The plan would have to call for the passing of ownership to another for no consideration or for the bidding off of the ownership interest with the proceeds going to the corporation, not its prior owners, the Banowsky family.

New value exception An exception to the absolute priority rule in a Chapter 11 case enabling holders of equity interests in a bankrupt debtor to retain their interests even though senior claim holders will not be paid in full.

Most courts recognize an exception to the harsh absolute priority rule. This exception is known as the **new value exception**. Under that exception, if the plan calls for the owners of the debtor to invest new capital in the debtor in cash or property in an amount at least equal to the value of their interests, then the plan can be approved even though the unsecured claims in the objecting class are paid less than full value. But the new capital requirement is strictly construed to include only the contribution of cash or property having actual value. A proposal to provide "services" or "expertise" to the corporation in exchange for stock will not be deemed new value for this purpose.

EXAMPLE

In a bankruptcy court recognizing the new value exception, the plan could call for the impairment of the objecting class of unsecured creditors by paying them less than 100 percent and for the members of the Banowsky family to contribute new capital to the corporation in exchange for a continuing ownership interest. But the new capital will have to be cash or property having actual value, and the contributions of each family member will have to equal or exceed the value of their interests at the time the Chapter 11 petition was filed.

3. The Confirmation Hearing

These confirmation issues are raised at the **confirmation hearing**. Once the court confirms the plan, an **order confirming plan** is entered based on Official Form 315 (Document 17 in the BBF case file).

P-H 25-p: Was the BBF plan confirmed under §1129(a) or §1129(b)?

4. The Effect of Plan Confirmation

The terms of a confirmed plan bind the debtor, any successor to the debtor created in the plan, the owners, and all creditors, per §1141(a). Property of the estate immediately vests in the **reorganized debtor** upon confirmation, per §1141(b), and is free and clear of all liens, claims, and interests, except as allowed by the confirmed plan per §1141(c).

Discharge Permanent relief from debt pursuant to order of the bankruptcy court.

Section 1141(d)(1) provides that confirmation of a plan operates as a **discharge** of all debts arising before the date of confirmation if the debtor is an entity. The idea is that the debtor now operates solely within the terms of the confirmed plan as to its preconfirmation obligations. However, §1141(d)(3) provides that an *entity* Chapter 11 debtor whose plan calls for effective liquidation of the business and the ceasing of operations will *not* receive a discharge of any debts if any of the grounds set forth in §727(a) for denial of a discharge to a Chapter 7 debtor are present. (See Chapter Twelve, Section B, and Illustration 12-b.) Moreover, BAPCPA added new §1141(d)(6), which provides that a corporate debtor receives no discharge as to an obligation owed to a government entity for money, property, services, or an extension of credit obtained by fraudulent pretenses or by the use of fraudulent financial statements in violation of §§523(a)(2)(A) or (B).

Section 1141(d)(2) provides that an *individual* Chapter 11 debtor cannot receive a discharge in Chapter 11 from any nondischargeable debt listed in §523 (see Chapter Twelve, Section A, and Illustration 12-a). BAPCPA added new §1141(d)(5) to make a Chapter 11 discharge for an individual operate much like the discharge received by a Chapter 13 debtor under §§1328(a) and (b): No discharge is received by the individual until completion of the plan payments unless the individual qualifies for a **hardship discharge** (see Chapter Sixteen, Section E).

Notwithstanding the entry of the confirmation order, the bankruptcy court retains authority to issue any other order "necessary to administer the estate" under Bankruptcy Rule 3020(d). This authority includes the postconfirmation determination of objections to claims or adversary proceedings, which must be resolved before a plan can be fully consummated. Sections 1106(a)(7) and 1107(a) of the Code require the reorganized debtor (or trustee if one was appointed) to file periodic reports on the progress made in implementing a plan after confirmation.

5. Postconfirmation Modification of a Chapter 11 Plan

Section 1127(b) provides that at any time after confirmation and before **substantial consummation** of a plan, the reorganized entity debtor can ask the court to modify the plan. Upon the filing of a motion for modification, the court will conduct a hearing on the request and can order a postconfirmation modification of the plan "if circumstances warrant such modification." Under §1127(e), an individual Chapter 11 debtor can seek modification at any time prior to completion of all payments called for in the plan and without regard to whether there has been substantial consummation.

Section 1121(f) provides that the proposed modification of the plan cannot be approved unless it complies with the various requirements of Chapter 11 including the disclosure and approval procedures of §§1121 through 1128. However, §1121(d) provides that any holder of a claim or interest that voted to approve the original plan will be deemed to approve the proposed modification unless it notifies the court of a change in its position within the time set by the court to do so.

P-H 19-q: What kinds of postconfirmation events might cause BBF to seek modification of the BBF plan?

6. Revocation of an Order of Confirmation

Revocation of an order confirming a plan requires a showing that the order "was procured by fraud," according to §1144, and an action to revoke an order of confirmation (an adversary proceeding per Bankruptcy Rule 7001(5)) must be instituted by a party in interest within 180 days after the order is entered. If the court does revoke the order of confirmation, any discharge made effective by the confirmation is revoked.

F. ▶ Postconfirmation Dismissal or Conversion of a Chapter 11 Case

Recall the discussion of the grounds for seeking dismissal of a Chapter 11 case or conversion of the case to a Chapter 7 liquidation in Chapter Eighteen, Section

C. Several of the grounds for dismissal or conversion we saw in Illustration 18-a involve cause arising after confirmation of the plan, including the revocation of an order of confirmation, the inability to effectuate a substantial consumation of a confirmed plan, or a material default by the debtor with a term of the confirmed plan.

EXAMPLE

Assume that BBF's plan of reorganization is confirmed but that its new business plan does not produce the income flow projected in its disclosure statement (Document 12 in the BBF case file), so that payments called for under the plan to begin nine months following the date of confirmation never begin. Or assume that the new business plan is successful for a couple of years and then falls apart, causing BBF to default on plan payments. These are the types of occurrences that may give rise to a motion by BBF to modify the plan or to a motion by creditors to dismiss or convert.

G. ▶ Consummation of the Plan of Reorganization

Pursuant to Bankruptcy Rule 3022, when the case has been fully administered the court will enter an order closing the case.

CHAPTER SUMMARY

The DIP has the exclusive right to file a proposed plan of reorganization during the 120 days following filing of the petition, and if it does so, no competing plan may be filed until 180 days postpetition. The plan must create classes of creditor and equity claim holders. Those in each class must have substantially similar claims. Undersecured claims may be treated in two different classes: one for secured and one for unsecured. Creditors holding unique claims may be placed in a class by themselves for administrative convenience.

A class of claims or interests is impaired if the plan proposes to alter the underlying rights of the holders. A Chapter 11 plan can propose to modify the rights of a secured creditor other than one holding a mortgage in the residence of an individual debtor to the same extent as allowed in a Chapter 13 case. Nonpriority unsecured claims may be modified in whole or part and discharged under the plan. Administrative operating expenses must be paid in full on the effective date of the plan and priority tax claims must be paid within six years of assessment.

To ensure that those voting on the plan understand it, the plan proponent must file a disclosure statement containing adequate information regarding the plan and the debtor. The court conducts a hearing on the adequacy of the disclosure statement. If the disclosure statement is approved by the court, it will issue an order establishing dates for distribution of ballots, setting time limits for voting on the plan, and setting a date for a confirmation hearing. Holders of allowed claims and interests can vote for or against the plan and good faith solicitation of support or opposition to the plan is allowed. Approval of a plan depends on its approval by the classes created by the plan. Approval of the plan by a class requires both approval by at least two-thirds of the dollar amount represented in the class and by more than one-half the creditors in the class. An undersecured creditor may make the §1111(b)(2) election to have its claim treated as secured up to the full amount owed.

A plan may be confirmed by the court in either of two ways. Confirmation under §1129(a) is used where all classes of creditors and claims, including any impaired class, approve the plan and other criteria are satisfied, including the best interests of creditors, good faith, lawfulness and feasibility tests, and the required treatment of priority claims. Confirmation under §1129(b), cram down confirmation, used when all impaired classes have not accepted the plan, requires that the various §1129(a) tests be satisfied and that at least one impaired class have approved the plan, that the plan not unfairly discriminate against objecting classes, and that the plan be fair and equitable to objecting classes. The fair and equitable requirement of §1129(b) can be satisfied for secured claims if the plan proposes to pay the full value of each secured claim. The fair and equitable requirement of §1129(b) can be satisfied for unsecured claims if the plan proposes to pay the full amount of the objecting claims in deferred installments over the term of the plan or if the plan proposes that equity holders receive nothing under the plan and retain no ownership interest in the reorganized debtor, the absolute priority rule. Some courts mitigate the harsh absolute priority rule with the new value exception.

Once the plan is confirmed, an order of confirmation is entered. The court retains postconfirmation authority to enter any order necessary to administer the case. A plan may be modified upon motion at any time before substantial consummation. An order of confirmation can be revoked upon motion made within 180 days and a showing that confirmation was procured by fraud. A Chapter 11 case can be dismissed or converted to a Chapter 7 liquidation for cause occurring postconfirmation as well. When the Chapter 11 case has been fully administered, the court will enter an order closing the case.

REVIEW QUESTIONS

1. Explain the 120-day exclusivity period of Chapter 11. What is the earliest date that a nondebtor can file a proposed plan? Under what circumstances must nondebtors wait 180 days postpetition to file a proposed plan?

2. What is the requirement for placing more than one claim or interest together in a single class by a Chapter 11 plan? How is it that an undersecured claim can be placed in more than one class?

3. What does it mean to say that a class of claims or interest is impaired under Chapter 11?

4. Summarize the various ways that a secured debt can be modified by a Chapter 11 plan.

5. What is a disclosure statement? Who prepares it? What kinds of information must it contain?

6. Explain the §1111(b)(2) election available to an undersecured creditor. Why would an undersecured creditor *not* make this election?

7. Explain the §1129(a) confirmation procedure. What role do the best interests of creditors, good faith, lawfulness and feasibility tests, and the required treatment of priority claims play in that procedure?

8. In a §1129(b) cram down confirmation, explain how a plan can meet the fair and equitable treatment requirement for a secured claim and for an unsecured claim. Summarize the absolute priority rule and the new value exception to it.

9. Summarize changes that can be made in a Chapter 11 plan or the case itself postconfirmation.

10. Under what circumstances can an order of confirmation in a Chapter 11 case be revoked? What timeframes are applicable to a motion to revoke confirmation? What is the procedure for seeking a revocation of plan confirmation?

WORDS AND PHRASES TO REMEMBER

absolute priority rule	gap period
administrative convenience	good faith
administrative expenses	hardship discharge
ballot	impaired (claim)
best interest of creditors test	indubitable equivalent
classes	insiders
conclusively presumed	interests
confirmation	new value exception
confirmation hearing	nonrecourse
cram down confirmation	order confirming plan
credit-bid	pay through
dirt for debt	prime rate
discharge	reorganized debtor
disclosure statement	replacement cost
discounted present value	ride through
discriminate unfairly	sale free and clear of liens
election of remedies	substantial consummation
exclusivity period	substantially similar
fair and equitable	undersecured claim
feasibility test	§1111(b)(2) election

TO LEARN MORE: A number of TLM activities to accompany this chapter are accessible on the companion web site for this textbook at http://aspenlawschool.com/books/Parsons_Debt4e/.

Chapter Twenty:

Bankruptcy Under Chapter 12, Chapter 9, and Chapter 15 of the Code

In this chapter we take a brief look at the three remaining bankruptcy proceedings authorized under the Code: the Chapter 12 reorganization proceeding for those who qualify as family farmers or family fishermen, the Chapter 9 adjustment of debts for a municipality, and the Chapter 15 cross-border bankruptcy case. These are all specialized types of proceedings and are filed much less frequently than the Chapter 7, 13, and 11 cases we have studied.

KEY CONCEPTS

- To qualify under Chapter 12, debtors must satisfy total monetary debt limitations, more than 50 percent of which must come from a family farming or commercial fishing operation; there are also fixed debt and income source limitations
- In Chapter 12, a standing trustee is appointed, but the debtor continues to operate the farming or fishing business as a debtor in possession
- The Chapter 12 debtor must file a debt adjustment plan with the petition or within 90 days thereafter
- The automatic stay goes into effect upon filing of a Chapter 12 petition and includes a co-debtor stay as in Chapter 13
- Unlike Chapter 13, Chapter 12 grants the debtor, as debtor in possession, all of the turnover and avoidance powers of a Chapter 7 bankruptcy trustee
- Unlike Chapter 13, a Chapter 12 plan may cure an arrearage or modify future payments due on secured debt over a term in excess of the plan
- In contrast to Chapter 13, Chapter 12 contains no prohibition on the strip down of an undersecured mortgage on real property or on a vehicle under the 910-day rule
- Chapter 9 is designed to provide temporary protection from creditors to a political subdivision or public agency or instrumentality of a state while it develops a plan for adjustment of debts
- A Chapter 15 case allows representatives of foreign insolvency proceedings to have the proceedings recognized in U.S. bankruptcy courts, and grants certain other powers provided to debtors and creditors under the Code
- Recognition of the foreign proceedings as main or nonmain proceedings significantly impacts the powers of the foreign representative to administer the debtor's estate

A. **The Chapter 12 Reorganization for a Family Farmer or Family Fisherman with Regular Annual Income**

1. History, Purpose, and Qualifications to File Under Chapter 12

Sunset clause A legislative enactment that expires of its own terms at some point in the future.

The Chapter 12 bankruptcy was created by Congress in 1986 exclusively for family farmers *with a regular annual income* in response to a time of economic hardship for the nation's farmers. The chapter was enacted with a **sunset clause**, pursuant to which it would expire at a specific time if not renewed. However, it was renewed several times and finally made a permanent part of the Code by BAPCPA, which expanded it to also cover family fishermen *with a regular annual income*.

P-H 20-a: Why do you think §109(f) references the family farmer or family fisherman's regular "annual" income? In contrast, §109(e), dealing with Chapter 13, only references individuals with regular income. How often do most debtors with regular income get paid or receive income? How often do most farmers get paid or otherwise receive income? If a Chapter 12 debtor only receives income once or twice a year, how might that impact the terms of the debt adjustment plan the debtor proposes?

A "family farmer" who may qualify for relief under Chapter 12 is defined in §§101(18) and (19) as an individual or an individual and spouse engaged in a **farming operation** (see §§101(20) and (21)) either as individuals, a partnership, or a closely held corporation. A "family fisherman" who may qualify for relief under Chapter 12 is defined in §§101(19A and B) as an individual or an individual and spouse engaged in a **commercial fishing operation** either as individuals, a partnership, or a closely held corporation. Thus, Chapter 12 allows qualifying entities to file as well as individuals.

Like Chapter 13, Chapter 12 imposes debt limitations on those seeking to qualify for relief, and the dollar amounts of those limitations are subject to adjustment every third year as mandated by §104. As of April 1, 2016, those filing for Chapter 12 relief as a family farmer can have no more than $4,153,150 in total debt while those filing for Chapter 12 relief as family fishermen can have no more than $1,954,550 in total debt. In addition to the debt limits, Chapter 12 contains debt and income source limitations. Per §§101(18) and (19A), at least 50 percent of the family farmer's total fixed debts and at least 80 percent of the family fisherman's total fixed debts (excluding debt on the debtor's principal residence) must be related to the farming or the commercial fishing operation. Additionally, more than 50 percent of the gross income of the individual or the husband and wife for the preceding tax year (or, for family farmers only, for each of the second and third prior tax years) must have derived from the farming or commercial fishing operation. For a good discussion of what constitutes income from a farming operation, see *In re Jessen*, 82 B.R. 490 (Bankr. S.D. Iowa 1988), highlighted below.

Large corporate farming or fish harvesting/processing businesses will usually not qualify for Chapter 12 and will proceed under Chapter 11 to reorganize. And many smaller, family-operated farming or fishing businesses that do qualify under Chapter 12 will opt to proceed under Chapter 13 because they don't need the expanded debt adjustment tools that Chapter 12 provides, as discussed below. But in some situations a Chapter 12 case can be quite advantageous over a Chapter 13 or a Chapter 11 for the individual, partnership, or closely held corporation that qualifies to file under Chapter 12. While in most federal districts very few if any Chapter 12 cases are filed each year, for those who work for attorneys in rural areas where family farming is still common or in communities located on our mighty rivers and teeming seashores where fishing for a living is still a way of life, a basic understanding of the Chapter 12 bankruptcy is essential.

P-H 20-b: Access the statistics and data tables page maintained by the Administrative Office of the Federal Courts at www.uscourts.gov/statistics-reports/case-load-statistics-data-tables and determine how many Chapter 12 cases have been filed in your federal district in the last two to three years. Compare what you find with the number of Chapter 13 and Chapter 11 cases filed in that district during the same time period.

Notice that the debt limits set out in §§101(18) for the family farmer and (19A) for the family fisherman are considerably higher than those set out in §109(e) for individuals filing under Chapter 13. This is one of the significant advantages of Chapter 12 for a qualifying individual debtor. Individuals qualifying as family farmers or family fishermen often carry considerably more debt than most individuals because they are operating a business. Thus, even though they are individual debtors, Chapter 13 is foreclosed to them because their debt exceeds the limits for that chapter. An individual qualifying as a family farmer or family fisherman whose debts exceed the debt limits set for Chapter 12 filing will file for reorganization under Chapter 11 of the Code.

In fact Chapter 12 was designed to be something of a hybrid between Chapter 13 and Chapter 11 of the Code although it has more in common with the former. It is designed to accommodate the economic realities with which farmers and fishermen live and to facilitate their adjustment of debts in ways that are less complex (or expensive) than those designed for businesses under Chapter 11 and to some extent more practical and streamlined than those for individual debtors under Chapter 13.

Per §109(g), like individuals filing under any other chapter of the Code, a debtor cannot file under Chapter 12 (or any other chapter) if during the preceding 180 days a prior bankruptcy petition was dismissed due to the debtor's willful failure to appear before the court or comply with orders of the court or was voluntarily dismissed after creditors sought relief from the bankruptcy court to recover property upon which they hold liens. In addition, the individual debtor who files under Chapter 12 must comply with the BAPCPA-imposed requirement that he or she receive credit counseling from an approved credit counseling agency within 180 days preceding the filing of the petition per §§109(h)(1) and 111.

PROTECTING THE FAMILY FARMER

Prior to enactment of the Chapter 12, bankruptcy laws in this country did not, for the most part, single out farmers much less fishermen for special treatment in bankruptcy. The Bankruptcy Act of 1898 did make farmers immune from involuntary bankruptcy. An amendment to the Bankruptcy Act in 1933 passed during the ravages of the Great Depression and Dust Bowl added temporary Section 75 to the Act intended to enable farmers in default on the mortgages securing their farms to modify the payment schedules in order to retain possession and avoid foreclosure. Section 75 proved generally unworkable since it required the agreement of mortgagee banks that were also struggling to survive. The Frazier-Lemke Farm Bankruptcy Act of 1934 strengthened Section 75 by mandating a five-year delay in foreclosure on farms in default so long as the farmer made rental payments. At the end of the five years the farmer was given the option to remain in possession as a paying tenant following foreclosure or to buy back the foreclosed property at its then appraised value over six years at 1 percent interest. Section 75 expired in 1949 when, in more prosperous times, Congress did not renew it. The hyper-inflation of the late 1970s followed by the savings and loan crisis of the mid-1980s led to a severe tightening of credit that impacted negatively on small farmers whose way of life depended on the regular securing of credit (often in excess of the debt limits set for Chapter 13) and whose numbers were steadily dwindling anyway. Those concerns led to Congress enacting Chapter 12 on a temporary basis in 1986 applicable only to the family farmer. Chapter 12 was scheduled to expire in 1993 but its duration was extended several times by Congress before being made permanent by BAPCPA in 2005. At that time, Chapter 12 was expanded to include family fishermen because, like the family farmer, many such fishing operations regularly incurred debt in excess of the Chapter 13 limits and some did business as entities, disqualifying them from Chapter 13 relief.

2. Filing the Chapter 12 Case

A Chapter 12 case is commenced in the same way as a Chapter 13, by filing a petition with a bankruptcy court, using Official Form 101 for individual filers and Official Form 201 for entity filers. A husband and wife filing individually may file a joint petition.

Like the individual Chapter 7 debtor and the Chapter 13 debtor, per Bankruptcy Rule 1007(b), the individual Chapter 12 debtor must also file a list of creditors, along with the various schedules of assets and liabilities, a statement of financial affairs, and the other statements and documents discussed in Chapter Eight, Section B, except for the Statement of Intent (Official Form 108). Section 521(a)(2) requires the filing of a Statement of Intent only of an individual Chapter 7 debtor. Like the Chapter 13 debtor, the Chapter 12 debtor's proposed plan will indicate how the debtor intends to deal with property that is subject to a security interest. Entity Chapter 12 debtors must file the various lists, schedules, and statements we considered for the Chapter 11 entity debtor in Chapter Seventeen, Section B.

Significantly, the individual Chapter 12 debtor is not required to complete and file either Official Form 122C-1 or 122C-2 to determine the applicable commitment period or projected disposable income. In a Chapter 12 case those determinations will be made by examination of the debtor's Schedules I and J together with the proposed plan itself. And since the debtor is operating a farming or fishing business, there will be tax returns that can be examined during the plan confirmation process as well.

3. The Chapter 12 Trustee and the Debtor as "Debtor in Possession"

Pursuant to §1202, a trustee is appointed in every Chapter 12 case. In most districts the U.S. Trustee has designated a standing Chapter 12 trustee pursuant to 28 U.S.C. §586(b) who will fulfill this role, as does the standing Chapter 13 trustee in cases filed under that chapter (in many districts the standing Chapter 13 trustee will also serve in Chapter 12 cases).

The duties of the Chapter 12 trustee are very similar to those of the trustee in a Chapter 13 case. (See Illustration 13-a and compare with the duties of the Chapter 12 trustee set out in §1202(b).) Significantly, the Chapter 12 trustee, like the Chapter 13 trustee, does not collect and liquidate the property of the estate as does the Chapter 7 trustee pursuant to §704(a)(1).

Since the Chapter 12 debtor is engaged in operating a farming or commercial fishing business, the debtor is considered a **debtor in possession** as in a Chapter 11 case and charged under §1203 with continuing that operation during the bankruptcy proceeding. Pursuant to §1204, a party in interest may request that the bankruptcy court remove the debtor as a debtor in possession "for cause," which can include fraud, dishonesty, incompetence, or gross mismanagement of the business. In that case the trustee will operate the business.

Of the grounds for removal of a Chapter 12 debtor in possession under §1204, the most frequently litigated is "gross mismanagement." What constitutes mismanagement may vary considerably depending on the eye of the beholder and the qualifying concept "gross" can make it difficult for the complaining party in interest to prevail on that ground.

HIGHLIGHTED CASE ●

IN RE JESSEN

82 B.R. 490 (Bankr. S.D. Iowa 1988)

OPINION: JACKWIG, Chief Bankruptcy Judge.

On July 8, 1987 the following matters came on for hearing in Council Bluffs, Iowa:

1. Motion to dismiss and/or to remove debtors as debtors in possession filed by the Production Credit Association of the Midlands (PCA) and the Federal Land Bank (FLB) on June 15, 1987;

. . .

5. Motion to dismiss filed by the standing Chapter 12 trustee on July 2, 1987.

FACTS

1. The debtors' 1986 federal tax return shows the debtors received income from the following sources:

Source	Amount
Wages	$35,256.00
Interest Income	758.00
Sealing of Grain	21,936.00
Cash Payment	2,981.00
Cash Rent	22,660.00
Executor Fee	1,975.00
Total	$85,566.00

2. For twenty-four years prior to 1985, the debtors actively engaged in farming.
3. In order to supplement farm income, Charles Jessen obtained off-farm employment as a custodian in December of 1984.
4. Unable to obtain operating financing, the debtors leased much of their land on a cash rent basis in 1985 and 1986.
5. Approximately 280 acres remained uncultivated in 1986.
6. Earl Phippen, the uncle of Charles Jessen, died on July 10, 1985.
7. Earl Phippen's last will and testament was filed with the Iowa District Court for Audubon County on July 17, 1985.
8. In the will, Earl Phippen devised 160 acres of land located in Audubon County to Charles Jessen.
9. On April 7, 1986 Charles Jessen executed and filed a disclaimer to the 160 acres in the estate proceedings.
10. The debtors filed a petition for relief under Chapter 12 on April 17, 1987.
11. The trustee estimates that the value of the land less encumbrances is $33,880.00.

DISCUSSION

The . . . issues include: whether the debtors are eligible for Chapter 12 relief; whether Charles Jessen's disclaimer of the 160 acres and failure to cultivate 280 acres in 1986 are grounds for removal of the debtors as debtors in possession or for dismissal of the case . . . .

A. Chapter 12 Eligibility

The PCA, the FLB and the trustee contend that the debtors are not eligible for Chapter 12 relief. Specifically, they argue that the cash rent is not derived from a "farming operation" and therefore the debtors do not satisfy the 50 percent income test set out in 11 U.S.C. section 101(17)(A). Further, the PCA and the FLB maintain that the income received from sealing corn should not be considered "gross income" for eligibility purposes.

11 U.S.C. section 109(f) states that "[o]nly a family farmer with regular income may be a debtor under Chapter 12 of this title." 11 U.S.C. section

101(17)(A), which defines "family farmer" in the context of an individual or individual and spouse, requires in part that:

> [an] individual or individual and spouse engaged in a farming operation . . . receive from such farming operation more than 50 percent of such individual's or such individual and spouse's gross income for the taxable year preceding the taxable year in which the case concerning such individual or such individual and spouse was filed;

A "farming operation" is defined in 11 U.S.C. section 101(20) as including "farming, tillage of the soil, dairy farming, ranching, production or raising of crops, poultry, or livestock, and production of poultry or livestock products in an unmanufactured state."

A number of cases have examined the meaning of "farming operation" in general and as it relates to the income test found in section 101(17)(A). This court in *Matter of Burke*, 81 B.R. 971 (Bankr. S.D. Iowa 1987) reviewed some of those cases and determined that the decisions generally have fallen along two lines. One line of cases, represented by *Matter of Armstrong*, 812 F.2d 1024 (7th Cir. 1987), cert. denied, 108 S. Ct. 287 (1987), views "farming operation" narrowly. For the *Armstrong* majority, a critical question is whether the activity under consideration exposes the debtor to the risks inherent in agricultural production. The other line of cases interprets "farming operation" in a broader fashion. Those courts look to the "totality of the circumstances" in determining whether the debtors or the family members or relatives in the case of a corporation or partnership are engaged in farming and whether, in the case of an individual or an individual and spouse, the income test is met. This court adopted the latter approach in the *Burke* decision.

With respect to cash rent arrangements, this court stated:

> Income received from a cash rent arrangement will be farm income in the case of an individual or individual and spouse only if the evidence reveals that past farming activities have been more than short term or sporadic and that any cessation of farming activities is temporary. Consideration will be given to the reason for the cessation (inability to obtain operating credit versus new non-farm venture); the extent of the cessation (leasing a portion of the farm in an effort to scale back the operation versus leasing the entire farm); and the relationship to the tenant (leasing to family members as opposed to leasing to nonrelated individuals or entities).

Burke, at 976-77.

Under the totality of the circumstances, the debtors in this case have established that the cash rent is derived from a farming operation. The debtors had been actively engaged in farming for twenty-four years prior to curtailing their farming operation in 1985. Thus, their past farming activities cannot be characterized as short term or sporadic. The debtors ceased actively farming because they were unable to obtain operating credit. The fact that these debtors leased much of their farm and sold their equipment does not obviate finding the rent was from a "farming operation." The record reveals that the PCA cut off operating credit in December of 1984 and the debtors were unable to find operating credit elsewhere. Therefore, maintaining more than a small portion of the farm was an impossibility.

Finally, the record does not address the relationship between the cash rent tenants and the debtors. However, a finding for the debtors is warranted even if it is assumed the tenants were not related to the debtors. Apparently, the debtors have access to relatives' equipment and their son farms a portion of their land on a crop share basis. They cannot be viewed as having abandoned farming on a permanent basis. Under the facts of this case, finding that the cash rent is derived from a farming operation does not abuse the Congressional intent underlying 11 U.S.C. §101(17)(A) in particular and Chapter 12 in general.

Accordingly, the debtors have established that more than 50% of their income is derived from a farming operation in which they are engaged.

B. Gross Mismanagement

The PCA and FLB maintain that the debtors should be removed as debtors in possession or that the case should be dismissed because a portion of the farm remained idle during 1986 and Charles disclaimed his inheritance. The PCA and FLB assert these actions constitute gross mismanagement.

11 U.S.C. section 1204(a) provides that a debtor may be removed as a debtor in possession "for cause, including . . . gross mismanagement of the affairs of the debtor, either before or after the commencement of the case." 11 U.S.C. section 1208(c)(1) states that a case may be dismissed for "gross mismanagement, by the debtor that is prejudicial to creditors." The PCA and FLB do not cite nor does the court find any cases that have examined the term "gross mismanagement" as used in sections 1204 and 1208. The legislative history of Chapter 12 and in particular, section 1204, indicates that Congress envisioned that a trustee would substitute for a removed debtor in possession and that this transfer of duties was modeled after provisions in Chapter 11. H. Conf. R. No. 958, 99th Cong., 2d Sess. 49, reprinted in 1986 U.S. Code Cong. & Admin. News 5227, 5246, 5250. 11 U.S.C. section 1104, which governs appointment of trustees in Chapter 11 cases, states in part:

> (a) At any time after the commencement of the case but before confirmation of a plan, on request of a party in interest or the United States trustee, and after notice and a hearing, the court shall order the appointment of a trustee—
>
> > (1) for cause, including . . . gross mismanagement of the affairs of the debtor by current management, either before or after commencement of the case . . . .

Courts interpreting this provision have recognized that appointment of a [Chapter 11] trustee is an extraordinary remedy. Appointment of a trustee may prevent reorganization because the administrative expenses associated with the appointment are paid by the estate. Accordingly, the parties seeking the appointment bear the burden of proving the appointment is justified. Use of a gross mismanagement standard implies a recognition that every bankruptcy reorganization involves some degree of mismanagement. Given the clarity of the legislative history, the similarity of the language used in sections 1104 and 1204 and the financial burdens that accompany having a trustee operate a farm, the court concludes that the aforementioned principles apply in a Chapter 12 context.

Under these standards, the PCA and the FLB fail to shoulder their burden. With respect to the uncultivated land, the evidence is clear that the debtors were unable to farm because of a lack of operating credit. Moreover, they attempted to rent the land. A prospective tenant was lined up but he eventually declined to lease the land because of the dispute between the debtors and the FLB. There is little more the debtors could have done to ensure that the land was cultivated. The fact that land remained idle was not the result of gross mismanagement.

Likewise, Charles' decision not to disclaim his inheritance does not constitute "gross mismanagement." The disclaimer was made pursuant to Iowa Code section 633.704(1). Under Iowa law, a disclaimer takes effect against creditors. [Citation omitted.] Contrary to the PCA's and FLB's contention, Charles had no obligation to accept the inheritance and apply it to debt.

The court's findings concerning "gross mismanagement" as used in section 1204 applies to "gross mismanagement" as used in section 1208(c)(1). Generally in rehabilitation cases, the burden of proof in a motion to dismiss rests with the moving party. [Citations omitted.] . . . PCA and FLB have failed to carry this burden.

POST-CASE FOLLOW-UP

Does the narrow or broad view of what constitutes a farming operation seem truer to the definition under the Code? Determine if the courts of your federal district or circuit have adopted one or the other of these views in a Chapter 12 case. Does the court's discussion of what constitutes "gross mismanagement" remind you somewhat of the business judgment rule in corporate law? Not every court would agree with this one on the issue of the debtor's disclaimer of the inheritance. Is it really determinative on the issue of mismanagement that the debtor had no obligation to accept the inheritance? Should that be the test? Compare *In re Kloubec*, 247 B.R. 246 (Bankr. N.D. Iowa 2000) (Chapter 12 debtor's disclaimer of inheritance valued at $85,000 one day before petition filed treated as fraudulent transfer as to creditors; involuntary conversion of case to one under Chapter 7 per §1208(d) based on fraud).

In re Jessen: Real Life Applications

1. Assume a federal district has adopted what *In re Jessen* describes as the narrow view of what constitutes a farming operation under §101(21). The following debtors in that district would like to file under Chapter 12. Most of their income over the past three years has derived from the following sources. Which do you think will qualify as Chapter 12 debtors?

   a. Debtor raises cattle sold for slaughter delivered to buyer twice a year at the then current market price and grows corn harvested once a year in the fall.

    b. Debtor grows wild flowers on 400 acres during a four-month growing season to sell to commercial florists in the region. Land is idle the remainder of the year.

    c. Debtor conducts tours of caves on 3,000 acres of former dairy farm that has been in the family for 100 years.

    d. Debtor sells off farm equipment used on 5,000-acre farm that is under option to be purchased by a real estate developer within the next 24 months.

2. The Chapter 12 debtors in the following cases have committed the acts described. Creditors in each case have filed a motion to remove them from management of their farming operations as debtors in possession. In each case, decide whether the court is likely to grant the motion.

    a. Debtor turned down offer from a real estate developer that would have provided debtor more than enough cash to pay all debts.

    b. Debtor stopped growing profitable alfalfa crop on half of the farm acreage to introduce new organic potato crop not expected to be profitable until after term of the plan but then expected to produce twice the profits as alfalfa.

    c. Debtor stopped growing profitable corn crop on 5 percent of farm acreage in order to make a gift of that acreage to newly married daughter and her husband.

    d. Debtor stopped growing crops on 90 percent of farm land in order to begin giving cave tours on the land to the public in expectation of greater profits.

    e. To reduce labor costs debtor replaced 10 percent of seasonal harvesters with undocumented immigrants paid less than minimum wage.

The debtor in possession or trustee charged with managing the debtor's business is required by Bankruptcy Rule 2015(b) to:

- keep a record of receipts and the disposition of money and property received;
- file the reports and summaries required by §704(a)(8) of the Code (periodic reports and summaries of the operation of such business, including a statement of receipts and disbursements, and such other information as the U.S. Trustee or the court requires) including a statement, if payments are made to employees, of the amounts of deductions for all taxes required to be withheld or paid for and in behalf of employees and the place where these amounts are deposited; and
- give notice of the case to every entity known to be holding money or property subject to withdrawal or order of the debtor, including every bank, savings or building and loan association, public utility company, and landlord with whom the debtor has a deposit, and to every insurance company that has issued a policy having a cash surrender value payable to the debtor, except that notice need not be given to any entity who has knowledge or has previously been notified of the case.

Often the local rules of the bankruptcy court where the Chapter 12 case is pending or guidelines adopted by the U.S. Trustee in the district will contain special reporting and operating requirements for the Chapter 12 debtor in possession. Common requirements at the beginning of a case are that the debtor immediately close all bank accounts and reopen them in the name of the debtor as debtor in possession since, as in Chapter 11, the debtor in possession is considered a new and different entity from the prepetition debtor. The same is required for credit cards and financial records.

P-H 20-c: As an example of local rules or guidelines adopted for Chapter 12 cases, see Operating and Reporting Requirements for Chapter 12 Cases issued by the U.S. Trustee for the Southern District of California at http://www.justice.gov/ust/r15/docs/chapter12/chapter_12_orr.pdf. See if your federal district has adopted local rules or guidelines for filing Chapter 12 cases.

---

4. The Automatic Stay, First Meeting of Creditors, and Filing Proofs of Claim in a Chapter 12

Upon the filing of the Chapter 12 petition, the **automatic stay** of §362 goes into effect and operates the same way as in a Chapter 13 case. As in Chapter 13, there is a **co-debtor stay** prohibiting creditors from seeking to collect a consumer debt from any individual who is liable along with the debtor. See §1201(a). At this time, you may want to review the discussion of how the automatic stay operates in a Chapter 13 case, including the co-debtor stay on consumer debt, discussed in Section C of Chapter Thirteen.

Pursuant to Bankruptcy Rule 2003(a), the first meeting of creditors is to be conducted by the trustee between 21 and 35 days after filing of the petition. In order to participate in distributions under the plan, unsecured creditors must file a proof of claim within 90 days following the date first set for the first meeting of creditors per Bankruptcy Rule 3002(c). A governmental unit that is a creditor has until 180 days following the filing of the petition to file its proof of claim per §502(b)(9).

5. Property of the Estate and the Debtor's Turnover and Avoidance Powers

The definition of property of the estate in §1207 is the same as in a Chapter 13 case. At this time you may want to review the discussion of that concept in a Chapter 13 case in Chapter Thirteen, Section D.

Significantly, §1203 bestows on the Chapter 12 debtor in possession all of the powers of a Chapter 11 trustee, which includes the avoidance and turnover powers discussed in Chapter Ten, Sections D and E, and in Chapter Eighteen, Section E. That stands in contrast to the failure of the Code to bestow such powers on a Chapter 13 debtor as discussed in Chapter Fifteen, Section B. It also can be a consideration in the decision of an individual debtor qualified to file under either Chapter 13 or Chapter 12 to choose the latter.

6. Treatment of Claims in a Chapter 12 Plan

Per §1221 the debtor must file a proposed Chapter 12 plan with the petition or within 90 days following. The Chapter 12 plan works very much the same as a Chapter 13 plan regarding treatment of secured, priority, and unsecured claims. Like a Chapter 13 plan, it will last three to five years unless it calls for earlier payment of 100 percent of priority and unsecured claims. All priority claims must be paid in full unless the priority creditor agrees to different treatment of its claim or, in the case of a domestic support obligation, unless the debtor contributes all disposable income per §1222(a)(2)(4). Unsecured claims do not have to be paid in full so long as the plan commits all the debtor's disposable income to such claims over the term of the plan and as long as the unsecured creditors receive at least as much as they would receive if the debtor's nonexempt assets were liquidated under Chapter 7. See §1225. For purposes of Chapter 12, "disposable income" is defined in §1225(b)(2) as income not reasonably necessary for the maintenance or support of the debtor or dependents or for making payments needed to continue, preserve, and operate the debtor's business.

Significantly, Chapter 12 offers debtors more powerful debt restructuring tools than does Chapter 13. Sections 1222(b)(5) and (9) allow a Chapter 12 plan to cure an arrearage or modify future payments due on secured debt over a term in excess of the plan.

EXAMPLE

Assume a debtor qualifies to file for relief under either Chapter 13 or Chapter 12. He owns a vehicle that is collateral for a loan from Bank on which he makes monthly payments of $400. The value of the vehicle exceeds the balance owed on the debt so the Bank is fully secured in the vehicle. Debtor has 40 more scheduled payments on the debt at the time he decides to file for bankruptcy relief. Debtor would like to retain the vehicle by paying the Bank the full amount of its secured claim. However, in order to successfully fund either a Chapter 13 or 12 plan he needs to adjust those payments downward. In a Chapter 13 case he can propose a plan to adjust the payments to Bank downward during the term of the plan but only so long as he pays the full amount of the claim during the term of the plan. So he might propose that the payments be lowered during the first three years of the plan but rise during the final two years so that the full claim is paid off. But in a Chapter 12 he has more flexibility. He can propose a plan to adjust the payments to Bank downward during the entire term of the plan even though the full claim is not paid off during the term of the plan. As you would expect, any amounts still owing on the claim at the conclusion of the plan are excepted from the discharge received by the debtor per §1228(a)(1).

In addition, Chapter 12 contains no prohibition on the strip down of an undersecured mortgage on real property used as the debtor's principal residence, unlike the prohibitions on such strip downs for Chapter 13 debtors (compare §1222(b)(2) with §1322(b)(2)). Chapter 12 contains no limitation like the 910-day rule on the strip down of an undersecured claim involving a motor vehicle as collateral or the one-year rule on the strip down of an undersecured claim involving collateral other than a motor vehicle (compare §1325 with §1225). Moreover, the Code's general adequate protection standard of §361, which comes into play in motions to lift the automatic stay under §362, is declared inapplicable in a Chapter 12 by §1205(a) and the Chapter 12 debtor has other options to satisfy that standard, including paying only "reasonable rent customary in the community" as adequate protection payments for farmland.

These more flexible debt adjustment tools, along with the higher debt limits discussed earlier, are what really separate Chapter 12 from Chapter 13 and make the former more advantageous to debtors seeking to restructure their debts and who meet the Chapter 12 definition of a family farmer or fisherman.

7. Confirming the Chapter 12 Plan

The standards for **confirmation** of a Chapter 12 plan under §1225 are substantially the same as those for a Chapter 13 plan as discussed in Chapter Sixteen, Section B. Per §1224 the confirmation hearing is to be conducted within 45 days following the filing of the proposed plan by the debtor. As in a Chapter 13 case, the most common objections to confirmation of a Chapter 12 plan are that it fails to commit all of the debtor's disposable income to payment of unsecured claims or that proposed payments to unsecured creditors under the plan are less than those creditors would receive in a Chapter 7 liquidation. If the proposed plan is filed before the first meeting of creditors, these disputes can often be worked out at that meeting so no formal objection to confirmation is filed with the court. Section 1223 authorizes the debtor to propose modifications to the plan at any time before confirmation.

If the debtor is unable to obtain confirmation of a plan he may ask that the case be converted to a Chapter 7 liquidation per §1208(a) or it will be dismissed. As in a Chapter 13 case, §1226(a) directs that plan payments received by the trustee prior to confirmation are to be retained by the trustee until confirmation or dismissal of the case. If no plan is confirmed (and the case is converted or dismissed), §1226(a) mandates that payments in the hands of the trustee be used to pay allowed administrative expenses and fees under §503(b) including of course the trustee's percentage fee with any balance paid to the debtor. If the conversion or dismissal occurs after a Chapter 12 plan has been confirmed, the same issues regarding proper distribution of the payments in the hands of the trustee are raised as discussed in Chapter Sixteen, Section F, in connection with *Harris v. Viegelahn*, 135 S. Ct. 1829 (2015).

Section 1230(a) provides that on motion filed by a party in interest within 180 days following entry of an order confirming a Chapter 12 plan, that order of confirmation can be revoked upon a showing that it was procured by fraud.

8. Living with a Chapter 12 Plan

Once the court confirms the plan, the debtor is obligated to make the periodic payments called for to the Chapter 12 trustee who will then distribute funds received to creditors in accordance with the terms of the plan per §1226(a). While we think of these distributions as being made monthly, for the family farmer or fisherman whose income is regularly received quarterly, semi-annually, or even annually, the payments to the trustee and disbursements to creditors will typically follow that schedule as well.

Under §364(b), during the term of the plan, a Chapter 12 debtor cannot obtain credit or incur unsecured debt other than in the ordinary course of business without prior court approval. Per §364(c), court approval must be sought in order to obtain credit or to incur new debt having priority over certain administrative expenses. Section 364(c) also requires court approval before the debtor can obtain credit or incur debt secured by a lien on property of the estate.

Section 363(b) authorizes (and requires) a debtor to seek court approval for the use, sale, or lease of property of the estate that is not in the ordinary course of business of the debtor.

EXAMPLE

Assume a farmer debtor in Chapter 12 decides to lease a portion of his farm-land next season rather than planting it himself as he has always done. Since this use of the land that is property of the estate is arguably not in the ordinary course of business of this debtor, he should seek court approval for the land lease before entering into it.

Like a Chapter 13 plan, a Chapter 12 plan can be modified after confirmation. See §1229. The debtor, the trustee, or the holder of an allowed unsecured claim can request postconfirmation modification based on changed and unforeseen circumstances as in the case of a Chapter 13 plan (discussed in Chapter Sixteen, Section D).

9. Conversion or Dismissal of a Chapter 12 Case

Under §1208(a) the Chapter 12 debtor has an absolute right to convert the case to a Chapter 7 liquidation at any time. Under §1208(b) the debtor can move to dismiss the case at any time and the court is to grant the motion unless the case was converted to Chapter 12 from Chapter 7 or Chapter 11. §§1222(a)(1), 1227. In any event, failure to make the plan payments may result in dismissal of the case. 11 U.S.C. §1208(c). In addition, under §1208(d), the court may dismiss the case or convert the case to a liquidation case under Chapter 7 of the Bankruptcy Code upon a showing that the debtor has committed fraud in connection with the case. See, e.g., *In re Kloubec*, 247 B.R. 246 (Bankr. N.D. Iowa 2000), discussed in the post-case follow-up to *In re Jessen*.

Section 1208(c) authorizes the bankruptcy court to dismiss a Chapter 12 case on a number of grounds summarized in Illustration 20-a.

Section 1208(e) authorizes the bankruptcy court to dismiss the case or convert it to a Chapter 7 liquidation upon a showing that the debtor has committed fraud in connection with the case.

10. The Chapter 12 Discharge

As in Chapter 13 and Chapter 11 cases, the Chapter 12 debtor receives a **discharge** under §1228(a) only after completion of all payments under the plan. Like the Chapter 13 debtor, the individual Chapter 12 debtor who owed a domestic support obligation must also certify that all such payments called for in the plan or otherwise due through the date of confirmation have been paid.

The §523(a) debts excepted from discharge that we considered in connection with Chapter 7 (see Chapter Twelve, Section A) apply too in a Chapter 12 case per

Illustration 20-a: GROUNDS FOR INVOLUNTARY DISMISSAL OF A CHAPTER 12 CASE

- Unreasonable delay or gross mismanagement by the debtor that is prejudicial to creditors
- Nonpayment of any required fees and charges
- Failure to timely file a plan
- Failure to commence making timely payments under a confirmed plan
- The denial of confirmation of a plan and the denial of a request made for additional time for filing another plan or a modification of a plan
- A material default by the debtor with respect to a term of a confirmed plan
- The revocation of the order of confirmation
- The termination of a confirmed plan by reason of the occurrence of a condition specified in the plan, other than completion of payments under the plan
- Continuing loss or diminution in value to property of the estate with no reasonable likelihood of rehabilitation
- Failure of the debtor to pay any domestic support obligation that first becomes payable after the date of the filing of the petition

§1228(c)(2). Also excepted from discharge are secured claims involving payments extending beyond the term of the plan including those that were modified in the plan per §§1222(b)(5) and (9).

Section 1228(b) authorizes the bankruptcy court to grant the Chapter 12 debtor an early **hardship discharge**. The Chapter 12 hardship discharge works the same way as the Chapter 13 hardship discharge discussed in Chapter Sixteen, Section E.

B.   The Chapter 9 Adjustment of Debts of a Municipality

Chapter 9 bankruptcy filings are rare. Between 1981 and 2015 there were only 67 Chapter 9 filings nationwide (35 of those, however, were filed between 2008 and 2015, fallout from the Great Recession). Thus, most legal professionals working in the bankruptcy field will never encounter a Chapter 9 case, even in a long career. But when they do occur, the cases tend to be significant events on a local and even a statewide or national level.

1. Purpose and Scope of Chapter 9

Chapter 9 is designed to provide the financially distressed **municipality** temporary relief from its creditors while it develops a plan for adjustment of debts. Per §109(c)(1), only a municipality may seek protection under Chapter 9. Section 101(40) of the Code defines a municipality as a "political subdivision or public agency or instrumentality of a state" and that has been construed to include:

- cities
- counties
- townships

- school districts
- public improvement districts
- quasi-public bodies such as bridge authorities, highway authorities, and gas authorities

Interestingly, §109(c)(2) requires that a municipality filing for Chapter 9 relief be specifically authorized by the state in which it is located to do so. Section 903 preserves the authority of states to limit or qualify the power of a municipality to file. Conversely, municipalities can only file under Chapter 9; no other provision of the Code is available to them. Thus, if a state does not authorize municipalities to file for Chapter 9 relief they must seek such relief under state law or seek special state legislation for relief. Currently, 24 states allow municipalities to file under Chapter 9. Some of those require the municipality to seek specific authorization from the state before filing, and at least one (Iowa) permits filing only if the insolvency is caused by involuntary debt (e.g., a court judgment entered in a liability suit).

WHY LET STATES DECIDE WHETHER TO ALLOW MUNICIPALITIES TO FILE UNDER CHAPTER 9?

Federalism A principle of government whereby a national government agrees to share power with political subdivisions such as states or territories; adopted in the Tenth Amendment to the United States Constitution.

What is the policy behind Congress's decision to let states decide whether municipal entities can file under Chapter 9? Is it ultimately a policy issue or a constitutional one arising under the principle of **federalism** in the Tenth Amendment to the Constitution, which reserves to the states a large measure of sovereignty over their internal affairs? The original congressional act seeking to regulate bankruptcy proceedings (a Chapter 10 filing under the old Bankruptcy Act) for governmental entities was struck down by the U.S. Supreme Court for Tenth Amendment reasons in *Ashton v. Cameron County Water Improvement Dist. No. 1*, 298 U.S. 513, 532 (1936). A subsequent 1937 act was upheld only two years later in *United States v. Bekins*, 304 U.S. 27, 54 (1938), and is the source of modern-day Chapter 9.

Additional §109(c) requirements for filing a petition in Chapter 9 require that the municipality be insolvent as that term is defined in §101(32)(C), that it desire to effect a plan to adjust its debts (i.e., no involuntary filing is allowed), and that it meet at least one of the following criteria:

- It has obtained the agreement of creditors holding at least a majority in amount of the claims of each class that it intends to impair under its Chapter 9 plan;
- It has negotiated in good faith with creditors but failed to obtain the agreement of creditors holding at least a majority in the amount of the claims of each class that the debtor intends to impair under its plan;
- It has been unable to negotiate with creditors because such negotiation is impracticable; or
- It reasonably believes that a creditor may attempt to obtain a preference.

WHY DO MUNICIPALITIES FAIL?

Prior to the Great Recession, the largest municipal bankruptcy in American history was the 1994 Chapter 9 filing of Orange County, California, the third most populous county in the state of California and the sixth most populous county in the nation. Triggered by risky investment strategies by the county treasurer, who was later indicted and convicted of six felonies, the county was unable to service its debt, sending the national municipal bond market into chaos. You can read a good history of the Orange County bankruptcy at www.ppic.org/content/pubs/op/op_398op.pdf. Fallout from the Great Recession has included several municipal filings, including that by Harrisburg, Pennsylvania, in October 2011; Jefferson County, Alabama, in November 2011; Stockton, California, in June 2012; and Detroit, Michigan in July 2013, now the largest municipal filing in the nation's history both by debt ($18-20 billion) and population (750,000). Unlike Orange County, these filings were triggered by falling tax revenues over an extended period of time as effects of the Great Recession persisted, juxtaposed against an inability to reduce the cost of government services.

---

2. Filing the Case and Notice to Creditors

Like proceedings under other chapters of the Code, a Chapter 9 case is initiated by the municipality filing a petition (Official Form 201) per §301(a) and the commencement of the case constitutes an order for relief in the case per §301(b). The municipality must also file a list of creditors per §924 at the time the petition is filed or within the time ordered by the court per Bankruptcy Rule 1007.

In all other cases under the Code, the clerk of the bankruptcy court where the petition is filed will assign a new filing to a particular judge. However, §921(b) mandates that the chief judge of the court of appeals for the federal circuit in which the filing occurs designate the bankruptcy judge to preside over the case. This provision reflects the political sensitivity of a municipal filing as well as concerns about the experience and qualifications of a judge who would preside over a filing potentially having momentous public consequences.

Notice of the filing must be given by the clerk of the bankruptcy court to the listed creditors as required by §923. In addition, the notice must also be published "at least once a week for three successive weeks in at least one newspaper of general circulation published within the district in which the case is commenced, and in such other newspaper having a general circulation among bond dealers and bondholders as the court designates."

Section 921(c) authorizes the filing of objections to the petition that will typically arise out of the qualifications for a municipality to file (e.g., Is the debtor a true municipality? Is the debtor insolvent? Does the state authorize the filing?). The bankruptcy court can dismiss the Chapter 9 petition if it finds, after notice and a hearing, that the petition was not filed in good faith or that the qualifications for filing are not present. Section 930 authorizes the court to dismiss the petition for cause, which can include:

- lack of prosecution;
- unreasonable delay by the debtor found to be prejudicial to creditors;
- failure to propose or confirm a plan within the time fixed by the court;
- material default by the debtor under a confirmed plan; or
- termination of a confirmed plan by reason of the occurrence of a condition specified in the plan.

3. The Automatic Stay and Creditor Claims

The automatic stay of §362 of the Code is applicable in Chapter 9 cases per §901(a). The stay blocks all collection actions against the debtor and its property. Section 922(a) actually expands the scope of the automatic stay in Chapter 9 cases by prohibiting actions against officers and inhabitants of the debtor if the action seeks to enforce a claim against the debtor.

EXAMPLE

The stay prohibits a creditor from bringing a mandamus action (an action to compel a government officer to perform his duty or to cease from violating it) against an officer of a municipality on account of a prepetition debt. It also prohibits a creditor from bringing an action against a resident of the debtor municipality to enforce a lien on or arising out of taxes or assessments owed to the debtor.

Per §922(d), a Chapter 9 petition does not operate to stay application of pledged special revenues to payment of indebtedness secured by such revenues.

EXAMPLE

A bond trustee may continue postpetition payments from pledged funds to bondholders without violating the stay.

Section 925 provides that a creditor is required to file a proof of claim in the Chapter 9 case only if that creditor is not listed on the list of creditors filed by the municipality, or if the listed claim is shown as disputed, contingent, or unliquidated, or if the claim is listed in an incorrect amount.

4. Postpetition Operation of the Debtor Municipality

Chapter 9 does not use the phrase "debtor in possession," but that idea is very much a part of the postpetition procedure in a Chapter 9. The powers of the bankruptcy court to oversee or interfere with the operations of the municipality are extremely limited. No bankruptcy trustee is appointed unless the debtor refuses to pursue a turnover or avoidance action under §§544-545 or 547-550, in which case the court can appoint a trustee under §926(a) for the limited purpose of pursuing such action. There is no property of the estate concept in a Chapter 9 as there is in other chapters of the Code, thus no estate for the bankruptcy court to administer. Pursuant to §903, the Chapter 9 filing does not limit or impair the power of the state to control or regulate the municipality as by legislation or agency rule.

Section 904 specifically limits the power of the bankruptcy court to interfere with:

- any of the political or governmental powers of the debtor;
- any of the property or revenues of the debtor; or
- the debtor's use or enjoyment of any income-producing property unless the debtor consents or the plan so provides.

This makes it clear that the debtor's day-to-day activities are not subject to court approval, the debtor may borrow money without court authority, and the court cannot interfere with the debtor's use of its property and revenues. The case cannot be converted to a liquidation proceeding.

Subject to court approval, the municipality can adjust burdensome contractual relationships under the power to reject executory contracts and unexpired leases like a debtor in Chapter 11. The debtor has the same avoiding powers as debtors in other cases under the Code and disputes arising from such claims will be resolved by the bankruptcy court. Interestingly, a municipality debtor can reject collective bargaining agreements and retiree benefit plans as part of its plan for adjustment of debts without going through the special procedures for approval for such a proposal in Chapter 11 cases.

A municipality can borrow money during a Chapter 9 case as an administrative expense per §901(a). It can obtain credit as it does outside of bankruptcy and the bankruptcy court has no supervisory authority over the amount of debt the municipality incurs in its operation. The debtor municipality can employ professionals without court approval, and the professional fees incurred are reviewed only within the context of plan confirmation.

The U.S. Trustee does not supervise the administration of a Chapter 9 case as that office will in other cases under the Code. No first meeting of creditors is held. A creditors' committee is appointed by the U.S. Trustee and §901(a) gives it most of the same powers it has in a Chapter 11 case pursuant to §1103 including:

- selecting and authorizing the employment of one or more attorneys, accountants, or other agents to represent the committee;
- consulting with the debtor concerning administration of the case;
- investigating the acts, conduct, assets, liabilities, and financial condition of the debtor;
- participating in the formulation of a plan; and
- performing such other services as are in the interest of those represented.

Conversely, as will be discussed in more detail below, if certain requirements are met, the debtor's plan is binding on dissenting creditors.

Parties in interest in a Chapter 9 case may include not just creditors but also municipal employees, organizations of employees of the debtor (unions), local residents, nonresident owners of real property, taxpayers, securities firms, local banks, and federal agencies such as the U.S. Department of Treasury and the Securities and Exchange Commission.

5. The Chapter 9 Plan for Adjustment of Debts

Section 941 mandates that the debtor municipality file a plan for adjustment of its debts with the petition or at such later time as set by the court. Unlike a Chapter 11, no creditor or other party in interest can file a competing plan.

As already indicated, the municipal debtor has much more flexibility in proposing a Chapter 9 plan than a Chapter 11 debtor does in proposing a plan under that chapter of the Code. A major source of revenue for most municipalities is **municipal bonds**. There are two general types of municipal bonds. A **general obligation bond** (GOB) is backed by the full faith and credit of the issuing municipality and bond buyers can look to all the revenue and assets of the municipality for payment of principal and interest when due. A **special revenue bond** (SRB) is payable out of revenue from a specific public project (e.g., a city parking garage or city park).

The two types of bonds receive different treatment in the Chapter 9 case and in the Chapter 9 plan. GOBs are treated as general debt in the Chapter 9 case. The municipality is not required to make payments of either principal or interest on account of such bonds during the case. The obligations created by GOBs are subject to negotiation and possible restructuring under the plan of adjustment. Per §928, SRBs must remain secured by the specified revenue source and must be serviced during the case so long as revenue is received from the specified source. Holders of special revenue bonds can expect to receive payment on such bonds during the Chapter 9 case if special revenues are available.

Per §926(b), holders of either GOBs or SRBs are exempt from §547 preference liability regarding prepetition payments as are holders of promissory notes issued by the municipality regardless of whether the prepetition payment was made while the debtor was insolvent.

6. Confirmation of a Chapter 9 Plan

The standards for confirmation of a Chapter 9 plan are similar in only some ways to those that apply to confirmation of a Chapter 11 plan. Section 943(b) provides that the bankruptcy court must confirm the Chapter 9 plan if all of the following conditions are met:

- All amounts to be paid by the debtor or by any person for services or expenses in the case or incident to the plan have been fully disclosed and are reasonable;
- The debtor is not prohibited by law from taking any action necessary to carry out the plan;
- Except to the extent that the holder of a particular claim has agreed to a different treatment of such claim, the plan provides that on the effective date of the plan, each holder of a claim of a kind specified in §507(a)(1) will receive on account of such claim cash equal to the allowed amount of such claim;
- Any regulatory or electoral approval necessary under applicable nonbankruptcy law in order to carry out any provision of the plan that has been obtained is expressly conditioned on such approval;
- The plan is in the best interests of creditors and is feasible; and
- The plan complies with the provisions of Chapter 9.

The requirement that the plan be in the "best interests of creditors" means something different under Chapter 9 than it does under Chapter 11. As we have seen, in a Chapter 11, a plan is said to be in the "best interest of creditors" if creditors would receive as much under the plan as they would if the debtor were liquidated (§1129(a)(7)(A)(ii)). But there is no liquidation of assets in a Chapter 9 to pay creditors so "best interests of creditors" in the Chapter 9 context is generally interpreted to mean that the plan must be better than other alternatives available to the creditors. See 6 Collier on Bankruptcy §943.03(7). The courts generally apply the test to require a reasonable effort by the municipal debtor that is a better alternative for its creditors than dismissal of the case.

Section 943(b)(1) also requires as a condition for confirmation that the plan comply with the provisions of the Code made applicable by §§103(e) and 901(a). The most important of these for purposes of confirming a plan are that §1129(a)(8) requires that the plan has been accepted by each class of claims or interests impaired under the plan (the legal, equitable, or contractual rights of such claims are altered). Unimpaired classes need not accept for the plan to be approved. If any class of impaired claims does not consent, the plan may still be confirmed via §§1129(a)(10) and 1129(b) if at least one impaired class accepts the plan. The plan can be crammed down on other impaired classes if that one impaired class accepts and the court finds that the plan does not unfairly discriminate against nonconsenting impaired classes and is otherwise fair and equitable.

7. The Chapter 9 Discharge

Per §944(b), a municipal debtor receives a discharge in Chapter 9 of debts the plan proposes to discharge after:

- confirmation of the plan;
- deposit by the debtor of any money or property to be distributed under the plan with the disbursing agent appointed by the court; and
- a determination by the court that securities (e.g., bonds) deposited with the disbursing agent to be distributed under the plan are valid legal obligations of the debtor.

Per §§901(a) and 1144, at any time within 180 days after entry of the confirmation order, the court may, after notice and a hearing, revoke the order of confirmation if the order was procured by fraud.

C. ▶ Cross-Border Insolvency Under the Bankruptcy Code

Simply put, a **multinational business entity** is one that does business in more than one country. Almost all major enterprises are multinational, as are numerous mid-sized and smaller entities. Multinationals encounter financial difficulties just like purely domestic ones. Up to this point in the book, we have been dealing with bankruptcy court supervision in a single jurisdiction—the United States—where access to and control over estate assets, creditors, and other parties in interest is assumed. But what happens in the case of a multinational enterprise undergoing insolvency proceedings in one country that has assets and or creditors in other countries? Clearly, there is the need for coherent and effective administration of the debtor's estate. How can the insolvency court or tribunal in one country exercise jurisdiction over assets and creditors in other countries?

Cross-border insolvencies are increasingly common, and increasingly complex. Without some workable international insolvency arrangement, cross-border insolvency runs the risk that local law and local interests will predominate over the interests of foreign parties, making it difficult to administer the estate in a transparent and efficient manner.

EXAMPLE

> Lenders might not be confident that their security interests are adequately protected, creditors might not be sure that terms negotiated with the debtor in one country would be honored in another, and vendors, employees, and other parties might not be confident that new agreements made as part of restructuring would be enforced by courts in other countries. Circumstances such as these can hamper international restructuring and reorganization, and cause more multinationals to fail as a result.

Countries have acted through the United Nations and other organizations to address the need for international comity in multinational bankruptcy cases. This section deals with how the U.S. Bankruptcy Code and courts accommodate cross-border insolvency.

1. UNCITRAL Model Law on Cross-Border Insolvency

All industrialized nations have some form of domestic business insolvency laws. The current German Insolvency Law (*Insolvenzordnung*) has been in effect since 1999, and places much significant responsibility on directors to commence insolvency proceedings when facing illiquidity, including possible criminal sanctions for failure to timely do so. The Spanish Insolvency Act, Ley 22/2003 (*de 9 de julio, Concursal*), saw major revisions in 2014 allowing for modification of secured debt and cram down vote of a majority of creditors to bind secured creditors. Prior to the revisions, dissenting secured creditors were not bound by restructuring agreements among other creditors, and as a result, up to 90 percent of all insolvency proceedings before the revisions went into liquidation. Russia's insolvency law, Federal Law No. 127-FZ "On Insolvency" (2002), was likewise revised in 2015 to reduce the ability of debtors to collusively appoint their own trustee, while giving creditors greater participation and enforcement rights. Canadian insolvency law is not codified in a single statute, and instead the Canadian parliament has enacted a number of statutes. Chief among these is the Bankruptcy Insolvency Act (BIA), which governs bankruptcies by individuals and enterprises, and provides for, among other things, suspension of enforcement of certain collection actions (similar to the automatic stay) and priority of payment to creditors. The Companies Creditor Arrangement Act (CCAA) supplements the BIA and is intended for use in large corporate restructuring. Among other provisions, the CCAA allows for the appointment of a monitor to help facilitate negotiated agreements between debtors, creditors, and other parties.

So how do domestic insolvency tribunals deal with the vast complexity of overlapping insolvency regimes? The task of administering an insolvency estate with assets in multiple countries was made easier with the enactment of the **United Nations Commission on International Trade Law** (UNCITRAL) **Model Law on Cross-Border Insolvency** (Model Law). Three years in the making, the Model Law was ratified by the United Nations in 1997. See UNCITRAL Model Law on Cross-Border Insolvency with Guide to Enactment, U.N. Sales No. E99.V.3 (1997), enacted by G.A. Res. 52/158, U.N. Doc. A/Res/52/158 (Jan. 30, 1998), reprinted in Ch. App. 13, available at http://www.uncitral.org/uncitral/en/uncitral_texts/insolvency/1997Model.html.

To date, 19 countries, including the United States and Great Britain (but not Russia), have adopted the Model Law. (For a current list of countries that have adopted the Model Law, see www.uncitral.org/uncitral/en/uncitral_texts/insolvency/1997Model_status.html.) The European Union (Denmark and Great Britain excepted) has adopted similar cross-border insolvency regulations. Council regulation (EC) No. 1346/2000 of 29 May 2000 on insolvency proceedings. A summary and links to the EU regulations are available at http://europa.eu/legislation_summaries/justice_freedom_security/judicial_cooperation_in_civil_matters/l33110_en.htm.

The Model Law is intended to cover the following four situations:

Foreign representative In a Chapter 15 case, the person authorized to represent a debtor or the tribunal in a foreign bankruptcy proceeding.

- requests for recognition and assistance in a forum country by a **foreign representative** (person authorized to represent the debtor or tribunal) in a foreign proceeding;
- requests from the forum country to foreign courts to grant recognition of the forum country proceeding;
- coordination of concurrent proceedings in two or more countries; and
- participation by foreign parties in a case pending in the forum state.

UNCITRAL Guide to Enactment, ¶20.

2. The Chapter 15 Cross-Border Bankruptcy Proceeding

Chapter 15 Purpose and Overview

Assume that Global Holdings Ltd. (Global) is multinational company based in Oslo, Norway, with shipping and cargo storage interests throughout the world. Global is the parent company of GH America Co. (GHA), a shipping container company incorporated in Delaware, U.S.A. Global also has another subsidiary, Global Netherlands Ltd. (GN), a shipping company headquartered in Amsterdam that is currently in insolvency proceedings in the Netherlands. On September 1, a GN vessel, GN-1, was seized by creditors of GHA (GHA Creditors) while at dock in Port Newark, New Jersey in order to satisfy an outstanding judgment. In fact, GN-1 is the secured collateral of certain creditors of GN (GN Creditors), and its operation provides substantial cash flow to GN. Illustration 20-b shows the configuration of the parties.

What remedy is there for the GN Creditors? Clearly, the Model Law would mandate recognition of the Netherland court's insolvency jurisdiction over GN and its assets. But how can the GN Creditors invoke that jurisdiction in U.S. courts?

Illustration 20-b: CONFIGURATION OF THE PARTIES

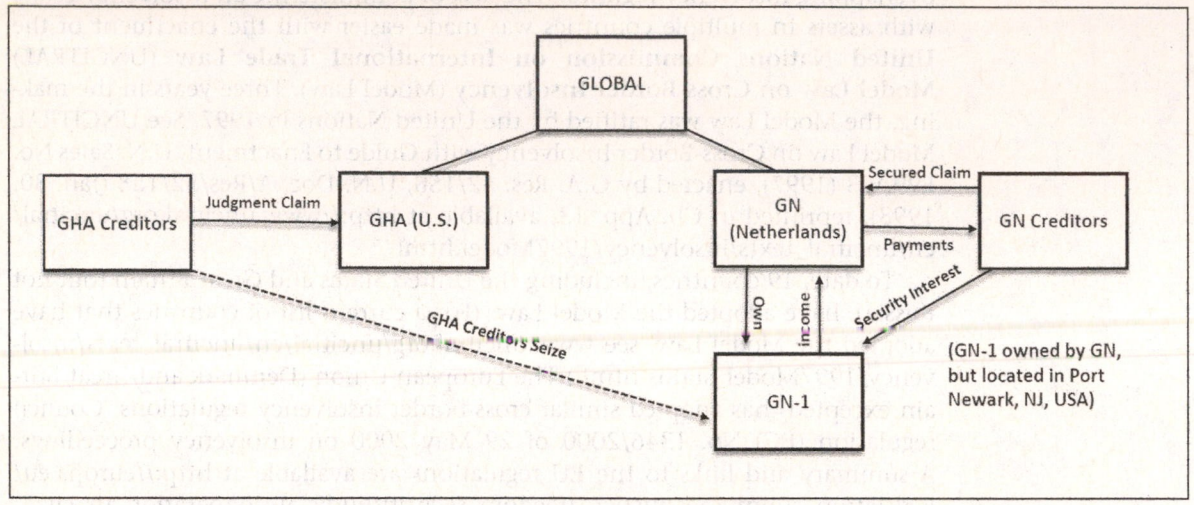

Chapter 15 of the U.S. Bankruptcy Code was enacted in 2005 in order to implement the UNCITRAL Model Law within the United States. If you compare Chapter 15 with the Model Law, you will see that much of Chapter 15 adopts verbatim the English language text of the Model Law.

Chapter 15 applies in the same four procedural situations listed above to which the Model Law applies. §§1501(b)(1)-(4). Moreover, it is rare among U.S. statutes in that it contains a detailed description of its underlying objectives, which include cooperation between U.S. courts and foreign courts, greater legal certainty for trade and investment, fair and efficient administration of cross-border insolvencies, protection and maximization of the value of the debtor's assets, and facilitation of the rescue of financially troubled businesses in order to protect investment and preserve employment. §§1501(a)(1)-(5). Additionally, Chapter 15 is to be interpreted by U.S. courts in light of its international origins and in a manner consistent with foreign insolvency statutes. §1508.

Foreign proceeding In a Chapter 15 case, a bankruptcy proceeding pending in a foreign country.

Chapter 15 allows for recognition of foreign insolvency proceedings (**foreign proceedings**) in U.S. bankruptcy courts (§1515), and authorizes the bankruptcy court to grant foreign debtors, creditors, and other parties in interest many of the powers provided in the Code (§§1519 and 1521). Pursuant to §1505, bankruptcy courts may appoint persons to represent U.S.-based bankruptcy estates in foreign countries, as well as recognize representatives of foreign proceedings. §1512. Among other powers, a foreign representative appearing in a Chapter 11 case has standing to bring avoidance actions for fraudulent conveyance, preference, and state-law fraudulent transfer law (§1523), and may intervene in a U.S. federal or state court case in which the debtor is a party. §1524.

Section 1512 provides that once the foreign proceeding is recognized, a foreign representative may participate as a "party in interest" in any U.S. bankruptcy case. Foreign creditors are granted the same rights as domestic creditors to participate in a case regarding the debtor. §1513. Foreign creditors who are known to the debtor have the right to receive notice of the commencement of the case, deadlines for filing proof of claim, and all other notices. §1514. While relief under Chapter 15 is to be consistent with applicable foreign statutes, the interests of creditors, domestic or foreign, must be adequately protected. §1522.

Section 1506 states that courts may refuse to take an act that would be "manifestly contrary" to U.S. public policy, but the public policy exception is to be applied narrowly.

EXAMPLE

> The fact that bankruptcy court recognition of foreign law might deprive a party in the United States of the right to jury trial was held not to violate fundamental U.S. policy. *In re Ephedra Products Liability Litigation*, 349 B.R. 333, 336-337 (Bankr. S.D.N.Y. 2006); see also *In re Metcalfe & Mansfield Alternative Invs.*, 421 B.R. 685, 699 (Bankr. S.D.N.Y. 2010) (courts may enforce foreign judgments that might not otherwise be enforced in the United States). Thus, Chapter 15 seeks to observe American legal norms, while linking U.S. insolvency administration as seamlessly as possible with the rest of the world.

Commencing a Chapter 15 Bankruptcy Case

A Chapter 15 bankruptcy is commenced by filing a petition for recognition of a foreign proceeding (Official Form 401) with a U.S. bankruptcy court per §§1504 and 1515. For purposes of Chapter 15, a "foreign proceeding" is a judicial or administrative proceeding in a foreign country in which the assets or affairs of the debtor are subject to control by a foreign court for the purpose of reorganization or liquidation. §101(23). To qualify, the U.S. bankruptcy court will look to see whether the foreign proceeding is, in fact, authorized under a law related to insolvency or adjustment of debts, that the debtor's assets are subject to the foreign court control, and that the proceeding is intended for the purpose of liquidation or reorganization. See, e.g., *In re Betcorp*, 400 B.R. 266, 285 (Bankr. D. Nev. 2009). Thus, a foreign receivership or collection proceeding does not qualify for recognition under Chapter 15. *In re Gold & Honey, Ltd.*, 410 B.R. 357, 371 (Bankr. E.D.N.Y. 2009) (Israeli receivership does not qualify as a foreign proceeding).

The petition for recognition must be filed on Official Form 401, and all supporting documents must be translated into English. §1515(c). The petition for recognition is filed by a foreign representative (also known as the petitioner), and accompanied by a proof that the representative has been authorized by the foreign court to appear in the U.S. bankruptcy court. §1515(b). This must be a certified copy of the order from the foreign court appointing the petitioner as the representative. §1515(b)(1). The petition should also include a description of all foreign proceedings related to the case, and identifying all foreign trustees, administrators, parties, or litigants related to the case. §1515(c).

The petition is served on the debtor, known creditors, and any party against whom relief may be sought. Bankruptcy Rule 1019. The court will enter the order granting recognition after notice and hearing if all the requirements under §1515 are satisfied. In emergency circumstances, the court may grant relief without a hearing (§102(1)) but otherwise a decision on recognition requires a hearing and must be made promptly. §1517(c). Between the time a petition for recognition is served but before the court has made a decision, the court may, upon request of the foreign representative, grant a stay of execution against the debtor's assets (having the same effect to stop creditor enforcement as per the automatic stay under §362), and entrust the representative to administer the assets of the foreign bankruptcy estate. §1519(a).

Sections 1516(a) and (b) provide that if the correct materials have accompanied the petition, then the court is entitled to presume that the documents are authentic, and that the petitioner is authorized by the foreign court to represent the foreign proceeding. On the other hand, the court may later withdraw recognition if, upon challenge by a party in interest, the court later determines that "grounds for granting it were fully or partially lacking or have ceased to exist." §1517(d).

It should be noted that serving as the authorized representative of the foreign proceeding does not, by itself, subject the representative to jurisdiction in U.S. courts for any other purpose not connected with the Chapter 15 case. §1510. However, this does not shield the representative from state or federal jurisdiction that may be acquired separately and not related to the Chapter 15 proceedings.

Eligibility and Venue

As with all other chapters in the Code, §109 governs who may be a debtor in a Chapter 15 bankruptcy. Section 109(a) provides that only a party that resides or has a place of business or property in the United States may be a debtor. The provision is broadly interpreted, since many foreign entities do not own tangible property in the United States. See, e.g., *In re Octaviar Admin. Pty Ltd*, 511 B.R. 361 (Bankr. S.D.N.Y. 2014), in which the court found that claims and causes of action, as well as an undrawn retainer in possession of counsel, were sufficient to constitute property for purposes of §109(a).

Bankruptcy venue may include anywhere in the United States where the debtor has its principal place of business or principal assets, or the state or federal district where an action is pending against the foreign debtor. 28 U.S.C. §§1410(1)-(2). If none of these apply, the case may be filed where venue would be "consistent with the interests of justice and convenience of the parties, having regard to the relief sought by the foreign representative." §1401(3).

Main and Nonmain Proceedings, and the Importance of COMI

The bankruptcy court may recognize the proceedings as a **foreign main proceeding**, or as a **foreign nonmain proceeding**. There are important differences in the powers of a debtor depending on whether the foreign proceedings are recognized as a main proceeding or a nonmain proceeding. If granted recognition as a foreign main proceeding, the representative is authorized by §1520 to operate the business of the debtor and control its assets. In addition, the automatic stay under §362 applies without further order of the court, although creditors are entitled to adequate protection for their collateral, and can file for relief from stay. The debtor in a main proceeding may also use or sell property under §§363(b) and (c), which, as we saw in Chapter Eighteen, Section D, can sometimes result in complete liquidation of the debtor. If the proceeding is a nonmain proceeding, the representative must separately request imposition of the stay and authority to administer and dispose of assets, and to grant other powers to which a representative in a main proceeding is otherwise entitled per §1521.

A foreign proceeding is eligible to be recognized as a foreign main proceeding if it is pending in the country where the debtor has its **center of main interest**

(COMI) per §1517(b)(1). It will be recognized as a foreign nonmain proceeding per §1517(b)(2) if the debtor has ongoing operations in that country. The Code does not define COMI, but these terms are based on Article 2(b) and (c) of the Model Law, and mirror the EU insolvency regulations. EU Insolvency Regulation, Ch. 1, Art. 3. As such, U.S. courts have struggled to come up with a specific test to determine COMI. The Second Circuit in *Morning Mist Holdings, Limited v. Krys (In re Fairfield Sentry Limited)*, 714 F.3d 127 (2d Cir. 2013), noted as much, but held that as a threshold matter, Chapter 15 creates a rebuttable presumption that the country where a debtor has its registered office will be its COMI. Id. at 133. However, the inquiry does not stop there:

> Various factors, singly or combined, could be relevant to such a determination: the location of the debtor's headquarters; the location of those who actually manage the debtor (which, conceivably could be the headquarters of a holding company); the location of the debtor's primary assets; the location of the majority of the debtor's creditors or of a majority of the creditors who would be affected by the case; and/or the jurisdiction whose law would apply to most disputes.
>
> This nonexclusive list is a helpful guide, but consideration of these specific factors is neither required nor dispositive.

Id. International law can also play a role in determining COMI under Chapter 15. The EU Regulation enacting the European Union Convention on Insolvency explains that COMI "should correspond to the place where the debtor conducts the administration of his interests on a regular basis and is therefore ascertainable by third parties." EU Regulation, Preamble ¶13. While not a dispositive rule for U.S. bankruptcy courts, it underscores the importance of factors that indicate regularity and ascertainability. See *In re Sphinx, Ltd.*, 351 B.R. 103, 118 (Bankr. S.D.N.Y. 2006) (holding that "in keeping with its international context, Chapter 15 directs courts also to obtain guidance from the application of similar statutes by foreign jurisdictions").

Comity and Limitations on the Powers of Foreign Representatives

Chapter 15 envisions broad cooperation between domestic bankruptcy courts and foreign representatives and foreign courts. The bankruptcy court may give "additional assistance" to the representative under the Bankruptcy Code or other laws of the United States as necessary to effect the purposes of Chapter 15 per §1507. Bankruptcy courts and trustees are authorized to communicate and cooperate "to the maximum extent possible" with the foreign court and/or the foreign representative per §§1525, 1526. This cooperation can take the form of appointing examiners, coordinating the supervision and administration of the debtor's affairs, approving or implementing agreements, and coordinating concurrent proceedings involving the same debtor per §1527.

In cases where a foreign insolvency is already underway, the U.S. court may only administer assets in the United States (§1528) and these are to be coordinated with the foreign proceeding (§1529), or, if applicable, multiple foreign proceedings (§1530).

One of the factors that has helped make cross-border insolvencies possible is the creation of **protocols**. In the *Lehman Brothers* bankruptcy case, for example,

Protocols Agreements reached by parties in individual cross-border cases dealing with hearings and meetings, information sharing, remote appearances, allocation of payments, etc.

which dealt with affiliated debtors in Australia, Germany, Hong Kong, the Netherlands, and Singapore, parties reached agreements dealing with hearings and meetings, information sharing, remote appearances, allocation of payments, and other matters. *In re Lehman Brothers Holdings, Inc.*, Case No. 08-13555 (Bankr. S.D.N.Y. 2006), Debtor's Motion Pursuant to Sections 105 and 363 of the Bankruptcy Code for Approval of a Cross-Border Insolvency Protocol, Docket No. 3647. Section 1527(4) allows for such forms of cooperation, and Bankruptcy Rule 5012 provides for procedures to establish protocols in a given case.

Comity The recognition and enforcement by courts of one jurisdiction of the laws and judicial decisions of another.

While Chapter 15 endeavors to achieve a high degree of **comity** (the recognition and enforcement by courts of one jurisdiction of the laws and judicial decisions of another), §103(a) provides certain rights and powers that are not given to parties under Chapter 15 without specific authority by the court. Of key importance are the fraudulent and preferential avoidance provisions of §§544 through 551. These sections allow a debtor or bankruptcy trustee to set aside certain prebankruptcy transfers if the transfers are fraudulent or prejudice the rights of creditors, or if the transfers unfairly favor one creditor to the detriment of others. For example, as you may recall from our discussion in Chapter Ten, Sections D and E, and in Chapter Eighteen, Section E, under §547, a transfer made to a creditor within 90 days prior to the bankruptcy can be avoided (recovered) by the debtor unless the creditor can assert one of the preference defenses available under §547(c). Preference actions are often a significant component of a business bankruptcy and can bring substantial sums back into the debtor's estate. The lack of this power for a representative of a foreign proceeding is a significant departure from the normal powers available to the bankruptcy trustee in Chapter 7 and to the debtor in possession or bankruptcy trustee (if one is appointed) in Chapter 11 cases.

There are other bankruptcy powers that are not provided under Chapter 15 including the broad powers to assume, reject, or assign executory contracts under §365 of the Code. The provisions of §§507 and 503 that deal with allowance and priority of claims also do not apply in Chapter 15, presumably because the foreign bankruptcy proceeding is governed by its own claims regulations.

CHAPTER SUMMARY

Chapter 12 bankruptcy is limited to those who qualify as family farmers or family fishermen with regular annual income. Qualifications to file include a debt ceiling, and certain percentages of the debtor's income and debt must be related to the farming or fishing operation. The debt ceiling for filing a Chapter 12 is considerably higher than that for filing a Chapter 13 making Chapter 12 an alternative to the more complicated Chapter 11 for qualifying debtors with too much debt to file under Chapter 13.

Although a bankruptcy trustee is appointed in a Chapter 12 case, the debtor retains possession of the property and continues to conduct farming or fishing operation as a debtor in possession. On motion of an interested party the court may remove the debtor as debtor in possession for fraud, dishonesty, incompetence, or gross mismanagement and turn over the control of the farming or fishing operation to the trustee. Courts are reluctant to grant such motions on the grounds of gross mismanagement due to the increase in administrative expenses and recognition that there is always some degree of mismanagement.

The automatic stay, including co-debtor stay, and property of the estate concepts work the same in Chapter 12 as in Chapter 13. The Chapter 12 debtor in possession enjoys the power to initiate turnover and avoidance actions to enhance property of the estate, making it distinctly advantageous over a Chapter 13 for qualifying debtors.

The debtor must file a proposed Chapter 12 plan with the petition or within 90 days following. Generally, a Chapter 12 plan operates very similarly to a Chapter 13 plan. Disposable income under Chapter 12 is income not reasonably necessary for the maintenance or support of the debtor or dependents or for making payments needed to continue, preserve, and operate the debtor's farming or fishing operation.

Unlike a Chapter 13 plan, a Chapter 12 plan can propose to cure a deficiency beyond the term of the plan. A Chapter 12 plan may also strip down an undersecured mortgage on the debtor's principal residence. There is no 910-day rule prohibiting strip down of undersecured debt secured by vehicles in Chapter 12 and no one-year rule prohibiting strip down of undersecured claims involving collateral other than a motor vehicle.

Chapter 9 is a debt adjustment proceeding for a municipality that includes political subdivisions of the state as well as state agencies. For reasons of federalism, the state must specifically authorize the political subdivision to file under Chapter 9.

The automatic stay goes into effect in a Chapter 9 and the debtor may continue day-to-day postpetition activities without court approval. Only the debtor can propose a debt adjustment plan, which is to be approved by the court on a finding of best interests of creditors.

Under Chapter 15, a foreign representative may petition a bankruptcy court to recognize the foreign insolvency proceedings. Once the court enters an order recognizing the proceedings, both the debtor and creditors are entitled to many of the powers and protections of the Code.

The representative of a foreign main proceeding is granted certain powers, including the protection of the automatic stay under §362, authority to manage the debtor's assets similar to a DIP, and the right to use and sell property as provided under §363.

Whether a foreign proceeding is main or nonmain depends upon whether the proceeding is pending in the debtor's center of main interest (COMI). This requires a fact inquiry of many elements by the bankruptcy court, but starts from a presumption that the debtor's headquarters or place of incorporation is its COMI.

There are certain powers under the Code that are not granted to a foreign representative. These include preference avoidance under §547 and assuming or rejecting contracts and leases under §365. In addition, §§503 and 507 dealing with allowance and priority of claims do not apply in Chapter 15.

REVIEW QUESTIONS

1. Debtors engaged in either of what two businesses can file for relief under Chapter 12? Why might some debtors who qualify to file under Chapter 12 be unable to file under Chapter 13?

2. What advantages does a Chapter 12 filing provide to an individual debtor over a Chapter 13 filing assuming the debtor qualifies to file under either?

3. On what basis can a trustee be appointed in a Chapter 12 case? Who has the burden of showing that grounds for a trustee are present in a particular case? Why are courts hesitant to replace the debtor in possession with a trustee in a Chapter 12?

4. On what basis can a bankruptcy court convert a Chapter 12 case to one under Chapter 7 over the objection of the debtor? Name four bases on which a Chapter 12 case can be involuntarily dismissed.

5. Give four examples of "political subdivision or public agency or instrumentality of a state" that come within the Code's definition of municipality for purposes of Chapter 9.

6. Explain why Chapter 9 allows states to authorize (or not authorize) municipalities within its borders to file under that chapter.

7. How is the scope of "parties in interest" broader in a case under Chapter 9 than in a case under other chapters of the Code? Explain the limited role of the U.S. Trustee and bankruptcy court itself in a Chapter 9 case.

8. What is the UNCITRAL Model Law on Cross-Border Insolvency? Name two countries that have adopted it. Name one country that has not.

9. Who is a "foreign representative" in a Chapter 15 case? Does that mean the same thing as the debtor?

10. Explain the difference between a main proceeding and a nonmain proceeding in a Chapter 15 case. What difference does the distinction make to the debtor and the foreign representative in the case?

WORDS AND PHRASES TO REMEMBER

automatic stay
center of main interest (COMI)
co-debtor stay
comity
commercial fishing operation
confirmation
debtor in possession
discharge
farming operation
federalism
foreign main proceeding
foreign nonmain proceeding
foreign proceeding
foreign representative

general obligation bond
hardship discharge
Model Law on Cross-Border
  Insolvency
multinational business entity
municipal bond
municipality
protocols
special revenue bond
sunset clause
United Nations Commission on
  International Trade Law
  (UNCITRAL)

TO LEARN MORE: A number of TLM activities to accompany this chapter are accessible on the companion web site for this textbook at http://aspenlawschool.com/books/Parsons_Debt4e/.

[As noted in the preface and text of the textbook, the case studies used in the appendices are entirely fictional and hypothetical. Though the hypothetical case studies used are set in actual federal districts, the names, location, and circumstances of debtors, creditors, trustees, lawyers, judges, and all other persons or entities described in these case studies are a product of the author's imagination, are fictitious, and any resemblance to actual persons living or dead or to any entity is entirely coincidental. Similarly the information contained on the documents that are listed in the case file index below and posted on the companion website is likewise fictional and hypothetical. The Official Bankruptcy Forms in effect during June 2016 have been used to prepare those documents and no attempt has been made to conform them to the local rules or customary practices of the named court.]

Appendix A

▶ In re Marta Rinaldi Carlson Chapter 7 Bankruptcy

[Inactive File]

ASSIGNMENT MEMORANDUM

TO: Paralegal
FROM: Carolyn A. Thomas, supervising attorney
RE: Marta Rinaldi Carlson
DATE: June 1, 2016

Marta Rinaldi Carlson is an executive assistant at Tomorrow Today, Inc. (TTI). She resides at 301 Pugh Street in Roseville, Minnesota.

Marta was one of the original employees of TTI, hired as a secretary to Howard Kine, a computer software genius and TTI shareholder. At Kine's urging, Marta obtained an associate's degree from Capital City Community College in computer science. She then transferred to Columbiana State University and has been pursuing her bachelor's in software engineering. Marta needs only 20 more semester hours to complete her degree, which she hopes to do in 18 months. Kine told Marta that once she receives that degree, he will recommend that TTI promote her from executive assistant to computer software engineer. Marta makes $48,000 per year at TTI as of January 1, 2016. Throughout 2015 she made slightly less than $40,000 per year ($3,333.28 per month). If she can secure the computer software engineer position, her pay should jump to the mid-50 thousands. But that is at least 18 months away.

Completing her education has been a long, hard road for Marta. At 37, when she began her college work, she had been out of school for 20 years, since completing high school. Now 40, she works full time for TTI so she must attend school at night. She has two children: a son, Chris, who is 14, and a daughter, Adela, who is 11. Marta and her husband, Eugene, separated around the time she began college in 2012 and the divorce became final about two years ago.

From a financial standpoint, when Marta and Eugene were together, they were a typical middle-class family. They had a house mortgage that was always paid on time, they had a couple of credit cards on which they carried a little higher balance than they should have, and they rarely put any money into savings. But the bills got paid, vacations got taken, both Marta and Eugene drove late-model cars, purchased with affordable loans, and everybody in the family had all the accoutrements of American middle-class life.

All that changed with the divorce. Six months after the decree became final Eugene lost his job as an assistant manager of a mid-sized regional retail discount chain when it was bought out by a national concern. He was able to find lower-paying work in retail sales for a while but then his health failed and he was diagnosed with leukemia. Today Eugene survives only on Social Security disability payments. The divorce decree required him to pay Marta $2,000 per month in child support and to keep Marta and the kids covered under his health insurance policy. Eugene is now $15,000 in arrears on his child support obligation and unable to provide health insurance coverage. Consequently, Marta pays to have herself and the two children covered under TTI's group policy. Unfortunately, the prospects of Eugene ever being able to make up the arrears or to resume child support payments are remote.

Two months after the divorce, Adela got sick with what Marta thought was an intestinal flu. The 11-year old had bouts of nausea and diarrhea that would last three to four days, resolve, and then recur a week later. The third time it happened, Adela was hospitalized for almost a week. The doctors diagnosed irritable bowel syndrome related to stress from the separation and divorce of Adela's parents. Medication was prescribed but did no good at all. Finally, Marta took her daughter to a gastrointestinal specialist in another city, who diagnosed Giardiasis, a condition caused by a waterborne, intestinal parasite. Though no one can say for sure where the child picked it up, it was probably on a swimming trip with friends to a popular swimming hole at a local lake. By the time the correct diagnosis was made, Adela's condition was serious and she had to undergo surgery to remove a portion of her large intestine, followed by an extended hospitalization. The infection was eventually checked but Adela still has to take very expensive medications and follow a strict diet. She will be under a doctor's watchful care for several years. Between the high deductible on her TTI policy and the limited coverage provided for several of the tests and procedures conducted on Adela, as well as the medications she is taking, Marta has unpaid medical bills totaling more than $60,000 and growing. Eugene remains unemployed and is unable to help financially.

In addition to Adela's health problems, Marta has been faced with responsibility for healthcare costs associated with her widowed 73-year-old mother, Estell Rinaldi. Six years ago Estell was diagnosed with Alzheimer's. She was able to live in her home for a year after the diagnosis but finally sold the home and went into a nursing facility, Pine Ridge Nursing Home. Although Marta had hoped that the proceeds from her mother's home, in addition to her remaining savings, would be enough to pay for the nursing home care, she was asked by the nursing home to sign a personal guaranty, promising to pay any costs her mother's assets and government assistance did not cover. She did so without consulting an attorney. A little over a year ago, her mother's assets were depleted and Marta began receiving bills from the nursing home. Her mother finally passed away two months ago, but the accumulated bills from her care, for which Pine Ridge Nursing claims Marta is responsible, total more than $45,000. Marta is disputing that claim against her, contending that when her mother's assets ran out, she advised the nursing home that she would not be able to pay anything and that she was verbally told by the home's administrator that she would not be billed anything on the guaranty because the government would pay all costs from that point on. Pine Ridge has filed suit to collect the indebtedness from Marta. She has answered the complaint denying any liability on the guaranty and alleging affirmatively, in the alternative, that a portion of the nursing home's claim against her represents sums the government has paid to Pine Ridge.

Eugene's unemployment has caused Marta other further financial problems. Under the divorce decree, he was ordered to assume liability for the accumulated credit card debt of the couple, which totaled more than $40,000 at the time. He made very few payments on the outstanding balance of that debt and Marta is now being dunned for it. With interest and late fees, the total balance owed to two different card providers is more than $50,000.

Marta has had to borrow money to finance her college education. She took out one loan from Columbiana Federal Savings & Loan in the principal amount of $5,000 for her community college expenses and has just begun paying that back. She took out a second loan from First Patriot Bank for $10,000 to finance her studies at Columbiana State University. Under the terms of that student loan, repayment will not begin until three months after she graduates. Both student loans are guaranteed by the federal government.

Six years ago, Eugene and Marta bought the house where Marta now lives with her children. They paid $200,000 for it, borrowing $150,000 from Capital Savings Bank (CSB). The loan was for 30 years at a fixed rate of interest at 6.5 percent per annum. The monthly payments to CSB, with taxes and insurance, total $965. Three years ago, Eugene and Marta took out a second mortgage on the house when they borrowed $50,000 from Dreams Come True Finance Company (DCT) to finance a business venture for Eugene that ultimately failed. The DCT loan was for 15 years at 8 percent interest and required monthly payments of $477.

In the divorce, Marta was awarded the house and Eugene quitclaimed his interest in it to her. The divorce decree provided that Marta was to assume responsibility for the remaining mortgage payments to CSB, though Eugene remained on the promissory note to CSB. Eugene was to assume responsibility for the remaining mortgage payments to DCT, though Marta remained liable on that note. Marta knew it would be a stretch for her to make the mortgage payments to CSB on her salary alone, but she decided it was worth the risk in order to keep her children in their home. The current principal balance on the loan from CSB is $142,500; the current principal balance on the loan from DCT, which has been in default for some time now, is $37,500. Marta is two payments behind to CSB and three behind to DCT. A realtor has told Marta that the house has a market value of $255,000. DCT has declared default on its loan and is preparing to foreclose on the home.

Marta is maxed out on the Capital City Bank Visa card issued in her own name following the divorce. Her balance on the card is $8,200, on which she manages to make no more than the minimum payment each month. She drives a four-year old Toyota Camry, which is titled in her name only. The book value of the car is $8,500 and she owes a balance on it of $1,750 to Automotive Financing, Inc. (AFI), which holds a security interest in the car. Her monthly payments to AFI are $210 and she is two payments in arrears at this time. She has no savings except her 401k plan at TTI, which has a current balance of $7,600.

Her 14-year-old son, Chris, has had his own problems since the divorce. His grades have dropped and he's started running with a group of friends Marta is not happy with. Eugene rarely sees either child, electing not to exercise his visitation rights most months. Last month Chris and another juvenile were arrested for malicious destruction of property. Marta had to come up with $500 to pay a lawyer who did manage to keep Chris from being sentenced to a juvenile facility. When Chris began experiencing problems after the divorce, Marta took him to Crisis Counseling Center, which billed her $1,250. Her insurance did not cover the counseling and she has been unable to pay the bill. That debt has been turned over to a collection agency. She is getting two to three phone calls a week from the collection agency asking when the bill will be paid.

Marta's own health has deteriorated since her financial problems began following the divorce. She suffers from chronic indigestion, which she suspects is an ulcer, but she has put off going to a doctor because she just can't afford it.

Since Chris turned 14, Marta has tried to minimize her child care costs by allowing the children to come home by themselves after school. But she still needs a sitter when Chris has school sports activities or trips and can't watch Adela or when she is out of town overnight herself. She will provide you with the estimate of her monthly child care expenses.

We are going to file a Chapter 7 bankruptcy for Ms. Carlson. Please contact her and begin gathering the additional specific information needed for the petition and schedules.

CASE FILE INDEX

[The documents listed in this index for the Chapter 7 bankruptcy case of *In re Marta Rinaldi Carlson* are available on textbook's companion web site at http://aspenlawschool.com/books/Parsons_Debt4e/.]

1. Fee agreement between Marta Rinaldi Carlson and Carolyn A. Thomas, Attorney at Law with Notice to Individual Consumer Debtor under §342(b) and Disclosure Pursuant to §527(a)(2) and Disclosure Pursuant to §527(b)
2. Voluntary Petition in Chapter 7
3. Application to Pay Fee in Installments and Order Granting Application
4. List of Creditors
5. Motion for Additional Time to File Schedules, Statement of Affairs, and Other Documents with Notice of Motion
6. Order granting Motion for Additional Time to File Schedules, etc.
7. Schedule A/B
8. Schedule C
9. Schedule D
10. Schedule E/F
11. Schedule G
12. Schedule H
13. Schedule I
14. Schedule J
15. Summary of Your Assets and Liabilities and Certain Statistical Information
16. Declaration About an Individual Debtor's Schedules
17. Statement of Financial Affairs for Individual's Filing for Bankruptcy
18. Debtor's Statement of Intent for Individuals Filing Under Chapter 7
19. Form 122A-1 Chapter 7 Statement of Your Current Monthly Income
20. Statement About Your Social Security Numbers
21. Disclosure of Compensation of Attorney for the Debtor
22. Payment Advices or Other Evidence of Payment Received from Any Employer within 60 Days Before the Filing of the Petition
23. Notice of Chapter 7 Bankruptcy Case
24. Motion for Order of Contempt for Violation of Automatic Stay and for Damages with Notice of Motion
25. Order on Motion for Order of Contempt, etc.
26. Trustee's §704(b)(1) Report
27. Proof of Claim with Attachment
28. Objection to Claim with Notice of Objection
29. Motion for Authorization to Hire Professional and to Approve Fee with Notice of Motion
30. Order on Motion for Authorization to Hire Professional and to Approve Fee
31. Complaint for Turnover of Property or Money Judgment for Its Value
32. Objection to Claimed Exemption with Notice
33. Certification About a Financial Management
34. Notice of Intent to Abandon Property with Notice
35. Motion for Permission to Sell Property Free and Clear of Liens with Notice of Motion

Extra Material:

1. Alternative Form 122A-1 Chapter 7 Statement of Your Current Monthly Income (assuming Marta Carlson had annual income of $84,000)
2. Form 122A-2 Chapter 7 Means Test Calculation (assuming Marta Carlson had annual income of $84,000)

Appendix B

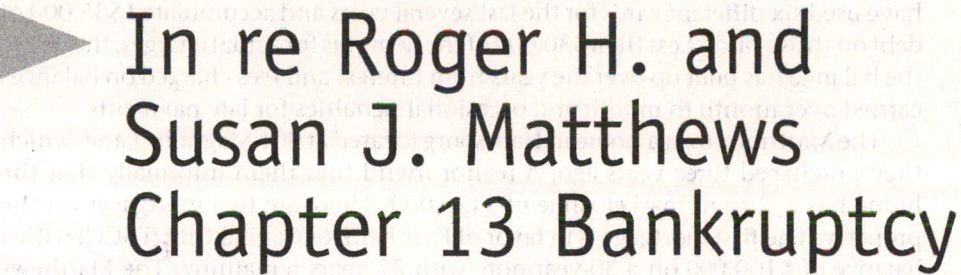

In re Roger H. and Susan J. Matthews Chapter 13 Bankruptcy

[Inactive File]

Assignment Memorandum

TO: Paralegal
FROM: Edmond J. Montgomery, supervising attorney
RE: Roger H. and Susan J. Matthews
DATE: June 1, 2016

Roger Matthews is 33 years old and works for City Plumbing Company in Harrisburg, Pennsylvania. Roger has a high school diploma, almost two years of college, and a certificate in plumbing from Columbiana College of Technology. He brings home $2,400 a month based on a gross salary of $36,000 per year. Roger's wife, Susan Matthews, is 32 years old and works as the librarian for Heart and Soul Academy, a private school in the area for kindergarten through eighth grade. Susan has a bachelor's degree in library science from Columbiana State University. She brings home $1,733 a month based on a gross salary of $26,000 per year.

Roger and Susan have been irresponsible in their credit card spending. They have used six different cards for the last several years and accumulated $35,000 of debt on those cards. Less than $30,000 of the debt was for actual charges; the rest of the balance has built up over the years from interest and fees charged on balances carried over month to month and occasional penalties for late payments.

The Matthews own a home in Harrisburg located at 901 Magnolia Lane, which they purchased three years ago. A realtor friend told them informally that the home has a current market value of $120,000. There are two mortgages on the property. The first mortgage is in favor of First Bank of Capital City (FBCC) with a balance of $100,000 on a 30-year note with 27 years remaining. The Matthews pay FBCC $850 per month and are one payment in arrears. The second mortgage is in favor of Capital Savings Bank (CSB) with a balance of $30,000 on a $35,000 home improvement loan the Matthews took out a year ago (thus the Matthews have no equity in their home). They have 48 months of payments remaining on the second mortgage. The Matthews pay CSB $700 per month on the second mortgage and are current on those payments.

The Matthews own three vehicles. Roger drives a YR-3 Ford F-150 truck worth $7,500, on which they owe $9,000 to Automotive Financing, Inc. (AFI), which holds a lien on the truck. The Matthews make payments of $360 per month to AFI on the truck. Susan drives a YR-4 Honda Civic worth $8,000, on which they owe $7,500 to Columbiana Federal Savings & Loan (CFSL), which holds a lien on the Civic. The Matthews make payments of $240 per month to CFSL on the Civic. They also own a YR-8 Chevrolet Malibu worth $2,000, on which they owe $5,000 to Car World (CW), which holds a lien on the Malibu. The Matthews make payments to CW of $120 per month on the Malibu. The Matthews are current on all three car payments but are pretty sure they will surrender the Malibu to CW since it is an extra vehicle.

Roger and Susan have two daughters: Carrie is 7 years old and her sister, Elizabeth, is 11 months. Medical expenses incurred in connection with Elizabeth's birth are the straw that broke the camel's back for the couple financially. Susan experienced complications with the pregnancy and, although the baby is fine, the unpaid doctor and hospital bills for Susan still total $25,000. Susan was out of work during the last three months of last year due to her health problems and the baby's birth, which devastated the couple's cash flow. Susan returned to work in January but they are too deeply in the hole financially to catch up. Susan's mother is keeping the baby during the day and Carrie after school to spare them child care expenses, but she's not going to be able to do that after July of this year.

Roger and Susan also borrowed $2,500 from Capital City Finance Company (CCFC) last year to finance a vacation they couldn't otherwise afford. The couple granted a security interest in Roger's plumbing tools to secure the loan from CCFC, the balance of which is $2,000. They are supposed to pay $50 a month to CCFC on this loan but are now three months in arrears. At about the same time, Roger was assessed $1,000 in taxes, penalties, and interest by the IRS as a result of unreported income from YR-2 when he did some independent plumbing work for a local contractor.

I have drawn up the following informal budget for the Matthews, which we will use in fashioning a proposed plan of reorganization for them under Chapter 13.

Monthly prepetition budget for Roger and Susan Matthews:

Net monthly income:

Roger:	$2,400
($3,000 per month minus withholding of $600 in taxes)	
Susan:	$1,733
($2,167 per month minus withholding of $360 in taxes and $74 health insurance premium)	
Total net monthly income	$4,133

Living expenses:

Food		475
Home maintenance		75
Clothing		175
Dry cleaning/laundry		25
Gas/transportation		150
Utilities, phone, and cable		500
Electric & gas	$ 315	
Water & sewer	$ 50	
Phones	$ 70	
Cable & Internet	$ 65	
Insurance (auto)		60
Medical/dental		100
Charitable contributions		50
Entertainment/recreation		50
Miscellaneous		100
Total living expenses		$1,760

Payments on secured debt:

House payments	1,550
(FBCC $850, one payment behind)	

(CSB $700, current)
Car payments   720
(AFI for YR-3 Ford F-150 truck $360, current)
(CFSL for YR-4 Honda Civic $240, current)
(C-W for YR-8 Chevy Malibu $120, current)

Total payments on secured debt .... $ 2,270

Total payments on living expenses and secured debt .... $ 4,030

Available to pay other debt .... $ 103

Debt not being paid:

Credit cards   35,000
Doctor & hospital   25,000
Tax bill from YR-2   1,000
CCFC secured loan   2,000

Total debt not being paid $63,000

CASE FILE INDEX

[The documents listed in this index for the Chapter 13 bankruptcy case of *In re Roger H. and Susan J. Matthews* are available on the textbook's companion web site at http://aspenlawschool.com/books/Parsons_Debt4e/.]

1. Joint Petition in Chapter 13
2. List of Creditors
3. Schedule A/B
4. Schedule C
5. Schedule D
6. Schedule E/F
7. Schedule G
8. Schedule H
9. Schedule I
10. Schedule J
11. Summary of Your Assets and Liabilities and Certain Statistical Information
12. Declaration re Schedules
13. Statement of Financial Affairs
14. Form 122C-1 Chapter 13 Statement of Your Current Monthly Income and Calculation of Commitment Period
15. Statement About Your Social Security Numbers
16. Disclosure of Compensation of Attorney for the Debtor
17. Payment Advices or Other Evidence of Payment Received from Any Employer within 60 Days Before the Filing of the Petition
18. Chapter 13 Plan
19. Notice of Commencement of Case
20. Debtor's Certification of Completion of Postpetition Instructional Course Concerning Personal Financial Management
21. Order Confirming Chapter 13 Plan
22. Wage Orders

Extra Material:

1. Alternative Form 122C-1 Chapter 13 Statement of Your Current Monthly Income and Calculation of Commitment Period (assuming the Matthews had combined annualized CMI of $95,000)
2. Form 122C-2 Chapter 13 Calculation of Your Disposable Income (assuming the Matthews had combined annualized CMI of $95,000)

[As noted in the preface and text of the textbook, the case studies used in the appendices are entirely fictional and hypothetical. Though the hypothetical case studies used are set in actual federal districts, the names, location, and circumstances of debtors, creditors, trustees, lawyers, judges, and all other persons or entities described in these case studies are a product of the author's imagination, are fictitious, and any resemblance to actual persons living or dead or to any entity is entirely coincidental. Similarly the information contained on the documents that are listed in the case file index below and posted on the companion website is likewise fictional and hypothetical. The Official Bankruptcy Forms in effect during June 2016 have been used to prepare those documents and no attempt has been made to conform them to the local rules or customary practices of the named court.]

Appendix C

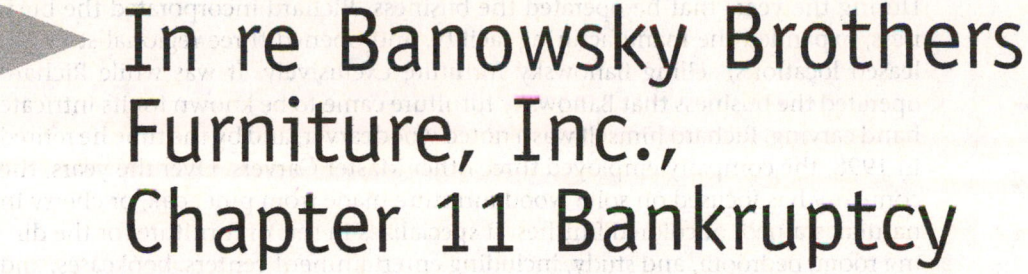

In re Banowsky Brothers Furniture, Inc., Chapter 11 Bankruptcy

[Inactive File]

Assignment Memorandum #1

TO: Paralegal
FROM: James W. Forsyth, supervising attorney
RE: Banowsky Brothers Furniture, Inc.
DATE: May 10, 2016

In 1931, as the Great Depression tightened its grip on America, Philip Banowsky, the grandfather of Charles and Timothy Banowsky, lost his job as local manager of an insurance company in Charlotte, North Carolina and turned to the only other thing he knew: furniture making. He started his business, Banowsky & Son Fine Furniture, in his Charlotte garage and the handmade wooden furniture he produced not only kept his family fed but also gained a reputation for being very well made and sturdy. When Philip passed away in 1960, his son, Richard, took over the business and relocated to High Point, North Carolina, known as "the furniture capital of the world." Richard built a small factory building in High Point where the company both made and sold furniture directly to the public. During the years that he operated the business, Richard incorporated the business, expanded the manufacturing facility, and opened three regional stores in leased locations, selling Banowsky furniture exclusively. It was while Richard operated the business that Banowsky furniture came to be known for its intricate hand carving. Richard himself was a noted woodcarver, and by the time he retired in 1998, the company employed three other Master Carvers. Over the years, the company has focused on solid wood furniture made from pine, oak, or cherry in natural, stained, or colored finishes. It specializes in sets of furniture for the dining room, bedroom, and study, including entertainment centers, bookcases, and corner pieces.

When Richard's two sons, Charles and Timothy, took over the business in 1998, they changed the name to Banowsky Brothers Furniture, Inc. and expanded the family business further by negotiating contracts with two chain department stores, Sherman Department Store and Maddens Home Furnishings, to carry BBF furniture in their stores. In 2010 the brothers undertook a major modernization of their factory by doubling the size of the facility and by purchasing computer-operated robot systems for material handling and product finishing. They went to computer-aided design/computer-aided manufacturing (CAD/CAM) systems to operate all new routers, panel saws, and other production equipment. The brothers also leased two new regional store locations, for a total of five, in addition to the showroom that is part of the furniture factory building. This 2010 expansion was funded by a master loan from Capital City Bank (CCB), which already held a mortgage in the factory property, and the balance owing was refinanced as part of the master loan. The amount of the master loan was $2 million, to be repaid over 25 years. In addition to the mortgage, CCB took a security interest in BBF's inventory, including furniture in process, accounts receivable, and cash, to secure repayment of the loan, the current balance of which is $1.5 million. Both Charles and Timothy have personally guaranteed the debt owed by the business to CCB.

The new computerized systems were purchased from New Century Automation (NCA), which also financed BBF's purchase of new production equipment, including routers, panel saws, and so forth. The total purchase price was $500,000 to be paid over a 12-year term. NCA retained a security interest in the CAD/CAM systems as well as the production equipment to assure repayment. The current balance owed to NCA is $425,000.

All of BBF's other assets—six vehicles, office furniture, fixtures, supplies, and nonproduction equipment—are subject to a security interest in favor of Columbiana Federal Savings & Loan, which is owed $175,000.

The Banowsky brothers had hoped that their 2010 modernization and expansion would accomplish two major goals: to reduce high labor costs in the production of their furniture and, at the same time, increase their cash flow by shortening the production period, thereby expanding the sales outlets for their products. That is not what happened, however. The transition from labor-intensive material handling and furniture production did not go well due to poor training and problems with the systems, which kept them offline for long periods. Additionally, beginning in 2011, company sales began to flatten out rather than rise, even as raw material prices began to soar. The wood used by the company has always been purchased in the United States, which, in recent years, has been a profitable selling point. But the cost of domestic supplies has risen steadily while the competition from foreign furniture makers, who benefit from cheaper sources of wood and far lower labor rates, continues to cut into BBF's sales.

For all these reasons, the gross income of the corporation has fallen steadily over the past several years. Last year the corporation actually operated at a loss and it appears it will do so again this year. BBF is in arrears on its payments to both CCB and NCA. If CCB forecloses on the mortgage or NCA repossesses the CAD/CAM systems and production equipment of BBF, the corporation will be out of business. BBF's unsecured trade debt is badly in arrears and now totals more than $350,000. Two trade creditors have filed lawsuits against BBF to collect the amounts owed to them. Two critical suppliers have put BBF on notice that they will no longer sell to BBF on credit and will demand cash on delivery. BBF has already closed four of its five leased retail locations. The company also has an unpaid corporate income tax bill to the state in the amount of $27,000.

There are five shareholders in BBF. In addition to Charles and Timothy, who each hold 25 percent of the stock in the corporation, their father and mother, Richard and Virginia Banowsky, each own 20 percent and a sister, Beverly Banowsky Davis, owns the other 10 percent. Richard and Virginia, though no longer involved in the business, depend on the income from the corporation to support themselves in retirement. Things have gotten so bad that Charles and Timothy have not drawn any salary or other compensation from the company in more than a year, and no dividend has been declared or other distribution made to any shareholder since 2014.

BBF has decided to file for Chapter 11 reorganization. I need your assistance in preparing the petition and schedules. Please contact Charles Banowsky and begin gathering the necessary information.

ASSIGNMENT MEMORANDUM #2

TO: Paralegal
FROM: James W. Forsyth, supervising attorney
RE: Banowsky Brothers Furniture, Inc.
DATE: June 1, 2016

Charles and Timothy Banowsky have concluded that there is no future for BBF in continuing with the company's traditional furniture business. They believe that the same market trends that have created the current financial emergency for the company (rising prices of domestic wood and foreign competition benefiting from lower material and labor costs) will continue and accelerate. The other owners of the corporation are in agreement. Consequently, they are putting together a plan pursuant to which the company will import teakwood and rubberwood from a supplier in Hong Kong, China, and begin to manufacture various home and office furniture for sale in primarily Asian markets through Furniture Internationale SE (FI), an Italian company based in Milan, Italy.

FI distributes various lines of furniture featuring unique national emblems and characteristics through a network of dealers located in the urban areas of China, Japan, Korea, and other Asian locations. The selling point of the various lines of FI furniture is that they are made of materials preferred by the customers in the targeted markets but reflect the character of foreign exotic places for those customers. The targeted urban markets reflect the explosion of middle class wealth in those markets, particularly China. BBF will supply FI with what will be called the American Patriot Line of furniture for distribution in these markets. Furniture made by BBF will take advantage of its established reputation for high-quality hand carving, which will feature American emblems recognized worldwide such as the stars and stripes of the American flag, the American eagle, the Statue of Liberty, the White House, Mount Vernon, Monticello, the Alamo, etc.

To pursue this new business plan, BBF will no longer use any significant quantity of domestic wood. It will no longer distribute or sell its furniture products domestically. It will be able to utilize most of its current production equipment and systems. It will need to keep the three Master Carvers it currently employs and add as many as three more within the next 12 months. Once the conversion begins, BBF estimates it will be six months before any significant cash flow is received. But FI has been in business for 12 years and its record for producing profits with its other national lines of furniture, based to date on Italian, English, French, and Mexican characteristics, has been impressive. FI has assisted BBF in developing this business plan and has helped BBF locate a company, New Era Capital Alliance based in Montreal, Canada, willing to provide venture capital for the undertaking.

These decisions will guide the formulation of our plan of reorganization for BBF, which I hope to have ready to file immediately following the §341 meeting, assuming we obtain the make-or-break first day orders and prevail on other post-petition operational motions that become necessary. At that point, I will need your assistance in putting together the disclosure statement and plan.

CASE FILE INDEX

[The documents listed in this index for the Chapter 7 bankruptcy case of *In re Banowsky Brothers Furniture, Inc.* are available on the textbook's companion web site at http://aspenlawschool.com/books/Parsons_Debt4e/. The required list of creditors, List of 20 Largest Unsecured Creditors, Schedules A/B, D, E/F, G, H, Summary of Schedules, Declaration re Schedules, and Statement of Financial Affairs are excluded from this list and from the documents exhibited on the companion web site.]

1. Voluntary Petition in Chapter 11
2. Corporate Resolution
3. Corporate Ownership Statement
4. List of Equity Security Holders
5. Statement of Current Income and Expenditures
6. Motion for Immediate Authorization to Hire Attorney for Debtor
7. Motion for Immediate Authorization to Use Cash Collateral and for Expedited Hearing with Notice of Motion
8. Motion for Immediate Authorization to Pay Prepetition Claims of Critical Vendors with Notice of Motion
9. Motion for Immediate Authorization to Pay Prepetition Priority Claims for Employee Benefits and Wages
10. Notice of Appointment of Creditors' Committee
11. Motion for Authorization to Reject Prepetition Executory Contract with Notice of Motion
12. Disclosure Statement
13. Plan of Reorganization (Proposed)
14. Notice of Hearing on Adequacy of Disclosure Statement
15. Order Approving Disclosure Statement and Setting Time for Ballot Distribution and Confirmation Hearing
16. Ballot
17. Order Confirming Plan

Glossary

All section references are to the Bankruptcy Code. Italicized words refer to other defined terms. The parenthetical at the end of each definition references the chapter(s) where the concept is introduced or receives primary attention.

Abandonment. The trustee's releasing of any claim by the estate to property deemed burdensome or of inconsequential value to the estate per §544 of the Code. See *surrender*. (Ch. Eleven and Eighteen.)

Absolute priority rule. The principle applicable in Chapter 11 cases that no junior class of claims or interests in a *plan of reorganization* should receive any distribution until senior classes are paid in full. (Ch. Nineteen)

Acceleration clause. A common provision in a promissory note and other installment contracts making all future installments immediately due and payable upon the debtor's default. (Ch. Two)

Adequate protection. The protection that must be provided by the bankrupt estate to a creditor whose interest in property is threatened by the estate's continued possession and use of the property. Provision of such assurance may be made in various ways per §361 but is recognized by the Code as a condition to the estate's continued possession and use of the property. In the context of the assumption or assignment of an executory contract the debtor or assignee must provide the other party to the contract, called adequate assurance of performance. (Ch. Nine, Eleven, Fifteen, Seventeen, Eighteen, and Nineteen)

Administrative expenses. Postpetition expenses incurred in preserving the property of the estate and in administering the estate by the trustee or debtor in possession. Governed by §503, such expenses are granted a first priority in estate distribution by §507. (Ch. Eleven and Nineteen)

Adversary proceedings. Certain disputes defined by Bankruptcy Rule 7001 that arise in a bankruptcy case and are resolved by the procedures governing a formal civil lawsuit. Cf. *contested matter*. (Ch. Six)

After-acquired property. Property acquired by a debtor that automatically becomes subject to a preexisting security interest (lien) of a creditor. See *floating lien* and *future advance*. (Ch. Two)

After notice and a hearing. A Code procedure requiring notice to parties in interest of the motion, objection, or intended action, but requiring a hearing only if a party in interest requests one. (Ch. Six)

Allowed claim. A creditor's claim that is acknowledged as being owed by the estate under §502. (Ch. Ten)

Alternative dispute resolution. Methods of resolving disputes outside of the litigation process (e.g., mediation or arbitration). (Ch. Four)

Ancillary proceeding. A bankruptcy case filed in a bankruptcy court in the United States that is related to the primary case filed in another country. Governed by new Chapter 15 of the Code. (Ch. Twenty)

Antecedent debt. A debt that was existing prior to a transfer from the debtor in satisfaction of the debt. Relevant to *fraudulent transfer* law and a *preferential transfer* under §547 of the Code. (Ch. Five and Ten)

Applicable commitment period. The required duration of a Chapter 13 plan between 3-5 years. Determined by the debtor's income as compared to the applicable *state median family income*. (Ch. Fourteen)

Arbitration. A form of alternative dispute resolution in which the disputing parties agree that a third-party *arbitrator*, or panel of arbitrators, may hear the dispute informally and render a decision (arbitrator's award). May be binding or nonbinding. (Ch. Four)

Article I courts. In the federal court system, courts created by Congress under Article I of the Constitution for some specialized legislative purpose involving resolution of disputes over public rights; do not enjoy plenary Article III powers; judges of these courts do not have lifetime tenure. See *Article III courts*, *private rights*, and *public rights*. (Ch. Six)

Article III courts. In the federal court system, courts existing under Article III of the Constitution having plenary judicial powers to resolve disputes involving both public and private rights; judges of these courts have lifetime tenure. See *Article I courts*, *private rights*, and *public rights*. (Ch. Six)

Artisan's lien. The right of one who performs work on the personal property of another to retain possession of the property as security for payment for the work done and to sell the property and apply the proceeds to the amount due. A common law lien in some states, statutory in others. (Ch. Three)

Asset buyers (or debt buyers). Persons who purchase delinquent or charged-off accounts from creditors for a fraction of the face value of the debt and then seek to collect it themselves or resell to another asset buyer. (Ch. Two)

Asset protection (self-settled) trust. A trust permitted in a handful of states whereby the settlor can convey his own property into trust and name himself as the beneficiary to receive distributions of principal or interest as proscribed in the trust document, yet prevent his creditors from seizing trust assets not yet distributed. Previously available only as questionable foreign asset protection trusts or offshore trusts. (Ch. Five)

Assignment for the benefit of creditors. A state law insolvency procedure involving the assignment of the debtor's property to a trustee empowered to liquidate the property and distribute the proceeds to creditors who are given notice and elect to participate. (Ch. Six)

Attachment. The creation of a security interest (lien) in favor of a creditor in property of the debtor. See *perfection*. (Ch. Two)

Attorney's charging lien. A nonpossessory lien imposed on a judgment or settlement amount due the client for the amount owed the attorney. (Ch. Three)

Attorney's or accountant's retaining lien. The right of a licensed professional to retain possession of a client's personal property until the client pays the amount owed or provides other security. (Ch. Three)

Automatic perfection. The perfection of a security interest (lien) immediately upon its attachment. (Ch. Two)

Automatic stay. The prohibition on creditors continuing collection efforts against a debtor that arises automatically upon the debtor's filing of a bankruptcy petition per §362 of the Code; enforceable by the contempt powers of the bankruptcy court. Expires automatically on personal property 45 days following the first meeting of creditors in individual Chapter 7 cases unless the debtor *redeems* the property or *reaffirms* the debt. (Ch. Nine and Thirteen)

Avoidance power. 1. The trustee's powers under the Code to set aside certain prepetition transfers of property of the estate. 2. The right of an individual debtor to set aside a lien in property of the estate to the extent it impairs an exemption in that property. See *preference, fraudulent transfer*, and *exempt property*. (Ch. Ten)

Badges of fraud. In the law of fraudulent transfer, certain recognized circumstances from which the inference may fairly be drawn that a transfer was made with intent to defraud creditors. (Ch. Five and Ten)

Balance sheet test. A test of *insolvency* whereby a debtor's liabilities exceed his assets. (Ch. Five and Ten)

The Bankruptcy Abuse Prevention and Consumer Protection Act of 2005 (BAPCPA). The 2005 statute that amended the Code in numerous ways including introducing the means test for Chapter 7 filers. (Ch. Six)

Bankruptcy Appellate Panel (BAP). A court made up of bankruptcy judges appointed in some federal circuits to hear the appeal of rulings by other bankruptcy judges in lieu of the District Court. (Ch. Six)

Bankruptcy petition preparer. One who prepares a bankruptcy petition for a fee and who is not an attorney or working under the supervision of an attorney. (Ch. Eight)

Best interests test. A test for confirmation of a plan of reorganization under Chapter 11 or 13 of the Code that requires a showing that unsecured creditors will receive at least as much under the plan as they would have received in a Chapter 7 liquidation. (Ch. Sixteen and Nineteen)

Bifurcated claim. Description of the treatment of the bankruptcy claim of a secured creditor whose dollar claim exceeds the value of the collateral securing the claim. See *secured debt*. (Ch. Ten and Fifteen)

Budget and credit counseling agency. An entity approved by the U.S. Trustee to provide prepetition credit counseling or predischarge financial management services to consumer debtors. See *credit counseling agency*. (Ch. Seven)

Bulk Sales Act. Article 6 of the *Uniform Commercial Code* providing a nonbankruptcy procedure for the sale of all or substantially all of the assets of a business outside the ordinary course of business. Repealed in most states. (Ch. Six)

Business bankruptcy case. A bankruptcy case in which the debtor is an entity or an individual with primarily business debts. (Ch. One and Six)

Business judgment rule. A rule applied by the bankruptcy court to a *trustee*'s decision to assume or reject an *executory contract* pursuant to which the court will not interfere with the trustee's decision if it was made in good faith and reflects reasonable business judgment. (Ch. Eighteen)

Car title loan. Loan in which a consumer signs title to his vehicle over to the lender to secure a similar short-term loan, often at a predatory rate of interest. (Ch. Two)

Case Management/Electronic Case Files (CM/ECF). The current system for filing documents with a bankruptcy court electronically. Access to case filings available through Public Access to Court Electronic Records (PACER). (Ch. Six)

Cash collateral. Cash or *cash equivalents* that are part of the property of the estate and which are subject to a security interest in favor of a creditor. (Ch. Seventeen)

Chapter 13 plan. A plan proposed by a Chapter 13 debtor. (Ch. Fifteen and Sixteen)

Chapter 20 case. Practitioner's term for a Chapter 13 bankruptcy case filed by a debtor within 4 years of receiving a discharge in a Chapter 7 case (7 + 13 = 20). (Ch. Thirteen)

Claim bifurcation. The splitting of a claim in bankruptcy between its secured portion equal to the value of the property securing the claim and its unsecured portion. (Ch. Ten and Fifteen)

Claims bar date. The deadline set for creditors in a case to file proofs of claim. Claims not filed by the bar date may be disallowed or *subordinated* to other claims. (Ch. Ten)

Claims docket. A list of claims filed in a bankruptcy case. (Ch. Ten)

Classes (of claims or interests). Designated groupings of creditor claims or equity interests with members of each class receiving equal treatment. (Ch. Fifteen and Nineteen)

Co-debtor stay. The Chapter 13 rule that the automatic stay extends to co-debtors of the Chapter 13 debtor. (Ch. Thirteen)

Collateral. The property subject to a consensual or nonconsensual security interest (lien). (Ch. Two)

Commercially reasonable manner. The standard governing the creditor's sale of repossessed property. What is commercially reasonable depends on the prevailing circumstances surrounding the sale and what is common or usual in the market for goods of that kind. (Ch. Two)

Common law lien. A nonconsensual lien recognized by case law; sometimes called an equitable lien. (Ch. Three)

Composition agreement. A contract made between a debtor and his creditors pursuant to which partial payment is made and accepted in full satisfaction of claims. See *extension agreement*. (Ch. Four and Six)

Community property. A form of concurrent ownership between married couples in which all property acquired by either spouse during the marriage, however titled, is deemed to be owned by both. See *concurrent ownership, joint tenancy, tenancy by the entireties,* and *tenancy in common*. (Ch. Five)

Concurrent ownership. Ownership of property by two or more persons simultaneously. See *community property, joint tenancy, tenancy by the entireties,* and *tenancy in common*. (Ch. Five)

Confirmation. The court's formal approval of a plan of reorganization under Chapter 11, 12, or 13. See *confirmation hearing*. (Ch. Sixteen and Nineteen)

Consensual lien. A security interest (lien) in property voluntarily granted by a debtor to a creditor in a contract such as a mortgage instrument or security agreement. (Ch. Two)

Consent decree. A final judgment entered by agreement of the parties. (Ch. Five)

Consolidation. The joining together of two or more bankruptcy cases involving interrelated debtors into one case for joint administration. (Ch. Six)

Constitutional jurisdiction. The issue of whether a bankruptcy court, as an Article I court, can enter final judgment in disputes traditionally within the province of Article III courts. (Ch. Six)

Constructive fraud (presumed fraud). A means of finding fraud based on inference from circumstances rather than proof of actual intent. (Ch. Five and Ten)

Constructive trust. An equitable remedy pursuant to which one who has wrongfully obtained title to or possession of property is deemed to hold that property in trust for the benefit of the true owner. (Ch. Three and Five)

Consumer bankruptcy case. A bankruptcy case in which the debtor is an individual with primarily *consumer debts*. (Ch. Six)

Consumer debt. Debt incurred for personal, family, or household purposes. (Ch. One, Six, and Seventeen)

Consumer Financial Protection Bureau. Federal bureau created in 2010 and charged with developing regulations regarding consumer credit and loan transactions. (Ch. Four)

Contemporaneous exchange for equivalent value. A transaction supported by adequate present consideration. (Ch. Five and Ten)

Contempt. Power of a court to declare one subject to the court's order in violation of it. Enforceable by fines, penalties, and incarceration. See *automatic stay*. (Ch. Nine)

Contested matter. A proceeding arising in a bankruptcy case that is initiated by motion or objection or statement of intent to act. Cf. *adversary proceeding*. (Ch. Six)

Contingent claim. A claim the enforceability of which depends on the happening of an uncertain future event. Also called an unmatured claim. (Ch. One and Two)

Core proceeding. A proceeding in a bankruptcy case involving the determination of rights under the Code or issues arising in a bankruptcy case as suggested by the list in 28 U.S.C. §157(2). Final orders may be entered by a bankruptcy court in a core proceeding. (Ch. Six)

Co-signer. One who signs a promissory note as a form of security for the lender, making himself primarily liable for the debt of another. (Ch. Two)

Cram down (strip off or strip down). The right of a bankruptcy debtor to reduce the value of some secured claims to the present value of the security without creditor consent. Cf., *lien stripping*. (Ch. Eleven, Fifteen, and Twenty)

Cram down confirmation. Confirmation of a Chapter 11 plan of reorganization over the objection of one or more classes. (Ch. Twenty)

Credit-bidding. Also called bidding in, the practice of a creditor secured in property foreclosed on or repossessed bidding the amount owed at the foreclosure/repossession sale and receiving credit for the amount owed against the sales price. In bankruptcy, specifically authorized in 11 U.S.C. §363(k) when property of the estate is sold. (Ch. Two, Fifteen and Eighteen)

Credit counseling agency. A company that provides budget counseling and financial literacy services to debt-strapped individuals or businesses; may also negotiate a debt management plan with creditors of client. See *debt relief agencies* and *budget and credit counseling agency*. (Ch. Four and Seven)

Creditors' committee. A committee of creditors appointed by the U.S. Trustee in Chapter 11 cases and sometimes in Chapter 7 cases to represent the interests of all creditors. (Ch. Seventeen)

Cross-border case. A bankruptcy case involving debtors, assets, and creditors in more than one country. Governed by new Chapter 15 of the Code. See *ancillary proceeding*. (Ch. Twenty)

Cross-collateralization. An arrangement whereby a creditor agrees to extend postpetition credit to a debtor in exchange for which property of the estate is pledged to secure both the postpetition and prepetition claims of the creditor. (Ch. Eighteen)

Cure. The payment of an arrearage to bring the defaulting party into compliance with its obligations under a contract. (Ch. Eleven and Fifteen)

Current monthly income. The income of a consumer debtor calculated by averaging the debtor's income from all sources for the six months preceding the filing of the petition. (Ch. Seven and Fourteen)

Custodian. A person authorized to have possession of a debtor's property for a specific purpose as in a trustee, receiver, or assignee for the benefit of creditors. (Ch. Ten)

Debt collection companies. Private businesses involved in prelitigation debt collection activities on behalf of creditors, usually for a percentage of what is collected. (Ch. Four)

Debt collectors. Under the FDCPA businesses the principal purpose of which is to collect debts owed to consumers and individuals who regularly collect or attempt to collect such debt. (Ch. Four)

Debt relief agency. Under the Code, one who provides any bankruptcy assistance to an assisted person in return for the payment of money or other valuable consideration. See *credit counseling agency*. (Ch. Four and Eight)

Debtor in possession. The legal status given a debtor filing a Chapter 11 or Chapter 12 case because the debtor retains possession of property of the estate. (Ch. Seventeen and Twenty)

Deeming. Code process where certain determinations are deemed made unless a timely objection is filed (e.g., claims deemed allowed absent objection per §502(a)). (Ch. Ten, Fifteen, and Eighteen)

Deficiency (judgment). The amount of a debt that remains owing after the property securing the debt has been liquidated. (Ch. Two)

Discharge hearing. The formal hearing conducted by a bankruptcy court to determine whether a debtor is entitled to an order of discharge. See *discharge* and *hardship discharge.* (Ch. Twelve and Sixteen)

Discharge in bankruptcy. Permanent relief from debt pursuant to order of the bankruptcy court. See *nondischargeable debt* and *exception to discharge.* (Ch. Twelve and Sixteen)

Disclosure statement. A detailed summary of the Chapter 11 debtor's financial and operational history and prospects sufficient to enable holders of claims and interests to make an informed judgment of a proposed plan of reorganization. (Ch. Nineteen)

Discovery in aid of execution (postjudgment). The right of a judgment creditor to engage in discovery for the purpose of locating assets of the judgment debtor on which to execute. (Ch. Five)

Disposable income. 1. The income of a garnishee a statutory percentage of which is subject to garnishment. (Ch. Five) 2. The income that a bankruptcy debtor has available to pay creditors after deducting income necessary for the support or maintenance of the debtor and his dependents. (Ch. Seven and Fourteen)

Domestic support obligation. An obligation to pay alimony, child support, or maintenance. (Ch. Three, Eleven, and Twelve)

Due on sale clause. A provision in a mortgage or security agreement providing that if the debtor sells the property pledged as security for repayment without the creditor's consent, a default has occurred and the entire amount due becomes immediately due and payable. (Ch. Two)

Election of remedies. The doctrine recognized in some states requiring a secured creditor to choose between exercising a right of foreclosure on secured property or suing the debtor for a judgment, but disallowing both foreclosure and a suit for deficiency judgment. (Ch. Two and Nineteen)

Electronic vehicle titling (E-Title). System for registering vehicles with the state electronically pursuant to which no paper title is issued unless requested. (Ch. Two)

Equitable lien (also called common law lien). A lien created by court rulings rather than by statute (e.g., vendor's lien). (Ch. Three)

Equitable subordination. The inherent power of a bankruptcy court as a court of equity to order that a claim be subordinated to others of the same rank due to inequitable or dishonest conduct of the claimant. (Ch. Ten and Eleven)

Equity. 1. An ownership interest in property unencumbered by any security interest or lien. Also called owner's equity. 2. The body of rules and principles developed historically by courts whereby they are authorized to provide relief when remedies at law are inadequate. (Ch. One and Two)

Equity of redemption. A mortgagor's right to prevent the sale of real property in foreclosure by paying the entire indebtedness owed prior to the foreclosure sale. See *redemption*. (Ch. Two)

Equity security holder. The holder of an ownership interest in an entity debtor (e.g., shareholder in a corporation, member of a limited liability company, or partner in a partnership). (Ch. Eighteen)

Evidentiary hearing. A court hearing at which sworn testimony is taken and exhibits may be offered. Governed by the Federal Rules of Evidence. (Ch. Six)

Examiner. A person appointed by a bankruptcy court to investigate specific aspects of a Chapter 11 debtor's conduct or management of the estate. (Ch. Seventeen)

Exclusivity period. The period of time in which a Chapter 11 debtor has the exclusive right to propose a plan of reorganization. (Ch. Twenty)

Execution. The satisfaction of a final judgment by the seizure and sale of non-exempt property of the debtor. (Ch. Five)

Execution grace period. The period of time between entry of a final judgment and the date on which the judgment creditor can begin execution on the judgment. (Ch. Five)

Executory contract. An agreement that is so far unperformed by the parties to it as to constitute a material breach. (Ch. Seventeen and Eighteen)

Exempt property. 1. Property of a debtor that cannot be seized by a judgment creditor. (Ch. Five) 2. Property of an individual debtor in bankruptcy that the debtor is allowed to keep and that cannot be made available to his creditors. See *declaration of exemptions* and *wild card exemption*. (Ch. Eight)

Extension agreement. An agreement made by a debtor with his creditors whereby the creditors consent to an extension of time for the debtor to pay. Often reached in conjunction with a *composition agreement*. (Ch. Six)

Fair and equitable. A test for cram down confirmation of a Chapter 11 plan requiring a showing that all classes and claims are treated in a fair and equitable manner. (Ch. Twenty)

Fair Debt Collection Practices Act (FDCPA). 15 U.S.C. §1601, et seq. Federal statute regulating *debt collectors*. (Ch. Four)

Family farmer. A debtor engaged in farming operations and who otherwise meets the requirements to be a debtor under Chapter 12. (Ch. Twenty)

Family fisherman. A debtor engaged in a commercial fishing operation and who otherwise meets the requirements to be a debtor under Chapter 12. (Ch. Twenty)

Feasibility test. A test for confirmation of a plan of reorganization requiring a showing that the debtor has a reasonable prospect of completing the plan. (Ch. Sixteen and Twenty)

Federalism. A principle of government whereby a national government agrees to share power with political subdivisions such as states or territories; adopted in the Tenth Amendment to the United States Constitution. (Ch. Twenty)

Fiduciary capacity (duty). Description of one providing services for another that include a high duty of loyalty, confidentiality, and trust. (Ch. Twelve)

Fieri facias. See *writ of execution*.

Final judgment. An order or decree entered by a court finally resolving the issues before it. (Ch. Five)

Financing statement. A document filed in a designated public office to perfect a security interest in personal property under Article 9 of the *UCC*. Also called a UCC-1. (Ch. Two)

First day orders. Practitioner's phrase for orders commonly sought immediately upon filing of a Chapter 11 case. (Ch. Seventeen)

First meeting of creditors. The meeting of creditors of a bankrupt debtor required by §341 of the Code called by the U.S. Trustee. The debtor may be questioned under oath at the meeting. (Ch. Nine, Thirteen, Seventeen)

Floating lien. A security interest (lien) that attaches automatically to property of the debtor acquired after the date the security interest was created. See *after-acquired property* and *future advance*. (Ch. Two)

Foreclosure. The process by which the holder of a mortgage in real property takes possession of the property following default by the mortgagor. The property is normally sold and the proceeds applied to the costs of foreclosure and underlying debt. In some cases the property is retained in satisfaction of the debt. A foreclosure may be consensual (power of sale foreclosure) or judicial (court ordered). (Ch. Two)

Foreign judgment. A final judgment entered in a state other than the state in which it is enforced. See *Uniform Enforcement of Foreign Judgment Act*. (Ch. Five)

Fraudulent transfer (or conveyance). A transfer of property by a debtor with actual or constructive intent to defraud his creditors by delaying or hindering their collection efforts. (Ch. Five and Ten)

Fresh start (clean slate). The opportunity provided to a debtor following a discharge in bankruptcy. (Ch. Six)

Future advance. A loan or credit extended to a debtor that is subject to a previously created security interest in property of the debtor. (Ch. Two)

Gap period. The Code's description of the period of time between the filing of an involuntary petition and the entry of an order for relief or appointment of a trustee. Claims arising in the gap period are gap claims and have a certain priority under §507. (Ch. Eleven)

Garnishment. A method of executing on a final judgment pursuant to which property of the debtor in the hands of a third person or a debt owed by a third person to the debtor is levied on. (Ch. Five)

Good faith. Generally, honesty in fact and compliance with the letter and spirit of the Code. (Ch. Twelve and Sixteen)

Guarantor. One who guarantees the debt of another. The guarantor is *secondarily liable* for the debt. (Ch. Two)

Hardship discharge. An early discharge granted at the discretion of the judge in a Chapter 13 or Chapter 11 case. See *discharge*. (Ch. Sixteen and Nineteen)

Healthcare services lien. A nonpossessory lien imposed on amounts due to a patient from a third party responsible for the patient's medical condition to secure amounts owed to the healthcare provider. (Ch. Three)

Home equity loan. A loan in which the borrower pledges the *equity* in his home as security for repayment. (Ch. Two)

Homestead exemption. The exemption available to a debtor to protect the equity in his primary residence. (Ch. Five and Eight)

Impaired (class or claims). A class created in a Chapter 11 or Chapter 9 plan whose claims are not to be paid according to their contractual terms. (Ch. Nineteen)

Insider. A person in close relationship with a debtor such that he may be assumed to have superior access to information and be subject to special treatment. Includes relatives of an individual debtor and owners, officers, and directors of entity debtors. (Ch. Five, Ten, and Nineteen)

Insolvency. The inability to pay debts as they come due (the *equity test*) or the state of having total liabilities in excess of total assets (the *balance sheet test*). (Ch. Five and Ten)

Installment note (payments). A promissory note calling for payment of the amount owed in periodic (e.g., monthly, quarterly, annually) payments. (Ch. Two)

Intentional fraud. To act (as in the transfer of property) with the actual intent to defraud a creditor. See *badges of fraud* and *constructive fraud*. (Ch. Five and Ten)

Interest. The cost of using another person's money or property. Usually assessed at a percentage of the amount borrowed *per annum*. The interest rate over the term of the loan may be fixed or variable. (Ch. Two, Five, Ten, and Nineteen)

Involuntary case petition. A Chapter 7 or 11 case initiated by the creditors of the debtor. (Ch. Eight and Seventeen)

Joint administration. Where two or more bankruptcy cases involving affiliated debtors are ordered to be administered jointly to save administrative costs. (Ch. Seventeen)

Joint tenancy. A form of joint ownership of property that includes a right of survivorship. (Ch. Five)

Judgment debtor/creditor. Once a final judgment is entered by a court awarding a money judgment to one party, the party to whom the judgment is awarded is the judgment creditor and the one against whom it is awarded is the judgment debtor. (Ch. Two)

Judgment lien. A judicial lien created on all real property owned by a judgment debtor in the county where the final judgment is recorded or docketed. In some states the lien attaches to personal property of the debtor as well when the judgment is recorded as is a UCC financing statement. (Ch. Three and Five)

Judgment proof. Condition of a debtor who has no assets that might be seized to satisfy a final judgment. (Ch. Five)

Judicial lien. Lien obtained by court action, whether judgment, levy, sequestration, or other legal or equitable process or proceeding. (Ch. Three and Five)

Judicial lien creditor. Priority status of a creditor in property that has been seized pursuant to a writ of execution to satisfy a judgment in favor of that creditor. (Ch. Three and Eleven)

Judicial repossession. A post-default process by which a secured creditor obtains possession of collateral or forecloses on a mortgage by a court order. (Ch. Two)

Jurisdiction. In general, the power of a court to hear and decide a particular case. (Ch. Six)

Landlord's lien. Where recognized, right of landlord to seize and sell tenant's personal property left on the premises to satisfy unpaid rent; requires express consent. (Ch. Three)

Levy. Seizing or taking control of a debtor's property pursuant to a lien or writ of execution. (Ch. Five)

Lien. Generally, another word for a security interest. Sometimes used narrowly to refer only to nonconsensual secured claims created by law or court order, e.g., mechanics' lien, artisan's lien, judicial lien. (Ch. Two and Three)

Lien of levy. The lien existing in favor of a judgment creditor against the property of the judgment debtor seized pursuant to a writ of execution. The judgment creditor then has the status of a *judicial lien* creditor as to such property. (Ch. Three and Five)

Lien stripping (or strip down or write down or strip off). Procedure attempted by debtor to reduce lien on property to value of secured claim and retain property with ride through. See *ride through*. (Ch. Eleven, Fifteen, Nineteen, and Twenty)

Line of credit. A loan in which the borrowed funds are not immediately advanced to the borrower but are put at the disposal of the borrower to draw down on as needed. (Ch. One and Two)

Liquidated claim (debt). A claim that has been reduced to a dollar amount. See *unliquidated claim*. (Ch. One)

Liquidation. The sale or other disposition of a debtor's nonexempt assets for the purpose of distribution to his creditors in exchange for a discharge of most unpaid debts. Chapter 7 is a liquidation proceeding. (Ch. Six)

Lis pendens (L. suit pending). Public notice that a lawsuit is pending regarding title, possession, or other rights to real property. Given by filing or recording notice of pendency in land records for county where the property at issue lies. Understood to create a lien on the realty that will act as a cloud on title until removed. (Ch. Three)

Local rules. Supplemental rules of procedure and practice that prevail in a particular court. (Ch. Six)

Luxury goods or services. Undefined phrase but includes goods or services not reasonably necessary for the maintenance or support of the debtor or a dependent. Purchases of same within 90 days preceding the petition are presumed fraudulent and nondischargeable. Presumption rebuttable. (Ch. Twelve)

Marshalling of assets. Requirement that a judgment creditor executing on property of the judgment debtor seize and exhaust property in a certain order, e.g., all nonexempt personalty before nonexempt realty. (Ch. Two and Five)

Materialman's lien. A statutory lien on realty available to a party who has supplied materials for the improvement of the realty. Sometimes called a construction lien. See *mechanic's lien*. (Ch. Three)

Means test. A test for Chapter 7 filers introduced by BAPCPA intended to determine whether the debtor has sufficient *disposable income* to enable the debtor to repay some or all of his debts in a Chapter 13 case. Test raises *presumption of abuse* when debtor's current monthly income exceeds the applicable state *median family income*. Unless rebutted, presumption of abuse mandates dismissal or conversion of case to Chapter 13. (Ch. Seven)

Mechanic's lien. A statutory lien on realty available to a party who has supplied services or labor for the improvement of the realty. Sometimes called a construction lien. See *materialman's lien*. (Ch. Three)

Median family income. State-by-state statistics compiled by the U.S. Census Bureau every ten years when a constitutionally mandated census is taken and set out by family size. (Ch. Seven and Fourteen)

Mediation. A form of *alternative dispute resolution* in which an impartial person serving as *mediator* uses back and forth dialogue with the disputing parties to assist them in reaching a settlement. (Ch. Six)

Mortgage. The pledging of liquidation of real property as security for a debt. Created by execution of a document called a mortgage, deed of trust, or security deed. (Ch. Two)

Necessity doctrine. The court-made rule that a Chapter 11 debtor may pay certain prepetition debts to critical vendors or essential employees if necessary for the business to survive. (Ch. Eighteen)

New value exception. An exception to the absolute priority rule in a Chapter 11 case enabling holders of equity interests in a bankrupt debtor to retain their interests even though senior claim holders will not be paid in full. Equity holders must contribute new capital to the debtor at least equal to the value of their interest. (Ch. Nineteen)

No-asset case. A Chapter 7 liquidation case in which there are no assets available for distribution to creditors. (Ch. Six and Nine)

Nonattorney bankruptcy petition preparer. Nonattorney who assists a debtor in preparing petition and schedules for bankruptcy filing. (Ch. Eight)

Noncontingent claim. A claim that is not subject to any future contingency. Also called a matured claim. (Ch. One and Two)

Non-core proceedings. Disputes governed by nonbankruptcy law the outcome of which may affect the administration of a bankruptcy estate. Such disputes fall within the nonexclusive jurisdiction of the bankruptcy court and no final order may be entered on them by the bankruptcy court without the consent of all parties. Absent that consent, such matters are heard by the district court. (Ch. Six)

Nondischargeable debt. A debt excluded from discharge under §523. (Ch. Twelve and Sixteen)

Nonrecourse secured note. A secured debt for which the debtor has no liability beyond the value of the property securing the debt. No deficiency judgment may be brought after foreclosure or repossession. (Ch. Two and Nineteen)

Notice and a hearing. Code procedure requiring notice of motion, objection, or intended action be given to parties in interest, but requiring a hearing only if a party in interest contests or objects. (Ch. Six)

Notice of intended action. Procedure authorized under the Code for giving parties in interest notice of the intent to take some action (e.g., intent to abandon property). Often joined with notice and a hearing procedure. (Ch. Six)

Operating reports. Periodic reports (usually monthly) of business activity required of a debtor in possession in Chapter 11 or 12 cases and of a trustee operating a business as part of a Chapter 7 liquidation. (Ch. Seventeen)

Order for relief. The formal beginning of a bankruptcy case. 1. In most districts the filing of a voluntary petition constitutes the order for relief; in others a formal order approving the filing of a voluntary petition. 2. A formal order that is always entered approving the filing of an involuntary petition. (Ch. Nine)

Oversecured debt. A secured debt where the value of the collateral exceeds the amount owed. (Ch. Two)

Owner's equity. See *equity*.

Party in interest. An important but undefined term in the Code, interpreted generally to refer to any person or entity having a stake in the outcome of a matter arising in a bankruptcy case (e.g., debtor, bankruptcy trustee, U.S. Trustee, creditors, and equity security holders). (Ch. Six and Seventeen)

Pawn shop loan. A short-term loan taken by a consumer who pledges some kind of personal property as security for repayment and gives pawn lender possession. Loan is made in an amount equal to a reduced value of the property pledged (usually 30–50%) and entitles lender to sell the property for full value if loan is not paid by due date. (Ch. Two)

Payday loan. Variously also called cash advance, check advance, postdated check loan, deferred deposit check loan, or deferred presentment loan; a high interest, short-term loan in which the borrower typically gives the lender a postdated check for the amount borrowed plus interest and fees. If the amount borrowed is not repaid by the date of the check, the lender will cash it in payment. See *car title loan*. (Ch. Two)

Perfection. Making a security interest in property enforceable against and superior to the rights of other creditors to the property. Normally accomplished by filing or recording required documents in a designated public office or by taking possession of the property. (Ch. Two)

Perpriority. A priority granted to the holders of some claims that is superior even to other priority claims. For example, (1) the priority some states grant tax liens in the debtor's property (Ch. Three); and (2) in bankruptcy, the priority over administrative expenses that can be granted to a creditor in exchange for giving post-petition credit to the estate pursuant to §364. (Ch. Eleven and Eighteen)

Personal defenses. A defense to liability unique to the circumstances of the principal debtor and which do not go to the merits of the underlying transaction such as discharge in bankruptcy or lack of capacity due to age or disability. Sureties and guarantors cannot successfully assert personal defenses of the principal debtor as a defense. (Ch. Two)

Personal jurisdiction. The *due process* requirement that a defendant have sufficient minimum contacts with a forum to enable a court in that forum to enter a final order binding on a named defendant. (Ch. Six)

Plan of reorganization. A plan proposed under Chapter 11. Cf. *Chapter 13 plan*. (Ch. Seventeen, Eighteen, and Nineteen)

Possessory liens. Types of statutory or equitable liens that attach to property in the possession of the lien holder (e.g., artisan's lien). Some liens are *nonpossessory* (e.g., *mechanic's* and *materialman's liens*; *lien lis pendens*). (Ch. Three)

Postjudgment asset discovery. The right of a judgment creditor to discover assets of a judgment debtor subject to execution following entry of the final judgment using interrogatories, document requests, and depositions. (Ch. Five)

Postjudgment interest. Statutory interest that runs on a final judgment from the date entered until paid is postjudgment interest. (Ch. Five)

Postjudgment motions. Motions the losing party may file in the trial court seeking to invalidate or amend a final judgment or a new trial. (Ch. Five)

Postpetition interest. Interest accruing on claims after debtor files a petition in bankruptcy. (Ch. Eight)

Preferential transfer. A payment or other transfer of an interest in the debtor's property that results in the creditor receiving the payment or transfer being unfairly advantaged compared to other creditors. May be avoidable pursuant to §547. (Ch. Eight)

Prejudgment interest. Interest on an amount owed calculated from due date through date of judgment. Within the trial court's discretion to award. (Ch. Five)

Prepackaged Chapter 11. A Chapter 11 proceeding in which the plan of reorganization has been drafted and informally approved by creditors prepetition. (Ch. Seventeen)

Prepetition credit counseling. Counseling that an individual debtor must receive from an approved *credit counseling agency* as a qualification for filing for bankruptcy relief. (Ch. Seven)

Present value. Calculation of the current value of property for purposes of determining the value of a secured claim in bankruptcy. Normally based on replacement cost of the property considering its age and condition. (Ch. Ten, Fifteen, and Nineteen)

Presumption of abuse. The presumption of inappropriate filing of a Chapter 7 case for the debtor who fails the *means test.* The presumption, once raised, must be rebutted by showing *special circumstances* or the case will be dismissed or converted to a case under Chapter 13. (Ch. Seven)

Primarily/secondarily liable. One who is primarily liable for the debt of another is liable without regard to whether the lender pursues collection from the other first (e.g., a *co-signer* or *surety*). One who is secondarily liable for the debt of another is liable only if the lender first pursues collection from the other (e.g., a *guarantor*). (Ch. Two)

Prime rate. The interest rate that commercial banks charge their best customers. (Ch. Fifteen)

Priming lien. A senior security interest granted to a creditor as an inducement to provide postpetition loan or credit to a Chapter 11 debtor and which is superior to a prepetition interest in the same property. (Ch. Eighteen)

Priority. 1. The ranking of security interests (liens) in the same property. 2. The ranking of approved claims in a bankruptcy case in the order in which they will be paid. (Ch. Two and Eleven)

Priority claim. An unsecured claim entitled to a certain order of preferment and payment under §507. (Ch. Eight, Eleven, and Fifteen)

Private rights. Rights existing between private parties arising from state law (e.g., contract and tort law). See *Article I courts, Article III courts,* and *public rights.* (Ch. Six)

Proceeds. Money or property received in exchange for an asset. (Ch. Two)

Professional. A person retained by the estate with the permission of the bankruptcy court to provide services for estate administration (e.g., appraiser, surveyor, realtor, auctioneer, accountant, or attorney). (Ch. Nine)

Promissory note. A contract containing an enforceable promise by one person (the maker or payor) to pay another person (the payee) a certain sum of money, the principal. The note may be payable installments (an installment note) or in full on a fixed date in the future (a balloon note). The note may be secured by property of the debtor or unsecured. (Ch. Two)

Proof of claim. The writing that a creditor submits as evidence of its claim against the estate. (Ch. Ten)

Property of the estate. All property in which the debtor holds a legal or equitable interest at the commencement of a bankruptcy case per §541. In a Chapter 13 case, property acquired by the debtor postpetition is included as well per §1306. (Ch. Ten, Thirteen, and Seventeen)

Public Access to Court Electronic Records (PACER). See *Case Management/Electronic Case Files*. (Ch. Six)

Public rights. Rights arising between parties as a result of specific government regulation. See *Article I courts*, *Article III courts*, and *private rights*. (Ch. Six)

Punitive damages. Damages intended to punish the wrongdoer in order to deter similar conduct in the future. (Ch. Nine)

Purchase money mortgage. A mortgage held by the seller rather than a third-party lender. A form of self-financing by seller. (Ch. Two, Three, and Ten)

Purchase money security interest (PMSI). A security interest in personal property created by loaning or extending credit to a debtor for the express purpose of purchasing the property. When the property is consumer goods, the PMSI is automatically perfected. (Ch. Two and Ten)

Reaffirmation agreement. The bankruptcy debtor's agreement with a creditor to pay the creditor a debt that could have been discharged in bankruptcy. (Ch. Eleven)

Reasonably equivalent value. Its absence is one of the tests to see if a transfer of property is constructively fraudulent as to creditors of the transferor under the Uniform Fraudulent Transfer Act and under §548 of the Code. Determined primarily by fair market value of the property at the time of the transfer. (Ch. Five and Ten)

Receivership. Proceeding in which a person is appointed to take control of a debtor's property and manage it under court supervision. (Ch. Six)

Recording statute. The state law controlling how mortgages are perfected thus determining the priority among mortgages or liens on the property. States have, variously, race-notice, pure notice, or pure race recording statutes. (Ch. Two)

Redemption. 1. In nonbankruptcy law, a debtor's right to buy back property that has been repossessed or foreclosed on. Not available in all states. See *equity of redemption*. (Ch. Two) 2. The right of a Chapter 7 *individual consumer debtor* under §722 of the Code to buy back collateralized *consumer property* that has either been claimed as *exempt* by the debtor or abandoned by the trustee by paying the creditor the *present value* of the property. (Ch. Eleven)

Referral jurisdiction. A description of the subject matter jurisdiction of U.S. bankruptcy courts, which depends on referral from the U.S. district courts. (Ch. Six)

Rejection (of contract). The bankruptcy estate's optional repudiation of an executory contract with the result that the debtor has no remaining obligations under it and the other party has an unsecured claim for prepetition obligations. (Ch. Eighteen)

Relation back. The retrospective effect given to some liens giving them priority from a date prior to their perfection. (Ch. Two and Ten)

Removal (jurisdiction). The transfer of bankruptcy proceedings from the U.S. district court to the bankruptcy court. (Ch. Six)

Rent-to-own agreement. A contract in which the buyer leases the property until the final payment at which time the seller/lessee conveys title to him. (Ch. Two)

Reorganization proceeding. The rearrangement of a debtor's finances under a court-approved plan as an alternative to liquidation. Cases under Chapters 11, 12, and 13 are reorganization proceedings. Cf. *liquidation* and *straight bankruptcy*. (Ch. Six)

Revolving credit. A credit arrangement whereby funds are borrowed only when the borrower chooses up to the limits of the approved credit limits. (Ch. Two)

Ride through (or pay through or pay and ride). Where a debtor retains possession of pledged collateral through a bankruptcy case by continuing to make payments to the secured creditor. (Ch. Eleven and Fifteen)

Right to redeem. See *redemption*.

Rule 2004 examination. The examination under oath as in a deposition of any person in connection with any matter related to a bankruptcy case. (Ch. Six and Nine)

Safe-harbor provision. A provision in a statute or regulation that exempts a person from liability for certain conduct. (Ch. Nine)

Sale free and clear of liens. The sale of property of the estate that is subject to a secured claim to enable the bankruptcy estate to realize the equity in the property in excess of that claim. Per §363, the sale may be authorized over the creditor's objection. (Ch. Eleven and Eighteen)

Secured debt (secured claim/secured creditor). A debt the payment of which is secured by real or personal property giving the secured creditor recourse against the property in the event of a default. See *bifurcated claim* and *unsecured debt*. (Ch. Two)

Security agreement. A contract creating a security interest. (Ch. Two)

Security interest. A property interest granted by a debtor to a creditor in property of the debtor authorizing the creditor to seize and sell the pledged property to satisfy the debt obligation in the event of a default. (Ch. Two)

Self-help repossession. The right of a secured creditor granted under a security agreement or mortgage instrument to repossess collateral or foreclose on a mortgage without a court order. See *judicial repossession*. (Ch. Two)

Separation of powers. The constitutional doctrine forbidding any one of the three branches of government from assuming powers granted by the Constitution to another branch. See *constitutional jurisdiction*. (Ch. Six)

Setoff. The principle that when two people owe each other a debt, the debts may cancel each other out except to the extent one debt exceeds the other. (Ch. Ten)

Sheriff's sale. The sale by public auction or private sale of property of a debtor levied on pursuant to a writ of execution. (Ch. Five)

Single asset real estate debtor. A Chapter 11 debtor whose primary business is the operation of a single piece of income-producing property and which derives substantially all of its income from that property. (Ch. Seventeen)

Slow pay motion. A motion made by a judgment debtor seeking court permission to pay a judgment in installments less than the amount that would be withheld by a lawful garnishment. (Ch. Five)

Small business debtor. A Chapter 11 debtor engaged in commercial or business activities that has aggregate noncontingent liquidated debts not exceeding $2,566,050 (as of April 2016) and who elects to have its case treated as a small business case for expedited administration. (Ch. Seventeen)

Special circumstances. Unique financial circumstances of a Chapter 7 debtor involving additional expenses or adjustments of *current monthly income* for which there is no reasonable alternative, which may be sufficient to rebut the *presumption of abuse*. (Ch. Seven)

Spendthrift trust. A trust arrangement that prohibits alienation of trust property the effect of which is to protect the property from dissipation by the beneficiary or seizure by creditors of the beneficiary. (Ch. Five and Ten)

Standard of review. The standard utilized by higher courts in reviewing decisions of the bankruptcy court; normally such decisions will not be reversed unless clearly erroneous. (Ch. Six)

Standing trustee. A person appointed by the U.S. Trustee to serve as trustee in all Chapter 12 and 13 cases filed in the district. Cf. *trustee panel*. (Ch. Thirteen and Twenty)

Statement of individual Chapter 7 debtor's intent. Form required of individual debtor in bankruptcy indicating debtor's intent to surrender property pledged as collateral, redeem it, or to reaffirm underlying debt secured by such property. (Ch. Seven, Eight, and Eleven)

Statutes of limitation. Statutory time limitations placed on the right to bring a lawsuit. (Ch. Five and Nine)

Statutory lien. A lien created by statute rather than by contract or court order. (Ch. Three)

Stay. See *automatic stay*, *co-debtor stay*, and *stay bond*.

Stay (supersedeas or appeal) bond. A bond in the form of cash, property, or surety contract sufficient to cover the amount of a judgment plus accrued interest during the appeal posted by a party seeking to stay execution as a condition to obtaining such stay. (Ch. Five)

Stay of execution. A halt or freeze on the judgment creditor's right to execute on a final judgment. (Ch. Five)

Strong-arm clause. Practitioner's phrase for the trustee's avoidance powers under §544 of the Code. (Ch. Ten, Thirteen, Seventeen, and Twenty)

Sub rosa **(L. under the rose).** Practitioner's term for an operating motion in a Chapter 11 that is effectively a plan of reorganization and for a plan of reorganization that is effectively a liquidation. (Ch. Seventeen)

Subject matter jurisdiction. A court's power to hear and decide certain types of cases. (Ch. Six)

Subordination. The treatment of a claim in a less favored way than others either by consent of the creditor or by court order as a matter of equity as where the creditor has filed a claim after the *claims bar date* or has acted dishonestly or in bad faith to the detriment of junior claim holders. See *equitable subordination*. (Ch. Ten and Eleven)

Substantial abuse. The abuse of the letter and or spirit of Chapter 7 justifying the dismissal of the case. (Ch. Twelve)

Substantial completion. The date that construction on real property is substantially done. Triggers applicable time limitations for filing mechanics' and materialman's liens. (Ch. Three)

Substantive consolidation. Where two or more bankruptcy cases involving closely affiliated debtors are ordered to be consolidated into a single case, and any technical distinctions between the debtors is ignored and they are treated as a single entity. (Ch. Seventeen)

Sunset clause. A legislative enactment that expires of its own terms at some point in the future. (Ch. Twenty)

Surety (agreement or bond). A contract pursuant to which a surety makes itself primarily liable to a named principal for a debt owed to the principal by a named obligee. (Ch. Two)

Surrender (property). The act of relinquishing property to another (e.g., the debtor surrendering secured property to the secured creditor). (Ch. Seven and Eight)

Tenancy by the entireties. A form of concurrent ownership of property between a husband and wife where each has a right of survivorship. See *concurrent ownership, joint tenancy*, and *tenancy in common*. (Ch. Five)

Tenancy in common. A form of concurrent ownership in which each owner has an undivided interest in the property; no right of survivorship. See *concurrent ownership, community property tenancy by the entireties*, and *joint tenancy*. (Ch. Five)

Till tap. The direct seizure of cash from the cash register of a business pursuant to a writ of execution. (Ch. Five)

Trust. A legal arrangement where the owner of property (trustor, grantor, or settler) conveys property (trust principal or res) into the hands of a *trustee* charged with holding and administering the property for the benefit of named beneficiaries. (Ch. Five)

Trustee. 1. In the context of a mortgage, the person to whom a power of sale foreclosure is transferred by the mortgagor for the benefit of the lender. 2. In the context of an express or constructive trust, the person to whom the trust property is conveyed to hold title for the benefit of the trust beneficiary. 3. Under the Code, the individual appointed by the U.S. Trustee (or elected by creditors in a Chapter 7 case) who is charged with administering the bankruptcy estate; the bankruptcy trustee. (Ch. Two, Three, Nine, Thirteen, Seventeen, and Twenty)

Trustee panel. Persons approved by the U.S. Trustee to serve as trustees in Chapter 7 or 11 cases in a district. Cases are normally assigned to panel members on a rotating basis. (Ch. Nine, Thirteen, Seventeen, and Twenty)

Turnover. The surrender of estate property to the trustee by the debtor or other person. (Ch. Ten)

Undersecured debt (claim/creditor). A secured debt where the value of the collateral is less than the amount of the debt. See *secured debt* and *unsecured debt*. (Ch. Two, Eleven, and Fifteen)

Undue hardship. Test for discharge of student loan obligation in bankruptcy. (Ch. Twelve)

Unfair discrimination. In a plan of reorganization, the unjustified different treatment of similar claims. (Ch. Nineteen)

Unfair or deceptive act or practice. Prohibited conduct by debt collectors under the FDCPA. (Ch. Two)

Uniform Arbitration Act. Uniform statute enacted in approximately 35 states setting forth procedures governing arbitration proceedings. (Ch. Six)

Uniform Commercial Code (UCC). A uniform code adopted in whole or part in all states covering contracts for the sale or lease of goods, negotiable instruments, security interests in personal property, and other commercial transactions. (Ch. Two and Ten)

Uniform Enforcement of Foreign Judgment Act. State statute regulating the enforcement in one state of a final judgment entered in another. (Ch. Five)

Uniform Fraudulent Transfer Act of 1984 (UFTA). The more current uniform act regulating the recovery of fraudulent transfers. In effect in most states. (Ch. Five and Ten)

Unimpaired (class of claims or interests). See *impaired (class* or *claims)*.

Unliquidated claim (debt). A claim that has not been reduced to a dollar amount. (Ch. One and Two)

Unsecured debt (claim/creditor). A debt enforceable only against the bare promise of a debtor to pay and not secured by any property of the debtor or guaranty of a third party. (Ch. One, Two, Eight, Ten, and Fifteen)

U.S. Trustee. Appointed official in federal districts responsible for appointment and supervision of bankruptcy trustees and general oversight of bankruptcy cases in that district. (Ch. Six)

Validation notice. Required language in communication from a debt collector governed by the FDCPA to a debtor regarding the debtor's right to demand verification of the debt. (Ch. Four)

Vendor's lien (or mortgage lien). An *equitable lien* afforded to sellers of real property on the real property sold even in the absence of a mortgage. (Ch. Three)

Venue. The appropriate bankruptcy court in which a particular case should be filed. (Ch. Six)

Wage earner plan. Informal and inaccurate name for a Chapter 13 plan. (Ch. Thirteen)

Wage order. A court order in a Chapter 13 case directing the employer of the debtor to pay a certain amount of the debtor's wages to the standing trustee to fund the plan. (Ch. Fifteen)

Warehouseman's lien. The right of a party who has transported or stored personal property of another to retain possession of and sell that property to satisfy an unpaid obligation. (Ch. Three)

Warrant of distress. A court order authorizing a landlord to seize property of the tenant to satisfy amount due but unpaid under the lease agreement. See, *landlord's lien*. (Ch. Three)

Wild card exemption. Practitioner's phrase for §522(d)(5) allowing an individual debtor a general exemption in any property up to a stated value. (Ch. Eight)

Workout. A negotiated arrangement done outside of bankruptcy under which a debtor and his creditors agree to terms of payment. Also called a composition and extension. (Ch. Six)

Writ. A court order directing an official, such as a sheriff, to take some action (e.g., to levy an execution). (Ch. Five)

Writ of attachment (or sequestration). A prejudgment court order directed to an official such as the county sheriff directing the official to seize property of a defendant and to hold the same pending outcome of the litigation. (Ch. Five)

Writ of execution. A court order directed to an official such as the county sheriff directing the official to seize property of a debtor and to liquidate it for the benefit of a creditor. See *fieri facias*. (Ch. Five)

Writ of garnishment. A court order directing a person in possession of the property of a debtor (e.g., an employer) to deliver that property to the clerk of the court for payment to a creditor. (Ch. Five)

Writ of possession. A court order directing an official such as a sheriff to take possession of property from the one currently in custody of it for the benefit of another with a superior right to it. (Ch. Five)

100 percent plan. A Chapter 13 plan in which unsecured claims are paid in full. (Ch. Thirteen, Fourteen, and Fifteen)

§1111(b)(2) election. The right of an undersecured creditor in a Chapter 11 case to demand that the plan treat its claim as secured up to the full amount owed. (Ch. Nineteen)

1,215-day rule. Rule applicable to claiming the homestead exemption in bankruptcy providing that if the debtor has not owned his principal residence for more than 1,215 days preceding the filing of the petition he cannot exempt more than $160,375 of equity in it (as of April 1, 2016) regardless of any applicable state homestead exemption law. (Ch. Eight)

▶ Table of Cases

[Principal case names are italicized]

Index